# Does God Exist?

# HANS KÜNG

# Does God Exist?
*An Answer for Today*

# Translated by Edward Quinn

COLLINS
St James's Place, London, 1980

William Collins Sons & Co. Ltd
London · Glasgow · Sydney · Auckland
Toronto · Johannesburg

The original German edition of this book was published
under the title *Existiert Gott?*
© R. Piper & Co. Verlag, Munchen, 1978.

First published 1980

ISBN 0 00 215147 2

Printed in the United States of America
by R. R. Donnelley and Sons Company,

Ad maiorem Dei gloriam

# Acknowledgments

This book was originally intended to be complementary to *On Being a Christian*. It emerged first of all from the necessity of keeping the earlier book to a manageable size and then grew in response to the need of entering more deeply into the question of God and of carrying out thoroughly a discussion with atheism and nihilism. What became increasingly clear to the author during the long years following his student days is recapitulated in the present book.

A number of colleagues have helped me with their advice: this I have acknowledged in the sections I asked them to read. But I want to thank Professor Walter Jens, as I did in *On Being a Christian*, for giving a critical reading also to this manuscript and for his suggestions for its improvement. I must likewise thank Professor Ludger Oeing-Hanhoff, whose judgment, based on his outstanding knowledge of the history of philosophy, was of the greatest importance throughout the whole book. I am grateful also to Frau Gudrun Oeing-Hanhoff for her attention to the emergence of the manuscript and for her devoted and accurate work on the corrections.

Among my academic assistants, I must first of all thank Dr. Karl-Josef Kuschel who stood by me with untiring energy, night and day, critically and loyally. Dr. Hermann Häring deserves gratitude for the way in which he made time—although fully occupied with the publication of his own considerable work—to go through the manuscript, scrutinizing it at every point. Dr. Georg Kraus, in addition to reading the manuscript, undertook with extraordinary energy the often wearisome task of verifying quotations, searching in libraries, assisting in drawing up the bibliography; as his successor, Dr. Urs Baumann checked the final proofs. The preparation of the manuscript was once more in the reliable hands of Dr. Margret Gentner, who—with Frau Ruth Sigrist assisting in the typing in Tübingen and Frau Marlis Abendroth-Knüsel in Sursee—spared no effort patiently and expertly to prepare the pages in every chapter, which I had repeatedly retouched. Not least, however, must I thank Frau Marianne Saur-Kemmler for her splendid work on a discriminating index of some sixteen hundred names and whose judgment in reading the various versions of the manuscript was also valuable to me in a different way.

I would not like to miss the opportunity of thanking heartily Frau Renate Böhme—as representative of many who worked for me with extraordinary devotion in the Piper-Verlag—for taking care of the production of the book. Finally, in connection with the fifth centenary celebration of the University of Tübingen, it is appropriate to give a very special mention to the entire university library, which cannot be too highly praised and on which I have made frequent demands, this time in areas far beyond its excellent theological department.

*Tübingen, January 1978.*

# Contents

# Contents

# Abbreviations

CC      *Corpus Christianorum seu nova Patrum collectio* (Tournai/ Paris, 1953 onward)

CSEL    *Corpus Scriptorum Ecclesiasticorum Latinorum* (Vienna, 1866 onward)

DS      Denzinger/Schönmetzer, *Enchiridion symbolorum, definitionum et declarationum de*

# The aim of this book

Does God exist? This question implies another: Who is God? The book is meant to give an answer to both questions and to give reasons for this answer. The question mark will be taken seriously, but that will not be the end of it.

Yes to God? For many believers, this has not been obvious for a long time. No to God? Neither has this been obvious for a long time to unbelievers.

Yes or no? Many are at a loss between belief and unbelief; they are undecided, skeptical. They are doubtful about their belief, but they are also doubtful about their doubting. And there are many who are even proud of their doubting. Yet there remains a longing for certainty. Certainty? Whether Catholics, Protestants, Orthodox, whether Christians or Jews, believers in God or atheists—the discussion today runs right across old denominations and new ideologies.

We may, however, really begin to wonder if Christianity has not come to an end. Is it not all over with belief in God? Has religion any future? Can we not have morality even without religion? Is not science sufficient? Has not religion developed out of magic? Will it not perish in the process of evolution? Is not God from the outset a projection of man (Feuerbach), opium of the people (Marx), resentment of those who have fallen short (Nietzsche), illusion of those who have remained infantile (Freud)? Has atheism not been proved and is nihilism not irrefutable? Have not even theologians finally given up proving God's existence? Or are we supposed to believe even without reasons? Simply believe? Can we not doubt everything except mathematics and what we can observe, weigh and measure? Would not the ideal be mathematical certainty? Or is there simply no ground for certainty?

And even if God existed, would he be personal or impersonal? To describe him as "personal" would be naïve; but an "impersonal" God would be an abstraction. Or ought we perhaps to prefer the wisdom of the East? The silence of Buddhism before the ineffable Absolute? In the last resort, are not all religions the same? Would it not be more intellectually honest to stop short at the God of the philosophers? Why should the God of the Bible be better? God as world creator and world completer? What do we know, anyway, about the beginning and the end? And even more, what can we make of the Christian God: Father, Son and Holy Spirit—the Trinity? What is all this that we are supposed to believe?

Yet, why, then, believe in God? Why not simply in man, society, the world? Why in God and not simply in human values: liberty, fraternity, love? Why add trust in God to trust in ourselves, prayer to work, religion to politics, the Bible to reason, the hereafter to the here and now? What is belief in God supposed to mean, anyway? What can it mean today?

We are not deluding ourselves. Atheism today demands an account of our belief in God as it never did in the past. In the course of modern times, this belief has been increasingly on the defensive and today has often been silenced, at first with a few people and then with more and more. Atheism as a mass phenomenon, however, is a phenomenon of the most recent times, of our own times. The question is forced upon us: How did it get so far? What are the causes? Where did the crisis break out?

These are difficult but fascinating problems in which the French Revolution is just as much involved as the theory of relativity, natural science as much as politics, epistemology as much as psychoanalysis, history of religion and criticism of religion— Is there anything at all that is not involved? But how can everything be answered at once—in view of the immense amount of material that has been deposited by the current of modern times, in view of all the questions and problems that must all be answered simultaneously if they are to be answered effectively? This may also serve to explain the size of the present book.

To find a reasoned answer, we have to look back to the beginning of modern times. But we are not writing a history of philosophy, showing how philosophers beget philosophers and ideas give birth to ideas. We are giving an account not of a history of ideas but of concrete human beings made up of flesh and blood, with their doubting, struggling and suffering, their belief and unbelief, with all the questions that still stir us today. It is amazing to see how many have wrestled with the question of God, from Descartes, Pascal and Spinoza by way of Kant and Hegel up to Vatican I and Karl Barth, to William James, Teilhard de Chardin, Whitehead, Heidegger and Bloch. Augustine and Aquinas are involved in this history just as much as the Reformers, Jansenism and the Enlightenment, as later Comte and Schopenhauer, Darwin and Strauss, positivism and existentialism and finally the linguistic philosophy of Carnap and Wittgenstein, the Critical Theory of Adorno and Horkheimer in Frankfurt and Popper's and Albert's critical rationalism.

If we continually turn to history, this is not in order to set out facts, to honor great minds, to tell stories—in a word, not for the sake of the past, but in order to create a distance from the present and at the same time to come closer again to it. We are giving an account of the past in order to understand the present better, to understand ourselves in all our dimensions: mind and heart, consciousness and subconsciousness, history and society, science and culture.

Does God exist? We are putting all our cards on the table here. The answer will be: "Yes, God exists." And as human beings in the twentieth century we certainly can reasonably believe in God, even in the Christian God. And perhaps more easily today than a few decades or even centuries ago. For, after so many crises, it is surprising how much has been clarified and how many difficulties in regard to belief in God have been cleared up —even though some people are still not aware of the fact. Today there is no necessity to be against God merely because we are for geocentrism and evolution, for democracy and science, for liberality or socialism. No, we can be forthrightly for true freedom, equality and fraternity, for humanity, liberality and social justice, for humane democracy and controlled scientific progress, just because we believe in God. Some time ago, an English Nobel prizewinner is supposed to have answered the question whether he believed in God: "Of course not, I am a scientist." This book is sustained by the hope that a new age is dawning when the very opposite answer will be given: "Of course. I am a scientist."

When it is appropriate, we shall not hesitate to profess our faith. But there will be no eulogizing, no preaching. The reader has the right first of all simply to be informed and oriented in regard to the present state of the question. But he should also receive answers: unequivocal though incomplete answers. They should provoke a free decision, for or against, a rationally justifiable decision. And perhaps also the revision of a decision.

One last point. The books *On Being a Christian* and *Does God Exist?* are mutually complementary and—we hope—merge smoothly one into the other. When repetitions seemed appropriate, particularly of course toward the end of these books, no attempt was made to avoid them. It should be possible to read and fully understand each book for its own sake. In the present work, the important thing for me was to set out as lucidly and consistently as possible the meaning of belief in God in its totality, even if in some particular questions this meant pointing to different ways of thinking, rather than producing ready-made solutions. This approach to

belief in God as a whole offers so many possible points of entry, all leading to the center, that the reader may certainly do what the author himself never hesitates to do with books of this kind: he may begin wherever
it suits him.

# A. REASON OR FAITH?

God's existence is questioned today. But our problem is not simply to cope with this question. There remains the struggle of a different kind with the insecurity of human existence, which has existed from time immemorial. And since the emergence of modern, rational man, there has been an almost desperate struggle with the problem of human certainty. Where, we wonder, is there a rocklike, unshakable certainty on which all human certainty could be built?

# I. I think; do I therefore exist?
# René Descartes

It is not surprising that mathematicians in particular have always had a special interest in an unconditional, absolute certainty in the realm of life and knowledge. Accustomed to demands for certainty, they could not fail to be fascinated by the evident, *a priori* conclusions, independent of experience, that can be reached in mathematics. Ought it not to be possible outside the admittedly very abstract field of pure numbers and pure possibilities, ought it not to be possible also in the concrete reality of life, to ascertain the truth with quasi-mathematical certainty, so that it is immune from all the fluctuations of private and public opinion? In the modern age, mathematical certainty, excluding all doubts, became the object of the philosophers' yearning. With the new ideal of knowledge, a new age, an age of calculation, of experimenting, of method, of exactitude in the natural sciences, came into existence.

## 1. The ideal of mathematical certainty

There is no one who personifies the modern ideal of absolute mathematical-philosophical certainty better than the brilliant inaugurator of analytical geometry *and* modern philosophy. His name, "Cartesius," became synonymous with *clarté*, a geometrically exact clarity of thought. But the man himself, as person and philosopher, nevertheless remained a great mystery. Was this René Descartes (1596–1650) originally a physicist or a metaphysician? Was he a good Christian or a "Cartesian" rationalist? Was he a modern apologist for the traditional faith or an initiator of modern unbelief, rightly placed on the Índex by Rome and condemned by the Dutch Reformed Synod?

### Necessity of an exact method

This pupil of the Jesuits, sickly from his youth onward, accustomed all his life to lying in bed till late in the morning, invited at the age of fifty-four by Queen Christina of Sweden to travel in the care of an admiral with a warship to ice-cold Stockholm in the grip of winter, contracted a fatal pneumonia when he had to appear at 5 A.M. each day to discuss philosophy with the Queen. From the very beginning, Descartes felt as much repelled by the traditional, scholastic textbook philosophy as he was attracted by mathematics "because of the certainty and evidence of its reasonings." What was the use of a philosophy with a basis of natural science that had been proved with increasing clarity (by Copernicus, Kepler and Galileo) to be unreliable? This was the question he had to face.

Descartes justifies his departure from tradition in an account of his life that is both intensely personal and carefully composed, written with supreme detachment and literary brilliance. This comes at the beginning of his first publication, *Discours de la méthode* ("On the Method of rightly directing one's Reason and of seeking Truth in the Sciences"), to which he added the Dioptrics, Meteors and Geometry as "essays in the method."[1] Coming after *L'Institution de la religion chrétienne* (1560), by the Reformer Jean Calvin, this second literary monument of French prose to become a classic contributed in no slight degree to the abandonment of Latin as the language of educated people. For us, however, it is useful particularly for the problems of the present time that this founder of modern thought was able to describe "what paths I have followed, and to represent my life as it were in a picture; in order that everybody may be able to judge."[2] Descartes—and this is why he is the first personality with whom we shall be particularly concerned—compels us modern men to reconsider thoroughly the question especially of the existence of God, the relationship of faith, reason and certainty, theology, philosophy and the natural sciences.

The outwardly docile, aristocratic student, treated with deference, but secretly a rebellious admirer of Galileo, found himself at the end of his studies entangled in so many doubts and errors that he gave up formal study entirely. Unlike the scholars in their ivory towers, he "resolved not to seek after any science but what might be found within myself or in the great book of the world. So I spent the rest of my youth in travel, in frequenting courts and armies, in mixing with people of various dispositions and ranks, in collecting a variety of experiences, of proving myself in the circumstances where fortune placed me, and in reflecting always on things as they came up, in a way that might enable me to derive some profit from them."[3] The two books in which medieval man had sought truth—the book of nature and that of the Bible—appear to be replaced here by those of modern man: the book of the world and that of his own self.

After taking a degree in law, he then opened up the "great book of the world," at first in Paris: as a financially independent cavalier, a good dancer, rider, swordsman, gambler, but secretly preoccupied with mathematical and philosophical problems. And after that he was continually traveling in Holland, Germany, Austria and Hungary as a soldier, a respected, unpaid volunteer with the rank of officer—at the same time, however, less an "actor" than a "spectator," with a special liking for his quiet winter quarters, where he had time for reflection.

It was in such winter quarters, in Ulm, on the Danube, on November 10, 1619, during a night of mental exaltation and stirring, prophetic dreams, that a decisive turning point came in Descartes's life. On the twenty-three-year-old there dawned—as he thought, from above—the light of a marvelous insight: as a germinal idea for his future work, the revelation of a *science admirable*, the ideal of a new, homogeneous, universal science that could expound clearly and unequivocally, with the aid of the mathematical-geometrical method, the laws of both nature and the mind, of physics as well as metaphysics. Whatever Descartes may have thought about it all, a new age had dawned, in which mathematics and natural science would play a very different role. Did not all developments up to that point, did not the way of thinking introduced by Copernicus, Kepler and Galileo, call for a comprehensive, mathematically certain systematization in a philosophy of nature and the mind?

This overwhelming experience of his vocation so gripped him that, in the very same night, he vowed to make a pilgrimage to Loreto, in Italy— something that simply does not fit in with the clichés about Descartes the rationalist—and, after abandoning his career as an officer, actually carried out his promise in the course of a great journey through half Europe. Later, in 1627, when he had finally settled again in Paris, he entered for the first time publicly into philosophical discussion. On the occasion of a lecture by a Monsieur de Chandoux in the presence of the Apostolic Nuncio, he expounded the principles of a new philosophy, which, he claimed, could lead to a firm and certain knowledge.

Cardinal Pierre de Bérulle was present on this occasion. This great founder of the Oratory and of French spiritual theology (*École Française*), unlike the Roman theologians, had adopted a friendly attitude toward Galileo's opinions and now evidently set his hopes on the young Descartes. On the latter he officially placed the obligation of dedicating himself to the *new philosophy*. Did not Christian faith, too, need a new foundation, a new philosophical substructure for theology, a new Aristotle? Here a new alliance could be established between the new, allegedly un-Christian, mathematical-mechanistic science and philosophy on the one hand and the representative particularly of a spiritual theology on the other hand—against the traditional (abstract) textbook theology and against the nature mysticism of the Renaissance (latently neopagan in the eyes of the Oratorians). How very different might the history of Christendom have been if in Rome the opportunity had been seized for an understanding between theology and natural science! Descartes was to be the first outstanding thinker of modern times, whose work—unlike the new philosophical attempts of the Renaissance—was to make a lasting impression on the modern consciousness.

Among the papers found after Descartes's death, in Stockholm, were the "Rules for the direction of the mind" (*Regulae ad directionem ingenii*, 1628),[4] which had been written down in Latin with a lengthy commentary twelve months after the discussion in Paris. This first philosophical work of Descartes, although incomplete, gives systematic expression, with an incisiveness scarcely surpassed afterward, to the original scientific intentions laid down at least in outline in his "conversion" and shows him to be the initiator of the modern theory of knowledge.*

The rules begin:

*Rule 1*
*The aim of our studies must be the direction of our mind so that it may form solid and true judgments on whatever matters arise.*[5]
*Rule 2*
*We must occupy ourselves only with those objects that our intellectual powers appear competent to know certainly and indubitably.*[6]
*Rule 3*
*As regards any subject we propose to investigate, we must inquire not what other people have thought, or what we ourselves conjecture, but what we can clearly and manifestly perceive with intuition or deduce with certainty. For there is no other way of acquiring knowledge.*[7]
*Rule 4*
*There is need of a method for investigating the truth about things.*[8]

Rules 4 to 21 are concerned with this method and become increasingly mathematical-geometrical rules as they continue. What matters to Descartes is not a metaphysics but a uniform *method*, free from inconsistencies: the mathematical method, which holds simultaneously for all fields of knowledge—against all possible prejudices and habits, against everything that impedes evidence. How is philosophy finally to emerge out of darkness into light, from the insecurity of contradictory opinions to clarity, evidence, certainty, unless the certainty—and that means the exact

---

* *Wissenschaftstheorie*. A discerning reviewer has recently questioned the translation of this term as "philosophy of science" in the title of Wolfhart Pannenberg's *Wissenschaftstheorie und Theologie* (Geoffrey Turner, in *New Blackfriars*, Oxford, England, July 1977). He thinks that "philosophy of knowledge" would be a better rendering. Probably there is no single term in English that covers the various possible meanings of the German. For a start, "science" in English usually refers to the natural sciences, distinguished in German as *Naturwissenschaften*, from *Geisteswissenschaften*, or "humanities," literally "mental sciences." *Wissenschaft* in German has retained the medieval sense of *scientia*, meaning both knowledge and science as a branch of learning. But, with the rise of natural science, there emerged also the modern problem of knowledge. Things were no longer what they had seemed to be. And Descartes set out to show how the mind could gain certain knowledge in this strange new world. The problem has remained at the center of philosophy till the present time. In this context, therefore, "theory of knowledge" seems the most suitable rendering. When we come to deal with those philosophers concerned exclusively with the validity of the conclusions of natural science, it will be more appropriate to speak of "philosophy of science." (Translator)

method—of mathematics or, more precisely, of geometry is transferred to philosophy? Mathematics alone makes possible that clear and secure form of argument that reaches the definition of an unknown factor by starting out from known factors, which advances to more difficult and complex solutions from simple and easily understood reasons. In mathematics, in geometry, Descartes had in fact found the *key ideas of his new philosophy*, which would set the trend for the whole subsequent period and its mathematical-technical understanding of reality:

the idea of a higher plane of truth, that of evidence free from doubt or error, of clear and well-differentiated concepts;

the idea of a knowledge based not on uncertain sense data, distorted images or recognized authorities but on understanding, which alone produces certainty;

the idea of methodical thinking, proceeding by evident steps from the known to the unknown, from the simple to the complex;

the idea of an analogy between the order of mathematics and the order of nature, which obeys mathematical laws, is revealed by mathematics and thus can be controlled by mathematics.

Reduction of all problems to such mathematical types: unlike the theologian Bonaventure, who in the Middle Ages attempted a "reduction of the arts (sciences) to theology,"[9] the philosopher Descartes attempted in a modern way a "reduction of the sciences" to mathematics; the "spirit" of the mathematical method was to permeate all the other sciences. What I know "clearly and distinctly" is true. After Descartes, *clare et distincte* became a kind of slogan, far beyond France, for philosophy, natural science and the intellectual life as a whole.


## The self-assured individual

The ancient Pythagoreans had long before dreamed of the possibility of finding the harmonic system of numbers in the whole universe. But now an individual thinker, relying wholly on himself, invoking the "liberty proper to the human mind,"[10] was undertaking much more. Regardless of all previous thinking, philosophical traditions or schools, political or ecclesiastical authorities, he wants to investigate in complete freedom what man can really know and how far he is able to reach truly substantiated judgments. In brief, here is a *radical new substantiation of philosophy and of human knowledge by one individual.* Because of the diversity of opinions among scholars and also among nationalities, even in regard to morality and ethics, he found himself "as if forced to become my own guide."[11] Descartes's epistemological reflections had ultimately a practical objective: not only knowledge for its own sake, but—as against the sterile scholastic speculations—at the same time and above all for the sake of life, for the benefit of mankind, of all individuals. Theory, then, is not, as it was for Aristotle (and to some extent for Aquinas), the supreme goal of life, but—here, too, functional in a highly modern sense—a means of realizing a (rational) practice, which for its own part should make man wiser and more competent.[12]

After practical experience of exploring the world—and scarcely any philosopher ever saw so much of countries, people, great events, or ever acquired so much knowledge of the world and human nature—Descartes now turned to the study of his own self. Alone and secluded, he maintained that buildings devised by one architect working alone are usually more beautiful and more harmonious than those on which several have worked, making use of old walls originally built for other purposes. He now did little reading. His indifference to history, also to the ancient languages and especially to his own (scholastic) tradition, to which he remained more attached than he was aware, adopted on a universal scale, would have led to a breakdown of memory.

In a new age, however, he wanted to make an entirely new start: he wanted deliberately to set aside his previous opinions in order to replace them by better or even to take them up again, when he had tested them with his own reason. It needed a radical break with the past, and also with Aristotle and Aquinas, in order—as is clearly stated in the first rule of the *Discours*—"never to accept anything as true if I had not evident knowledge of its being so" and thus "to embrace in my judgment only what presented itself to my mind so clearly and distinctly (*si clairement et distinctement*) that I had no occasion to doubt it."[13] That is to say: anything that had thitherto been undoubted, unassailable authority was now put in doubt. But was this not bound to lead to conflicts with theology and the Church, perhaps even with the state?

In order to be undisturbed and independent in his great task, Descartes moved out of Richelieu's Paris—where the air was more likely to drive him to "wild fantasies" than to philosophical ideas—in the year when he had written down his "Rules" (1628), into the familiar, peaceful, rich and freer, "heretical" Holland. There, using accommodation addresses because of ecclesiastical and political pressures, he frequently changed his place of residence, devoting his life wholly to his scholarly aims. He stayed there as a prosperous gentlemen—with his maid, by whom he had a daughter, who to his great sorrow died at the age of five—for over twenty years, apart from three journeys to his French fatherland, until his final journey to Sweden. Leading a very regular life—after adequate sleep, food, work in the garden, riding—he devoted himself intensively from afternoon until late into the night to all possible mathematical, physical, physiological and philosophical problems as well as to extensive correspondence, and also to the technical realization of his ideas (making spectacles, wheelchairs, pumps), to autopsies to find cures for blindness and finally, with advancing age, to the possibilities of prolonging life. The application of modern algebraic arithmetic to ancient geometry was of permanent importance: algebraized analytical geometry, which provided the mathematician with a modern tool for the very first time. Algebra thus became a key not only for finding a particular proposition but for reaching any proposition desired.

For the first five years in Holland (1628–33), Descartes worked mainly at his physics. Although never a coward, he was very cautious and often all too diplomatic in his dealings with people: when he heard of Galileo's condemnation by the Roman Inquisition in 1633, he held back the post-Copernican "Treatise on the World or on Light" (*Traité du monde ou de la lumière*), even though it was ready for the printer. This was one of the innumerable consequences of the case of Galileo—still minimized in ecclesiastical circles—which, together with other acts of the magisterium (the most notorious in Descartes's time were the burning of Giordana Bruno at the beginning of the century, the condemnation of Copernicus as early as 1616 and the lifelong imprisonment of the anti-Aristotelian philosopher Tommaso Campanella by the same "Holy Office"), was to burden and poison relations between Church and theology on the one hand and philosophers and natural scientists on the other up to the present time.

The condemnation of Galileo, approved by Pope Urban VIII himself, carried out in the Catholic universities by the Roman authorities making use of inquisitors and nuncios as instruments of power, was only apparently a defense of the Bible. In reality it was mainly a defense of the Graeco-medieval world picture and particularly the authority of Aristotle, with whose teachings on physics, biology and philosophy the biblical world picture was identified. But, in all this, what had to be defended was the legally assured supremacy of theology in the hierarchy of the sciences, the authority of the Church in all questions of life and finally—purely and simply—blind, obedient submission to the Church's doctrinal system. This Roman declaration was regarded in theology as a factually infallible and irreformable decision and nipped in the bud the modest attempts of open-minded theologians as in the thirteenth century to rethink the biblical message in the light of a new Weltanschauung.

A historical opportunity had been missed, and from that time onward, despite cautious attempts at reconciliation, the Catholic Church has largely been regarded up to the present time as an enemy particularly of the natural sciences. It is this that makes Bertolt Brecht's *Life of Galileo*, even for us today, a drama full of scientific, social, political and moral tension. Galileo's condemnation and the consequent loss of the world of science has not unjustly been ranked with the East-West schism and the Western divisions in faith as one of the three greatest disasters in Church history.[14] It played an essential part in opening that gap between the Church and modern civilization which is still far from being bridged. But it was a personal tragedy for Galileo that he and many like-minded persons did not succeed in convincing the Church's magisterium of the truth of his conclusions and in making the Church and the new sciences allies, as they had been in the Middle Ages.[15] "To want to draw from Sacred Scripture the knowledge of truths which belong solely to the human sciences and have no bearing on salvation is to use Scripture for a purpose for which God did not intend it and consequently to abuse it."[16] Descartes wrote this in 1638, and not even the Second Vatican Council, in the present century, ventured to state the fact so clearly in its Constitution on Revelation.

As a result, therefore, of Galileo's condemnation, Descartes's work remained a torso for his contemporaries. The treatise on the world (together with the treatises on man and on the formation of the fetus) was not published in Paris until fourteen years after his death:[17] a new model —deviating considerably, however, from the Bible—of a world not interpreted any longer according to a sanctified tradition but explored by observation and examination of nature and its phenomena. The origin of suns, stars, earth, moon, he explained by the vortex theory: the earth moves around the sun. Immediately after Galileo's condemnation, Descartes no longer wanted to publish anything. Nevertheless, he hoped for a revision of the Church's judgment. But it was only a century after Descartes's death—much too late—that the condemnation of Copernicus was lifted (1757), and only in 1822 was Galileo's work removed from the Index of Prohibited Books. *Pensiamo in secoli,* "We think in centuries," they say in Rome.

Descartes, however, finally published his *Discours de la méthode,* but without the appendixes on geometry and optics (the explanation of the telescope and the famous law of refraction), without creating a sensation. Originally, the title (recalling the November night in Germany) was to have been: "The project of a universal science that could raise our nature to its supreme perfection."[18] It was only the Latin "Meditations on the foundations of philosophy" (1641),[19] in which Descartes as both physicist and metaphysician seeks with the aid of his new, exact method to establish an indubitable solution to the questions of both God's existence and the nature of the human soul, that provoked vigorous opposition on the part of Catholic and Protestant theologians and philosophers but also helped to bring his philosophy to fruition. In order to complete its presentation, Descartes then published in Latin—his great ambition was to have the work used in schools—his *Principles of Philosophy* (1644).[20] This work is dedicated to Princess Elizabeth of Bohemia (of the Palatinate), as intelligent as she was beautiful, with whom Descartes felt closely linked in his later life and to whose suggestion his last work, "On the Passions of the Soul" (1649),[21] published immediately before his journey to Sweden, owes its origin.

Even in Protestant Holland, protected by high-ranking patrons from being arrested or having his books burned, Descartes was sometimes accused of atheism, Pelagianism, as well as skepticism. Yet he had himself expressly attacked "the skeptics, who doubt just for the sake of doubting and affect to be always undecided"; for him, on the contrary, the "whole aim was to reach security, and cast aside loose earth and sand so as to reach rock or clay."[22]

## 2. The fundamental certainty of reason

But how is a person to get his feet on firm ground? The path that Descartes had clearly outlined in his *Discours* as one that he had tested and discovered by experience, he follows in his *Meditationes* systematically and more thoroughly, intent on proving the existence of God and the nature of the human soul. What appears in the *Discours* as a history of his own mind is presented and developed in principle in the *Meditationes* as the history of the mind as such.[23] It is the adventurous route of methodical (accomplished at a regular pace of thought) and radical (going to the roots) and therefore universal (all-embracing) *doubt*. The same procedure is repeated in the *Principles*.

### In what sense we can doubt everything

How, then, in the midst of all actual and possible errors, is man to reach permanent and firm ground? "Some years ago now I observed the multitude of errors that I had accepted as true in my earliest years, and the dubiousness of the whole superstructure I had since then reared on them; and the consequent need of making a clean sweep for once in my life, and beginning again from the very foundations, if I would establish some secure and lasting result in science."[24]

It is better, of course, as Descartes observed, "to postpone" this "clean sweep of all [one's] opinions" to one's "mature age."[25] In order to accomplish this, Descartes did not merely retire outwardly but provided himself with the security of rules of method and some moral rules:[26] despite his doubts, there had to be a "provisional code of morals," a veritably conformist temporary morality, which he later declared to be definitive. So now he goes—undaunted but, like someone alone in the darkness, slowly, step by step, so as not to fall[27]—along the dangerous path of doubt, which should lead him—as he hopes and expects—not to despair but to a certainty free from all doubts.

This doubting person soon observes that it is possible to doubt about all things "and especially material things."[28] To make clear how dubious everything is, it is not necessary to go to endless trouble in testing everything in detail: "When the foundation is undermined, the superstructure will collapse of itself; so I will proceed at once to attack the very principles on which all my former beliefs rested."[29] This takes place in four stages:

*First consideration:* Sense perception is unreliable. Since the senses are sometimes deceptive, we can never entirely trust them. The certainty of the external world as a whole is dubious.[30]

*But:* There may be uncertainty about very small or remote objects, but not about myself, about the fact that I am sitting here, with my hands and my whole body.

*Second consideration:* Sleeping and waking can never be distinguished by any certain signs. What we experience in waking we can also experience in dreaming: the very fact that I am sitting here with my hands and my whole body. Might not all this be a dream (hallucination, delusion)? Even my bodily existence, therefore, is uncertain.[31]

*But:* All these details may well be uncertain, but not corporeal nature in general, its extension, quantity, size, number, place and time. Whether dreaming or not, two and three always add up to five, and squares always have four sides.

*Third consideration:* Everything might be deception. If we are already so much deceived, why should we not be deceived about that which seems to us the most certain? Even the most universal basic concepts and principles of nature, even the truths on which all knowledge is based are doubtful.[32]

*But:* Such uncertainty on man's part is indeed conceivable but only on the assumption that the supremely good God has created man to be deceived and wrong. This is contrary to God's goodness.

*Fourth consideration:* Instead of God, there might be a deceiving spirit. May we not suppose for a while "not that there is a supremely good God, the source of truth; but that there is an evil spirit (*genius malignus*), who is supremely powerful and intelligent, and does his utmost to deceive me"?[33] Everything, then, outside me and about me would, then, in fact be "mere delusive dreams."[34]

Although he rejects the arbitrary God of Nominalism, Descartes does not hesitate radically, if merely "fictively," methodically, to doubt the truth of the Creator. Thus universal and radical doubt throughout everything has gotten at and touched the roots of previous certainty: the certainty of God as the deepest ground of all certainty of the self. But if doubt goes so deep, how are we to avoid despair? Does this method not lead at least to total skepticism?

### The Archimedean point

If we do not in any way evade the problem of doubt, but stand up to it to the very end, how are we to reach any certainty at all? "Yesterday's meditation plunged me into doubts of such a gravity that I cannot forget them, and yet do not see how to resolve them. I am bewildered, as though I had suddenly fallen into a deep sea, and could neither plant my foot on the bottom or swim up to the top. But I will make an effort, and try once more the same path as I entered upon yesterday; I will reject, that is, whatever admits of the least doubt, just as if I had found it was wholly false; and I will go on until I know something for certain—if it is only this, that there is nothing certain. Archimedes asked only for one fixed and immovable point so as to move the whole earth from its place; so I may have great hopes if I find even the least thing that is unshakably certain."[35]

Is there, then, this one point, directly certain and obvious, which could sustain the whole structure of human knowledge? Yet all certainty appears to have been destroyed. But—and here comes the great surprise—it is precisely this universal and radical doubt that itself begets the new fundamental certainty: "But immediately upon this I noticed that while I was trying to think everything false, it must needs be that I, who was thinking this, was something. And observing that this truth 'I am thinking, therefore I exist' was so solid and secure that the most extravagant suppositions of the sceptics could not overthrow it, I judged that I need not scruple to accept it as the first principle of philosophy that I was seeking."[36]

And this *je pense, donc je suis,* formulated already in the *Discours,* which becomes in Latin the famous *cogito, ergo sum,* Descartes expounds in the *Meditationes,* on the assumption that God might deceive him: "If he deceives me, then again I undoubtedly exist; let him deceive me as much as he may, he will never bring it about that, at the time of thinking (*quamdiu cogitabo*) that I am something, I am in fact nothing. Thus I have now weighed all considerations enough and more than enough; and must at length conclude that this proposition 'I am,' 'I exist,' whenever I utter it or conceive it in my mind, is necessarily true."[37] The goal appears to have been attained. Clearness and distinctness are manifested here not only in the mathematical-geometrical sphere of abstract numbers and relations but in concrete life, in actual existence. Since there is nothing indubitable on the side of the object, the doubting subject is necessarily thrown back on himself.

"I think, (therefore) I am." The "therefore" (*donc, ergo*)—used only incidentally—does not imply a syllogistic argument, but the insight directly involved in the act of thinking: "I am a thinking, a conscious being." As long as I am doubting, I am thinking and I must exist as the doubter and the thinker. Thus, throughout all doubt, the Archimedean point had been found. The fact of one's own existence—and not only of one's thinking—is the basis of all certainty. From this firm and immovable point, Descartes now sets in motion all the basic questions of philosophy: the three great questions about the self, about God and about material things.

a. The nature of the *self* or of the human mind:[38] for Descartes, it consists wholly and entirely in thinking, understood in the widest sense of the term (*cogitare, cogitatio*=consciousness). To this self, the "thinking being" (*res cogitans*), belong the attributes of thinking and also of feeling or sensation and of willing, in the same way as color or weight belongs to the things of the physical world, whose nature consists in extension (*res extensa*).

b. But how does the self come to the existence of *God?* This is Descartes's new starting point: not from the world, but wholly and entirely from the self. In two ways:

First of all *causally*, in the scheme of cause and effect.[39] For Descartes it is unquestionable that man finds present in himself the idea of a perfect, infinite being. Where does this idea come from? Not from man himself, for, as doubting, thinking being, what he knows is precisely his imperfection and finiteness. But the imperfect and the finite—here, with the concept of the efficient cause between finite and infinite, Descartes takes up Neoplatonic trains of thought—cannot be the sufficient reason for the perfect. For—since the idea is not nothing—this idea of perfection and infinity must have as its real author an actual being corresponding to it, a truly infinite being: God. The idea of perfection and infinity cannot have been produced by us; God himself has planted it in us. The idea of God is an innate, or congenital, idea in man.

Then *ontologically* from the idea to existence:[40] Descartes goes back to the famous argument of Anselm of Canterbury, known from Kant's time onward as the ontological argument, now, however, based on the presupposition of his principle of clear and distinct knowledge. That which we know clearly and distinctly to belong to the true nature of something must in fact belong to it. But the idea of God cannot be confused with just any sort of idea. We know clearly and distinctly that God is the most perfect being and that his existence also belongs to his perfections: the supremely perfect being cannot be without the supreme perfection. Thus in the very idea of God as the most perfect being is involved also the fact that he exists.

But how can we be sure that we are not deceiving ourselves in this conclusion or that we are not being deceived by a fraudulent spirit? Descartes's answer is that if God were a deceiving spirit, he could not be the most perfect being. For deception and fraud are signs of weakness and imperfection. The concept itself or the idea of the perfect being therefore includes not only the existence but also the truthfulness and goodness of God. A deceiver-God is impossible.

The idea of God, then, is not derived from knowledge of the world. Knowledge and faith appear to be sharply separated, and this should really have permitted a free development of both natural science and theology. The conclusion of the third meditation testifies that the contemplation of God is admiration, adoration, joy: "So far as the eye of my darkened understanding can bear it," this contemplation provides "the greatest joy of which we are capable in this life."[41]

c. From this point, the step to the *material things*[42] of the world is no longer difficult. If God is truthful and good, man can be certain of himself and the material things around him. God in his truthfulness and goodness guarantees also the reliability of the reason he has created, if it is rightly used—that is, clearly and distinctly. I can be certain that what I perceive clearly and distinctly (that is, not simply all secondary qualities of matter such as color, shape, solidity) is not delusion, not semblance, but true, and consequently exists. At the same time, it also becomes clear and distinct that the nature of material things is really different from the nature of the human mind. The human mind (the self, the soul) is characterized by thinking, material things by extension. In the material field, God must be understood as first cause of all motion.

## 3. Reason as basis of faith?

"Here, we may say, we are at home, and like the mariner after a long voyage in a tempestuous sea, we may now hail the sight of land; with Descartes the culture of modern times, the thought of modern Philosophy, really begins to appear, after a long and tedious journey on the way that has led so far."[43] This is how Hegel in his lectures on the history of philosophy, more than two hundred years later, greets the advent of Descartes. In fact, despite all opposition, Cartesianism became very much more than a school. It became a movement, a way of thinking, a mental attitude, a matter of education as a whole. Its history is largely identified with the history of philosophy as such. Not only rationalism, psychologism and particularly idealism, on the right, but—as a result of his sharp division of body and soul as of two substances—also on the left, empiricism, mechanism and even materialism all invoke Descartes. What Descartes's genius held together was afterward dissipated. It was not Descartes's system that set the trend for the future, influential as it was; what systems do not become "historical" sooner or later! What set the trend for the future were his scientific attitude, his style of thinking, his method.

## From certainty of the self to certainty of God

With Descartes, European consciousness in a critical development reached an *epochal turning point*. Basic certainty is no longer centered on God, but on man. In other words, the medieval way of reasoning from certainty of God to certainty of the self is replaced by the modern approach: from certainty of the self to certainty of God.

Here is a Copernican turning point—no less important than that relating to earth and sun. Instead of theocentrism we now have a solidly based anthropocentrism. Man stands at the center and indeed on his own feet. With the utmost energy, resolution and discipline, Descartes set out methodically from man, from the subject, his freedom, reason, certainty, and was thus the first person to substantiate philosophically the autonomy of science. He has rightly been called the "Father of modern philosophy," the "Father of modern thought."

For with him begins the priority of the subject over the object, of consciousness over being, of personal freedom over cosmic order, of questioning in immanent rather than transcendent terms. With him begin both modern philosophical anthropology and an independent theory of knowledge, a theory of method and a philosophy of science—all of which as philosophical disciplines now got the better of metaphysics, which had occupied the first place in the Middle Ages.

And now that man has fortunately won his certainty of the self, has he not also gained the rocklike, unshakable certainty on which all certainty, even the certainty of faith, can be built? Descartes answers the question decidedly in the affirmative. And with him, the philosophical national hero, wide clerical circles—from Bossuet and Malebranche by way of the Oratorians and Benedictines to the Jansenists and Protestants—began to think that this very philosophy of reason and freedom, oriented to the future and accessible to all men—precisely this philosophy of Descartes, at once critical, optimistic and universal—was most suitable to serve in a new age as a philosophical foundation of the Christian religion.

In fact, however much of a philosophical revolutionary Descartes was, *he had no wish to be a religious reformer.* In contrast to former interpreters of Descartes, with a rationalistic, positivistic, neo-Kantian or even Thomistic outlook—who saw in him primarily not the metaphysician but the physicist (and epistemologist)—the latest interpreters (Gouhier, Laporte, Alquié)[44] attach more importance to Descartes as a metaphysician and wholly religiously oriented person. Descartes obviously saw no contradiction between his vision of a methodical-rational universal science and theological-ecclesiastical doctrines and practices. Unlike the "Enlighteners" and defenders of natural religion after him, he always maintained unequivocally the Christian revealed faith. He was a Christian, even if not a very zealous one. Philosophy leads to the threshold of religion but does not seek to abolish it.

Descartes was by no means, as Maxime Leroy once held,[45] an unbelieving philosopher using a mask to cover his fear. Some interpreters—particularly in Germany up to Karl Jaspers[46] and Wilhelm Weischedel[47]—under the influence of Leroy and ignorant of the tradition to which Descartes belonged, have not sufficiently appreciated all that deserves to be considered in the light of recent French studies together with his new philosophical projects: his Catholic education at La Flèche; his pilgrimage to Loreto after discovering his vocation at a crucial stage in his life and thought; his acquaintance with Bérulle and other Oratorians (such as Gibieuf) and his lasting friendship with Mersenne, of the Friars Minims, his point of contact with all the scholars of the day who were also working for a reconciliation of theology with the new natural science; his explicit attachment to the traditional Christian faith in the rules laid down for a "provisional morality" during the period of his methodic doubt; the affirmation in his letters of his attachment to the Church, even when it was not necessary to mention this; his efforts for a new Catholic understanding of the Eucharist; his loyal profession and practice of the Catholic faith in Protestant surroundings; finally, his death—in accordance with his own teaching—in complete submission to God's Providence. The French ambassador in Stockholm is reported to have said to those present at the bedside after Descartes's death that his friend was "retiring, content with life, satisfied by men, full of confidence in the mercy of God, eager to see unveiled and to possess a truth which he had sought throughout his life."[48] The Swedish Queen, Christina, daughter of the great Gustavus Adolphus, ascribed to Descartes as her teacher a part in her "glorious conversion" to the Catholic faith. Four years after Descartes's death, in Stockholm, she renounced the throne (1654).

Naturally, modern interpretations of Descartes continue to differ considerably from one another. "But this much at least is certain: Descartes is no longer to be understood merely as a natural scientist, using metaphysics merely as a cloak and a methodical instrument for destroying the scholastic conceptual scheme. There is no longer any problem about Descartes's *sincérité* in questions of religion."[49]

That does not mean, however, that Descartes advocated or wanted to advocate any Christian philosophy. There is nothing specifically Christian about his philosophy: Jesus Christ does not appear to have played any part in it. The submission of his *Meditationes* to the Sorbonne, the theological faculty of the University of Paris, need not have been merely a tactical move, a measure of caution, but was more probably a gesture to gain the support for which he hoped from the Sorbonne and if possible from the Church for his teaching. Certainly he was more concerned to enlist support for his new philosophy and thus also for his post-Copernican physics—the conclusions of which he made known only in part—than of defending belief in the existence of God or the immortality of the soul, of which surprisingly little is said in the *Meditationes*. Nevertheless we cannot overlook the basic apologetic trend of his writing, against the freethinkers (philosophical, moral and sociological *libertins*), which he combines with opposition to scholasticism as a source of false physics and of many errors. Even after Galileo's condemnation, Descartes hoped that the time for Aristotelian-scholastic physics, metaphysics and theology had passed and that the hour had come for a new philosophy, his philosophy. And even though Descartes did not practice a Christian philosophy, *he did practice philosophy as a Christian.*

The question may be raised, however, as to how *reason and faith,* radical rational analysis and the "higher" certainty of Christian faith, can be combined. Is there not a contradiction here? There might seem to be one if we did not know Descartes's views on the question. The position adopted in his earliest book, *Rules for the Direction of the Mind,* is typical also of the later Descartes. In commenting on rule 3, on certainty through clear and manifest intuition or through certain deduction (what we might describe more strictly as "induction"), he says: "These are the two most certain ways to knowledge; and on the side of the mind no more must be admitted; all others must be rejected as suspect and liable to mislead. This, however, does not prevent our believing that divine revelation is more certain than any knowledge; for our faith in it, so far as it concerns obscure matters, is an act not of the mind but of the will; and any intellectual foundations that it may have can and must be sought chiefly by one or other of the two ways I have mentioned. Perhaps I shall later on show this to be so at greater length."[50]

How, then, is certainty of faith related to certainty arising from the manifest intuition of reason? For Descartes, *faith is an exception to the general rules of evidence.* Faith exhibits the greatest certainty of all, although—unlike philosophy or natural science—it relates not to an evident but to an obscure content, which surpasses reason. How is this possible? Because faith is an act not of the perceiving mind, of the intellect, but of the will, which, disposed by God's revelation, can assent even without evidence. The foundations of this faith should of course be established rationally by intuition or deduction. This remains Descartes's basic response in the very rare texts where he expresses himself spontaneously on this question. In the *Meditationes* it becomes still more clear that it is God's grace which disposes man to assent, not, however, by diminishing his freedom, but by increasing and strengthening it.[51]

It is only in private and public statements provoked by others that clearer trends can be perceived:[52]

a. The two cognitive powers (the natural light of reason and the light of faith stemming from divine grace) and the two spheres of knowledge (the realm of clear and distinct ideas and the realm of revelation) are absolutely distinct: there is neither mingling of the two nor any mutual opposition, but a parallelism and a proper distance between them.

b. Consequently there is nothing specifically Christian in Descartes's philosophy: when it is concerned with God, it is always with the God of the philosophers and not the God of the fathers and of Jesus Christ.

c. Yet there is no contradictory double truth, but a harmony of philosophy and revelation, in which Descartes sees his philosophy as more in accordance than—for instance—the Aristotelian with Christian revelation.

If we are to see clearly the situation at the present time, the question must be asked: How does Descartes reach this definition of the relations between reason and faith? To what tradition does he belong? It was only with difficulty that Descartes was able to admit that he, too, the great innovator, had learned from others. But it is precisely in the light of the tradition to which he belonged that a number of "contradictions" can be clarified.


## Neither freethinking nor Augustinism

Did Descartes perhaps belong to the *freethinking tradition,* as some philosophical interpreters think? Descartes was a liberal man, he associated with many *libertins,* he knew their views. Undoubtedly, the skeptical basic attitude of the French Renaissance thinkers—as found in Michel de Montaigne's *Essais* (1552–88) and his friend Pierre Charron's *De la Sagesse* (1601) and also Franz Sanchez's *Tractatus de multum nobili et prima universali scientia, quod nihil scitur* (1581)—formed the background in the light of which Descartes's methodical doubt and thought are to be understood.

*Nevertheless,* this methodical doubt must itself be very clearly distinguished from the purely negative doubt of skepticism. Descartes did not wish to persist in doubt, but to emerge from doubt—which proves to be the error-destroying force of truth itself—to unambiguous and unshakable certainty, to the foundation of a new certainty of God. "What do I really know?" is Montaigne's standpoint, not Descartes's. No one ever had any right to question the sincerity of Descartes's belief in God.

Neither did Descartes maintain any theory of two truths that need not be mutually consistent. His theory aims at unity and implies not opposition but harmony between reason and faith. Unlike the Averroists, of the thirteenth century, the Renaissance philosophers of the sixteenth and the freethinkers of the seventeenth century, he did not see any contradiction between classical antiquity and Christianity; he had little interest in Plato, Aristotle, Epictetus or Epicurus; he did not want any *philosophie renaissante* but a *philosophie nouvelle.* It is not surprising, then, that the freethinkers never invoked Descartes but were reserved in their attitude toward him.

Or does Descartes belong to the Augustinian tradition, as some—especially theological—interpreters insist? Descartes knew several important representatives of Augustinism in France, notably Bérulle and members of the Oratory. He was united with them in opposition to scholastic philosophy and to Aristotle as also against the nature mysticism of the Renaissance. Moreover Descartes's philosophy exhibits important elements of Platonic-Neoplatonic-Augustinian philosophy: especially the intuitive, immediate vision of innate ideas and the proof of God from the impossibility of conceiving the imperfect without assuming the existence of the perfect; also—as found especially in Augustine's work—the study of the self, doubt, and the recourse to the *cogito:* "If I err, I exist," "If I am deceived, I exist," as it is stated briefly and incisively in Augustine's *The City of God*.[53]

*Nevertheless,* unlike Augustine, Descartes does not particularly stress either the limitations of reason or the dignity of faith. The influence of Bérulle should not be exaggerated. Descartes, already firmly fixed in his opinions, was in close contact with him for a period only of four months (Bérulle died in 1628). In general, it can be said that Augustinism and Cartesianism often converge, but there is no reason to derive the latter from the former. When Descartes's attention was drawn by a number of correspondents to parallels with Augustine's *cogito*, he showed little interest, did not consult Augustine's work, and merely suggested that anyone—and particularly Augustine—could easily light on the same idea. We know nothing about Descartes's reading of Augustine.

Despite similar features in his system, Descartes, anyway, had a completely different conception of philosophy. Like the rest of the Fathers of the Church, Augustine is unaware of any autonomous philosophical system; he knows nothing of two sciences distinct from one another (philosophy and theology), two organs (reason and faith), two ways (thought and action). He sees everything in a grand philosophical-theological unity of reason and faith, where philosophical truth is one with revealed truth, where, on the one hand, philosophical arguments can be used in interpreting the Bible and, on the other, biblical quotations can be used in philosophical reasoning. But Descartes carefully separates reason and faith, philosophy and theology, rational arguments and biblical texts. His philosophical works never display religious feeling; still less do they pass over into prayer, as Augustine's quite naturally do. Descartes's *Discours* and Augustine's *Confessiones* are brilliant autobiographical justifications of each author's way of life. But we need to read only a few pages of either to sense a completely different mental atmosphere. Between them lies not only a millennium but a whole world.

## Thomistic heritage

Does Descartes, then, belong perhaps to the *Thomistic tradition*?[54] He must certainly have become acquainted with it when he studied philosophy at the Jesuit-run Collège Royal of La Flèche: the order's founder, Ignatius of Loyola, had himself imposed on his followers the obligation of following Aquinas in their theology. In this respect we must not overlook the role of Spanish baroque scholasticism, which was very influential in Europe at the time—at La Flèche, especially the system of the Jesuit Francisco Suárez—as the link uniting medieval scholasticism with modern philosophy. But this had little to do with the question of the fundamental relationship between reason and faith. Descartes, always very polite, complimented his Thomistic teachers: "I must do my teachers the honour of saying that I do not think there is anywhere in the world a place where philosophy is better taught than at La Flèche."[55] In fact, in his statement of problems, his conceptuality, language, style, his desire for system, history had a much greater influence on the founder of modern philosophy—contemptuous as he was of history—than either he or his followers appreciated. Certainly there was discontinuity, but—as so often—against a background of continuity.

What is indisputable is the fact that Descartes—this man of few books—had with him even in his later years a *Summa Theologiae* and needed only to consult the first pages of the second section of the second part to find the principles of a solution to the question of reason and faith. Descartes refers expressly to Aquinas, particularly when speaking of faith and its mysteries.[56] The Cartesian thesis on faith as an act of will is also close to Aquinas' view that the assent of faith "is caused, not by thought (*cogitatio*), but by the will."[57] Particularly on the relations between reason and faith, philosophy and theology, Descartes is much closer to Aquinas or at any rate to Thomism than to the very different system of Augustine and Augustinism. Cartesianism and Thomism clearly divide the two ways of knowing (natural reason and grace-inspired faith), two planes of knowledge (natural truth and grace-given revealed truth), two sciences (philosophy and theology). And yet there is no contradiction, but a fundamental harmony, between them. Two spheres, even—as it were—like two floors of a building: clearly distinguished in their scope; the one with higher certainty, unequivocally superordinated to the other as its basis; but both linked in harmonious contiguity and bound in principle to collaborate. We must be careful not to talk hastily of contradictions, in the work either of Aquinas or of Descartes.

It must be admitted, however, that Descartes's definition of the relations between reason and faith resembles the position only of a somewhat *simplified* Thomism. If we examine Aquinas' own writings, we find in his system as a whole nothing like so rigid a separation of the two planes of knowledge and the two sciences as in later Thomism. It is necessary therefore to insist, as against Descartes,

that faith needs a solid, rational foundation and permeation;

that the act of faith—although elicited by the (blind) will in face of non-manifest truths of faith—remains in fact an act of the (percipient) intellect;

that rational knowledge as a whole may not be rationalistically narrowed in its scope, still less understood in merely mathematical terms.

These differences, however, involve little change in the essential state of affairs. In the two-floor theory of reason and faith, Descartes is basically following the Thomist line. With that established, our questions must now be directed forward.

Clarity as ideal of theology

From Descartes it is possible to draw lines backward to Aquinas or to
Spanish baroque scholasticism as mediating the teaching of Aquinas. But
the lines forward are no less important: to the Neo-Thomism that
emerged in Italy a century after Descartes's death and came to prevail
everywhere—apart from the Tübingen school—in Catholic theology in
the nineteenth century and to the First Vatican Council, of 1869 to 1870,
where it was dominant.

Thomas Aquinas in his day was not an uncontroversial figure as a theologian. He was frequently denounced, attacked as a modernist by traditionalist (Augustinian) theologians, recalled from Paris by his own
(Dominican) Order and finally forthrightly condemned by the ecclesiastical authorities in Paris as a defender of the (mainly philosophical-Aris-
totelian) *nouvelle théologie*. But by Descartes's time he had become
purely and simply the theologian of the Order, the *Doctor communis* and
finally a Catholic classic author. After the period of rehabilitating and
defending Aquinas (John Capreolus, †1444, was his most important advocate), there came, at the end of the fifteenth century, the period of
commentaries on the *Summa Theologiae* (the first commentator on the
whole *Summa* being Cardinal Cajetan, the classical interpreter of Aquinas
and the opponent of Luther).[58] Francisco de Vittoria, Father of Spanish
scholasticism, introduced the *Summa Theologiae* as the textbook at the
University of Salamanca—which thus became the point of origin of
Spanish scholasticism—and wrote a commentary on it. In the year of Descartes's birth, 1596, the University of Louvain joined the movement, and
in 1617—the year before Descartes entered military service in Holland—
set up a seven-year course of study of the *Summa Theologiae* with two
specially created professorships to cover the course. Up to 1924, ninety
commentaries on the whole *Summa* were published (also 218 on the first
part and eighty-nine on the second section of the first part, above mentioned).

In both *classical Thomism* and the *Neo-Thomism* of the nineteenth and
the present centuries, interpreters diverged considerably from their master
(so much so that some German authorities have distinguished between
*thomanisch* and *thomistisch*). And although the conclusions of natural
science (condemned at this stage) and of modern philosophy were at first
opposed and then simply ignored, while Thomism was turned from the
avant-garde of the thirteenth century into the arrière-garde of the seventeenth, the rationalist spirit of the age personified in Descartes demanded
its tribute also from Thomism. Descartes's modern philosophical equipment was used as a means by which the traditional medieval view of
Christianity could continue to be defended. While a lack of historical

sense involved a failure to appreciate the development of Aquinas' own teaching, there could now be observed in the formal aspects of theology a new effort to build up the logical-rational structure of proofs (retaining, however, the medieval syllogistic or disputation form), to gain greater exactitude in terminology (but with a rigidity not found in Aquinas), to suppress biblical-theological discussions (as contained even in the *Summa Theologiae*) in favor of one's own speculations, for which the Bible had to serve as a quarry for digging out quotations (*locus theologicus*).

Aquinas himself, of course, was mainly interested in the rational clarification of questions of faith. But, as Aquinas took up Greek intellectualism and in some ways surpassed it, so now classical and Neo-Thomism took up the intellectualism of Aquinas. Interest, however, was now centered much more on the genesis of faith, questions were concentrated on the function of rational motives of credibility, and a rational theory of the act of faith was worked out under the heading of "analysis of faith." In Aquinas' conception of faith—which would now be called "mystical"—there was no special problem as to how the authority of God as revealer can itself be the immediate and ultimate motive for the assent of faith.

This question now became increasingly—as Kleutgen, the influential neo-scholastic council theologian of Vatican I, says—"the cross or torment of theologians,"[59] or—according to a neo-scholastic of our time—"one of the most difficult questions in the whole of theology."[60] Concepts central to Descartes's philosophy—such as reason, freedom, certainty, evidence, rationality—were now applied to the analysis of the act of faith.[61] And as the attempt was made to produce clear and distinct ideas by a vivisection of the act of faith, so, too, by a rational analysis of the collaboration between divine predestination and human free will an explanation was sought of the exact functioning of the various types of grace in man, of the causality of the sacraments, and later also of the inspiration of the biblical writers. All in all, this is a rational-deductive syllogistic theology, attaching great importance to the scientific spirit and method, although its apparently highly reasonable conclusions today scarcely arouse even historical interest.

It is, however, easy to see how the triumphs of mathematics and of the experimental "exact" sciences connected with it, and thus finally also the Cartesian demand for rational method and mathematical-geometrical clarity, certainty, evidence—the Cartesian spirit of the age as a whole—influenced Thomistic theology and philosophy to no small degree, despite or even because of the latter's defensive attitude toward the new world picture and the new science. Not that theology—even according to Descartes himself—could simply take over the mathematical-geometrical ideal of knowledge and science for its realm of "obscure" truths of faith. Incidentally, like Copernicus and Galileo before him, Descartes in 1663 had his works placed posthumously on the Index of Prohibited Books by the Roman Holy Office, *donec corrigatur,* "until corrected," which seems to be demanding too much of a dead man.

Catholic and Protestant theology subsequently came to be inspired more by Leibniz, the initiator of an autonomous German philosophy, and by Christian Wolff, the popular philosopher of the German Enlightenment, both of whom, however, had adopted Cartesian rationalism in its essentials—despite many corrections—and were glad to hand it on to the theologians. Like Descartes, both men were simultaneously mathematicians and philosophers and practiced philosophy in mathematical terms; their thought was also wholly ecumenically oriented: Leibniz expressly exerted himself for the unity of the churches, Wolff was friendly with the Jesuits. And it was especially the latter's clear, rich and comprehensive rationalist system which on the one hand adopted many conclusions of scholasticism and on the other transmitted many rationalistic impulses to modern scholasticism. This is likewise true of the "Roman School," even though it has scarcely been possible hitherto to establish a direct genealogy from the Jesuits of the eighteenth century to those of the nineteenth who dominated the First Vatican Council with their Thomistic theology. Among the latter were G. Perrone, who played an essential part in preparing both the definition of the Immaculate Conception and the First Vatican Council, and his students and colleagues J. Kleutgen, C. Schrader, and J. B. Franzelin. In this connection it is important to note that the real inspirers of Italian Neo-Thomism, which started at an earlier date than German, L. Taparelli (†1862) and M. Liberatore (†1892), were partly under the influence of rationalism.[62]

Neo-scholasticism, then (and with it also Vatican I), as distinct from high scholasticism, was marked by the spirit not only of the Restoration and Romanticism but also—which has often been overlooked—by the spirit of rationalism, the object, in other respects, of vigorous protests. Only in this way can it be understood why there was so much interest in clear and distinct propositions, in definitions as far-reaching as possible of the Church's official teaching, and a system as "self-contained" as possible. But the leading philosophers of the time had meanwhile progressed far beyond such naïve rationalism.

Vatican I, which took no notice of the new world picture, regarded itself as providing in its definitions a *via media* between rationalism and fideism. This was the attitude behind Chapter Four of the Constitution *On the Catholic Faith,* definitively edited by Kleutgen, the Jesuit mentioned above. This chapter, "On Faith and Reason,"[63] would have been acceptable to Descartes, at least for its definition, in the proper Thomistic spirit, of a twofold order of knowledge: above the natural sphere of natural truths (including the knowledge of the existence of God), which are known by natural reason, there is a supernatural sphere of revealed divine truths, which are mysteries of faith and are known only by divine faith.

3. *Reason as basis of faith?*

Faith and reason do not contradict one another, but—here Descartes would have been more reserved—can provide mutual aid. Reason establishes the foundations of faith and—enlightened by faith—works out the science of theology. Man can know the one true God and Creator with certainty by the natural light of human reason.[64] On the other hand, faith frees reason from errors, protects it, and equips it with manifold knowledge.

Finally the same council—and this likewise is linked with Descartes's *clare et distincte*—also defined papal infallibility: that the Pope as supreme pastor and teacher of the Church can make statements on matters of faith and morals which, in virtue of the special assistance of the Holy Spirit, are *a priori* absolutely true. Thus the attempt was made with the aid of clear and distinct propositions—even infallible propositions—to guarantee and secure for faith that higher certainty which was admitted also by Descartes. This is theology in the sense of Cartesian science: a system—supernaturally secured, of course—of absolutely true propositions, from which all other propositions can be conclusively deduced and which are consequently indirectly also certain.[65] All this is, however, contrary to the intentions of Descartes, who had a horror of speculative theology and—out of respect for faith—just did not want his philosophical method to be applied to theology.

It was entirely logical for the popes after Vatican I to promote Neo-Thomism (tied incidentally to the medieval world view) with all the abundant means of power at their disposal: an encyclical on Aquinas, the nomination of Aquinas as authentic Doctor of the Church and patron of all Catholic schools, a new critical edition of his works, the imposition of twenty-four obligatory, normative philosophical (!) basic theses, the continual threat of sanctions, often cruelly carried out with every means against deviationists (the "modernists" in particular), finally the legal regulation in the Code of Canon Law (1918) that philosophy and theology in Catholic seminaries were to be studied "according to the method, teaching and principles of the Angelic Doctor, St. Thomas Aquinas."[66] This is how heretics become Doctors of the Church.

And Descartes? In the light of the development of Neo-Thomism, it was not surprising that scarcely anyone remembered that Descartes's works were on the Index, and he was treated with benevolence. There was too much in common: not only a similar relationship between reason and faith but, generally, the liking for rational demonstration, strict method, evident foundations, clear and distinct ideas, intellectualism and rationalism. Thus finally Descartes was granted what he had longed for in vain in his lifetime: the admission of his method into the traditionally Thomistic Jesuit schools, from one of which he had himself come. "Because of the fame of the Cartesian method even modern scholastics appeal to the certainty of truth derived from knowledge either of the data of consciousness or of one's own existence."[67] This was what one heard at the Pontifical Gregorian University. Not of course that so universal a doubt can be permitted. That is why a clarification was added at once: the Cartesian method certainly, "but not in the Cartesian sense."[68]

That these clear and distinct definitions of Vatican I—beginning with that of infallibility—and Neo-Thomism were anything but clear and distinct has been visibly demonstrated by the discussions to which they gave rise and particularly by Vatican II together with its effects. But critical questions must now be put especially to Descartes.

### 4. Shattered unity

There are many questions that could be put to Descartes—and indirectly also to Thomism and scholasticism as a whole. It is scarcely possible to distinguish clearly between separate groups of questions as belonging to different planes and systems, as the concern of philosophers or theologians. But we are not attempting here a general criticism of Descartes's philosophy, which is highly complex and remains ambiguous in many respects, even though he himself was able to set out his thought biographically in an exciting and challenging way, as his life's destiny. All that we are attempting is to add a few notes to his philosophy within the scope of the problems relating to faith and reason. Nevertheless, it seems desirable not to start out theologically—"vertically, from above"—but to begin with mainly philosophical questions. And here, too, our main interest is not historical but topical: These questions have often persisted in a form that has scarcely changed even up to the present time—not least in contemporary rationalism, positivism and materialism.

### Split reality

The book of nature is written in mathematical letters; it is the object of that part of mathematics—geometry—that deals with bodies. In his comprehensive mathematical-geometrical world view, Descartes drew the conclusions from the scientific discoveries and insights of Copernicus, Kepler and Galileo. By doing so, he determined the average person's concept of "reality" up to the present time. In the Middle Ages, the main question was expressed in terms of finality: Why does a thing exist? In modern times, it is expressed causally: How does a thing come to be, in what does it consist, and what laws does it obey?

Descartes makes it clear in principle that this world is matter, and matter must be understood as something existing independently. It is not—as in Aristotelian-scholastic philosophy or even in the more or less pantheistic Renaissance philosophy (for instance, of Campanella)—mixed with any kind of indeterminable, obscure, immaterial forces or forms (as when matter and form are said to be the constituent elements of all things) or with concealed quasi-psychological properties or qualities (for instance, the inherent trend in heavy bodies to their "natural place" as the explanation of free fall or even nature's "abhorrence of a vacuum"). But matter must be understood as in modern physics, as structured according to its own strict laws, which are evidently spatiotemporal, quantitative, and therefore mathematically perceptible, purely mechanical laws. Only what can be grasped mathematically can be relied on. Descartes laid the way open for natural science to proceed consistently, restricting itself to what can be quantified and measured. His was the first comprehensive cosmological theory, based admittedly on mechanistic principles. In its *a priori* rational deductions, unrelated to experience, it was frequently abstruse, very inadequate, and often false in its conclusions. It retained its importance for natural science until Isaac Newton's formulation of the principles of classical physics, established empirically by induction and verified (to which both Locke and Kant were oriented). Newton's *hypotheses non fingo* ("I don't make up hypotheses") was directed against Cartesianism—theorizing more than investigating, from astronomy to chemistry—which had already become a new mechanistic scholasticism.

Descartes demands a radical methodical *separation* between the *spatio-temporal-quantitative* on the one hand and the *emotional-mental* on the other. Matter must not be understood multivocally, as formerly, but strictly unequivocally: as (mathematically determinable) extension, extended substance (*res extensa*). It is contrasted with consciousness, with thought in the widest sense of the term, with the thinking substance (*res cogitans*). Matter is matter in extension, spatial matter, occupied space, and therefore there is no space without matter—a view that was soon to be refuted by physics—no empty space, no vacuum. We have thus already discovered the consequences of this distinction, conceptually indeed very clear and in many respects useful for natural science, but doing violence to reality as a whole.

A distinction between consciousness and the spatial existence of things was necessary and helpful. But a separation between thinking substance and extended substance, permitting no gradual transition and no inner unity, was bound to have serious consequences:

a. *for the relationship between body and soul:* Taking the soul out of matter involved a dematerialization of the soul. The *body* must now be understood as matter (to be known), which is constituted by extension, that is, as occupied space: (together with the circulation of the blood and the nervous system) it is the object of mechanics. Life is nothing but spatial movement, the body a machine, biology mechanics. The *soul,* on the other hand, must be understood as (knowing) mind, which is constituted by thinking, in the widest sense of the term, that is, as consciousness, as the self: it is the object of philosophy. Through the mind, which is pure thought, which can abstract from everything, man is free—which, however, means that human freedom is defined merely negatively and remains empty.

Both—body and soul—are therefore absolutely distinct, separate from each other, and they do not have a single attribute in common. They are coordinated merely externally by the Creator, for the preservation of life: united but not one. The *unity* between the two "substances," apparently peculiar to man, thus becomes the great riddle, which is scarcely solved by Descartes. How can a mental and a material principle, a "thinking thing" and an "extended thing," each with completely opposite qualities, form a unity? Can a purely external interaction be sufficient?

In fact, Descartes found himself compelled—contrary to his theory of a clear separation of the two substances—to accept *in the case of man* an interaction between the physical and psychical spheres: one of the weakest points of his philosophy. Oddly enough, the point of intersection was supposed to be the pineal gland, the point in the brain where the soul (present, of course, in the whole body) could be particularly effective. For *animals*, however, the distressing consequence is inescapable: they must be denied consciousness, soul, any psychical element. Their instinctive behavior takes its course systematically without adaptation to changing conditions (as with man—for instance—in his speech): their cries are merely reflexes like the reactions of a spring when released. Animals are merely something extended, a kind of clockwork, soulless machines (*machines animaux*). By comparison, of course, with artificial machines constructed by man, they are higher, better machines, equipped with very much more subtle mainsprings (which can perhaps be found with persistent dissection), since they are produced by the Creator himself, the great mechanic, watchmaker, architect. Here, then, we see the formation of the mental attitude of the pure technician, who has no love for nature, but wants to control it with the aid of his reason. In this century only man is important: apart from Spinoza, the feeling for nature of former times (and later times) is lacking everywhere—even in the theater and the arrangement of gardens.

b. *for the relationship between subject and object:* The dualism between thinking substance (the human mind) and extended substance (the world of bodies) acquires a decisive importance for the modern understanding of reality within the subject-object scheme. The subject as pure thought, surmounting sensation, also lacks sense experience and is estranged from nature. Hence arises that gulf between self-understanding and understanding of the world, between existence and nature, which is characteristic of modern thinking: an interpretation of nature without mind and of mind without nature, an estrangement between the natural sciences and the humanities. Thus reality is torn apart into an unrelated subject and an isolated object, into a worldless subjectivity and an objectivity conceived in terms of single objects. At this point we must also raise the question whether such a separation between subject and object can ever be realized strictly and consistently. Even in natural science, is the object ever known otherwise than in the mode of the subject: that is, never simply objectively, but always subjectively colored—according to the way the question is put, in the light of the method adopted and of the subject's horizon of meaning?

We shall continually be coming across the negative results of this disruption of reality. This Cartesian dualism provides—albeit in differing ways—the starting point for philosophical rationalism and idealism on the one hand and philosophical empiricism, materialism and positivism on the other. But here, too, are the roots of the very questionable separation —admittedly existing from the time of Aquinas—and double-tracking of thinking and faith, philosophy and theology, study and piety, later also of inwardness and outward display, spirituality and materiality, concern for the soul and concern for the world, even, in the last resort, of unworldly belief in God and unbelieving worldliness, of an unreal God and godless reality. Can all the problems emerging here be solved without finding a new, albeit differentiated unity?

## Mathematics as the ideal of truth

Descartes's penetrating distinction between thinking and extended substance, like all simplifications, certainly had its great—particularly methodological—advantages: the purely geometrical, scientific treatment of extended substance (matter) had an enormous influence on the development of scientific and technical thinking. This much must be clearly recognized: only in the light of the mathematical notion of truth was it possible securely and deductively to construct a physics, mechanics, and in the last resort a natural science as a whole, such as the time required. We can calculate with numbers. The conditions of order and measure, investigated by Descartes, which are common to algebra and geometry and made possible his ingenious "analytical geometry," are very close to the modern abstract structural concept of mathematics.

The question remains, however: Clear and distinct as it may seem at first sight and practicable as it has proved to be in mechanistic natural science, does *mathematical truth* provide a basis for the formation of the concept of *truth as such*? Is truth in any case simply the indubitably clear and distinct understanding—for instance—that $2+2=4$? What must first be noted critically here with reference to philosophy we shall afterward find confirmed in a sensational way with reference to mathematics itself.

It cannot be denied that the knowing subject and the object to be known must be seen in their historical context, that objective knowledge is always dependent on the way the question is stated, on the method adopted, and on the standpoint of the subject. This means that any cognitive act establishes its object. An object is only an object when it is the object of a subject. Cognition never means that the object is known simply as it is. Cognition always stresses a particular aspect of reality and leaves many other aspects obscure. It includes and excludes, limits and delimits. Even objective knowledge is historically conditioned, provisional, and in principle never complete. It is to the credit of Immanuel Kant's critique of reason and knowledge that people have come to consider methodically the conditions on which objective knowledge is possible for human reason.

The more abstract the situation in which knowledge occurs, the more clear and distinct this knowledge can be. Mathematical knowledge—at least in the first place—is so clear and distinct because the degree of abstraction is correspondingly high. It is possible, however, to limit and delimit even the most fully living object of knowledge, to fit it in, so to speak—as any spatial object can be fitted in—to geometrical figures. In this way, a mathematical-geometrical clarity and distinctness, is attained; but, as a result of such geometricizing, the living object loses its concreteness and vitality. Any abstraction and reduction for the sake of clarity and distinctness is at the expense of concrete substantiality and fullness. Kant in his day drew attention to the fact that concrete knowledge is richer than mathematical. Clarity and unclarity cannot be so unequivocally distinguished in real life. There is a continual transition from the obscurity to the clarity of the image, with infinitely many degrees and stages.

In his demand for clarity and distinctness, Descartes started out from a naïve, static conception of subject and object. He had not considered the historical dynamism either of the object or of the subject. After Kant, it was mainly Hegel who drew attention to the dubiousness of such a staticism and separation of object and subject and demanded instead a dialectical knowledge of the truth which would attempt to do justice to the dynamism of object and subject (which cannot be separated in knowledge).[69] What is meant by dynamism of the object? What I know is not something that passes by as in a vehicle, but it is moved in itself and is therefore quite unlike the geometricized Cartesian object. What is meant by dynamism of the subject? I myself, I who know, am not unmoved, not static like the camera on its stand, but in my knowing I am moved myself in harmony with the moving object.

Knowledge and science can do justice to this unending dynamism of subject and object only by being involved in the whole movement and by not clinging to apparently manifest, fixed definitions and clear theses. This is what rationalism does—and truly not only that of Descartes but also that of Neo-Thomism—and it therefore fails completely to see reality in all its historical vitality, animation, concreteness, fullness. For Hegel, therefore, it was not a mere fancy or a game with the number three when his circling thought advanced in both small things and great in triple steps (or in a triangular movement). Behind it lay the basic insight—which has never been forgotten since that time—that I cannot state the truth absolutely clearly and distinctly merely in *one* sentence, but really need three, dialectically affirming, denying, surpassing: this is how it is, and yet not so, in fact there is more to it. And so on. In this sense truth lies in the totality, not in the individual steps, theses, propositions or elements of which it is made up.

The criticism expressed in regard to clarity as the ideal of science is not meant to deny the importance of a critically considered *striving for clarity*, without which not only natural science but also philosophy and theology would be abandoned to confusion and destruction. But no amount of striving for clarity will provide philosophy and theology with the kind of clarity that mathematics and the particular sciences based on a division of labor can offer in their own fields, as long as the latter take as given at least the object and mode of investigation without further questioning. There are several kinds of certainty, dependent in each case on the particular source. The certainty of mathematics or of natural science is merely an abstract, limited and relative certainty. It is not to be regarded as absolute.

We shall return later to the questions arising from positivism, analytic philosophy and critical rationalism. For the moment, we need only point out that there is a difference between philosophy and theology striving for the clarity and distinctness that is possible in their propositions, and their claiming that their propositions exhibit a definitive clarity and distinctness, that a quasi-mathematical evidence and certainty have been attained. There is a difference between attempting to grasp their material at every point in precise concepts and putting it on ice in clear propositions. There is a difference between clearly indicating the obscurities and incomprehensibilities and thus being able to state clearly what is unclear and, on the other hand, refusing to admit obscurities and incomprehensibilities and thus attempting to remove them by unclear distinctions. There is a difference between wrestling for the truth while remaining open to the greater truth of the future and—by claiming to know everything—shutting up the truth and oneself in the golden cage of a closed system, tied now to the present and soon to be tied to the past. In brief, there is a difference as to whether philosophy and theology in particular are committed to the clarity of rationality or to the pseudo clarity of rationalism.

## Consistent mathematics?

Rationalism has very recently discovered its limitations not only in philosophy and theology but—surprisingly enough—in mathematics itself. The very notion of mathematical truth has itself become questionable.

Among mathematicians, there is now a saying that God exists, because mathematics contains no contradictions; and the devil exists, because it cannot be proved that there are no contradictions.

It was only late, about two hundred years after Descartes's death, that mathematics reached an earth-shaking crisis which deprived mathematicians—despite numerous further successes in detail—of the confidence that they would really attain to truth with the aid of mathematics. Up to that point its progress had seemed constant, rectilinear and unstoppable. And its application to gravitational astronomy, acoustics, optics, electricity, and indeed to all branches of natural science and technology had produced truly fantastic successes for modern man. Why should Descartes's dream of a universal science of mathematics not have become reality? The great philosopher and mathematician Gottfried Wilhelm von Leibniz, invoking the medieval polymath Raymond Lulle (particularly the latter's *Ars Magna*), who in turn had been influenced by the Arab mathematicians, had worked at a uniform mathematical language and postulated "a characteristic of reason in virtue of which the truths of reason would be attainable up to a point by calculation, just as in arithmetic and algebra, so too in any other field where conclusions are reached by inference."[70]

Modern mathematical logic, which emerged in the nineteenth century, attempted to realize the Cartesian-Leibnizian idea and thus became involved in increasing difficulties. *Set theory*, produced by Georg Cantor (1854–1918), fundamental to modern mathematics, shattered in the second half of the nineteenth century the consistency and incontestability of mathematics. For the further development of set theory led to *antinomies*, paradoxes, contradictions: certain statements connected with the concept of infinity could be mathematically both proved *and* refuted. We may cite as an example the famous logical-mathematical antinomy of the "set of all ordinal numbers" (according to Russell and Burali-Forti). To every set of ordinal numbers there exists an ordinal number greater than all the ordinal numbers occurring in that set. Consider the set of *all* ordinal numbers: the corresponding ordinal number must lie *outside* that set (for it is as such greater than all the members of the set); but—and this can be proved immediately—it must lie *inside* the set (for this is the set of *all* ordinal numbers). Thus coping with the numerous logical-mathematical and also linguistic (semantic and syntactic) antinomies brought on a crisis in the foundations of mathematics. Attempts were made to cope with it by various methods or modes of thought, so that finally three different standard interpretations—each consistent in itself but contradicting the rest—and at the same time three schools of mathematics emerged: logicism (J. G. Frege, Bertrand Russell, A. N. Whitehead), intuitionism (L. E. J. Brouwer), formalism (D. Hilbert, H. Weyl). Neither logicism—which traces mathematics back to logic—nor intuitionism (constructivism)—which attempts to construct logic in the light of certain basic mathematical insights—nor, finally, formalism—which strives to develop both logic and mathematics in a purely formal way—has been able to prevail hitherto.

Hence, according to the mathematician Hans Hermes, "in view of the great role which mathematics plays in our modern world picture," it is in fact "of considerable philosophical interest that mathematicians have shown by purely mathematical methods that there are mathematical problems which cannot be treated with the tool of mathematical calculation."[71] Following E. L. Post, Hermes speaks of limits imposed by the laws of nature on man's power of mathematicizing: of a "law of nature on the limitations of the mathematicizing power of *Homo sapiens*."[72]

Today therefore mathematicians themselves are demanding a "mathematics without illusions": "We might find cause for regret in the present state of mathematics. Its claim to truth has had to be abandoned. Efforts to eliminate its paradoxes and to establish the consistency of its structure have hitherto failed. There is no longer any agreement on the axioms to be used. Without counting the variety of algebras and geometries, the fact must now be accepted that we are free to appeal to the axiom of our choice and to the hypothesis of the continuum or to reject them. From these different possible choices equally diverse mathematical systems can arise. There is disagreement now even on the methods of argument. . . . The assumption of flawless reasoning must be abandoned. Finally, the prevailing concept of mathematics as a collection of superstructures, each founded on its own set of axioms, is incapable of including everything that mathematics ought to include. . . . Since the diversity of algebras and geometries was recognized over a century ago, each has had to choose for himself. Shrewd mathematicians knew what to choose."[73]

The question of the ultimate foundations and the ultimate meaning of mathematics, then, remains open today. For the time being we do not know in what direction to look for the definitive solution or whether a definitive answer can be found at all. "Perhaps mathematics is a creative activity like language or music, essentially original and whose historical decisions defy a complete, objective rationalization."[74]

For everyday mathematics the basic questions may be as unimportant as basic philosophical questions for human life. Calculation continues and truly—in both pure and applied mathematics—with impressive successes. Natural science and technology live on it. One thing, however, is important for our problems here: as a result of the crisis, the universal claims of mathematical-scientific thought have been shaken to their foundations. If the concept of mathematical truth itself has become questionable, the orientation of any kind of science to the ideal of mathematical truth can scarcely be justified. The result, then, of our mathematical reflection is the same as that of our philosophical reflection: today less than ever is there any excuse for making mathematical method and mathematical truth into absolutes.

## Conclusive proof of God?

Descartes's ingenious proofs of God, drawn not from the cosmos but from the human subject, from human consciousness, have been criticized in a variety of ways in the course of the history of philosophy. Rightly enough, the causal argument has come in for less criticism than the ontological. Two brief observations may be made on these:

a. *On the causal argument.* Even Descartes's contemporaries objected that the proof of God appealing to clear and distinct knowledge is in the last resort not conclusive but rests on a vicious circle. The Jansenist Arnauld explained his criticism in this way: "My sole misgiving is that I cannot see how he avoids a vicious circle when he says that, unless God exists, we cannot be certain that the things we perceive clearly and distinctly are true. But on the other hand we cannot be certain that God exists unless this is clearly and evidently perceived by us; therefore, before we can be certain that God exists, we must be certain that whatever is clearly and evidently perceived by us is true."[75] In his response, Descartes proved convincingly that his argument was not circular: the *cogito* is not dependent on the existence of God. But does this mean that God's existence is proved?

b. *On the ontological argument.* The conclusion from the idea of the perfect being to its real existence is scarcely convincing today. From Kant's time particularly, the objection has continually been raised that from the concept of God we can conclude only to the possibility and not to the reality of God. In just the same way, we can conclude from the concept of a hundred thalers merely to the possibility and not to the reality of a hundred thalers. Here, too, contemporaries—like Caterus, who appeals to Aquinas—recognize the weakness of this argument: "Even if it is granted that the very notion of a supremely perfect being implies existence, it does not follow that this existence is actually something in the nature of things, but only that the concept of existence is inseparably connected with the concept of a supreme being."[76] The ontological argument remained convincing only as long as a Platonic-Augustinian realism of ideas could be assumed: that is, on the assumption that ideas had a reality of their own. For Descartes the idea was by no means a mere thought, an empty term, "only" a concept, but reality. From that standpoint it was of course possible to conclude from the reality of the idea to the reality of existence.

Evidently it is easier to reach certainty of the self from a certainty of God presupposed by faith than conversely to gain certainty of God from a philosophically proved certainty of the self. But this is connected with Descartes's definition of the relations between faith and reason as a whole. On this, again, we must raise some critical questions within the wider historical context.

Two floors? Aquinas and the consequences

A *new appreciation of reason* in relation to faith, of "natural" truth in relation to revealed truth, of philosophy in relation to theology, had begun to make its way as early as the high *Middle Ages:*

introduced in the twelfth century by the acceptance in Europe of *Aristotle,* who had hitherto been known only indirectly to medieval scholars but was now becoming rapidly known—despite ecclesiastical prohibitions—through translations from the Greek and through the mediation of Arab-Jewish philosophy, and was finally made compulsory reading;

provoked by the unavoidable controversy with a more advanced *Arab-Jewish philosophy,* especially with the strong defender of the autonomy of reason and philosophy as against the absolute claims of Islamic religion, "the commentator" *tout court* on Aristotle, the Arab Averroës, from Córdoba;

supported by the universities now beginning to flourish—especially in Paris and Oxford but also in other, recently founded universities—and by the scholarly involvement of the religious orders in competition with the secular clergy and with each other.

It became increasingly impossible to appeal in matters of faith solely to authority (the Bible, the Fathers of the Church, councils or popes—often mutually contradictory). If clarity was to be achieved, it had to be by making bold use of reason and conceptual analysis. And this in fact was what was done with considerable objectivity and logical acumen, even though frequently uncritically and with an unhistorical interpretation of authoritative statements. In the new situation, therefore, it was a historical necessity for Albert the Great, philosopher, theologian and natural scientist, to assist in the establishment of Aristotle—the greatest Greek philosopher after Plato. The result was a new universality of interest, a new autonomy of thought, a new preoccupation with natural science.

And it was even more a historical necessity for Albert's disciple, likewise a Dominican, *Thomas Aquinas,* as intermediary between the ancient Platonic-Augustinian tradition and the new Aristotelianism, to create with great boldness and objectivity a new synthesis for the new age: ingeniously devised, with methodical strictness and didactic shrewdness, thitherto unparalleled in its unity and integrity, in the form of *two* Summas, one philosophical-theological against the Arabs, the "pagans" (*Summa Contra Gentiles*), and the other theological-philosophical for the Christian faith (*Summa Theologiae*).

Under the influence of Aristotle, knowledge gained by human reason was now evaluated quite differently from formerly: as against faith it has its own autonomy, its own laws and its own field of action. An enormous craving for knowledge, for learning, had been roused. Formerly reason had been proved to be justified alongside faith; now—as Aquinas explained in the Introductions to the two Summas—faith had to be justified alongside reason. It was clear to Aquinas that philosophy had its own justification, from the very nature of the order of creation, and not by permission of the Church.

This philosophical-theological system of Aquinas, however, owed much more than most Thomists even today will admit to the *Greek world picture*. This picture, Aquinas took over almost uncritically (even the idea of the generation of man by man and the sun): the four elements of which all mixed bodies consist; the seven planets (including sun and moon) moved and guided (if not directly animated) by pure spirits (angels); finally, the three heavens. All these made up a perfect world order, unchangeable from beginning to end, strictly hierarchical, with grades of being rising upward in increasing perfection, geocentric (oriented to the earth) and anthropocentric (planned wholly with reference to man). With the aid of the Platonic idea of an immutable, static order of things, an all-embracing interpretation of the world emerged in the light of the Christian faith and at the same time a complete interpretation of the faith in the light of the geocentric world view. The Bible is understood cosmically and the cosmos biblically; Christian faith guarantees the world picture and the world picture guarantees Christian faith. Theology and cosmology, the order of salvation and the order of the world, appear to be in perfect harmony. Medieval theology is determined by the Graeco-medieval world picture down to the last detail: knowledge of God from the order of creation, a widely accepted astrology, a hierarchy of angels corresponding to the heavenly spheres, the number of the elect (replacing the fallen angels), the origin and nature of man as consisting in body and soul, original state and original sin, descent of Christ from heaven to earth and to the underworld and his ascension to heaven, grace and seven sacraments, hierarchical order in Church and state, an ethic of order and obedience, end of the world and bodily resurrection. But what will become of this medieval theology when the medieval cosmology, so closely linked with it, breaks down as a result of the Copernican revolution?[77]

Nevertheless, at least for the next two centuries, this finely balanced synthesis between reason and faith, nature and grace, philosophy and theology, secular and spiritual power, persisted. At the same time, it was clear what was subordinated to what. Aquinas was a medieval man not only in the light of his world picture but also of his faith: for him it was a natural assumption that reason is subordinated to faith, nature to grace, philosophy to theology, state to Church. Nothing in the lower sphere, in philosophy or other sciences, would or could ever contradict a truth of the higher sphere.

But the tension of this wholly Christian medieval synthesis was very heavily charged, and a dynamic historical development unleashed a thitherto unparalleled, all-embracing *movement of secularization and emancipation*. The latter was by no means a movement of apostasy from the Christian faith. But in the end—contrary to the intentions of those who prepared and unleashed it—it found expression in the revolt of what had now become the autonomous "natural" basis of reason against the "supernatural" superstructure of the Christian faith, and thus burst open the comprehensive synthesis of reason and faith. For the autonomy of a neutral order of nature and reason—made possible even in the Middle Ages with the aid of Aristotelian philosophy—led by way of humanism and the Renaissance and indirectly also by way of the Reformation to the emergence of modern autonomous man, of his science and philosophy, of his natural law and autonomous ethics: in other words, precisely to the emergence of that autonomy that Descartes for the first time attempted to substantiate, independently of Christian faith, consistently in philosophical terms, on the basis of the thinking individual's certainty of himself.

What was the consequence of all this for the relationship between subject and object, reason and faith? Subject and object—as we saw—were torn apart and existed unconnected alongside each other: there was a cleavage between self-understanding and understanding of the world, between interiorized piety and exteriorized worldliness. Subsequently reason and faith were narrowed down, became isolated, separated from each other and became appreciably more dogmatic: on the one side there was a dogmatic refusal to know, a claim to know better or even to know everything, on the part of an unbelieving rationality, and on the other, dogmatic belief in authority, belief in the Bible, belief in the Church, on the part of an anti-rational piety.

The way was thus open for the *philosophie des lumières*, the "Enlightenment": the belief in enlightenment by the light of a reason that had now become autonomous and opposed to all traditional belief in authority; the strongest European intellectual movement since the Reformation; the expression of a new rational-optimistic-active awareness of life. According to Kant's classic definition, the Enlightenment was "man's emergence from his self-inflicted tutelage."[78] It became established first in tolerant Holland, where Descartes had found hospitality (Spinoza, Bekker, Bayle), and in England (Locke, Newton), then in France in a sharp confrontation with the Church (Voltaire, the Encyclopedists), and finally in less aggressive forms in Germany (Leibniz, Thomasius, Wolff, Lessing). Order, hierarchy, authority, discipline, Church, dogma, faith, still highly esteemed in the seventeenth century, came to be detested in the eighteenth. As formerly educated men had followed Bossuet, now they came to think like Voltaire. The great controversy had begun on God, Providence, authority, the foundations of morality and social life, on Christian faith and rational "natural religion," traditional theology and autonomous philosophy.

What had been wholly and entirely affirmed in the Christian synthesis

of Aquinas was respected by Descartes, even if he remained cool and aloof,
but completely neglected by some of his successors on the left. Those who
were busy in the substructure came increasingly to the conclusion that it
was possible to live and work quite well within this substructure and that
they were not really dependent on the superstructure. Descartes had provided new and better foundations for the substructure, but, out of
religious and traditional motives, left the superstructure unshaken, although weakly supported, and always respected it. He was, however,
scarcely interested in its renewal. This attitude could not fail to be noticed, and his successors simply drew the obvious conclusions: the superstructure is unimportant for the substructure and in any case in philosophical terms absolutely irrelevant. But here we must put some questions
to Descartes, which might be turned back in a different form also to
Aquinas.

a. *With reference to the superstructure:* Descartes's theory of two floors
implies conclusions that he himself did not want to draw or even to
admit. And anyway, if in the light of his own consciousness man can erect
such a solid foundation for his knowledge and action, in fact a whole
structure of knowledge and even a universal science, why should he want
any more? Why should he not resolutely and consistently cast off all the
prejudices of faith and rid himself of all authority in order to live solely
by the light of pure reason, where everything will turn out well. Why
should a rational person like this want to be a Christian at all? Being a
Christian really seems to be a superfluous appendage, an external attribute, an irrational superstructure of man's existence.

To be more precise, cannot such a rational person be religious in his
own way? Does not self-confident modern man know, by reason, of
God's existence, even of his goodness, truthfulness and other important
attributes: all as a result of his own original rational analysis? This God of
the philosophers he has in common even with non-Christians. Why
should he have any need, then, of the God of Abraham, Isaac and Jacob,
the Father of Jesus Christ? Would it not be logical to follow up the methodical dissociation—which functions so well—with a real dissociation
from the biblical God?

Why, then, should an intelligent person take refuge in mysteries of
faith and in faith's certainty, when he knows all that is essential from his
own resources? Is not the truth of faith, which is supposed to produce for
us a "higher" certainty of faith, so "dark" for our understanding that it
can be accepted only under the influence of grace and by a sheer act of
blind will? Is it not therefore something wholly arbitrary in itself, behind
whose deficiencies of clearness and distinctness there may lurk a banality
or an absurdity or even—as in Descartes's own hypothesis—an evil spirit?
Is not all this more of an illusion than a higher certainty? In virtue of his
method of universal doubt, should not our philosopher, anyway, have

questioned also the authority of the Church, of the state, of faith, of individual articles of faith, instead of simply allowing them to remain precariously existing, unquestioned and uncomprehended?

And finally, have we not a kind of negative confirmation of the suspicion that there is nothing real behind the truth of faith when even the existence of a God of the philosophers can scarcely be convincingly proved from isolated human consciousness? Have we not someone here who has methodically investigated whether it is possible to do without God and has involuntarily made it clear that all goes well for the man who is certain of himself even without God: not only without the God of the philosophers but even more without the God of the Bible, without any faith, Church, theology, Christianity at all?

There were not a few at that time who were quick to draw the obvious conclusions. Certainly the relevance of these questions needs no commentary. And the following questions are equally relevant.

b. *With reference to the substructure:* "Common sense is the best distributed thing in the world," says Descartes—ironically, as so often?—at the opening of the first part of his *Discours de la méthode*. This provokes questions in the opposite direction. What is the situation on the lower plane, the plane of reason? Is everything there as rational as it ought to be in the light of Descartes's conception of reason? Is man actually nothing but thought? Even if we leave aside the unconscious, can even consciousness as a whole be reduced to thinking? Undoubtedly, Descartes's assimilation of the soul to consciousness has made its mark on the modern concept of psychology. But does not consciousness include in addition to and together with rational thinking also willing and feeling, imagination and temperament, emotions and passions, which just cannot be attributed rationalistically to pure reason, but have their own reality, often opposed to reason? Can truth, then, be known truly only *more mathematico*, so that whatever is less clear and distinct is *a priori* uninteresting? Does not a dogmatic hubris of reason—which in the last resort perhaps also rests on irrational grounds—create a false self-assurance and a blindness in regard to the total reality of the world and man?

Consequently the question may be raised: Cannot even that truth which was known clearly and distinctly in an abstract and general way become utterly obscure and indistinct in a particular situation on the plane of concrete existence? Are there not people who perceive their existence more or less clearly and distinctly in the midst of doubt and yet deny that existence—people who are aware of the reality of their existence even while they are doubting, but cannot accept themselves? I doubt, but what I am may still not be true; I do not merely doubt, I despair; and therefore the saying could be given a nihilistic turn: *cogito, ergo NON sum*. And this occasionally may be understood radically and even carried out in suicide.

From this aspect of concrete existence, is it not in the first place a question of being or not being, of life or death? Was the path of methodic doubt not a very narrow track, the path—that is—of intellectual, conceptual certainty? Would not someone actually radically doubting be bound to doubt precisely this certainty? Would he not therefore have to begin at a much deeper level and ask not only about the truth of our rational thinking but about the rationality of reason as a whole? Not only about overcoming doubt but about overcoming despair? Not only about the reality of God and the world but about the reality of one's own existence as experienced in doubting and thinking? Can modern man, in particular, still reach certainty in the Cartesian, intellectual way?

But at this point we can break off. In the concrete, even in his philosophy, was not Descartes engaged in practice, rather than theoretical reflection? In the concrete situation, did he not act even when he did not by any means see clearly and distinctly, even when he was not absolutely certain what was the right thing to do? In practice did he not assume the rationality of reason from the very beginning? Prior to and in the midst of all his doubting, did he not trust in the truth and certainty that he was absolutely intent on establishing by his methodic doubt? Did not doubt produce truth as its fruit only because that doubt was rooted in the truth from the very beginning? Did not Descartes accept his existence before he perceived it afresh as a result of his doubt? Did he not already believe in the existence of God before he began to prove it? Had he not an enormous confidence in reality as a whole, which itself made possible his radical, universal, methodic doubt and made it seem meaningful to him? Were not all his doubting and thinking, his intuitions and deductions, permeated by an *a priori*, a *prior confidence*, which he took for granted in practice? And was he not able to practice this confidence so obviously because he knew that he was protected precisely as a thinker by that Christian faith which he would never have exchanged—as Karl Jaspers would have wanted him to do[79]—for a universal "philosophical faith"? *In practice*, then, it was a question less of reason as a presupposition of faith than of faith as a presupposition of reason. Paradoxically enough, Descartes's everyday practice seems to us to lead to the opposite of his own theory. And perhaps it is all this which makes him seem to some people so enigmatic and inconsistent: simultaneously a freethinker hostile to authority and a loyal churchman supporting authority, skeptic and Christian, Protestant philosopher and devout Catholic, rational and yet not wholly rational, a philosopher behind a mask.

This much at least has become clear: conceptual certainty, however methodically sought, is still a long way from existential security. In his new certainty, Descartes had a genuine sense of mission and even of victory. He was absolutely convinced that he was in possession of the truth and became passionately involved—which some interpreted as ambition and will to power—on behalf of his philosophy of certainty, which for all its novelty he regarded as conclusively valid for everyone. Highly honored by the Queen of Sweden, he expected to return home from Stockholm as a victor to his fatherland. But this did not happen. It was not until sixteen years after his death that his body was brought back to Paris and buried at Sainte Geneviève du Mont. On his tombstone are the words: *In otiis hibernis componens mysteria naturae cum legibus matheseos, utriusque arcana eadem clavi reserare posse ausus est sperare* ("On quiet winter nights he would discover parallels between nature's mysteries and the laws of mathematics and look boldly forward to the time when one and the same key might unlock the secrets of both").

Was his hope—or ours—fulfilled? At least the state of the question has become clear and distinct. But, for all that we have learned from Descartes, a number of essential questions remain unanswered. Perhaps, then, we shall make more progress if—without forgetting Descartes—we proceed watchfully on another path, under the guidance of his great contemporary and antipode, Blaise Pascal, for whom all these questions became questions of life and destiny.

# II. I believe; do I therefore exist?
## Blaise Pascal

Certainty of knowledge is a long way from security of life. Not that we need to be always looking death in the face. By thinking, by clear and distinct thinking, it is possible—perhaps—to gain conceptual certainty, but never existential security. And "pure" mathematics in particular, with its absolute certainty, often contributes—as soon as it is "applied"—as much to the insecurity as to the security of human life. When modern "pure" mathematics especially—in its innumerable applications to new weapons and techniques, including the atom bomb—becomes so to speak "impure," the contradictions between conceptual-mathematical certainty and existential (and social) security become crystal clear: contradictions that have led to great suffering for many besides Albert Einstein and Robert Oppenheimer (to mention only two prominent individuals). This is a problem that became increasingly urgent from the time when it became clear that not only mathematics and natural science but every science— from formal logic to theology—can become an applied science and thus an exercise of power.

## 1. The relativity of mathematical certainty

Four years after Descartes's memorable enlightenment and his discernment of the possibility of a *science admirable*, the second great mathematical-philosophical genius of this epoch was born. Blaise Pascal (1623–62) might have been the greatest Cartesian of them all, if only he had not already shown as an infant prodigy that his talents were far from being restricted to a gift for geometry. Within him the *homo mathematicus* of the exact sciences was in conflict with the *homo religiosus* of the Christian faith. He matured early and wore himself out quickly, dying completely exhausted at thirty-nine. But it was precisely this discordant existence which made Pascal—even more than Descartes—the prototype of modern man.

### Convergences and divergences

Among the great men of seventeenth-century France, it would be impossible to find two who were at once so similar and so dissimilar as Descartes and Pascal. It may throw light on problems that are still pressing even today if we briefly outline these resemblances and differences.

Like Descartes, Pascal was a genius as a mathematician, as a physicist and as an engineer. Like Descartes also, he was a modern man of the world, a brilliant man of letters and a profound thinker.

He was a *mathematician* of genius. His father and tutor wanted to keep him away from mathematics, so that he could concentrate first on Latin and Greek. But his elder sister Gilberte gives a detailed account of the twelve-year-old boy drawing triangles and circles in charcoal on the tiles in his spare time and thus working out independently the basic laws of geometry, being surprised by his father when he was proving the thirty-second proposition of Euclid.[1] The story has been dismissed as a legend, but it is not at all improbable and there are other achievements which are certainly not mere legends.

At the age of sixteen he was recognized as one of the leading mathematicians of his time when he developed in an essay on conic sections what came to be known as "Pascal's Theorem," or the "mystic hexagram": the opposite sides of a hexagon inserted in the circumference of a circle meet at three points which are a straight line (the "Pascal line"). At a later stage, prompted by observation of dice playing and dice players, he contributed in a variety of works to the foundation of the calculus of probabilities, which is important today for all possible sciences from atomic physics to actuarial theory. He conceived his *Histoire du roulette* during a night when he was kept awake with a raging toothache, reflecting on the problem of the cycloid (the curve described by a point on the rim of a wheel as it moves forward) and coming close to the discovery of the infinitesimal calculus (calculation with infinitely small units). It was in the margin of his copy of the *Roulette* that Leibniz recorded his first thoughts on the infinitesimal calculus, which he worked out independently of Newton and about ten years after the latter.

He was a *physicist* of genius. It was, again, at the age of twelve that Pascal wrote his essay on acoustics (*Traité des sons*) after noting that the sound emitted by a pewter plate when struck by a spoon stopped as soon as he touched the plate with his finger. Over ten years later, after receiving an incomplete account of the attempts by Torricelli—a student of Galileo's—to measure the pressure of air, he carried out an experiment in an improved and much more varied and controlled form. As a result of this and other crucial experiments with a tube of mercury (later called a barometer), he produced an irrefutable proof of the existence of empty space (a fact previously disputed on account of nature's supposed abhorrence of a vacuum). He stated the result as a general law (that liquid and air are to be treated as mobile substances) and formulated the theory of hydrostatic equilibrium. After all that, he went on to invent the hydraulic press and put it to practical use.

He was an *engineer* of genius. He invented not only the hydraulic press but—at the age of nineteen—also the first calculating machine to function, in order to help his father, a very busy tax commissioner in Richelieu's service. He obtained a patent for the model, the prototype of our computer, which he had produced in more than fifty variations in the course of two years of intensive work. He printed prospectuses and made plans for production in bulk but failed at this point because of the lack of capable mechanics and because of the high costs of production. It is not surprising that the man who invented the calculating machine and conducted the sensational air-pressure experiments on the summit of Puy de Dôme, near his home town, Clermont-Ferrand, was called the "young Archimedes" of Paris. Even in his last years, he worked out a plan for bus traffic across greater Paris and founded his own bus company with coachmen driving the buses at a charge of five *sous* for each passenger—all of which increased his fame even more than the calculating machine had.

He was a modern *man of the world*. Like Descartes, he came from a wealthy family, managing his father's property shrewdly to the end, and he had access in Paris to exclusive social circles. His charming younger sister, Jacqueline, also regarded as an infant prodigy because of her poems, appeared in a play performed by children in Richelieu's presence and thus regained the latter's favor for her father, who had fallen into disgrace after opposing the Cardinal Minister's financial policy. It was on the same occasion that Pascal came to the notice of Richelieu. More important to Pascal, however, was the circle—somewhere between a family and a learned society—of men of various callings who met together regularly—in an age before the organization of natural science—under the leadership of the always friendly, devout Marin Mersenne, a member of the strict order of Minims (founded by St. Francis of Paola in 1435), to discuss all possible problems of geometry, physics, literature, philosophy and theology.

Mersenne endeavored to combine Christian faith with geometry and, although he stood up for Galileo, Campanella and Descartes, was not challenged by either political or ecclesiastical authorities. Possessed of encyclopedic knowledge, he kept up a lively, learned correspondence with scholars of all kinds in the whole of Europe: from Torricelli, in Italy, to the English philosopher Thomas Hobbes and the Dutch mathematician, physicist and astronomer Christian Huygens (famous for his wave theory of light and the invention of the pendulum clock, the latter being admired as a wonder of the world and a model of the world machine produced by the Divine Clockmaker). To Pascal it seemed quite natural, at the age of sixteen, to be accepted by this circle. But, at the same time, his manifold social connections brought him into contact with such notorious *libertins* as Antoine Gombaud, Chevalier de Méré, who advocated religious indifference and propagated and exemplified the ideal of the *honnête homme*. It was De Méré who impressed Pascal with the importance of Montaigne's *Essais*. Like Descartes, Pascal was regarded as a man of wit and taste, skeptical in regard to customs and prejudices.

He was a brilliant *man of letters*. Although neither (nor even Molière) was a member of Richelieu's recently founded Académie Française, Pascal together with Descartes did more than anyone else at the time to contribute to the renown of French prose, particularly academic prose, which is distinguished, by its simplicity and elegance, from the complicated and obscure style too often adopted by scholars elsewhere even today. The works of Descartes and Pascal—who both also wrote good Latin—became classics of the French language, bearing the stamp of an instinctive literary and aesthetic assurance, the result of the great care taken by the authors to give form to their ideas and to strive continually for readability. Pascal's terse, vivid style was in fact that of one who was both scholar and poet: it combines clarity and rhythm, precision and poetry, and appeals at once to head and heart. His writings on mathematics and physics are distinguished by the same admirable lucidity and smooth brilliance as his writing on philosophy and theology. His *Pensées* are among the most important works of world literature. But more especially as an often merciless polemicist and pamphletist, making use of every means of irony, wit and satire, he had no equal in his day: a model for Voltaire, who described Pascal's *Lettres Provinciales* as the "first book to be written by a genius of prose." Pascal was regarded then as the "first journalist" of French literature—which is high praise in that country, where good stylists even in science are admired.

He was a profound *thinker*. Like Descartes, Pascal produced few books and, after his very private education by his father, he enjoyed the utmost freedom and was not tied to any particular calling or mission. Like Descartes, he possessed an extraordinary gift for analytic discrimination, which was made even more effective by his brilliant use of language. Like Descartes, he had a positive passion for thinking: "Man is only a reed, . . . but he is a thinking reed."[2] Consequently he largely shares the Cartesian dualism in regard to mind and matter, soul and body. Like Descartes, Pascal also despised scholasticism, considering that the Bible had no more authority than Aristotle's physics in modern physics. But also like Descartes, he found himself confronted as an apologist by *libertins*, freethinkers and atheists. And like Descartes, he had a flair for tracking down the problems of man, and in this respect he advanced perhaps farther than the former to the ultimate ground of human existence.

It is at this very point that *divergences* appear. They bring out clearly the difference between these contemporaries, despite all their similarities.

When geniuses meet, it is not always the signal for displays of mental lightning: human sympathy is one of the conditions for understanding. When the great "geometer" in Holland, Pascal's elder by a generation, heard of the "mystic hexagram" of the infant prodigy in France, he remarked somewhat coolly that the father must have discovered it. Nevertheless, urged by their mutual friend Mersenne, the noble Descartes (both he and Pascal were sons of ennobled officials), during one of his rare visits to Paris, on September 23, 1647, together with Roberval—the mathematician of the University of Paris—and a large retinue, was brought to the young genius—very sickly even then but completely self-confident. But Professor Roberval thrust himself forward in the conversation and Descartes had to leave for a dinner, having time only to advise Pascal as a patient to use his own prescription: long sleep in the mornings followed by a cup of broth. But next day he returned, alone. He was particularly interested in Pascal's air-pressure experiments, especially in the problem of the vacuum: there seemed to be no place for a vacuum in the Cartesian world, which consisted everywhere of extended and—where necessary—very fine matter.

He was distrustful, and Pascal remained cautious. They were not enemies, but neither did they become friends. But there was certainly mutual respect and perhaps also admiration. For his large-scale series of very varied experiments, stretching over months, Pascal had the considerable resources of his father at his disposal and made known the results gradually in booklets generally intelligible to the admiring public; he was undoubtedly much more important as experimenter, organizer, constructor and also as writer. Was the older man jealous of the very successful, spoiled young man? Certainly this played a part. At any rate, Descartes claimed in the following year that he had anticipated the great barometer experiment on Puy de Dôme. The question of who was first became an occasion for continual disputes at that time among aspiring scholars in the still largely unworked field of natural science. Descartes claimed that he had advised Pascal to make the experiments with the mercury tube simultaneously in the valley and on the mountain, in order to prove that the height of the column of mercury was dependent on the column of air resting on it. Pascal vigorously disputed the claim.

Was it, then, a question of jealousy? Certainly not merely that. Here were two men who belonged to the same period, the same country, working in the same fields of knowledge, whose lives admittedly did not run parallel with each other but converged, drew toward each other and then —not finding a point of intersection—diverged again, drew away from each other. Why? What were the essential reasons for these divergences?

## The logic of the heart

In mathematics, physics and philosophy, Descartes is the man of method. He had been educated methodically and systematically in the Jesuit college (in classical literature, natural science, mathematics, philosophy) and he remained methodical throughout his life. He followed a daily rhythm in his life which was always the same, maintaining imperturbably a balance between the claims of mind and body. He investigated methodically first the world and then his own self. He devoted his first publications to the question of method. He was concerned with practice oriented to learning. He left nothing to chance. He avoided difficulties. He needed to be undisturbed, to lead a life without conflict. He proceeded step by step from problem to problem, always resolutely keeping the whole scheme in mind, and thus developed his method into a system. He crowned his work in philosophy and natural science with a comprehensive synthesis.

Pascal, coming between two sisters (their mother died three years after his birth), educated entirely at home, was in both life and learning a man of deep feeling: feeling in the best and broadest sense, of profound experience, sensitivity, endurance, of suffering and passion. From youth onward he was frail and, after his hectic two years' work on his calculating machine, when he was just twenty-one, he had his first breakdown: from then onward he scarcely spent a single day free from pain. A complex genius of the utmost bodily and mental sensitivity, he not only did not refuse suffering but accepted and even heightened it, finally almost pathologically bringing on his own suffering. Far from frightening him, difficulties only spurred him on to deeper involvement. Even in mathematics and physics he was passionately involved, but he always maintained an unerring scientific objectivity; he could work on arithmetical or geometrical problems or at his calculating machine like someone possessed. This man, who never attended school or university but had received his education from his highly cultured father, was interested only in great, difficult, "insoluble" problems; he rushed from one question to another without working out a total plan, even in mathematics and experimentation relying independently on the inspiration of the moment. Given more to aphorisms than to systems, he scarcely bothered about a comprehensive synthesis. It is true that toward the end of his life he was continually making notes for a large philosophical-theological work, but after his death all that was found was a large pile of slips of paper and half pages, snatches of ideas, smaller or larger fragments. These were posthumously published in various arrangements as *pensées*, and they have since provided mankind with more food for thought than all the solid philosophical and theological manuals of that time.

Pascal knew quite well his own value and often vacillated between proud self-confidence and touching unselfishness, between modesty and aggressiveness. Only slowly did he learn to control his sarcasm, his impatience and anger. He never considered himself a saint, although his sister built up a pious and edifying account of his sanctity. Nevertheless, he might well have been canonized if he had not rendered himself suspect of heresy. In this respect at least he resembled his rival, Descartes. He, too, had his work placed on the Index of Forbidden Books by the institution that unfortunately must be mentioned once more: the *Sanctum Officium Sanctissimae Inquisitionis* (the Holy Office).

The world itself therefore seemed different to Descartes and Pascal, for each looked at it differently even in the light of scientific knowledge. Pascal's completely unbiased proof of the possibility of a vacuum also meant an impressive victory of the new mathematical-empirical method of investigating nature, over that of the traditional physics and metaphysics, which had upheld a whole series of physical-metaphysical dogmas, like the dogma—going back in fact to Aristotle—that nature abhors a vacuum (or that about the privileged status of the circle, dethroned in physics by Kepler's discovery of the elliptical planetary orbits). That dogma of nature's abhorrence of a vacuum, which had been accepted even by Descartes and Galileo, confusing the vacuum with nothingness, before Newton's insight into the nature of gravitation, was one of the basic hypotheses of the traditional explanation of nature. In his answer to Père Noël, rector of the Jesuit school in Paris, Descartes's teacher and friend but tied to the metaphysically oriented method of interpreting nature, Pascal makes clear the foundations of the new method of natural science: the truth of physics rests either on the evidence of ideas or the evidence of the facts, and it is found in one of two ways, by mathematical deduction or by experiment.[3] Pascal speaks even more clearly of method in physics in the famous fragment of an introduction to the treatise on the vacuum: "The elucidation of this difference (between natural science and theology) cannot but make us pity the blindness of those who cite only authority as a proof in matters of physics instead of reasoning or experience and to be shocked by the malice of others who use only reasoning in theology instead of the authority of Scripture and the Fathers."[4] But is not this an oversimplified view of the difference between natural science and theology?

In any case, the difference between Pascal and Descartes, particularly in the matter of scientific method, has now become clear. Although in principle Descartes insists on experience, in practice he proceeds largely deductively, starting out from mental constructs. Experiment is useful to him in order to prove and confirm the truth in individual cases, rather than to discover it. In his ideal picture of an absolutely clear and distinct science, everything had to be derivable from a few clearly established principles or axioms. In natural science, unlike mathematics, he had no tool with which to build the new structure of science from experience. Pascal begins more decisively with experience and looks for the causes of certain effects. And while Descartes, in stating the principles of his preconceived scientific structure (such as the equation of matter with extension, making motion the result of pressure or a push, dualism of body and soul, the function of the pineal gland), often displays a boldness that cannot stand up to empirical verification, Pascal is often excessively cautious in testing the principles from which he wants to start out. The air-pressure experiments prove this. He avoids apodictic assertions and awaits the outcome of the experiments. He shows boldness in drawing conclusions from established principles, but these can and should be verified again in the light of experience. He is not inclined to adopt a system that can be rapidly constructed. It was only with the subsequent generation of scholars—Newton, Boyle, Huygens—that the preconditions for such a construction were present.

But more than scientific knowledge was involved here. It was a question of *human cognition* as such, human consciousness as a whole. Descartes had identified the soul with consciousness and reduced all its functions to thinking. Pascal was too fine an observer, not only of nature but also of the human psyche, to agree to such a reduction, despite his insistence on the importance of thought. At first he had nothing against Descartes's emphasis on reason. He was himself too rational for that: as a mathematician, physicist and engineer, he could hardly fail to be. Nevertheless, reason alone is not sufficient: precisely because he was a mathematician, physicist and engineer, Pascal was not a rationalist. Not that he had anything against discursive reason, but was there not also an intuitive apprehension? He had nothing against the slow process of analytic-synthetic construction on the part of the intellect, but was there not also simple, swift affection? He had nothing against logic, but was there not also instinct?

Thus, sound reasoning (*raisonnement*) must be combined with sensitive feeling (*sentiment*). Both have their limits: "Those who are accustomed to judge by feeling have no understanding of matters involving reasoning. For they want to go right to the bottom of things at a glance, and are not accustomed to look for principles. The others, on the contrary, who are accustomed to reason from principles, have no understanding of matters involving feeling, because they look for principles and are unable to see things at a glance."[5] Mind, reason—that is, logical reasoning—on the one hand must therefore be distinguished from feeling, instinct—that is, intuitive sense—on the other: both can be shaped or corrupted by the company we keep (*conversations*).[6]

*Sentiment*, "feeling," here has evidently nothing to do with sentimentality or mawkishness, which was completely alien to Pascal. The word "heart" (*coeur*) summarizes better than "feeling" that which Pascal opposed to "reason" (*raison*). Neither does "heart" mean the irrational-emotional factor as opposed to the rational-logical; it is not "soul" as contrasted with "spirit." The heart—of which the bodily organ is a symbol—means the personal, spiritual center of man, his innermost operative center, the starting point of his dynamic personal relationships with other people, the precision instrument by which he grasps reality in its wholeness. "Heart" certainly means the human mind: not, however, mind as purely theoretical thinking, as reasoning, but as spontaneously present, intuitively sensing, existentially apprehending, totally appreciating, and indeed in the widest sense loving (or even hating). It is in this light that we can rightly understand Pascal's perhaps most quoted but not easily translated play on words: *Le coeur a ses raisons, que la raison ne connaît point; on le sait en mille choses,* "The heart has its reasons of which reason knows nothing: we know this in countless ways."[7] This, then, is the logic of the heart: the heart has its own reason.

Even at this stage it is clear that this great mathematician has perceived the whole *relativity of purely rational, mathematical certainty:* "We know the truth not only through our reason but also through our heart."[8] With the heart, in intuitive immediacy, we perceive first principles: the existence of space, time, motion, number. And even though reason cannot prove these things, it will try in vain—like the skeptics—to dispute them. Does reason itself, then, presuppose some knowledge? "It is on such knowledge, coming from the heart and instinct, that reason has to depend and base all its argument. The heart feels that there are three spatial dimensions and that there is an infinite series of numbers, and reason goes on to demonstrate that there are no two square numbers of which one is double the other."[9]

Principles, then, are sensed intuitively with the heart, but propositions are logical conclusions established by reason: "and both with certainty though by different means."[10] Does not all this make clear the limits of reason? "It is just as pointless and absurd for reason to demand proof of first principles from the heart before agreeing to accept them as it would be absurd for the heart to demand an intuition of all the propositions demonstrated by reason before agreeing to accept them. Our inability must therefore serve only to humble reason, which would like to be the judge of everything, but not to confute our certainty. As if reason were the only way we could learn!"[11] Could the importance *and* limits of purely rational certainty be more clearly stated?

Descartes had transferred to the other sciences the "spirit" of the analytical method used in geometry, in mathematics. But the very people who have had a mathematical-geometrical training should appreciate the importance of the fact that, in addition to the *esprit de géométrie,* the spirit of mathematics, there is also—again almost untranslatable—the *esprit de finesse.* This is an exacting term, usually rendered "intuitive mind": it suggests a delicate sensitivity, sure instinct, tact, flair, discernment, perhaps even shrewdness. In other words it enables us to perceive more acutely, more closely, more discriminatingly, more sensitively, more subtly.

Pascal thought that all "geometricians," all mathematicians, ought also to have intuitive minds, and on the other hand all those who have intuitive minds should also be "geometricians," mathematicians. But "the reason why certain intuitive minds are not mathematical is that they are quite unable to apply themselves to the principles of mathematics, but the reason why mathematicians are not intuitive is that they cannot see what is in front of them; for, being accustomed to the clear-cut, obvious principles of mathematics and to draw no conclusions until they have clearly seen and handled their principles, they become lost in matters requiring intuition, whose principles cannot be handled in this way. These principles can hardly be seen—they are perceived instinctively rather than seen—and it is with endless difficulty that they can be communicated to those who do not perceive them for themselves. These things are so delicate and numerous that it takes a sense of great delicacy and precision to perceive them and judge correctly and accurately from this perception: most often it is not possible to set it out logically as in mathematics, because the necessary principles are not ready to hand, and it would be an endless task to undertake. The thing must be seen all at once, at a glance, and not as a result of progressive reasoning, at least up to a point."[12]

Intuitive minds, accustomed to judge only spontaneously, are taken by surprise when they are confronted with the definitions and principles of geometry: "Intuitive minds which are merely intuitive lack the patience to go right into the first principles of speculative and imaginative matters which they have never seen in practice and are quite outside ordinary experience."[13] But mathematicians should not make themselves ridiculous by trying to deal geometrically with questions requiring intuition: "Mathematicians who are merely mathematicians therefore reason soundly as long as everything is explained to them by definitions and principles, otherwise they are unsound and intolerable, because they reason soundly only from clearly defined principles."[14]

Against this background we can perhaps understand why Pascal had planned in his greatest work to write a highly critical chapter against the most outstanding representative of the *esprit de géométrie*. This seems to be the meaning of the note: "Write against those who probe science too deeply. Descartes."[15]

## 2. *The fundamental certainty of faith*

The ideal of mathematical evidence can at best be attained only in mathematics. None of the other, less abstract, less formal human sciences, from the empirical disciplines to philosophy, can approach this (abstract, formal) certainty. And Descartes's vision of a universal science, covering all the problems of human life, proved increasingly unrealizable, so that Cartesians who at first had been enthusiastic were driven finally to skepticism or even to fideism.[16] Pascal, who had never been merely a mathematician or a physicist, turned in his later years away from "studying abstract sciences" to "the study of man":[17] "One must know oneself."[18] Thus he became one of the early great investigators of the self. He was concerned not with abstract human nature as understood by traditional philosophy or theology, nor even with man as a thinking being in Des-

cartes's sense. What interested him was the wholly concrete, historical
human being, as he lives in his world, in his everyday existence. He
wanted to take the measure of this human being in his heights and
depths. In this respect he was really impressed—unlike Descartes—not
mainly with the uncertainty of human knowledge but—as we saw in our
criticism of Descartes—with the utter insecurity of human life as such.


## Man's greatness and wretchedness

In the completely full, static, hierarchically ordered, geocentric and
anthropocentric world picture of the Middle Ages, man had his own quite
definite place: the firm ground of the earth under his feet and the secure
celestial spheres—the dwelling place of God and his angels—above his
head, himself safe at the very heart of all creation. But now it had become
clear that this picture was completely wrong. This firm and well-ordered
world structure had fallen to pieces as a result of the discoveries of Copernicus, Kepler and Galileo. God seemed to be homeless, the angels to have
become superfluous. The new mechanistic physics and gravitational astronomy ("celestial mechanics"), only to be perfected very much later by
Newton, showed that man is alone in a world in which abysses, immensi-
ties, are opened up both above and below him. A feeling of confusion and
insecurity was spread not only among churchmen and theologians but
among thinking people everywhere.

Pascal took very seriously man's forlornness in the infinitely imperme-
able universe, out of which no Creator's voice can be heard: "The eternal
silence of these infinite spaces fills me with dread."[19] Nevertheless he refused to isolate man from the world and interpret him, as Descartes had
done, merely in the light of consciousness. For him, man is not *a priori*
confronted by the world but is in the world. And in this world, which
remains always incomprehensible to him, man ought first of all to try to
understand himself in all his contradictoriness. For what is it that characterizes man's situation when seen in all its *cosmic dimensions?* His state is
one of contrasts, tensions, fundamental disproportion, complete incongruity. His mathematical insights helped Pascal to understand this human
situation.

If we look from man's standpoint into the distance—into the macrocosm—the earth and in the end even the sun shrink to a small point,
the whole visible world becomes an inconspicuous mark in the broad, incomprehensible cavity of the universe. What is man in face of this
infinity? Compared to the universe, man is nothing.

On the other hand, if we look from man's standpoint into the
microcosm, into the tiny organisms, everything can be divided and again
divided, even the atom, in which an infinity of universes is opened up,
each with its firmament, its planets, its earth, with the same relationships

as the visible world: an infinity of the small, which ends in nothing but which we can never fathom. What is man in relation to this negative infinity? Compared with nothing, man is a universe.

This, then, is the disproportion, the incongruity, the greatness and wretchedness of man in the world: "A nothing compared to the infinite, a whole compared to the nothing, a middle point between all and nothing, infinitely remote from an understanding of the extremes; the end of things and their principles are unattainably hidden from him in impenetrable secrecy. Equally incapable of seeing the nothingness from which he emerges and the infinity in which he is engulfed. What else can he do, then, but perceive some semblance of the middle of things, eternally hopeless of knowing either their principles or their end? All things have come out of nothingness and are carried onwards to infinity. Who can follow these astonishing processes? The author of these wonders understands them: no one else can."[20]

Infinities in space and also in time—of hours, days, years—an infinity of numbers, geometrical propositions, scientific principles. Here is revealed man's radical insecurity in the world, where we drift uncertainly and where everything slips away from us in a flight without end: "We burn with desire to find a firm footing, an ultimate, lasting base on which to build a tower rising up to infinity, but our whole foundation cracks and the earth opens up into the depth of the abyss. Let us seek neither assurance nor stability; our reason is always deceived by the inconsistency of appearances; nothing can fix the finite between the two infinites which enclose and evade it."[21] So insecure is man, this "thinking reed," that "a vapour, a drop of water is enough to kill him."[22] Nevertheless, "if the universe were to crush him, man would still be nobler than his slayer, because he knows that he is dying and the advantage the universe has over him. The universe knows none of this."[23]

If we consider man's existence not in its cosmic but in its everyday dimensions, this insecurity is seen in a different form. Pascal, moving in higher and even the highest circles, knew the life particularly of the materially secure and socially respected classes. In Paris he had his *période mondaine* and devoted himself to what the strict Jansenist morality of Port-Royal condemned as "worldly vanities." He was, then, anything but an unworldly moralist with vague ideas about real life. He saw from direct and close observation, as some theologians could never have seen, that even worldly people are not necessarily bad, but can show in their mode of life that formation of mind and heart, that *esprit de finesse* which he so admired: the ideal of the *honnête homme*. They were people to be respected, talented in every way, frank and magnanimous, supremely tactful, assured in their behavior in all life's situations and with firm convictions on all questions.

But Pascal caught sight also of the concealed insecurities, doubts, weaknesses of these people who seemed so secure while being at once dependent and independent, unbelieving and believing, undaunted and frightened. He analyzed their imbalance—a psychological exposer of people before Kierkegaard, Dostoevsky, Nietzsche, Kafka, Freud—mercilessly laying bare in all possible situations their habits, vacillations, self-love, aversion to the truth, injustice, pride, vanity. He exposed particularly the worldly people who to all outward appearances are guided often more by presumption than by reason; whose friendships would all be broken if each one knew what his friend had said about him; who would be glad to be cowards if at the same time they could earn the reputation of being heroes; who are easily consoled because they are upset by any triviality; who, because they are not able to overcome death, misery, ignorance, have agreed not to consider these things. In haste, continually on the move and fully occupied with both serious and nonserious matters, they are always looking for new diversions for the sake of diversion: "Here is this man, born to know the universe, to judge everything, to rule a whole state, wholly concerned with catching a hare."[24] Should he really be concerned about a hare or about a small sum won by gambling?

These are dubious activities. What is concealed behind all the diversions, behind hunting and dancing, gambling and sport, behind the social whirl, amorous adventures and acceptance of offices? If we look behind all the masks, we find in the last resort nothing but a fear of being alone: "The sole cause of man's unhappiness is that he does not know how to stay quietly in his room."[25] All the intrigues and bustle—including heroic deeds in war—are supposed to divert man from the menacing silence in which he is confronted only with himself: "Man finds nothing so intolerable as to be in a state of complete rest, without passions, without occupation, without diversion, without effort. Then he feels his nullity, loneliness, inadequacy, dependence, helplessness, emptiness. And at once there wells up from the depths of his soul boredom, gloom, depression, chagrin, resentment, despair."[26]

Who has not known such moods? And how many there are who say: "I do not know who put me into the world, nor what the world is, nor what I am myself. I am terribly ignorant about everything. I do not know what my body is, or my senses, or my soul, or even that part of me which thinks what I am saying, which reflects about everything and about itself, and does not know itself any better than it knows anything else. I see the terrifying spaces of the universe hemming me in, and I find myself attached to one corner of this vast expanse without knowing why I have been put in this place rather than that, or why the brief span of life allotted to me should be assigned to one moment rather than another of all the eternity which went before me and all that which will come after me. I see only infinity on every side, hemming me in like an atom or like the shadow of a fleeting instant. All I know is that I must soon die, but what I know least about is this very death which I cannot evade. Just as I do not know whence I come, so I do not know whither I am going. All I know is that when I leave this world I shall fall for ever into nothingness or into the hands of a wrathful God, but I do not know which of these states is to be my eternal lot. Such is my state, full of weakness and uncertainty."[27]

In fact nowhere is the bleakness of human existence more clearly manifested than in the constant menace of death, which is often so distant when it seems close and close when it seems distant: "The last act is bloody, however fine the rest of the play. They throw earth over your head and it is finished for ever."[28] Pascal shows sympathy for those people who are suffering in their doubts and seriously looking for a way out. But he has no patience with those who boast of their doubts and continue to live superficially and thoughtlessly, never reflecting on these elemental questions of human living and dying, and who imagine that they are sure of themselves because they have read something in the Bible or occasionally talked to a priest about matters of faith.

Are not the basic problems as Pascal sees them reopened at a very much deeper level than in Descartes's work? What is mainly involved is not the uncertainty of human knowledge but the insecurity of human life: man's basic forlornness, his perilous state, his incapacity, discordance, "disproportion." Kierkegaard, Heidegger and Sartre have analyzed even more closely this condition of man: "inconstancy, boredom, anxiety"[29] and especially his mortality. It is true of course that Pascal always stressed man's *grandeur* as well as his *misère*. The greatness of man even in his wretchedness consists in the fact that he is aware of his wretchedness: "Man's greatness comes from knowing he is wretched: a tree does not know it is wretched. Thus it is wretched to know that one is wretched, but there is greatness in knowing one is wretched."[30] Thus all man's wretchedness itself proves his greatness: "It is the wretchedness of a great lord, the wretchedness of a dispossessed king."[31]

Against this background, it can be understood that Pascal, who never in his life found a worthy partner to his conversation, was not necessarily being arrogant when he dismissed Descartes in short order as "useless and uncertain."[32]

## What cannot be doubted

It is strange to find Descartes in particular, who struggled as no one else ever did to find basic *certitude*, described as *inutile et incertain*. Nevertheless, in view of man's basic insecurity, can the *cogito* really be useful? Pascal was not prepared to take even Descartes's methodical doubt entirely seriously.

With regard to Descartes's statement of the problem,[33] Pascal found himself confronted by two basic positions: either acquiescence in *skepticism* (of the *pyrrhoniens*, named after the ancient skeptic Pyrrho) or taking refuge in *dogmatism*. This would mean for the skeptics—and here Pascal outlines what is in effect Descartes's methodical doubt—that, apart from revelation and faith, there is no certainty whether man was created by a good God, by an evil spirit or by chance; whether the natural principles of the true and good can be regarded as true, false or uncertain; whether even that half of our life in which we think we are awake is not also a dream. But, for the dogmatists, it would mean that we cannot doubt natural principles if we speak in good faith and sincerely.

How, then, is man to decide? For he must decide: neutrality is not possible. Any one who does not decide becomes *ipso facto* a skeptic: "What is man to do in this state of affairs? Is he to doubt everything, to doubt whether he is awake, whether he is being pinched or burned? Is he to doubt whether he is doubting, to doubt whether he exists?"[34] Pascal is convinced that "no one can go that far, and I maintain that a perfectly genuine sceptic has never existed. Nature backs up helpless reason and stops it going so wildly astray."[35] Total skepticism comes up against the spontaneous protest of human nature. In fact the skeptic's whole life contradicts his fundamental doubt.

Or is man to become a dogmatist? "Is he, on the other hand, to say that he is the certain possessor of truth, when at the slightest pressure he fails to prove his claim and is compelled to loose his grasp?"[36] Dogmatism comes up against the menacing opposition of human reason. In fact the dogmatist bases his conclusions on foundations that prove on critical scrutiny to be nonexistent.

Neither dogmatism nor skepticism can be strictly proved: as it is not certain that everything is certain, neither is it certain that everything is uncertain. Human existence is seen in all its discordance and perilous condition: "What sort of a freak then is man! How novel, how monstrous, how chaotic, how paradoxical, how prodigious! Judge of all things, feeble earthworm, repository of truth, sink of doubt and error, glory and refuse of the universe!"[37]

Who can clear up this immense confusion where reason blocks dogmatism and nature blocks skepticism? Is not this the absolute end of philosophy? But here Pascal reaches a wholly surprising turning point: what amounts to a dictatorial appeal to recognize that the solution of the contradiction simply cannot be expected from man and that he has to look elsewhere, to something that transcends him: "Know then, proud man, what a paradox you are to yourself. Be humble, impotent reason! Be silent, feeble nature! Learn that man infinitely transcends man, hear from your master your true condition, which is unknown to you. Listen to God."[38]

But is not man at this point expected to make a leap, a leap in thought? Pascal would not only admit this, he really challenges man to make the leap, *to take the risk of believing in God*, in whose light alone both the greatness of man (as a result of the original goodness of God's creation) and the wretchedness of man (as a result of man's lapse into sin) can be explained. According to Pascal, it is not philosophy but the Christian message which provides the answer to the enigma of discordant human nature. The knot for the understanding of our discordant existence lies hidden at too great a height—or, better, too great a depth—for us to get at it with our reason: "Consequently it is not through the proud activity of our reason but through its simple submission that we can really know ourselves."[39]

The question is thrust upon us: How did Pascal come to this view, so very surprising for a modern mathematician, physicist and engineer? Four years after Descartes's death, Pascal, too—also during a November night and after a long case history—had his "vision." It is here that we come across the ultimate reason for their divergences. In the same year, Pascal had presented to the Paris Academy his works on the arithmetical triangle and on the calculation of probabilities, but he had also gone through a profound internal crisis—which had evidently been impending for a long time—involving emotional unrest, fear, sickness, disgust with worldly pursuits and simultaneously numerous conversations with his favorite sister, Jacqueline, a kindred spirit, who had worked with him for a long time but then, against his wishes, become a nun and entered the Jansenist center of Port-Royal; she expected to be able to offer a dowry to the convent, and this, too, Pascal found unwelcome. But she, too, seems to have known nothing of that decisive and ultimately not wholly explicable conversion experience, the climax and solution of the crisis.

It was only after Descartes's death that a servant found the carefully written small sheet of parchment (together with an outline on paper) that Pascal had evidently kept sewn up in the lining of his coat until the time of his death.[40] It was very precisely dated and timed: "The year of grace 1654. Monday, 23 November. . . . From about half past ten in the evening until half past midnight." This was not the rational vision of a *science admirable*, to be judged solely according to the logic of the intellect. It was the supremely ecstatic *and* supremely conscious experience of a new certainty of the heart rising out of genuine fears and not merely methodical doubts, recorded in stammering words and with dashes between the phrases. This certainty he evidently wanted to be able to recall with the aid of the notes he always carried on his person.

What was afterward called Pascal's reminder note, the *Memorial*, begins with the word *FEU* ("FIRE"), written in capitals. Although it is often overlooked by interpreters, the reference is quite clearly to the vision of Moses at the burning bush, where the "God of Abraham, God of Isaac, God of Jacob" was revealed.[41] So, too, the continuation in Pascal runs as in the Book of Exodus, but with a very significant contrast: " 'God of Abraham, God of Isaac, God of Jacob,' not of philosophers and scholars."

Pascal adds: "God of Jesus Christ. . . . He can only be found by the
ways taught in the Gospel. . . . He can only be kept by the ways taught
in the Gospel."

Pascal, then, has found for himself the ultimate ground of certainty, on
which there can no longer be any doubt, on which all certainty can be
built: not one's own self-awareness, not a concept, not any sort of an idea
of God, not the God of philosophers and scholars, but the real, living
God of the Bible. Immediately after this comes the word, twice repeated,
*certitude, certitude.* After the flight from God, there is now fundamental
certainty arising from trustful submission to the God who is revealed and
historically present in Jesus Christ. That is fundamental certainty, not
simply from thought but from faith. As antithesis to Descartes's *cogito,*
Pascal's position might almost be formulated as *Credo, ergo sum* (I believe, therefore I exist).

This certainty is obviously not an irrational certainty. Pascal extols at
the same time the "greatness of the human soul." It is a certainty not
simply of reason thinking mathematically, clearly and distinctly but of the
intuitively and totally feeling, suffering heart. Hence after "certainty"
comes the word *sentiment.* And as a result of this, an overwhelming
"joy," "tears of joy," and a "peace" conquering all forsakenness. For Pascal, the consequence was "sweet and total renunciation." Hard and rigid
as he could be, he added as a warning to himself on the parchment sheet:
"Total submission to Jesus Christ and my director. Everlasting joy in return for one day's effort on earth." The conclusion of the *Memorial* is a
verse of a psalm: "I will not forget thy word.[42] Amen."

It has now become clear to Pascal that man apprehends God only with
the heart: "It is the heart which perceives God and not the reason. That
is what faith is: God perceived by the heart, not by the reason."[43] Not
that reason should be depreciated or abused: "There is nothing so consistent with reason as this denial of reason."[44] For "reason's last step is the
recognition that there are an infinite number of things which are beyond
it."[45] Both, then, are necessary: "Submission and use of reason; that is
what makes true Christianity."[46]

For Pascal, what matters from now on is essentially the true Christian
God, not the abstract, remote God of the philosophers and scholars. And
he finds it unpardonable that Descartes in his philosophy did not bother at
all about this true Christian God: "I cannot forgive Descartes: in his
whole philosophy he would like to do without God; but he could not help
allowing him a flick of the fingers to set the world in motion; after that he
had no more use for God."[47] At this decisive point, therefore, Descartes
and Pascal part company. For Pascal, it is clear and distinct that "knowing God without knowing our own wretchedness makes for pride. Knowing our own wretchedness without knowing God makes for despair.
Knowing Jesus Christ strikes the balance because he shows us both God
and our own wretchedness."[48] The rest of Pascal's fragments hang on this
balance: on the Old Testament (law, prophecies, the hidden God), Jesus

Christ (fulfillment of the prophecies, miracles, redemption and grace, morality and ways of salvation), the Church (foundation, continuity, infallibility), and the mystery of divine love.

## 3. *Faith as the basis of reason*

Unlike Descartes, Pascal did not found a school. His comprehensive work "The Truth of the Christian Religion" remained a torso. These *pensées*—his ideas, flashes of insight, aphorisms, outcries, together with his acute analyses and fragmentary but fully worked out comments, often leading to misunderstanding—did not form and could not be made into a system. They never became material for teaching and study, as Descartes's system did. And yet these sketches, so coherent in themselves, have not only continually roused the interest of historians but have had a disturbing influence on Catholics and Protestants up to the present time. Catholic theology played for safety apparently by simply ignoring these *pensées*, like so much else in modern times, and to its own disadvantage. Pascal's insights passed it by and exercised their influence elsewhere, so that even today this layman is in a better position than the theologians and philosophers of the schools of his own or later times to frighten the life out of those whom Schleiermacher called "the educated among the despisers of religion."

The court bishop Bossuet, the most popular and most influential theologian and preacher of seventeenth-century France, is today of merely historical interest; so, too, is his great antipode, the more spiritualized, mystical bishop and theologian Fénelon. Pascal, on the other hand, remains not a dead classical author but a living, relevant figure. He has stimulated not only rationalists of all times from Voltaire and the Encyclopedists to Aldous Huxley, the militant anticlerical Albert Bayet as well as the Marxists Henri Lefebvre and Lucien Goldmann, but also the devout papalist Count de Maistre, who prepared the way for Vatican I, and Charles Maurras, the right-wing rationalist and founder of the *Action Française*; finally, too, our valiant Thomists Jacques Maritain and Charles Journet. He has fascinated not only countless philosophers and theologians but more especially writers from Chateaubriand to Charles Péguy: "After three centuries he is with us, alive and involved in our controversies. Even his slightest thoughts disturb, enchant or irritate us; he is swiftly understood, when he gives merely a hint, much better than he was in his lifetime."[49]

## Reasonable reason—credible faith?

Pascal did not want to return to the time before Descartes under any circumstances. He was not less, but even more, critical than Descartes;

reason, freedom and certainty were equally important to him. But he saw
Descartes's limitations more closely than his contemporaries. Just because
he was more critical, he could not be convinced that the rational self-cer-
tainty of the human subject alone provided a firm, unshakable foundation
on which all certainty—including the certainty of Christian faith—might
be built. For him, there were "two excesses: to exclude reason, to admit
nothing but reason."[50]

Pascal, then, was more discriminating: "One must know when it is
right to doubt, to affirm, to submit. Anyone who does otherwise does not
understand the force of reason. Some men run counter to these three
principles, either affirming that everything can be proved, because they
know nothing about proof, or doubting everything, because they do not
know when to submit, or always submitting, because they do not know
when judgement is called for."[51]

The *rationality of reason* therefore cannot simply be assumed: "It
would surely be enough if reason were reasonable. It is quite reasonable
enough to admit that it has so far found no firm truth, but it has not yet
given up hope of finding one."[52] But this is in vain. "Would you not say
that this magistrate, whose venerable age commands universal respect, is
ruled by pure, sublime reason, and judges things as they really are, without paying heed to the trivial circumstances which offend only the imagination of weaker men? See him go to hear a sermon in a spirit of pious
zeal, the soundness of his judgement strengthened by the ardour of his
charity, ready to listen with exemplary respect. If, when the preacher appears, it turns out that nature has given him a hoarse voice and an odd
sort of face, that his barber has shaved him badly and he happens not to
be too clean either, then, whatever great truths he may announce, I wager
that our senator will not be able to keep a straight face."[53] And as the
tone of the speaker can substantially change the sense of what he says, so,
too, affection or hatred may change completely the dispensation of justice: "An advocate who has been well paid in advance will find the cause
he is pleading all the more just. The boldness of his bearing will make it
seem all the better to the judges, taken in by appearances. How absurd is
reason, the sport of every wind!"[54] And cannot the same thing be said of
any of men's actions? We might even say: "All man's dignity consists in
thought, but what is this thought? How silly it is!"[55]

The *credibility of faith*, however, is also something that cannot be assumed. Neither can we dispense with reason and rationality and build up
faith merely on authority: "Hearsay is so far from being a criterion of belief that you should not believe anything until you have put yourself into
the same state as if you had never heard it. It is your own inner assent
and the consistent voice of your reason rather than that of others which
should make you believe. . . ."[56] If antiquity were the criterion of belief,
then the ancients would have had no criterion. And if it were universal
consent, then faith would depend on men. To believe only on authority is

false humility, it is pride. Therefore: "Raise the curtain. You are wasting your time, one must either believe, deny or doubt. . . . Denying, believing and doubting are to men what running is to horses. Punishment of sinners: error."[57] Even in faith, then, there is no certainty entirely free from doubt. In faith, we must commit ourselves to something uncertain.

Pascal attaches great importance to the observation that certainty is lacking not only in questions of religion but also in most important questions of ordinary life, and decisions must constantly be made in face of uncertainties: "If we must never take any chances we ought not to do anything for religion, for it is not certain. But how many chances we do take: sea voyages, battles. Therefore, I say, we should have to do nothing at all, for nothing is certain. And there is more certainty in religion than that we shall live to see tomorrow. For it is not certain that we shall see tomorrow but it is certainly possible that we shall not. We cannot say the same of religion. It is not certain that it is true, but who would dare to say that it is certainly possible that it is not? Not when we work for tomorrow and take chances, according to the rule of probability already demonstrated."[58]

But what is meant here by "the rule of probability"? In a much discussed fragment on "the wager" (*le pari*), Pascal applies the basic idea of the calculation of probabilities (*la règle des partis*) to the question of the existence of God. As in coin-tossing (cross or script, head or tail?)— and Pascal had experience of the gaming table—two possibilities are offered from which to choose: God is or he is not. Two possibilities are uncertain: "Reason cannot decide this question. . . . How will you wager? Reason cannot make you choose either, reason cannot prove either wrong. Do not then condemn as wrong those who have made a choice, for you know nothing about it."[59]

This is the essential point. One *must* choose. Not choosing is itself a choice: "*Il faut parier*, you must wager. There is no choice, you are already committed."[60] But what are the odds? In accordance with the rules for the calculation of probabilities, Pascal indicates the possible gain or loss: from the nature of the factors opposed to one another (infinite and infinitely happy life or nothing) and from the greatness of the commitment (finite commitment for infinite), and thus in view of the whole import of this decision, the odds in favor of belief in God's existence are infinitely better than those in favor of unbelief. In fact, if we consider the matter more closely, the odds on unbelief or belief are as "nothing to infinite" (the title of the fragment is *Infini-rien*). That is: you lose nothing in any case by believing in God, but you can gain everything.

The question has continually been disputed, whether the wager argument is central or peripheral to Pascal's thought, whether it is an ingenious way of reasoning or merely a game. The detailed working out of the argument is less important than what Pascal regards as the substance. There is no question at all of a new mathematically oriented proof of

God's existence, as some interpreters have thought (speaking of an "existential" proof of God or a "games proof" in the light of the "games theory"). What it really means is that in the question of the existence or nonexistence of God the object is not to seek a judgment of pure reason but to provoke a decision of the whole person: a decision that cannot be proved by reason but that can be justified at the bar of reason. A calculated risk: man should take at least as much care over this basic decision as he would for a decision at the gaming table or in regard to life as a whole. From this standpoint, the argument of the wager is of the greatest importance.

"I marvel at the boldness with which these people presume to speak of God. In addressing their arguments to unbelievers, their first chapter is the proof of the existence of God from the works of nature."[61] Such proofs of God can at best convince those who already believe but not unbelievers. These weak arguments will only confirm the latter in their contempt for religion, as Pascal knows from reflection and experience. "It is a remarkable fact that no canonical author has ever used nature to prove God. They all try to make people believe in him."[62] Is not the God of Scripture a hidden God and are not men, "since nature was corrupted, left to their blindness, from which they can escape only through Jesus Christ, without whom all communication with God is broken off?"[63] Pascal thinks that all the weight has to be laid on original sin (through Adam) and redemption (through Jesus Christ).

Not only proofs from nature, however, but the metaphysical proofs as a whole seem to Pascal to be of little use: "The metaphysical proofs for the existence of God are so remote from human reasoning and so involved that they make little impact, and, even if they did help some people, it would only be for the moment during which they watched the demonstration, because an hour later they would be afraid they had made a mistake."[64] How, then, are we to come to God? "We know God only through Jesus Christ. Without this mediator all communication with God is broken off. Through Jesus we know God. All those who have claimed to know God and prove his existence without Jesus Christ have only had futile proofs to offer."[65]

It thus becomes clear that Pascal's view of the relationship between reason and faith is quite different from that of Descartes. Despite his appreciation of the *esprit de géométrie* and his use of it in geometry, mathematics, exact sciences, Pascal disputes the claim of reason and mathematical-rational thinking to sole authority. Apart from geometry, mathematics and the exact sciences, and particularly in religious questions, what is needed is the *esprit de finesse*, a sensitively apprehending, intuitive act of the whole person (of the "heart"). It is not in the rarefied atmosphere of rational arguments or counterarguments that the decision of faith occurs, but at a deeper level in man, where instincts and feelings, attachments and aversions, also play a part and where passions can influence or even obstruct reason in its decision for faith.

In view of man's basic discordance, his perilous condition and insecurity, Pascal attaches little importance to a firm, unshakable certainty of self as the basis of certainty of God. What is important for him is *not* the path *from conceptual certainty of the self to conceptual certainty of God, but* the path *from existential certainty of God to existential certainty of the self.* True self-knowledge on the part of man in his wretchedness and greatness is concretely possible only as a result of knowing God by acknowledging him in faith. In this respect, in contrast to Descartes, the specifically Christian factor lies at the center of things: Jesus Christ, in whose light Pascal tried to see man and God and to whom he devoted a large part of his *Pensées.* It should always be a question of the living God of the Fathers and of Jesus Christ.

In Pascal's thought, then, faith is not an exception to the universal rules of evidence. On the contrary, it is (abstract) mathematical evidence that forms an exception within the field of concrete human knowledge (never completely sure of the future) and concrete human action operating with probabilities. Like the rationality of reason, so, too, the credibility of faith may not simply be assumed in concrete existence.

In this view, a Cartesian-Thomistic separation of the two cognitive powers (reason and faith) and the two spheres of knowledge (reason and revelation) cannot be defended in the light of either reason or faith: from the very outset, reason has to do with faith and faith also has to do with reason. Reasonableness and credibility involve each other. For Pascal, however, in the last resort, reason is not the basis of faith, but faith is the basis of reason.

In order to see the present situation clearly, the question must now be raised as to how Pascal reached this definition of the relationship between reason and faith. To which tradition does he belong? This is easier to ascertain with Pascal than with Descartes.

## Neither freethinking nor Thomism

There are some things that Pascal took over from other people, but he transformed everything by his genius: "Let no one say that I have said nothing new; the arrangement of the material is new. In playing tennis both players use the same ball, but one plays it better."[66] Like Descartes, Pascal is quite unmistakably and agreeably his independent self. And if we speak here at all of his belonging to a tradition—although he never went to school and did little reading—this is not to say that he was dependent on certain models and schools of thought, but that he freely appreciated certain important ideas, themes, impulses. "Pascal's originality did not consist in discovering everything completely on his own, but in fusing and combining with the aid of a rigorous method and his imcomparable gifts of synthesis and vitality all that came to him from the four corners of heaven," writes Ferdinand Strowski.[67] He took up a variety of initiatives and was able to combine them into a unity through a novel way of thinking that always gave vital expression to the contrasts: thus establishing a standpoint beyond dogmatism and skepticism, idealism and naturalism, rationalism and irrationalism.

Pascal adopted from the freethinking tradition more than he permits us to see in the *Pensées*. He had learned much, especially from Montaigne (and the latter's friend Charron), whom he criticized severely in the *Pensées*: he had learned from Montaigne's skepticism but also from his language, his all-round observations of the limitations of human nature and not least from his knowledge of Greek and Roman literature and philosophy—on which Pascal was badly informed. The society of the Chevalier de Méré—who accused Pascal of an all-too-mathematical attitude toward everything—and of the young, very rich Duc de Roannez—who admired him—brought home to him the living reality of the *esprit de finesse* and the educational ideal as a whole, of the self-assured, highly cultured, courteous *honnête homme*. This had been given literary form for the first time a century before by Count Baldassare Castiglione, in his work *Il Cortegiano*,[68] in the spirit of the Italian Renaissance and inspired by ancient models: the unimpeded development of all talents and abilities had been recommended in Aristotle's *Ethics*. The ideal of the "courtier," courteous in every respect, then lived on in national variations, in the Spanish *caballero*, the German *Mann von Welt* and most permanently—long after the French Revolution—in the English "gentleman." French civilization gave European status to the ideal of the *honnête homme* from Pascal's time for the following centuries.

Pascal entered into a lively discussion particularly with the Epicurean stoic-skeptical philosophy of the *libertins* and atheists. The negative label of *libertins* was attached to all "strong" or "free" minds who expressed themselves more freely, more forcefully, more skeptically on religion and politics—a dangerous procedure at the time of the Cardinals Richelieu and Mazarin. Open "atheism" was scarcely tolerated. A few years before Pascal's birth, the Italian pantheistic nature philosopher Lucilio (he called himself Julius Caesar) Vanini, who had given up his Catholic faith in England, was accused of atheism and blasphemy and executed in particularly cruel circumstances in Toulouse in 1617.

In Pascal's time, "atheists" was a name used to discredit all those who ridiculed (mostly only in talk) religion, pope, politicizing cardinals and worldly clerics. It is only in this way that Mersenne's round figure of fifty thousand atheists in Paris can be explained. But it was at this time, of the Thirty Years' War of "religion," of unscrupulous absolutist power politics both at home and abroad, and of a Church with a baroque, triumphalistic façade supporting the throne, that the militant atheism was prepared that found expression a couple of decades later in literary form and reached its climax in the blood and terror of the French Revolution. Pascal entered at an earlier date and more seriously than others into discussion with libertinism and atheism: believing in God, believing in Christ and even—with reference to so many dogmas—believing in the Church. *Bon chrétien, catholique, apostolique et romain*, as he describes himself in his will.[69] Perhaps also a good Thomist?

If we merely look at his education and training, temperament and style, it is obvious that there is no need to prove that Pascal did not belong to the Thomist tradition. It is true that he cited Aquinas, in his defense of the Jansenists against the Jesuits, on the paramount importance of grace. But this was a matter of tactics. Neither Aquinas nor Thomism plays any part in the *Pensées*. Aquinas is mentioned only on two occasions and merely incidentally, with reference to human vanity.[70] In particular, Pascal has a completely different view of the relationship between reason and faith, philosophy and theology.

## Augustinian heritage

On one point there is no dispute: namely that Pascal received his main theological inspiration—apart from the Bible, which he seems to have studied closely only after his "conversion"—from the *Augustinian tradition*. At the same time that the seventeen-year-old boy published his sensational paper on conic sections, there appeared a book of a very different kind: the *Augustinus*, of Cornelis Jansen, Flemish theologian and Bishop of Ypres, who had died two years earlier. Six years after this, Pascal's whole family spent three months under the guidance of two noblemen who provided medical care for their father after his accident, studying the writings of the Abbé Saint-Cyran, head of the movement stemming from the same "Jansenius" and adopting his interpretation of Augustine. On the death of his father, Pascal wrote an oddly impersonal letter of consolation, couched in theological terms and ending with a paraphrase of Augustine, to his family.[71] He always regarded Augustine's sudden conversion as a model for his own. Pascal was bound to feel that he had a close affinity with Augustine, originally a very worldly person, a profound thinker and acute dialectician, talented psychologist, brilliant stylist and finally a passionately committed believer. And in the subsequent graceless dispute on grace between "Jansenists" and Jesuits, he was convinced that he had behind him that Augustine who had authoritatively solved the problem of grace and free (or unfree) will. "God has ruled his Church well by sending him [Augustine] earlier, and endowed with authority."[72]

For our problem of the relationship between *reason and faith* Pascal also was greatly influenced by Augustine. Attention has rightly been drawn to the parallels between Descartes's *cogito* and Augustine's: the fight against skepticism and the affirmation of the necessity of systematic thinking are in fact common to Augustine and Descartes. But Pascal's affinity with Augustine goes much deeper, particularly in regard to basic certainty.[73]

For both Augustine and Pascal, doubt arises from *profound existential distress*. It is not a question merely of the logic of abstract thought but of the tragedy of the concrete individual. This doubt is not merely methodic-conceptual but vitally existential. For Augustine, the *cogito* was not—as it was for Descartes—merely the first step in an ordered sequence of thought, but the painful experience—after his disappointment with Mani-chaeism—of a doubt akin to despair: a remedy against the menace of skepticism, undoubtedly familiar to him from the Greek Middle Academy. And Pascal? While Descartes tried out his methodic doubt sitting behind his stove, Pascal—as he says himself—was on his knees before and after his remarks on the wager.[74]

Both Augustine and Pascal see salvation not in a universal rational or—still less—geometrical-mathematical method but in an *open-mindedness of the whole person to reality as a whole*. For both Augustine and Pascal, thought is no less important than it is for Descartes, but man's mind is essentially more than merely thinking reason. Pascal belongs to the tradition of the *philosophia* or *theologia cordis*, the philosophy or theology of the heart, which—prepared by Plato and Paul—stretched from Augustine by way of Bernard, Bonaventure, Dante, medieval mysticism, to Teresa of Ávila, François de Sales and finally to Bérulle—the theologian of the French Oratory—with Gibieuf and Condren.[75]

For both Augustine and Pascal, final existential certainty is rooted not in the *cogito* of pure reason but in the *"credo" of the biblical message*. The radical remedy for skepticism is the biblical faith guaranteed by the Church. "I would not believe the gospel if I were not moved to do so by the authority of the Catholic Church," says Augustine.[76] For him, what is decisive is *crede, ut intellegas*, "believe, in order to know."[77] For Pascal, too, what is important is the *soumission*, the "submission" of reason: belief on authority (of God, Scripture, the Church). But it is precisely in this way that the truths of faith can be made intelligible, at least up to a point.

For both Augustine and Pascal, it is never a question of an irrational but always of a *rationally justifiable faith*; not rationalism, but rationality; not blind, but reasonable, submission. That is why *intellege, ut credas*, "know in order to believe," precedes *crede, ut intellegas*.[78] Precisely for this important viewpoint, Pascal appeals expressly to Augustine: "St. Augustine.[79] Reason would never submit unless it judged that there are occasions when it ought to submit. It is right, then, that reason should submit when it judges that it ought to submit."[80]

For both Augustine and Pascal, faith is necessary not only in regard to questions of Christian revelation but also in regard to questions of every-day life. Here, too, Pascal expressly invokes Augustine in support of his view: "St. Augustine saw that we take chances at sea, in battle, etc.—but he did not see the rule of probability which proves that we ought to."[81] So also, then, not only for Pascal but even earlier for Augustine, the prin-ciple holds that, as faith has to do with reason, so reason also has to do with faith.

With both Augustine and Pascal, we find a *Christocentrism governing all reality*. Many of Pascal's statements about the central importance of Jesus Christ could also have been composed by Augustine and are possibly inspired by him: "For man the way to the God of man would lead through the God-man. This is the mediator of God and man, the man Christ Jesus. For he is mediator by the very fact of being man; because of this too he is the way. . . . He is the sole way, well fortified against all errors."[82]

Is it possible, then, in this Augustinian-Pascalian view, to settle faith and reason on two floors as simply as it is done in the Thomistic-Car-tesian tradition, as if they had nothing to do with each other? In fact, Thomism and Augustinism are different in principle in regard to the rela-tionship between reason and faith, philosophy and theology. We might describe the position systematically, confirming in the light of Pascal's ap-proach what Descartes said.

*Thomism and Descartes* maintain the clear and distinct separation of the two spheres: two cognitive powers (reason and faith), two planes of knowledge (natural truth and revealed truth), two sciences (philosophy and theology). In regard to things as they really are, reason has a very large field for its own activity, where it can use its own resources to acquire knowledge: the existence and attributes of God, creation and providence, the soul and immortality, are natural truths that can be known even with-out revelation. What is known (*scitum*) cannot be what is believed (*creditum*), and what is believed cannot be something known. Faith in the strict sense is required only for the apprehension, the acceptance as true, of certain higher, revealed truths. The mysteries, for instance, of the Trinity and of God's becoming man surpass human reason and are super-natural truths, knowable only by revelation.

Because of this dual possibility of knowing God and the dual form of truth about God, philosophy (including philosophical teaching on God) and theology must be separated, even though they both speak—albeit in different ways—about the same God. In this respect, philosophy starts out from creatures, theology from God. Nevertheless, since both faith and reason, philosophy and theology—rooted in the one truth of God—are mutually compatible, they could and should provide mutual support, as already mentioned. It is understandable that in such a theory of two floors, the principle *intellego, ut credam*, "I know in order to believe," should be mainly stressed.

*Augustinism and Pascal* maintain the comprehensive and complete unity of the two spheres: faith and reason, philosophy and theology, are intertwined: we are thinking when we are believing and believing when we are thinking. What is known (*scitum*) and what is believed (*creditum*), therefore, cannot be adequately distinguished from each other. A clear and distinct division of the two planes of knowledge, as with two floors, is uninteresting, in the last resort impossible and in any case dangerous to faith: all truths are interconnected and one cannot be known without the other. It is not primarily a question of accepting certain articles of faith as true but of a confident submission to God and his word.

Because of this grand unity of reason and faith, in which philosophical truth is one with revealed truth, philosophy and theology are not to be divorced: we must be distrustful of a supposedly "pure" philosophy. In this view, only philosophy grounded in Christian faith is true philosophy. Such a "Christian philosophy" is therefore not grounded in thinking as such but is reflective self-interpretation of the Christian faith, especially in regard to God and the human soul. Consequently, submission to divine authority is prior to all searching and researching. It is understandable that in this view—as opposed to the Cartesian—the principle *credo, ut intelligam,* "I believe in order to understand," should be mainly stressed.

### Faith as ground of theology: Augustine and the consequences

From Pascal, lines cannot merely be traced back to Augustine and the Augustinian tradition. No less important are the lines that can be traced forward, especially to Protestantism and to Catholic Jansenism.

Although a very controversial figure in his own day, Aurelius Augustinus, the one true genius among the Latin Fathers of the Church, became *the* teacher of the Christian West. He had produced the most important synthesis before Aquinas of Christian faith and Greek (Neoplatonic) thought. It was through him especially, in whom patristic theology reached its brilliant culmination, that the theology of the Greek and Latin Fathers continued to live and to exercise an influence in the Middle Ages.

From the "Sentences" of Peter Lombard (†1160) especially, consisting largely of quotations from Augustine, the great medieval scholastics derived a markedly Augustinian theology. Consequently Augustine, together with a mainly Neoplatonic system of thought, dominated the method and content of scholastic philosophy and theology until well into the thirteenth century. And even after the acceptance—already described —of the whole of Aristotle by Albertus Magnus and Thomas, the Franciscan school under Bonaventure—he and Aquinas being the foremost

teachers at the University of Paris—tried to orient itself to Augustine especially in epistemology and psychology, giving priority to the good over the
true, the will over the intellect, love over perception.

Of course, this Franciscan Augustinism, which increasingly incorporated
also Aristotelian ideas, had only a short-term success (with the aid of condemnations) against the consistently applied Aristotelianism of Aquinas.
Bonaventure and Aquinas died in the same year (1274). Conservative
Augustinism, however, now increasingly anti-Thomist, was absorbed by
the "more modern" Scotism (of the Franciscan *doctor subtilis*, Duns
Scotus, †1308) and ended finally in the Ockhamism (of the English
Franciscan theologian William of Ockham, †1347) to which Luther
probably owed the first shape of his theology. But medieval mysticism
particularly and also political theory continued to be very much under
the influence of Augustine (*civitas Dei* and *civitas terrena* being seen as
exemplifying the relationship between *sacerdotium* and *imperium*). In
Western theology as a whole, it is possible to follow his traces at every
step. In St. Peter's, in Rome, he is seen together with Ambrose and the
Eastern Doctors of the Church, Athanasius and Chrysostom, carrying
lightly the gigantic *Cathedra Petri*, suspended under the Holy Spirit in
the alabaster window. This creation of Bernini was transferred from the
baptistery to this position in 1656, the year in which Pascal, invoking the
same Augustine, published his anti-Jesuit *Lettres Provinciales*—which
were to be condemned a year later by the *Cathedra Petri*.

Theological Augustinism today is understood not so much as the heritage of Augustinian theology common to all theological schools but as
the strict Augustinism associated with the theology of grace (especially of
predestination to glory or damnation), with obvious consequences for the
relationship between reason and faith. This strict Augustinism continually
came into conflict with ecclesiastical authority. It was condemned in the
ninth century in the form of the predestinationism taught by Gottschalk
of Orbais,[83] who was then kept in prison until his death. It was again condemned in the fourteenth century in the theories of the Englishman John
Wyclif, whose bones were disinterred some decades after his death on the
orders of the Council of Constance and had to be burned.[84] His disciple
Jan Hus, in Bohemia, had been assured of a safe-conduct at the same
council but was promptly burned. The two men are regarded as the most
important precursors of the Lutheran Reformation.

Was the *Reformation* the vanguard of the modern age, bringing with it
what we know as modern freedom, as Feuerbach assumed?[85] Or was it the
rear guard of medieval religious attitudes, temporarily holding up the secular emancipation movement of the Renaissance and then being superseded by more radical forces, as Nietzsche held?[86] As a movement at the
turn of an era, the Reformation was both in one: it had two faces. Its
specific importance, however, both for that time and for today, lies in the

fact that it was an unparalleled new awareness of the original meaning of
Christianity after fifteen hundred years of very complex Church history,
which we in the Catholic Church began to consider seriously only after
Vatican II.

The Reformation itself—in view of all the doubts and tribulations
caused by the tempestuous transition from the Middle Ages to modern
times—meant a search for a *new certainty*. But the solutions were mutually opposed:[87]

*Luther* gained certainty through a radical new awareness—contrary to all
ecclesiastical authorities and traditions—of the Christian *faith*, a certainty
of conscience, of faith, of salvation;

*Descartes*, a hundred years later, as we saw, gained certainty through a
radical new awareness—contrary to all authorities and traditions whatsoever—of human *reason*, a certainty of knowledge, of science, a basic certainty.

Luther's new awareness both prepared the way for Descartes's new
awareness and presented an obstruction to it from the outset. It was only
the new awareness brought by the Reformation to the Christian faith—
and not the Roman Catholic solidly defensive strategy in support of a medieval Christendom and medieval religious attitudes, as it was developed
between Trent and Vatican I and brought to an end with Vatican II—
which made possible a constructive discussion with the modern age. And
all this despite the fact that the Reformers' opposition to Aristotelianism,
scholasticism, Aquinas himself, to modern worldliness and rationality,
even as early as Luther, frequently took the form of opposition to the
"whore reason" as such.

In this epoch-making controversy, the Reformers considered themselves
to be without exception the true disciples of Augustine. They saw their
struggle against the Roman theory of justification by works, the glorification of the Church and the Renaissance papacy as a continuation of
Augustine's passionate struggle against Pelagianism, which had stressed
human works at the expense of God's grace. According to Luther, Calvin
and the other Reformers, man gains certainty, the certainty of his salvation, not by all the prescribed or recommended pious works but "by faith
alone" (*sola fide*), which corresponds to "by grace alone" (*sola gratia*).
This, they claimed, was the authentic teaching of Paul on man's justification and also the teaching of Augustine. For the Reformers, Augustine
was, among the Fathers, what Paul had been among the New Testament
witnesses. And some later Protestant theologians, too, strode in their
theology—often in seven-league boots—from Paul to Augustine and from
Augustine across the "Dark Ages" to Luther. But in their theory of nature
and grace, reason and faith, free will and predestination, the Reformers
were undoubtedly closer to Augustine than were their Thomist, their
Scotist and afterward their Jesuit opponents.

Thus Protestantism, especially where it felt strictly bound by the Reformation principle of appealing to the gospel, continued even into the nineteenth and twentieth centuries to be strongly marked by Augustinian influences. On the other hand, a number of Augustinian ideas found a place in French fideism and traditionalism in the nineteenth century—notably in the work of De Bonald and De Lamennais, the latter being entirely under the influence of Pascal. It often seems as if Pascal's *Pensées* were remembered more in Protestant than in Catholic theology, even though the former scarcely refers to them. If we take only one prominent witness for the nineteenth and one for the twentieth centuries, we can say that this is true first of all for that wholly and entirely extraordinary prophet in "Christian" Denmark of the nineteenth century who wanted to bring back Christianity into Christendom: *Sören Kierkegaard.*

Kierkegaard obviously did not know Pascal's work at first hand: he quotes him only once and then indirectly, through Feuerbach.[88] But, like Pascal, he, too, philosophized in the light of the wretchedness of his own existence and could not be satisfied with an objectively uncommitted knowledge in the spirit of Descartes, nor even with an idealistic dialectic of consciousness on the speculative heights in the spirit of Hegel. Like Pascal, Kierkegaard, too, wanted, not a general, theoretical *introduction* to Christianity, but the individual's existential *practice* in Christianity. A person should not simply devoutly accept a historical, philosophical or dogmatic truth, not simply admit its truth, but should live as a Christian, not only thinking or possessing Christian truth, but doing it, being it. This is the way in which man is to be helped toward a Christian existence. The passion for this way of existing—and here Pascal would agree—is faith.

It is not surprising that this Lutheran, thinking in the light of his personal-existential understanding of faith, who faced squarely the philosophy of natural reason introduced by Descartes and completed by Hegel, the philosophy of the Enlightenment and of Idealism, should have grappled in particular with Descartes's *cogito*. This he did in his witty but unfortunately uncompleted and then posthumously published little book *Johannes Climacus or De omnibus Dubitandum Est.*[89] In this early work (presumably 1842–43), which brings out very clearly his own intentions, Kierkegaard attempts to take the philosophers at their word. Doubting ought not to be an intellectual conceptual experiment or an inconclusive, theoretical "dialecticizing." Doubting ought to mean taking human existence quite seriously in practice. Modern philosophers—runs Kierkegaard's critique—dispense themselves from any serious existential doubt mainly by appealing to Descartes's conquest of doubt: "Why do these thinkers [Hegel and Spinoza] speak as though they themselves had not doubted? Has Descartes done it and disposed of the matter on behalf of us all, as Christ was crucified [for us all]?—Is this a philosophical question—or a practical one?—It must certainly have been with Descartes."[90]

Thus, wholly in the spirit of Pascal, Kierkegaard attempted to turn Descartes's methodic doubt into a radical doubt related to the concrete and discordant existence of the individual—whom he continually invokes— and to bring about a crisis for Descartes's purely conceptual certainty: we must at some time doubt seriously, absolutely seriously, to the point of despair. And we simply cannot despair impersonally. A distinction like that of Descartes, between doubting in theory and not doubting in practice, is not consistent. Theoretical doubt is partial, but despair is total. There is, of course, no way out of a serious universal doubt adopted for the sake of an intellectual self-assurance: "Thus the philosophers are worse than the Pharisees, of whom we read that they bind heavy burdens and do not themselves lift them with a finger. Which is the same as saying that though they do not lift the burdens themselves, yet the burdens can be lifted. But the philosophers demand the impossible. And if perchance some young person exists who thinks that philosophizing is not talking or writing, but making an honest attempt to do what philosophy tells him to (viz., to doubt everything), they let him waste years of his life in the attempt. And when it turns out that he was attempting the impossible, he has been so deeply affected that perhaps his rescue becomes impossible."[91]

The alternative resulting from this is "either" to despair "or" to risk the leap into faith: "What I am interested in is myself. It is really Christianity which has brought this ethical doubt into the world, because in Christianity this self acquires importance. Doubt is not conquered by the System, but by Faith, even as Faith has brought Doubt into the world. If the System is to calm Doubt, it must be by standing higher than both faith and doubt. But in that case doubt must first of all be conquered by faith. For you cannot leap over the middle term."[92]

Later social-political-religious upheavals and disasters have made relevant to our own times the insights of Kierkegaard—this early precursor of existential philosophy and existential theology—into the profound insecurity of human existence. But, for the liberal philosophy and theology of the nineteenth century, he remained a strange outsider, without followers. Optimistic, intellectual Protestantism, wholly in the tradition of the Enlightenment and Idealism (more Schleiermacher's than Hegel's), was only now approaching its culmination. "Natural theology" flourished not only in Catholicism and at Vatican I but also—in different forms—in Protestantism.

It was only after the First World War had discredited liberal theology and Karl Barth had begun to develop a "theology of crisis" or "dialectical theology" that a turning point came. Upset by the miserable state of preaching and under the influence especially of Kierkegaard, but also of Plato, Kant, Dostoevsky and Franz Overbeck, Barth broke with Schleiermacher and liberal theology, took up again the Reformation interests and stressed these in relation to the new world situation and the new conditions in Church history. Jesus Christ did not merely bring a new form of religious experience or piety, but as the Crucified and Risen he is the revelation of the God who is "wholly other." This Jesus Christ, attested by Scripture and proclaimed by the Church as God's word made flesh, is God's *sole* revelation for the salvation of the world.

In this polemical confrontation with liberal theology, Barth, of course, goes far beyond the Reformers and even beyond Pascal and Kierkegaard: any other possibility of a revelation is excluded. Man cannot of himself establish a relationship with God but must allow God to bestow it on him. In this way, an uncompromising challenge is offered not only to neo-Protestantism (from Schleiermacher to Harnack) but most of all to Roman Catholicism (at Vatican I), both of which agree in accepting a "natural theology" independent of faith. Now as never before, "by Scripture alone," "by grace alone," "by faith alone"—all concentrated in "by Christ alone"—are taken seriously even in major questions of politics, where Barth, in virtue of his theological position, took up the "Churches' struggle" against National Socialism's "blood and soil" natural theology and the "political theology" of the "German Christians" who supported it: with this aim he organized also the "Confessing Church."

The first article of the Barmen Declaration, the confessing Church's profession of faith, drawn up by Barth in 1934, states: "Jesus Christ, as attested to us in Holy Scripture, is the one Word of God that we hear, that we have to trust and obey, living or dying. We reject the false doctrine that the Church can and must acknowledge as the source of its proclamation, over and above this one Word of God, also other events and powers, figures and truths, as God's revelation."[93] What is to provide man (and the Church) with decisive support in life's insecurity—individual, social and political? Nothing but God's word and grace and on man's side—without any false security of knowledge—trusting faith.

The whole of Christian theology, as Barth developed it systematically in his "Church Dogmatics" (from 1932), must be exclusively and consistently the teaching of Jesus Christ as God's living word spoken to us.[94] In the third part of his many-volumed *Dogmatics*, on Creation, Barth expounds at length his reaction to the Cartesian *cogito* in the light of this fundamental principle.[95]

In the *Church Dogmatics*, Barth avoids any discussion with Pascal, who was too much a man of the Church,[96] but makes a close analysis of Descartes's six *Meditationes* and then formulates his critique of the *cogito* wholly on the lines of Kierkegaard. He maintains that Descartes did not actually doubt his own existence but merely toyed with the idea of doubting it: "Let us suppose that he really considered the possibility of the nothingness of his whole life as a scholar dedicated to the service of reason, with all his attempts at theoretical destruction and construction, with all the Catholic-humanistic equipment with which, 'between the lines,' he orientated himself and carried through his work, with all his plans and achievements, his hopes and fears. . . . Let us suppose that in view of this possibility, he not only seriously doubted but fell into despair. Obviously this did not happen."[97]

Descartes would have doubted seriously only if he had doubted his own existence in face of the revelation of this God and Creator—and not merely in face of a philosophical God, the "inoffensive product of his own mind." "In the recognition of this God the possibility of his own nothingness, and then also of the nothingness of his own thinking and of the whole external world, must have irresistibly impressed him."[98]

As with Pascal, so, too, with Barth, in view of the limits of our reason seen in the light of the living God of the Bible, it is a question of *credo, ergo sum:* "We emphasise that this awareness of creaturely existence rests wholly and exclusively upon God's self-communication in revelation. It is wholly and exclusively an echo and response of the creature to what is said to him by his Creator. . . . It is recognition in the form of acknowledgment, recognition under the law of faith and obedience. This character formally distinguishes it from all recognition based upon the consciousness of the ego, the world and God."[99]

This was the development in Protestant theology. But what was the fate of Augustinism in Catholic theology?


## Conflict of faith with faith: Jansenism

After the Reformation even more than before it, Catholic Augustinism tended to be thrust into the background. The fact that the Reformers appealed mainly to Augustine—after Paul—made any sort of Augustinism uncongenial and suspect in the Catholic Church. It is true that the moderate Augustinism of the Hermits of St. Augustine, with its stronger emphasis on grace and faith, played a considerable part even at the Council of Trent, especially in the decree on justification (and predestination), which was of central importance for the Reformation. It was mainly the Augustinian General, Cardinal Girolamo Seripando (†1563, in Trent), who exercised this influence; but even he did not escape the charge of having conceded too much to Martin Luther, his contemporary and fellow religious.

The "younger Augustinian school," also resident in Italy, founded by Pascal's contemporary Henricus de Noris and continued by Augustinian hermits, had to defend itself continually against charges of heresy. It was only as a result of a letter from the enlightened Pope Benedict XIV that the Spanish Inquisition—after resisting the papal directive for ten years—finally struck Noris' name from its Index. From that time onward, the Augustinian doctrine of the cooperation of God's efficacious grace with man's weakened freedom could be upheld, alongside the Thomist view, with its emphasis on grace efficacious of itself prior to any free consent (the Dominican Dominic Bannez was its chief defender), and the Jesuit view emphasizing free will, which by its consent alone makes possible the efficacy of prevenient grace (its chief defender being Luis Molina, who gave his name to the Jesuit system of Molinism).

The discussions between strictly Augustinian and "progressive" Aristotelian-humanistic theology went less smoothly at the University of Louvain than in Italy. The first phase ended with the condemnation of Michael Baius, a defender of Augustinism, in 1567.[100] During the second phase, Leonard Lessius, an extreme Molinist but at first more courageous than other theologians in defending Galileo, was condemned and later rehabilitated by Louvain; his opinions expressed in *De gratia efficaci*, in 1610, were contested by some of his fellow Jesuits. Finally a decree of the Inquisition in 1611 required all publications on grace to be first submitted for approval.[101]

It was from the University of Louvain that the very complex theological-moral-political reform movement of "Jansenism" started out a little later. The goal of Professor and afterward Bishop Jansen and his French friend Jean Du Vergier de Hauranne (later Abbé de Saint-Cyran), universally respected, devout and zealous for reform but hostile to the Jesuits from their early acquaintance (1614–17), was the reform of post-Tridentine scholastic dogmatic and moral theology, in the spirit of Scripture and the Fathers (especially Augustine). But, after Jansen's death, the publication of his three-volume *Augustinus*, or "doctrine of Saint Augustine on the health, sickness and healing of human nature,"[102] led to the great controversy on grace, which was carried on mainly in France and could not be brought to an end even with the aid of papal condemnations.

Two parties engaged in the controversy: on the one side Augustinian Jansenism defending Augustine's view of grace and the stricter moral and disciplinary ideals of the early Church; on the other side Molinism, defended by the Jesuits, stressing man's free will and advocating a more liberal morality and sacramental discipline. The controversy was carried on even in the salons and the theater. Pierre Corneille, creator of French classical tragedy, was inclined to Molinism; Jean Baptiste Racine, who brought that tragedy to its peak, an orphan educated in Port-Royal and desirous of being buried there, was inclined to Jansenism. Pascal had come into very close contact, as we saw, with what was later to be called "Jansenism," in his early twenties (at his "first conversion"), but without at that time changing his way of life. The decisive turning point of 1654, however, brought him into the closest contact with the convent of Port-Royal in Versailles (and its branch foundation in Paris), the center of Jansenism in France and the residence at that time of his sister Jacqueline.

A stricter observance had been introduced there by the abbess, "Mère Angélique" Arnauld, whose family was closely associated with Port-Royal and whose father, as public prosecutor, had won a case against the Jesuits.

It was Saint-Cyran who introduced the Jansenist doctrine of grace into the convent and who, as spiritual director and inspirer of Port-Royal, became head of the Jansenist movement in its early stages. But it was more a common attitude than a common doctrine that kept together this small, silent group of nuns and hermits who, however, soon gained numerous sympathizers among Gallicans, members of the Paris Parliament (supreme court) and influential ladies. For the frivolous society in the Versailles of Louis XIV, Port-Royal was at hand as a warning and a challenge. But for the absolutism of Church and state, which could not tolerate the slightest deviation from the existing system, despite the small numbers, it was a harassment and a threat.

The Jesuits, scenting Calvinism in Port-Royal and in Jansen's work, attacked the *Augustinus.* The youngest brother of the abbess, Antoine, "the Great Arnauld," professor at the Sorbonne, defended it, although very academically and ponderously. The Jesuits, for their part suspected of Pelagianism, brought about the intervention of Rome.

Why did this bulky and little-read work of "Jansenius" seem so dangerous? His *Augustinus* is an organized attack on the increasing importance attached to human agencies from the period of Humanism and the Renaissance, even in scholastic theology, and fostered especially by Jesuit theologians. Continually invoking Augustine, he emphasizes Scripture and the Fathers (Augustine again) instead of philosophy, God's grace instead of human freedom, faith instead of reason. In his unfathomable predestination, God decides as he will from eternity, regardless of merits, to whom he is to give grace and glory and to whom not. Through original and inherited sin, man's nature is corrupted, his will weakened, he is irresistibly determined by love for the earthly, by evil desire (concupiscence). Unless God's love or grace, likewise irresistible (*gratia victrix*), overcomes concupiscence, man can do nothing pleasing to God. The possibility of a "pure" human nature, without either grace or sin, is rejected. Is it so surprising that the Jansenists, although they wanted to be loyal Catholics, were accused of Calvinism?

The practical consequences of this anthropological pessimism were considerable: they included a demand for a return to the strict faith and life of the early Church, for moral rigorism even going as far as rejection of the arts (music, comedy, but not tragedy), and more difficult conditions for confession and communion. In addition, as a result of papal condemnations, they adopted an anticentralist (Gallican) attitude: for the authority of the bishops and parochial clergy against the religious orders under Roman direction; rejection of papal infallibility; permissibility of state intervention in certain ecclesiastical affairs.

Naturally it is impossible here to examine how far the *Augustinus* of Louvain correctly interpreted Augustine of Hippo. There can of course be no doubt today that even Augustine himself in his defensive, anti-

Pelagian, later phase maintained views on predestination to damnation, original sin and irresistible grace[103] that provide abundant material for the Jansenist interpretations (not supported by the New Testament); at a later stage, even the Jansenists tried to show more open-mindedness by borrowing from Aquinas—who could scarcely be regarded as a Molinist.

Finally, five propositions made up by the Jesuit Nicolas Cornet, which the Sorbonne refused to condemn since the author was not known, were condemned as heretical in Rome by Innocent X in 1653.[104] This amounted to defining, against Jansenius, that it is possible to observe God's commandments, that it is possible to resist God's grace, that man is free from inward coercion, that Jesus' death was salvific for all men. The whole controversy was subsequently centered not so much on the book of Jansenius as on the condemned propositions taken from it. The French Jansenists admitted that the propositions were heretical and that the Pope was competent in the "question *de jure.*" But they disputed the claim that these propositions could be found in the *Augustinus:* the Pope could not decide the "question *de facto.*" It is true that the propositions do not occur in so many words in the *Augustinus,* but is not their sense to be found there?

Nevertheless, the Jesuits did not rest until the Sorbonne condemned Antoine Arnauld, in January 1656, after lengthy proceedings followed with great excitement by the public. Only then—at the request of Arnauld, who supplied him and his assistant Nicole with the material—did Pascal intervene in a very different spirit in the controversy. Only ten days afterward, an anonymous broadsheet appeared and created a sensation: the first "letter to an (imagined) friend in the provinces." The subsequent *Lettres Provinciales*[105]—displaying a new mastery of irony and satire and written in a succinct, polished, serene style—were eagerly devoured by the public and at the same time made the mathematician, who had just decided on a retired life in Port-Royal, into a passionately committed, great albeit anonymous publicist. He had taken up residence under another name in the King David Inn, near the Sorbonne and quite close to the Jesuit college. If it had been possible to prove his authorship of the letters, he would certainly have been sent to the Bastille.

The first three letters are directed against the Sorbonne. The irritated theologians, with little concern for correct procedure, thereupon dismissed their colleague Arnauld from office; the printers of the letters were prosecuted, some of them kept in prison for months, and Port-Royal's schools—which were in competition with the Jesuit schools—were closed. Meanwhile in Rome the Jesuits were pressing for a definitive condemnation. Consequently, Pascal wrote the next letters directly against them, the chief opponents: against their lax, hypocritical morality and their confessional practice (letters 4–10), their politics and power-seeking, their *esprit de corps* and their use of unspiritual means for spiritual ends (letters 11–16), finally even against the powerful Jesuit confessor of the young Louis XIV, François Annat (letters 17–18).

Complaints about the "Provincial Letters" were widespread. The members of the Company of Jesus, organized in the spirit of absolute military obedience—unlike the older orders, actively entering into the midst of the world—had established themselves increasingly close to the power centers as confessors in the princely courts, in schools and universities, in science and arts: with a keen sense of what was practically possible, with understanding for the weaknesses of people in high positions, in dogmatic and moral theology optimistically and opportunely stressing man's freedom under the influence of God's grace. With the aid of selected quotations from original works, especially from the widely circulated "Confessor's Manual," drawn up by the Spanish Jesuit Escobar[106] from the writings of twenty-four authorities of the Order, Pascal showed how everything was permitted in various and especially tricky "cases" (*casus*): *escobarder* entered into the French language as a synonym for "equivocate," "quibble," "split hairs." There were many rejoinders (including slanderous attacks on himself and the nuns of Port-Royal), but none of them significant. Casuistry acquired a bad name from that time onward, and Pascal's letters undoubtedly provided the intellectual preparation for the dissolution of the Society of Jesus a hundred years later by Clement XIV (under pressure from the Catholic powers of France, Spain and Portugal and from interested ecclesiastical and curial circles). On the other hand, the stubborn, harsh rigorism of the Jansenists, which seemed to allow people no pleasure and not to recognize the necessity of a more humane Christian ethic, won little sympathy. And at some points in his argument Pascal exaggerated and, in any case, made too many generalizations.

Meanwhile the decisive factor was that power was in the hands of the opponents. Pope Alexander VII confirmed the bull of his predecessor, Innocent X, and now declared expressly that the five propositions were taken from the book of Jansenius and had been condemned wholly in the sense intended by the author.[107] In the following year (1657), the *Lettres Provinciales* were put on the Index of Forbidden Books. But the decrees of the Holy Office were not recognized in France. Later, however, the *Lettres* were condemned also by the Paris council of state and were symbolically torn to pieces and burned by the public executioner at the crossroads at Croix du Tiroir at midday, October 14, 1660. Pascal kept up the struggle for a time with the *Écrits*[108] subscribed by the parish priests of Paris and mainly directed against the *Apologie pour les casuistes*, by the Jesuit Pirot, who himself was condemned by the Sorbonne for his moral laxism and whose work was likewise finally put on the Index by Rome. Further *Écrits sur la grace*[109] exist only as drafts and were not published by Pascal; they would scarcely have escaped condemnation. But the five propositions together with the assertion that they were contained in Jansen's *Augustinus* now became a test of faith. At the orders of the French bishops in 1666, monks and nuns together with priests inclined to Jansenism had to subscribe to them on pain of excommunication.[110] Port-Royal at first attempted a casuistic solution. In a proud letter, worthy of her brother, Jacqueline Pascal urged people to refuse to sign: if bishops had only the courage of girls, then girls ought to have the courage of bishops. But then she, too, yielded and, on the advice of Arnauld, signed with the others. She died a few weeks later.

The conflict went on for a long time in various phases in which unfortunately Port-Royal also became fixed on the controversy about the five propositions supposedly not contained in the *Augustinus*—vigorously criticized on this account a few years later by Jean Racine[111]—and visibly became more rigidly sectarian. Finally the *Roi-Soleil*, for political reasons—in this matter at one with the Pope—struck the definitive blow. He banished Arnauld and his comrade-in-arms Paschasius Quesnel and in 1710 had Port-Royal razed to the ground by his dragoons; not even the graves were spared. But even after this the disputes continued, with fresh condemnations of Jansenism (101 propositions of Quesnel in 1713[112]) and then also of laxism,[113] and ended only with the French Revolution, which had been brought on by state and Church together, and where the Jansenist spirit still influenced the *Constitution civile* for the reorganization of relations between Church and state. Meanwhile "Jansenist" remained in France a label for people who wanted to be Catholic and at the same time puritanically Protestant. More recently Georges Bernanos and François Mauriac were suspected of latent Jansenism.

And Pascal himself? He was strictly opposed to any compromise and felt that the diplomatic tactics of Arnauld and Nicole in subscribing with secret reservations to their condemnation were untruthful. There could be no hair-splitting with Rome's words: if Jansenius—and with him Augustine and Paul—were right, then the Pope and with him the contemporary Church were wrong. Pascal was prepared to take his stand even publicly against Rome and the bishops.[114] But the majority of the friends of Port-Royal were opposed to him, appealed finally to the infallibility of the Church and declared themselves ready to subscribe to the unconditional condemnation.

Disappointed at the attitude of his friends, Pascal had fainted during the vigorous discussion with them and from then on maintained silence. He had only a few months to live. He withdrew from the narrower circle of Port-Royal and tried again to dedicate the remainder of his life to God. As soon as he had published his articles on the cycloid and other works on geometrical problems—at least according to his sister's account—he had finally even given up mathematics as something unnecessary. But even his keen mind could find no solution to the dilemma facing his conscience of remaining loyal to Pope and Church and at the same time to his personal conviction. Here the conflict was no longer between faith and reason but between faith and faith.

In a note on a slip of paper, he had appealed to a higher court against the placing of his *Lettres* on the Index: "If my letters are condemned in Rome, then what I condemn in them is condemned in heaven. To your court I appeal, Lord Jesus. *Ad tuum, Domine Jesu, tribunal appello.*"[115] Certainly Pascal never became an ecclesiastical conformist, as some tried to represent him after his death: he never made any retraction. Nor is it correct to say that he simply rose above the confrontation. The Jansenists tried to forget their dispute with him and remained his friends, constantly in touch with him. But the debate had become fruitless for Pascal and he thought he could continue it only on a higher plane. This he meant to do in his great work the "Apology for the Christian Religion," for which two dozen bundles of notes were found after his death: what we know as the *Pensées.*

Pascal's bodily powers had visibly declined: tuberculosis, cancer or some other illness? There are learned medical treatises on the subject, but none of them solve the problem. He willingly put up with the numerous medicines, bleedings, purgings, by the best doctors in Paris, but they only weakened him even more. He himself had shortened his life by his ruthless penitential practices, continually fighting against the contradictions of his own ego. He had sold his valuable furniture and other possessions and distributed the money to the poor. As already mentioned, six months before his death, he made time to organize the first bus company for Paris and in his will bequeathed the income from this source to the hospitals of Paris and Clermont. The child of a destitute family he had taken into his house fell ill with smallpox. Because of the danger of infection, his sister Gilberte took Pascal into her care, but she would not allow him to be transferred to the hospital for incurables, where he wanted to go to await the end. He was in great torment to the very last day as a result of being refused Viaticum, because the doctors did not think the time had come. His parish priest finally gave him Holy Communion when he was already in his last agony, and had to answer for this to the sharply anti-Jansenist Archbishop of Paris. In this emergency the priest produced evidence that Pascal had broken with Port-Royal, and this the Archbishop—contrary to his promise—triumphantly published. Pascal had indeed wanted to maintain the harmony of his personal faith with the faith of the Church (now defined against him). But how could he give a sign of submission to the official faith of the Church without giving up his personal faith? Pascal died convinced that he was a loyal Catholic, only thirty-nine years old, on August 9, 1662, nine months after Port-Royal's subscription to the condemnation of Port-Royal. His last words were: "May God never abandon me."

## 4. *Tracks of atheism*

We might hesitate a little before putting critical questions to Pascal, for whom—in view of his way of life and suffering—the questions that had to be put to Descartes became questions of life and death. But, since we are not passing judgment here on Pascal, only trying to clarify the modern problems of reason and faith, and since these crictical questions are to be put not only to him but to the whole Augustinian-Reformation tradition, we cannot dispense ourselves from the task. But we can no more enter into a general criticism of his philosophy than we did with regard to Descartes. And it is even less possible than it was with Descartes to make a clear-cut distinction between philosophical and theological questions in Pascal's work. But, just as with Descartes, so also with Pascal, it can be seen how these questions have persisted to the present time in what is often only a slightly different form. They are therefore not primarily historical but still highly relevant questions. It is here not least that we find, even before the French Revolution, the tracks that were to lead to modern forms of atheism: to humanistic, political and scientific atheism. As with Descartes, we begin with questions that might seem to the superficial observer to have little to do with the problems of faith and reason or with the question of God and which nevertheless are of the utmost importance for the decision today for belief in God or atheism.

## Questions of morality: humanistic atheism?

It has been said that Pascal's last years were his greatest. This was the period of the *Pensées,* which more than anything else established his world fame; the period of the passionate fighter with the frail figure, who could no longer walk without a stick and could scarcely bear to travel; the period of the unsparing devotion of a "moralist" who in that century was not satisfied with moral meditations in the style of La Rochefoucauld's maxims, La Bruyère's portrayal of manners or La Fontaine's fables, and who was still less prepared to accept that discrepancy between doctrine and life which Rousseau permitted in the following century, but who tried radically to put in practice the implications of his moral theory. It would be utterly banal to explain this unusual, truly "abnormal" life simply as the result of his sickness and—since, to adapt Shakespeare, genius and madness are closely related*—to dismiss the challenge of Pascal's pathos as "pathological." Whatever psychopathic factors may have been in-

---

* "The lunatic, the lover, and the poet,
  Are of imagination all compact."
  A *Midsummer Night's Dream,* Act V, Scene 1. Translator

volved, Pascal was in every respect a shrewd, very sober analyst and as such always to be taken seriously.

Nevertheless the *questions* must be raised. Even at his first turning to inwardness (his "first conversion"), did not Pascal display the rigorous intolerance of a new convert toward the ex-Capuchin Jacques Forton, Sieur de Saint-Ange? The latter seemed to Pascal to be propagating an alliance of faith with rational thought too much and God's grace too little and, after a personal discussion with him, Pascal denounced him to the archbishop and did not let go until he had retracted. A tragic prelude to what Pascal himself was to experience at the hands of the Inquisition? Even at this early stage, do we not perceive signs of the pride, fostered by the Jansenists, of belonging to the "elect" or "enlightened"?

And after his "second conversion," did not Pascal practice an extremely rigorous ascetical self-torment and a spirituality hostile to the senses? Does not his idea of man's strict renunciation and humiliation before God bear the mark more of Saint-Cyran and Jansen than of the gospel? Do we not find here an ancient sickness of intellectuals and aristocrats, the *taedium vitae*, the weariness and disgust of life, which—following in Pascal's tracks—can be found again in Jean Paul Sartre's analyses of boredom (*ennui*) and loathing (*nausée*)? In order to be perfect in the sight of God, must we renounce all amenities, neglect the body, even be dirty (Jacqueline Pascal objected vigorously to this, at an early stage)? In order to be disciples of Jesus Christ, instead of bearing as a cross the sufferings of every day, must we impose on ourselves extraordinary sufferings— following the example of the ancient monks and penitents of the desert? Must we deny ourselves such superfluities as pictures, wall hangings, favorite foods? Must we find terribly bitter medicines tasty, secretly wear a spiked belt on the naked body and press it into the skin when thoughts of pride or worldly pleasure occur? Must we also give up the most innocent friendships, repel even a sister's love, on the ground that we must not commit ourselves to human beings? Must we understand self-abasement as self-destruction instead of service to our fellow men? Must we dismiss servants, do our own cleaning, and refuse medical attention simply because poor people cannot afford these things? In brief, must we hate our own selves in order to love God with all our heart? Does not the Christian way lead to God by turning to the other person, rather than by annihilation of the self? Is not loving our neighbor (as we love ourselves) the fulfillment of loving God?

Does not all this reveal, particularly at the end, a certain inconsistency which always appears when an attempt is made to fulfill Jesus' requirements too literally and anachronistically in a wholly different world and time? There is imitation instead of correlation: copying/simulating instead of following Christ in our own way in a new situation in a new age. This is particularly important with reference to the three traditional "evangelical counsels," of poverty, obedience, celibacy. What is the position if someone sells horses, coaches, Gobelins, silver and precious furniture and yet keeps—perhaps must keep—his house? If someone breaks with his family in order to live in primitive simplicity and yet continually returns to claim their help when he is in need? If he vows obedience to his confessor but refuses it to the Pope on the grounds that his conscience demands obedience to God? If someone voluntarily renounces marriage but then—as in the case of Pascal's niece, a boarder in Port-Royal—wants to forbid it to others, describes it as the most dangerous and the lowest of all Christian ways of life and at the same time becomes so prudish that he cannot bear to hear beauty praised or to see children fondled?

These questions of ours are concerned *not with the person* but with the facts. What we have said—based on the records of Pascal's life—is obviously not meant as a judgment on his personal conscience and his personal attitude. No one has a right to make such a judgment, especially in view of the indescribable suffering of this man who was so acutely sensitive in mind and body. After his twenty-fourth year (his second breakdown in health came a few months before Descartes's visit) he was incapable of any regular work and yet—without ever playing the "eternal patient" or acting like Molière's *malade imaginaire*—continued to be present and active in the world of learning and in society until, after bearing within himself the germ of death for a long time, he died completely worn out by mental exertion and bodily asceticism.

*Asceticism instead of love?* Disregarding Pascal's person, we must be clear about the true meaning of Christian asceticism. In modern times, these external practices (of renunciation, mortification, self-denial) at the expense of humanity and our fellow men—as will become clearer in connection with Feuerbach and Nietzsche—have undoubtedly completely repelled many with humanist inclinations from belief in God and Christianity. For God seemed to be possible only at the expense of man—being a Christian only at the expense of being human. All this prepared the way for the rise of humanistic atheism. Phenomena found among the Jansenists (the world-forsaking "Catholic puritans") were also found in a different form among Protestant puritans and Pietists—who for the most part were not world-forsaking—with their belief in election, proselytizing zeal, and their depreciation of the body and sexuality, worldly joys, pleasure, theater. Against all these tendencies it must be said that there are in fact many examples of external asceticism or self-denial by special accomplishments even in non-Christian religions, but they have scarcely anything to do with the life and teachings of Jesus of Nazareth, who—for Christians—should be the norm, the standard.[116]

## Questions of politics: political atheism?

The fact must not be overlooked that Pascal, particularly in the final period of his life, practiced love of neighbor in an extraordinary way, mostly in the form of anonymous works of Christian charity, in daily service to the poor. As we heard, he received a poor family into his house; he also continued to help a fifteen-year-old country girl whom he had found begging, and he constantly gave money to the poor and hungry and at the same time (after selling so much of his furniture) went to the limits of what was financially possible.

And yet here, too, *questions* must be raised. When the burden of taxation imposed by Richelieu led to a great rebellion even in Rouen, put down with great bloodshed, could not the young Pascal have done something more sociologically effective than construct a calculating machine for his father, who had been sent there as tax commissioner? And under the dictatorship of Richelieu's successor, Cardinal Mazarin, would he not have done better to join the revolt—the *Fronde*—against the central authority in Paris? But of course Pascal had no sympathy for the revolt, since he had a horror of civil war as the greatest of all evils.

But had this intellectual, moving in the ruling circles, any idea at all of the social and political problems created by the subjects of these rulers in the outwardly brilliant France of Louis XIII and Louis XIV? Did he not seem to be living in a completely unspoiled world? Would he not otherwise have had to speak quite differently not only of the individual but also of the social *misère* of man, of men, which supplied the dynamite for the great explosion a century later: not only of man's lowliness but of his abasement, enslavement, pauperization? In these thirty, forty years of incessant warfare—religious wars, fiscal wars, peasant wars, cabinet wars— brutally carried out for reasons of state, supposedly absolute but in fact serving very definite interests, ought he not to have protested in a very different way and pleaded—against the misunderstood *grandeur* of the nation—for peace at home and abroad? Ought not this man, who considered it dangerous to tell the people that the laws were unjust, instead of talking merely in a general way about law and laws, to have clearly named the true culprits, to have pointed out the power seekers and the self-seekers? Under the influence of individualistic, interiorized Jansenistic piety, was he not all too naïve in seeking the solution simply in faith? Even after his conversion, was he not occupied merely with general questions of practicing the faith and with a socially irrelevant love of neighbor instead of political enlightenment and action? These are questions that even non-Marxists may and should raise.

But here, too, it is a question *not of the person* but *of the facts*. We should not try to judge Pascal from an unhistorical perspective. Under the dictatorships of Richelieu, Mazarin and finally Louis XIV, who all made use of spying and sudden arrests to shut out promptly any sort of opposition, it was not only dangerous but in fact impossible to name the people, who incidentally were only too well known. Even Saint-Cyran, once a friend of Richelieu, but allegedly more dangerous than six armies, long before the great theological controversies, was arrested on the orders of the same Richelieu and released again only five years later, after Richelieu's death. The seventeenth century was not as ripe as the eighteenth for social revolutionary activity on the grand scale, but only for political conspiracies and smaller revolts in the provinces. And to have joined the (last) "Fronde" of the great noble families against the absolutist kingship would have meant merely replacing one domination by another, exchanging Cardinal Mazarin for Cardinal de Retz, who could certainly compete with the former in greed for power, lack of scruple, and cunning. Both came, incidentally, from Macchiavelli's country, where the Renaissance had produced a policy—prevailing in France with the absolutism of Richelieu—unaffected by considerations of religion or morality, based solely on calculations of the prospects of success.

Did Pascal see through these connecting links, especially the continual misuse of religion for the interests of naked power? He certainly was not living in isolation, nor was he so unpolitical as he might seem to superficial readers of his "thoughts." A number of his *pensées* on laws and power make it clear that he thought more than he was able to say. According to him, the power of kings is based on reason, but also on the stupidity of the people. Thus the greatest and most important thing in the world is founded on weakness but nevertheless can be surprisingly secure because nothing is so certain as the fact that the people will be weak.[117] On this last point in particular Pascal was mistaken.

*Love of neighbor instead of political commitment?* Again disregarding the person of Pascal and merely in order to establish the facts, it must be observed quite generally that the failure especially of the Catholic Church to meet sociopolitical problems with more than pious words, almsgiving and individual charity, seriously discredited belief in God at an early stage. Both the social implications of Jesus' proclamation, behavior and fate and also the socioethical potential and sociological relevance of the Christian message as a whole were completely neglected.[118] The association of spiritualized, individualized belief in God with the oppressive political claims of princely absolutism made that belief increasingly incredible to the rising bourgeoisie, particularly in France. The Enlightenment here more than elsewhere—rooted in the earlier Enlightenment of the early-capitalist upper-Italian Renaissance cities, which had grown rich on the Eastern trade—acquired simultaneously both a political and an extremely antireligious character.

Opposition to belief in God increased because it was used by princes ruling by God's grace, by cardinals, bishops and priests as a means of preventing the diffusion of the "light of reason" and of keeping the people in tutelage and servitude. After churches and clergy had come to be the main support of the unsocial, corrupt and bankrupt *ancien régime*, the cry of the Jacobins "Priests to the lampposts"—at the end of the outwardly devout French "century of the saints"—was not really surprising. For the first time in world history, atheism had become a political program. It was almost exactly a hundred and thirty years after Pascal's death, on November 10, 1793, that the Christian God was deposed in Notre Dame, in Paris, by the party of the Hébertists and atheistic Reason proclaimed as antigoddess; the Christian calculation of time was abolished, and the revolutionary calendar, beginning with 1792, introduced. The calendar soon disappeared, but *political atheism* did not: it was rediscovered in new forms, not only bourgeois liberal but also proletarian socialist. We shall have to deal with this again, particularly in connection with Karl Marx.

## Questions of science: scientific atheism?

As against Descartes, Pascal rightly carried the problem of conceptual certainty over to the very much more fundamental problem of existential insecurity, imbalance, peril: man looks not only for conceptual certainty, he wants existential security. And Pascal saw the solution—as opposed to purely mathematically rational apprehension—in the dimension of intuitive, integral sensitivity, of *sentiment*, the *esprit de finesse*, of the "heart." His Archimedean point he found between dogmatism and skepticism, in faith in the biblical God, the credibility of which can be justified at the bar of reason: an existential certainty of the self that is rooted in an existential certainty of God. Man therefore should think in believing and believe in thinking.

But here, too, *questions* emerge. Must we devalue the mathematical-scientific conclusions of reason in order to revalue the faith of the heart? Was it really right for Pascal, after playing with science as a precocious child, to neglect this science when he grew older, almost as an adult throws away a toy for which he is too old? Was it right for him, on the threshold of the greatest scientific discoveries, not to want to "probe science too deeply"? Or must we give up the study of the mysteries of nature in order to get on the track of the divine mysteries? May we at most have recourse to mathematics—as Pascal did at the end—as to a necessary evil (like sexual desire), perhaps as a pain-killer for incurable toothache? Did not God himself—as Descartes thought—give man reason, the power to think, to study, to discover in microcosm and macrocosm, and indeed to be able to make calculating machines and conduct pressure experiments? Must we really reject science in order to devote ourselves to the service of God? Must a person cease to be a "philosopher and scholar" in order truly to believe in God, to be a Christian?

In his last years, did not Pascal in practice increasingly allow reason to be overpowered by faith, stressing only man's nothingness and the limitations of reason and acknowledging the sole authority remaining for him, that of faith? Is Christian revelation, in practice, therefore the sole source of truth and certainty, as Kierkegaard later insisted and as Karl Barth attempted to think out fundamentally and dogmatically? On the whole, then, this means a depreciation of human reason, also of human freedom and indeed of man himself, which can be justified vis-à-vis neither the Creator nor his creature. In the age of absolutism, did this amount to a new absolutism of faith? And thus a reason that abdicates? A thinking that is given up? A renunciation of philosophy as the legitimate end of all philosophy? "To have no time for philosophy is to be a true philosopher"?[119]

And does not this depreciation of reason and philosophy involve also a serious depreciation of the philosophical understanding of God, which does not do justice either to the history of philosophy and religion or to the biblical faith? Did not Pascal separate the God of philosophers and scholars so clearly from the God of Jesus Christ that he could no longer find any truth at all in the former? Why should not even the God of the philosophers be able to tell man something about his greatness and wretchedness? Without conceptual reflection on the biblical image of God, are we not reduced to an anthropomorphic, naïve belief in God, which is too much to ask of modern thinking man? Does it not lead—as it did in particular with Pascal after a sensational miraculous cure of his niece in Port-Royal with the aid of a thorn supposedly from the crown of thorns—to a crude belief in miracles, relics and prophecies, which was questioned even then and which today is no longer maintained by any serious biblical scholars? Why should it not be possible—without empty compromises—to find a way between this rigid separation of the philosophical from the Christian understanding of God on Augustinian lines, which Pascal (and after him Kierkegaard and Barth) carried out, and that harmonization on Thomist lines which Descartes (and with him baroque scholasticism and neoscholasticism) practiced? Should not philosophy, then, mean for faith something other than merely a lapse from faith or an impediment to faith? And is not faith also something other than merely a discrediting of reason and an abolishing of philosophy? And finally, should not the world religions be more positively evaluated than they were by Pascal, Kierkegaard and Karl Barth and at the same time more critically than is usual in Thomism and Neo-Thomism?

If we ask about the theological background of this depreciation of reason, freedom, philosophy and science, we come up against the general defamation of the desire for knowledge (*libido sciendi*) which, for Augustine and Jansen, together with the desire for pleasures of the flesh (*libido sentiendi*) and the desire for power (*libido dominandi*), form the three types of irresistible evil desire, or concupiscence. We find here the theological interpretation of man between Adam and Christ, which assumes

three clearly distinguished stages, states or natures of man, as described in
the very title of the *Augustinus*. There is first the integral "innocent nature" of Adam before the first sin, which nature must necessarily be
equipped with God's grace. Then there is the corrupt, "fallen nature" of
Adam after his sin, subject to that triple concupiscence. Finally, we have
redeemed, "purified nature," healed by infallibly efficacious grace, which,
however, is granted only to the elect and leaves the others—even children
who die without baptism—in eternal damnation. The virtues of the pagans are brilliant vices, unredeemed humanity is a *massa damnata*.

Today at least we must ask quite clearly if this whole conception of
man is not associated with an idea of paradise and original sin, of a
golden age and a mythological lapse into sin, that—from the modern
viewpoint on both biblical and scientific primitive history—has never
been realized—the world from the very beginning in a perfect, unchangeable, static, paradisiac order and the first (and sole) human couple directly
created by God with grandiose natural, preternatural and supernatural
gifts? A kind of superman, free from concupiscence, suffering and mortality, endowed with higher knowledge infused by God and with sanctifying
grace not only for himself but also for posterity? And then this whole
beautiful original order destroyed by a lapse of this one human couple
into sin and man from that time onward deprived of all preternatural
and supernatural gifts? An original sin conveyed to all men by sexual
desire as inherited sin and supposed to result for all in a weakening if
not corruption of human nature, reason and freedom? With regard to
the origin and evolution of the world and man, has not science established
the very opposite of such a perfect original state of the world and man:
that there is no place in the scientific understanding of the world for a
story of paradise and of the sin of a single human couple, if this is understood as a historical account and not as a statement of principles?

In such a theology, is not even the advent of Jesus Christ interpreted
too much in the light of this initially perfect order, which is destroyed
and then has to be restored by him: the descent—completely intelligible
against the background of the older world picture—of a Son of God from
heaven to earth and even into the underworld and then again the journey
up into the same heaven? And together with this Christology, an anthropology that in all three stages or states is associated with a hypostasized,
impersonally understood "created grace" that—contrary to the whole biblical understanding of grace—is detached from and made independent of
God's gracious benevolence: grace—understood more in Stoic than in
Christian terms—as "power," almost as supernatural fuel?

All this, it must be said, is a very burdensome traditional and especially
Augustinian heritage, which Pascal accepted by way of Jansenism, which
is found also with the Reformers and with Protestant theologians standing by the Augustinian-Reformation tradition. This is a situation that in
any case makes it impossible simply to replace Thomas by Augustine,

Spanish baroque scholasticism by Luther or Calvin, Vatican I by Kierkegaard or Barth.

Here, too, it is a question *not of the person but of the facts.* We certainly cannot identify Pascal's opinions in all points with those of Jansen and Port-Royal. In the *Lettres Provinciales*, it was not merely for tactical reasons that he objected to being regarded as a Jansenist. Some interpreters of Pascal are also doubtful whether the two last chapters in particular of the Brunschvicq edition ("The Miracles" and "Polemical Fragments") should be included in the great work, the "Apology for the Christian Religion." They were perhaps simply material for further writings against the Jesuits, some of this possibly drawn from Saint-Cyran and Nicole. The nature of the fragments makes it difficult to sort out and decide which are Pascal's very own theological opinions. Neither can Pascal in any case be identified with hostility to science. In his early contacts with Jansenists, he just did not adopt their rejection of science. And he could never maintain it consistently to the end. Did he merely relapse occasionally? In his last years, he composed a book for geometry lessons in Port-Royal. Perhaps it could more correctly be said that he lived to the very end in an unsettled inward conflict between science and religion, the spirit of research and the love of God.

*Religion instead of science?* Again disregarding Pascal's person, we must insist on the fact that Christian faith does not demand this kind of hostility to reason, philosophy and science. On the contrary, it is an attitude that has very seriously compromised belief in God in modern times.

If the new developments in natural science and philosophy had not been resisted both by apologetic-defensive appeals to the authority of God, the Bible, the Church, the Pope, and mostly by inquisitorial offensive measures, only to be continually losing ground in one skirmish after another; if faith had not been made absolute, isolated and apparently immunized, then abandoned to an unworldly inwardness; would it not, then, have been possible, as in the high Middle Ages, in the light of Christian faith—as Copernicus, Kepler, Galileo, Mersenne, Descartes and others hoped—opportunely to accept influences and conclusions from the new science? To interpret it comprehensively and—when necessary—to criticize it and bring out its relativity? All this for the sake of a deeper, comprehensive understanding of natural science *and* the Christian faith? Was the unparalleled mastery of the world by modern science and technology necessarily bound to result in the denial of God? Must this occur merely because natural science cannot verify God like other objects, cannot analyze or in the end manipulate him and can nevertheless function splendidly without him?

A precondition, of course, for a different approach would have been a new critical understanding of the Bible in the light of the discoveries in astronomy and physics and increasingly in biology and medicine. A balanced literary criticism of the Bible could have helped in this respect. In Paris, a largely unknown contemporary of Descartes and Pascal, Richard Simon (1638–1712), who entered the Oratory as a young cleric in the year of Pascal's death, founded modern biblical criticism long before Lessing and Reimarus. He was the first Christian author to discover—from what he had learned from the *Tractatus theologico-politicus*[120] of the Jewish philosopher Baruch Spinoza (1632–77) and from a rabbi in Paris—that the Pentateuch (those "five books of Moses," which continually provoked conflicts with the natural sciences) was made up from various literary sources, and to attempt to harmonize the conclusions of his critical exegesis with dogma.

Pascal still regarded the Bible as a book written in code, full of symbols, allegories and enigmas, which all had to be deciphered by the allegorical method used long before by Origen and Augustine, by the ancient and medieval theologians and also latterly by Jansen. Simon, however, thought nothing of this method, which had been practiced by pre-Christian rabbis and especially by Philo of Alexandria, unhistorically spiritualizing and reinterpreting the texts. He studied Hebrew zealously and took considerable pains to understand the individual texts, which for the contemporaries of the biblical writers were certainly not in code but completely intelligible. He suspected also the anonymity and pseudonymity of numerous Old Testament books, the significance of the interpolations and the variety of styles. But when he published his *Critical History of the Old Testament*,[121] some fifteen years after Pascal's death, he met with serious hostility, especially on the part of Jacques Bénigne Bossuet, powerful preacher and Bishop of Meaux, a very influential theologian under Louis XIV and later author of the anti-Roman Gallican Articles of the Church of France. Once more, the problem was "solved" in an authoritarian-inquisitorial manner. In the very year of its publication, Simon's book was suppressed and he himself was turned out of the Oratory. He continued to work tirelessly until his death and published his suppressed work and all his later books in heretical Amsterdam,[122] but had no successor in Catholicism.

The opportunities for Christianity in regard to modern science were by no means merely hypothetical. In fact they were very great, as is shown by the fact that both Descartes and Pascal, as also Copernicus, Kepler, Galileo and Newton, the leading representatives of the new mathematical-mechanical natural science, were not only believers in God but professing Christians. And even Voltaire, who popularized Newton's world picture on the continent, and likewise d'Alembert and Diderot, with their Encyclopedia—the great work of the French Enlightenment—propagated the new mechanistic world view not as atheists but as Deists, believing in a Creator—however remote—and Ruler of this world machine. Nevertheless, not only the ancient-medieval idea of a God *above* the world but also the modern, enlightened idea of a God *outside* the world proved to be inadequate. This Deism, not accepted by theology, which still needed God in the physical world—as with Newton—to correct the distortions of the planetary orbits, now developed consistently into a *scientific atheism*, which did not need God either physically for the explanation of the world or even morally for the conduct of life.

Descartes's dualism, between mind and matter, between God as above the world and the world machine, which made possible a purely mathematical-mechanistic natural science, resulted—as already noted—in the disruption of philosophy into materialism and idealism. But in the long run this dualism satisfied neither side: the world should be explicable in the light of a uniform principle. And while on the Cartesian right the attempt was made to explain everything uniformly in the light of the eternal divine idea (as in the various forms of idealism from Malebranche and Spinoza to Schelling and Hegel), on the Cartesian left everything was increasingly interpreted in the light of "divine" eternal matter. This became evident in the various forms of materialism that now began to appear.

The term "materialism" was used for the first time, twelve months before Pascal's death, by Robert Boyle, the English founder of chemistry as a science, who attacked and destroyed Aristotle's theory of the four elements but defended the Christian faith against atheism.[123] The word came into general use in the subsequent decades. But the way was prepared by the long tradition of Franco-British freethinking on the part of Jean Bodin, Lord Herbert of Cherbury, Anthony Collins, then of Thomas Hobbes and Pierre Bayle and finally of Voltaire and the Encyclopedists, for Julien Offroy de La Mettrie in the following century to draw the logical conclusions and profess a completely atheistic materialism. What was rejected here was not only—as by the Deists—the God of the Fathers and of Jesus Christ but also—as against the Deists—the God of the philosophers and scholars. La Mettrie, dismissed as an army doctor in France because of his materialistic atheism but received in Prussia by Frederick II and even accepted into the Berlin Academy of Sciences, in his main work, on *Man as Machine*,[124] published in Holland, did no more than consistently apply to man Descartes's mechanistic idea of animals as complex machines (contrary to Descartes's intentions). For La Mettrie, even human thinking and indeed the whole human psyche—which in fact is completely dependent on bodily processes—must be explained by the mechanism of the nervous system. Thus consciousness within being and the mind within the infinite world of bodies are not incomprehensible residues but are explicable in the light of being, of corporeal reality, of matter. Morality still makes sense: it is the art of enjoying life. But religion is weighed in the balance with hygiene—and found wanting: it turns out to be unimportant for our well-being.

The materialistic-atheistic trend was continued after La Mettrie's death

—for which Frederick the Great himself composed the memorial address —by Baron P.-H. d'Holbach, who was born in the Palatinate but settled in Paris. Twenty years before the great revolution, he published under a pseudonym his comprehensive dogmatics of atheism. His *System of Nature or the Laws of the Physical and the Moral World*[125] explains matter and mind, physics and ethics, as identical and religion as harmful: priests must be replaced by doctors. The survival of the soul after death is as absurd as the possibility that a clock shattered into a thousand pieces could continue to strike and count the hours.

Atheistic materialism had the immense advantage in the arguments that it seemed continually to be confirmed by the conclusions of mechanistic natural science. The better this science came to understand matter and its unlimited possibilities, the more superfluous God or belief in him became for it. When finally Pierre-Simon de Laplace, as the "Newton of France," completing Newton's work in his *Celestial Mechanics*,[126] was able to explain even the irregularities in the planetary orbits (of Saturn and Jupiter) as self-correcting, recourse to a world Creator and world Ruler was also seen from that time onward to be definitively unnecessary. When presenting his first volume to Napoleon, Laplace could rightly answer his questions about the place of God in this creation: "Sire, I had no need of this hypothesis."

Thus the whole solar system turned out to be mechanically stable and the universe an immense self-regulating machine existing of itself for unlimited time. And—against all opposition from Church, theology and state, the whole authority-accepting world—natural science without God had definitively become possible. In this science, God must not—indeed could not and might not—play a part any longer, if its method was to remain neat and exact. What the great revolution had achieved only temporarily, mechanistic science, not held up by any statement of faith, had achieved for itself: the abolition of God. From now on religion was not a scientific but only a private affair. And for many people, science had replaced religion even in the private sphere. But the news of the death of God was to reach the mass of educated people only a few decades later.

But before we come to deal with the problems as they developed after the French Revolution, we must draw up a brief inventory of the material related to the problems of the relations between reason and faith.

# III. Against rationalism for rationality

If the observer looks back over the dramatic history of reason and faith in modern times, which led to the elimination of God from politics and science, his impressions are bound to be conflicting. In the course of this history, what was "inevitable" and what was not? Is the trend of this historical process irreversible, completed once and for all? Or has belief in God still a future? Has it perhaps a new future, particularly if we take for granted and recognize the modern process of secularization and emancipation?

## 1. The epistemological discussion

In the last part of this chapter, we can make only a provisional inventory: a kind of consolidation of the material relating to the problems of reason and faith, of modern science and theology. Unless we are completely mistaken, it seems that the general outlook for epistemology in the present century, after some clouds at the beginning, is now brighter. At any rate, after testing thoroughly some extreme possibilities, there are concrete indications of a new awareness on both sides and a better understanding between theology and natural science. It is worth while to cast a brief glance at the latest developments in the theory of knowledge,[1] in order then to deduce some fundamental conclusions with reference to modern rationality.

## The empirical and the "mystical": Ludwig Wittgenstein

Between the two world wars, leading epistemologists—combining Cartesian rationalism and British empiricism—defended the thesis that only propositions of mathematics and logic, together with those of the empirical sciences, can be meaningful: propositions that go beyond these must be described *a priori* as senseless.

This in the first place was the view of *Ludwig Wittgenstein* (1889–1951), a Viennese industrialist's son, a talented aeronautical engineer, who came to Cambridge to study mathematics and became friendly with Bertrand Russell. As a volunteer and officer in the First World War, he was taken prisoner in Italy and used his time there to complete his inspired, one-sided *Tractatus Logico-Philosophicus*.[2] The "whole meaning" of this extraordinarily influential "logical-philosophical treatise," which is meant to be an analysis of the logical structure of language, can be summarized—according to the author's preface—in two propositions.

*Proposition I:* "*What can be said at all can be said clearly.*"[3] Thus Wittgenstein had followed Descartes's rational path to clear and distinct "ideas" or—better—"propositions," "statements," "words," but had far outstripped Descartes, who had left to faith and theology their own "ideas," although these were far from clear and distinct. For the young Wittgenstein, combining the linguistic criticism of the British empiricists with the mathematical logicism of Russell, the "right method of philosophy" would really be "to say nothing except what can be said, i.e., the propositions of natural science, i.e., something that has nothing to do with philosophy: and then always, when someone else wished to say something metaphysical, to demonstrate to him that he had given no meaning to certain signs in his propositions."[4] Propositions that go beyond logic or natural science are consequently to be described forthrightly as senseless: "Most propositions and questions, that have been written about philosophical matters, are not false, but senseless."[5] Consequently:

*Proposition II:* "*Whereof one cannot speak thereof one must be silent.*"[6] Of course, Wittgenstein was often misunderstood, as if he had claimed that anything that could not be expressed meaningfully in mathematical-scientific terms did not exist, was absurd. Wittgenstein's opinion, however, was, "We feel that even if *all possible* scientific questions be answered, the problems of life have still not been touched at all. Of course there is then no question left, and just this is the answer."[7] What is beyond the limits of language, what cannot be thought and cannot be said, can still exist: "There is indeed the inexpressible. This *shows* itself; it is the mystical."[8] What does this mean?

The existence of the world is inexpressible: "Not *how* the world is, is the mystical, but *that* it is."[9]

The meaning and the value of the world are inexpressible: "The sense of the world must lie outside the world. . . . *In* it there is no value—and if there were, it would be of no value."[10]

Consequently the ethical also is inexpressible: "Hence also there can be no ethical propositions."[11]

Life and survival are inexpressible: "The solution of the riddle of life in space and time lies *outside* space and time."[12]

Finally God, too, is inexpressible: "God does not reveal himself *in* the world."[13] Is Norman Malcolm, Wittgenstein's interpreter and a personal acquaintance, right when he says: "Obviously the *Tractatus* is a thoroughly metaphysical work; this is not a minor tendency of the book"?[14] Certainly "Wittgenstein did not reject the metaphysical; rather, he rejected the possibility of *stating* the metaphysical."[15] But this means for Wittgenstein that the experience of the "mystical" cannot be given expression. And this has devastating consequences for theology and philosophy.

In the face of such a claim on the part of scientific thought, is *theology* as mere "mysticism" on the lines of Asiatic philosophers of religion simply to point by purely negative statements to a wordless experience? Or should it, even as "dialectical theology," in the style of the young Barth, get right away from modern thought and—following Kierkegaard—take refuge in a paradoxical faith that cannot be rationally justified? Not only theology, however, but also any *philosophy* that claims to be more than a "critique of language"[16] and a logical clarification of ideas is condemned to silence by Wittgenstein. And in so far as propositions of the *Tractatus* go beyond this, even they must be "surmounted" as "senseless" in order to see the world rightly.[17] So radical is Wittgenstein: "Whereof one cannot speak thereof one must be silent." This last proposition of the *Tractatus* holds also for the treatise itself.[18]

What remains theoretically for the "problems of life"—and this must be clearly recognized—is speechlessness. And—in this respect like Albert Schweitzer after the negative result of the liberal quest for the historical Jesus—Wittgenstein drew from this fact the surprising conclusion that he had to devote himself no longer to philosophical theory but to a life of practical work. He decided to lead a simple life and was active for many years as a village schoolteacher, leading a kind of monastic life, in Lower Austria; then, without entering the order, he worked as assistant gardener in a Benedictine monastery, sleeping in a toolshed; finally he worked as an architect. Only in 1929, when his views had fundamentally changed, did he return to Cambridge under pressure from his friends, but even there still maintaining his monastic way of life. He promptly took his Ph.D. and then gave lectures, which, however, often turned out to be monologues or duologues. We shall have to take note of his later development.[19]

## Logic and theory of knowledge against metaphysics?
## Rudolf Carnap

The inexpressible, "mystical," in Wittgenstein's thought *and* life has often later been simply neglected. This happened at the very place where his *Tractatus* otherwise had its greatest influence: in that *Vienna Circle*, founded in 1922 by Moritz Schlick,[20] a student of Max Planck, composed of philosophers, mathematicians and natural scientists, which published in 1929 a manifesto, "Scientific Theory of the World—the Vienna Circle."[21] Here, too, it was claimed that only propositions of mathematics and logic,

which in fact are purely formal, without empirical content, and propositions of the empirical sciences, which can be tested by experience, can be
meaningful. On the other hand, there is no mention here of the inexpressible, "mystical." The Vienna Circle therefore strictly insisted on the
*verification principle,* attributed to Wittgenstein:[22] Those propositions
alone are not meaningless which can be proved true, "verified," by observation of the facts (*Sachverhalte*).*

For this rationalist-empiricist program, empiricists like Hume and Mill
were invoked, philosophers of science like Helmholtz, Mach, Poincaré and
Einstein, logicians like Leibniz, Frege, Russell, Whitehead and of course
Wittgenstein, finally social philosophers like Feuerbach, Marx and
Spencer. But there was no appeal to the great German tradition, not even
to Kant, and the movement, then, on the whole was not taken seriously
in Germany. The aversion of the Viennese to "metaphysics" was shown
especially in their attitude toward German idealism (and with it to the
"philosophy of life" or "existence"), in which they perceived—not incorrectly—a stronghold of hostility to modern science and an instrument of
social and political reaction. A turning point in philosophy was seen to be
emerging. Only now, with the turning of philosophy to language, to
mathematics, to natural science, had the Enlightenment reached its goal;
only now would absolute clarity prevail and rationality find its fulfillment.
There would be no false consideration for tradition, no false consideration
for ordinary language. But there would be objective analysis of reality to
be achieved with the assistance of new, neutral, historically unburdened,
unambiguous signs and symbols that would make possible a yes or no and
thus a definitive settlement of long-outstanding problems. Philosophy
would be reduced to logic and linguistic analysis, metaphysics definitively
overcome, theology declared *a priori* senseless. The "search for a rock-bot-
tom foundation of science and philosophy" as we found it in its modern
form first in Descartes is therefore found not only in transcendental philosophy, in phenomenology, in Heidegger's fundamental ontology and in
the older positivism but also in analytic philosophy: "for its effort to replace ordinary language with a precise scientific language satisfying all requirements for exactness is nothing more than the old ideal of the absolute expressed in a typically modern form. Instead of absolute knowledge,
there is now absolute exactness."[23]

A year before the manifesto, one of the most important representatives
of the Vienna Circle, *Rudolf Carnap* (1891–1970), a student of the mathematician and logician Gottlob Frege, had produced an extremely ambi-

---

* In his Introduction to Wittgenstein's *Tractatus* (p. 9), Bertrand Russell writes:
"Facts which are not compounded of other facts are what Mr. Wittgenstein calls
*Sachverhalte,* whereas a fact which may consist of two or more facts is called a
*Tatsache:* thus, for example, 'Socrates is wise' is a *Sachverhalt,* as well as a *Tatsache,*
whereas 'Socrates is wise and Plato is his pupil' is a *Tatsache* but not a *Sachverhalt.*"
Translator.

tious work on the "logical structure of the world."[24] Descartes's dream seemed to be fulfilled here. Moved by the ethos of a genuine "scientific approach," Carnap considered that he was putting into effect Leibnizian ideas: of a universal mathematics (*mathesis universalis*) and art of combination (*ars combinatoria*), as also of a universal science (*scientia generalis*) and a symbolic language (*characteristica universalis*). In their *Principia mathematica*,[25] Whitehead and Russell had worked out the most comprehensive system of a "symbolic logic" (logistics) oriented to mathematics. Carnap then wanted to combine this mathematical logic with the reduction of all reality to that which is "given" in experience ("given" as understood by Ernst Mach, the philosopher of science, Schlick's predecessor, and by the neopositivist Poincaré).

An analysis of reality as a whole is sought with the aid of the mathematical-logical theory of relations on an empirical basis: the undecomposable units from one's own stream of experience ("autopsychological elementary experiences"[26]) are taken as basic elements. Then, from certain fundamental or root concepts, all concepts with an empirical content (perceived in the first place intuitively) of the natural and the human sciences are rationally deduced in the form of a genealogy. That is to say, a genealogy "constructed" by logical-mathematical formulas: autopsychological, physical, heteropsychological and cultural objects.[27] The great aim, admittedly in the still distant future, is to reconstruct rationally all scientifically possible statements in an all-embracing, logically connected uniform science. Anyway, Carnap's constructional system aims programmatically at "a rational reconstruction of the entire *formation of reality*, which, in cognition, is carried out for the most part intuitively."[28] In this connection, all objects are to be characterized by purely structural (formal, logical) properties, all scientific statements to be reshaped into purely structural statements: that is, a total structuralism.[29]

*What are the consequences for philosophy?* Unlike his great precursor the mathematician, philosopher and theologian Leibniz, who was quite capable of combining the scientific approach with the Christian faith, Carnap declared categorically in his Preface the "requirement of scientific strictness" that "all of metaphysics was banished from philosophy, since its theses cannot be rationally justified."[30] Just as from physics, so, too, from philosophy "a purely empirical-rational justification"[31] must be demanded. Hence the radical "call for clarity, for a science that is free from metaphysics."[32] Nonrational, nonscientific, but in fact metaphysical concepts are—for example—"reality (in the sense of independence from the cognizing consciousness)" and also "things-in-themselves."[33] And the self? "The existence of the self is not an originally given fact."[34] "The *sum* does not follow from the *cogito*; it does not follow from 'I experience' that 'I am,' but only that an experience is."[35] Instead of Descartes's "I think," it would be better to say with Russell, "It thinks within me"— and then Carnap would "strike out the 'within me.'" This means strict objectivity without any subjectivity. Only in this way can the progress of science be guaranteed.

*What are the consequences for religious faith?* In a section on "faith and knowledge," at the end of his *Logical Structure of the World*,[36] Carnap suggests a compromise for the peaceful coexistence of the two very diverse fields. Only rational (formal or empirical) science can be called knowledge. Religious faith, like nonrational intuition, if it does not mean simply accepting certain propositions as true, cannot be called knowledge. Like poetry and love, it belongs to "the nonrational areas," to vital feelings and emotions. These areas on the one hand and science on the other "can neither confirm nor disprove one another."[37] "There is no road from the continent of rational knowledge to the island of intuition."[38]

But even in his more popular "Pseudoproblems in Philosophy," of the same year, 1928—partly influenced by Wittgenstein's conception of metaphysical, unverifiable, senseless propositions—Carnap turned from peaceful coexistence and skeptical neutrality to the cold war and to the "condemnation of all theses about metaphysical reality."[39] Carnap now began to wonder about the origin of "magic (as theory), mythology (including theology), and metaphysics." Instead of expressing their content "through artistic media or through the practical conduct of life," the attempt was made to give them "the form of a theory that has no theoretical content."[40] Subsequently Carnap vigorously defended his program, not least against Heidegger's work "What is Metaphysics?" and such "senseless" propositions as "Nothing negates itself." He advocated the "conquest of metaphysics by the logical analysis of language" and—taking his starting point now not from psychic experiences but from physically verifiable events (physicalism)—"the language of physics as the universal language of science."[41]

In England, in addition to Bertrand Russell,[42] A. J. Ayer[43] in particular defended similar directly antimetaphysical and antitheological opinions. These theories became widespread in Poland (A. Tarski), Scandinavia and the United States in the form of *logical positivism*, which assumes as the ultimate basis of its argumentation a *positum*, something "posited," "given," in sense experience. This sense experience is no longer regarded as the starting point and sole content (as in the older, empiricist positivism of Comte, who in 1830 coined the word "positivism") but as the means of controlling the truth of statements (logical neopositivism or logical empiricism). These scholars were deeply impressed by the successes of natural science and mathematics, fascinated by an "objective," "exact," "precise," "formalized" science. They were quite certain about a number of points.

Only by a methodic orientation to the natural sciences as a whole and by *testing and verifying* all statements *empirically* is it possible to make any decisive progress even in philosophy and finally to inaugurate a new, fully rational epoch. That alone, therefore, can be regarded as real and meaningful which gives expression to a fact, which is accessible to direct observation and can be tested by experiments.

They also thought that it was only by making use of the purely formal sign language of mathematics—that is, of an *artificial or symbolic language*—that absolute clarity of thought could be attained. In this way an unexceptional method, transparent structure and an unambiguous account of the data of experience, even a single "language of science," a model language, which can be used as a better test of one's own theories —all become possible. This is the birth of the modern *theory of knowledge*. It renders philosophical argumentation more precise, substantiates and tests empirical scientific theories. It investigates and clarifies the propositions about the world established by the sciences but sets up none of its own. Theory of knowledge is metatheory, a theory about theory, a science of science.

Carnap's "faith" that the approach that seeks clarity at every point "will win the future"[44] was discredited with the oncoming of National Socialism and Fascism. In 1935 Carnap emigrated to the U.S.A. Schlick was shot dead by a former student, a psychopath, for motives that were not clear. At the latest in 1938 after the occupation of Austria, the rest of the members of the circle emigrated to England or America. The sale of the "subversive" publications of the (largely Jewish) circle was forbidden. The Vienna Circle had been dissolved, but its influence rapidly increased, especially in the English-speaking countries.

This way of thought, however, involved unresolvable *internal conflicts*, dilemmas, which led to a crisis in the program of logical positivism. It had to be corrected at every point and finally proved to be impossible to carry out in the light of its original concept. It was the logicians themselves in their intellectual honesty and unsparing self-criticism who set in motion a dramatic transformation process. Carnap especially—completely familiar with the construction of scientific languages, like an airplane designer constantly improving and developing his types—was very ready to listen to objections and suggestions for improvements. Over and above all this, by his own counterarguments, he made a substantial contribution to the revision, correction or even the abandonment of his former views. For him, science meant not an infallible Weltanschauung but continual progress as a result of constant correction. From the very beginning, he never regarded his first works as definitive but only as first projects and essays calling for further developments. He did, however, try to keep to his basic model even though he was later occupied—after his studies of semantics[45] —especially with the problems of probability and induction.[46]

As a theologian, one can only *agree* with many of Carnap's *concerns*. In philosophy and theology there have been many sins against the commandment of clarity, transparency and objectivity. And more than in the natural sciences, an attitude of piety toward tradition meant that long-obsolete pseudo problems continued to be discussed instead of being discarded.

But even at an early stage, apart from detailed logical objections, decisive objections particularly of a philosophical character were raised precisely against the basic conception of this "scientific faith" or "scientism." By what right are the norms of an artificial language (oriented to logic and mathematics) imposed on ordinary language (even though this is defective in some respects)? Can any scientific language be entirely without everyday prescience? Is not the formalized language of science constantly thrown back on ordinary language? Is it possible at all to define unambiguously the basic concepts of research even in natural science (the atom, for example)? Are they not so dependent on the continually changing developments in research that the attempt to find unambiguous concepts can never entirely succeed (the very word "atom," which means "indivisible," has been discredited by research)? Is is possible in mathematical-scientific knowledge and research wholly to exclude the subject—that is, subjective conditions and assumptions, standpoints and perspectives—in order to attain a pure objectivity? Must every science really take the mathematical-scientific method as the sole legitimate guiding idea? Has not the homogeneous scientific language that was once sought—and with it homogeneous science—meanwhile been clearly shown to be an illusion? Can philosophy today still work out in a theory of knowledge a methodological foundation for natural science? Must not philosophy today be content—as the Tübingen philosopher Walter Schulz demands, following Edmund Husserl—to "get acclimatized" as far as possible to the empirical sciences, without claiming to provide a theoretical foundation, in order "to perceive what happens in these sciences themselves"?[47]

But shall we not have to ask further whether it is legitimate to exclude certain questions from the outset as "senseless," if it is quite impossible to define empirically-mathematically what "sense" or "meaning" really is? By what right is empirical, sense experience in particular set up as a criterion of meaning? Is this not itself a "meta-physical" and therefore "senseless" proposition, a declaration that two thousand years of critical thinking in metaphysics are "senseless"? Is it possible at all by such sleight of hand to achieve a "conquest of metaphysics by the logical analysis of language"? Is any kind of metaphysics really nothing more than conceptual poetry? Are metaphysical propositions really only pseudo propositions; concepts like the absolute, the unconditioned, the being of the existent, the self, only pseudo concepts? And is the word "God" not really different from a meaningless, invented word like "babig," for which no criterion of meaning is available?[48] Is even the distinction between theism, atheism and agnosticism meaningless? Because of the successes of mathematics and natural science, do we actually have to accept the "death of God in language"? Must a modern logic and theory of knowledge necessarily set out to be antimetaphysical and antitheological?

The philosophical, social and political aversion to German idealism (together with Heidegger's existential philosophy and its linguistic obstinacy) and more especially the "resurrection of metaphysics" (as developed by Peter Wust[49]) in the wake of Schopenhauer, Nietzsche and Klages, was very understandable in the thirties. Today, despite the breakdown of the neopositivist program, belief in facts and rationality has largely become the spirit of the age. A dissociation from Carnap's antimetaphysical texts is now becoming noticeable, as Günther Patzig explains in a postscript to the new edition of Carnap's "Pseudo Problems in Philosophy," since on the one hand belief in the "merely beneficial effects of science" has been shaken and, on the other hand, "the battle against that kind of metaphysics which Carnap especially opposed . . . has been fought."[50] Metaphysics today no longer attempts to be an "*ideological superstructure* of science, but the *indispensable foundation* of the sciences."[51] Metaphysics of this kind by no means claims to make empirically verifiable statements, but to produce conditions under which empirical statements are possible.

Today, therefore, many logicians and epistemologists will agree with Wolfgang Stegmüller, who is continuing in a critical spirit Carnap's tradition in Germany, when in his appreciation of Carnap and the Vienna Circle he distinguishes clearly between the important work of individual defenders of modern empiricism on logical-scientific questions on the one hand and the polemical attitude of empiricism to metaphysics as a whole on the other: "The two are really independent of each other. . . . But as a matter of fact, a Thomist, say, or a modern ontologist can accept the results of research into the construction of semantical systems, the confirmability of empirical sentences, the possibilities of rendering more precise the rules of inductive inference and so forth, without assuming that metaphysics is meaningless."[52]

All things considered, was the positivist "perception" that metaphysical problems are merely "senseless pseudo problems" not perhaps merely wishful thinking? This precisely was Karl Popper's objection at an early stage: "This wish . . . can always be gratified. For nothing is easier than to unmask a problem as 'meaningless' or 'pseudo.' All you have to do is to fix upon a conveniently narrow meaning for 'meaning,' and you will soon be bound to say of any inconvenient question that you are unable to detect any meaning in it. Moreover, if you admit as meaningful none except problems in natural science, any debate about the concept of 'meaning' will also turn out to be meaningless. The dogma of meaning, once enthroned, is elevated forever above the battle. It can no longer be attacked. It has become (in Wittgenstein's own words) 'unassailable and definitive.' "[53]

## The universal claim of scientific thought? Karl Popper

As we saw in our critical questions to Descartes, the development of mathematics itself led at a very early stage to those antinomies, paradoxes, inconsistencies, that deeply shook the foundations of mathematics and logic and thus questioned the very roots of the universal claims of mathematical-scientific thinking.[54] But now the verification principle itself, at first so illuminating, led quite generally in epistemology to difficulties that made logical positivism as a whole seem questionable.

The main blow had in fact been delivered as early as 1935 by *Karl Popper*, who—despite his acquaintance with several members of it—never belonged to the Vienna Circle but paradoxically enough was at first frequently taken for a positivist. Only in our time has Popper become popular even in Germany, as an alternative to the total explanations—for many becoming increasingly dubious—of positivist "scientism" and of both orthodox and more recent Marxism. With his important book "The Logic of Scientific Discovery," which analyzes closely the rules for establishing scientific hypotheses and theories, he laid down even then the foundations of a critical rationalism or rational criticism. How does a researcher pass from statements of individual experience to setting up a theoretical system? How does scientific progress come about?

Popper makes it clear that logical positivism leads to absurdity. The verification principle, which is so important to it, the radical demand for verifiability in experience, would not only eliminate metaphysical statements; it would at the same time *destroy* also empirical hypotheses and therefore *scientific knowledge as a whole*: "Positivists, in their anxiety to annihilate metaphysics, annihilate natural science along with it."[55] Why? Because most of the propositions even of natural science are not empirically verifiable and consequently would have to be rejected as pseudo statements and "metaphysics." "For scientific laws, too, cannot be logically reduced to elementary statements of experience."[56] That is why Popper opposes Wittgenstein: "If consistently applied, Wittgenstein's criterion of meaningfulness rejects as meaningless those natural laws the search for which, as Einstein says, is 'the supreme task of the physicist.' "[57] If, for example, a proposition like "all copper conducts electricity" is to be verified, then all the copper in the whole universe would have to be tested in regard to this property—which is obviously impossible. That is, natural laws—which are also meant to make possible decisive predictions for the future—are not verifiable.

And what of the "principle of induction," which, starting out from individual experiences, concludes to the existence of general laws, thus permits an "inductive" confirmation of scientific theories? Hume already had expressed it in a different form: a universal proposition can never be verified by observations. Nor is the much-used concept of the probability of hypotheses a means for judging their truth.

Popper later defined his position *historically* both with reference to *Descartes* and with reference to the *empiricists* (especially Bacon[58]). Both fought against authority and tradition and based knowledge on the immediate certainty of man himself: whether, as with Descartes, on the *cogito* and the rational insights following on this, or, as with the empiricists, on sense impressions. Both sides regarded their basic truths as manifest, evident, and consequently as immediately certain. According to Popper, both sides therefore remained tied to the *model of religious revelation*. They merely replaced one authority—the Bible and Aristotle—by another: that of reason or that of the senses. For them, all that is important is to derive assured conclusions from those ultimate certainties: whether by deduction, as with Descartes, or by induction, as with the empiricists.

According to Popper, however, there are *no such ultimate "manifest" certainties either of reason or of the senses* from which we could start out: it is not without good reason that such certainties have regularly been called into question by the opposite side. Even immediate sense perception involves an interpretation. Consequently our knowledge always begins with conjectures, assumptions, patterns, hypotheses, which must be exposed to scrutiny. For Popper, the assumption that there exists an ultimate substantiation of propositions of science no longer open to criticism is a belief that ends in an insoluble trilemma. This he explains in the light of the philosophy of Jakob Friedrich Fries (1773–1843): either a simply asserted dogmatism or a recourse to a never-ending series of new substantiations (*regressus in infinitum*) or a psychologism generalizing individual experiences.[59]

For Popper, therefore, theories are not simply derived inductively from experience. They are first of all free, creative projects that have only hypothetical validity and need to be tested. For this, a "critical method" is necessary: "the method of trial and error." The thesis that "we can learn from our mistakes" is the theme of the essays and lectures in the book *Conjectures and Refutations*.[60] Against all claims to infallibility on the part of a dogmatic infallibilism, he puts forward a fundamental fallibilism.[61]

But under these conditions is it possible at all to test scientific hypotheses or universal "all-propositions" (for example, "all swans are white")? Certainly not by verification. We simply cannot examine all the swans in the universe. But we can use the method of *falsification*. We can attempt to refute, to falsify this hypothesis. How? We must start out from certain "basis statements" or "singular statements," which speak of individual observed and verifiable occurrences or qualities (a single black swan, which can be observed in Australia, suffices for falsification). But even these basis statements are themselves interpretations, explaining observations with the aid of universal concepts (swan, black, white). It is possible, however, to deduce from such basis statements a universal statement of existence ("there are nonwhite swans"), which logically contradicts the original hypothesis ("all swans are white" = "there are no nonwhite swans"). The latter is thus unequivocally refuted, falsified. A singular proposition therefore can negate, but cannot establish, a universal proposition.

But when is a hypothesis proved to be *true*? Popper does not like the word "true" (or "false"); he prefers "corroborated." When, therefore, may a hypothesis, an empirical theory, be regarded as *corroborated?* When it has withstood all previous attempts at falsification. This, however, holds only provisionally: "I hold that hypotheses cannot be asserted to be 'true' statements, but that they are 'provisional conjectures.' "[62] "The old scientific ideal of *episteme*—of absolutely certain, demonstrable knowledge—has proved to be an idol . . . every scientific statement must remain *tentative for ever*. It may indeed be corroborated, but every corroboration is relative."[63] Only in this way is progress made in knowledge and science: not by confirmation of theories, but by refutation; not by verification, but by falsification.

What does Popper conclude from all this in regard to the *verification criterion?* Such a criterion may *not* be used as a positivistic *criterion of meaning:* not as a rule for distinguishing between propositions meaningful or meaningless in themselves, which then call for another criterion to distinguish between meaning and meaninglessness. *But* only as a rational *demarcation criterion:* to distinguish between both logical-mathematical and empirical-scientific, admissible or non-admissible propositions. Such a rational but not positivistic demarcation criterion leaves scope also for meaningful "nonphysical," in the widest sense "meta-physical" propositions: propositions, that is, that are beyond the scope of natural science. In principle, therefore, a rational analysis of metaphysical questions is possible.

Popper, however, when young, had studied Spinoza's Cartesian ("geometrical") ethics and his treatise on Descartes's *Principles of Philosophy* and thereby acquired "a lifetime's dislike of theorizing about God."[64] Consequently he severely restricts the function of *metaphysics:* to theories that are something like all-too-generalized preliminary forms of scientific theories (often myths) and should gradually find access to the sciences and there likewise be open to falsification. As against some speculative-idealist systems or even mythical-poetical theories of being, these restrictions are understandable. Against logical positivism, on the other hand, Popper in any case insists:

that a homogeneous science with a homogeneous language is nonsense;

that philosophy cannot be reduced merely to "logical analysis" or "linguistic analysis";

that language must not be restricted to mathematical symbols and calculations;

that there is not only one (mathematical-scientific) method of attaining salvation;

that "unclear" concepts cannot always be avoided at the beginning of the formation of a theory;

that there are legitimate, genuinely philosophical problems that cannot be clarified with the means at the disposal of natural science.

Such a genuinely philosophical problem, for Popper, is especially the *"problem of cosmology"* (understood in the widest sense), "in which all thinking men are interested: the problem of understanding the world—including ourselves, and our knowledge, as part of the world."[65] Linguistic analysis must be seen within this framework: "all science is cosmology, I believe."[66] "Understanding the functions of language" is part of the task of natural science and philosophy, "but explaining away our problems as merely linguistic 'puzzles' is not."[67] According to Popper, it cannot be denied "that purely metaphysical ideas—and therefore philosophical ideas —have been of the greatest importance for cosmology. From Thales to Einstein, from ancient atomism to Descartes's speculation about matter, from the speculations of Gilbert and Newton and Leibniz and Boscovich about forces to those of Faraday and Einstein about fields of forces, metaphysical ideas have shown the way."[68]

Hence Popper's concept of science is far removed from that of logical positivism: "Our science is not knowledge (*episteme*): it can never claim to have attained truth, or even a substitute for it, such as probability."[69] In fact, Popper permits himself the statement: "*We do not know; we can only guess.* And our guesses are guided by the unscientific, the metaphysical (though biologically explicable) faith in laws which we can only uncover-discover. Like Bacon, we might describe our own contemporary science—'the method of reasoning which men now ordinarily apply to nature'—as consisting of 'anticipations, rash and premature' and as 'prejudices.' "[70] "But these marvellously imaginative and bold conjectures or 'anticipations' of ours are carefully and soberly controlled by systematic tests."[71] The tests must be continually repeated: "It is not his *possession* of knowledge, of irrefutable truth, that makes the man of science, but his persistent and recklessly critical *quest* for truth."[72] Against all dogmatism —that is, by continual criticism and rational control—an increasingly close approach to the truth and greater resemblance to the truth.

Throughout his life, Popper has upheld substantially his fallibilist-reformist basic theory. Unlike the logical positivists, as professor for many years at the London School of Economics he was open-minded toward the natural and the human sciences and thus alert to sociological and historiographical problems. He later expanded his theory of knowledge into a theory of society and history. Against all totalitarian-utopian doctrines of salvation on the right (Plato and Hegel) and on the left (Karl Marx), he pleaded impressively for a democratic "open society," to be improved not by a revolutionary upheaval but step by step, with the aid of realistic, reformist "social technology" and "piecemeal technology."[73] At the same time, however, the transformation of Popper's critical "design of knowledge" into a critical "design of society" has frequently come up against the charge of abstractness, impracticality, insubstantiality.

Thirty-five years after his *Logic of Scientific Discovery*, in a preface to the third German edition, Popper defined his epistemological standpoint between skepticism and rationalistic positivism as still equally:

against the epistemological pessimism of the skeptics: "an approach to the truth is possible";[74]

against the epistemological optimism of the positivists: "certain knowledge is denied to us. Our knowledge is *critical guesswork, a net of hypotheses, a web of surmises.*"[75]

Today we can recognize, with the Australian philosopher John Passmore, that "logical positivism is dead, or as dead as a philosophical movement ever becomes."[76] In his autobiography, under the heading "Who Killed Logical Positivism?"[77] Popper answers: "I fear that I must admit responsibility. Yet I did not do it on purpose."[78] The ultimate reason for its demise did not lie so much in its grave mistakes as in "a decline of interest in the great problems: the concentration upon *minutiae* (upon puzzles) and especially the meaning of words; in brief, its scholasticism."[79]

In the theory of knowledge, Popper rightly found the problem of the *growth* of our knowledge far more important than the construction of complicated, difficult, artificial language models, to be used only by specialists and surprisingly impoverished by comparison with everyday speech. In investigating scientific progress, he took for granted from the outset the hypothetical character of all scientific theories as an obvious consequence of Einstein's theory of relativity: he saw that even the best-tested theory—such as that of Newton—cannot be regarded as more than a hypothesis and an approach to the truth. The fact, however, that progress in science comes about decidedly not through continuous change or even through continual falsification but through revolutionary processes has been the subject of theoretical reflection only in very recent times. And at the same time, Popper's falsification theory also has largely proved to be "provisional." What Popper continually avoided has happened: his falsification theory has been exposed to falsification and has in fact been falsified.

## Scientific revolutions: Thomas S. Kuhn

Popper himself observed occasionally that a theory could by no means be regarded as falsified merely because of isolated contrary basis statements: a theory is superseded only when it is replaced by a better one. But does this really come about as a result of strict rational scrutinies and tests, as Popper assumes? In order to establish this, logical-critical discernment is not sufficient: we must go back to the concrete history of science, to psychology and sociology. It was Thomas S. Kuhn, the American physicist and historian of science, who first made a comprehensive study of "the structure of scientific revolutions"[80] and thus inaugurated something like a "new philosophy of science,"[81] which considers not only the logical but also the *historical-hermeneutic* and particularly the *psycho-*

*logical-sociological* problems of scientific progress. Kuhn's heretical main thesis is that radically new theories arise neither by verification nor by falsification but by the replacement—in individual cases, highly complex and protracted—of a hitherto accepted explanatory model (paradigm) by a new one. Before returning to theology, we must now pay special attention to this process of *"paradigm change,"* which is neither simply irrational nor completely rational and is often linked with violent conflicts. How do we *really* make "progress" in natural science?

There is obviously progress in *"normal science"*: "research firmly based upon one or more past scientific achievements, achievements that some particular scientific community acknowledges for a time as supplying the foundation for its further practice."[82] Today such achievements are described in detail in scientific textbooks, elementary or advanced. Formerly the same function was fulfilled by the famous classics of science: Aristotle's *Physics*, Ptolemy's *Almagest*, Newton's *Principia* and *Opticks*, Franklin's *Electricity*, Lavoisier's *Chemistry*, Lyell's *Geology*, and so on. The great theoretical constructions provide "models" for everyday scientific practice from which particular coherent traditions of scientific research emerge: they serve as "paradigms." Ptolemaic (and later Copernican) astronomy, Aristotelian (and later Newtonian) dynamics, corpuscular (and later "wave") optics, and so on, were or are such paradigms on a grand scale, and every student must examine them thoroughly if he is to be able at all to enter into scientific discussion. The importance of the textbooks in this respect cannot be overlooked. In practice, students accept such paradigms less as a result of proofs than because of the authority of the textbook and the teacher. In addition to these greater paradigms, which stand for an entire constellation of beliefs, values, techniques, there are also concrete "puzzle solutions," which can be described as paradigms.[83]

Normal scientific research is not very concerned to produce anything radically new but is more inclined to suppress novelties. The real interest of research lies in finding additional material to make the traditional model more precise, to confirm and secure it, to extend its scope: in other words, in a cumulative growth of knowledge. Normal research consists, in practice, not in a continuous effort at falsification but in *puzzle solving,* that is, in "the solution of all sorts of complex instrumental, conceptual, and mathematical puzzles. The man who succeeds proves himself an expert puzzle-solver, and the challenge of the puzzle is an important part of what usually drives him on."[84]

If *anomalies*—new, unsuspected phenomena—are detected in a science, an attempt is made first of all to fit these into the existing paradigm and not to falsify the latter. For scientists at first show no slight resistance to anything new, to any anomaly and its empirical or theoretical recognition, which might result in a change of the paradigm, of its categories or of its operation. Instead of falsifying the theory, an attempt is made to correct it, to modify it, to formulate it in a new way. The scientists often simply wait or even try to discredit the discoverer morally as a disturber of the peace.

But the increasing precision and expansion of the existing paradigm, the increasingly strong specialization and professionalization, the increasingly exact information and the growing complexity of the theory: these are the very things that lead not to the consolidation of the paradigm but —ironically enough—slowly to its undermining. For instance, the more the movements of the stars were studied and corrected in the light of the Ptolemaic system, the more material was produced to refute that system. And the same thing happened not only with the Copernican revolution but also with the Newtonian, the chemical and the Einsteinian revolutions. "The more precise and far-reaching that paradigm is, the more sensitive an indicator it provides of anomaly and hence of an occasion for paradigm change."[85] The process may be tedious, protracted and complex. And there are transitional periods in which at first only the stereotypes of the old model begin to break up. But the critical state of the traditional theory increasingly comes to light. A period of pronounced insecurity generally precedes the emergence of new theories, which in the end leads to the destruction of the paradigm. In a word, *crisis* is the usual *condition for the rejection of a hitherto accepted paradigm.*

According to Kuhn, then, *neither* the *verification* nor the *falsification* procedure can explain the really far-reaching upheavals in science. With acute psychological perception, he defends his claim that, as soon as a paradigm has proved itself, scientists are rarely interested in seeking alternatives. And even when anomalies occur, they are not treated as counter instances that falsify the traditional theory: "Once it has achieved the status of paradigm, a scientific theory is declared invalid only if an alternate candidate is available to take its place. No process yet disclosed by the historical study of scientific development at all resembles the methodological stereotype of falsification by direct comparison with nature. . . . The decision to reject one paradigm is always simultaneously the decision to accept another, and the judgment leading to that decision involves the comparison of both paradigms with nature *and* with each other."[86]

The transition to a new paradigm simply does not come about step by step, as suggested in Popper's *The Logic of Scientific Discovery*. It is a *scientific revolution*. The process is not cumulative, as in normal science, but revolutionary. The established and the future paradigms are mutually incompatible: the old must yield to the new. Now we can perceive what was behind both the case of Galileo and that of Darwin. Established and familiar concepts are changed. Norms and criteria are displaced. Theories and methods are shaken. Whether in the macrocosm or in the microcosm, whether in astronomy, physics, chemistry or biology, the total world view is changed: "Led by a new paradigm, scientists adopt new instruments and look in new places. Even more important, during revolutions scientists see new and different things when looking with familiar instruments in places they have looked before. It is rather as if the professional community had been suddenly transported to another planet where familiar objects are seen in a different light and are joined by unfamiliar ones as well. Of course, nothing of quite that sort does occur: there is no geographical transplantation; outside the laboratory everyday affairs usually continue as before. Nevertheless, paradigm changes do cause scientists to see the world of their research-engagement differently. In so far as their only recourse to that world is through what they see and do, we may want to say that after a revolution scientists are responding to a different world."[87]

What conclusions can we draw from all this? The development of the *theory of knowledge* over the past fifty years has led from the hyper-Cartesian rationality of an abstract positivistic logic and linguistic analysis, by way of countless internal corrections, back again to the dimensions of history, of the subject, of the social group and thus to the necessity of history, psychology, sociology and even "metaphysics."[88] Obviously, no single simple criterion, no single specialized method, no single rigid theory, no single homogeneous language as a way of reflecting the world, no single great paradigm, is adequate to judge this entire rational-irrational process of scientific progress. The "logic of scientific discovery" and of scientific progress cannot be brought under such purely rational control. The logical-critical approach is too narrow, and in its pronounced antidogmatism leads to a new dogmatism, which is not open to criticism.[89]

In this way it has become abundantly clear that there is now less excuse than ever for making the mathematical method and mathematical truth absolute (monism of method), and some arguments of Paul K. Feyerabend—the *enfant terrible* of critical rationalism—are worth considering even if it is impossible to share his anarchical attitude to method ("anything goes").[90] Not only in physics but in natural science generally, great care is taken today—differently from formerly—not to regard as absolute either the method applied or the truth perceived. Classical physics still started out from the assumption that nature can be known as it really is and that all physical processes can in principle be calculated in advance. As a result of new discoveries in connection with the theory of relativity and quantum mechanics, modern physics starts out from the assumption that the conclusions of classical physics hold not in themselves but only under certain conditions and not in others: that we are by no means dealing with an occurrence completely determined in every way; that, even in experiments in physics, the method changes the object and reproduces only one perspective and one aspect; that the chemical-physical method—for instance—perceives only one aspect of a living organism and tones down other aspects.

Hence today, in physics, chemistry, biology and other natural sciences, it is customary to speak not of universally valid truths copying reality but of hypothetically valid "projects" and "patterns" that hold only in virtue of certain conditions and within certain limits, while fully permitting the coexistence of other projects and patterns. The result is not an image of nature but only the ascertainment of certain functions and relations, often unimaginable and expressible only in formal mathematical language. That is, an absolutely objective truth is not envisaged but only one that is relatively objective. In perspectivity and variability, any number of methods and aspects, projects and patterns, are possible in regard to the one reality, which itself always remains infinitely richer and more complex than all the statements—even the most exact—about it.

In addition, however, to the epistemological relativizing of scientific knowledge, a *social-critical de-ideologizing*—as practiced, for instance, by Jürgen Habermas—must also be considered.[91] In this respect, critical sociological theory is assisted by the general social-economic development, which vividly reveals the problems of technological progress and the "limits of growth." Natural science is by no means merely ideologically neutral, simply ascertaining the data, the facts, in an entirely objective fashion and without making value judgments. Natural science and scientists also are secretly—if often unconsciously—guided by certain ideas of value and *interests*, as well as being concerned with efficiency, economy, controlled disposability, technical exploitability. Even in this respect, then, the objectivity of natural science is not absolute but conditioned by the whole reference system, by sociological interests and by the method adopted. The frequently invoked objective restraints are often only the restraints of a particular method. But scientific research in practice mostly disregards its reference system: the point, the values and the goals of its activity. These questions are often expressly left to others. Scientists consider themselves competent not in regard to values but only in regard to facts.

But there are many scientists today who raise these wider questions. Is everything that is done by science and technology *ipso facto* meaningful? Should everything be done that can be done, that is technically possible? Is any kind of scientific-technological progress as such an aid to man's freedom, maturity, humanity?

It is in fact necessary, for the interests guiding scientific research, for both the initial methodological assumptions and in the end the practical results to be explicitly stated and considered and not neglected or disguised. A purely technical elucidation must itself be elucidated. Only in this way will both science and technology not be ideologically misled. Only in this way will they avoid being pressed to serve the weighty interests of economic or political powers or even simply an unrestrained social technology with vast equipment to deprive men of their legal and political rights. Only in this way, finally, will the "cybernetic dream" of a total regulation of society, a rational administration of the world by technological control, be prevented from becoming reality. In brief: ideological scientism—the dogmatic faith in science, in *scientia*—must be abandoned.[92]

## Theology and changes in the world picture

Are there "scientific revolutions" also in philosophy and theology? As a natural scientist, Kuhn does not deal with this question. It is, however, scarcely possible to deny it. Certainly not for *philosophy*, where—for instance—in connection with Descartes or Kant we speak of a "Copernican turning point." But neither is it possible to deny the existence of revolutions in *theology*, which involve the replacement of one paradigm by another more frequently than people have been or are aware. It is true that "revolutionary" is not a word that is very popular in theology, still less in the official Church: the very one-sided emphasis is always on continuity, identity, and—up to our own times—even infallible teaching. But—to say nothing of the great Greek theologians Clement and Origen—did not even Augustine produce what in many ways was a new pattern of interpretation, a new paradigm?[93] Was not—as we saw[94]—the acceptance of Aristotle in the philosophy and theology of the Middle Ages by Albertus Magnus and Thomas Aquinas also a scientific revolution? And was this not particularly true of Martin Luther in relation to the Middle Ages? And in turn, finally, the reaction of the Enlightenment and historical-critical theology to the Reformation?

The *parallels between theology and natural science* are often amazing. In theology, too, we have a "normal science," normal theology with its classical authors, textbooks and teachers, with the gradual cumulative growth of knowledge and the solution of outstanding problems or "puzzles."

Here, too, of course, new difficulties emerge, and at first an attempt is made to fit them into the old paradigm, but this turns out to be impossible.

Here, too, we find stubborn resistance to everything—adaptations, modifications, new formulations—that might result in a change or replacement of the established paradigm.

But we also find that, as the established paradigm is made more perfect scientifically, the acquisition of new data begins slowly to undermine it: there are transitional periods of dissatisfaction in which ties and rules are loosened; traditional schools are reduced in number, and there is competition between the many new approaches; but some retreat to a waiting position, while "disturbers of the peace" are morally discredited or simply—as far as possible—reduced to silence.

Finally, as elsewhere, it is a question here not of getting at the truth bit by bit but of an open crisis as the precondition of a far-reaching revolutionary change of certain former basic assumptions and the necessity of a new paradigm that enables everything to be seen in a new light.

For some people, changes in theology may be less apparent than those in physics; and in any case the differences are considerable. But the *"doubts of faith"* on the part of theologians appear sometimes to correspond to the doubts that—though rarely admitted—disturb the "faith" of those great physicists who have not simply been content with "normal science" and the accepted system. It was not a theologian talking about theology, but a physicist—Albert Einstein—talking about physics, who said: "It was as if the ground had been pulled out from under one, with no firm foundation to be seen anywhere, upon which one could have built."[95] And again it was a physicist who wrote to a friend about his science: "At the moment, physics is again terribly confused. In any case, it is too difficult for me, and I wish I had been a movie comedian or something of the sort and had never heard of physics." This was written by Wolfgang Pauli in the months before Heisenberg's paper on matrix mechanics pointed the way to a new quantum theory.[96]

And just as the "religious doubts" of theologians and physicists may correspond to one another, so, too—despite the differences—may their difficulties about "conversion" to a new paradigm: a conversion that cannot be extorted from either the theologian or the physicist. The discussions between the two parties or—better—language worlds, between the "puzzle solvers" and the "paradigm testers," the defenders of the old and those of the new models, from the very outset are often not so much serious scientific, rational discussions as skillful attempts at recruitment, persuasion and conversion, to get the other side to adopt one's own so illuminating assumptions, from which everything else is supposed to follow. The origins, careers and personalities of the participants are involved here as much as the nationality, reputation and teachers of the "innovator." In addition to these sociological and psychological factors, what is most relevant to the claim of the defenders of the new paradigm is their ability to solve the problems that brought the old one into a crisis, not least to render attractive the greater simplicity, transparency, universality and elegance of the new solution. But objective discussion is difficult. Difficulties of translation lie behind the difficulties of communication between the two language worlds. For someone who has grown up in the older language world and in normal science to be convinced, he needs a translation in order to learn something of the strength and weakness of the new paradigm. But, behind the translation, there must be conviction and, behind conviction, conversion. In the last resort, then, *it is always faith that must decide* which paradigm is to guide research on the problems in the future: a decision to be made—particularly in the first stage of the discussion—by both theologian and physicist, as a matter of trust: They "must have faith that the new paradigm will succeed with the many large problems that confront it, knowing only that the older paradigm has failed with a few. A decision of that kind can only be made on faith."[97]

And again—despite all the great differences—the more exact *process of paradigm change* is similar in theology and physics. At the beginning, a new paradigm candidate has very often only a few advocates, and these are often young (or even outsiders). Only in the course of time, as research into the paradigm progresses, are scientists increasingly converted. But often it is just the most experienced older scientists, who researched the established model, who keep up a lifelong resistance, and it may take a generation before the whole scientific community goes over to the new paradigm. Might it not be said of theologians, as Max Planck said of physicists when he looked back over his whole life: "A new scientific truth does not triumph by convincing its opponents and making them see the light, but rather because its opponents eventually die, and a new generation grows up that is familiar with it"?[98]

In theology as in physics there are in principle *three ways of getting out of the crisis.*[99]

*Either* normal science, contrary to all appearances, still proves to be capable of coping with the crisis-provoking problems and of improving the existing paradigm.

*Or* these problems resist even apparently radically new approaches, so that for the time being they are shelved (in theology and in the Church this was in fact often achieved only by brutal persecution of heretics and suppression of discussion, latterly in the struggle against Catholic "modernists" at the turn of the century and the *nouvelle théologie* in mid-century).

*Or* a new paradigm candidate turns up and is accepted in a process that involves "handling the same bundle of data as before, but placing them in a new system of relations with one another by giving them a different framework."[100]

*After the victory of the new paradigm,* scientific textbooks, commonly understood descriptions and philosophical interpretations are wholly or partly rewritten and form the (new) tradition for the next period. They record "the stable *outcome* of past revolutions and thus display the bases of the current normal-scientific tradition."[101] At the same time, however, they inevitably conceal the role and often even the existence of the scientific revolutions: they amount, then, to reinterpretations or even false interpretations of history, rendering the revolutions invisible and subsequently making them seem to be an extension of existing knowledge. Churches and theologians are like nations and scientists: they do not like to be told too much about human subjectivity and irrationality, about omissions, mistakes and errors within their own field. More elevating is the history of their own heroes, a history that is harmonized, idealized and transfigured—as if the building of science had been erected stone by stone, in accordance with a plan.

A final parallel between theology and science deserves to be stressed. As in natural science, so too in theology, it is a question of "the same bundle of data as before," which, however, are placed "in a new system of relations with one another." Neither in physics nor in theology is there any question simply of a total break, but there is simultaneously a *fundamental continuity* despite all the discontinuity. In theology, very much more than in the natural sciences (which are essentially unhistorical, mentioning their fathers and heroes only in introductions and marginally), it is therefore not simply a question of inventing a new tradition. It is more a question of a new formulation of the old tradition, in the light, however, of a new paradigm: "Novelty for its own sake is not a desideratum in the sciences as it is in so many other creative fields."[102] "As a result, though new paradigms seldom or never possess all the capabilities of their predecessors, they usually preserve a great deal of the most concrete parts of past achievement and they always permit additional concrete problem-solutions besides."[103]

For theology, the problem of continuity appears at a much deeper level. For what is involved here is something that Kuhn avoids mentioning up to the very last pages, even the word: "truth."[104] It is a question indeed of the "truth of life" or—as Wittgenstein says—of the "problems of life." For the natural scientist generally starts out less directly from the problems of life: "Unlike the engineer, and many doctors, and most theologians, the scientist need not choose problems because they urgently need solution. . . ."[105] And because the theologian is more directly concerned with the problems of life, he must also be more concerned about recognition, not only by the experts but by the wider public. Even "the most abstract of theologians is far more concerned than the scientist with lay approbation of his creative work, though he may be even less concerned with approbation in general."[106] As a scientist, then, Kuhn has no answer to the very obvious vital question of the whither of the vast process of development of both science and the world as a whole: "Inevitably that lacuna will have disturbed many readers."[107] But neither has he any answer to the vital question of the whence: "Anyone who has followed the argument this far will nevertheless feel the need to ask why the evolutionary process should work."[108]

Here, then, for Kuhn also, the question arises that for Popper is the "metaphysical" problem of "cosmology": "The world of which that [scientific] community is a part must also possess quite special characteristics, and we are no closer than we were at the start to knowing what these must be."[109] On the last page of his fascinating book, Kuhn then observes: "That problem—What must the world be like in order that man may know it?—is as old as science itself," but, for the scientist, "it remains unanswered."[110] Could theology perhaps provide further help here?

## 2. *Interim results I: Theses on modern rationality*

Obviously, not only philosophy and theology but also the natural sciences have great difficulties with changes in the world picture. Neither natural science alone nor philosophy and theology alone can solve these difficulties. More than ever, they are dependent on mutual collaboration. Today more than ever—after so many prejudices have been cleared up and so many misunderstandings on both sides removed—such collaboration can be possible and fruitful. Thus we have no longer a mutual hostility, nor—as in recent times—merely a peaceful coexistence, but a meaningful *critical-dialogic cooperation between theology and natural science* in face of the one world and the one humanity.

### Correcting course

There may be scientists who say that philosophical-theological questions are no concern of theirs and are uninteresting, just as there may be philosophers and theologians who say that mathematical-scientific questions are no concern of theirs and are uninteresting. But the questions are not thereby settled; they are merely suppressed as a result of ignorance or arrogance. As the philosopher and the theologian in practice live every day by the "functioning" of mathematics and the natural sciences, so the mathematician and the scientist live in practice—admittedly in a very different way—by the reality that makes possible and sustains the world of their phenomena.

The presupposition for a new critical-dialogic collaboration between theology and natural science is, of course—apart from critical queries addressed directly to natural science and technology[1]—a *radical course correction of Church and theology.* What the seventeenth century—the "century of genius" which we have been considering—demanded and what has been overdue since the nineteenth century (with the theory of evolution) must finally be realized not only in word but also in deed. The medieval world picture must be abandoned and the modern world picture consequently adopted, the result of which for theology itself will undoubtedly be the definitive transition to a new paradigm.

A methodical reorientation has undoubtedly been going on for a long time, but it must be consistently and comprehensively carried out. Such a *consistent reorientation*, then, must no longer be delayed by more fighting retreats and concealment tactics either in the theology of God or in the theology of man's original state and original sin, in Descent and Ascent Christology, in questions of ethics and sexual morality or in the theology of the "Last Things" (death, devil, judgment, hell and heaven). This course correction was and is indicated for any traditional theology, especially, on the one hand, for that Protestant fundamentalism that remains tied to the words of the Bible and, on the other, for that traditional scholastic theology discussed here, which—apart from the great controversy on grace—from Spanish baroque scholasticism to the neoscholasticism of the present century has been content, after (wrongly) invoking Aquinas, largely with repeating and summarizing high scholastic theology, commenting on this and substantiating it.[2] This medieval theology, becoming increasingly remote from the Bible and the world, suffered an obvious and irreparable fiasco, in the Catholic Church of the present time, at the Second Vatican Council, where it utterly failed to solve theological, ethical, pastoral, or sociological problems some of which had been outstanding for centuries. But in the Roman Curia and in some of the ecclesiastical educational establishments under its control, this theology continues to lead an increasingly anachronistic existence, with very negative consequences for the Catholic Church and for Christendom as a whole.

Generally, however, contemporary theology is obviously moving in another direction. The first acceptance of a new paradigm by theology took place a long time ago and among many people, in connection with the acceptance of the modern world picture and the development of the historical-critical method: admittedly in exegesis and Church history, and also in ethics and practical theology, more than in dogmatics, which is more closely tied to ecclesiastical tradition. But even more-traditional theologians cannot speak as they did two hundred years ago about the Bible and tradition, creation and consummation, messianic titles and miracles, heaven and hell, and many other things. Unless we are completely mistaken, in present-day theological discussions it is a question of that "transition to maturity" which, according to Kuhn, represents the real "transition from the pre- to the post-paradigm period in the development of a scientific field," in which what changes "is not the presence of a paradigm but rather its nature. Only after the change is normal puzzle-solving research possible."[3]

For all the more far-sighted in theology and Church there can be no doubt about the necessity of *persistence*. It is no longer sufficient to permit a conservative disposition, anxiety about faith and a long-cultivated tradition (and this holds also for Protestant and Orthodox churches), to lead us to pass over in silence the definitive collapse of the ancient and medieval world picture, simply to ignore the obsolete world horizon of the traditional doctrinal statements, and thus in practice to offer a bisected scholasticism.[4] In the present state of upheaval, anyone who adopts a dogmatic, ostrich-like policy, putting his head in the sand of tradition (which has been happening for a long time), seeking to get away from embarrassments and contradictions, is throwing away all credibility for theology and Church:

As if the biblical message itself did not have to be detached from its time-conditioned ideological framework and repeatedly translated for each new age.

As if medieval scholasticism had not been based on Greek metaphysics, which was essentially connected with Greek physics and the ancient world picture.

As if the Roman magisterium (Pope, Holy Office, Congregation of the Index, Biblical Commission) had not continuously overlooked these ideological connections and consequently, from the condemnation of Copernicus and Galileo, both with reference to the interpretation of Scripture (especially the Book of Genesis) and with reference to the conclusions of modern science (as in the theory of evolution), up to Pius XII's encyclical *Humani Generis* (1950), made wrong decisions on matters of faith, which could not be admitted for fear of questioning infallibility.

As if questions still unsettled today—for instance, with reference to "paradise," "original sin" and Christology—were not connected with the failure to cope with the ancient and medieval world picture.[5]

As if the wrong decision of Paul VI's encyclical *Humanae Vitae* (1968), with reference to birth control, had not been based on the idea of an unchangeable cosmic order that had to be observed unconditionally (described as natural law).[6]

As if finally the encyclical on celibacy (1967), the Roman study document on demonology (1975), the document on masturbation and homosexuality (1976) and the defamatory statements about women and the prohibition of ordination of women (1977),[7] with so many other things, were not also the expression of outdated medieval thought.

The practical importance of this question becomes clear from what has been called in various countries the "Catholic education deficit."[8] Examples can be found up to the present time: i. among the educated classes there is a far greater percentage of Protestants than of Catholics; ii. Catholics are particularly underrepresented among those who take up a scientific career; iii. Catholics in strikingly large numbers avoid scientific-technical studies and prefer the humanities. What are the reasons for this situation? Politics hostile to the Church and the inferior social position of Catholics—which, however, themselves are the result of factors at work within the Church—provide a partial explanation. But ideological inhibitions are also involved, in particular the problematic, historically conditioned relationship of the Church to modern science. In recent years, however, at least in Germany and the U.S.A., there have been welcome signs of a change of trend.

A consistent course correction will take place only when wrong decisions and wrong attitudes on the part of the Church and theology are honestly admitted: when theological teaching is adjusted and fitted in to the new world picture, not only when it is too late to do anything else, not only provisionally, but when the Christian message as a whole is thought out afresh within the framework of the new, historical-dynamic world view. At the same time, it should not be a question of substantiating again a new fashionable theology with the aid of some new opinions, slogans and labels, but of developing theology as a whole clearly and consistently in an established harmony with the relatively assured data of natural science. The hot and later the cold wars between theology and natural science therefore must not now be followed by a lifeless, unconnected coexistence but by constructive debate—without paper or iron curtains—about the one world and the one humanity, about truth, unity, the value and meaning of the whole. This is a task, of course, that is far beyond the resources of a particular individual or a particular group. As a contribution to such a joint rethinking, it is intended in this book to describe a few, but essential, basic ideas with reference to an image of God that can be justified at the present time.

Although we have hitherto been concerned with questions that are merely preliminary to the question of God, the importance of what is involved here has become very clear. Some of the problems raised have more or less solved themselves in the course of the historical-systematic presentation, but the most important are still unsettled and must be kept in mind. But before we pursue the problems further—centered after the French Revolution mainly on the question of God itself—we must draw up, as announced, a brief interim balance in the light of the dual perspective developed up to now. What conclusions can be drawn at the present stage in the light of the *perspective of Descartes and Pascal* and of the traditions they represented and that can be perceived even up to the present time?

In Protestant theology also, the necessity of a constructive confrontation of the two traditions is seen today more clearly than it was some decades ago. We can certainly agree with Gerhard Ebeling's intentions when—admittedly without recalling the problems of natural science or those of Pascal—he says: "In the entanglement of the traditions relating to the problem of certainty, theology must be the advocate of the confrontation of both modes of certainty. It must consequently accept in a critical spirit its responsibility for both sides, as represented by the names of Luther and Descartes. It must present an independent account of Luther's heritage before the forum of modern thought shaped by the influence of Descartes. But it must also put to the test what is known as 'the spirit of modern times' before the forum of the certainty of faith. Properly understood, however, these are not two separate events."[9]

We are attempting a comparison in recapitulatory and combined theses. The interests of Descartes *and* Pascal will be expressly taken up on each occasion in a *couple of theses*. This confrontation therefore means anything but an irreconcilability in principle between two fundamentally opposed positions, or between what C. P. Snow called "the two cultures," as was recently asserted polemically against the "myth of philosophy."[10]

Obviously, from the time of Plato and Aristotle up to analytic and social-critical philosophy there have been numerous polarizations. Obviously, there are differences between mysticism and scholasticism, classical and modern education, humanities and natural sciences. Obviously, there are contrasts between rationality and experience, explanation and understanding, judging and valuing, *esprit de géométrie* and *esprit de finesse*. But should not some sort of collaboration, of communication, be possible between the two forms of thought? Provided the differences are maintained and observed between the various spheres, aspects and strata of reality, a *differentiated synthesis* cannot *a priori* be excluded and is even possible in one and the same person. Pascal in particular "believed in a possible union or reconciliation of the two disparate attitudes" and indeed "might be regarded as an example of a successful synthesis of both types of mind," although—as we saw[11]—"in his person the one type of mind gradually came to prevail over the other."[12] Our dual theses on modern rationality deal first in general with modern science, then with the relationship between theology and natural science and finally—only in a preparatory form—the relationship between science and the question of God.

## Modern science

Man has learned to use his reason over an increasingly wide area. But does he live only by reason?

- *It was right in principle and historically necessary for man, encompassed by doubt, to learn to make a better use of reason, in order, enlightened by science, to investigate without prejudice and systematically nature and its laws, finally also himself and sociological conditions in all their aspects.*
- *Despite the justification in principle and the historical necessity of autonomous rationality and scientific knowledge, for the sake of full human existence and genuine enlightenment, rationality must not be regarded as absolute. In addition to reason, we must also take into account willing and feeling, imagination and temperament, emotions and passions, which cannot simply be reduced to reason: in addition to methodical-rational thinking (l'esprit de géométrie), also intuitive-total apprehension, sensing, feeling (l'esprit de finesse).*

The ideal of modern science consists in adequate method, clarity, exactitude: that is, in the last resort, mathematicizing of the problems. Can all dimensions of the human be grasped in this way?

- *For scientific investigation in all fields, a secure, neutral and adequate method is required, proceeding according to its own laws. For the application of this method, criteria such as clarity and distinctness, exactitude, efficacy and objectivity are appropriate. In the world of what is quantitative and measurable, the spirit of geometry, objectivity, neutrality and freedom from values must prevail. Problems must be mathematicized, quantified and formalized as much as possible.*

- *Despite the recognition of the mathematical-scientific ideals of clarity and distinctness, of exactitude, efficacy and objectivity, we may not extend the mathematical-scientific method—as if it had an exclusive claim—to the human mind as a whole, which is in fact more than mathematics. Mathematicizing, quantifying and formalizing are not adequate for the understanding of the world of the qualitative and of such specifically human phenomena as smiling, humor, music, art, suffering, love, faith, in all their dimensions. What is actually measured may not be identified with the phenomenon under consideration. There is not merely one—the mathematical-scientific rationality. Even in science, there are many methods and not merely one: the choice of method depends on the particular set of problems. Objectivity, neutrality and freedom from values have a meaning in science only if we always remain aware of the whole system of reference and of the interests behind the quest for knowledge, of the methodical assumptions, of the practical results and of both personal and social responsibility. Methods and science should not be ends in themselves but means to the humanizing of man.*

As long as it does not become an ideology, theory of knowledge can be a help also in philosophy and theology so far as these are meant to be sciences. Criticism, therefore, must be accepted, but not destruction.

- *It is legitimate to construct a purely formal logic, linguistic analysis and a theory of knowledge and at the same time to ask about the verification or falsification of empirical propositions. It can be helpful to philosophy and theology only if they make use of logic, linguistic analysis and theory of knowledge while seeking to formulate their problems as unambiguously as possible, to gain a clear understanding of their specific procedure, to render concepts more precise, to use an exact, scientific language and to examine critically the various attempts at a solution. In this sense, theology, too, if it claims to be a science, must be pursued rationally—that is, critically and in a spirit of intellectual responsibility.*

- *Formal logic, linguistic analysis and theory of knowledge, however, may not—any more than theology—be made into a uniform science with universal claims. The problem of verification or falsification of statements must be seen within the whole context of history, society and their hermeneutics. It cannot be helpful to theology and philosophy to be broken up into logic, linguistic analysis and theory of knowledge, to be so absorbed in the question of method as never to catch sight of their "material" and to see their sole purpose in rationally critical de- struction. Theology, too, is pursued with intellectual responsibility as a science only if—in addition to a critical function—it accepts also a ra- tional and justifiable affirmative function.*

## Relationship of theology to natural science

Natural sciences attempt to advance their knowledge to the point of mathematical certainty. Are there no limits to natural science?

- *Exact research, from atomic physics to astrophysics, from microbiology to genetics and medicine, can be pursued to the point at which the greatest possible mathematical certainty is attained. Mathematically oriented science, then, has its complete justification, its autonomy and inherent laws, which no theologian or churchman may dispute by ap- pealing to a higher authority (God, Bible, Church, Pope). Against any sort of patronizing by theology and Church, it must be emphasized that a demarcation between mathematical-scientific and metaphysical-theo- logical statements is right and necessary.*

- *If questions of natural science are—rightly—treated according to the methods and style of natural science, then—on the other hand—ques- tions of the human psyche and society, questions of law, of politics, of history, questions of aesthetics, of morality and religion, must also be treated according to the methods corresponding to their object and in their own style. No matter how rightly we stress the autonomy and the inherent laws of natural science, the problems of its foundations may not be passed over in silence, the hypothetical character of its laws may not be overlooked and its conclusions may not be regarded as absolute: together with the possibilities of natural science, its limitations must also be seen. As against any sort of patronizing by mathematics and nat- ural science, it must be observed that there is no mathematical-scientific criterion in the light of which metaphysical-theological statements can be described as senseless (or pseudo problems).*

Natural science as a foundation? Yes, if it is not made into the whole.

- *Natural science rightly became the foundation of modern technology and industry, and indeed for the modern world picture, for modern civi- lization and culture as a whole.*

- *But natural science is an appropriate foundation for the modern world picture, modern civilization and culture only if the foundation is not made the whole structure; only if the relativity, provisional character and social contingency of each and every world picture, of all projects, patterns and aspects, are seen; if, in addition to the methods of natural science, those of other sciences, of the human and the social sciences and also of philosophy, even of theology—again in a very different way —are permitted to count. Any science that claims to be absolute puts itself in question.*

It is a question of truth. Who possesses it definitively?

● *Natural scientists also recognize today that they have no final, definitive truths to offer: they are prepared to revise a formerly adopted standpoint and, if the occasion arises, even to withdraw it.*
● *Theologians, too, aspiring to definitive truth, do not possess this truth definitively. They must also constantly seek the truth afresh, they can only approach closer to it, learn by trial and error and must therefore be prepared to revise their standpoint. In theology, too, the scientific interplay of project, criticism, countercriticism and improvement should be possible.*

But is the term "science" itself unambiguous? If theology seeks to be a science, what would be the consequences?

● *Definitions of terms like "science," "philosophy," "metaphysics" amount largely to agreements (conventions, traditions). The term "science"—as in English—may largely be confined to mathematical-logical statements and to those of natural science.*
● *Just because definitions of "science," "philosophy," "metaphysics" have largely a conventional, traditional character, the term "science" may also be used for nonmathematical statements and statements other than those of natural science: that is, for meta-empirical-theological statements. If, however, theology claims to be a science (or "academic discipline"), it must submit to certain scientific principles of concept formation and substantiation and may not offend against these as it is concretely worked out by not explaining newly introduced concepts or by not substantiating assertions.*

## Science and the question of God

May modern science leave out God?

● *If modern science wanted to proceed with methodical irreproachability, it necessarily had to leave out God, for he cannot be empirically verified and analyzed like other objects.*
● *Precisely because subject and object, the method and the object, of science, are closely interwoven, a distinction must nevertheless be made between the phenomenon perceptible to natural science and the reality in itself. No method (or project, pattern, theory), however secure, ade-*

quate, exact, may be regarded as absolute; the perspectivity and variability particularly of the mathematical-scientific methods demand constant awareness of their limits, especially in respect of the ever-greater total reality.

The estrangement between theology and natural science was disastrous. Self-criticism on the part of theology and the Church is necessary. Can the question particularly of the ultimate reality and of reality as a whole be simply eliminated?

- *In the light of the biblical belief, it was not necessary in principle for Christian theology and the Church to be opposed from the very beginning to the findings of the rising natural sciences. It would have been possible at an early stage to distinguish between the biblical world picture and the biblical message, as the results produced by natural science and scientists themselves suggested.*

- *If it wants to remain faithful to its method, natural science may not extend its judgments beyond the horizon of experience: neither a supercilious, skeptical indifference to knowledge nor a claim to know everything better is appropriate. A possible all-embracing, absolutely primal and ultimate reality, which we call God and which—because unascertainable and unanalyzable—cannot be manipulated, must be methodically eliminated from consideration in the natural sciences. Nevertheless, with reference to reality as a whole and to man himself, the question of the ultimate and primal meanings and standards, values and norms, and thus of an ultimate and primal reality as such, cannot be a priori rejected. Open-mindedness toward reality as a whole is required in principle on the part of the natural scientist. Philosophers of science also and epistemologists recognize today beyond the field of scientific knowledge the wider "meta-physical" question of the "problems of life" (Wittgenstein), of "cosmology" (Popper), of the "world" (Kuhn).*

Was the development to modern atheism necessary? Have not theology and natural science overstepped their limits?

- *According to the ideas of the natural scientists of the sixteenth and seventeenth centuries, Christian theology and the Church should have become allies of the new science; but, because of their failure to do so and because of their failure in regard to the new philosophical and social-political developments, they contributed substantially to the establishment of both scientific and political atheism: in the eighteenth century among individual precursors, in the nineteenth among large numbers of educated people, in the twentieth even among large masses in East and West.*

- *There was, however, no necessity in principle for autonomous reason, for modern natural science, increasingly so to generalize their conclu-*

*sions as to leave no place for a belief in God and in practice largely to substitute belief in science for belief in God. The God of the Bible is not identical with the God of the ancient world picture or with the God of Greek philosophy.*

To sum up: What are we pleading for? We are pleading with Descartes and his followers decidedly *for critical rationality*, but with Pascal and his followers equally decidedly *against an ideological rationalism*. Hence the idea of critical rationality must be entirely approved; but the ideology of a critical rationalism, absolutizing and mysticizing the rational factor, must be rejected. Ideology is understood here critically as a system of "ideas," concepts and convictions, of interpretative patterns, motives and norms of action, which—mostly governed by particular interests—produces a distorted picture of the reality of the world, disguises real abuses and replaces rational arguments by an appeal to emotion. Rationalistic ideology is characterized by rationalistic dogmatism and rationalistic intolerance.

## Complexity and unity of reality

Theology, too, must stand for critical rationality. Theologians, too, should be aware of their debt to the tradition of critical thought: the boldest among them have played no small part in antiquity, the Middle Ages and modern times, in enlightening men in regard to mythologies, ideologies and obscurantisms of every kind. On the other hand, philosophy and natural science can also be opposed to an ideological rationalism. It would never have occurred to the great initiators of the Enlightenment —to such philosophers as Descartes, Spinoza and Leibniz, as also to Voltaire, Lessing and Kant, or to such scientists as Copernicus, Kepler, Galileo, Newton and Boyle—simply to deny the existence of another dimension beyond that of mathematical-scientific reason. At least in this respect, the great rational thinkers have wrongly been described as "rationalists," representatives of an "ism" with blinkers narrowing their vision of reality in its wholeness.

Genuine rationality is not to be equated with one-sidedness and one-dimensionality. As opposed to the ideology of rationalism, the multiple dimensionality and the *complex stratification of reality* must be kept in mind from the outset: "What is real can be encountered in wholly different ways and consequently can also bear a wholly different character. The reality of the atomic physicist is different from that of the Platonist, the reality of ordinary life is different from that of religious experience. Considered in its content, reality is fissured: it is differentiated on each occasion according to the aspect that comes into view. Obviously there is not simply 'reality,' but very different planes of reality. But this means that we cannot and may not make a particular aspect into absolute reality, for then the other aspects will revolt." That is how the philosopher Wilhelm Weischedel expresses it.[13]

Despite all the complexity of reality, we may not explain the various strata and planes of reality as so many different realities. Despite the multiple dimensionality of reality, we may not overlook the unity in the various dimensions. In all the planes and strata, dimensions, aspects and differentiations, it is a question of the *one* reality, which—as we have sufficiently seen—can be split up only at the expense of a full human existence in this world.

Against Descartes's dualism between subject and object, thinking and being, mind and matter, body and soul, as also between reason and faith, philosophy and theology, already criticized here, which was taken up by Pascal to far too great an extent and even intensified with reference to reason and faith, but this time giving faith the advantage instead of reason—against this dualism, the *unity and truth of reality* must once more be brought up for discussion: "The obsolence of the theological unity of reality expressed in Aristotelian terms certainly does not settle the question of the unity and truth, the salvation and meaning of the whole. Only now does it cease to be a traditional postulate and become an open question which keeps time and the progress of human history in suspense, continually provokes new answers and makes all answers obsolete and temporary. Truth and the salvation of the whole is understood in the form of the open question. As long as this question is open and still is recognized everywhere as a question, science remains science. Kant justifiably declared that 'a religion which, without hesitation, declares war on reason, will not, in the long run, be able to hold out against it.' Yet it became evident that even reason, in its enlightening victory over what it called faith, could not hold out alone, but developed highly unreasonable forms of naïve credibility." So writes the theologian Jürgen Moltmann.[14]

How, then, is the open question of unity and truth, meaning and value, of the whole to be answered? How is a solution to be found for problems of life, of cosmology, of society, of the world? These questions are obviously connected with the question of God. We shall have to deal with this in the following sections. Here we have had to discuss first of all the fundamental relationship between reason and faith: that is, the framework of an answer. The framework must and will now be filled in, so as to provide a positive description of this relationship. To this end, one thing especially is necessary. The consequences of the modern development for the understanding of God must be resolutely drawn out. Are we not in absolute need of a new, a modern understanding of God?

# B. THE NEW UNDERSTANDING OF GOD

How is man to *think* of God in the one but multidimensional reality? This question, which has been at the center of philosophical thinking from time immemorial, has become increasingly acute from the time of Descartes and Pascal onward. After the Enlightenment and the French Revolution, the development of thought on the question of God reached a climax in German idealism. Both the Protestant-biblicist and the Catholic-traditionalist, as well as the deistic-rationalist images of God, were caught up in the crisis.

Theology was then involved in conflict—as we saw—not only with modern science but also with modern philosophy. What was the use of attempting—at this very late stage—to start out from a scientific world picture while sticking to a philosophically obsolete image of God? Has normal theology up to the present time paid sufficient attention to the significant developments that have taken place in modern philosophy and the history of ideas not simply to repel them but in order to share in the whole process of thought? These developments permit man to think of God, and particularly of the biblical God, on a grander scale than was possible in the time of the Greek and Latin Fathers or in the Middle Ages or even at the time of Descartes and Pascal. The gulf between normal theology and modern philosophy—and indeed modern thought as a whole—particularly in the understanding of God, has often been far too deep. But, as always, whether a decision today is made for or against God, it must be made realistically, not in the light of a Greek or medieval but of a modern understanding of God that is the fruit of long reflection.

# I. God in the world: Georg Wilhelm Friedrich Hegel

By way of introduction to this chapter, it must be repeated that what is intended here is not a history of philosophy, still less a history of ideas: only the continuation of the systematic clarification of the problem of God as it has developed in the course of history. In the first place, it is especially the philosophy of *Hegel* that will serve as a model for further discussion. In this philosophy, the epochal development that started with Descartes reached its completion, and in the light of this philosophy the later thrust of the problems will be checked: how far the assumptions of this thought are still valid today and how far a stage of thought was attained here from which there can be no return.

## 1. From deism to panentheism

Hegel's biography, his place in the history of ideas, his works, beginning with his diaries as a schoolboy in Stuttgart, his early writings as a theology student at Tübingen, as a tutor in Berne and Frankfurt, going on to his published works as a university teacher at Jena, secondary-school director at Nuremberg and professor at Heidelberg (*Phenomenology, Logic, Encyclopedia*), and thence finally to the great historical-philosophical lectures as full professor in Berlin (after the *Philosophy of Right*, the posthumously published lectures on the philosophy of world history, of art, religion, philosophy of history): all this in its continuity and discontinuity, in its interconnection and its breaks, the present author has surveyed elsewhere from the philosophical-theological standpoint, examining the very diverse implications and complications.[1] It would be fine if the same attention could be given to the treatment of the problem of God by such other important figures in the history of ideas as Lessing, Kant, Fichte, Schelling, Hölderlin, and Goethe.[2] But this is not possible, nor is it necessary, in view of the objectives of the present book. Within these limits, we may hope that the general picture will be clear even to the reader who is not familiar with the details.

Hegel is undoubtedly the most difficult among the notoriously difficult German philosophers. But at the end of this Section B, further aid will be provided once more in the form of an account of interim results.

If, then, anyone finds it too difficult to read all this section, he need not feel discouraged but is free to go straight on to these interim results. The same applies to a person who is less interested in following the path to the modern understanding of God and to the post-Hegelian turning to atheism. It would, however, be better for the reader to take time to acquire a better understanding perhaps by once more going over this section, which also involved the author in considerable exertions.

## Limits of the Enlightenment

It was in the year of the publication of the "dogmatics" of materialistic atheism, Holbach's *Système de la nature,* in Stuttgart, still under the *ancien régime,* that Georg Wilhelm Friedrich Hegel came into the world: this was 1770. A year before the outbreak of the French Revolution, this schoolboy, educated in a Protestant family but filled less with the spirit of the Reformation than with that of the Enlightenment, with an arid, intellectual approach to religion, entered the famous Protestant seminary in Tübingen to study theology—he was looking to a Christianity of natural reasonableness, protesting against obscurantism and superstition and wholly oriented to utility, virtue and happiness: it was now 1788. Finally, in the year when God was deposed in Paris, Hegel—who had not been a particularly overzealous student of theology—completed his course at Tübingen. During that period, he had not a high opinion of the apologetic-biblicist supernaturalism of his dogmatics professor, G. C. Storr,[3] head of the older Tübingen Protestant school, preferring to read Voltaire, Kant and especially Rousseau; together with his friends and fellow students Hölderlin and Schelling, he had taken part enthusiastically in debates in the Political Club and written such slogans as *In tyrannos, Vive Jean-Jacques,* and *Vive la liberté,* on the pages of visitors' books; toward the end, by such activities as planting a symbolic "tree of liberty" in Tübingen, he had provoked an inspection by the Consistory and a personal intervention by the feudal, absolutist ruler, Duke Karl-Eugen, in the refectory of the seminary. After all this, he took his master's degree in philosophy and passed the ecclesiastical consistorial examination: this was 1793—a year of terror for Europe.

Most of the leading brains even in Germany had at first been very enthusiastic about the Enlightenment and the *French Revolution:* not only Kant, Jacobi, Fichte, but also Klopstock, Herder, Wieland, Novalis, Schlegel; Schiller had even been offered the freedom of the city of Paris. But, just at the end of Hegel's time in Tübingen, the revolutionary dictatorship of the Jacobins had been set up in Paris: the murders in September 1792 had already considerably cooled down foreign sympathy for the revolution. In January 1793 Louis XVI had been executed. Then began the terror, under Robespierre's Committee for Public Security, with mass executions going into the thousands. All this amounted to a confirmation of the influential book by the liberal English statesman Edmund Burke *Reflections on the Revolution in France*,[4] which appeared in a German translation in the same year of terror and stood decisively for the freedom of the individual and justice in the state but against violent political subversion: an essential book for the historically potent early Romantic movement, which was just beginning. Like Herder, Schiller and others, so now Hegel, Schelling and Hölderlin also condemned the Jacobin terror, without, however, abandoning the aims of the revolution.

At the same time, our Tübingen students were concerned with more than politicosocial revolution: their interest was the *revolution of the spirit*. A cultural revolution? Certainly it was not simply a matter of a revolutionary political program, which anyway had little prospect of being realized in Germany. But they were interested in a comprehensive humanitarian sociopolitical program embracing all fields: science, literature and art, politics, philosophy, and especially religion. Their slogan was "the kingdom of God," a code word that amply covered whatever they wanted it to cover.[5]

It was particularly in this humanitarian sociopolitical perspective that religion played a decisive part for Hegel. For it had become clear to him even at the school in Stuttgart that the "common man," the average man, had to have a share in this bright new age, in the "Enlightenment." An abstract rational philosophy would not be adequate at this point. Religion was needed.[6] For this very reason, Hegel's attitude to religion during his student years was unambiguously critical. Criticism was not an argument against his religious commitment but a part of the latter: an attitude typical also of other German philosophers of the Enlightenment. His critique of religion was aimed not—as in France—at the abolition but at the renewal of religion in a modern, enlightened society: religion had to become a genuine "folk-religion."

By the end of his time in Tübingen, Hegel was already beginning to see more and more clearly the *limits of the Enlightenment*. He raised the question explicitly: "What constitutes folk-religion?" The answer is that it must be "based on universal reason," but at the same time "imagination, heart and sensuousness must not be left unsatisfied."[7] As against all forms of rationalism, he maintained: "Intellectual enlightenment makes people shrewder, but not better. . . . No book on morality, no intellectual enlightenment can prevent evil inclinations from rising up, from becoming rampant."[8] Hegel as a theology student was not a supernaturalistic pedantic theologian, but neither was he a rationalistic freethinker. He did not want an irrational tradition: in that respect he belonged to the Enlightenment. But neither did he want reason without tradition: in this respect he went farther than the Enlightenment. We can catch here the echo of Pascal against Descartes: "Wisdom is something different from enlightenment, it is different from reasoning. But wisdom is not science, wisdom is an elevation of the soul . . . it reasons little, nor does it proceed mathematically from concepts, through a series of syllogisms, in order to reach what it takes to be the truth, . . . but it speaks from the fullness of the heart."[9]

Some ideas, of which Pascal had been the sole defender in the previous century, had meanwhile in a variety of ways become common property and blended with others. In the new Hegelian emphasis against the Enlightenment, the *most diverse influences* could be seen at work: the folk spirit as with Montesquieu and Herder, Shaftesbury's altruism and the importance attached to feeling by Mendelssohn; the idealizing of Hellenism with Winckelmann, Wieland, Herder and Schiller, as well as Fichte's distinction between the religion of pure reason and true religion. But, above all—in some respects on the lines of Pascal—*Rousseau* must be mentioned here: not so much for his pessimistic view of civilization or his questioning of private property and science but—despite his connection with the Enlightenment—for his insistence on the vital union of reason and sensuousness; the rights of the heart, imagination and feeling; natural altruism (compassion, friendship, love); the antiauthoritarian tendency in education (leaving children to grow up); the sense of a superindividual unity (*volonté générale*); determination to renew society, from art up to politics and religion.

## All in God: Spinoza and his influence

Almost imperceptibly, over a long period, a significant change had come about in the intellectual climate and with it also a change in the understanding of God: *away from the deism of the Enlightenment to a basically pantheistic attitude.* A completely new sense of life had been established: a sense of life and nature, of the world and God, heralded by Lessing, fostered by Kant, coming to fruition in the literary movement of *Sturm und Drang* (storm and stress), but ultimately going back mainly to Spinoza.

As early as the rationalism of the seventeenth century and the Enlightenment of the eighteenth, there had been marginally new attempts at a wide-ranging reconciliation, stimulated by undercurrents of medieval mysticism persisting at the dawn of modern times, especially with Giordano Bruno and then—more effectively for the future—with Spinoza. The Iberian Jew *Baruch* (Benedict, the blessed) *Spinoza* (1632–77), was certainly the most abused philosopher and religious thinker of early modern times. In Amsterdam he had had a rabbinical education; but he had also acquired a knowledge of Latin philosophy and literature and, as an autonomous and independent thinker, became an outsider for the Jewish community, resembling in this respect another great outsider, his neighbor in the Jewish quarter of Amsterdam, the painter Rembrandt.[10] In

1656—the year when Pascal's "Provincial Letters" were condemned—
Spinoza came under major excommunication on account of his serious errors and was expelled from the Amsterdam synagogue. He turned down a
professorship in Heidelberg, offered by the Elector Palatine—brother of
that Elizabeth of the Palatinate to whom Descartes had dedicated his
"Principles of Philosophy"—because he wanted a quiet life and intellectual freedom. In his peaceful country retreat, he devoted himself entirely to philosophical reflection, earning his living by grinding and
polishing lenses. In the sole work (*Tractatus theologico-politicus*[11]) published (and repeatedly condemned) in his lifetime (anonymously and
with a fictitious place of publication), he proved to be one of the first resolute defenders of liberty of thought and faith. But, at the same time, he
thus became the precursor of modern biblical criticism, regarding the
Bible not as God's inspired, inerrant book but as the often contradictory
document of genuinely human Jewish faith.

Quite unlike Descartes, from whom he had learned so much, Spinoza
placed God as the absolutely certain at the beginning of philosophy.[12]
Spinoza's God does not live apart from the universe: God is in the world
and the world is in God. Nature is a particular way in which God himself
exists; human consciousness is a particular way in which God himself
thinks. The individual self and all finite things are not autonomous substances but only modifications of the *one and only divine substance*. God,
then, all in all—a purely immanent, not a transcendent, God? For
Spinoza, God is transcendent only in the sense that his infinitely many attributes—apart from extension and thought, in Descartes's sense—remain
inaccessible to us. God is not a cause outside and beyond this world but
the inward cause of all things and cause of himself.

This impersonally conceived God of Spinoza is of course not the Creator of the world, and the philosopher's contemporaries were absolutely
right to ask if this was still the God of Abraham, Isaac and Jacob. But
Spinoza believed—he was firmly convinced—in a greater God than did
believers in the Bible. Despite his rejection by Jews, Catholics and Protestants, he remained unshakably loyal to his conviction and drew his
strength from that yearning—transcending all perishable things—for the
eternal, the "intellectual love of God," and hoped to die into the all-one
God-Nature.

In his "History of Philosophy," Hegel says of Spinoza: "To be a follower of Spinoza is the essential commencement of all philosophy. For,
when man begins to philosophize, the soul must commence by bathing in
this ether of the One Substance, in which all that man has held as true
has disappeared; this negation of all that is particular, to which every philosopher must have come, is the liberation of the mind and its absolute
foundation."[13] But the difficulties arising out of this understanding of
God, which sees the world and all its wretchedness as taken up into God,
are nowhere more apparent than in Hegel's work.

In his own time, however, Spinoza, with his ontological-ethical pantheism, was too far advanced to be able to win followers. But, after Lessing, at the time of Goethe, Fichte, Schelling and Hegel, "Spinozism" was to become the more or less secret refuge of all those who sought an all-embracing unity. And even earlier, with the Cartesians, in Malebranche's occasionalism and especially with Berkeley, the being and operation of God were understood as a being in the human mind. And the question continued to be raised: Is this still the God of the Fathers, the God of Jesus Christ? But now no one was interested in the God *above* man or even in the God *outside* man but in the God *in* man. That is, God in all things and all things in God.

Like Herder, Fichte and Schiller, so too Hölderlin, Schelling and presumably also Hegel came under the influence of Spinozistic-pantheistic ideas while they were still in Tübingen. But three figures, who were responsible for the turnabout in Germany, must be mentioned here at least briefly: Kant, Lessing and Goethe.

From the time of *Kant's* critique of the proofs of God—however little they were understood in detail—to educated people it seemed to be proved that God's existence could not be proved, that God therefore was not a matter of knowledge. In Germany—unlike France—at first God was scarcely denied, but he increasingly became the very questionable ultimate horizon of the world vision. Instead of speaking of God as the thinking and operating world Creator and world Ruler of the great world clockwork, people began to talk increasingly of the "Deity." And the latter is beyond all finite determinations of human thought, beyond all human statements. "The Father, Creator of heaven and earth," became the all-embracing "Absolute."

At the same time, *Lessing*—the greatest controversialist of German classical literature and publisher of the scandalous "fragments" by Reimarus (which started the "quest for the historical Jesus"*)—had, so to speak, posthumously drawn the attention of the intellectual avant-garde to the ideas of Spinoza. His rationalist Berlin friends were profoundly shocked when, four years after his death (1781, the year of Kant's "Critique of Pure Reason"), Friedrich Heinrich Jacobi ("Letters to Moses Mendelssohn on Spinoza's Doctrine")[14] gave a brief account of a private conversation with Lessing shortly before the latter's death: in 1780, in his own words, he had abandoned the orthodox ideas of God. In fact, he had invoked Spinoza while rejecting God as personal cause of the world, understanding him as a kind of soul of the universe encompassing the world as the One and the All. Jacobi thus charged Lessing with pantheism and consequently also with determinism, atheism, fatalism. This was the open-

---

* The English title of Albert Schweitzer's *Geschichte der Leben-Jesu-Forschung*, first published in Tübingen, 1906. The English translation appeared in 1910 (London/New York); a new edition came out in 1911; it has frequently been reprinted. Translator.

ing of the "pantheism controversy." Lessing's friend Moses Mendelssohn, a follower of Wolff and collaborator of Friedrich Nicolai—leader of the Berlin rationalists—was unable to dissipate the doubts. Lessing had been a Spinozist. From that time onward, he was regarded as the founder of the peculiarly German variety of a dynamic (Leibnizian) pantheism.

*Goethe's* religious influence was exercised indirectly, through his poetry; but it was all the more effective at that time and subsequently because of the uncontroversial and harmonious way in which it was conveyed and what might be called its natural worldliness. Under Pietist influence at first and more than reserved throughout his life toward the radical French Enlightenment—after encountering Herder's understanding of nature and history and coming to terms with Lavater's Christ-piety—the Goethe of *Sturm und Drang* had struggled to reach his own understanding of the divine. For Goethe, God is not the architect, creator or ruler of the world. His God is the unfathomable primal reason of all things, the all-encompassing and all-sustaining, creative fantasy and constructive universal nature. Soon Goethe also was to be accused of atheism.

This countermovement to the rationalistic-deistic Enlightenment was strengthened by Hamann's religious thought, Herder's philosophy of history and Jacobi's philosophy of feeling. As against the Enlightenment's solidarity with civilization, the stress was laid again, from Rousseau's time onward, more on solidarity with nature. And even to the point of the arrangement of gardens and parks, French geometric rationalism was replaced by a more organic (English) style. Herder, Goethe and Hölderlin restored to nature the divine character of which it had been deprived as a result of its scientific interpretation by the Enlightenment. This restoration of the divinity of nature found philosophical expression particularly in the early works of Schelling. A sense of the living, comprehensive totality of all that exists, a sense of nature understood as life, of life understood as divine, now came to prevail.

Despite—or, rather, because of—the political weakness of the "Holy Roman Empire of the German Nation" under the hegemony of Napoleonic France, the focus of philosophical-cultural discussion toward the end of the eighteenth century had plainly shifted from France to Germany. The fifty years from Lessing's death and Kant's "Critique of Pure Reason" (1781) to the deaths of Hegel and Goethe (1831–32) were filled with a breathtakingly rapid development and an abundance of problems thitherto rarely observed in the history of human ideas (perhaps not even in the similarly crowded history of classical Greek philosophy). Nor should the fact go unmentioned that European music reached its peak in Vienna at the same time. It was also in the year 1781 that Mozart came to Haydn in Vienna, in 1787 Beethoven came to see Mozart, and after that came Schubert. But the classical period likewise came to an end by 1827–28, with the deaths of Beethoven and Schubert.

And *Hegel?* What might be called his apprenticeship lasted for seven long years. From Tübingen, he went as a private tutor first to Berne and then to Frankfurt. It was only in 1801, at the age of thirty-one, that he qualified at Jena as a teacher in philosophy, while his friend Schelling had become professor of philosophy there at twenty-three. What had been prepared in Berne became obvious in Frankfurt. For Hegel, too, there had been a turning away from the rationalist and then also from the Kantian separation of God and man. For him, too, a turning toward a unity of infinite and finite, divine and human, to a unity of life, of mind, even of the divine. For Hegel also, then—as with Lessing and Goethe—a definitive abandonment of dualistic deism, which had thrust God into a distant transcendence and saw in him merely an Opposite (ob-jectum) set up over against man and the world, lacking any connection or fellowship with these.

Was Hegel therefore a *pantheist?* It is better not to talk of pantheism in the strict sense, which makes all things God. For Hegel does not deify the empirical world, he does not make everything God, as if the finite were simply absorbed in the infinite. But we may certainly speak of a pan-en-theism in the widest sense, of a vital unity of all being in God: a differentiated unity of life, of love, of all-embracing Spirit—these three notions are typical of Hegel's Frankfurt period. God as Opposite seems to be conquered by Deity as all-encompassing. Consequently, in describing the relationship between God and man, personal categories are now avoided as much as possible.

Nevertheless the fact cannot be overlooked that there is a vast difference between the "theologian" of Frankfurt and the "philosopher" of Jena. The great themes of Tübingen, Berne and Frankfurt were folk-religion and Christianity: there he had even written a life of Jesus in the spirit of Kant; he had written about the positivity of the Christian religion, the spirit of Judaism and Christianity. All these theological themes seem now to be completely replaced by other, secular themes: logic, metaphysics, philosophy of nature, philosophy of spirit, and the problems resulting from these.

Now, in Jena, there is found in Hegel's work the clearly conceived and theoretical principle of unity: *mind-monism,* which sees the (divine) mind as the One, all-encompassing. Here also is found his understanding of the contrariety of all life: the *dialectic,* logical thinking and real happening in opposites which produce something new. The dialectic, then, is also simultaneously a method of thought, a form of systematic description and a metaphysical-real process of being and eternal coming-to-be of all life. Hegel *and* Schelling are in debt mainly to Fichte for the break-through to this systematic-universal design, to the formation of both monism of mind and the dialectic. Fichte had, of course, left Jena before Hegel's arrival and gone to Berlin. All this was the result of a second un-fortunate conflict that must be recalled here: after the pantheism conflict, we now have the atheism conflict.

## 2. Atheism?

The philosopher *Johann Gottlieb Fichte*, eight years older than Hegel, had also been first a student of theology and then a private tutor; soon after Hegel's departure from Tübingen, he became Professor in Jena. Following the lines of Lessing's last secret thoughts and the ideas of the young Goethe, he had *at first* been fascinated by the identity of all things in God in Spinoza's sense: God understood not as a living personality with free will but as eternally necessary being. This Deity certainly is not simply the universe. But the Deity does in fact think and posit the universe in virtue of eternal necessity. For Spinoza, individual things are no more than modifications of God. But, for the early Fichte, individual things are thoughts in the great thought of the universe, thought by God. In this light, the world appears as a totality interlinked in itself, and man as fatalistically determined by the primal thought of the Deity. Providence becomes fate, sin the necessary consequence of finiteness. These ideas are still found in 1790 in Fichte's "Aphorisms on Religion and Deism."[15]

But *then* it was Kant's practical philosophy that diverted Fichte from this kind of identity. Kant liberated him from the fatalistic view of God and the world and made him see the dignity of the free, responsible moral personality. From that time onward, what mattered to Fichte was that man should seize on the faith in his human destiny, which is revealed in the moral sense of duty, as something final and absolute. What is man's destiny? To be a free moral personality firmly rooted in himself. It is only in the light of this ethical starting point that we can judge the system that Fichte first outlined in his "Science of Knowledge," in 1794.[16] But, in view of these assumptions, how could he be accused of atheism?

### Fichte and the atheism controversy

In 1798, in his article "On the Ground of our Faith in a Divine World Government," Fichte had declared: "That living and active moral order of things is God: we need no other God and can comprehend no other."[17] On this account, Fichte was *accused—certainly unjustly—of atheism*: for at heart this profound and passionate thinker was an inwardly devout, religious man; by his statement, he really meant the One and All, which as moral ground conditions, sustains and realizes a world of freedom.[18] And yet he was *not entirely unjustly* suspected of atheism. For, from the time of his turning away, under Kant's influence, from fatalistic Spinozism and his turning to a moral primal certainty, he seemed to have eliminated any relationship to God. Why?

In the early period of the "Science of Knowledge," the idea of God is little more than a marginal concept: an absolute that is not personality, not self-consciousness, and still less creator of the world. Should a concept of God be formulated at all? Fichte was content to suggest that belief in God is an immediate, original certainty that is rooted in feeling (a theory that Schleiermacher made immensely popular). At the same time, he defined the substance of this religious faith in the light of Kant's idea of the supreme good: God as the moral order of things, through which—by doing good—the ideal kingdom, the "kingdom of God," is unconditionally brought about.

In his distress, in 1799 Fichte addressed a passionate "Appeal to the Public": "a work that we beg you to read before it is confiscated."[19] But, after he had himself threatened to resign in a hastily written letter, the appeal could not prevent his dismissal. His Excellency, Johann Wolfgang von Goethe, whose Faustian profession of faith—"I have no name to give it; feeling's surely all"[20]—Fichte had quoted at the end of the article under attack, voted for his dismissal. Schiller, whose "Words of Faith"[21] had also been quoted, took up an ambiguous attitude. And who came to the help of Fichte? Oddly enough, the Upper Consistory councilors in Berlin unanimously prevented any kind of measures against Fichte's writings and—just as Frederick the Great had protected the atheistic materialist La Mettrie—Frederick William III now provided a refuge for the philosopher who had been rejected everywhere else: "If it is true that he is involved in hostilities with God, God can settle that: it has nothing to do with me."[22]

Fichte's last word in this scarcely friendly conflict was his work on "The Vocation of Man" (1800):[23] together with Schleiermacher's "Monologues" and Schelling's "System of Transcendental Idealism," of the same year, one of the great dowries of the dawning nineteenth century. Recapitulating and making more intelligible the system of his "Science of Knowledge," Fichte presents it in three steps: from "doubt" (Spinozism as dogmatism) by way of "knowing" (Kant's criticism as epistemological idealism) to "believing." Fichte's moralism appears as a religion of duty, based on conscience. Two years later, Hegel reacted critically especially to this work, under the influence of Schelling, who had dissociated himself in Jena from Fichte, whom he had at first greatly admired. In his work "Faith and Knowledge," Hegel deals with the "reflexion philosophy of subjectivity in the totality of its forms, as Kantian, Jacobian and Fichtean philosophy" (1802).

## Postatheistism

Almost a century before Nietzsche's announcement: "God is dead! God remains dead! And we have killed him,"[24] Hegel, in his "Faith and

Knowledge," gives the title of "Death of God" to the history of modern times, at the same time invoking Pascal. What are we to make of Hegel's attitude to atheism?

a. *Hegel scrutinized modern atheism closely.* For him, the statement "God is dead"—a quotation from a Lutheran hymn in the context of Christ's death on the cross—is not a pious phrase emerging from an orthodox theological background but a harsh historical experience: an "infinite pain."[25] Clearsighted and alert, he perceived exactly the historical context in which must be seen this basic feeling of the religion of modern times that God is dead. In his article on the nature of philosophical criticism, Hegel reacted sharply to the basic dualism of the modern development: Cartesianism (with its separation of extension and thought, of world machine and the mind above the world) is merely its philosophical expression, and both political and religious revolutions merely its external aspect: "Here was a dualism spreading universally in modern civilization, a dualism that meant the end of all the older ways of life and of which the silent transformation of the public life of men and also the many political and religious revolutions were nothing but the multicolored external aspects. It was this dualism that Cartesianism expressed in philosophical form. Philosophy therefore had to find ways of escape from Cartesianism, just as every aspect of living nature had to react against the whole civilization that it expressed."[26]

Hegel naturally had no desire to charge Fichte with atheism, but he does bring out a conceptual connection between Fichte's position and atheism. What is faith, forced so strongly on the defensive from the time of the Enlightenment, to do to withstand the domination of the understanding? It will retire—with the approval of Fichte, as well as Kant and Jacobi—into "pure" *Protestant interiority,* unclouded by any objectivity: into the inwardness of emotion, of feeling, of man's self-assured subjectivity. But—Hegel argues—precisely by this retreat into Protestant subjectivity—generally speaking, the Pietist alternative—faith surrenders objective reality, the reality of the world and of man, to atheism.

And Fichte's philosophy in particular never gets beyond the "ought" in the realization of subjectivity. With him also, self-assured human subjectivity will not abandon its assumed absoluteness and cannot reach a knowledge of the Absolute by reason. That is to say, the *dualism* between infinite God and finite man is not overcome and unity is not attained. But if infinity is opposed in this way to finiteness, "the one is as finite as the other."[27] All the modern philosophers mentioned, then, "have in common this basic principle of the absoluteness of the finite and of the resultant absolute opposition of finiteness and infiniteness, reality and ideality, sensible and suprasensible, with the truly real and absolute seen as totally outside this world."[28] It is therefore this dualistic conflict, as still found also in Kant, Jacobi and Fichte, that is behind the basic modern feeling of the death of God, the loss of God both inside and outside man, which Pascal deplored at an earlier stage: "The religion of modern times rests on the feeling that God himself is dead (which was expressed—so to speak— merely empirically in Pascal's words: *'la nature est telle quelle* marque *partout un* Dieu perdu *et dans l'homme et hors de l'homme'*)."[29]

b. *Hegel understood modern atheism as postatheistic.* For Hegel, there is no going back behind the Enlightenment. From the time that a critique of religion by the notion of reason has become necessary, it is all over with the old, naïve immediacy of faith. The understanding has a right to critical reflection as long as it is not made into an absolute. Hegel therefore by no means simply rejects the philosophy of subjectivity of his predecessors. At this point, nevertheless, against all subject-object separation, the unity of thinking and being is assumed and realized—admittedly only on the subjective side. And if in this way the unification of finite and infinite is only a purely subjective unity, nevertheless Fichte's "philosophy of infinity is closer to the philosophy of the absolute than is that of the finite."[30]

But Hegel's concern is with this "philosophy of the absolute." If human subjectivity is made absolute, it can lapse into nihilism: to the "abyss of nothingness in which all being is absorbed."[31] Consequently not only a subjective but a *real unity of finite and infinite* must be achieved. This means a unity in God himself, *in the Absolute.* This unity in the divine Absolute cannot be attained by a rationalistic-deistic juxtaposition of the finite and the infinite but by the preserving "pan-en-theistic" sublation* of the finite in the infinite.

Even at this point, it becomes clear that, according to Hegel, philosophy must take up the *cause of Christian theology.* For Hegel sees the sublation of the finite in the infinite depicted, "presented" (*vorgestellt*), in Jesus Christ, his death and resurrection. The Christian view is that in Christ, God himself died, but also rose. In philosophical terms, this means that the infinite pain of the loss or death of God is sublated in God himself, "as moment of the supreme Idea."[32] How is this divine dialectic to be understood?

According to Hegel, the *death* of Christ must not be understood in a merely moral sense, as a "sacrifice of empirical being,"[33] but must be understood in a truly philosophical sense as the externalization and alienation (*Entäusserung*) of the divine Absolute itself. This is God's "absolute freedom" but, then, also his "absolute suffering." God externalizes himself

---

* At the risk of seeming to explain the *obscurum per obscurius*, it seems best to follow the practice of most Hegelian scholars in translating the verb *aufheben* by "sublate" and the noun *Aufhebung* by "sublation." Derived from the past participle of the Latin *tollere*, which means both "to remove" and "to elevate," it is an exact equivalent of the German word as used by Hegel to mean at once "canceling," "preserving," "elevating" and "transfiguring." Translator.

into the world. In virtue of such a philosophical understanding of the Absolute as the unity of the infinite with the finite, philosophy will not merely recall the "historical" Good Friday (that particular event). It will in fact "reproduce" the truly "speculative (historical-eternal) Good Friday . . . in the whole truth and harshness of its godlessness."[34]

On the heights of speculative philosophy, then, the atheistic basic feeling of modern times must be understood as an interpretation of the Good Friday event. The historical Good Friday of the Godforsakenness of Jesus must be understood in speculative philosophy, where faith and reason are found together and reconciled, as the Good Friday of the divine Absolute itself and thus as the Good Friday of the Godforsakenness of all that is. It is only this christological interpretation that reveals the "whole seriousness" and the "deepest reason"[35] of godlessness.

c. This and other surprising texts on the death of God make it understandable why the *"Death of God theologians,"*[36] who turned up sporadically especially in the U.S.A. and Germany in the 1960s, after invoking Nietzsche, appealed especially to Hegel. Dorothee Sölle, in her "Atheistically Believing in God," admits that "in the quest for models and starting points of such a theology . . . our attention is attracted especially by Hegel."[37] These theologians certainly have Hegel behind them when— like Hegel, with the utmost sincerity, genuine commitment and resolute identification with his secular contemporaries—they take completely seriously the secular world which considers itself atheistic: that in the modern, markedly scientific conception of reality God no longer plays any creative or conserving role and that we must live (in Bonhoeffer's words[38]) "as if God did not exist" (*etsi Deus non daretur*). They are also right to insist on the problems created by a supramundane, supernatural and in this sense "theistic" image of God, while looking for a point at which God could be relevant to this world and at the same time upholding the idea of the Christian God revealed in the death of Jesus. Nevertheless, there should be no equivocation here and no playing with words like "atheism" (a-theism). Hegel himself anyway cannot be claimed as a supporter of atheism in the usual sense of the term, the denial of any God. As Bonhoeffer also adds, after saying we must live as if God did not exist: "And this is just what we do recognize—before God."

The "death of God" is not the end. Hegel does not proclaim a "gospel of Christian atheism" but—as we might say—a "Christian sublation of atheism." Not an "atheistically believing in God" but a "postatheistically believing in God." It is precisely because Good Friday is the death of God that the *resurrection* follows from it. For the very fact that it is the Good Friday of God himself means that the infinite pain may be understood "as moment but also then no longer as moment of the supreme Idea."[39] Because it is the Absolute itself, it "can and must" rise out of the abyss of nothingness, transcending itself as it were, as "the supreme totality in all its seriousness and from its deepest roots, both all-encompassing and rising to the purest freedom of its form."[40] Thus the Godforsakenness of the world is encompassed by the Godforsakenness of Jesus—understood as the Godforsakenness of God himself—but then also turned around and transcended.

## The primacy of God

What is it, then, that excites and thrills Hegel about the modern complex of problems? It is a question of *one* reality. In the last resort, in all problems of man and the world, it is a question of *God himself*. As Hegel declared with brutal clarity in the Jena article on "common sense," he wants nothing other than simply that which "at the present moment is primarily the interest of philosophy: that is, once again to put God absolutely in the first place, at the apex of philosophy, as the sole ground of all things, as the sole principle of being and knowing, after he has been long enough placed *alongside* other finitenesses or wholly at the end as a postulate that starts out from an absolute finiteness."[41]

Hegel speaks with mingled compassion and irony about an all-too-reasonable reflective philosophy that reduces the problematic of God to the problematic of man: to what is called in naïve reflection "man." He does not want to commit himself to what "can be the aim of such a philosophy: to know not God but what is called 'man.' This 'man' and 'mankind' are its absolute standpoint, that is, as a fixed, invincible finiteness of reason. . . ."[42]

Despite all the discontinuity in the setting of the themes, is not the continuity also clear at this point between the philosophical Hegel of Jena and the theological Hegel of Tübingen, Berne and Frankfurt? The great difference, of course, is that he is now *determined on a comprehensive system*. By "system," Hegel does not mean anything like a one-sided philosophy of mind. The natural sciences will be incorporated as concretely as possible into the system. In Jena he was occupied—as he had been at an earlier stage—with mineralogy, botany, physiology and medicine; he was also a member of various scientific societies. He had qualified as a university teacher with a dissertation on the planetary orbits—evidence, in fact, not only of his continued lively interest in mathematics and natural science but also of his opposition to the abstract, mechanistic atomism of the purely mathematical conception of nature.[43] Hegel, then, worked out his first projects of a system as generally as possible, in connection with his lectures. These became known as the Jena systems.[44] Not in a rigidly mathematical but in a lively dialectical universal system, *everything individual* was to be understood *as moment of the uniform dialectical evolution of the whole*, of the divine "Absolute Spirit" itself: the Absolute

Spirit which represents a unity of subject and object, being and thought, real and ideal.

Hegel thus attempted to describe—so to speak—"God's course of life": the self-externalizing course of God into secularity (philosophy of nature) and through secularity to the complete achievement of self-awareness by spirit (philosophy of spirit). In this process, the immense richness of the world is taken up into the notion of God and likewise developed out of it, and a new awareness of God and the world is made possible. Undoubtedly a tremendous revaluation for the world and man. But is it also an enrichment for God? At any rate, as Hegel also sees, there is a danger: the *danger of the alienation of the notion of God*. Where are the limits to be drawn?

Both the pantheism and the atheism controversies had pointed very clearly to the dangers. And the humbled Fichte would have been the last not to have understood them. Those limits that Schelling—for example— had clearly marked out in 1800 in his audacious "System of Transcendental Idealism," in order to protect the notion of a living God in a "system of Providence, that is, of religion," had certainly been recognized also by Fichte and by Hegel.

On the right, there is *no* question of *fatalistic pantheism*, according to which "all free actions and consequently also the whole of history" must be assumed to be "purely and simply predetermined": this would mean "a completely blind predetermination" by a "fate."

On the left, there is *no* question of *irreligious atheism*, according to which "in all deeds and actions there is no law and no necessity": this would mean setting up a "system of absolute lawlessness."

What is *affirmed*, however, is the "*Absolute*," which is the common "ground of harmony between freedom and the intelligent agent."[45]

Of course, there were many possible opinions as to how this Absolute should be more closely defined in its relationship to the world and especially to human freedom; and Fichte, Schelling and Hegel soon began to disagree about it.

# II. God in history

Despite all that they still had in common, Fichte, Schelling and Hegel followed very different paths after Jena. Hegel himself thought that the difficulties between atheism and pantheism could best be overcome if the life, the "spiritedness" (*Lebendigkeit*), of God himself was taken seriously. If God—that is—was seen in his life's *course:* in the light not only of the finite, human subject (Kant) or of an absolute subject (Fichte) or of an absolute identity of subject and object (Schelling) but also of the dialectically understood Absolute Spirit. For him, this means that God must be seen as one who goes through a *history* and reveals himself in this history: in becoming who he is.

## 1. Phenomenology of spirit

For a whole week in October 1806, Hegel went around devastated Jena carrying in his coat pocket sheets of paper that were to shape the destiny of Geman philosophy. They contained the last part of the "Phenomenology of Spirit," completed in unusual haste during a restless night by a tormented author not only disturbed by the political events of the time but also pressed by a very impatient publisher. The next day, as usual with lightning speed, Napoleon fought and won the battle before Jena. And Hegel then saw "the Emperor—this world soul . . . riding out through the city to reconnoiter: it is indeed a wonderful sensation to see such an individual, here concentrated at one point, sitting on a horse, surmounting and ruling the world."[1] But Hegel himself had been plundered, and it was only some days later that he was able to send his manuscript to the publisher in Bamberg.

### The absolute in consciousness

The "Phenomenology of Spirit"[2] is perhaps at once Hegel's most brilliant and most obscure book: a pioneer work in which his whole philosophy is already present. It recapitulates with pervasive industry Hegel's previous development and gives to it a rich, concentrated and powerful if not wholly unambiguous expression in a first broad outline: boiling and bubbling, sometimes and especially in the second part overflowing and yet in the last resort held together in disciplined passion. All things considered, a work of youthful exuberance but already bearing many signs of maturity: despite all the changes of internal perspective, all the lack of uniformity in its accomplishment and all the unnecessary linguistic complication, it remains a profound work of consummate thought.

Hegel also is a descendant of Descartes. The path that man's natural understanding has to follow here must be "looked on as the path of *doubt,* or more properly a highway of despair."[3] For the person should be led from the natural standpoint of common sense—which is so often wrong—to the genuinely scientific standpoint: he should rise *from the immediate sense impression through all forms of consciousness to self-knowing spirit.* Consequently this "phenomeno-logy of spirit" must be understood in the light of its definitive form as the "science of the manifestation of spirit" in its diverse forms. Hegel describes patiently, stage by stage, how natural consciousness reaches absolute consciousness or—better—how it becomes aware of absolute knowledge, which it is already itself in secret. This "path of the soul"[4] therefore may not be interpreted psychologically or pedagogically. It must also be understood philosophically and historically. This educational path of individual consciousness—as Hegel himself makes clear in the course of the further development of his thought in a way he had not himself expected—is simultaneously the way of manifestation of Absolute Spirit itself in its diverse forms in world history. The essential background of this phenomenology of spirit is that absolute knowledge and human knowledge from the very outset are not separate but are linked in a still unexplicated unity. And the path of experience followed here involves reciprocity: human consciousness becomes aware of the Absolute, and the Absolute becomes aware of itself in human consciousness.

Is all this pure *speculation?* No—and yes. No: in the sense that—according to Hegel—the philosopher must not devote himself to theoretical structures devoid of reality, must not deduce reality "from above." Yes: in the sense that he must be watching—literally, "speculating"—and then forthrightly describe reality as it is manifested to him in its history, as he experiences it out of the whole abundance of the thoughts of his theoretical and practical, ethical, juridical, religious, philosophical consciousness. For consciousness is known through the world, and at the same time the world is known through consciousness: a necessary history of experience which—wholly in the modern tradition of Descartes, Kant and Fichte—starts out everywhere consistently from the human subject and in the light of this subject experiences the world (nature, society, civilization). Ex-perience of the world from the re-collection of consciousness: a far

reaching, inward going of the spirit, as Martin Heidegger has made clear
from his own standpoint in his article on Hegel's notion of experience.[5]
For Hegel, then, starting out from the individual subject simply does not
mean subjectivist individualism: there is always a reference to the world.

Connected with the reference to the world is the fact that the recol-
lecting, outreaching experience is not exhausted—as it was with Descartes
—in an initial "methodical" doubt but dwells on the doubt, from which
in a vital antithetic movement the continually new dialectical *sublation*
proceeds. What is the meaning of this term *Aufheben,* which has become
so famous as a result of Hegel's use of it and which is scarcely translatable
into other languages? From the triple sense of the term, Hegel draws these
conclusions: the truth regarded as absolute must continually be *discarded;*
but, in being discarded, it must at the same time be *taken up* afresh—as
relative moment—and *raised up* into a higher unity. Hegel scarcely uses
the words "thesis-antithesis-synthesis," so often ascribed to him. But what
is meant anyway is the affirmation of a truth that turns into a denial and
then again into a transcending of both affirmation and denial. In very ordinary terms, it might be expressed: so—and yet not just so—but so! In
this way, rigid conceptual thinking is turned into a living, mental dynamism. Human consciousness thus shares in the dynamism of the divine
Absolute itself, which is not emptiness and solid substance but a subject
and spirit moving vitally through all contradictions.

The "Phenomenology," then, is concerned with the history of the subject, in which the subject is continuously being corrected by the particular
object and the object by the subject: a mental process going on in constantly differing contradictions and negations, at increasingly higher levels,
in increasingly concrete forms of consciousness and finally even world
figures. In this "Phenomenology," therefore, we have first the chapters on
consciousness/self-consciousness/reason, on which follow (although not
originally planned) the chapters oriented to world history on spirit,
religion and absolute knowledge. According to Hegel, reason must necessarily be manifested, must "appear," in time. Phenomenology is now better understood as the history of the manifestation of spirit. In this way, it
becomes clear that it is a question here not merely of a psychological
movement of consciousness but also of a logical, cosmic, sociopolitical,
world-historical, even religious movement—but one that in the last resort
is philosophical. Religion also—as always—has a twofold meaning: self-
revelation of infinite spirit in finite spirit and simultaneously contemplative absorption of finite spirit in infinite spirit. This is how the dialectical process—likewise philosophical in the last resort—of self-knowledge
occurs: human consciousness becoming conscious of itself in the Absolute
and the Absolute in human consciousness. Who would have thought at
that time that criticism later would set in precisely at this point and that
the result would be—with Ludwig Feuerbach—the turning to atheism?

## Dialectic in God himself

In this whole painful-tragic and yet not pan-tragic but ultimately victorious history of the manifestation of spirit, throughout all positions and negations, externalizations and interiorizations, it is a question of a powerful, *all-embracing process of reconciliation*. It is a question of reconciling the opposites emerging in modern times from the standpoint of consciousness, in which, however, the whole of world history is reflected: the subjective line of Descartes and Kant is consistently extended into the area of world history.

And what is the purpose of the all-round reconciliation of phenomenology? It is aimed at reconciliation between stoicism and skepticism, faith and enlightenment, rationalism and romanticism. But also at reconciliation between master and slave, idea and feeling, desire and necessity, between the law of the heart and the law of reality, virtue and the course of the world. Finally, it is also aimed at reconciliation as a whole between exterior and interior, in itself and for itself, object and subject, being and thought, here and hereafter, finite and infinite, all at the end "sublated" in absolute knowledge—that is, in spirit knowing itself as spirit. All this, Hegel works out in many hundreds of pages. It is—as Hegel called it in old age—his "voyage of discovery"[6] through the realm of spirit, which is revealed as the dramatic odyssey of the divine Spirit itself in this world and in its history. With Faustian restlessness and continually newly fulfilled, consciousness has passed through history, outpacing the finite on all sides, in order thus in a variety of adventures and struggles to reach the infinite, by which it has been encompassed from the outset: an arduous journey of the ex-periences of spirit ascending in spirals or triangular movements. It is the history of the divine Spirit itself, described by the philosopher faithfully hour by hour as he heard the clock striking. In this sense, phenomenology is a theological philosophy of history and a philosophical theology of history.

Hegel could maintain that in his work nothing had been lost of what modern times had brought to the deepening of the (Christian) understanding of God. Had he not defined this new reality of God and reality of the world, the new God-being-in-the-world and world-being-in-God, without lapsing into fatalistic pantheism or irreligious atheism? On the contrary, in his phenomenology two things had become simultaneously clear: how God is the world and yet how he is not simply the world, since the world can be so terribly ungodly and nevertheless remain the outward form of God.

Looking back on his phenomenology, however, in the light of its end, how did Hegel reach this position? By way of *development*: the world is not simply God, but it is *God in his development*. This God externalizes

himself to the world in development, in history, *and* leads the world as
nature and finally as spirit through all stages up to himself and to his
infinity and divinity. All this in a mighty, all-encompassing circular movement, like that described long before by the Fathers of the Church and
the medieval scholastics: *exitus a Deo—reditus in Deum,* outgoing from
God—return to God. Or—better—as Hegel expresses it: outgoing of God
and return of God himself.

The difference is significant. The traditional dualistic paradigm has
been overcome here in an up-to-date, modern way: not only the external
dualism between heaven and earth, which natural science had relativized,
but also the internal dualism—as seen by philosophy and theology—between God and man. The Deity encompasses everything but without
removing the distinction. Quite the contrary: the distinction is seen even
in God himself. The life of God really consists in the struggle with his opposite: a conflict of God with himself in the course of which the world
comes to be from God and the reconciliation of the world comes to be in
God. In this way, the dualism is cleared up in God himself. The idea of
an unclouded life of God, always the same, the idea of the one development of God, Hegel regards as merely edifying or even insipid, unless it is
understood as an internal *dialectic of God himself:* "The life of God and
divine intelligence, then, can, if we like, be spoken of as love disporting
with itself, but this idea falls into edification, and even sinks into in-
sipidity, if it lacks the seriousness, the suffering, the patience and the
labour of the negative. *Per se* the divine life is no doubt undisturbed identity and oneness with itself, which finds no serious obstacle in otherness
and estrangement, and none in the surmounting of this estrangement.
But this 'per se' is abstract generality, where we abstract from its real nature, which consists in its being objective to itself, conscious of itself on
its own account (*für sich zu sein*); and where consequently we neglect altogether the self-movement which is the formal character of its activity."[7]
The term "estrangement" or "alienation," which became so important
later for Marx's theory of society, belongs for Hegel wholly and entirely to
a theological context.

The fact that God himself is seen in this dialectical alienation and in
the overcoming of alienation has tremendous consequences for the notion
of God. The notion of God thus includes the *negative as moment in God*
and his development: the seriousness, the pain, the patience and the labor
of the negative. In order to give expression in the very name to this
purification and deepening of the notion of God, Hegel prefers to speak
of God as *spirit.* "Spirit" expresses the fact that God is a God who comes
to be: a self-developing, a dialectical, self-externalizing God, coming to
himself out of alienation.

Development—dialectic—spirit: in the light of this God, all the contrarieties of the world and society can be comprehended in their interconnection and in their necessity. In the light of this God, the tragic,

unhappy disruption of reality on its various levels can be healed and transfigured by the negation of negation. Hegel's consciousness suffered more than any other philosophical consciousness before his time from the unreconciled state of reality and especially of modern human society. And to him in particular it had become clear that all the lower levels of alienation are only the anticipation and the consequence of the supreme level; true reconciliation is possible only if a reconciliation is achieved between finite and infinite, the world and God.

Certainly Hegel's first total philosophical project is in many ways, from both the philosophical and the theological aspects, a problematic enterprise. But his "Phenomenology of Spirit" remains a splendid and often fruitful attempt at a comprehensive reconciliation between philosophy and theology, insight and revelation, enlightenment and dogma, reason and history, research and faith, being human in a modern way and being more profoundly Christian. Hegel could rightly ask if, in the last resort, this was not, all in all, a reconciliation in which Christianity seemed to have excelled—in fact, "sublated"—itself? Many educated Christians, philosophers and theologians at that time were grateful to Hegel for it.

In any case, we do justice to Hegel only if we do not forget that he is arguing substantially in the light of a different, transformed, deepened, modern notion of God. And we can scarcely oppose him simply by invoking the God of the Fathers and of Jesus Christ, if we do not at least take into account how much of the biblical image of God belongs to a particular world picture.

Hegel was determined to take absolutely seriously the Copernican turning point: in the physical world, that of Copernicus himself, in the mental, that of Descartes and later of Kant. He was a modern thinker through and through, who had *finally left behind the image of God belonging to a past age.* He had left behind the old naïve, anthropomorphic image of someone dwelling, in a literal or spatial sense, "above" the world (God in heaven), with whom we are in obvious, continual contact. But he had also left behind the more recent rationalistic, Deistic image of a being existing in an intellectual or metaphysical sense "outside" the world (world-architect, clockmaker God), in an extramundane "beyond," without whom in practice we can get along very well. In that sense, Hegel—like Spinoza, Lessing and Goethe—was actually interested only in God *in* the world and in the world *in* God.

As we saw, according to Hegel such a view had really nothing to do with atheism. Nor—despite his concentration on the one world—had it anything to do with naturalism. Certainly Hegel, like so many poets and thinkers at that time, felt that he had been freed from the former fear of the world and the later horror of the world: Pascal's dread in the face of the empty spaces of the universe. He felt liberated for a new world religiosity, world piety and even world passion. The earlier feeling for nature, which had grown distrustful and in the rationalistic Enlightenment had largely disappeared, seemed to have returned with Romanticism as a new feeling of trust in nature. It was not a question merely of perceiving individual living creatures. Nature was now understood in its totality as something living, united in itself, akin to man, even spiritual. Religious feeling in fact was not reassured until the earthly world had acquired a deeply rooted divine character.

Hegel, however, was definitely concerned with more than nature. He was determined that God himself should be accepted for what he is; that he should not simply be finitized, materialized, rigidified, as in the former images of a supramundane or extramundane God. That is why he describes him as the "Absolute" or as "Absolute Spirit," who is beyond all finite determinations. That is why he understands God not as "supreme being," above, outside, beyond this world, nor as alongside or opposite this world: not, then, in the last resort merely a part of reality as a whole, a finite alongside finite. And that is also why Hegel understands God positively as the all-pervading infinite *in* the finite, as the ultimate reality in the world, in the heart of things, in man himself, in world history. God as the inexhaustible ground of all being. God as the here-hereafter, as transcendence in immanence.

## 2.  *System in history*

Meanwhile Hegel had gone to live in Bamberg (an important publishing center at the beginning of the nineteenth century). Up to then he had tried in vain to get a full professorship in Heidelberg, Erlangen and Berlin. He was in fact appointed as extraordinary professor at Jena in 1805, after asking for Goethe's support in a letter written in 1804, in which he described himself as "the eldest of the non-salaried teachers* of philosophy" in the university. After the battle, however, conditions in Jena and at the university had become really unpleasant. So Hegel was very glad to be able to take over the vacant post of editor of the *Bamberger Zeitung*. But not for long. He was soon longing to be released from the "newspaper-galley,"[8] and he jumped at once at the offer of a post much more in accord with his philosophical bent. In 1808 he became director of the gymnasium in Nuremberg. It was at this time that he wrote, in addition to a propaedeutic for the pupils at the gymnasium—on whom he made considerable demands—a great *Science of Logic*.[9] Starting out from the dialectic of being, nothing and becoming, Hegel deals in three large sections with the logic of being, of essence and of the notion: an order of pure essences or—as Hegel is convinced—God in his eternal being before the creation of the world.

* *Privatdozenten*

It was only in 1816 that he received the long-desired call: to the University of Heidelberg. At forty-six he was now teaching for the first time as full professor, well equipped in every way, able to present his ideas in a comprehensive, precisely formulated system. These two years at Heidelberg, before he was called to Berlin, thus became the years of the "Encyclopaedia of the Philosophical Sciences in Outline. For use with his lectures" (1817).[10]

## The new synthesis

Is there not, however, too much speculative deduction in this system of Hegel? This is a question raised not only by empiricists. Anyone who has followed the development of Hegelian philosophy even a little knows that Hegel's system, as he first substantiated it afresh after the arduous ascent of his phenomenology (from immediate experience to absolute knowledge), on the ridgeway of his logic (by the explication of the pure notion), and then recapitulated in the *Encyclopaedia*, contrary to first impressions, is not at all a facile, *a priori* construction. Certainly it was planned willfully, extremely schematically outlined and very broadly drawn, in fact given an encyclopedic form. But this was possible only because of the immense detailed work of *Hegel the empiricist*—not generally known to the empiricists—which had preceded it: acute observation of natural and mental reality; industrious preoccupation over decades with the empirical sciences; untiring remodeling of categories and terminology; vital reconstruction and new construction of the system as a whole and in detail. "You know that I have been far too busy not only with ancient literature but also with mathematics, recently with analytical geometry, differential calculus, natural history, chemistry, to permit myself to get involved with the humbug of philosophy of nature, to philosophize without knowledge and by sheer fantasy and to take whims even of pure lunacy for ideas. This might count at least negatively as a recommendation": so Hegel, director of the gymnasium in Nuremberg, wrote—with an allusion to Schelling's philosophy of nature—to the famous rationalist theologian H. E. G. Paulus, in Heidelberg.[11]

Only if we know the immense preliminary work of this unwearying searcher—his portrait shows his large, frank eyes—shall we rightly estimate Hegel's importance as the universal systematizer of modern times. In every field of knowledge—stones or plants, Kepler's laws or Newton's theory of light, from electricity to association of ideas, even to police and property—he was a match, if not for any specialist, then certainly for any polymath. But what distinguished him from men like Varro, in antiquity, or Vincent of Beauvais, in the Middle Ages, what put him more on a level with Aristotle and Leibniz, was the depth of his insight, which he

combined with breadth of vision and which made him become not a collector but a thinker and indeed more of a coherent encyclopedic thinker
than Leibniz and more of a theological thinker than Aristotle.

We may well wonder therefore with Karl Barth[12] why Hegel did not
become for Protestant theology what Aquinas had been for Catholic.
Why—after the early idealism of Kant's criticism and the various inspired
or near-inspired ventures and projects (Fichte, S. Maimon, the young
Schelling, Jacobi)—did not Hegel become what Aquinas, after early scholasticism, learning from Christians and non-Christians, Jews and Arabs,
had been for the Middle Ages (and on a lower plane and—compared
with Hegel—less original, Christian Wolff for the Enlightenment): the
*doctor communis*, the "universal teacher," who had sifted the material
stacked up by history within and more especially outside the walls, arranged it conceptually in a new form and worked out scientifically and
creatively the new comprehensive synthesis that had become necessary,
the great new paradigm.

Hegel had a sure sense of what was in the air. And what Aquinas
modestly and silently accomplished, Hegel—as we can see even from his
various inaugural addresses and introductions to his books—declared
programmatically: that a new age had dawned, that the older syntheses
were no longer adequate, that the time had come for a new recapitulation. Was not everything prepared for this? What had to be done was
to open courageously the doors prematurely closed or that had perhaps
never before been opened to fuller truth. All that was necessary was to be
in possession of the new key. Aquinas, the theologian, in his own time
had found that key—passed on by the Muslim Arabs and by Albertus
Magnus—in Aristotle and had thoroughly cleansed this Aristotelianism as
he understood it from surviving pagan elements. Hegel's up-to-date *passe
partout* was the gift of his idealist brethren: the dialectical method.
Firm, supple and thus at the same time irresistible, but not easy to han-
dle, this thinking in creative antitheses seemed to Hegel to be the generous gift of the Spirit to the new age, to open not only one closed door but
all of them. This, the dialectical method, adopted by Fichte and trans-
posed into the Absolute, is—as we saw in examining Hegel's phenomenology—more than a mere intellectual implement. It is life, principle of
life, self-movement, the specific dynamism of the divine Spirit itself. It
contains the *passe partout* within itself. It presses for totality, for a universal system.[13] "Unless it is a system, a philosophy is not a scientific
production."[14] Only in a system—which is in fact organized spirit comprehending itself—is truth liberated—and this becomes much clearer now
than in the first Jena projects or in the "voyage of discovery" of the *Phenomenology*—from contingency and disconnectedness and the development displayed in its strict *necessity*.

Compared with a medieval *Summa*—which was anyway not intended
merely for class work—the *Encyclopaedia* is a relatively small book. All

that was provided by the latter was an "outline," a "textbook," for use in connection with lectures:

In the *first* part, *Logic*,[15] a smaller, corrected edition of the earlier, larger *Logic*, written in Nuremberg, on the same basic plan, of being-essence-notion, again culminating in the "Absolute Idea."[16]

Then, in the *second* part—based on the "externalization" of the Idea in nature—*Philosophy of Nature*:[17] mechanics, physics, organics.

Finally, in the *third* part—based on the return of Spirit from nature to itself—*Philosophy of Spirit*, likewise in three parts:[18] Subjective Spirit (in anthropology, phenomenology or theory of consciousness, and psychology), Objective Spirit (in law, morality of conscience, moral life or social ethics), Absolute Spirit (in art, religion and philosophy).

In this way, Hegel—this genius of dialectical synthesis—created a system containing an amazing abundance of material, far-reaching in scope and with a uniformity worked out to the last detail, on a scale never before offered to Christianity: a *summa universalis* and—for that very reason—supremely a *summa theologica*. Compared to most of the theological productions at that time, this was a work thought out completely in accordance with the spirit of the age. Hegel was not a man with both feet in the Middle Ages or in the Reformation period, as were quite a few contemporary theologians in both the Catholic and the Protestant camps. Nor did he place one foot in earlier and the other in modern times, as did a good number of "intermediary theologians." He had both feet firmly and securely planted in the modern age: he resolutely professed his faith in a *philosophia perennis* that had not ceased to be perennial or to make progress either in the thirteenth or in the seventeenth or in the eighteenth century. Testing everything was Hegel's way, while keeping the good in all things.

Here—as many theologians also felt at the time—was a miracle in the age of an unbelieving philosophy, hostile to revelation. It was a system—as we saw in the interpretation of the Good Friday event—in which Christianity was neither disposed of polemically nor left aside in indifference, but sympathetically grasped and brilliantly accommodated, "sublated" in the very best sense of the word. It was a system—unlike former systems—that did not combine merely antiquity and Christianity but also Renaissance and Reformation, Enlightenment and Romanticism, finally older times and the modern age as a whole. The system reconciled in principle all conceivable opposites in Absolute Spirit and in all this was meant to be nothing other than a cognizant, philosophical religion: Christianity conceiving and knowing itself. Ought not Christendom—then involved in conflict between rationalists and theologians of pure feeling and finally in the mortal struggle against the aggressive modern spirit as such —to have seized with enthusiasm on this liberating Christian system? Certainly much would have had to be corrected in detail (as Hegel was magnanimous enough to admit), but could there not have been a grateful recognition of the fact that what was offered here to Christianity in the tempests of the time, in a way both traditional and modern, was not a straw to clutch at but a well-constructed new instrument of systematic security and strict necessity?

## The new philosophy of history

So Hegel came to occupy Fichte's professorial chair. Heidelberg had become too narrow for him, and in the midst of revolts in the universities by student fraternities, gymnasts and others intoxicated by the idea of freedom, in 1817, the year of the publication of the *Encyclopaedia*, he was invited by Prussia's first *Kultusminister*, Altenstein, to that rising state, devoted alike to military and educational pursuits: to the University of Berlin, founded in 1810 within the framework of Humboldt's educational reforms (other names associated with the post include Schleiermacher, Niebuhr, F. A. Wolf, Savigny, Fichte).

In his inaugural lecture, on October 22, 1818, in Berlin, Hegel declared: "I may be permitted to wish and hope to succeed, on the path on which we are starting, in winning and earning your trust. But in the first place I can demand only one thing, that you bring with you trust in *science, faith in reason, trust and faith in yourselves. Courage for truth, faith in the power of the mind,* is the first condition of *philosophical study;* man should respect himself and *consider himself worthy of the highest.*[19]

His wishes and hopes were soon abundantly fulfilled. At an early stage, he was not only professor but also head of a school, greatly admired and surrounded by many supporters; he had considerable influence in appointments to positions of state and was able to make a number of journeys abroad. At the same time, he had ample opportunity quietly to expand his system on all sides. The foundation had been laid down, the total plan worked out, in the *Encyclopaedia*. Hegel of course could not know that the *Grundlinien der Philosophie des Rechts* ("Outlines of the Philosophy of Right")[20] was to be the last great work that he himself would prepare for publication.

More important for us, however, are the lectures on the philosophy of history, to which the *Philosophy of Right* leads up and to which he devoted the greater part of his energies in Berlin. He proceeds by way of philosophy of world history, philosophy of art, philosophy of religion and finally philosophy of philosophy (history of philosophy). Only a few comments can be made here on these "applications" of the system, which are integral parts of the system itself and—drawn from the transcripts of his students—occupy many volumes in Hegel's collected works.

Hegel's *Philosophy of World-History*[21] is not meant to be just any kind of study of world history, but an explicitly philosophical-speculative reflection on history. "Whoever looks at the world rationally will find that it in turn assumes a rational aspect; the two exist in a reciprocal relationship."[22] Examined in this way, world history shows clearly enough that it is reasonable to assume "*that the world is governed by providence, . . . that the world's events are controlled by divine providence.*"[23] The events of world history are for "the glorification of God," seeing them as ruled by the Spirit we "do honour to God."[24] World history, then, is the realization of the kingdom of God on earth. But what of all the disasters, wars and revolutions? Throughout all these things, the philosopher's contemplative eye sees the unimpeded march of the free, good, but also cunning World Spirit. Forms and figures, nations, even the great world-historical individuals, must disappear: they *must* disappear in order to make a new place. The divine Spirit marches on and yet preserves everything it lets fall in the best possible form in the new place. At every time, the Spirit is present with the whole plenitude of eternity and consequently every time is the complete end of time. Every time has its good side—if it is considered as the *Kairos*, the "favourable moment" of the all-recovering World Spirit. Even the worst disasters have a good sense. Genuine pessimism is elevated and transfigured in the optimism of the Spirit.

For *God himself is in history*. Throughout all wretchedness, all negations, the divine Spirit unfolds all his riches in time. Since God in his passage through history takes all wretchedness on himself, evil, the negative in world history, is from the outset encompassed by good. World history is the "Golgotha of Absolute Spirit," as Hegel said at the end of the *Phenomenology*.[25] He seeks deliberately to surpass in historical terms the abstract "justification of God" produced by Leibniz with his secular piety: "From this point of view, our investigation can be seen as a theodicy, a justification of the ways of God (such as Leibniz attempted in his own metaphysical manner, but using categories which were as yet abstract and indeterminate). It should enable us to comprehend all the ills of the world, including the existence of evil, so that the thinking spirit may be reconciled with the negative aspects of existence; and it is in world-history that we encounter the sum total of concrete evil. (Indeed, there is no department of knowledge in which such a reconciliation is more urgently required than in world-history. . . .)"[26]

In view of all this, what is the *function* of philosophy of history? "Philosophy, therefore, is not a means of consolation. It is more than that, for it transfigures reality with all its apparent injustices and reconciles it with the rational; it shows that it is based upon the Idea itself, and that reason is fulfilled in it."[27] A theodicy—that is—no longer with the unhistorical categories of Leibniz but really in the concrete history of the world, organically throughout the great ages of the world. In a mighty East-West movement of growing freedom, from the oriental world as the age of childhood (China, India, Persia, Asia Minor, Egypt) to the Greek world as the age of youth and to the Roman as adult manhood and thence finally to the Germanic world as the ripe old age of mankind:

dawn—Middle Ages—modern times. All irreversibly eschatologically oriented to the final end of history: the reality of freedom purely and simply. Equipped with seven-league boots, the philosopher follows in great marches along this path, follows this movement of the World Spirit.

Both analytically and synthetically, Hegel thinks of political history—which clearly has priority here—in connection with the history of civilization and of religion. He combines his intuitive-integral view of spirit with a profusion of polyhistorical detailed knowledge and thus presents the history of mankind in its intellectual context: as a single unconscious-conscious, mysterious development toward an increasingly profound awareness, to increasingly great perfection, to true freedom. This world history, however, is by no means an innocuous, harmonious development (a charge made against Hegel by Schopenhauer and others). Hegel was not a naïve believer in progress, and he lived with the experience of an antagonistic society. For him, world history was a sacrificial slaughtering block, a violent dialectical sequence of stages of decline and ascent. At the same time, each stage has its definite, specific principle in the spirit of each and every nation, in which the actions of its tools, of particular individuals and of the great world-historical personalities, are sublated: that is, in the "national spirit" (Volksgeist), which, by ascending, reaching its zenith and descending again, continually reaches its home in the universal World Spirit. But it is the philosopher who is permitted, in this continuous world court of world history, to pronounce the judgments that have been passed on nations and states, their victories and defeats, their rise and decline.[28]

Hegel's philosophy of world history can be regarded as the foundation for the subsequent *historical presentations of art, religion and philosophy*. For it is from the national spirits, in which world history concretely takes place, that civilization proceeds: the world forms of art, religion and philosophy.[29] As perfect will took shape in the absolute state, so then perfect vision in absolute art, perfect sensitivity and feeling in absolute religion, perfect thought in absolute philosophy. These three world forms constitute various spheres of the one historical development of God in the world: a process of becoming conscious on the part of spirit, a process that is grasped in the three sciences of philosophy of art, philosophy of religion and history of philosophy.

## The new philosophy of religion

For Hegel, in all these sciences historical development and systematic presentation coincide. In Hegel's system, they thus form both the continuation of the *Philosophy of World-History* and the working out of the systematization explained in the *Encyclopaedia*. Philosophy of right culminates in philosophy of world history, and both describe systematically and historically *objective spirit* (after the *Encyclopaedia,* Hegel never discussed in detail *subjective spirit* in anthropology, phenomenology or psychology). Philosophy of art, philosophy of religion and history of philosophy are now supposed to represent—always systematically and historically—the three moments of *Absolute Spirit.* A very brief survey will provide an outline of the content of the transcripts of very varied quality by Hegel's colleagues and published in several volumes.

*Philosophy of art*[30] deals
first generally with the idea of the beautiful as such, the beautiful in nature and the beautiful in art, the Ideal;
then with the systematic basic notions in the historical development of the Ideal to the particular forms of the beautiful in art, from the symbolic (oriental) by way of the classical (Greek) to the romantic (Christian) art forms;
finally with the historical development of the hierarchy of the arts from the most external (architecture) by way of sculpture, painting and music to the most internal (poetry).

*Philosophy of religion*[31] deals
first generally with the notion (ground, knowledge and reality) of religion and especially its purely ideal moments: God in his universality as absolute substance, then creation and revelation as absolute difference, finally elevation to God in proofs of God and in cult (faith) as absolute reconciliation;
then with particular, or finite, religion: excluding any paradisial original state, the dialectical-ascending development from the nature religions (Deity as force of nature) by way of the religions of spiritual individuality (from Judaism as the religion of sublimity by way of Hellenism as the religion of necessity and beauty to Romanism as the religion of utility) up to the highest form of religion, assuming all preliminary forms, Christianity;
finally, with the Christian or absolute religion: the absolute, eternal Idea is,
in and for itself, God in his eternity, on the ground of thought, which is the kingdom of the Father (Trinity);
in the separation and creation of the world, in the sphere of externalization and presentation, which is the kingdom of the Son (creation and evil);
in the sublation of separation, in the process of reconciliation, which is the kingdom of the Spirit (death and life of the God-man, Spirit and Church).
    The most profound and ultimate meaning of philosophy of religion is of course that it points not to itself but beyond itself. This is not to say that it does not contain the ultimate and entire truth in itself. But it does not contain the latter in its final and definitive form. It only points to

truth in its final and definitive form: to philosophy, compared to which even religion presents only a provisional form. But concrete philosophy is philosophy in its development from its beginnings to its present culmination. It is this development which Hegel describes for us in his *History of Philosophy*.[32] This "philosophy of philosophy" deals with the history of the rise of problems and systems: after Chinese and Indian philosophy as preliminary stages, the philosophy of the Greeks up to the end of antiquity; then medieval philosophy up to the Reformation and finally modern philosophy, which—after Bacon and Boehme—definitely begins with Descartes: "With him thought began to go into itself. *Cogito ergo sum* are the first words of his system; and these very words express the difference between modern philosophy and all that had gone before."[33]

Countless great names pass under review here, countless ideas are developed, tested—and surpassed—until Hegel makes a clean break with the past. The "result," the "present standpoint":[34] on the mighty peak, with three thousand years of spirit's ascent behind and beneath him, stands Hegel! "To this point the World-spirit has come, and each stage has its own form in the true system of Philosophy; nothing is lost, all principles are preserved."[35] Hegel inherits the whole heritage. And looking back over the millennia of "the strivings of spirit" and its "earnest work," he observes: "So great was the effort made by mind to know itself" (*tantae molis erat, se ipsam cognoscere mentem*).[36]

A proper appreciation of Hegel's grandiose conception of the philosophy of history is not possible here.[37] Do not the philosophy of art, of religion, of the history of philosophy—all interwoven from the outset with each other in a differentiated unity—reveal clearly with all the consequences what we underlined earlier in connection with his system? Mediating in the centuries-old conflict between idea and history, Hegel gave a surprisingly compact, inexhaustibly profound and consciously *Christian view of history*. Hegel's whole thinking aims at being historical thinking, his historical thinking at being religious thinking. His religious thinking, of course, is meant to be understood philosophically and speculatively in the light of the incarnation of God: not as a timeless, static metaphysic of ideas, but as a comprehensive, dynamic Christian philosophy of history. Hegel's onto-theo-logy has been manifested as a mighty historical theodicy (justification of God), which, at the same time along the whole line and in all its strata, is meant to be a comprehensive divine historiodicy (justification of history).

It was at this time that a more than two-thousand-year-old world picture was finally shattered and the older image of God and man was seen as historically transitory. Human history had been stripped of its magic and mystery and become secularized; new economic-sociological conditions, a revolutionary new "civic" society, had been formed. The French Revolution had left scarcely any political, moral or religious institution unshaken; the Enlightenment and the conflict it produced between faith and reason had spread far beyond the educated classes to the ordinary people; not only state and society but also Christianity and churches had suffered an immense loss of integrating power, and anti-Enlightenment, subjective romanticism was scarcely in a position to restore it.

It was at this time that Hegel's achievement made a tremendous impression on many people who wanted in intellectual honesty to be both human and Christian, enlightened and devout, rooted in tradition and progressive. Here a wholly and entirely modern philosopher, rising above criticism and also defense of religion, in a grandiose compact system, had produced a visualization of Christian truth to which even critical modern man could give his assent. An assent that was not merely a naïve belief in authority but one that was philosophically substantiated and thought out to the last detail. Instead of the modern schizophrenia of faith and enlightenment, a differentiated unity of philosophy and theology. Instead of the alternative of rationalism or emotional religion, a reason that united understanding and feeling. Instead of orthodox biblicism or a philosophical natural religion, a systematic effort to produce an up-to-date biblical hermeneutic.

Anyone who reads for himself the texts from Hegel's *Philosophy of Religion* and compares them with earlier passages on the subject will recognize that the author—who was admittedly not an exegete but a systematizer—had taken very much greater pains in interpreting Scripture particularly in this work. He tried here to be more precise about a number of difficult points that had not been clearly expounded in the earlier works and in the main published works: in his teaching on the Trinity, on good and evil in man, on the generation of the Son and the creation of the world, on the uniqueness of Christ (description of his message and fate), finally on the meaning of the Spirit and the Church. His philosophy of religion is certainly anything but orthodox dogmatics, but it is also anything but superficial rationalism. It is a new paradigm, a new paradigm-candidate. But will it be successful?

*Compared with normal theology*—and this may be of interest not only to theologians—this philosophical-theological view of history, reached as a result of unsparing mental effort, presents some striking features:

Hegel's God is not a spirit beyond the stars, working on the world from outside, but the mind permeating all minds, in the depth of human subjectivity.

His teaching on the Trinity is not an unrealistic conceptual arithmetic, but a trinitarian "economy" related to the world, salvation history.

The creation of the world is regarded not as an abstract, arbitrary volition but as rooted in God's nature: not as a kind of emanation (from the perfect to the imperfect, with a paradisial golden age at the beginning), but as evolution (from the imperfect to the perfect, although without evolution of species).

Providence is not attributed to a despotic God, nor is it proved in an abstract, unhistorical fashion, but is observed speculatively in the concrete course of history.

The non-Christian religions are evaluated not as purely negative or neu-tral-irrelevant phenomena but as pre-Christian religions approaching the one true God "from shadows and symbols,"* as pro-visional forms already announcing the perfect.

The Christ event is not minimized in a pietistic spirit as the object of pri-vate devotion or theologically appropriated for the institutional Church, but is shown as a world event of the Spirit in its significance for mankind as a whole.

The negative aspects of reality—sin, suffering and death—are not trivi-alized by a supratemporal, abstract theodicy but depicted by a theology of the death of God in a concrete justification of God and man as overcome painfully and victoriously by God himself in history.

According to Hegel, therefore, the philosophical observer of history will not reject as illusions the contradictions, antagonisms and disasters in the history of the world and of man, but neither will he face them in bewil-derment. He will neither be content to abandon all hope of under-standing the world tragedy nor revolt in unreasonable indignation against the superficial meaninglessness. Instead he will calmly accept history just as it happens, because reason tells him of the ultimate reasonableness of history, which is at present beyond our understanding. Could not such an attitude be a middle way between the superficial reasoning of the Enlight-enment and the pious irrationalism of Romanticism, neither of which does justice to the reason in all unreason? Should faith have anything to fear in all this if it is understood reasonably, understood in the light of the reason of God himself?

The time, however, that lay ahead of Hegel scarcely looked reasonable. With the revolutions in France, Belgium and Poland, and the disturb-ances in Germany in 1830, it seemed as if the tempestuous years of the turn of the century had returned. Hegel had not reckoned with this. "What had never happened to him in forty years occurred now for the first time," writes the philosopher Franz Rosenzweig: "He had to deny re-ality the clear and definite answer of spirit to its unspoken question. The man who—as 'secretary of the world spirit'—had followed with under-standing and approval, step by step, the course of the revolution, the rise and fall of Napoleon, the restoration of the only community of states, averted his gaze from the new 'jolt' produced by history; he heard it, but could not see it, could not interpret it."[38]

But, while the future was taking this unexpected new turn in history, Hegel's end was approaching closer than he or anyone else suspected.

---

* *Ex umbris et imaginibus in veritatem:* Cardinal Newman's chosen epitaph for his grave at Edgbaston. Translator.

Cholera had broken out in Germany in the summer of 1831 but then declined. On November 10, he opened the lectures of the new term on philosophy of right and history of philosophy. Three days later, he was taken ill, and on the following afternoon he passed away painlessly in a gentle sleep. The cause of death, according to the doctors, was "cholera in its most intense form." The last work on his desk, intended for publication, remained a torso: its title was "Proofs of God's Existence." Hegel, then, without having wrestled with death, passed away peacefully at the peak of his life, without having seen the discomforts of age and declining fame, without having suspected the failure of his school. "Nothing about him was outmoded when he died," says his distinguished interpreter Kuno Fischer.[39]

The news of Hegel's death created immense surprise in Berlin. The funeral procession was enormous. As he had wanted, Hegel was buried next to Fichte. Germany had lost its leading philosopher, one of its great philosophers, overnight. An age—Goethe was to die a few months later—was coming to an end.

# III. Secular and historical God

The significance of Hegel's philosophical reflection on history far surpassed what had been described from Voltaire onward as "philosophy of history." After the Enlightenment, after Hamann and Herder, this philosophy in fact reached such a climax in Hegel's work that even the largely anti-Hegelian understanding of history on the part of Marx, Kierkegaard or Dilthey, as also the historiography of the nineteenth century, continued to bear the Hegelian stamp. History, it might be said, is *the* great theme of Hegelian philosophy as a whole. What was slowly prepared in the early writings and essentially came to fruition in Jena; what was developed in the *Phenomenology* in a brilliant survey in the light of consciousness and then laid down quite precisely in the pure thought of the *Logic*; what was presented in the *Encyclopaedia* as a universal system and applied in the *Philosophy of Right* to sociological reality—all this had been made concrete in a unique way in the great lectures on philosophy of history, under the headings of world history, art, religion and history of philosophy; history as realization, as dialectical process, as self-presentation and self-revelation of the Absolute. By installing history in the Absolute and turning the Absolute itself into history, Hegel went far beyond what "philosophy of history" had thitherto meant and stimulated awareness of what was later to be called "historicity" and especially "historicity of truth": these terms—particularly with Hegel—are not *a priori* to be connected with the idea of relativism, of the rejection of all permanence and of a universal insecurity. Nevertheless, questions arise at this point.

## 1. The irremovable difference

"True refutation must engage the force of the opponent and must place itself within the compass of his strength; the task is not advanced if he is attacked outside himself and the case is carried in his absence."[1] This is the advice given by Hegel with reference to Spinozism.

### Identity of finite and infinite?

It has always been a notoriously difficult task to criticize Hegel and nevertheless do him justice. But, in that case, how is a fundamental criticism possible? Whatever objection he raises, the critic thinks he can hear Hegel's answer in the form of a further question: "Did I not say this myself and allow for it?" Certainly Hegel's system leaves much to be desired, and yet it includes so much. This is the fundamental difficulty of any criticism of Hegel: it results directly from the comprehensive reconciliation of all opposites in Hegel's Absolute Spirit. It is better, then, from the outset to charge Hegel with one-sidedness than to accuse him purely and simply of negation in the interpretation of certain aspects of reality.

Nevertheless, among Hegel's critics today—both philosophical and theological, Marxist and Christian—there can be seen a certain *negative agreement against Hegel's speculative identity of finite and infinite*. The identity proclaimed at the time seems to many today to have been a beautiful, idealistic dream. This became obvious at an early stage in view of Kierkegaard's counterdialectic of the irremovable human existence of the individual and particularly and even more in view of the Marxist confrontation with unreconciled sociological reality and with the actual alienation of the working man. The criticism therefore is concerned not only with secondary points but with the heart of the system: Hegel's theory of "Absolute Spirit," which in the light of the dimension of the problem is called in turn Absolute Idea, Absolute Notion, Absolute Self-consciousness, the Self or even God.

The basic question may be raised in the form of the question of the universal and the particular, of the abstract and the concrete, of subject and object, at *each* of the innumerable stages of the Hegelian dialectic of spirit: since each of these stages must be understood as a realization of the concrete-speculative, differentiating-synthesizing process of Absolute Spirit. But the question becomes more acute as the dialectic progresses, and is raised in all its explicitness when the talk is of "absolute religion" and "absolute knowledge." It can be formulated here both in terms of being (ontologically) and in terms of cognition (noetically) as the question of identity (of identity and nonidentity) of finite and infinite spirit, of God and man (or world).

Hegel certainly noted the difference between finite and infinite spirit, between man (or world) and God. But he tried to "sublate" them in the absolute knowledge of Absolute Spirit. On this point, however, the very varied criticism of Hegel is unanimous. And it is significant that Richard Kroner, Hegel's skillful interpreter and defender, should say: "*Philosophy misunderstands itself if it puts its own reflective work of reconciliation above that of religion, if it imagines that it has finally reconciled consciousness by itself: as reflection, what it really understands is the impossibility and even the absurdity of a state of complete reconciliation. Philosophy misunderstands itself if it imagines it has achieved absolute reconciliation simply by thinking of the total self-realization* of spirit as the latter's progressive self-understanding. . . .*"[2]

Ultimately such criticism will always reach the conclusion one way or another that the *sublation of opposites in Absolute Spirit* remains *merely a demand and a claim:* "In the Hegelian system the all-embracing reconciliation is in fact always merely intended, but never attained and accomplished in practice, for we human beings remain finite. Finiteness and infinity, faith and knowledge, God and man, were the determining factors of Hegelian philosophy. The solution could not be maintained, the questions persisted, but it will remain to Hegel's credit that he reopened these questions in great depth."[3]

Meanwhile it might be fruitful to supplement Hegel's *dialectic of cognition* by a *dialectic of love*.[4] Did not the young Hegel himself, as his early writings show, manifest an original mental experience of love: of the love that unites without dominating or being dominated, that allows the other person to count *as* another and indeed wills and approves this? Anyone, therefore, who demands in the light of the young Hegel an extension of the dialectic of cognition by a dialectic of love is not introducing anything alien, any criticism from outside into Hegel's thought. The subject-object realization of spirit as such would then be a corealization; it would not be seen one-sidedly merely under the aspect of cognition. Freed from its internal constriction, it would be consistently explicated in its whole structure. Together with the intellectual-cognitive moment, the existential-volitive moment would be involved, love and freedom would become effective.

In the light of all these reflections, a *post-Hegelian notion of God*, in the best sense of the term, would be desirable—and in two senses:

a. There can be no going back behind Hegel to a naïve-anthropomorphic or even rationalist-deistic image of God, of a supramundane or extramundane God who exists along with and over against this world and man. Against all *biblicistic* appealing to the biblical God and all *traditionalistic* appealing to the traditional Christian God, we must abide by the post-Copernican, modern understanding of God in the *world*, transcendence in *immanence*, the hereafter in the *here and now*.

b. We must go beyond Hegel to God, who is seen in a new way to be a *living* God. The dialectic of love creates new space for God to be God, for God's freedom, God's love, and all that which is one-sidedly appropriated in the constricted dialectic of cognition. Against all *modernistic* appealing to the God of modern philosophers, we must maintain in a new way what was a pre-Copernican concern: *God* in the world, *transcendence* in immanence, the *hereafter* in the here and now.

### Everything reasonable?

Is it not obvious now that the internal difficulties of the Hegelian basic conception become particularly apparent in his philosophy of history? How could Hegel so easily overlook the blood and tears, hunger and misery, crises and disasters, the injustice and mindlessness of world history? At this point anyone begins to ask, "Why?" At this point also a philosophy of history must face the question; here it is put to the test. In detail the range is endless—of *chance, arbitrariness, injustice, unreason.* And in a truly dramatic description, Hegel points with "profound pity" to "a most terrifying picture . . . as we look upon history as an altar on which the happiness of nations, the wisdom of states and the virtue of individuals are slaughtered. . . ."[5]

What does Hegel do about it? He does not want to refer directly to this terrifying empirical reality: he has "rejected the path of reflection as a means of ascending from the spectacle of historical detail to the universal principle behind it."[6] He appeals instead to the *cunning of reason,* the cunning of the rational World Spirit, which maintains and preserves itself: despite and within this whole terrible machinery of unreason. We may wonder whether there lies behind Hegel's historical-philosophical optimism what amounts to a tragic view of life.[7] Finally, however—since he cannot purely and simply deny unreason—there is no other course left open to him than to compromise in practice between the lofty speculative course of World Spirit and inferior empirical, irrational world history.[8]

This vast conception deserves to be spared all-too-trivial objections. Undoubtedly Hegel was dependent on the state of knowledge in his time, but he always strove for historical exactitude and tried to present the true facts in the right context. But the critical *question* remains: How can world history still be regarded as the speculative history of rational World Spirit if in this process of self-perfecting of spirit toward greater freedom so much refuse—of individuals, nations, whole epochs—is left behind?

And even though Hegel, with the "cunning of reason," produced perhaps his most brilliant sleight of hand (parallel, incidentally, to Leibniz's attempt at a solution of the problem of evil), we may wonder if this "cunning of reason" is not in fact the Achilles' heel of Hegel's philosophy of history. Is not Hegel at this very point defending a dualistic, rather than a speculative, conception? The ultimately irrational conception of a self-outwitting of the absolute Subject in so far as it is also Object of its cunning?[9]

This means, however, that even with Hegel's stupendous knowledge of almost all areas of life, even with his brilliant synthesis unparalleled in its extent, his supreme formal technique and well-thought-out detail, he still *could not show the whole historical reality as speculative-rational.* What did he do about it? Warding off the difficulties only with an effort, he surreptitiously turned the original dialectical mind monism of his philosophy of history into a disguised dualism, while at the same time continuing to proclaim the triumph of his original conception and behaving as if nothing had been changed.[10]

What, however, could be carried out more or less without compromise in pure logic became increasingly difficult in the further development of spirit in nature and history. Hegel was faced with a dilemma essentially the same as that which had faced Spinoza. Hegel would really have liked speculatively simply to deny empirical-concrete reality, but—being himself an empiricist and realist—the longer he tried to do so the less he succeeded. Then, in the light of his original conception, he would have had no option but to draw it into the majestic course of the Absolute. But this was something on which Hegel could never wholly make up his mind: it would have meant including chaos in God and turning everything into God. His position is summed up by Iljin: "Hegel's philosophy sways unceasingly between *dualism in a disguised form* and *the attempt to 'expunge' the empirical-concrete* by his own power."[11]

This means that mind monism, from what is at first considered to be an accomplished philosophical fact, becomes the creative task of the slow being and coming-to-be of the divine, which philosophy must unhurriedly follow. The originally rationalistic pan-logism becomes a rational-irrational pan-teleologism. It cannot be proved that everything is logical, reasonable; it is easier to show that everything is teleological, oriented to a goal. This means that not everything is reasonable, but it can become reasonable. The dialectical, organic self-thinking of reason becomes the organic, creative reason of God. God creates even where reason—in nature and history —breaks down and does not think of itself. Panentheism as God's form of being becomes the task of God's creative activity. Logos theodicy becomes telos theodicy. Which means in effect that the maximal Hegelian program is given a minimal execution.

The very next generation after Hegel—and not only Marx but also especially the future historians such as Ranke, Droysen and Burckhardt— was no longer able to see everything working reasonably in world history or the whole of history as the progressive, dialectical self-unfolding of spirit.[12] The facts spoke a language other than that of Hegel's systematization.

## Everything necessary?

The accusation has often been made against Hegel that his thinking is forced to conform to a system. To this he would reply that it is not a question of his, of Hegel's, system (he is said to have told a lady admirer in awe of his genius: "What comes from myself in my books is false"). It is a question of the absolute system, *the system of the Absolute itself*: God as he is in himself, as he externalizes himself and returns to himself, the system of this God in the world. This *enkyklo-paideia*, this "in-circle teaching," in which each part of philosophy is "a circle rounded and complete in itself" and the whole is "a circle of circles,"[13] understood in a properly philosophical sense, represents nothing other than the history of the Absolute itself—with the philosopher thinking about it and with it—a history whose necessity in detail throws light on the freedom of the whole. In this sense, Hegel's system does not exclude freedom but assumes it in its necessity.

And yet the question is thrust upon us: Is the God of this systematization not his own prisoner? Must not this God be forced—if not by someone else, at least by himself—to develop in one way and not in another? Must he not by his very nature function and differentiate himself into finiteness according to an encyclopedic scheme comprehensible to man? Is this God not confined within the necessity of a system of knowledge? In a closed system that is certainly not meant to be a rigid construction but the fullness of vital movement, and yet, as the necessary self-movement of the divine-human Notion, as the applied absolute Method, moves on inexorably in rigid three-part time? A dialectic which does not hold back from any abyss, since it is hurled into each one and—by affirming the negation—lifted out far beyond it? A dialectic that boldly gives way to the antithetical contradiction in order by this very fact—by the negative power of error and malice—to be raised up into the full synthetic truth that overlooks nothing? Is this steady three-part rhythm of the system not highly problematical? Not simply because objections could be raised against the triad as such, not because the triads might be replaced by tetrads or because some pedant could find fault with individual triads. But because this grandiose three-part rhythm also tries systematically to appropriate even God in order to reinterpret that which—in the light of the Bible—is to be understood only from man's sin and God's free grace: to turn this into a dialectical logical consistency and necessity of the divine Notion and of human consciousness, an immanently necessary turning to evil and in turn to the still better good.

It is, then, already clear that *theological criticism* of Hegel's system is bound to sharpen philosophical criticism. In the light of the biblical message, there are a number of aspects that can scarcely be justified:

Father, Son and Holy Spirit understood as personal symbols for the immanent movement of the absolute divine Notion, progressing in triple dialectic; creation made eternally necessary, as a symbol for the dialectical transition of God himself to being otherwise, within the self-movement of spirit;

man's fall into sin (which is involved in the finiteness of consciousness) and consequently the redemption (as a life process that requires no forgiveness) rationalized as immanently logical;

an incarnation of God understood according to the stringent system of Absolute Spirit (identity—nonidentity—identity of identity and nonidentity); proclaiming a more ideal than real elimination of contradictions and liberation of man: an interpretation without a change of reality; a freedom and salvation that leave the ethical aspect predominantly to Objective Spirit (the state) and that exist in a purely intellectual-speculative sense;

acceptance of a Church that in its consciousness dominates and over-
reaches its Head and Lord and that in the end is outmaneuvered by the
secular institution of salvation of the state;

a belief in progress that, in view of the sinful-stationary world and the
profoundly unjust world court of world history, amounts to a justification
of the status quo;

an external revelation that must be regarded as preparatory and provisional and therefore to be discarded in the authentic worship of philosophy.

Certainly the God of Abraham, Isaac and Jacob, the God of Jesus
Christ in particular, the Christian God of grace especially, may not be understood as a God conformed to a system; but *neither* may he be understood *as a God of unsystematic arbitrariness*. In his article on Kant and
the question of a gracious God, H. Blumenberg sharply criticized the
image of God of late-medieval nominalism which "pressed to extremes
the features of absolute sovereignty and despotic arbitrariness"; he criticized also Luther's *mutabilissimus Deus* ("most changeable God") and
Jansenius' God as *ipsissima Libertas* ("freedom itself").[14] Such a God,
who "sends" good or evil as he chooses, can become morally intolerable.
And even in antiquity, philosophers strove in the name of morality to
deprive the gods of power, a tradition that can be traced up to Nietzsche,
Sartre and Camus. The protest—whether that of Ivan in Dostoevsky's
*The Brothers Karamazov*, that of Orestes in Sartre's *Les mouches* or that
of Dr. Rieux in Camus's *La Peste*—against a despotic, unreliable, arbitrary God, is justified.

The critics of Hegel's insistence on conformity to a system therefore
cannot be regarded as defenders of a God of freedom as opposed to a God
of reason. An isolation of the divine will as an authority outside reason
and indifferent toward it, as in nominalistic and often also in Reformation and Jansenistic theology, is of no help; neither is an isolation of divine reason as a very schematic principle of cosmic order, as with many
English, French and German rationalists.

Here too—as we made clear in connection with the *Phenomenology*
but now in a more practical-ethical sense—there can be no going back behind Hegel. The God of the Fathers and of Jesus Christ, the God of grace,
is not God as understood in a naïve, biblicistic way, as an almighty absolute ruler who deals with the world and with man with unrestricted power
wholly according to his whims. Neither is the God of grace the same as
the God understood in a rationalistic-deistic sense as a kind of constitutional monarch who is bound for his part by a constitution based on
natural and moral law and who has now largely withdrawn from the concrete life of the world and man. What is really meant by the God of
grace is that God who himself is living *in* the world, not discoverable and
yet present, immanent and transcendent, here and now but also hereafter,
close yet distant; who precisely as holding, sustaining, encompassing, is al-

ways ahead of us in all life and movement, marching on and falling back; who precisely in what *does not have* to be but actually *is*, who simply in his free grace also according to the Bible is not the irrational, but the reliable, the steadfast, the faithful God.

## 2. God in coming to be

Any critique of Hegel today will certainly recognize that it is impossible simply to adopt his system of mind monism and its ontic-noetic constraints which cover up the difference between God and man. But neither would we want to do what some philosophers and theologians have done: merely to select at random particular marginal Hegelian elements or even to make use of them in the interest of apologetics. What we must do is to try again, as suggested in Hegel's own words at the opening of this section, to "engage the force of the opponent" and—precisely on the question of the understanding of God—place ourselves "within the compass of his strength." "Who knows," asks Karl Barth with reference to a theology that rejects Hegel, "whether it was not in fact the *genuinely* theological element in Hegel which made it (theology) shrink back?"[15] And perhaps in this sense the very last, enigmatic phrase with which Barth closes his penetrating description and criticism of Hegelian philosophy might still come true: Hegel—"a great problem and a great disappointment, but perhaps also a great promise."[16] What might be regarded as a negative foil to Hegel's philosophy may help us in the first place to get a better view of the positive-theological element as it finds expression in recent developments.

### Progress without God? Auguste Comte

World history, then, can be interpreted otherwise than as the history of God in the world: that is, atheistically as the history of humanity. This was done by someone who was a contemporary but did not know Hegel: the French philosopher *Auguste Comte* (1798–1857), the very talented student of the École Polytechnique who had given up his Catholic faith at the age of thirteen. Comte was not the inventor of "positivism" and "sociology," but he was quite probably responsible for the names. With his six-volume *Cours de philosophie positive*,[17] which began to appear in the last year of Hegel's life, he proved to be an important systematizer, attempting, like Hegel, to bring the whole history of humanity into a homogeneous system of thought. All this was a theoretical preparation for a practical reformism that tried to go beyond the traditionalism of the conservatives and the Jacobinism of the progressives, in order "positively" to realize the ideas of the French Revolution.

Like Hegel, Comte also saw everything as developing, and stressed the necessity of order together with progress. He, too, saw development taking place according to strict laws and moving forward in three-part time. He, too, stressed the parallels between the development of humanity and that of the individual. He, too, put the community before the individual, the general before the personal. He, too, assumed—admittedly as only just emerging—a state of rational moral maturity on the part of humanity.

In his belief in progress, wholly oriented to positive science, Comte, however, was thinking not of the absolute but of the relative, in the light of the facts, of the data, of positive reality, compared with which anything metaphysical seemed to him purely fictitious. Here there was no Absolute Spirit developing in the history of the world to increasingly higher forms. Instead it was *humanity*, this great universal being, which was developing in *three stages* to positivity: upon the theological-fictive poetry of myth on the part of a predominantly militarized society, there had followed the abstract metaphysics of the juridically oriented society; and finally the positive science of facts would be established in an industrial society. According to Comte, therefore, the traditional God is not replaced by *Raison* in Robespierre's sense, this *Raison* as *Être suprême* of Year II after the great Revolution, but by the *Grand Être*, mankind wholly in general. Man now stands in the place of God and his Providence: man who sees in order to foresee, foresees in order to plan, and plans in advance in order to take possession of the world (*voir pour prévoir, prévoir pour prévenir, prévenir pour pourvoir*).

Comte, then—especially in his last phase, after a love affair with Clothilde de Vaux—developed in place of belief in God the new *religion de l'humanité*, the main object of which is humanity; the norm, love of one's fellow man; the basis, social order; and the goal, human progress. Comte, herald and prophet of the new, positivist Weltanschauung, regarded himself in the end as the high priest of a new, secular church, of a new *religion without God*, the organization, hierarchy and ceremonial of which were to be reproduced from those of the Catholic Church (Comte had been greatly impressed from the very beginning by the Catholic papal ideologist Joseph de Maistre). This church, of course, was never founded —apart from small positivist associations. This Catholic without Christianity never gained any support, and only a couple of dozen friends came to his funeral.

Comte's historical constructions, with their systematic constraints, just like those of Hegel, were disavowed by the strictly historical research of the subsequent time. Instead of giving an account of the actual course of events, they postulate a logical necessity. Comte's law of three stages—the way for which had been prepared by Turgot and by Comte's teacher Saint-Simon—is today merely of "historical" interest. Neither the positivist philosophy of history of Comte nor the speculative of Hegel was able to establish itself as a new paradigm for historical science.

Nevertheless Comte proved to be a prophet of the new age, since he had worked out more clearly and systematically than others the positivistic foundations of the coming technocratic age: science and technology as the historical forces that necessarily bring about the definitive progress of humanity and a new, better social order. This, however, was not so much a scientifically substantiated theory as a *simple belief in science and technology* (scientism), which in our time is seen to be profoundly shaken. In the age of oil, raw-material, atom and environment crises, only naïve people believe in the necessary progress of humanity through technology. All this puts in question that sociological positivism of Comte, which could not be maintained even in its logical variants, as we saw in connection with the Vienna Circle.[18]

Consequently, in the present century, important thinkers particularly in the fields of mathematics and natural science are working out alternatives to science without religion and progress without God. They want to see God in the very midst of progress and God himself in progress. Despite all the differences, they are closer to Hegel and show the relevance of his ideas for the present time. Of these, we must consider in particular Teilhard de Chardin and Alfred North Whitehead.

## The God of evolution: Pierre Teilhard de Chardin

"First, in spite of certain appearances to the contrary, the 'Weltanschauung' I offer in no way represents a fixed and closed system. There is no question here (for such a thing would be absurd) of a deductive *solution* to the world, in the manner of Hegel, of a definitive framework of truth—it is simply a cluster of axial lines of progression, such as exists and gradually comes to light in every evolutionary system."[19] This is what the French Jesuit *Pierre Teilhard de Chardin* (1881–1955) wrote in his extraordinarily concentrated essay, produced toward the end of his life, *Comment je vois* ("My fundamental vision"): "an authentic and complete summary of my present intellectual attitude to the world and to God— the essence of my faith."[20] This great geologist and paleontologist made the evolution of nature and the cosmos his vast field of operation and tried to bring together in a unity of thought his scientific knowledge and theological ideas.

What is to be made, however, of the "certain appearances" of *a resemblance of his Weltanschauung to that of Hegel*? It may be noted that Teilhard, constantly suspected of heresy, attempts to correct this idea in the very first sentences of his exposition. In fact, Hegel—also an empiricist—does not want simply to "deduce" a "solution" for the world. But neither does Teilhard—also a speculative thinker—establish his "metaphysics" without "deductions." And—as the Protestant theologian S. Daecke has brought out—it is quite possible that Teilhard did not adopt

Hegelian intentions merely "unconsciously."[21] For, with both Hegel and Teilhard, we find 1. the surmounting of dualism (two-world system) and the unity of reality; 2. a secularization of God and deification of the world; 3. evolutionary-historical thinking and God's coming to be: "According to Teilhard also the history of God takes place in world history, in the natural history of the cosmos and in the intellectual history of humanity. Teilhard speaks here of a 'theogenesis' and 'Christogenesis' that is realized in and with the 'cosmogenesis' and the 'noogenesis.' With these ideas, Teilhard is close to Hegel in two ways. Firstly because he thus touches on Hegel's understanding of God as coming to be and world process and—secondly—because for him also there is a close connection between thinking and being."[22]

If we look more closely at Teilhard's "fundamental vision," the *convergences* are even more surprising. With Hegel also, within the cosmic process there is an irreversible progressive movement: something like an "involution" of the universe into increasingly complex forms, which ends in a kind of "superreflection" (Hegel's "absolute knowledge"). With Hegel, too, there is a universal cosmic process of unification: a process of convergence and concentration, of personalization, spiritualization, socialization and totalization. With Hegel, too, God is understood in trinitarian terms as precondition of creation; man as being that knows that it knows; evil as unavoidable byproduct of creation. For Hegel, too, there is "no God (up to a certain point . . .) without creative union. No creation without incarnational immersion. No incarnation without redemptive repayment."[23] Creation, incarnation and consummation as "the three fundamental 'mysteries' of Christianity," which "are seen to be simply the three aspects of one and the same mystery of mysteries, that of pleromization, or unifying reduction of the multiple."[24]

It is, however, at this very point that the *differences* between Teilhard and Hegel become apparent. With Teilhard—as we quickly perceive when we read the three sections in "My fundamental vision"—his "physics" is different, so, too, his "metaphysics" and even more his "mysticism" (piety). The essential difference amounts to this: 1. Teilhard's evolutionary thought does not take the form of an idealist philosophy of history "from above," in the light of the divine Idea, but follows the line of Darwinian evolutionary biology, in the light of matter and life, "from below," an upward and forward movement of the world—toward God; 2. quite unlike Hegel, who saw the consummation as already present in his system, Teilhard is open to a future and a consummation still to come.

In this sense, Teilhard's evolutionary thinking is oriented to cosmogony, to the evolution of the world. For the world appears to this thinker as a gigantic evolutionary process that ripens to its fulfillment, groping forward step by step in the course of billions of years, through the increasing complexity and interiorization of matter. In this view of the world, even man himself is not yet finished. He is a being that comes to be: becoming human, anthropogenesis, is not yet completed. He is drifting toward Christogenesis and Christogenesis finally to its future fullness, its "Pleroma" in the "Omega point," where the individual and collective adventure of man finds its end and fulfillment, where the consummation of the world and the consummation of God converge. This "Pleromization," this coming to fullness, this forward and upward evolution of cosmos and man, culminates in the universal cosmic Christ, who, for Teilhard, is in person the unity of the reality of God and the reality of the world. All this, for Teilhard, is a vision not of pure reason but of perceptive faith, a faith that he professes in the opening sentences of his paper "Comment je crois":

I believe that the universe is an evolution.
I believe that evolution proceeds toward spirit.
I believe that spirit is fully realized in a form of personality.
I believe that the supremely personal is the universal Christ.[25]

Behind Teilhard's whole effort—again, so very different from that of Hegel, the philosopher—is the *pastoral concern* of a theologian who is confronted with the modern, largely scientifically, technologically oriented age. As both scientist and priest—a tension he endured throughout his life —he was aware of his exceptional position at that time. He was convinced that modern science not only does not contradict revelation but leads directly to Christianity: "The originality of my belief lies in its being rooted in two domains of life which are commonly regarded as antagonistic. By upbringing and intellectual training, I belong to the 'children of heaven'; but by temperament, and by my professional studies, I am a 'child of the earth.' Situated thus by life at the heart of two worlds with whose theory, idiom and feelings intimate experience has made me familiar, I have not erected any watertight bulkhead inside myself. On the contrary, I have allowed two apparently conflicting influences full freedom to act upon one another deep within me. And now, at the end of that operation, after thirty years devoted to the pursuit of interior unity, I have the feeling that a synthesis has been effected naturally between the two currents that claim my allegiance. The one has not destroyed, but has reinforced, the other. Today I believe more profoundly than ever in God, and certainly more than ever in the world."[26]

But Teilhard had to admit that "Christianity, in spite of a certain renewal of its grip on backward-looking (or undeveloped) circles in the world, is decidedly and obviously losing its reputation with the most influential and most progressive portion of mankind and ceasing to appeal to it. Not only among the Gentiles or the rank and file of the faithful, but even in the religious orders themselves, Christianity still to some degree provides a *shelter* for the 'modern soul,' but it no longer *clothes* it, nor *satisfies* it, nor *leads* it. Something has gone wrong—and so something, in the area of faith and religion, must be supplied without delay on this planet. The question is, what is it we are looking for?" Teilhard's answer is contained in the very title of the article written shortly before his death "The God of Evolution": "I mean the rise (irresistible and yet still unrecognized) over our horizon of what one might call a God (*the* God) of evolution."[27]

What is the meaning of this term, *"God of Evolution"*? Certainly not —as with Hegel—an identification of God with evolution (world). Theogenesis, God's coming to be, in Teilhard's sense, does not mean a theogony in mythological terms, not an emergence of God, with a God coming to be who does not yet exist. Although God comes to be in the process of evolution, he who comes to be is nevertheless he who is from the beginning. And although God is future, he who will come is already here in the present. In this sense, Teilhard corrects the Hegelian positions.

God is not evolution, but God is *in* evolution—in two senses:

A God *from within*: God should no longer be understood as efficient cause of his creation, as having created the world as it were "from outside." But within the process of evolution as a kind of "formal" cause that coincides with "the centre of convergence of cosmogenesis": which accelerates creation evolutively-dynamically as it were "from within."[28]

A God *ahead*: God should no longer be conceived—as in philosophy and theology from Aristotle's time onward—*a retro*, in the light of the origin of things. But—precisely as "Prime Mover" of the world—*ab ante*, in the light of the goal: as he who is "ahead" of creation and draws it to himself.[29]

For Teilhard, this God of the future is not an abstract God of the philosophers, but the God of Jesus Christ, acknowledged in faith: "An inevitable 'implosive' meeting; and its probable effect will soon be to weld together science and mysticism in a great tide of released evolutive power centred around a Christ at last, two thousand years after Peter's confession, identified by the work of centuries as the ultimate summit (that is, the only possible God) of an evolution definitively recognized as a moment of convergence.

That is what I foresee.

And that is what I am waiting for."[30]

On Teilhard's desk, after his death, a litany was found that had been written two years earlier on both sides of a picture of the radiant heart of Christ—a recollection of an overwhelming experience in prayer of the eighteen-year-old boy shortly before his entry into the order, reminding us also of Pascal:

> *The God of evolution*
> *The Christic, the Trans-Christ*
> *Jesus* $\begin{cases} Heart\ of\ the\ world \\ Essence \\ Motor \end{cases} \begin{cases} \\ of\ evolution^{31} \end{cases}$

Scientists—as we shall see—will not be able to follow Teilhard in some of his bolder scientific hypotheses, and theologians will find some of his often one-sidedly formulated theological views too extreme or—with reference to Jesus' life and crucifixion—unsatisfactory. And today possibly both sides will reject particularly his optimism and belief in progress—apparently the result of inadequate reflection on the problem of evil. Nevertheless Pierre Teilhard de Chardin can never be adequately praised for his achievement of being the *first* to have united theology and science brilliantly in his thought and *provoked both scientists and theologians to become aware of their common problems.* He did not want any superficial "concordism" between Bible and natural sciences and decisively rejected "certain infantile, over-hasty reconciliations, which fail to distinguish between planes and sources of knowledge, and so produce constructions which can only be unstable, because grotesque."[32] But he wanted a deep, inward "coherence," so "as to form a positively constructed whole in which the parts support and complement one another ever more effectively."[33]

Nowhere is this more movingly expressed than in Teilhard's "Hymn to Matter": "Blessed be you, perilous matter, violent sea, untameable passion. Blessed be you, mighty matter, irresistible march of evolution, reality ever new-born. Blessed be you, universal matter, immeasurable time, boundless ether, you who by overflowing and dissolving our narrow standards of measurement reveal to us the dimensions of God. I acclaim you as the divine *milieu*, charged with creative power, as the ocean stirred by the Spirit, as the clay moulded and infused with life by the incarnate Word. You I acclaim as the inexhaustible potentiality for existence and transformation wherein the predestined substance germinates and grows. I acclaim you as the melodious fountain of water whence spring the souls of men and as the limpid crystal whereof is fashioned the new Jerusalem. I bless you, matter, and you I acclaim: not as the pontiffs of science or the moralizing preachers depict you, debased, disfigured—a mass of brute forces and base appetites—but as you reveal yourself to me today, in your totality and true nature. Raise me up then, matter, to those heights, until it becomes possible for me to embrace the universe."[34]

Up to the present time, the ecclesiastical authorities have not thanked Teilhard for his work of conciliation. And even the Second Vatican Council was unable to decide either in his or Galileo's case clearly to make amends to those who had been wrongly condemned, persecuted and calumniated. The suffering of this theological thinker also remains, then, as shocking evidence of the incompetence of the Roman system and of the persistence to a large extent even at the present time of an antimodernist mentality, searching out heretics and persecuting dissidents. It cannot be passed over in silence here.

Teilhard entered the Society of Jesus at the age of eighteen, in 1899. In 1926 his superiors deprived him of his chair at the Institut Catholique and afterward suppressed all his philosophical-scientific writings. Even in 1947 he was forbidden to deal with philosophical themes at all. He became totally isolated: in 1948 he was forbidden to accept an appointment at the Collège de France; in 1951 he was exiled from Europe to the research institute of the Wenner-Gren Foundation, in New York. Even in the year of his death he was forbidden to take part in the International Congress for Palaeontology. Only a few people who happened to be in the vicinity followed the coffin when he was buried (on Easter Sunday) in the cemetery of a Jesuit novitiate (now closed) on the Hudson River, a hundred miles from New York; later visitors had great difficulty in finding the grave.

It is true that Cuénot lists 380 works of one kind or another. But Teilhard had been allowed to publish only strictly academic scientific studies. Throughout his life, he was never granted the sight of even one of his main works in print. On December 6, 1957, a decree of the Holy Office (now Congregation for the Doctrine of Faith[35]) required Teilhard's books to be removed from libraries and forbade their sale in Catholic bookshops and their translation into other languages. But, after his death, ownership of the manuscripts passed as a bequest—with the approval of the order—to his secretary, Jeanne Mortier, and were thus withdrawn from the control of the Roman Inquisition. How much this theologian might have achieved if his obedience to the Church had not been so shamefully exploited! And how much his scientific work might have gained and how many partialities, defects and inconsistencies might have been removed if it had been continually exposed to public criticism during his lifetime!


## God in process: Alfred North Whitehead

After growing up in a strictly Anglican household, *Alfred North Whitehead* (1861–1947) began his career as mathematician and logician at Cambridge, where—as already mentioned—he published with Bertrand Russell (his one-time student) the monumental *Principia Mathematica*; then, in London, he was mainly engaged in working out a philosophy of science. Finally, in the third phase of his life, at the age of sixty-three, as professor of philosophy at Harvard (from 1924 onward), he devised a comprehensive metaphysical system.

As Teilhard links theology, so Whitehead links philosophy closely with modern scientific thought. He, too, sees the whole of nature as a gigantic process in which endless numbers of tiny units ("events" or—as Whitehead says later—"actual occasions") enter into active relations with others and grow together in infinitely many small processes of becoming (to a "concrescence of prehensions"). For him, too, modern man has gained a wholly new awareness of the dynamism of nature: he has a wholly new, serious appreciation of the reality of time (theory of relativity) and of the potentialities of what is new, of the dynamic character of reality as a whole. But, unlike Teilhard, who understood this dynamism of nature as a movement through various phases, as the linear "upward" course of cumulative evolution, Whitehead understood it as life pulsating in all possible forms, not oriented to a goal: a creative forward movement, an endless time without a culminating point.

The *metaphysical system* of this outstanding mathematician, as expounded particularly in his difficult philosophical major work *Process and Reality*, works with forty-five highly original categories (eight Categories of Existence, nine Categoreal Obligations, twenty-seven Categories of Explanation, one Category of the Ultimate). This universal, formal method enables Whitehead to give expression to his early interest in mathematical-logical systems and also to his interest in theories of electromagnetic fields and particularly in the notion of energy flow. Important statements by Plato and Aristotle about ideas, Leibniz's theory of dynamic atoms (monads) and even William James's and John Dewey's experimental-empirical pragmatism, all exercise an influence here. Bergson's theory of the all-embracing *élan vital*, that vital moving force that thrusts forward the development of organisms in an *évolution créatrice*, is involved as much as Hegel's metaphysics and understanding of God—as mediated by the English Hegelian Francis Herbert Bradley (1846–1924).[36] These influences are often overlooked by American "process theologians." Particularly with reference to the relationship between God and the world, Whitehead is essentially concerned with what he himself calls "a transformation of some main doctrines of Absolute Idealism onto a realistic basis."[37] Whitehead has of course been criticized for not accepting any fundamentally different kinds of entities in the world—organic and inorganic, mental and material—but ascribes the same general character to all that is. For this reason, Whitehead was able to use and generalize psychological terms (for example, "feelings") in order to explain biological and even physical processes; in his system, therefore, "feelings" are ascribed even to stones. But is it so obvious that all the various experiences—physiological, psychological, even moral, aesthetic, religious—are visualizations of the same basic principles?

Our interest, however, lies in the *understanding of God*. Whitehead tries to avoid the partialities of traditional "attempts at a solution" of the relationship of God and world, transcendence and immanence. The oriental notion of an impersonal order—that is, the absolute immanence of God—seems to him one-sided. Admittedly, he also regards as one-sided the Semitic notion of God as a personal being—that is, God's absolute transcendence. And finally he considers the pantheistic notion one-sided, with its understanding of the world as a phase of the being of God, which means a lapse into extreme monism. He thinks that Christianity has been right not to accept any of these clear but all-too-simple alternatives. It is important, however, for Whitehead not only to avoid the partialities of the three notions but really to bring them together in a unity of thought, in order to render the notion of God intelligible today in a "metaphysical rationalization."[38]

It cannot, of course, be said that the classical theology of the Fathers of the Church and of the Middle Ages did not also strive to bring together God's transcendence *and* immanence, God *and* world, in a unity of thought. For this theology, too, God is neither simply an impersonal order nor simply the individual person who creates the universe. But theology before Hegel tried to effect a static reconciliation, while Whitehead— after Hegel and on the same lines as Hegel—attempts a dynamic reconciliation. Hence he understands religion as a whole historically and phenomenologically as religion coming to be: as what he called—in the title of his Lowell Lectures, in Boston in 1926—"religion in the making," with reference to the four elements of religion (ritual, emotion, faith, rationalization of faith). In particular, he sees God himself as God in process, but now tries—and this becomes much more clear in his Gifford Lectures, in Edinburgh, *Process and Reality*, 1927–28—not only to assert but to *justify rationally God's coming to be.*

The world is essentially a world in transition. But God is the reality that is the antecedent ground of the whole process, in which the ideal forms of all "entities" enter into the temporal world. Therefore "God, who is the ground antecedent to transition, must include all possibilities of physical value conceptually."[39] *God's nature must therefore be understood as "dipolar."*[40] In the "classical" final chapter of *Process and Reality*, therefore, Whitehead distinguishes between a "primordial" and a "consequent" nature of God.[41]

What is the meaning of this conceptual-ideal *"primordial nature"* of God? At the "beginning," God is "the unlimited conceptual realization of the absolute wealth of potentiality."[42] In this respect, he is not "before" but "with" all creation; in this respect, he is "deficiently actual" and even "devoid of consciousness."[43] This conceptual "primordial nature" of God recalls Plato's world of real ideas, which Augustine placed in the mind of God; but we are reminded even more of Hegel's *Logic*, in which God is seen as being explicated before the creation of the world in purely logical categories.

What is meant by the physical-real *"consequent nature"* of God? At the "end," God is "the realization of the actual world in the unity of his nature."[44] The wealth of conceptual potentialities is realized in the world, but only incompletely, and this has repercussions on God himself. By the creative act, the world of ideas is—so to speak—objectivized in God. In this sense, God is now determined, fully realized and conscious. In a further analysis, this everlasting "consequent nature" of God is delineated by Whitehead in metaphors of tender care by which nothing is lost, of considerate wisdom and infinite patience. God is thus seen as the "poet of the world": he realizes his "vision of truth, beauty and goodness,"[45] patiently leaving an all-encompassing reasonableness to have its effect and thus uniting in harmony the real processes of the temporal world with his infinite original conception of the world.

Like Teilhard, Whitehead decisively rejects the concept of the "unmoved mover," which Christianity and also Islam took over from Aristotle, but he also rejects the understanding of God as a sovereign ruler or as an unmerciful moralist. And although, as a philosopher, he scarcely stresses the Christological factor—in contrast to Teilhard's Christocentrism—even he, under the influence of Christianity, can speak of a God characterized by love, even of God as "a fellow sufferer who understands":[46] something that could not easily be justified philosophically, but only in Christian terms. For Whitehead, the authentic Christian understanding of God does not fit into the scheme of the three main types: "It dwells upon the tender elements in the world, which slowly and in quietness operate by love; and it finds purpose in the present immediacy of a kingdom not of this world. Love neither rules, nor is it unmoved; also it is a little oblivious as to morals."[47] Thus Whitehead's understanding of God—which he regards as the authentic Christian idea—in accordance with his general metaphysics and in contrast to Teilhard, is not oriented to the future, but concentrated on the present: love "does not look to the future; for it finds its own reward in the immediate present."[48]

In his metaphysical reflection, Whitehead thinks of God wholly in Hegelian terms—even though without the claim of absolute knowledge—as dialectical *unity of permanence in flux and flux in permanence.* That is, actuality in permanence as it characterizes God's primordial nature needs to find fulfillment in flowing. On the other hand, actuality in flowing as it characterizes God's consequent nature needs permanence as its fulfillment. Thus the profound unity of God and the world becomes apparent: "The consequent nature of God is the fluent world become 'everlasting' by its objective immortality in God."[49] On the other hand, "the objective immortality of actual occasions requires the primordial permanence of God, whereby the creative advance ever re-establishes itself endowed with initial subjective aim derived from the relevance of God to the evolving world."[50] So God and the world find mutual fulfillment.

Whitehead recapitulates his understanding of God in a number of closing *antitheses:* according to him, their apparent self-contradiction is turned into contrast by the shifts of meaning:
"It is as true to say that God is permanent and the World fluent, as that the World is permanent and God is fluent.
It is as true to say that God is one and the World many, as that the World is one and God many.
It is as true to say that, in comparison with the World, God is actual eminently, as that, in comparison with God, the World is actual eminently.

It is as true to say that the World is immanent in God, as that God is immanent in the World.

It is as true to say that God transcends the World, as that the World transcends God.

It is as true to say that God creates the World, as that the World creates God."[51]

Here obviously *questions arise about Whitehead's system*. Not only that he uses the Old and New Testaments selectively and on the other hand disregards conclusions of classical Christian theology on God, conclusions that cannot be neglected with impunity. But, also and above all, he oversimplifies in his thought the relationship between God and the world, reducing it to complete reciprocity. Is the problem really solved by regarding God and the world as eternally related to one another, as ultimately interchangeable factors, so that in the end it is just as true that God is before the world as that the world is before God? The problem lies precisely in this "just as true."

The suspicion arises here that Whitehead is insisting on conformity to a system as a result of his aversion to the notion of a creator, even though the latter does not imply irrationality, contingency or arbitrariness. This is certainly the reason for Whitehead's assertion of a primordial nature of God without any consciousness, which, however, can scarcely explain the emergence of consciousness in the world. Here, finally, we have the explanation for the neglect of a real consummation of the world in the future, which is what the biblical message—quoted by Whitehead—of the kingdom of God really means.

We may wonder if Whitehead—for all his dissociation from Hegelian speculation—is not claiming to know too much about God's nature. Does he not create a "poet of the world" in his own image and reduce God by psychologizing and aestheticizing him to the human level? Does not his process theory, like Teilhard's evolutionary theory, go too far in minimizing evil, guilt, sin, unreason, in the world? Does not, therefore, his magnanimous and spacious harmonizing of all opposites without looking to an omega point—in this respect quite unlike Teilhard's theory—prove in fact to be all too optimistic, too much directed to the stabilization of a system? And with regard to our problem in this book, we must ask above all if Whitehead's undefended "antitheses" on God and the world, his bold statements on God as "poet of the world" and "fellow sufferer"—however much his thought has stimulated particularly American process philosophy and process theology[52]—are not in fact mere assertions? For all the emphasis on a realistic basis and all claims to "rationality," is there not, in the last resort, too much Hegelian speculation in the sense of "absolute idealism"?

"A royal contempt for argument" is precisely the charge that Karl Popper levels against Whitehead, regarding the latter, with Arnold J. Toynbee, as one "of the most influential irrationalist authorities of our time" but also as "one of the few Neo-Hegelians who know how much they owe to Hegel."[53] As an example of Whitehead's "dogmatic method," he points to that closing chapter of *Process and Reality*, on "God and the World," which we analyzed above, and in particular the recapitulatory antitheses: these Popper regards not as contradictions but as purely dogmatic assertions: "But like all Neo-Hegelians, he adopts the dogmatic method of laying down his philosophy without argument. We can take it or leave it. But we cannot discuss it."[54]

Of course, Popper deals with Whitehead here only on the logical plane, so that the confrontation remains superficial and insubstantial. As a logician, Popper does not raise the question of God, which the mathematician Whitehead took so seriously—a fact that is connected with the limitations of Popper's epistemological method already discussed[55]—and consequently the two are bound to be talking at cross-purposes. Popper is right, however, to insist on arguments with reference to the question of God. For us, this means that we shall have to face the problem of atheism in all its radicalness. Before that, however, we must examine the results of the whole discussion on the new understanding of God, leaving out the special problems arising from the peculiarities of individual thinkers.

## 3. Interim results II: Theses on the secularity and historicity of God

Does God exist? The question is still far from being decided. This much, however, must have become absolutely clear in this chapter: whether the answer is "Yes" or "No," the question at least must be correctly stated. That is, it must be stated for modern man, without Greek, medieval or early-modern assumptions, but in a form that can be understood today, adapted to present-day modes of thinking, in accordance with the stage now reached in the history of ideas.

### Correcting course

Here, too, one thing can be said in advance. It is not only between theology and natural science that we must seek something more than an amicable juxtaposition. In view of the one world and of the one humanity, a new, meaningful, *critical-dialogic collaboration* must be sought also *between theology and both modern philosophy and modern thought as a whole.*

Is not a radical course correction on the part of Church and theology required here? Has not the change from the older paradigm already set in? What has been emerging from the turn of the eighteenth century into the nineteenth must be realized not only verbally and halfheartedly but also practically and consistently toward the end of the twentieth. A *con-*

*sistent, methodical rethinking* is also necessary here: not only with reference to the antiquated world picture but—as we saw—also with reference
to the antiquated image of God that is still linked with this world picture.
And this must not be delayed either in neoscholastic textbook theology or
in Protestant fundamentalism by further fighting retreats or concealment
tactics. Not only in theology as a whole but also in individual sermons and
religious instruction, it ought to be clearly and distinctly stated that modern man need no longer imagine or think of God in the same way as ancient or medieval man.

Is it, then, sufficient, while taking for granted the modern world picture, to appeal with Pascal and many others simply to the God of
Abraham, Isaac and Jacob, the God of Jesus Christ, the biblical God?
This we have already found questionable in the preceding chapter. Or, on
the other hand, while taking for granted the modern world picture, is it
sufficient with Descartes and many others simply to ignore the biblical
God and to allow only for an abstract God of philosophers and scholars,
for a philosophical God? This, too, proved in the preceding chapter to be
scarcely satisfactory.

Hegel—in this sense contrary to both Descartes and Pascal—sought, instead of a cleavage, a *reconciliation* of faith and knowledge, of a philosophical and a biblical God. And in this respect we must agree with him
in principle. But Hegel found this reconciliation by transforming faith
into knowledge, the biblical God into a philosophical Absolute. And in
this respect we could not agree with him either philosophically or theologically. What in fact has become clear, particularly with Teilhard and
Whitehead, is that, no matter how close the unity, there is everywhere an
*irremovable difference between the divine and the human:* in both the
ontic and in the noetic-ethical respect. This means:

In the *ontic* perspective, as opposed to a monistic dialectic of *being*
that takes place wholly within the one Absolute Spirit,
in philosophical terms, the contrast between divine and human nature
must be taken seriously. In theological terms, this contrast would have to
be portrayed as a contradiction between a gracious God and sinful man.
In the biblical understanding, there is no speculative necessity to outmaneuver and render superfluous God's free grace.

In the *noetical-ethical* perspective, as opposed to a monistic dialectic of
*knowledge* that takes place wholly within the one absolute knowledge,
in philosophical terms, the contrast between divine and human knowledge must be taken seriously. In theological terms, this contrast would
have to be portrayed as a contradiction between divine revelation and
human unbelief. In the biblical understanding, there is no absolute knowledge to outmaneuver and render superfluous trusting faith.

And yet, despite all critical demarcation and correction, as far as we are
concerned one thing is decisive. Even though, as against Hegel's
identification of God and man (or world), intended from the beginning

and proclaimed at the end, we must insist on an irremovable difference, we must *never again abandon Hegel's fundamental insights into the relationship between God and man:* insights that were also accepted by Teilhard and Whitehead.

It should not be forgotten that, on the plane of religion—not of philosophy—despite his emphasis on unity, Hegel, too, insists on an ultimate difference. And this difference between God and man is stressed more, rather than less, by the later Hegel. Ernst Bloch rightly observes that "Hegel's emphasis on the object, in the sense of the Father and the supreme Object" (that is, the emphasis on the contrast) increased in later years, and Hegel's last lectures on the proofs of God's existence scarcely underline any longer the transposition of substance into subject, but stress instead God's aseity, a being of God dependent only on itself.[56] And after having to describe the parting of the ways between Hegel and his former friends and kindred spirits Schelling and Fichte, we may round off the picture by pointing out how they finally came together again: despite all the differences, Hegel moved—without admitting it—in the same direction as Fichte and Schelling, away from an initial philosophy of identity to a much more serious acceptance of the irremovable basic limits.[57] One important demarcation therefore must be maintained: instead of an *identification*, a *correlation* (as with Teilhard and Whitehead) must be asserted between God and man, between divine and human reason:

- *There is no equation between God and man. Even though God and man are not to be separated from each other, neither are they to be identified: they are not to be equated, but related. Man and God do not merge into each other; God is never a product of man. Despite all the unity, therefore, the difference between divine nature and human nature is irremovable.*

- *There is no equation between divine and human nature. Even though divine reason and human reason are not to be separated from each other, neither are they identical. They are not to be equated, but related. Human reason and divine reason do not merge into each other; God's thought is never a product of human thought. Despite all the unity, therefore, the difference between divine knowledge and human knowledge is irremovable.*

But precisely if—unlike Hegel—for the sake of God and man, we maintain the irremovability of the divinity of God and the humanity of man and thus do not reduce religion to a philosophy of identity, then we can recognize that Hegel is largely right when he both completes and surmounts the notion of the God of Greek metaphysics and—for genuinely Christian motives—tries to take seriously the unity of God and the world, God's coming to be and dialectic in God, as perhaps no other philosopher before or after him. Neither from Hegel nor from Teilhard or Whitehead can the system as a whole, the "vision" of a whole, be taken over: the objections to all of these are numerous. But, particularly in the light of Hegel, Teilhard and Whitehead, especially today the secularity and historicity of God must be freshly considered.


## Secularity of God

Classical Greek metaphysics as taken over by Christian theology was a first, but for us inadequate, step toward surmounting the naïve-anthropomorphic understanding of God (for example, in Homer): an insistence on the fundamental difference between God and the divine on one side and the world and man on the other.

It was *Plato* who mediated between Heraclitus' philosophy of becoming and Parmenides' philosophy of being by introducing into the history of Western thought that momentous dualistic division of reality that has confronted us so often: the partition between the untrue, bad, disintegrated, sensible world of becoming (in Heraclitus' sense) and the true, one, mental world of being (in Parmenides' sense), in a word, the metaphysical. For the understanding of God, this means a clear division: between the divine world of ideas, with the supreme idea of the Good, and the phenomenal world of the senses, which consists of evil matter.

*Aristotle*, then, succeeded in bringing down from heaven the supramundane divine ideas of Plato and relocating them in the things of this world. But, in this way, the distance to the First Principle of the world becomes even more difficult to bridge. Apart from the divine impulse to set the world in motion, God and the world live from eternity merely in juxtaposition. God thinks only himself; he is thought of thought. This God does not know the world, nor does he love it: there is no causal activity, no Providence, no establishment of a moral order and no system of laws that might be traced back to him. All this because Aristotle thought he owed it to the ab-soluteness, the de-tachedness of his God, which permits no real relation, no actual reference to another. For any genuine relationship to the world would imply a defect (*potentia*) in this pure divine Being (*actus purus*).

*Plotinus*—the third in the triple star of classical Greek philosophy—likewise sees the divine One as separated from the world. The world is not known by this God. It has flowed out from unity: it is efflux, refuse. Matter, the body, is the bad, from which man must free himself.[58]

Christian theology—it is not necessary to substantiate this in detail—corrected Greek dualism in a variety of ways; for the classical theology of the Fathers of the Church and the great patristic age, God is immanent in the world by the very fact of being transcendent to it. Nevertheless, throughout history, Christian theology has remained tied to dualism in many ways: according to this theology also, a real relationship to the world would make God dependent on the world. As we saw, Descartes even sharpened this dualism and prepared the way for the Deism of the Enlightenment, which, again, completely separated God and the world. After others, it was *Hegel* finally—with Fichte and Schelling—who sought a reconciliation. Teilhard and Whitehead were the first to see God and the world in the light of the modern homogeneous scientific world picture without dissolving the difference in their unity. Despite the reservations we have expressed in regard to Hegel's identification of God and world, faith and knowledge, this development brought us to a stage of thought behind which modern theological thinking must not be allowed to fall. At this point, we may briefly recapitulate:

- *God is not a supramundane being, above the clouds, in the physical heaven. The naïve, anthropomorphic idea is obsolete. God is not in any literal or spatial sense a "supreme being" living "above" the world (the "higher world").*
  *For man's being and action, this means that God is not an almighty, absolute ruler exercising unlimited power just as he chooses over world and man.*
- *God is not an extramundane being beyond the stars, in the metaphysical heaven. The rationalistic-deistic idea is obsolete. God is not in any mental or metaphysical sense "outside" the world, existing as an objectivized, materialized Opposite in an extramundane beyond (the "world beyond").*
  *For man's being and action, this means that God is not now—so to speak—a constitutionally reigning monarch who is bound, for his part, by a constitution based on natural and moral law and who has largely retired from the concrete life of the world and man.*
- *God is in this world, and this world is in God. There must be a uniform understanding of reality. God is not only a (supreme) finite—as a part of reality—alongside finite things. He is in fact the infinite in the finite, transcendence in immanence, the absolute in the relative. It is precisely as the absolute that God can enter into a relationship with the world and man: a relationship not in the sense of weakness, of dependence, of relativity in a bad sense, but of strength, of unlimited freedom, of absolute sovereignty. God is therefore the absolute who includes and creates relativity, who, precisely as free, makes possible and actualizes relationship: God as the absolute-relative, here-hereafter, transcendent-immanent, all-embracing and all-permeating most real reality in the heart of things, in man, in the history of mankind, in the world.*
  *The Absolute in the world is therefore at once sustaining the world, maintaining the world and escorting the world: at once depth, center and height of world and man.*
  *That is, a world-immanent world preeminence of God: a modern, secular understanding of God.*

*For man's being and action, this means that God is the close-distant, secular-nonsecular God, who precisely as sustaining, upholding us in all life and movement, failure and falling, is also always present and encompassing us. "God is beyond in the midst of our life," as Bonhoeffer puts it.*[59]

● *"Secularity," then (as a "transcendental" concept transcending the categories), is used of both man and world on the one hand and God on the other, not equivalently (univocally), nor unequivalently (equivocally), but as similar in a still greater dissimilarity (analogously): analogy of secularity.*

This is how the relationship between God and world, God and man, appears today.[60] In the light of this *secularity of God*, the *biblical message* of a God who does not exist in isolation from the world but acts in the midst of the world, can be understood better than in the light of classical Greek or medieval metaphysics.


## Historicity of God

In yet another respect, classical Greek metaphysics as adopted by Christian theology was a first, even though for us, again, an inadequate, step to overcoming the naïve, anthropomorphic understanding of God: as already indicated, it stressed also the fundamental difference between being and becoming.

*Plato*—between Heraclitus and Parmenides—understood the division between the divine world of ideas and the nondivine world of sense essentially as a separation between the changeable reality of this world in time and space and the extratemporal and extraspatial, eternally unchangeable reality above the heavens. Sharply criticizing the capricious and temperamental gods of Homer, he saw the divine primordial principle as absolutely unmoving and unchanging. This primordial principle, he regarded as the unceasingly radiant, intelligible sun, the idea of the Good at the pinnacle of the pyramid of ideas, self-sufficient.

*Aristotle* certainly understood the divine mind as pure actuality. But he made this mind so rigidly unchangeable and so radically exclusive of any movement that it could know only itself and could sustain no action or deed in regard to anything else. Any movement would mean change, and any change would imply a not-yet, an unactualized potentiality, a defect, which would contradict the absolute perfection of the Deity. In the extreme transcendence of perfect divinity as unmoving mover and thinker of itself, the Greek fear of becoming is only too clearly manifested. Becoming is imperfection.

*Plotinus* largely overcame the Platonic rigidity by a system of grades of being flowing out of one another. But, for him, too, the supreme principle of all being, the divine One, remained in absolutely rigid unchangeability, so that even life had to be denied to it.

*Christian theology* corrected the Greek idea of unchangeability up to a point; for the classical theology of the Fathers of the Church and the great patristic age, God is always the living God. This claim, however, is often implicitly contradicted as a result of the way in which this theology remains tied to the Greek idea of unchangeability: here, too, a real change would seem to imply a defect in God. Descartes, with his new theory of motion in the material world, did not produce any solution to the problem of God. After the Enlightenment (and Leibniz's dynamic monadology), philosophers turned first of all to the coming to be of the cosmos (the young Kant), the coming to be of the history of mankind (Lessing), the coming to be of the history of nature and of mankind (Herder). But it was *Hegel* (after Fichte and Schelling) who first made the historical starting point fruitful philosophically for the understanding of God, and in the light of it projected a consistent, comprehensive philosophy of becoming, of life, of development, of history. And it was Teilhard—and Whitehead also up to a point—who first saw in the light of the biological process of evolution the significance for God himself of the development and progress, the coming to be and self-explicating, the ascending and advancing, of the world. Despite all the reservations expressed in regard to Hegel's identification of God and the world process, here, too, a stage of thought was attained in regard to these problems behind which modern theological thinking must not be allowed to fall. Once again, we may briefly recapitulate:

- *God is not the absolutely immovable and unchangeable, who knows only himself and cannot sustain any deed or action in regard to another. He cannot be found in an unchanging, eternal "metaphysical" world set apart from the changing, temporal "physical" world.*
  *There is no nonhistoricity of God: therefore no Greek-metaphysical concept of God.*
  *For man's being and action, this means that God is not an unmoved mover and not an unchanging idea of the good unrelated to man and the world in their historicity.*
- *God is not static being itself, excluding any coming to be and any genuine future: not a God who knows and loves the world while remaining immovable and unchangeable in himself. He is not to be found in a suprahistorical sphere, from which he would intervene miraculously in the history of the world and man.*
  *There is no suprahistoricity of God: therefore no medieval-metaphysical concept of God.*
  *For man's being and action, this means that God is not a suprahistorical person who, by virtue of his creative power, descends on and*

*overpowers historical man and the nations even against the order and laws of the world and nature.*

- *God is the living God, always the selfsame, dynamically actual and continually active in history. Precisely as the eternally perfect, he is free to seize the "possibility" of becoming historical. "Possibility" therefore does not mean unfulfilledness, potentiality, but powerfulness, superabundance, omni-potence. God is thus the eternal, who founds, sustains and completes history, the historical primal reason and primal meaning of the whole reality of world and man.*

  *The eternal God in history is therefore at once basic historicity, powerfulness in history and ultimate historicity: at once origin, center and future, Alpha and Omega of world and man.*

  *That is, a power of God over history immanent to history: a modern, dynamic understanding of God.*

  *For man's being and action, this means that God is the living God who in all his indisposability and freedom knows and loves man, acts, moves and attracts in man's history.*

- *"Historicity," then (as a "transcendental" concept transcending the categories), is used of both man and world on the one hand and God on the other, not equivalently (univocally), nor unequivalently (equivocally), but as similar in a still greater dissimilarity (analogously): analogy of historicity.*

So this is how the relationship between God and world, God and man, appears today.[61] In the light of this *historicity* of God, the *biblical message* of a God who by no means persists unmoving and unchanging in an unhistorical or suprahistorical sphere, but is alive and active in history, can be understood better than in the light of classical Greek or medieval metaphysics.

This may suffice for our second account of interim results. The fact that we have already advanced a very long way in the positive exposition of a modern understanding of God will not have escaped the reader's notice. Nor will it have escaped his notice that, as indicated, we have all the time assumed the existence of God. But does God exist at all? Is his existence really proved or established, or is it merely asserted?

For it must be remembered that in Germany after Hegel the atheism that had been established in France even before Hegel was ready with its further skeptical question and gained its whole force and its classical form by referring to Hegel and even invoking him. The question then runs: This God, about whom philosophers and theologians up to the present time are supposed to be so well informed—does he really exist? Consequently it is time for us—naturally with the newly acquired image of God in the background—to enter into the argument with atheism.

# C. THE CHALLENGE OF ATHEISM

Socrates was condemned to death as *atheos*, as "godless." But he had by no means rejected any kind of God; he had rejected, like many other educated Greeks, only the customary veneration of the gods of the Greek *polis*. Atheism properly so called does not deny merely a plurality of gods or merely a particular way of worshiping God or even simply a personal, "theistic" God. It denies any God and any divine reality, whether understood mythologically, theologically or philosophically. In both antiquity and the Middle Ages, there were very few who upheld atheism in this sense: a total view of reality assuming that it is possible to do without any God at all.

It was only with the radicalized French Enlightenment—in the aftermath of secularization and the Church's compromising of belief in God by its struggle against both modern science and modern democracy—that atheism, as we saw,[1] became more widespread at first among the educated classes. The new defenders of atheism in the nineteenth century felt, however, that they were far above this "common atheism." In fact, it was only with Feuerbach and Marx and later—supported by atheistic natural scientists—with Nietzsche and Freud that atheism became a Weltanschauung, threatening belief in God and Christianity at their roots, penetrating all classes of the population and finally reaching global dimensions beyond the frontiers of Europe. Modern man's self-understanding thus came to be atheistically determined to a considerable degree. Not only the political mass movements of National Socialism in Germany and of Communism in the Soviet Union, in Eastern Europe and China were and are atheistically oriented. Belief in science and technology in Western Europe, North and South America, Australia and Japan also bears the stamp of atheism. At the present time, atheistic ideas of Marxist or non-Marxist origin are finding their way into such hitherto underdeveloped areas as the Near East, Black Africa, Indonesia and even India. Anyone, therefore, who wants to justify belief in God before the world and his own reason must do so in face of this widespread atheism.

# I. God—a projection of man?
# Ludwig Feuerbach

Friedrich Engels, faithful comrade-in-arms of Karl Marx, wrote in 1886 about the abrupt turning to atheism in the Hegelian school: "Then came Feuerbach's *Essence of Christianity*. At a stroke it demolished the contradiction by raising materialism again without more ado to the throne. Nature exists independently of all philosophy; it is the foundation on which we human beings, ourselves products of nature, have grown up; apart from nature and man nothing exists and the higher beings produced by our religious imagination are merely the weird reflections of our own nature. The spell was broken, the 'system' burst open and thrown aside, the contradiction—existing merely in imagination—dissolved. To get any idea of all this, one must have experienced for oneself the liberating effect of the book. Enthusiasm was universal; for the time being we were all Feuerbachians. How enthusiastically Marx welcomed the new view of things and how much—despite all critical reservations—he was influenced by it, we can read in *The Holy Family*. . . . The Hegelian school was dissolved, but Hegelian philosophy had not been critically vanquished. . . . Feuerbach breached the system and simply threw it aside."[2]

Whether Engels is correct in detail in his account, based on his memories over forty years, of the role that Ludwig Feuerbach[3] really played in the Berlin circle of Young Hegelians (Bruno Bauer, Max Stirner, Karl Marx), is a matter for discussion. The claim has been made lately—but it is scarcely justified—that it was not *The Essence of Christianity*, but *Principles of the Philosophy of the Future*, published two years afterward (1843), that turned Marx into a convinced Feuerbachian.[4] We are not concerned, however, with settling these questions of historical detail, although in practice we often have to make up our own mind about them. Neither are we concerned with the philosophy of Feuerbach (and especially the later Feuerbach) in general, although, again, we must keep in mind the new interpretations and the many revaluations of it.[5] Feuerbach, anyway, is the most important representative before Marx of the left-wing criticism of Hegel and is just as important for the interpretation of Hegel as for the study of Marxism. Feuerbach is invoked by such diverse thinkers as Karl Barth for the criticism of anthropocentric Protestant theology,[6] Martin Buber for the understanding of the I-Thou relationship in his dialogic philosophy,[7] and Karl Löwith for his analysis of the individual in the role of fellow man.[8] What interests us here is Feuerbach's critique of religion, his atheism and its substantiation.[9]

## 1. Anthropological atheism

Theology and atheism are close to one another. And if there are atheists who became theologians, there are also theologians (even before the Tiflis seminarist Josif Vissarionovich Dzhugashvili, later to become famous as Stalin) who became atheists. *Ludwig Feuerbach* (1804–72) says of himself and thus describes his whole intellectual development: "God was my first thought, reason my second, man my third and last thought."[10]

## From theologian to atheist

*God* was Feuerbach's *first thought:* the young Feuerbach was a theologian. It was the youthful wish of the quiet model schoolboy, baptized as a Catholic (probably in urgent necessity) but brought up as a good Protestant, son of a well-known jurist, zealously studying Greek, Hebrew and the Bible, even at his secondary school, to become a Protestant pastor: "from the standpoint," however, "of a *rational* religiosity."[11] From 1823 onward, he studied theology in Heidelberg but was not satisfied either by the narrow-minded, idealless Protestant orthodoxy or by the rationalistic, arbitrary interpretation of Scripture on the part of the exegete and church historian H. E. G. Paulus. Finally he attended regularly only the lectures on dogmatics by the speculative systematizer Karl Daub, who had been influenced by Hegel and drew Feuerbach's attention to Hegel as philosopher. Everything was now drawing him to Berlin, where, together with Hegel, famous theologians—the Hegelian systematizer Marheinecke, the church historian Neander and Hegel's theological antipode Schleiermacher—were also teaching. Since two of his likewise highly talented brothers at the University of Erlangen were leading members of a widespread secret student organization (one of them spent a long time in prison), the Prussian police tried at first to prevent him from studying in Berlin. The democratic opposition to the reactionary political system between the fall of Napoleon in 1815 and the French July revolution of 1830 was in fact recruited in Germany mainly from the universities. After the murder of the conservative dramatist August von Kotzebue, in 1819, by the revolutionary theology student K. L. Sand, the Karlsbad decrees were drawn up, at Metternich's instigation. These included supervision of universities, dismissal of revolution-minded teachers, prohibition of student fraternities, preliminary censorship of periodicals and all publications with fewer than twenty printed sheets. In the end, however, Ludwig Feuerbach was admitted.

*Reason* was Ludwig Feuerbach's *second thought*: the theologian became a Hegelian. Oscillating between philosophy and theology and inwardly torn apart, "longing for truth, that is, unity, decisiveness, absoluteness,"[12] Feuerbach came in 1824 to Hegel's lectures. Hegel soon put him right "in head and heart" and "made him see" in a unique way "what a teacher is," his "second father,"[13] although Feuerbach only once had any personal conversation with him, in a wine tavern, and on that occasion was too shy to produce any very coherent statements. But, for him, it was now clear: "I knew what I ought to do and wanted to do: not *theology*, but *philosophy*. Not to babble and rave, but to learn. Not to believe, but to think."[14] And for philosophy, this meant not only individual reason but a universal reason transcending all particular individuals. "On the infinity, unity and community of reason"[15] was the title of the dissertation he submitted for his doctorate in philosophy (at the University of Erlangen, because of the Bavarian university statutes and personal financial reasons). He qualified also at Erlangen and as an unsalaried teacher (*Privatdozent*) gave lectures on Descartes and Spinoza, on logic and metaphysics. Inwardly, however, he began slowly to break away from Hegel, as is already apparent in the letter he sent to Hegel along with his dissertation.[16]

*Man* was Feuerbach's *third and last thought*: the Hegelian becomes an atheist. Feuerbach wants to follow Hegel's path consistently to the very end. The old split between here and hereafter must be removed, not only—as with Hegel—in thought, but in reality, so that humanity can again concentrate wholeheartedly on itself, on its world and on the present time. Instead of immortal life in a hereafter, a new life here and now; instead of immortal souls, capable human beings healthy in mind and body. A year before the death of Hegel—for whom man as spirit, elevated above finiteness and dependence, is immortal—the student of Hegel publishes anonymously his revolutionary *Thoughts on Death and Immortality, with an appendix of theological-satirical epigrams*,[17] against the idea of a personal God and the selfish belief in immortality. The antitheological, rationalist book, with its appendix of cheeky and often silly verses and trivial rhymes, is confiscated and prohibited, the author made the subject of a police inquiry. Feuerbach writes to his sister: "I am in bad odour, they say I am a horrible freethinker, an atheist, and—as if that were not enough—Antichrist in person."[18]

Not hitherto much of a speaker and not particularly successful as a lecturer, after three years of waiting around and three vain applications (vain because of his book on immortality) for an extraordinary professorship in Erlangen, Feuerbach retires definitively from the university in 1836. He maintains that he was born to be a philosopher, not a professor of philosophy; nevertheless he takes the trouble to apply for professorships in Berne, Berlin, Bonn, Jena, Marburg and Freiburg im Breisgau. All in vain. Faced with the very difficult choice of a calling—editor, school-teacher, private tutor, librarian or emigrant (like Heinrich Heine) to Paris, Greece or even America—he is rescued by an attractive woman. Berta Löw, daughter of a porcelain manufacturer, enables the brilliant, good-looking man with the serious, gentle features, from 1837 onward, to lead the contemplative life of a private scholar in the midst of nature, oc-cupying rooms in the tower of her castle near the village of Bruckberg (between Ansbach and Nuremberg). Now, as he writes, he can "step, cleansed from a filthy bachelor existence, into the healthy bathwater of the holy state of matrimony."[19]

Retired, living a simple and disciplined life, Feuerbach could now de-vote himself entirely to philosophy: in order to grasp the problems of the present in the light of the consideration of the past. Following the con-tent and method of Hegel's history of philosophy, in a Spinozistic-pantheistic spirit, on the path to materialism, he catches up again with the history of modern philosophy. At the same time, it becomes increas-ingly clear to him that reason and faith, philosophy and theology, En-lightenment and Christianity, cannot be reconciled, but in fact are deeply opposed to one another. He publishes in rapid succession his *History of Modern Philosophy from Bacon of Verulam to Benedict Spinoza* (1833),[20] then as a continuation the *Description, Development and Cri-tique of Leibnizian Philosophy* (1836)[21] and finally *Pierre Bayle* (1838).[22]

## Conflict about Hegel: religion preserved or dissolved?

Feuerbach came into contact with French atheism through its precursor *Pierre Bayle* (1647–1706), the "unattached, uncommitted skeptic." Al-though not himself an atheist, Bayle—a member of the Reformed Church who had studied Descartes in Geneva—regarded Deism as a halfhearted affair: how could the traditional Christian religion be rejected as unrea-sonable while God's existence was accepted as reasonable? Feuerbach is quite fascinated by the way in which this "hyperbolically caustic critic"[23] analyzes the "conflict of God and world, heaven and earth, of grace and nature, spirit and flesh, reason and faith"[24] and also the contradictions in both Catholicism (between spirit and flesh: celibacy) and Protestantism (between reason and faith), the way in which he simply reserves judg-ment on the question of the existence of God and is even the first Euro-pean to assert the possibility of a society of atheists. For the atheist need not by any means be an immoral person; he may possibly be closer to a god than the superstitious Christian. It is precisely dogmatic superstition which is the devil in the human mind. Thus Bayle, wanting to keep only to the facts, completely relativizes religion to the advantage of morality, which he regards as innate and, as such, capable of being formulated in clear, universally valid propositions. Bayle was dismissed by members of the Reformed Church as professor in Rotterdam, and all his works were placed by the Roman Church on the Index of Prohibited Books.[25] Despite his doubts, he himself remained a faithful Calvinist to the time of his death in Rotterdam. Feuerbach, on the other hand, now strengthens considerably the doubts raised by Bayle, drawing on his own arguments from history and natural science, and passionately rejects both the Christian religion as a necessary element in education and theology as a science.

Yet Feuerbach's *Bayle* was merely the "prelude to a greater work," which he begins at once to prepare, not, however, without first *settling publicly with his teacher Hegel*. Hitherto he had frequently defended Hegel's philosophy against attacks from orthodox Protestantism and the followers of Schelling: by reviews in the "Halle Yearbooks"[26] supported— against the "right-wing" Old Hegelians in Berlin (and their Berlin "yearbooks")—by the Neo- or Young Hegelians under the leadership of Arnold Ruge. A final defense, which was at the same time a parting from Hegel, took the form of a pamphlet by Feuerbach—in connection with the dispute between the diocese of Cologne and the Prussian Government about the Catholic education of children of denominationally mixed marriages —against Heinrich Leo, leader of anti-Catholic Protestant orthodoxy, who had attacked the left-wing "Hegel-lings" as atheists. There Feuerbach defended the incompatibility of philosophy and Christian faith and the replacement of the idea of God by the idea of the human race.[27]

Now, however, in the *Critique of Hegelian Philosophy*,[28] he directly attacks the foundations of the Hegelian system. He objects to the view of Hegelian philosophy as ultimate and supreme and therefore as absolute; but he also objects to making Christianity into an absolute (the human race cannot possibly be fully realized in Christ as a single individual). Against Hegel's idealism and break with sense experience, Feuerbach demands a realistic and—in the widest sense of the term—"materialistic" theory of knowledge: despite the appeal to sense perception, Hegel's philosophy does not start out from sense perception itself, but only from the idea of sense perception. But, in this way, the secondary is made primary, consciousness made absolute as opposed to being, and the dialectical method is subordinated to the system. Instead of reality (nature) being the canon for philosophy, philosophy would become the canon for reality: "Philosophy is the science of reality in its truth and totality; but the embodiment of reality is *nature* (nature in the universal sense of the term). . . . Only a return to nature can bring us salvation."[29]

Almost a hundred years after the Enlightenment in France had been radicalized in atheistic materialism, there appeared also in Germany, in the forties, a *religious and political radicalism* that prepared the way for the revolution of 1848. In Germany, too, religion, Church and theology had been the main supports of an absolutist system, their professions of faith the state religion. This radicalization could be observed particularly *in the Hegelian school,* where the split came at first on religious and philosophical grounds but later took on a political character.

The question came to a head: What had really been Hegel's ultimate intention? In the last resort, how were philosophy and theology related to each other? After Hegel's death, both philosophers and theologians put forward very varied conjectures. Two trends eventually made their appearance in the interpretation of Hegel's speculative Christianity:

*either* as an attempt to justify rationally and to interpret in a profoundly speculative way the truths of Christian faith, in order to make them acceptable, intelligible, apparent and even—in a higher sense—reasonable to modern man: religion, that is, *positively elevated and preserved* in philosophy (so thought the "right-wing" Hegelians, invoking numerous explicit statements of Hegel himself);

*or* as an attempt to present the truths of Christian faith as merely pictorial, imaginative, provisional, inadequate forms of the real, self-conscious, complete, definitive truth, the truth in fact of philosophy, of speculative reason and its absolute knowledge: *religion,* that is, *ultimately negatively canceled and dissolved* in philosophy (so thought the "left-wing" Hegelians, conjecturing Hegel's secret intentions).

If Hegel was understood in the second way, it was possible sooner or later to draw the conclusion that he himself, as a pantheist, had been "at bottom" an atheist: then, quite consistently, by appealing to Hegel, the Christian religion would have to be replaced by philosophy.


## Precursor of atheism in Germany: David Friedrich Strauss

The occasion of the split between right- and left-wing Hegelians had been a theological work: *The Life of Jesus Critically Examined* (Vol. I, 1835), by the Hegelian *David Friedrich Strauss* (1808–74), who had become *répétiteur* at the Tübingen Protestant seminary in the year after Hegel's death but was promptly dismissed when he brought out his second volume, in 1836. Strauss was by no means an atheist, but more a passionate, shrewd introvert and debater than a speculative thinker or constructive systematizer. Influenced by the great Tübingen church historian and exegete Ferdinand Christian Bauer, who had resolutely applied the historical method to the field of New Testament studies, he was the first to formulate in all its sharpness the thesis that still holds the attention of New Testament scholars even today: the thesis of the fundamental difference between the Jesus of history (the "historical individual") and the Christ of (ecclesiastical) faith (the "idea of the God-man").

In the light of Hegelian philosophy, Strauss was convinced that the biblical statements must be seen as mythical ideas, the mythical drapery of an essentially philosophical statement: myths, understood as the narrative, historical-style clothing of primitive Christian ideas, shaped in the casually composed saga, in the consciousness of the Spirit-filled primitive community, to which Hegel himself had ascribed a fundamental importance for Christian faith. Strauss's intention should not be misunderstood. His merciless philological criticism of the biblical texts was quite definitely not meant to destroy the substance of Christian faith but to bring out its authentic, unmythological—that is, philosophical—truth. On the secure foundation of Hegel's speculative Christology (the idea of the God-man), he thought he could carry out undisturbed an unrestricted historical critique: a radical "demythologizing" not only of the beginning and the end but of the whole life of Jesus, of both discourses and miracles. The result was a critical destruction of the story of Jesus from his supernatural conception and birth up to his resurrection and ascension.

This demythologizing, Strauss carries out with the utmost exactitude in his two volumes. He had originally intended to add large second and third parts to his own speculative Christology, but in the end he disposed of it in a mere six pages.[30] It was precisely by starting out from Hegel's *idea of the God-man* that Strauss became skeptical about the possibility of this idea's being fully realized in a single human being. To whom should the features reasonably be ascribed that are lacking in a single individual and that Christian faith unjustifiably attributes to the one God-man, Jesus, if not to *humanity as a whole?* Of whom should this unity of human and divine nature, of which Hegel spoke so emphatically, be predicated otherwise than of humanity itself, of the human race? Strauss, then, agrees with the speculative Christology of the God-man, but only with the shattering correction that he calls the "key to the whole of Christology" and that was to provide also the key for Feuerbach's interpretation of Christianity: "In an individual, a God-man, the properties and functions which the church ascribes to Christ contradict themselves; in the idea of the race, they perfectly agree. Humanity is the union of the two natures— God become man, the infinite manifesting itself in the finite, and the finite spirit remembering its infinitude. . . ."[31]

Through the history of Jesus, it was this universal idea that entered into consciousness—no less and no more. After the death of Jesus, however, there followed the mythologizing by the Christian community: "Just as Plato's God looked to the ideas when he formed the world, so the Church was unconsciously influenced by the idea of humanity in its relationship to divinity, when the person and fate of Jesus provided the occasion for it to outline the picture of Christ."[32] Thus with Strauss already—stimulated by Hegel's idea of the universal divine manhood—Christology (the doctrine of the one God-man, Jesus Christ) is turned into anthropology (the doctrine of the divinity of humanity). Even in Strauss, then, the tendency is apparent that will come to fruition with Feuerbach and still more so with Marx: to put the human species, humanity, human society, in the place of God.

Is it surprising that Strauss provided an occasion for the discernment of spirits in Germany? His *Life of Jesus* provoked forty-one pamphlets by named authors and nineteen anonymous, as well as an incalculable number of articles in periodicals.[33] Strauss was accused not only of destroying Christian faith but also—and wrongly—of atheism. With his first work, like Feuerbach, he, too, ruined for his whole lifetime any chances of an academic career. But it was Feuerbach who interpreted in an openly atheistic sense the idea of the human species as replacing the God-man.

The Prussian state reacted to religious and political radicalism by more severe censorship and by appointing conservative professors in Berlin. In particular, ten years after Hegel's death, Friedrich Wilhelm von Schelling, his old Tübingen friend and later determined enemy, was appointed in 1841 to the chair of philosophy at Berlin and held it until 1846. In the fight against religion and—after the hope of liberalization under the new Prussian King, Friedrich Wilhelm IV, had proved deceptive—then quite openly also against the reactionary state, the left-wing Hegelians found that they were forced to have recourse to the arguments of French materialism and atheism and thus to reject with increasing explicitness Hegel's idealist system.

Thus *Feuerbach* found himself involved in a *double confrontation:*
against *Christian theology* (for him, mythology), which sacrifices philosophy to religion and swallows any old wives' tale as if it were fact;
against *Hegelian philosophy*, or speculation, which sacrifices religion to philosophy and tries to deduce the articles of Christian faith as necessary logical-metaphysical truth.
Speculative philosophy allows religion to say only what it has thought out itself and said far better. But Christian theology allows religion to speak in place of reason.

In the year of Schelling's appointment to Berlin, 1841, that "great work" was published that made even Strauss appear to be compromising between philosophy and religion and that was enthusiastically welcomed in the circle of the radical Berlin Young Hegelians as the consistent completion and surpassing of the Hegelian philosophy of religion. This was *The Essence of Christianity*, to which Ludwig Feuerbach, contrary to his original intentions, signed his full name.[34] Feuerbach's self-confidence increased considerably as a result of this success: he now felt that he was "the ultimate philosopher pushed to the absolute limit of philosophizing."[35]

So now, in Germany, as with the radicals of the French Revolution (the *Montagnards*="mountain party"), the *Montagne* is proclaimed and the "banner of atheism and mortality hoisted," as the leading Young Hegelian, Arnold Ruge, already mentioned, describes the new situation:

"God, religion and immortality are deposed and the philosophical republic, men, proclaimed as gods. . . . So we have 1. Old doctrinaires, 2. Straussians, 3. atheists or those who call Strauss a 'goddam parson.' "[36] Bruno Bauer, Ludwig Feuerbach and Karl Marx now plan to publish an "Archive of Atheism," and Marx will see to the French edition of *The Essence of Christianity*. The Young Hegelian school also is now split. This, then, is the dramatically changed situation—only ten years after Hegel's death.

## God as reflection of man

With Feuerbach, the tremendous danger to belief in God and Christianity presented by Hegel's identification of finite and infinite consciousness, of man and God, becomes apparent. We need only change our standpoint and everything appears to be reversed. For then finite consciousness is not "elevated" into infinite, human spirit into Absolute Spirit, but—on the contrary—infinite consciousness is dissolved into finite, Absolute Spirit into human spirit. And this is just what Feuerbach does. He does not want "drunken" speculation, he wants "sober" philosophy. So he abandons the "absolute standpoint" and with it the "absurdity of the absolute." In this way, human consciousness is turned away from the (divine) infinite into the human consciousness of the infinity of (its own, human) consciousness: "Consciousness of God is self-consciousness, knowledge of God is self-knowledge."[37] Idealist pantheism (panentheism) is overturned into "materialistic" atheism.

In a most impressive way, in passionate, not ironic, language, Feuerbach now applies this insight critically to Christian theology as a whole. What is the mystery of theology? "*Anthropology* [is] *the mystery of theology*."[38] Here "anthropology" is understood as a term of combat: an appeal to go forward into a more real reality than that with which Christian theology and idealist speculation think they have to be occupied. This is "the task of the modern age": "the realization and humanization of God—the transformation and dissolving of theology into anthropology."[39] Feuerbach therefore wants to establish a consistent anthropological philosophy.

Quite unlike Hegel in his idealist style, the post-Hegelian philosopher has to start out—and not only in thought—not with the hypostatized consciousness, with the idea, but with the concrete, solid, sensible reality that cannot be reduced to "spirit." Not like the idealist, with the suprasensible, but like the realist, with the empirical: with the "materials," with the "senses."[40] We must "*open* the *eyes*" of religion—and also of speculative philosophy and theology—"or rather turn its gaze from the *internal towards the external*."[41]

It becomes increasingly clear to Feuerbach that reality means primarily the sensible and that even the mind—as universal unity of the senses—

must be reduced to sense. Seen in this way, for all his ethical idealism Feuerbach theoretically defends with increasing clarity an admittedly differentiated sensualistic "materialism," which, however, is very different from the mechanistic materialism of a La Mettrie or Holbach: an unmechanistic, anthropological materialism that explains world and man purely from themselves and by themselves.[42]

It is not God, but man, who is now the starting point of all philosophizing: "The first object of man is man."[43] Its concern is "no abstract, merely conceptual being, but a *real* being, the true *Ens realissimum*—man."[44] Man, for Feuerbach, however, is simply not—as understood repeatedly from Descartes onward—rational man, uprooted from nature, abstracted from his sense life. He is the true, real, whole, concrete, sensual, physical human being. Like Pascal and Rousseau, Feuerbach stresses—in addition to reason—will and heart, feeling and love. At the same time, however, he sees man not only as an isolated individual but in community: in the unity of man with man; the "I" needs to be complemented by the "Thou." Finally he evaluates man with reference not only to the "Thou" but to the totality of human beings, to the human species as such: that is, to the nature not only of this human being or that but to the universal, specific nature of man. For the other human being always represents the "universal human being," the whole human species, which alone is perfect man and the criterion of man and truth. So, then, the "universal man," the human species, is the supreme being and the measure of all things. Is this not a humanism *par excellence*? Anthropological philosophy means a philosophy of man for man: man as the supreme being of man.

And *God?* What follows, from all this, for the notion of God? The essential presupposition is that "the consciousness of the infinite is nothing else than the consciousness of the *infinity of the consciousness.*" That is: "In the consciousness of the infinite, the conscious subject has for his *object the infinity of his own nature.*"[45] This, then, is how the notion of God emerges, and it seems entirely understandable. Man sets up his human nature out of himself, he sees it as something existing outside himself and separated from himself; he projects it, then, as an autonomous figure—so to speak—in heaven, calls it God and worships it. In a word, the notion of God is nothing but a *projection of man:* "The *absolute* to man is *his own nature.* The power of the *object* over him is therefore the power of *his own nature.*"[46]

The knowledge of God, then, is a gigantic floodlight. God appears as a projected, hypostatized reflection of man, behind which nothing exists in reality. The divine is the universally human projected into the hereafter. What are the attributes of the divine nature: love, wisdom, justice . . . ? In reality, these are the attributes of man, of the human species. *Homo homini Deus est,* man is God for man: here lies the whole mystery of religion.

This becomes particularly clear with the personal ("theistic") God of Christianity, independent and existing outside man. This God is nothing other than the specific notion of man, given independent existence, the personified nature of man. Man "contemplates his nature as external to himself"; God is the manifest interior of man, his expressed, "relinquished self."[47] The attributes of God are really the attributes of the objectified nature of man. It is not, as in the Bible, that God created man in his own image. But, on the contrary, man created God in his own image. God as a ghostly Opposite, existing outside man, simulated by man himself. Man a great projector, God the great projection. Just test it . . . and it disappears.

God is intellectual being, spirit. In this very way, God appears as a pure *projection of human understanding*:[48] God is nothing but the objectified universal nature of human intelligence. Not God but human intelligence actually proves to be the criterion of all reality: as true autonomy, independence, unity, infinity and necessity (Hegel's "Absolute Spirit" is human reason set free from the limitations of individuality and corporality). Of course, God as purely intellectual being would satisfy only man's intellect. But religion has more to say about God.

God is morally perfect being. In this very way, too, God clearly appears as a *projection of the human will*:[49] God is nothing but the personified law of human morality, man's moral nature made absolute. Not God but man's own conscience is judge of his innermost thoughts and sentiments. Anyway, even an absolutely perfect being, with his legal demands, would leave man cold and empty in the torment of his consciousness of sin and his sense of futility, would seem to him heartless. But religion says still more about God.

God is love. And again, in this very way, God appears indisputably as a *projection of the human heart*:[50] God is nothing but the objectified universal nature of human love, he is not only a moral but a truly human being. God is not love, but love is God. Human love—and indeed sensual love, which has flesh and blood, which idealizes matter and materializes spirit—is supreme, absolute power and truth.

This, then, is the key with which the mystery of God is opened up once and for all: God—in every respect the mighty reflection of man projected to heaven, to which there is no corresponding being apart from that of man projecting himself. In chapter after chapter, excitedly and yet wearily but in fact very persistently, Feuerbach hammers his new creed into the reader and thus applies his basic insight to the Christian dogmas as a whole, the explanation of which we can now almost work out for ourselves:

What is the mystery of the Incarnation, of *God's becoming man*? The incarnate God is only the manifestation of man become God. The mystery of God's love for man is nothing but the mystery of man's love for himself. It is at this very point that God is more than a God of pure intellect and law. The Incarnation is the manifestation of the humanly tender heart.

What is the mystery of the Passion, of the *suffering* God? It is the mystery of human compassion. Man's suffering for others, compassion as such, is divine.

What is the mystery of the *Trinity?* It is the mystery of social life: in the divine Trinity is mirrored the community of I, Thou and unity in spirit.

What is the mystery of the Logos, of the *divine* Word? It is nothing but the mystery of the divinity of the redeeming, reconciling, gladdening, liberating human word.

What is the mystery of the *resurrection of Christ?* It is nothing but man's satisfied longing for immediate certainty of his personal immortality.

And so on. By making God personal, man celebrates the independence, absoluteness, immortality of his own personality. In prayer, man worships his own heart and venerates the omnipotence of feeling. Baptism and Eucharist are a solemn recognition of the divine healing power of nature, of the objects of sensual pleasure. Faith in divine providence is a manifestation of faith in man's own worth, the faith of man in himself. My own interest is declared as God's interest; my own will as God's will; my own ultimate purpose as God's purpose. . . .

## The secret of religion: atheism

Has not Feuerbach in his interpretation of religion gone far beyond that of the Enlightenment? Religion is not to be explained superficially— as it was then—as priestly fraud, a great illusion. Religion must be understood at a deeper level: man himself is the beginning, center and end of religion; religion is man's self-worship. Consequently religion is an odd mixture of truth and falsehood. For "religion, at least the Christian, is the *relation of man to himself,* or more correctly to his own nature." Therein lies its truth. But unfortunately religion is also man's "relation to it (his nature), viewed *as a nature apart from his own.*"[51] Therein lies its untruth. Or, in other words, the truth of religion consists in the equation of divine and human predicates; its untruth, in the attempt to distinguish these.

And what are the consequences of this untruth? The continually increasing and intensified *alienation and impoverishment of man.* Religion is clearly seen as self-emptying and self-estrangement, not of God—as Hegel thought—but of the individual human being himself. The more man becomes religious, the more he divests himself of his humanity. Man endows God with the treasures of his inner life: the poor man has a rich God. But because God and man are seen as two instead of one, the result of religion is the torn, disrupted, self-estranged, inwardly impoverished human being.

What, then, is necessary? What else but that God and man should again become one? What else but to cancel and reverse the continual self-estrangement and impoverishment of man? That is: "The reduction of the extrahuman, supernatural, and antirational nature of God to the natural, immanent, inborn nature of man."[52] For from the outset the course of the development of religion has been for man increasingly to deny more to God and to award more to himself; at the beginning he ascribed each and every thing to God; in the course of history, less and less. This process must be brought to its end, so that man's alienated wealth may be returned to him in full and the partition between God and man completely canceled. It must therefore be accepted in principle that what is made a predicate in religion (intelligence, morality, love, suffering) must again become the subject. And on the other hand, what is now the subject in religion (that is, God) must become the new predicate. No longer, then, should we say, "God is intelligence, morality, love, suffering," but, on the contrary, "Intelligence, morality, love, suffering are divine."

*Atheism* therefore is "the secret of religion."[53] But the fact cannot be overlooked that the denial here is for the sake of an affirmation. This atheism is anything but mere negation; it is in fact an absolutely positive assertion. This atheism is *true humanism*. God (the pseudo nature of religion) is not simply to be denied, but the real nature of man (the true nature of religion) is to be affirmed, extolled, loved. Indeed, it is through atheism that the true divine dignity that theism has taken away from man is to be restored to him: instead of "atheism," it would be better to speak of "*anthropotheism.*" It thus becomes clear that "quite simple, natural truths lie behind the supernatural mysteries of religion."[54] "They are not foreign, but native mysteries, the mysteries of human nature."[55] All that is needed is a faithful, correct translation of the Christian religion from oriental imagery and metaphor into proper German, merely historical-philosophical analysis, and the riddle of the Christian religion is solved. Religious reality is reduced to human. The basis of religion is seen to lie in interpersonal human relationships and contacts. Man's nature is deduced not from the divine hereafter but from the real here and now.

Thus, in a new age, philosophy (as anthropology) becomes the new, true, atheistic "religion." Why wander so far afield when the good is so near? To be quite practical, this is what we really need: love of man finally instead of love of God, man's faith in himself instead of belief in God, complete involvement in this world instead of concern for the next.

In this sense, then, Feuerbach was producing as early as 1843 a destructive, revolutionary "political theology," regarding the antireligious struggle as a political necessity: "For the rest, I stick to my position. For Germany —at least for the time being—theology is the only practical and effective vehicle for politics."[56] Later, in his *Lectures on the Nature of Religion*, he formulated his task very clearly in this way: "The purpose of my writings, as also of my lectures, is to turn men from theologians into anthropologists, from theophiles into philanthropists, from candidates for the here-after into students of the here and now, from religious and political lackeys of the heavenly and earthly monarchy and aristocracy into free, self-confident citizens of the world."[57]


## 2. Critique of Feuerbach

Feuerbach had "now taken Strauss's place as the scarecrow of Christians," as Ruge wrote to him in 1842.[58] But does not his conception seem amazingly obvious and convincing? There can scarcely be a reader of Feuerbach who has not at least stopped short and said something like "Surely, that's true; his opening seems thoroughly plausible; his key fits." In this light, the enthusiasm of the young Engels becomes so much more explicable. Coming from Protestant orthodoxy and pietism, under the influence of Strauss's *Life of Jesus* and of Schleiermacher during his stay in Berlin, he had turned to pantheism and joined the Young Hegelians, and now, after reading the *Essence of Christianity*, he had his atheistic "revelatory experience." Even today—it is scarcely necessary to stress the fact—Feuerbach is anything but passé. From that time onward there has been no form of atheism that did not draw on Feuerbach's arguments. Even today, then, we must ask seriously if Feuerbach's critique of religion is not really justified.


## Background of anthropological criticism of religion

Feuerbach's critique of religion must be seen within the whole context of his work. It must neither be overestimated nor underestimated.

It should not be *overestimated*. Feuerbach's work may not be reduced simply to criticism of religion, as it is to a large extent in both Marxist and non-Marxist literature. The later Feuerbach in particular is more than a critic of religion and more than a philosopher of religion. His anthropological (sensualistic but not mechanistic) materialism and his by no means naïve, realistic epistemological involvement in sensuousness have recently been stressed by neo-Marxism, under the programmatic title of "emancipatory sensuousness," more or less as an autonomous and fruitful starting point. The aim is to submit to criticism, from within, from its own sources, the increasingly dogmatically fossilized and technocratically constricted Marxism and to develop it in such a way as to establish a new theoretical-practical relationship to subjectivity, humanity, nature, world.[59] The attempt, however, has met with more rejection than agreement in both Marxist and non-Marxist circles.[60] We shall have to return to this question when we come to deal with Marx.

It should not be *underestimated*. Feuerbach's critique of religion, of course, must not be dialectically played down, nor may his harsh, determined atheism be evaded, as happens on the part of a Marxist-revolutionary (or even, today, an ecclesiastical-conformist) "political theology," which, however, is less a theology than a "critical theory of history" at the service of the proletarian class struggle.[61] Appealing to Feuerbach's *Sinnlichkeit* (primarily understood as *sensualité* instead of *sensibilité*) and to Wilhelm Reich's demand for sexual liberation as a precondition for social revolution, this type of "political theology" is presented as a new solution. Between "theology" and Feuerbach's "antitheology," we have a "countertheology," describing itself as "destructive," that has "to formulate the definite criticism of 'religious ideology' and remove the physical and mental fears on the part of the individual of freedom and happiness"[62]—a countertheological *discours post-Feuerbachien de la foi chrétienne*, which, however, despite its justified concerns (mental and social liberation), does not seem either to Marxists or to non-Marxists to be sufficiently challenging or to take seriously enough especially Feuerbach and his atheism.[63]

This atheism in particular, which is of central importance for Feuerbach, must not be played down, but seriously discussed. And the decisive question, which has often been passed over even in recent discussion of Feuerbach—because of embarrassment?—is whether Feuerbach's atheism has really been convincingly substantiated. A number of arguments must be examined.

### Infinity of human consciousness?

Feuerbach justified his atheism *phenomenologically*, in the light of consciousness: "Religion is consciousness of the infinite; thus it is and can be nothing else than the consciousness which man has of *his own*—not finite and limited, but *infinite* nature."[64]

And in fact does not consciousness of an infinite imply a kind of infinity, that is, an orientation (intentionality) toward the infinite? Can we not and must we not speak of an *intentional infinity* of the human consciousness? On the basis of this orientation of our human consciousness, knowledge, aspiration (described as a "natural desire" by scholastic theologians) to the infinite, some theologians (with the help of a "transcendental deduction") have tried to establish the existence of a divine Infinite, independent of our consciousness, knowledge, aspiration. In the light of Feuerbach's critique, this seems scarcely convincing. For why should it not be possible for our consciousness, knowledge, aspiration to be oriented to nothing, to a sham and not to a real infinite? Certainly the intentional infinity of our consciousness is still *no proof* of the existence of an infinite reality independent of our consciousness.

There is a further question that cannot be suppressed. Is this intentional infinity of consciousness perhaps an argument *against* the existence of such an infinite reality? That is, does it not imply something about the nonexistence of an infinite independent of our consciousness? Feuerbach, for his part, continually asserted this, but never proved it. The question must in fact remain open. The only conclusion that logically follows from Feuerbach's argument is that the orientation of human consciousness toward an infinite does not provide any evidence of the existence or nonexistence of an infinite reality independent of consciousness.

Is it possible, however, perhaps to ascribe to man not only an intentional but a *real infinity*? Even Feuerbach did not directly assert a real infinity of the human individual. But he did assert a real infinity of the "highest powers" determining man and his nature, which "are the *absolute nature* of man as man, and the basis of his existence." "Reason (imagination, fantasy, understanding, opinion), Will, Love (or heart), are not powers which man possesses, for he is nothing without them, he is what he is only by them; they are the constituent elements of his nature, which he neither *has* nor *makes*, the *animating, determining, governing powers—divine, absolute powers*—to which he can oppose no resistance."[65]

But a real infinity of the human being or of the human species and its powers or even—as Feuerbach later maintained—of nature as a whole cannot be accepted without question: least of all in the light of Feuerbach's fundamental accentuation of the sensuousness and consequently the finiteness of reality. Nowhere did Feuerbach substantiate such an infinity of the human powers, of the human being or of the species or even of nature, which would then have no limits of space or time, no beginning and no end. He assumes it: it appears to be a pure postulate.

Feuerbach often speaks of the individual man as if the latter were man in general, universal man, the universal human being. But here we must raise another question: Is not Feuerbach himself uncritical in regard to his own designs and projections? Is the real man not the individual man, this often so limited and not at all good, in any case—as even Feuerbach stresses—mortal and therefore finite man? Is the "universal human being" not an abstraction? Is not Feuerbach himself here projecting something out of himself that does not exist in reality? Is not therefore this very man in general, is not this *universal human being, a pure projection* objectified and given independent existence by Feuerbach? Can the projection of such a ghostly human being guarantee the humanism to which Feuerbach rightly attaches so much importance?

In fact Feuerbach could not even get the left-wing Hegelians to accept his ill-defined notion of the universal human being. And even before Marx, but too readily overlooked by Marxists in their preference for Marx, the young Hegelian Max Stirner, himself more an existentialist than—as is always maintained—an individualist or anarchist, rejected Feuerbach's generic man and thus also rejected the early Marx in his book *The Ego and His Own*.[66] Friedrich Engels, quoted at the opening of this chapter, later regarded as not worth mentioning what he had himself written to Marx on November 19, 1844: "Stirner is right to reject Feuerbach's 'man,' or at least his *Essence of Christianity*; Feuerbachian 'man' is derived from God. . . . 'Man' is always a ghostly figure unless his basis is in empirical man."[67]


## The end of Christianity?

Feuerbach justified his atheism also in the light of his philosophy of history. He proclaimed with great suggestive force that the age of Christianity had irrevocably passed and that we were living in a "period of the decline of Christianity";[68] "Faith has been replaced by unbelief, the Bible by reason, religion and Church by politics, heaven by earth, prayer by work, hell by material wretchedness, the Christian by man."[69]

Even without detailed proof, it is easy to perceive how much in this theory is quite simply true. Has not the secularization process of modern times, which led to the autonomy of the world's structures, acquired a formerly unsuspected breadth and depth? Has not traditional Christianity reached a severe crisis as a result of the acknowledged complicity of Church and theology? And from the Enlightenment onward has not belief in God itself become largely incredible and atheism finally a mass phenomenon?

Some Christians hope for a reversal of this secularization process, but if we are realistic we must recognize that this is not to be expected. All that can be expected is its completion in universal atheism. Here, too, questions arise from the other side.

*First of all*, in the complex problems of secularity must we not *distinguish between secularization and secularism?* That is, between the modern process of secularization and the worldliness of the world on the one hand and on the other secularism as an ideology that associates the world in its worldliness and its structures with fundamental atheism? Are there not countless modern men who definitely approve modern secularization but equally definitely reject atheistic secularism? Can the secular believer in God not perhaps affirm the secularization process, precisely because of this belief, just as well as or even better than the secularistic atheist?

*Further*, has Feuerbach's *prophecy of the decline of Christianity been fulfilled?* Has belief in God disappeared in the past hundred years and atheism become common property, as Feuerbach prognosticated? Is this true in the West; is it true in the East? Even without Auschwitz and the Gulag Archipelago, in East and West, has not atheism lost credibility: in both natural science and medicine, in both politics and culture?

*Finally*, can we declare *a priori* that Christian faith and the Christian community will not emerge—as often before—purified and strengthened, from this crisis? Might not *belief in God acquire a new attractiveness in the future?* Particularly for someone who has seen and experienced atheism with all its consequences in his own life or social milieu? At a time when the churches are losing their public, political and cultural influence, could personal faith in God not become more free and thus gain a less strained credibility? Must reason and Bible, politics and religion, work and prayer, earth and heaven, necessarily exclude one another? Cannot the Christian, too, be human, perhaps even "more human"? Do not some of Feuerbach's objections strike us today as anachronistic or even comic, as for instance when he claimed, a hundred and fifty years ago, to have proved that "Christianity has in fact long vanished, not only from the reason but from the life of mankind, that it is nothing more than a *fixed idea*, in flagrant contradiction with our fire and life assurance companies, our railroads and steam-carriages, our picture and sculpture galleries, our military and industrial schools, our theatres and scientific museums"?[70] Really?

The conclusion can scarcely be avoided that Feuerbach's *historical-philosophical thesis* also proves to be an *assertion that does not seem to be justified: an extrapolation into the future that* even today, in retrospect, *cannot be verified.* Indeed, in view of the obvious political misuse in orthodox communism of Feuerbach's critique of religion and in view of the continued existence of religion, theology and Christianity, we shall have to reflect on the problems today from the opposite standpoint: "If criticism of religion is a thorn in the flesh of theology, so too theology is a thorn in the flesh of the consequences of this criticism, in as much as theology insists on the fact that the political and social definition of man is not the whole truth about him. This theological understanding of the human reality not only makes it impossible to isolate the set of problems indicated by the theme 'Feuerbach and theology,' but points to the conditions under which criticism of religion may reach its own end in theology."[71]


God—wish or reality?

Feuerbach justified his atheism—and in this respect it has had its most enduring influence—mainly *psychologically.* The notion of God is seen as a psychological product of man. Religion appears to be unmasked as soon as it is recognized that "no powers, causes, reasons, are at work or become objectified in religion except those which are involved in anthropology as a whole."[72] According to Feuerbach, religion is based mainly on the feeling of dependence, which, however, is a purely intramundane and intrahuman affair (as dependence on nature); it is likewise based on wholly understandable human wishes and needs, in the last resort in man's all-round drive for happiness: "What man *is in need of*—whether this be a definite and therefore conscious, or an unconscious need—that is God";[73] or, more positively, "What man wishes to be, he makes his God."[74] Religion is thus fundamentally a product of man's instinct for self-preservation, of human egoism. It is, however, man's fancy that posits as real the object of these powers and instincts, needs, wishes and ideals: which makes it appear as a real being. But appearances are deceptive, and religion makes out that this appearance is reality. The idea of God is nothing but human fantasy.

Is this psychologically justified projection theory not more than plausible? There has never been any dispute about the fact that belief in God can be interpreted and even deduced psychologically. From the psychological standpoint, the powers and functions assumed by Feuerbach are undoubtedly involved in belief in God and in religion. It cannot be denied that the feeling of dependence, the most varied wishes and needs, and most of all the drive for happiness and self-preservation, play a fundamental role in religion. At the same time, it must be admitted that imagination also plays a part in any cognitive act, that I know anything at all in my own way, and that in all cognition I place—project—something of myself into the object of my perception. We must really insist that it is to be hoped that not only the mind but also the heart, the whole man, are involved in knowing God. The reality of these psychological factors is quite obviously the reason why Feuerbach's psychological explanation of religion is so striking at first glance and also continually freshly fascinating.

But here, too, questions that cannot be dismissed arise from the opposite standpoint. Does the psychological explanation alone tell us everything about the very complex phenomenon of belief in God? If it is admitted that psychological factors play a considerable part in belief in God, does this mean *ipso facto* that these psychological factors are not directed to a real object, a reality? Certainly the possibility cannot be excluded (and this much must be said in the light of Feuerbach's thesis against all-too-nimble "transcendentally" deducting theologians) that in reality there is no object corresponding to the various needs, wishes and instincts (brought under the heading of "natural desire"). But on the other hand neither can the possibility be *a priori* excluded (and this must be said against atheists who merely make assertions) that there is actually something real (how it is to be defined must remain an open question here) that corresponds to all these needs, wishes and instincts.

To put the question more concretely: might not our *feeling of dependence* and our *instinct for self-preservation* have a very *real ground*; might not our *striving for happiness* have a very *real goal*? And if, as with all knowledge, so, too, with my knowledge of God, I put—project—into the object much of myself, does this alone prove that the object is merely my projection, my fantasy, and otherwise nothing? Might not perhaps some real object, some sort of reality, correspond to all our wishing, thinking and imagining? If I speak in a human way about God, does that mean that the God of whom I speak is merely something human?

"If the gods are products of wishful thinking, it does not follow that they are merely such: we cannot conclude from this either to their existence or to their nonexistence," explains E. von Hartmann: "It is quite true that nothing exists merely because we wish it, but it is not true that something cannot exist if we wish it. Feuerbach's whole critique of religion and the proof of his atheism, however, rest on this single argument; that is, on a logical fallacy."[75] This is more than an argument in formal logic. I can also deduce psychologically my experience of the world, but this implies nothing against the existence of a world independent of me, as the reference point of my experiences. And I can *deduce psychologically my experience of God*, but *this still implies nothing against the existence of a God independent of me*, as the reference point of all my needs and wishes. In a word, something real can certainly correspond in reality to my psychological experience; a real God can certainly correspond to the wish for God.

We cannot avoid the conclusion that Feuerbach's *atheism, from this third psychological viewpoint*, also remains *a pure postulate*. It is not sufficient continually to present supposedly merely human definitions of religion, without proving that these definitions are merely human, while simply expounding them and commenting on them. Psychological arguments alone cannot in principle bring us to the reality of transcendence but must remain neutral in regard to the latter. At the same time, the criticism could be reversed. Once again the question may be raised here whether, particularly with Feuerbach's interest (understandable for a variety of reasons) in a definitive atheism, the wish might be father to the thought. Atheism itself would, then, be a projection of man. The critic of projection himself becomes *suspect of projection*.

We should not, of course, be too hasty in drawing conclusions. All the apt criticism of Feuerbach's phenomenological, philosophical-historical and psychological justification of atheism still does not amount to a positive proof of belief in God. In fact we are faced with the disturbing question: Are perhaps theism and atheism both irrefutable but both also indemonstrable? Have we not reached a great standoff, a stalemate?

## 3. Critique of the critique

Feuerbach's atheism was more intuitively grasped than scientifically substantiated. But, despite his dubious arguments, his atheistic critique of religion formed an unprecedented threat to any kind of belief in God and thus to the whole of Christian theology at its roots, a threat that is not to be minimized even today. Theologians often seem to find it difficult, or are even afraid, to face directly such naked atheism, to come to grips with it. They prefer to avoid it, to refuse to recognize it as a fact, to play it down dialectically.

## Atheism—permanent challenge

Such theological artifices, however, must stop short at Feuerbach. Here we have reached the limits of "interpretation." Feuerbach is not a person who "atheistically believes in God"; he is not a "countertheological political theologian"; still less—despite the good will that cannot be denied to him—is he an "anonymous Christian." Precisely as humanist, he is utterly unambiguously a decided and professing unbeliever, non-Christian and antitheologian. In this respect, Feuerbach himself maintains: "My atheism [is] merely the unconscious and actual atheism of modern humanity and science, made conscious, untwisted and openly declared."[76]

For all Feuerbach's prophetic passion, all his quasireligious language and all his theological terminology, what he offers is definitively atheism. For the first time in the history of humanity, we are faced with a fully considered, absolutely determined, unreservedly professed and—this, too, is important—*planned atheism, kept up to the very end:* an atheism that cannot in any way be subsequently theologically reinterpreted and appropriated. This consistent atheism represents a permanent challenge to any belief in God.

Feuerbach remained to his death an anthropologist who, however, had never gotten away from theologizing throughout his life. What he had written in 1841, at the height of his fame, was true: "So I feel even now that my new work, instead of bringing my antitheological writing to an end forever—as I had planned and anticipated—will only drive me more and more into it."[77] In later years, it is true, as has been checked, after his first, second and third thoughts (God, reason, man), he had yet a fourth (the sensuous), fifth (nature) and sixth (matter), and committed himself with his notorious proposition "Man is what he eats"*[78] to the crude scientific materialism of the 1850s and 1860s. But in all this he remained the antitheologian, continually attempting to justify atheism from different standpoints and to work for the dissolution of religion. In this respect, of course, in his later publications he never got beyond the standpoint developed in *Essence of Christianity* and in *Principles of the Philosophy of the Future* (1843).

But very soon, because of his cult of the universal nature of man, Feuerbach was discarded first by Stirner and then by Marx as "religious" and caught up by the general political and social development. He did in

---

* It is impossible to reproduce in English the play upon the words *ist*="is" and *isst*="eats": *Der Mensch ist, was er isst.* Translator.

fact, as a "communist" (instead of "egoist"), support the revolution when it broke out in 1848. But, when the leader of the Baden revolt, Gustav Struve, asked him to take up arms on the side of the people, he replied: "I am now going to Heidelberg to lecture on the nature of religion to the students, and when in a hundred years' time a few grains grow up out of the seed I sow there, I shall have done more for the betterment of mankind than you with your blasting and bombarding."[79]

At the invitation of the student body, Feuerbach lectured in fact in the Heidelberg town hall—the university closed its doors to him—for students, townsmen and workers, on "the nature of religion."[80] But his popularity was linked with the now collapsing movement of 1848. He was and remained a theorist: "We have not yet reached the transition from theory to practice, for the theory is still lacking, at least in its definitive and fully developed form. Doctrine is still the main thing."[81]

After one term, Feuerbach returned depressed to Bruckberg to study the natural sciences again (chemistry, physiology) and especially to work on his *Origin of the Gods*. But this "theogony according to the sources of classical, Hebrew and Christian antiquity," his chief work in the 1850s, drew scarcely any attention. Feuerbach was forgotten—and isolated— more quickly than he deserved to be. To his great distress, the study room in the castle, which had been his world for twenty-four years, was no longer at his disposal. The porcelain factory, in which he had invested all his resources, went bankrupt. He had to leave with his wife and daughter: "My parting from Bruckberg is a parting of the soul from the body. Today I signed my tenancy agreement with H.v.B. and with that perhaps also my death sentence."[82] Assisted by private and public donations, he lived out the final years of his life in Rechenberg, a village near Nuremberg, in wretched conditions, utterly impoverished, lethargic and finally weakened by a stroke. He was longing for rest: "How the blasted dogs are barking again. My existence in Rechenberg is really a dog's life."[83]

But he would admit no compromise with belief in God: "As a *young* man I celebrated *death*, as an *old* man I celebrate *life*."[84] His last work, *Deity, Freedom, Immortality*, appeared in 1866. After another stroke and a long period of apathetic vegetating, he died, on September 13, 1872, at the age of sixty-eight. He was buried in Nuremberg. Twenty thousand people attended the funeral of this man who had led such a lonely life. At the graveside, one of his last friends said: "What was it that enabled him to fulfill this lifetime's task which he accomplished for mankind, what enabled him to achieve this vast work and this gigantic deed, what was the innermost drive or impulse of his nature which made him do all this? *It was his great, unsullied, unerring love of truth*."[85]

With Feuerbach's death, the questions that this truly existential thinker had raised were still far from being settled. And even after the evidence produced here to show how his atheism is ultimately without justification, his critique of religion is still in substance by no means out of date. On the contrary, it is precisely by completing a criticism of the foundations that we can face more freely the unsettled questions of this critique of religion. For Feuerbach's critique is not a transitional stage, now definitively behind us, but the shadow constantly following theology. Some of the unsettled questions may be briefly noted in what follows.

### What remains of Feuerbach's critique of religion?

A *first point:* Ludwig's brother Edward, a jurist, asked him to be godfather to his son, but at the same time seized the opportunity to criticize Ludwig's *"opposition to Christianity, which to my mind is the basis of the moral education of the human race and for any higher education."*[86] Feuerbach answered that he regretted Edward's "infatuation with the ghost of Christianity, which asserts itself only by political and literary feats," and his demand for "a special supernaturalist pardon for his child, over and above the *natural,* straightforward education of man to man."[87] A deputation of the Heidelberg Workers' Education Association, on the other hand, at the end of his course of lectures, presented a public address of gratitude to "Herr Dr. Feuerbach," ending with the words: "We are not scholars and therefore are not able to appreciate the academic value of your lectures. But this much we feel and know, that the imposture of the parsons and religion, against which you are fighting, is the ultimate foundation of the present system of oppression and worthlessness under which we are suffering; and that consequently your teaching, which replaces faith by love, religion by education, parsons by teaching, can alone be the secure foundation of that future for which we are striving. . . ."[88]

Here we find clearly stated Feuerbach's very serious *questions* to religion and theology. Have not Church and theology frequently defended *God* at the *expense of man,* the hereafter at the expense of the here and now? Did not Feuerbach rightly—although often giving a distorted picture as a result of his completely arbitrary use of biblical and ecclesiastical texts and facts—uncover the great weakness of historical Christianity: a weakness we have frequently noted here, especially in connection with Pascal, Jansenism, and also with Augustine and Protestant pietism and puritanism? Is there not a broad dualistic (Neoplatonic) tradition that devalues nature, the present world and the body, running through the whole history of Christianity? A devaluation in particular of corporeal-sensual man (and especially of woman) in order to exalt God? A spirituality hostile to the senses, expressed in a strict renunciation and humiliation of man before God that is not supported by Jesus' own teaching, often also in neglecting and punishing the body and in rejecting friendship, Eros and sex? All things considered, more a destruction of the self than a turning to the Other, an asceticism at the expense of humanity and of human fellowship? Does it not seem at every point here that God is possible only at the expense of man, being a Christian only at the expense of being human?

A *second point:* On October 11, 1867, Father Ildephonsus Müller, Benedictine Subprior of Mariastein, wrote full of respect for Feuerbach as a "man of character who is in the habit of expressing his personal conviction freely and frankly": "My dear sir, you will find it understandable and also pardonable that this very forthrightness, combined with so many other qualities of mind and heart, has often roused in me the wish, *Utinam cum sis talis, noster esses*" ("Being what you are, if only you were one of us")! And he adds: "Incidentally I am firmly convinced that, if you had devoted yourself from youth onward to the study of *Catholic* theology, our Church would number you among its greatest apologists of modern times. I can well understand that Protestantism—what is called Protestant Christianity—could not appeal to you, could not quench your thirst for truth, and it would be a miracle if *you* had found satisfaction there."[89]

There is no occasion for us here to make the same recommendation to Feuerbach. But here, too, *questions* arise—which are not to be understood in a narrowly denominational sense. Was Feuerbach not right to see his philosophy as the end phase of a Protestant *theology* that—as he thought —*long before his time had become an anthropology*, so that he needed only to understand and appropriate its real intentions? Does not the danger become apparent at this point of a theology in Schleiermacher's style, which makes the reality of God dependent on the religious experiences and emotional needs of the devout human subject? But is not the danger also evident of a contemporary "political theology," which reduces theology to a "critical theory of history" or of "society"? Is it not clear at this point how close we are to atheism if we do not distinguish between theological and anthropological propositions, if we identify man's interest with God's, if we one-sidedly stress God's nonobjectivity, almost see God as absorbed in our neighbor and the mystery of being simply as the mystery of love?

A *third point:* Our friendly Benedictine, Ildephonsus Müller, more or less confirms Feuerbach's critique of belief in God when he naïvely and ingenuously makes this belief the satisfaction of a need (only to be achieved in the Catholic Church): "But how you can find full satisfaction in pantheism, materialism or any other purely philosophical system is and remains a puzzle to me. For the human heart has undeniable needs for which this earth will always remain fallow land. Only Christianity as it lives on in the Catholic Church, continually active and bestowing life, can provide all-round satisfaction for these needs."[90]

But even with this well-meant Catholic opinion, offered with the best intentions, *questions* arise that, however, are not to be addressed only to the Catholic Church. Was not Feuerbach right to expose great weaknesses in Christian talk about God, both naïve and speculative?

*The weaknesses in the first place are those of an all-too-naïve, anthropomorphic talk about God*, his words and deeds, in metaphors, formulas, predicates, that are actually more appropriate to the reality of man than to the reality of God. Have not Christians throughout history often adjusted God to their own needs, longings and purposes, and reduced him to the demands of their often banal everyday reality? Have they not frequently in practice created God "in their own image" and put themselves in his place? Have they not talked about God and meant by this their own interests, proclaimed God and at the same time secured the fulfillment of their own wishes? Must such a materialized God, pinned down and directed to our own interests, not necessarily be suspect as a projection and thus come in for Feuerbach's critique of religion?

But the *weaknesses are also those of philosophical-speculative talk about God*. Did not Feuerbach make it clear that the answer to the all-too-anthropomorphic talk about God cannot be—as Hegel brilliantly attempted to describe it[91]—the dialectical self-movement of spirit canceling the opposition between the world and God? Not, therefore, as against the former, all-too-superficial *vis-à-vis*, now a pantheistic or pantheizing unity canceling all contrast between divine and human nature, between divine and human knowledge? Instead of the former, all-too-human God, not now an all-too-inhuman God? And has not Feuerbach also made it clear how a speculative or even mystical unification canceling all contrasts between God and man opens the way to a reversal of above and below, of the positions of God and man, and thus makes possible an interpretation oriented not only toward pantheism but also toward atheism? With Feuerbach's effective turning from pantheism to atheism, has it not become clear how important it is for the relationship between God and man to remain an irreversible state of affairs and to retain the character of an encounter? And is it not true that wherever God was misunderstood, man also has been misunderstood?

The root problem of the conflict between Feuerbach and theology is thus laid bare. It is a question of correctly defining the relationship between theology and anthropology. Against Feuerbach's claim to have dissolved theology into anthropology, theology *does not attempt to dissolve anthropology into theology, but asserts the objective priority of theology over anthropology*: not to weaken the reality of being human, but to add to it. Theology must dispute with Feuerbach about man because it is wholly and entirely concerned with God. And it must dispute with him about God because it is wholly and entirely concerned with man. Whether, however, we should go as far as Martin Buber, who accused Feuerbach of a "reduction to the unproblematic human being," we may leave open. But we must agree with Buber in so far as he sees the controversy with Feuerbach essentially as a conflict about the "real human being." "But the real human being, the person who is faced by a being that is nonhuman, who is continually overpowered by it as by an inhuman fate and who nevertheless dares to know this being and this fate, is not unproblematic; in fact, he is the beginning of all problems."[92]

Karl Barth has drawn the attention of both sides here to the essential dimensions: "The true man, if he is to be thought of in completely existentialist terms, should surely be individual man. Like all the theologians of his time, Feuerbach discussed man in general, and in attributing to him divinity in his sense had in fact not said anything about man as he is in reality. And Feuerbach's tendency to make the two largely interchangeable, so that he speaks of individual man as if he were man in general and thus dares to attribute divinity to the individual, is evidently connected with the fact that he does not seem sincerely and earnestly to have taken cognizance either of the wickedness of the individual or of the fact that this individual must surely die. If he had been truly aware of this, then he might perhaps have seen the fictitious nature of this concept of generalized man. He would then perhaps have refrained from identifying God with man, the real man, that is, who remains when the element of abstraction has been stripped from him. But the theology of the time was not so fully aware of the individual, or of wickedness or death, that it could instruct Feuerbach upon these points. Its own hypotheses about the relationship with God were themselves too little affected by them. In this way they were similar to Feuerbach's, and upon this common ground his rivals could not defeat him. That was why the theology of his time found it ultimately possible to preserve itself in the face of him, as it had preserved itself in the face of D. F. Strauss, without summoning an energetic cry of 'God preserve us!' "[93]

The atheistic critique of religion practiced by Feuerbach really came to fruition in the hundred years after his death. Despite all his failures, Feuerbach finally became the "Church Father" of modern atheism, the inspirer of Gottfried Keller, of the young Richard Wagner, of Friedrich Nietzsche; admittedly also the inspirer of a bourgeois, mediocre "freethinking" and even of groups with cremation as the main point of their programs. But he attained world significance through Karl Marx.

# II. God—a consolation serving vested interests?
# Karl Marx

Was it Karl Marx or Feuerbach himself who wrote, a year after the appearance of *The Essence of Christianity* (1841), the famous words? "And I advise you speculative theologians and philosophers: get rid of the notions and prejudices of previous speculative philosophy if you want to make a different approach and get at things as they are, that is, at the truth. And for you there is no other way to truth and freedom except through the 'stream of fire,' through Feuerbach. Feuerbach is the purgatory of the present time." The expression *Feuer-bach* (fire stream), used in the most important recent editions of Marx,[1] has become classical in orthodox Marxism. But presumably the short article "Luther as arbiter between Strauss and Feuerbach," signed by "Not a Berliner," was not written by Marx, who never directly quotes Luther elsewhere. More probably it was by Feuerbach, who at that very time was intensively occupied with Luther, was fond of describing himself as "Luther II," and published at the same time *Provisional Theses on the Reformation of Philosophy*,[2] deliberately imitating Luther's theses, ascribing a similar "world-historical" importance to his work for religion, theology and philosophy.[3] Hence the disputed article has appeared recently in editions of Feuerbach.[4]

As always, what "truth and freedom" mean—to which the way through the "fire stream" was supposed to lead—was even then differently defined by Feuerbach and by Marx. The latter, in a first letter from Paris, tried to suggest his own view to Feuerbach: "In these writings, you have provided —I don't know whether intentionally—a philosophical basis for socialism, and the Communists have immediately understood them in this way. The unity of man with man, which is based on the real differences between men, the concept of the human species brought down from the heaven of abstraction to the real earth, what is this but the concept of *society!*"[5]

In this section, too, we are not concerned with the often very controversial questions of historical detail, nor with the genesis and systematics of Marxist thinking in general. Once again, what interests us is the critique of religion: atheism and its substantiation.

## 1. Sociopolitical atheism

The year 1841 was a year of destiny also for the Young Hegelian Marx. At twenty-three, after six years of study, he obtained his doctorate for a dissertation on a theme of ancient atheistic philosophy: *The Difference between the Democritean and Epicurean Philosophy of Nature.*[6] This was completed in Berlin, but—since the author had a bad reputation there as a, member of the left-wing liberal Doktorclub—submitted in Jena. In the Preface, there is a profession of atheism, quoting the Promethean "I hate the pack of gods" and proclaiming human self-consciousness as the supreme and sole deity. Although he continued to work in the spirit of Hegel, Marx was already very much under the influence of Feuerbach and more especially of Bruno Bauer, unsalaried lecturer for theology in Berlin and an atheist at the time. Bauer moved to Bonn, where he qualified again and Marx himself would have liked to qualify under him. But, after moving to Bonn, Marx then went home to Trier—not until three years after the death of his father—to settle some family affairs.

## From Jew to atheist

Born a Jew, brought up as a Christian, finishing off his education as an atheist: these are the three phases in the development of the youthful Karl Marx.

*As a Jew,* Marx had been born in Trier in 1818, in the midst of the period of the political restoration, when the "Holy Alliance," devised by Metternich, the Vienna chancellor of state, in the name of legitimacy, legal order and religion, was trying to suppress the civic freedoms won through the French Revolution. Although his parents came from highly respected rabbinical families, the father—a liberal lawyer—had turned to Protestantism shortly before Karl's birth; it was only about seven years later—when Karl was six years old—that the children followed and finally also the wife. Conversion for the successful, politically opportunist advocate and prosperous owner of a large house and a number of vineyards—in view of all the countless scandalous difficulties for Jews in professional life—was an act of understandable adjustment and social integration. For the man under the influence of the French Enlightenment, conversion was also a deliberate act of emancipation; although remaining in contact with his rabbi brother and the members of the Jewish community, the father even read to his children not from the Bible but from the works of Voltaire, Racine and especially Rousseau. He and, even more, his wife remained believers in God. But could it have had no significance for the religious attitude of the young Marx that his scarcely impressive, subservient father and his nervous, unintellectual mother—hardly ever mentioned later by him—endowed him with alienation, so to speak, in the cradle? Künzli, the Basel sociologist, writes: "Marx was not alienated only as a Jew from his non-Jewish milieu but also as a baptized Christian from his own Judaism. . . . But Marx had evidently gotten into the habit at an early stage of suppressing anything that might touch him too closely, and the basic experience of alienation did not keep him awake at night with thoughts of despair: what he did was to sublimate, rationalize, objectify everything as a philosophical—and later economic—problem. But all this was an unconscious process."[7]

*As a Christian* of Jewish origin and Protestant denomination, the more than usually talented and rather aggressive nephew of the Chief Rabbi of Trier, during his early schooldays and his time at the secondary school in that ultra-Catholic city—even though we do not want to make too much of his psychological biography—was nevertheless an "alien," or at any rate without many friends: in 1835, when he took his final examination, out of thirty-two pupils, twelve—mostly from the country—were studying theology. For this examination, the boy who was never to practice a profession wrote a German essay on "Reflections of a Young Man on the Choice of a Profession."[8] Here he linked two "interests—our own perfection and the welfare of mankind"—in a strikingly direct way as the "chief guide which must direct us in the choice of a profession."[9] Working for the welfare of mankind, of course, did not mean for him—as it would have meant for the dozen pupils just mentioned—active work in the Church. He had also to write on a social theme from a religious standpoint. The title of this essay was "The Union of Believers with Christ according to John 15:1–14, showing its basis and essence, its absolute necessity and its effects."[10] It was an essay composed—as was then customary in Protestant circles—in the spirit of an idealist humanism, in which the talk is generally of the "Deity" and its "voice." In his closing sentence, Marx's view of Christianity—evidently not a revolutionary but a passive enduring Christianity —is vividly illustrated: "Once man has attained this virtue, this union with Christ, he will await the blows of fate with composure, courageously oppose the storms of passion, and endure undaunted the wrath of the iniquitous. . . . Who would not bear suffering gladly, knowing that by his abiding in Christ, by his works, God himself is glorified. . . ."[11]

As an *atheist*, Marx returned, in 1841, to his home town. In the Bonn of the romantic Biedermeier period, he had begun his career as a student, spending money riotously, in "wild goings-on,"[12] beer-drinking gatherings with his friends from Trier, sometimes locked up for the night in prison, getting involved in a shady pistol duel in Cologne. After that, in Berlin, he took his studies more seriously. Stirred by the debates in the left-wing Hegelian Doktorclub, in addition to attending the particularly crowded lectures on jurisprudence (especially with the left-wing Hegelian Eduard Gans), he studied history and philosophy privately. His attempts at literary work should not be forgotten, out of which various trifling poems have been preserved. It was here, in the circle of the Berlin Young Hegelians, that Marx became an atheist. In connection with Feuerbach, we mentioned earlier the post-Hegelian development to atheism: "Bruno Bauer (and Marx and Christiansen) and Feuerbach will proclaim or have already proclaimed the *Montagne* and hoisted the banner of atheism and mortality."[13] In his dissertation for the doctorate, this became perceptible for the first time. Epicurus is applauded, because he blamed "those who believe that man needs heaven."[14] But precisely this Promethean atheism, proclaimed in the Preface, was now to darken the future of the young doctor of philosophy.

In this circle—to which Arnold Ruge, Ludwig Feuerbach, Max Stirner, Moses Hess and later also Friedrich Engels belonged—Marx as a student had found a friend especially in the unsalaried lecturer already mentioned, Bruno Bauer, inspirer of the circle, then the head of that radical "Mountain Party." This theologian, formerly a right-wing Hegelian and editor of the *Zeitschrift für spekulative Theologie*, who had at the time vigorously attacked Strauss's *Life of Jesus*, had meanwhile switched to the left. In the same year, 1841, he invoked Hegel—anonymously, however, unlike Feuerbach, in the guise of an indignant pietistic believer in the Bible— the pantheist as a secret "atheist and anti-Christian." This was in the book *The Trumpet of the Last Judgment on Hegel, the Atheist and Anti-Christian. An Ultimatum.*[15] In the end—under the influence of the French materialists and Marx—he disputed not only the existence of God but also the historical core of the Gospels and the historical existence of Jesus of Nazareth.

It was in any case not surprising that Bauer, biblical critic and unsalaried lecturer in theology, in the following year, 1842, was refused the professorship in the Protestant theological faculty of the University of Bonn to which he aspired, and was deprived of his academic license to teach.[16] This—together with the prohibition of the liberal press by the Prussian Government—was the signal to the Young Hegelians of Berlin for a more intense political radicalism. Religious criticism, even that of Feuerbach and Stirner, was increasingly replaced by political and social criticism. From humanistic atheism in Germany also—in confrontation with the "Christian state"—there emerged a *political atheism*.

For Marx especially, who presumably had collaborated on Bauer's *Trumpet*, the latter's removal from the university was a profound shock. While he was still a student, some of the members of the Doktorclub had prophesied a great future for Marx. What would happen to him now as Dr. Marx but with no prospect of a university career? As the founder of "true socialism," later to be known as the "Communists' rabbi," Moses Hess, had written to a friend, "You can prepare yourself for making the acquaintance of the greatest and perhaps the *only real philosopher* now living. . . . Both by his natural tendency and as a result of his philosophical training, he goes not only beyond Strauss but even beyond Feuerbach—and that means a great deal. . . . Dr. Marx, as my idol is called, is still a very young man (about twenty-four years old) who will strike a final blow at medieval religion and politics; he combines the most caustic wit with the most profound philosophical seriousness. Imagine Rousseau, Voltaire, Holbach, Lessing, Heine and Hegel combined in one person—I

say '*combined,*' not 'thrown together'—there you have Dr. Marx."[17]
Would everything have been different if Dr. Marx, Dr. Bauer, Dr. Feuerbach, Dr. Strauss, had been able at the proper time to become established as university professors?

## From atheist to socialist

Without professional and financial backing—his father dead, his mother practically the sole heiress, with no publications to show apart from two poems—Marx, at the age of twenty-four, at Bauer's instigation, took over the well-paid post of editor-in-chief of the recently launched liberal-democratic *Rheinische Zeitung* and thus came into contact for the first time with the social question. He soon began to have considerable difficulties with the censorship on account of critical social-political articles on wood-stealing and the situation of the Mosel wine growers and peasants. He was finally compelled to dismiss the leading member of his editorial staff, who had come under the influence of the Young Hegelians. He stuck to his *atheism,* even to political atheism. But in his paper he turned decisively against communism and socialism, even accepting the break with his now increasingly radicalized Berlin friends, also, surprisingly, with Bruno Bauer; the Doktorclub had meanwhile been turned into the still more radical association of the "free ones." In a letter to Ruge explaining his plans, Marx dissociated himself from the radicals: "I stated that I regard it as inappropriate, indeed even immoral, to smuggle communist and socialist doctrines, hence a new world outlook, into incidental theatrical criticisms, etc., and that I demand a quite different and more thorough discussion of communism, if it should be discussed at all. . . . Finally, I desired that, if there is to be talk about philosophy, there should be less trifling with the *label* 'atheism' (which reminds one of children, assuring everyone who is ready to listen to them that they are not afraid of the bogeyman) and that instead the content of philosophy should be brought to the people. *Voilà tout.*"[18] Despite all its restraint, the paper was suppressed by the Prussian Government two months later.

Once more without a profession or income, Marx now finally married—in church—Jenny von Westphalen, the friend of his youth, half sister of the later Prussian Minister of the Interior, to whom he had become engaged seven years earlier—at that time, probably out of fear, behind the back of the now deceased Baron von Westphalen, whom he had honored as a father. This charming, sympathetic, distinguished woman identified herself completely with his views and from then onward followed the more than difficult path through material poverty and mental distress together with her frequently selfish, exacting husband: wife and secretary at the same time, responsible for house and children and also both writing down his manuscripts and dealing with his extensive correspondence.

Marx saw no future for himself in Germany and left with his young wife for Paris in 1843.

*Paris*—this meant for Marx:

a comfortable *bourgeois existence,* now also with a daughter, free—as a result of donations from Germany—from material cares;

friendship with the poet *Heinrich Heine,* who was more inclined to the nonviolent socialism of an F. N. Babeuf (demanding equality of possessions as well as equality in law) and who owed to Marx his turning to political poetry and the first publication of parts of his social-critical *Germany, a Winter's Tale;*

friendship again with *Georg Herwegh,* now a lyrical poet, who had been expelled at the same time as Strauss from the Protestant seminary in Tübingen, with whom Marx richly enjoyed the social life of Paris, for whose sake he even broke abruptly with Arnold Ruge—the man who had so often supported Marx and, now also in Paris, had started with him the *Deutsch-französische Jahrbücher* (only one issue appeared).

*Paris*—this, however, also meant the following for Marx:

Here he came into closer contact with the ideas of the prerevolutionary *early socialism* of Fourier, Saint-Simon, Owen, Cabet, Blanc and in particular made the personal acquaintance—through the anarchist Bakunin—of P. J. Proudhon ("Property is theft"), against whose book *The Philosophy of Poverty,* which seemed to Marx too conciliatory, he later wrote a violent but not very effective pamphlet, *The Poverty of Philosophy.*

Here for the first time Marx came into contact with a living *revolutionary tradition:* under the influence of *Moses Hess*—now also resident in Paris —and his social-revolutionary *Philosophy of Action* (Praxis),[19] he dissociated himself from the reformist, democratic humanism of Ruge and Feuerbach.

Here for the first time—not least as a result of reading the sensational, sentimental novel *The Mysteries of Paris,* by Eugène Sue—Marx's attention (like that of the great Paris public as a whole) was drawn to the *wretchedness of the industrial proletariat.*

Here for the first time—through the friendship now beginning with *Friedrich Engels,* the son of a manufacturer—he became intensely occupied with the study of political economy, heard of a "Union of Communists" in London and in Switzerland, and took part—without actually joining the organizations—in the meetings of secret communist associations ("workers' societies," somewhat fanatical groups mainly of German-speaking workmen).

Here came the great *showdown* with another tried friend, *Bruno Bauer,* who became a conservative politician in his third phase. Marx composed his shapeless book, tackling all possible philosophical, political and economic themes, *The Holy Family, or Critique of Critical Criticism. Against Bruno Bauer and Company.*[20]

In a word: it was in Paris that Marx first became a *socialist and commu-*

*nist,* that he perceived with his peculiar power of creating utopias the enormous possibilities of an organized workers' movement and became the theorist of the proletariat.

For the question that concerns us, however, this means that Marx was *an atheist long before he became a communist.* His anticapitalist attitude was not a presupposition but a confirmation of his atheism. The atmosphere in both home and school, then decisively the philosophical climate among the radical Young Hegelians in Berlin, his preoccupation with the atheistic tradition and especially the influence of the atheists Bauer and Feuerbach—all this led to that materialistic atheism that Marx soon came to take for granted but that was bound to exercise a special influence on a genius who combined a high degree of rationality and a capacity for acute analysis with unusual impulsiveness and readiness for practical commitment. From then onward, atheism determined not only Marx the analytical scholar but also Marx the political fighter and prophet. Marx's greatest achievement was to have recognized at an early stage, less from social sense than from intellectual analysis, the historical role and dynamism of the workers' movement and to have given it an appropriate program. It was through him that atheism became largely and for a long time the obvious ideological foundation for socialism.

## Dialectical materialism instead of idealism

Atheism and communism: here we have the new humanism. As Marx expresses it in his *Economic and Philosophical Manuscripts,* composed in Paris, "atheism is humanism mediated with itself through the supersession of religion, whilst communism is humanism mediated with itself through the supersession of private property."[21]

Before he went to Paris, Marx had scarcely bothered to deal academically with *economic questions.* But *Friedrich Engels* now appeared on the scene to convince him of the importance of political economy.[22] This manufacturer's son from Barmen, two years younger than Marx, had become a Young Hegelian in Bruno Bauer's circle in Berlin during his military service and had paid a visit later to the office of the *Rheinische Zeitung* but was not very cordially received. Now, however, on a ten-day visit to Paris from Manchester, he came into very close contact with Marx and thus laid the foundations of a lifelong collaboration. As always, Marx now threw himself enthusiastically into the task of becoming familiar with the literature on economics, studying and making excerpts from the works of Adam Smith and his French systematist Jean-Baptiste Say, David Ricardo and John Stuart Mill. But he did not produce the great systematic work of political economy that Engels expected from him; he let himself be diverted by controversy—in particular by his work against "Bauer and Company," which Engels regarded as completely superfluous.

It was only in 1932 (after being published in part in Russian in 1927) that these "Paris Manuscripts," which Marx had collected in 1844 under the title "Toward a Critique of Political Economy" (collections of material, outlines of individual chapters), were published. These *Economic and Philosophical Manuscripts*, as they are mostly known today, on the wages of labor and alienated labor, profit of capital, private property and communism, and finally on the Hegelian dialectic and philosophy as a whole, have been regarded from that time onward as the birth certificate of what is now called "scientific socialism." Here for the first time it was a question of alienation, understood in a philosophical sense, through wage labor and private property and its cancellation through the communist society. These *Economic and Philosophical Manuscripts*, together with the article (published in the sole issue of the *Deutsch-französische Jahrbücher*) "Critique of Hegel's 'Philosophy of Right,' Introduction,"[23] also represent the sole independent attempt in the whole of Marxist literature to justify philosophically the Marxist theory of religion. All that follows is nothing more than the expansion or application of the sociophilosophical interpretation of religion worked out here.

Marx's life was accompanied by (often abrupt and ruthless) showdowns with friends, comrades-in-arms and rivals. However we react—sympathetically or unsympathetically—to these sudden turnings of friendship into enmity, one thing is clear: Marx very often establishes his position from contraposition, his own theory from controversy; he gains his inheritance by fighting for it; he develops by judging. But in regard to two figures, from whom he likewise definitely dissociated himself, he maintained respect and even admiration as long as he lived: Hegel and Feuerbach. Why?

Marx must have become acquainted with *Hegel's philosophy* in the first place mainly through Bruno Bauer and Eduard Gans and possibly studied it closely only in Paris. In any case it is from this time that we have to date not only an excerpt from the last chapter of the *Phenomenology of Mind* (on absolute knowledge and religion)[24] but also an incomplete manuscript, *Critique of the Hegelian Dialectic and Philosophy as a Whole*,[25] a *Critique of Hegel's Constitutional Law*, likewise only begun,[26] and finally—the only *publication* in this connection—the article above mentioned, *Critique of Hegel's "Philosphy of Right,"* which did not get beyond the "Introduction." Evidently Marx had planned a comprehensive treatment of Hegel. But, like most of his greater works, it remained a fragment. And yet this compact and brilliantly formulated introductory article comprising only a few pages contains more explosive force than the completed anti-Bauer work, *The Holy Family, or Critique of Critical Criticism*, in many hundreds of pages. The Great Soviet Encyclopedia rightly says of it: "Here we find the basic theses of Marxist theory in which religion is considered as a distorted, fantastic reflection."[27]

If, however, we want to understand the critique of Hegel and his philosophy of religion, we must never forget *how much Marx owed to Hegel:*
What would his materialism be without *dialectic?* It simply would not be
dialectical materialism. And it was from Hegel that Marx took over the
dialectic, the "algebra of revolution" as it was later known in Russian socialism.

And what would his materialism be without *history?* It simply would not
be historical materialism. And it was from Hegel, too, that Marx had
learned how to see history, the coherent-dialectical consideration of world
history.

And it was from Hegel[28] that Marx learned to appreciate, in a way that
was quite new by comparison with the traditional view, the *social nature*
of man, the importance of the factor of *labor* for man's self-understanding, the perception of man's *alienation* and of so much that made earlier
materialism seem primitive, a "mechanistic materialism." All this, however, with a difference that changes everything.

Marx rejected idealism, which, however, constitutes the very heart of
the Hegelian system. This he did *under the influence of Feuerbach:*
"Feuerbach is the only one who has a *serious, critical* attitude to the
Hegelian dialectic and who has made genuine discoveries in this field. He
is in fact the true conqueror of the old philosophy."[29] What is Feuerbach's "great achievement"? According to Marx:

"(1) the proof that philosophy is nothing else but religion rendered into
thought and expounded by thought, i.e., another form and manner of existence of the estrangement of the essence of man; hence equally to be
condemned;

"(2) the establishment of *true materialism* and of *real science*, by making
the social relationship of 'man to man' the basic principle of the
theory. . . ."[30] Hence: dialectic, certainly; not, however, the abstract,
unreal dialectic of a divine idea, but, on the contrary, the actual concrete
dialectic of matter, dialectical *materialism;*

history, certainly; not, however, the abstract, unreal history of an absolute
spirit, but, on the contrary, the concrete, actual history of the true subject
of history, of man, of human society, of the proletariat, materialistic *socialism.*

Concretely this means that man is not primarily consciousness, but
being, matter, body. All of which is neglected by idealism. His world is
not merely a world of abstract ideas, but a world of concrete social conditions. His work is not primarily the self-reproduction of consciousness, but
the practical labor of the workman. His alienation is not that of thought,
but brutal estrangement in the labor process. And the removal of this alienation, again, must take place not only in thought but in the practical
life of society as it really is.

In regard also to *religion and criticism of religion*, Marx in principle is against Hegel and on the side of Feuerbach. Marx does not only approve the new starting point—at man, at the real facts, at the sensuous reality of the present world, at being instead of consciousness—but he also approves completely of Feuerbach's critique of religion. Even more, according to Marx, Feuerbach has completed this critique once and for all: "For Germany the *criticism of religion* is in the main complete, and criticism of religion is the premise of all criticism."[31] In this objective, historical sense also, therefore, atheism precedes communism. And it should be noted that, for Feuerbach, religion, theology and atheism were still the object of continual discussion. But, for Marx, atheism is no longer something that needs to be justified or seriously discussed; it can be taken for granted.

For Marx it is quite obvious that *God is a projection of man:* "Man, who looked for a superhuman being in the fantastic reality of heaven and found nothing there but the *reflection* of himself, will no longer be disposed to find but the *semblance* of himself, only an inhuman being, where he seeks and must seek his true reality."[32]

For Marx, it is quite obvious also that *religion is both the product and the alienation of man:* "The basis of irreligious criticism is that *Man makes religion,* religion does not make man. Religion is the self-consciousness and self-esteem of man who has either not yet found himself or has already lost himself again."[33]

But how, then, are man and his reality to be understood?

### Feuer-bach to Marx?

For all the points of agreement, Marx at an early stage had also strong *reservations in regard to Feuerbach.* These reservations are confirmed in the *Theses on Feuerbach,* composed a little later in Brussels, not published by Marx at the time (but only, after Marx's death, by Engels). Nevertheless, we should not regard Feuerbach merely as the "stream of fire" leading to Marx, as he is regarded in orthodox Marxism. Feuerbach was not only the precursor, preparing the way, but also occasionally the companion of Marx on that way. Even with Feuerbach—especially in his *Principles of the Philosophy of the Future*—we find the beginnings of a new appreciation of man's historicity, sociality and practice. But— measured against Marx—they remain merely beginnings. Even Feuerbach's critique of religion was meant to be understood in a political and social sense and, according to the letter of Marx to Feuerbach from Paris mentioned above, his *Principles of the Philosophy of the Future* and *Essence of Christianity* "provided a philosophical basis for socialism."[34] But, with Feuerbach, there is not yet any penetration of the problems as a whole or any comprehensive social criticism. A brief statement of the concrete points of agreement or difference, which are not always appreciated, may be worthwhile.

1. Does Feuerbach recognize the *sociality of man?* Marx: "Feuerbach resolves the religious essence into the *human* essence. But the human essence is no abstraction inherent in each single individual. In its reality it is the ensemble of the social relations" (sixth thesis on Feuerbach[35]).

Certainly, *even Feuerbach* sees man as a communal and even social being—in fact, as the human species—and tries to fathom man from the nature of natural relationships. But his notion of man as species reflects only the natural relationships between individual human beings and with nature, and neglects the sociological context.

*Marx, on the other hand,* tries to fathom man from the nature of social conditions. He examines the actual sociological reality, analyzes its driving forces and laws, provides a concrete political-economic analysis of the material social conditions, the role of labor, of production, the emergence of the conditions of production, of social organization as a whole.

2. Does Feuerbach recognize the *historicity of man?* Marx: "Feuerbach, who does not enter upon a criticism of this real essence, is consequently compelled to abstract from the historical process and to fix the religious sentiment (*Gemüt*) as something by itself and to presuppose an abstract —*isolated*—human individual . . ." (sixth thesis on Feuerbach[36]).

Certainly, *even Feuerbach*—unlike Hegel—wanted to be oriented to the concrete, empirical and indeed to the sensual, corporeal, concrete human being. But man, for him, is seen nevertheless as the universal species man, outside the world and its history.

*Marx, on the other hand,* tries to understand man essentially in historical terms, within the great process of world history and against the background of the particular historical period. He is not, like Feuerbach, a believer in universal progress, but he is aware of progress in accordance with sociological necessities and laws.

3. Does Feuerbach recognize the importance of the *practical activity of man?* Marx: "The chief defect of all hitherto existing materialism—that of Feuerbach included—is that the thing (*Gegenstand*), reality, sensuousness, is conceived only in the form of the *object* (*Objekt*) or of *contemplation* (*Anschauung*), but not as *human sensuous activity, practice,* not subjectively. . . . Hence he does not grasp the significance of 'revolutionary,' of 'practical-critical' activity. . . . In practice man must prove the truth, that is the reality and power, the this-sidedness (*Diesseitigkeit*) of his thinking" (first and second theses on Feuerbach[37]).

Certainly, *even Feuerbach* advocates human emancipation. For him this is linked with understanding of human nature, human ideals, the organization of human relationships, and is characterized by bourgeois ideas of reform and morality. But Feuerbach consequently expects social reorganization mainly through enlightenment, changed awareness, freedom from religious and moral constraints and the regaining of human relationships both with men and with nature. He appeals, therefore—without any substantial practical results—to the individual member of bourgeois society and to his quest for happiness, which must be realized in the other person and must also constantly be limited by the other person's justified quest for happiness: the conquest of selfishness (according to him, finding expression particularly in religion) through love for man.

*Marx, on the other hand*, analyzes human emancipation as a social question from the economic, political and ideological standpoints. For him, emancipation is a problem not of selfishness but of economic constraints and social classes. What is required is not a new relationship of man to nonhuman nature but a commitment to practical politics. Marx expects social reorganization as a result of revolutionizing society from the bottom upward. He appeals, therefore, to the working class—which alone is capable of this task—and demands practical political struggle: the class struggle of the exploited proletariat against the exploiting bourgeoisie. In contrast to earlier forms of socialism, this means the liberation of the working classes by the working classes. Socialism must become proletarian, so that the proletariat will become socialist. All things considered, then, the practical—that is, socialist-revolutionary—emancipation of man: concretely, the communist revolution.

Unlike Feuerbach, then, Marx is not concerned with a cult of the abstract "man," who would be the core of a new religion. He is interested in a science of man as he really is in his concrete social development, which represents the theory for a new sociological—and for him this always means revolutionary—practice. And in this very way, Marx substantially deepened the Feuerbachian critique of religion.


## Opium of the people

For Marx, it is clear that we cannot speak merely in general about human nature with reference to religion. We must attempt to clarify the concrete social and political conditions for the emergence and existence of religious ideology and practice with its degrading consequences for man. Consequently the decisive question for Marx—unanswered by Feuerbach —is, How did man's religious self-alienation, rightly noted by Feuerbach, come about, and how can it be overcome? If we are to answer these two questions—and Marx does so at the beginning of his article *"Critique of the Hegelian Philosophy of Right. Introduction"* in language of almost Lutheran vigor—we must take the factors of society and of practice much more seriously than Feuerbach did. And we must do so with reference to both the emergence and the conquest of religious alienation.

1. How does *religious alienation* come about? Religious alienation must be explained in the light not simply of man in the abstract but of the *concrete sociological conditions.* This means that the fact that man—as Feuerbach, according to Marx, rightly sees—projects religion out of himself, is explained—as Feuerbach does not see—in the light of the inverted social world: "But *man* is no abstract being encamped outside the world. Man is the *world of man,* the state, society. This state, this society, produce religion, an *inverted world-consciousness,* because they are an *inverted world.*"[38] Inverted, unjust, inhuman society produces man's inverted—that is, religious—consciousness.

Religious alienation is in need, therefore, not only of general, rationalistic criticism but of *practical criticism* of the unjust and inhuman social conditions that produce religion and that religion, in its turn, also sanctions, supports, justifies, keeps alive by the consolation it offers: "Religion is the general theory of that world, . . . its moral sanction, its solemn complement, its universal source of consolation and justification. It is the *fantastic realization* of the human essence because the *human essence* has no true reality. The struggle against religion is therefore indirectly a fight against *the world* of which religion is the spiritual *aroma.*"[39]

And yet religion—and this is often overlooked in interpretations of Marx—must not be seen merely in negative terms. It is not only a *consequence* but also—and in this light Ernst Bloch will try to discover the "red thread" of protest running through the whole Bible and the whole of Church history[40]—a *protest* against inhuman social conditions: "*Religious* distress is at the same time the *expression* of real distress and also the *protest* against real distress. Religion is the sigh of the oppressed creature, the heart of a heartless world, just as it is the spirit of spiritless conditions."[41]

In Marx's opinion, however, this protest of religion remains ineffectual and helpless, since religion diverts attention from the present world and its transformation and puts us off with a promise of the hereafter. Thus religion, in the end, simply has the effect of a sedative or a narcotic, producing illusory instead of real happiness: "It is the *opium* of the people."[42] It is this very phrase—so often misunderstood in Marxism and which is found also in Moses Hess[43]—that distinguishes Marx as an ideological critic from a naïve rationalist. Religion is not simply the invention of swindling priests or rulers. Religion is the utterance of suffering humanity in its quest for consolation. As it is called in the same social-psychological context: "the sigh of the oppressed creature." The phrase is suggested by Feuerbach, who in his chapter on prayer seeks to interpret God as "the echo of our cry of anguish," "the uttered sorrow of the soul," "a tear of love, shed in the deepest concealment, over human misery," and makes use in this connection of a saying of the mystical visionary of the Reformation Sebastian Franck: "God is an unutterable sigh, lying in the depths of the heart."[44]

2. How does the *abolition of religious alienation* come about? Abolition, too, must emerge from concrete social conditions and from practice. There would be no point in merely depriving men of their opium and leaving unchanged the circumstances that make the pain-killer necessary: "To abolish religion as the *illusory* happiness of the people is to demand their *real* happiness. The demand to give up illusions about the existing state of affairs is the *demand to give up a state of affairs which needs illusions*. The criticism of religion is therefore *in embryo the criticism of the vale of tears*, the *halo* of which is religion. Criticism has torn up the imaginary flowers from the chain not so that man shall wear the unadorned, bleak chain but so that he will shake off the chain and pluck the living flower."[45]

From the criticism of religion, the criticism of politics must follow and thus in the end the practical revolution, which is realized by history itself but prepared by philosophy: "The *task of history*, therefore, once the *world beyond the truth* has disappeared, is to establish the *truth of this world*. The immediate *task of philosophy*, which is at the service of history, once the *holy form* of self-estrangement has been unmasked, is to unmask self-estrangement in its *unholy forms*. Thus the criticism of heaven turns into the criticism of the earth, the *criticism of religion* into the *criticism of law* and the *criticism of theology* into the *criticism of politics*."[46]

The revolutionary imperative is therefore clear: "The criticism of religion ends with the teaching that *man is the highest being for man*, hence with the *categorical imperative to overthrow all relations* in which man is a debased, enslaved, forsaken, despicable being, relations which cannot be better described than by an exclamation of a Frenchman when it was planned to introduce a tax on dogs: 'Poor dogs! They want to treat you like human beings.' Even historically, theoretical emancipation has specific practical significance for Germany. For Germany's *revolutionary* past is theoretical, it is the *Reformation*. As the revolution then began in the brain of the *monk*, so now it begins in the brain of the *philosopher*."[47]

Marx, then—like Feuerbach earlier—is a kind of second Luther, but with certain differences: "It was no longer a case of the layman's struggle against the *priest outside himself* but of his struggle against his *own priest inside himself*, his *priestly nature*."[48] Here it is a question of the emancipation not of the princes but of the people. The term "proletariat" turns up for the first time. The proletariat will bring about "the complete rewinning of man."[49] The closing lines of this article have the tone and character of a prophecy: "In Germany *no* kind of bondage can be broken without breaking *every* kind of bondage. The *thorough* Germany cannot make a revolution without making a *thoroughgoing* revolution. The *emancipation of the German* is the *emancipation of the human being.* The *head* of this emancipation is philosophy, its *heart* is the *proletariat.* Philosophy cannot be made a reality without the abolition of the proletariat, the proletariat cannot be abolished without philosophy being made a reality. When all inner requisites are fulfilled, the *day of German resurrection* will be proclaimed by the *ringing call of the Gallic cock.*"[50] The sole great hope, then, is the proletarian revolution. The German and the French minds, German philosophy and French socialism, must come to terms with it.

We now understand better the meaning of the frequently quoted eleventh thesis on Feuerbach: "The philosophers have only *interpreted* the world, in various ways; the point, however, is to change it."[51]


## Economic justification of atheism

It was long after he had left Paris that Marx wrote in his notebook the theses against Feuerbach. The attack of the German opposition forces in Paris had become too much for the Prussian Government. After their periodical, *Vorwärts*, had welcomed an attempt—which miscarried—to shoot the German king, Heine, Bakunin, Ruge and Marx were expelled from France. Only Marx obeyed the order—within twenty-four hours. So Marx was in Brussels from the beginning of 1844 and—again well supported with donations and provided with a house where he lived plainly—plunged into tremendous activity both literary and political: philosophical and economic studies and in particular—in addition to the answer to Proudhon mentioned above—a renewed, oversized attack on his former friends, on "modern German philosophy, according to its representatives Feuerbach, Bruno Bauer and Stirner, and German socialism, according to its various prophets," with the title of *The German Ideology.* Not being able to find a publisher, however, he had to abandon the manuscript "to the gnawing criticism of the mice."[52] It was published only in 1932.[53]

In the year 1847, on the eve of the new revolutionary movement in Europe, Marx and Engels, in Brussels, now intervened directly in the *workers' political movement.* With their "Communist Correspondence Committee" and their "Communist Party" (consisting at the beginning of only seventeen members, all German), they joined the admittedly small but internationally organized League of the Just (previously, League of the Despised). This organization, under the leadership of the tailor Wilhelm Weitling, adopted a moralizing, visionary and Christian socialist attitude in the spirit of the early socialist Babeuf, and demanded an unbloody revolution, community of goods and a "Guarantee of Harmony and Freedom" (the new title of Weitling's expanded version of his program: "Humanity as it is and as it ought to be"). Marx—often intolerant, dictatorial, even malicious in the company of colleagues like Weitling—worked resolutely to establish a close international organization of a self-confident proletariat under his own leadership.

In London in 1847, the first congress of the League of the Just decided to exclude Weitling's supporters, to change the name to the Communist League, to set up a new organization and in particular to commission Marx and Engels to work out a "Profession of Communist Faith." After petty internal conflicts and intrigues, this profession finally appeared in February 1848 in English, French, German, Italian, Flemish and Danish, published under the title of the *Manifesto of the Communist Party*. In that same February, in Paris, the new revolution took place: the bourgeois king, Louis-Philippe, was deposed and the Second Republic proclaimed; riots occurred in Brussels, and the workers—with Marx's explicit approval —demanded weapons. On March 3, 1848, Marx was expelled by the King of Belgium but at the same time invited to Paris by the provisional revolutionary government.

"A spectre is haunting Europe—the spectre of Communism."[54] These are the opening words, more ironic than menacing, of the *Manifesto*, which for the first time provides a compact theoretical justification of the revolutionary emancipation program for the working class. Making a sharp distinction between the bourgeoisie on the one hand and the various reactionary, conservative and utopian forms of socialism on the other, it provides a brief synthesis of what was later to be called "dialectical and historical materialism." Apart from a short, sharp diatribe against "clerical socialism,"[55] which had been allied with feudalist reactionary socialism, little is said about the criticism of religion: "What else does the history of ideas prove, than that intellectual production changes in character in proportion as material production is changed? The ruling ideas of each age have ever been the ideas of its ruling class. . . . When the ancient world was in its last throes, the ancient religions were overcome by Christianity. When Christian ideas succumbed in the eighteenth century to rationalist ideas, feudal society fought its death battle with the then revolutionary bourgeoisie. The ideas of religious liberty and freedom of conscience merely gave expression to the sway of free competition within the domain of knowledge."[56]

And now? The bourgeois charge that communism abolishes eternal truths like freedom and justice, abolishes religion and morals, receives the cool response that the history of society has hitherto taken the form of successive social class antagonisms, but what has been common to all epochs is the exploitation of one class by another. The communist revolution, however, will make a radical break with the traditional conditions of ownership (private property) and of society (class society), so that the traditional "forms of consciousness," such as state, religion and morality, will "completely vanish."[57]

Even in *The Communist Manifesto*, therefore, there is no invitation to direct, violent persecution of religion and Church, but an unambiguous demand for "the forcible overthrow of all existing social conditions." This is the promise with which the manifesto ends: "Let the ruling classes tremble at a Communistic revolution. The proletarians have nothing to lose but their chains. They have a world to win. WORKING MEN OF ALL COUNTRIES UNITE!"[58]

Was the promise already fulfilled in 1848? Whether Marx expected it, is disputed. Metternich had been chased out of Vienna on March 19, and the revolution broke out in Berlin on the next day. Marx left Paris for Cologne but decided there that the time for a proletarian revolution had evidently not yet come. The *Neue Rheinische Zeitung*, which he had set up, and directed in an authoritarian way, sailed on for a time at least not under the communist but under the democratic (and strictly anti-Russian) flag, and supported not a proletarian but the bourgeois revolution. It was only after the greatly strengthened restoration had taken place, thirteen months later, when expelled from Prussia—on account of the increasingly radical policy of the paper and his involvement in revolutionary activities—that Marx, on May 16, 1849, showed his true colors. In the last issue, printed wholly in red, he waved the blood-red flag of revolutionary violence, not shrinking—and this must not be overlooked—even from the use of terror: "We are ruthless, we expect no consideration from you. And when our turn comes, we shall not disguise terrorism."[59]

Marx, now destitute, returned with his family to Paris, only to be banished shortly afterward to the provinces. He decided to go to *London* in August 1849. There—apart from a very few interruptions—he spent the last three decades of his life. The first years in London were the most depressing in his life: in regard to money, accommodation, food and health. His wife, already pregnant again on arrival in England, had to bear the main burden, which brought her to the verge of collapse. Three of their children died in the midst of the hardships of the first years of exile. He (or frequently Engels for him) wrote articles for the main American newspaper, the New York *Tribune*, organized correspondence and conferred with the whole world. At the same time, he began to receive generous financial support from his friend Engels, who had meanwhile taken over his father's prosperous textile factory. So, once again, with all the money he needed coming to him in the form of donations or bequests, he was able to live quite comfortably but disturbed by the inevitable disputes between various social groups among the emigrants and by serious difficulties with his wife and daughters (and a boy said to be his illegitimate son). Working at home and—after the opening, in 1857, of the circular reading room—in the British Museum, he took up his studies again. He got through an enormous amount of literature of every kind, in order to support his ideas and theories on the philosophy of history and on politics with economic facts and to clarify the function of the proletariat on its way to the future. He was not so much a practitioner of politics as a theorist of political practice.

Ten years after his arrival in London, there appeared the work for which Engels had been so long waiting, the first fruits of Marx's economic studies—but only in part. This was no more than the very first section of the *Critique of Political Economy*, including, however, in its Preface an account of the author's own development as a thinker and his famous compact summary of the theory of historical materialism; here, too, is found a first, brief description of his theory of value.[60] Its content is substantially the same as that of the first section of the first volume of Marx's great main work, *Das Kapital*, which—after lengthy preparation, often interrupted for a variety of reasons—was published, in 1867, in Hamburg, without provoking any notable response at the time. In this opening section of a work that is critically and soberly analytical but also proclamatory, prophetic, accusing, Marx returns to his *critique of religion* under the heading of "The Mystery of the Fetishistic Character of Commodities."[61] While formerly the arguments had been political and humanistic, now, in *Das Kapital*, they are *political and economic*. Socioeconomic alienation is really the basis of religious and political alienation. For the materialistic basis—the conditions of production or ownership changing independently of man—determines the sociological situation at any particular time and man's consciousness as a whole: law, state, religion and philosophy, the entire ideological "superstructure." In the light of the critical analysis of capitalistic society and economy, the two basic questions of Marx's critique of religion raised at an earlier stage can now be given a more exact answer.

1. How does *religious alienation* come about? Since, as a result of the division of labor, the means of production (together with the products) have become the private property of individuals, the workers in the modern industrialized and technicized process of production have nothing but their sheer labor—as a "commodity"—to offer. The price they receive for this, the *quid pro quo*, is their wage. But—and this is decisive—they do not receive the full wage: the value of the product of their labor afterward in exchange, in the market. The owners of the means of production, that is, skim off the "surplus value" (the difference between the wage and the exchange value of the product of labor), so that their capital is continually increasing at the expense of the real producers, the workers. "Capital," as money producing money, thus becomes the characteristic feature of the "capitalist" economic and social system. But, in the process of exchange, the product of their own labor becomes for wage earners an alienated, branded "commodity": something separated from them, made independent, exchangeable, mysteriously increased and heightened in value, amounting even to a kind of sensuous-suprasensuous

fetish (from the religious standpoint, an object that is considered and venerated as the seat of higher powers).

Are not these conditions analogous to those in the "nebulous world of religion"? "In that world, the products of the human mind become independent shapes, endowed with lives of their own, and able to enter into relations with men and women. The products of the human hand do the same thing in the world of commodities. I speak of this as the *fetishistic character* which attaches to the products of labour, so soon as they are produced in the form of commodities. It is inseparable from commodity production."[62]

As long as economic alienation continues in commodity fetishism, religious alienation, with its divine figures, will continue in their nebulous world. Corresponding to the economic and social development at any particular time (Marx distinguishes Asian, ancient, feudal, and modern-bourgeois ways of production or forms of society), there were also various forms of religious alienation. Thus, individualistic Protestantism forms a striking counterpart to the capitalism of bourgeois society, with its individual mode of production and the isolation of the producers of commodities (linked only through the market), the workers. Here, long before Max Weber, Marx had drawn attention to certain connections between Protestantism and the "spirit of capitalism."

2. How does the *abolition of religious alienation* come about? Religious alienation will be abolished only when relations between human beings again become intelligible and reasonable as a result of new modes of production: "Such *religious reflexions* of the real world will not disappear until the relations between human beings in their practical everyday life have assumed the aspect of perfectly intelligible and reasonable relations as between man and man, and as between man and nature. The life process of society, this meaning the material process of production, will not lose its veil of mystery until it becomes a process carried on by a free association of producers, under their conscious and purposive control."[63]

And how will these intelligible and reasonable conditions of production be attained? By the abolition of the division of labor and the disappearance of private property. With the continually increasing accumulation and concentration of capital in fewer and fewer hands, there is a continous augmentation and impoverishment of the proletariat. This will go on until, in this necessary dialectical process, the great upheaval of the communist revolution occurs: expropriation of the expropriators, socialization of the means of production; dictatorship of the proletariat as interim stage on the way toward the introduction of the complete communism of the classless society in which division of labor and economic alienation have been abolished and the state (the instrument of oppression used by the ruling class), national antagonisms (to be overcome by the International) and in the end also religion (a consoling remedy now become superfluous) die out.

It has, again, become clear that there is no need of an active struggle against religion, nor does it have to be exterminated by force. There will simply be no more need of religion. Religious consciousness will die of itself as soon as the new, communistic social order is introduced—the realization of the true human being in the realm of freedom.

### Atheism as Weltanschauung: from Engels to Lenin

Was the socialist revolution on the way? In highly industrialized England, the very place where the upheaval ought to have taken place first, according to Marx's economic theory, it seemed less likely than ever. Marx himself was evidently prevented not only by sickness and external difficulties from continuing *Das Kapital*. Only after Marx's death did Engels (and after him Karl Kautsky and Eduard Bernstein) publish as additional volumes of *Das Kapital* the material collected many years before but never given a definitive form by the author. Why it was left incomplete is disputed again particularly today. Certainly the orthodox theory, that Marx was prevented by sickness and poverty, is too simple. Did Marx himself perhaps see that economic and political developments had in practice rendered his theories obsolete and that he would have to be continually revising his work?[64]

This much at least is certain: Marx remained tirelessly active right up to his last years, not only studying but also publishing and agitating. He analyzed acutely the economic and political causes and effects of Louis Bonaparte's *coup d'état*.[65] A large public meeting in London in 1863 on behalf of oppressed Poland led, in the following year, to the fulfillment of Marx's invitation "Working men of all countries unite!" An International Workers' Association was founded, becoming known in history as the "First International." Marx—who had dissolved the Communist League as early as 1852 and now became corresponding secretary of the International for Germany—wrote for it both the magisterially argued "Inaugural Address" and the "Provisional Rules."[66] But, as he became increasingly remote from conditions in Germany without becoming an Englishman, he had no decisive influence either on the rising trade-union movement in England or on the social-democratic workers' movement in Germany. He rejected both the Universal German Workers' Union of the socialist reformer Ferdinand Lassalle and the ideas of the anarchist Bakunin. Although he did not support from London the bloody revolt of the Paris Commune in 1871, he wrote afterward a brilliant pamphlet about it: *The Civil War in France*.[67] By 1871, when the seat of the General Council was moved, at the suggestion of Marx and Engels, to New York as a result of internal dissensions and external inefficiency, the First International had practically ceased to exist.

The more the advent of the socialist revolution was delayed, however, and an all-subverting revolutionary project seemed impossible, the more the need of a theoretical substitute became evident: a binding doctrine, comprehensive teaching, an all-embracing Weltanschauung. And the more the workers' movement at the same time—in Germany especially after 1870[68]—as a party of millions of men, became organized and consolidated, the more it needed not only organizational but also ideological integration and strengthening by a common Weltanschauung. Dialectical and historical materialism could be helpful in this respect. *Friedrich Engels* took on this work, which was wholly in accordance with his personal inclinations.

In 1878, Engels presented the public with the results of his labors: *Herr Eugen Dühring's Revolution in Science*.[69] The attack on the "universal system" of the temporarily influential Berlin lecturer was more or less incidental. While another philosophical work by Engels, *Dialectic of Nature*, remained incomplete and was only published in 1925 in Moscow, the *Anti-Dühring* became in effect the program of dialectical materialism (*Diamat*) as a universal Weltanschauung. It was more widely read than *Das Kapital*, has had considerable influence in the present century on all forms of social democracy, and became the classical philosophical textbook of the whole communist movement. With reference to the critique of religion, Engels went beyond Marx in two respects:

he looked for support from the *natural sciences*, regarding theories such as that of the conservation of energy and especially Darwin's discovery of the evolution of species as a splendid confirmation of Marx's discovery of the law of the material evolution of society;

he looked for support from the *history of religion*, regarding ethnological studies on primitive religion as helpful in confirming historical materialism.

It may be useful by way of illustration to quote here an exceptionally long passage in which Engels attempts to describe the historical development of religion on the basis of historical materialism (we shall stress the particular phases by breaking down the passage into paragraphs and by making use of italics).

"All *religion*, however, is nothing but the fantastic reflection in men's minds of those external forces which control their daily life, a reflection in which the terrestrial forces assume the form of supernatural forces. In the *beginnings of history* it was the *forces of nature* which were first so reflected, and which in the course of further evolution underwent the most manifold and varied personifications among the various peoples. This early process has been traced back by comparative mythology, at least in the case of the Indo-European peoples, to its origin in the Indian Vedas, and in its further evolution it has been demonstrated in detail among the Indians, Persians, Greeks, Romans, Germans and, so far as material is available, also among the Celts, Lithuanians and Slavs.

"But it is not long before, side by side with the forces of nature, *social forces* begin to be active—forces which confront man as equally alien and at first equally inexplicable, dominating him with the same apparent natural necessity as the forces of nature themselves. The fantastic figures, which at first only reflected the mysterious forces of nature, at this point acquire social attributes, become representatives of the forces of history.

"At a still further stage of evolution, *all the natural and social attributes of the numerous gods* are transferred *to one almighty god*, who is but a reflection of the abstract man. Such was the origin of monotheism, which was historically the last product of the vulgarized philosophy of the later Greeks and found its incarnation in the exclusively national god of the Jews, Jehovah. In this convenient, handy and universally adaptable form, religion can continue to exist as the immediate, that is, the sentimental form of men's relation to the alien, natural and social, forces which dominate them, so long as men remain under the control of these forces. However we have seen repeatedly that in *existing bourgeois society* men are dominated by the economic conditions created by themselves, by the means of production which they themselves have produced, as if by an alien force. *The actual basis of the reflective activity that gives rise to religion therefore continues to exist, and with it the religious reflection itself.* And although bourgeois political economy has given a certain insight into the causal connection of this alien domination, this makes no essential difference. Bourgeois economics can neither prevent crises in general, nor protect the individual capitalists from losses, bad debts and bankruptcy, nor secure the individual workers against unemployment and destitution. It is still true that man proposes and God (that is, the alien domination of the capitalist mode of production) disposes.

"Mere knowledge, even if it went much further and deeper than that of bourgeois economic science, is not enough to bring social forces under the domination of society. What is above all necessary for this, is a social *act*. And when this act has been accomplished, when *society, by taking possession of all means of production and using them on a planned basis*, has freed itself and all its members from the bondage in which they are now held by these means of production which they themselves have produced but which confront them as an irresistible alien force; when therefore man no longer merely proposes, but also disposes—only then *will the last alien force which is still reflected in religion vanish; and with it will also vanish the religious reflection itself*, for the simple reason that then there will be nothing left to reflect."[70]

This view of history and religion has repeatedly been compared to the three-stage scheme of the French positivist Auguste Comte: from the religious-fictive by way of the abstract-metaphysical to the scientific-positive (atheistic) world view.[71] In its arguments against religion, this Marxism is in fact largely in agreement with positivism. But, since the traditional Church and theology had either fought against or ignored natural science and its conclusions, it was easy for Engels and after him—for instance—Karl Kautsky, the distinguished Austrian social democrat, and finally also for Lenin, to appeal to natural science and especially to Haeckel's materialistic theory of evolution, rather than Darwin's, in order to oppose the Marxist Weltanschauung as "science" to "unscientific" religion. At the same time, Engels himself had stressed the parallels between proletarian socialism and primitive Christianity,[72] and the "proletarian philosopher," Joseph Dietzgen, a friend of Marx and Engels, had commended socialism itself as the "new religion": "Yes, *social democracy is the true religion, the only saving Church*, in as much as it strives after the common goal, no longer by way of fantasy, no longer with petitions, desires, sighs, but in a real and effective way, really and truly, by the social organization of manual and mental work. . . . Social democracy lives in *faith* in the victory of the truth, in *hope* of redemption from material and mental bondage, in *love* for men's equality."[73]

Here it becomes clear how much the Marxist Weltanschauung serves in practice as *an atheistic substitute for religion or an atheistic substitute religion*. At the same time, the content of this explicitly materialistic Weltanschauung agrees to a surprising extent with the likewise materialistic and not (as required by the scheme of historical materialism) idealistic Weltanschauung of the "bourgeoisie."

But while Marx (and also positivism) assumed that religion would become superfluous simply as a result of social developments, later Marxists, no longer so sure of this, have actively fought against religion as a hostile Weltanschauung. It was above all Vladimir Ilyich Ulyanov, better known as *Lenin*, whose unhappy experiences of state and religion in Czarist Russia (his brother Alexander had been executed in connection with the murder of Czar Alexander II on March 1, 1881: an event that deeply shook Lenin) had filled him with an indescribable hatred for everything religious, who argued and agitated most vigorously against religion. For him, religion was no longer, as it had been for Marx, "opium of the people," to which the people abandoned themselves to alleviate their misery. Religion for Lenin was—more on the lines of the pre-Marxist Enlightenment—"opium *for* the people" (deliberately handed out by the rulers): "Religion is opium for the people. Religion is a kind of spiritual intoxicant, in which the slaves of capital drown their humanity, and blunt their desire for a decent human existence. But a slave who has become conscious of his slavery, and who has risen to the height of fighting for his emancipation, has half-ceased to be a slave. The class-conscious worker of today, brought up in the environment of a big factory, and enlightened by town life, rejects religious prejudices with contempt. He leaves heaven to the priests and bourgeois hypocrites. He fights for a better life for himself, here on earth."[74]

Even at that time, then, Lenin had demanded from his supporters a coherent atheistic Weltanschauung. As far as the state is concerned, religion is indeed a private affair. But it is not at all so for the party, one of the objects of which "is precisely to fight against all religious deception of the workers."[75]

For tactical reasons, however—despite all organized propaganda for it—atheism should not be mentioned at all in the party program itself, nor should it be made elsewhere a main concern. The first thing is not the struggle against religion. What comes first is the class struggle, in which all—Christians and even priests dissatisfied with the regime—are welcome to take part: "A union in that genuinely revolutionary struggle of the oppressed class to set up a heaven on earth is more important to us than a unity in proletarian opinion about the imaginary paradise in the sky."[76]

In his main philosophical work, *Materialism and Empiriocriticism*, Lenin confirmed his view of religion and at the same time rejected any complementation of Marxism by other philosophical trends such as neo-Kantianism, positivism or empiriocriticism. But he was shrewd enough, even after the October Revolution, to tolerate supporters of deviationist ideological trends in important positions in party and government. Nevertheless there could be no doubt about the party line and Lenin's wholly personal view of religion. Nowhere did he express more clearly his decided rejection of Christianity than in a letter in 1913 to the writer Maxim Gorky, who was inclined toward religious socialism (belonging to a group that claimed to be "God-seeking" or "God-creating") and tried to reconcile Marxism with religion: "The 'popular' conception of little gods and of the Divine is the result of 'popular' ignorance, exactly as is the 'popular' conception of the Tsar, of goblins, of dragging wives by the hair. How you can call the 'popular' conception of God a 'democratic' one is absolutely beyond me."[77]

From such a solid verbal rejection of Christianity to a solid practical *persecution* was only a short step. We cannot give an account here of the long trail of suffering the Russian Orthodox Church—which, admittedly, shared the responsibility for the wretched prerevolutionary conditions—and of the Russian Christians which began especially with the regime of Stalin. The question of freedom of religion and human rights is connected with the communist system as a whole. Is this system the realization of that humanism out of which all Marx's thought was developed? Is this the kind of society, which is truly social, for which he had hoped up to the time of his death?

On the Church's side, for a long time only the dangers and not the positive concerns of socialism were recognized. In 1878, Pope Leo XIII published his encyclical *Quod Apostolici Muneris*, against the "plague" of socialism, which was working for the overthrow of society, rejecting all existing laws, all authority, all subordination and inequality, and even the marriage bond and the right of ownership and which must therefore be extirpated.[78] And Marx himself? At that time, he was largely inactive, a sick man, living quietly as a pensioner and moving within a small circle; he had to stay from time to time in health resorts. After his wife's death, in 1881, his life consisted in little more than a chain of sufferings stoically endured, which became even more acute a year later as a result of the death of his eldest daughter. Marx was a broken man and he never recovered. On March 14, 1881, Engels discovered him dead in his armchair.

## 2. *Critique of Marx*

In any critique of Marx and Marxism, we must avoid Christian self-righteousness. Has not Christianity also—contradicting of course its original message—perhaps often become a Weltanschauung manipulated in an absolutist, centralist and even totalitarian way? It has been asserted—and not only by evil tongues—that Soviet communism and Roman Catholicism in particular hate each other so much because they are so much alike. Gustav A. Wetter, former rector of the Pontifical Russian College, in Rome, one of the foremost authorities on communist ideology, as a Catholic theologian has very clearly set out in his well-known book *Dialectical Materialism*[79] the unmistakable phenotypic *resemblances between the Roman Catholic and the Soviet communist systems*.

Like Roman Catholicism, Soviet communism starts out from the assumption that the world is evil and needs "redemption." "Revelation," given in the fullness of time or at the climax of the dialectical development, is recorded also for communists in four canonical texts (Marx, Engels, Lenin and any particular successor). It is preserved, protected and interpreted by the infallible magisterium of the party, by the Holy Office of the politburo and by the supreme, infallible party secretary in person. It is not the function of the individual philosopher to enrich, increase and criticize this body of doctrine but solely to teach people its application to all spheres of life and to take care of "pure doctrine" by unmasking heresies and deviations. The party's infallible magisterium publicly condemns heresies. Once it has spoken, the dissident heretic has to submit, practice self-criticism and recant his errors. If he neglects his duty, he is "excommunicated," shut out. Thus the party proves to be the "pillar and ground of truth," the bulwark of orthodoxy. While on the defensive, this orthodox communism has at the same time an offensive missionary policy. As the sole true and saving doctrine, it strives of its very nature to spread by every means throughout the world, and to send out missionaries everywhere from its propaganda center. Outside it there is no salvation. It demands strict organization, blind obedience, party discipline. Everything is under the great leader, who is almost the object of a cult, venerated with attestations of devotion, with grand marches, parades and pilgrimages to his tomb.[80]

## Background of the sociopolitical critique of religion

Even Karl Marx's atheism must be understood as humanism. A humanism of course that does not consist in abstract postulates like those of Feuerbach, but is to be realized historically in a humane society: *a humanism in the real world*. In later years also Marx continued to strive for a real humanism.

In his mainly philosophical early works, under the influence of Hegel and Feuerbach, Marx uses a more or less *humanistic terminology and form of argument*. In the later works, especially in *Das Kapital*, he argues in economic and political terms and avoids—in order to distinguish his socialism from other forms of socialism—the humanistic terms and phrases which now seem to him ineffectual.

The *humanistic intention*, however, remains. Instead of the inhuman conditions of capitalist society, truly human conditions are to be created. There must no longer be a society where great masses of human beings are degraded, despised, pauperized, exploited; where commodity value is the supreme value, money (as commodity of commodities) is the true God, profit, self-interest and selfishness the motives of action: where—that is—capitalism in practice functions as a substitute for religion. But there must be a society where every human being can be truly human, a free, upstanding, dignified, autonomous being realizing all his potentialities: that is, the end of the exploitation of man by man. The humanity of conditions, of society and thus of man himself—according to Marx, this and nothing else is the point of the revolution by the abolition of division of labor, abolition of private property and dictatorship of the proletariat. This and nothing else is the essence of the classless, communist society of the future, of which Marx gives only a tentative outline: the society where state and religion will wither away. All this amounts to a socialized and democratized humanism or—in fact—a humane socialism and a humane social democracy.

With regard to this sociopolitical program, it may be briefly noted that important *elements of the Marxist theory of society* have also been generally *adopted* even in the West.[81] Everywhere today man is seen not as he was in individualistic liberalism but as a social being. Today our standpoint is very different from that of idealist thought: we concentrate on concrete sociological reality, which has to be changed, on the actual alienation of man in inhuman conditions, on the necessity of verifying every theory in practice. The central importance of work and the working process for the development of mankind and humanity is appreciated and the influence of economic factors on the history of ideas and ideologies investigated down to the last detail. The world-historical relevance of the rise of the working classes in connection with socialist ideas is recognized also in the West. Even non-Marxists are sensitive to the contradictions and structural injustices of the capitalist economic system and use for their analyses the critical instruments prepared by Marx. Thus the unrestrained economic liberalism of the time of Marx and Engels, "Manchester liberalism," with its *laisser-faire*, for which the satisfaction of wants is a means to the maximization of profits for personal gain and the state is merely a kind of night watchman,* has been largely superseded by more truly social forms of economy and society (admittedly with increasingly powerful state intervention).

Today, wherever there is freedom of criticism and Marxism is not dominant as a dogmatic system, the *weaknesses* are perceived *of the Marxist theory of society and history* to the extent that it claims—as it does unfortunately in all communist states—to be a total explanation of reality and an atheistic Weltanschauung.[82] It is not a "bourgeois" prejudice simply and objectively to observe that Marx was mistaken in his basic assumption that the situation of the proletariat could not be improved without revolution. He did not recognize the new possibilities of the trade union movement, the improvement of working conditions by new technical methods of production, the opportunities of social intervention on the part of the state (welfare state) and all the other things that have improved the real income of the workers and turned them in practice into a bourgeoisie (Marx never made use of wage statistics). With all the (partial) accumulation of capital (by national and multinational concerns), the Marxist idea of a progressive proletarianization of the workers in a gigantic revolutionary reserve army, out of which through a dialectical subversion the revolution would necessarily emerge as the transition to socialism, then to communism and to the realm of freedom—this idea has not been verified in practice. The theory of surplus value (produced by the worker, skimmed off by the capitalist), lying behind this idea—for popular Marxism at least, the cornerstone of the Marxist economy—is still repeated by orthodox Marxists but criticized by other Marxist economists and completely rejected by non-Marxists. The theory of the struggle between two classes has proved to be too simple as a scheme of interpretation of the course of the history of mankind and particularly of the analysis of the complex social stratification of the present time—a proletariat turned bourgeois, persistence of the old middle classes (farmers and peasantry, craftsmen, neglected in Marx's theory) and the emergence of new classes (technicians, managers). The economic theory of history in-

---

* *Nachtwächterstaat*, a word coined by Lassalle to denote a liberal state taking great care not to intervene in economic matters. Translator.

volved in historical materialism rests in fact to a considerable degree on subsequent artificial reconstructions of history and on false assumptions.[83] And this affects not least the problem of religion. Is this very atheism, which claims to be so obvious and so sure of itself, really substantiated?

## Is religion a human fabrication?

It is clear from what we know of Marx's life that what faced him in the first place was the question of God, and only after that the social question. It was not the wretchedness of the proletariat but left-wing Hegelian philosophy which was responsible for his atheism. In other words, his atheism was not based on his socialism or communism but preceded these. His wholly personal view was that the atheistic critique of religion was the presupposition of all criticism. Marx *took over the decisive arguments for his atheism* in substance *from Feuerbach*. He was firmly convinced that with Feuerbach the critique of religion had been completed and atheism solidly established. Marx as critic of religion does not really get beyond Feuerbach as critic of religion, in his substantiation of atheism.

This means, however, when we come to criticize Marxist atheism, that the reasons that had to be cited against Feuerbach's atheism, especially his psychological and historical-philosophical arguments, are valid also against Marx's atheism. And since Feuerbach's atheism has turned out in the last resort to be a hypothesis that is not conclusively proved, Marx's atheism, too, can be seen as a *hypothesis that in the last resort is not conclusively demonstrated.*

Marx of course had asked what lay behind Feuerbach's psychological projection hypothesis and tested it sociopsychologically with reference to its sociological conditions. In this way, he could have given greater depth to his hypothesis from the standpoint of political humanism and political economy. But even he did not thereby provide an independent justification of the projection theory. For Marx had *assumed* this projection theory (apparently irrefutably substantiated by Feuerbach) and asked and then shown how it could be explained politically, humanistically and economically. But it was precisely this atheistic assumption which had proved even with Feuerbach to be in the last resort unsubstantiated.

It is to Marx's indisputable credit to have brought out how much economic changes affect the world; how much the development of technology and of new conditions of production is responsible for the actual alienation of man and especially of the modern wage earner; how great, as a whole, is the influence of economics on the history of ideas and also on the history of religion. But we saw clearly in connection with *Feuerbach* that no conclusion about the existence or nonexistence of God can be drawn from the indisputable influence of *psychological factors* on religion and the idea of God. Consequently there is no need of any further explanation if we say exactly the same with reference to Marx: from the undeniable influence of *economic and sociological factors* on religion and the idea of God, *we can likewise draw no conclusion about the existence or nonexistence of God.*

We may, however, briefly examine what is meant by the saying: "Man makes religion." Marx never defined his concept of religion. It can be admitted that the proposition is true if by religion we mean religious ideas and ways of life: that is, human teachings, dogmas, prayers and hymns, rites and institutions. But is it also true if by religion we mean the essential content, the real concern of religion—that is, God himself? Man produces his own ideas of God (and ideas of the world), but does this mean that God himself (or the world itself) is the product of man's own mind? Does it not mean arguing from the idea of God, not to his existence but to his nonexistence: a kind of ontological argument in reverse?

Certainly man thinks of God, produces his own ideas, images, concepts of God. But this does not prove that God is *merely* a product of human thinking and imagination. Admittedly, ideas of God are the work of man. But this does not prove that God himself is a human fabrication. Admittedly, ideas of God change with economic conditions and in that sense God is a "reflection" of man. But this certainly does not prove that God is no more than an appearance.

Even if it can be proved (and this is easier today than it was in Engels' time) that the image of God in an ancient-Hellenistic, feudal or bourgeois society is essentially Hellenistic, feudalistic or bourgeois in character, color and imprint, it by no means follows that this image is a pure illusion, this notion of God merely a projection, this God a nonentity. Perhaps God is wholly different from all these images and each age proclaims him differently. Nevertheless, he can—perhaps—exist. Or perhaps he really does not exist in fact, but this conclusion cannot strictly be drawn from the influence of economic and social factors on the image of God and the notion of God. *The question*—here, too, the counterargument must not be overstretched in favor of the existence of God—*must consequently remain open.* Marx's atheism, established before any economic critique, likewise proves to be a pure hypothesis, an unproved postulate, a dogmatic claim.

From the very beginning—as is evident from his upbringing and education—Marx was actually never very interested in the nature and self-understanding of religion, of Christianity or of Judaism. All that really interested him—and even then intensely only during his time in Berlin, Paris and Brussels—was the role that religion played in practice in the social process. There was no proportion even then between his slender knowledge of theology, philosophy of religion and history of religion and the enormous implications of his criticism. Otherwise he would himself certainly have pursued the question—which Max Weber and other sociologists of religion later examined closely—as to whether, in addition to all the influence of the economic and sociological basis on the religious "superstructure," there might also be observed conversely an influence of religion on the economic-sociological basis.

Feuerbach had undoubtedly developed his critique of religion far more thoroughly than Marx did with his programmatic but more proclamatory and aphoristic than argumentative utterances. Yet Marx—from the viewpoint of the working classes, exploited also by religion and Church—had the advantage of greater vividness and thus of direct, realistic plausibility. The polished brilliance of his language and the dialectical acuteness of his ideas gained him superiority over friends and foes. His conception of religion in particular was linked with a broad view of history that had drawn its suggestive force less from the study of concrete historical facts than from Hegel's world-historical dialectic, materialistically inverted. A number of questions arise at this point.

Was not Marx so much *under the spell of Hegel* that—for this very reason—the question of substantiating his dialectical and historical materialism simply could not occur to him? Obviously he was content to accept as evidence for its truth the fact that he had succeeded, in connection with Feuerbach, in standing Hegel's massive idealist system "on its head,"[84] turning it into a materialist system: according to him, this was bound to result more or less automatically in the irresistible "process of decomposition of Absolute Spirit," as if overcoming Hegel's philosophy meant *ipso facto* overcoming also belief in God.

Did Marx not feel that he was on the right way simply because he regarded himself as covered by the *sense of time cultivated by the Young Hegelians?* For his atheism, Marx could appeal essentially to Feuerbach and his own practical experiences. It was only decades later that Engels attempted to provide an additional ideological substantiation of something that had been settled irrevocably from the outset.

Marx, then, had not so much rationally substantiated this materialistic atheism as a scientist as proclaimed and announced it as a prophet in scientist's clothing: an odd sentence here and there, the unpublished "German Ideology," a few pages of lengthier commentary from the *Critique of Hegel's Philosophy of Law* and from the *Critique of Political Economy*. Marx rightly recognized how much economic conditions affect the reality of man and the world but also and more particularly of politics, art, literature, science, technology, law, morality, philosophy, religion (known as the "superstructure"). But he was wrong to make out of this an ideological economism: making the economic aspect absolute as a total explanation of reality, which cannot be consistently maintained any more than the *a priori* constructed "necessary" system of idealism, which he merely reversed. Thus in the last resort the Utopian revolutionary always turned out to be stronger in Marx than the realistic scientific analyst. And this is especially true of the picture he outlined of the future: a future without religion.

## Future without religion?

Acute and realistic as Marx's analyses of the society of his own time often were, most of his prognoses for a society of the future soon proved to be distorted, unrealistic and downright false. This we have already seen when considering the background of Marx's critique of religion. Thus his prognoses for the future—particularly of religion—are unbalanced from the outset. We may ask whether here, too, perhaps, revolutionary ideology and a revolutionary will had far too great an influence on Marx's scientific analyses and conclusions.

*What is this future, religionless, socialist society supposed to look like?* According to Marx, certainly not like the paradise on earth of which Lenin spoke, nor like a land of milk and honey without existential human problems. But certainly it must be a kingdom of freedom and of human self-realization, where—despite all individual peculiarities—there is in principle no inequality or oppression of human beings, classes and nations, where the exploitation of men by men has come to an end, so that the state can lose its political function as controlling power and religion becomes superfluous.

This is the idea. But it is obvious that, while Marx's diagnosis is often cogent, his therapy is not. In his published works, he refuses to give details about the future. All that seems to interest him is that which is attainable by revolution: the complete abolition of private ownership and of the division of labor and consequently the complete overturning of social conditions. But what then?

Marx discredited socialism as it was before his time—"crude communism"—and its idealist conception of man as utopian, as unrealizable. How could we ever want to change conditions in society without first changing man, without the "new man," able to develop fully his human existence in free, universal activity and to enjoy rational human relationships with other people? But if we then point to all these brilliant analyses of society and ask about these changed sociological conditions themselves, instead of concrete sociopolitical projects, models, plans, and even details, we receive highly abstract, indefinite, vague, in fact *Utopian, effusive answers.*

We find one of these answers in the Paris Manuscripts, which had not been published at the time: "Assuming that we had been engaged as human beings in producing things, each of us in his production would have affirmed himself and the other person in two ways. 1. In my production I would have objectified my individuality, its peculiar character, and consequently both enjoyed an individual expression of life during the activity and experienced in contemplating the object the individual joy of knowing my personality as an objective power visible to the senses and therefore existing beyond all doubt. 2. In your enjoyment or your use of my product I would have had the immediate pleasure of being aware that in my work I had both satisfied a human need and objectified the essence of man and thus provided an object appropriate to the requirements of another human being. 3. For you I would have been the mediator between you and the human race, that is, I would have been known and perceived by you yourself as an extension of your own being and as a necessary part of yourself: in other words, I would know that I had been authenticated both in your thought and in your love. 4. In my individual expression of life I would have created directly your expression of life, that is, in my individual activity I would have authenticated and realized immediately my true nature, my human, my common nature. Our products would thus be so many mirrors in which our nature would find a reflection of itself."[85]

There is a passage in *The German Ideology*, also unpublished at the time, where the unrealistic, purely Utopian character of this godless future is made even more clear: "For as soon as the distribution of labour comes into being, each man has a particular, exclusive sphere of activity, which is forced upon him and from which he cannot escape. He is a hunter, a fisherman, a shepherd, or a critical critic, and must remain so if he does not want to lose his means of livelihood; while in communist society, where nobody has one exclusive sphere of activity, but each can become accomplished in any branch he wishes, society regulates the general production and thus makes it possible for me to do one thing today and another tomorrow, to hunt in the morning, fish in the afternoon, rear cattle in the evening, criticise after dinner, just as I have a mind, without ever becoming hunter, fisherman, shepherd or critic."[86]

Even later—admittedly in more general statements—Marx continued to look forward to this Utopia of a new "humane society" in which—as we heard—"the relations between human beings in their practical everyday life have assumed the aspect of perfectly intelligible and reasonable relations as between man and man, and as between man and nature," so that such "religious reflexions of the real world" can disappear.[87] In the *Communist Manifesto* we read: "In place of the old bourgeois society, with its classes and class antagonisms, we shall have an association, in which the free development of each is the condition for the free development of all."[88]

We may wonder how Marx, the realistic analyst, could entertain such unrealistic and optimistic ideas of a Utopian future.[89] The explanation is not simply that the prophetic revolutionary has here taken over from the level-headed scholar. What is perfectly clear is that Marx precisely in his analyses—which were certainly not false—took seriously only the *negative* trends in *capitalism*, radicalized and dramatized these, then extrapolated them into the future, while on the other hand perceiving only the *positive* aspects in *socialism*. In the concrete:

a. According to him, the *development of technology* on the one hand will lead capitalism into a disastrous crisis and on the other hand will put at the disposal of socialism in the large industries ready-made patterns of a highly collectivized planning and control that only need to be adopted by the proletariat in the revolution for enough to be produced—without skimming off the surplus value—to satisfy all needs.

b. But, at the same time, a *change* will take place in man's *moral nature*. As a result of the socialist revolution, the class antagonisms intensified to the extreme in capitalist society and the alienation of man, which is linked with these, will be abolished, and man's nature will be so greatly changed that the new socialist man will voluntarily accomplish as much as he is able to accomplish and at the same time will not demand more than he needs. All this is in accordance with the principle: from each according to his ability, to each according to his need.

In this way, Marx—more like a man of the Enlightenment than of his own day, in his optimistic belief in man as essentially good but spoiled by social influences—was able to develop his ideas of the Utopian future beyond the Utopias of the "Utopian" socialists whom he criticized and who continued to invent new institutions to maintain order. For him,

*the state becomes superfluous*, as a product of the class struggle, disappearing with the class struggles in their last stage, in communism;

*religion becomes superfluous*, as a product and visible expression of economic-social alienation, disappearing likewise with the abolition of alienation.

## Promise without fulfillment?

With regard to religion, a purely hypothetical question must be raised first of all. Marx has analyzed the function of religion within the bourgeois, capitalist society of the nineteenth century. But what is the place of religion in a postbourgeois, socialist society? For Marx it is clear that religion will no longer exist after the abolition of private ownership and class antagonisms in the postbourgeois socialist society. But we must ask then: Is it not an *a priori* risky and little-justified extrapolation to conclude that religion will die out even under completely different social conditions? The other hypothesis never occurs to Marx, namely, the possibility of a new kind of religious and Christian attitude in a postbourgeois socialist society: a possibility that seems to modern Marxists to provide an opportunity even of reconciling Christianity and socialism. The thesis of the dissolution of religion as maintained by Marx is therefore suspect from the outset, as being not a scientific prognosis but an arbitrary assumption. Wishful thinking? But let us examine it more closely.

In his one-sided extrapolation of a stateless and religionless future, Marx has in fact overlooked two factors:

a. A highly developed technology and our highly complicated modern science in particular demand to an increasing extent division of labor, super- and subordination, structuring of society and thus a legal system and the state as guarantor.

b. Even in a communist state, man remains man. His ever-present alienation, weakness and malice are obviously not merely the result of private ownership and the class struggle, and his religion, too, is possibly not the result of his economic-social alienation. To recognize this is not to abandon the struggle for humanity in a society suffering from alienation, but to make it possible to allow from the very outset for the limits that will confront any reform or revolution in man himself. At this point, the question arises: Can man himself make man into man or does it need more than man for this? Does the "kingdom of freedom" come as the kingdom of man's evolutionary or revolutionary self-perfecting or . . . as kingdom of God?

Marx expected the advent of the "kingdom of freedom" in his own time. But in this *"early expectation" he was disappointed*. The collapse of the capitalist system, from which the communist mode of production was expected to emerge in the revolutionary dialectical upheaval, was expected by Marx possibly as early as 1848, then by the fifties, then the seventies, and prophesied by Engels for the turn of the century particularly in the highly industrialized countries (England and Germany). But it did not take place. Significantly enough, the socialist revolution was successful only in backward agrarian countries, supported by intellectuals and peasants—and even then only by violence and terror. In most of the Eastern-bloc states, it is upheld only by Soviet military power.

"Capitalism"—an ambiguous term—despite all the persisting serious defects, has turned out to be open to correction to a large extent. It has not only created empirical social analysis and thus a system of control and correction, but at the same time has effected far-reaching social reforms, beginning with the prohibition of child labor and going on to legal provision for the aged and to various forms of codetermination. The broadest strata of the population were liberated by this "network of social security" from the pressures of poverty and even assured of a formerly unimaginable measure of prosperity. Today we speak of a "social market economy"— a market economy with some state intervention—more appropriately than of "capitalism" (as opposed to a "socialist planned economy").

However that may be, hitherto, neither in the West nor in the East, neither in economic theory nor in political practice, has a different economic and social system been developed that could remove the defects of the market economy without producing other, worse evils. Neither the orthodox centrally planned economy nor a soviet democracy, still less the short-lived and hastily constructed, empty and wishful formulas of individual radicals, have produced any evidence that they are better able to guarantee freedom and democracy, justice and prosperity.[90] Nowhere on the horizon is there any sign of the advent of the free, classless, communist society; nowhere is either the state or religion withering away.

*Nowhere is the state dying out.* The excessive power of the state in the communist society carries a threat that is quite different from that in the Western democracies: in the former, the identification of state and party results in a socialist *étatisme* with state capitalism and a "new class" of party managers at the expense of the working population. There is a sardonic joke passed around widely in the East to the effect that "in capitalism the domination of men by men prevails, but in socialism it is the other way around." Individuals are put off with an appeal to a distant, future happiness of mankind, and in the "meantime" are enclosed in a merciless system, bound by harsh norms of work and achievement to increase production, to fulfill and to overfulfill plans. The newspapers in the "workers' paradise" are filled to satiety with these things. *Before* the communist revolution, it was possible to ask seriously if *religion* was the opium of the people. But now, sixty years *after* the communist revolution has been achieved, we must ask in all sincerity if the *revolution* is the opium of the people.[91]

*Nowhere is religion dying out.* Developments precisely in the socialist states have thoroughly discredited Marx in his Utopian idea—inspired by Feuerbach—of a "fading out of religion" after the revolution. Not being able to trust in such a "decease" of religion, militant, aggressive atheism was accepted into the doctrine and practice of the Communist Party of the Soviet Union and other Communist parties and religion and churches were exposed to the Stalinist terror and the post-Stalinist repression aiming at their extirpation. Stalin's successors have not only not given up but intensified and refined unobtrusively the struggle against religion. The Stalinist antireligious legislation has remained in force, antireligious propaganda has been reorganized, atheistic education intensified: the prohibition of religious instruction of young people even in the parishes remains, atheism is an obligatory subject in the universities and institutes of higher studies, increasing numbers of churches are closed, seminaries for students for the priesthood have been closed down until now only three are left. This *chronique scandaleuse* of the Communist Party of the Soviet Union could easily be continued: a violation of human rights to an extent unparalleled in history. Solzhenitsyn's "Lenten Letter" to the Patriarch of Moscow in 1972[92] testifies to the persistently grave situation of Christians in the Soviet Union; it is the same with the letter of the two Russian Orthodox priests to the Plenary Assembly of the World Council of Churches in Nairobi in 1975, which—without naming the culprits—

finally stirred the Council to react to the situation of Christians in the Soviet Union but which drew down on the priests personally immediate punitive measures.

Nevertheless, over sixty years after the October Revolution, after indescribable persecutions and both direct and indirect vexations of churches and individuals, Christianity is more a growing than a declining factor in the Soviet Union. According to the latest (perhaps exaggerated) statistics, every third Russian (Russians represent about half of all Soviet citizens) and every fifth adult Soviet human being is said to be in one form or another a practicing Christian.[93] The Soviet society is certainly not the socialist society that Marx expected.

"There is scarcely anything which has been declared dead as often as religion," says Thomas Luckmann, the sociologist of religion: "Certainly different religions have come and gone in the course of the history of humanity. But in all societies from the most primitive to the most modern there have been systems of symbols, given social form, more or less fixed, more or less obligatory, which linked the world orientation, the authorization of natural and social institutions and interpretations transcending the individual (related, for example, to the family or clan) with practical instructions on the conduct of life and personal obligations—admittedly with doses varying at different times. Religion in *this* sense, as 'social product,' as 'awareness of transcendence emerging from real knowledge,' to adopt two of Marx's phrases relating to religion—has been wrongly declared dead. Religion in *this* sense is evidently not—as Marx assumed—linked to a particular form of society."[94]

For us, of course, there arises at this point the further question: Have we said all that is to be said today about Marx and religion?

### 3. Critique of the critique

Marx's atheism appears to be no more substantiated than Feuerbach's. But does this dispose of his critique of religion? Not at all. It contains too much that is true. Instead, then, of regarding it as an interim stage, easy to see through and to pass through, it is better to regard it as a warning dark shadow continually accompanying belief in God.

### What is left of Marx's critique of religion?

The far-reaching *justification of Marx's critique of religion* becomes clear from the course of our previous reflections. We saw in connection with Pascal[95] how much even committed Christians at a time of continual political misuse of religion in the interest of naked power have been concerned more with men's individual needs than with their social wretchedness. Is it not true that theology and Church have been more interested in the baseness and sinful state of the individual than in the degradation, enslavement and impoverishment of whole classes? That they felt more committed to a socially irrelevant love of neighbor than to political enlightenment and activity? Did we not have to point to the fact that the failure especially of the Catholic Church in face of sociopolitical problems—which were met at best with pious phrases, almsgiving and individual acts of charity—discredited belief in God at an early stage and that in the French Revolution atheism became a political program for the first time in world history: a politically motivated militant atheism, at first bourgeois, liberal and later proletarian-socialist in character?

And did not Christianity in the nineteenth and even in the twentieth centuries display a one-sidedly bourgeois character? Did not the ruling religion largely appear to be the religion of the ruling classes? Did it not consist in consoling people with promises of the hereafter, in distorting consciousness, in adorning chains with flowers instead of breaking them? Did not the official churches in the nineteenth century frequently capitulate before social problems? We must not deceive ourselves: this is not by any means merely a matter of historical reminiscence. Even at the Catholic Synod in Germany in 1975 there was a very serious debate as to whether the Church at that time was capitulating before the labor question.[96]

We would largely have to agree with Marx, not in regard to "social principles" in general but certainly in regard to a number of historical expressions of Christianity—he had in mind particularly the Prussian state church—when, in answer to an article on social reform by the Magdeburg consistorial assessor H. Wagener, he wrote on September 12, 1847, in the *Deutsche-Brüsseler Zeitung*:

"The social principles of Christianity have now had eighteen hundred years in which to be developed and need no further development by Prussian consistorial councillors.

"The social principles of Christianity justified slavery in antiquity, glorified medieval serfdom and can be used likewise in an emergency to defend—albeit with some show of regret—the oppression of the proletariat.

"The social principles of Christianity preach the necessity of a ruling and an oppressed class and offer the latter only the pious hope that the former will be benevolent.

"The social principles of Christianity place in heaven the consistorial council's compensation for all infamies and in this way justify the persistence of these infamies on earth.

"The social principles of Christianity explain all mean tricks played by the oppressors on the oppressed either as just punishment for original sin and other sins or as trials which the Lord in his infinite wisdom imposes on the redeemed.

"The social principles of Christianity preach cowardice, self-contempt, degradation, servility, humility, in a word, all the qualities of the rabble, while the proletariat will not submit to being treated as a rabble and regards its courage, its self-confidence, its pride and its sense of independence as far more necessary than its food.

"The social principles of Christianity are servile and the proletariat is revolutionary."[97]

*The Communist Manifesto* had been published in 1848, but it was only in 1891 that the first papal encyclical on the social question—Leo XIII's *Rerum Novarum*—appeared. "Forty years too late," as someone said, making use of the title of the second social encyclical, Pius XI's *Quadragesimo Anno* (1931). But the Protestant churches in Germany for the most part began to face the problem at an even later stage. They were largely socially paralyzed by the caesaropapist state-church establishment, with its association of throne and altar; by the involvement of religion, politics and industry in the rise of capitalism; by political-religious education for such civic virtues as peace and order, against any change of the supposedly God-given social system; by the individualistic orthodox-pietist idea of religion as a matter of saving souls; by the idealist theology of the intellectuals, uninterested in the real requirements of life. Thus the Protestant Church and theology likewise scarcely recognized the importance of industrialization, the epoch-making rise of the proletariat and the urgency of the social question.

All this of course disregards the exceptions, both Catholic and Protestant, which stood out precisely because of their rarity and marginal character and are frequently recalled today in order to cover up the social failure of the churches and of theology at the time.[98] Certainly even Marx could not overlook the slowly growing awareness of social responsibility particularly within the Catholic Church, with its greater freedom from state control (but soon to be involved in the *Kulturkampf* of the seventies). Two decades after the Brussels article, under the influence of a journey through Germany in autumn 1869, in a letter to Engels he notes with some irritation: "On this tour through Belgium, followed by a stay in Aachen and a journey up the Rhine, I have become convinced that the clergy, especially in the Catholic districts, must be vigorously attacked. I shall work for this through the International. The dogs (for example, Bishop Ketteler in Mainz, the clergy at the Düsseldorf Congress, and so on) are toying where they think fit with the labour question. We worked for them in fact in 1848, but they enjoyed the fruits of the revolution in the period of reaction."[99]

This quotation shows indirectly that *Marx's critique of religion, however well justified, was one-sided*. Marx never seriously came to terms with the biblical understanding of God and man and with the message of Jesus Christ and consequently was not at all familiar with the "social principles of Christianity" (he was even inclined to think that the first Christian communities practiced cannibalism when they met for the eucharist[100]). Hence, in his presentation, Christianity appears as a power ideology determined purely by economic and political interests, with a Church subordinated to the state, justifying all injustice in the here and now with an illusory promise of happiness in the hereafter. What is properly and specifically Christian remained alien to Marx throughout his life. It is possible to see Christianity and the Christian message, being a Christian and even the Christian Church, in a wholly different way.[101] What is certain is that Christianity and its "principles" must not be confused with the ecclesiastical systems of Byzantinism, of medieval Roman Catholicism or of the Protestant state-church establishment. And even there, considerable social achievements must be noted: not only provision for the poor, schools, homes for the aged and orphans, but also even the reclamation by the monasteries of large areas of Central and Eastern Europe, as well as handing down the agricultural methods and the crafts of antiquity, its art, literature and philosophy to the Middle Ages.

Marx, however, drew conclusions about the essence of Christianity and religion from certain patterns of behavior on the part of the clergy, theology and the Church; about the normal situation from undeniably abnormal conditions; about the function of religion as such from its dysfunction. Today, however—and this is to the credit of Marx's critique—no Christian would seriously dispute the following:

Christianity, which has supported the weak with consolation and help, cannot be a cringing, servile morality.

Christianity, which for a long time tolerated ancient slavery and then later Germanic serfdom, by its very nature cannot under any circumstances justify oppression and discrimination.

Christianity, which in the Middle Ages associated with the feudal lords and in the nineteenth century with the rich, can no longer act generally as representative of the interests of those who happen to be in power.

Christianity, which in the nineteenth century did not seriously cope with the social question, cannot in principle be an unsocial institution.

Christianity, which undoubtedly has economic aspects, is not by any means necessarily and exclusively the reflex and product of economic conditions.[102]

Although in his article on Hegel's philosophy of right he had clearly indicated the *function of religion as a protest*, Marx was never interested in analyzing this function. Only his disciples, from Karl Kautsky to Ernst Bloch, did so systematically, in order to take over Christianity and its revolutionary potential in their Marxism. There is undeniably a powerful critical (and "Utopian") undercurrent in the history of Christianity. Christian impulses were of the greatest importance not only for the social betterment of the lower classes in antiquity and the Middle Ages but also for the peasant wars and the rise of the modern industrial society. And as can be seen from Marx's own account, the social reforms that orthodox Marxism—speculating on the impoverishment of the proletariat and on the revolution—opposed in principle were suggested and carried out to a considerable extent by responsible Christian politicians and clerics. The opposition also to a reign of terror like that of National Socialism (and today of communism) was substantially supported by active Christians. Similarly the peace and emancipation movements of the twentieth century (civil-rights movement in the United States, women's movements, national independence in Africa and South America) are largely inspired by practicing Christians. Such impulses for a humane society can renew the face of Christianity also in the future and change it finally "up to recognizability" (to adopt Ernst Bloch's expression). In this connection, the question of the relationship of Marxism to atheism and Christianity becomes so much more pressing. Must Marxism necessarily be atheistic? Can a Christian be a Marxist? Is Marxism at all open to correction?

## Christianity and Marxism

Among neo-Marxists, the attempt has recently been made—as we have seen—to use Feuerbach to correct Marx. According to them, there were elements in Feuerbach—neglected by Marx—that could really provide a *corrective* to a totalitarian and increasingly technocratic Marxism. Even though now sensuousness as such is regarded more as a conservative than an emancipatory force (morality being regarded mainly as an emancipatory force[103]), we can approve the Feuerbach interpretations—for instance —of Alfred Schmidt[104] (and in another respect, of Martin Buber and Karl Löwith) from two viewpoints.

Firstly, Feuerbach's interest in *man's noncognitive powers*, too little considered by Marx: heart, imagination, love. Feuerbach rightly takes man's sensuousness and materiality, the significance of the other person and of human fellowship much more seriously than Marx: as the necessary precondition of a new society and a new freedom.

Secondly, Feuerbach's *positive evaluation of nature apart from man*, which for Marx is merely the object of man's control and the material of social work. Feuerbach rightly sees that nature and freedom are not hostile to one another, and he stresses the reconciliation of man and nature. This is a permanent warning against all excessive self-esteem on the part of the technological society, against the separation of politics and nature, morality and nature, against the utilitarianism of overheated practice, against the destruction of the natural foundations of man's life and the life of human society.

But there remains a *question*, which should in fact be put to both Marx *and* Feuerbach: In order to correct a totalitarian Marxism, in addition to the questions about the individual human being and nature, ought not also the question to be raised afresh about the meaning, ground and support of the whole (man and nature): that is, the question about God? But at this point we can hear the dogmatic response: Marxism is *necessarily atheistic*. Is this true?

It is true of *orthodox Marxism*. For Marx and the classical Marxist authors, Engels, Lenin and Stalin—in their personal life, in their culture, in their system and in their practice—atheism was and remained of central importance and essentially connected with their theory of society and history. In their view, religion and science are two mutually exclusive methods of grasping reality. Hence Lenin writes, with reference to Engels: "If objective truth exists (as the materialists think), if natural science, reflecting the outer world in human 'experience' is alone capable of giving us objective truth, then all fideism is absolutely refuted."[105] It is true that economic alienation precedes religious objective-historical alienation, but the conquest of alienation as a whole must begin with the understanding of religious alienation, that is, with the atheistic critique of religion. "The critique of religion is the precondition of all criticism," wrote Marx; for Lenin, too, the struggle against religion is the "ABC of *all* materialism, and consequently of Marxism."[106] The intellectual proletarian elite that prepares and inaugurates the socialist revolution must be atheist. The atheism of the masses will follow on the economic and political upheaval. Orthodox Marxism is therefore necessarily atheistic. This continues to be the standpoint of both official Soviet Russian Marxism-Leninism and Chinese Maoism.

But is this true also of a *revised Marxism*? A revised Marxism could be nonatheistic if it distinguished between dispensable and indispensable elements. The critique of religion is then no longer the precondition of all criticism. It would then no longer be—as with the classical atheist writers —a central element in Marxism but marginal and open to modification. Such an understanding of Marxism—denounced in Moscow as "revisionist"—is found in fact today even among individual Communist parties, among individual less-orthodox party theorists, and not least in Europe and South America among those forces that are aiming at a practical alliance between Christians and Marxists. The Communist Party of Italy, like other Eurocommunist parties, rejects not only the idea of a Catholic state but also Soviet state atheism—at least for the sake of winning votes—and invites practicing Christians to join the Party, without pressing for a profession of atheistic materialism. Hence today there are differing interpretations of Marxism: in addition to Soviet, Maoist, Spanish or Italian communistic interpretations, there are also social-democratic, existentialist, structuralist; finally, in addition to all atheistic interpretations, there is also a Christian interpretation of Marx. But which is the Marxism of Marx himself?

If we look at the social conditions of the workers especially in the southern—unfortunately mostly Catholic—countries, we can understand why here in particular many active Christians, laymen and priests, support Marxism; why especially in South America there should be a powerful movement of "Christians for socialism"; why in Italy at a meeting of worker-priests (140 in Modena in 1976) the "Internationale" was sung and the "Christ of the Factories" proclaimed as different from the "Christ of the Curia," and so on? Here the failure of the institutional Church and also of the "Christian" parties becomes obvious. Marxism seems to many Christians the one real hope of removing the indescribable social abuses in these countries and of bringing about a more just and humane social order.

Can a *Christian*, then, be a *Marxist*? *Must* he not, indeed, be one?[107] For so many committed Christians even in Central Europe, this "must" is no longer a question. They are even now taking the second step on the way of reconciliation of Christianity and socialism, from "dialogue to alliance."[108] Nevertheless, we must again issue a warning against hastily drawing the wrong conclusions.[109] In view of the sociopolitical and theological complexity of the problems in various countries and continents, an answer to this explosive question—if it is both theologically and politically justified—today more than ever must involve careful distinctions. The answer will have to be very differently phrased in the light of the situations in the particular countries or political blocs: it will have to be different in the socialist countries from what it is in the countries of the Western world and again different there from what it is in the Third or Fourth World.[110]

A guideline may be helpful here. We have already seen how essential elements of the Marxist theory of society were accepted even in the West as independent of Marxist atheism, while other elements have turned out to be questionable even in the East. The longer we think about it, the more clearly total rejection or total acceptance is seen to be a false choice. In the last resort, the answer to the question depends on the exact definition of what one understands by "Marxism." "Marxism" is sometimes understood simply as a social science with a generally positive trend or as ethical, economic, communal, "revolutionary" humanism, which does not exclude belief in God.[111] Free democratic socialism (continental social democracy, the British Labour Party) emerged in the form of "revised" socialism as a result of the division in socialism that started in the 1890s (with Eduard Bernstein, following Lassalle rather than Marx). This represented a moderate trend as opposed to the radical, communist trend, turning away from the Marxist promises of the future to a practical social policy for the present time. At the same time, there was a change of attitude to the class struggle, private property and nationalization, and also to the materialist conception of history and its determinist theory of the inevitability of the historical process. Here atheism is abandoned as a party doctrine and numerous practicing Christians collaborate in these "socialist" parties.

A *social commitment* is required of the Christian in any case, even if no particular solution or party can be prescribed for him. We are not going to defend either socialism or capitalism here, still less to produce propaganda for a definite party. But two things must be clearly stated by way of a conclusion (regardless of any unpopularity to left or right): *a Christian can be a socialist* (against the "right"), *but a Christian is not bound to be a socialist* (against the "left"). In other words, a Christian has various political options. He can take quite seriously his commitment to social justice and yet need not see the remedy in the *nationalization* of industry, rural economy and where possible also of education and culture —which is what is meant by socialism in the strict sense. As a Christian, he can also favor a market economy with a measure of state intervention. But, whatever his attitude to these questions, a person will in any case be taken seriously as a Christian only if Christ and not Marx is for him the ultimate, decisive authority in such questions as class struggle, use of force, terror, peace, justice, love.[112]

Certainly on all these questions not only can Christians learn from Marxists, but Marxists can also learn from Christians. What has been openly discussed for a long time in Western Marxism cannot simply be passed over in silence today even in Eastern Marxism-Leninism. The question, for instance, of the *meaning of life, and other "moral" questions,* are discussed today even in certain Soviet publications. Dogmatic Marxism-Leninism sees the meaning of life in work, militant solidarity and dialogic existence, which are supposed to lead to the development of personality, to moral contentment and to a human happiness that is admittedly beyond our control. But vis-à-vis ultimate questions of meaning, vis-à-vis the question of dying and death—the point at which there is an end of all perfecting of personality and of all happiness—this dogmatic Marxism-Leninism in the last resort seems incapable of offering the individual a conception of the sense of life, free of internal contradictions and humanly stimulating, going beyond all contingent happiness.[113] The meaning given generally by the communist society (progress, nationalization, humanization, classless society) obviously cannot replace the meaning of individual life.

Hence orthodox Marxism-Leninism—as a comprehensive atheistic Weltanschauung, as we saw more a product of Engels and Lenin than of Marx—is still committed to atheism as to an infallible dogma that is absolutely binding for the programs of by far the most Communist parties. But the attempt is being made not only in Italy, Spain, France and South America to detach Marxist theory from atheistic ideology. Even in the Eastern states, the successes and failures of Marxism have led to new forms—not foreseen by Marx—of specifically class alienation of the individual being reflected openly or secretly in socialist society. Such progressive Eastern Marxists as the Pole Adam Schaff[114] and the Czech Milan Machovec[115] (the latter, of course, reduced to silence after the "Prague Spring") have discussed even the "private" questions, formerly suppressed with the aid of economic pressures, with which religion was and presumably will remain competent to deal: the questions of personal guilt and personal destiny, of suffering and death, justice and love on the part of the individual and in the last resort also of mankind as a whole, the question of its ultimate whence and whither. All these are questions to which it is scarcely possible to give a satisfactory answer from the standpoint of an atheistic, materialistic Weltanschauung.

## Verification in practice

It is not necessary to be a Marxist in order to see that there is a limit to all rational arguments against the Marxist critique of religion: a limit is imposed by practice.
However effectively we prove that religion is not simply opium of the people, when this is the way it works in practice all arguments are of little use.
However clear our exposition that religion does not simply reflect the conditions of earthly domination, when it does so in fact all exposition is of little help.
However well we establish the principle that God cannot be understood as guarantor of existing social injustice, when he is in fact invoked as such all theology to the contrary is of little use.
Positively this means—and according to Marx, this, too, is a matter of theology—that *the truth of belief in God must be proved, tested, verified in practice*. It must be proved in practice that religion is not opium, that it does not serve earthly power or sanction injustice. A merely theoretical, meditative argument without practical criticism and change of existing conditions is without probative force.
For the Christian belief in God in particular, this means that there must be practical proof
that Christian faith has social-ethical potential and social-critical relevance,
that Christianity requires a readiness for change and active commitment,
that the expectation of the kingdom of God does not exclude but includes the emancipation of the weary and heavily burdened.
In this way, Christian faith can enter into peaceful competition with the atheistic Weltanschauung of Marxism. As the well-known expert on Marxism Iring Fetscher expresses it:
"1. Against the Marxist thesis that religion always emerges out of social conditions in which man is a wretched and enslaved being and which for

individuals remains opaque, unintelligible, the Christian answer can be: 'Very well, then, let us settle it by a wager, in Pascal's sense. We *know* that religion is something more than a mere consequence of human misery and the lack of transparency of social relationships; but, if you are sure that the situation is different, then *prove* that religion dies out *automatically* when optimal (or "ideal") social conditions are created, in which all men can be made happy. But in that case you must not weaken the probative force of this empirical argument by proceeding *directly* against believers and their Church with all possible kinds of social and political pressures. The Church will not oppose efforts to establish conditions of true justice and freedom. On the contrary. . . .'

"2. As against the *later Marxist critique of religion*, however, contemporary theology and epistemology can produce convincing arguments. It can be shown that Christian faith is by no means tied to a medieval world picture, that modern theology does not impose any limits to scientific research, but simply declares its concern for the interests of man and his personal dignity in face of an unscrupulous use of scientific knowledge. At the same time, we can point to the understanding of science on the part of practically all the important contemporary scientists, who are well aware how little science is able to answer questions about the meaning of human existence, about the value of life and about our moral duties."[116]

The first group of problems—Christian faith and the modern world picture—has already been discussed in detail here.[117] But the second needs a closer investigation. For science has not always been aware of its exact limits. In the last years of the lives of Marx and Engels, natural science did indeed seem to be becoming increasingly a new, atheistic Weltanschauung. And this was the assumption with which Sigmund Freud began his epoch-making studies and enlarged the critique of religion by a further dimension: the psychoanalytic.

# III. God—an infantile illusion? Sigmund Freud

After the failure of the political revolution of 1848, it was Feuerbach who prophesied another—successful—revolution, which would be accelerated by the natural sciences, the radical, corrosive, destructive natural sciences —especially chemistry. Although reactionary governments with their limited range of vision had not noticed the fact, the natural sciences had "long before dissolved the Christian Weltanschauung in nitric acid."[1] The philosopher, himself drawn to the natural sciences but continually coming back to theology, insisted that philosophy should be linked no longer with theology but with natural science. After a hymn of praise to Copernicus, the "first revolutionary of modern times,"[2] he recommended Jakob Moleschott's chemical study *Lehre der Nahrungsmittel. Für das Volk* ("Theory of Foodstuffs. For the People"). It was Moleschott, together with Karl Vogt and Ludwig Büchner among other young scientists, supported by Feuerbach's philosophical critique of religion and immortality, who brought to fruition in the nineteenth century a specifically *natural-scientific materialism.*

Hegel and Schelling's speculative, idealist philosophy of nature was finally superseded by exact, inductive research in the laboratories. German idealism had played down the importance of the materialistic projects of Democritus and Lucretius in antiquity, of La Mettrie and Holbach at the time of the French Enlightenment, but these projects now found approval also in Germany, particularly among natural scientists. And the tempestuous development of the natural sciences, together with their subsequent technicalization and industrialization in France, England and Germany, seemed to confirm materialism at every stage. The attempt to produce a primary organic material (uric acid) from inorganic materials had already succeeded (F. Wöhler in 1828). Experiments on animals also proved the dependence of mental processes on bodily functions.

In the year 1854—the same year Pius IX, in Rome, defined Mary's immaculate conception—at the "thirty-first assembly of German natural scientists and doctors in Göttingen" an open conflict broke out, a conflict that was not, however, on a high philosophical or scientific level. This was the famous *"materialism controversy,"* between the medical specialist Rudolf Wagner, working in the field of anatomy and physiology, and the physiologist Karl Vogt. Wagner wanted to defend by philosophical and theological arguments the descent of all men from a single pair of human beings and also the existence of a special, invisible, weightless "soul substance," against recent physiological theories.[3] When attacked, Vogt sharply discounted the traditional conception under the heading Blind Faith and Science,[4] assuming on the other hand that there were several original human couples and comparing the relationship between brain and thought to that between liver and bile or between kidneys and urine. A confrontation of this kind—with obscurities, exaggerations, downright errors and even coarseness on both sides—would scarcely be possible in a debate today. But who was right at the time?

## 1. *Psychoanalytic atheism*

To the general public then, it seemed that the materialists had won the battle. After the controversy, it was clear that religious persuasions had no place in questions of natural science or medicine. The interconnection of mechanical and natural laws had to be investigated to the very end, without philosophical or theological reservations; there was no activity of consciousness without cerebral activity, no soul existing independently of the body; religion had nothing to do with science and—if it counted at all—was a private affair. Two years before the Göttingen discussion, the physiologist Moleschott had published *Der Kreislauf des Lebens* (The Cycle of Life),[5] and a year after it, in 1885, Ludwig Büchner, a doctor, produced his *Kraft und Stoff* ("Force and Matter").[6] More than twenty editions of the latter made it the militant bible of the new scientific-materialistic world view. According to Büchner, the world as a whole and also the human mind are explained by the combined activity of materials and their forces. God is superfluous.

A year after the appearance of that book, on May 6, 1856, Sigismund Freud was born (he used the name "Sigmund" continuously after leaving school) in the small Catholic town of Freiberg, in Moravia (now in Czechoslovakia), where there were only 2 per cent Protestants and about the same number of Jews.[7]

## From natural scientist to atheist

Leaving Darwin aside for the time being, it was mainly the epoch-making progress of the two basic medical sciences of anatomy and physiology (including pathology) that favored a kind of *medical materialism*. Only a decade after the materialism controversy—during which time the family of the wool merchant Jakob Freud, with the four-year-old Sigmund, had moved to Vienna because of business difficulties and remained in very

cramped conditions—Feuerbach, in one if his last works, *Über Spiritualismus und Materialismus* (On Spiritualism and Materialism) praised—
of all people—the Reformer Martin Luther: because the latter had allowed his son Paul to study medicine and so to be in a position to deny
the immortality of the soul. The Reformation was thus seen as the beginning of German materialism. For Feuerbach at any rate it was clear at
this time that the medical man is by nature a materialist.[8]

In fact, medicine in particular was of the greatest importance for materialistic atheism in the second half of the nineteenth century. This
atheism was found not only in the Marxist and non-Marxist workers'
movements but primarily among the "enlightened" bourgeoisie, who had
become increasingly estranged from both the Church and Christianity.
From Feuerbach therefore the way led not only to the Weltanschaauung
of dialectical materialism (Engels, incidentally, opposed Büchner's mechanistic, undialectical materialism) but also—by way of mechanistic or
even materialistic medicine—to Sigmund Freud's psychoanalysis. The fact
is also important that Feuerbach upheld the fundamental significance of
human sexuality and openly denounced idealistic-spiritualistic psychology,
with its corresponding prudery: this, too, contributed substantially to the
breakdown of the considerable inhibitions preventing the scientific and
medical investigation of sexuality.

According to Ernest Jones, Freud's student and author of a three-
volume biography running to more than fifteen hundred pages, the boy
"grew up devoid of any belief in a God or Immortality, and does not appear to have felt the need of it."[9] This is a surprisingly sweeping statement for which Jones, who sometimes goes on at great length about the
most trivial details concerning his hero, can produce no evidence. In fact,
all that he has himself to say about the young Freud's attitude to religion
proves the opposite: "Freud himself was certainly conversant with all Jewish customs and festivals."[10]

Sigmund's father, Jakob Freud, a patriarchal figure, had been educated
as an orthodox Jew and, despite his liberal, aloof attitude to Jewish tradition, unlike Karl Marx's father was never converted to Christianity.
When he was seventy-five, he gave his son a Bible for his thirty-fifth
birthday, with an inscription in Hebrew:

"My dear Son
"It was in the seventh year of your age that the spirit of God began to
move you to learning. I would say the spirit of God speaketh to you:
'Read in My book; there will be opened to thee sources of knowledge of
the intellect.' It is the Book of Books; it is the well that wise men have
digged and from which lawgivers have drawn the waters of their knowledge.
"Thou hast seen in this Book the vision of the Almighty, thou hast
heard willingly, thou hast done and hast tried to fly high upon the wings

of the Holy Spirit. Since then I have preserved the same Bible. Now, on your thirty-fifth birthday I have brought it out from its retirement and I send it to you as a token of love from your old father."[11]

Freud's mother called down the blessing of the Almighty on her son when he set up in practice, but Jones implies only that she "preserved some belief in the Deity."[12] Nevertheless it was she who instructed him in the Jewish faith. Such instruction of course might be of very dubious value, as is clear from Freud's later recollection: "When I was six years old and was given my first lessons by my mother, I was expected to believe that we were all made of earth and must therefore return to earth. This did not suit me and I expressed doubts of the doctrine. My mother thereupon rubbed the palms of her hands together—just as she did when making dumplings, except that there was no dough between them—and showed me the blackish scales of *epidermis* produced by the friction as a proof that we were made of earth."[13]

In any case, Freud himself admits that reading the Bible had made a strong impression on him as a young man: "My deep engrossment in the Bible story (almost as soon as I had learnt the art of reading) had, as I recognized much later, an enduring effect on the direction of my interest."[14] Professor Hammerschlag, who had taught him biblical history and Hebrew, remained throughout his life the most important of his older friends and one of the few "of whom Freud has no word whatever of criticism, and Freud was not sparing in this."[15]

Present-day psychoanalysts, however, will scarcely be able now to find out how far experiences in early childhood and the very complicated family relationships influenced the religious attitude of little Sigmund. It should be observed that, after the death of his first wife, by whom he had two children, Freud's father, Jakob Freud, at the age of forty (and already a grandfather) married a Jewish girl who was not yet twenty. A year later, she brought Sigmund into the world as the first of her eight children. Freud was an uncle from his birth onward, his playmate, almost the same age and the stronger of the two, being his nephew, son of his half brother Emanuel and grandson of Jakob. Forty years later, after the death of his father, Freud's unsparing selfanalysis revealed the peak of a neurosis: an unconscious jealousy of and aversion to his father, who personified for him authority, refusal and compulsion; at the same time a passion for his youthful mother; in a word, what he called an Oedipus complex. From then onward, in order to prevent further children, he rigorously avoided all sexual activity. This fact led not a few of his critics to attribute his evaluation of sexuality to "sexual congestion."[16] In any case, he himself attributed his unshakable self-confidence, his inner security, to his relationship with his mother: "If a man has been his mother's undisputed darling he retains throughout life the triumphant feeling, the confidence in success, which not seldom brings actual success along with it."[17]

Two kinds of "antireligious" experiences, however—like his aversion to music—made a deep impression on Freud at an early age: his experiences of ritualism and of anti-Semitism.

Experiences of Catholic *ritualism:* the old nanny, efficient and strict, who looked after him during his earliest years, was a Czech Catholic who implanted in the small boy Catholic ideas of heaven and hell, probably also of redemption and resurrection, and used to take him with her to Mass in the Catholic church. At home afterward he would imitate the liturgical gestures, preach and explain "God's doings."[18] Could this have been the source of Freud's later aversion to Christian ceremonies and doctrines? At any rate it cannot be accidental that his first essay on religion, in 1907, bore the title "Obsessive Actions and Religious Practices."[19] There he describes "obsessional neuroses as a pathological counterpart of the formation of a religion" and—conversely—religion itself "as a universal obsessional neurosis."[20]

Experiences with Catholic *anti-Semitism:* Freud considered himself a Jew and was proud of the fact. But he had to suffer for this, although he was quite clearly first in his class at secondary school and rarely had to face tests there. As an outsider at primary and secondary school, his position was similar to that of Karl Marx: he had only a few non-Jewish friends; humiliations of all kinds at the hands of anti-Semitic "Christians" were his daily lot. He would have preferred, like his nephew John, to be educated in the more liberal atmosphere of England. But he lost much of his respect for his father when he learned at the age of twelve that Jakob Freud had simply swallowed the insult when a boy had thrown his new fur cap into the mud and shouted: "Get off the pavement, Jew."[21] Such experiences unleashed in Freud feelings of hatred and revenge at an early date and made the Christian faith completely incredible for him. It was no better at the university: "Above all, I found that I was expected to feel myself inferior and an alien because I was a Jew. I refused absolutely to do the first of these things."[22] He was sixty-nine when he recorded this in his *Autobiography.*

Nevertheless, these negative experiences with religion, however much they discredit Christianity, need not have shaken Freud's (Jewish) faith in God. How did this come about?

When he went to the university, at the age of seventeen, Freud chose his calling only after some hesitation and certainly regardless of economic considerations. Although he had no particular inclination for it, he finally decided to become a doctor. According to his own later admission, this was not the result of a "craving to help suffering humanity" but due to his "need to understand something of the riddles of the world in which we live and perhaps even to contribute something to their solution."[23] Desire for knowledge, then, was the decisive factor: "The most hopeful means of achieving this end seemed to be to enrol myself in the medical faculty; but even after that I experimented—unsuccessfully—with zoology and chemistry, till at last, under the influence of Brücke, who carried more weight with me than anyone else in my whole life, I settled down to physiology, though in those days it was too narrowly restricted to histology."[24] Here he found men whom he "could respect and take as models."[25]

Thus Freud, too, had found his "second father." What Hegel had been for Feuerbach in Berlin, Brücke was in Vienna for Freud. We thus come to the chief promoters of the very successful physical, *mechanistic* physiology, in that school of medicine, led by Helmholtz, that had emerged from a club of young physicists and physiologists in Berlin in the 1840s. They had been for the most part students of the great physiologist Johannes Müller and afterward became lifelong friends, exercising an influence on the researchers of the next twenty or thirty years far beyond Germany: Hermann Helmholtz, Emil Du Bois-Reymond, Carl Ludwig and Ernst Brücke himself, the model of a disciplined, incorruptible, serious natural scientist. Freud remained in Brücke's institute for six years and even then was reluctant to leave it.

Helmholtz, at one and the same time physicist, mathematician and biologist—"one of my idols," said Freud in 1883[26]—at the age of twenty-six had helped to obtain recognition for the law of the conservation of energy, discovered in 1842 by the physician and physicist Robert von Mayer and then given precise expression in a general formula: the sum total of energy remains constant in any isolated system no matter what changes take place in the individual energy components (mechanical, electrical, radiant, chemical). This law of conservation (the first law of thermodynamics) made it possible to assume a unity of all natural forces. Together with the law of entropy (heat can never be totally converted into energy), it is the most fundamental of all laws of nature. It was only now that the mechanistic theory of the human body, sustained by Descartes, was also able to exercise its full influence—but, as earlier with La Mettrie, at the expense of the human mind. The human organism, like inorganic nature, had to be understood from the interplay and transformation of physicochemical forces or energies. Helmholtz—incidentally also inventor of a lens to focus the vessels of the retina (ophthalmoscope) and author of a wide-ranging work on acoustics embracing physics, physiology, psychology and aesthetics—succeeded in measuring the velocity of transmission of stimuli in nerve fibers.

As early as 1842, Du Bois-Reymond, researcher of animal electricity in muscles and nerves, had written: "Brücke and I pledged a solemn oath to put into effect this truth: 'No other forces than the common physical and chemical ones are active within the organism. In those cases which cannot at the time be explained by these forces, one has either to find the specific way or form of their action by means of the physical-mathematical method or to assume new forces equal in dignity to the chemical-physical forces inherent to matter, reducible to the force of attraction and repulsion.'"[27] In this way, physicalist physiology completely got rid of the idealist philosophy of nature (*Naturphilosophie*). And it eliminated all traces of that "vitalism" belonging to the Aristotelian and scholastic tradition which assumed that organisms had been endowed by the Creator with immaterial factors, substantial forms, ends, purposes (entelechies) and therefore with higher plans and ultimate objectives. What was now favored was a purely causal, deterministic explanation in the light of chemical-physical factors (that is, like the artificial production of uric acid, already mentioned).

Psychoanalysis, too, as Freud was to say later, "derives all mental processes . . . from the interplay of forces which assist or inhibit one another, combine with one another, enter into compromises with one another, etc."[28] Dispensing with an anatomical basis, Freud applied principles of this physicalist-physiological science empirically to clinically observed psychological processes, the human psyche being understood as a kind of machine, as a "mental appliance." "Psychic energy" (energic cathexis and countercathexis, influx and discharge of energy, excitation, tension and displacement, and so on) thus became one of Freud's main ideas. In connection with the analysis of dreams as wish fulfillment, he was indeed able to introduce once more the terms "end," "objective," "purpose"; but he did not abandon the deterministic assumptions he regarded as equally valid for psychical and for physical phenomena. For him, then, what appear to be the most obscure and fortuitous mental phenomena are wholly within the world of sense *and* wholly determined.

It is understandable that many people now see the universal panacea for all the sufferings of the time in natural science and not in religion, politics or philosophy. A method of investigation was turned into a Weltanschauung: people "believed" in it. Freud also had an infinite reverence for this science as personified by his teacher, Brücke, and the latter's assistants. He, too, "believed" in it. For him, it meant in any case the transition to atheism, if not for a time even to radical materialism, which, however, such eminent scholars as Du Bois-Reymond and probably also Brücke rejected. But there is no direct evidence of this transition in Freud's own writings. This is odd. Freud, who otherwise relates the most intimate details of his life, does not say a word about this transition to atheism. Did he perhaps resist it? If we want to understand Freud's critique of religion, we must go farther back and trace more precisely his path to psychoanalysis.

## From physiology to psychology

Since Freud did not feel drawn to practical work as a doctor either before or after his examinations (he graduated as a doctor in 1881), he continued his scientific research and laboratory work. The object of his investigations here was the spinal cord of one of the lowest forms of fish. His theoretical work in the physiological institute did not of course provide him with an adequate livelihood. Brücke, therefore, advised him to take up medical practice. For better or worse, from 1882 Freud worked in various departments of the Vienna General Hospital but especially in *neuropathology* with the famous psychiatrist Meynert. But theory continued to be his main interest. While working intermittently at the laboratory of cerebral anatomy and at the children's clinic, he extended his investigations from animal nerve cells and nerve fibers to the human central nervous system. Right up to the 1890s, he published a whole series of works, including, in 1891, the most important of his neurological studies, on brain paralysis in children.[29]

He now obtained what he had sought for so long. From 1885, he had been a nonsalaried teacher (*Privatdozent*) of neuropathology at the University of Vienna. The following year, at the age of thirty, he finally entered private practice as a specialist for nervous disorders. The opening took place on Easter Monday, of all days: an "act of defiance," recalling the Easter feasts with his Catholic nanny, to whom he later ascribed a large part of his psychological difficulties.[30] However that may be, Freud was now finally able to marry, after four years' delay and almost daily correspondence with his distant fiancée (more than nine hundred love letters). The latter was Martha Bernays, from a well-known Jewish family in Hamburg who, however, were not at all happy about a marriage with the impecunious and professionally not very successful and even "pagan" Freud. Freud had to put up with a Jewish marriage rite and to learn the Hebrew texts, despite his lifelong horror of ceremonies—particularly religious ceremonies. Under his influence, however, his wife gave up orthodox Jewish customs, although she never denied her Jewish origins. It was a happy marriage: it bore fruit in three sons and two daughters and formed for Freud a strong counterbalance to the unceasing difficulties in his profession.

There certainly was no lack of these. The anti-Semitic attitude prevailing in Vienna, Freud's glaring failure (afterward concealed) in the matter of the medicinal use of cocaine, finally the increasingly widespread prejudices of his professional colleagues against Freud's unusual discoveries in connection with hysteria and hypnosis (regarded in Vienna from the outset as "unserious" themes, even as "unauthentic" phenomena)—all these formed unsurmountable obstacles to a call to an official teaching post at the university.

Shortly before the opening of his private practice, however, Brücke had enabled him to obtain a travel scholarship to go to the "Mecca of neurology," the Paris nerve clinic under the great Jean Martin Charcot. There he began to take an interest in hysteria (also among men) and hypnosis (as a healing method): the first beginnings of his *investigation of the soul*, the turning from neurology to *psychopathology*. When he returned to Vienna, Freud met with opposition: hysteria in men? hysterical paralyses produced by hypnotic suggestion? No one wanted to believe this. But he began gradually to expand his discoveries to form a method of systematic research.

In 1889, Freud learned from the specialists in Nancy (Liébault, Bernheim) the technique of hypnotic suggestion, but in practice this did not satisfy him any more than experiments with electrotherapy. It was only the experiences of his older medical friend Josef Breuer with an intelligent young woman suffering from hysteria (the famous case of Fräulein Anna O = Bertha Pappenheim) that brought him farther. He began to see and to treat hysteria and its symptoms as products of emotional shocks (traumas). The patient had forgotten, "repressed" them; now the patient had to recall them under hypnotic suggestion in order to "abreact" instead of repressing them. Thus the patient could gradually be healed of the unconscious stimulus (later called a "complex") which had remained untreated, and of his morbid symptoms; but this could not happen without a certain "transference love" for the doctor (not admitted by Breuer at the time. Breuer and Freud called this process the *method of catharsis* (purification).[31]

Freud's transition from physiology to psychology now became increasingly decisive. It was first given shape in 1895 in his "Project of a Psychology"[32] (which was made known only to a Berlin doctor, Wilhelm Fliess): a description of psychological processes but still in purely physiological terminology (as quantifiable states of the nerve cells or "neurons"). Five years later, in *The Interpretation of Dreams*, he described psychological processes still with the aid of numerous individual features and structural characteristics from physiology but without proving the existence of a physical-physiological basis of the clinically observed psychological processes. Freud now increasingly gave a psychological meaning to physiological expressions. For there is a parallelism and interaction between physiological and psychological processes, which had not thitherto been explained.

How did Freud reach this stage? "I was always open to the ideas of G. T. Fechner and have followed that thinker on many important points," wrote Freud in his *Autobiography*.[33] In fact, in his basic psychological ideas, Freud leaned heavily on Fechner, the founder of experimental psychology (who himself derived many of his ideas from the philosopher and psychologist J. F. Herbart).[34] Fechner had at that time produced the only important counterdraft by a natural scientist against the materialism of Moleschott, Vogt and Büchner, and exercised a powerful influence on Freud's teachers, both the physiologist Brücke and the psychiatrist Meynert.

But the more independently Freud made use of the cathartic method in theory and practice, the more he found himself on a different path and became a revolutionary against the traditional dogmas of medicine. He had an unexpected experience, but one that was soon to be confirmed; he found that behind the manifestations of neurosis there are not just any kind of emotional stirrings, but as a rule present or former *sexual disturbances* (not so much actual seductions—a fact he established only at a later date—as sexual fantasies) are secretly at work. Freud went on, consistently, to investigate the sexual life of neurotics—which, again, hardly made his position in Vienna any easier. The consequences included the loss of a number of patients, the universal criticism of his professional colleagues, and especially the break in the twenty-year friendship with Breuer (1895), now compensated by his intense friendship with the above-mentioned Wilhelm Fliess.

## The realm of concealed wishes

Very much later, Freud was to make a critical analysis of religion, which would render him even more suspect in Catholic Vienna. He would ask about the sources of the inner strength of religious ideas. And his answer would be that they "are not precipitates of experiences or end-results of our thinking," but "illusions, fulfilments of the oldest, strongest and most urgent wishes of mankind. The secret of their strength lies in the strength of those wishes."[35] If we are not to misunderstand this basic answer of Freud to the question of the essence of religion, we must keep clearly in mind his new insights into the human psyche and also into the meaning of wishing. It is not only or even primarily a question of conscious wishes, of human consciousness. We are now coming close to what is really the essence of psychoanalysis.

Freud had discovered the dynamism of the human psyche, the interplay of forces especially of that mental stratum, often scarcely noticed and by some people completely denied, that is not accessible to direct knowledge: the unconscious, at first completely dark and—by comparison with conscious mental life—apparently arbitrary and unaccountable. His main insight was that all psychical activity is at first unconscious. Here we have the "primary" psychic processes; the conscious processes, on the other hand, are "secondary." Freud's epochal achievement, after infinite pains, was to make the *unconscious*—thitherto (in Romanticism, for instance) more suspected than investigated—*the object of methodical, scientific exploration* (distinguishing between the preconscious and the unconscious properly so-called, and very much later among the various agencies or systems of the psyche: ego, id, superego).

Freud discovered that, in the normal case, unconscious, repulsive instinctual impulses are rejected by consciousness, by the ego, after a more or less intense conflict: its energy is withdrawn or discharged. But, in certain cases, these instinctual impulses are not even brought into the conflict. Rejected by the ego from the outset through a primary defense mechanism, they are shifted, *repressed*—the sum total of energy remaining constant—with their full energy cathexis, into the unconscious. This

results in substitute satisfaction in the form of dreams or even bodily neurotic symptoms.

The task of *therapy*, therefore, is not simply to abreact the traumatic or
neurotic affects, but to expose them as repressions. They are to be raised
up into consciousness and, as a result of the collaboration of patient and
therapist, to be replaced by judgments that may mean the acceptance or
rejection of the previously rejected instinctual impulses. Thus Freud had
found his different path. It was to lead to the cure of mental illnesses by
laying bare unconscious, untreated traumatic experiences and affects, but
no longer as a result of hypnotic exploration ("reconnoitering" the psyche
in a state of hypnosis), which was often unsuccessful, nor (as Freud had
at first attempted) as a result of pressure and insistent interrogation on
the part of the therapist, but as a result of *the patient's own "free association."* This means that the patient is to say completely honestly everything—really everything—that comes into his mind at the moment, while
he is avoiding any deliberate objectives. What is repressed can thus be
brought into consciousness despite the resistance of the latter. The patient then comes to know himself to the very depths of his existence.
Freud gave the new procedure of investigation and healing the name of
*psychoanalysis.*

Freud, however, had recognized that the patient's resistance to admitting these things into consciousness can be laid bare and overcome only if
the analyst has mastered that particular art of interpretation (which has
to be acquired), which leaves to the patient the course of the analysis and
the arrangement of the material. There was one thing that Breuer had
not understood and consequently had not admitted: the factor of *"transference,"* the positive or negative emotional relationship of the patient to
the analyst which arises without the latter's wish, and also the reverse phenomenon, the *"countertransference,"* of the analyst onto the patient. But,
for Freud, transference now becomes the decisive turning point of the
therapeutic process. It makes possible both the doctor's influence and the
patient's resistance: something emerges that was later called a "working
agreement" or "therapeutic alliance." Only in this way—on the doctor, so
to speak, as the duplicate of a person formerly experienced—can the patient experience again his repressed positive or negative emotional relationships to important persons in the past (especially parents, brothers
and sisters). Only in this way is it possible to catch sight of the unconscious structures and dynamisms at work here and so to lay bare, interpret and formulate the unconscious motivations. Only in this way is it
possible to achieve a lasting transformation of the mental resources, the
disappearance of the morbid symptoms, together with a deactivation of
the transference. The patient ought to be able to love and work again.
This, according to Freud, is the goal of therapy.

But what is the best way to this goal? The main route of psychoanalysis, the *via regia,* the royal road into the dark realm of the uncon-

scious, is the *interpretation of dreams*. What seems at first to be a point-less dream certainly has a meaning if we look not simply at the conscious, "manifest dream content" but at the preconscious "latent dream thoughts" that are processed in the dream. If we investigate these, we find mainly traces left over from the person's waking life ("day's residue"). Alongside these, however, there is often a very repulsive, formerly re-pressed wish/impulse that is really what shaped the dream and summoned up the energy for its production. It makes use of the day's residues as ma-terial in order—when the repressive resistance of the ego is shut off during sleep—to press forward into consciousness with the aid of the dream. But, because of the dream censorship of the ego (the residue of the repressive resistance), the preconscious dream material must be changed, di-minished, condensed, displaced, distorted and eventually dramatized. This is the process of "dream work": it leads to the typical "dream distortion" and permits it to be seen clearly as a substitute, and compromise, forma-tion.

As early as 1895, Freud had discovered the element of meaning in the dream: *"Dreams are wish fulfillments."*[36] That is, dreams—like the neu-rotic symptoms that at first are equally unintelligible—are *disguised* fulfillments of a wish that is *repressed* and therefore needs interpretation. Repressed traumas can thus be analyzed and understood with the help of dreams. Or even with the help of small slips and symptomatic actions of everyday life (slips of the tongue, of the pen; misreading, misplacing, for-getting resolutions, names, experiences), which are by no means acciden-tal but bring to light unconscious processes, as Freud explained in 1904 in a book that was the first of his to become popular: *The Psychopathology of Everyday Life*. But the book that remains fundamental and that Freud always regarded as his most important is *The Interpretation of Dreams*, published, like Harnack's *Essence of Christianity*, in 1900,[37] at first com-pletely ignored by the general public and destructively criticized in spe-cialist reviews. It was hardly a good start for the father of psychoanalysis. In the course of six years, only 351 copies of this most original and impor-tant work of Sigmund Freud were sold. In the same year, 1900, three peo-ple attended his course of lectures on dreams.

Nevertheless, from the standpoint of the understanding of dreams, psy-choanalysis no longer appeared to be merely an auxiliary science to psy-chopathology. It provided a starting point for a more thorough under-standing of the mental life also of the normal, healthy human being. With the aid of dream interpretation in particular, the analysis could pen-etrate to the forgotten material of the years of childhood. While looking for sexual conflict situations, from which repressions result, Freud came to the investigation of the earliest years of childhood, which—by no means sexually "innocent"—proved to be highly significant for the person's de-velopment as a whole. If we do not want to misunderstand from the out-set Freud's theory of *infantile sexuality*—which seemed very shocking at the time—we must know what he meant by the often misinterpreted term "libido." Libido (which is also to be found even in children) is the energy of the sexual instincts: it is not, however, linked solely with the genital organs, but represents a more comprehensive pleasure-seeking bodily function (sensuality in the widest sense of the term); it is common to both children and adults, normal and abnormal people, and thus includes also all merely tender or friendly feelings (all kinds of "love"). Why did he extend so widely the meaning of the term "sexuality"? For Freud, it was possible only in this way to elaborate a comprehensive theory of sexuality: its wish fantasies (later especially the Oedipus complex); its various early phases (autoerotic, oral, anal, genital); its fixations at certain stages of development; its regressions to these stages in the event of repression; its sublimation or applicability for numerous cultural achievements.

These, then, are the two most important of Freud's scientific achievements: his theories of the unconscious and of the way it works ("primary process," interpretation of dreams) and of the libido (infantile sexual life). For both these epochal discoveries, Freud's self-analysis (undertaken systematically from 1897) played a decisive role. At the same time, as already mentioned, he discovered in himself an early-childhood passion for his mother and jealousy of his father: a universally human characteristic, as he thought, given expression at an early date in the myth of King Oedipus, who, without knowing it, had killed his father and married his mother.[38]

In 1905, Freud summed up the essentials of his surprising conclusions on human sexual life in *Three Essays on the Theory of Sexuality*,[39] a work that appeared in later editions continually corrected and with additional material (from 1908 it included direct observation of children). Freud regarded this, together with *The Interpretation of Dreams*, as his most important books. Finally, in 1916–17, he was able to produce his *Introductory Lectures on Psycho-Analysis*[40]—a large synthesis consisting of three parts, "Parapraxes," "Dreams," and "General Theory of the Neuroses"—which was supplemented in 1933 by *New Introductory Lectures on Psycho-Analysis*.[41]

Freud now was no longer isolated, as he had been during the decade after the separation from Breuer. In 1902 he had at last received the title of professor (extraordinary), so important for medical men in Vienna (but it was only in 1920 that he became full professor). His students and comrades-in-arms increasingly rallied to his support: at first a small group in Vienna; then the great Swiss psychiatrists Eugen Bleuler and C. G. Jung, with whom Freud founded a psychoanalytical review, followed shortly by a second and a third; finally the International Psycho-Analytical Association was set up, in 1910, with a number of local groups and with Jung as its first president. In the previous year, Freud and Jung, who were still being ostracized and vilified in Germany, had gone as visiting lecturers to Worcester, Massachusetts, and there met the Harvard neurologist J. J. Putnam and the philosopher William James. And when subsequently, after Bleuler, Jung, too, and Alfred Adler separated from Freud and founded their own schools of depth psychology, psychoanalysis had become sufficiently established in its theory, practice and organization so that Freud could get on not only with expanding the psychoanalytical doctrinal system itself (with reference to the Oedipus complex, narcissism, theory of instincts and its application to psychoses) but also with transferring its assumptions and conclusions to other fields of emotional and mental happenings.

With the interpretation of dreams (and especially with the theory of the Oedipus complex), psychoanalysis had long before *crossed the frontiers of medicine*. And Freud himself, for whom psychoanalysis had become his whole life, now showed how widely its applications could be extended, in a variety of greater and smaller works, including essays on a childhood memory of Leonardo da Vinci, delusion and dreams in Wilhelm Jensen's *Gradiva*, Michelangelo's "Moses," a childhood recollection of Goethe from *Dichtung und Wahrheit*, and Dostoevsky and parricide. Psychoanalysis was now applied to literature and aesthetics, mythology, folklore and educational theory, prehistory and the history of religion. It was no longer a therapeutic procedure, but an instrument of *universal enlightenment*.

After an unavoidably lengthy preparation, we have thus reached once again our proper theme, the theme to which Freud, too, had now found his way at the end of his long road from cerebral anatomy and cerebral physiology by way of psychopathology to his new form of psychology ("metapsychology"): the critique of religion.

Two questions have been kept alive continuously by the various branches of the modern scientific study of religions, and these also occupied Freud: what is the origin and what is the nature of religion? The two questions are connected.

## What is the source of religion?

First of all we must look at the *historical background*. For Freud, the question of the origin of the various religions was quite obviously *psychological* in character. For Christian and Jewish *theologians*, for centuries it had been a dogmatic question: the pagan religions were distortions, degenerations of the original, pure, revealed religion (with a primordial revelation), as a result of man's sin as described in the Bible. But, for the rationalist "enlighteners" of the eighteenth century also—David Hume in England, Rousseau, Voltaire and Diderot in France, Gotthold Ephraim Lessing in Germany—it was a dogmatic question: the various religions were distortions and degenerations of the originally pure religion of reason, with its clear belief in God, freedom and immortality—distortions brought about by priestly inventions and popular customs. It was only with the rise of a *science of religion*, in the nineteenth century, that the question of the origin of religion became a historical, philological, ethnological, psychological question. Even in classical Greece, of course, there had been an interest in the history of religions; but a science of religion as a specific field of study has existed only from the nineteenth century onward. In this field, primitive religion itself became a problem.

*Philologists* of all kinds—Sinologists, Indologists, Iranists, Assyriologists, Egyptologists, Arabists, Germanists, both classical philologists and Old- and New-Testament exegetes—were now concerned to bring to light the numerous missing religious documents of the literate peoples and to throw light on the close connection between religion and language. By a comparative study of the ancient myths and fables, such German philologists as Jakob Grimm and Wilhelm Schwartz hoped to be able to reconstruct the primitive Germanic religion and even the oldest Indo-European religion. The myth researcher Adolf Kuhn, who also drew on Indian sources, and F. Max Müller, the real founder of the "science of religion" (and responsible also for the use of the term *Religionswissenschaft*)—these two saw natural phenomena behind all myths and thus reconstructed a poetic religion of nature. Is this historical truth?

British *anthropologists* and *ethnologists*—by virtue of their philosophical tradition and the cosmopolitan-colonial interests during the rise of the Empire—took a different view. The earliest religion was not to be speculatively constructed in the light of ancient mythological traditions, but investigated empirically: by direct study of the religions of the uncultured, illiterate ("primitive") peoples ("nature-peoples") on the spot. Ethnology (anthropology) and the science of religion (history, phenomenology, psychology and sociology of religion) could subsequently be separated in theory but scarcely in practice. People were now—at the time of Darwin—wanting to see "evolution" everywhere; the interest can even be seen in the work of the later Engels.

"At the same time, the theories of Darwin, which were then of topical interest, strongly attracted me, for they held out hopes of an extraordinary advance in our understanding of the world."[42] This is how Freud, when he was almost seventy, described his schoolboy attitude and his resolve to study medicine. Charles Darwin, in the meantime, had brought to fruition the *idea of evolution* not only in biology and the natural sciences but also in *ethnology, in the new science of religion and history of religion*, in an epoch-making fashion. The theological scheme of a beginning on the heights, a pure monotheism and a paradisiac state of human perfection (as presupposed by the theory of degeneration) was replaced by a scientifically corrected scheme of a beginning in the depths: a primitive human state with an elemental belief in "powers" or spirits, which only gradually developed into something higher (theory of evolution).

The idea of evolution as such was not new. It had its starting points in Greek antiquity (in the work of Empedocles and Lucretius) and became acclimatized, especially from Leibniz's time onward, in both German idealism and French positivism. The philosopher and sociologist *Herbert Spencer*, Darwin's English contemporary and the leading philosophical advocate of evolutionism in the nineteenth century, had proclaimed, even before Darwin, development from lower to higher grades as the basic law of all reality and made it the foundation of his *System of Synthetic Philosophy*.[43] On the ethnological plane, the theory of evolution was established by *E. B. Tylor*, specialist in cultural anthropology and first professor of the subject at Oxford.[44] Religion, too, it was claimed, had developed straightforwardly from the Stone Age up to the present time, uniformly throughout the same phases in small steps from lower to higher forms—naturally, at differing paces in various areas. Thus all that needed to be done was to investigate the religion of the "primitive" nature-peoples and its survivals in later religions, and the earliest religion would be found.

From Tylor onward, it was assumed that *animism* represents the first stage or—better—merely the threshold of religion. It was understood as a belief, existing in a pure or hybrid form, in anthropomorphically conceived "souls" or—later—"spirits" (from the Latin *animi*, independently existing souls): a belief that everything is ensouled. Belief in souls or spirits was then followed by polytheistic belief in gods and finally by monotheistic belief in one God. The psychologist and philosopher Wilhelm Wundt provided a psychological foundation for this view of the animistic origin of religion.[45] Later there were some, with R. R. Marett in England,[46] who assumed a preanimistic preliminary stage. Preanimism is here regarded as a minimal definition of religion: a stage at which man, before coming to believe in particular spirits, believes in a mysterious, supposedly impersonal animating force or "power" (Melanesian "mana") in all things. On the one hand, there is belief in the existence of souls in all things (animism) and, on the other, belief that there is life in all earthly things (animatism).

The Scotsman W. Robertson Smith,[47] however, had brought out the fact that it was not so much belief in spirits or gods, as the sacred action, the rite, the cult, that was fundamental to religion. For him, therefore, *totemism*, veneration of an animal, as he had found it in a primitive Australian clan and as it had been known among all peoples, was the original religion. The clan regards itself as related to a particular totem, an animal (or—later—a plant or natural phenomenon), or even as descended from it ("totem" = kinship). The totem animal protects the group and may not be injured or killed; members of the same totem group are not permitted sexual intercourse with one another, but only outside the group (exogamy). Thus the primary ethical precepts follow from totemism: prohibition of murder and incest; according to Robertson Smith, these are the two prevailing "taboos" (a Polynesian word for "marked off," "prohibited," that is, "untouchable"). Once in the year, the totem animal is ritually killed and devoured in order to renew the strength of the clan or tribe. From this quasi-sacramental totem meal have emerged both the veneration of divine beings (at first in animal form) and also sacrifice.

According to the evolutionary scheme, the life of the nature peoples cannot be imagined as anything but primitive: gloomy and even—as some have thought—almost without speech (communication taking place only by gestures and grunts). Consequently any cult at the level of animism or totemism can be no more than *magic* (or sorcery), taking the form of actions and especially words that are as it were automatically effective and are supposed to coerce the forces of nature. It was thought that belief in spirits and gods and therefore in *religion* developed only with increasing awareness of the ineffectiveness of magic, especially in the face of death. And eventually, very much later, as a result of further corrections in attitudes, rational, scientific thinking—*science*—emerged.

The well-known triadic scheme of world history associated with Hegel and Comte now appears in another guise. Magic, religion and science are seen as stages in an evolutionary scheme of the history of religion. The theory was supported with an enormous amount of factual material by J. G. Frazer, the British ethnologist and investigator of religion, who under the influence of Robertson Smith and Wilhelm Mannhardt[48] distinguished between imitative and sympathetic magic.[49] Does it not all seem clear and logically conclusive?

It was precisely this *ethnological explanation of religion* and this evolutionary scheme of the early classical writers on the history of religion that Freud adopted. He was directly prompted to do this by C. G. Jung's comparative studies of religion and the latter's large work *Symbols of Transformation*;[50] but, for his own part, he relied especially on Robertson Smith, Frazer and also Marett. Freud at first was concerned simply to corroborate from the history of religion the thesis he had put forward as early as 1907: that religious rites are similar to neurotic obsessive actions. This he did in four essays published as a book with the general title of *Totem and Taboo* (1912).[51] Whether investigating the horror of incest (first essay), taboo prohibitions in general (second essay), animism and magic (third essay) or even totemism (fourth essay), he finds everywhere a similarity between the customs and religious attitudes of primitives on the one hand and the obsessive actions of his neurotic patients on the other: everywhere a survival of primitive mental life up to the present time. Nevertheless, Freud now modifies his earlier, provocative statement to the effect that religion is a universal obsessional neurosis. Despite any similarity between obsessional neurosis and religion, the former is in fact a *distortion* of the latter: "It might be maintained that a case of hysteria is a caricature of a work of art, that an obsessional neurosis is a caricature of a religion and that a paranoic delusion is a caricature of a philosophical system."[52]

But Freud wanted to do more than simply draw attention to this similarity. He wanted to produce a *"psychogenesis of religion,"* the basic conception of which had been fixed in his mind from the outset: "I am reading thick books without being really interested in them, since I already know the results; my instinct tells me that. But they have to slither their way through all the material on the subject."[53] Where had Freud obtained his results? He drew them from his total psychoanalytical view and from the clinical experiences he put forward after discussing the various unsatisfying theories meant to explain totemism.

In his observation of small children, he had been particularly impressed by the fact that they like animals at first but begin to show fear of them at a later phase of development. If animal phobias of this kind are examined in children or even in those adults who have retained their childish phobias in a neurotic form, the reason is found to be a fear of one's own father, which, however, is projected onto the animal as a father symbol. Why? The child really wants to respect and love its father and yet fears him at the same time. This fear, however, is not consciously worked up but thrust by consciousness into the unconscious. It survives there and turns up again in a different form. An animal takes the place of the father. Yet the ambivalent feelings, both love and fear, are really directed toward the father; the animal is merely a substitute.

This psychoanalytical explanation Freud now applied to totem belief in the last of his four essays. Under the title "The Return of Totemism in Childhood," he attempted to give a psychological explanation of religion. The same ambivalence of feelings can be observed in behavior toward totem animals: killing is prohibited, but the animal is sacrificed. The members of the totem group therefore behave toward the totem animals as children and neurotics do toward the animals they come across. For the former also, the animal is a symbol for the father, more precisely a symbol for the primogenitor.

This means that behind totemism, this transitional stage even for more advanced peoples, what is secretly at work is nothing but the *Oedipus complex,* with its double content: attachment to the mother and death wish to the father, who is seen as a rival. And the very core of totemism— the totem meal in which the totem animal as a sacred object is ritually killed and devoured annually, then mourned and finally celebrated in a feast—makes it clear that killing the father is the starting point of totemism and thus of the formation of religion as a whole.

Is it possible, however, to *provide historical evidence of such a parricide?* Freud appeals here to Darwin's "assumption" that human beings originally lived in packs or hordes (comparable to a herd of deer), all the females being under the domination of a strong, brutal, jealous male. Freud persisted later in this view, which he had developed in *Totem and*

*Taboo*, without correcting or amplifying it. He sums it up in his *Autobiography* in this way:

> The father of the primal horde, since he was an unlimited despot, had seized all the women for himself; his sons, being dangerous to him as rivals, had been killed or driven away. One day, however, the sons came together and united to overwhelm, kill and devour their father, who had been their enemy but also their ideal. After the deed they were unable to take over their heritage since they stood in one another's way. Under the influence of failure and remorse they learned to come to an agreement among themselves; they banded themselves into a clan of brothers by the help of the ordinances of totemism, which aimed at preventing a repetition of such a deed, and they jointly undertook to forgo the possession of the women on whose account they had killed their father. They were then driven to finding strange women, and this was the origin of the exogamy which is so closely bound up with totemism. The totem meal was the festival commemorating the fearful deed from which sprang man's sense of guilt (or "original sin") and which was the beginning at once of social organization, of religion and of ethical restrictions.[54]

Thus religion is based entirely on the Oedipus complex of mankind as a whole.

For Freud, the origin of religion is therefore explained psychologically. The formation of religion is built on the father complex and its ambivalence: "After the totem animal had ceased to serve as a substitute for him, the primal father, at once feared and hated, revered and envied, became the prototype of God himself. The son's rebelliousness and his affection for his father struggled against each other through a constant succession of compromises, which sought on the one hand to atone for the act of parricide and on the other to consolidate the advantage it had brought. This view of religion throws a particularly clear light upon the psychological basis of Christianity, in which, as we know, the ceremony of the totem meal still survives with but little distortion in the form of Communion."[55]

Unlike Judaism, Christianity admits parricide into religion. According to Freud, Paul came to the conclusion that we are unhappy because we have killed God the Father. We were redeemed from this sin only by the fact that Jesus Christ as Son sacrificed his life. The Son even takes the place of the Father: "Christianity, having arisen out of a father-religion, became a son-religion. It has not escaped the fate of having to get rid of the father."[56] Fear of the primordial father has been maintained in the most varied forms in Christianity.

A present-day reader (in this respect like most readers at the time, except of course in psychoanalytical circles) may regard this interpretation of the origin of religion as highly fictional, as a fantasy product unworthy of a scholar. He should remember two points:

*Firstly,* Freud was writing at a time of great enthusiasm for the new evolutionary explanation of the world and religion, when the joy of discovery led to the construction of bold outlines of grades, phases and even the detailed courses of the evolution of religion, so that it was possible to assume all the more imperturbably an animistic or totemist phase as the first stage of religion. Things became different later, of course.

*Secondly,* Freud himself, looking back over the theories he had worked out, spoke very clearly of "hypotheses," "visions," "assumptions," "attempts." But, despite their historical disputability and the universal criticism also of ethnologists and experts in the study of religion, he continued to uphold these views. Why?

At bottom, Freud had only a secondary interest in the historical question. For him, as we saw, the *theory of religion was established in essentials from the very outset,* and he attempted then to support it with the aid of material from the history of religion. Even before seriously investigating the sources of primitive religion, in his article on Leonardo da Vinci (1910), he had anticipated the result of a psychoanalytical interpretation of religion: "Psycho-analysis has made us familiar with the intimate connection between the father-complex and belief in God; it has shown us that a personal God is, psychologically, nothing other than an exalted father, and it brings us evidence every day of how young people lose their religious beliefs as soon as their father's authority breaks down. Thus we recognize that the roots of the need for religion are in the parental complex."[57]

The roots of the need for religion: from the psychological standpoint, the question of the origin of religion is closely linked with that of its essence.

## What is religion?

Four years before his death—in a "Postscript" to his *Autobiography*—Freud remarked that a "significant difference" was to be observed in his writings over the previous ten years, making much of what he had done in the past seem like a "detour": "My interest, after making a lifelong *detour* through the natural sciences, medicine and psychotherapy, returned to the cultural problems which had fascinated me long before, when I was a youth scarcely old enough for thinking."[58]

Religion takes first place among these problems of youth and age. Freud's main critical work on religion, *The Future of an Illusion*, in 1927, was the first of a series of studies that became his main preoccupation for the rest of his life, among them being *Civilisation and Its Discontents* (1930)[59] and eventually his last great work, *Moses and Monotheism*

(1939).[60] He deals with religion also at the end of the *New Introductory Lectures on Psycho-Analysis* (1933).[61]

What is religion? Freud now looks beyond religious rites and asks, What are "religious ideas"? He gives an exhaustive account of these in his *The Future of an Illusion*. What is new is that religion is no longer analyzed merely as historical, but mainly as a contemporary social phenomenon. "Religious ideas are teachings and assertions about facts and conditions of external (or internal) reality which tell something one has not discovered for oneself and which lay claim to one's belief."[62] But *what is the basis of this claim?* According to Freud, three answers are given to this question, answers that are mutually contradictory and as a whole inadequate.

*The first answer* is that we should believe without demanding proofs. Freud in turn asks, "Why?" and suggests that it is because we are really aware of the fact that the claim is uncertain and without foundation.

*The second answer* is that we should believe because our forefathers believed. Freud points out that our ancestors believed a great deal that we could not possibly believe today.

*The third answer* is that we should believe because we possess proofs handed down to us from primeval times. Freud asserts that the writings from which these proofs are drawn are untrustworthy, full of contradictions, frequently revised and often downright false, and to invoke divine revelation is itself a proof that their doctrine is not authenticated. And if it is claimed that there are proofs from the present time—those of the spiritualists, for instance—is it not clear that the great spirits whom they invoke, together with their trivial and silly answers, are so like themselves that it is easy to see the information for what it really is, the product of people who provide no evidence in their own persons of a spiritual reality independent of the body, of an immortal soul?

The "singular conclusion" to be drawn is that the most important statements, which are supposed to solve the riddles of the universe for us and to reconcile us all to our suffering, are "the least well authenticated of any."[63] They are and evidently always were undemonstrable.

And yet we may wonder if it can be true that there is no reality at all behind religion. Despite defective authentication, have not religious ideas exercised the strongest influences of all on human beings? Where did they acquire their force? This, too, is a question that must be approached psychologically: the psychological origin of religion explains its essence. Freud now applies to the phenomenon of religion the model of wish fulfillment discovered in dreams and neurotic symptoms. After gaining a deeper understanding of the structure of the unconscious, of instincts and dreams, we can now understand much better what we first heard from him about this subject, and it must now be stressed that *religious ideas* are "not precipitates of experiences or end-results of our thinking," but "*illusions, fulfilments of the oldest, strongest and most urgent wishes of mankind.* The secret of their strength lies in the strength of those wishes."[64] Which wishes? The wishes of the childishly helpless human being for protection from life's perils, for the fulfillment of justice in this unjust society, for the prolongation of earthly existence in a future life, for knowledge of the origin of the world, of the relationship between the corporeal and the mental. Also according to Freud, it is a question of projections (the dependence on Feuerbach is obvious): "The unclear, inner perception of one's own psychical apparatus stimulates thought illusions that are naturally projected outward and—characteristically—into the future and into a hereafter. Immortality, retribution, the whole hereafter, are such representations of our psychical interior . . . psychomythology."[65]

Yet all these wishes are *infantile wishes,* rooted in "conflicts of childhood arising from the father-complex" and "never wholly overcome."[66] These are childhood conflicts in two senses, of the human individual and of the human race. The conflicts emerge therefore from the very earliest times of mankind: for the childhood of the individual is a reproduction of the childhood of mankind, the ontogenesis of the human individual a reproduction of the phylogenesis of the human race. In both cases, longing for a father is the root of religious needs; in both cases, the Oedipus complex plays the main part. In *The Future of an Illusion,* therefore, Freud did not revoke the historical-ethnological explanation of totemism and religion given in *Totem and Taboo.* In fact, he confirmed it, stressing the *childish helplessness* of the individual human being and of mankind as a whole in the face of the immense dangers threatening us from outside and from within ourselves. What has this helplessness to do with religion?

It is culture that creates and produces religious ideas in the individual. Like all other cultural attainments, religion springs from the necessity of defending oneself against the superpowers of nature and fate. How? Because impotent man in his perplexity and helplessness tries to get in contact with these superpowers and to influence them: in a word, naïvely and childishly to humanize and personify them. But, since he cannot associate with these menacing superpowers as with his equals, they acquire paternal characteristics: the need for protection and the longing for a father thus turn out to be identical. This means that impotent man creates gods for himself, both to be feared and to be won over: ambivalent nature gods of fear and comfort.

Yet even when man gradually comes to appreciate the regularity and laws of natural phenomena, these gods do not lose their function. For "man's helplessness remains and along with it his longing for his father and the gods."[67] The *gods* retain their *triple function*: to banish the terrors of nature, to reconcile men to fate and death, and—since any culture is based on the necessity of work and the inhibition of instincts—to compensate men for all the suffering and privation of a common cultural life. With increasing knowledge of nature's laws, anyway, people concentrate their religious ideas on this third, moral function. The gods are supposed to offer men a higher purpose in life, an intelligence or providence above the world, a divine sanction for the moral precepts, a life after death. In this way, the wisdom, infinite goodness and justice, and finally—with the Jews—the uniqueness of the divine being are made clear to men. Only at this stage, in regard to the one God, can a true child-father relationship emerge. For those people who are incapable of interiorizing the moral rules governing interpersonal relationships, the threat of divine penalties provides an additional motivation. But, for the others, such a threat is no longer necessary; on the contrary, if it is extended beyond the original, elementary precepts (prohibition of murder and incest) to all possible small, individual precepts, it is even harmful.

Religion, then, arose out of the oldest, strongest and most urgent wishes of mankind. *Religion is wishful thinking, illusion.* "Illusion" means that religion is not a deliberate lie in the moral sense or—and Freud stresses this—error in the epistemological sense; nor is it necessarily illusory in the sense of being unrealistic or contradicting reality. Illusion— and this is typical—is motivated by the need of wish fulfillment: it is a product therefore of sensual-instinctual life and needs for its deciphering the decoding technique of applied psychology.

For Freud, all religious doctrines are illusions. They are undemonstrable, and therefore no one can be compelled to believe them. It is true that they are also irrefutable. And for that very reason, they are certainly not credible. Some of them indeed, from the psychological standpoint, are so improbable that they amount to delusions (here Freud's old idea of rites as obsessive actions is extended to religious doctrines). But religious doctrines differ from illusions, because—as we saw—they are not necessarily false. For it might be that. . . .

It should be noted that Freud is concerned only with the psychological nature of religious ideas (as illusions), not with their truth content (as reality): "To assess the truth-value of religious doctrine does not lie within the scope of the present enquiry. It is enough for us that we have recognized them as being, in their psychological nature, illusions."[68] Of course, Freud makes no secret of the fact that the psychological derivation of religion has powerfully influenced his attitude to its truth content, especially since we know today more or less at what times and for what motives particular religious doctrines have emerged: "We shall tell ourselves that it would be very nice if there were a moral order in the universe and an after-life; but it is a very striking fact that all this is exactly as we are bound to wish it to be. And it would be more remarkable still if our wretched, ignorant and downtrodden ancestors had succeeded in solving all these difficult riddles of the universe."[69]

## Education for reality

Would it not be sad, however, *if religion*, which has done so much for civilization, *were to disappear?* Could man sustain at all the great hardships of life without the consolation of religion? Freud coolly answers that religion has had time in the course of millennia to show what it could do for men's happiness. Obviously it did not do enough, for the majority of people are still unhappy in this civilization of ours. But was not religion the support of morality? That is true, but it was at the same time the support of immorality. In order to preserve the submissiveness of the masses toward religion, great concessions were made to man's instinctual nature.

In our time, however, the influence of religion is increasingly declining. The reason for this is "the increase of the scientific spirit in the higher strata of human society." "Criticism has whittled away the evidential value of religious documents, natural science has shown up the errors in them, and comparative research has been struck by the fatal resemblance between the religious ideas which we revere and the mental products of primitive peoples and times. . . . In this process there is no stopping."[70] According to Freud, religion, as the universal human obsessional neurosis stemming in the last resort from the Oedipus complex, is inexorably disappearing.

If, however, we want to forestall the dangers of such a process of dissolution, especially for the morality of the uneducated and oppressed masses, a thorough revision of the relations between religion and culture is needed: a new, rationally substantiated Weltanschauung that leaves out God and admits the purely human origin of all cultural institutions and regulations. This means a wholly rational justification of the prohibition of murder and of all cultural regulations, not in virtue of divine revelation but on the basis of social necessity. However overwhelming our feelings, our instinctual wishes, they must be controlled: by intelligence, by reason, which must no longer be stultified by early training, by religious prohibitions of thinking and the inhibition of sexual thoughts. Consequently an attempt should be made at nonreligious education. One thing we must not do: that is, to abolish religion by force and at one stroke.

"*Education for reality.*" Both for the individual human being and for mankind as a whole, religion is a pubertal, transitional phase of human development. Neither as an individual nor as a species can man remain a child forever. He must grow up; he must master reality with his own resources and with the aid of science and at the same time learn to resign himself to the inescapable necessities of fate. To leave heaven to the angels and the sparrows (Freud quotes the poem *Deutschland, ein Win-*

termärchen, by his fellow unbeliever, Heinrich Heine), abandon expectations of a hereafter and concentrate all the resources thus released on
earthly life—this is the task of the mature, adult human being. "Of what
use to him is the mirage of wide acres on the moon, whose harvest no one
has ever yet seen?"[71]

Admittedly, even this rational procedure may leave scope for illusions.
But these illusions can be corrected and—unlike those of religion—they
are not delusions. In the long run, it is impossible to resist reason and experience, and the opposition of religion to both is striking. No, the voice
of reason can still secure a hearing despite all unreason. Our God—Logos
—gradually realizes the wishes permitted by nature. *Faith in science*, in
knowledge acquired by verifiable experience, provides a support that is
lacking to the believer in God: "We believe that it is possible for
scientific work to gain some knowledge about the reality of the world, by
means of which we can increase our power and in accordance with which
we can arrange our life. If this belief is an illusion, then we are in the
same position as you. But science has given us evidence by its numerous
and important successes that it is no illusion."[72] At the end of the book,
Freud repeats this with unusual passion: "No, our science is no illusion.
But an illusion it would be to suppose that what science cannot give us
we can get elsewhere."[73]

Half a century later, in the *New Introductory Lectures on Psycho-Analysis* (1933), Freud returns to the relationship between religion and science: in the last chapter, "The Question of a *Weltanschauung*." Is psychoanalysis itself a Weltanschauung? Freud's answer is quite clearly
negative, and he sums it up at the end: "Psycho-analysis, in my opinion,
is incapable of creating a *Weltanschauung* of its own. It does not need
one; it is a part of science and can adhere to the scientific *Weltanschauung*."[74]

But it is precisely *religion* that *is the greatest opponent of this scientific
Weltanschauung:* "Of the three powers which may dispute the basic positions of science, religion alone is to be taken seriously as an enemy."[75]
Not art, not philosophy, but religion is the "immense power which has the
strongest emotions of human beings at its service," and "it constructed a
*Weltanschauung*, consistent and self-contained to an unparalleled degree,
which, although it has been profoundly shaken, persists to this day."[76]
Never did Freud speak more clearly of the "grandiose nature of religion"
and of "what it undertakes to do for human beings" by simultaneously exercising three functions: "It gives information about the origin and coming into existence of the universe, it assures them of its protection and of
ultimate happiness in the ups and downs of life and it directs their
thoughts and actions by precepts which it lays down with its whole
authority."[77] At one and the same time, therefore, it provides information and consolation and imposes demands.

But never did Freud submit religion to such close criticism as he did here by gathering together and expanding with concentrated force, systematically and consistently, what he had written twenty years before in his book on totemism and six years before in his treatment of religion as illusion: "In summary, therefore, the judgement of science of the religious *Weltanschauung* is this. While the different religions wrangle with one another as to which of them is in possession of the truth, our view is that the question of the truth of religious beliefs may be left altogether on one side. Religion is an attempt to master the sensory world in which we are situated by means of the wishful world which we have developed within us as a result of biological and psychological necessities. But religion cannot achieve this. Its doctrines bear the imprint of the times in which they arose, the ignorant times of the childhood of humanity. Its consolations deserve no trust. Experience teaches us that the world is no nursery. The ethical demands on which religion seeks to lay stress need, rather, to be given another basis; for they are indispensable to human society and it is dangerous to link obedience to them with religious faith. If we attempt to assign the place of religion in the evolution of mankind, it appears not as a permanent acquisition but as a counterpart to the neurosis which individual civilised men have to go through in their passage from childhood to maturity."[78]

Against any kind of religion, Freud declares himself in favor of a "scientific *Weltanschauung*." Admittedly, with an appropriate dose of skepticism, for—after a brief discussion also of nihilism and Marxism— the *New Introductory Lectures* conclude: "A *Weltanschauung* erected upon science has, apart from its emphasis on the real external world, mainly negative traits, such as submission to the truth and rejection of illusions. Any of our fellow-men who is dissatisfied with this state of things, who calls for more than this for his momentary consolation, may look for it where he can find it. We shall not grudge it him, we cannot help him, but nor can we on his account think differently."[79]

After this destructive criticism, is it not surprising that Freud, from his eightieth year, continued to study religion intensively and even devoted to it almost the greater part of the remaining five years of his life? Is it not surprising also that he reflected again on the origins of the Jewish and the Christian religions, in order now to bring out not only the psychological but also the historical truth, particularly of monotheistic religion: to show how this also rests on the unconscious memory of actual events? At the same time—incidentally, with considerable hesitation—he committed himself to a very bold reconstruction of the Moses legend. According to this, Moses was an Egyptian who had accepted the monotheistic faith of the Pharaoh Ikhnaton and converted the Jews to it; he was killed in a rebellion, leaving the Jewish people with a lasting unconscious sense of guilt. The murder of the prophet in monotheistic religion corresponds to the murder of the primordial father in totemism and the murder of the Son of God in Christianity—all consequences of the Oedipus complex.

Originally entitled "The Man Moses. A Historical Novel," this work was published in three separate papers. Part of the third was read by his daughter Anna at the Paris International Psycho-Analytical Congress, 1938. In 1939 the work appeared in German with the title "The Man Moses and Monotheistic Religion." It was the year when World War II broke out and also the year when Freud died.

## 2. Critique of Freud

Freud himself in his main critical work on religion raised the question "whether the publication of this work might not, after all, do harm. Not to a person, however, but to a cause—the cause of psycho-analysis."[1] In fact for a long time and not least under the influence of the churches, psychoanalysis has been identified in public opinion with irreligiousness and sexuality, with the breakdown of religion, order and morality.

But, despite all the "noise" of opponents—which was to be expected— and all the difficulties created for his fellow workers, "some of whom do not by any means share my attitude to the problems of religion," Freud maintained his standpoint: "In point of fact psycho-analysis is a method of research, an impartial instrument, like the infinitesimal calculus, as it were. . . . If the application of the psycho-analytical method makes it possible to find a new argument against the truths of religion, *tant pis* for religion; but defenders of religion will by the same right make use of psycho-analysis in order to give full value to the affective significance of religious doctrines."[2] This is what in fact happened. It was not least the differing approaches to sexuality and religion that led Freud and his friends—particularly Adler and Jung—to part from and later to oppose one another.

### Adler and Jung on religion

"Depth psychology" (like "schizophrenia" and "ambivalence") is an expression that we owe to the famous Zürich psychiatrist Eugen Bleuler, who was Jung's teacher. What was and remained common to Freud, Adler and Jung—the famous "triple star" of depth psychology—in contrast to all former psychologists, was their theoretical and practical concern with the "depths" of the human psyche, with the "underground" of human behavior; that is, with the unconscious. This was to be understood scientifically, methodically rendered accessible and opened up therapeutically, particularly by means of dream analysis but increasingly also by other therapeutical methods and especially with the aid of various tests. It thus became possible to obtain a deeper insight into human reality, with scarcely foreseeable consequences for the individual and for society not only for medicine, psychiatry and psychology but also for educational theory, the human sciences, the science of religion and for human behavior as a whole.

Freud's theory, however, had raised very serious questions, particularly for his friends who had gone their own way. Is it right to understand the unconscious so very negatively as a reservoir of repressed wishes? Is it right to consider instinct in a mechanistic sense merely from the standpoint of causality? Is it right to ascribe all intentions beyond the instinct for self-preservation to sexual wishes, to the libido, even if with Freud we understand "sexual" in a broader sense? Is it right to understand the individual structure of the psyche merely retrospectively, in the light of past events, instead of prospectively, in the light of a meaning and purpose in life that a person has decided for himself or adopted from elsewhere?

In 1911 *Alfred Adler* (1870–1937), a practicing physician, gave four lectures under the heading of "A Critique of the Freudian Sexual Theory of Mental Life."[3] Like Freud, Adler was of Jewish descent, but a convinced socialist and later a friend of Trotsky; for a decade or so he had been a member of Freud's circle of friends and was now president of the Vienna group of the Psycho-Analytical Union. The lectures led to his being "excommunicated," together with seven other doctors, from the group around Sigmund Freud. A year later, in his work on *The Neurotic Constitution*,[4] he laid the foundations of the "Individual Psychology" with which his name was to be associated in the future. The object of his teaching and the goal of his psychotherapeutic practice (and later particularly of his educational theory) was the integral, free, purposeful "individual," responsible for his actions. Unlike Freud's analyzing, dissecting method, Adler's approach is directed more to the human being in his wholeness and to the project of his life plan in this world.

For Adler, the starting point of his scientific theory and the explanatory principle of mental disorders is not the conflict between the ego and the sexual instinct but the striving for superiority, which is likewise found already in the child as it builds and destroys and struggles for recognition by adults—the "striving for power," as Adler's most outstanding student —Fritz Künkel—put it. From the investigation of "organ inferiority,"[5] Adler came to discover the "inferiority feeling."[6] Neuroses therefore are not to be interpreted causally, as the consequences of infantile and unconsciously operative traumas, but purposively, as the expressions of an "inferiority feeling" that is continually nourished by new negative experiences of life, preventing the person from reaching his goals, and which is "compensated"—often "overcompensated"—by the "instinct to dominate." As opposed to the innumerable false adjustments, the common feature of which is the "ego-centering" ("ego attachment") of human experience and behavior as a whole, Adler insists that the authentic normal state is the centering on the group in "community feeling" ("social interest") and on the given task at any particular time (the requirement of "striving for perfection" or—according to Künkel—of "objectivity"). There can be no happiness for the individual at the expense of others, but—without wanting to hunt it down or extort it—only together with others. The "inferiority feeling" must be overcome by "community feeling." This, then, is the objective of a "comparative individual and community psychology."[7]

Carl Gustav Jung (1875–1961), even before his collaboration with Freud (from 1907), was well known as a psychiatrist because of his experimental studies of affectively toned complexes.[8] Twelve months after Adler's departure, he, too, separated from Freud, because—as he showed in his early work Symbols of Transformation (1912)[9]—he rejected the latter's sexual theory and conception of the libido. In 1914, Jung retired from the presidency of the International Psycho-Analytical Society and later cut himself off completely from it. Subsequently he attempted to overcome Freud's and Adler's lack of balance by a greater differentiation and a more comprehensive grasp of the problems and to analyze the human psyche—this totality of all psychic processes, both conscious and unconscious—in the whole complexity of its relationships and potentialities. Hence, in contrast to Freud's "psychoanalysis" and Adler's "individual psychology," he called his theory "Analytical" or "Complex Psychology."

According to Jung, libido must not be regarded (as it is still largely understood) exclusively as man's sexual drive. It must be seen as undifferentiated psychic energy which is governed especially by the laws of conservation of energy and of entropy, by causality, but also by finality, and which lies behind the four mental processes (thinking, feeling, sensation, intuition). Consequently, four basic types of psychic function are to be distinguished: the rational, evaluating functions of thinking (distinguishing true from false) and feeling (distinguishing pleasant from unpleasant); the irrational, purely perceptive functions of sensation (concerned with external data) and intuition (concerned with the internal, the recondite, the essential). At the same time, two modes of approach or reaction must be noted: a person is either extraverted (influenced mainly by objective factors) or introverted (influenced mainly by subjective factors). On the basis of these differing modes of functioning and reacting, Jung establishes his eight "psychological types":[10] the extraverted and introverted thinking, feeling, sensation, intuitive types. With each of these types, one function is the "superior function" (for example, thinking) and its opposite pole is the "inferior function" (for example, feeling), the latter being powerful in the unconscious and (especially in the second half of life) seeking a compensatory balance; the remaining two functions count as "auxiliary functions."

According to Jung, the dark side of the soul, its "shadow," should be made conscious, "accepted" and involved in personal responsibility; the element of the opposite sex in a person (for a man the "anima," for a woman the "animus") also should be differentiated and realized in us; the "persona," the face, which we show (as protection or mask) to others, should be brought into the right relationship to our ego. Only in this way, in the process of coming to be himself (individuation), does a person develop his individual self, which is responsible for the integration and stability of the personality: the unity of the person in an authentic combination of consciousness and the unconscious. Neuroses are disturbances of this individuation process.

Adler's and Jung's corrections and further developments—which are important for the understanding of religion—must be noted here. At the same time, it cannot be our task to judge among Freud, Adler and Jung or among their schools, or to examine the repercussions of the work of Adler and Jung on Freud. Otherwise, it would be necessary to explain a number of things: how Freud almost from the beginning distinguished between the sexual and the self-preservation instincts (later known as the ego instinct) but examined only the sexual instinct at length, then later (tacitly admitting that Adler was right) turned his attention to the aggressive character of these instincts; how finally, after further modification of his theory of instinct, he conceded a fundamental and autonomous status to the phenomena of aggression and obstructiveness by distinguishing between two types of instinct: life instinct (libido) and death instinct (destruction, aggression), the great powers Eros and Thanatos.[11]

In particular it cannot be our task to discuss the great specific themes of Adler's individual psychology: for instance, the mother's oversolicitude and her pampering of the child, the dethronement of the firstborn and the conflicts among brothers and sisters, the project of a life plan already present in childhood and directed to a fictive goal, the revolt of women in "masculine protest," striving for recognition as an attempt to conquer the feeling of insecurity and inferiority. Neither can it be our task to get involved in the controversy about certain theories of Jung in the field of depth psychology: in addition to those mentioned above, the theories of the individual and the collective unconscious, of the archetypes, of the symbols and myths. For our consideration, all that is really important is the *complex of problems relating to religion*; and it is just at this point that both Adler and Jung differ essentially from Freud.

*Adler* does not start out from the father complex in his analysis of religion. In fact, with an explicit allusion to Freud's "drive psychology," he dissociates himself from this standpoint. He sees in this "mechanistic view" an "illusion," since "it is without goal and direction."[12]

The point at which Adler really starts out in his definition of religion is the "constant inferiority feeling of distressed humanity." "God, eternally complete," says Adler, "is to date the most brilliant manifestation of the goal of perfection" of man. Concretely: "The idea of God and its immense significance for mankind can be understood and appreciated from the viewpoint of Individual Psychology as concretization and interpretation of the human recognition of greatness and perfection, and as commitment of the individual as well as of society to a goal which rests in man's future and which in the present heightens the driving force by enhancing the feelings and emotions."[13]

It thus becomes clear that, for Adler, religion and individual psychology meet in "the goal of perfection of mankind." He can be tolerant in regard to religion as long as it serves this purpose: "I would acknowledge as valuable any movement which guarantees in its final goal the welfare of all."[14] This is the attitude of a man who regards his individual psychology as "the heir to all great movements whose aim is the welfare of mankind."[15] For, despite all his tolerance in regard to religion, it is quite clear to Adler that God is an idea, albeit the supreme and greatest idea, of mankind, the idea of perfection for which man is longing. But also for Adler, the ultimate reality is man. Man is the center of reality, and it is the function of individual psychology "to make him the center."[16] Thus, although unattainable, the goal is set for mankind in a continually ascending, vast evolutionary process. "Whether one calls the highest effective goal deity, or socialism, or"—as Adler does—"the pure idea of social interest, . . . it always reflects the same ruling, perfection-promising, grace-giving goal of overcoming."[17]

Ernst Jahn, a student of Adler and theologian, clearly perceived the problem becoming apparent at this point, and insisted on it in replying to Adler: "This is the question that is not fully clarified: Is God an idea, a goal, or reality? The Christian interpretation is that God is neither idea nor goal. He is reality. Ideas and goals can be determined by the power of human thinking. But God's being is not tied to human thought processes. God is not the result of thinking. God is overwhelming reality."[18] Of course, one may ask how Jahn can be so certain. For Adler, the psychologist, God "is a gift of faith."[19] Unlike Freud's psychoanalysis, faith does not lack "the goal which signifies life," but—since God is not scientifically demonstrable—what is lacking is the "causal foundation."[20] For Jahn, the theologian, it is the very opposite: "Faith is a gift of God."[21] But is not this really wishful thinking? Freud's radical question has not yet been answered.

*Jung* expressly dissociates himself from the atheism of Freud's work on religion as illusion. Younger than Freud by a generation, he says that the latter's standpoint "is based on the rationalistic materialism of the scientific views current in the late nineteenth century."[22] At the time when that book was published, he turned clearly against "medical incursions into religion and philosophy, to which doctors naively believe themselves entitled (witness the explanation of religious processes in terms of sexual symbols or infantile wish-fantasies)."[23] While Freud uncompromisingly rejects religion as such and Adler benevolently tolerates it,

Jung's attitude is in principle friendly toward it. But how far does this friendliness extend?

Jung alone of the three concentrates seriously on the psychological dimension of the contents of religious faith: the doctrine of God (Trinity), Christology, Mariology, sacraments and especially confession and Mass—all these are examined in lengthy studies.[24] At the same time, however, his standpoint is exclusively psychological-phenomenological. In other words, he is asking not about historical but only about psychological truth: "When psychology speaks, for instance, of the motif of the virgin birth, it is only concerned with the fact that there is such an idea, but it is not concerned with the question whether such an idea is true or false in any other sense. The idea is psychologically true in as much as it exists. Psychological existence is subjective in so far as an idea occurs in only one individual. But it is objective in so far as that idea is shared by a society—by a *consensus gentium*."[25] But can psychological truth (that is, psychological existence) be so clearly distinguished from actual, historical truth? Erich Fromm in his criticism of Jung's view of religion rightly observes: "Even the practising psychiatrist could not work were he not concerned with the truth of an idea. . . . Otherwise he could not speak of a delusion or a paranoid system."[26]

Later, Jung became more clearly aware of the limits of his psychological method. Psychological research does not at all mean a "psychologizing, that is, an annihilation of the mystery": "To treat a metaphysical statement as a psychic process is not to say that it is 'merely psychic,' as my critics assert—in the fond belief that the word 'psychic' postulates something known. It does not seem to have occurred to people that when we say 'psyche' we are alluding to the densest darkness it is possible to imagine. The ethics of the researcher require him to admit where his knowledge comes to an end. This end is the beginning of wisdom."[27] But it is still not clear whether God is regarded as a part of the human psyche or as distinct from it.

Despite all his skepticism in regard to ecclesiastical and denominational Christianity, Jung himself always wanted to remain a Christian. In the last year of his life, he wrote to a Belgian theologian: "To be exact, I must say that, although I profess myself a Christian, I am at the same time convinced that the chaotic contemporary situation shows that present-day Christianity is not the final truth. Further progress is an absolute necessity since the present state of affairs seems to me unsupportable. As I see it, the contributions of the psychology of the unconscious should be taken into account."[28]

Adler and Jung, in their view of religion, relativized Freud's critique of religion in important points. But even Jung's more friendly approach to religion still leaves unanswered Freud's fundamental question: Despite its positive function, is not religion nevertheless merely wishful thinking?

However significant the idea of God may be in psychological terms, is not God a "purely psychological" reality? Or—to adopt Jung's terminology— if God is undoubtedly "psychologically existent" (that is, a "psychological truth"), subjectively in the human individual, objectively in a larger group, does he also exist independently of our consciousness, of our psyche? Before turning again to this question—with which we were earlier concerned in the debate with Feuerbach and Marx—in its psychological aspect, we must first examine Freud's answer to the question of the origin of religion, which prepares the way for his answer to the question of its essence.

## The disputed origins of religion

Nowhere did Freud find so little support than for his views on ethnology and the history of religion. The reason why ethnologists and anthropologists did not deal adequately with his theses from the very beginning may have been because they were all convinced that there was no point in serious discussion, that Freud had misunderstood the material. As always, the theories based on the history of religion, which Freud used to substantiate what we saw to be his preconceived opinion of the Oedipus complex as the origin of religion, are scarcely defended in their pure form by experts in the field of religious studies today. Neither the animistic nor the preanimistic, neither the magical nor the totemistic theory of the origin of religion succeeded in gaining acceptance.

*What was questioned* was not primarily the abundant factual material that had been collected by such reputable researchers as Tylor and Marett, Frazer and Robertson Smith. It was the interpretation of this material that came under criticism: for example, the conception of *mana* as an impersonal fluid power outside the control of individuals, animatism attributing life to all things, or the linking of totemism with exogamy. Above all, the incorporation of the very heterogeneous material into a preconceived *evolutionary scheme* was questioned.

Obviously, no serious scholar today disputes the evidence of evolution in the history of religion. Even religions have gone through a process of development. To that extent, Freud, with the ethnologists, has proved to be right against all theologians thinking in terms of a static and immobile reality. Nevertheless, all serious scholars today question the imposition of a doctrinaire, systematic evolutionism on the history of religion. Religions have developed in a wholly and entirely unsystematic pluriformity. This means that in many religions, in their primitive phases, magic and belief in souls or spirits certainly played a prominent part; certainly some ancestors were worshiped as divine beings; certainly in many cases the worship of a totem animal passed over into worship of gods. But the claim that preanimism or animism or totemism was everywhere the original form of religion is a dogmatic postulate, not a historically proved fact.

What have by no means been proved are the assumptions behind the evolutionary scheme: that religion ever developed uniformly; that any particular religion passed through the various phases; that religion generally developed out of magic, ideas of holiness from taboo, belief in spirits from belief in souls, belief in gods from belief in spirits, belief in God from belief in gods. Even what is presumed to be the most primitive stage—belief in souls or spirits—is not found among all nature peoples and particularly not in the supposedly oldest cultures. In the light of ethnology, history of religion and development psychology, animistic ideas are not original, but later, derived phenomena. From this very fact, it becomes clear why the alleged sequence of the various phases could not hitherto be proved in the case of any single religion. The individual phenomena and phases interpenetrate. Instead of talking about phases or epochs, it seems more appropriate now to speak of strata or structures, which in principle can be found in all phases or epochs.

Today we have grown distrustful of beautifully worked out structures, and we are inclined to question their *problematic assumptions*. Is it so certain that the Western type of intellectual with all his enlightenment is really superior to the people—especially the "primitives"—whose lives are governed by these religions but whose knowledge is so much more vital and existential? Is it so certain that there is no reality at all behind the religious belief and action of these "primitives" and that their whole attitude arises from a mistake (which needs to be clarified)? Are religions *a priori* less true than science? Or has science perhaps reached the limits of its resources at this point when it tries to probe a living religion and the wholly different knowledge of "primitive" human beings with the aid of "mathematical," rational knowledge? Is there any justification at all for seeking in principle to explain religious factors in the light of nonreligious, to explain religion in the light of magic? Is this the way to advance toward an understanding of what is genuinely religious? And does the relationship between lower and higher cultures coincide with the relationship between lower and higher religions? Is it possible at all to distinguish so sharply and unequivocally between primitive and higher religions?

In the very year when *Totem and Taboo* was published, one of the founders of modern sociology—Émile Durkheim[29]—with an eye particularly on certain primitive Australian peoples, objected to the picture presented at the time of primitive religion as an empty, abstruse tissue of superstition. Even the primitive religions had a core of reality, which, however, Durkheim found not in a divine power but in society: in the clan, the symbol or emblem of which is the totem.

The evolutionary scheme was first directly attacked by the Scots writer

Andrew Lang.[30] The anthropologist Wilhelm Schmidt followed him with an enormous, twelve-volume work on *The Origin of Religion*,[31] using the method of Frobenius and others in an attempt with his students to demonstrate the thesis that the oldest religion was not animism, preanimism or totemism, but "primitive monotheism." Here an anti-evolutionary scheme was set up against the evolutionary scheme. It certainly seems possible to show that there were primitive tribes who believed not in spirits but in a "High God" (primordial or universal Father as father of the tribe or of heaven), although the latter, oddly enough, had little or no place in worship and apparently as "originator" merely represented an answer to the question about the source of things. These high gods might be something primary and not merely derived from lower grades. But their antiquity and their nature are disputed by scholars. There is a lack of clarity especially about the questions whether these "primitive peoples" are really primitive in a historical sense, whether such a supreme God excludes other gods (monotheism) or includes them (henotheism), whether his nature is to be understood as active or as passive (and thus superfluous).

But however much the studies of Lang, Schmidt and lastly of the German ethnologist A. E. Jensen[32] have shaken the evolutionary scheme, they have not proved *the central thesis* they were meant to prove: namely, that the primordial religion is precisely this high-god religion and not animism. The theological interest behind the anti-evolutionary scheme was obvious. This thesis of primitive monotheism was intended to demonstrate historically the fact of a "primitive revelation," a consideration that has in fact been an obstacle to scholarly discussion.

It has become increasingly clear that *neither the theory of degeneration* from a lofty monotheistic beginning *nor the evolutionary theory* of a lower animistic or preanimistic beginning can be definitively historically proved. Both are essentially dogmatic systems, the first in the guise of a theologically inspired natural science and the other in the guise of rationalistic natural science. Not only has the *primordial religion* not been found. Scientifically it simply *cannot be found*. Hence—and a consensus is already emerging on this point—the search should be called off. The Indian expert on comparative religion M. Dhavamony, rightly says: "We cannot show historically that one form of religion is earlier than another. Animism, pre-animism, manism, fetishism, totemism, primitive monotheism and so on have all had their day as theories of the origin of religion."[33] People have come to realize—and this of course must count also for Freud's theory—that the sources necessary for a historical explanation of the origin of religion are simply not available. Contemporary nature peoples are not historically "primitive peoples": like civilized people, they have a long, albeit unwritten history behind them. As Freud himself actually indicated, as far as the origin of religion is concerned we cannot get beyond historical and psychological "hypotheses," "visions," "presumptions," "essays."

On the other hand, *theology* must frankly admit today that historically *nothing is known about the beginning of religion.* The statements of the Book of Genesis about a primordial, paradisiac state of the world and of men are meant to be not "recollections of primeval times" but a message in poetic form about the greatness of the one Creator, about the essential goodness of his creatures, about man's freedom, responsibility and sin. Serious theology today has no longer any difficulty in accepting an evolution of the world and of man from lower forms. Hence the interest of theology in the thesis of a "primitive monotheism" has perceptibly declined. In view of the state of the sources, any attempt at a synthesis between the biblical accounts and ethnological findings has become pointless. Fortunately, an easing of dogmatic restraints can be felt everywhere, both on the part of theology and on the part of ethnology and the science of religion.

Recent manuals on the history of religion often dispense with a chapter on a primordial or *the* primitive religion. Instead of this, we find one or mostly several chapters on the various *primitive religions.* It has even been suggested that we should begin straightway, quite concretely, with Polynesian, North Indian and African religion; but such a procedure might lead us to overlook the common features that exist, despite everything, in the various primitive religions.[34] At any rate, the various cultures or (to use Ruth Benedict's term) "patterns of culture" must be understood in themselves[35] and the various religions in each case in the light of their own assumptions. Studies of religion today have concentrated on this approach.

Religions are increasingly examined in their own specific forms by intensive field studies, with the aid of philology, psychology, sociology, ethnology, archeology, history of art, folklore. The "functionalistic" anthropology of Bronislaw Malinowski[36] has done a great deal to assist such field studies. It describes how the various institutions of a primitive culture "function," so that a viable whole emerges. When considered together, very odd and apparently pointless customs of the "primitives" have revealed their function. Hence the task of a modern science of religion is seen to consist not in *a priori* fabrications, not in classifying religions into "higher" and "lower," not in value judgments on particular religions, but in bringing out the diversities among all the similarities, in analyzing the functions perceptible against the mysterious background, in respecting the religions in all their diversity of experience.

Meanwhile all the investigations have made one thing clear, that in the whole long history of mankind *no people or tribe* has been discovered *without any traces of religion.* Even in the case of Neanderthal man a hundred thousand years ago, ideas of a future life are perceptible in his grave furnishings; and even Heidelberg man one hundred fifty thousand years ago appears to have offered a sacrifice of first fruits. Religion has always existed. It has been present always and everywhere. In fact, in the study of the history of religion there has occurred what amounts to a reversal in the formulation of the problem. As Bronislaw Malinowski puts it: "Tylor had still to refute the fallacy that there are primitive peoples without religion. Today we are somewhat perplexed by the discovery that to a savage all is religion, that he perpetually lives in a world of mysticism and ritualism. If religion is coextensive with 'life' and with 'death' into the bargain, if it arises from all 'collective' acts and from all 'crises in the individual's existence,' if it comprises all savage 'theory' and covers all his 'practical concerns'—we are led to ask, not without dismay: What remains outside it, what is the world of the 'profane' in primitive life?"[37] Can we not understand that some of the authorities on the subject, precisely as a result of their understanding of the history of religion, maintain that religion will also exist forever? Is religion, then, an eternal yearning of mankind?

One of the most outstanding present-day authorities on religion, Mircea Eliade, has expressed his surprise that Freud's *Totem and Taboo*—this *roman noir frénétique*—could have had such "incredible success" among Western intellectuals, even though the leading ethnologists of Freud's own time—from W. H. Rivers and F. Boas to A. L. Kroeber, B. Malinowski and W. Schmidt—had proved "the absurdity of such a primordial 'totemic banquet.'"[38] It was in vain that all these scholars had brought out the fact that totemism was not found at the beginnings of religion, that it is not universal and that not all peoples have passed through a totemistic phase; that, among the many hundreds of totemistic tribes, Frazer himself had found that only four were aware of a rite that resembled a ritual killing and eating of a "totem god"; that this rite therefore has nothing to do with the origin of sacrifice, since totemism does not occur in the oldest cultures.

According to Eliade, Freud's genius must not be judged in the light of the "horror stories" that are put forward in *Totem and Taboo* as objective historical facts. What is more important is that psychoanalysis has once and for all won the battle against the older psychologists. Consequently of course—and also for many other reasons—it became a "cultural fashion." And because it was the fashion, Freudian ideology even in its uncertain elements was accepted as proved by the Western intelligentsia after 1920. But if we look into this "cultural fashion" with the means and methods of psychoanalysis itself, according to Eliade, "we can lay open some tragic secrets of the modern Western intellectual: for example, his profound dissatisfaction with the worn-out forms of historical Christianity and his desire to violently rid himself of his forefathers' faith, accompanied by a strange sense of guilt, as if he himself had killed a God in whom he could not believe but whose absence he could not bear. For this reason I have said that a cultural fashion is immensely significant, no matter what its objective value may be; the success of certain ideas or ideologies reveals to us the spiritual and existential situation of all those for whom these ideas or ideologies constitute a kind of soteriology."[39]

## Religion—merely wishful thinking?

Historically and biographically, there can be no doubt that Freud was an atheist from his student years. He was an atheist long before he became a psychoanalyst. Consequently his atheism was not based on his psychoanalysis but preceded it. This, too, is what Freud constantly maintained, *that psychoanalysis does not necessarily lead to atheism*. It is a method of investigation and healing and can be practiced by both atheists and theists. And for that very reason, Freud the atheist defends himself against the charge of extrapolating an atheistic "Weltanschauung" from a "neutral working tool." Methodological "atheism" must not be turned into ideological atheism; psychoanalysis cannot be made into a total explanation of reality.

Freud *took over from Feuerbach and his successors* the essential *arguments for his personal atheism*. As he says, both modestly and correctly, "All I have done—and this is the only thing that is new in my exposition —is to add some psychological foundation to the criticisms of my great predecessors."[40] Feuerbach, as we saw, had already produced a psychological substantiation of atheism: wishes, fantasies, or the power of imagination are responsible for the projection of the idea of God and of the whole religious pseudo or dream world. Like Marx's opium theory, Freud's illusion theory is also based on Feuerbach's projection theory. What is essentially new is merely Freud's psychoanalytical reinforcement of Feuerbach's theory.

But this means also that the arguments against Feuerbach's (and Marx's) atheism, particularly against the evidence drawn from psychology and philosophy of religion, are valid also against Freud's atheism. And in so far as Feuerbach's (and Marx's) atheism turned out in the last resort to be a hypothesis that had not been conclusively proved, so, too, must *Freud's atheism* now be regarded in the last resort as a *hypothesis that has not been conclusively proved*.

Of course, Freud had asked about the background of Feuerbach's psychological projection theory and applied the tests of depth psychology to its unconscious assumptions. Hence he was able to reinforce this hypothesis in the light of the history of religion and of the psychology of religion. But he did not thereby produce—any more than Marx did—an independent argument for the projection theory. For Freud *had taken for granted* the projection theory (apparently irrefutably substantiated by his "great predecessors") and then asked and tried to show how it could be explained in the light of the history and the psychology of religion. And it is precisely this assumption that turns out in the last resort to be unproved.

It is to Freud's immense credit that he worked out how much the unconscious determines the individual human being and the history of mankind, how fundamental even the earliest childhood years, the first parent-child relationships, the approach to sexuality, are also for a person's religious attitudes and ideas. But we saw very clearly in connection with *Feuerbach* (and Marx) that from the indisputable influence of *psychological* (or economic and social) factors on religion and the idea of God no conclusions can be drawn about the existence or nonexistence of God. Hence there is really no need of further explanation if we now say much the same about *Freud:* from the indisputable influence of *depthpsychological, unconscious* factors on religion and the idea of God, *no conclusions can be drawn for the existence or nonexistence of God.*

We may put this more concretely in summary form with reference to Freud's main statement on the critique of religion: "Religious ideas are fulfillments of the oldest, strongest and most urgent wishes of mankind." This is quite true, and the believer in God can say the same. At the same time, he will also admit:

Religion, as Marx shows, can certainly be opium, a means of social assuagement and consolation (repression). But it need not be.

Religion, as Freud shows, can certainly be an illusion, the expression of a neurosis and psychological immaturity (regression). But it need not be.

All human believing, hoping, loving—related to a person, a thing, or God —certainly contains an element of projection. But its object need not, for that reason, be a mere projection.

Belief in God can certainly be very greatly influenced by the child's attitude to its father. But this does not mean that God cannot exist.

Consequently the problem does not lie in the fact that belief in God can be psychologically explained. It is not a question of a choice between psychology and not psychology. From the psychological standpoint, belief in God always exhibits the structure and content of a projection and can be suspected as a mere projection. It is the same with lovers: every lover necessarily projects his own image of her onto the beloved. But does this mean that his beloved does not exist or at any rate does not exist substantially as he sees her and thinks of her? With the aid of his projections, may he not even understand her more profoundly than someone who tries as a neutral observer to judge her from outside? The mere fact of projection therefore does not decide the existence or nonexistence of the object to which it refers.

It is at this point that the Freudian conclusion from the abnormal to the normal, from the neurotic to the religious—however well justified— finds its essential limitations. Is religion human *wishful thinking?* And must God for that reason be merely a human wishful construction, an infantile illusion or even purely a neurotic delusion? As we argued against

Feuerbach, a real God may certainly correspond to the wish for God. This possibility—to be discussed more closely at a later stage—is one that even Freud did not exclude. And why should wishful thinking be absolutely universally discredited? Is not wishing wholly and entirely human, wishing in small matters or in great, wishing in regard to the goods of this world, in regard to our fellow men, to the world and perhaps also in regard to God?

Of course, religious belief would be in a bad way if there were no genuine grounds for it or if no grounds remained after a psychoanalytic treatment of the subject: however devout its appearance, such a faith would be immature, infantile, perhaps even neurotic. But is a faith bad and its truth dubious simply because—like psychoanalysis itself—it also involves all possible instinctual motivations, lustful inclinations, psychodynamic mechanisms, conscious and unconscious wishes? Why in fact should I not be permitted to wish? Why should I not be allowed to wish that the sweat, blood and tears, all the sufferings of millennia, may not have been in vain, that definitive happiness may finally be possible for all human beings—especially the despised and downtrodden? And why should I not, on the other hand, feel an aversion to being required to be satisfied with rare moments of happiness and—for the rest—to come to terms with "normal unhappiness"? May I not feel an aversion also in regard to the idea that the life of the individual and of mankind is governed only by the pitiless laws of nature, by the play of chance and by the survival of the fittest, and that all dying is a dying into nothingness?[41]

It does not follow—as some theologians have mistakenly concluded—from man's profound desire for God and eternal life, that God exists and eternal life and happiness are real. But some atheists, too, are mistaken in thinking that what follows is the nonexistence of God and the unreality of eternal life. It is true that the wish alone does not contain its own fulfillment. It *may* be that nothing corresponds to the oldest, strongest and most urgent wishes of mankind and that mankind has actually been cherishing illusions for millennia. Just like a child that, in its solitude, forsakenness, distress, need for happiness, wishes wholeheartedly, longs, imagines, and fantasizes that it might have a father in some distant Russian camp, cherishes illusions, gives way to self-deception, pursues wish images, unless, unless . . . ? Unless the father, long assumed to be dead, whom the child knows only from hearsay, had by some chance remained alive and—although no one believed it any longer—was still existing. Then—then indeed—the child would actually be right against the many who did not believe in the father's existence. Then there would in fact be a reality corresponding to the child's wishful thinking and one day perhaps might be seen face to face.

Here, then, again, as earlier with Feuerbach and Marx, we have reached the crux of the problem, which is not at all difficult to understand and in the face of which any kind of projection theory, opium theory or illusion theory momentarily loses its suggestive power. *Perhaps* this being of our longings and dreams does *actually* exist. Perhaps this being who promises us eternal bliss does exist. Not only the bliss of the baby at its mother's breast—which, according to Freud, permanently determines a person's unconscious—but a quite different reality in the future that corresponds to the unconscious and conscious strivings precisely of the mature, adult human being and to which the oldest, strongest, most urgent wishes of mankind are oriented. Who knows?

Freud's explanation of the psychological genesis of belief in God is not a refutation of that faith. He analyzed and deduced religious ideas psychologically. And this is just what theologians and churchmen should never have forbidden him—or Feuerbach at an earlier stage—to do. For the psychological interpretation of belief in God is possible and also legitimate. But is the psychic aspect itself the whole of religion? It should be observed that Freud has not in fact destroyed or refuted religious ideas in principle, and neither atheists nor theologians should ever have read this into his critique of religion. For, by its very nature, psychological interpretation alone cannot penetrate to the absolutely final or first reality: on this point it must remain neutral in principle. From the psychological standpoint, then, the question of the existence of God—and even the positive force of the argument must not be exaggerated—must remain open.

*Freud's atheism,* of which he was firmly convinced long before any of his psychological discoveries, thus turns out to be a *pure hypothesis,* an unproved postulate, a dogmatic claim. And at bottom Freud was well aware of this. For religious ideas, though incredible, were for him also irrefutable. In principle they might also be true. Even for him, whatever may be said about their psychological nature by no means decides their truth content and truth value. We heard his answer: "We tell ourselves, it would indeed be fine . . . but. . . ."

### Faith in science?

For Freud, belief in God is replaced by belief in science, "our god logos,"[42] in which he finds the "sure support" that—according to him—is "lacking" to believers in God.[43] We saw how emphatically Freud, fully aware of the inadequacy of man and of his progress, nevertheless confessed his *faith:* "We believe that it is possible for scientific work to gain some knowledge about the reality of the world. . . ."[44] And how emphatically he forswore unbelief: "No, our science is no illusion."[45]

Obviously, man cannot avoid setting up at least as a fiction such a supreme value (in Freud's case, science) without expressing any opinion about the reality of this value. Here the only question that arises is: Can belief in science replace *belief in God?* We need not repeat what we had to say from Pascal's standpoint on the modern ideal of knowledge, natural science and the question of God: certainly not against a critical rationality, but definitely against an ideological rationalism.[46] In any case, as against Feuerbach[47] and Marx,[48] we then had to draw attention to the fact that neither in the West nor in the East has belief in God yet disappeared to make way for science. Particularly after the experience of National Socialism and of Communism, modern atheism has lost much of its credibility. But, for innumerable people in the world as a whole, belief in God has also gained a new future, particularly in our time. Both Feuerbach's anthropological atheism and Marx's sociopolitical atheism, as well as Freud's psychoanalytical atheism, are still far from gaining universal acceptance. Freud's thesis, then, of the *supersession of religion by science* also turned out to be an *assertion* that does *not* appear to be *proved*: an extrapolation into the future that even today, in retrospect, cannot in any way be verified.

On the other hand, we have long ceased to take every *advance in science*—as it was taken in Freud's student years—as contradicting belief in God. And among natural scientists and psychologists also, the question is asked whether the core of belief in God has really been affected by the progress of science up to now and by the corrections that this progress necessarily involved. Is there really an essential contradiction between science and belief in God?

Meanwhile, however, the very progress of science has involved it in a crisis far greater than what Freud—for all his skepticism in regard to progress—anticipated. The indubitable progress of science itself in all fields leads many today, particularly in industrial nations, to doubt this *faith in science*, which Freud also had held: the belief that science and the technology resulting from it automatically imply progress and thus provide the key to that universal happiness of mankind which—according to Freud—is not provided by religion. On the other hand, it is possible today to point to the ambivalent character of this progress of science and technology, which so easily evades any kind of human control and now spreads a fear of the future often amounting to apocalyptic terror.[49] Freud himself had only a limited confidence in progress. He was not certain of the future of our civilization; he regarded as highly dangerous the force of the death instinct and the excessive accumulation of the potential of aggression; for him, the struggle between reason and destruction was far from being decided.[50]

The ideology maintaining that the progress of scientific development leads of itself to a more humane outlook has now been shattered anyway. This progress has been in many ways a destructive influence, a rationality bearing irrational features, a god logos that has increasingly turned out to be an idol. Consequently even scientists think that belief in science as a total explanation of reality, as a Weltanschauung, must be abandoned.

Nevertheless, it would be wrong in principle to exploit the now widespread skepticism in regard to science and technology for theological advantage. Not every step away from scientific credulity is a step toward theistic piety. Skepticism toward science and technology is far from being a foundation for belief in God. Theologians must recognize the fact that today there are many people who reject an ideologizing of science as a total explanation of reality but are equally skeptical when it comes to belief in God. There are many people today who no longer fight passionately for their atheistic convictions but are even less inclined to speak out passionately for a belief in God. Between skepticism and affirmation, we now find all too often an atheism that is not indeed militant but practical, everyday, and banal.

Today there are only a few scientists who—like Freud—publicly acknowledge their unbelief. But neither are there too many who publicly bear witness to their belief. Religion, faith, God—for many, all this seems singularly faded, taboo, left undecided: they remain uncommitted. Belief in God is regarded as a private affair that does not concern anyone else. As far as religion is concerned, is there not in many cases a widespread easygoing tolerance, leaving everyone to believe just what he happens to believe?

It would not be entirely irrelevant to raise the question: Are we perhaps faced here with a repression phenomenon that naturally has its own, and not least historical, roots? The unnecessary controversies, already mentioned, between Church and science explain at least up to a point why scientists today prefer to be silent, rather than to speak of God. We have observed that sexuality can be repressed. Hence it is possible to ask if perhaps the future, fear and hope, the question of the meaning of life, even religious feeling, can also be repressed. One should not appeal too hastily to objective science, to impartial reason. Even scientific reason can be corrupted: by all kinds of wishes, instincts, inclinations, childhood fixations, prejudices. And this occurs particularly at the point where it is not a question of "exact" (mathematical, scientific, technological, "pure") conclusions, but of their assumptions and applications, especially where the problems of one's own life are involved. Atheists accuse religion of being wishful thinking. But we for our part may ask whether *atheism*, too, might not be *wishful thinking, projection.* Raising the question, of course, is not the same thing as answering it.

## Repressed religious feeling?

For Freud personally, so far as this is of interest here, the problem became acute. Was there perhaps a repression problem involved in the atheism he maintained to the end? This closing question of the present critique, which we raise with the utmost caution, is not meant in the last resort to interpret Freud's criticism of religion in terms of individual psychology and so neutralize it. Nevertheless there is food for thought in the fact—as we have seen—that Freud was not brought up without religion. He has testified in his *Autobiographical Study* to the fact that he was quite familiar with the Bible, but, oddly enough, in a sentence that was added only in 1935.[51] He also admits that in his early years he had a strong bent toward speculation on the riddle of the world and of man, but again, oddly enough, he resisted this inclination: "As a young man I felt a strong attraction towards speculation and ruthlessly checked it."[52] Thus he "secretly nursed the hope" of arriving by a detour through physiology at his "original objective, philosophy": "for that was my original ambition, before I knew what I was intended to do in the world."[53] At the age of forty he wrote about his *yearning for knowledge* to his friend Fliess: "As a young man my only longing was for philosophical knowledge, and now that I am changing over from medicine to psychology I am in the process of fulfilling this wish. I became a therapist against my will."[54]

Evidently the young Freud was preoccupied with questions that can be called philosophical, ideological or religious. And evidently Freud in his old age—as he has told us himself, everything in the meantime had been merely a "detour"—returned to the questions of his youth and became intensely occupied until his death mainly with problems of religion. In this respect, from his youth onward and from his first biblical studies, nothing fascinated him more than the "founder" of that religion—the Jewish— from which he came. As early as 1913, for three lonely September weeks, he stood every day contemplating the statue of Moses by Michelangelo in San Pietro in Vincoli, in Rome, in order to write his early (anonymously published) work on this figure. And he wrote the last great work of his life also on the history and significance of this same Moses. What was the source of this fascination?

Undoubtedly Freud was one of the great moralists of mankind. He was not at all a sexual libertine, as many thought at the time and as some suspect even today. In his whole way of life and in his sexual life in particular, he observed an extremely strict morality. In fact he was not without a deep-rooted prudery, and his morality displays some very strict, even legalistic, somber features.

His theory of man had nothing to do with "pansexualism" or "making the most of one's instincts." On the contrary, for Freud, all human civilization rested essentially on the renunciation of instinct, on subduing the infantile pleasure principle in favor of the reality principle. There is litttle mention in his work of either "joy" or "beauty." The ethical requirements, which he wanted to see substantiated purely rationally, without the aid of religion, were noticeably identical in content with those of the Mosaic decalogue. And it can scarcely be doubted that, while he speaks himself of the strict education that made its mark on his childhood and in which a father complex had been observed as a result of his self-analysis, he had remained unconsciously indebted to the ancient Mosaic legalism.

His atheism, on the other hand, is not original, but—as we saw very clearly—adopted: not connected with the psychoanalytic method, which he developed under the enormous influence of supposedly atheistic natural science, now for him replacing the Jewish belief in God. Belief in God, however, was not simply replaced by scientific arguments but by another faith, the quasi-religious faith in science. For Freud personally, then, *psychoanalysis*, too, was far more than merely a method of research and healing: it was the basis of an atheistic Weltanschauung, a kind of *substitute for religion*.

At the same time, it is striking that Freud's atheism in particular—as he said himself—was not shared by many of his friends, even though they had in common with him important convictions in the field of depth psychology. And also many of his own students, who adopted his psychoanalytic method in its entirety, did not—as he himself admitted—adopt his atheism. Thus Freud's atheism remains his wholly personal basic attitude and has nothing to do with psychoanalysis as such. Is it not possible, perhaps, that we are faced here with the phenomenon of a Jewish religious feeling repressed for understandable reasons?

We need not settle the question here. In any case, we have the greatest respect for the life and work of this singularly consistent scholar. We have the greatest respect, too, for his long-drawn-out *dying*. Death released him from cruel suffering that had endured for years: a cancer of the palate borne for sixteen years with heroic equanimity and necessitating more than thirty operations.

But his death, too, raises questions: the death of this man to whom Max Schur, the family doctor of his last ten years, dedicated his recollections.[55] We see with amazement the powerfully charged emotional role that personal death played for this man, with his austere science and absolutely clear rationality. He had wrestled with this problem throughout his life and never really mastered it: beginning with an almost obsessive "preoccupation with the prospective dates of his death,"[56] partly nourished from sources of Jewish superstitions about "attacks of fear of death,"[57] particularly in connection with his fifty-first year, and continuing to his feeling of the "guilt of the survivor" at his father's death.[58] All this belongs to the very personal background of someone who eventually saw the whole reality of man as marked by the mutual antagonism of the instincts of Eros and Thanatos, the life and the death instincts.

Unbroken despite all his suffering, Freud continued to work to the end. In 1938, the invasion of Austria by the Nazis forced him to leave Vienna and emigrate to London. But his illness followed its inexorable course. At the end of August 1939, the cancer had eaten a way through the skin from the mouth cavity. A mosquito net had to be stretched over his bed, because the smell attracted flies. The war began, and Freud heard the first air-raid warnings. Aged eighty-three, he died at three o'clock in the morning of September 23, 1939, after the doctor, with his consent, had eased his passing with an injection of morphine. As early as 1915, Freud had written in his "Thoughts for the Times on War and Death": "Towards the actual person who has died we adopt a special attitude: something like admiration for someone who has accomplished a very difficult task."[59]

## 3. Critique of the critique

Freud's atheism seems to be no better substantiated than that of Feuerbach or Marx. But does this mean that his critique of religion can therefore be dismissed? Again, no more than that of Feuerbach or Marx. This critique, too, must be understood less as an interim stage to be quickly passed through than as a warning shadow accompanying belief in God. The much quoted "revolution of psychoanalysis," Freud's inspired discovery and methodical, scientific probing of the dynamic reality of the unconscious, has had lasting effects also on religion and belief in God. Whatever may be thought of individual elements of the psychoanalytic theory, which he later continued to improve and modify empirically and conceptually, from Freud onward all that is human, all man's conscious individual and social activity, even his religion and his belief in God, must be seen as essentially connected with that region of the psyche that has its own laws and yet remains beyond deliberate control and direct observation: the unconscious, the deepest stratum in man.

## What remains of Freud's critique of religion?

"Freud has already reinforced the belief of unbelievers; he has scarcely begun to purify the faith of believers," writes the French philosopher Paul Ricoeur.[1] Theologians can actually learn from Freud: his critical writings on religion amount to a single plea for *honesty in dealing with religion.* In this respect, we hear of "every possible sort of dishonesty and intellectual misdemeanour." Philosophers (and, I might add, theologians) "stretch the meaning of words until they retain scarcely anything of the original sense."[2] There are those who "give the name of 'God' to some vague abstraction which they have created for themselves."[3] Or they "persist in describing as 'deeply religious' anyone who admits to a sense of man's insignificance or impotence in the face of the universe."[4] Freud himself in any case professes atheism unequivocally and, in his sincere critical attitude to religion, is prepared to put up with the most "disagreeable reproaches": "If a man has already learnt in his youth to rise superior to the disapproval of his contemporaries, what can it matter to him in his old age when he is certain soon to be beyond the reach of all favour or disfavour?"[5]

What is involved here, however, is more than merely intellectual probity: it is a question of *critical rationality*. Certainly there can be no belief in science in the sense of making reason absolute: this objection in the spirit of Pascal had to be raised *against* Freud. But, on the other hand, there must be no skepticism in regard to science in the sense of making faith absolute: this must be said in the spirit of Descartes *for* Freud.[6] We saw in connection with Pascal, Jansenism, Kierkegaard and Barth how Christians and theologians have been repeatedly in danger of devaluing the conclusions of reason in order to revalue faith: a specific form of hostility to reason which does not seem in any way to be required by Christian faith. Must we cease to be philosophers and scholars in order truly to believe in God? Did not Pascal, Kierkegaard and Barth allow faith to overwhelm reason in this way? Did they not in practice make Christian revelation the unique source of truth and certainty? Against both Protestant biblicism and Catholic traditionalism, therefore, must not a radical correction of their course be required from Church and theology? Instead of hostile, polemical, mutual opposition, or even agreement to differ while maintaining peaceful coexistence, must there not now be a critical-dialogic cooperation between theology and science, particularly between theology and natural science? Consequently all that was said at an earlier stage from the standpoint of Descartes and the tradition he represents, supporting in principle the modern ideal of knowledge, natural science and the new setting of the problem of God, and everywhere here in favor of a critical rationality without ideological rationalism—all this largely amounts to a justification of Freud's method of psychology oriented to natural science.

In any case, Freud was absolutely right to object to the idea of *credo quia absurdum*: as if religious doctrines were wholly beyond the claims of reason, completely above reason. As if their truth needed only to be inwardly perceived and not understood. He calls such a *credo* "an authoritative statement" without "binding force" and goes on to ask: "Am I obliged to believe *every* absurdity? And if not, why this one in particular?"[7] There is no appeal to an authority above reason: "If the truth of religious doctrines is dependent on inner experience which bears witness to that truth, what is one to do about the many people who do not have this rare experience? One may require every man to use the gift of reason which he possesses, but one cannot erect, on the basis of a motive that exists only for a very few, an obligation that shall apply to everyone."[8]

Freud rightly objects to the widespread attitude or philosophy of "as if," which means that the groundlessness, even the absurdity, of religious doctrines is perhaps appreciated, "but for a variety of practical reasons we have to behave 'as if' we believed in these fictions."[9] We practice a religious conformism or opportunism mainly because of the incomparable importance of religion "for the maintenance of human society."[10] To a person not corrupted by such a philosophy, religion would seem to be disposed of as soon as its absurdity and irrationality had been recognized: "It cannot be expected of him that precisely in treating his most important interests he shall forgo the guarantees he requires for all his ordinary activities."[11] Even children, if they were more rational, would listen to a fairy story and then raise the question: Is that true?

But, over and above the general requirement of intellectual honesty and critical rationality, it must be said that the *relative justification of Freud's specific critique of religion* can no more be disputed than that of similar attempts on the part of Feuerbach and Marx. What Feuerbach wanted from the philosophical standpoint and Marx from the sociopolitical, Freud sought from the standpoint of depth psychology: emancipation, comprehensive liberation, more humanity on the part of man. It meant in particular opposition to tutelage, domination, oppression by religion, Church, God himself. Was all this entirely wrong? In order to bring out its concrete meaning, a few points may be mentioned here—which incidentally can be illustrated also from the work of Adler or Jung.

Freud rightly criticizes *defective forms of religion*. Christians should admit in a spirit of self-criticism:

When religion is completely concentrated on the "wholly Other," contact with reality is inevitably lost. Religious questions thus easily become a form of self-deception and escapism. Religion becomes an infantile commitment, regardless of reality, to a tyrannical superego; God becomes a displacement substitute.

When religion relies solely on wish fulfillment and not on intrinsic truth, it is reduced to pure satisfaction of needs. Such a religion is undoubtedly a return to infantile structures, a regression to childish wishing.

When religion is manifested in rigid fidelity to the letter, in a legalistic conscience, in obsessive, pedantic and petty repetition of certain prayers, formulas and rites, religious ideas come close to delusive fabrications, religious observances to substitute satisfaction as a result of obsessive cultic repetition. Such religious practices, which have become pointless or inadequately motivated, are often defensive and protective measures dictated by fear, guilt feelings, tormented conscience, against certain—often unconscious—temptations and threatening punishments: just like the private ritual (for example, ablutomania) of the obsessional neurotic.

Freud also rightly criticizes *the churches' misuse of power*. The facts are well known:

What an abundance of examples of arrogance of power and *misuse of power* can be found in the history of the churches: intolerance and cruelty toward deviationists, crusades, inquisition, extermination of heresies, obsession with witches, struggle against theological research, oppression of their own theologians—right up to the present time.

What *activity of the superego* on the part of the churches can be seen through the centuries: dominating souls in the name of God, exploiting the dependence and immaturity of poor sinners, requiring submission to the taboos of untested authority, continually suppressing sexuality and displaying contempt for women (in the law of celibacy, in excluding women from ministries in the Church).

What an amount of *ecclesiogenic neuroses:* neuroses as a result of the constraints of the ecclesiastical system, clerical domination, confessional practice, sexual repression, hostility to progress and to science. There is no need to reopen here the *chronique scandaleuse* of Christianity and the churches.[12]

Finally, Freud rightly criticizes the *traditional image of God.* People are still too little aware of some of the ways in which it has been formed:

Often enough, a believer's image of God springs not from original insight and free decision but from a vindictive or kind *father image* imprinted at an early age.

Often enough, early-childhood experiences with adults who appear as "gods" are *transferred to God* both positively and negatively, so that behind the image of God the image of one's own father becomes visible even though the latter image has long been forgotten or repressed (it is the same with the mother image as reflected in the Mother of God or in Mother Church).

Often enough, the vindictive Father-God is deliberately *misused* by parents *as a means of education,* in order to discipline their children, with long-term negative consequences for the religious attitudes of those children as they grow up.

Often enough, *religion and sexuality* (the latter frequently repressed by religion) are *knit together* from the very beginning in such a way that what appear to be religious conflicts are really only fixations on the earliest experiences in the family.


## Importance of psychotherapy for religion

In his critical analysis, Freud cultivated a brilliant artistic style, making use in both theory and practice of *all the possibilities of language.* According to H. M. Gauger, this can be seen from three aspects:[13]

*Stylistic-aesthetic:* Using a style midway between the passionate and the prosaic, he gives vivid expression to his interests and views.

*Heuristic:* Proverbs, common phrases, "transparent words," are used to make the speaker conscious of what have hitherto been unconscious, buried planes of meaning.

*Therapeutic:* In the cooperation between patient and therapist, language is almost the sole or at least the fundamental therapeutic tool. For language is the "phenomenon of consciousness, which is constitutive for 'becoming man.' . . . Language makes man possible."[14] Not only man's "ego," however, but also his "superego" is linguistically structured, formed by the acquisition of language in internalizing speech patterns already existing and largely imprinted by parents. "For it is worth noting that we understand what we call 'conscience'—so to speak—vocally-acoustically, by analogy with speech; it seems like a voice speaking to us within us and even as the voice of another person, a stranger in ourselves."[15] Language, finally, is important also for the third, unconscious factor of the psyche, the "id." Language plays a decisive role in all dreamwork and consequently in all rendering conscious and processing of repressions. For Freud, the conscious "ego" thus comes to be from the unconscious "id" by a linguistic process.

Should not theologians particularly and pastors in their practical work, who *ex professo* have to deal with the "word," learn from Freud the complex significance of language: for preaching, discussion, exhortation, confession of sin or faith—language as liberating, consoling, meaning-endowing power, which can help both self-understanding and the understanding of others, both self-acceptance and the acceptance of others?

Psychologists and theologians, doctors of souls and pastors have every reason today to enter into close cooperation. Fortunately, *both sides* have made considerable progress in this respect.

*Psychoanalysts* today increasingly criticize the relegation of psychoanalysis to the realm of the natural sciences. This criticism is voiced not only by those who follow the more recent political, sociocritical trend but also by those who adopt the orthodox individual-psychological approach. In addition to sexual impulses, they recognize also numerous intellectual and even religious impulses, queries, problems, which are not to be repressed but must be admitted.

But *theologians and pastors* today are increasingly discovering the critical potential of psychoanalysis for Church and theology. They recognize psychoanalysis not only as a better auxiliary science for the Church but as an independent critical authority to which theology must render an account of the reality reference of many of its statements, an account that can also make an effective contribution to a faith that is no longer infantile but adult. It will also clarify the content of faith, notably such important concepts as sin and guilt, justification and forgiveness, corporality and sexuality.

According to Freud, man should become aware of himself by learning to control his instincts, to bear the burden of his history and master the problem of his sense of guilt. Involved in the "reality principle" is an ethical appeal that coincides also with the great humane intentions of the Christian faith. Thus the discussion with Freud becomes a demand on the Christian understanding of man, to see man also in his psychical reality as a free, mature, realistic and assured person, for whom everything depends on learning to accept himself, coming to terms with the truth of his past, looking for the causes of his failure and sin and mastering them.

In this way, Christian faith and psychoanalysis might become partners in pursuit of the same humane goal.

Nevertheless the *limitations* must be observed. The competence of the *psychoanalyst* remains restricted to the field of psychological reality. Psychoanalysis therefore may not reduce all reality to the psychical sphere if it is to avoid the danger of a "reductionist hermeneutic."[16] Psychoanalysis can remove neurotic guilt feelings, but it cannot liberate a person from real guilt. It can relieve psychosomatic illnesses, but it cannot answer ultimate questions about meaning and meaninglessness, living and dying. Its aim is to bring things into consciousness, not to forgive; it is healing, not salvation.

Of course, the ultimate questions call for an answer, to satisfy both the sick and the healthy. The problems of neuroses themselves are very often linked with more fundamental problems of life and lead the patients sometimes to ask what is the point of a cure. A psychoanalysis that is not merely skeptically and resignedly backward-looking, but progressively and communicatively forward-looking, will not be able simply to suppress the question of the meaning of living and also of suffering and dying. But the psychotherapist must then know that he will be able to answer such questions, which concern man as a whole, only if he deliberately goes beyond the limits of his science and appeals to some sort of (religious or nonreligious) faith.

The *theologian*, for his part, will have to be reserved in regard to psychological questions. He is not an expert and he is simply not equipped to be an arbitrator in the various therapeutical controversies. He should not seek to judge theories that belong strictly to the field of psychology, but he should certainly take note of the problems associated with psychological theories that are relevant to religion. Nor, of course, can he evade the arduous task of examining from the standpoint of religion certain conclusions of psychoanalysts and the criticism of their opponents.

Is one-sidedness the price of genius? Some of Freud's apparently exaggerated views, which he links with his psychoanalytic theory, may be of a personal character and are perhaps rooted in his own psychological development, even in neurosis. But even if in practice he is often very dogmatic and unwilling to make formal corrections, even if he neglects or depreciates what is opposed to his teaching, he is right in his positive claims. Critique and countercritique[17] may be briefly illustrated with reference to some points that are important also for religion and religious attitudes.

## Critique and countercritique

a. *The critics assert* that Freud *overstretched* the concept of *libido* and, regardless of the consequences, extended it indiscriminately and automatically to all possible expressions not only of sexuality but also of sympathy, friendship, parental, filial and self-love, and of religious feeling, with the result that sexuality seemed to be everywhere present and everywhere active.

*In concrete terms,* the objection is raised that sexuality can scarcely be granted such psychical universality. Other instinctual and personality factors, the whole complexity and multiple polarity of the instinctual and personality structure, need to be considered. Even with the small child, sucking, eating, running, produce pleasure, but those feelings of pleasure are not sexual in character. Sexual themes can be perceived everywhere in dream symbolism only if they are seen from the outset against a sexual background. Not everything that is forgotten is also repressed, not every slip is Freudian. Dreams are far from being always fulfillments of unfulfillable wishes. Behind them lie not only sexual wishes but a broad spectrum of emotions, affections, moods, sensations, instincts, images, as equally important motifs, which are not open to any systematic interpretation. Dream material consists of the problems left over from daily life, of feelings unsatisfied in daily life. Sexuality and love, sexual charm and personal charm, although often linked, must be distinguished in principle. The transference of theories of natural science, of physiology and brain mechanism, to mental happenings that are seen as the functioning of a reflex machinery, reaches its limits at the point where specifically human needs are involved, which transcend all physiologically programmed instincts.

*Nevertheless,* it remains true that man in his whole conscious life— including his religious life—is constantly decisively influenced also by unconscious but very dynamic experiences and recollections, materials and trends, psychical factors—among which sexuality has a primary role—all pressing into the light of consciousness. Disturbed sexuality is the cause of many neuroses that also find religious expression (for example, pathological scrupulosity, aggressiveness, sanctimoniousness and fanaticism). Sexuality acquires a truly ubiquitous virulence if it is not processed and integrated into the personality structure.

b. *The critics assert* that Freud *exaggerated the experiential and environmental factors of early childhood* by comparison with the innate dispositions (genetic constitution, influences in the mother's womb and in the process of being born).

*In concrete terms,* the objection is raised that an exclusive significance can scarcely be attributed to sexually characterized childhood traumata. The significance of traumatizations and aberrations in early childhood should not be exaggerated; the conflicts of puberty, on the other hand, which are decisive for the formation of the adult, must not be underestimated. As early-childhood sexual interest, not oriented expressly to any immediate sexual goal, and adult sexuality are qualitatively different, so, too, there are other conflicts at later stages of development that cannot simply be reduced to early-childhood experiential and environmental factors. Dreams process what are predominantly current occasions and material and not merely those that go back to early childhood.

*Nevertheless*, it cannot be disputed that, in addition to all the contents later repressed for a variety of reasons (conscience, environment, authority), there are also instinctual wishes and conflicts from early childhood that determine a person's thinking, feeling, willing and acting, and also his religious attitudes. Only too often, the decisive problems and difficulties of a whole life result from the unprocessed events of early childhood, even though the person concerned is unaware of the fact.

c. *The critics assert* that a normally functioning sexual life does not exclude neurotic disorders that may be due to *other than sexual causes*. Consequently the free activity of sexuality is just as likely as its repression to produce *conflicts* in a person. Even psychoanalytic treatment can have negative consequences: insecurity in instinctual behavior, disorders in the sense of discretion, unresolved transferences especially in analyses continued over years (fixation on the person of the doctor), complete relativization of ethical values or dogmatic rigidity.

*In concrete terms*, the objection is raised that Freudian therapy can scarcely be regarded as the only possible method of mastering mental conflicts. The positive vital, ethical, even religious objectives cannot be neglected, and there must be an appeal to awareness, responsibility and will. A gradually increasing cooperation on the part of the patient and mutual discussion should be sought, and a shortening of the treatment (otherwise it would be available only to the rich) made possible (short-term therapy for the numerous current conflicts and neuroses that are not deep-rooted, possibly group therapy). Some rightly ask for a synthetic-intuitive approach to supplement the analytical, dissecting operation: for self-discovery, for the reconstruction of an integrated personality and for rousing productive forces and trends, so that the person may again find his way into life and integration into society (psychosynthesis, psychagogy).[18] This means prospective orientation, directed not merely backward but forward, in which the psychotherapist's positive view of life—acting as a partner in the discussion—plays a major part. Religion can be extremely important at this point.

*Nevertheless*, the fact must not be overlooked that education for absolute sincerity also in regard to sexuality is important particularly for morality. "Know thyself" can become the basis of the reconstruction of the personality. If certain conflicts are solved, this does not mean that their source can be ignored. With conflicts that emerge as a result of compromises between unconscious instinctual wishes or between the conscious and the unconscious (rejected and disguised but half-accepted instinctual wishes), a more mature solution of the conflict must be brought about by rendering conscious the unconscious motivations. The patient should learn either to satisfy in reality the repressed impulses (including those which are sexual in origin) or—if they cannot be satisfied—to sublimate them; or he might even renounce satisfaction more successfully than before, so that the symptoms of his illness disappear and the way is laid open to new development and the full use of his vital energies.

d. *The critics assert* that the *Oedipus complex* (on the man's part) and —correspondingly—the *castration complex* (on the woman's part) *have not been shown* either clinically or ontogenetically or phylogenetically *to be universal phenomena.*

*In concrete terms,* the objection is raised that an incestuous tie with the parents has never been shown either by ethnologists or psychologists to have been a normal occurrence in childhood. There is no evidence of the existence as a general rule of positive sexual ties to the parent of the opposite sex or of jealousy toward the parent of the same sex. The decisive factor in the creation of neuroses is not so much the child's pleasure-seeking, as those adverse conditions that give it the feeling of insecurity, helplessness and defenselessness. Sexual difficulties often turn out to be more the effect than the cause of the neurotic constitution. Fixations of incestuous childhood relationships therefore should not be generalized and distorted into a coarsely sexual form. We must not simply impose a dogmatically preconceived scheme on all possible observations and facts.

*Nevertheless,* it remains true that Freud's theories of the Oedipus or castration complex brought to light material that is important for all human conflicts. Feelings and affections for those people with whom the child enters into a relationship at an early—still more, the earliest—stage (mother and father) are and remain of fundamental importance for the person's whole life.

In view of what has to be said at a later stage, a brief critical comment on this point may be in place here. Does not the *Oedipus complex,* too, need *demythologizing,* and not merely in the light of the history of religion? It is not of course to be eliminated, but it certainly needs intelligent interpretation.

Literally understood, the Oedipus complex seems like a myth to many psychologists. And it is impossible to deny *a priori* what A. Hoche, the dream researcher, speaking perhaps for many others, expresses humorously if a little one-sidedly: "The procedure of the psychoanalysts, who discover in their cases what dogma has projected into them, reminds me of the fathers who give their children the impression that they are surprised and pleased to find the Easter eggs that they themselves had hidden. . . It is strange that, after sincerely trying for many years, I have not yet suc ceeded in finding anyone who desired his mother and wanted to kill his father. Other experienced colleagues have fared no better. The Oedipus complex travels around in literature like the Flying Dutchman on the high seas: everyone talks about it, some believe in it, but no one has seen it."[19]

Nevertheless, if it is demythologized, the Oedipus complex expresses a truth. In connection with Freud's famous *Three Essays on the Theory of Sexuality*, psychoanalysts tried to investigate closely the very early development processes in the human child, the "emergence of the first objective relationships": both by reconstruction on the basis of an analysis of later phases and by direct observation of children. Alongside the innate dispositions, the first objective relationship—that is, of the newborn child to its *mother* or her substitute—is of fundamental importance for the development of the personality: "for the newborn, the surround consists, so to say, of one single individual, of the mother or her substitute."[20] The infant spends the first year of its life in union, in symbiosis, with the mother, as it were in a "closed system."

The appearance, however, of a second relationship—normally with the *father*—is no less important. For it is through him that the triangular child-parents relationship emerges. The "closed" mother-child relationship is opened, the symbiotic relationship situation is expanded to a community of three, in which competition and conflict play an important part. And whether we call the conflict within the *three-person relationship* "Oedipus complex" or not, it is impossible to dispute the existence of the essential objective content of this term: "What takes place in the period of the Oedipus complex (from the second to the sixth years of life) between these three persons, as experienced and mastered by the growing child, contributes decisively to character formation. In other words, the definitive foundations of all later modes of feeling, thinking and action are laid down during this period. . . . If the experiences of the Oedipus phase are not mastered, then neurotic symptoms are later practically the rule."[21]

Is not all this very important for the psychological understanding of religion? We must not lose sight in particular of this last group of problems. But, on the other hand, might not religion also be very important for psychotherapy?

## The importance of religion for Jung, Fromm, Frankl

For Freud, religion still had the function of a "universal obsessional neurosis." For *C. G. Jung*, on the other hand, it was precisely the want of religion, of a living religion, that was the cause of many neuroses. It seemed to him that "side by side with the decline of religious life, the neuroses grow noticeably more frequent."[22] For Freud, then, religion produced neurosis and was itself a neurosis substitute, but for Jung it produced a cure for neuroses and prevented the rise of neuroses. Jung had observed: "Among all my patients in the second half of life—that is to say, over thirty-five—there has not been one whose problem in the last resort was not that of finding a religious outlook on life. It is safe to say that everyone of them fell ill because he had lost what the religions of every age have given to their followers, and none of them has been really healed who did not regain his religious outlook. This of course has nothing to do with a particular creed or membership of a church."[23]

What is to be solved is not only the organization of the instincts but also the *question of the meaning of life.* Jung sees in the psychoneurosis, in the last resort, "the suffering of a soul which has not discovered its meaning."[24] But what will happen when someone "has *no love,* but only sexuality; no faith, because he is afraid to grope in the dark; *no hope,* because he is disillusioned by the world and by life; and *no understanding,* because he has failed to read the meaning of his own existence"?[25] Here, according to Jung, is revealed a complex of problems that we simply cannot take too seriously and that brings the doctor of souls into the closest contact with the pastor. Here it is not only a question of repressed sexuality, even if the sexual sphere is in fact disturbed. Here it is a question of the meaning of life, by comparison with which the disturbance of the instinctual sphere may be secondary. "That is why I regard the religious problems which the patient puts before me as authentic and as possible causes of the neurosis."[26]

At the same time, it is of the utmost importance—so to speak, "the essence of the moral problem and the acid test of one's whole outlook on life"[27]—that a person learn *to accept himself:* to accept himself also with his darker side, with all the irrational, meaningless, evil elements. But, at this very point, it is not sufficient, with Freud, to make the darker side and the evil elements conscious through psychoanalysis: "Freud has unfortunately overlooked the fact that man has never yet been able single-handed to hold his own against the powers of darkness—that is, of the unconscious. Man has always stood in need of the spiritual help which his particular religion held out to him. . . . Man is never helped in his suffering by what he thinks of for himself: only suprahuman, revealed truth lifts him out of his distress."[28]

*Erich Fromm,*[29] the German-American psychoanalyst, of Jewish descent, born 1900 in Frankfurt am Main, attaches more importance than Freud and Jung to the fact that man must be seen not merely abstractly or in the inner workings of his mind as *homo psychologicus* but—as Adler also sees him—in his essential relatedness to the world and thus increasingly—as the young Marx saw him—in his sociopsychological dimension. Freud and Marx should be considered together: this becomes increasingly clearly Fromm's concern.[30] For man's passions cannot be derived directly and solely from biologically preexisting instincts: they are formed sociobiologically from the setting of the relationship of human needs to the environment and are thus essentially the consequence of social and cultural conditions.

The *psychoanalyst* himself is also involved in this relationship to the world. His thinking and feeling are *influenced by his Weltanschauung and his system of values*. His interpretations differ according to the kind of person he is. Two basic attitudes must be observed here.[31] There are psychoanalysts who act as "adjustment advisers": for them, the primary goal of life and also of psychoanalysis is "social adjustment," adaptation to the existing social structures. Other psychoanalysts regard themselves as true "doctors of souls": for them, the primary goal is the "cure of the soul," that is, the optimal development of a person's potentialities, the realization of his individuality and his moral-intellectual integrity in the unfolding of a fruitful affirmation of life, of love.

Starting out in this way, how does Fromm regard *religion?* He makes this clear in his lectures under the title of *Psychoanalysis and Religion,* which represent a consistent continuation of his work on the *Psychology of Ethics.*[32] Psychoanalysis, he maintains, which is concerned with human individuality and integrity, is *not irreconcilably opposed to a genuine humanitarian* (not authoritarian) *religion.*[33] For such a humanitarian religion is certainly not simply to be derived from a supernatural power to which man has to submit: absolutely speaking, it does not need a God beyond the world on whom alone the acceptance of life could be based. But neither is it simply to be traced—as Freud traced it—to a superego, a supposedly authoritarian conscience. As if conscience could not also provide a balance and be a calming influence; as if it could not help man to overcome estrangement and nonidentity. On the contrary, with both genuine religion and psychoanalysis, it is a question of knowledge of the truth, the freedom and independence of man, his capacity for love, of the social conditions in which these things can flourish, of the knowledge of the difference between good and evil and of listening to one's conscience.

According to Fromm, the attitude—"religious" in the widest sense of the term—of wonder, of rapture, of becoming one with the universe, is found also in psychoanalysis: a process of breaking through the barriers of the conscious ego and of contact with the hitherto excluded unconscious, advancing toward a surrender to a framework of orientation that transcends the individual, to an unconditional assent to life. This unconscious, however, is not to be understood either with Freud as the repressed, negative, "evil," or with Jung as practically a source of revelation and as a symbol for God. Our unconscious, shaped individually in the system of the passions, is from the very beginning in contact with its environment and reacts to it by affirming or denying: it begins already to realize productively or negatively man's need for roots, identity, effectiveness and devotion, and therefore contains at one and the same time the lowest and the highest, the worst and the best, the acceptance and rejection of life, all possible wishes, misgivings, ideas and insights, which must not be repressed but permeated and integrated with the supreme values of the religions. *The unconscious* thus becomes *the point at which positive human possibilities can be realized.*

There is, then, no irreconcilable opposition between psychoanalysis and religion, no threat to genuine, humanitarian religion from psychoanalysis. For Fromm, the question is not—as it was for Freud—that of religion or no religion, but, of what religion? For Fromm, then, it all depends on what you mean by "religion."[34] Certainly psychoanalysis presents a *threat to the "scientific-magical" aspect* of religion: the unverifiable hypotheses about nature and its creation. But *there is no threat to the "experiential" or "semantic" aspect:* religious feeling and devotion and symbolic language in life and customs. Even if a psychoanalyst like Fromm is unable to make any positive statements about God, it is at this very point that psychoanalysis can help toward a deeper appreciation of the profound wisdom embodied in religion.

*Neither is* the *"ritualistic" aspect* of religion *threatened.* It is true that Freud rightly observed a parallelism between certain religious rites and neurotic obsessional actions. But he and a number of psychoanalysts overlooked the fact that, in addition to irrational rites that have a repressive and obsessive character, neglect of which leads to fear and feelings of guilt, there are also rational forms of worship, which promote life and which without compulsion "express our devotion to dominant values by actions shared with others."[35] Together with secular rites (forms of greeting, clapping by way of applause, reverence for the dead, etc.), there are also meaningful religious rites: "A religious ritual of washing can be understood as a meaningful and rational expression of an inner cleansing without any obsessional or irrational component, as a symbolic expression of our wish for inner purity performed as ritual to prepare for an activity requiring full concentration and devotion. In the same way, rituals such as fasting, religious wedding ceremonies, concentration and meditation practices can be entirely rational rituals, in need of no analysis except for the one which leads to an understanding of their intended meaning."[36] According to Fromm, even modern man has a need for ritual which is largely underestimated.

Admittedly, despite Fromm's positive appreciation of the function of religion in the individual and sociocultural spheres, one thing must be noticed. Fromm, like Adler, makes *no concessions to belief in God* as experience of a reality existing independently of man and the world. For him, too, at the heart of the question of religion the ultimate reality is not God but man. The question raised is about the function of belief in God, not about the reality of God. Hence, according to Fromm, what is important is not so much the affirmation or denial of God, of whom we know nothing, but the affirmation or rejection of certain human attitudes. A human attitude that Fromm would call "religious" in the humanitarian sense should be developed: instead of deifying things or aspects of the world, there should be an attitude of love and reasonableness. But will not any serious believer in God agree at least with Fromm's rejection of modern idolatry: "It is not only pictures in stone and wood that are idols. Words can become idols; leaders, the state, power and political groups may also serve. Science and the opinion of one's neighbors can become idols, and God has become an idol for many."[37] Certainly we can agree with Fromm that God, too, can become an idol. But cannot God be seen differently even by a psychoanalyst?

In this respect, *Viktor E. Frankl*—born in 1905 in Vienna, often described as the founder of a "third Viennese trend in psychotherapy (logotherapy)" and influential especially in the U.S.A.—also goes beyond Jung and Fromm. According to him, man is determined not only by an unconscious instinctual element (Freud) or even an unconscious psychical element (Jung) but also by an unconscious spiritual element or an unconscious spirituality. According to Frankl, the psychotherapist in his everyday practice is continually faced with ideological, spiritual questions that, as such, must be taken absolutely seriously. They are not to be *a priori* unmasked as sublimations of the libido (Freud) or interpreted as the impersonal expressions of a collective unconscious, as archetypes (Jung). These are questions that are summed up in that of the meaning of human life, completely neglected by Freud and all-too-hastily psychologized by Adler and Jung. A cure is possible—that spiritual orientation that man needs for his health and for directing his life—not from the soul, the "psyche," but *only from the spirit, from the "logos."* Consequently, religious feeling in particular is not to be repressed. Hence Frankl demands a psychotherapy oriented to the spiritual and to the conscious— but unforced—"will to meaning (logos)." Psychoanalysis must progress to existential analysis, secular confession to medical pastoral care, psychotherapy to *logotherapy*. Frankl, too, proceeds empirically. With conscience as a model and with the aid of existential-analytical interpretations of dreams, with numerous examples from his own practice, he attempts to convince the reader of the reality of an unconscious religious attitude and relatedness to God.

Of course *questions* arise here as to whether it is possible to conclude so quickly from the "facticity" to the "transcendental quality" of conscience: from the voice of conscience to a "trans-human agent" that is even of "a personal nature" and indeed to an "unconscious God."[38] In the light of this religious position, does not Frankl pass judgment too hastily on "irreligious man," who cannot get beyond conscience in its "immanent facticity"?[39] Where Fromm is too detached in a negative psychology (theology?), does not Frankl press too ardently for a positive theology (psychology?)? And where Freud sees only the manifestation of the instinctual—in fact, the sexual—element, Frankl sees the manifestation of the spiritual and even the religious.

This much, however, must be granted to Frankl: decades before the sense of futility threatened to become a mass neurosis, he demanded more clearly than any other of the great psychotherapists that psychotherapy face the spiritual questions, particularly the *question of meaning* and eventually also the *question of God*, in order not to evade the confrontation with theology.[40]

Meanwhile, however, *psychoanalysts even of Freud's school* have increasingly paid attention to what Jung and Frankl pointed out at an early stage. In Freud's Vienna before the First World War—there, too, a period of "Victorian" prudery—the problem of repressed sexuality was rightly placed at the center of therapeutical efforts. At that time, the "id" needed an intensive analysis. But now the "ego" is drawing renewed attention to itself. The sociocultural conditions of most neuroses should not be overlooked. Should we not now consider also the problem of *repressed religious feeling?*

From the middle of the present century, the *problem of man's identity* has been in the foreground. In this connection, we may refer to Erik Erikson's *Childhood and Society* (1950)[41] and Rollo May's *Man's Search for Himself* (1953).[42] As a result of his own clinical experiences and those of his colleagues, May observed at that time: "The chief problem of people in the middle decade of the twentieth century is *emptiness*."[43] He added: "The human being cannot live in a condition of emptiness for very long: if he is not growing *toward* something, he does not merely stagnate; the pent-up potentialities turn into morbidity and despair, and eventually into destructive activities";[44] "the experience of emptiness . . . generally comes from people's feeling that they are *powerless* to do anything effective about their lives or the world they live in."[45] Some years later—after the student revolts had broken out in force—May could write: "The cultural values by which people had gotten their sense of identity had been wiped away. Our patients were aware of this *before* society at large was, and they did not have the defenses to protect themselves from its disturbing and traumatic consequences."[46]

Does it in fact require today the enormous courage of a Freud to oppose a stale sexual morality and sexual prudery? Is it not the spiritual that is repressed today, more than the sexual? In addition to repression, is not the control of sexuality—insufficiently stressed by Freud—also a genuine problem? In our present-day, consumer society are not the specific behavior disorders to be found in the comfort-seeking and self-indulgent attitudes and in addictions of all kinds, from cigarettes to drugs? And is it a question today merely of regaining the capacity for enjoyment and achievement and not, rather, of regaining a true sense of life and a purpose in life?

No, the *typical neurosis of our time* is not the repression of sexuality and guilt, but *lack of orientation, absence of norms, meaninglessness, futility*, and consequently the *repression of morality and religious feeling*. Psychotherapists of the most diverse trends today increasingly deplore "the proliferation of the pleasure-principle together with the simultaneous neglect and repression of spiritual and religious principles."[47] The whole development—including the problem of the addiction particularly of educated young people for quasi-religious ideologies up to the point of terrorist anarchy—is connected in no small degree with the breakdown of religious beliefs and the abandonment of religious rites. Do not these things in particular foster man's individuation and self-discovery, as factors of order could they not offer orientation, and by the fostering and guidance of sensitivity and emotionality could they not contribute to creativity, to an extension of awareness? Might they not help toward a working over of the past and even toward an authentic "regression"? For a regression wrongly understood, particularly in the religious sphere, can be a disastrous flight; that is, when someone falls back into infantile patterns of behavior that are not appropriate to his present age and his present situation in life. But a regression rightly understood, with the aid of certain religious practices (prayer, worship, examination of conscience, confession), can be supremely helpful for a healthy person and can smooth the path to progression and maturity, in as much—that is— as he reexperiences, positively assimilates and reintegrates into his self-identification what has been forgotten or repressed.

*Freud*, the atheist, undoubtedly rejected Christianity in principle. But was he so remote from it in practice? "As you admit, I have done a great deal for love": this is what he wrote as early as 1910 to Pastor Oskar Pfister, the only theologian with whom he remained in intellectual contact throughout his life.[48] In Freud's system at that time, however, there was no place for any concept except that of sexually defined love, the all-embracing libido. It was only at the end of his life that Freud acknowledged nonsexual love.[49] At that point, man became for him more than the mechanistically understood system driven by the ego instinct and libido, *homme machine*, basically isolated and egoistic, which he had constructed under the influence of Brücke and the earlier physiologists. He now saw man as a being essentially related to others, driven by vital instincts demanding union with others. Life and love belong together and are more deeply rooted than all sexuality.

As late as 1930, in his *Civilisation and Its Discontents*, Freud had described the Christian commandment of love of neighbor as "not reasonable," as "unpsychological" and "impossible to fulfil."[50] Three years later, in view of the darkening world situation with Hitler's seizure of power, in an open letter (not published in Germany) to Albert Einstein, Freud called for love "without a sexual aim" as an indirect way of opposing war: "There is no need for psycho-analysis to be ashamed to speak of love in this connection, for religion itself uses the same words: 'Thou shalt love thy neighbour as thyself.' "[51]

What Freud admitted here in theory—love of neighbor—he had practiced for a long time, admittedly without knowing why. As early as 1915, he wrote to James Putnam, the Harvard neurologist: "When I ask myself why I have always behaved honourably, ready to spare others and to be kind wherever possible, and why I did not give up being so when I observed that in that way one harms oneself and becomes an anvil because other people are brutal and untrustworthy, then, it is true, I have no answer."[52]

Is there really no answer?

## 4. Interim results III: Theses on atheism

Anyone who looks back over our lengthy critical-constructive treatment of atheism can scarcely accuse us of having placed the modern critics of religion in what *Theodor W. Adorno*—distinguished as both philosopher and sociologist and founder, with *Max Horkheimer*, of the "Frankfurt School" and its "Critical Theory"—has described as a "distorted situation." In his essay "Reason and Revelation," he makes clear the dilemma facing the critic of religion. The controversy about revealed religion, he claims, was settled in the eighteenth century. The critic may now simply repeat the very complete series of arguments produced by the Enlightenment, and then he is saying presumably only what has long been known. Or he may be content with these familiar arguments, and then he comes under suspicion as an old-fashioned eighteenth-century type of rationalist. This situation could be exploited by the defenders of religion.

Nevertheless, even in the face of the criticism not only of revealed religion but of religion in general, which reached its peak only after the Enlightenment, in the nineteenth and twentieth centuries, we had no wish to evade at all costs the question of truth, as Adorno complains, in order, "instead of objectively reflecting on truth or falsehood, to make the age as such responsible for the decision and wherever possible to play off what belonged to the day before yesterday against what belonged to yesterday."[1] Radical criticism of religion cannot really be outmaneuvered. Not with the argument that we know it already and it is therefore false. Nor by "adapting ourselves to the present religious need, which is so singularly and explicably connected with the prevailing positivism."[2] That is why we repeatedly resisted the temptation "to leap abruptly from the continuing nominalistic situation into realism, by-passing the world of ideas existing in itself, which is thus turned for its own part into a product of pure subjectivity, of what is called decision, but is really whim."[3] As if God really existed simply because man uses the name, the word, "God," or thinks of the idea of God. We then had to consider with the utmost seriousness the reasons that seemed to tell against his existence. Now we are in a position to draw out some of the lines indicated by contemporary critics of religion and eventually also to link them together. Which conclusions should be stressed?

## Correcting course

The early rationalist criticism of religion in the eighteenth century, the classical criticism of religion in the nineteenth and early-twentieth centuries, and more recent criticism have one thing in common: rejection of religion as a whole is connected with rejection of institutionalized religion, rejection of Christianity with rejection of Christendom, *rejection of God* with *rejection of the Church*. This was true already of La Mettrie and Holbach; it was true especially of Feuerbach, Marx and Freud. And this precisely is true also of present-day criticism of religion, also—for instance—of Adorno, Horkheimer and Hans Albert.[4]

In an interview shortly before his death, Max Horkheimer, the philosopher and sociologist above mentioned, with a clarity unparalleled thitherto in the "Frankfurt School," made a decidedly positive assessment of religion and theology as a possible instrument for the criticism of unjust social conditions. This surprised many who had come to know and admire him as a Marxist philosopher, ideological critic, social analyst and father of the "Critical Theory." Above all, the programmatic description of religion as an expression of the "longing for the Wholly Other" led many to think that here was an old man who had become resigned and lost his critical powers. The cliché of the obstinate atheist converted on his deathbed turned up.

Now, however, when, with the appearance of the *Notizen*,[5] Horkheimer's later work is definitively available, his statements on religion can no longer be isolated but must be seen in continuity with his and Adorno's "Critical Theory." There can in any case be no question of a modification of his former criticism of religion, still less of ingratiation with ecclesiastical institutions. On the contrary, his charge against the Church and theology is unmistakable. The Christian religion has not understood how "to translate its conviction of the existence of an all-bountiful God into practice in the course of the history that it has dominated and on which it has made its mark."[6] For "its representatives have not made credible the assumption of an all-bountiful God, nor have they acted in the spirit of a divine Creator and Founder, but frequently perpetrated cruelties and abominations which placed religion at the disposal of evil human instincts. The Crusades and the burning of witches are sad examples of this. The vexation of oppressed human beings in unworthy conditions was diverted—precisely with the aid of established religion—to defenceless victims and objects of aggression. Out of this practice there arose a serious threat to religion."[7]

We have drawn attention elsewhere to the striking phenotypical similarities particularly between Roman Catholicism and Soviet Communism with regard to ideology, organization and power structure.[8] Can we charge these critics of religion and the churches with being—so to speak—blind in the left eye and seeing one-sidedly only the defects and aberrations in religion and Christianity? The same critic continues: "Communism, too, has experienced a similar fate. Communism, which set out to establish a peaceful unification of all countries and—for the time being—of all the people in the one country and to abolish the class society, set up in all the countries under its control a class domination far stricter than that of the non-Communist world. Here, too, the aggressiveness of oppressed human beings is diverted to external threats and enemies—that is, to countries in which there is no flagrant class domination of that kind."[9]

There is one striking feature of contemporary criticism of religion. No matter how much the Church and Christendom are criticized, the person of Jesus Christ always remains beyond criticism and is even invoked as an authority against the former: "Anyone who does not see from the Gospel that Jesus died *in opposition* to his modern representatives is unable to read. This theology is the most cruel mockery which ever befell an idea."[10] Would not God perhaps look different if he were seen in the light of the concrete Jesus instead of that of the concrete Church? As Horkheimer, again, says, "The man at the stake, on the gallows, on the cross, is the symbol of Christianity. Who is to be regarded as my neighbor is not for the prevailing system to decide: the prison, the gas chamber, are at least no more remote from the disciples of the Divine Delinquent than are headquarters. It was for the sake of their souls that the barbarian rulers, the men of quick decisions, the commanders and their associates, were received with love. In the first place, the Covenant affected the poor in spirit, whose lives were not primarily oriented to wealth, dominion, political expediency, not even to prestige. In the first centuries of the Christian era, when the emerging peoples outside and the increasing barbarity of the struggle with them shook the self-confidence of the Senate and people within, the proclamation of the goal hereafter gave a new meaning to life for the enslaved masses and the distressed people under their masters."[11]

How closely the question of God and that of the Church are connected can be observed continually among both Christians and atheists. Can the theologian in particular overlook this fact? Some older spiritualizing or aestheticizing theologians on the one side and some younger sociocritical theologians on the other are agreed, oddly enough—the former on the high-altitude flight of mysticism, the latter gliding over the sociopolitical program—in neglecting the concrete, earthly Church and especially what seem to be commonplace, practical, structural questions. This is a more congenial and also more opportunist way out, often dictated by fear of disciplinary measures. But the fact cannot be overlooked that, for both atheists and Christians, theological questions of faith and practical questions of Church structures—quite generally, *theory and practice*—go together. If the churches are not credible in their practice—and for many today they do not seem to be—who is to speak up for God publicly and credibly before the whole world?

Of course, we are not going to talk here about an undifferentiated unity of theory and practice. Certainly theory may not be separated from practice. But neither can practice be separated from theory. Theory and practice do indeed go together. But theory may not be reduced to practice, nor may practice be reduced to theory.[12] We shall have to go into the problems of pragmatism for their own sake later. But here two points should be noted.

a. *Practice is not the criterion of the truth of theory*. Truth cannot be equated with practical utility, practicability, exploitability; it cannot be sacrificed to tactics, nor abandoned to utilitarian pragmatism. Hence, practical people should not be hostile to theory, as if thinking itself were not action and theory not a form of practice capable of itself of producing practical change. In fact, even a theory that is not followed up can be true; a message, too, that meets with little or no faith can still be right. Success is not a criterion of truth.

b. *Theory, however, must lead to practice*. Theory has to be proved in practice, it must be practically verified. Theorists, then, must not dissociate themselves from practice, as if science had nothing to do with life, reflection nothing to do with action, thinking with getting things done, theoretical with practical reason, knowledge with interest.

A *course correction* is therefore urgent not only for the Church's theological theory but *also for the Church's practice*. Applied to belief in God, this would mean especially:

- *Belief in God is proved in practice:*
  *Believers in God who live in a truly human way are an argument for that belief. But the reverse is also true:*
  *Believers in God who do not live in a truly human way are an argument against that belief.*
- *Nevertheless, the criterion of the truth of belief in God is not simply practice:*
  *Believers in God who do not live in a truly human way cannot make that faith untrue in itself. But the reverse is also true:*
  *Believers in God who live in a truly human way cannot make that belife true in itself.*

- *The question of God and the question of the Church, the under-standing of God and reform of the Church, theo-logy and ecclesio-logy, therefore go together:*
  *The question of God is certainly more important than the question of the Church, but the question of the Church frequently distorts the question of God.*[13]
  *The Church, existing for the proclamation of God, by its teaching and practice can compromise belief in God. But, if credible, it can also by its teaching and practice keep open for man the question of God and reinforce or freshly awaken belief in God.*[14]

But do we not often get the impression that too little is known in the churches today about how to speak of God firmly and convincingly? Our discussion with atheism in particular may provide some guidelines for this.

## The question of truth

Ever since the Enlightenment, the traditional faith of the Church has been attacked in the name of critical reason. On the part of the churches, however, this faith has often been defended by an equally rationalistic appeal to reason, and thus the argument has been brought down to the level of the opponent—at the expense of faith. But in our changed situation, after all the political, economic and social upheavals, confidence in the power of reason has for a long time been less obvious than it seemed at the time of the Enlightenment. Instead of an optimism of reason, a pessimism of reason is now widespread; instead of rationalism, we have irrationalism. On the part of the churches, therefore, the attempt has frequently been made to exploit the crisis of reason to the advantage of faith. With the aid of rational reflection, theologians fight against rational reflection. Reason is knocked down by reason, in order to justify faith. It is precisely against this attitude, as opportunist as it is shortsighted, that *Theodor W. Adorno* raises his objections, which may be summed up under two headings.

a. *Instead of raising the question of the truth of religion,* an appeal is made in theology and in the Church to the *need* (admittedly widespread) *of religion:* "It is not the truth and authenticity of revelation that is decisive, but the need of orientation, the recourse to what solidly exists; also the hope, simply by willing it, of being able to breathe a meaning into the disenchanted world, so that we no longer suffer as mere spectators staring at its emptiness."[15]
*But:* "The sacrifice of the intellect, which was once made—as in the case of Pascal or Kierkegaard—by the most advanced consciousness and at the cost of little less than a whole life, has meanwhile been socialized, and anyone who makes the sacrifice is thereby relieved of the burden of fear

and trembling."[16] Adorno in particular has analyzed the situation more clearly than others in his *Dialectic of Enlightenment*.[17] As a result of the triumph of human rationality, the Enlightenment made possible a progressive control of nature—what Max Weber called the "disenchantment of nature." But, at the same time, through rationalizing, mechanizing, industrializing, together with the simultaneous atomizing of the individual and the deindividualizing of whole societies, it has brought infinite suffering and disaster to human beings in a "managed world." How much is now blamed on rationality itself, on reason as such! But, according to Adorno, people overlook the fact that we suffer not from too much but from too little rationality: that the Enlightenment was not driven too far for the benefit of mankind but was broken off too soon.

b. *Instead of appealing to the truth of religion*, in both theology and the Church, the appeal is made to the *necessity of commitments*: "The heteronomous is chosen—so to speak—from a precarious autonomy."[18]

*But:* "At the present time, despite all secularity, there are too many, rather than too few, commitments."[19] And behind this craving for commitments there is concealed not only the weakness of the ego (Freud) but frequently also a capitulation to the existing inhuman conditions and even their fetishizing (Marx). As if man were simply not capable of humanity: "What Thomas Mann—reacting against Spengler—once called the 'defeatism of humanity' has become universal. Turning to transcendence serves as a cover for immanent, sociological hopelessness."[20] Here, then, a pact is made with fear. And yet: "The victories that religion gains in the name of such fear are Pyrrhic victories. If religion is accepted for the sake of something other than its own truth content, it is undermined."[21]

As a theologian, must one not agree with this criticism? Does not this critique of religion rightly challenge theology not to be satisfied with second-rate motives of faith, but to raise with the utmost clarity the *question of truth?* We offer the following observations, therefore, as an echo of Adorno's criticism and as recalling those of Feuerbach, Marx and Freud:

- *Belief in God can never be a question merely of some kind of (individual or social) human needs, which are supposed to call for religion. Instead, it must be a question of the full, strict truth of belief in God: not of its usefulness but of its truth content. Otherwise faith, adopting the wrong defense against unbelief, becomes superstition.*
- *Belief in God must never be a question merely of irrational feelings and sentiments, but neither can it be a matter merely of teachings, dogmas, formularies, to be transmitted automatically. It must be a question of continual effort in seeking to think out afresh the truth of belief in God. Otherwise faith, adopting the wrong defense against rationalism, becomes merely an emotional faith or a faith in the letter.*

- Rationality *must not—as in rationalism—be made absolute or be isolated: there must be no intellectual pride.*
  *But neither may rationality—as in irrationalism—be passed over or sacrificed: there must be no intellectual sacrifice.*
  *Instead, rationality must be taken seriously as one factor—but only as one factor—within reality as a whole.*

All this should mean that our earlier plea for a critical rationality without ideological rationalism[22] has made a considerable advance. With reference to the relations between reason and faith—which must be more closely defined at a later stage—it can now be observed that the two go together in principle. They cannot simply be separated, but neither can they be simply identified. It is wrong to say either "we must simply believe" or "we can know everything."

But if with belief in God it is a matter of the whole, strict truth, it must obviously be the same with *atheism.* And consequently, with reference to Feuerbach, Marx and Freud, we may recapitulate our conclusions:

- *All* proofs or arguments of the eminent atheists *are certainly adequate to raise doubts about the existence of God but not to make God's nonexistence unquestionable. Neither a philosophical-psychological (Feuerbach), nor a sociocritical (Marx), nor a psychoanalytical (Freud) interpretation of belief in God can decide on the existence or nonexistence of a reality independent of our thinking, willing and feeling, of psyche and society.*
- *The constantly varied* arguments, based on philosophy of history or of culture, for an end of religion *involve an ultimately unsubstantiated extrapolation into the future. Neither the "nullification of religion" by atheistic humanism (Feuerbach)*[23] *nor the "withering away of religion" to be brought about by atheistic socialism (Marx)*[24] *nor the "supersession of religion" by atheistic science (Freud)*[25] *has proved to be a true prognosis.*
- *The continually varied* individual- or social-psychological arguments for religion as projection *are based on a postulate that is neither methodically nor objectively substantiated. Feuerbach's projection theory,*[26] *Marx's opium theory*[27] *and Freud's illusion theory*[28] *were not able to prove that God is merely a projection of man or merely a consolation serving vested interests or merely an infantile illusion. "Only" propositions or "nothing but" propositions must therefore be distrusted.*
- *Atheism, too, lives by an* undemonstrable faith: *whether it is faith in human nature (Feuerbach)*[29] *or faith in the future socialist society (Marx)*[30] *or faith in rational science (Freud).*[31] *The absolutizing of sensible experience (Feuerbach), of the sociological process (Marx), or of scientific development (Freud), remains a dogma of humanist, socialist, psychoanalytical antidogmatism. The question, then, can be*

*asked of any form of atheism whether it is not itself an understandable projection of man (Feuerbach), a consolation serving vested interests (Marx) or an infantile illusion (Freud).*

● *But, just because atheism turns out in the last resort to be unsubstantiated, this does not by any means show that belief in God is substantiated. Is it possible, then, to justify, to verify, on the other hand, belief in God? We seem to have reached an impasse.*

In fact, the existence of God is questioned; but so, too, is his nonexistence. Belief in God seems to be unproved, but neither is atheism proved. Is it perhaps impossible to verify that God is either living or dead? In the light both of philosophy (Feuerbach) and of sociological criticism and sociological theory (Marx), and also of psychology and depth psychology (Freud), the question of God still appears to be an open question.

## Against a theological withdrawal strategy

Time was when God was seen as the one immediately responsible for everything that could not be explained. When science made possible the knowledge of intramundane events in the light of their own natural causes, without any need to appeal to God as an explanatory hypothesis, God seemed to have become superfluous. Weather and victory in battle, sickness and healing, the happiness and unhappiness of individuals, groups and nations, are not explained by modern men in terms of God's direct and immediate intervention but by natural causes operating within the framework of nature's laws.

This exclusion of God from the world understandably created difficulties for theology and required the latter to go through a new process of learning. But what was not understandable was the odd *theological strategy of defense and withdrawal,* yielding ground only involuntarily and bit by bit: repeated useless rearguard actions that demanded sacrifices from innumerable people in theology and Church. We may recall briefly what happened.[32]

When God's direct intervention was no longer needed to explain the inexplicable happenings in daily life, there was a withdrawal to the point at which God was necessary to direct the planetary orbits. When it became possible to explain the planetary orbits by gravitation, there was a further withdrawal to the point at which God's direct intervention seemed to be required to explain the still not explicable deviations in their orbits (Newton). And when even these deviations came to be explained and God appeared to have no function in the present universe (Laplace), there was a fresh withdrawal. It was now time to concentrate on the beginning of the world and, against Darwin's theory of evolution, fiercely to defend a literal understanding of the biblical accounts of creation.

The treatment of the *case of Darwin,* particularly in the Catholic Church, was quite as symptomatic as the treatment of Galileo. As early as 1860, a year after the appearance of Darwin's epoch-making work (and the year of publication of the German translation), at the Particular Council of Cologne, the German bishops officially opposed the theory of evolution, explaining that the origin of the human body from the higher animal forms was contrary to Scripture and had to be rejected as incompatible with Catholic dogma.[33] The majority of Catholic theologians and later also the Roman magisterium took the same line. Theological dissenters were subsequently intimidated, compelled to withdraw their books and thus reduced to silence. The suffering of a Pierre Teilhard de Chardin, who tried in our time to reconcile theology with evolutionary thought, alone speaks volumes. As recently as 1941, almost a century after the publication of Darwin's *Origin of Species,* in an address to the Pontifical Academy of the Sciences, Pius XII declared that the origin of human life from animal ancestors was completely unproved and—we are reminded of *Humanae Vitae* and the pill—that further investigations would have to be awaited.[34] Only in the (completely reactionary) encyclical *Humani Generis* (1950) did the same Pope admit expressly, with many warnings, that the still wholly uncertain problem of an evolution of the human body might be further investigated scientifically and theologically (naturally, under certain conditions). For it had to be maintained that the human soul was directly created by God and that the whole human race originated from a single human couple (monogenism): in every case, the judgment of the Church's magisterium had to be obeyed.[35]

Thus the claim that the whole world was directly created by God was withdrawn, and it was then maintained that life (as opposed to inorganic matter) originated by direct creation. After this, direct creation was restricted to man (as opposed to animals) and finally—or so it seems today —it was accepted that no sort of direct intervention in the evolution of the world and of man need be involved. Is this credible belief in God?

It seemed as if there was a desire to rehearse—so to speak—the first chapters of the Bible and on each occasion to repeat constantly the same mistake: after Genesis 1 (creation of the world in six days) and Genesis 2 (creation of the one human couple), now Genesis 3 (the first sin, original sin, the devil), the point at which certain hierarchs and theologians even today, uncomprehending as ever, want to uphold dogmatically the old, traditional ideas. The same can be said of the New Testament with reference to Christology (from preexistence and virgin birth by way of nature miracles up to the descent into hell and ascension into heaven). This continually repeated strategy of defense and withdrawal, unfortunately, provides some justification for the comment of the English philosopher Anthony Flew on the treatment of the hypothesis of God: "A fine brash hypothesis may thus be killed by inches, the death of a thousand qualifications."[36]

Not least because of this deplorable strategy of defense and withdrawal, "natural theology" along with conservative biblical exegesis has fallen into discredit among modern theologians. To quote now a witness from the sociological camp opposed to the "Frankfurt School," an atheist defender of the "critical rationalism" inspired by K. R. Popper, *Hans Albert* observes with satisfaction: "For the most part they do not want to know much about natural theology, and this is associated with the fact that such a theology has been made obsolete as a result of the progress of science."[37]

Such a "natural theology as a constituent of a cosmological theory"[38] is in fact obsolete. But does this mean that all the preoccupations of the former "natural theology" are also obsolete? Albert himself warns theologians: "The unpleasant consequences of this situation are overlooked. As long as we think we need a natural theology as a relevant explanatory constituent of a cosmology, we continue to have reasons also for believing in the existence of God. That is to say, the idea of God is not without a function within the framework of the accepted world picture, even though strict proofs of God are bound to miscarry, simply because a proof cannot guarantee any meaningful statements. But as soon as a natural theology turns out to be superfluous, the maintenance of the old idea of God—however much certain human needs seem to speak in favor of it— is objectively nothing more than a constituent part of a questionable ideological strategy, of an *ad hoc* procedure, which must necessarily lead to 'scandals,' 'paradoxes' and 'dilemmas.' "[39]

Adorno had also criticized a religion and theology that evades confrontation with the findings of natural science: "There was a time when religion was not so fastidious, and with good reason. It insisted on its truth even in the cosmological sense, because it knew that its claim on that of the material-concrete content could not be set apart without being damaged. As soon as it relinquishes its objective content, it is liable to evaporate into pure symbolism, and this strikes at the very life of its claim to truth."[40]

What is to be said of this from the theological standpoint? It is clear from all that has been said up to now—especially in the first chapter, on reason, faith and world picture[41]—that there is no question here of defending a theology that evades confrontation with the conclusions of natural science. Nor, of course, one that capitulates to them. In particular, we are not going to raise questions about God without reference to the world (acosmic questions), concentrated solely on human existence (existential questions). If God today is no longer seen as an immediate, universal or partial *cosmic principle of explanation* of particular sequences of events in the universe, *neither* can he be regarded merely *as a principle of existential interpretation*, intended simply to assist the individual human existence to a proper self-understanding. God must be considered *in relation to the totality of man and the world*. The solutions of a "natural theology" can be rejected, but not its problems. Indeed, albeit from a different standpoint, its real preoccupations must be thought out afresh. Here we shall only make a few provisional distinctions in response to the objections raised by the critics of religion.

- *No science—neither theology nor any other—has as its object all aspects of the world, of human life and action. If, then, other scientists—natural scientists, psychologists, sociologists—are rightly concerned mainly with analyses of data, facts, phenomena, operations, processes, energies, structures, developments, so, too, the theologian is rightly concerned with questions of* ultimate or primary *interpretations, objectives, values, ideals, norms, decisions, attitudes. These often tormenting but perhaps also liberating questions about an ultimate or primary why and wherefore, whither and whence, of man and the world cannot be declared illegitimate—to appease the atheist, often more emotionally than rationally.*

- *The questions of theology, then, do not affect merely one section of all that makes up man and the world. They affect the most fundamental of all aspects of what constitutes man and the world. From this one aspect, theology examines all the strata of human life and action. If, under the one basic aspect, reality in its wholeness comes to light, theology must raise all questions related to man and the world.*

- *Undoubtedly obsolete is the question about the* God of the old world picture, *who was understood as the Almighty, immediately responsible for everything, or—later—as the still partly responsible miracle-working helper in distress and ready to fill in the gaps:*
  *the God—that is—who is to be invoked in nature and history only at the point at which we can get no farther with our human science and technology or at which we can no longer cope with our personal life;*
  *the God—that is—who, as a result of mental-material progress, has become increasingly intellectually dispensable, practically superfluous and consequently increasingly incredible.*

- *What is by no means obsolete, however, is the question about the* God of the new world picture, *who is to be understood as the transcendent-immanent, all-embracing, all-permeating, most real reality in man and in the world:*
  *the God—that is—who can be the answer to the questions of ultimate and primary interpretations, objectives, values, ideals, norms, decisions, attitudes, to the questions of the ultimate or primary why and wherefore, whither and whence, of man and the world;*
  *the God—that is—who as the Unconditioned involves us unconditionally, quite personally in the midst of and through all the relativities*

*in the world, who sustains us, supports and embraces us (infinitely distant and yet closer than we are to ourselves) as ultimate and primary ground, support and goal of all reality, who thus has a claim on us which demands response, responsibility, action, and who—for this very reason—may also be invoked.*[42]

The question about this God of the new world picture is not obsolete. But just because the question is not obsolete, it has not yet found an answer. The question is still no more than a question.

## For a serious theology

Theologians sometimes seem to have a strange fear of speaking about God, although the term "theologian" itself means "one who speaks about God." They avoid as much as possible the name of God and prefer to speak of man, whom they know better, although it would, then, be more honest to call them not "theologians" but "anthropologists," "those who speak about man."

Committed atheists are understandably irritated when theologians defend a completely vague, overstretched, *eroded concept of God* and blur the frontiers between belief in God and atheism. We noted Freud's exasperation in this respect. *Hans Albert*, too, charges theology with being a playground for lovers of dishonest "immunization strategies," by which the concept involved, and particularly the idea of God itself, "is so completely drained of meaning that it cannot be incompatible with any possible fact."[43] In this respect, too, he is aiming—although wrongly—at theologians as distinguished as Bultmann, Tillich and Niebuhr, but also at a German philosophy allegedly infected by irrationalism. The "special strategy" or "special pleading" of theologians, for which even they would have no other use in ordinary life, consists "in suspending the methodology of critical examination" in regard to certain religious beliefs. They speak simply of "faith" or of "scandals," "paradoxes," "dilemmas" of faith.[44] Could not any kind of nonsense be asserted in this way?

As "one of the most curious strategies for immunizing the idea of God which has lately become fashionable," Hans Albert mentions "the *defamation* of that concept of faith which concentrates 'merely' on the *acceptance* of a statement *as true*."[45] On the contrary, Albert rightly maintains: "The mere acceptance as true of the thesis that a God exists who possesses certain attributes or intervenes in a certain way in world events may not in practice often satisfy believers, but it is certainly a minimal implication of any faith within which it is possible meaningfully and significantly to speak about God."[46] Theologians are not speaking meaningfully and significantly about God when they use " 'God' as a metaphor for interpersonal relationships . . . or merely as an expression."[47] Or is there perhaps the possibility of a "theo-logy" without *Theos*, of an atheistic theology?

Albert accuses this kind of theology of an ambiguous-sounding "crypto-atheism." The belittling or even elimination of this problem of God's existence is not by any means a symptom of a preference for a higher or less crude form of belief in God. On the contrary, it is "a sign that people are either not clear about the important consequences of their own theory of the world or even that they have *gone over in fact to atheism* while wanting to preserve the old façade with the aid of theistic language, possibly in order not to have to give up the opportunities offered in working with an old tradition."[48] Or is God perhaps (as the theologian Fritz Buri puts it[49]) "the mythological expression for the absoluteness of being personally responsible"? It might be possible to hear Freud speaking in Albert's answer: "An idea of God that has only moral and rhetorical functions is a very dubious affair, particularly if it becomes for those addressed in these terms a question of understanding how far they are capable of seeing through the way it is used."[50] In this way—or even on the pretext of the "impossibility of objectifying God"—theologians could "continue to talk of God, unembarrassed and undisturbed," without linking with this term assertions that "have even a trace of content." The theologians "do not seem in the least disturbed" by the fact that they talk in the same way also of other arbitrarily chosen mythological beings, of witches, devils and gods.[51] Is God, then, no more real than gods, witches and devils?

Theologians who claim to be modern should in any case not talk around the problem of God's existence, whenever it turns up, in such a way "that we cannot be at all clear about what the theological—or, sometimes, philosophical—author really thinks."[52] In the face of this "elaborately constructed immunization machinery" of a specific theory of knowledge put forward particularly by Protestant theologians, in which we hear of subject-object disruption, nonobjectifiability, unobjective talk, of ciphers of being and so on, without any perceptible effort to consider the conclusions of logic, semantics, linguistics or modern epistemology, we must ask "whether in this respect even the more or less unconcealed dogmatism of Catholic thought might perhaps be preferable."[53] The Catholic theologian might prefer to answer this question in the negative, at least in so far as Albert takes "dogma" to mean a thesis "immune from criticism."[54]

But there is food for thought in the fact that even a theologian of the caliber of Gerhard Ebeling, a disciple of Bultmann, who certainly does not want to replace theology by anthropology, entered with notable commitment into discussion with Hans Albert but excluded from the very beginning the question of God, which was so important for his atheist partner. Only subsequently did he incorporate a thesis—one out of seventy—one that scarcely did justice to Albert's queries.[55] Would he not have to admit that Albert was right in saying that his " 'talk of God' also up to a point 'is left ontologically hanging in the air,' " in so far as he evades the question of God's existence, even belittles it, and at the same time continues to operate with the "infinite contentiousness and ambiguity of the vocable 'God' "?[56] It is scarcely possible to contradict Albert when he observes: "Even someone who, as a theologian, *speaks* of God 'with reference to human existence' will presumably agree that this God also exists, so that he comes quite spontaneously to the problem of God's 'objective' existence—unless he is using the 'ambiguous vocable' in that more or less metaphorical sense that is typical of modern crypto-atheism."[57]

Certainly the theologian—we may be permitted to say this—has no easy task today. Both the development of the secular world and of science and the rise of secularism and atheism that is linked with it face him with an enormous challenge: a *challenge to critical theological self-awareness.* The task today—after so many missed opportunities—is not easier than that of the Greek and Latin Fathers of the second and third centuries in their discussion with Hellenism, or that of Scholasticism confronted with Aristotelianism in the thirteenth century, or that of the Reformers of the sixteenth century in the face of humanism and the Renaissance. Today particularly this theological task can be accomplished effectively only if—as required indirectly by Feuerbach and Marx and later by Freud, Adorno, Horkheimer and Albert, and here at least attempted—it is done with the greatest possible *intellectual honesty:* against the background of this world as it really is, with the aid of the sciences and experiences of our time, with an eye on the practice of the individual, the Church and society. But in all this with continually fresh concentration on the great "cause" of theo-logy, on God himself. The more the theologian knows of this world, through the natural sciences, psychology, sociology, philosophy, art, literature and—today less than ever to be forgotten—history, but perhaps most of all through his own experiences, so much the more comprehensively will he be able to fulfill his theo-logical task. But the theologian also—singulary enough—can "worry about so many things" and forget the "one thing necessary."[58]

Particularly in view of the largely justified objections of religious criticism to dishonest theological apologetics and in view of a "plea for critical rationalism,"[59] Catholic, Protestant and Orthodox theology needs today a "plea for a critical theology," for an absolutely honest, sincere, *serious theology:*

- *Serious theology does not claim any elitist, privileged access to truth: It cannot in any case be meant to be intelligible only to believers. It claims only to be scholarly reflection on its object, with a neat method appropriate to this object, the suitability of which, as in other sciences, should be proved by results.*

- *Serious theology does not claim any complete, total possession of the truth, nor any monopoly of truth:*
  *It cannot in any case be a comprehensive ideological system, worked out to the last detail, which would ultimately render superfluous any further reflections on the part of sociologists, psychologists, economists, jurists, medical experts, scientists.*
  *It claims only to be scholarly reflection on reality from one particular standpoint, which, however, is one legitimate standpoint among others.*
- *Serious theology consequently cannot in any case be content to be graciously tolerated in an undefined, detached, special field (say, of "religious truth" analogous to "poetic truth"):*
  *In theological science, the rules are no different in principle from the rules of other sciences. Here, too, irrationality, unjustified reactions, subjectivist decisions, cannot be permitted. Strictly to be rejected are any kind of protection against arguments, information, facts; unconditional authorization of existing intellectual and social situations; biased justification of certain dogmas, ideological structures, forms of social domination.*
- *Serious theology, therefore, even within the Church, can never be concerned with putting a premium on "simple faith" or with cementing an "ecclesiastical system," but, again—always and everywhere—only with the whole and entire truth:*
  *In theological science, we cannot neglect consideration of critical arguments by appealing to some authority within the system, we cannot evade the competition of ideas, suppress temptations to doubt, exclude possibilities on the part of certain persons or in certain situations.*

The theologian cannot permit anyone to prevent him from fulfilling his task. Not even the leaders of his Church, to whom he is bound by a sense of loyalty. The theologian should struggle—as is his joyous duty and obligation—unpretentiously in serious study to find honest answers that he can justify to Church and society: undaunted in freedom, but at the same time in solidarity with his community, bound by its great tradition, loyal to its leaders and teachers. Precisely in this way, he will be increasingly concerned with the great "cause" of theology without ever being able to claim infallibility for his own part.

## Atheism to be taken seriously

As "the last stand in the retreat of Protestant theology," Horkheimer also criticizes the position of the "progressive Protestant theologians" who, without God—"the dogma that must be valid if their own talk is not to be in vain"—"ascribe to the life of the individual the significance proper only to himself." This they do by recalling their religious heritage and defining as "love" what they hold to be "more than worldly in worldly life." Horkheimer comments: "Love, however, in the abstract, as it occurs in recent works, remains as obscure as the hidden God whose place it is meant to take."[60]

As opposed to any vague approach to atheism, it seems to us that both the new solidarity between believers in God and atheists, and the enduring distinction between belief in God and atheism must be taken seriously:

a. The new *solidarity between believers in God and atheists*: If we look critically at practice, we get the impression that it has become clear also to critical atheists and agnostics that we can bring to the discovery of truth on the one side not only the positive aspects of atheism and on the other side not only the negative aspects of belief in God. In this sense and only in this sense is "the opposition between atheism and theism no longer relevant."[61] For:

*Belief in God and atheism* each has its *own debit account*: "In European history at any rate bad and good have been brought about by both, both have their tyrants and their martyrs. What remains as a hope is the effort being made to ensure that in the world period now dawning of blocks of controlled masses there will still be some who resist like the victims of history, one of whom was the Founder of Christianity." Thus Horkheimer.[62]

But *atheism and belief in God* each has also its own *credit account*: "In the critique of political economy, the theory of Marx and Engels, psychoanalysis, in those so-called nihilistic works that are on the blacklists in both East and West and rouse the anger of the mighty as the provocative speeches of the Founder once roused his contemporaries, no less than in some theological projects, the idea of a truer reality has taken shape." Again Horkheimer.[63]

A belief in God that "uses eternal justice as a pretext for temporal wrong" is "as bad" as an atheism "that allows no scope for the idea of an Other."[64] Has it been sufficiently realized on both sides that the *situation with regard to belief in God and atheism has fundamentally changed?*
*Formerly it was atheism that required courage*: "Time was when atheism was a testimony of inward independence and indescribable courage. It is still so in the authoritarian and semiauthoritarian states, where it is regarded as a symptom of the hated spirit of liberalism."[65]
*Today*, however, *belief in God often requires more courage*: "Under totalitarian rule of whatever kind, which today forms a universal threat, sincere theism usually takes a stand."[66] In this respect it must be noted that " 'atheism' includes a variety of meanings, while the term 'theism' is definite enough to stamp as hypocrites all those who hate others in its name."[67]

b. Although a not unimportant solidarity can be seen in practice between belief in God and atheism or, better, between believers in God and atheists, nevertheless the vitally important *distinction* in principle between believers in God and atheists or, better, *between belief in God and atheism*—the acceptance or rejection of the reality of God—must not be played down. The atheistic critique of religion continues to offer a serious challenge to theology which the latter must meet in an appropriate way:[68]

- *Atheism may not be indiscriminately morally condemned as deliberate apostasy from God:*
  *It is not always the result of a fully considered—still less malicious—decision against God but often of merely half-considered participation in the philosophical, scientific, cultural spirit of the age: more a drift away from faith than an abandonment of faith, sometimes admittedly also a process of repression, with all its negative consequences. It is not always the individual fault of modern man but at least also the historical fault of generations, more historical repression than real sin.*
- *Neither may atheism be theologically appropriated as hidden "belief in God":*
  *The atheists' conviction must be respected and not played down speculatively. As if their atheism were not genuine, as if their unbelief were belief, as if atheists were "secret" believers in God. As if Feuerbach, Marx and Freud, together with the atheists of today, were simply "anonymous Christians"—an idea that would seem to them, if not arrogant, then at least comic.*
- *Finally, atheism is not to be toyed with, flattered, acquiesced in:*
  *"A-theism" (denial of an independent, personal God), casually propagated, leads to atheism (complete denial of God). A God who dies has never existed; it is possible to speak of the "death" of God in theological terms at best noetically: an expression in fact of God's absence, of his dying in human experience.*

But what if God really did not exist and never had existed? The question is open now as it was before. We must ask ourselves very seriously: What would it mean for mankind if all signs of religion, from the graves of the Stone Age, the cave drawings of Altamira and the pyramids of Egypt, up to present-day grave tokens of death and eternal life, had really been set up for a nothing? If all the wonderful churches and temples from Salamanca to Agra—the finest works of art ever produced by mankind—had really been built for a nothing? If all the great thinkers from the ancient Hindus and Greeks up to the moderns had really been thinking about a pure nothing? Would the world, would our situation not be different if in place of God there were a bare nothing?

# D. NIHILISM—CONSEQUENCE OF ATHEISM

Is "God" perhaps just a word, like any other? Can we ask lightheartedly if God exists, in the same casual way as we ask if there are flying saucers or a Loch Ness monster? Does it make any difference to man if God does not exist? Does it really? Is the difference perhaps greater than Feuerbach, Marx or Freud surmised? Does atheism, thought out to the very end and consistently realized, not finally lead to the reassessment of all values, to the destruction of existing morality and thus to nihilism? In the last resort, then, is not Friedrich Nietzsche right? Has he not in fact long been proved right in the present century: this philosopher who was also a prophet and who made such an impact not least on writers, philosophers and composers, that he has decisively contributed to the shaping of European intellectual history in the twentieth century?

# I. The rise of nihilism: Friedrich Nietzsche

Just before his mental breakdown, *Friedrich Nietzsche* (1844–1900)[1] had written a survey of his life and work: *Ecce Homo. How One Becomes What One Is* (1889). He recalls that, after his "deadly attack" on the old David Friedrich Strauss and the latter's "new faith," a certain Professor Hoffmann, from Würzburg, a disciple of the philosopher Von Baader, had predicted for him a "great destiny": "bringing about a kind of crisis and ultimate decision in the problem of atheism whose most distinctive and relentless type he divined in me."[2] Decision? Against whom? Against "the theologians and all that has theologian blood in its veins—our entire philosophy."[3] This was what Nietzsche wrote about the same time in a work that he likewise did not publish himself: *The Antichrist. A Curse on Christianity*. Was it only against the theologians? No, for in the same breath Nietzsche also attacks the self-sufficient, optimistic atheism of "our naturalists and physiologists," which he can regard only as a bad "joke": "they lack passion in these things, they do not *suffer* from them."[4] On the other hand, Nietzsche, the theologian's son, declares: "One must have seen the fatality, . . . one must have experienced it in oneself, one must have almost perished by it, no longer to find anything funny here."[5] Nietzsche had little time for the rationalistic, optimistic belief in progress cherished by the educated middle classes of his century, which was then a strong and—as it is again today—widespread phenomenon. We must examine the situation more closely.

## 1. Critique of culture

Nietzsche remained skeptical especially in regard to the idea of progress, this great idea of the nineteenth century propagated—as we saw—mainly by natural scientists: "Mankind does *not* represent a development of the better or the stronger or the higher in the way that it is believed today," he holds. " 'Progress' is merely a modern idea, that is to say a false idea. The European of today is of far less value than the European of the Renaissance; onward development is not by *any* means, by any necessity the same thing as elevation, advance, strengthening."[6] Nietzsche wanted especially to "reflect" on "how far Christian assumptions and inter-

pretations live on under the formulas of 'nature,' 'progress,' 'improvement,' 'Darwinism,' in the superstition of a kind of connection between
happiness and virtue, between unhappiness and guilt. That absurd *trust* in
the course of things, in 'life,' in the 'instinct of life.' "[7] We must now return to Darwin.

## Darwin's evolutionary thinking

In 1859, Freud was three years old; two years earlier, Feuerbach had
published his great atheistic *Theogonie* and immediately afterward had to
leave his beloved Bruckberg forever; Marx had finally brought out as a
brochure the *Critique of Political Economy*, for which Engels had been
so eagerly waiting, and Nietzsche—just fifteen—had entered the famous
humanistic gynmasium of Schulpforta, in East Prussia: in the same year,
in London, Charles Darwin published his epoch-making work *On the Origin of Species by means of natural selection, or the preservation of
favoured races in the struggle for life*[8] (a German translation appeared in
1860). The English edition, of 1,250 copies, was sold out on the first day
and was enthusiastically welcomed by the protagonists of atheism: by
Feuerbach and Marx, and later by Freud. Marx, living in the same city,
even wanted to dedicate to the now world-famous author the English edition of the first (or the second) volume of his own *Das Kapital*; but Darwin remained aloof and politely declined the offer, pointing out, however,
that atheistic propaganda was detrimental to intellectual freedom.

What, then, was so extraordinarily alarming about the theories of this
doctor's son, born in 1809 in the English county of Shrewsbury, who was
driven by the experience of two surgical operations from the study of
medicine to that of theology; who then, however, turned to natural science and as unpaid scientific researcher spent five years (1831–36) in
sailing around the world in the *Beagle*; who was thus able to study and
collect plants, animals, fossils and geological data in South America, the
Pacific islands, and Australia; who—despite chronic headaches—carried
out innumerable investigations (from the origin of the volcanic islands
and coral reefs to the fertilization of orchids and the activity of earth-
worms) and published his theory only after twenty years of empirical
verification? What, then, is so extraordinarily alarming about the *Darwinian theory?* Mainly the following conclusions:
*First*: Animal and plant species can be changed. They are not, as the biblical account suggests, created independently of one another, nor—
consequently—are they, as Linnaeus' theory of fixed species assumes, immutable.
*Second*: Affinities between species and mutation of species can be observed. Present-day species, as we find from appropriate investigations of
their condition both in their domesticated state and in their natural free-

dom, are descended from other species, most of which are extinct but can sometimes be found in fossilized form.

*Third:* The struggle for existence is nature's principle of life. It is this that brings about a natural selection or selective breeding: the survival of the fittest (the strongest, best, best-adapted), the variations of which are increased and accumulated according to the laws of heredity. The result is the elimination of the weaker and less adapted species.

*Fourth:* The whole vast history of nature's evolution, stretching over millions of years, has followed purely causal, mechanistic laws without preestablished goals and ends: from the most simple (possibly from a single primordial organism) to increasingly complicated and more perfect forms.

*Fifth:* Man, too, is variable in bodily structure and embryonic development and turns out to be descended from older and inferior forms of life, but he has stood the test of the struggle for existence better than these. All this, however, Darwin expounded only later in his *Descent of Man* (1871).[9]

Oddly enough, the Darwinian solution—leaving aside Herbert Spencer, the philosopher of evolution already mentioned[10]—was prepared mainly by an economist (and former clergyman). As early as 1798, in his *Essay on the Principles of Population*,[11] Thomas Robert Malthus (1766–1834) had opposed the idea of a "natural" stable economic development and any prospect of progress toward Utopia with his theory that the provision of foodstuffs does not increase at the same pace as the growth of population, the result of which must be—in his view—overpopulation and mass destitution unless births are restricted by the practice of continence. Shortage of food was thus seen to lead to the struggle for existence. Darwin applied Malthus' theory to the world of plants and animals as a whole and thus reached his idea of natural selection. The natural scientists also had themselves been preparing the ground for Darwin: Charles Lyell in geology, J. B. de Lamarck and Erasmus Darwin (grandfather of Charles) in biology. But it was only Charles Darwin who succeeded—as a result of his own observations with an overwhelming abundance of morphological, embryological, biogeographical and paleontological material—in working out inductively an evolutionary model at once striking and universally intelligible for plants, animals and men: a scientifically substantiated theory.

As a result, therefore, of his universal explanation of evolution from the primordial cell up to man, Darwin had in the end become the "Copernicus of biology." Unfortunately also—as above mentioned—he became the occasion for a *second "Galileo case."* It was not without reason that Ernst Haeckel, Darwin's most important follower in Germany, placed Galileo's retort, *E pur si muove*, as a motto, on the title pages of the two volumes of his *General Morphology of Organisms*.[12] It would be superfluous to draw up a list of conservative Christians, theologians and ministers of Anglican, Protestant and Catholic provenience who protested and agitated against the new theory as obviously opposed to the Bible and tradition. As earlier vis-à-vis the new physics and astronomy, so now the biblical message was again identified with a particular scientific theory and—on the supposedly firm basis of a biblical or traditional faith—pernicious "evolutionism" was attacked and a "fixism" in harmony with the Bible and tradition defended. This happened especially with the methods practiced in the various churches from the seventeenth century onward, methods already mentioned in connection with Galileo and Darwin:[13] with books, pamphlets, articles, caricatures and everywhere in sermons and religious instruction.

But—so ran the objection at the time—in view of this theory of evolution, which revolutionizes everything, can we simply ignore the serious *consequences for faith and morals* and for religion as a whole?

Is not a primacy ascribed here to biology and organic thought as it was formerly to Cartesian geometry and then to Newtonian physics, and all this, again, at the expense of religion? Is not this an ideal of science to be set before the numerous sciences newly emerging, to which, however, theology of its very nature cannot respond?[14]

And if even in the biological field all species change to such an extent and continually give way to new ones, must it not be the same also in the mental and social sphere for all human ideas and ideals, institutions, organizations and structures, as indeed seems to be suggested by the vast development of modern industrial society in the nineteenth and twentieth centuries? In both the mental and the social spheres, then, the same confusing complexity of species, the same entanglement of connections and processes of development? With these blurred frontiers is it possible at all to distinguish in principle between truth and untruth? Or is it merely a question of distinguishing historically between new and old, the modern and the antiquated?

With all the necessary concentration on empirical study of the individual stages of evolution, evolutionary mechanisms, evolutionary truths, are we not going to be put off still more from seeking the primary and ultimate grounds, goals, truths? Instead of belief in a divine purpose and plan in nature and history, the mechanism of chance will be set up as the standard: through it even an emergence of the primordial organism in a physicochemical process becomes conceivable, and man, too, can be understood wholly "from below," from matter, from the cosmos, from the animal.

An *integrated, comprehensive scientific "Weltanschauung"* seemed to have become possible. In Darwin the two great scientific trends of the nineteenth century—natural science and the human sciences, which at first had developed on completely separate lines—came together. Nature and history were seen to be evolving in a single mighty natural-historical process which by the smallest steps over vast ages had produced all the wealth of the world and the abundance of its living beings. Progress thus became the law of history and of nature. The last relics of the medieval world order had disintegrated: there could be no more talk of an immutable, static, hierarchically organized and anthropocentric world order perfect from the very beginning. The hypothesis of God was not necessary to explain the origin either of life or of man. Man, hitherto the "image of God," was now seen as the image of the animal.

Did this completely new situation mean that Christian Church and theology were finished? Certainly there were numerous theologians who passionately defended the old, biblical faith, without, however, taking seriously the new, evolutive understanding of the world. And there were theologians—admittedly a small number—who adopted enthusiastically the new understanding of the world, without, however, being able also to preserve the old, biblical faith. But there were scarcely any who could convincingly bring the old faith to bear on the new understanding of the world, who could "translate" the old faith into the new understanding. It was only in the course of time and in fact only from Teilhard de Chardin onward that theologians increasingly began to observe what *new opportunities for the old faith* were offered in particular by the evolutive understanding of the world: opportunities for

a deeper understanding of God—not above or outside but in the midst of the world and its evolution;[15]

a deeper understanding of *creation*—not as contrary to evolution but as making evolution possible;

a deeper understanding of the special position of *man*—not as independent of the animal, of his history, of his behavior, but as a being of body and mind in his unique relationship with God.

In 1882 Charles Darwin was buried in Westminster Abbey, quite close to the grave of Sir Isaac Newton. By that time, he had on his side all the leading biologists and a large part of the educated world as far as the fact of evolution was concerned, even though his theory of the factors involved in evolution was later corrected in many respects (in "Neodarwinism," for instance, in regard to the theory of the inheritance of acquired characteristics taken over from Lamarck). Nevertheless, the scientific-theological dogma of the immutability of species had definitively broken down, and continuous change was set up as cosmic law.

The debate on faith, however, now raged right across Europe: between radicals, freethinkers, anticlericals of all kinds, on the one side, and traditionalist, biblicist, fundamentalist Anglicans, Protestants and Catholics, on the other. Unlike "Darwin's bulldog," Thomas H. Huxley (grandfather of the writer Aldous Huxley and of geneticist Julian Huxley), Darwin himself—personally a modest and cautious, sober-minded man of absolute intellectual integrity—kept out of the conflict. Although reviled as such, he was by no means an atheist. After his great voyage, however, he could not accept either the biblical miracles or the idea of the eternal damnation of unbelievers. At the time of the publication of *The Origin of Species,* he still believed, in a theistic or deistic sense, in a Deity that had created the primordial organisms from which all life then evolved. But, as his autobiography (first published in unabridged form in 1958)[16] shows, he seems finally (also as a result of the failure of theology) to have accepted a kind of agnosticism: "The mystery of the beginning of all things is insoluble by us; and I for one must remain an Agnostic."[17]

Many Darwinians, of the first generation anyway, expressly professed atheism, especially in the form of a coherent atheistic ("pantheistic") "monism," as against discordant Christian "dualism." Among these was Ernst Haeckel (1834–1919), already mentioned, much disparaged by theologians, the main protagonist and propagandist in Germany of the Darwinian theory of evolution. Two years after his main theoretical work, *General Morphology* (1866), there followed his universally understandable *Natural History of Creation,*[18] a description of the evolution of the world as a whole from primordial fog right up to mental processes, a description that—even before Darwin—consistently incorporated man into the process of evolution (there were ten editions, and translations into twelve languages). Very much later, he published directly ideological works, the most notable at the turn of the century being *The Riddle of the Universe* (1899), in which he writes with an almost religious fervor about man, soul, world and God (three hundred thousand copies were sold in Germany, and the book was translated into fifteen languages).[19] By contrast with the materialists mentioned earlier, Moleschott and Büchner, Haeckel, like Darwin himself, was not merely a constructor of theories but an acutely observant empiricist and a scholar involved in intensive research. His biogenetic basic law, according to which the evolution of each single human individual (ontogenesis) repeats the evolution of the whole human race (phylogenesis), was adopted—as we learned— also by Freud.

Haeckel's solution of the "riddle of the universe," however—like Thomas H. Huxley, he thought that natural science was the means of solving the supreme questions of life—strikes natural scientists today as a little naïve. His monism, mainly inspired by Goethe, "recognises one sole substance in the universe, which is at once 'God and Nature'; body and spirit (or matter and energy) it holds to be inseparable."[20] In his often hurtful polemic he not only argues for the descent of man from the "ape" but dismisses even the purely spiritual and yet personal God as a "gaseous vertebrate."[21] His profession of "atheism," of a "godless world-system," is unambiguous: "There are no gods or goddesses, assuming that god means a personal, extramundane entity. This 'godless world-system' substantially agrees with the monism or pantheism of the modern scientist."[22] He quotes Schopenhauer with approval: "Pantheism is only a polite form of atheism. The truth of pantheism lies in its destruction of the dualist antithesis of God and the world, in its recognition that the world exists in virtue of its own inherent forces. The maxim of the pantheist, 'God and the world are one,' is merely a polite way of giving the Lord God his *congé.*"[23] And what is the "ample compensation for the anthropistic ideals of 'God, freedom, and immortality' which we have lost"? According to Haeckel, "the sincere cult of 'the true, the good, and the beautiful.' "[24]

Haeckel extols as "the greatest theologian of the nineteenth century" David Friedrich Strauss, known to us as the author of *The Life of Jesus* (1835–36): "His last work, *The Old Faith and the New* (1872, ninth edition 1877), is a magnificent expression of the honest conviction of all educated people of the present day who understand this unavoidable conflict between the discredited, dominant doctrines of Christianity and the illuminating, rational revelation of modern science."[25] In fact, in his later years, Strauss had begun—as also the later Friedrich Engels ("Anti-Dührung")—in a rather different way—to orient his "new faith" to such an optimistic mechanistic, evolutionary Weltanschauung. No one blamed him for this more than Friedrich Nietzsche. The latter devoted the first of his "Thoughts out of Season" to this "David Strauss, the Confessor and the Writer," who had thitherto been celebrated as a freethinker, and exposed him to public ridicule by an unparalleled philosophical-literary critique.[26]

## Strauss's Philistine optimism

Feuerbach died in the year 1872; Marx had been waiting in vain for five years for an appropriate response to Volume 1 of *Das Kapital*, which in the end had not been dedicated to Darwin (the latter had published in the previous year his *Descent of Man*); Freud, before leaving school, decided under the influence of the impressive Darwinian theory to study medicine; in the same year, Strauss, at the age of sixty-six, published a summary—again, widely noted—of his Weltanschauung at the time, under the title "The Old and the New Faith."[27] Strauss's "new faith" showed unmistakably how far its author had departed from the old, biblical faith and now also from philosophical idealism and gone over to the camp of mechanistic-evolutionary atheism: "God" identified with the "universe," the origin of the latter described with the help of Kant and Laplace and its evolution with the help of Darwin. Strauss wanted to answer with the utmost clarity, for himself and—as he said—for countless others ("we"), four great questions: Are we still Christians? Have we still a religion? What is our conception of the universe? What is our rule of life?

Strauss—"we as honest and sincere men"—clearly answers "No" to the first question: "We are no longer Christians."[28] The second he answers equivocally-unequivocally: "We demand for our universe the same piety as that which the old-style devout person had for his God. When our feeling for the universe is hurt, our reaction is essentially religious. And if we are then asked if we still have a religion, our answer will not be a blunt denial—as it once was—but either 'Yes' or 'No,' depending on what is understood by 'religion.' "[29] A year later, in his *Thoughts out of Season*, Nietzsche commented on this *Weltanschauung of contemporary* "Culture-Philistinism": "At bottom, therefore, the religion is not a new belief, but, being of a piece with modern science, it has nothing to do with religion at all."[30] In fact, according to Strauss, the heaven of the new believers is here on earth, the Christian hope of an immortal life is an illusion, Jesus is an eccentric enthusiast, his resurrection a world-historical humbug, the self-denial of the ancient anchorites and saints a kind of hangover—Nietzsche fastidiously refuses to judge these views.[31] But it seems to him impossible then to describe as a religion "that feeling for the 'All' that the old believer demanded for his God." It is no more than an indigent, feeble, cold, "double-distilled emergency-belief" of which even Strauss wanted to say as little as possible, in order instead to "present his recently acquired biological knowledge." "The more embarrassed he may happen to be when he speaks of faith, the rounder and fuller his mouth becomes when he quotes the greatest benefactor to modern men— Darwin. Then he not only exacts belief for the new Messiah, but also for himself—the new apostle."[32]

Nietzsche finds Strauss's "shameless Philistine optimism" particuarly offensive. He regards it, however, as derived less from Darwin than from Hegel (and Schleiermacher) at an earlier stage: "for he who has once sickened on Hegel and Schleiermacher never completely recovers."[33] In view of this "incurable optimism," it is possible to understand "Schopenhauer's solemn utterance to the effect that optimism . . . seemed to him not merely an absurd *but a vicious attitude of mind*, and one of scornful irony towards the indescribable sufferings of humanity."[34]

Strauss, the "Philistine captain," however, "with a certain rude self-satisfaction, swathes himself in the hirsute garment of our Simian genealogists, and extols Darwin as one of mankind's greatest benefactors."[35] But after he has answered his third question ("What is our conception of the universe?"), he solves the fourth ("What is our rule of life?") without reference to the third: "Our perplexity is great when we find him constructing his ethics quite independently of the question, 'What is our conception of the universe?' "[36] In the treatment of the four main questions, there is no logical consistency, "because the third question has nothing to do with the second, nor the fourth with the third, nor all three with the first."[37] Here Strauss, who is always railing against parsons, miracles and the resurrection, ought to have had the courage to draw the ethical conclusions from the Darwinian theory and develop "a genuine and seriously constructed ethical system, based upon Darwin's teaching." How? "In this department he had an opportunity of exhibiting native pluck; for he ought to have turned his back on his 'We,' and have established a moral code for life out of *bellum omnium contra omnes* and the privileges of the strong."[38]

Obviously Strauss has not yet even learned "that the preaching of a morality is as easy as the establishment of it is difficult."[39] According to Darwin, man as "a creature of nature" evolved to what he is "by the very fact that he was continually forgetting that others were constituted like him and shared the same rights with him; by the very fact that he regarded himself as the stronger, and thus brought about the gradual suppression of weaker types."[40] And in view of "all ruin and irrationality, all evil" in the world, Nietzsche simply does not want to talk of a *"rationale* of all becoming and all natural laws," nor will he venerate the universe in a religious way in a new metaphysic and address it as "God."[41] Strauss, that is, does not venture to be honest and tell men: " 'I have liberated you from a helpful and pitiful God; the Cosmos is no more than an inflexible machine; beware of its wheels, that they do not crush you.' He dare not do this. Consequently, he must enlist the help of a witch, and he turns to metaphysics."[42]

But, for this very reason, Strauss's book is useful not only as a "pocket-oracle of the German Philistine," welcomed by students as a "canon for strong intellects" and by some even as a "religious book for scholars."[43] It is suitable especially for the "scientific type," in whose heart, according to Nietzsche, there lies a paradox, which consists precisely in having a great deal of time for what is unimportant and none at all for what is important: "It seems to him justifiable to spend his whole life in answering questions which, after all is said and done, can only be of interest to that person who believes in eternal life as an absolute certainty. The heir of but a few hours, he sees himself encompassed by yawning abysses, terrible to behold; and every step he takes should recall the questions, Wherefore? Whither? and Whence? to his mind. But his soul rather warms to his work, and, be this the counting of a floweret's petals or the breaking of stones by the roadside, he spends his whole fund of interest, pleasure, strength, and aspirations upon it."[44] But Pascal—as we also may recall— "suggests that men only endeavour to work hard at their business and sciences with the view of escaping those questions of greatest import which every moment of loneliness or leisure presses upon them—the questions relating to the *wherefore*, the *whence*, and the *whither* of life."[45]

It is a pity for Strauss, thinks Nietzsche. A pity for this gradually undermined and ultimately destroyed nature, "a nature strongly and deeply scholarly and critical, . . . in fact *the real Straussian genius*": "Once upon a time there lived a Strauss, a brave, severe, and stoutly equipped scholar, with whom we sympathised as wholly as with all those in Germany who seek to serve truth with earnestness and energy, and to rule within the limits of their powers. He, however, who is now publicly famous as David Strauss, is another person. The theologians may be to blame for this metamorphosis; but, at any rate, his present toying with the mask of genius inspires us with as much hatred and scorn as his former earnestness commanded respect and sympathy."[46] The first Strauss was the Strauss of the "Life of Jesus": he had helped Nietzsche finally to make the great decision of his life clearsightedly between theology and philology or, rather, between belief in God and atheism.

But what a coincidence at the end! Nietzsche's *Thoughts out of Season* was scarcely published when he and Overbeck, in Basel, were overwhelmed by the news that Strauss was "mortally ill and in the greatest distress"[47] in his birthplace, Ludwigsburg. In all probability, Strauss had been unable to read Nietzsche's "deadly" literary attack. He died at the beginning of the following year, on February 8, 1874.

## Nietzsche's beginnings

The year 1882 was the tenth anniversary of Feuerbach's death; it was the year before Marx died and the year when Engels published his "Development of Socialism from Utopia to Science";[48] twelve months earlier, Freud had graduated in Vienna and was now a confirmed atheist, practicing in the General Hospital. And it was in the same year that Nietzsche publicly proclaimed his *Requiem aeternam deo:* "God is dead. God remains dead. And we have killed him."[49]

But had this herald of the death of God—like Feuerbach before him—not begun as a good Christian and theology student? "When the candidates for confirmation went in twos to the altar, where they knelt to receive their consecration, Nietzsche also knelt, and as his closest friend, I knelt with him. I remember well the sense of holiness and detachment from the world that filled us during the weeks before and after confirmation. We would have been quite prepared there and then to die in order to be with Christ, and all our thinking, feeling and activity was resplendent with a more than earthly serenity—this of course was an artifically reared little plant, which could not endure very long." This is the account by Nietzsche's friend Paul Deussen of how they were confirmed together at Easter 1861.[50]

There is no doubt that the future atheist and anti-Christian had been for many years a well-behaved, very devout Christian child, as befitted someone brought up in the tradition of the parsonage. It may have surprised a number of people to have found in library catalogues the name of Friedrich Nietzsche followed by titles like "Gamaliel, or on the perpetual duration of Christianity, for instruction and reassurance in the present ferment in the theological world" and "Contributions to the promotion of a rational way of thinking about religion, education, duty of subjects and human life." The author, however, was the busy pastor and superintendent Friedrich August Ludwig Nietzsche,[51] grandfather of little "Fritz," who attacked the new freethinking in the period after the French

Revolution and defended zealously all that his grandson was to reject so passionately. Nietzsche's father, Karl Ludwig Nietzsche, was also a pastor, musically gifted, but more sensitive and rather fanatical; he married a (seventeen-year-old) pastor's daughter who, a year later, on October 15, 1844, in the country parsonage of Röcken, near Lützen, presented him with her firstborn, Friedrich Wilhelm. But, only five years later, the child lost his father, who died of softening of the brain. The family moved to the town of Naumburg, where the serious, sensitive model boy with his early musical and literary inclinations and good knowledge of the Bible (he was nicknamed the "little pastor") understandably had difficulties in adapting himself and making contacts and now grew up wholly in the care of women: in addition to his young mother, there were his sister Elisabeth, two years his junior, who idolized him throughout her life, as well as two devout aunts and a grandmother, who dominated everything. The family atmosphere and his *education solely at the hands of gentle, pious women could have been a first factor in the genesis of Nietzsche's anti-Christianity.* Christianity always seemed to him a soft, feeble, unmanly, decadent affair; in practice, he never got to know its pristine strength and depth.

The youngster, destined from youth onward for the ministry of preaching, composing a motet and writing poems at the age of ten, stood out even at the higher-grade boys' primary school by his sense of being different and his eagerness to know everything. What Jaspers called the "distinctive feature of Nietzsche's life," "his *being an exception,*"[52] developed at an early stage. When he was selected for the gymnasium, with its great traditions in the former Cistercian abbey of Schulpforta, near Naumburg, having an aversion to "boring" mathematics and a preference for Greek, he received a thorough training in the humanities and especially in classical philology. These studies gained a new depth through the private literary and musical association "Germania," which he and two of his friends founded and where he became acquainted for the first time with a piano arrangement of Richard Wagner's *Tristan.* His own compositions and poems, Sallust, Rousseau, Byron, Jean Paul and especially the Tübingen poet Hölderlin—who was not at all appreciated by Nietzsche's teachers and who became insane at an early age—all these captivated him more than anything to do with Christianity.

His excellent philological training increased his remoteness from the traditional belief of his family; it was obvious, too, that the critical-historical method would be bound to influence his understanding of the New Testament. Two years before leaving the gymnasium, already imbued with a sense of superiority and solitude and tormented by severe headaches, he composed a philosophical essay for his "Germania," which anticipates many of his later themes and reveals serious doubts about his childhood faith: "There will be great upheavals as soon as the masses have grasped the fact that the whole of Christianity rests on assumptions; the existence of God and immortality, the authority of the Bible, inspiration and other things will always remain problems. I have tried to deny everything; but it is easy to tear down and not so easy to build up. And even tearing down looks easier than it is; we are so determined inwardly by our childhood impressions, the influence of our parents, of our education, that those deeply rooted prejudices cannot be eradicated easily by rational arguments or by a simple act of will. The power of habit, the need of something higher, the break with the existing order of things, the dissolution of all forms of society, the doubt as to whether mankind can have been led astray by an illusion for two thousand years, the sense of one's own presumption and foolhardiness: all this is involved in an indecisive battle until finally painful experiences, sad events, lead our hearts back to the old childhood faith."[53] Back to the old childhood faith? Another great solitary—Kierkegaard—always impressed by his father's faith, found his way to a renewed, adult faith. Nietzsche did not.

In the same year, Nietzsche read the "Church History" and the "Life of Jesus," by Karl August von Hase,[54] the "witty advocate of ideal rationalism," and recommended his sister to read it, at which his mother and his similarly strictly orthodox Aunt Rosalie took great offense. So he then kept his critical ideas and doubts to himself and his two friends and became increasingly estranged from his mother, who cared for him but did not understand him. For her sake, after taking his leaving examination (for which he submitted a concluding, or "valedictory," Latin essay on Theognis of Megara), he registered at the age of twenty at the University of Bonn for the study of philology *and* theology. But he was now quite clear that his profession was to be classical philology. A poem of this autumn, 1864, to the incomprehensible "unknown God" that he had lost and wanted to recall shows the great internal tension between his incapacity to believe any longer and his desire nevertheless to continue to believe:

> *Once more before I wander on*
> *and turn my eyes to distant lands,*
> *in solitude I raise my hands*
> *to you on high to whom I fly,*
> *whom in my heart's profundity*
> *I hallowed altars to implore*
> *that evermore*
> *your voice might call again to me.*

> *On them is glowing, inscribed deep,*
> *the word: Unto the Unknown God.*
> *His am I, although in the sinners' squad*
> *until this hour I did keep:*
> *his am I, and I feel the chains*

*that in my fight I can't untie*
*and, though I fly,*
*force me to serve the god again.*

*I want to know you, Unknown One,*
*you that are reaching deep into my soul*
*and ravaging my life, a savage gale,*
*you Inconceivable and yet Related One!*
*I want to know you—even serve.*[55]

Like Marx in his time, Nietzsche studied only for two terms at Bonn; he, too, was a member of a student association and spent much of his time in drinking, fencing, riding, dancing, heaping up debts—a wasted time, as he later observed. And theology? "I took an interest in theology only in so far as I was attracted by the philological aspect of gospel criticism and the study of New Testament sources. . . . I still imagined at that time that history and historical research could provide a direct answer to certain religious and philosophical questions."[56] Nietzsche never really studied theology.

As noted earlier, it was David Friedrich Strauss, with his "Life of Jesus," who helped Nietzsche finally to see his position clearly. That was the time—"I was then twenty years old"—when he, too, "like every young scholar and with the clever dullness of a refined philologist, savoured the work of the incomparable Strauss."[57] In the Easter holiday of the following year, once more at home, Nietzsche seemed very much changed. For his mother a whole world collapsed when he announced that he had definitively abandoned the study of theology, at the same time vigorously attacking Christianity and refusing to go with his mother and sister to the Communion service. After this big scene, with many tears and violent talk, his mother stipulated only that his doubts were never again to be mentioned in her presence; she left her son—throughout her life her beloved problem child—to go his way, without preventing him but also without understanding him. In addition, therefore, to family and education, *critical philological study* was the *second factor* that had a decisive influence on the genesis of Nietzsche as atheist and anti-Christian.

After moving from Bonn to the University of Leipzig, Nietzsche changed his life fundamentally. He broke with the student association, "Frankonia"; formed a friendship with Erwin Rohde, the philologist (incidentally, he was in love—as often later, at a distance—at this time with an actress); and established contact with the great philologist Professor Friedrich Wilhelm Ritschl, a teacher who gave him great encouragement and at whose suggestion he published not only his work on Theognis but also other philological essays which had attracted notice. But Nietzsche, now an atheist and deprived of his former intellectual supports, was anything but happy: "At that time I was—so to speak—hanging in the air, particularly after a number of painful experiences and disappointments, without principles, without hopes and without a friendly memory."[58]

And who helped him? A wealthy Danzig merchant's son, endowed with pessimism in his cradle—so to speak—tormented from the age of six with vague fears and suspicions, even when young on journeys with his parents meditating pessimistically on human beings and making a striking impression by his passionate sensitivity (his compassion, for instance, for the galley slaves of Toulon). A little later, weighed down by the early death of his father and complete rejection by his mother, Adele, who enjoyed life and engaged in literary activity in Goethe's Weimar, this man discovered consolation for his life and death in an affinity with the ancient Indian Upanishads (a Persian compendium of the Vedanta philosophy, published in Latin). After some business activity, at the age of twenty, he caught up with secondary school and university studies (with a special interest in Plato, Kant and Goethe's theory of colors) and as nonsalaried lecturer in Berlin stubbornly and arrogantly tried—in vain, of course—to compete with the famous Professor Hegel. This was the man who finally —after complaining bitterly about university philosophy and especially Hegelianism—became a free-lance writer in Frankfurt, gained increasing fame only in the last lonely and gloomy years of his life and had been dead for five years when Nietzsche discovered his main work quite by chance in a Leipzig secondhand bookshop and then greedily devoured it in a few days. The name of this philosopher was *Arthur Schopenhauer* (1788–1860). Schopenhauer's philosophy is the *third factor* that can explain Nietzsche's anti-Christianity.

Schopenhauer's pessimistic sense of life and the world, however, made its mark on too many people, especially artists, writers and musicians (from Jakob Burckhardt to Max Horkheimer, from Richard Wagner to Hans Pfitzner), not to be given special attention here—even apart from the connection with Nietzsche. To quote only two Nobel prizewinners for literature: Thomas Mann wrote in 1918: "Before my eyes there floats the small room high up in the suburbs where, sixteen years ago, I lay stretched out on an unusually long easy chair or settee, reading *The World as Will and Idea*. Lonely, erratic youth, craving for the world and for death, drinking up the magic potion of this metaphysic which in its deepest nature is eroticism and in which I recognized the spiritual source of the Tristan music."[59] And André Gide in 1924: "When I read Schopenhauer's *The World as Will and Idea*, I thought at once: so that's it."[60]

## Schopenhauer's pessimism

The main work of this proud, distrustful, irritable, sarcastic philosopher, with his contempt for the world and for men, *The World as Will and*

*Idea,*[61] was completely in accord with Nietzsche's basic mood at the time: "Imagine what an effect the reading of Schopenhauer's main work was bound to have in these circumstances. . . . Here every line was a cry of renunciation, denial, resignation; here was a mirror in which I caught sight of the world, of life and of my own feelings, in terrible grandeur. Here the totally disinterested solar eye of art stared at me, here I saw sickness and healing, exile and a place of refuge, hell and heaven. I was violently seized with a need for self-knowledge and even self-erosion. . . ."[62]

And indeed where were those questing bourgeois intellectuals, scientists and artists to flee after the foundations of their Christian belief in God and their idealist mentality had been undermined and destroyed by Feuerbach and his followers, by scientific materialism and Darwinian evolutionism, and when nevertheless they still did not want to follow in the tracks of Marx to become militant socialists? Where were they to acquire new foundations, where could they gain a new, sustaining understanding of the self and the world of equal or possibly higher value, if not from this independent thinker—atheistic and yet not superficial, anti-Hegelian and yet not materialistic, deeply pessimistic and yet also supremely aesthetic? This man who started out from immediate, painful experience of life and nevertheless surveyed the history of philosophy and united in an original way Kantian criticism and Goethean intuition? Who so completely matched the sense of life of late romantics like Nietzsche and Richard Wagner and—in contrast to many German professors of philosophy—fascinated everyone by the simplicity, vividness, flexibility and temperament that made him such a master of the German language? Schopenhauer's philosophy became a *substitute for religion:* "It was atheism that led me to Schopenhauer," admits Nietzsche.[63]

But how did Schopenhauer provide Nietzsche with that intellectual backing that he so urgently needed after losing his faith in God, if he was to cope with life at all? According to Schopenhauer, the materialism of a Moleschott or a Büchner was a philosophy for barbers' apprentices or trainee chemists who tried impudently and presumptuously to get at the nature of things and of the world with the aid of anatomy and physiology: it was not an alternative to the idealism of a Fichte, Schelling or Hegel (although the last named is still accused in the preface to the second edition, in 1844, of "empty bombast and charlatanism").[64] Like so many after Hegel, Schopenhauer goes back to Kant. "The world is my idea": with this first, quite general principle and after invoking Descartes, Berkeley, Kant, and also the sages of India, Schopenhauer begins his *The World as Will and Idea.*[65] This means that what are immediately present to me are not things themselves but my ideas of things: not the tree, but my idea of the tree; not the sun, but the eye that sees the sun, and even the eye only as an idea. It might also be said that the whole world contained in our ideas and even our own body is—in the first place—nothing but a world of appearances beyond which human knowledge and science do not extend. Kant was right: we know "appearances," "phenomena," not "things in themselves," still less an Absolute, least of all God.

But, in this world of appearances, does not man need something more: the *meaning, significance, nature of the whole?* According to Schopenhauer, this need must be satisfied by the human subject himself: in a free interpretation of human existence that, however, must be tested in a scientific explanation as comprehensive and coherent as possible of the phenomena in the world as a whole. How is this to be done?

Man as a corporeal being experiences his body in two ways: outwardly as object of the idea, inwardly as expression of the will. According to Schopenhauer, the word "will" must be understood in a broad sense. Man knows or—better—feels his innermost nature as that *will to live* that impregnates and permeates all individual organs, impulses, instincts, wishes, yearnings, passions, up to cognition. Compared to this will, the knowing intellect is derived, subsidiary, secondary; its role is merely to serve. It is not by knowing (here Kant was right) but by willing (Kant did not see this), that we come into contact with the "thing in itself." So the will to live, as I experience it in my own body, is also the "key to the nature of every phenomenon in nature."[66] What gives internal coherence to the world of our ideas—from the force of gravity to human self-awareness, from natural forces, from the growth of plants, the instinct of animals, to man's instinct for self-preservation—is not Spirit, not an Absolute, not God. Schopenhauer's intellectual honesty prevents him from introducing any kind of pantheistic trimmings. "The world is my will": this is how Schopenhauer formulates his second, complementary principle.[67] How is this to be understood?

The innermost nature of all phenomena is a primarily unconscious will, "which, considered purely in itself, is without knowledge, and merely a blind incessant impulse."[68] It is this urge to live, this primordial will, that appears in all appearances: the world of the idea exists as will making its appearance. The world is "in its whole nature through and through *will*, and at the same time through and through *idea*."[69] What for Kant remains in a vacuum as a pure unknown, undetermined and unexplained, is thus clearly defined by Schopenhauer. The will is the "thing-in-itself." The "will to live"—a pleonasm for Schopenhauer—is "the thing-in-itself, the inner content, the essence of the world."[70]

This will, one and the same in the variety of its appearances in space and time, is, however, a primordial will without cause, without rest, without goal. The conviction, prevailing from the ancient Greeks onward, that the world had a rational explanation was now for the first time seriously questioned: the essence of the world is not ratio, logos, idea, reason, Absolute Spirit or transcendental Subject, but drive, instinct, life, will. No meaning can be perceived in this groundless and motiveless will to live, in either the restless drive of nature or the chaotic movement of history. Everywhere, we find only the unceasing, primitively dark, blind, shapeless, discordant pressures of a vitality, a continual rise and decline, a living, suffering, dying and new life on the part of individuals—without fulfillment. The one primordial force, in the process of its self-realization, in all the various stages of its appearing, splits into infinitely many wills, which are everywhere involved in unceasing conflict: a reciprocal opposition in the inorganic field, a struggle for existence also among organisms, a continual argument especially in the world of men—all of which can easily be proved empirically.[71]

Schopenhauer describes this human existence, which he felt to be an "unpleasant business," in the light of his own personal suffering, in colors that remind us of Pascal: a finite, thrown into infinite space and infinite time, without any firm, absolute where and when. A life that is death from the very beginning, clamped down between fulfilled desires and boredom: so "that the game may be kept up of constant transition from desire to satisfaction, and from satisfaction to a new desire, the rapid course of which is called happiness, and the slow course sorrow, and does not sink into that stagnation that shows itself in fearful ennui that paralyzes life, vain yearning without a definite object, deadening languor."[72] Man is "the most necessitous of all beings": "left to himself, uncertain about everything except his own need and misery."[73] What nevertheless keeps him constantly moving is the fear of death and consequently his striving for existence, for a life that, however, is still essentially suffering, from which man tries again to free himself by securing his existence and is thus presented with renewed boredom and discontent.

It has become clear that the one discordant and suffering primordial will, immanent in everything, is for Schopenhauer the metaphysical basic principle explaining everything, which is supposed to give man the answer to his metaphysical need for the meaning, significance, nature of the whole. Behind everything, there is *not a God but the groundless and motiveless primordial urge to live*, for which, however, we should not use "negative conceptions, void of content," such as "absolutes," "infinites" and "supersensibles"—all really amounting to "cloud-cuckoo-town."[74] Genuine philosophy does not ask about "the whence, the whither, and the why of the world, but always and everywhere demands only the what."[75] This, then, is what Schopenhauer's metaphysics looks like: a philosophy of will in the spirit of Romanticism, but with an original association of Platonic, Kantian, Goethean and ancient Indian ideas, all under negative, irrational, atheistic, pessimistic auspices.

The deep and comprehensive *pessimism* rooted in Schopenhauer's life is substantiated metaphysically by the philosopher. All wishing and desire is derived from the primordial will, which is in conflict with itself, boundless, restless, insatiable. What is all existence but a striving arising from want; what is it but suffering? What is every life story but a story of pro-

found suffering? In detail often a comedy, in its totality a tragedy. Human
life? A business in which the proceeds do not cover the costs. Social life?
A hell where human beings are both tormented souls and tormenting
devils. What is all the progress and development of mankind? An absurd
going around in circles. Despite all the optimistic attempts by Leibniz to
prove it otherwise, this world is not the best but the worst of all possible
worlds. Despite all Hegel's cunning, optimistic philosophy of history, this
world process is without reason, without meaning or goal. Schopenhauer
comments: "The said philosophers and glorifiers of history are accordingly
simple realists, and also optimists and eudaemonists, consequently dull
fellows and incarnate philistines; and besides are really bad Christians; for
the true spirit and kernel of Christianity, as also of Brahmanism and Buddhism, is the knowledge of the vanity of earthly happiness, the complete
contempt for it, and the turning away from it to an existence of another,
nay, an opposite kind. This, I say, is the spirit and end of Christianity, the
true 'humour of the matter'; and not, as they imagine, monotheism; therefore even atheistic Buddhism is far more closely related to Christianity
than optimistic Judaism or its variety Islamism."[76]

But how, then, is *liberation from suffering,* how is *redemption,* possible?
According to Schopenhauer, only by man's self-redemption. And how is
this attained? *Art* is a beginning. Schopenhauer became closely involved
in the visual arts, in poetry and music, and also with the diverse forms of
the sublime, attractive and beautiful. Art brings release from the burden
of existence, with all its suffering, by leading us beyond the knowledge of
the individual to pure contemplation of the nature of things: that other,
unbiased, disinterested contemplation of the world, as it takes place (in
addition to philosophical knowledge) in the vision of the artist (genius)
and also of the person contemplating art. Art elevates the person who
loses himself entirely in the object beyond limited, painful individuality to
the universal, to the eternal form, to the contemplation of ideas: those
primordial forms of all things for which the various arts provide the material embodiment.[77] This occurs in a unique fashion in *music,*[78] the most
perfect, purest and most penetrating of the arts. It is music which gives
expression not only to the primordial forms or ideas existing in the
primordial will prior to all realization but to the primordial will itself and
thus to the pure nature of the world. Anyone who has read Schopenhauer's remarks on music will scarcely be surprised that in the light of
such a metaphysic of art, art in particular and especially music—and most
of all the music of Richard Wagner—could become a substitute for
religion for many educated people.

But even art, music itself, for Schopenhauer, is only an initial redemption, a constantly elusive repose, a transitory appeasement, lasting often
only for a moment. Complete redemption comes about only when the
will to live, this source of all suffering, is seen through in theory by the intellect and rejected in practice by the will. Self-knowledge and denial,

therefore, alone offer man scope for the exercise of genuine freedom. According to Schopenhauer, this freedom exists not in individual deeds (there is no freedom of choice) but only at the roots of man's nature, in the primordial will. Definitive redemption is a matter not of art but of ethics: an *ethic of renunciation and compassion*.[79] It is here that Schopenhauer the atheist sees the ethical core of Buddhism *and* Christianity, the latter being for him originally a religion of asceticism: "Certainly the doctrine of original sin (assertion of the will) and of salvation (denial of the will) is the great truth which constitutes the essence of Christianity, while most of what remains is only the clothing of it, the husk or accessories. Therefore Jesus Christ ought always to be conceived in the universal, as the symbol or personification of the denial of the will to live, but never as an individual, whether according to his mythical history given in the Gospels, or according to the probably true history which lies at the foundation of this."[80]

What, then, is the important thing? Lacking all desire and utterly resigned, to die to oneself and renounce everything to which the heart clings, but at the same time also to show compassion and relieve the suffering of others. This is substantiated more in Buddhist than in Christian terms. The principle of individuation, the space-time separation of one individual from another, as it is shown by the world of ideas, must be overcome by understanding of the nature of the world: the world as will, in which everything is one. Consequently the suffering of another person is also my suffering. Consequently, against the egoism of the individual, from which all evil arises, there is required that compassion in which man is aware of his oneness with all living beings (including animals) and their suffering and out of which comes the good that is expressed in justice and especially in unselfish love. The more a person knows that as an individual he is only a transitory appearance of the one will to live and the more therefore he denies for his own part his individual will to live, so much the more does he attain to the complete dissolution of egoism, to true resignation and holiness; so much the more there occurs in him the redemption of the world and of himself; so much the more does he enter into the All-and-One.

That is why asceticism is also necessary; voluntary suppression of the natural instincts (especially of the sexual instinct), mortification of desire and will, and thus finally "a peace that cannot be shaken, a deep rest and inward serenity."[81] Schopenhauer is full of praise for the Christian and Buddhist ascetics. He cannot praise sufficiently these beautiful souls, saints, who overcame the world, who are greater than all world conquerors. But, in addition to the voluntary asceticism of the saints, there is also a second, more usual way to salvation: suffering as imposed by fate and often bringing about a complete change of mind, rejection of the will to live, complete resignation and holiness, and even supreme gladness in death (not suicide).

In this way or in another, then, man gains an attitude of lack of desire. Anyone who gets so far cannot be shocked at his own death, even by nothingness; he will calmly submit entirely to it. Only then is the spell broken, only then is the cycle of life, suffering, death and life again stopped; only then is individuality overcome and the will to live abandoned. With the abandonment of the will, all manifestations of life are also dissolved. For without the will there is no idea, no world.

What remains? "Before us there is certainly only nothingness."[82] The *true goal of world and man*, then, is not any kind of Brahma or Nirvana but, whether we like it or not, *nothingness*: "Rather do we freely acknowledge that what remains after the entire abolition of will is for all those who are still full of will certainly nothing; but, conversely, to those in whom the will has turned and has denied itself, this our world, which is so real, with all its suns and milky ways—is nothing."[83] Nothing—this is the very last word in Schopenhauer's great work.

Who can be surprised that this work did not fit in with the times? It appeared in 1819, but after eighteen months scarcely a hundred copies had been sold; the rest—in considerable numbers—were later pulped. Over the next eighteen years, the disappointed author published nothing more. In 1831 he fled from Berlin—which he hated—because of an outbreak of cholera, which snatched away his less nervous great antagonist, Hegel; in 1833, at the age of forty-five, he settled finally in Frankfurt, in order to live in accordance with his principles as a hermit solely for his science. All his publications from that time onward were at bottom commentaries on his main work: thus *On the Will in Nature* (1836),[84] then *The Two Fundamental Problems of Ethics* (1841, on freedom of the will and on compassion as the foundation of morality),[85] and thirdly what he described as "short philosophical essays" under the title of *Parerga and Paralipomena* (secondary works and remains),[86] with *Aphorisms on the Wisdom of Life* as centerpiece[87]—that book, published in 1851 without payment, which finally brought about a change in public favor and became and remained Schopenhauer's most popular book.

A conflicted personality, this philosopher, who was a stranger among people and on his daily two-hour forced marches with his poodle had become one of the sights of Frankfurt; who, in the concrete, bestowing his universal compassion only on his dog, hated the world and yet—coming from a wealthy family—loved good food and fine clothes; who despised human beings and especially (after some liaisons and frustrated marriage projects) women and yet throughout his life longed for recognition and a wife; who rejected the will to live but—fearing suffering and death—wanted to go on until he was ninety. He died of pneumonia on September 21, 1860, at the age of seventy-one. In the study where he died, portraits of Descartes, Shakespeare, Goethe and Matthias Claudius were hanging; on his desk there was a bust of Kant; in the corner, however, on a marble console, was a gilded statuette of the Buddha. In the last conversation before his death, with his friend, executor and later biographer, the lawyer and writer Wilhelm von Gwimmer, Schopenhauer declared his joy especially in the fact "that his apparently irreligious teachings 'worked as a religion,' filled up the place left empty by the loss of faith and became the source of innermost reassurance and satisfaction."[88] As he passed away, he also declared "that for him it would be an act of charity to come to absolute nothingness; but death offered no prospect of that. But, however it might be, he had at least a pure *intellectual conscience*."[89]

## Nietzsche's own way

Schopenhauer's theory of redemption and ethics—determined in the last resort not by Christian but by Buddhist spirituality—is a further great example of a modern atheistic "religiosity," which was also able to an increasing extent to attract a veritable congregation of supporters: "apostles" and "archevangelists," as the philosophical "founder of the religion" called his first disciples. And Nietzsche? For him, too, this teaching occupied "the place left empty by the loss of faith" when, after studying intensely only Plato among the philosophers, as a student in Leipzig, he discovered for himself five years after Schopenhauer's death this atheistic "gospel" of denial and renunciation (not to say *dys-angelion*, "bad news"). But it did not by any means become for him, as Schopenhauer had hoped, a "source of innermost reassurance and satisfaction." On the contrary, merciless self-analysis, asceticism, hatred of self, even self-torment, for two weeks, with never more than four hours' sleep, were the result. This, however, did not last. But the passion for philosophy had now been roused in him; the lone wolf Schopenhauer had responded to the lone wolf Nietzsche.

If we leave aside F. A. Lange's *History of Materialism*,[90] which oriented him on the history of philosophy and on Darwinism, Nietzsche's high regard for Schopenhauer was decisively confirmed by the thirty-one years older and already very famous "tone poet" *Richard Wagner*—after Schopenhauer, his second great Leipzig discovery—whom he found to be a fascinating personality when he was able to meet him at a very private *soirée* in Wagner's sister's house. Wagner admitted frankly his regard for Schopenhauer: "the only philosopher who had perceived the essence of music."[91] As early as 1854, Wagner, who had been originally an enthusiastic Feuerbachian, had the libretto of the *Ring des Nibelungen* sent to his philosopher with the handwritten dedication "with admiration and gratitude," which Schopenhauer answered by correcting a few verses and explaining that for his own part he was indebted to Mozart and Rossini. It was not *The Ring*, however (often wrongly criticized as "rhymed Schopenhauer"), but only *Tristan* that was written by Wagner in the spirit of Schopenhauer when he depicted the world's pain and redemption in terms of universal extinction.

What Schopenhauer had been in philosophy, Wagner now became in music for Nietzsche: "genius" and idol of his heart—at least for the time being. Philology increasingly seemed to him merely a matter of fate. But as a complete surprise—Nietzsche had really wanted to study chemistry in Paris—the twenty-five-year-old, without a doctorate or teaching qualification, on the recommendation of his teacher Ritschl, received in 1869 an appointment as professor of Greek language and literature at the University of Basel. The young scholar—as also his inaugural lecture on "Homer and Classical Education"—was received in a very friendly way in Basel; he made the acquaintance—among others—of the great historian of art Jakob Burckhardt, whose series of lectures in 1879, published as *World-Historical Meditations*, created great interest, and also later of the young skeptical theologian and Church historian Franz Overbeck, who almost alone remained his friend to the very end.[92] But, apart from three months' service as a nationalist spirited volunteer medical orderly in the Franco-Prussian War (his earlier voluntary military service, as artilleryman, came to an end as a result of a riding accident), Nietzsche in the next three years made the short journey from Basel to Lucerne as often as possible to the Villa Tribschen, close to the Lake, where Richard Wagner resided and composed, living with the thirty-two-year-old Cosima von Bülow, wife of Wagner's friend, the conductor Hans von Bülow, daughter of Franz Liszt and of the French Countess Marie d'Agoult. Their young friend was welcome there at all times, and there were always two rooms at his disposal. Nietzsche, however, does not seem to have made any deeper impression on Cosima, whom he greatly admired but who was completely fascinated by Richard. Although repeatedly mentioned in Cosima's diaries (not published until 1976–77,[93] scarcely anything is recorded about conversations with him.

What was more natural than that the young Nietzsche in the first period of his creative work, at the beginning of the eighteen seventies, should have attempted, on the foundation of an aesthetic irrationalism of feeling, *to combine Schopenhauer's metaphysic of the will with Wagner's theory of art? The Birth of Tragedy out of the Spirit of Music*,[94] published in 1871, his first year in Basel, was such an attempt. The much admired world of Greek antiquity—he maintains—was not merely "simplicity and calm grandeur" (Winckelmann) but profound discord between two life forces (Schopenhauer): a perpetual conflict between the *Apollonian*, the principle of measure and order (= the world as idea), and the *Dionysian*, the principle of destruction and of tempestuous creative power (= the world as will). Out of this wrestling—directly out of the ecstatic choral dance of the Dionysus cult and thus out of music—emerges the greatest achievement of Hellenism: tragedy. But the Dionysian spirit is soon crushed by the intellectualistic Socratic spirit of science and enlightenment. Only in Romanticism is it resurrected: in Schopenhauer's philosophy and Wagner's music, the expression of a universal, new cultural beginning.

This interpretation of Greek art and contemporary culture, both new and questionable, was presented by a classical philologist, to the horror of all classical philologists of his time. For Nietzsche, the consequence of producing this work—especially after the pamphlet by the young, later highly distinguished classical philologist Ulrich von Wilamowitz-Möllendorf, against Nietzsche's "Philology of the Future"*[95]—was that in the eyes of his colleagues as serious philologists he was once and for all "academically dead." His lectures were attended by no more than four listeners, one of them a paperhanger who scarcely understood Greek. He was and remained deeply affected by the reaction of his professional colleagues, including Ritschl.[96] Even at that time, of course, Nietzsche despised pure philology and history, giving unmistakable public expression to his views in the *Thoughts out of Season,* which soon followed: on "David Strauss" (1873), then especially on the "Use and Abuse of History" (1874), on "Schopenhauer as Educator" (1874) and a little later on "Richard Wagner in Bayreuth" (1876). Nietzsche the *philologist* had now become Nietzsche the *philosopher* and—also in Basel—tried, unfortunately in vain, to get another professorship, in order as professor of philosophy to be able to proclaim his aesthetic-heroic Weltanschauung against all philistinism in life and scholarship. From that time onward, pre-Socratic Greece—as a substitute for primitive Christianity?—offered a model and standard of true humanity. The Dionysian aspect in particular—delight in the irrational, in life, in the power of instinct, in wild, primitive frenzy, in the shapeless chaos emerging from the primordial ground of everything creative—remained from that time onward one of Nietzsche's fundamental categories.

Even in his first period of creativity, however, Nietzsche had increasingly *dissociated himself from Schopenhauer.* His esteem had always been less for the philosophical system as a whole than for the man, with his absolute truthfulness, pure intellectual conscience and courageous thought, the educator in self-criticism, self-discipline, self-defense, hardness, simplicity and healthy pessimism, and finally the great stylist and aesthete who defended the special way of the natural genius as opposed to the average man, the philistine. By contrast to Kant, Schopenhauer is the poet; by contrast to Goethe, he is the philosopher. Nietzsche, however, now dissociated himself from Schopenhauer's rejection of willing and living, since he was beginning to defend a Dionysian, frenzied assent to absolutely all

* *Zukunftsphilologie,* used here as an adverse critic once used *Zukunftsmusik* as a description of Wagner's work, later adopted by Liszt as a rallying cry for Wagner's supporters. Translator.

manifestations of life: the ideal of a Germanic Hellenism was less Schopenhauer's ideal than Nietzsche's. And at the same time, Nietzsche's explicit criticism was directed to a central point: Schopenhauer's basic intention to replace the Kantian "thing in itself" simply by the "will" and his way of imposing far too definite predicates on what is absolutely inconceivable lead to the world's being fitted far too conveniently into a system. "Schopenhauer wanted to find the $x$ in an equation, and the result of his calculation was that $x$ turned out to be the very fact that he did not discover it."[97] But "the errors of great men are honorable, since they are more fruitful than the truths of small men."[98] Nietzsche dissociated himself clearly also from Schopenhauer's relatively positive (atheistic) appreciation of (ascetic) Christianity: "It is also certain that he was mistaken about the *value of religion for knowledge*." Now, certainly, Schopenhauer would agree that "*no religion, directly or indirectly, either as dogma or as allegory, has ever contained a truth.*"[99]

The *dissociation from Wagner* and his now wedded (second) wife, Cosima, was more cruel, beginning with their move from Lucerne to the very different atmosphere of Bayreuth (1872): the spatial dissociation soon became a personal dissociation. Sensitivity on both sides, but especially Nietzsche's vulnerability, his clear feelings of rivalry and his deteriorating state of health all played a part. But the decisive reason for the break was something else. Wagner had been an active revolutionary in 1839 (in Leipzig) and in 1849 (in Dresden, with Bakunin) and was the author of *Art and Revolution* (1849),[100] but he was now turning to Christianity. As Nietzsche wrote twelve years later in his book *Nietzsche contra Wagner*, about that first Bayreuth summer festival: "It was indeed high time to say farewell: soon after, I received the proof. Richard Wagner, apparently most triumphant, but in truth a decaying and despairing decadent, suddenly sank down, helpless and broken, before the Christian Cross."[101] When Wagner, at a subsequent meeting in Sorrento, talked excitedly about the composition of his Christian *Parsifal*, Nietzsche became silent, suddenly excused himself and disappeared in the dusk—never to meet him again. When a copy of *Parsifal* was sent to him, two years later, Nietzsche answered with the book he had started to write when he left Bayreuth, the greater part of which he wrote in Sorrento and which had just been published, *Human, All-Too-Human*,[102] where Wagner is mentioned only as "the artist." Nor did Nietzsche ever see Cosima again. The break was definitive; it was the parting of the ways. Wagner regarded himself increasingly as the guardian of the Holy Grail of German art, continued to build up Bayreuth, the pilgrimage center of a secular, aestheticizing substitute religion in which he was elevated to the status of a messianic savior figure. After Wagner's death, Cosima, endowed with infallible authority, administered the sacred estate.

With his health seriously deteriorating (violent headaches and pain in the eyes, continual vomiting, attacks of depression), in the following year,

1879, Nietzsche, at the age of forty-five, had to seek permission to retire as professor at the university. A great deal has been written about Nietzsche's *illness*, which released him without a sharp break from his profession as a philologist—which he had never liked—and from his former milieu, forcing him to inactivity and to his own thinking.[103] It is in any case a complex phenomenon: headaches and eye pains from youth onward; chest injuries through a riding accident during his military service (1868), then dysentery in the Franco-Prussian War (1870), and after that, abdominal complaints; psychological disturbances perhaps as a result of the parting from Wagner and his wife, and later frustrated marital projects. Particularly serious was the syphilitic infection, clearly attested during his student days, although the exact date is disputed.[104] But, however much sickness and pain were Nietzsche's constant companions from 1870 onward and however inexorably his bodily disintegration advanced in the 1880s—despite temporary recovery, occasional euphoric moods and periods of extraordinary creativity—the writings even of the last period cannot be regarded as the works of a lunatic. Such a "diagnosis" would be far too convenient.

With *Human, All-Too-Human* (1878), this "book for free spirits," sent ironically to Wagner, Nietzsche, as a "spirit freed" in manner and matter from idealism, Christianity, Schopenhauer and Wagner, had finally "taken possession of himself": from now on going his *own way* unmistakably as thinker and writer. A predominantly aphoristic style was the appropriate form of expression for the sick man, continually seeking relief in various places from Genoa and Venice to Naumburg and Sils-Maria, in the Upper Engadine, finding it difficult in his illness to get on with desk work but on journeys and walks tirelessly entering into his notebook innumerable stray thoughts, observations, ideas, perceptions. It was a smooth, flexible style, making use of the finest nuances of language, without any sort of pedantry: both scholarly and artistic, ironically and intellectually aloof and psychologically ingenious. The style was based on the literary model of great Frenchmen: Michel de Montaigne, La Rochefoucauld and La Bruyère, also Chamfort and Stendhal and other *esprits forts*. But there are others who should not be forgotten: Gotthold Ephraim Lessing and Nietzsche's friend Paul Rée, with his *Psychological Meditations*,[105] in which self-love is commended. There is no doubt that *Human, All-Too-Human* was a worthy gift for the centenary of Voltaire's death, a man who by contrast to his successors was above all what Nietzsche thought himself to be, "a *grand seigneur* of the spirit."[106] "For my generation," declares the poet Gottfried Benn, Nietzsche "was the earthquake of the epoch and—after Luther—the greatest genius of the German language."[107]

Where others saw the ideal, Nietzsche saw only the human, all too human. His *faith in culture, in the modern age, was shattered.* We live—

he claimed—in an age of internal disintegration, of uncertainty, of the loss of mental resources, when intoxication and sensation drown the dreariness and boredom of life, in a word, an age of decadence. And Wagner's music is a symptom of it.[108] The Schopenhauerian-Wagnerian pre-Socratic, who praised beautiful feeling and Dionysian enthusiasm, had become the critical-negative Socratic and skeptical-rational intellectual. Deliberately bearing onward "the banner of enlightenment, the banner with the three names, Petrarch, Erasmus, Voltaire,"[109] with unerring sharpness he submitted not only eudaemonistic, philistine morality but "idealism" as a whole, to ruthless criticism: "errors" like "the ideal," "the genius," "the saint," "the hero," "faith," "conviction," "compassion," "the thing in itself" and thus Christianity and metaphysics (possible in itself but no longer necessary or credible) as a whole—that "second actual world" we know in dreams and the "distinction between soul and body" in man.[110] He talks about "first and last things," "the history of moral sentiments," "the religious life," "the soul of artists and authors," and "the signs of higher and lower culture," or about "man in society," "wife and child," "the state," "man alone by himself":[111] in all this—without speculation, empirically-inductively analyzing and testing the truth content—Nietzsche starts out from realities instead of idealities and thus even at this stage, with his truly psychological perception, proves to be the most important but also the most dangerous diagnostician of modern man. This very work tends with an "uncompromising *difference of outlook*" to "the inversion of customary valuations and valued customs," as Nietzsche himself observed subsequently in his preface to the second edition: "In the background of his (the liberated spirit's) activities and wanderings—for he is restless and aimless in his course as in a desert—stands the note of interrogation of an increasingly dangerous curiosity. 'Cannot *all* valuations be reversed? And is good perhaps evil? And God only an invention and artifice of the devil? Is everything, perhaps, radically false? And if we are the deceived, are we not thereby also deceivers? *Must* we not also be deceivers?'—Such thoughts lead and mislead him more and more, onward and away. Solitude encircles and engirdles him, always more threatening, more throttling, more heart-oppressing, that terrible goddess and *mater saeva cupidinum*—but who knows nowadays what *solitude* is?"[112]

The two other books of this period, which have been misleadingly described as Nietzsche's "most positivistic" works, certainly belong to what his critics at the time called "a school of suspicion." These are also books of aphorisms: *The Dawn of Day. Reflections on Moral Prejudices* (1881) and *The Gay Science* (1882). With *The Dawn of Day*[113] begins Nietzsche's great campaign against morality as prejudice, as decadence, as contempt for life and the body, as self-destruction. Here, already, we find in practice a standpoint beyond good and evil, with the aim of giving positive approval to a "revaluation of all values," as Nietzsche, again in retrospect, clearly observes: "In a *revaluation of all values,* in a liberation from all moral values, in saying Yes to and having confidence in all that has hitherto been forbidden, despised, and damned. This Yes-saying book pours out its light, its love, its tenderness upon ever so many wicked things; it gives back to them their 'soul,' a good conscience, the lofty right and privilege of existence. Morality is not attacked, it is merely no longer in the picture. . . . This book closes with an 'Or?'—it is the only book that closes with an 'Or?' "114

After *The Dawn of Day,* Nietzsche regarded *The Gay Science*115—that Provençal *gaya scienza* of the singer, knight, free spirit, in which one dances right over morality ("Songs of Prince Vogelfrei")—especially as a decisive step toward an internal and external "recovery." In any case, Nietzsche wrote this book in a new mood of elation. His state of health had perceptibly improved during his first stay in Sils-Maria, in the high-lying Swiss valley of the Engadine, two thousand meters above sea level. Here there dawned on him the key idea for his *Zarathustra,* who is then introduced also, at the end of the fourth book,116 for the first time, while the work as a whole provides a prelude for themes from *Zarathustra:* themes, however, of a very ambiguous gaiety, basic themes of a counterreligion.

## 2. *The counterreligion*

"The greatest recent event—that 'God is dead,' that the belief in the Christian God has become unbelievable—is already beginning to cast its first shadows over Europe." This is how Friedrich Nietzsche opens the fifth book, "We fearless ones," of his *The Gay Science,* with a section on "the meaning of our cheerfulness."1

But how many are there now who have any forebodings of the *more distant consequences* of this tremendous event? How many know at this stage what will be the results of this by way of inconceivable loss of confidence, collapse of morality, cataclysm and ruin, by way of gloom and eclipse, in the *distant* future? Must not the horror of it all disturb their bourgeois self-satisfaction? Nietzsche has no illusions on this score: "For the few at least, whose eyes—the *suspicion* in whose eyes is strong and subtle enough for this spectacle, some sun seems to have set and some ancient and profound trust has been turned into doubt; to them our old world must appear daily more like evening, more mistrustful, stranger, 'older.' But in the main one may say: The event itself is far too great, too distant, too remote from the multitude's capacity for comprehension even for the tidings of it to be thought of as having *arrived* as yet. Much less may one suppose that many people know as yet *what* this event really means—and how much must collapse now that this faith has been undermined because it was built upon this faith, propped up by it, grown into it; for example, the whole of our European morality. This long plenitude and sequence of breakdown, destruction, ruin and cataclysm that is now impending—who could guess enough of it today to be compelled to play the teacher and advance proclaimer of this monstrous logic of terror, the prophet of a gloom and an eclipse of the sun whose like has probably never yet occurred on earth?"[2]

There are few, then, who have any suspicion of it. And even for these, cares and fears are only slight. Why? They can see only the *immediate consequences* of this tremendous event. And for their own *immediate* future they see emerging an indescribable illumination, delight, relief, encouragement, a new dawn, a free horizon, the open sea: "Are we perhaps still too much under the impression of the *initial consequences* of this event—and these initial consequences, the consequences for *ourselves*, are quite the opposite of what one might perhaps expect. They are not at all sad and gloomy but rather like a new and scarcely describable kind of light, happiness, relief, exhilaration, encouragement, dawn. . . . Indeed, we philosophers and 'free spirits' feel, when we hear the news that 'the old god is dead,' as if a new dawn shone on us; our heart overflows with gratitude, amazement, premonitions, expectation. At long last the horizon appears free to us again, even if it should not be bright; at long last our ships may venture out again, venture out to face any danger; all the daring of the lover of knowledge is permitted again; the sea, *our* sea, lies open again; perhaps there has never yet been such an 'open sea.' "[3]

Yet Nietzsche even in this work is interested mainly in making people consider also the *more remote consequences* of the death of God. And he does so quite differently and more comprehensively than—for instance—Feuerbach. At the opening of the fifth book, "We fearless ones," stands the warning of the Vicomte de Turenne, Marshal of France: *Carcasse, tu trembles? Tu tremblerais bien davantage, si tu savais, où je te mène.* "You tremble, carcass? You would tremble a lot more if you knew where I am taking you."[4]

## Against inconsequential atheism

"The decline of the faith in the Christian God, the triumph of artificial atheism," according to Nietzsche, "is a generally European event in which all races had their share and for which all deserve credit and honor."[5] What follows from such atheism if we assume with Schopenhauer—according to Nietzsche, "the *first* admitted and inexorable atheist among us Germans"—"the ungodliness of existence . . . as something given, palpable, indisputable"?[6] What follows? "*Schopenhauer's* question immediately comes to us in a terrifying way: *Has existence any meaning at all?* It will require a few centuries before this question can even be heard completely and in its full depth."[7] We must also go far beyond Schopenhauer's youthful, hasty and—unfortunately—Christian answer to "his horrified look into a de-deified world that had become stupid, blind, mad, and questionable, his *honest* horror."[8] His answer was still "a way of remaining stuck in precisely those Christian-ascetic moral perspectives in which one had *renounced faith* along with the faith in God."[9] So where do we stand?

Nowhere did Nietzsche announce more dramatically the remote consequences of atheism than in the well-known parable of the "madman," that vision of a keen-sighted prophet "who lit a lantern in the bright morning hours" and proclaimed the *death of God*. It should be observed that this proclamation of the death of God is not addressed primarily to theologians. It is meant for those superficial atheists—we may recall "our naturalists and physiologists" who "lack passion in these things"—who do not know what it means to have lost God and who respond to the seer's cry, "I seek God! I seek God!" with "much laughter": "Has he got lost? . . . Or is he hiding? Is he afraid of us? Has he gone on a voyage? emigrated?"[10] What is stigmatized here is the careless, irresponsible atheism that does not see the consequences.

But people cannot avoid their responsibility, even though—according to Nietzsche—they do not know what they have done. "Whither is God," cried the "madman" and "pierced them with his eyes": "I will tell you. *We have killed him*—you and I. All of us are his murderers. But how did we do this?"[11] Can this be without *consequences?*

No, what might at first seem to be open sea, broad horizon, new dawn, seems quite different to the seer, probing into the future, judging the present. What can be expressed only feebly in concepts, the "madman" describes in *three* impressive, powerful metaphors: "How could we drink up the sea? Who gave us the sponge to wipe away the entire horizon? What were we doing when we unchained this earth from its sun? Whither is it moving now?"[12]

"God is dead. God remains dead":[13] an event of vertiginous impossibility and of meaninglessness which threatens everything. Theologians have tried subsequently to render this parable innocuous by getting rid of the metaphor of the unchained earth or by reducing that of the horizon wiped away to a symbolic revocation of the Anselmian proof of God.[14] But this cannot be justified either from the history of the text or from the wording and context of the three mutually complementary and interpretative metaphors.[15] No, even Nietzsche's atheism and particularly this must be taken wholly seriously in theological terms.[16] Nietzsche denies God—any God, and the Christian God in particular. He does not want subsequently to be appropriated as a "God-seeker." Like Schopenhauer before him, Nietzsche stands for "an unconditional and honest atheism" which forbids itself the *lie* in faith in God": and this in virtue of that "scientific conscience" and "intellectual cleanliness" that in the last resort amount to a sublimation of "the concept of truthfulness understood ever more rigorously" and "the father-confessor's refinement of the Christian conscience," so that it is "Christian morality itself" that "really triumphed over the Christian God."[17] What he praised in Schopenhauer is true also of Nietzsche: "The ungodliness of existence was for him something given, palpable, indisputable; he always lost his philosopher's composure and became indignant when he saw anyone hesitate or mince matters at this point. This is the locus of his whole integrity."[18]

What is important here is the fact that Nietzsche, when talking about the death of God, does not restrict himself to the purely psychological observation: "There is no God. I do not believe in any God." He is stating what he regards as a basic fact, to be used for the interpretation of the totality of man and the world, which carries within itself important consequences for the further course of the age. God's death means the *great collapse*. Desolate emptiness: the sea drunk up. A living space without prospects: the horizon wiped away. Unfathomable nothingness: the earth unchained from the sun. For man himself a desperate, aimless fall, which must tear him apart: "Whither are we moving? Away from all suns? Are we not plunging continually? Backward, sideward, forward, in all directions?"[19] Here chaos opens up, the deadly coldness and night of nihilism: "Is there still any up or down? Are we not straying as through an infinite nothing? Do we not feel the breath of empty space? Has it not become colder? Is not night continually closing in on us?"[20]

Feuerbach's relief at the death of God seems to be dangerously innocent and naïve as compared with the deep horror to which the "madman" gives expression here: "Do we not need to light lanterns in the morning? Do we hear nothing as yet of the noise of the gravediggers who are burying God? Do we smell nothing as yet of the divine decomposition? Gods, too, decompose. God is dead. God remains dead. And we have killed him. How shall we comfort ourselves, the murderers of all murderers? What was holiest and mightiest of all that the world has yet owned has bled to death under our knives: who will wipe this blood off us? What water is there for us to clean ourselves? What festivals of atonement, what sacred games shall we have to invent?"[21]

"Festivals of atonement?" "Sacred games?" Some have turned all this into an apologetic argument for the existence of God—completely against Nietzsche's own intentions. Nietzsche here is not recalling God. More prophet than diagnostician, behind the mask of the "madman," he proclaims the death of God not simply in order to describe the spiritual situation of man and world but to make men aware of the fact and so to change the situation. In modern linguistic theory, talk of this kind is said to have performative character. Nietzsche wants to make people aware of the vast consequences of the murder of God, and he himself is prepared to accept the consequences: "Is not the greatness of this deed too great for us? Must we ourselves not become gods simply to appear worthy of it? There has never been a greater deed; and whoever is born after us—for the sake of this deed he will belong to a higher history than all history hitherto."[22]

In his *The Gay Science*, Nietzsche does not yet explain the meaning of "becoming gods," of this "higher history." But he will soon do so. Here first of all it is a question of proclaiming the death of God, without any positive alternative. But even at this point Nietzsche is far ahead of his own, superficial times: "I have come too early," says the "madman" after reducing his audience to silence and shattering his lantern to pieces: "My time is not yet. This tremendous event is still on its way, still wandering; it has not yet reached the ears of men. Lightning and thunder require time; the light of the stars requires time; deeds, though done, still require time to be seen and heard. This deed is still more distant from the most distant stars—*and yet they have done it themselves.*"[23]

At the close of this section of *The Gay Science*, he adds a punch line by way of criticism of the churches: "It has been related further that on the same day the madman forced his way into several churches and there struck up his *requiem aeternam deo*. Led out and called to account, he is said to have replied nothing but: 'What after all are these churches now if they are not the tombs and sepulchers of God.' "[24]

From all this it is evident that, according to Nietzsche, not only belief in God but also all the *consequences of belief in God must be overcome.* God is dead, but he casts a long shadow: "After Buddha was dead, his shadow was still shown for centuries in a cave—a tremendous, gruesome shadow. God is dead; but, given the way of men, there may still be caves for thousands of years in which his shadow will be shown. —And we—we still have to vanquish his shadow too."[25] To achieve God's death completely in theory and practice, "new struggles" are needed.[26]

Hence Nietzsche's frequent "let us beware" of a deified nature. We should not believe in any ultimate order, functionality, finality, either in an organic or in a mechanistic sense: "The total character of the world, however, is in all eternity chaos—in the sense not of a lack of necessity but of a lack of order, arrangement, form, beauty, wisdom, and whatever other names there are for our aesthetic anthropomorphisms."[27]

Hence even at this stage we are shown Nietzsche's now increasingly violent struggle against morality, as he formulates it in "granite propositions" at the end of the third book of *The Gay Science*:

"*Ultimate skepsis.* —What are man's truths ultimately? Merely his *irrefutable* errors.

"*Where cruelty is needed.* —Those who have greatness are cruel to their virtues and to secondary considerations.

"*With a great goal.* —With a great goal one is superior even to justice, not only to one's deeds and one's judges.

"*What makes one heroic?* —Going out to meet at the same time one's highest suffering and one's highest hope.

*"In what do you believe? —*In this, that the weights of all things must be determined anew.

*"What does your conscience say? —*'You shall become the person you are.'

*"Where are your greatest dangers? —*In pity.

*"What do you love in others? —*My hopes.

*"Whom do you call bad? —*Those who always want to put to shame.

*"What do you consider most humane? —*To spare someone shame.

*"What is the seal of liberation? —*No longer being ashamed in front of oneself."*[28]

According to Schopenhauer, in his altruistic, social attitude, all morality culminates in compassion. It is this very compassion that Nietzsche selfishly and aristocratically rejects from the outset.

## The superman as antitype

How can the shadow of God be obliterated, how can his traces be effaced, all consequences of belief in God eliminated? Only when man himself rises above himself, enters in fact into a "higher history," becomes equal to the "gods." And it is just this that is the great theme of the first part of that work which recapitulates all the earlier writings and provides the foundation of all the later ones, the work in which Nietzsche no longer merely writes or speaks but proclaims and preaches: *Thus Spoke Zarathustra.*[29]

This book, "for everyone and no one," was written at a time when the author was again severely handicapped physically and psychologically, when he was—if it were possible—even more lonely than ever before. It was in Rome in 1882 that he fell head over heels in love with the young Russian Lou von Salomé, as attractive as she was shrewd, later to belong to the circle of Freud's friends. With her and his friend Paul Rée, Nietzsche traveled to Lucerne, there visiting Tribschen, with all its memories, enthusiastically recalling the time spent with Richard Wagner and Cosima and revealing to Lou his innermost philosophical thoughts. Alone once again, in Naumburg, he composed Lou's "Prayer to Life" and then celebrated a reunion with her near Bayreuth (not *in* Bayreuth, not with Wagner, not at the premiere of *Parsifal*). But this, perhaps the most serious of Nietzsche's love affairs, ended disastrously: there was the rivalry with his friend Rée, also in love with Lou; his jealous sister indulged in indescribable intrigues; Nietzsche himself was not entirely honest and suffered from inhibitions, even asking Rée to court Lou for him. Out of all this came finally Nietzsche's break with his sister and mother, his separation from Rée and—above all—his estrangement from Lou, his student and admirer, who, however, had turned down his proposal of marriage. Nietzsche fled to Italy, to Rapallo, near the foothills of Portofino. He wrote to Peter Gast: "This winter was the worst in my life."[30]

But, at this very place, at breathtaking speed, in ten days of euphoric inspiration—he spoke even of "revelation"[31]—Nietzsche wrote the first part of *Zarathustra*: the *anti-Bible of an antireligion*. It was not written by Nietzsche the prose writer—who as such even today is beyond criticism —but by the poet, polemicist, preacher, prophet, who hoped with his religious language and bibilical passion to outdo the Bible and eradicate all religion: all this—particularly today—gives the impression of rhetorical exaggeration, theatricality, often of bombast. But, whatever may be thought of the manner—the *how*—the matter—*what* he said—was and remains worth considering. And what did he say? *Two great leading conceptions—superman* and *eternal return*—expressed in an abundance of parables and metaphors dominate the discourses of "Zarathustra": that pre-Christian founder of Persian religion whom Nietzsche made the central figure of his work because he was the only one who taught that the supreme virtue was "to speak the truth and to *shoot well with arrows*";[32] but he was also the first to preach the dualism of good and evil and therefore was now to be the first to announce its overcoming.

And Zarathustra then spoke to the people: "*I teach you the Superman. Man is something that should be overcome. What have you done to overcome him?*"[33] The *overcoming of man by man* is the theme of the first book, the *Superman* the *first leading conception of Zarathustra* as a whole.

Here Darwin—or at least some of his general, prevailing ideas—comes very clearly into his own. As man should transcend the ape, the Superman should transcend man: "You have made your way from worm to man, and much in you is still worm. Once you were apes, and even now man is more of an ape than any ape. . . . Behold, I teach you the Superman."[34] The goal of evolution is and ought to be not a God and his kingdom but the Superman and his dominion: "The Superman is the meaning of the earth. Let your will say: The Superman *shall be* the meaning of the earth!"[35] The Superman—with his earth without heaven, his here without hereafter, his world without afterworld, his body without spirit-soul— *after God's death*, he is to take *God's place*:
"I entreat you, my brothers, *remain true to the earth*, and do not believe those who speak to you of superterrestrial hopes! They are poisoners, whether they know it or not.
"They are despisers of life, atrophying and self-poisoned men, of whom the earth is weary: so let them be gone!
"Once blasphemy against God was the greatest blasphemy, but God died, and thereupon these blasphemers died too. To blaspheme the earth is now the most dreadful offence, and to esteem the bowels of the Inscrutable more highly than the meaning of the earth.
"Once the soul looked contemptuously upon the body; and then this contempt was the supreme good—the soul wanted the body lean, monstrous,

famished. So the soul thought to escape from the body and from the earth."[36]

Thus, as the "madman" demanded, the conclusions are resolutely drawn from the great achievement of the death of God. It is true that man cannot cope with the death of God, but the Superman can do so. He is the goal of the unchained earth, he can drink up the sea into himself, he is to act as enkindling and destructive lightning: "Behold, I teach you the Superman: he is this sea, in him your great contempt can go under . . . he is this lightning, he is this madness! . . . What can be loved in man is that he is a *going-across* and a *down-going*."[37]

Thus the Superman, who is both the strong and the wise, the destroyer and the lover, will be the new type. For the sake of this grandiose future of man, which has not yet been realized anywhere, there follows the *critique of traditional virtues and the existing order of things*. Against the despisers of life and of the body, against the teachers of virtue and the priests, against the poets and saints, against the afterworldsmen and preachers of death, against the compassionate and the rabble, against the ancient delusion of good and evil:

praise of life, of the body, of health, of the joys of the flesh;

praise of the passions, turned into virtues and joys;

praise of war, struggle, hatred, hardness and obedience;

praise of powerful natures, warriors and soldiers, as opposed to all unteachable scholars;

praise of the aristocratic few, as opposed to those far too many superfluous people and their democratic state;

praise of the transvaluation of values, of the new law tables instead of the old, of love for the most distant instead of love of neighbor;

praise finally of the *will to power*, which is the true purpose of life, which all will to truth has to serve: "Where I found a living creature, there I found will to power; and even in the will of the servant I found the will to be master. . . . And life itself told me this secret: 'Behold,' it said, 'I am *that which must overcome itself again and again*.' To be sure, you call it will to procreate or impulse towards a goal, towards the higher, more distant, more manifold: but all this is one and *one* secret. . . . And you too, enlightened man, are only a path and footstep of my will: truly, my will to power walks with the feet of your will to truth!"[38] Here everywhere Darwin was tacitly accepted as godfather: the power of life and its evolution; the struggle for existence, which only the hardest survive; selection and selective breeding of the fittest. Whatever Strauss had neglected— Nietzsche thoroughly made up for it.

### The most abysmal thought

The Superman was the first great leading conception of *Zarathustra*. It was only in the third part, written in 1884 in Nice, that Nietzsche revealed his *second leading conception,* in fact the essential basic conception of his work, as it came like a flash of lightning to the lonely wanderer lost in thought at the lake and on the woodland paths of the Engadine: *the eternal recurrence of the same.* Nietzsche himself tells the story: "The fundamental conception of this work, the idea of the eternal recurrence, this highest formula of affirmation that is at all attainable, belongs in August 1881: it was penned on a sheet with a notation underneath, '6000 feet beyond man and time.' That day I was walking through the woods along the lake of Silvaplana; at a powerful pyramidal rock not far from Surlei I stopped."[39]

As early as *The Gay Science,* as we heard, he had hesitatingly announced in advance the fundamental idea that had then dawned upon him in all its ambivalence of supreme affirmation *and* supreme negation: "What, if some day or night a demon were to steal after you into your loneliest loneliness and say to you: 'This life as you now live it and have lived it, you will have to live once more and innumerable times more; and there will be nothing new in it, but every pain and every joy and every thought and sigh and everything unutterably small or great in your life will have to return to you, all in the same succession and sequence—even this spider and this moonlight between the trees, and even this moment and I myself. The eternal hourglass of existence is turned upside down again and again, and you with it, speck of dust!' Would you not throw yourself down and gnash your teeth and curse the demon who spoke thus? Or have you once experienced a tremendous moment when you would have answered him: 'You are a god and never have I heard anything more divine.' "[40]

In the first case, then, supreme *negation:* "If this thought gained possession of you, it would change you as you are or perhaps crush you. The question in each and every thing, 'Do you desire this once more and innumerable times more?' would lie upon your actions as the greatest weight."[41]

Or perhaps, nevertheless, supreme affirmation? "Or how well disposed would you have to become to yourself and to life *to crave nothing more fervently* than this ultimate eternal confirmation and seal?"[42] Eternal recurrence—a highly discordant idea.

Three years passed before Nietzsche expounded the fundamental conception that had flashed upon him in the Engadine, but which he obviously could not easily develop. In the third part of *Zarathustra,* however, it is introduced effectively but in a completely negative way right at the beginning, within the framework of a gruesome argument with a dwarf under the heading of "The Vision and the Riddle": "Behold this gateway! . . . it has two aspects. Two paths come together here: no one has ever reached their end. This long lane behind us: it goes on for an eternity. And that long lane ahead of us—that is another eternity. . . . The name of the gateway is written above it: 'Moment.' . . . From this gate-

way Moment a long, eternal lane runs *back*: an eternity lies behind us.
Must not all things that *can* run have already run along this lane? Must
not all things that *can* happen *have* already happened, been done, run
past? . . . Must we not all have been here before?—and must we not return and run down that other lane out before us, down that long, terrible
lane—must we not return eternally?"[43] An idea that is difficult to cope
with. At the end, the shepherd has to bite the head off the snake, which
had crawled into his mouth while he was asleep, but then he is
transfigured, illuminated, and able to laugh.

The real "revelation" of this teaching, however, comes only after the
important section on the "Old and New Law-tables": "I, Zarathustra, the
advocate of life, the advocate of suffering, the advocate of the circle—I
call you, my most abysmal thought."[44] A thought which produces healing
but also "Disgust, disgust, disgust—woe is me!"[45] It is interpreted in the
words of the animals:
"Everything goes, everything returns; the wheel of existence rolls for ever.
Everything dies, everything blossoms anew; the year of existence runs on
for ever.
"Everything breaks, everything is joined anew; the same house of existence builds itself for ever. Everything departs, everything meets again; the
ring of existence is true to itself for ever.
"Existence begins in every instant; the ball There rolls around every Here.
The middle is everywhere. The path of eternity is crooked."[46]

This, then, is Zarathustra's destiny: "Behold, *you are the teacher of the
eternal recurrence*."[47] As such, he, too, should himself "convalesce," "decline" and "return." Here, too, however, the ambivalence remains: "Alas,
man recurs eternally! The little man recurs eternally! . . . And eternal recurrence even for the smallest! that was my disgust at all existence! Ah,
disgust! Disgust! Disgust!"[48] On the other hand, "new songs" and "bearing his destiny" should bring him "comfort" and "convalescence."[49] Consequently Zarathustra passes on to a "second dance song": a song to eternal "life," the life "beyond good and evil," which means life, suffering,
passing away and coming to be, and thus indeed eternity:

> The world is deep,
> Deeper than day can comprehend.
> Deep is its woe,
> Joy—deeper than heart's agony:
> Woe says: Fade! Go!
> But all joy wants eternity,
> —wants deep, deep, deep eternity![50]

Thus the third part of *Zarathustra* culminates and ends in the great
"Song of Yes and Amen," with the refrain of the "seven seals": "Oh how
should I not lust for eternity and for the wedding ring of rings—the Ring
of Recurrence! . . . *For I love you, O Eternity!*"[51]

In regard to the essential point of eternal recurrence, the fourth part of *Zarathustra* does not go beyond the third. Once again "The Intoxicated Song"—"whose name is 'Once More,' whose meaning is 'To all eternity!' "—is sung.[52] But here hardness is preached, against the temptation to the "ultimate sin" of becoming weak through suffering and pity: "My suffering and my pity—what of them? For do I aspire after *happiness*? I aspire after my *work*."[53]

As soon as he had completed the third part, Nietzsche wrote to Rohde: "I think that with this Z. I have brought the German language to its perfection. After *Luther* and Goethe there was only a third step to take; my old and dear comrade, see if ever strength, flexibility and sonority were so closely united in our language."[54] Later, when looking back in *Ecce Homo*, Nietzsche placed *Zarathustra* even above Shakespeare, Dante and the poets of the Vedas; an incipient megalomania becomes apparent here. Objectively, however, he brings out in concentrated form what he regards as essential: that this work as a negation of all existing order is nevertheless wholly and entirely a work of Dionysian affirmation of all things: "The psychological problem in the type of Zarathustra is how he that says No and *does* No to an unheard-of degree, to everything to which one has so far said Yes, can nevertheless be the opposite of a No-saying spirit; how the spirit who bears the heaviest fate, a fatality of a task, can nevertheless be the lightest and most transcendent—Zarathustra is a dancer—how he that has the hardest, most terrible insight into reality, that has thought the 'most abysmal idea,' nevertheless does not consider it an objection to existence, not even to its eternal recurrence—but rather one reason more for *being himself* the eternal Yes to all things, 'the tremendous, unbounded saying Yes and Amen.' 'Into all abysses I still carry the blessings of my saying Yes.' *But this is the concept of Dionysus once again.*"[55]

Nietzsche had every reason to assume that he had written a work of the century. So much the worse was his experience. Even *Zarathustra* made no impression. From the start, he disagreed with his publisher, who did not regard it as a profitable venture and delayed publication. In the event, it did not sell. The fourth part, Nietzsche had privately printed: an edition of forty copies. Nietzsche's health deteriorated again: "Except for these ten-day works"—the three parts of *Zarathustra*, each written in a ten-day period, according to Nietzsche's autobiography—"the years during and above all *after* my Zarathustra were marked by distress without equal. One pays dearly for immortality: one has to die several times while still alive."[56] But Nietzsche was convinced that he had accomplished his *positive* task: "*saying Yes* to the point of justifying, of redeeming even all of the past. . . . Zarathustra has mastered the *great nausea* over man, too."[57]

Certainly: "Among the conditions for a *Dionysian* task are, in a decisive way, the hardness of the hammer, the *joy even in destroying*."[58] There is the *negative* task, then, its negative side. We thus reach

Nietzsche's later years. Outwardly they brought few events: summer in Sils, winter mostly in Nice and then in Turin, at the same time constant disagreements with his mother and sister (now—to Nietzsche's great irritation—married to the Berlin schoolmaster, Wagnerian and anti-Semite, Dr. Bernhard Förster). Inwardly, however, these years brought the drama to its climax.

## 3. What is nihilism?

"The task for the years that followed now was indicated as clearly as possible. After the Yes-saying part of my task had been solved, the turn had come for the No-saying, *No-doing* part: the revaluation of our values so far, the great war—conjuring up a day of decision."[1] Nietzsche here indicates the direction of the work of his later years, an indication that has all too often been neglected in discussions of the period.

In fact, in the next three years, the last before his breakdown, one book appeared after another, an *internecine war* without equal. In essentials, all negations are already present in *Zarathustra*: there is not a motif that is not audible there, not a shadow that does not fall there. But Nietzsche now wants to lay the greatest stress on the counterpoint, to bring out the diversity of the shadows and thus clarify their meaning. Consequently, coldness, skepticism, mistrust, malice, dominate these later works, not the light and warmth of *Zarathustra*. With all the resources of style and language, in an elaborate mixture of psychological clearsightedness and sarcasm, wittily, ingeniously and brutally, he laid bare, tested, sounded, and finally dropped or threw away everything that had thitherto been regarded by Europeans—even when they had long ceased to be Christians—as true, good and humane. Neither Socrates nor Plato, neither Descartes nor Kant, neither Buddhism nor Christianity, are spared. Least of all, the object of Nietzsche's love-hate attitude, Richard Wagner: although he died in Venice in the year of the publication of *Zarathustra* (1883), Nietzsche stubbornly pursued him far beyond the grave: "*artist of decadence, he has made music sick, actor in music,*" unsuccessful genius and even neurotic. It was five years after Wagner's death that Nietzsche wrote his pamphlet *The Case of Wagner. A Musician's Problem*[2] and, recapitulating his earlier writings, *Nietzsche contra Wagner. Out of the Files of a Psychologist.*[3]

## Descartes, Pascal and the controversy over fundamental certainty

"Beyond good and evil": this motif, too, was continually heard in *Zarathustra* and now becomes the theme of a separate, deliberately destructive work (1886). Even this "prelude to a philosophy of the future"[4] is meant to be "in all essentials a *critique of modernity*," and also of the modern sciences, arts, culture and even of politics. But against *what*, precisely? Against "our famous 'objectivity,' for example; 'pity for all that suffers'; the 'historical sense,' with its submission to foreign tastes, grovelling on its belly before *petits faits*, and 'being scientific.'"[5] At the same time, "pointers" are to be given "to a contrary type that is as little modern as possible—a noble, Yes-saying type." The book is to be—we may recall the line from Castiglione's *Cortigiano* to the Chevalier de Méré and to Pascal[6]—"a school for the *gentilhomme*, taking this concept in a more spiritual and radical sense than has ever been done."[7]

Nietzsche once declared that the Germans had "never gone through a seventeenth century of hard self-examination, like the French,"[8] and he mentioned the names of La Rochefoucauld and Descartes, in other passages also that of Pascal. Three hundred years later, Nietzsche fully caught up with this self-examination. And in this respect it is significant that he pressed on to the point from which we thought it right to start out historically in order to understand the modern question of God: Descartes's *cogito* as the ground of all certainty: "I think, therefore I am." Nietzsche's interest is blatant. All previous *foundations of human knowledge* are to be *undermined* by depicting them as *prejudices of faith*: "Prejudices of the Philosophers," as he entitles the first part of his book *Beyond Good and Evil*. And in fact, on our long and unavoidable road through modern times, we have reached that ground of the problems of faith and knowledge at which we aimed from the beginning. If a fundamental answer to the question of God is conceivable at all today, it can only be against this background. For that very reason, Nietzsche's *negative* arguments must be taken completely seriously. How does Nietzsche's "hard self-examination" compare, then, with that of Descartes or Pascal?

Nietzsche reduces "the old theological problem of 'faith' and 'knowledge'" to the problem of "instinct and reason." From Plato onward, he claims, philosophers and theologians have given the priority over reason in moral questions to "instinct," or—as Christians call it—"faith," or—as Nietzsche himself calls it—"the herd."[9] With the one great exception of *Descartes*: "the father of rationalism (and consequently the grandfather of the Revolution), who recognized only the authority of reason." But—Nietzsche's praise is quickly followed by a rebuke—"reason is only an instrument, and Descartes was superficial."[10] Superficial?

As we saw,[11] Descartes, the great master of *certitude*, was described as *uncertain* by Pascal, who was likewise concerned about (higher) certitude; to the latter, Descartes's *cogito* scarcely seemed to provide a secure foundation for knowledge. Nietzsche knew and appreciated Pascal, regarding the latter as his early predecessor, as "psychologist" and explorer of the depths and abysses of the self. Skepticism, passionate thinking, urge for truth, aversion to authorities, and a sharp pen were typical also of him.

Nietzsche linked him with Schopenhauer, to follow Epicurus and Montaigne, Goethe and Spinoza, Plato and Rousseau, in a list of the four pairs of thinkers "who responded to me in my sacrifice" and whom he constantly had in mind.[12] They were more important to him than any living persons. Almost in every one of his works, Nietzsche grapples with Pascal, whose cruel destiny, on the edge of a precipice, was imprinted vividly on his mind. Even on the verge of his breakdown, he wrote to Georg Brandes, his Danish admirer: "Pascal I almost love, for he has given me infinite instruction; he is the only *logical* Christian."[13] That man's problem is not only the uncertainty of reason but also the insecurity of human existence as a whole; that man is not only reason but also heart, feeling, instinct, at bottom even a chimera, a monster, a chaos, a subject of contradiction: all this—with Pascal against Descartes—was also the view of Friedrich Nietzsche.

But *Pascal's solution*—a leap into faith in the God of the Bible—was completely *unacceptable* to Nietzsche. Here he was on the side of Descartes once more: he praises Pascal indeed as a genuine Christian (= ascetic), but for that very reason "the most instructive victim of Christianity, murdered slowly, first physically, then psychologically—the whole logic of this most gruesome form of inhuman cruelty."[14] Pascal believed in his own depravity, because he "believed his reason had been depraved by original sin while it had only been depraved by his Christianity."[15] For Nietzsche, this was completely out of the question: the sacrifice of reason, the "Pascalian *sacrifizio dell'intelletto.*"[16]

But can reason and Descartes's *cogito* for their part produce fundamental certainty? No. Nietzsche thinks he has *seen through Descartes.* Only "harmless self-observers" could still "believe 'immediate certainties' exist, for example 'I think' or, as was Schopenhauer's superstition, 'I will': as though knowledge here got hold of its object pure and naked, as 'thing in itself,' and no falsification occurred either on the side of the subject or on that of the object."[17] For Nietzsche, an immediate certainty is a contradiction in terms: "Let the people believe that knowledge is total knowledge, but the philosopher must say to himself: when I analyse the event expressed in the sentence 'I think,' I acquire a series of rash assertions which are difficult, perhaps impossible, to prove—for example, that it is *I* who think, that thinking is an activity and operation on the part of an entity thought of as a cause, that an 'I' exists, finally that what is designated by 'thinking' has already been determined—that I *know* what thinking is."[18]

Instead of that immediate certainty "in which the people may believe in the present case," the philosopher therefore is presented with a series of metaphysical questions, "true questions of conscience for the intellect": "Whence do I take the concept thinking? Why do I believe in cause and effect? What gives me the right to speak of an 'I,' and even of an 'I' as cause, and finally of an 'I' as cause of thought?"[19] Nietzsche argues in a very similar way also against Schopenhauer's "I will" and in particular against the theory of "freedom of will."[20]

But Nietzsche goes beyond this to criticize also "belief in 'synthetic judgements' *a priori*" in Kant's sense,[21] and "belief in 'substance,' in 'matter,' in the earth-residuum and particle atom"[22] as understood by the natural scientists, and most of all "soul atomism": "that belief which regards the soul as being something indestructible, eternal, indivisible, as a monad, as an *atomon: this* belief ought to be ejected from science."[23] For physics as a whole is "only an interpretation and arrangement of the world . . . and *not* an explanation of the world; but in so far as it is founded on belief in the senses, it passes for more than that and must continue to do so for a long time to come."[24]

Here everywhere Nietzsche raises the *question of truth, of the value of truth as such,* more radically than anyone before him: "Granted that we want truth: *why not rather* untruth? And uncertainty? Even ignorance?"[25] It is only in the light of a "faith," that philosophers reach their "knowledge," reach something that is at last solemnly baptized as "the truth." What sort of a faith is this? What sort of a "basic faith"? It is a faith that is by no means obvious: "*the faith in antithetical values,*" especially the basic antitheses between good and evil, true and false. But, according to Nietzsche, these are precisely what we are absolutely bound to doubt. And yet not even philosophers who were followers of Descartes did so: "It had not occurred to even the most cautious of them to pause and doubt here on the threshold, where however it was most needful that they should: even if they *had* vowed to themselves '*de omnibus dubitandum.*' "[26]

According to Nietzsche, there are two things about which we must decidedly doubt: "firstly whether there exist any antitheses at all, and secondly whether these popular evaluations and value-antitheses, on which the metaphysicians have set their seal, are not perhaps merely foreground valuations, merely provisional perspectives, perhaps from below, as it were frog-perspectives, to borrow an expression employed by painters."[27] The most deliberate thinking on the part of a philosopher is still secretly guided by his instincts. Behind all logic, there are value judgments, even physiological requirements to maintain a particular kind of life; and the true "interests" of a scholar usually lie by no means in the drive for knowledge but in something completely different: in the family, in making money, in politics. In any case, despite all the value that some ascribe to the true, the truthful, the selfless, it must be said "that a higher and more fundamental value for all life might have to be ascribed to appearance, to the will to deception, to selfishness and to appetite."[28]

Is, then, the falsity of a judgment not an objection to a judgment? No: "The question is to what extent it is life-advancing, life-preserving, species-preserving, perhaps even species-breeding."[29] The falsest judgments might possibly be for us the most indispensable. Beyond good and evil, therefore, means in the first place *beyond true and false.*

## Overcoming morality

For Nietzsche, the question of truth is reduced in the end to a *psychological question.* But what does "psychology" mean here? He conceives it as "morphology and the *development-theory of the will to power*" and thus as "the road to the fundamental problems."[30] Thus psychology becomes "the queen of the sciences."[31] Against all "the power of the moral prejudices" and all "unconscious resistances," such a "physio-psychology" must prevail: "a theory of the mutual dependence of the 'good' and the 'wicked' impulses," even "a theory of the derivation of all good impulses from wicked ones."[32] In fact, it might even be necessary to approve "the emotions of hatred, envy, covetousness, and lust for domination as life-conditioning emotions, as something that must fundamentally and essentially be present in the total economy of life, and consequently must be heightened further if life is to be heightened further."[33]

Beyond good and evil means beyond true and false. But also conversely, beyond true and false means *beyond good and evil.* The epistemological problems appear as the reverse side of the ethical-moral problems. In a second destructive work, *On the Genealogy of Morals,* this psychology is applied in the form of a "polemic."[34] This consists of three independent sections. First the psychology of Christianity: "the birth of Christianity out of the spirit of *ressentiment.*"[35] Then the psychology of conscience: conscience is not "the voice of God in man" but "the instinct of cruelty that turns back."[36] Finally the psychology of the priest: "the tremendous power of the ascetic ideal . . . the *harmful* ideal par excellence."[37] In fact: "three decisive preliminary studies by a psychologist for a revaluation of all values."[38]

The third destructive work against morality is *Twilight of the Idols or How to Philosophize with a Hammer.*[39] For Nietzsche, the whole book is a *"grand declaration of war,"* this time not against "idols of the age," of modern times, but against "*eternal* idols which are here touched with the hammer as with a tuning fork."[40] Nietzsche comments: "If you want a quick idea how before me everything stood on its head, begin with this essay. What is called *idol* on the title page is simply what has been called truth so far. *Twilight of the Idols*—that is: the old truth is approaching its end."[41]

The consequences are obvious. The end is coming for "virtually every morality that has hitherto been taught, reverenced and preached."[42] Why? Because that morality "turns precisely *against* the instincts of life" and represents "a now secret, now loud and impudent *condemnation* of these instincts. By saying 'God sees into the heart' it denies the deepest and highest desires of life and takes God for the *enemy of life*."[43] What Nietzsche wants, on the contrary, is "naturalism in morality," which can also be called "*healthy* morality" in so far as it "is dominated by an instinct of life."[44] Such an unmoral morality, such as immoralism, affirms whatever is useful to life. "We others, we immoralists, have on the contrary opened wide our hearts to every kind of understanding, comprehension, *approval*. We do not readily deny, we seek our honour in *affirming*."[45]

Finally, the recapitulation and culmination of Nietzsche's discussion of morality, and at the same time the last work that he himself prepared for publication, is *The Anti-Christ*. It was truly "a curse on Christianity."[46] Or—more precisely—Christianity itself as "the *one* great curse, the *one* great intrinsic depravity, the *one* great instinct for revenge for which no expedient is sufficiently poisonous, secret, subterranean, *petty*."[47]

Annihilation of Christianity: this is Nietzsche's objective as he deals in anger, hatred and pride, with Christianity—linking it with Buddhism and Judaism—in its great, negative historical development, as a religion that misunderstood its own founder from the very beginning. Jesus, the "bringer of glad tidings," who "died as he lived, as he *taught*,"[48] was only afterward turned by Paul and the early Church into a savior figure. The fact can scarcely be ignored that "the church is precisely that against which Jesus preached—and against which he taught his disciples to fight."[49] It is scarcely surprising that Nietzsche in this context also should once again sharply criticize the Christian *idea of God* which he had already constantly attacked: "The Christian conception of God—God as God of the sick, God as spider, God as spirit—is one of the most corrupt conceptions of God arrived at on earth: perhaps it even represents the low-water mark in the descending development of the God type. God degenerated to the *contradiction of life*, instead of being its transfiguration and eternal Y*es!* In God a declaration of hostility towards life, nature, the will to life! God the formula for every calumny of 'this world,' for every lie about 'the next world'! In God nothingness deified, the will to nothingness sanctified!"[50]

Even here, however, despite such outrageous negations, Nietzsche's affirmations cannot be overlooked. He himself states this quite emphatically in the pathetic final section of his autobiography, *Ecce Homo*, written very shortly afterward and already betraying a pathological strain. In "Why I am a destiny," he certainly recognizes his destructive power. He feels that he is "the first immoralist" and "annihilator *par excellence*":[51] "I am no man, I am dynamite."[52] But Nietzsche has no desire to be merely a naysayer. After "the mendaciousness of millennia," he feels that he is "the first *decent* human being." "I contradict as has never been contradicted before and am nevertheless the opposite of a No-saying spirit. I am a bringer of glad tidings like no one before me; I know tasks of such elevation that any notion of them has been lacking so far; only beginning with me are there hopes again."[53] Nietzsche then—although he does not want to be the founder of a religion, to address the masses, to have "believers"—has "a terrible fear that one day I will be pronounced *holy*. . . . I do not want to be a holy man; sooner even a buffoon. . . . Perhaps I am a buffoon. . . . Yet in spite of that—or rather *not* in spite of it, because so far nobody has been more mendacious than holy men— the truth speaks out of me. But my truth is *terrible;* for so far one has called *lies* truth. *Revaluation of all values:* that is my formula for an act of supreme self-examination on the part of humanity, become flesh and genius in me."[54]

This is the point to which Nietzsche pressed his questioning of the traditional values of morality, religion and culture. What follows? First of all, Nietzsche's treatment of a concept that, through him, became a key concept of the history of thought in the nineteenth century: the concept of nihilism. He deals with the concept in his *later* work, in particular in the unpublished writings that have been the subject of more fierce discussion among experts than almost any other philosophical literary remains.

It was Peter Gast, Nietzsche's friend for many years, who published—in accordance with the intentions of Nietzsche's sister, Elisabeth Förster-Nietzsche—the unpublished "major work" of the philosopher and even substantially expanded it in a second edition: *The Will to Power. Attempt at a Revaluation of all Values* (1911).[55] This work has often roused greater interest among both Nietzsche enthusiasts and Nietzsche opponents than the works released by Nietzsche himself for publication. Today, however, after many years of research carried out after the death of Nietzsche's sister (1935), by Karl Schlechta (editor of the edition used here) in the Nietzsche Archives, in Weimar, one thing is certain: there is no "major work" composed by Nietzsche himself; *The Will to Power* is not simply an unpublished work by Nietzsche. The intentions of his sister were certainly not those of her brother; the decisive letters of the brother to his sister, which provide evidence of a relationship of trust and a very high degree of agreement with her or even contain negative judgments on such of Nietzsche's friends as Overbeck, Rée, Lou Salomé, have been proved to be the forgeries of the jealous and egotistical Elisabeth.[56] Erich F. Podach has sharply criticized numerous German experts on Nietzsche who have put up for decades with these editorial whims and fostered the formation of legends.[57]

In the light of historical criticism, therefore, what Nietzsche has bequeathed to us is no more than a collection of all kinds of notes and sketches with very varied plans and titles for the arrangement of the material ("Will to Power," "The Eternal Recurrence," "Revaluation of all Values"): *Unpublished Material of the Eighties* is the title of Schlechta's edition, without an obvious structure and based on purely philological criteria.[58] Admittedly, different compilations can be made out of this material, either in the style of Förster-Gast or even in the very different form adopted by Friedrich Würzbach.[59] But, in this respect, any sort of systematic treatment remains the work of the editor. What Nietzsche's genius might have made of it must remain once and for all an open question.

This of course does not mean that we must be content with the unarranged material, as Schlechta thought, interpreting everything in the light of Nietzsche's breakdown, finding there "no *new* central idea," warning people against "rooting around in the rubbish."[60] The possibility certainly cannot be excluded that Nietzsche would have been capable of completing his work, which he regarded as a unity. And if the great themes are kept up and all the themes—as we have stressed—are heard in *Zarathustra*, it is only at this point that they are brought out in more detail and frequently varied. We have kept, therefore—unlike other systematic presentations[61]—strictly historically to the works released by Nietzsche for publication and only now—without attempting any compact systematization of the unpublished material—come to the themes developed by Nietzsche at the end. For our statement of the question, the problems of *nihilism* are foremost, as they began to be thought out systematically only at this stage by Nietzsche. He himself says in this connection: "*On the genesis of the nihilist.* —It is only late that one musters the courage for what one really knows. That I have hitherto been a thorough-going nihilist, I have admitted to myself only recently: the energy and radicalism with which I advanced as a nihilist deceived me about this basic fact. When one moves toward a goal it seems impossible that 'goal-lessness as such' is the principle of our faith."[62] Here what is raised is not only a personal problem of Nietzsche but a universal problem of modern humanity, which theologians have far too often played down with an appeal to "faith."

## Origins of nihilism

We have seen that Nietzsche's faith in civilization, culture, progress, modernity, had long been shattered. After his separation from Wagner and Cosima, he was firmly convinced that he was living at a time of uncertainty, collapse, nullity, that is, of *decadence* and therefore of "waste, decay, elimination."[63] The question had already occurred in *Human, All-Too-Human*: "Cannot all valuations be reversed?"[64] And in *The Gay Science*, the "madman" had prophesied that the earth-shaking consequence of the death of God would be "straying as through an infinite nothing."[65] From that time onward "nihilism" was Nietzsche's great "question mark,"[66] the "questionable character" that marked all things.[67] In place of what is customary and apparently securely existing, there appears with increasing clarity utter nothingness.

The *word* "nihilism" is found for the first time not—as is sometimes maintained[68]—in 1829 in Russia, entering into circulation through Turgenev's novel *Fathers and Sons* (1862), nor even, a little earlier, in Jean Paul's critique of Novalis, *Vorschule der Ästhetik* ("Primer of Aesthetics").[69] It was in fact used as early as 1799 in the letter of the philosopher Friedrich Heinrich Jacobi to his colleague Johann Gottlieb Fichte: "My dear Fichte, I really shall not be put out if you or anyone else want to call *chimerism* that which I am opposing to idealism, to what I prefer to call *nihilism.*"[70] That is to say, the idealist can indeed dismiss the reality of God, of other human beings, of things—according to Jacobi, immediately experienced by reason—as a chimera, as something merely imagined, at bottom as nothingness. But idealism for its own part, according to which reason perceives only itself and dissolves all that exists in the nothingness of subjectivity, is for Jacobi a nihilism, so that consequently a choice would have to be made between one nihilism and another.[71]

From that time onward, the word has been used regularly in discussions on idealism. Often a pejorative slogan and in any case used for a variety of things: atheism, pantheism, fatalism, decline of the West. Nietzsche, too, used it initially with little discrimination. Only in the unpublished work do we find him reflecting on all aspects of it. "What does nihilism mean?" asks Nietzsche here, and his answer now runs: "*That the highest values devaluate themselves.* The aim is lacking; 'why?' finds no answer."[72] In another fragment, he expesses it more precisely: "*Radical nihilism* is the conviction of an absolute untenability of existence when it comes to the highest values one recognizes; plus the realization that we lack the least right to posit a beyond or an in-itself of things that might be 'divine' or morality incarnate."[73] It can be said—and this, too, will be explained in the following pages—that, according to Nietzsche, *nihilism means the conviction of the nullity, of the internal contradiction, futility and worthlessness of reality.*

Nietzsche sees this nihilism as coming in the twentieth and twenty-first centuries: "What I relate is the history of the next two centuries. I describe what is coming, what can no longer come differently: *the advent of nihilism.* This history can be related even now; for necessity itself is at work here. This future speaks even now in a hundred signs, this destiny announces itself everywhere; for the music of the future all ears are cocked even now. For some time now, our whole European culture has been moving as toward a catastrophe, with a tortured tension that is growing from decade to decade: restlessly, violently, headlong, like a river that wants to reach the end, that no longer reflects, that is afraid to reflect."[74] Indeed, it must be said: "Nihilism stands at the door," and we can only ask: "Whence comes this uncanniest of all guests?"[75]

But was it not Nietzsche himself who introduced this uncanny guest into our society? So some say. Nietzsche would strictly reject this charge.

For nihilism is coming *with historical necessity.* "Why has the advent of nihilism become necessary?" Nietzsche answers: "Because the values we have had hitherto thus draw their final consequence; because nihilism represents the ultimate logical conclusion of our great values and ideals."[76] What does this mean?

Man's values and ideals—truth, justice, love, morality, religion—do not exist anywhere as such. They are entirely the product of man's invention and definition; Man projected them originally into things and thus created values and ideals in accordance with his life's needs: "All these values are, psychologically considered, the results of certain perspectives of utility, designed to maintain and increase human constructs of domination—and they have been falsely *projected* into the essence of things."[77] At a very early stage, however—historically perceptible already in Socrates and then in Plato—these values and ideals were hypostatized: the good or true "as such," the "idea" of the good or the true. But the needs of life were forgotten. From now on values and ideals are regarded as "in themselves," absolute, detached from the realities and needs of life. The highest values become religious and even metaphysical factors: "The supreme values in whose service man *should* live, especially when they were very hard on him and exacted a high price—these *social values* were erected over man to strengthen their voice, as if they were commands of God, as 'reality,' as the 'true' world, as a hope and *future* world."[78]

Of course, "now that the shabby origin of these values is becoming clear, the universe seems to have lost value, seems 'meaningless.'"[79] The result is that, precisely in their *hypostatization,* precisely as absolute moral and religious values, these supreme values are turned against the needs of life, becoming the expression of remoteness from life, estrangement from life, hostility to life—in a word, decadence. All morality, therefore, is an "instinct of decadence,"[80] an "instinct of denial of life."[81] In fact, "such a total aberration of mankind from its basic instincts, such a total decadence of value judgments—that is the question mark par excellence, the real riddle that the animal 'man' poses for the philosopher."[82]

For Nietzsche, then, it is clear that, behind the absolutized values to which morality aspires . . . there is simply nothingness. As oriented to unreal values (God, the hereafter, true life, virtues), *all morality* is turned toward nothingness, it is itself *nihilistic.*

This holds especially for *Christian morality* and indeed for the Christian religion as such, which for Nietzsche is reduced in essentials to morality: "The whole absurd residue of Christian fable, conceptual cobwebspinning and theology does not concern us."[83] Is not this Christian morality—very much more than Buddhism, the second great nihilistic religion—the stock example of the hypostatization of values? Plato, of course, had already placed all values in an eternal, unchanging, higher world: in the world of eternal ideas, the supreme ideas of the good, of the divine itself. Christianity likewise set up absolute values and—over and above these—made man himself an absolute value: "Christianity is Platonism for 'the people.'"[84] Hence Christianity more than any other religion has sinned against life by its morality. Christian morality is "a capital crime against life,"[85] and God himself has "degenerated to the *contradiction of life.*"[86] In so far as Christianity is oriented wholly to antilife, unreal values, especially to God, at once the supreme and absolutely unreal value, Christianity is a *"nihilistic* religion."[87] Paradoxically enough, it is the truthfulness that itself emerges from Christianity that has brought to light the nullity of Christianity and established atheism. "In God nothingness is deified, the will to nothingness sanctified."[88]

"Those who have abandoned God cling that much more firmly to the faith in morality."[89] In this atheistic and consequently futile and insupportable situation, it is understandable that modern man should have produced in place of the old superhuman meaning and support a new, purely human meaning and support: *substitute authorities.* "The nihilistic question 'for what?' is rooted in the old habit of supposing that the goal must be put up, given, demanded *from outside*—by some *superhuman authority.* Having unlearned faith in that, one still follows the old habit and seeks *another* authority that can *speak unconditionally* and *command* goals and tasks. The authority of *conscience* now steps up front (the more emancipated one is from theology, the more imperativistic morality becomes) to compensate for the loss of a *personal* authority. Or the authority of *reason.* Or the *social instinct* (the herd). Or *history* with an immanent spirit and a goal within, so one can entrust oneself to it. One wants to get around the will, the willing of a goal, the risk of positing a goal for oneself; one wants to rid oneself of the responsibility (one would accept fatalism). Finally, *happiness*—and, with a touch of Tartuffe, the *happiness of the greatest number.*"[90]

But can these substitute authorities provide an ultimate meaning and support? "Every purely moral value system (that of Buddhism, for example) ends in nihilism: this is to be expected in Europe. One still hopes to get along with a moralism without religious background: but that necessarily leads to nihilism."[91] And what about the modern sciences, natural and historical sciences, which are not bound by any morality? They help actively to bring on this nihilism. For they are supposed to be carried on "without moral prejudices." They are supposed to be "value-free" sciences, which are not concerned with the meaning of nature, the meaning of history, the meaning of the whole. In that sense we cannot fail to notice in them—and also in value-free and morality-free economics, politics, art—a "nihilistic trait."[92]

What was prepared so long and in so many ways is slowly dawning in our time. This whole immense development makes us fully aware of the hitherto concealed nihilism, and this means: "Everything lacks meaning," "meaninglessness," "yearning for Nothing";[93] "belief in valuelessness," "in vain so far";[94] "radical repudiation of value, meaning and desirability";[95] "rebound from 'God is truth' to the fanatical faith 'All is false.' "[96] This, then, is the "nihilistic belief," "that there is no truth at all."[97] "The philosophical nihilist is convinced that all that happens is meaningless and in vain."[98] "The pathos of 'in vain,' " according to Nietzsche, "is the nihilists' pathos—at the same time, as pathos, an inconsistency on the part of the nihilists."[99] Has it not now become clear what it means: nihilism is the conviction of the nullity—that is, of the internal contradiction, meaninglessness and worthlessness—of reality? In this reality, there is no connection, no meaning, no value: everything is void.

If a person becomes aware of the nullity of reality, his hitherto concealed, implicit nihilism is turned into an explicit but still in many ways "incomplete nihilism."[100] He attempts to avoid the consequences, but—in view of the vast emptiness—involuntarily makes the problem all the more acute by his delaying tactics and "ways of self-narcotization" (music, work, science, enthusiasm for persons or times).[101] Complete nihilism is not thereby held back.

## Was Nietzsche a nihilist?

What, then, is to be done? Nietzsche now makes his own, very special contribution. We cannot slow down nihilism; we must put up with it and endure it. This is Nietzsche's demand: the *nihilism of weakness must be turned into a nihilism of strength.* The nihilism of *weakness* is a "weary nihilism that no longer *attacks.*"[1] Its most famous form—here, too, Nietzsche's appraisal differs substantially from that of Schopenhauer—is Buddhism: this is "*a passive* nihilism,"[2] which represents a sign of disappointment, of the "*decline and recession of the power of the spirit.*"[3] The former values and goals are simply not believed any longer and are decaying. Nihilism of *strength,* on the other hand, is "a sign of *increased power of the spirit.*"[4] The former values and goals are no longer adequate to its new power; on the other hand, it is not yet strong enough "to posit for itself, productively, a goal, a why, a faith."[5] It reaches its *maximum* of relative strength as a violent force of *destruction*—as active nihilism."[6] But the "most extreme form of nihilism would be the view that *every* belief, every considering-something-true, is necessarily false because there simply is no *true world.* Thus: a *perspectival appearance* whose origin lies in us (in so far as we continually *need* a narrower, abbreviated, simplified world)."[7] "As the denial of a truthful world, of being," nihilism "might be *a divine way of thinking.*"[8]

Nihilism, however, is *not only a way of thinking.* It is not only a contemplation of the "in vain"; it is not merely "the belief that everything deserves to perish." On the contrary, *practice* is required: "One helps to destroy. —This is, if you will, illogical; but the nihilist does not believe that one needs to be logical. . . . The reduction to nothing by judgment is seconded by the reduction to nothing by hand."[9] In this slow and complex process of reducing morality to nothing by action—according to Nietzsche, a play with a hundred acts—there must be no consideration of human beings, of oneself or of others. Here one cannot hesitate ruthlessly "to offer *human sacrifices,* to risk every danger, to take upon oneself whatever is bad and worst: the *great passion.*"[10]

And yet all this negation is only transitional; destruction is merely the precondition of new creation, the great No a preparation for the great Yes: "We do not yet know the 'whither' toward which we are driven once we have detached ourselves from our old soil. But it was from this same soil that we acquired the force which now drives us forth into the distance, into adventures, thrusting us into the boundless, the untried, the undiscovered—we have no choice left, we have to be conquerors once we no longer have any country in which we are at home, in which we would want to 'preserve' things. A concealed Yes drives us that is stronger than all our No's. Our strength itself will no longer endure us in the old decaying soil: we venture away, we venture *ourselves:* the world is still rich and undiscovered, and even to perish is better than to become half-hearted and poisonous. Our strength itself drives us to sea, where all suns have hitherto gone down: we *know* of a new world. . . ."[11]

Here is the answer to the "madman's" questions about the sea drained out, the horizon wiped away, the unchained earth. In the concrete, this means that the devaluation of all values must be followed by a "countermovement" in the form of a "revaluation of all values."[12] As urged in *Zarathustra,* instead of the old tables of values there must be new ones.

What kind of *new values and ideals* are these to be? Not, in any case, the antilife, metaphysical, moral, religious values. But now the vital, natural, naturalistic values, the values of life: "*Fundamental innovations:* In place of 'moral values' purely *naturalistic values.* Naturalization of morality. . . . In place of 'metaphysics' and religion, the *theory of eternal recurrence* (this as a means of breeding and selection)."[13]

Thus we come again to the theory of *eternal recurrence,* with which *Zarathustra* had ended. It is the answer to nihilism, freshly discovered by Nietzsche. It is both the *most extreme form and the overcoming of nihilism,* making possible a crossing from "a No, a will to negation," to an "affirmation of the world as it is, without subtraction, exception or selection":[14] "affirmation of life even in its strangest and sternest problems, the will to life rejoicing in its own inexhaustibility through the *sacrifice* of its highest types, . . . *to realize in oneself* the eternal joy of becoming—that joy which also encompasses *joy in destruction.*"[15]

According to Nietzsche at this stage, *life* in all its contradictoriness therefore is what is really true. Life is the—completely relative—criterion of the true or the false. Hence the true is what serves life, the life of the individual. Life understood—now, in Nietzsche's later phase, increasingly relying again on Schopenhauer and accepting Burckhardt's emphasis on historical personalities—as blind, instinctive, creative-destructive *will to power:* "My formula for it is: Life is will to power."[16] This inexhaustible, eternally rising and declining, recurring life, this will to power finding expression and continually breaking through in instinctual life, in organic functions, indeed in all active forces, is now in fact the great antimetaphysician's metaphysical fundamental principle, the symbol of which is Dionysus: "Do you know what 'the world' is to me? . . . A monster of energy, without beginning, without end, . . . that does not expend itself but only transforms itself, . . . enclosed by 'nothingness' as by a boundary, . . . a sea of forces flowing and rushing together, eternally changing, eternally flooding back, with tremendous years of recurrence, with an ebb and flood of its forms; out of the simplest forms striving toward the most complex, out of the stillest, most rigid, coldest forms toward the hottest, most turbulent, most self-contradictory, and then returning home to the simple out of this abundance, out of the play of contradictions back to the joy of concord, . . . as a becoming that knows no satiety, no disgust, no weariness: this, my *Dionysian* world of the eternally self-creating, the eternally self-destroying, . . . do you want a *name* for this world? . . . *This world is the will to power—and nothing more.* And you yourselves are also this will to power—and nothing besides."[17] And for Nietzsche—unlike Schopenhauer—the important thing was "a *justification of life,* even at its most terrible, ambiguous, and mendacious; for this I had the formula '*Dionysian.*' "[18]

Was Nietzsche, then, a nihilist? We must distinguish. He only diagnosed the destruction of values, only caught sight of the rise of nihilism and loudly proclaimed it earlier than others—and in this sense he was *not a nihilist.* But the pastor's son, admirer of Schopenhauer and friend of Wagner also experienced nihilism in his own body more cruelly than others and affirmed it, so that it became his permanent destiny—and in this sense *he was a nihilist.* If you like, then, patient, diagnostician and therapist of the fatal disease of nihilism in the one person. Nothing, absolutely nothing, in his life turned out to be lasting: not the pious training by his mother, not the strict discipline of Schulpforta, not his classical education under Professor Ritschl, not the aesthetic Weltanschauung of a Schopenhauer or a Wagner. Thus in the end everything broke down around him: truth, morality, religion, belief in God, Christianity as a whole, and even belief in humanity, reason, in human science, philosophy, culture, development and progress. What was left to him except to learn "to live alone 'without God or morality' "?[19]

Did he not do everything to cope with this destiny? As free spirit and precursor of the future superman, he made the superhuman effort to face

the nothingness lurking in all things. With the great instinct of the creator, he progressed from the devaluation to the revaluation of all values,
from total denial to total affirmation. To the affirmation of life and its
contradictions, its absurd circling, of the blind will to power. He loved his
destiny—*amor fati*—as well as he could and endured in solitude what—
according to him—the future would bring to all. Alone—without wife,
students, disciples, without a calling, without a circle of friends or a fixed
domicile—he sacrificed himself and dared to go through everything in
order to announce it in advance to others: "as a spirit of daring and experiment that has already lost its way once in every labyrinth of the future;
as a soothsayer-bird spirit who *looks back* when relating what will come;
as the first perfect nihilist of Europe who, however, has even now lived
through the whole of nihilism, to the end, leaving it behind, outside
himself."[20]

Had Nietzsche really left nihilism behind and outside himself? Doubts
arise at this point. Nietzsche had forebodings of his own decline at an
early stage. Seven years before it, he had warned Overbeck's wife, Ida, to
give up the idea of God and at the same time gloomily observed: "I have
given it up, I want to create something new, I will not and may not go
back. I shall perish by my passions, they toss me hither and thither; I am
continually disintegrating, but it does not matter."[21] In the seven years
between the breakdown of his love affair with Lou von Salomé and his
mental derangement, does he not seem to have looked for someone who
might have helped him out of the labyrinth into which he had ventured?
The woman perhaps for whom he—here, too, like Schopenhauer—had
yearned throughout his life: an *Ariadne* who could have led him out of
this labyrinth, as in the Greek legend? Ariadne plays a mysterious, background role in the *Dionysus-Dithyrambs*, those last great free rhythmic
poems from the years 1884–88 about the God Dionysus, suffering infinitely and yet rising again, which Nietzsche produced in a fair copy and
prepared for publication in Turin immediately before his breakdown (his
last year of sanity was one of unparalleled creative frenzy). Here—"between birds of prey"—he, who "had lately been so proud, . . . had lately
been the solitary without God, sharing his solitude with the devil, the
scarlet prince of wantonness," had to recognize:

> *Now—*
> *bent between*
> *two nothings,*
> *a question mark,*
> *a weary riddle—*
> *a riddle for* birds of prey . . .
> *—they will soon "solve" you,*

> *they hunger now for your "solution,"*
> *they flutter now around you, their riddle,*
> *around you, the hanged one!*
> *O Zarathustra!*
> *Self-knower!*
> *Self-hangman!*\*22

On this occasion he took out again the sorcerer's song from the fourth book of *Zarathustra*, thus showing how little the solitary could forget the God he had given up. This song of complaint is now put into Ariadne's mouth. The complaint is addressed to the cruel hunter behind the clouds, unnamable, veiled, terrible, the moral hangman-God, who malignantly, jealously, shamelessly listens to everything in the heart and steals it, to the still *unknown God.*

This God, now in the role of Ariadne, is importuned for love:

> *Offer me love—who still warms me?*
> *Who still loves me?—offer me hot hands!*
> *Offer me coal-warmers for the heart. . . .*

But this God draws back when he should yield:

> *Offer, yes yield to me,*
> *Cruelest enemy—*
> *Yourself!*
>
> *He is gone!*
> *He himself has fled,*
> *My last, sole companion,*
> *My great enemy,*
> *My unknown,*
> *My Hangman-God!*

This God is nevertheless called back, both pain and happiness:

> *No! Come back,*
> *With all your torments!*
> *All the streams of my tears*
> *Run their course to you!*
> *And the last flame of my heart—*
> *It burns up to you!*
> *Oh, come back,*
> *My unknown God! My pain! My last . . . happiness!*23

---

\* There is a play upon words here which cannot be conveyed in the English translation: *lösen*, the verb, and *Lösung*, the noun, mean "to solve" and "solution"—as in solving a riddle—but also to loosen, detach, remove. The birds of prey will "pick off" the man hanging on the gallows. Translator.

As he did not get away from Wagner, his supposed adversary, neither did Nietzsche get away from a quite different supposed adversary, from God. A promethean will to the godless superman and at the same time a repressed, consuming yearning for the rejected, unknown God, mistaken for an enemy? At the close of this dithyramb, however, before Ariadne there appears Dionysus "in emerald beauty," bringing to an end the temptation of yearning for God. How? Dionysus asks Ariadne . . . for her love. It is notable that Nietzsche added this conclusion only in the new version. Who is Ariadne? A great riddle. In *Ecce Homo* Nietzsche wrote at the same time: "The answer to such a dithyramb of solar solitude in the light"—that Roman "night-song" of the desire for love in *Zarathustra*— "would be Ariadne.—Who besides me knows what Ariadne is!—For all such riddles nobody so far had any solution; I doubt that anybody ever saw any riddles here."[24] And yet Nietzsche himself gave away this riddle in his last letter, of January 6, 1889, to Jakob Burckhardt, when he was already out of his mind: "The *rest* for Frau Cosima—Ariadne." This was not a chance remark. Some years earlier he had spoken of her as the "most sympathetic woman I have met in my whole life."[25] And in those same January days, Cosima Wagner herself also received a note on a large sheet of handmade paper: "Ariadne, I love you. Dionysus." The sender was Friedrich Nietzsche.

*Disaster finally struck* on January 3, 1889.[26] On that day Nietzsche— then forty-five—left his house in Turin and found a coachman brutally mistreating his horse on the Piazza Carlo Alberto. Sobbing, he threw himself on the animal's neck, attracting a group of onlookers, among them fortunately his landlord, who was able with considerable effort to get him back home. Three days later, in Basel, Nietzsche's most constant friend, the theologian Franz Overbeck, was alerted by Jakob Burckhardt, who had received Neitzsche's letter from Turin and could interpret it only as the writing of a lunatic: Nietzsche was quite certain that he had been "sacrificed" and identified himself not only with Dionysus—dismembered and yet bearing new life—but finally also with the Crucified and even with God himself. As the "Crucified," he had written letters to the King of Italy, to the Cardinal Secretary of State Mariani and to various friends. On the following day, when Overbeck in his turn received a letter signed by Dionysus, he did not hesitate any longer. He got in touch with Professor Wille, the director of the psychiatric clinic in Basel, traveled to Turin and with great difficulty brought Nietzsche from Italy to Basel. It was Overbeck also who informed Nietzsche's mother, the simple, limited pastor's widow, now showing a touching concern for her son. She came to Basel at once and wanted without more ado to take him back to Naumburg and care for him there. But Overbeck and Wille were able to have Nietzsche first transferred to Jena, to Professor Binswanger's clinic for nervous diseases. There he found the rest and care that at least improved his physical condition, so that his mother herself moved to Jena and was able finally to look after him, being replaced later by his self-important sister, who was even then "organizing" the Nietzsche Archives. Nietzsche lingered in his madness for ten years. He died about midday on August 25, 1900, at the age of fifty-six. He was buried in Röcken, his birthplace, next to his father, Pastor Karl Ludwig Nietzsche.

# II.  Conquest of nihilism?

Nietzsche's "curses" on Christianity provoke hasty, perhaps far too hasty defensive reactions. It is easy to avoid his often one-sided, unjust and unrestrained criticism by personalizing and psychologizing his "case." But as we saw with Feuerbach, Marx and Sigmund Freud a personal and often dramatic destiny behind every criticism, every rejection, every rebellion, in regard to religion, so too with Friedrich Nietzsche. And as the lives of those three great figures of world history compelled our respect, so, too, does the life of this pastor's son who broke with everything—regardless of the cost—that tied him to the past; who followed his philosophical path with absolute honesty and without a trace of opportunism; who had few friends and for the most part was not understood even by them—still worse, seemed to have friends who ignored his writings.

Does not all this make understandable something of the increasing aggressiveness, loudness and also coldness in this man who became more and more lonely, caught in a vicious circle of self-isolation and isolation by others? Even his friends kept quiet about his philosophy, and the universities took no notice of it at all: "Nevertheless it is true that almost every letter that has reached me for years now strikes me as a piece of cynicism: there is more cynicism in being kind to me than in any hatred. . . . I tell everyone of my friends to his face that he has never considered it worth while to *study* any of my writings: I infer from the smallest signs that they do not even know what is in them. As for my *Zarathustra*: who among my friends saw more in it than an impermissible but fortunately utterly inconsequential presumption? . . . Ten years —and nobody in Germany has felt bound in conscience to defend my name against the absurd silence under which it lies buried: it was a foreigner, a Dane, who first possessed sufficient refinement of instinct *and courage* for this, who felt outraged by my alleged friends. . . . At what German university would it be possible today to have lectures on my philosophy, such as were given last spring in Copenhagen by Dr. Georg Brandes who thus proved himself once again as a psychologist?"[1] Considered in this way, was it entirely due to Nietzsche himself, fatally wounded, that he had to go so early from the midst of his work on his way to lunacy?

Yes, it is here that the real *tragedy of Friedrich Nietzsche* lies: "It is a singular thought that a healthy Nietzsche, not infected by a prostitute with venereal disease, would most probably never have left the realm of books and lecterns, of lecture halls and libraries," writes Walter Jens. "As Kant developed the *Critique of Practical Reason* in his study in Königsberg, . . . as Marx in the British Museum thought out a philosophy which aimed at sublimating theory in practice, so too might the third of the three great philosophical practitioners with some luck have expounded in the lecture hall his philosophy of the revaluation of all values. In conversation with students, and not talking to himself in hotel rooms. Nietzsche's real tragedy lay in the fact that he who was so worthy and conventionally correct was denied the dialogue of the schools, was permitted to exercise an influence only indirectly through his books, through inadequate substitute lecture courses. This is the reason why he envied Socrates—and even Bismarck, who at least had a Reichstag before which he could expound his ideas. Nietzsche was a pastor without a pulpit, a professor without a chair."[2]

## 1. Critique of Nietzsche

Nietzsche would have liked to remain a professor. A professor, rather than God. His last, confused, pathetic letter to the brilliant citizen of Basel Jakob Burckhardt, on January 6, 1889, two days after his breakdown, reveals the unfulfilled wish of the godless person whose megalomania born out of great distress had finally turned into delusions of divinity: "Dear Professor: In the end I would much rather be a Basel professor than God; but I have not dared push my private eogism so far as to desist for its sake from the creation of the world. You see, one must make sacrifices however and wherever one lives."[3] No one should exploit an end like this for apologetic reasons. It raises questions certainly—but on both sides.

### Eternal recurrence of the same?

"There is far too much fuss about Nietzsche. The literature on Nietzsche is to a large extent not much more than hot air, music hall entertainment and attempts to create interest. It is time to stop playing about with the deeper sense, the non-sense and the manic sense of Nietzsche's thought. Nietzsche has caused enough mischief. He thought that wherever Germany reached, it ruined culture. It would be more correct to say that wherever Nietzsche reached, he ruined philosophy. A young man who tries to make his first contact with philosophy by studying Nietzsche will never learn to think clearly, soberly, critically and above all objectively, but will soon begin to lose balance and increase his subjectivity, to talk pompously and issue orders. This is the very opposite of philosophy. But, although things are not as they should be, the fact is that Nietzsche acquired an enormous following and that we can practically speak of a Nietzsche movement." This is the opinion of the Catholic philosopher Johannes Hirschberger.[4] It is possible to see the argument about Nietzsche in this way and . . . to get out of it.

Certainly—and here Hirschberger is right[5]—we should be more reserved and skeptical than ever today in regard to the various *Nietzsche movements* of the present century. For:

The time is past for an *aesthetic, artistic interpretation of Nietzsche* like that adopted by the Stefan George circle (K. Hildebrandt, E. Bertram) at the beginning of the century, recommending to the Germans the heroic-aesthetic Greek conception of tragedy as an educational ideal.

And in particular, the *political-national Nietzsche interpretation* of popular Nazi propaganda after 1933 and its academic version (especially A. Baeumler) has been discredited. Who could still glorify today the blond beast and the brutality of the superior race or even merely heroic activism, instinctive vitality, permanent struggle, desire for sacrifice and extinction?

But is the *philosophical, existentialist interpretation*—for example of Karl Jaspers—out of date? Here it is scarcely possible to agree with Hirschberger in his one-sided interpretation of Jaspers. Jaspers' own interpretation of Nietzsche is also sometimes one-sided and attempts to harmonize too much, but it may well come closer than earlier interpretations to the authentic Nietzsche. Presumably also closer than the highly individual interpretation by Martin Heidegger, who—after turning from the analysis of human existence to thought about being itself—explained Nietzsche—for him, the last representative of a metaphysic (of the "will to power" and the "eternal recurrence of the same")—wholly in the light of his own understanding of being.[6]

Undoubtedly, the extreme diversity of the interpretations of Nietzsche is based on Nietzsche's own work. Many statements contradict one another and make it easy to take out and isolate certain strands of thought from their context. Nevertheless, as opposed to neoscholastics all too certain of their own understanding of being and unable even to see nihilism as a genuine problem, it has to be clearly stated that *the challenge of nihilism must be taken seriously*. What is involved here is not a "fuss about Nietzsche" but the serious crisis of the foundations of naïve metaphysics.

Neither can we get out of the essential argument by using justifiable objections as *excuses:*

an excuse—for instance—to point out scientific, sociological, psychological, philosophical-theological inaccuracies in Nietzsche's work and to criticize his defective methodology and lack of philosophical training: Nietzsche was quite aware of his very limited knowledge especially of the natural sciences and even of philosophy, but compensated for many a deficiency by his brilliant critical intuition;

an excuse to check in detail all possible contradictions in Nietzsche's writings: with such extensive work, mainly consisting of aphorisms and in the end only of unpublished notes and momentary insights, this is too easy a game, for Nietzsche's work must be understood as a whole;

an excuse quickly to pin down Nietzsche to a contradiction in his basic conception: to the assertion—for instance—that the idea of recurrence and the idea of the superman are mutually contradictory, the answer can be briefly made that even the superman, even Zarathustra, comes again;[7]

an excuse finally to take seriously only the negative, destructive aspects— the absolute meaninglessness of the world and the will to nothingness—in his controversial unpublished work "The Will to Power" may not be dismissed—as Karl Schlechta, for example, dismisses it[8]—as a "makeshift bit of information."

Unlike Schlechta, Wilhelm Weischedel has stressed the positive aspect of Nietzsche's thought—not entirely incorrectly—in such a way as to suggest that the latter did not consistently maintain the meaninglessness of things, that he stabilized the idea of eternal recurrence as ultimate meaning, assimilated eternal becoming to eternal being and thus avoided nihilism instead of overcoming it.[9] A nihilist, however, has little difficulty in admitting contradictions. Nietzsche's fundamental principle, the "will to power," is contradictory by its very nature. Anyone who takes seriously Nietzsche's description of life as a pulsating, active coming to be, complex and contradictory in itself, will not necessarily see here a want of consistency; for the *idea of the eternal recurrence* is not meant to be a coherent principle of becoming or being, but merely an expression of the absurdity of the whole happening. It does not mean that Nietzsche has avoided nihilism. Certainly we may ask whether he has gone through it. The idea of the eternal recurrence is and remains in fact *ambivalent*: "Existence as it is, without meaning or aim, yet recurring inevitably without any finale of nothingness. . . . This is the most extreme form of nihilism: the nothing (the 'meaningless') eternally!"[10]

Lou von Salomé, to whom Nietzsche first entrusted the recurrence idea, tells us of this ambivalence: "For me the hours are unforgettable in which he first entrusted to me the idea, as a secret, as something whose verification and confirmation he regarded with unspeakable dread: he spoke of it only in a faint voice and with every sign of deepest horror. He suffered in fact so deeply from life that the certainty of the eternal recurrence of life must have held something terrible for him. The quintessence of the theory of recurrence, the radiant apotheosis of life, which Nietzsche later advanced, forms such a contrast to his own cruel experience of life that it strikes us as a weird mask. To become the preacher of a doctrine that is bearable only to the extent that love for life prevails, that can have an elevating effect only when the idea of man soars up to the deification of life: this must truly have formed a terrible contradiction to his own innermost experience, a contradiction that finally crushed him. All that Nietzsche thought, felt, lived, after the emergence of his recurrence idea, springs out of this conflict within him, moves between 'cursing with grinding teeth the demon of life's eternity' and the expectation of that 'great moment' that will give force to the words: 'you are a God and never did I hear anything more divine!' The higher he rose—as a philosopher—to the full exaltation of the glory of life, the more deeply he suffered—as a human being—under his own theory of life."[11]

On the substantiation of the recurrence idea, Lou von Salomé adds: "At that time . . . the recurrence idea had not yet become a conviction for Nietzsche, but only an apprehension. He intended to make the proclamation of it dependent on whether and how far it could be scientifically justified. We exchanged a series of letters on this subject, and from Nietzsche's remarks there always emerged the erroneous opinion that it would be possible, on the basis of physical studies and atomic theory, to gain for it a scientifically unshakable foundation. It was at this time that he resolved to study exclusively natural sciences for ten years at the university of Vienna or Paris. Only after years of absolute silence, if the success he feared came to pass, he would then go among men as the teacher of the eternal recurrence."[12]

Nietzsche's apprehension, that the disastrous idea would prove in the light of the atomic theory to be correct, was not confirmed. But "what had been expected to become scientifically proved truth took on the character of a mystical revelation, and from then onward Nietzsche made the foundation of his philosophy as a whole not science but inward inspiration—his own personal inspiration."[13] Even Nietzsche's friend Peter Gast adopted an attitude of reserve toward the recurrence idea. Overbeck regarded it as an eccentricity. Could it have prevailed? Karl Jaspers examined closely and differentiated Nietzsche's arguments for the recurrence theory and found every one of them unconvincing.[14] We cannot but agree with what he wrote some years later: "But no one has ever yet really believed in the eternal recurrence, in Nietzsche's Dionysus and the superman. The extraordinary vagueness of terms like 'life,' 'strength,' and 'will to power' seems to give them a constantly shifting meaning."[15]

Nietzsche wanted to leave nihilism behind him but not to return to the Judeo-Christian conception of history as a meaningful, coherent, continuous, purposive happening. He took the alternative of recourse to myth. To that one *primeval myth of mankind* the general version of which is found in both the oldest Indian and the oldest Germanic tradition: "Belief in the periodic destruction and creation of the universe is already found in the *Atharva-Veda*. The preservation of similar ideas in the Germanic tradition (universal conflagration, Ragnarok, followed by a new creation) confirms the Indo-Aryan structure of the myth. . . ."[16] This myth is found again not only in Buddhism and Jainism, but also—probably under Eastern influence—in the pre-Socratics, so highly appreciated by

Nietzsche, especially clearly in primitive Pythagoreanism, modified in Plato and again very clearly in neo-Pythagoreanism, with many repercussions then in the Middle Ages and modern times (in Nietzsche's time in physicalistic-mechanistic form in Louis A. Blanqui, Gustave Le Bon, Jean-Marie Guyau). According to the Romanian-born American expert on comparative religion Mircea Eliade, this myth is "a supreme attempt toward the 'staticization' of becoming, toward annulling the irreversibility of time."[17]

Of course, *this cyclical theory cannot be proved.* And up to a point, it can be a matter of indifference to us. For whether a person exists once or an infinite number of times in exactly the same way, he is not aware of it and so it all comes to the same thing. Certainly no one has any doubts about a certain periodicity in nature according to which essential sequences such as the movements of the stars, the seasons, day and night, are continually repeated; but what are not repeated here are precisely the concrete details. But the theory of the eternal recurrence goes far beyond all this and is scientifically completely unverifiable: the claim is made that every event in the universe in all its details and in its whole cosmic coherence will occur in the future and has occurred in the past an infinite number of times in exactly the same way. The American philosopher Milič Čapek says of this theory: "The assumption of a completely identical repetition of cosmic situations makes the theory intrinsically unverifiable. . . . The eternal return is rejected by all thinkers who insist on the irreversibility of becoming, on genuine novelty, and the immortality of the past."[18] The eternal recurrence is a myth, and in practice it was useful to Nietzsche as a substitute for religion after he had lost all religion: to use his own words, as "religion of religions."[19] This "religion of religions," which is to absorb, dissolve and sublimate all religions, is of course understood in an atheistic sense. Of course?

### Atheism justified?

Did Nietzsche really substantiate his atheism? We raised this question with Feuerbach, Marx and Freud, and it had to be answered in every case in the negative. Feuerbach's atheism was a Hegelianism stood on its head, Marx's critique of religion presupposes Feuerbach, and Freud, for his part, presupposes all his great comrades in unbelief of the nineteenth century. Nietzsche was no different. If we look dispassionately behind the mask of the prophet, visionary, emotional thinker, preacher, his atheism also was *not really justified, but assumed as a datum.*

"Men have created God";[20] "A people . . . projects its joy in itself, its feeling of power on to a being whom one can thank for them":[21] here speaks a docile student of Ludwig Feuerbach. Christianity? Nothing but imaginary causes, nothing but imaginary effects, nothing but imaginary beings, imaginary natural science, imaginary psychology. Here the philosopher anticipates what the psychoanalyst will later closely examine. For him, Christianity is a purely fictitious world. But this world "is distinguished from the world of dreams, very much to its disadvantage, by the fact that the latter *mirrors* actuality, while the former falsifies, disvalues and denies actuality."²² Here, too, however, there is no real substantiation, but only assertion.

It must be observed anyway that Nietzsche was not at all interested in justifying his atheism. He was not concerned with proving the nonexistence of God, at any rate not with a historical refutation of belief in God. For, with him—just as with Feuerbach, Marx and Freud—the answer to the question of the source of belief in God also disposed of the belief itself. This fact was established for Nietzsche at an early stage, as is evident from his *The Dawn of Day* (1881): "*The historical refutation as the decisive one.*—Formerly it was sought to prove that there was no God —now it is shown how the belief that God existed could have *originated*, and by what means this belief gained authority and importance: in this way the counterproof that there is no God becomes unnecessary and superfluous.—In former times, when the 'evidences of the existence of God' which had been brought forward were refuted, a doubt still remained, viz. whether better proofs could not be found than those which had just been refuted: at that time the atheists did not understand the art of making a *tabula rasa*."²³

*What*, according to Nietzsche, is the *source of* belief in God? His explanation involves a distinction; it has a cognitive and a practical aspect: interpretation of inexplicable natural processes on the one hand, justification of moral action on the other. Essentially, however—for Nietzsche—belief in God comes from two sources: man's sense of power and sense of powerlessness, both feelings being understood as psychological processes that have to be clarified in their "psychological logic." For "when a man is suddenly and overwhelmingly suffused with the *feeling of power* . . . it raises in him a doubt about his own person: he does not dare to think himself the cause of this astonishing feeling—and so he posits a stronger person, a divinity, to account for it. *In summa:* the origin of religion lies in the extreme feelings of power which, because they are strange, take men by surprise. . . . Religion is . . . a sort of feeling of fear and terror at oneself—But also a feeling of extraordinary happiness and exaltation."²⁴ Feelings of power, then, on one side and feelings of powerlessness on the other. For, out of the feeling of self-denial and decadence, man "ejects from himself all his denial of himself, of his nature, naturalness and actuality . . . as God."²⁵

For Nietzsche, belief in God is thus revealed as error, religion is unmasked as invention, atheism as self-evident—with the appropriate consequences. At the same time, he very decisively rejects belief in God that has a Christian origin. Nietzsche regards it as settled that God does not exist, but even if the existence of God could be proved it would make no difference: the *God of Christianity remains unacceptable*. "What sets *us* apart is not that we recognize no God, either in history or in nature or behind nature—but that we find that which has been reverenced as God not 'godlike' but pitiable, absurd, harmful, not merely an error but a *crime against life*. . . . We deny God as God. . . . If this God of the Christians were *proved* to us to exist, we should know even less how to believe in him."[26] The nature of God is—so to speak—the counterproof to God's existence.

But, as we saw, there remains for the atheist an ultimate doubting and yearning that is evident not only in "The Sorcerer's Song" and later "Ariadne's Lament." Nietzsche's godlessness was shock, torment and yearning, all in one. In the unpublished work especially, we find notes like "At bottom, it is only the moral god that has been overcome. Does it make sense to conceive a god 'beyond good and evil'?"[27] Nietzsche, continually asking what is behind anything new, seems here to be thinking of an eternal recurrence in a pantheistic context. On another occasion, he speaks of God as the distinctness of the will to power: "The sole way of maintaining a meaning for the concept 'God' would be: God *not* as the driving force, but God as a maximal state, as an epoch—a point in the evolution of the will to power."[28] But what sort of a God would this be? It is impossible to build up an argument from such isolated and ambiguous statements, still less can they be used to question Nietzsche's atheism. It is much more important, particularly for Christians, to take quite seriously Nietzsche's critique of belief in God and of Christianity as a whole. It is not so much Nietzsche's positive "solutions"—will to power, Dionysian life, eternal recurrence, superman: all substitute products for the dead God—which offer a challenge to Christians, but his radical questioning, accomplished with the deliberate will to godlessness and pure worldliness: "*If* there were gods, how could I endure not to be a god! *Therefore* there are no gods."[29]

## 2. *What Christians can learn*

Certainly Christians do not need to accept all that Nietzsche produces by way of criticism. And with all due respect for his passion for truth, Nietzsche's truths are often half-truths. His knowledge of theology and Church history does not come up to the seriousness of his charges. Many passages, especially in the historically and exegetically oriented *Antichrist*, are more like pamphlets than records of cool investigation: Nietzsche's indignant and contemptuous language is meant to wound. His slips are sometimes embarrassing, generalizations and labels abound, anti-Christian fanaticism clouds his judgment. Even his compliments on the antidemocratic order of precedence of the Roman hierarchy, their will to power and their aristocratic, lordly manners, and even on Jesuits, celibacy and confession, are questionable. Particularly questionable are his invectives against Luther as the corrupter of the pagan Renaissance, the plebeian and hooligan, the most eloquent and most presumptuous peasant in Germany, who approached all cardinal questions of power shortsightedly, superficially and recklessly: "Luther, this calamity of a monk, restored the church and, what is a thousand times worse, Christianity, at the very moment *when it was vanquished.*"[1] What is to be said about all this? Detailed refutations would fill volumes and yet would not be worthwhile. For it is a question not of details but of the whole. Isolated positive statements on the Church and priests simply do not count by comparison with Nietzsche's wholly destructive criticism of Christianity as it has come to be.[2]

## The only true Christian

Here in any case is a decisive rejection of Christianity, but surprisingly enough we find respect for him whose person and cause Christianity invokes: *Jesus of Nazareth.* Certainly he, too, in the end is rejected by Nietzsche as the—admittedly "most interesting"—*decadent,* but without the tirades of hate and feelings of disgust usually linked with matters of Christianity. In his attempt at a critique of the Gospels, Nietzsche thought he could establish a fundamental contradiction: Here we have "the mountain, lake and field preacher, whose appearance strikes one as that of a Buddha on a soil very little like that of India"[3] and on the other hand "the aggressive fanatic, the mortal enemy of theologian and priest."[4] Nietzsche thinks that this fanatic type only later "overflowed on to the type of the Master" as a result of Christian propaganda.[5]

What really interests Nietzsche about Jesus is "the problem of the *psychology of the redeemer.*"[6] Concepts such as "hero" and "genius" do not suit him: "a quite different word would, rather, be in place here: the word idiot."[7] There is an odd agreement here with Dostoevsky's interpretation of Christ, and Nietzsche had perhaps read Dostoevsky's novel *The Idiot.* "Idiot" means "instinctive hatred of *every* reality, as flight into the 'ungraspable,' into the 'inconceivable,' as antipathy towards every form, every spatial and temporal concept, towards everything firm, all that is custom, institution, Church."[8] For the "good news" of this "bringer of glad tidings" consists in the fact that there are no longer any antagonisms. The barriers have fallen between Jews and non-Jews, foreigners and natives, even between God and man. Such concepts as guilt, punishment and reward do not exist: "Blessedness is not promised, it is not tied to any conditions: it is the *only* reality—the rest is signs for speaking of it."[9] The kingdom of heaven of this "great symbolist" is "a condition of the heart —not something that comes 'upon the earth' or 'after death.' . . . It is everywhere, it is nowhere."[10] Hence it is practice, not belief, that distinguishes Christians: no resistance to evil, no defense of one's rights despite calumny and scorn, passive acceptance of everything that happens. That is why this Jesus of Nazareth died on the cross as he lived: "he entreats, he suffers, he loves *with* those, *in* those who are doing evil to him . . . *Not* to defend oneself, *not* to grow angry, *not* to make responsible. . . . But not to resist even the evil man—to *love* him. . . ."[11]

This is not an unsympathetic picture of Jesus of Nazareth. It is clear to Nietzsche that the message of such a "symbolist *par excellence*"—who spoke only of innermost reality, of life, truth, light, and for whom all other reality had value only as a sign or a parable—cannot be reduced to formulas, dogmas and doctrines. It is clear too that the disciples understood him only when they could fit him into the well-known categories: prophet, Messiah, future judge, moral teacher, miracle man. But even that was a distortion, a misunderstanding. And the whole history of Christianity, which became increasingly vulgarized, barbarized, absorbed the doctrines and rites of all the subterranean cults of the Roman Empire, turned out to be the history of "progressively cruder misunderstanding of an *original* symbolism."[12] Jesus' living practice was turned into a faith and this faith into a doctrine. Think, for instance, of what Christians (especially Paul) have made of the cross. In the sign of this cross—which, for Jesus, was precisely the most severe test of his love—revenge, retribution, punishment, justice, were preached and the glad tidings turned into tidings of woe. It was now that the type of Jesus the fanatic was created: "Now all that contempt for and bitterness against Pharisee and theologian was worked into the type of the Master—one thereby *made* of him a Pharisee and theologian."[13]

Is this a picture only in black and white? Certainly from the present-day standpoint we must judge critically this style of historiography and exegesis. But is it not more important for Christians—who see themselves in the light of their Christ Jesus—to note with what respect the person, the message of Jesus Christ is brought out here, even though we cannot agree with the picture as a whole? In individual features—to the shame of many Christians—is not the message perhaps more credibly proclaimed by this atheist and nihilist than it is by these Christians themselves? How many Christians even ask about the authentic, original Christianity? The main charge brought by Nietzsche deserves all our attention: "I shall now relate the *real* history of Christianity.—The word 'Christianity' is already a misunderstanding—in reality there has been only one Christian, and he died on the Cross. The 'Evangel' died on the Cross. What was called 'Evangel' from this moment onwards was already the opposite of what *he* had lived: 'bad tidings,' a *dysangel*. It is false to the point of absurdity to see in a 'belief,' perchance the belief in redemption through Christ, the distinguishing characteristic of the Christian: only Christian *practice*, a life such as he who died on the Cross *lived*, is Christian . . ."[14]

And we may hear and wonder at the words in *The Antichrist*: "Even today *such* a life is possible, for *certain* men even necessary: genuine, primitive Christianity will be possible at all times."[15] Are not Christians challenged here continually to compare their claim critically with reality, to make theory and practice coincide credibly, to judge themselves by the source, by Jesus himself?


## Being Christian and being human?

*The Antichrist* is obviously more anti-Christian than anti-Christ: a provocation for Christians which can be salutary. We need only recall some typical headings to find sufficient material for critical reflection.

*First:* How much is true in Nietzsche's *critique of the Church?* Church as power structure over men's souls, a kind of pseudo state? Church in opposition to the gospel of Jesus and to honest, straightforward humanity? Church in conflict with all human greatness, intent on making itself indispensable? Church as a center of psychological forgery, devaluing the natural virtues of life and intruding into people's private life? Churches as sepulchers of God, estranged from life, immobile, rigid . . . ?

*Secondly:* How much is true in his *critique of the priesthood?* Priests as the great haters in world history? The smartest, conscious hypocrites? Poisoners of life, parasites who live on men's sins, feelings of fear and feelings of guilt? Who fear both sensuality and science, suppress both liberty and life? Priests—far too long wrongly regarded as the supreme type, the ideal, of man . . . ?

*Thirdly:* How much is true in Nietzsche's *critique of the idea of God?* That idea of God which is born out of resentment and plebeian morality, the one above this pitiful loafer morality of good and evil? That idea of God from which all that is strong, brave, heroic, proud, has been eliminated and which has made God into a God of the weak, sick and decadent, a poor man's God, a sinner's God, a sick man's God? How much is true in the critique by Friedrich Nietzsche, who sees an abuse of divine dexterity in all talk of "grace," "providence," "experience of salvation"? Who finds "absurd" a God who cures a cold at the right time or gets us into the cab at the very moment of an outbreak of heavy rain? A God, that is, who is more of a "servant," "postman," "Santa Claus": when all is said and done, a word for the most stupid kind of all coincidences? Must it not be admitted that this critique of God is made for man's sake: to protect human identity against a paralyzing knowledge, a petty moral supervision, an oppressive love of God? Did Nietzsche not get rid of God for man's sake: godlessness not as an end in itself but as a precaution against a belief in God that depreciates human existence? Cannot the immediacy of human existence be threatened by an alienation brought about by religious influences?

Nevertheless, something more has to be said: *If* Christianity really *were* as Nietzsche saw it, then it could be and would have to be rejected today, and for good reasons;

*if* "God" were merely the counterconcept to life, and in it everything detrimental, poisonous, slanderous, the whole mortal enmity to life, were brought into a horrible unity;

*if* the concept "beyond" or "true world" had been invented in order to devalue the only world that exists, in order to have no goal, no reason, no function left for this earthly reality;

*if* the concept "soul" or "spirit" or, still more, "immortal soul" had been invented in order to despise the body, to make it sick, "holy," in order to approach with an appalling superficiality all the things that deserve to be taken seriously in life, that is, the questions of sustenance, a place to live, treatment of the sick, cleanliness, weather;

*if*, instead of health, "salvation of the soul" were sought, as a manic-depressive condition, a *folie circulaire*, alternating between spasms of penance and redemption hysteria;

*if* both the concept of "sin" and that of "free will" had been invented in order to confuse the instincts and to make mistrust of these into a second nature;

*if* the mark of real decadence were involved in the concept of the "selfless" or of "self-denial";

*if* self-destruction were made into a stamp in general use, into a "duty," into "holiness," into the "divine" in man;

*if*, finally, the concept of the "good man" implied taking the side of all the weak, the sick, the failures, all those suffering from themselves, against the people who say Yes, who are certain of the future, who are guaranteed the future;

*if*, then, all that were Christian morality,[16]

*then*—yes, then—we would have to subscribe along with Nietzsche to Voltaire's *Écrasez l'infâme!* Then—yes, then—we would have to be with "Dionysus versus the Crucified."[17] Then it would no longer be possible to be Christian, but only anti-Christian.

But how often has Christianity—in certain forms of Protestantism and Catholicism—actually been presented as it was seen by Nietzsche, who had gotten to know Christianity mainly in a Protestant parsonage, a Christian boarding school and through Schopenhauer's philosophy? And how often is it preached, commended, lived, in this way even today in the churches?

All that we can say here is that Christianity does not have to be seen in this way. Indeed, it cannot be seen in this way if Jesus Christ is rightly understood. For in this light it is impossible to be a Christian without being human, to be a Christian at the expense of being human, to be a Christian alongside, above or below being human. Being a Christian must be radically, truly humanly being human, so far—that is—as it can fully incorporate the human, all-too-human in all its negativity.[18]

### 3. What non-Christians can learn

Non-Christians? Can even non-Christians learn from Nietzsche? The question might surprise anyone who was far too sure of knowing where he stood with Nietzsche. The question should surprise anyone who is not clear about the consequences of getting involved with Nietzsche. Nietzsche pierced through to the foundations of human knowledge and questioned them as no one had done before him. No one has equaled him in the acuteness, depth, and radicalness of his thought: not Feuerbach, not Marx and not even Freud; at most, Pascal. Ought not the consequences particularly of the nihilism analyzed by Nietzsche to have been considered at the opportune time?

## Consequences of private nihilism

After all we have had to say about Nietzsche's struggle against Christianity, one thing is crystal clear. With all the passion that was in him, Nietzsche opposed a particular kind of human being: the sick, suffering, inferior, mediocre human being. The latter is the type of decay, disintegration and weakness. At this very point, therefore, we have a revaluation of values, the will to power. Nature, seen from the Darwinian standpoint, is the model on which Nietzsche bases his picture of man: "The grandiose prototype: man in nature—the weakest, shrewdest creature making himself master, subjugating the stupider forces."[19]

As we have seen, Nietzsche nowhere saw the type he despised more fully realized than in Christianity, with its "God on the Cross," where "everything that suffers, everything that hangs on the Cross" is declared "divine."[20] And who would say—particularly as a Christian—even today that this picture by Nietzsche of a suffering, guilty, inferior, feeble "typical" Christian is merely a caricature? Of course Christians, too, have learned something. Even within Christianity, today, there is no question of building up the hypocritical, the weakly, the mediocre, the frustrated, the guilty. But—and this question must in turn be put to Nietzsche—what of the opposite type, which—after the publication of *Zarathustra*—he never tired of propagating, commending, celebrating as an alternative: the superman? Is it, then, the superman or at least the man of power who should be sought and bred today? Who despises the mob and counts himself among the physically and mentally strong, the distinguished, aristocrats, privileged? Who, while certainly also ruthless toward himself, wants to exterminate whatever is mediocre and to cultivate whatever promises hardness and cruelty? Who as a beast of prey with the motto "live dangerously" pursues his interests regardless of the victims, if this only feeds power, is useful to life, is of service to the rulers? Who simply withstands his destiny right up to pointless extinction?

In the second half of the twentieth century, this type of man has become only too well known: men without God, whose relationships with one another are concretized even into the private sphere, determined by functional and practical values, guided by power interests, the weak everywhere being the victim of the stronger, superior, less scrupulous. The horizon of meaning is in fact effaced, there are no longer any supreme values, reliable guiding principles, absolute truth. In practice, does this not mean that a nihilism of values is determining human behavior? Has that not come to pass which Nietzsche foresaw—more clearsightedly than many before him? But it is often a mild, concealed, unemotional nihilism, without the passion of a Zarathustra but no less dangerous. Many today are distrustful toward a loud, public nihilism, and no politician, anyway, could afford to indulge in it. But people permit themselves a mild, private nihilism, often guilelessly, innocently, perceiving the consequences only at a very late stage. For, after so many taboos were broken in the war years and subsequently, so many traditions disappeared, conventions were dropped, humanisms were emptied of meaning, despite all the prosperity and better education, in many families parents no longer know to which values, guiding principles, ideals, norms, to which truth, they should cling and to which they should educate their children: devaluation (often without any revaluation) of values, the loss of which can then be noted, but can be canceled only with difficulty. In education, culture, economy, science, politics, "an incomplete nihilism" lived in a middle- or upper-class style, feeble and only half affirmed: "we live in the midst of it."[21]

Sometimes, however, more is involved. Nihilism presents many faces, from bored, intellectual skepticism to brutal political anarchism. Undoubtedly it is not only because of a whole packet of social factors but in the last resort also because of a nihilistic lack of orientation and lack of norms, that there has been an alarming increase in the number of thefts, robberies, crimes of violence, murders, by children, young people, students (more and more of them female), that the number of drug addicts, dropouts, suicides has risen tremendously in the past decade, that susceptibility to ideologies has often amounted to mania. The "meaning deficit" and "meaning vacuum" in the Western affluent society, for a long time now, has not only provided the middle classes with intellectual titillation in the "theater of the absurd" of a Ionesco or a Beckett, has not only been diagnosed and deplored by psychotherapists and psychiatrists.[22] It is beginning to be a political fact.

Has Nietzsche, then, been proved right? As we saw, in many ways certainly with his analysis. Was Nietzsche right? Not with his alternative. For just as the weakling type, of Christian provenance—as Nietzsche saw him—cannot be, may not be, the model for being truly human, neither can the superman, of secular provenance. These are not true alternatives. Can weakness be overcome only by hardness? Are there no intermediate hues, no gradations, no mean? Are compassion, goodness, mercy, indulgence, fellowship, love, something that can only be denounced as weakness? Is there not also a mercy that comes from strength, a compassion from fullness, a goodness from the greatness of a man? Indeed, is not this perhaps the very goal that men should seek today, precisely as Christians, precisely in the light of belief in God? If not moralism, then perhaps morality? If not idealism, then perhaps ideals? If not sanctimoniousness, then perhaps religion.

## Consequences of social nihilism

The devastating crisis of meaning today not only affects the individual but has also gripped society and its institutions: marriage and family, school and university, even the state itself. The question may occur to some people: What has all this to do with a "permissive society," in which nothing is true and everything is allowed, in which no deeper meaning can be seen, in which everyone may be permitted everything? On the other hand, public discussion of human rights, of fundamental values, of commercial and political morality, shows that now, as before, there is undeniably a genuine need of norms, values, orientation, meaning. In this respect, of course, Nietzsche had developed his own sociological ideas.

"Temporary preponderance of the social value-feelings comprehensible and useful: it is a question of creating a *foundation* upon which a *stronger* species will ultimately be possible.—Standard of strength: to be able to live under the reverse evaluations and to will them again eternally. State and society as foundation: world-economic point of view, education as *breeding.*"[23] Three important aspects of Nietzsche's picture of society are combined in this note: education as breeding, the world-economic point of view of a total society, social value-feelings useful as precondition of the creation of a stronger species of man.

Nietzsche attached little importance to *education.* For education means being concerned with the mediocre, with human beings *en masse*, raising them up to a higher level. He wants nothing of this: the gulf between the species must be widened; "establish distances"—this is the solution.[24] The lower species is the base on which the higher stands, on which alone the higher can perform its task. And what is due to the higher is nothing for the lower. "That which is available only to the *strongest* and most fruitful natures and makes *their* existence possible—leisure, adventure, disbelief, even dissipation—would, if it were available to mediocre natures, necessarily destroy them—and actually does. This is where industriousness, rule, moderation, firm 'conviction' have their place—in short, the 'herd virtues': under them this intermediate type of man grows perfect."[25]

Where education is not desired, *breeding* must take its place. What Nietzsche wrote about this became the prescription followed by the National Socialist ideologists, blinded by their biology of race, fifty years later: "A question constantly keeps coming back to us. . . . Is it not time, now that the type 'herd animal' is being evolved more and more in Europe, to make the experiment of a fundamental, artificial and conscious *breeding* of the opposite type and its virtues? And would it not be a kind of goal, redemption, and justification for the democratic movement itself if someone arrived who could make use of it—by finally producing beside its new and sublime development of slavery (that is what European democracy must become ultimately) a higher kind of dominating and Caesarian spirits who would stand upon it, maintain themselves by it, and elevate themselves through it? To new, hitherto impossible prospects, to their own prospects? To their own tasks?"[26] These ideas of Nietzsche were not disposed of when National Socialism came to its disastrous end. They are again relevant today in view of microbiological discoveries concerning the manipulation of genes.

When such a doctrine of contempt for man is preached, it is not difficult to *justify war*, the sacrifice of the many, endurance at all costs: "One must learn from war: (1) to associate death with the interests for which one fights—that makes *us* venerable; (2) one must learn to sacrifice *many* and to take one's cause seriously enough not to spare men; (3) rigid discipline, and to permit oneself force and cunning in war."[27]

In the present century, we have seen all these ideas exploited in the most cruel, albeit one-sided fashion, particularly when a real "superman" finally appeared. In the person of a German, which was not exactly what Nietzsche had expected. For Nietzsche was an antinationalist and European, despiser of German philistinism, squareness, beeriness, nationalistic blustering, and at the same time an admirer of Latin form, French wit and Mediterranean mentality. Allowing for all this, Nietzsche must still be described as one of the—involuntary—precursors of National Socialism (and Italian Fascism, which people like to forget today), which—understanding and misunderstanding—put into practice essential ideas of Nietzsche.[28]

It was clear that Nietzsche could not think anything of *democracy* or parliamentary government, nor could he think anything of socialism. The people? From the time of his early preoccupation with the Greeks, Nietzsche was fascinated by the idea of the elite, now with the power elite. The Revolution? For him it had only one good aspect: it produced Napoleon. Otherwise the result was a *"social hodge-podge"*: "the establishment of equal rights, of the superstition of 'equal men.' "[29] Universal suffrage, parliamentary government? For Nietzsche, this is the tyranny of mediocrity, the rule of inferior human beings. All that could so long be kept under now comes to the top: "the slave instincts, the instincts of cowardice, cunning, and *canaille* in those orders that have long been kept down."[30] Walter Jens is right when he says: "While Kant and Hegel, Goethe and Heine, knew the age in which they lived and expected from the French Revolution or the Prussian court, from America or the republican spirit, influences that characterized their epoch . . . while they were contemporaries, exchanging ideas with kindred spirits and opponents, Nietzsche lived alone, by himself, in a no-man's-land, in a realm of shades: blind not only in a physical sense. No Marx ever encountered him. The manner in which he describes socialism—'tyranny of the stupid,' 'the herd animal itself as master,' 'a hopelessly sour affair'—displays pure ignorance. Nietzsche—it must be said—did not know what he was talking about."[31]

Also, did Nietzsche know what he was talking about when he compared the practical value of men—of the inferior men, it should be noted, not of the superior men—with the function of a machine? "The task is to make man as useful as possible and to approximate him, as far as possible, to an infallible machine: to this end, he must be equipped with the virtues of the machine (he must learn to experience the states in which he works in a mechanically useful way as the supremely valuable states; hence it is necessary to spoil the other states for him as much as possible, as highly dangerous and disreputable)."[32] Did Nietzsche know what he was talking about when he demanded "the production of a synthetic . . . man for whose existence this transformation of mankind into a machine is a precondition, as a base on which he can invent his *higher form of being*"?[33] Did he know what he was talking about when he preferred to express his contempt for inferior human beings in a metaphorical language of industrial technology: "Lunatics, criminals, and 'naturalists' are increasing: sign of a growing culture rushing on precipitately—i.e., the refuse, the waste, gain importance—the decline keeps pace."[34] There is no doubt that we have here an anticipation of what Fritz Lang, in his famous film of the twenties *Metropolis*, evoked in expressionistic imagery, and Aldous Huxley, in *Brave New World*, in the early thirties, developed in the shape of a negative Utopia: The mob has to function in the style of a machine, the rule of an aristocratic-technocratic elite has been set up, the superman created.

And Nietzsche himself? What a contrast between this man and his work, this message and this messenger. It must be made quite clear that here is someone who proclaims a philosophy of world-historical import with great visionary force, with the passion of a world-surveying prophet and the gestures of the founder of a religion—and is himself an unknown retired professor of ancient philology, traveling restlessly from place to place, barely managing to live in modest rooms of a hotel or bakehouse.

Here is someone who proclaims the message of absolute hardness, ruthless cruelty and the extermination of all that is ailing and weak—and has himself been a sick man since his student days, needs the help of the very people he despises, depends on the compassion of the very people he opposes, is continually troubled about his food and mode of life, following planned diets, drawing up climatological graphs and even forging medical prescriptions. Here is someone who proclaims the doctrine of the superman, of light and of life—and never comes out of his own shadowy world, lives unsuccessfully remote from the reality of his time, conversing only with hotel guests and especially with his books. What a contrast! An essentially tender, vulnerable, rather timid, effusive person, whom everyone—even the most simple people—found agreeable. And yet this hatred for people, particularly the weak and inferior. An absolutely intellectually honest thinker. And yet he prefers to adopt an aristocratic, upper-class manner and to talk about his supposed descent from a noble Polish family, instead of admitting his origin from a Protestant pastor's family. A divided personality? Yes, in many respects: thinker, psychologist, rhetorician, preacher, but also actor in the grand manner, all in one person, whose thought is challenging in its radicality, whose destiny is shattering in its severity, whose teaching, however, is alarming in its consequences.

## 4. *Interim results IV: Theses on nihilism*

We have traveled a long way in our investigation of the approaches to the problem of God in modern times: from Descartes and Pascal by way of Hegel to Feuerbach, Marx and Freud, and now to Nietzsche—to mention only our "main stations," where we stayed longer to get our bearings, looking backward, sideways and forward. But all this was necessary for the clarification of modern questions; in this respect, even theologians have often talked superficially and in clichés. Does it not seem, however, that Nietzsche marks an end and perhaps also a turning point in the debate on atheism? With Nietzsche, we have advanced finally to the radical questioning and also the calling into question of modern times. And "to be or not to be" really is the question here: nihilism or . . . ? This in particular is the question of the present century. Is it sufficient here simply to appeal to belief in God? We want to avoid hasty conclusions and to advance methodically, clearly, step by step. Where do we stand now?

### Correcting course

Each of the three previous summaries indicated the necessity of a correction of course on the part of theology and Church:

in Part A, as a kind of "consolidation" in the preliminary field of reason and faith: a new critical-dialogic cooperation of theology (Church) and *natural science;*

in Part B, in view of a modern understanding of God: a new critical-dialogic cooperation of theology (Church) and *both modern philosophy and modern thought as a whole;*

in Part C, in view of the justified concerns of atheists: a correction not only of theological theory but also of the *Church's practice.*

In this Part D now—in view of radical nihilism—it has become clear that a *basic correction* is required of theology: not a new basis but a correction of the basic orientation. After Nietzsche, talk about *God* must take place *against the background of nihilism*—the most extreme opposite position to belief in God—and this necessitates in the end fresh thinking on the question with which we started, at the beginning of the modern age, with Descartes and Pascal: the *question of fundamental certainty.*

On what, on what ultimate certainty, are all our knowledge, action, living, based? This we, too, asked from the very beginning: on a certainty of reason or a certainty of faith?

On the certainty of reason! This was and is the cry of some on the side of Descartes. *Cogito, ergo sum;* I *think*, therefore I am: man is primarily thinking reason. On what can we rely in the last resort if not on the certainty of subjective human consciousness, of human reason? It is a question of the logic of clear thinking. Of what use to man is all the certainty of faith without the fundamental certainty of reason?

But: of what use to man is all the certainty of reason without the sustaining certainty of faith? This was and is the cry of others, on the side of Pascal. *Credo, ergo sum;* I *believe*, therefore I am: man is certainly more than thinking reason. On what can we rely in the last resort, in view of the unreliability of reason, if not on the certainty of personal Christian faith, if not on the certainty of the revelation of God himself? It is a question not only of the logic of abstract thinking but of the tragedy of the concrete human being.

Yet, with Descartes, it must be said that, without thinking, man never reaches faith. Pascal would say that this is true but with thinking alone man does not reach the truth.

But there is more to it. According to Descartes (and Aquinas), the important thing is clearly to separate faith from reason. As reason can supply faith with a foundation, so faith can give to reason a final elevation and perfection. What is to be known and what is to be believed must be distinguished. What is known must be presupposed to what is believed. *Intelligo ut credam;* I must know in order to believe.

On the other hand, according to Pascal (and Augustine), although faith and knowledge must be distinguished, they must certainly not be separated. As faith always has to do with reason, so reason always has to do with faith. What is to be known and what is to be believed can never be adequately distinguished. We think in believing and believe in thinking. *Credo ut intelligam*; I must believe in order to know.

And Nietzsche? On which side of this dispute does he stand? For Nietzsche's *nihilistic negation challenges both sides* and indeed radically: the certainty of faith from which he came and the certainty of reason to which he aspired but did not find his way. As we saw, he passionately rejected the credo of Christian faith and buried in skepticism the *cogito* of human reason. His conclusion was that there is no fundamental certainty. Nothing is certain.

Nihilistic negation, however, affects not only subjective certainty: the certainty of the thinking or believing subject. It *affects also any objective certainty*, that which we can tacitly assume as certain in every cognitive act: the *supposed fundamental certainty of being and of evident first principles of being*, as asserted in the classical philosophy of being. In particular, *ens est ens, ens non est nonens*; being is being, being is not not-being —to cite here the two fundamental principles of the philosophy of being, the principles of identity and contradiction. Are not these principles evident to all men (*principia per se nota omnibus*)? Must they still be proved? Is not the relationship between subject and predicate immediately obvious in such propositions? Has not man a natural certainty (*habitus principiorum*) in this respect?

There is no doubt that more than two thousand years of the history of the Western mind have been marked with such an objective philosophy of being. With the foundations laid by the ancient Greeks, it was developed by Augustine and the medieval scholastics, handed down by the baroque scholastics in modern times, reinterpreted by such other philosophers as Leibniz, Kant and Hegel, and finally restored—frequently in a very much weaker state—against all idealistic philosophy of consciousness by the neoscholastics of the nineteenth century. It was called *philosophia perennis* and sometimes also the natural philosophy or metaphysics of common sense. The debate proceeded.

Against the defenders of the *cogito* and the credo, the neoscholastic philosophers of being objected that both *cogito* and credo are merely subjective, subjectivist positions. I can become certain of the truth not from (thinking or believing) consciousness but only in the light of being, of objective reality, of objective principles.

But the defenders of the *cogito* and the credo from the very beginning pointed out, against the philosophy of being, that we simply cannot grasp a purely objective truth. Being can be known only from being conscious, in the light of consciousness. The standpoint of the subject plays an essential part always and everywhere in the act of cognition. Subject and object, subjective and objective, being conscious and simply being, from the very outset cannot be adequately distinguished but are in reciprocal relationship. The subject-object scheme is more than problematical.

Nevertheless, neoscholasticism, with the aid of this philosophy of being, attempted to establish an evident objective substructure for faith. Following on the naïve metaphysics of medieval scholasticism, there emerged a general ontology or theory of being, culminating in a "natural theology" or philosophical theory of God, the latter being the presupposition for faith. All this, as we saw, means two clearly distinguished cognitive powers (reason and faith), two planes of knowledge (natural truth and revealed truth), two sciences (philosophy and theology). It is this scheme that lies behind the definitions of Vatican I (1870) on the relations between faith and reason.[35] It is a system impressive in its clarity, compactness and consistency. Only a person who is familiar with this philosophy and has at some time tested it thoroughly in order to base his faith and his theology on its so "objective," so "natural," so "rational" foundations, knows also what dangerous illusions of certainty a basis allegedly so rational, so obvious, so clear, can produce.

Nietzsche, for his part, cast doubts not only on "immediate certainties" of the subject, like the *cogito* and the credo, but also on the "immediate certainty" of being and the supposedly evident first principles of being. He not only doubted particular ways of attaining certainty; he disputed also their common intrinsic assumption; for, according to him, there is no perceptible meaning in things. The old controversy about the locus of ultimate certainty—whether in faith or thought, whether in subject or object, whether, finally, in the process of alienation and return of Spirit to itself—this controversy is now reduced *ad absurdum*. Its basis is withdrawn. For it is pointless to continue the debate when we can no longer be sure that such loci of certainty can exist at all. The *doubt about the validity of particular certainties* is radicalized: it has now become a *doubt about the possibility of being certain at all*.

This means that nihilism raises radical doubts even about the certainty of the first principles of being. They cannot be the basis of any further controversy; their meaning has been shaken. What is the point of trying to make the world and life intelligible with the aid of the principles of being if the latter are themselves no longer self-evident? It is not worthwhile to reflect on their explicability, since any explanation ends in inconsistent nonsense.

Hence, the supposedly clear principles of being neither prevented nor even delayed the rise of European nihilism. But this means that the whole basis must be freshly considered if theology is to be carried on not only in well-protected church circles but also in the face of nihilism in the world of today. In order to show that we cannot avoid a basic correction, we shall confront the fundamental principles of the traditional philosophy of being with the corresponding negations of nihilism in systematic conciseness.

## Reality in doubt

Even the nihilist obviously does not deny that this sheet of paper is a sheet of paper and this book in my hand is a book; he does not deny that it *is*. For him, too, this is simply given, a datum, a fact, an actuality, a true state of affairs: an unquestionable reality. But, admitting this unquestionable facticity, it is only at this point that the radical questions of the nihilist begin. For if he begins to ask, to inquire what is behind it all, this facticity—of the world, of others, of myself—which seems so unquestionable, is by no means so self-evident. To the nihilist, it is the totality that is suspect; reality as a whole and especially his own life seem to him profoundly unstable, fragile and ephemeral: fleeting, empty, ineffective, discordant, in the last resort useless, pointless, worthless—in a word, null. And this "nihilist's faith" has its effect on all and sundry. Anyone who is convinced of the nullity of his own life and of reality as a whole, who has passed with Nietzsche through the "school of suspicion," will observe everywhere instability, fragility, transitoriness, fleetingness, emptiness, ineffectiveness, discordance, in the last resort uselessness, pointlessness, worthlessness—in a word, nullity. For, all that is could also not be. This possibility of not-being, which has its effect and manifests itself in everything—this nullity continually puts reality profoundly in question. It constitutes the basic questionability of reality.

These apparently simple but fundamental questions thus reveal their hidden depth—or shallowness. However unquestionable as a fact the individual thing may be even for the nihilist, what is questionable for him is the totality: the wholeness of reality and that of his own life. And these questions of his, aiming at the whole, thus indirectly affect also the individual. Is there any truth at all? Is the world really good? Is man at bottom not contradictory, not divided? Human life thus characterized by non-entity, an ultimate pointlessness and worthlessness: that is, nullity? And in this sense is what is simply given, the purely factual, actual—is this truly real? Is the world of the factual, this "bare" reality, "true" reality?

It should not be said that the linguistic usage is unclear from the outset. In what follows, we shall use the expression "reality" not *only* for facticity, actuality, but for all strata, planes, dimensions of that which is. We are not using it, as some linguistic analysts use it, only for "facts" (= "true" or "real states of affairs").[*36] This usage may be suitable for the construction of a "normative language,"[37] or a logical scientific language with a view to a "process of interpersonal verification,"[38] but even there—as we saw in connection with Carnap and Popper[39]—it has its great prob-

---

* Here the author explains that the German *Tatsache*, like the English "matter of fact," is derived from the Latin *res facti*. Translator.

lems. This usage cannot be normative for us if only because of the fact—
which its advocates admit—that it contradicts not only the traditional understanding of "reality" but also the use of this word in both ordinary
conversation and educated speech. According to this, more limited, usage,
for which the "preferred field" is the "past,"[40] that is, what has happened,
what has come to be, we cannot even speak of "future" reality, of "strata
of reality," of "social reality" and the like,[41] since it is not simply a question of facts here.

Such a usage in any case is inappropriate for dealing with the *problems
of nihilism*, which aims not only at facticity but at reality as a whole. The
great tradition of the West had indeed given its answer to the question of
reality by conceding to reality as a whole, to the world, man, things, all
that is, not only being but also a fundamental being one, being true,
being good. Projection, Nietzsche would say, an interpretation imposed by
a lingering faith. For can it still be said that to individual being and to
being as a whole (= the totality of what is) being (= *Dasein* or "being
there," existence) belongs? Yes, says the traditional philosophy of being,
each individual existent and also the totality of all that is, being, is in
principle, in so far as it *is*, identical with itself (= one, *unum*), meaningful (= true, *verum*), valuable (= good, *bonum*). Today—against the
background of nihilism—this is a bold thesis: fundamental identity
(unity), meaningfulness (truth), valuability (goodness), belong to everything that is and in so far as it *is*. These three concepts really represent
the incontestable, indisputable, self-evident *peculiarities, basic characteristics and basic features of everything that is and of being as a whole*.
Being one, being true, being good, are immediate implications, necessary
aspects of the concept of being and really interchangeable (convertible).

This is certainly a long tradition. The doctrine had its foundations in
Plato's theory of ideas, in Aristotle's metaphysics and in Plotinus' philosophy of the One, and was then systematically developed by Augustine, the
Arab Avicenna and the scholastics Albert and Thomas: to the concepts of
the one, true and good, there were often added those of the beautiful, of
essence, of "something" (*aliquid*). But, in particular, the one, the true
and the good, as the three classical "transcendentals," surpassing (*tran-
scendere*) and embracing all individual orders and categories of being,
were transmitted through the perspicacious Spanish baroque scholastic
Francisco Suárez, to later scholasticism and also to the German philosophy of the Enlightenment, especially to Christian Wolff. Leibniz used
them in his theory of monads; Kant, however, saw in them only logical
preconditions for any knowledge of things; but Hegel in his logic developed them afresh as the primordial determinations of being.[42]

All this, Nietzsche put into question by his nihilism. The contrasts between true and false, good and evil, one and not-one, being and not-being,
cannot be taken for granted, but we must look beyond these contrasts

from a standpoint within the Dionysian becoming: the irrational is the "true," and frenzy is "true" life. What does this mean for Nietzsche with reference to those three "transcendentals"?

a. *No unity:* Man deludes himself when he assumes a *"totality,* a *systematization,* indeed any *organization* in all events and underneath all events."[43] "Underneath all becoming there is no grand unity,"[44] "any comprehensive unity in the plurality of events is lacking."[45] "The overall character of existence may not be interpreted by means . . . of the concept of *unity."*[46]

b. *No truth:* The nihilist has become aware of the fact that "we have sought a 'meaning' in all events that is not there: so the seeker eventually becomes discouraged":[47] "meaninglessness,"[48] "absolute *meaninglessness."*[49] Neither may "the overall character of existence be interpreted by means . . . of the concept of *truth."*[50] The nihilist's assumption is "that there is *no truth,* that there is no absolute nature of things nor a 'thing-in-itself.' "[51]

c. *No goodness:* After "the long waste of strength, the agony of the 'in vain,' insecurity, . . . one realizes that becoming aims at *nothing* and achieves *nothing":* "valuelessness,"[52] "absolute *worthlessness."*[53] Nor— finally—may "the overall character of existence be interpreted by means of the concept of *'aim.' "*[54]

This in fact is the meaning of nihilism as insight into the nothingness, contradictoriness, meaninglessness, worthlessness, of reality. "Briefly: the categories 'aim,' 'unity,' 'being,' which we used to project some value into the world—we *pull out* again; so the world looks *valueless."*[55] Thus the very face of being—without its basic characteristics and basic features— seems to be completely destroyed. These *"categories of reason"* refer *"to a purely fictitious world."*[56] In the concrete, this means that " 'beautiful and ugly,' 'true and false,' 'good and evil'—these distinctions and antagonisms betray" completely superficial and relative "conditions of existence and enhancement."[57] On the other hand, it is essential "to demonstrate the absolute homogeneity of all events and the application of moral distinctions as *conditioned by perspective;* to demonstrate how everything praised as moral is identical in essence with everything immoral and was made possible, as in every development of morality, with immoral means and for immoral ends—; how, on the other hand, everything decried as immoral is, economically considered, higher and more essential, and how a development toward a greater fullness of life necessarily also demands the *advance of immorality.* 'Truth' is the extent to which we permit ourselves to understand this fact."[58]

After Descartes and Pascal and through the whole modern period up to Nietzsche, man's nullity, his many-sided threatenedness and corruptibility, insecurity and uncertainty, unprotectedness and forlornness, became increasingly clear. In view of this, who would still venture to make a naïve appeal in the manner of the older philosophers and theologians to the *alleged evidence of first principles of being?* After Nietzsche's protest, finally, against "immediate certainties," for instance, the "natural" certainty of the principles of identity and contradiction? The radical nihilist asserts precisely that nothing has any support, meaning or value. The totality is not coherent, meaningful, valuable. All that is, all being and being as such, is null, insubstantial, meaningless, worthless. All that is, is good for nothing, explains nothing, aims at nothing, and indeed is nothing. Being in its entirety is nothing. Reality in the last resort is nullity and nothing but nullity.

Radical nihilism is not to be avoided—as, for example, Dieter Arendt tries to do on the lines of dialectical materialism against idealism, existential philosophy and nihilism—by denying an ontological nothingness and thinking that nihilism has thus been overcome.[59] Certainly nothingness may not be ontologized, that is, made independent, hypostatized, mythicized, as if it were nevertheless a being. There is no "absolute" nothing, as —so to speak—a negative God.

But the nullity of all that is, and of human existence in particular, is a fundamental problem that even the materialist cannot evade: this nullity encompasses all that is implied by transitoriness, corruptibility, forlornness, finiteness.[60]

What does all this mean for the question of God? We shall come to this later. In order to deal with these, more *general,* questions we must leave aside for the time being the question of God and atheism. The alternative is not, as is often asserted, "either belief in God or atheism." Otherwise all atheists would be nihilists, which they are not. Nihilism, as understood in the present debate, is certainly atheistic; but not every form of atheism is simultaneously nihilistic. The answers to atheism and to nihilism must therefore be distinguished. In this fourth interim summary of results, we are not yet dealing with the problems presented by atheism, with the question God or not God. Our concern is with the more wideranging problems of nihilism: with the question *to be or not to be.* These are the findings:

- *Reality—all that is—is threatened by the nullity present everywhere, the possibility of not being, transitoriness, corruptibility, finiteness. This is what constitutes the uncertainty of reality. The question of the being or not being of the existent cannot be dismissed.*
- *A denial of being—by insisting on the nullity of all that is—is possible, so that everything, the self and the world, would have to be regarded in the last resort as chaotic, absurd, illusory, null.*
- *There is consequently nothing about which it is impossible to doubt or even despair. Doubt—not only methodical (Descartes) but also existential (Pascal)—does not begin only with the question of God. It begins with the question of being. It begins with the uncertainty of human*

*existence and of reality as a whole. It is futile to look for a manifest foundation of reason on which faith could be based ("natural theology"). In the face of nihilsim, such a justification of faith would offer merely a pseudo foundation for pseudo certainty.*

It can now be seen that no proposition on being is conclusive, obvious. All *principia per se nota* are abstract and in the concrete can be *principia ignota* or *negata*. All "philosophical or metaphysical certainty" must be seen against the background of a fundamental existential insecurity of human existence.

## Nihilism—possible, irrefutable, but unproved

The chances of nihilism must therefore be considered, objectively and impartially:

- *Nihilism is possible. The thoroughgoing uncertainty of reality itself makes nihilism possible, whether in practical life (practical nihilism) or in philosophical or unphilosophical reflection (fundamental nihilism).*

If hitherto no unity, truth, goodness of reality could be proved, it is in fact possible that they do not exist. Factual existence can be meaningless existence. Doubt can develop not only a creative but also a destructive force, and thus doubt (possibly merely methodical) can become existential despair. It might be said: "*Cogito, ergo non sum*—I do indeed think, but really I am not." The "death instinct," which Freud thought he could establish and the existence of which is questioned by many psychologists, might represent a problem not so much of the instinctual structure as of the existential threatenedness of life. If, then, nihilism is possible, it can, however, also be maintained:

- *Nihilism is irrefutable. There is no rationally conclusive argument against the possibility of nihilism. It is indeed at least possible that this human life, in the last resort, is meaningless, that chance, blind fate, chaos, absurdity and illusion rule the world, that, in the last resort, everything is contradictory, meaningless, worthless, null.*

It is, of course, claimed that the statement that everything is contradictory, meaningless, worthless, null, is a contradiction in terms. But this formal logical argument against nihilism is scarcely convincing. The assertion that everything is contradictory, meaningless, worthless, null is not a contradiction in terms. For the very fact that this statement is made about the nullity of all being, for the nihilist is itself meaningless and worthless.

It is also said that suicide is a necessary consequence of nihilism. But even this practical argument against nihilism is not convincing. For the

nihilist, life is not an absolute value. Consequently it is a matter of indifference whether he abandons it or—in apathy, irony or defiance—goes
on living. He is more likely to refrain from suicide: for this might be
understood as a final meaningful act. But if nihilism is irrefutable, the opposite can also be maintained:

- *Nihilism is also* unprovable. *There is no rational argument for the necessity of accepting nihilism. It is indeed also possible that this human
  life is not, in the last resort, meaningless, that not only chance, fate, absurdity and illusion rule the world, that by no means everything is contradictory, meaningless, worthless, in the last resort, null.*

Who could have proved the opposite? As we saw, Nietzsche's brilliant
rhetoric can easily be blinding; it reveals experiences but does not provide
substantiation. Also, if it has to be admitted that reality is uncertain and
that the being of the existent can be denied, then it must be admitted
that what can be denied is also in fact being. It is indeed uncertain, but is
it for that reason *a priori* nothing? If being were *a priori* nothing, the
nihilist would not need to deny it and to keep on denying it. If being
were simply nothing, it would not endure denial at all but would dissolve
into nothing. But language itself betrays the nihilist: "Being *is* not-being"
or "I *am* not." The formal logical argument is not thereby justified, but
the value is seen of the insight into the fact that being, despite all the
menace of nothingness, continually puts up fresh resistance to any kind of
absolute denial, any total reduction to nothing, by man. It is true that
being does not impose itself, conclusively, obviously, as being. But, in the
very moment it is denied, it seems by its resistance to that denial to
manifest itself as being. So then: to be or not to be?

- *If, then, in the last resort, there is no rational argument for the impossibility of nihilism, so, conversely, neither is there any for its justification.
  If it is possible that everything, in the last resort, is contradictory,
  meaningless, worthless, null, so, too, the opposite is not a priori impossible: that, in the last resort, everything is nevertheless identical, meaningful, valuable, real.*

This, then, is the outcome of the controversy. Nihilism is unprovable, but
so is its opposite. A very desperate stalemate situation? Perhaps.

We at any rate have advanced to the ground of the problems for our
setting of the question. Have we perhaps reached a turning point?

# E. YES TO REALITY—
# ALTERNATIVE TO NIHILISM

To be or not to be—that is the question, that is the *basic question*. Can nihilism be overcome and, if so, how?

"The academic expert, concentrated on his special field (mathematics, history, natural science), does not like to be told *that basic assumptions of his thinking are metaphysical in character*; the metaphysician does not like to be told *that his mental activity rests on a prerational, primordial decision*; philosophers of all types—apart from skeptics—do not like to be told *that the kinds of skepticism that are to be taken seriously are irrefutable*; and skeptics themselves, of all shades, do not like to admit *that they cannot prove their standpoint*. Such a complex assessment more or less provokes the indignant protest: 'This cannot possibly be your *last word*. One way or another, there must be a solution of some kind.' To which I can only reply: 'The solution is in your hands, at any time. Make up your mind. Decide.'" The words are those of Wolfgang Stegmüller, one of the leading logicians and epistemologists of our time.[1]

# I. The basic attitude

The turning point is becoming clear. With all the clarifications and discriminating answers with reference to reason and faith, understanding of the world and understanding of God, atheism and belief in God, produced up to now, questions were piled up on questions, until we advanced to the point at which we came face to face with the complete uncertainty of reality as a whole. Doubts were heaped on doubts until we caught sight of the utter dubiousness of all that exists, of the unreality of reality. We have thus come up against the ground of all questions, the basic question. We did not want to leave anything unquestioned, to conceal anything apologetically, to appeal to any authority beyond further appeal. We tried to think critically and self-critically, in order to perceive and to be certain of the foundation of our knowledge and faith. But with what success? Are we not threatened with failure?

Or is there an ultimate certainty that can be opposed to nihilism? Despite all appearances, despite all the uncertainty of reality and despite the dubiousness of all that exists, should it not be possible now to place our feet on firm ground, to establish a fundamental certainty such as we have been seeking continuously from the very first page onward, from the dawn of modern times with Descartes and Pascal? Might it be possible to find a basic certainty to conquer and to transcend in depth the one-sided, unsatisfactory positions of both the *cogito* and the credo, and also that of *ens est ens?* After the detailed historical-systematic analyses, we can proceed more synthetically in this section, while assuming a knowledge of some of the theories and texts from past and present.

## 1. Clarifications

From the discussions with and about nihilism, it has become clear that in principle I can adopt a positive or negative attitude to uncertain reality, can regard it as real or unreal. Even the nihilist, who in principle adopts a negative or indifferent attitude to uncertain reality, cannot overlook the fact that there are other people who—wrongly, according to him—in principle adopt a positive attitude to this uncertain reality. For the time being, we shall continue our analysis on the assumption that in prin-

ciple I can adopt a positive or a negative attitude toward uncertain reality.
But what is the self, what is the reality, presented to me here? Which "reaction," which "attitude," is meant?

## Which self?

First of all, it is a question of my own attitude toward reality. This
question about reality is about myself. But—and this became clear as
against Descartes—I am never merely reason. Even in the midst of doubt,
I am never merely thinking. Humanity never means merely rationality.
Even if we abstract from a "third dimension," of "feeling," not all
processes of the human mind can be distributed between two faculties—
as it were, two arms of the soul—as they seemed to be predominantly
with Descartes and in later Thomism. *Reason* and *will* cannot be separated like two different substances, but at best distinguished as two
different basic functions of the one human being. That is, there is no such
thing as an isolated *cogito*.

Despite his indisputable intellectualism, unlike some Thomists,
Aquinas himself makes intellect and will wholly and entirely coordinated
factors. Even considered subjectively, from the standpoint of the mind's
resources, there is an interlocking: in every genuine human act, the will
must bring the intellect into activity (*exercitium*). And at the same time,
the intellect must direct the (blind) will to a particular object (*specifica-
tio*). But there is an interlocking also considered from the standpoint of
the object: what is true for the intellect becomes for the will something
good. And at the same time what is good for the will is for the intellect
something true.[2] For Aquinas, therefore, between intellect and will, true
and good, there is a reciprocal priority and completion.

Today, admittedly, there is less inclination to talk of "powers" or
"faculties of the soul." Psychologists insist that with will and intellect we
are dealing with underivable primordial phenomena, which are not
explicable either physiologically or psychologically. For this reason, the
verb "willing" is frequently preferred to the noun "will." As opposed to
"will," "willing" is observable, empirically perceptible. Willing means the
deliberate (not impulsive or unconsidered) decision for a particular orientation of action (a way or mode of action[3]). But, in this sense, willing is a
decision not merely of an isolated will but of the whole individual, of myself.

It is a question therefore of myself. More precisely, it concerns my
whole person, intellect and will, feeling and instinctual structure, mind
and body, head and heart: heart—that is—understood as Pascal understood it, as the center of my person. It is a question of myself *with my
whole subjectivity*.

Certainly we can distinguish between "functional" and "essential" questions, between technical-rational and total-personal questions. But, in life in the concrete, everything is interconnected. "Calculating" thought in Heidegger's sense, related to what is feasible, calculable, correct, cannot in ordinary life be completely distinguished from "reflective," "essential" thinking, which is intent upon being and truth. Universally valid, unhistorical, timeless truths, whose accuracy can be proved (in terms of mathematics or physics), are linked in the concrete human being with those vital, concrete, historical truths that cannot be proved in the same way.

Whether I will it or not, subjective ties—also interests, instincts, emotions, passions, attitudes—just like social conditions, have a decisive influence on my knowledge, its assumptions and its consequences. Every human being is in many ways preformed. Even in his most elemental experiences and knowledge ("I am," "something is"), his subjectivity is involved. Being human is never merely being reasonable, never merely rationality, not even critical rationality. It is therefore by no means always stupidity or malice if reason does not everywhere prevail; this became clear even for natural science in Kuhn's *Structure of Scientific Revolutions.*[4]

*Objective and subjective,* insight and feelings, rational and irrational, *cannot be neatly divided* in the human being. Always and everywhere, I see, know and judge in the light of what I am myself, in my whole concrete existence: placed in a quite definite situation, consciously or unconsciously dependent on certain experiences and encounters, traditions and authorities, habits of thought and schemes of values, involved in one set of social conditions or another, characterized by quite definite interests. All this makes me see one thing and not another, makes my perception, cognition, memory, feeling, appreciation, selective, discriminating, even conditioned by my perspective, my standpoint.[5] But there is no one absolute human standpoint. In the light of my subjectivity, the direction of my perception and imagination continually determines the selection of what in fact is perceived or even remembered. I myself give color and emphasis to reality. Thus, up to a point, I "make" my truth: from universal truth "in itself," in my perception, cognition, feeling, appreciation, I make the concrete truth "for me." This also holds for my elemental experience of being and my basic attitude to reality.

## Which reality?

Reality? This is all that is real, all that is: all being, the totality of beings, in this sense existent being as a whole. What reality is, will not be closely examined here. Reality cannot be defined *a priori.* For the all-embracing, by its very nature, is not definable, not delimitable. At the end of the first part of this book, we saw how complex and multidimensional this concept is. We shall only recall briefly what is meant here concretely by reality, so that we are not talking abstractly or pointlessly.

Reality is primarily the *world* and all that constitutes the world in space and time, macrocosm and microcosm, with their abysses. The world in its history, in past, present and future. The world with matter and energy, with nature and culture, with all its marvels and horrors. Not an "unbroken world," anyway, but the real world in all its uncertainty: with all its concrete conditions and natural disasters, with its actual misery and all its pain. Animals and men in their struggle for existence: rise and decline, "devouring" and "being devoured." The whole world, so difficult to accept in its ambivalence, as Dostoevsky describes it in his novel *The Brothers Karamazov*. There the skeptical Ivan Karamazov says to his younger brother Alyosha, who believes in God: "Would you believe it, in the final result I don't accept this world of God's, and, although I know it exists, I don't accept it all. It's not that I don't accept God, you must understand, it's the world created by *Him* I don't and cannot accept."[6]

Reality means especially *human beings* in the world: human beings of all groups and classes, of all colors and races, nations and regions, individuals and societies. Human beings: the most distant and particularly our neighbors, who often seem to us the most remote. Human beings who are indeed human, all too human. Not by any means ideal humanity, but humanity that includes all that we would prefer to exclude when we sing: "You millions, I embrace you. This kiss is for all the world."* Including, too, all those who make life hell for us, on a grand or a small scale. *L'enfer, c'est les autres*: "Hell . . . is other people"; this is the main theme of Jean Paul Sartre's play *Huis clos*, about three people condemned to remain together in a room under the constant glare of an electric light:[7] a kind of association whose breakdown Sartre analyzes from every possible standpoint in his great philosophical work *L'être et le néant*.[8]

Reality means above all *myself*, I who as subject can become object to myself. I myself with mind and body, with disposition and behavior, with weaknesses and strengths. Certainly not an ideal human being, but a human being with his heights and depths, with his bright side and his seamy side, with all that which C. G. Jung calls the "shadow" of the person, with all that he has pushed off, suppressed, repressed—what Freud with the aid of analysis tried to restore to consciousness and make acceptable. Also, a human being who is always splitting up into the various roles he has to play in society, who always has to fulfill particular social functions that society expects of him.[9] We often accept the world more easily than ourselves, as we happen to be or as we are made by others. "I am not Stiller" is the opening of a novel, *Stiller*, by the Swiss writer Max Frisch,

---

* *Seid umschlungen Millionen. Diesen Kuss der ganzen Welt.* From Schiller's *Ode to Joy*, sung as the climax of Beethoven's Ninth Symphony.

the story of a man who stubbornly refuses to accept himself: because he wants to escape from the images that others have made of him; because he wants to shake off the roles that other people compel him to play; because he suffers from the inability to be as he wants to be but only as he is expected to be. Against this background of the typical identity and role problems of modern man, a person's acceptance of himself becomes a grave problem. As C. G. Jung says: "Perhaps this sounds very simple, but simple things are always the most difficult. In actual life it requires the greatest art to be simple, and so acceptance of oneself is the essence of the moral problem and the acid test of one's whole outlook on life."[10]

On this "acceptance of oneself," on the task of being oneself, Romano Guardini wrote a long time ago, invoking Pascal:

"The task can become very difficult.

"There is resistance to having to be oneself. Why should I? Did I ask to be? . . .

"There is the feeling that it is not worthwhile to be oneself. What do I get out of it? I am bored with myself. I loathe myself. I can't stand myself. . . .

"There is the feeling of deceiving myself; of being closed up within myself. I am only so much and would like to be more. I have only this talent and would like greater, more brilliant gifts. I must always do the same thing. I always come up against the same limits. I always commit the same errors, experience the same failure. . . .

"Out of all this an infinite monotony can arise; a terrible weariness."[11]

But—as we pointed out at an earlier stage—*self and world* may *not* be *understood simply as subject and "confronting" object.* Subject and object cannot be detached from one another and thought of in isolation. There is no purely objective knowledge—as Kant made clear and modern physics confirms—not even in natural science. This is not to say that all the fundamental categories of the world, such as space, time and causality, could be reduced to pure subjectivity: in this respect, modern physics has not confirmed Kant. But the most exact science today starts out from the assumption that what we are dealing with is never the world in itself, but always the world as it appears to us. The world as we know it, then, is not anything either purely objective or purely subjective, but the common product of our subjectivity and the existent in itself. This means that—despite all the differences—subject and object are continually referred to one another, tied to one another, are in a *dialectical "reciprocal relationship,"* in a "dialectical interweaving."[12]

Thus in principle there is no subject without object, no object without subject. The subject-object scheme is not adequate to describe reality. The question about reality is also always a question about the questioner. As a subject, I am not merely confronted by an object; as subject, I am myself also my own object. For this reason, I can never wholly objectify myself and the world, any more than I can ever myself become pure sub-

ject. I myself am a part of the world and the world is a part of myself. If,
then, we speak here of reality, we never mean something that is found
only on one side or the other, we never mean merely the subjective or
merely the objective. If we speak here of reality, we always mean something that combines and embraces subject and object, consciousness and
being, self and world. In this sense, we speak concisely of the reality of
self and world.


## 2. *Reaction to reality*

Reality itself demands a reaction. Within reality I must take a stand,
live, act and take up a position as a human being. Every human being decides for himself his *fundamental attitude* to reality: that basic approach
which embraces, colors, characterizes his whole experience, behavior,
action.[13] In this respect it is a question of a *free reaction* within certain
limits. For we must first of all bear in mind the principle that reality does
not thrust itself on us conclusively, self-evidently, as what it is. It thus
leaves scope—within limits, as we shall see—for a free decision without intellectual or moral coercion. Such a reaction does not mean adopting a
dogmatic attitude. Nothing more is assumed than uncertain reality itself.
Nothing more is "implied." I am simply allowing reality—of which I am a
part—to have its effect on me. I am not postulating or demanding anything, but reality itself invites me, challenges me. It demands my answer,
my reaction, my free reaction. But what does that mean?


## Freedom within limits

*Absolute freedom?* This was an exaggerated claim made by existentialists, especially the young Jean Paul Sartre, in opposition to the denial
of freedom in materialism and mechanistic natural science and also to the
suppression of human freedom implied in a particular understanding of
God. Man, so often degraded to an object by science and in life, so often
also humiliated by religion, was to be given back his dignity. And this dignity—so runs the main thesis of Sartre, the atheist—lies in his freedom,
which constitutes man's being or existence, which is not dependent on
success and is even increased by real impediments. "I *am* my freedom. No
sooner had you created me than I ceased to be yours," retorts Orestes to
Zeus in Sartre's play *The Flies*.[14] And again, in his programmatic essay
*Existentialism and Humanism*, we read: "There is no determinism—man
is free, man *is* freedom."[15]

But was not the criticism of Sartre by Christians and atheists justified?
Can man's being, his existence, be simply defined as freedom, merely as

freedom? Does this freely projected existence—as Sartre's freedom thesis also runs—really precede any human essence or nature? Is this existence really undetermined, this freedom completely unrestricted, man's responsibility total? Is man really the free inventor and creator of all values, of morality and the meaning of life? Unrestricted, absolute freedom leads, as Hegel—at first an enthusiastic supporter of the French Revolution—explains in the *Phenomenology of Mind,* to the terror of the guillotine: "The terror of death is the direct apprehension of its negative nature."[16] The alternative, which Sartre expounds in his main work, *Being and Nothingness,* is not convincing: "Man is wholly and forever free or he is not free at all."[17] Is not our experience different: we are free and yet not free?

*Relative freedom?* Today we can afford less than ever to forget the true element of the existentialist philosophy of Heidegger, Jaspers, Marcel and Sartre, or even of the philosophy of Rousseau, Kant, Fichte, of the later Schelling and Bergson, as opposed to any denial of freedom in a philosophical, physiological, psychological or sociological determinism. Within certain limits of the human, which Sartre in the end had to admit in the form of an unchangeable "human relativity" (*condition humaine*),[18] Orestes is right: "For I, Zeus, am a man and every man must find his own way."[19] Against all false self-assurance and bourgeois complacency, it must be stressed that the man who is not what he is, is abandoned to himself; he will be as he has projected himself. He must realize himself, and only in this realization is his freedom fulfilled. In this restricted sense, the statement in Sartre's programmatic essay is correct: "Man is nothing else but that which he makes of himself."[20] And Sartre is also right in seeing individual acts as the expression of a more fundamental choice: "I may wish to join a party, to write a book or to marry—but in such a case what is usually called my will is probably a manifestation of a prior and more spontaneous decision."[21] This prior decision he calls *choix originel* or *choix fundamental.*[22] "It is a choice of myself in the world and by the same token it is a discovery of the world."[23] For Sartre, this is the fundamental act of existence and freedom that makes its mark on all particular acts and gives them meaning. The fundamental choice, in which I decide about my being, precedes all acts of the will. It is one with the consciousness that I have of myself.[24]

This fundamental decision will have to be understood in a way different from that in which Sartre understands it: an act of freedom certainly; not, however, in the sense of a completely undetermined, free project, but in the sense of the acknowledgment of unchangeable—by no means merely external—human relativity; an act of freedom, anyway, that can be directed not only to being but also to nothingness. Sartre's existentialism pays too little attention here to the nihilistic alternative.[25] Nevertheless it is actually a question of a free choice of man vis-à-vis the world. A free reaction to reality as a whole, in the fundamental question of being or not-being: this we call the *fundamental decision*.

It was Kierkegaard who made the concept of "decision" (or "choice"), which had always been used in both the legal-ethical and the religious spheres, into a basic philosophical concept, to be used to characterize human existence. In this respect, he exercised a powerful influence on such philosophers as Heidegger, Jaspers and Sartre and also on such theologians as Barth, Gogarten and Bultmann.[26] The early Kierkegaard used the term in a subjectivist sense for the isolated existence of the individual human being: "I choose the absolute. And what is the absolute? It is I myself in my eternal validity. Anything else but myself I can never choose as the absolute."[27] The later Kierkegaard used the term "decision" predominantly in a specifically Christian sense. In the "most decisive moment of actual danger to life"—and this is the test case—according to him, there is "only *one* name that a man might wish to name; one consolation that he would want to seek, that of Jesus Christ"; it is man's "task" to "maintain this eternal decision of inwardness in time and to preserve the impression of this decision."[28]

But neither the purely subjective nor the specifically Christian meaning of decision is what is meant here by fundamental decision. What is meant is man's decision in regard to reality as a whole: his basic reaction to his own existence and to the world.

The most recent conclusions especially of American and German behavioral science have of course established more clearly than we had formerly realized the fact that man is *preformed in two ways*: both by environmental influences and by inherited dispositions.

Man is *environmentally controlled*, molded by influences, dependent on circumstances, conditioned in a variety of ways, and thus his behavior is largely predictable. The behavioral scientists—such as those American *behaviorists* who demand a human being programmed for the good— make use of this. The radical behaviorist B. F. Skinner even demands— and this appears as an extreme counterposition to Sartre—a standpoint "beyond freedom and dignity."[29] The unrestrained freedom drive of autonomous man, which is responsible for so much individual and social evil, must be replaced by scientific control of human behavior and directed with the aid of a comprehensive "behavior technology."

But even Skinner does not deny human freedom. In fact, man is not *only* environmentally controlled, not *totally* conditioned, not *completely* predictable. Undoubtedly, the environment shapes man and his will. But, at the same time, man and his will shape the environment in so far as he is an autonomous system confronting the environment. Despite all environmental conditioning and in face of traditional prejudices, there is no doubt that I can break into freedom and change my behavior accordingly.

I can also believe in the freedom of others to consider my arguments, perhaps accept them and likewise change their behavior. In brief, I can realize the autonomy of the inward man and also invite others to do so.

The opponents of the American behaviorists, however, the German behavioral scientists and ethologists of the school of the Nobel prizewinner Konrad Lorenz, are right in claiming—incidentally Skinner does not deny this—that man as a phylogenetic construction is already *genetically preprogrammed:* in his forms of behavior, modes of action, reactions, driven and controlled by inherited programs. Innate dispositions are of fundamental importance for individual and social behavior.[30] But the ethologists point out that innate dispositions operate only as one particular factor and not as an inescapable fate to be endured and accepted. As Irenäus Eibl-Eibesfeldt, a disciple of Lorenz, says: the one-sided view "that man is programmed only by learning is false, just as false as it is to assert that man is preprogrammed all along the line."[31]

We should be quite clear about the fact that a human being totally preprogrammed by his genetic constitution or totally conditioned by his environment would no longer be human: he would be a beast or a robot. Within the limits of innate dispositions and environmental determinants, man is free: free as opposed to dependent on power and force, free in the sense of self-determination, of autonomy.

## Experience of freedom

Both behaviorists and ethologists, both psychoanalysts and Marxist sociologists, should note that any kind of *absolutizing of correct but individual conclusions* leads eventually to misunderstanding of freedom and humanity, as Karl Jaspers explained, to the "dilapidation of man's image" and thus to the "dilapidation of man himself": "All secular dependencies and biological processes of evolution affect what might be called the material of man, not man himself. It cannot be foreseen how far research will progress in the knowledge of the evolution of this human material. And there is scarcely any field of study that would be more breathtaking and exciting for us. Any knowledge of man, if it is absolutized and understood as knowledge of man as a whole, causes freedom to disappear. So it is also with theories of man as outlined appropriately for limited horizons by psychoanalysis, Marxism, race theory. They disguise man himself as soon as they want to do more than investigate aspects of his appearance."[32]

Scientific research *never* perceived *more than aspects of man:* "Research certainly shows us many odd, surprising things about man, but the clearer it becomes, the more aware it is that it can never make man as a whole into an object of research. Man is always more than he knows of himself. This holds both of man as such and of every individual human being. We can never take stock, never be fully informed, either of man as such or of any individual human being."[33] But the person himself is absolutely certain of being fully human and thus precisely of his human freedom: "Each and every one of us is certain of what man is in a way that comes before and after study. It is a matter of our freedom, which is aware of being tied to conclusive knowledge but is itself never embraced by the latter as an object of knowledge. For, as far as we investigate ourselves, we fail to discern freedom but only our way of being, our finiteness, form, relationship, causal necessity. But it is in the light of our freedom that we are aware of being human."[34]

As far as the *knowledge of human freedom* is concerned, this means that man's freedom cannot be presented simply objectively, like other objects: it is a thoroughly debatable, uncertain factor. Neither can it be verified or proved scientifically from outside. But I myself can become aware of this freedom. I can perceive it inwardly. In the last resort, it is not an external proof of freedom, but my own, inward *experience of freedom*, that tells me that I am free. It is an experience not of thinking but of *doing*. Precisely in the accomplishment, I can experience directly the fact that I will this but could also act otherwise, that I do now act otherwise, that I am free. This is an experience not only of doing but also of not doing, of failing, of *becoming guilty*. In the accomplishment, I can also immediately experience the fact that I have not done something but could have done it; that I have made a promise but not kept it; but that I require acknowledgment of guilt from the other person when I was not guilty; for anyway, this was wholly within the scope of his freedom. . . . What would morality be without responsibility, what would responsibility be without freedom?

In my whole person, I experience myself as the source of my will to be in this way and not otherwise. This freedom of mine is not merely a property of my willing or even merely of my action, but of my being. Am I in this respect simply dependent on the strongest motive, which necessarily prevails in my mental association mechanism? So runs the secular version of the Augustinian-Jansenist theory—which we met at an earlier stage—that the human will is necessarily determined by whatever happens to be the stronger "attraction" (*delectatio victrix*) at the moment: either irresistible evil concupiscence or irresistible grace.[35] But even in theology and, again, in psychology, this kind of predetermination was more asserted than proved. For do I not also have a part in deciding the weight to be attached to individual motives? Do I not decide even criteria and standards? Do I not describe as the "stronger motive" that which I myself allow to become the stronger? In the end, do I not decide myself whether and when to act in this way or another? No matter how much I am outwardly and inwardly determined in my whole existence, I am nevertheless aware that, in the end, it depends on me whether I speak or remain silent, stand up or remain seated, whether I prefer or choose this or that article of clothing, this or that dish, this or that journey. . . . Man remains— despite all causal laws—a free being and as such profoundly incalculable. So often he says No, when a Yes is expected; and Yes, when a No is feared.

In the end, however, it is in a quite different way that I have to face the *fundamental question* presented here, where what is involved is not simply this or that but uncertain reality as a whole, my fundamental atti- tude to the uncertain reality of myself and the world. It is at this very point that I can become aware of *my freedom to say Yes or No.* This fun- damental decision in regard to uncertain reality of course does not need to be the result of reflection, and certainly not of any sort of philosophical reflection. From childhood onward, as we shall see, man slowly grows into it. It can also be made later, more or less consciously, in the midst of daily life. It becomes for him a particular attitude to life, to the world, to real- ity. But, in the face of the threat so often concretely experienced in ordi- nary life by the nothingness, transitoriness, decay, forlornness, finiteness of all that is human and earthly, even the person who passes his life in men- tal indolence and superficiality is continually forced—whether he reflects on it or not—to make a decision. What had hitherto been lived through without reflection must now be deliberately appropriated and resolutely accepted. Even slight disturbances can raise the great question: What, in principle, is my approach to life, positive or negative? What is my atti- tude to my own existence and to my milieu? How do I react to my fellow men and to society? What do I make of the world as a whole and of its history? What is my attitude *to reality altogether?*

● Vis-à-vis reality as a whole, it is a question not only of the more or less significant individual decisions of life, which are means to an end. It is a question of the free but not arbitrary, responsibly effected, considered or unconsidered, fundamental reaction to reality: the positive or nega- tive fundamental decision that determines, characterizes, colors man's fundamental attitude to reality as a whole: the fundamental attitude to oneself, to other human beings, to society, to the world. It is thus a question of man's total experience, behavior and action.

The terminology need not worry us too much. Other names can be given to this fundamental decision. For instance: "life decision," in which a per- son's whole attitude to life is involved;
"fundamental choice," in which I choose what world, society, people and I myself mean to me;
"fundamental option," on which all my individual options, the whole complex system of my views, opinions, convictions and expectations, are based;
"primary resolution," which affects all my perception, feeling, thinking

and action and in regard to which all my other decisions are secondary. "cardinal determination," on which my life (cognition and feeling, behavior and action) hinges;

the great "Either/Or" (of Kierkegaard), in which a radical decision is made about my life in the world (what Ignatius Loyola, in a religious context, in the *Exercises,* called *electio*).


## The fundamental alternative

We can say Yes or No to uncertain reality. Such a fundamental decision and fundamental approach always involve a *risk.* If everything is transitory, decaying, finite, null, who can tell me what is right? If it is a question of the totality, who is there who can himself weigh the import of the decision? If it is a question of the ground and meaning of life, who can protect me from disappointment and failure, who can guarantee success and happiness?

Reality itself does not extort a Yes or a No, a positive or a negative fundamental attitude. It is not—and this has to be admitted all over again—self-evident; the whole is not transparent. Should I, then, surrender myself to what is not obvious, demonstrable, calculable? Is there not every reason for "suspicion" (in Nietzsche's sense), doubt and mistrust?

This really is a *matter of trust or mistrust,* in which I stake myself without security or guarantee. We may paraphrase the verb "to trust" in a variety of ways:

either I believe that reality sustains me and I trust it—or not;
either I commit myself in principle to reality and rely on it—or not;
either I regard reality therefore as trustworthy and reliable—or not;
either I express my trust in reality—or not.

Whatever way this fundamental decision goes, whatever kind of fundamental attitude is adopted, it is *inescapable.* Man is free. But he is not free to be free: "You must wager. There is no choice, you are already committed," said Pascal.[36] Jean Paul Sartre says that man is "condemned" to freedom,[37] while others say that he is "called" to freedom. But, whether condemned or called to freedom, in the long run it is impossible to remain undecided in regard to reality, to hover between nihilism and nonnihilism. Either-or: to see or not to see! A person who will not see is not indifferent, but blind.

And not to choose is itself a choice. A choice not to choose, a disguised choice, which means either winning or losing. And since it is a question not of a selection of a particular thing or of a single existent, not of a particular decision, but of the choice of my life, of the fundamental decision and fundamental attitude in regard to my life and to the life of others, to the world as it is, to reality as a whole; since it is a question, then, of the reaction to the totality of what exists, apart from which nothing exists, there remains only the choice between affirmation and denial. In this vote of confidence, abstention means refusal of trust, a vote for mistrust. In this respect, anyone who does not—at least as a simple fact—say Yes, is actually saying No.

- *Since uncertain reality—that of myself or that of the world—is not manifested conclusively, obviously, as what it is, it can be interpreted in the sense either of being or of not-being: the existent, then, appears to me either in a fundamental identity, meaningfulness, valuability, actuality, or on the other hand in a fundamental discordance, pointlessness, worthlessness, nullity.*
- *In this basic question, the fundamental alternative is a (considered or unconsidered) Yes or No to reality in principle: an unforcible and unprovable trust or mistrust in the reality of the world and of my own self.*
- *Since in this fundamental alternative it is a question of trust or mistrust in principle, we can speak of* fundamental trust *or* fundamental mistrust *corresponding to the fundamental decision and the fundamental attitude. That is, not merely a trust (or mistrust) in this or that person, in this or that thing, but the fundamental trust (or mistrust) in myself, in other human beings, in the world, in uncertain reality as a whole, which lies behind—and alone makes possible—any individual trust at all.*
- *A fundamental trust in reality by no means excludes mistrust in a particular case and therefore is not to be confused with credulity or uncritical optimism.*
  *A fundamental mistrust in regard to reality perhaps does not exclude trust in a particular case and anyway is not to be equated with ill humor or a superficial pessimism.*

Here, too, what is important is not the terminology, but the reality. Fundamental trust or fundamental mistrust can be given a variety of names, and each expression has its own emphasis and hazards. Instead of "fundamental trust" or "fundamental mistrust," we can also speak of

"primordial trust" or "primordial mistrust," trust or mistrust purely and simply (not to be misunderstood in a religious or mystical sense);

"trust in life" or "mistrust of life," a basic confidence or want of confidence in life in its general meaning, including world and man, in the "course of things" (not to be misunderstood in a subjectivist or psychological sense);

"trust in being" or "mistrust of being," a fundamental commitment or noncommitment of oneself to all-embracing being (not to be misunderstood in an objectivist or ontological sense);

"trust in reason" or "mistrust of reason," a fundamental commitment or noncommitment of oneself to the reasonableness of reason (not to be misunderstood in a rationalist or positivist sense).

No one can evade this fundamental decision and fundamental attitude. Not even the "critical rationalist."[38] For if I am a rationalist, how am I to prove or establish the fact that my *ratio* is rational, my reason reasonable? As we saw, even the reasonableness of reason is often uncertain. And it is not an *argument* of reason, but a *trust* in reason (fundamental trust), that—not surprisingly, as it seems to us—even critical rationalists must simply assume as the basis of their entire system. Karl Popper saw this clearly and admitted it: "Rationalism appreciates argument and theory and verification by experience. But this decision for rationalism cannot in its own turn be justified by argument and experience. Although it can be discussed, it rests ultimately on an irrational decision, on faith in reason. And this decision for reason is not a purely intellectual but a moral decision. It influences our whole attitude to other human beings and to the problems of social life. It is closely linked to a faith in the rational unity of man, in the value of every man."[39] A surprising admission for a critical rationalist! How is it to be understood?

According to Popper, a "self-sufficient," "comprehensive" or "uncritical" rationalism, as supported by Descartes and many modern scientists, is "logically untenable."[40] A rationalistic approach, which seeks to base every assumption on an argument or on experience, cannot in its own turn be supported by arguments or experience. But "a modest and self-critical rationalism which recognizes certain limitations," such as Popper advocates, must adopt, without rational reflection, "some proposal, or decision, or belief, or behaviour; an adoption which may be called 'irrational.' Whether this adoption is tentative or leads to a settled habit, we may describe it as an irrational *faith in reason*."[41] A "choice," that is, which "is not simply an intellectual affair, or a matter of taste," but "a moral decision" which "will deeply affect our whole attitude towards other men and towards the problems of social life."[42] No wonder that, for Popper, "the conflict between rationalism and irrationalism has become the most important intellectual, and perhaps even moral, issue of our time."[43]

But we must ask how it is possible to speak of a "critical rationalism" if its foundation is—and remains—irrationalism. For this "irrational faith in reason" must be *constantly* assumed. Is not rationalism based on an irrational foundation simply an unfounded rationalism? Popper replies: "I freely admit that in arriving at my proposals I have been guided, in the last analysis, by value judgments and predilections."[44] Does not this really mean that, in view of its negative consequences, irrational rationalism is an irrationalism subsequently rationalized?[45] And did not Popper himself have to admit, "to that extent, a certain priority of irrationalism"?[46]

We can agree with Popper that "the foundation is shaky."[47] The structure of objective science, he says, "does not rest on rock bottom," but "rises, as it were, above a swamp. It is like a building erected on piles. The piles are driven down from above into the swamp, but not down to any natural or 'given' base."[48] The very fallibility of reason in all fields—even in mathematics, logic and natural science—so strongly emphasized by Popper and Hans Albert, manifests that uncertainty of reason which gives rise to the question of the fundamental reasonableness of reason. And not only the reasonableness of reason, but also the reality of reality—disputed as it is by nihilism—is in question here. But neither Popper nor his followers ever really come to grips with nihilism on the question of the reality of reality (in this second volume of *The Open Society*, with which we are concerned here, Nietzsche is scarcely mentioned). Are we to abandon our usual procedure and dispense with any critical examination of the constantly assumed reasonableness of reason and reality of reality? Are we not to attempt a rational answer particularly to this basic question, while attaching so much importance to rational thinking, logical arguments and conclusions from experience in much more trivial matters?

"For me, rationalists ought to be more rational," we might say, to vary appropriately a well-known Barthian saying. If we are more rational than the rationalists, we shall simply not describe such a fundamental decision as "irrational," as we shall make clear at a later stage. For the time being, it is sufficient to observe that even the rationalist cannot evade the "choice," the "option," the "decision," between trust in reason and mistrust of reason, between fundamental trust and fundamental mistrust.

It has now become clear that the fundamental decision is a venture of freedom. But freedom does not mean irrational, random choice. Because the fundamental reaction is free, it by no means follows that it is a matter of indifference what choice is made. Neither does the possibility of a variety of fundamental decisions, fundamental approaches, fundamental attitudes, mean that they are all equally irrelevant. Not every direction is the right one. But we reach the decisive point when we ask: Which direction is the right one?

# II. Fundamental mistrust or fundamental trust

Right up to the time of his breakdown, Nietzsche was looking for an Ariadne to lead him out of life's labyrinth. Is there really no answer, even for the victims, to the prospect of disaster? Another approach has been suggested in our own times:

> I don't know Who—or what—put the question, I don't know when it was put. I don't even remember answering. But at some moment I did answer Yes to Someone—or Something—and from that hour I was certain that existence is meaningful and that, therefore, my life, in self-surrender, had a goal.
>
> From that moment I have known what it means "not to look back," and "to take no thought for the morrow."
>
> Led by the Ariadne's thread of my answer through the labyrinth of Life, I came to a time and place where I realised that the Way leads to a triumph which is a catastrophe, and to a catastrophe which is a triumph, but the price for committing one's life would be reproach, and that the only elevation possible to man lies in the depths of humiliation. After that, the word "courage" lost its meaning, since nothing could be taken from me.

The words are by Dag Hammarskjöld, Secretary General of the United Nations, written at Pentecost 1961, four months before his death, on the Congo border, when carrying out a peace mission.[1] The fundamental alternative, already visible in Nietzsche's early work, here receives a fundamentally different answer.

## 1. Confrontation

In order to speak completely unambiguously at this central point of our discussion, we shall first of all set out the two positions antithetically. At the same time, we have no intention of dividing people into sheep and goats or of making a moral judgment on their decision for or against reality. That is to say, the fundamental alternative between Yes or No to uncertain reality is not *a priori* to be identified with the moral alternative phrased in such expressions as "love explaining everything" or "selfishness obscuring all clarity"; "a will loving and sincere and a mind clear and serene" or "obstinacy and blindness"; "chivalrous, idealistic high-mindedness" or "selfish and distrustful mean-mindedness." These expressions are found literally in *Ungewissheit und Wagnis* ("Uncertainty and Risk"), by Peter Wust,[2] the Catholic philosopher, who also makes an insidious appeal to the "bright radiance of objective evidence" and "what we might call the curtained window of our mind." Admittedly, Wust was analyzing the basic alternative of "primordial trust" and "primordial mistrust" at a time when most Catholic neoscholastics and even most psychologists showed no understanding of the depths of the problems of uncertainty and risk.[3] We do not intend here, however, to deal with the psychological genesis of fundamental trust and fundamental mistrust or to analyze the process of decision primarily in psychological terms. Although psychological and moral aspects will be involved in what follows, any moralizing or psychologizing of the basic problems would be wrong. Here, first of all, the alternative must be brought out in a fundamental confrontation.

## No to reality

We begin with the negative fundamental attitude. What does fundamental mistrust mean? What is the meaning of primordial mistrust, mistrust of life, mistrust of being, mistrust of reason? In the first place, here is a concise answer, to be followed by a more detailed explanation:

- *Fundamental mistrust means that a person in principle says No to the uncertain reality of himself and the world, closing his eyes to reality, without being able to maintain this attitude consistently in practice. This negative fundamental attitude implies a nihilistic fixation on the nullity of reality and an abysmal uncertainty in regard to all human experience and behavior.*

Three aspects can be seen:

a. *Man is not by nature inclined to say* No. Something in him, he himself, resists a fundamentally negative decision. He has to overcome his resistance. For, as such, his eye is meant to see, his intellect to know, his will to strive. Man is not by nature blind to a fundamental identity, meaningfulness and value of the uncertain reality of himself and the world; he is not against accepting the existent as being instead of mere appearance. And even a bitter protest against reality is often a way of clinging to this reality.

But man is nevertheless free, free even to say No. The challenge of skepticism and the temptation to nihilism are genuine and serious. They are based, as we saw, on the fact that it is possible to concentrate on the thoroughgoing uncertainty of reality. Despite the inclination of his reason and despite the openness of his existence, man can stubbornly and willfully close his eyes to the reality of himself and the world and explain the existent as mere appearance. He can take the risk of a fundamental mistrust of life, reason, reality as a whole; he may have no trust in the course of things but only what Nietzsche called a "nihilist's faith."

b. *Reality remains closed against fundamental mistrust.* That is one possibility. I can react negatively. I can encounter uncertain reality with a fundamental mistrust and then recognize no genuine being in myself, in the world, in the existent at all. I then see only the nullity of reality: under its appearance, not being but nonbeing. Thus—despite all possible admissions in detail—I say No in principle to uncertain reality. In this fundamental mistrust, what becomes apparent to me is nullity instead of reality:

absolute disunion instead of identity, reality as chaos;
absolute meaninglessness instead of meaningfulness, reality as absurdity;
absolute worthlessness instead of value, reality as illusion.

And even for my own uncertain existence, what is apparent is the triumph of nullity over reality:
of fate and death over identity;
of emptiness and meaninglessness over meaningfulness;
of sin and failure over the value of my life.

Thus the uncertain reality to which I completely close my mind shows me only its nullity. Reality is closed up against my mistrustful fundamental attitude, which in fact determines my whole experience and behavior. This, then, is the doubtful venture of fundamental mistrust, the result of which is that I am fixed in a nihilistic attitude. In my stubbornness and willfulness, I enter into the abyss of *uncertainty*, into the forlornness of doubt, the fear arising from despair, against which even apathy, irony and heroic defiance cannot prevail.

c. *The No cannot be consistently maintained in practice.* Certainly it can be said that everything is absurd, but individual steps are reasonable. But a trust in the individual case is not consistent with mistrust in principle. How can it be meaningful to take a single step if the whole journey is absurd? This alone shows that the No cannot be consistently maintained in practice. If someone as a nihilist chooses nothingness, in practice he must be continually making inroads on being. If someone wants to live as a nihilist, he cannot live on nothing either corporeally or mentally. Even the most mistrustful person must be trustful from time to time. And the author who writes about the absurdity of being still lives—among other things—on his literary fees. There are even many people who live not only in but on absurdity. The bad compromises of nihilism and the fundamental discrepancy between theory and practice, despite all irony and all defiance, are unavoidable. There is a certain tragicomedy about all this, which makes a truth out of absurdity and also displays the characteristics of what Sartre called *mauvaise foi:*[4] an illogical, inconsistent, distorted existence.* Does not the No to uncertain reality thus clearly appear as a pseudopossibility?

## Yes to reality

Now, by contrast, we have the positive fundamental attitude. What does fundamental trust mean? What is the meaning of primordial trust, trust in life, trust in being, trust in reason? Here, too, in the first place, is a concise answer:

- *Fundamental trust means that a person, in principle, says Yes to the uncertain reality of himself and the world, making himself open to reality and able to maintain this attitude consistently in practice. This positive fundamental attitude implies an antinihilistic fundamental certainty in regard to all human experience and behavior, despite persistent, menacing uncertainty.*

Again three aspects can be seen:

a. *Man is by nature inclined to say Yes.* He is not indifferent in regard to such a decision. Placed between chaos and cosmos, between absurdity and intelligibility, between value and lack of value, between being and nonbeing, I find that I am handicapped. Naturally I would like to see, to understand, to strive, to be successful and happy. I am drawn toward being. Reality itself—the reality of the world and myself—has an effect on me. Its identity, meaningfulness and value are thrust on me.[5]

But I remain free. I can say No, can stifle all trust with skepticism, can obstinately and willfully close my eyes to reality. Without willingness there is no understanding, without openness there is no reception. And even if I say Yes, the temptation to say No persists.

b. *Fundamental trust makes us open to reality.* This is the other possibility. I can react positively. I can encounter uncertain reality with a fundamental trust and then recognize genuine being in myself, in the world, in the existent as such. I then see reality despite all nullity, being and not nonbeing behind all sham. Thus, without cheap optimism, I say in principle Yes to uncertain reality. In this fundamental trust, despite nullity, reality becomes apparent to me:

---

* Philip Mairet translates this term by "self-deception," as generally "preferable to the literal meaning of the words." It is a question of the "contradiction of the self by itself." (*Existentialism and Humanism,* Introduction, p. 16.)

despite all disunion a concealed identity, reality as one;
despite all meaninglessness a concealed meaningfulness, reality as true;
despite all worthlessness a concealed value, reality as good.

And even for my own uncertain existence, despite all nullity, reality is apparent:
identity despite fate and death;
meaningfulness despite emptiness and meaninglessness;
the value of my life despite sin and self-rejection.

Thus, uncertain reality, to which I am completely open, throughout all nullity shows its reality to me. Reality reveals itself to my trusting fundamental attitude, which in fact determines my whole experience and behavior. This, then, is the hopeful venture of fundamental trust, the result of which is that I am open to the world and man. Despite all menacing uncertainties, I gain a *fundamental certainty*, which doubt and fear, and even nihilism, can challenge but cannot conquer against my will. I alone can withdraw my Yes.

c. *The Yes can be consistently maintained in practice.* While the No to reality gets entangled in ever greater contradictions, the Yes—as acceptance of uncertain reality—can survive and endure throughout all trials. It is quite possible to combine fundamental trust with mistrust in the individual case. For fundamental trust can also accept the element of truth in fundamental mistrust—the nullity of reality—while, on the other hand, fundamental mistrust cannot recognize any element of truth in fundamental trust, any reality in all the nullity. Hence the attitude of fundamental trust, and this alone, is open to reality in its uncertainty. Certainly a fundamental trust cannot be maintained without continual difficulties and doubts, without danger of embitterment and disappointment, but in continual fidelity to the fundamental decision that has been made. Obviously reality does not reveal itself abruptly, but only step by step; being is seen through the veil of nothingness. But reality continually makes possible a new stand and a new start. In this sense, fundamental trust means hope, not just this or that particular hope but a *fundamental hope* sustained through all disappointments, which is the condition of the possibility of truly human life and the opposite pole to despair.

## No stalemate

By comparing the three aspects in each case, it has become clear that we cannot speak of a stalemate between Yes and No, fundamental trust and fundamental mistrust. By nature, man is inclined not to the No but to the Yes, which reveals reality to him instead of closing it up and which can also be maintained consistently in practice. But the confrontation may now be brought to a head by the observation that *an essential reason-*

ableness, an essential rationality, is proper to fundamental trust. At this point, we would like to take a further step—one that is of interest perhaps not only to specialists—on the way to an epistemological explanation of the foundations.

What is meant by *essential rationality?* A distinction must be made here. We must not oversimplify and deny any sort of reasonableness or rationality to fundamental mistrust. For even mistrust starts out, not unreasonably, from the indisputable uncertainty of reality. But in the light of this starting point, this beginning, we can speak only of an initial and in this sense contingent (or accidental), even *feigned rationality* on the part of fundamental mistrust. For, in its realization, fundamental mistrust persists in this uncertainty, which in itself is bound to appear as absolute chaos, absurdity and illusion, which of its nature cannot permit the emergence of any reasonableness at all, cannot permit the appearance of any essential rationality. We saw that to anyone who regards reality merely with mistrust, its identity, meaning and value will not be revealed. An *essential* rationality can be made possible only by reality itself as it is revealed—this, too, we have seen—in fundamental trust. If someone regards reality trustfully in principle, it will reveal to him identity, meaning and value. That is why an *essential* rationality belongs to fundamental trust. We can therefore formulate a thesis to be discussed more closely in what follows:

- *Fundamental trust manifests its essential reasonableness in its realization. Such a positive fundamental attitude is rationally justifiable.*

This does not mean that we are now taking back what we conceded—because we had to concede it—to nihilism. The fact remains that nihilism, fundamental distrust, cannot be shaken by rational arguments. It rests on a fundamental decision and cannot—as explained—be refuted rationally. By comparison, fundamental trust is never unassailable by rational arguments or firmly secured against crises.

Nevertheless, as we explained as against Popper, this fundamental trust is *by no means irrational.* This is linked with the character of the choice. The fundamental choice does not lie between two equal possibilities. The choice is not between red and green, or even between white and black, but as it were between light and nonlight, brightness and complete darkness. Nor is it the famous choice of Hercules at the crossroads. For here a choice has to be made not between vice and virtue, inclination and duty, but between being and not-being. Not-being, however, is neither a reality nor a (real) possibility, but unreality and a (certainly conceivable) impossibility. Yet (and this is the enigma of human freedom) the choice of this unreality and impossibility is possible, albeit with contradictory consequences. Hence the fundamental decision is not a choice between two equal possibilities, but—seen more closely—one between reality and a possible impossibility. Anything, therefore, but a stalemate.

If, then, I do not close my eyes to uncertain reality but lay myself open to its influence; if I do not evade the being in the appearance, but take the risk of yielding and surrendering, I perceive *not before, nor indeed only afterward*, but simply by doing it, that I am doing what is right, what is most reasonable. For what cannot be proved or experienced in advance (in that sense, there is neither argument nor experience) I experience *in the very act of trusting*. The existent manifests being as long as I do not blind myself to it. In all its uncertainty, reality reveals itself and manifests its identity, meaningfulness and value. And at the same time, in all the uncertainty even of my own reason, I experience the fundamental reasonableness of my reason. I thus perceive the reasonableness of reason not as a premise *before* my decision (in this, Popper is right), nor even as a consequence *after* my decision (here Popper is wrong), but *in the realization* of my decision. How can this reasonableness, this rationality, of fundamental trust in its realization be more closely defined?

We cannot but agree with Hans Albert (here following Popper) when he says that a "substantiation" in the strictly logical sense (in accordance with the methodological principle of sufficient reason) is lacking in the Cartesian fundamental question of the foundation of our knowledge. It is impossible "to go back with the aid of logical methods—that is, with the help of logical arguments—to secure and therefore indubitable reasons" as a basis of our knowledge and action.[6] Here Albert rightly invokes Pascal against Descartes.[7] For if someone demands a logical justification for *everything*, he must either be continually looking back and asking for the causes of the causes (in an infinite regress) or be going around in circles and assuming as justified the very principle that needs justification (in a vicious circle), or he must break off the process of justification and declare an intuition marked by evidence (in experience of one kind or another) to be the Archimedean point of knowledge; this last alternative amounts to dogmatism, a dogmatic assertion the truth of which is supposed to be certain and to have no need of justification. In a word, if anyone tries to justify everything strictly logically, if he wants (deductively, inductively or transcendentally) to provide himself with rational support, to be free of all doubt, he will land himself in the Münchhausen trilemma from which he cannot raise himself by his own bootstraps. This means for us:

● *The trusting Yes in principle to uncertain reality is not supported by any external rationality. I cannot establish objectively, as it were from outside, the foundation of my positive fundamental attitude. To begin with, there is nothing that can be shown to be obvious or reasonable that might, then, guarantee the foundation of my trust and make it beyond all doubt. There simply is nothing of this kind, nothing that could be assumed as the Archimedean point of thought. For, since it is a question of reality as a whole—that is, of the totality of all that exists—outside which there is nothing but nothingness itself, all external argu-*

*ments are ruled out. And any attempt at a rational demonstration of the Yes in principle to the fundamental reasonableness of my reason, implicit in the Yes to reality, can end only in a vicious circle. The reasonableness of reason can actually be accepted only in a resolute trust, to which there is always the alternative of fundamental mistrust.*

"Decide," says Wolfgang Stegmüller;[8] Karl Popper speaks of "faith in reason."[9] Long before this, Hegel had demanded "faith in reason, trust and faith in oneself . . . , courage of truth, faith in the power of the Spirit, . . . as the first condition of philosophical study."[10] But why is this decision not, as Popper thinks, irrational? The problem of the Archimedean point of all knowledge can be described (with Albert also against Popper) as a problem wrongly stated. The impossibility of a logical justification, however, does not mean (with Popper against Albert) that the problem of the reasonableness of reason may be evaded. For Albert's "idea of critical examination"[11] itself presupposes—as Popper rightly sees—a trust in reason. Although we cannot attempt a logical justification of fundamental certainty, we are not dispensed from the obligation of rendering a rational account of it. The rational foundation of our fundamental certainty can be perceived in the light of reality itself in fundamental trust, without being caught in the trilemma mentioned above. If I commit myself trustingly to reality despite its uncertainty, I am not simply questioning in a circle, nor am I continually going farther back with my questions, nor do I dogmatically assume anything as obvious. I neither have recourse to an ultimate indubitable datum nor take an intuition to be revelation. My process of knowing does not come suddenly to an end at this point, leaving me free from all doubt. On the contrary, I must constantly take into account the persistent uncertainty of reality, while nevertheless committing myself to it in all its uncertainty; in this very way, I experience, I know, the reality of reality and the reasonableness of reason. For us, this means:

● *The trustful Yes in principle to uncertain reality is distinguished by an intrinsic rationality. I can experience the firm foundation of my fundamentally positive attitude to reality. For reality manifests itself throughout all uncertainty and permits my fundamental trust in it (not blind confidence) to be seen as justified. In other words, in my very trust in being—which is not mere credulity—in the midst of all the real menace of the nullity of being, I experience being and with it the fundamental justification of my trust. Likewise, in my trust in reason—which, again, is not credulity—and in the confident use of reason, despite all the real menace of unreason, I experience the fundamental reasonableness of reason. Like other basic experiences (for example, love and hope), the basic experience of trust is apparent only in its realization, through practice. It is only in the realization that I experience the justification of my Yes to (persistently uncertain) reality.*

Hence it is a question here not—as Albert fears—of a self-fabricated and thus worthless security, turned into a dogma, assumed to be immune from any possible criticism and supposed from the outset to be assured against the risk of failure. There is no question of replacing knowledge by sheer decision or of defending irrational decisions. But this is not a reason for dispensing with the critical examination of the foundations of our knowledge. We simply must not—as Albert thinks—"sacrifice the quest for certainty and put up with permanent uncertainty."[12] It simply is not the case that "the striving for certainty and the quest for truth are in the last resort mutually exclusive."[13] This kind of "pseudocritical antidogmatism," as Albert has to admit, "includes a complementary dogmatism within itself"; his critical rationalism lacks "internal consistency."[14]

- *Thus my fundamental trust turns out to be a trust based on reality itself and thus justified at the bar of reason, a trust that does not guarantee from the outset any obvious, self-fabricated security, but a certainty which dawns upon a person in the very act of trusting.*
- *The fundamental Yes to reality, then, can be defined more precisely as a trust neither rationalistically demonstrable nor irrationalistically unverifiable, but more than reasonable—that is,* superrational—*and which for that very reason is a* rationally accountable, *not unreasonable but completely* reasonable *risk, which, however, always remains a risk.*
- *Consequently there is a middle way between an irrational "uncritical dogmatism" and a "critical rationalism" that also, in the last resort, rests on irrational foundations: the way of critical rationality.*

Both "uncritical dogmatism" and "critical rationalism" are inadequate to meet the challenge of nihilism. In practice, anyway, all arguments against nihilism are of very limited value. What is directly helpful is only trust practiced by each person for himself and continually undertaken afresh. However useful the theories and however helpful exercises on dry land may be, I can learn to swim only in the water: I must take the not irrational but utterly rationally justifiable risk and commit myself to the insecure watery element that will sustain me if I allow myself to be sustained. Similarly, against nihilism, living testimony to reality can be indirectly helpful. If another person despite all uncertainty says Yes to reality and lives out convincingly his positive fundamental attitude, he can rouse in me a willingness for the same fundamental trust. The risk taken by the other person is an invitation to me to take the same risk, just as the person who jumps first into the water shows that it will also sustain me. Of course each individual must himself swim. The risk undertaken by the other person does not relieve me of taking my own risk.

Thus it is now finally clear that there can be no talk of a real stalemate situation, that a Yes or a No cannot be a matter of indifference. Instead of the rationally unaccountable risk of an ultimately irrational and not consistently sustainable fundamental trust, the Yes to reality is the rationally accountable risk of a superrational and consistently sustainable fundamental trust. To quote Dag Hammarskjöld again:

> *You dare your Yes—and experience a meaning.*
> *You repeat your Yes—and all things acquire a meaning.*
> *When everything has a meaning, how can you live anything but a Yes?*[15]

But does this mean that fundamental trust is the great, positive achievement that man has to produce?

## Gift and task

Trust cannot be extorted. For my own part, I give my trust to another person, but only because the latter inspires trust in me. How is this reciprocity to be understood, in interpersonal trust, in fundamental trust?

Niklas Luhmann, interpreting trust against the background of his functional theory of systems, purely sociologically as "a mechanism of reduction of social complexity," rightly sees the problem of interpersonal trust as a "problem of hazardous advance concession."[16] Trust implies a pledge, a venture, a risk. Personal trust, he thinks, "cannot be demanded. It has to be given. Relations of trust consequently cannot be prepared by demands, but only by advance concessions, by the fact that the initiator himself accords trust."[17] But, for my own part, can I give my trust to another person if the latter does not seem trustworthy? The other must make my trust possible by his own trustworthiness.

Similarly, *fundamental trust*—which implies much more than Luhmann's "trust in systems" (reliance on the functioning of system mechanisms and institutional structures such as money, political power, truth[18]) —includes a pledge, a venture, a risk. But neither can fundamental trust be simply agreed, willed, produced, made. *Reality itself must make my trust possible* despite all uncertainty. And in fact:

It is uncertain reality itself which invites and challenges me to commit myself in principle to it and to rely upon it; to believe that it sustains me and to trust it; to accept its reliability and trustworthiness and to declare my trust in it.

It is with uncertain reality itself that the initiative lies—so to speak—to manifest to me its concealed identity, meaningfulness and value and thus at the same time the concealed identity, meaningfulness and value of my own existence.

It is uncertain reality itself which thus creates a basis of trust for the relationship of trust and which can make possible a certain atmosphere of trust, a genuine familiarity or sense of security.

● *Fundamental trust is* a gift. *Reality is given to me from the start: if I commit myself trustingly to it, I get it back filled with meaning and*

*value. My own existence is given to me from the start: if I commit my-*
*self trustingly to it, I can experience the meaning of my life. My reason,*
*too, is given to me from the start: if I commit myself trustingly to it, I*
*can experience its reasonableness. And my freedom is given to me from*
*the start: if I commit myself trustingly to it, I can experience it as real.*

Like Gabriel Marcel in France,[19] the Tübingen philosopher and educationist *Otto Friedrich Bollnow*[20] has made greater efforts than others to
overcome a one-sidedly heroic, hopeless existentialism. Under the
influence of the life philosophy of F. H. Jacobi and W. Dilthey and of
the argument both with Heidegger and H. Lipps and with Sartre and
Camus, Bollnow has worked out with his students[21] the anthropological
significance of trust—all too rarely considered[22]—as counterbalance to
fear and anxiety.[23] It was Bollnow, too, in the course of his anthropological study, who insisted on the character of fundamental trust as something given. How is trust in life and the world, now largely lost, to be restored to modern man? "It is of no avail for a person to attempt with all
his will power to bring it about. And the more desperately he strives to do
so, the more it eludes him and becomes unattainable, only to return when
he least expects it. This universal trust in life is like a mood that comes
over a person and fills his life with gladness, revealing meaning and value
where previously there seemed to be only the empty desert of absolute
pointlessness. He is filled with a new sense of security in life. . . . This
new trust is like a gift that accrues to the person. It might almost be possible to speak of a favor or a grace, as long as the term is used only very
cautiously to describe the phenomenon of trust coming upon a person
without being produced by him and as long as no attempt is made to go
beyond this and provide a dogmatic interpretation."[24] In a later chapter,
however, this character of fundamental trust as gift, favor or grace will be
considered more closely; not dogmatically, but certainly theologically.

A second point must be considered immediately if misunderstandings
are to be avoided: *What comes as a gift to man must be turned into a*
*task of man.* To quote Bollnow once more: "Real trust, however, must be
seized, and man must accept the risk that is irrevocably contained in it. In
this respect, man must exert himself. . . . Of course, it is a virtue of a
special kind, one that cannot be produced by man's deliberate effort, but
in which something is added to this effort, coming to it as a gift, where—
that is—effort and gift interpenetrate one another in an indissoluble
way."[25] Some of Bollnow's statements with reference to that "gladdening
mood that comes upon man" may strike people today as too optimistic,
too emotional, too unpolitical. All this may seem as remote as that "unbroken world" (*heile Welt*) of the poet Werner Bergengruen (used as
the title of a volume of poems in 1952), who, together with Rilke, was
left out of the new edition of Bollnow's *Neue Geborgenheit* in 1972 as
"not typical of later developments" and replaced by a section on Ernst

Bloch's *Prinzip Hoffnung*. One thing can never be too clearly understood today:

- *Fundamental trust is a task. Fundamental trust in uncertain reality, in my existence, in my reason and in my freedom, must be proved in practice. Fundamental trust as risk does not permit any flight into the atmosphere and idyll of an unbroken world. Precisely because of the uncertainty of reality, there is required both a critique and a change of those social conditions that are continually shaking afresh men's trust in the solidity of their institutions, authorities and systems, and often make fundamental trust itself seem dubious. What we had to say in connection with Marx need not be repeated here.*[26]

The decision for persistently uncertain reality therefore may *not* be understood as *taken once and for all*. If someone says No, he can later say Yes; and also, if someone says Yes, he can later say No. Even fundamental trust, then, is always threatened, can be revised, must be ratified, sustained, lived, acquired, endured, against all pressing doubts, in new situations, by a new decision. Trust in reality, once declared, can be revoked. There is no unquestionable security. Throughout his life, man remains fixed in the indissoluble opposition between trust and despair, hope and hopelessness. "To be, or not to be: that is the question," and not only in the situation of the prince of Denmark hesitating in face of death.[27] In face of the dubiousness of the world, of society, of time—"The time is out of joint"—the responsibility lies with man, "born to set it right."[28]

## 2. Concretion

What has been explained hitherto in terms of a basic confrontation will now be given more concrete shape in various respects after considering a number of scientific conclusions. We should never come to an end, of course, if we were to get involved in the many studies in psychotherapy that mention trust directly or indirectly[29] or in the variety of studies from the social, behavioral and educational sciences that deal with trust in the sphere of interpersonal relationships.[30] And in the present context it would not be worthwhile to go into the demand by Wolfgang Klafki, even in educational theory, for "operationalizing," which is supposed to make the phenomenon of trust (genesis and structure, assumptions and effects) measurable for the purposes of empirical investigation and verification; previous attempts, as Claus Narowski persuasively explains,[31] started out from an inadequate notion of trust, did not use unambiguous indicators of measurability and made the whole possibility of operationalizing phenomena like trust seem very dubious.

It might, however, be worthwhile first of all to give concrete expression to fundamental trust *from the standpoint of development psychology*, in order later to explicate it in epistemological terms. Although at first we had to carry out strictly the fundamental confrontation between the two possible reactions to uncertain reality, there was no question in this respect of an arbitrary conceptual construction or of speculation impossible to verify in experience. However much a complete psychologizing of the two attitudes had to be avoided at that point, it is all the more important now to examine the psychological aspects particularly of fundamental trust. Consequently we have to ask two questions: From the psychological standpoint, how does fundamental trust arise in man? How far is it and how far does it remain important for man throughout life?

## On the emergence of fundamental trust in the young child

Fundamental trust is not something that is simply waiting to be picked up by man. As we learned, it is a gift and not to be taken for granted. But it is not a gift that drops straight down from heaven and overpowers man. It presupposes the more or less normal physicopsychical development of the person. The psychosomatic preconditions of fundamental trust must be formed in the small child. Three phases can be distinguished.

*Phase I: before birth.* We would be overlooking the cruel reality of life if we did not observe that fundamental trust can arise in a human being only with difficulty or not at all if the child's *innate dispositions* have been impaired. This can happen in a variety of ways: by heredity (damaged genes or chromosomes), by intrauterine influences during pregnancy (if the mother is ill), by influences in the birth process (less as a result of the birth trauma, asserted by Rank but disputed by many, than as a result of organic injuries).

There are two aspects that deserve serious thought. The responsibility of parents for fundamental trust begins long before birth. But also, however carefully parents exercise their responsibility, there are occasions when they cannot prevent the newborn child from being without any basis for human trust, and for some parents the presence of an abnormal child raises and leaves open in a veritably dramatic way the question of the identity, meaning and value of human life.

*Phase II: after birth.* Fundamental trust can also arise only with difficulty and perhaps not at all if the child has been injured in *early infancy* by *psychogenic illnesses.* As early as 1905, in his *Three Essays on the Theory of Sexuality,* Freud had used in this connection the term "choice": for the choice of the people involved in some kind of relationship with the child (father, mother or their substitutes), whom Freud, oriented as he was to the natural sciences, called "objects." Thus Freud created at that time the term "object choice," but without examining empirically the problems of the earliest reciprocal relationships between subject and object, particularly between child and mother. The psychoanalysts were the first to attempt—solely with the aid of the Freudian method of analysis of later phases—a reconstruction of the processes in the infantile phase. René A. Spitz, the American psychiatrist, was the first within the Freudian school to proceed experimentally—instead of by reconstruction—by direct observation of (several hundred) infants (with the aid of tests, films, records and interviews with parents and nurses).[32]

We do not need to go into Spitz's individual statistics, his psychological interpretations and etiological classifications of the psychogenic infantile illnesses (emotional deficiency diseases). But the generally recognized results of his observations are important for the question of fundamental trust. The comparison of babies cared for by the mother with those taken away from the mother and looked after by uninterested and overworked nurses (in a foundling home) shows strikingly the devastating psychical and physical consequences of a partial or total withdrawal of love (emotional deprivation). From the most diverse phenomena, it becomes clear "that the normal mother-child relationships have an effect that goes far beyond bodily needs, sustaining life and providing protection against illness, while the complete withdrawal of love leads to a progressive deterioration. Deterioration in children is directly related to the length of the period of withdrawal of love to which the child is exposed. This clinical picture is described in specialist literature as 'hospitalism' and forms the object of many scientific studies."[33] Depending on the stage of development, Spitz has observed the following disturbances: loss of weight, arrested development, refusal of contact, sleeplessness, rigid facial expression, motor retardation, inability to assimilate food, self-aggression (tearing hair out), up to complete deterioration (marasmus) and death. Hence, according to Spitz, with these neglected children, three developments are possible, all of which—we must conclude—exclude a fundamental trust from the very outset: "They turn the aggression remaining after the withdrawal of love against themselves and die; in the milder cases, normal bodily activity remains, but the free-roaming aggressive drive turns them into imbeciles; if they succeed in avoiding these two fates, they become dissipated youngsters filled with hatred—at the end of this road is crime."[34]

On the other hand, if the mother-child relationship remains intact, the mother or her substitute is then—as has been established meanwhile by many other studies—the decisive agent for mediating reality to the child. For she represents for the child its whole environment, mediates both the optical, acoustical and tactile perceptions and the various emotions, and is thus a decisive factor for all later social relationships. The importance of the emotional climate is empirically demonstrable: "In the first six months of life, supported by its mother's attitude and emotional climate, the child gradually acquires an increasing degree of security. The security, the safety, of its existence forms the springboard from which the rapid development in the second half year can start and the measure of this security determines the pace of the development. The affective signals that the child has received from its mother, their quality, their consistency, the certainty and reliability which these signals convey to the child, guarantee its normal psychical development. These affective signals given by the mother are determined by her unconscious attitude; she is only partially aware of what she is doing."[35] The psychoanalyst Spitz does not speak directly of "trust," but in his later summary he does speak of an "atmosphere of security, which is provided by stable and consistent object relations."[36]

*Phase III:* Even *after the first half year*, the mother-child relationship is of fundamental importance—for the motorial behavior, for the play and exploration behavior, for the social behavior of the child. *Franz Renggli*, the biologist (student of the well-known Basel biologist Adolf Portmann) and psychoanalyst, has recently summarized impressively the diverse and yet parallel conclusions of the behavioral sciences, psychoanalysis and ethnology,[37] and at the same time provided a synthesis of the far-reaching sociocultural consequences of the mother-child relationship in the first year of life. From the studies considered by Renggli, it is clear that the mother provides for the young child what amounts to a secure base or— we might say—a *basis of trust for all exploration of the world.* "When the child is able to crawl, it does not always remain in close contact with its mother but begins to move increasingly away from her, in order to investigate its surroundings or to make contact with other persons. At the same time, distances from the mother become greater in the course of its development; in the second year of life, the child can already move about out of sight of its mother. Nevertheless, from time to time—the intervals of course become longer as it grows older—the child returns to the mother to see that she is still there. This tendency to move away from the mother to explore the surroundings is shown by the child only when the mother is safely present, that is, when it can at any time return to her as its *secure base.* If on the other hand the mother goes away, the child begins to scream: it shows its fear of separation."[38]

With regard to social behavior in the first year of life, H. E. Schaffer and P. E. Emerson have observed certain regularities: a child that has a strong bond with its mother is inclined to establish relationships or even bonds with other people and vice versa.[39] The negative course, according to M. D. S. Ainsworth, means that the less secure the child's bond is with its mother, the more obstacles it finds to forming relationships with other people, since it is wholly occupied with constructing at least a reliable mother relationship.[40]

After at first trustingly opening out to the mother, the young child begins gradually to detach itself from her and to open out to people, things, the world. As the Tübingen pediatrician Alfred Nitschke expresses it: "As the child trustingly opens out in the bond of love with its mother, experiencing a unique sense of belonging to another person, it opens out also as an independent human being to the world. . . . The mother in her loving care for the child provides a realm where everything is trustworthy, reliable, clear. Whatever is included in this realm becomes something belonging to the child, meaningful, alive, familiar, close and accessible. Trust has an enormous power to open a person out. Even things—not only human beings—reveal their nature, their organization, their hidden meaning. It is from this source that the powers of discernment arise, enabling the child to gain access to the world, to people and to things."[41]

From trusting in its mother (or her substitute), in a complex process—we cannot here go into the position of the father[42] or into a number of highly interesting details (for instance, the significance of skin contacts) —the child comes to form an *at first naïve, unquestioning,* but soon continually imperiled *fundamental trust.*[43] But, the longer it continues, the more the child's spontaneous, unquestioning behavior will be jeopardized and, often, shattered. Even at an early stage and increasingly later, serious crises of trust can arise, as is evident—among other things—from the increasing number of suicides on the part of schoolchildren. Also at an early stage, young people today experience failure at school, higher education and life, and may face a hopeless future because of unemployment, betrayed friendships and the first great disappointments in love, failure in their calling, loss of health, the often intolerable burden of existence. Sooner or later, from the unquestioned, uninhibited, spontaneous trust of the child, at first wholly dependent on the mother, through a series of crises, the mature fundamental trust must come to be: the *considered, critical trust* in reality *of the now independent adult.* The more time passes, the less possible it will be, without *a deliberate decision,* to adjust to life, to the world, to reality. This decision must be continually freshly proved and freshly established. Without mature fundamental trust, it is impossible to withstand life's crises.

## Fundamental trust as lifelong task

Reaction to reality occurs in the midst of human existence itself, obviously, however, from the very beginning not in an isolated human existence but constantly afresh *in relationship to another human being.* Which means that this reaction occurs not only in human consciousness (idealist philosophy), nor merely in human existence against the background simply of the universal fellowship of humanity (existentialist philosophy), whether of an anonymous "one" (Heidegger) or even of a negative relationship to our fellow man (Sartre). In order to cope with reality, man needs more than a universal coexistence. He needs a genuine personal "thou," a need to which—according to analyses of the concept of "thou" made by F. H. Jacobi, J. G. Fichte and W. von Humboldt[44]—Feuerbach[45] at an early stage and more recently E. Rosenstock,[46] Ferdinand Ebner,[47] Martin Buber,[48] and Gabriel Marcel[49] have drawn attention. Man needs not only an "it," not only another thing or another person merely as not the self. He needs a "thou," another self, capable of freedom, help, loyalty, goodness, understanding, and becoming "thou" when addressed: a "thou" accepting trust and bestowing it. Certainly, not all human beings can meet together in this way, but everyone must meet some others or at least one other human being in this wholly and entirely personal way if he is continually to gain afresh and also maintain trust in uncertain reality as a whole.

Even for adults, *without trust a decent human life is not possible:* "Trust is the indispensable precondition of all human life. It is only on the basis of a trust that life is possible at all. On the other hand, mistrust makes life grow stale and in the end entirely cease," says Otto Friedrich Bollnow,[50] acutely aware that we are living at a time that is largely—and unfortunately in many ways understandably, as we saw in connection with Marx, Freud and Nietzsche—characterized by a loss of trust: in the field of human relationships, not only in regard to others but also in regard to oneself (with one's disguised will to power, one's sublimated sex drive) and in the end also in regard to the existing social authorities, institutions and structures. Certainly criticism in all fields and especially criticism of society—this should have become clear in the course of this book—is constantly necessary. Nevertheless it is true that, without trust, there can be no common human life, no friendship, love or marriage, nor any psychotherapeutic treatment, no business life, no politics, science or culture. There must be trust in human beings with whom I have to deal, in conditions in which I work, in things on which I must rely, and even trust in grammar, in semantic and grammatical rules, without which language and human understanding are quite impossible. All this, Nietzsche indirectly confirms: "I fear we are not getting rid of God, because we still believe in grammar."[51]

*Maintenance and corroboration of trust:* The adult—no longer a child protected by its mother in a world of unquestioning trust—must continually freshly assert his trust in reality against all pressing doubts and temptations, he must decide afresh for a positive approach to reality. But the trustworthiness and reliability of another person cannot be proved or demonstrated by positive arguments, still less imposed when doubts persist; even the tenderest smile and the most expensive present can be deceptive. Here, too, it is necessary to take a risk, a risk that cannot be commanded but that—this does not need repeating—is not unreasonable and can be rationally justified. I must—so to speak—commit myself by trusting the other person in advance and take the risk of deciding if I am now to offer him, instead of aversion or indifference, trust, sympathy, or even friendship and love. "Trust me, let us trust each other," wrote even Friedrich Nietzsche when he was in love.[52] Apart from taking the risk of an encounter in trust, there is no human knowledge of the ultimate trustworthiness of the other person. But the encounter in trust changes the image of the other person and the image of the world. Trust has power to change, and reality in all its uncertainty is then seen not merely in its weird, threatening aspect but in its sustaining, sheltering, joyful character. That other person therefore is indisputably of decisive importance for the emergence *and* maintenance of human fundamental trust.

From the very beginning, as we saw,[53] psychoanalysis was criticized for seeking the decisive events for the development of the individual exclusively in early childhood. In the later phases of life also, there are decisive turning points; we may recall the recently much-discussed mid-life crisis. As Horst Eberhard Richter, the psychosomatics expert, has recently brought out,[54] a phenomenon such as the fear of isolation noted in small children in connection with hospitalism can be observed and has considerable social consequences in all age groups. Even within the Freudian school, efforts have been made for a long time to correct and supplement the classical teaching. *Erik H. Erikson*, the American psychoanalyst mentioned earlier, has attempted with the aid of epigenetic diagrams to analyze with the greatest possible discrimination the individual phases of human development, in order to describe more comprehensively the "growth and crises of the 'healthy' personality."[55]

For him, the first stage (more or less the first year of life) is essentially the *stage of basic trust*.[56] This basic trust—foundation of the sense of identity—must, however, be maintained afterward in continually new forms *throughout all sociopsychological conflicts:* over and over again, that is, "basic trust versus basic mistrust."[57] This basic approach is one that is shared by Irenäus Eibl-Eibesfeldt, the behavioral scientist and student of Konrad Lorenz, on the development of personal ties and primordial trust: "We display this basic attitude in innumerable situations of ordinary life, whether we are entrusting ourselves to public transport or asking someone for information. In principle, we expect good from our fellow men, and nothing creates more embitterment than disappointed trust. This primordial trust is the precondition for any positive approach to society, for any ability to identify with a community, for any social commitment. The ability to love human beings presupposes the capacity for friendship. In my opinion, this is a point that is not seen clearly by those who—with the highest motives—try to bring about the individual's adaptation to the mass society by preventing at the earliest stage the formation of personal relationships."[58]

For Erikson, basic trust is practically the *cornerstone of the psychologically healthy personality:* "For the first component of a healthy personality I nominate a sense of *basic trust*."[59] What does Erikson mean by this? "An attitude toward oneself and the world derived from the experiences of the first year of life."[60] He describes this basic attitude in these terms: "By 'trust' I mean what is commonly implied in reasonable trustfulness as far as others are concerned and a simple sense of trustworthiness as far as oneself is concerned."[61]

This attitude, established in the mother-child relationship and at first unconscious, becomes fully conscious only in adult crisis situations, in the face of the possibilities of basic mistrust: "When I say 'basic,' I mean that neither this component nor any of those that follow are, either in childhood or in adulthood, especially conscious. In fact, all of these criteria, when developed in childhood and when integrated in adulthood, blend into the total personality. Their crises in childhood, however, and their impairment in adulthood are clearly circumscribed. . . . In adults the impairment of basic trust is expressed in a basic mistrust. It characterizes individuals who withdraw into themselves in particular ways when at odds with themselves and with others. These ways, which often are not obvious, are more strikingly represented by individuals who regress into psychotic states in which they sometimes close up, refusing food and comfort and becoming oblivious to companionship. In so far as we hope to assist them with psychotherapy, we must try to reach them again in specific ways in order to convince them that they can trust the world and that they can trust themselves."[62]

Hence: "It is from the knowledge of such radical regressions and of the deepest and most infantile layers in our not-so-sick patients that we have learned to regard basic trust as the cornerstone of a healthy personality."[63] *Basic mistrust* thus forms a *lifelong counterpoint*: "It is against the combination of these impressions of having been deprived, of having been divided, and of having been abandoned, all of which leave a residue of basic mistrust, that basic trust must be established and maintained."[64] Here everywhere—to take up the slogan of H. E. Richter—it is a question not of "flight" but—particularly in modern society—of "holding one's ground."[65] According to Richter also, a basic trust in Erikson's sense is "indispensable" for the sake of human identity.[66] Andrew M. Greeley, the American sociologist, regards "the absence of trust" as "one of the critical problems in society": "To solve the kinds of problems of prejudice, war and pollution that face the world today, we may well need a new kind of human being, a human being whose strength and confidence are rooted in a strong, supporting network of friendship and who is able both to trust others and to radiate trust among those with whom he interacts."[67]

## 3. Explication

After the confrontation of the two fundamental attitudes to reality and the concretion especially of fundamental trust, we must now go on to the explication. Although they cannot be explained at length, some of the consequences *from the epistemological aspect* will certainly be adequately indicated. Epistemological considerations may appear to some to be far too "theoretical," abstract and unrealistic. But, by starting out in particular from the great problems at the beginning of modern science, from the fundamental questions of Descartes and Pascal, we made clear how eminently "practical," how concrete, even vital, such questions can be. Now it must be time to collect in this connection some important results that have emerged in the course of our lengthy investigations. For the initial question of the *cogito* and the *credo* has not yet been positively answered. Consequently, while interpreting and appropriating the conclusions of competent specialists, we shall first make some comments on the problem of the basis of science as a whole and then on the problem of the basis of ethics:

## Fundamental trust as basis of science

In the course of the dramatic development of the theory of knowledge,[1] *Karl Popper* especially made two things crystal clear. Firstly, that all methodological rules are free "conventions," so to speak, "the rules of the game of empirical science";[2] "thus it is *decisions* which settle the fate of theories."[3] Then, above all, that all rational thinking rests on a choice, a resolution, a decision, an attitude; in a word, on a "faith in reason."[4] But *Rudolf Carnap*, the logical positivist, in his early project of a universal syntax of arbitrarily chosen languages (1934) maintained that the principles and rules of argument of an artificial language are a matter of free "choice" and consequently any other "choice" must be tolerated.[5] "By this method, also, the conflict between the divergent points of view on the problem of the foundations of mathematics disappears."[6] According to Carnap, this "principle of tolerance relates not only to mathematics, but to all questions of logic."[7] "Before us lies the boundless ocean of unlimited possibilities."[8] At the same time, Carnap, citing Moritz Schlick, head of the Vienna Circle, tells us that even *Wittgenstein*, in opposition to his "former dogmatic standpoint, . . . for some time past, in writings as yet unpublished, has agreed that the rules of language may be chosen with complete freedom."[9] In the light of the history of science, *Thomas Kuhn* then showed that the "choice" between scientific theories or paradigms can generally be dependent not on logic and experiment alone but also on psychological and sociological factors. There is a whole "set of commitments without which no man is a scientist," a "strong network of commitments—conceptual, theoretical, instrumental and methodological."[10] Such commitments can be described "as beliefs in particular models."[11] And anyone who gets involved analytically with colloquial language instead of an artificial language must in fact trust in language, grammar and logic, as *W. Kamlah* and *P. Lorenzen* observe: "We begin 'trustingly in the midst' by always speaking from the very beginning and continuing to speak, that is, by using our *colloquial language.* Our skeptical mistrust is directed against *educated language.*"[12] And J. *Habermas,* discussing critical rationalism, admits: "I trust in the power of self-reflection."[13]

This brief account points unmistakably to the central importance of fundamental trust also for the theory of knowledge, a fact that oddly enough is overlooked precisely by such theologians as Pannenberg[14] and Peukert,[15] who are interested in the theory of knowledge. At the same time, the leading representative of analytical philosophy, Wolfgang Stegmüller, who was quoted at the beginning of this chapter, has worked out systematically the importance of "faith" for "knowledge." For him, it was important "to know where the frontier lies at which philosophy ceases to be meaningful. It is the point at which any conceivable theory 'comes to the end of its wisdom' and personal decision must intervene." That is what he wrote in Oxford in 1954 in the preface to *Metaphysik, Skepsis, Wissenschaft* ("Metaphysics, Skepticism, Science").[16] But what is the point at which philosophy "comes to the end of its wisdom"?

In his "New Introduction 1969: after fifteen years," Stegmüller explicitly reacts to the very questions that are of burning interest to us here and expresses himself on the problems of evidence in a way that is surprising for a logician but with which—after all that has been said—we can largely agree. According to him, any evidence or insight rests on a decision of conscience: "On the contrary, it is my opinion precisely *that the problem of whether here and now we are presented with a genuine insight that must be accepted and recognized, can be solved only by a personal decision of my conscience, for which I am responsible only to myself.*"[17] There are questions that cannot be decided "by pure reflection."[18]

The objection may be raised, however, that personal conscience is competent only for ethical questions. According to Stegmüller, this is by no means true: "My personal conscience is the supreme authority not only in *ethical* decisions but also in *apparently* wholly desubjectivized objective, scientific, material questions. This is a decision in the *practical,* nontheoretical sense."[19] But is this not "existentialism"? Stegmüller is not impressed: "In a discussion, I was once faced with the objection: 'By putting a private decision of conscience before *all* scientific reasoning, you are exposing yourself as a disguised existentialist.' There is nothing that I can say against such an objection except *that I do not regard it as an objection.* I would reply: 'If you want to understand *this*—among other things —as a position in existentialist philosophy, then you are merely pointing to a core of truth in this philosophy.' "[20] In fact, we might add, here is the point at which these two great trends of contemporary philosophy meet: existentialist philosophy, with its emphasis on decision, and analytical philosophy (theory of knowledge), with its emphasis on knowledge.

Stegmüller, who thinks he can perceive the mythological origins of the notion of evidence, brings Descartes especially—in addition to Aristotle—into the discussion: In modern times, "the problem in its disturbing vehemence has been perceived most acutely by *Descartes*."[21] Unlike Aristotle, however, Descartes did not emphasize mainly the apodictic (necessary) evidence of universally comprehensible principles of being, but started out from the "primordial" truth of the *cogito*, "*that the problem is insoluble at the human level*." "In order nevertheless to reach something like a solution, he had to put up with the famous *Cartesian circular argument*. In this *theoretically hopeless situation*, he could see only one possibility, which he expressed in these terms: In order to be certain that I am not being deceived by an evil spirit when I am faced with what seems to be evident, I must first of all assure myself that there is a good God who has created me and who has no intention of deceiving me. At the same time, to prove God's existence I must draw on that kind of *unmistakable evidence* of which I can be certain only after making assumptions, *after* I have acquired the knowledge that I was not created by an evil spirit."[22]

In a detailed analysis of the "philosophical foundations of logic and mathematics,"[23] Stegmüller confirms what he has worked out up to that point and states his conclusion in this way: "A 'self-guarantee' of human thought, in whatever field, is excluded. We cannot reach any positive result if we are completely free from presuppositions. We must believe something before we can justify something else."[24]

But Stegmüller sees the problem at the same time in a broader metaphysical framework and there—"at the most decisive point of all our reflections"—states his thesis, which is likewise at first negative: "*The problem of evidence is absolutely insoluble; the question whether there is insight or not is absolutely impossible to decide*."[25] Why? Stegmüller says: "*All arguments for evidence involve a vicious circle and all arguments against it are self-contradictory*."[26] Thus:

If someone argues *for* evidence, he is involved in a circle, since he must assume evidence from the very first moment of his argumentation: "If someone maintains that there is evidence and thinks he is giving reasons for this, he is himself disguising the fact that he is merely expressing his belief in the evidence."[27]

If someone argues *against* evidence, he is contradicting himself, since he, too, must assume that his arguments are evident: "Anyone who fights against it and at the same time likewise offers reasons for his opposition is only expressing his unbelief and belying himself, since he could not even attempt to argue if he really did not believe in evidence."[28]

From these negative findings, there follows Stegmüller's positive conclusion: "We can believe or not believe in insight, but we cannot justify this belief or unbelief unless we mean by 'justifying' producing certain motives for doing or not doing something. It is a 'prerational primordial decision' that has to be made here and in fact on every single occasion when something is supposed to become known."[29]

But is not the problem thus pushed off from the "theoretical" to the "practical" plane, so that "pure whim becomes the supreme arbiter in the question of insight"?[30] Stegmüller's answer is quite unequivocal: "A personal decision of conscience for which I am responsible only to myself is obviously *not* an arbitrary decision."[31] Obviously? We cannot of course be satisfied with this answer. For Stegmüller, here at least, does not suggest any reasons why a wholly personal decision of conscience is not an arbitrary decision. Might not the concept of intrinsic rationality, developed above, give us further help in this respect?

As always, however, we cannot but agree with Stegmüller's final conclusion: "that the problem *cannot be settled* on the basis of *theoretical* reasoning alone."[32] As we distinguished between neoscholastics and nihilists, so Stegmüller places his solution between "the reflection of the theorizers of evidence" and the "arguments of the skeptics."[33] He both confirms and surpasses Kant: "*We must not deny knowledge to make room for faith. Instead we must believe something from the outset in order to be able to talk of knowledge or science at all.*"[34]

All knowledge thus contains a "presupposition" that can be described as a "matter of faith": "The alternative usually understood as 'faith or reason,' implying the distinction between religious experience and scientific knowledge, is misleading."[35] Why?

In *science*, the *hypothesis* is the predominant factor, which must be "believed": "As already stressed, the business of scientific research, especially in the empirical sciences, consists mainly in advancing hypotheses provisionally confirmed up to a point. But, in the formalized disciplines also, in mathematics for instance, the hypothetical factor plays a major role in so far as, on the one hand, we must at first assume that certain propositions are theorems for which a proof can then be discovered and, on the other hand, that when a new system of axioms is advanced, for the time being it can only be assumed hypothetically that the system will not turn out to be contradictory; the assumption holds at least as long as it has not been proved on a 'finite basis' to be free of contradictions (but how rarely is such a proof established!)."[36]

In *religion*, on the other hand, *certainty* is the dominant factor: we "know" this certainty: "On the other hand, every religion has a theoretical content that can be expressed in propositions: 'there is only one God,' 'man has an immortal soul,' and so on. These statements here are by no means hypothetical assumptions but are put forward as certain propositions."[37]

Thus *the relationship between faith and knowledge is more or less reversed:* "In religion things are not 'merely believed' while in science they are 'known,' but on the contrary in science we are mostly content with a hypothetical, provisional belief—even though, as we have recognized, a little must become known—while within religion a great deal that can be expressed in theoretical statements is presented as acquired knowledge. For what is certain is described in ordinary language as knowledge. Hence we could with more justification reverse the above formula and say that in science things are believed, in religion we know (or claim to know)."[38] Do we claim to know? There will be more to be said about this later.

"Belief" or "faith" might be misunderstood here as specifically religious faith, belief in God or even biblical faith in God, and evidently Stegmüller's use of the term has been similarly misunderstood. But, on the other hand, the expressions he used at an earlier stage in this connection—"prerational decision,"[39] "prerational primordial decision,"[40] "prerational primordial resolution"[41]—as he writes himself, have also been misunderstood. We may suggest *instead:* a "rationally justifiable fundamental trust," which possesses an "intrinsic rationality."[42]

Here, however, we may simply note the fact that *Hans-Georg Gadamer,* the most important representative of hermeneutic philosophizing, in his main work, *Wahrheit und Methode,*[43] confirms from quite a different philosophical standpoint the existence of truth and certainty even without method, the existence of prescientific truth as presupposition of all science. Unfortunately, as a result of Gadamer's emphasis on all-embracing understanding, the factors of criticism and of the distinction of true and false are inadequately considered.[44] But even according to Gadamer there is a faith—we would call it trust—that precedes knowledge and science. As he says at the end of his book: "In understanding we are drawn into an event of truth and arrive, as it were, too late, if we want to know what we ought to believe."[45]

## Fundamental trust as basis of ethics

The same problems of the basis with which we dealt theoretically (but not without regard for practice) with reference to human knowledge as a whole can be explained practically (but not without regard for theory) with reference to *human action.* What conclusions can be drawn from the initial position then adopted about man's practical attitude to the same uncertain reality?

After the devastating effects of nihilism on both society and the individual, the decline especially of ethical values and norms,[46] a number of people are asking about these things today with greater awareness than formerly. And this is happening precisely in a democratic, ideologically neutral state which—unlike the totalitarian systems of whatever color —cannot lay down in an official, doctrinaire fashion a meaning of life and a way of life, supreme values and ultimate norms, and yet is dependent on values and norms. The need of commitment can no more be neglected than the question of truth.[47] Consciously or unconsciously, man has an elemental need of basic commitment, of a commitment to meaning, values and norms.

The unparalleled progress of the natural sciences and technology did not—as was widely expected—lead to the waning of this need for meaning, values and norms, but—in view of the increasing problems with technology—to its revival. Our experience is that man today can cope with everything possible . . . except himself. Natural scientists in particular are asking today about the meaning and limits of human achievement, about the meaning and limits also of scientific research and technological realization: "For hundreds of thousands of years, man has evolved in the face of the resistance of his environment, has oriented himself and adapted himself to it. With the decline of this resistance, he falls flat on the ground. . . . The new ethical situation consists in the fact that man in the future will have to struggle less with nature and more with himself. Obviously we can do more than we are permitted to do, and consequently we may not do all that we are able to do. Unfortunately, however, relevant and practicable norms scarcely exist at the present time and no one really wants to do anything about this unpopular business. Even religious bodies have become very reserved about binding statements on a material ethic and refer instead to subjective judgment, to freedom of conscience, overlooking the fact that the closeness of our life together today scarcely permits purely private decisions."[48] If this need is not satisfied—not even in the prepolitical field (religions, churches, groups)— and if nothing and no one provides a basic orientation, an order of values, a commitment to a meaning in life, we shall be threatened by a dangerous nihilistic *vacuum of meaning and norms*, which, after all the experiences of the present century, only very few people want or could want.

Consequently more people are again asking where an orientation can be found in the modern disorientation. Where can orientation be found as insecurity increases with the profusion of information about the most diverse and contradictory systems of values and norms, ideologies, philosophies and theologies, world views and religions, all of which seem to relativize radically one's own moral and religious standpoint? With the many legally guaranteed liberties, where is man's own personal freedom, his self-determination and self-formation, to be found? In the threatening arbitrary pluralism, where can the meaning and purpose of life be found? And particularly in the open (open to learning, open to the future, open to truth), liberal, democratic society, with its free interplay of mental and social forces, where is that minimal agreement to be found in values, norms and attitudes that is absolutely necessary for a decent common life and also for the functioning of a democratic state?[49] If we are not simply to have a subjectivistic license and a nihilism of order, recognizing absolutely everything, where are we to find goals, priorities, ideals, models?[50] If we are not to have an immoral aloofness, beyond good and evil, true and false, where shall we find decisive criteria for true and false, good and evil; where shall we find the ultimate orientation and absolute obligation for all the innumerable, unavoidable, relevant decisions of individual and political life?[51]

But does this mean that *only the believer in God* or even only the Christian *can have* aims and priorities, ideals and models, values and norms, *criteria for true and false, good and evil?* Can only the believer in God or even only the Christian live decently, in a truly human way, or simply morally? Does not man possess a real human autonomy that permits him occasionally even without belief in God to perceive his responsibility in the world? Finally, cannot even the atheist or agnostic have a genuine fundamental trust in reality? To deny this would mean ignoring the realities of our time and many of our contemporaries.

It cannot be denied that there are innumerable scientifically oriented people like *Bertrand Russell*, the English mathematician, philosopher and sociologist, who regarded his life as governed by "three passions, simple but overwhelmingly strong: the longing for love, the search for knowledge, and unbearable pity for the suffering of mankind."[52] In practice he was decidedly on the side of love and not hate, of cooperation and not competition, peace and not war, and precisely as an agnostic—in his book *Why I Am Not a Christian*[53]—expressed his fundamental trust in the form of a belief in "the good life . . . inspired by love and guided by knowledge."[54] He went on to explain this in more detail: "When I said that the good life consists of love guided by knowledge, the desire which prompted me was the desire to live such a life as far as possible, and to see others living it; and the logical content of the statement is that, in a community where men live in this way, more desires will be satisfied than in one where there is less love or less knowledge. I do not mean that such a life is 'virtuous' or that its opposite is 'sinful,' for these are conceptions which seem to me to have no scientific justification."[55]

There are innumerable socially committed people like the unorthodox Marxist philosopher *Ernst Bloch*. He, too, was an atheist who struggled throughout his life to remove the alienation between man and nature, to bring about a juster social order and the humanizing of man. On the very first page of his main work, *Das Prinzip Hoffnung,* he proclaims his fundamental trust in the form of a *docta spes*, a tried and continually tested hope in an antinihilistic, dialectical-materialist sense: "The important thing is to learn to hope. The work of hope does not give up; it is in love with success and not with failure. Hope, which rises above all fear, is neither passive as fear is nor—still less—entrapped in nothingness. Hope is passionately outgoing, it broadens men instead of narrowing them, can never know enough of what they are inwardly seeking or of what may outwardly be making demands on them. The work of hope requires men who can throw themselves actively into what is coming to be, into that of which they are themselves a part. It will not put up with a dog's life, it will not be content to be thrown merely passively into existing reality, into the unexamined or what is barely recognized. Work against fear of life and the stratagems of fear is directed against the causes of these things, largely very easily demonstrable, and it looks in the world itself for what will help the world; this can be found. How rich have been the dreams at all times, the dreams of a better world that might be possible."[56] And the last sentence of the first book runs: "Both human beings and the world carry enough of a good future; no plan is good in itself without this thoroughgoing belief in it."[57]

There are innumerable skeptics like *Albert Camus*, the French writer and philosopher, disappointed equally by Christianity's promises of the hereafter and by the Marxist promises, who nevertheless can express programmatically "beyond nihilism"[58] a fundamental trust in the form of a rebellion. For Camus cannot come to terms with a world "in which children suffer and die."[59] He knows that "we cannot prevent this world from being a world in which children are tortured."[60] But he knows also—being "pessimistic as to human destiny" but "optimistic as to man"—that "we can reduce the number of tortured children."[61] For him, then, "rebellion without claiming to solve everything can at least pretend to do so";[62] it means living for the "humiliated" and in "insane generosity," refusing "injustice."[63] According to Camus, "rebellion cannot exist without a strange form of love": "Its merit lies in making no calculations, distributing everything it possesses to life and to living men. It is thus that it is prodigal in its gifts to men to come. Real generosity towards the future lies in giving all to the present. Rebellion proves, in this way, that it is the very movement of life and that it cannot be denied without renouncing life. Its purest outburst, on each occasion, gives birth to existence. Thus, it is love and fecundity or it is nothing at all."[64] And the men who live this rebellion, according to Camus, "choose, and give us, by their example,* the only original rule of life today: to learn to live and die, and in order to be a man, to refuse to be a god."[65]

Do not these examples show that *fundamental trust can be the basis of an autonomous morality*, however its defenders may choose to follow it in their lives? At any rate, the times are past when theologians thought they could answer all possible questions about what is or is not permissible, peremptorily from the Bible (Protestants) or from human nature (Catholics), as often as possible in set propositions or categorical brief formulas. The problems and conflicts of modern humanity (overpopulation and birth control, economic growth and protection of the environment, appa-

---

* Published translation has "we offer as an example," but the French is *nous donnent*= "give us."

ratus of power and control of power, aggressiveness and sexuality) are too complex, the problems also of interpreting Scripture and of "natural law" are too complex, for us to be able to deduce easily from Scripture or from human nature perennially valid norms of human behavior. We cannot here go into the fundamental problems of justifying ethical norms, intensively discussed by moral philosophers: norms, that is, understood as universally binding rules of human behavior and living together and thus of being authentically human.[66] But—recapitulating what was said earlier[67] —we can now set out with reference to our problems three lines of thought, which, again, take into account the justified concerns of the atheists, especially Nietzsche but also Feuerbach, Marx and Freud.

a. *Today less than ever can we call down from heaven ready-made solutions* or deduce them theologically from an immutable universal essential nature of man. There is in fact what Nietzsche called a "genealogy of morals." From a historical standpoint, concrete ethical norms, values, insights, key concepts, have been formed in a supremely complicated group-dynamical and social-dynamical process—as creations of man. Morality did not drop down from heaven, but—like language is the product of development. When life's needs, human pressures and necessities appeared, then rules of action, priorities, conventions, laws, precepts, directives, customs—in brief, norms—for human action suggested themselves. Continually men have had and still have to test ethical solutions in projects and models and often to practice and prove them over generations. After periods of formation and familiarization, such norms become established and obtain recognition, but—as times change—they may again be eroded and begin to disintegrate.

b. Today more than ever, we have *to look for and work out "on earth" discriminating solutions* for all the difficult problems. We are responsible for our morality. We must start out from our experiences, from the diversity of life, and stick to the facts. Which means that we must obtain for ourselves reliable informations and certain knowledge and at all times make use of relevant arguments, in order to find verifiable aids to decision and in the end to reach practicable solutions. In that sense, we must, like Faust, "remain true to earth." No appeal even to the highest authority can deprive man of his intramundane autonomy: ethical self-legislation and self-responsibility for his self-realization and for the organization of the world.

c. Today more than ever, we must examine with as little prejudice as possible, *in accordance with strict scientific methods*, the manifold, changeable and complex reality of man and society with reference to its objective laws and future possibilities. Certainly scholars are not the only ones who can act ethically. Prescientific awareness of certain ethical norms obviously retains its fundamental importance even today. And many people in a particular situation spontaneously "do the right thing" without ever having read a treatise on moral theology or moral philosophy. Nevertheless, modern life has become too complex for a naïve blindness to reality to permit us to ignore the scientifically assured empirical data and insights when defining concrete ethical norms (for instance with reference to economic or political power, sexuality, aggressiveness). This is something to which we continually drew attention in connection with Marx and Freud. There can be no ethics as a science today therefore without close contact with the human sciences: with psychology and psychoanalysis, with social criticism and sociology, with behavioral science, biology, history of civilization and philosophical anthropology. The human sciences offer an increasing abundance of assured anthropological knowledge and information relevant to action: verifiable aids to decision, which of course cannot replace the establishment of ultimate foundations and norms of the human ethos.

If ethics is no longer based on a system of eternal, rigid, immutable norms, handed down and simply passively accepted, and there is now a conscious attempt to start out from concrete, dynamic, complex reality, then it presupposes this one thing: an assent to uncertain reality; despite all criticism in details, a *basic attitude of trust in principle* to this reality *as a foundation for all man's ethical behavior and action* in this reality. Hence:

● *Any acceptance of meaning, truth and rationality, of values and ideals, priorities and preferences, models and norms, presupposes a* funda-*mental trust in uncertain reality: by contrast with nihilism, an assent in principle to its fundamental identity, meaningfulness and value despite all discordance, meaninglessness and worthlessness; an assent in principle also to the fundamental rationality of human reason despite all unreason.*

From all this is it not clear how important are the consequences of fundamental trust for the justification of binding normative rules of human behavior? How fundamental is this trust for human action and for living together? How necessary for the *justification of ethical norms?*[68] These consequences may be briefly indicated:

● *Only if the reality of the world and man, as accepted in fundamental trust, is characterized by an ultimate identity, meaningfulness and value, can individual norms of genuinely human behavior and action be deduced in an appropriate way from this reality and—decisively—from the essential human needs, pressures and necessities, as they can be experienced in ordinary life and ascertained scientifically and empirically in a new way today with the aid of the human sciences.*

● *Such norms are of course neither purely logical propositions nor state-*

*ments of pure experience. Neither in general nor in particular are they purely rationally transparent, but only on condition of a positive, trustful approach of the whole person to reality as a whole and to man in particular. To a nihilist, on the contrary, the logic of their claim is neither ascertainable nor obvious.*

Assuming man's trusting acceptance of his existence, what, then, is the *basic norm of an autonomous human morality?*[60] At first, in negative terms:

*Good* is certainly not simply that which is accepted always and everywhere: neither traditionality nor universality solely in itself is a binding norm for man. The "good old rule" has often turned out to be antihuman.

*Good*, however, is not simply that which produces something new and special. Neither novelty nor originality solely in itself is a binding norm for man. What has been extolled as new has often turned out to be likewise antihuman. Now, in positive terms:

- Good *for man is that which—whether old or new, widespread or not— helps him to become truly man. The autonomous basic norm is that man should be man. Man should realize his being as man. Man should live humanly. That is morally good, therefore, which makes human life in its individual and social dimensions in the long run successful and fulfilled, which makes possible an optimal development of the person at all levels and in all dimensions. Consequently man should live his humanity at all levels (including the level of instinct and feeling) and in all dimensions (including his relatedness to society and to nature).*
- *In the light of this basic norm, it is possible for man, endowed with reason,* to distinguish between good and evil *and in both the individual and social spheres also to test by experience:*
  *ways, norms, structures, deeds, that* promote *man's identity, significance and value and thus enable him to* gain *a meaningful and fruitful existence;*
  *ways, norms, structures, deeds, that* prevent *man from achieving his identity, significance and value and thus deprive him of a meaningful and fruitful existence.*

From all this, the autonomy of the moral sphere should be clear in its concrete forms. A person should not simply realize an external principle or a universal norm but himself at all levels and in all dimensions and in this very way contribute to the self-realization of other human beings. Particularly within the ethical field, my self-realization and the self-realization of the other person and also our common responsibility for the world are indissolubly connected. It is precisely here—as we indicated—that fundamental trust is gift and task, basis and goal of human action. The appeal to fundamental trust implies also an element of *ideological criticism* of the social conditions that render impossible the creation of fundamental structures of interpersonal trust (in politics, at work, in the family).[70] We can recapitulate:

- *Man's self-realization, his becoming human and the humanizing of society are possible only on the basis of a positive attitude in principle to the uncertain reality of world and man. Only if man's self-realization and the humanizing of society are regarded as equally urgent tasks will this attitude be more than a congenial ideology hostile to change. The acceptance of autonomous norms of the human is thus the ethical expression of fundamental trust in the identity, significance and especially the value of the uncertain reality of world and man. Without this fundamental trust, autonomous ethical norms cannot be accepted as meaningful and justified.*

Hence: *no ethics without fundamental trust.* But does this also mean: *ethics based solely on fundamental trust?* We have seen that ethical behavior based solely on fundamental trust *is possible*, and believers in God in particular should not deny this for apologetic reasons. Human beings who live uprightly without belief in God can be a very salutary challenge to the faith of some believers in God; the latter should not misinterpret the virtues of pagans as the later Augustine did, calling them "splendid vices" although he had praised them and lived in the same way in his early years. Today it is obvious to anyone that there are upright men even outside the Church. There are good people who do not believe in God. There are atheists and agnostics of a liberal, Marxist, positivist or of any other type who try to live not nihilistically but in an authentically human way, that is, humanely and in this sense wholly ethically and morally. If they themselves reject belief in God, this does not mean that we can deny their fundamental trust, on the basis of which they try to live humanly and morally.

Only in the light of fundamental trust can the believer in God *evaluate objectively and justly* the positive fundamental approach and *ethical attitude of atheists and agnostics:* neither flattery nor condemnation is appropriate. Even believers in God—without either discrediting unbelievers as immoral or, still less, appropriate them as secret ("anonymous") believers[71]—can recognize without prejudice:

- *On the basis of fundamental trust, even an atheist can lead a genuinely human, that is, humane, and in this sense moral, life.*
- *In this very fact, man's intramundane autonomy becomes evident: his self-legislation and self-responsibility for his self-realization and his organization of the world.*
- *Even atheists and agnostics are not necessarily nihilists, but can be humanists and moralists, seriously concerned about humanity and morality.*
- *But, precisely for the sake of humanity and morality, we may expect the*

*atheist or agnostic to face the questions of the believer in God about his humanity and morality.*

These questions will have to be raised later, and fundamental trust will also have to be considered later in theological terms. But, first of all, for the sake of the matter in hand, we must press for clarity and discernment. Can and should fundamental trust be called "faith"?

## Fundamental trust and religious faith

Fundamental trust can be called "faith." Nevertheless, for the sake of clarity, *fundamental trust and faith should be distinguished.* Even authors who—unlike some other philosophers and theologians—have closely examined the basic problems discussed here are inclined to identify the two overhastily. In speaking of "philosophical faith," Karl Jaspers does not distinguish sharply enough between faith and fundamental trust.[72] Romano Guardini relates too hastily the "acceptance of oneself" (like Pascal) to the biblical God.[73] Wilhelm Weischedel, who asks only about the "whence" of the uncertainty and not about the "whence" of uncertain reality and opts for a suspension of decision, does not face the possibility of a fundamental trust.[74] Conversely, such an author as the psychiatrist Balthasar Staehelin interprets fundamental trust far too quickly in terms of mystical theology: for him, "primordial trust" is described polemically in an antirationalist spirit as "a sense of the unconditioned in one's own inwardness," as a "primary, intuitive, elementally religious certainty of faith,"[75] in which the person—wholly on the lines of the great (Christian and non-Christian) mystical tradition—finds that he is one with the "unconditioned," "ineffable," "absolute,"[76] in fact with "God";[77] thus "in principle every human being according to his second nature—even in its biological aspect"—would be "a mystic";[78] in fact "every human being is primarily and inescapably religious."[79] All this with a "scientific-empirical" appeal to dreams, mystical experiences (the great Ftan experience), parapsychology (psi phenomena), but without considering critically the possibility that these things might be projections.[80]

If we do not use the words "fundamental trust" (or "primordial trust"), on the one hand, and "faith," on the other, in the strict sense, a clarification of these complex and so long pending problems will be almost impossible. That is why we deliberately never describe fundamental trust as faith but reserve the latter term for faith in the strict sense: religious faith, faith in God or the Divine, and, in a special way, of faith in the God of the Bible. On this assumption, how can the relationship between fundamental trust and (religious) faith be more closely described?

Let us listen first to the psychologist again: "The psychological observer must ask whether or not in any area under observation religion and tradition are living psychological forces creating the kind of faith and conviction which permeates a parent's personality and thus reinforces the child's basic trust in the world's trustworthiness."[81] This terminology of Erikson is also inexact. Nonetheless, his description of *three distinct possible relationships* between fundamental trust and faith is helpful:

*First possibility:* There is a *fundamental trust that comes from religious faith:* "The psychopathologist cannot avoid observing that there are millions of people who cannot really afford to be without religion and whose pride in not having it is that much whistling in the dark."[82]

*Second possibility:* There is a *fundamental trust without religous faith:* "On the other hand, there are millions who seem to derive faith from other than religious dogmas, that is, from fellowship, productive work, social action, scientific pursuit, and artistic creation."[83]

*Third possibility:* There is a *religious faith without fundamental trust:* "And again, there are millions who profess faith, yet in practice mistrust both life and man."[84]

In itself, *religion can be very favorable to fundamental trust:* "It seems worth while to speculate on the fact that religion through the centuries has served to restore a sense of trust at regular intervals in the form of faith while giving tangible form to a sense of evil which it promises to ban. All religions have in common the periodical childlike surrender to a Provider or providers who dispense earthly fortune as well as spiritual health; the demonstration of one's smallness and dependence through the medium of reduced posture and humble gesture; the admission in prayer and song of misdeeds, of misthoughts, and of evil intentions; the admission of inner division and the consequent appeal for inner unification by divine guidance; the need for clearer self-delineation and self-restriction; and finally, the insight that individual trust must become a common faith, individual mistrust a commonly formulated evil, while the individual's need for restoration must become part of the ritual practice of many, and must become a sign of trustworthiness in the community."[85]

Erikson's inference is: "Whosoever says he has religion must derive a faith from it which is transmitted to infants in the form of basic trust; whosoever claims that he does not need religion must derive such basic faith from elsewhere."[86]

At a later stage, we must go beyond this psychological explanation and produce a clarification in principle of the relationship between fundamental trust and faith. But, before we come to that, we must first know more exactly what faith is.

## The persistent basic riddle of reality

With fundamental trust, man can establish a foothold in uncertain reality and gain basic certainty but cannot attain any definitive security. As we saw, the fundamental decision cannot be made once and for all but must be taken up again in every new situation. This emphasis on decision does not of course mean being forced into a decision on every occasion.[87] Not every state of affairs in which man is involved is a "situation" in the strict sense. What we are talking about here is a critical state of affairs, a state of affairs that provokes a crisis and calls for a decision. But, fortunately, our life consists not only of crises but also of the normal daily routine involving certain habits and plans, sustaining convictions and relationships (profession, partnership, friendship, marriage), where often patience and composure are more appropriate than continually new decisions. Decision therefore may not be made formal and absolute: no passion for decision for the sake of decisiveness (Heidegger), no demand for permanent decision as the supreme form of human existence, the consequences of which—as we know from experience—are all too likely to be activism, irrationalism, heroics, and even existentialist and political adventurism. As opposed to such a rigid, irrational insistence on decision, Bollnow rightly demands determination without reserve, backed up by the "counter virtues"—composure, availability, confidence, gratitude, patience and hope—in order in this way to find a "new security."

But do not these concepts also remain ambivalent and these countervirtues also problematic? Does not confidence easily become a way of postponing decisions? Does not "availability" (Gabriel Marcel speaks of *disponibilité*), this openness to all future possibilities, all too easily become vacillation here and now? Is it so simple in regard to the past to practice gratitude when we do not know where we really come from? And is it not too much to demand in regard to the present the practice of patience (with ourselves, with our work, with people, things, reality as a whole), when we do not know where we really stand? And, again, can we seriously hope in regard to the future, when we have no idea where we are really going? How are we to put up with this life when we feel that there is no one supporting us? How are we to find comfort when life is desolate, drifting to insignificance, replaceability, anonymity? The security bestowed by fundamental trust, in view of reality as it is, appears to be profoundly problematic and threatened: is it no more than a "sense of security that cannot be justified"?[88]

Is not our autonomous human action also problematic? Are not our rudimentary norms, in particular, ambiguous? Is not what is "human" and "humane," what humanly "goes," also ambivalent? Cannot man's optimal development be understood in sharply differing ways? And can "man," being human, the human as such, raise an absolute claim? Why can there be categorical requirements in the name of man? Why can there be an absolute obligation in a particular situation? In view of the problematic character of all norms and in view of man's enormously increased responsibility, the question of the ultimate foundation and the provision of norms of human behavior is perhaps more acute than ever before. Precisely as a result of the difficult empirical and technical problems, the question arises: In all individual and social planning, controlling, organizing, transacting, what are the grounds of the assumed rationality of reality and the continually questioned meaning of the whole?

It must now be obvious that the fundamental trust in the identity, meaningfulness and value of reality, which is the presupposition of human science and autonomous ethics, is justified in the last resort only if reality itself—of which man is also a part—is not groundless, unsupported and aimless.

The fact cannot be overlooked—and this much, again, must be conceded to nihilism—that if I trustfully affirm reality in its uncertainty, if I react positively to it, it *does not* on that account *lose its uncertainty*: the world, for the most part, appears more as the "broken" than as the "unbroken" world; man as a not at all rational *monstre incompréhensible* (in Pascal's description); the past as past, the present as ephemeral, the future as inaccessible, and consequently reality as a whole more appearance than being. And if uncertain reality can be shown completely in its fundamental identity, meaningfulness and value to the person who trusts in it, it appears so merely as a fact and ultimately without evident foundation. Are the identity, meaningfulness and value experienced in the act of fundamental trust really lasting? Or do chaos, absurdity, illusion, sickness, evil and death prevail in the end? Who will have the last laugh? Are those things from which we started out in our exposition—uncertainty and insecurity, forsakenness and exposedness, the desolation and the peril of my own existence—definitively overcome? Or have I perhaps not finally left behind me fate and death, emptiness and futility, guilt and self-rejection? Is the being of the world and self really stable and reliable? Does the whole possess stability? Is reality not fathomless, does it not hang—so to speak—in the air? On what and for what are we living? Do things just "go on," without ground, support or goal?

- *The uncertain* reality of the world and self justifies *trust in so far as its being really is. But it seems itself to be* without foundation *in so far as its being remains uncertain. Hence reality appears to be a riddle:*
  *founding, but itself unfounded;*
  *supporting, but itself unsupported;*
  *pointing the way, but itself without a goal.*
- *The uncertain reality of the world and self appears as* pure facticity, *which calls for an explanation. The mysterious fact that I exist, that things and people exist, that the world exists, that there is anything at all— this is the* basic riddle *of reality.*

At the end of this large section of the Yes to reality as the alternative to nihilism, we have to ask what all this means for nihilism itself. It means two things:

- *Nihilism is* factually overcome *by fundamental trust. Fundamental trust is based on reality; and in fundamental trust man can live and deal with reality in its uncertainty.*

- *But, despite fundamental trust, nihilism is not overcome in principle. The reality on which fundamental trust is based seems itself to be without foundation; and it is also in fundamental trust that man must live and deal with the uncertainty of reality.*

The enigmatic facticity—the groundlessness, unsupportedness and aimlessness of the world and in particular of my own existence—raises over and over again the question of the possible unreality of reality, of the nullity of the existent. Despite fundamental trust, the question *remains:* "To be, or not to be?" Is there no solution to this basic riddle of reality, which for man turns out to be constantly secretly present and dangerously virulent in the more delicate situations of life?

# F. YES TO GOD—ALTERNATIVE TO ATHEISM

"If I had to die now, I would say: 'Was that all?' And: 'That is not really how I understood it.' And: 'It was rather noisy.'" The words are those of the Berlin Jewish writer Kurt Tucholsky, who took his own life, in 1935, in despair at the successes of the National Socialists.[1]

Are there not many people who think the same way? If they are as honest as Tucholsky, life for them remains something not understood, a riddle. Is it possible to get at this basic riddle? We shall try to do so.

# I. Multidimensional man

The basic riddle of human life can scarcely be solved if the central question, the question of God, is not faced. Can modern science alone provide any further help at this point? "There is one thing I would like to tell the theologians: something that they know and others should know. They possess the sole truth that goes deeper than the truth of science, on which the atomic age rests. They possess a knowledge of the nature of man that is more deeply rooted than the rationality of modern times. The moment always comes inevitably when our planning breaks down and people ask and continue to ask about this truth. The present, bourgeois status of the Church is no proof that men are really asking about Christian truth. This truth will be convincing when it is lived." The words are those of Carl Friedrich von Weizsäcker, atomic physicist and philosopher, and they are addressed to theologians.[2] Has this moment arrived?

## 1. Transcendence?

The course taken by developments in science and technology, economics, politics and culture in the past quarter of a century is amazing. The developments cannot be described here, but a brief glance may be helpful.

### Retrospect and prospect

If we do not assume that religion simply falls from heaven, we must start out from the questions and hopes of modern man. That is why my book *On Being a Christian*, first published, in German, in 1974, began not with a theological study of God or of Christ but with an analysis of the two *great ideologies* that have dominated the past decades: the ideologies of *technological evolution* and of *politicosocial revolution*. A great deal could be conceded to both sides: on the one side, the enormous progress of modern science and technology; on the other side, the considerable humanistic potential that can be found even in a social-revolutionary ideology such as Marxism. But, even at that time, the ambivalence of these two ideologies had to be seen. In the one case, as in the other, our thesis is that the ideology of a technological evolution or of a political revolution, leading naturally to humanity, appears to be shaken.

This thesis was not disputed at that time; neither has it been refuted by subsequent events in society and politics. The signs of breakdown in the economic sphere have become clearer, the crisis in the political sphere has been more sharply outlined. And a great deal that could only be suspected then has today become certainty, even for the wider public: the extent of inflation and currency problems, unemployment and fear of the future, shortage of raw materials and energy gaps, the atomic danger and the overall threat to the environment, overpopulation and hunger, poverty and the suppression of human rights; the North-South conflict, the struggle for Africa, the unclarified situation in the Near and Far East, rearmament of the Eastern bloc, the military dictatorships in South America, the unstable democracies in Western Europe. Certainly democratic developments—as, for instance, in Spain, Portugal and Greece—are to be noted as positive achievements. But these can scarcely make a decisive change in the generally alarming total picture.

Nevertheless we will *not give up the hope* expressed at that time. To repeat what we said then with reference to both sides:

a. *What has to be given up* is only the *ideology of technological progress*, controlled as it is by vested interests, which fails to perceive the true reality of the world and rouses pseudorational illusions of practicability. Concern with science and technology and thus with human progress must continue. What has to be given up is only *faith in science* as a *total explanation of reality* (as a Weltanschauung) and in *technocracy* as a cure-all *substitute religion*.

Hence the *hope of a meta-technological society* is not to be abandoned, the hope of a new synthesis between controlled technical progress and a human existence freed from the constraints of progress: a more human form of work, more closeness to nature, a more balanced social structure and the satisfaction also of nonmaterial needs, of those human values, that is, which alone make life worth living and yet cannot be expressed in monetary terms.

b. *What has to be given up* is only the *ideology of politicosocial revolution*, which pursues social subversion with violence and sets up a new system of domination by men over men. Concern for a basic change in society must be continued. What must be abandoned is only *Marxism* as a *total explanation of reality* (as a Weltanschauung), *revolution* as a cure-all *substitute religion*.

Hence the *hope of a meta-revolutionary society* is not to be abandoned, a society beyond stagnation and revolution, uncritical acceptance of the facts and total criticism of the existing order. A hope therefore of a really contented existence, of a better society, of a realm of freedom, equality and happiness, a meaning in one's own life and a meaning in the history of mankind.

There is no need to be reminded of the fact that there are numerous technocrats who by no means make science and technology their religion. And there are also more and more Marxists in the West and even in the East who do not make Marxism their religion. The longer we consider it, the more clearly does it appear that total rejection *or* total acceptance of technological evolution and also total rejection *or* total acceptance of politicosocial revolution are false alternatives. Does not the evolution of society in West and East also call for a new synthesis? In the distant future, cannot the two perhaps be combined: the longing of a politicorevolutionary humanism for a fundamental change of conditions, for a better, more just world, for a really good life, and at the same time the demands of a technological-evolutive humanism for the possibility of concrete realization, for avoidance of terror, for a pluralistic order of freedom open-minded toward problems and not imposing a particular belief on anyone? Here is a liberating transcendence making possible in theory and practice a real alternative—and not only a nostalgia for the past or a superficial reformism[3]—to Marcuse's "one-dimensional man,"[4] to which otherwise there seems to be no genuine alternative.

## Transcending man: Ernst Bloch

"I am, but I do not possess myself; that is why we are only coming to be."[5] This is the opening sentence of the *Tübinger Einleitung in die Philosophie* ("Tübingen Introduction to Philosophy"), a course given in winter term 1961–62 by the Marxist philosopher *Ernst Bloch* (1885–1977), who left Leipzig for West Germany and did not return, after the Berlin Wall was built, settling down finally in Tübingen.

Man's *transcending* is the great theme of Bloch's thought: crossing frontiers, surmounting barriers, philosophy of the not-yet, all developed in an unusually rich work, overflowing with insights, ideas, thoughts, images, metaphors, stories, allusions, which is able to combine expressiveness of language with strictly philosophical sequences of thought and to incorporate both the natural history of man and the cosmos and the great tradition of philosophy, literature, art, music and religion.

Bloch's thought begins with man. Light is turned on life situations in all their complexity and diversity, to reveal what remains unsettled, undischarged, not yet finished, half done. Even childhood is included, with its wishes, dreams, longings, hopes. Considered in this way, every human life is seen to be unfinished, incomplete and—as distinct from animal life—never wholly fulfilled. Man has not sufficient; he wants more: this is the wholly elemental starting point of this way of thinking. Hence, for Bloch, man is primarily a defective being who, however, continually transcends himself as he overcomes his defects. Even the newborn child thrusts itself on its mother's breast in order to remedy its deficiencies: "The fact of being in want is the first thing that dawns upon us. All other instincts have their root in hunger; from that point, every instinct presses outward and around, seeking satisfaction in something appropriate to its nature and in something beyond its nature. That is to say, whatever lives must be intent on something or get moving toward and be on the way to something; the unquiet void satisfies outside the need that comes from within itself."[6]

Instinct therefore is what drives man forward. But necessity, too, does this. Necessity is the mother of invention and—Bloch thinks—it was necessity that first taught man to think, to make tools, to light fires, to build huts. At the same time, thought did not stand still. In ordinary life, there is much that rouses astonishment. For Bloch, as for Plato long ago, wonder is the beginning of all philosophy, wonder that leads to reflection. But wonder is the expression of not-knowing, of the not-yet. Thus man's instinct, necessity and wonder take him beyond the mere fact of being and in this way reveal his fundamental openness. According to Bloch, therefore, the "not" is part of man's very first experiences. Man is not as he might be: this is a basic experience. But this "not" is nothing definitive; it is the not-yet, which can be redeemed if man actively cooperates in the redemption.

"Who are we? Where do we come from? Where are we going to? What are we expecting? What is awaiting us?" With these universally human questions, Ernst Bloch began his main work, Das Prinzip Hoffnung ("Hope as Principle"), which he wrote during his stay in the U.S.A., 1938–47, and revised in the fifties after returning to Germany.[7] To these universally human questions he gives universally human answers. Even at this stage he made it clear that man, unfinished as individual and as society, in both thought and action, is continually freshly involved in surmounting, surpassing, transcending. Man lives by striving, lives on the future, lives determined by the future. His existence, both private and public, in the midst of evil, is pervaded with daydreams, dreams of a better life. And this dream, this yearning, this desiderium, according to Bloch, is the one sincere quality that belongs to all men; but it is the very thing that has not been investigated.

Bloch then—in the light of Marx's teaching but with rare breadth and depth of involvement—investigates dreaming as forward-looking, to what has not yet become part of consciousness, what has not yet come to be: that is, man's yearning, expectation and hope. In this respect, for Bloch, man's basic attitude to reality is one of docta spes, tested, founded, acquired, well-oriented hope, which can also integrate disappointment as the "creative minus."[8] But docta spes is also the great, always present and continually enduring principle of reality as a whole: "Expectation, hope, intention directed to possibilities that have not yet come to be: this is not only a basic feature of human consciousness but, concretely justified and understood, a basic category within objective reality as a whole."[9]

And this objective reality for Bloch—wholly different from what it was for Teilhard and Whitehead—is a cosmic process that is still open and in which man can creatively intervene. The world is a laboratory in which "possible salvation" can be outlined experimentally: "Nothing is more human than to go beyond that which is. It has been known for a long time that dreams are practically never fulfilled. The man whose hope has been tried knows this better than anyone; in this respect, too, hope is far from being firm assurance. Such a hope is also aware—by its very definition, so to speak—not only that saving power grows with the growth of danger but that danger also grows with the growth of saving power.* It is aware that obstructive forces are active in the world as a function of nothingness, that an 'in vain' is latent in objective, real possibility, which carries within itself unreconciled both salvation and disaster. The cosmic process is still nowhere achieved, but neither is it anywhere frustrated; human beings can be on earth the switchmen of its track, not yet decisively leading to salvation but neither yet decisively leading to disaster. The world itself in its totality remains the most intensively laboring laboratory of possible salvation."[10]

The world as laboratory is consequently full of aptitude for something, tendency to something, latency of something: "the utopian" in the wide, positive, world-oriented sense (not merely as a description of the ideal state, as in Thomas More's *Utopia,* Tommaso Campanella's *City of the Sun,* or Francis Bacon's *New Atlantis*). According to Bloch, an interweaving of having and not having, which characterizes all yearning and hope, has been operative in all the freedom movements of mankind: at an early stage in the Exodus theme and in the messianic passages of the Bible, in the myths of Prometheus and the recurring Golden Age, in such figures as Odysseus and Faust, Don Quixote and Don Juan, in the German peasant wars, in the American, French, German and Russian revolutions. It has been operative in philosophy: in Leibniz' concept of tendency, in Kant's postulates of moral consciousness, in Hegel's world-historical dialectic and particularly in the Marxist passion for practical change. Bloch thus distinguishes from every aspect the function of a Utopia and of conscious anticipation, on the basis of a general ontology of the not-yet, in connection with the categories of future, front, new, home, in comparison with archetypes, ideals, ideologies. And he describes and analyzes man's yearning and hope quite concretely in all possible fantasies: in the fairy-tale world,

---

* "Wo aber Gefahr ist, wächst
 Das Rettende auch."
 (Where there is danger, the saving power also grows.)
 Friedrich Hölderlin, *Patmos.*

in the film dream factory, in theatrical presentation, in wanderlust, in dancing; also in medical, social, technical, geographical, artistic utopias and consequently in fantasies of health and of a society without poverty, in the invented problems of leisure, in voyages of geographical discovery, in the real castles in the air produced by architecture, in the ideal land-scapes of painting, poetry, opera; finally in the images built up by hope against the most powerful non-Utopia, death. "Everywhere here the cen-tral point remains the problem of the desirable as such or of the *supreme good*."[11]


## Transcending without transcendence?

Socialism, by which he means the practice of the concrete Utopia, is and remains for Bloch the way to this "supreme good." This is certainly a very unorthodox, creative Marxism, with no time for the platitudes of a crude Marxist atheism. Behind superficial enlightenment and its No to what the name of God implies as a promise to mankind, Bloch sees "the rise of the all-too-complete instability of nihilism"; "the lack of fire for any whither, wherefore, altogether, end point, meaning."[12] Unlike that banal, insubstantial atheism, Bloch would want to take up—against the Church, constantly allied with the ruling class—the positive, revolutionary impulses of belief in God that he finds especially in the Bible, which of course must be submitted to a specific critical exegesis if we want to dis-cover, under all kinds of strata, deposits, disguises, the concealed factor of rebellion against a domineering, theocratic understanding of God. Instead of demythologizing, therefore, Bloch demands detheocratizing of the Bible.[13] The Moses impulse and the Christ impulse especially can be in-terpreted in a "forward" sense. The rebellious, prophetic and messianic el-ements of the Judeo-Christian religion in their latencies and tendencies can thus be made fruitful even for the present time: for the new socialist society, for the New Life, the utopian omega, the moment of fulfillment, for the kingdom of God without God.

"Where there is hope, there is also religion."[14] For Bloch—as distinct from Feuerbach and Marx—religion is the expression of hope or—better —it can be the expression of hope, for "the converse, 'where there is religion, there is also hope,' does not hold."[15] Religion arises from the ineradicable distinction between what is and what is not yet, between pres-ent and future reality, with reference to both man and the cosmos. For Bloch, "God" is a code name for the unfound, future human reality, the still-unknown human being; more precisely: the *"hypostatized ideal of the nature of man that has not yet come to be in its reality."*[16]

This seems to make absolutely clear the difference from belief in God, whatever its origin. What Bloch had always maintained as his thesis, he placed as an epigraph at the opening of his book *Atheismus im Christen-*

*tum* ("Atheism in Christianity"): *"Decisive: a transcending without transcendence."*

There are admittedly theologians who think that Bloch's kingdom of God is not really without God. Bloch would reject only the deistic God, the God of heteronomy, theocracy and man's alienation, the unreal God of theodicy. Bloch's continually professed atheism at bottom would not be really godless, would not be radical atheism.

If, however, we read Bloch without prejudice, it is absolutely clear that he rejects any kind of God. Bloch is not a nontheist, but an atheist. His truly radical atheism requires an abandonment of God himself, who for Bloch is dead together with religion, the heritage of which, however, he would like to take over. Without all the mythicizings, ideologies and illusions, creative Marxism ought to combine with itself the deepest latencies and tendencies of religion in the no longer alienated, godless human reality. "Kingdom of God?" For Bloch, this is the godless, socialistic kingdom of freedom—his great Utopia—in which man is naturalized and nature humanized, man and nature, logos and cosmos, reconciled; where God wholly in Feuerbach's sense has become man and nothing but man. Bloch, then, stands for a promethean-active, atheistic-utopian coming-to-be of man.[17]

The philosopher Ernst Bloch is undoubtedly an eminently fruitful partner in discussion with the theologian, more fruitful, perhaps, than most other contemporary philosophers. In such a discussion, of course, further weighty questions would arise.

Is Bloch's future Utopia (nowhere realized) of a socialistic kingdom of freedom, in which man and nature, logos and cosmos, are reconciled and man is really man, not merely a wishful projection, which—since God drops out—is guaranteed in the last resort only by the alleged necessity of an originally Hegelian-idealistic but now materialistic dialectic of history?[18]

In all future Utopias, does not man himself—as individual and society —remain the problem, since he seems to cope with everything in the world but not with himself? Is it sufficient to be emancipated from all ecclesiastical and theological dominances and to provide an autonomous, intramundane, instead of a religious, foundation for life plans and norms of action, in order to rescue the humanity of man? Has not recent history in particular made it clear that no kind of linear or possibly revolutionary transcending will lead us out of the one-dimensionality of our modern existence? In the last resort, is not man constantly dependent precisely on the forces and powers and their mechanisms that he released when he came of age and became autonomous?

Can, then, individual and social transcending reach its goal at all without real transcendence? And does Bloch's question about the wherefore and the whither not also provoke the question of the whence and why, a question that his materialistic dialectic is quite incapable of answering adequately? And if God has survived in a bourgeois form, why should he not be able to manifest himself again in a new form in a new age?[19]

But we shall not pursue these questions further. The essential answers have already been given in the chapter on atheism and particularly in the sections on Feuerbach and Marx.[20] Despite all the differences, Bloch's atheism also is based ultimately on Feuerbach's unproved and unprovable projection theory, on Marx's thesis of social alienation, and on the thesis defended by both these men, based on their philosophy of history, of the disintegration of religion to make way for an atheistic humanism—a thesis that has not yet been fulfilled. Bloch speaks of "religion in the heritage" (*Religion im Erbe*). Ironically enough, if we look at the history of Bloch's influence, we could reverse the phrase and speak of "Bloch in the heritage of religion." That is to say, through Bloch, religion itself has acquired new creative impulses—a fact that was first and most abundantly made clear by the Protestant theologian Jürgen Moltmann in his *Theology of Hope*. It is not least for this reason that religion is now even more unlikely to die out than it was at the time of Feuerbach and Marx.

What remains? Where is the common ground of Bloch's philosophy of hope and the Christian theology of hope? It is on this common ground that any further discussion must be based. This much can be said:

- *Man is restless, unfinished, not completely fulfilled.*
  *He is not the one he could be.*
  *Man—a defective being.*
- *Man is therefore constantly on his way, longing for more, seeking to know more, reaching out for what is different, for what is new.*
  *He is the one who constantly surpasses himself.*
  *Man—an expectant, hoping, yearning being.*
- *Wherever inhuman social conditions, political oppression, economic exploitation, social discrimination and violation of elementary human rights prevent man's striving to go beyond himself, he is frustrated in the realization of his being human and reduced to a subhuman state, the condition of a robot.*
- *Wherever finite, intramundane factors—formerly "the nation," "the people," "the race," or even "the Church," now "the working class," "the party" or "the true consciousness" of an intellectual elite—are made absolute and regarded as final emancipation, there is no true liberation of man, but totalitarian domination by men over men and thus new mistrust and hate, new fears and sufferings among individuals, groups, nations, races and classes: that is, no better society, no justice for all and no freedom for the individual, no true love.*
- *On the plane of the linear, horizontal, purely human alone, no truly qualitative ascent to a really different dimension seems possible: without genuine transcendence, there is no genuine transcending.*

● *For man continuously going on thinking and acting, for mankind as a whole, precisely in view of the improvement of social conditions, the question arises of the great wherefore and whither, and also the whence and why, of an ultimate meaning, supreme value, first cause.*

Certainly it cannot be overlooked that the idea of man as a restless, defective and consequently self-transcending being is not a specifically Marxist, still less Blochian, insight. It is—as Bloch himself makes clear in countless hints—part of ancient Jewish-Greek-Christian lore, newly discovered in the light of unworthy human conditions, thought out in an original way, sharpened under social criticism and brought to a head with a view to practical change, by the Marxist Bloch. Our question is: Must this insight, clarified by social criticism, necessarily remain atheistic, or does not this very clarification reveal a longing for a wholly Other?

## 2. The other dimension

Like Bloch, even though with many differences, but at any rate unlike some defenders of traditional sociology, the representatives in particular of the "Frankfurt School" already mentioned, especially Theodor W. Adorno and Max Horkheimer, have continually applied their Critical Theory in the light of social conflicts to the denunciation of injustice. They, too, from the very beginning were highly sensitive to all unavoidable suffering, which cannot simply be conceptually grasped and then abolished (with the aid of a "negative dialectic"): to unhappiness, pain, age, death of the individual, to the menacing end point of boredom in a totally managed world.[21]

Long before the disillusionment following on the failure of the student revolts,[22] Max Horkheimer especially, in statements scarcely noticed at the time, had pointed to the importance of a really different dimension for a philosophy of society.

### Longing for the wholly Other: Max Horkheimer

It is impossible to say anything positive about God, to depict the Absolute, thinks *Max Horkheimer* (1895–1973), this representative of a "negative theology" who is able to combine the Old Testament prohibition of images with Kant's critique of knowledge and modern agnosticism. But he also insists that, without the thought of God, there is no absolute meaning, no absolute truth, and morality becomes a matter of taste or mood.[23] Elsewhere he says: "It is useless to attempt to rescue an absolute meaning without God. . . . If God dies, eternal truth also dies."[24]

Horkheimer starts out from the *longing for perfect justice*, which is typ-

ical of man. But this is a justice that does not and cannot exist in our society and its secular history, a justice that transcends our society and all
intramundane Utopias. In this sense, it is unimportant to him whether
there is a God, whether we believe in God or not. But, from another aspect, it is important, since human actions and attitudes, in the last resort,
are theologically determined. "Remember," says Horkheimer in the course
of a discussion, "what we, Horkheimer and I, wrote in the *Dialectic of
Enlightenment*. There we said: 'Politics that does not contain theology
within itself, however little considered, may often be shrewd but remains
in the end no more than a business.' "[25]

This means that, according to Horkheimer, everything connected with
*morality* goes back in the last resort to *theology*: "From the standpoint of
positivism, no conclusions can be drawn about morality in politics.
Scientifically speaking, hatred is no worse than love, though its social
function may be different. There is no logically conclusive argument to
show that I should not hate, as long as I am not thereby placed at a disadvantage in my social life."[26] Without an authority transcending man, it
could in fact be said, in the spirit of George Orwell's *Nineteen Eighty-
four*, that war is neither better nor worse than peace, freedom neither better nor worse than oppression: "For how can it be proved exactly that I
should not hate if I feel like doing so. Positivism cannot find any authority transcending men, to distinguish between helpfulness and cupidity,
kindness and cruelty, avarice and unselfishness. Logic too remains silent, it
does not concede any precedence to moral sentiment. All attempts to justify morality by worldly prudence instead of looking to the hereafter—
even Kant did not always resist this inclination—rest on harmonistic
illusions."[27]

Religion, then, or at least the inner feeling that there is a God, must
mean something decisive: precisely for the realization of a more reasonable, more just society; for a plausible order of the existing state of affairs
(including at least the abolition of senseless cruelty); for the struggle on a
world scale of the great economic power groups, carried on with the wast-
age of so many good human resources, with the mobilization of so much
lying and hatred at the expense of human beings. There is such a thing as
a "longing for perfect justice." But this is the very thing that "can never
be realized in secular history."[28] And even if this were possible in the future, it would not compensate for past misery, and the distress in sur-
rounding nature would not be abolished.

Like Bloch's, Horkheimer's understanding of religion is in *continuity*
with that of Marx *and* at the same time goes *beyond Marx*. There is on
the one hand a continuity with Marx, who had spoken of religion as the
"sigh of the oppressed creature" and "the protest against real distress."
For Horkheimer, too, religion, in which are recorded the wishes, yearnings
and accusations of countless human beings in the face of unbounded
suffering and wrong, makes man aware "that he is a finite being, that he

must suffer and die; but that over and above suffering and death there is the longing that this earthly existence may not be absolute, not the ultimate reality."[29] But, on the other hand, there remains the "longing for the Other."[30] And for a "theology," this means "that the world is a phenomenon, that it is not the absolute truth, not the ultimate reality. Theology—I am deliberately expressing myself cautiously—is the hope that this injustice which characterizes the world is not permanent, that injustice will not be the last word . . . , that the murderer will not triumph over his innocent victim."[31] And this appraisal of religion with the reference to "the Other," "the absolute truth," "the ultimate reality," is a decisive step beyond Marx and Bloch. "That the reality known to us is not the ultimate reality," for Horkheimer, is a certainty even in the light of the epistemology of Kant and Schopenhauer. Admittedly he says also: "We cannot describe what the Absolute is and in what it consists."[32]

Can we really speak only in this negative way about the Absolute? This is a question we still have to examine. In this immediate context, Horkheimer's observation in any case is important, that even such dogmatic atheists as Schopenhauer are mistaken when they claim that "nothingness is the ultimate reality, which releases us from the misery of this world."[33] Even the concept of nothingness—like all the others—is subjective. Nevertheless or perhaps for that very reason, *the reality around us is not the ultimate reality.* Horkheimer quite rightly insists: "A genuine liberalizing of religion must concentrate on this insight. By comparison with this, questions about changing ceremonies and customs are far less important. The main thing seems to me to be the new version of man's understanding of God."[34] God as positive dogma, as object of knowledge and possession, of course divides men. On the other hand, the longing that the reality of the world with all its horror may not be the final reality is something that unites and binds together all men who will not and cannot come to terms with the injustice of this world: "God thus becomes the object of human longing and veneration. . . . A faith understood in this way is an indispensable part of what we call human culture."[35]

Is there a new version of the human understanding of God? Some would say that this is possible only in virtue of a new understanding of being.

## The question of being: Martin Heidegger

What is the meaning of being? For *Martin Heidegger* (1889–1976), this was the central question from the time when he started out at the age of eighteen to study theology after receiving from his friend and spiritual father in his home town of Messkirch, Conrad Grüber, later Archbishop of Freiburg, a copy of the dissertation by the philosopher Franz Brentano, "On the manifold meaning of the existent according to Aris-

totle" (published in 1862).³⁶ Heidegger, of course, was always one of the
most difficult philosophical thinkers—because of his way of formulating
problems and his highly individual language. Nevertheless we must
demand—at least from the reader interested in philosophy—some study
of an (extremely compressed) account of Heidegger together with theological questions raised by his work. Otherwise an important voice would
be unheard in our answer to the question of God in modern times.

The stone "is," the animal, the machine, the work of art, man "is,"
God "is." But what does "is" mean here, what does "being" mean? Does
being mean simply what "is there," what there is in the world, what occurs
or happens to be present there—the "existent"? This is the question that
led Heidegger to his early major work *Sein und Zeit* ("Being and
Time"), published in 1927: "The question, then stirring only obscurely
and uncertainly and helplessly, of the simple in the manifold, *remained*,
throughout many upheavals, labyrinths and perplexities, *the* persistent in-
centive for the work *Sein und Zeit*, which appeared two decades later."³⁷

Heidegger (who had been a Jesuit novice for a short time) had meanwhile given up Catholic theology and consequently also traditional metaphysics and its God. Under the influence of the Greeks, Kierkegaard, neo-
Kantianism, life philosophy and the phenomenology of his Freiburg
teacher Edmund Husserl (a student of Brentano), he had applied himself
to thinking out a more elemental, fundamental theory of being ("fundamental ontology"). From that time onward, his investigation was centered not on the existent as in the traditional ontology but on *being itself*
as the ground of all that is.

According to Heidegger, in the course of Western history, in thinking
and working, we have looked only to the individual existent and thereby
forgotten the decisive question: "What is it that makes the existent a
being at all?" This, he says, is being itself, which is distinct from all individual beings, from things and men, and also from the totality of all that
exists (= reality): a distinction that Heidegger calls the "*ontological
difference*" between being itself and all that is. It is true that traditional
ontology had also considered the existent in the light of being. But, according to Heidegger, being itself as distinct from all that is had not yet
been really considered. The sciences, too, in particular, as a result of increasing specialization, occupied with delimited realms of being, and still
more technology, with its mathematical thinking prevailing everywhere,
have only suppressed all the more the question about being itself and contributed substantially to the basic condition of modern times and especially of the technical world: the state of forgetfulness of being.

But how is being—which can be neither an individual existent nor the
totality of what is (= reality)—to be rediscovered and really conceived?
Heidegger answers that this is possible only in the light of man, who
somehow understands in his own existence what "being" means, even
though he does not reflect upon it. It is possible in the light of man, who

—as opposed to the animal—has an understanding of being and can also express it in language, in his ordinary activity, in his dealings with other men. For the distinctive feature of man's peculiar mode of being is the fact that he is not merely "there," "available," like a stone or a tree, a machine or a work of art. He "ex-sists." That is to say, he projects himself in freedom in virtue of his potentialities and thus realizes his existence in the midst of the world and among other human beings. We may not, therefore—as has been the custom in philosophy from Descartes onward —isolate man from things and people. Instead, he must be seen from the outset in his "being in the world" and in his "being together with others." It is just in this way that the otherwise closed world is opened to man, to his understanding, feeling and perception. And he succeeds in breaking through to the true understanding of being, which "reveals" itself to him.

According to Heidegger, then, the distinctive mode of man's being consists in the *"transcendence of human existence."* As Heidegger says elsewhere: "This projection (of existence) into Nothing on the basis of hidden dread is the overcoming of what-is-in-totality: Transcendence."[38] This means that man surpasses all individual existents. Not, however, with reference to a metaphysical world or a God, but *with reference to being,* which constitutes the horizon of all his understanding, feeling and perception and which—when he goes beyond all that is—appears to him first of all as not-being, as nothingness. That is why man is not barely available but is "being there" and "ex-sistence": a projection of himself into being, which is in some way understood or "there" in him.

It is not necessary here to describe how Heidegger—who, during his period of teaching at Marburg (1923–28), had a decisive influence on the theologian Rudolf Bultmann and his "existential" interpretation of the New Testament—analyzes what pertains to human existence, *what determines concrete human existence in its structures* (Heidegger's existential analytics or analysis of *Dasein*): man's entanglement in the daily routine and his existence as "care"; his exposure to the world, to the dictatorship of the anonymous and indefinite "one" among many, to averageness and unauthenticity. In addition, there are the basic categories of man, especially the basic experience of dread (under the influence of Kierkegaard), in which man is confronted with the uncertainty of all that is, with the nullity of the world and the inescapability of death; his "thrownness" into death and his being projected out into possible not-being, even into nothingness. But there is also man's potential, by a free decision and determination to the point of death, to take over his empty existence and to exist out of himself in order in this way to reach his true self.

Everywhere here, Heidegger wants not merely to give a psychological description of human life situations but to interpret in terms of fundamental ontology the special mode of being of human existence: *temporality*. At every moment of his present existence, man is determined by both his past and his future; this is the basic structure of human existence. This finiteness of temporality and thus also "being toward death" is for Heidegger the hidden reason for man's historicity. In this way, the question of being itself must be raised in the light of human existence, so that what we discover are not accidental structures but the structures of the human experience of being that are given with every existence ("existentials").

Heidegger—professor of philosophy in Freiburg from 1928 onward and rector of the university for a brief year after Hitler's seizure of power, unfortunately at first saw this understanding of the self and the world as developed in *Sein und Zeit,* this heroic determination even in the approach to death, realized in National Socialist ideology. Working with such guiding concepts as being, truth, people, leader, he opted publicly for Hitler (as rector, he was a party member) and racial science against superficial and powerless thinking. He soon realized his mistake, began to lecture on logic instead of political philosophy and refused an invitation to Berlin in autumn 1933; but, after the war, it cost him his professorship.[39]

As we saw,[40] Jean Paul Sartre, in *L'être et le néant* (1943), took Heidegger's analysis of existence as the starting point of his existentialist philosophy but went on in a different direction. Sartre, who had studied German philosophy in Berlin before the war, did not understand man's nature (like Heidegger) merely in the light of the existential interpretation of being. For Sartre, existence is prior to essence (or nature) and (unlike Heidegger) he interprets it in an atheistic sense. In 1946, Heidegger wrote an answer to Sartre's *L'existentialisme est un humanisme,*[41] which he sent to his French student Jean Beaufret and later published in an expanded form with the title *Über den Humanismus* ("Letter on Humanism").[42] From this, it is clear that Heidegger—who in his later years (emeritus professor in 1951) withdrew almost entirely from public life and spent most of his time in his hut in the Black Forest near Todtnau—dissociated himself completely from the existentialist fashion prevailing especially in France. *He had never shared this "existentialism"* concentrated entirely on man, nor did he ever want to be described as an "existentialist philosopher." For, from the very beginning, he was concerned less with man's being than with being as a whole, as can be seen quite clearly from the opening chapter of *Sein und Zeit,* on the priority of the question of being and the conclusion on the question of the meaning of being as such.

The second part of *Sein und Zeit* was announced but never published. Heidegger was now very fully occupied with the great philosophers from the pre-Socratics to Nietzsche and even more in philosophical argument with such poets as Hölderlin, Hebel, Rilke, George, Trakl and Benn; he felt increasingly that it was impossible to get from the existence of man to being itself. Hence in his later works[43] he accomplished a *"volte-face in his thought,"* no longer thinking of being in the light of man but *thinking of man and the world in the light of being.*

Heidegger does not want to be—like Jaspers—a philosopher of existence, but a thinker of being: at the service now of a new humanism "that thinks the humanity of man from nearness to being."[44] Man is not only understood—as hitherto—as "lord of being," but, in the light of being freshly understood, as "shepherd of being."[45] He is commissioned— especially by a new form of thinking—to "guard the truth of Being, in order that beings might appear in the light of Being as the beings they are."[46] It thus becomes clear that "what is essential is not man but Being."[47] Of course, man never gains the mastery over being. But, for its communication, its possible disclosure, its unconcealment—in other words, for its truth—being is dependent on man, by whom it is made evident: *man is the center of the illumination of being.* Hence, if it is understood existentially, in terms of transcendental philosophy, human existence is made possible only by being as such. Man and being are oriented to each other.

What is behind Heidegger's endeavors? In thinking of being itself, Heidegger is planning to overcome traditional metaphysics as represented —wholly determined by theology—with final stage by Hegel and—in Heidegger's opinion—not overcome even by Nietzsche. Why? For Heidegger, metaphysics—this onto-theo-logy[48]—throughout the centuries from Plato onward has maintained the separation between the physical-sensible and the metaphysical-suprasensible worlds. It has considered only the individual existent in relation to being and forgotten being itself. And in this sense, the history of being hitherto can be regarded as a history of forgetting being. This is the real decline of the West.

Heidegger can admit that Nietzsche was right: it is metaphysics itself that produced nihilism.[49] But even Nietzsche—despite his radical negativity—remains entangled in the metaphysical system. His program of the revaluation of all values is not an overturning and overcoming of all metaphysics but only a new (and, as Heidegger expects, final) metaphysics, a metaphysics of the "Will to Power" and the "eternal recurrence of the same." For Nietzsche, too, it remains hidden "how far the essence of man is determined by the essence of being."[50] Nietzsche thus repeats the old mistake of metaphysics: not considering being itself but only the being of the existent. And being itself, in its truth, eludes him also. In nihilism, according to Heidegger, there is no question at all merely of devaluing or revaluing being but of being itself, which—as a result of forgetting, even of forsaking being—amounts to nothing. The *overcoming of nihilism* cannot be brought about by man but only *by being itself,* which must, again, become evident. But to think of being itself demands a new kind of thinking, contemplative (or "essential") instead of calculating thinking.

And to think "objectively" of being itself means "to think of it in its difference from the existent and to think of the existent in its difference from being."[51]

Thus, contrary to all older objectivistic and also modern subjectivistic metaphysics, and also contrary to all existentialism and nihilism, the later Heidegger attempts to think of being itself, on which everything else depends: on the meaning of being, its comprehensibility, its possible disclosure, its truth. And this thought is expressed in a *language* that as it were speaks *out of being* and considers together (language as the "house of being") being (truth) and historicity. As Walter Jens expresses it, "Heidegger: an artist of thinking who had two languages at his disposal to make himself understood, the Greek of the pre-Socratic philosophers and the Latin of Scholasticism, and who then thought out for himself a third, highly artificial language: a German on the borderline between image and concept, with the aid of which, at the midpoint between poetry and theology, he attempted to give a name to a being that could not be grasped in a formula but only paraphrased and allusively evoked in continual fresh starts. As 'illumination' and as 'unconcealed,' as 'befitting' and as 'unique affair.'"[52] Hence:

*Being* understood as *history of being,* which is also "world history" and which nevertheless as ontological history must be clearly distinguished from intramundane ontic history.

*Being* understood as the *power of history,* which belongs to man as the mode of his existence, as temporal, historical, transitory.

*Being* understood as *being's destiny,* which man can never control.

*Being* understood not as isolated from time, as a static condition, but *as event in time,* which is not rigidity, abstraction, still less an empty formula, but an occurring, grounding, permeating, uncontrollably controlling, self-revealing and self-concealing, self-giving and elusive fullness and vivacity.

*Being* in its various epochs understood *as the all-embracing and illuminating basic event,* which is effective not by man's favor but of itself, and which carries its meaning within itself.

This being is continuously revealing itself in the world throughout the nothingness that is everywhere experienced. For all that is might also not be. Thus being, at once concealed and unconcealed, becomes evident, comes to light; and *nothingness,* at work everywhere with nullifying effect, appears as merely the *veil of being,* as the way in which being is manifested to man when he transcends the existent.

If we examine this almost mythological terminology and imagery relating to being, we may be tempted to wonder if Heidegger is not really talking about God here. But Heidegger makes it clear continually in his work: "'Being'—that is not God and not a cosmic ground."[53] With him, the question of God is deliberately left out of consideration. His philosophy is meant to be neither atheistic nor theistic. The whole effort of philosophy must be concentrated on bringing being itself, as distinct from the individual being, into consideration. It is only against the background of being as thus considered that even the *Holy* can be thought of as the essential realm of divinity. It is only then that questions may be raised *about the divine and about God*, who in any case could not be the "God of the philosophers," the God of metaphysics; for to him "man can neither pray nor offer sacrifice," before him he "can neither fall on his knees in awe nor sing and dance."[54] Looking back to his theological past, Heidegger observes: "Anyone whose experience of theology—whether that of Christian faith or that of philosophy—has grown from the soil of his own heritage, will prefer today to be silent in the field of thinking about God."[55] The question of God can be tackled only "when Being itself beforehand and after extensive preparation has been illuminated and is experienced in truth."[56] As he declared in his lecture in 1962 on "Time and Being," he thinks it is perhaps "more expedient to refrain not only from giving an answer but even from raising the question."[57] Are philosophers, then, to be silent and only theologians to speak about God?

## Silence before God?

Theologians should not put their trust uncritically in Heidegger. Since the end of the war, all too many, enticed by the siren sounds of existence and being, have danced to Heidegger's tune. To philosophical adherents there have been added, up to a point, theological Heidegger believers and Heidegger congregations. In a barren time, the thinker of being has been regarded as the high priest of a profound existentialist theology (by Protestants) and as the secret patron saint of a renewed Thomism (by Catholics).

But theologians should listen—albeit critically—to Heidegger and not only with reference to the rejection of a "Christian philosophy"—a tricky question for Heidegger—or to the forgetfulness of being, which prevails also in Christian theology. So many theologians, and preachers especially, have God's name constantly on their lips and speak of God as if they had him in their pockets. Vis-à-vis a thoughtless transmission of traditional ideas of God or even of thoughtless chatter about God's existence or his death, Heidegger's reservation about talking of God at all could lead both believers and unbelievers perhaps to a new reverence, a new respect for God. Talk of God that does not, in the last resort, *emerge from silence and lead again into silence* does not know with whom it is dealing. And good theology—from the Greek Fathers and Augustine by way of Aquinas and Luther up to the moderns—has always known that in regard to God himself it is more *theologia negativa* than *positiva* and can say what God is not better than what he is. *Theo-logia*, as talk of God, in the end will always be muted in the presence of the greatness of the mystery, which no objectifying, objective, representational thinking can dispose of and which does not permit itself to be disposed of.

But is *philosophy merely to be silent before God?* There are theologians —understandably belonging to the tradition of dialectical theology—who would like to impose silence on philosophy and who all too obviously applaud Heidegger's aloof reserve in regard to the question of God, in which in his turn he is partly influenced by dialectical theology. Which means that Heidegger is cited as a witness by the very people who have made him one. In this way, theology, especially Christian theology, is to be granted an exclusive right to speak of matters concerning God, a right supposed to be justified on the one hand by the alleged muteness of philosophy and on the other by the revealed word of God in Scripture.

But can the fact be overlooked that philosophy *has* spoken of God for two and a half millennia? That it did no harm at all to theology to listen —if not exclusively or primarily, at least up to a point—to this philosophical talk of God? What would the Greek theologians we have mentioned have been, what would Augustine and Aquinas have been, what would even the Reformers and their successors have been, without Greek and—later—modern philosophy? The philosopher Wilhelm Weischedel has recently produced an impressive account of the "God of the philosophers" and at the same time presented the question of God "as the central problem of philosophy," from Thales and Anaximander up to Nietzsche and Heidegger:[58] "Even where philosophical theology is in decline . . . , as that which must be overcome before everything else, it remains of decisive importance. Talk of God therefore is rightly considered as the essential problem of philosophy."[59]

If for theology nothing is more worthy of thought than God, why should philosophy be deprived by theologians or philosophers of the opportunity of thinking of God and—perhaps after a period of godlessness— again to speak of God in an entirely new way? What interest of theological science or pastoral practice can provide theology with an excuse for prohibiting philosophy from saying anything in regard to the question of God? The "decline" of philosophy is greatly deplored today[60] when there is violent disagreement about political and methodological questions, and it appears to be splitting up into the various sciences or being reduced to epistemology. Is this perhaps connected with the fact that it no longer dares to talk about what for thousands of years was its most distinguished "object"?

Certainly the time of dualistic metaphysics, which directed God into an afterworld or even proved him to be there, is past. But should it not be possible, particularly in the one, undivided reality, to point to the God who is in the world and to the world that is in God?

Certainly we may never talk of God in such a way as to reduce him to an object of our systematic knowledge, making him even—ascending the metaphysical scale of being—a supreme being, supreme value: that is, an objectified, represented and guaranteed God. But is this a reason for being content to invoke the vanished gods, as Heidegger—following Hölderlin—does in a very ambiguous way?

Certainly we cannot deduce God like any ordinary matter of fact from certain premises by a chain of inferences. But should it not be possible to reach God (as Heidegger suggests that being should be reached) in virtue of a number of indications by a *leap* of thought (which must, of course, be justified) or—better—of trust?

Certainly we cannot speak of God in the way that science speaks. But, for that very reason, should we not make a new attempt to find an adequate way of speaking about God, so that we are not entirely silent about him and so that theology can make faith articulate in thought?

Certainly the God of the Fathers and of Jesus Christ—the living, "more divine" God of faith, of freedom and of history, on whom Christian theology is supposed to reflect—is quite different from the God of the philosophers, before whom we really cannot dance and pray. But does this mean that the God of the philosophers must be a different God: an idol instead of the true God?

## Waiting for God?

"I am a Christian theologian," wrote the young Heidegger in 1920 to the philosopher Karl Löwith,[61] a confession that the later Heidegger would certainly not have made. In a lecture at that time, "Introduction to the Phenomenology of Religion" (1920–21), Heidegger had made use of the First Letter to the Thessalonians in order to examine closely the primitive Christian understanding of time (*kairos*), a study that was to have a considerable influence on *Sein und Zeit*.[62] Human existence always depends on decision. And throughout his life, Heidegger made a clear distinction between what Christianity had become (*Christentum*) as a metaphysical system and the original Christian spirit (*Christlichkeit*), based on faith (and the gospel): not philosophy but only theology can vouch for the latter and it must do so emphatically.[63]

Heidegger's inaugural lecture in Freiburg, on July 24, 1929, "What is Metaphysics?" had ended with a reference to the *"ground-question of metaphysics,* which is wrested from Nothing itself: Why is there any Being at all—why not far rather Nothing?"[64] Here (in a postscript written in 1943) Heidegger can even speak of "the marvel of all marvels": "Man alone of all beings, when addressed by the voice of Being, experiences the marvel of all marvels: that what-is *is*."[65] The basic question—aiming at "Being's favor"[66]—is a reformulation of the Leibnizian basic question, which, however, with Leibniz (we might say) aimed at God's favor: *Pourquoi il y a plutôt quelque chose que rien?* ("Why is there something rather than nothing?").[67] But can these two basic questions—the question of being and the question of God—be absolutely separated? And what of the old proposition *Ex nihilo nihil fit* ("nothing can come from nothing")? This, too, Heidegger reformulated: "*Ex nihilo omne ens qua ens fit* (every being, so far as it is a being, is made out of nothing)."[68] But, once again, do not these two propositions go together? Is being, being as event, as history of being, really self-explanatory?

These are the decisive *questions raised by theology in regard to Heidegger's philosophy.* Cannot God be considered in the light of the nature of being? If we understand being as history, as the opening up of primordial truth occurring in constantly new ways in the individual human being, if we recognize the original connection between being, truth and historicity, when we come to think of the history of being, is it so easy to reject the question of a divine being? Even though, according to Heidegger, what is presented to us is the "groundless" history of being, can the question of a power that explains being and history be rejected and suppressed in this way? If the divine can never *a priori* be adequately represented, can the fact be overlooked that being as historicity, as a question, points beyond itself to a whither of historicity and to a whence and thus to a primal reason as a possibility of events?

Heidegger is supposed to have said once: "My philosophy is a waiting for God."[69] And even in 1953 he declared: "Without . . . theological origins, I would never have entered on a life of thought. But the origin always remains future."[70] He hoped that one day the night of God's darkness would be overcome and *a new God* would appear *in the light of being.* If man then were to come into "nearness to Being," a decision might be made "as to whether and how God and the gods withhold their presence and the night remains, whether and how the day of the holy dawns, whether and how in the upsurgence of the holy an epiphany of God and the gods can begin anew."[71] To talk about this, of course, is not the business of philosophizing in the traditional sense: "The thinking that is to come is no longer philosophy. . . . Thinking is on the descent to the poverty of its provisional essence. Thinking gathers language into simple saying."[72]

Heidegger studied theological texts right up to his last years, even following attentively the debate on infallibility that started in Catholic circles in the early seventies[73] and expressly asking for a church burial (which could not have been taken for granted).[74] At this time of waiting, he adorns being itself with divine attributes and metaphors. He speaks of the revelation of being, its nonappearance and its illuminating-concealing advent; of its consolation and claim prevailing even today; of a being to which man belongs, with a voice to which he should listen even in the age of science and technology; on the truth of which he is intent as he pursues his pilgrimage; the history of which constitutes man's destiny. Is *being,* then, perhaps indeed the *veil of God?*

It may be doubted whether the forgetfulness of being on the part of philosophy ("leaving out being") is really worse—"uncanny . . . because more active and older"[75]—than the forsakenness of God ("absence of God").[76] Is it possible that Nietzsche, the "metaphysician," in this respect had a deeper insight than Heidegger, his interpreter? And conversely, according to Heidegger, should it not be a matter for theology—which is also charged by him, together with metaphysics, with forgetfulness of being—also "to think of being itself"[77] and precisely in this way to think of God, even though its most typical question is and must remain the question of God and not that of being? To think of God, who, according to Aquinas also, is not to be understood simply as supreme being or (as with Spinoza) as *causa sui* but certainly as the reality whose essence is pure being: "self-subsistent being itself"?[78] To think of God, who —perhaps even according to Heidegger—is even more hidden than being?

Certainly we shall have to face the question as to how a way from the finite event (despite the openness of being toward the unlimited, its advent in man is finite) to the infinite is possible. After all that we have heard about fundamental trust, it seems unlikely that pure reason will be successful in finding that way. At this point, reason must wait for a basic experience in which the veil is lifted. It is kept to the question of whether it will be lifted. All philosophically "pure" talk of God should not deny its hypothetical character, its suprarational assumptions. After all that we have already considered, pure reason must also be expected to commit itself to a qualified fundamental trust, in virtue of which—becoming itself more transparent—it can talk of God without relapsing into the dualism of traditional "meta-physics." It might thus perhaps come more close to that simple hearing and speaking sought by Heidegger. It might then find its way from the question to an answer in which the event of being as veil of God is perhaps not lifted but at any rate becomes transparent. These are the possibilities to which Heidegger draws our attention. Ludwig Weber says appropriately: "It is possible, anyway, to believe in a relationship of God to being as event in the form of a coordination or preordination. Again the question is raised as to whether the articulation of this belief means a relapse into metaphysics. In my opinion this is not so. For the question of being is not in the least affected by this belief but must be undertaken with all its consequences also by the believer. On the other hand, nothing is said that defines the relationship of God to being, to suggest that being could not be being as event. But it is true that God 'is' even more hidden than being."[79]

Of course the question is not now being or not-being, nor waiting for being or not-being. But, *waiting for God,* or waiting, vain, futile *waiting for Godot*—that is the question that Heidegger's philosophy in the last resort places before us, and theology should make every effort to examine it. Theology should not simply be silent before God but should talk about him afresh, without the framework of a dualistic metaphysics. At the same time, we must always remain aware of the *limits of Heidegger's phi-*

*losophy*—if only by recalling what we learned about transcending and transcendence from Bloch and Horkheimer. It is in this light that we can understand why Heidegger's waiting remained so oddly neutral and anemic. He was unable to make clear that this waiting was not merely thinking and meditating but could be man's concrete experience of life and suffering in history and society, for many even an inhuman suffering that tears all waiting away from its restrained neutrality. Here—in the opinion of many people—lie the limits of Heidegger's philosophy:

in a dangerous way—and the political consequences have become only too obvious—Heidegger ignores the *real history* of the world and of man in favor of a universal history of being and of man's historicity;

in a similarly dangerous way—and this affects his understanding of relatedness to the future—Heidegger ignores *real society* in favor of a universal being-together on the part of men and of a universal relatedness to being.

These limits, however, may be left to philosophical discussion. And it is precisely the question of the God who is more hidden than being, the question of the "more divine God,"[80] that permits us to raise the question of his existence in a new form. Does God exist? Indeed, is the term "God" a meaningful term at all? This is the problem as stated in analytical philosophy, which has largely replaced Heidegger's philosophy even in Germany.

## "God"—a meaningful term: Ludwig Wittgenstein

After all that we have heard, it may seem a little odd (not only to theologians) that, up to the present time, in certain philosophical schools and especially in analytical philosophy or linguistic analysis, discussion has centered, with a great display of erudition, not on whether God exists or does not exist but on whether "God" is a meaningful or meaningless term. How is this possible after the great minds of world history have wrestled for a lifetime particularly with the question of God, after the history of philosophy through two and a half millennia has turned mainly on this term, when even today there can be no doubt about the relevance of the term for the greater part of mankind? The riddle is quickly solved if we recall the fact that these discussions are the consequence of that positivistic theory of knowledge that had to be corrected in the course of its history. We heard about this at an earlier stage.[81] If we do not accept the empiricist verification principle of logical positivism, then from the very outset there is no basis for asserting the meaninglessness of all "metaphysical" terms and thus particularly of the term "God."

Here, too, lies the reason why the aggressive book *Language, Truth and Logic* (1936), produced by the then twenty-five-year-old Oxford lecturer A. J. Ayer,[82] which became the antitheological catechism of the logical analysts, is out of date. Out of date too is Anthony Flew's *Theology and Falsification* (1950),[83] along with John Wisdom's frequently reprinted parable of God as a gardener, nowhere palpable, nowhere visible, in the dim light of the primeval forest and consequently not verifiable. All this is as out of date as the antimetaphysical positions of the Vienna Circle, on which it depends.[84] Are ethical propositions merely "emotional expressions"? Is God a "nonsense"? This position is as unsound as it is radical. Discussion on Carnap's theories as early as the thirties showed the *untenability of the empiricist verification principle*.[85] And Ayer himself had to admit that ethical statements at least can be meaningful without being empirically verifiable, an admission that makes the empiricist criterion of meaning thoroughly questionable.

Other analysts,[86] such as the English philosophers R. B. Braithwaite[87] and R. M. Hare,[88] have drawn the conclusion that not only ethical but *also religious statements can be meaningful* without being empirically verifiable. Religious statements also, they think, are not meant to describe any "facts," to express any truth. Literally understood, they are neither true nor false, but meaningless. They are meaningful only in so far as they express certain attitudes to life and to the world: moral (expressions of man's ethical commitment: R. B. Braithwaite) or quasi-metaphysical (expressions of a particular view of reality, what R. M. Hare calls "blik").[89] With reference to Hare, the American theologian Paul van Buren[90] later interpreted New Testament statements of faith—appealing to Karl Barth's critique of a natural knowledge of God—simply as forms of expression for a particular attitude to life (Jesus' "contagious freedom"). But all these views, although they represent an obvious advance on Ayer and Flew, are still entangled in empiricist prejudices and at the same time contradict the self-understanding of the religions.

Of course, there can be no objection in principle if philosophers, instead of outlining a speculative system or an ideological synthesis, choose to occupy themselves simply and solely with analysis or "meta-analysis" (= analysis of the analysis) of "logic" and "grammar"—even of religious language—if they are concerned with a "therapeutic" analysis that is meant to describe (and not to explain) not the truth, not the what, but only the how, that is, the style and functioning, of religious language. On the contrary: in our very first chapter, we stressed the fact that linguistic analysis can help considerably to clarify even theology, with its often nebulous, antiquated or jargonistic, pseudo-profound language and its lack of logical transparency. There are, then, increasing numbers of linguistic analysts who reject or at least considerably modify the empiricist criterion of meaning, refuted already by Popper, as the sole legitimate principle of knowledge of reality. From this standpoint, they can easily see a meaning even in religious language and in the term "God." Linguistic analysis or analytical philosophy, established in England from the beginning of this century and in America from the forties, proves increasingly to be a methodological trend (a way of pursuing philosophy) embracing the most diverse ideological positions and not a uniform movement or theory even of a positivist character (concerned with "what" is pursued in philosophy).[91]

Ludwig Wittgenstein in particular, whom we got to know at an earlier stage as the central figure in this movement,[92] never described the "mystical," or particularly God, simply as absurd, as nonexistent. For him, God was not expressible, "inexpressible," and was part of what he called "problems of life." And when Wittgenstein returned from Austria to Cambridge in 1929, he had already thoroughly changed his views and begun to be doubtful about fundamental positions adopted in his *Tractatus Logico-philosophicus,* which he had first presented as a definitive solution. In his *Philosophical Investigations,* on which he was mainly working from the thirties until his death and which was only published after his death (1951),[93] it becomes clear that the world splits up not only into facts but also into things or events. Reality offers for analysis not merely a single possibility but several. An ideal uniform language to depict the world is impossible. Language itself is not absolutely clear, but ambiguous. Analysis does not lead necessarily to true reality. It is here that the difficulties really lie. "Philosophy is a battle against the bewitchment of our intelligence by means of language."[94] Such concepts as nothingness or spirit, for instance, are regarded as things; we think it is possible to participate in such universal essences as "horse" or "man."

What is to be done in this situation? According to Wittgenstein, the only possibility is to clarify and distinguish precisely the various meanings of words according to usage, function, role in the many areas of life. The meaning of words differs in each particular language world. There is not merely "language" in a general way. According to the various spheres of life or "forms of life," where in each case words are differently used, within a unity of language and activities there are *different "language games"* with different working rules. There is a great difference whether the word "thou" is used as a threat or as a term of endearment, whether one and the same statement is made in science, in ethics or in aesthetics, in a joke, in a police report or in the description of a dream. Hence, according to Wittgenstein, there is no transition from one speech level to another, there is no universal criterion of the meaningfulness of language. Every language game—which can, however, never be a private language— has its own criterion. Only if we describe and elucidate not the great speculations about ultimate reasons but the various language games as they are actually and underivably played, can we—according to Wittgenstein— get rid of the confusion in our minds and make philosophical problems disappear.[95]

Is the term "God" thereby saved? Some contemporary linguistic analysts, such as Norman Malcolm, G. E. Hughes, W. D. Hudson, P.

Winch, D. Z. Phillips,[96] with a more positive attitude to religion, perhaps make things too easy when they declare that religious language is simply and solely a language game that has been so long in use that it cannot be replaced by any other. Certainly religious terms have their own meaning and religious language has its own logic. But is religious language exempted from the universal rules of logic, which can scarcely be given up? Is it so certain that the religious language game is meaningful simply because it is a *fait accompli?* Is it so certain that it cannot be replaced by another language game, for instance by the ethical as with Braithwaite or the quasi-metaphysical as with Hare? If God did not really exist and religious language was consequently unrelated to anything (as some early logical positivists assumed as a result of their partly understandable negative attitude to religion), it could be very difficult, even impossible, to justify religious language as an autonomous, irreducible language game. For there is also an atheistic language game (or perhaps that of superstition or of magic, etc.), which is not justified merely because (likewise after long use) it is a *fait accompli.* Or are the two language games—the religious and the atheistic—supposed to be simultaneously legitimate and meaningful? And within the one religious language game would any possible superstition, however unreasonable, be supposed from the outset to be justified?

In brief, the question of truth cannot be avoided. And this truth can be tested by experience, as we shall see, by indirect verification through the experience of reality.[97] Man, endowed with reason, has a right to know whether his prayer and ritual are or are not related to a reality other than himself; whether traditional religious images of creation and consummation are not merely human inventions; whether the concept of God is nothing but a pure projection; whether religion as a whole, as Freud thought, is merely the strongest of all illusions. All meta-theology (theory of theology), reflecting on theology, is (like meta-language) nonsense if theology (or language) itself is without meaning. And theology would be without meaning if God did not exist.

M. J. Charlesworth is right: "In order to show that the concept of God is not an illusory one, we would need to demonstrate its instantiation in some way and not merely rest content with describing and analysing its *de facto* use in religious discourse."[98] Religion is not a more or less irrational, emotional, special field like—to recall Carnap—poetry or erotic literature. If God does not exist, the term "God" and the genuinely religious game is meaningless. But if God does exist—and this question of course remains open—the term "God," anyway, has meaning and the religious language game has its specific importance. Neither does this language game contradict that universal logic which in fact holds for all language games. It then has its own, intrinsic rationality. If God exists, the atheist—who rejects the religious language game—is cutting himself off from fundamental human experiences no less than someone whose prejudice prevents him from recognizing the aesthetic or ethical dimension of life. If God exists, this means for man an invitation to commit himself to the religious "form of life" in order to understand the religious language game. If he exists. . . .

Wittgenstein once admitted that the point of his *Tractatus* was ethical and that the more important part of the book was the part he had not written.[99] By this he meant—in the opinion of his biographer, David Pears—"that, among the things that cannot be said, those which he did not even try to put into words, religion, morality and aesthetics, are more important than the one he did try to put into words, philosophy. . . . The *Tractatus* is an attempt to say about all possible facts something which cannot really be said, because it is not itself factual, but which can be discerned through the world of facts."[100] Whether Wittgenstein stood for pantheism (or panentheism)—as Pears thinks he can establish by comparing the *Tractatus* with the *Notebooks*—or not, "there is a positive analogy between philosophy and religion."[101]

However we link together and fit into a whole (if this is possible at all) Wittgenstein's statements—often at once illuminating and obscuring, the product of wide-ranging and occasionally incoherent thought[102]—in the light of our own fundamental positions, observing the "limits of language" in our argument and yet transcending them in reasonable trust, we can possibly understand and also approve what Wittgenstein wrote in his notebook as early as June 11, 1916:

> *What do I know about God and the purpose of life?*
> *I know that this world exists.*
> *That I am placed in it like my eye in its visual field.*
> *That something about it is problematic, which we call its meaning.*
> *That this meaning does not lie in it but outside it.*
> *That life is the world.*
> *That my will penetrates the world.*
> *That my will is good or evil.*
> *Therefore that good and evil are somehow connected with the meaning of the world.*
> *The meaning of life, i.e. the meaning of the world, we can call God.*
> *And connect with this the comparison of God to a father.*
> *To pray is to think about the meaning of life.*[103]

And on July 8:

> *To believe in a god means to see that the facts of the world are not the end of the matter.*
> *To believe in God means to see that life has a meaning.*[104]

During the Second World War, Wittgenstein worked as a male nurse in a hospital and in 1947, at the age of fifty-eight, four years before his death, resigned his chair at Cambridge. Throughout his life, he personally defended religion against its destructive, positivistic despisers.[105] Religious dogmas, however, he continued to regard not as empirical hypotheses but as affecting our thoughts and actions in other ways. What was decisive for him was the difference they made to the life of the people who believed in them. From its great turning point in the First World War, Wittgenstein's life seems to be a testimony to this. Just before he lost consciousness, he cried: "Tell them that I've had a wonderful life!"[106]

Wittgenstein cannot be invoked anyway when the question of God is assumed to have been answered in the negative in contemporary analytical philosophy. Indeed, we must ask if it is a good thing for philosophy and "problems of life," philosophy and religion, to be separated in such a way that those great questions are scarcely raised in philosophical terms and the administration of the *great inherited estate of philosophy* is largely left to theologians.

At the present time also, many philosophers see that philosophy after the Second World War had acquired an unusual prestige as a result of the work of Heidegger and Jaspers, Sartre and Camus, Russell and Whitehead, Wittgenstein and Carnap, Adorno and Horkheimer, Marcuse and Bloch, but that today—despite the colossal business of learning carried on at the universities—it is faced by two dangers: on the one hand of being split up into the specialist sciences such as the natural sciences, psychology and sociology, which seem to have a more exact knowledge of man and the world than philosophy has; on the other hand, of disappearing in the increasingly abstract theory of knowledge, linguistic criticism and metatheories. We would prefer not to speak here of a "decline of philosophy" (C. Grossner)[107] or of the survival only of a "myth of philosophy" (W. Hochkeppel).[108] But at least we must point to a real danger when philosophy no longer raises at all the questions of the great whence and why: "The history of philosophy was once the great field of experiment for bold speculations, daring hypotheses and endless daydreams. Here for thousands of years the dough was kneaded and kneaded until it finally emerged as science. If it is true—to quote Jaspers once more—that 'in philosophizing itself' we have scarcely even gotten back to Plato—and there are many signs of this—where are we to find courage and hope for radical improvements? If, according to Adorno's 'protest against myth,' what is 'always the same is mythical,' why, then, do we still have today the myth of philosophy? And yet at the heart of this myth there lives the ineradicable wish and promise to come by reflection to understand the world in its total coherence, to become aware of its meaning and to reconcile nature and mind. This religious motive is the vital spark also of critical philosophy, even though at the present time it is almost extinguished under a mass of scholastic problems of detail. And it is clear that, if philosophy denies this residue, it is depriving itself of its ultimate meaning."[109]

There are signs today of a renovation of philosophy. Are we not—as is frequently stressed—waiting today for new values, patterns of interpretation and models? Are we not raising afresh the three great questions of Kant? Is there not perhaps a new philosophy of religion in the process of formation? Theologians should not be jealous if the most important heritage of the two and a half millennia of philosophy is not assigned solely to them. Neither should philosophers leave it entirely to theologians, even though it is not at all easy to manage and make fruitful. Is there not something invested here that could be considered in Bloch's thought on hope and in Heidegger's waiting for a new God? Ought we not—and this would be our modestly tentative invitation to philosophers —to *begin afresh to reflect together and also to talk together about the question of God?* Perhaps this book may help to break down some hitherto justifiable "antimetaphysical" and "antitheological" barriers to attempts at dealing again with this central theme.

We know all the objections raised by critics of religion from Feuerbach to analytical philosophy, even against the very term "God," which is so often misused. We have tried to take these objections seriously. And yet there is *no alternative to this term.* Despite all its monstrous misuse, it is irreplaceable. "How do you manage time after time to say 'God'? How can you expect your readers to accept the term in the sense in which you want it to be taken? . . . Which term in human language has been so misused, so stained, so desecrated as this?" To this question, Martin Buber, the Jewish philosopher of religion, replies: "Yes, it is the most loaded of all words used by men. None has been so soiled, so mauled. But that is the very reason why I cannot give it up. Generations of men have blamed this word for the burdens of their troubled lives and crushed it to the ground; it lies in the dust, bearing all their burdens. Generations of men with their religious divisions have torn the word apart; they have killed for it and died for it; it bears all their fingerprints and is stained with all their blood. Where would I find a word to equal it, to describe supreme reality? If I were to take the purest, most sparkling term from the innermost treasury of the philosophers, I could capture in it no more than a noncommittal idea, not the presence of what I mean, of what generations of men in the vastness of their living and dying have venerated and degraded. . . . We must respect those who taboo it, since they revolt against the wrong and mischief that were so readily claimed to be authorized in the name of God; but we cannot relinquish it. It is easy to understand why there are some who propose a period of silence about the 'last things,' so that the misused words may be redeemed. But this is not the way to redeem them. We cannot clean up the term 'God' and we cannot make it whole; but, stained and mauled as it is, we can raise it from the ground and set it above an hour of great sorrow."[110]

No, instead of not talking any more about God, or instead of talking about God as we have done hitherto, the really important thing for theologians and philosophers today would be to learn afresh to speak with care about God.

# II. Theological discussions

Does God exist at all? Must we simply believe it? We are constantly told to do so by all types of believers in God. But the response, that it is possible not to believe in God, comes not only from those who deny God but also from those who doubt his existence or who are still seeking him. Some Catholics suggest that we must first know God if we are to believe in him. But Protestants especially deny this and claim that we must first believe in God before we can know him. Belief in God is a matter of dispute between believers and unbelievers, between believers of one kind and believers of a different kind. The debate, both in Catholic and in Protestant circles, is extremely lively but also very complex. We shall try to sort it out. The reader who is less interested in these theological discussions may be content to look at the results summarized in a series of points at the end of this section.

The positions on the *question of fundamental certainty*, as we came to understand them from the beginning of modern times onward—fundamental certainty being based either on the *cogito* or on the credo—appear to have been eliminated in our answer about fundamental trust. But the same positions were taken up again and maintained even more strongly in regard to the *question of the certainty of God* and must be studied in greater depth here. Does certainty of God arise from reason or from faith?

## 1. Catholic or Protestant approach?

"To come to this question of the existence of God, it is a large and serious question, and if I were to attempt to deal with it in any adequate manner I should have to keep you here until Kingdom Come, so that you will have to excuse me if I deal with it in a somewhat summary fashion."[1] We certainly cannot deal with it as briefly as *Bertrand Russell* does in this lecture, but we must first hear a little more of what he says: "You know, of course, that the Catholic Church has laid it down as a dogma that the existence of God can be proved by the unaided reason. That is a somewhat curious dogma, but it is one of their dogmas. They had to introduce it because at one time the Freethinkers were in the habit of saying that there were such and such arguments which mere reason might urge against the existence of God, but of course they knew as a matter of faith that God did exist. The arguments and the reasons were set out at great length, and the Catholic Church felt that they must stop it. Therefore they laid it down that the existence of God can be proved by the unaided reason, and they had to set up what they considered were arguments to prove it."[2] Russell himself thought that these arguments did not prove it, and this was a decisive reason why he would not become a Christian. But what is the dogma about which Russell speaks here so vaguely?

## Knowledge of God by reason: Vatican I

Basically, certainty comes from reason, to which of course the certainty of faith must be added. This is the position quite clearly adopted by the First Vatican Council, in 1870. Hence the declaration: "If anyone says that the one true God, our Creator and Lord, cannot be known with certainty by the natural light of reason from created things, he is to be condemned."[3] How did the Council come to produce such a harsh theological proposition?

It was Pope Pius IX who formed the plan for a new council[4]—three hundred years after the Counter-Reformation Council of Trent—because of the Church's need to defend itself and to ward off opponents, "so as to provide in this extraordinary way for the extraordinary needs of the flock of Christ"[5] and "to bring necessary and salutary remedies to the many evils whereby the Church is oppressed."[6] This is how the situation was seen at that time in Rome. In modern times, one attack after another had been made on the bulwark of the Church. On Lutheranism and Calvinism there followed Jansenism, Gallicanism and princely absolutism; with the beginning of a new age came the French Revolution, the Napoleonic Wars and secularism; and after all these, atheistic materialism, liberalism and socialism. An immense number of completely new questions, problems and needs had arisen: innumerable educated people had left the Church, and the proletarian masses were increasingly abandoning it. Falling away from the Church in the Reformation period was followed—consistently, from the Roman viewpoint—by the falling away from Christ at the Enlightenment and finally by the falling away from God in the nineteenth century.

What was to be done? In Rome there seemed to be only one way to preserve the Catholic Church from the danger of falling apart as Protestantism had done. There had to be a consolidation around the Roman center and an unflinching rejection of the spirit of the age: opposition to the omnipotent modern states and to the revolutions of philosophers and writers and later of the proletarian masses endangering everything; opposition to enemies without and heretics within the walls. Among the here-

tics, the Jansenists were succeeded by the fideists and on the other hand
by the much more dangerous rationalists, who were ready to make compromises with modern philosophy and science.

Rome, then, had become involved in a stubborn confrontation with the
modern age, leading to a reaction in the form of a raging anticlericalism
and a *Kulturkampf*. People in the Roman Curia were increasingly unable
to perceive what was positive in the revolutions, what was true in modern
philosophy, literature, natural science, what was good in democracy and
national consolidation, in liberal tolerance and freedom and eventually
also in the socialist critique of religion and society. There was indeed a
religious revival (with new forms of piety and devotion, religious orders,
associations, missionary impulses, pastoral methods) at the time of restoration and Romanticism. But all this happened mostly in specifically
Roman Catholic forms, anti-Protestant, anti-Enlightenment, antimodern.
What prevented a more positive attitude toward the modern age were not
least the Papal States, the lamentable organization and wretched social
conditions of which inevitably placed the popes in an antidemocratic, antinationalist, antilaical, antiliberal, antisocial light. On the whole, there
was an orientation toward the past, toward restoration. It was the period
of the Neo-Gothic, Neo-Romanesque, Neo-Gregorian, Neo-Scholastic.
The new—what was really new—was condemned. In the course of the
first half of the nineteenth century, there had been such an immense
number of condemnations by the papal magisterium of the new errors
that Pius IX felt compelled, on the tenth anniversary of the definition of
Mary's immaculate conception, on December 8, 1964, to publish a comprehensive list, that famous-notorious "Syllabus" ("Collection of Modern Errors"),[7] which is a thoroughgoing rejection of the modern outlook
and culminates in the eightieth "error": "The Roman Pontiff can and
must be reconciled and come to terms with progress, liberalism, and modern civilisation."[8]

All this forms the background against which alone the First Vatican
Council can be understood: its complete failure in regard to practical
reforms (out of forty-six schemata on reform, four were discussed and
none adopted); its definition of papal primacy and infallibility, which was
supposed to preserve the Papal States from destruction; finally, its Dogmatic Constitution, "On Catholic Faith," against the errors of the time:
against materialism, deism, various forms of pantheism, against fideism,
traditionalism and rationalism. There was a desire especially definitively to
clarify the question of reason and faith, which had been violently disputed
from the period of the Enlightenment. The attempt was made—wholly
under the influence of neoscholastic theology, fostered especially by the
Roman Jesuits—to restore the medieval outlook, in particular that of
Aquinas, with the dual order of knowledge described in an earlier chapter:
the planes of reason and of faith, natural truth and revealed truth, philosophy and theology, on two clearly distinguished but simultaneously coor-

dinated levels.[9] In the light of this traditional, Thomistic position, the
Council did not need to develop any detailed teaching on reason and
faith, but could restrict itself to the rejection of what were regarded as
errors, to marking out two main fronts and placing itself in the center, between rationalism and fideism. What does this mean in concrete terms?

It means a *first demarcation. There must be no reduction of faith to
reason.* This is what radical rationalism did, upholding a reason without
faith and rejecting everything supernatural. But, in the Council's view,
this, too, was the effect of the moderate rationalism of those German theologians who allegedly met rationalism halfway (semirationalism).

The Bonn Catholic theologian *Georg Hermes* (1775–1831), highly esteemed by the Archbishop of Cologne at the time, attempted to make use
of Kant's philosophy to establish a new scientific foundation for faith and
theology. After his death (in the same year as Hegel's), he was summarily
condemned, in 1835, by Pope Gregory XVI, and his books were placed on
the Index.[10] The "Hermesian" professors of theology, who did not submit
to Rome, years later—when a more conservative archbishop was appointed to Cologne and when the situation in ecclesiastical politics
seemed more favorable—were removed from their chairs (F. X. Biunde,
J. J. Rosenbaum, J. H. Leutzen) or deprived of their ecclesiastical license
to teach and compelled to retire (H. Achterfeld, J. W. J. Braun).

Similarly the Austrian theologian *Anton Günther,* known as *Cartesius
correctus,* influenced by Descartes but also by Kant and German Idealism,
was condemned in 1857 by Pius IX, and his work was placed on the
Index. He had ventured to undertake a new justification of the Church's
teaching in a more or less speculative but also sharply antischolastic fashion, in the light of the philosophical trends of the time.[11] In the subsequent years, individual works defending Günther were also put on the
Index; such prominent Güntherians as P. Knoodt, J. B. Baltzer, T. W.
Weber and J. H. Reinkens joined the Old Catholics after the First
Vatican Council. For that council had again condemned both "Her-
mesianism" and "Güntherianism,"[12] which actually amounted to a
commitment on the part of Rome to neo-Scholasticism and prepared
the further phase in the struggle against dissident theologians who had
become involved in a constructive discussion with scientific trends of the
time and had worked for a reform of the Church.

But, for the Council, *a second demarcation* is linked with the first.
*There must be no reduction of reason to faith.* This in fact is what radical
fideism did, upholding in practice an irrational faith—a faith without
reason—and rejecting any natural knowledge of God. But, in the view of
Vatican I, this, too, was the effect of the radical traditionalism—especially
of certain French theologians—which was practically the same as fideism.

The Roman magisterium, however, proceeded only hesitatingly and

very much more considerately against these conservative, anti-Enlightenment traditionalists, who declared that individual human reason was incapable of knowing metaphysical and religious truths and appealed instead
—even for the knowledge of God's existence—to a "primitive revelation"
given by God to the first human couple, handed down orally through the
generations and guaranteed by the consensus of the human race.

Thus *Louis Gabriel Ambroise, Vicomte de Bonald* (1754–1840), royal-
ist philosopher of the Restoration, opponent of the separation of powers
and freedom of the press in the modern democratic state, who developed
traditionalism as a system, was not censured. And *Hugues-Félicité Robert
de Lamennais* (1782–1854), a Catholic theologian also influenced by De
Bonald, at first a papalist and infallibilist, who won European support for
traditionalism, was condemned only after he had turned to liberal democracy[13] and ended—unreconciled to the Church—as a deputy on the extreme Left. *Louis E. M. Bautain* (1796–1867), who had been influenced
by the Augustinian-Jansenist theory of grace, was repeatedly compelled to
subscribe to certain propositions;[14] the same thing happened to the later
spokesman for French traditionalism *Augustine Bonnetty* (1789–1879).[15]
The First Vatican Council finally condemned radical traditionalism,
which sought to make knowledge of God depend with absolute necessity
on a primitive revelation.[16]

From the two demarcations, what followed thirdly for the Council was
positively *reason and faith*.[17] There could be no contradiction,[18] but only
mutual dependence,[19] between reason and faith. This meant, in the first
place, a knowledge of God as found in creation, acquired by natural
reason, which belongs to man at every stage in his history from his original to his final state.[20] To what purpose? To provide a rational foundation
for the knowledge of the God attested and revealed in the Bible, the God
who is known only by divine faith. But it is only in virtue of the knowledge of God by natural reason that this Christian faith can be seen not to
be an irrational, intellectually irresponsible undertaking. Only in this way
is knowledge of God possible for every human being and not only for
Christians: knowledge of God, that is, as origin and end of all things.[21]

Against Russell it must be pointed out that Vatican I asserts not that
every human being actually knows God but that knowledge of God is possible in principle for every human being.[22] Neither does it assert that
God's existence can be proved, but only that it can be known from
created things.[23] Nor, finally, does it assert that even natural knowledge of
God is acquired in fact without God's grace; only that natural knowledge
of God comes about without divine revelation. Does this seem an ingenious solution to the problem of reason and faith? Is it a bad or a fair compromise?

Even at that time, of course, it could well have been asked whether this
"synthesis" of Vatican I was not too simple, more a superficial juxtapo-

sition of reason and faith than a genuine reconciliation. Anyway, the Council—broken off as a result of the outbreak of the Franco-Prussian War on the day of the definition of infallibility—had only a limited effect on almost all questions. Despite the definitions of the primacy and of infallibility, the Papal States were lost. Pius IX's liberal successor, Leo XIII (1878–1903), at once corrected to a surprising extent Rome's negative attitude toward democracy, liberal freedoms and the social question, as also toward exegesis and church history. A century later, Vatican II had to catch up with the practical reforms. The problems of "Catholic faith" in general and of reason and faith in particular arose again in a dramatic fashion soon after Vatican I in the fierce struggle of Pius X (1903–14), the successor of Leo XIII, against all those theologians who had dared to come to terms with the modern age and who were discredited simply by being called "modernists."[24] Typical in this connection is the tightening— not justified in the light of Vatican I—of the definition of the natural knowledge of God. The antimodernist oath, prescribed as binding on all the Catholic clergy up to Vatican II, among many other things requires a sworn statement that God's existence can not only be known with certainty but "even proved" (*adeoque demonstrari*).[25]

The theologically most important attack on the definition of Vatican I, however, came only after the purge of the modernists and then from outside. It was made by the Protestant theologian Karl Barth.


## Knowledge of God by faith: Karl Barth

As human beings, how can we speak, how can we preach about God? This was the question that stirred *Karl Barth* in the general political, economic, cultural and intellectual crisis after the disaster of the First World War. It stands at the beginning of his very first work, which was neither "scientific" nor "orthodox" but profoundly disturbing in its expressionistic style, the commentary on Paul's Epistle to the Romans,[26] which made the young pastor of the Swiss congregation at Safenwil famous at one stroke.

As we saw earlier in connection with Pascal and Kierkegaard,[27] for Barth (at that time together with his friends Emil Brunner, Eduard Thurneysen, Friedrich Gogarten and Rudolf Bultmann), optimistic, cultured Protestantism had been thoroughly compromised and with it its "liberal theology." Undecided, still "between the times" (the title of a periodical produced by him and his friends), he had begun to develop a "theology of crisis," later called *dialectical theology*, and thus initiated the great upheaval in Protestant theology in the twentieth century. In the many-sided crisis of the whole existing order, of institutions, traditions and authorities, for Barth a turning point was unavoidable: away from subjective experience and pious feelings and toward the Bible; away from history and toward God's revelation; away from religious talk about the notion of God and toward the proclamation of the word of God; away from religion and religiosity and toward Christian faith; away from man's religious needs and toward God, who is the "wholly Other," manifest only in Jesus Christ.

In the name of this wholly other God, in the name—that is—of the divinity of God, Barth protests decidedly *against "natural theology"* in its two great denominational theological forms, which are only superficially opposed to one another: *on the one hand* in the form of liberal *neo-Protestantism*, following Schleiermacher, wholly oriented to the devout, religious person instead of God and his revelation; *on the other hand* in the form of *Roman Catholicism*, following scholasticism and the First Vatican Council, coordinating God and man, involving an interplay of man and God, nature and grace, reason and faith, philosophy and theology.

This theological protest had decidedly *political consequences*. According to Barth, both liberal neo-Protestantism and Roman Catholicism had adopted an uncritical conformism and *come to terms with the prevailing political systems*, at first with imperial Germany and later with National Socialism. Did not the Protestant "German Christians" at that time see in National Socialism something like a new revelation and in Adolf Hitler a new Luther or even Christ, uniting Christianity and Germanity? Did not prominent advocates of the Catholic "two floors" theology think that National Socialism wanted to do on the natural plane what Christianity wanted to do on the supernatural plane? Here, according to Barth, could be seen the whole political danger of a "Christian" natural theology. And Barth then drew the appropriate concrete conclusions from this theological insight. After 1933 he organized the resistance of the "Confessing Church" to the National Socialist regime and in 1934 inspired the Barmen Synod, with its clear profession of faith in Jesus Christ, the "one Word of God," besides which no "other events and powers, forms and truths" can be recognized as God's revelation.[28] In 1935, Barth was expelled from his professorship in Bonn and sent back to his own country, Switzerland.

Under these circumstances, it seemed necessary radically to reject any form of natural theology: both neo-Protestant and Roman Catholic, both purely theological and political, both neopagan (autonomous) and Christian (nonautonomous). For Karl Barth, any natural theology is anti-Christian. And the analogy of being, which assimilates God and man in the name of the concept of being, is for Barth anti-Christian in an absolute sense. As he explains in the famous Foreword to the first volume of the monumental *Church Dogmatics:* "I regard the *analogia entis* as the invention of Antichrist and think that because of it one cannot become Catholic. Whereupon I at the same time allow myself to regard all other reasons for not becoming Catholic, as short-sighted and lacking in seriousness."[29]

Karl Barth's uncompromising "No" to natural theology struck even at his own Protestant fellow combatant and fellow countryman Emil Brunner, who in 1934 in his book *Nature and Grace*[30] had postulated a "point of contact" for revelation in man. Man's rationality, personhood and responsibility—all expressions of his created likeness to God—according to Brunner are preconditions for hearing the word of God.

*No:* this was the emphatic title of the angry work that Karl Barth wrote in the same year (in the Hotel Hassler, in Rome, with a view of the Vatican) against Brunner. No: for Barth, natural man is a sinner through and through, an absolutely rational and responsible sinner. And this sinful man's reason is blind to God's truth. Religious attitudes, knowledge of God, are certainly possible for man, he has a capacity for these things. But he does not reach his goal. For the God whom this human reason perceives in a natural knowledge—whether in philosophy or in theology or in the religions of the world—is nothing but a projection of man (in this respect, according to Barth, Feuerbach is absolutely right); he is the creation of man's ideological fantasy; he is not the one true Christian God; he is an idol, a substitute God, a counter-God. No, man cannot know the one true God. Unless . . . ? Unless God himself makes himself known, unless God himself shows himself, reveals himself to man. There is, then, no knowledge of God on man's part without God's revelation. God alone has the initiative. He is simultaneously the reality and the possibility of revelation. He does not need any "point of contact," any "organ" in man, for his revelation.[31]

From this point of view, it becomes clearer why Karl Barth directed this vigorous No, which he opposed to liberal theology and even to Emil Brunner, also against Vatican I, whose definition of the natural knowledge of God he submitted to a radical critique in his *Church Dogmatics*. For Barth finds even the statement of the question in Vatican I completely false in two respects:

a. The teaching of Vatican I means in practice a cleavage in the idea of one God into a "natural" and "supernatural" God. It lacks therefore the notion of the one true God.

Barth on the other hand wanted to start out unambiguously from the Christian idea of God, from the one trinitarian, true God: "Of this God and of His truth we have said that He is knowable only by the truth, i.e., only by His own grace and mercy."[32]

According to Barth, Vatican I likewise does not want to talk of another God or definitively only of a part of this one God: "But its procedure in the noetic question is different from in the ontological. To that extent it certainly intends to make a provisional division or partition in regard to the knowability of God, and this will inevitably lead to a partitioning of the one God as well."[33]

Scripture, according to Barth, knows only the one God of Abraham, Isaac and Jacob, the Father of Jesus Christ, and not a God of the philosophers or God only as Creator: "What word of Scripture can be legitimately understood if it is not understood as witness to the one God? How can that partition of God be effected from the Scriptures?"[34]

b. The teaching of Vatican I means in practice abstracting from the real gracious work and action of God for the sake of being in general, which God is supposed to have in common with us human beings and with all that is.

For Barth, on the other hand, God is certainly he who was, is and will be: that is, a supremely real being. But, precisely as being, he is always simultaneously the one who acts: "We asked about the knowability of this being, about the truth of the real being of the Subject of this history."[35] But it is quite impossible to draw from Vatican I the conclusion "that the God referred to is engaged in a work and activity with man, which is for man a matter of life and death, of blessedness and damnation, nay more, which is for God a matter of His honour and therefore of the miracle of His love, and from which we cannot abstract for a single moment when it is a matter of the relationship of God and man and in particular of the knowability of God. Apparently Roman Catholic doctrine can and must make this abstraction."[36]

But, in virtue of that analogy of being in which being is to be attributed to God albeit on a different level and in an analogical fashion also to man, are God and man to be seen together on a common and therefore neutral ground? To this analogy of being, Barth opposes an analogy of faith, which, however, includes the analogy of being: "If there is a real analogy between God and man—an analogy which is a true analogy of being on both sides, an analogy in and with which the knowledge of God will in fact be given—what other analogy can it be than the analogy of being which is posited and created by the work and action of God Himself, the analogy which has its actuality from God and from God alone, and therefore in faith and in faith alone?"[37]

There is no doubt that this theological stance of Karl Barth is marvelously consistent. Religion must be understood in the light of revelation and not vice versa. And what revelation is must be told us by God himself and is attested in the Old and New Testaments. But, in the light of the word of God attested in Scripture, according to Barth, any kind of natural religion or knowledge of God—whether in Christianity or outside it—is simply false belief or even unbelief, both theoretically and practically:
*in theory,* natural religion (in the form of religious dogmatics) is an obstinate and arbitrary human desire to give shape to the image of God: "*idolatry*";[38]

*in practice*, natural religion (in the form of religious morality) is an obstinate and arbitrary human desire to fulfill God's law: *"justification by works."*[39]

*How, then, are we to know God? Only in faith in the revelation of God himself attested in the Bible.* Against the background of Luther's skepticism in regard to the bewitching "whore reason" and the "charlatan Aristotle," this is the position of the dialectical theology of Karl Barth and in this question also of Rudolf Bultmann,[40] together with their large following in Protestant theology[41] to this day. Compared with the depth to which the question has been probed here, the internal Catholic disputes about grace and nature seem at first to be very innocuous. But let us examine them more closely.

## 2. Controversy on natural theology

How did Catholic theology react to Karl Barth's radical attack? At first —apart from such exceptions as Gottlieb Söhngen and the unforgotten Robert Grosche, with the review for controversial theology *Catholica*, which the latter founded in 1932—not at all. In general, things went on at first in a good neo-Scholastic way, while of course insights of theological outsiders at the time—such as Romano Guardini and John Henry Newman—were cleverly incorporated into the neo-Scholastic system.[42] But a great internal Catholic controversy about the "supernatural," after various detours, led eventually to an ecumenical clarification.

### Nature and supernature: *nouvelle théologie*

It was only toward the end of the Second World War that the two-floors theory came under serious criticism, first of all in France. The French Jesuit *Henri de Lubac*, a friend of Teilhard, had edited with his fellow Jesuit Jean Daniélou the series Sources Chrétiennes (texts of the Fathers of the Church with commentaries) and Théologie (historical and systematic monographs). Together with a number of other French theologians, in the light especially of the thought of the Church Fathers, he tried to point to an alternative to neo-Scholastic theology and to work this out in various directions. This trend soon came to be called the *nouvelle théologie*, numbering among its supporters also H. Bouillard, H. Rondet, Y. de Montcheuil, H. U. von Balthasar, M. D. Chenu, Y. Congar.

De Lubac's book *Le surnaturel*,[43] published immediately after the Second World War, unleashed the conflict. Like many French and German Jesuit theologians, influenced by the Catholic transcendental philosophy of Joseph Maréchal and appealing to the authentic Aquinas (free from neo-Scholastic interpretation), De Lubac attempted to overcome the cleavage between the natural and the supernatural planes (involving an "extrincism" of grace). Any created spirit is endowed by the Creator with a natural aspiration for the infinite, for the eternal beatific vision of God (*desiderium naturale beatitudinis*), which is unconditional but of itself ineffectual without God's cooperation. Consequently there can be no "pure nature" of man oriented solely to a purely natural final end (without the vision of God). This idea of a "pure" nature (order of nature) with a purely natural end emerged historically for the first time in the controversy with Baius and Jansenius in the sixteenth and seventeenth centuries, as a means of securing the gratuitousness (the supernaturality) of grace (which can be protected in other ways today); the aspiration to beatitude is in the last resort a gift of the Creator and is fulfilled only by God's gift. The idea of pure nature must therefore be abandoned. In fact, even Vatican I avoided the term "pure nature" and, in particular, left unanswered the question as to whether a "pure" nature is possible or, still less, actual, whether it is identical with the nature of the pagan or of the sinner (fallen nature). Had the solution of the problem of nature and grace been found?

*Pius XII* (1939–58) reacted to this "new theology" almost as sharply as Pius X—whom he had canonized—had reacted to modernism. No genuine discussion was even permitted to emerge. On August 12, 1950, four years after the appearance of De Lubac's *Le surnaturel*, came a kind of new "Syllabus," the encyclical *Humani Generis*, "on some false opinions that threaten to undermine the fundamentals of Catholic teaching." This encyclical condemned the methods and many of the conclusions of the new theology (and philosophy) that deviated from neoscholasticism. De Lubac's view of the supernatural was expressly rejected, and at the same time the teaching on the natural knowledge of God was emphasized: "It is not surprising that novelties of this kind have already produced their poisonous fruits in almost all fields of theology. Doubts are raised about the capacity of human reason, unaided by divine revelation and divine grace, to demonstrate from created things the existence of a personal God. . . . Others destroy the gratuitousness of the supernatural order, suggesting that God cannot create beings endowed with intellect without ordaining and calling them to the beatific vision."[44]

Pius XII's words were followed by deeds. Without any sort of legal process, Henri de Lubac and other French Jesuit theologians were dismissed from their teaching posts and in many cases expelled from the locality of their previous activity. They were forbidden to write on controversial matters and were unable to defend themselves in any way; as we saw, Teilhard de Chardin had been reduced to silence at an earlier stage.[45] Only Jean Daniélou, at that time notably progressive, a masterly conformist, was able to continue teaching in Paris and even to gain advancement (becoming cardinal under Paul VI). Fear descended on the once so promising ecclesiastical educational establishments in France, whose teachers are not protected by civil law. On November 1 of the same Holy Year 1950 (despite numerous theological misgivings outside and inside the Catholic Church), Pius XII defined the bodily assumption of Mary into heaven. And on the theological purge in the Jesuit order there soon followed—in connection with the prohibition of the worker-priests—the purge in the Dominican order, where such outstanding theologians as M. D. Chenu and Yves Congar had become deeply involved in seeking a new relationship of the Catholic Church to the world, to the workers and to ecumenism, and a thoroughgoing reform of the Church.[46] Here too, without any legal process, books were prohibited, writing prohibited, people were dismissed and transferred, even temporarily banished from their own country.

Thus, within a short time, all the leaders in French Catholic theology, which had barely recovered from the antimodernist campaign and together with French Catholic literature (represented by Péguy, Bernanos, Claudel, Mauriac) had made unparalleled advances, were reduced to silence by a Pope who for his own part had his innumerable encyclicals and addresses written by court theologians, mostly German Jesuits. It was only under the former nuncio in Paris, later Pope John XXIII, that a number of the disciplined theologians were called as advisers to the Second Vatican Council and so rehabilitated in practice but without any public admission of the enormous wrong that had been done to them. But French theology even today has not recovered from these disciplinary measures, the same measures which (despite the famous speech against the methods of the Holy Office delivered at the Council by the Cardinal of Cologne), even in the postconciliar period, have been and are taken (more circumspectly, of course) in particular and not unimportant cases.

In Germany, *Karl Rahner* in particular, at first the object of considerable hostility, had pressed forward with unusual courage in many theological fields and thus opened new doors to postwar theology, all this largely in agreement with the intentions of his French fellow Jesuits. He criticized the two-floors theory and insisted on the one and only actual order of salvation, with the one and only actual end for all men, the supernatural vision of God. But Rahner wanted to retain "pure nature" with a purely natural end to human life, albeit merely as a strictly hypothetical possibility. He held the view that every human being, whether a believer or not, is in fact oriented to the supernatural end and consequently bears from the very outset a supernatural imprint: not as a supernatural essential constituent (an "essential"), as De Lubac thought, but as a factual supernatural "existential." Rahner, too, subsequently got into serious difficulties with the Roman magisterium and was for a time placed directly under his order's Roman censorship.

The Swiss *Hans Urs von Balthasar*, who left the Jesuit order in 1950 but associated by his studies in Lyons with the French Jesuits and particularly with De Lubac, warned now by the encyclical *Humani Generis*, adopted a very discriminating attitude in his brilliant book, a model of ecumenical theology, *Karl Barth. Darstellung und Deutung seiner Theologie*.[47] As against Barth, he maintained the view that the authentic Catholic understanding of the analogy of being sees this as encompassed by the analogy of faith; this was the view upheld especially by the Munich theologian Gottlieb Söhngen in the early thirties against Barth. And with regard to the concept of nature so vehemently attacked by Barth, Balthasar maintained that as a theological concept it could not be deduced from the philosophical concept but could be known only in faith on the basis of the order of grace. Thus a concept of nature filled with content (concrete human nature) would have to be distinguished from a formal, abstract concept of "pure" nature; the latter would be a mere marginal and auxiliary concept, the content of which could not be made clear and precise.

This internal Catholic and ecumenical controversy was the background for my own dissertation on "justification," written toward the end of my studies in Rome and Paris, in which I discussed from the Catholic standpoint the teaching of Karl Barth. It was surprising to find in 1957 that not only my teachers in Paris—Louis Bouyer and Guy de Broglie—as well as Balthasar and Rahner, but also conservative Roman Jesuits belonging to the circle around Pius XII, showed an interest in this work that not only represented a fundamental agreement between Barth and the Catholic teaching—properly understood—on the justification of the sinner, the basic Catholic-Protestant controversial point, but also clearly expressed reservations in regard to the terminology of "natural" and "supernatural."[48] The work constantly avoided that terminology (instead of speaking abstractly about human "nature," the concrete terms "man," "sinner," "Christian," were used). And at the time, no one agreed more clearly on this point with the "particularly welcome contribution to the discussion" than another theologian of the younger generation, Joseph Ratzinger, who had been a student of Söhngen. Particularly with reference to the problem of the natural and the supernatural, he warned against wanting to assume the existence of magisterial "decisions that have not yet been made."[49] And he saw a new starting point for discussion precisely in the attempt "in a discussion that had become too much bogged down in abstract terms (nature, supernatural, analogy of being or of faith)" to point to "its concrete center," that is, to Jesus Christ: "from this point the discussion could and should in fact gain new life."[50]

After the death of Pius XII, in 1958—who had been able to endow his exercise even of the ordinary magisterium with an aura of infallibility—and after the summoning of the Second Vatican Council, the new controversy on grace was soon forgotten and the terminology of "natural" and "supernatural" fell out of use surprisingly quickly. When Henri de Lubac was eventually able, in 1965, at the end of the Council, to publish his defensive work, produced during the long years of ostracism, scarcely anyone was interested.[51] The same problems were now presented in a different way, and new problems had emerged for which the appeal formerly made by De Lubac and Balthasar to the theology of the Fathers and to Aquinas seemed neither necessary nor very helpful.

Here, too, inquisitorial methods and factual claims to infallibility—as so often in the modern age—delayed an objective discussion for a long time and prevented a genuine solution of the problem. What can be maintained today of *the fruits of this unfortunate internal Catholic controversy on grace* as an aid to dealing with the problems of natural theology?

a. There is in reality *only one single goal of salvation ordained by God* for all men (the beatific vision of God) and consequently only one single order of salvation ordained by God's grace.

b. A *"pure nature,"* not oriented to the vision of God, *does not exist*. It can at best be abstracted theologically from the existing order of grace (as an unclear and imprecise auxiliary theological construct).

c. There is therefore *no two-level reality*, consisting of a "natural" substructure of truths of pure reason and a "supernatural" superstructure of truths of pure faith; justifiable distinctions between nature and grace, reason and faith, philosophy and theology, must therefore be seen and made within the one, undivided reality.

d. The abstract, quasi-Aristotelian, ambiguous, iridescent *categories of "natural" and "supernatural"* have proved *inadequate* for a discriminating solution of the complex problems presented here.

e. Instead of abstract talk in terms of "natural" and "supernatural," there must be *concrete talk of man* (not of human "nature") *and of God* (not of a "vision of God"), which for Christians must be oriented to the authentic Christian message and to an understanding of modern man.

The analogy of being—as Balthasar's answer to Barth has shown—does not mean the assimilation of God and man on the same plane and is not the real point of controversy between Catholics and Protestants. Karl Barth tacitly dropped what he had thought to be the one serious reason for not being a Catholic. But he did not become a Catholic. He merely corrected himself—not formally but practically. Almost like the popes in so many things.

## Non-Christians' knowledge of God

*Rudolf Bultmann* had agreed from the beginning with Karl Barth in the claim that faith is the sole possible way of access to God, who is perceptible only through his revelation in the word of proclamation. "Nevertheless," for Bultmann, "the problem of natural theology does not thereby

cease to exist."[52] Why? For all his insistence on the divinity of God, Bultmann—as exegete and expert in the science of religion, under the
influence of Heidegger—was interested very much more than Barth in
human existence and in understanding it, a fact that led logically to his
later program of demythologization. But what made him think again
about the problem of natural theology? There are *three facts* that were
obviously not taken seriously enough by Barth and that can be admitted
by Bultmann himself—on the basis of Barthian assumptions—only with a
great deal of "dialectical" hither and thither, ifs and buts, and constantly
with further qualifications.

*The fact of understanding:* Even before the Christian proclamation
reaches him, has not man a prior knowledge, a prior understanding of
God?

*The fact of the world religions:* Is there not talk of God and talk to God
even outside Christianity?

*The fact of philosophy:* Does not philosophy, too, claim to be able to understand man's existence?

Oddly enough, Bultmann, as a New Testament scholar, manages not to
say anything at all about the classical texts on the *"natural" knowledge of
God in the New Testament.* As is well known, *Paul,* Apostle of the Gentiles, was confronted with the problem at an early stage. Of course, Paul
does not prove that God exists and is actually known by men. But, like
the whole of the Old and New Testaments and incidentally the whole
Catholic tradition and also (unlike Barth) the Reformers, he takes these
things for granted. Admittedly, the decisive chapters of the Letter to the
Romans do not contain any optimistic positive statements about the
pagan world in terms of the kind of natural theology that seems to be assumed in Vatican I. For Paul does not want people to persist in
paganism, but he invites them to faith in the salvific message of Christ.
Although the revelation of God in creation calls them to do so, the
pagans—so runs the global judgment of the first chapter of Romans—
have not honored God and thanked him, but kept truth "imprisoned."
But—and in this respect Vatican I is right against Barth—according to
Romans 1, it is quite clear that the pagans had a knowledge of the fact of
God without any special revelation. They know not only an "idol" but
the true God and "his everlasting power and deity."[53]

The third chapter of Romans also—unlike a Catholic natural theology
—can be summed up in the basic statement that *all* men, Jews and Gentiles, are under the dominion of sin[54] and need justification in Jesus
Christ.[55] But this does not mean that a judgment is passed on the salvation or damnation of individual pagans. For the question here is not—as
Barth claims, following the later Augustine—about the fate of the gentile
Christians, nor about the fate of individual pre-Christian pagans, but
about the responsibility and guilt of both groups of pre-Christian humanity, of (actual) pagans and Jews. In this connection, the more positive un-

dertone in Romans 2 is unmistakable. Paul's basic statement is, "Renown, honour and peace will come to *everyone* who does good—Jews first, but Greeks as well. God has no favourites."[56] Consequently, *in the last resort,* it is not important who has received a special revelation (the "law")—an offensive statement to every Jew. Whether with the law or without the law, "it is not listening to the Law but keeping it that will make people holy in the sight of God."[57] But how can people to whom the special revelation, the "law," has not been proclaimed, be said to "keep the law"? Paul's answer is that "they can point to the substance of the Law engraved on their hearts—they can then call a witness, that is, their own conscience."[58] Which means: "pagans who never heard of the Law, but are led by reason to do what the Law commands, may not actually 'possess' the Law, but they can be said to 'be' the Law."[59]

Precisely because Paul's positive statements on non-Christians are in a negative context—their inexcusability—it must be asked today, in view of a fundamental change in the setting of the question, whether they ought to be translated into our new situation. After all, we are not living now in immediate expectation of the end, like Paul, who therefore considered it necessary to preach the message within his lifetime to all men. Our world is no longer the limited, immediately visible Mediterranean world, as it was for Paul, who therefore considered it possible to preach the message within his lifetime to all men. Today we know that pre-Christian humanity was infinitely older and greater and that the whole inhabited world was infinitely wider than Paul and his contemporaries could even suspect. Historically and, still more, geographically, Christians have turned out to be a minority in mankind. Is all this to have no influence on our judgment of men whom the proclamation of the gospel has either never reached at all or not reached in the right way?

In the New Testament itself, a tendency toward a more positive interpretation can be perceived. We need only compare Paul with Luke, who lived a generation later and no longer started out in the light of the immediate expectation. Paul's missionary speeches in Lystra[60] and Athens,[61] as edited by Luke himself in his Acts of the Apostles, undoubtedly speak more positively about the pagans. Obviously, these speeches, too, are not exhortations to persist in paganism but appeals to the pagans to be converted to belief in the true God.[62] But there is at the same time an obvious effort to excuse the pagans as far as this is in any way possible. God "in the past allowed each nation to go its own way,"[63] he "overlooked that sort of thing when men were ignorant."[64] There is no more talk—as in Romans 1:20—about the pagans being "without excuse." In Lystra, the Lucan Paul says expressly that God did not leave the pagans "without evidence," since he distributes to them the gifts of creation and fills their hearts with gratitude and joy.[65]

Moreover in the Lucan description, Paul recognizes in Athens a religious concern, an awe in the presence of the gods[66] and in this respect —in their veneration of the unknown God—an obscure unconscious presentiment of God.[67] And if this presentiment was misguided (in temple worship,[68] in the failure to understand God's lack of need,[69] in the cult of images,[70] so that the pagans are "ignorant" and "must repent"[71]), they were nevertheless not godless or Godforsaken even without the Christian revelation. For God—as is clear even in Romans 1–2 and is here confirmed by the emphasis on the unity of the human race[72]—is close to every human being, "since it is in him that we live, and move, and exist, as indeed some of your own writers have said: 'We are all his children.' "[73] The Letter to the Hebrews, without mentioning a special verbal revelation, attests the faith of Abel,[74] Enoch,[75] and Rahab the prostitute.[76]

According to John's prologue, the divine Logos is already present in the creation, which comes to be through him, as life and light for men in the darkness.[77] The Creator is at the same time the Revealer. The Logos has a universal revelatory function: "The true light that enlightens *all* men was coming into the world."[78] But "the world did not know him."[79] Obviously, a distinction must be made here between the light occurring everywhere and at all times through the Word existing with God on the one hand, and on the other the calling of the community to God through the man Jesus.

## Tacit correction: Karl Barth again

In the last complete volume of the *Church Dogmatics*, the third part of his "Doctrine of Reconciliation," Barth returns to the question of natural theology, which he had treated so negatively and polemically against Catholic theology and Vatican I in his first volumes. Exactly forty years had passed since the first German edition of the *Epistle to the Romans* and exactly twenty-five years since the Confessional Synod of Barmen, and once again Barth developed his "hard," exclusive thesis: Jesus Christ "is the one and only light of life."[80]

But despite all the confirmation and the strengthening of the exclusiveness of the Christian revelation, after his many volumes on the theology of creation, Barth can no longer avoid the question of the relationship between the one and only light and the other lights, between the one and only word of God and the other words, which—as Barth now insists—are creaturely words and "yet true words"[81] or at least can be true words. We may wonder which are the words that create a problem here. Obviously not the words of the Bible or of the Church. For Scripture and Church proclamation, according to Barth—as he explained at length in the prolegomena to the *Church Dogmatics*[82]—are merely the two other, derived forms of the word of God. But what of the *"profane"* words and the *"lights"* of the created world; how are they related to the one word and the one light?

a. With regard to the *"profane" words* of non-Christians or even unthinking Christians: Jesus Christ is the one Word of God—for Barth, this is an exclusive proposition. Bible and Church are God's word—for him, this is not an exclusive proposition. That is to say, Jesus Christ is not confined either within the covers of the Bible or within the walls of the Church. As risen, he is Lord of the world and can raise up witnesses for himself even outside Scripture and the Church. If, of course, such "profane" words are to be just as true as the one word, they must say the same thing in their own language; they, too, must speak in some way about God's grace, forgiveness, sanctification, reconciliation, and about man's faith and obedience. According to Barth, the Christian community can confidently take into account such words outside the walls of the Church, since the cause of Jesus Christ does not depend only on the Church, since God in Christ has reconciled not only the Church but the world, since God is active also outside the walls of the Church. Of course, the true words heard from outside will never pronounce the word of the center. They can throw light only on one aspect and cannot invoke any mandate. The Church, however, should examine closely whether these words are related to the one word and whether the latter is not better and earlier attested than within, by the Church itself. The criterion of the examination is whether these words agree with Scripture and (with certain reservations) also with the Church's dogma, whether the fruits of these words outside are good and their effects in the community positive. In any case, they can be binding only to a limited extent.

b. With regard to the *"creaturely world,"* which "has its own *lights and truths* and therefore its own *speech* and *words"*: "Like its persistence, its self-witness and lights are not extinguished by the corruption of the relationship between God and man through the sin of man, his pride and sloth and falsehood. However corrupt man may be, they illumine him, and even in the depths of his corruption he does not cease to see and understand them. It is true that by the shining of the one true light of life, by the self-revelation of God in Jesus Christ, they are exposed and characterised as lights, words and truths of the created cosmos, and therefore as *created* lights in distinction to this one light."[83]

It is amazing how positively the former prosecutor of natural theology and the analogy of being speaks of the lights, words and truths of the created world. According to Barth, even "dangerous modern expressions like the 'revelation of creation' or 'primal revelation' might be given a clear and unequivocal sense in this respect."[84] Of course Barth tries to maintain his original starting positions. For him, in contrast to Paul's Letter to the Romans and the Acts of the Apostles, the lights, words and truths of creation do not reveal God's everlasting power and deity but only the lines, continuities, constants and systems of created being (such as existing for one another, rhythm and internal contrarieties, laws of nature and of mind, etc.). In contrast to Romans and Acts, the lights, words and truths of creation therefore reveal God not by their own light but only—so to speak—like taillights reflecting Christian revelation. Consequently it is not surprising that Barth in this section quotes a variety of texts but passes over in silence the classical passages on revelation in creation from Romans and Acts. Otherwise it would have been far too obvious how successfully (but in the last resort inconsistently) *Barth had corrected his former positions* but—unlike the later Augustine, with his *Retractiones* (or "withdrawals")—without publicly admitting it.[85]

If we want to take Barth's and also Bultmann's interests seriously and yet not stop there, we may regard the following points as *fruits of the discussion on dialectical theology*:

a. From beginning to end, the *Bible* attests not man's proof of God but God's self-evidence: his revelation.

b. According to the biblical understanding, therefore, *God encounters me in the word of proclamation*: God himself has the initiative in this respect; the encounter with him is his gift; we know him in so far as he makes himself known, in so far as he reveals himself.

c. What is expected from *man* here is *not a neutral reaction*: he is not expected to prove God, but to rely trustingly on God's word; we know him by recognizing him, we know because we *believe* (*credo ut intelligam*).

d. But this is not a reason for theologians to reject from the outset the *demand for confirmation of belief in God*. Not every attempt at a confirmation or a verification of talk about God is *ipso facto* a self-important desire to submit God to the control of reason; it is not an objectification, an objectivization of God.

e. From a theological and realistic standpoint, *God is at the beginning* of all things; he has the primacy. But *theologically and methodologically* we can begin with the *questions of modern man* and ask about God; the order of being and the order of knowledge do not need to correspond with one another.

f. The proclamation of the word of God must *not* be degraded *to a theology of pure need*, in which man's needs become the predominant aspect. *But the needs*, the fears and longings of man, can be the *methodological starting point* of the question about God, precisely in order to be able to criticize, correct and deepen the question in the light of the biblical message.

g. The *biblical message* is the *essential criterion* for all talk about God. But not all talk of God is dependent on the biblical message.

h. According to the evidence of the Old Testament and even more of the New, it is impossible to claim that the Bible adopts a purely negative attitude and an exclusive intolerance toward the non-Christian religions. The *God of the Bible* appears increasingly not only as God of the Jews and Christians but as *God of all men.*

i. The *negative statements* about the error, darkness, lying and sin of the non-Christian world are valid for that paganism which rejects the Christian message: there are no definitive judgments of damnation, but a clear *invitation to conversion.* The fate of people not confronted with the Christian message is only indirectly of interest to the Bible.

j. The *positive statements* of the Bible about the non-Christian world show that there is an authentic manifestation of God to all mankind. *Non-Christians, too, can know the true God*—which is what Scripture understands as the revelation of God in creation. In this sense, God is close also to non-Christians.

Christians talk of and to the true God. Can non-Christians also talk of and to the true God? Now we are suddenly beginning to talk so naturally about God, as if we were already certain that experiences of God on the part of Christians and non-Christians are more than experiences of the self; in other words, that the true God also truly exists. But does God exist?

Discussion on God's existence should be opened with anyone, with Christians or non-Christians, and it should be possible to include the experiences of the other party in the discussion. It is wholly and entirely a question of the truth of belief in God, as we insisted at an earlier stage when discussing atheism. But the *truth of belief* in God may not be merely asserted, it *must be confirmed.* We appeal to "revelation." But is revelation an unsubstantiated assumption and therefore perhaps only an illusion or an ideological superstructure? Or even simply an external didactic law that man, whether he understands it or not, must accept outright? Am I simply to dispense with my reason, simply sacrifice my understanding? No, theology cannot evade the demands for confirmation of belief in God:

- *Not a blind, but a* justifiable, belief: *a person should not be mentally abused, but convinced by arguments, so that he can make a responsible decision of faith.*
- *Not a belief devoid of reality, but a* belief related to reality. A *person should not simply have to believe without verification. But his statements should be verified and tested in contact with reality, against the background of the experience of the individual and of society, and should thus be covered by the concrete experience of reality.*

Does all this mean that the existence of God can be proved? Are there really proofs of God?

# III.  Proving God?

Proofs of God today have lost much of their force but little of their fascination. They continue to exercise a silent, secret attraction on thinking people. Does God exist? It must be possible to prove this. There must be a proof that is irrefutable, rational, obvious to everyone. It may be that the proofs of God have failed as proofs today, that they are perhaps dead. But even as failed and dead proofs, they demand respect from those born in later times. And quite a number of people have shown a melancholy defiance in the presence of the last remains of the proofs of God. It must still be possible. What is possible and what is not possible with reference to the proofs of God? This is the question to be discussed in the present section.[1]

## 1. Arguments for and against

The proofs of God have an *impressive tradition*. The greatest minds of humanity have been concerned with this. Their foundations were laid with the "pagans," Plato and Aristotle; they became acclimatized in Christianity, particularly through Augustine; then, in the Middle Ages, extensively systematized by Aquinas; and freshly thought out in modern times—in connection with Anselm's "ontological" argument—by Descartes, Spinoza, Leibniz and Wolff; but, after that, they were all involved together in a radical crisis and replaced by Kant with a moral "postulate," eventually reinterpreted speculatively by Fichte and Hegel and finally restored by neo-Thomism in neo-Scholastic form.

### Arguments for

What precisely is the question here? Not only that God is knowable in principle, as Vatican I defined. Nor on the other hand that God can be immediately experienced, as Pascal's *Memorial* suggests But that God's existence can be proved in principle and in fact:
Proofs of God seek to prove *God*. They have as their object not only—like fundamental trust—the reality of the world and man, reality as a

whole, but a possible primal reason, primal support and primal meaning of reality, which we call God.

Proofs of God seek to prove God's *existence*. They are not meant merely to say how we can talk of God, of his relationship to the world, to man, to knowledge and aspiration, but they are meant to answer the stern question of whether God is.

Proofs of God seek to *prove* God's existence. They are meant to offer not merely pointers, conceptual possibilities, probable conclusions, but a proof —that is, a train of thought inferring a proposition hitherto unknown from a logical connection of known propositions.

Proofs of God mostly start out from an immediately evident external or internal experience, in the light of which, by means of methodical reflection and strictly logical deductive thinking, they seek to make God's existence manifest. In this respect, a universal metaphysical principle has to serve as a bridge *from the world of experience to transcendental reality*, from the finite to the infinite. How is such a bridging possible?

It was possible for *Plato*, who was the first to use the term *theologia*, because he saw all things as participating in the eternal ideas and these again in the all-vivifying, single, supreme idea of the good: God, that is, as the good purely and simply, as the sun in the pure light world of ideas, the primal good, which is at the same time the primal beautiful, the absolutely one, the mind and maker of the world.

*Aristotle*, who put the proofs of God into strictly scientific form, started out from the analysis of empirical reality and asked about the efficient and final cause: God as first unmoved mover and end, God as pure reality, unalloyed actuality; the thought of himself to all eternity and primal reason of order in the world.

For *Augustine*, only the existence of a supreme, eternal, immutable primal truth can explain the unchanging truths in the human mind; only a divine artist can explain the work of art that is the world, only God as supreme good can fulfill man's insatiable desire for beatitude.

According to *Anselm of Canterbury*, however, and later also Descartes, Leibniz and Wolff, God's existence is proved not only from the existence, goodness and varying grades of things but from pure thought: from the idea of a most perfect or absolutely necessary being, an idea that necessarily includes the existence of this being.

And *Kant* finally no longer uses a theoretical proof, but "postulates" the existence of God in practice: as the condition for the possibility of reconciling morality with man's quest for happiness.

Aquinas, with recourse to Plato, Aristotle, Augustine and Anselm, had distinguished "five ways"[2] to God, which, however, up to a point can be reduced to one another. Today, substantially and terminologically following Kant, *four classical proofs of God* are generally distinguished; these are dependent on the various traditions and can be given concrete expression in a variety of ways. Here they are set out systematically:

a. The *cosmological* proof of God: this starts out from the phenomenon of movement, change, causality in the external world of experience. Then, since an infinite regression is pointless, with the aid of the principle of causality, the conclusion is drawn that there must be a *first cause*.

b. The *teleological* (physicotheological) proof of God: this starts out from the order, appropriateness, purposefulness, from the insistent dynamism of all natural happenings (more recently also of the human mind, which remains unfulfilled in the finite). Then, with the aid of the principle of finality, which assumes an intended purposefulness and excludes the possibility that everything happens by chance, the conclusion is drawn that there must be a *world orderer* and *world creator* (and likewise a supreme goal, a final end).

c. The *ontological* proof of God: this starts out from the idea of God (innate in every human being) as the most perfect and necessary being. Then, without recourse to empirical experience (= *a priori*), the conclusion is drawn that this being exists, since existence is simply involved in its perfection and necessity.

d. The *moral* proof of God: this starts out from the necessity of achieving agreement between morality (which is absolutely required) and man's aspiration to beatitude. In this light it is possible not strictly to demonstrate God's existence but to "postulate" it as practically, morally necessary: God as *condition of the possibility of the highest good*.

## Difficulties

If, however, all these proofs of God—or at least the first three—are supposed to be conclusive, why is not any single one of them universally accepted? Or are they perhaps not as conclusive for the intellect as—for instance—the proofs of the Pythagorean theorem or of the fact that the earth goes around the sun? Even neo-Scholastic defenders of the proofs of God no longer insist on their coercive force. "Coercive force," says H. Ogiermann, "has only a very relative value; in the philosophical field, particularly in philosophical theology, it can and may be completely lost. Thus even a theoretical knowledge of God leaves intact that which is absolutely essential to the religious person: the 'function' of free commitment."[3] And J. Schmucker, referring to the "practical effectiveness of the traditional proofs of God," speaks even of a "formal fiasco."[4] Against the exaggerations of a natural theology that assumes that it is possible to prove by pure reason the existence of God and even the attributes of his nature, objections have increased enormously.

a. Can a *proof* prove God? Can we deal with what are properly called —in Wittgenstein's term—"problems of life" as with technical or

scientific questions? In such questions of life, is it possible to get anywhere at all by a purely rational train of thought that concludes to a
hitherto unknown proposition from the logical connection of known propositions? Is it possible by logical reasoning to prove in particular the existence of God, so that at the end we gain not only probable but absolutely
certain understanding of the existence of God? Does not such a proof at
best become an ingenious cerebral thought-construct for philosophical and
theological specialists, which, however, for the average man remains abstract, opaque and uncontrollable, without convincing force or binding
character? Is not the application of the universally valid principle of
causality (and particularly the principle of finality) contested today in
both natural science (as physical law of causality) and philosophy? In
connection with the proof of God, do not such principles assume the very
thing that they are meant to prove? And by what right is a recourse to an
infinite series or even to the coincidence of pure facticity excluded? Is not
the world of phenomena as a whole perhaps the absolute? Cannot even
evolution, imperfection, finiteness, be part of the absolute? And for every
proof of God, cannot an equivalent counterargument be produced?

b. Can God still be God in a *proof?* Does it not mean that we are
treating God like a physical or mathematical object? Like a distant star,
the existence of which can be calculated in a spirit of objective neutrality,
without anyone ever having seen it? Do we really reach God with what
Newman called a "smart syllogism"? Is not God degraded by such a process of inference to any sort of thing which might be dis-closed, dis-covered
by human astuteness? An object—that is—as opposed to the subject, to
be brought to us externally and by a logical chain of arguments—so to
speak—from the beyond? Is a God objectified and proved in this way still
God at all?

c. Can *man's reason* reach so far? Have we not come to realize since
Kant's critique of pure reason that the range of our theoretical reason is
limited? Can pure reason advance at all beyond phenomena, the realm of
appearances, to "things in themselves"? Does it not remain tied to the
background of human experience, so that it can reach only illegitimately
beyond the bounds of possible experience? Or can empirical experience be
excluded from the human process of knowing in the way attempted in the
ontological argument? Is there not an unjustifiable inference from the
ideal order to the real, from the conceptual possibility (or conceptual necessity) of an absolutely perfect or necessary being to his real existence?
Have not the proofs of God's existence all been knocked out of our hands
as a result of Kant's critique of the ontological and also of the cosmological and teleological proofs of God by theoretical reason? In the metaphysical field, then, is reason able to do more than regulate and systematize (this much is not denied by Kant), without itself being able to draw
any conclusions about reality?

We cannot entirely close our minds to these objections and will have to admit:

- As *the discussion with nihilism made clear,*[5] *there is* no evident substructure of reason *on which faith could be based. It is not only at a "supernatural" superstructure that doubt is possible. It begins at the uncertainty of human existence and of reality as a whole.*
- *The* reality of God, *if he exists, is in any case* not directly "given" *in the world: God as a datum is not God. He is not among the objects that experience has no problems in discovering. There is no direct experience of God. Neither is there any immediate intuition of God (as claimed in the "ontologism" of Malebranche, Gioberti and Rosmini-Serbati).*
- Without recourse to empirical experience (= *a priori*), *solely from the* concept *of God (as of a necessary or absolutely perfect being), it is impossible to infer his necessary existence. The "ontological" proof of God (Anselm of Canterbury, Descartes, Leibniz), avoiding the digression by way of experience of the self and the world, presupposes a complete identity between the conceptual and the real orders.*[6]
- *With all* the proofs of God from experience (= *a posteriori*), *the question always arises whether they effect the transition from the "visible" to the "invisible," to the transcendence beyond experience. It is doubtful whether the variants of either the cosmological (God as efficient cause) or the teleological proof of God (God as orderer of the world or final cause) really reach an ultimate cause or goal not identifiable with myself, society and world (or whether they exclude an infinite regress).*
- *Belief in God cannot be proved to a person if the existential constituents are neglected, with the result that this person is dispensed from belief instead of being summoned to belief. In the light of our previous experiences, there is no purely rational demonstration of God's existence that could carry universal conviction.* Proofs of God *turn out in fact not to be coercive for everyone, whatever may be thought of the "possibility" of knowledge of God as taught by Vatican I. There is not a single proof that is universally accepted.*

### The nondemonstrable content

Nevertheless, we should not take the proofs of God too lightly. Despite all legitimate philosophical misgivings, they still present a challenge to thought that cannot be neglected. Even the philosopher Karl Jaspers insisted: "After Kant's brilliant refutation of all proofs of God, after Hegel's ingenious but facile and false restoration of the proofs, after the new interest in the medieval proofs of God, a new philosophical appropriation of the proofs of God is an urgent necessity today."[7]

It must be admitted that, in so far as they seek to prove something, the proofs of God are meaningless. But in so far as they bring God into the discussion, they are very meaningful. As definite answers they are inadequate, but as open questions they are irrecusable. There is no doubt that the *probative character of the proofs of God is finished* today, *but their content remains important* and it is precisely the nondemonstrable content of the proofs that is in question here. What does this mean? Here we may provide some preliminary indications of what will become clearer at a later stage.

The *cosmological proof of God* had asked about the efficient cause of all change and movement. But a first cause does not seem to be strictly logically demonstrable, since the bridge supposed to be provided by the principle of causality, together with its supports, gets lost in the incomprehensible infinite, of which it is by no means certain whether it is fullness or emptiness.

*Nevertheless,* there is food for thought here. Is the finite to get us bogged down in an infinite retrospective questioning? Does not the law of causality even with its limited scientific and philosophical application assume a connection—admittedly not demonstrable—between cause and effect in the world? Otherwise, would we not have to assume the groundlessness and instability of reality as a whole and therefore profess nihilism—which is an alternative to be taken seriously? In order therefore to clarify a connection between cause and effect, would it not perhaps be more reasonable to assume a first cause of all, a cause of all causes? And on closer reflection, if God is understood as ultimately founding and causing, would not the acceptance of a cause of all causes *ipso facto* mean (even though only under a certain dim aspect) the acceptance of God? This would be an acceptance (not unreasonable, but worth further reflection) of God's existence without a proof of God. In any case, this question is suggested by the cosmological proof of God, even though the latter cannot answer it conclusively for us.

The *teleological proof of God* had asked about the appropriateness and purposiveness of all things and especially of the human mind. But a supreme goal (or a supreme orderer) cannot be proved rationally in a universally convincing way, since the principle of finality also points to the incomprehensible infinite, of which, again, it is not certain whether it is fullness or emptiness, God or nothingness.

*Nevertheless,* there is, again, food for thought here. Is the finite to drive us to an infinite prospective questioning? May we not assume—as we assumed a connection between cause and effect in the world—also a connection between meaning and end, even though, once more, we cannot prove it? Otherwise, would we not have to assume the meaninglessness and aimlessness of reality as a whole and therefore profess nihilism—

again, an alternative to be taken seriously? In order, then, to explain a connection between meaning and end, would it not perhaps be more reasonable to assume a final end of the world and of man, an end of all ends? And on closer reflection, if God is understood as ultimately bestowing meaning and attracting, would not the acceptance of an end of all ends *ipso facto* mean (even though, again, only under a certain aspect) the acceptance of God? This would be an acceptance (not unreasonable, but worth further reflection) of God's existence without a proof of God. In any case, this question is suggested by the teleological proof of God, even though the latter cannot answer it conclusively for us.

The *ontological proof of God* asked about the existence of a most perfect or absolutely necessary being. But it cannot be proved that such a being actually exists, since merely conceiving the idea of something does not mean that the latter exists in reality.

*Nevertheless*, here, too, there is food for thought. Is there to be only the contingent without any necessity? Is it possible to think of laws of nature and still more of ethical norms without in some form transcending the empirical field? Does not the idea of a being than which nothing greater can be conceived, which is the absolutely necessary in all contingency, make clear that what is involved here is the knowledge of one that is wholly other? And is it not perhaps this very fact which constitutes the hard core, the fascinating power of the idea of God? And if it is not possible to deduce God's existence purely *a priori* from the idea of God, independently of our experience of the self and the world, is not at least an *a priori* of trust required for the acceptance of the reality of God as it is for the acceptance of reality as a whole? Ought not the argument that existence is involved in the very idea of God to be understood less as a proof than as an expression of trusting faith (as Anselm himself expressed it in the prayer accompanying his argument): a trusting faith that to my idea of a most perfect being there does also correspond a reality and that my thinking is oriented not to a nothingness but to a supreme fullness of being? Here, too, then, we have an acceptance (not unreasonable but worth further reflection) of God's existence without a proof of God. In any case, this question is suggested by the ontological proof of God even though in the end this proof also cannot answer the question conclusively for us.

Must we not turn our thoughts back at every point here? In every dimension, we are reminded of the *fundamental enigma of reality* as we came across it at the end of the chapter on fundamental trust: reality— that is—founding but itself without foundation, sustaining but itself unsustained, guiding but itself without a goal of its own. Here is the enigmatic fact—whence and wherefore?—that I exist, that things, human beings exist, that the world exists. Must not all this have something to do with an ultimate founding, sustaining, guiding factor? Is not the ground-lessness, unsupportedness, aimlessness of everything, is not nihilism, ulti-mately to be dispelled only because of the fact that at the frontier before the abyss instead of nothing we find God? But how is this God—who so obviously cannot be proved—actually to be found? Must we from the out-set refrain from a rational approach to him, throw ourselves blindly—so to speak—into his arms and then perhaps in this very way fall into nothing-ness? Believe? Has belief, then, nothing to do with thinking? Is belief without thought not unconsidered, unjustifiable belief? Or is belief in God to be something only for devout fanatics and not for thinking peo-ple?

The question therefore arises whether perhaps a way is laid open here, a way between the fronts. The *demarcations*, anyway, have now become sufficiently clear:

- *as against dialectical theology firstly: belief in God must not only be as-serted, it must be verified;*
- *as against natural theology now: belief in God is to be verified but not proved;*
- *The right way, then, would lie between the purely authoritative asser-tion of God in the spirit of dialectical theology and the purely rational proof of God in the spirit of natural theology, would lie between Karl Barth and Vatican I.*
  *Is there such a way?*


## 2. More than pure reason: Immanuel Kant

It was *Immanuel Kant* (1724–1804), so often quoted here, who at-tempted resolutely to follow the path between a dogmatic assertion of the existence of God and a rational proof. This great thinker grew up in a pietistic craftsman's family and—as is well known—in his whole life never left the province of Königsberg. It was only after some nine years of work-ing as a private tutor (at first with a country pastor of the Reformed Church) that he came to teach in the university; there he failed to gain a number of appointments and worked for some time as sublibrarian before being promoted, in 1770 (the year of birth of Hegel, Hölderlin and Bee-thoven), at the age of forty-six, to the professorship of logic and meta-physics. He now began to produce his really original works and to initiate the *Copernican turning point in the theory of knowledge*. No longer was it to be assumed "that all our knowledge must conform to objects," but "that objects must conform to our knowledge."[1]

This means that the starting point of knowledge is no longer the ready-made object, received passively and reflected in the human intellect. The starting point is the human intellect, which (together with the senses) actively imprints its pure forms (categories) on the sense data and thus sets up the object of knowledge for the very first time. What we have, then, is self-knowledge of human reason, of human cognitive power in all its dimensions. More precisely, self-knowledge of pure intellect and pure reason, in so far as these, with their "pure" concepts and ideas of themselves (*a priori*), constitute and regulate our experiences and their objects. This is Kant's preliminary transcendental setting of the question of the knowledge of objects and of the conditions of the possibility of knowledge as such. In this connection, Kant laid down a new solution also of the question of the knowledge of God, a solution that no one can ignore, not even the person who finally rejects it.

## Self-critique of reason

Because of his critique of the traditional proofs of God (in which he followed Moses Mendelssohn, the philosopher of the Enlightenment), Kant became known at an early date as the *Alleszermalmer* ("the man who crushes everything"), a judgment that has pursued him even up to the present time. At the same time, the younger Kant, known as the *precritical* Kant—trained in the philosophy of the Leibniz-Wolffian school and at first a very sociable person, full of the joy of life, and nothing like the prototype of the pedantic German professor so often caricatured later—had still retained something of the *proofs of God*. At first basing himself on Newton, occupied with questions of the origin and order of the world (for instance with the nebular theory of the origin of the stars, later adopted by Laplace), in his *Allgemeine Naturgeschichte und Theorie des Himmels* ("Universal History of Nature and Theory of the Heavens") (1755),[2] he explained the teleological proof of God, and then, in his *Der einzig mögliche Beweisgrund zu einer Demonstration des Daseins Gottes* ("The Only Possible Ground of Proof of God's Existence") (1763),[3] developed the ontological argument at length. At any rate, even at this stage Kant is not at all a narrow-minded rationalist; he admits to supporters of a philosophy of feeling and faith: "It is absolutely necessary to be convinced of God's existence; it is not equally necessary to demonstrate it."[4] Immanuel Kant stuck to this view even after he had been startled—especially by the British philosopher David Hume—out of the "dogmatic slumber" of rationalist metaphysics, to pour scorn and derision on this metaphysics—in *Träume eines Geistersehers, erläutert durch Träume der Metaphysik* ("Dreams of a Spirit Seer, elucidated by dreams of metaphysics")[5]—which, according to him, lives dreaming in another world.

The fact is still too little considered that even the precritical Kant and still more the Kant of the critique of religion⁶ was decisively influenced not only by the somewhat gloomy, pedantic pietism of his childhood and boyhood years but also by a Calvinistic understanding of God and creation.⁷ For Kant's discussion with Leibniz and especially Newton—who, for him, was throughout his life the personification of science—the ideas and phraseology of the Reformed dogmatic theologian J. F. Stapfer on the distance between God and man, on God's grandeur and the limits of reason, exercised a notable influence. Due to his *criticism*, the philosopher from Königsberg has continually been suspected of agnosticism and disguised atheism, although it was he in particular—between orthodoxy and free-thinking, between Franco-German rationalism and British empiricism—at a time of rising atheism, who protected belief in God against a "devouring" reason and tried to tie down the latter in its own chains. What is behind Kant's criticism is not—as is often assumed—a resignation in matters of reason, but the *conviction, based* ultimately *on ethics and religion, that limits must certainly be imposed on reason*. As he says in the Preface to the second edition to the *Critique of Pure Reason*, "I have therefore found it necessary to deny *knowledge*, in order to make room for *faith*."⁸ Even for the "critical" Kant—as for Rousseau, whom he greatly admired (and whose portrait was the only picture in his study)—faith is a truth of the heart or—better—of conscience, prior to and beyond all philosophical reflection and demonstration. Toward the end of the *Critique of Pure Reason*, he declares: "Belief in a God and in another world is so interwoven with my moral sentiment that as there is little danger of my losing the latter, there is equally little cause for fear that the former can ever be taken from me."⁹

It is not surprising that Kant, who as the great son of the Enlightenment irrevocably overcame the Enlightenment in his three critiques, set definite *limits* to the naïve omnipotence of *reason* with reference particularly to God, the wholly Other. Substantiation means demarcation. From the time of his *Critique of Pure Reason*, worked out so conscientiously over the course of a decade and published in 1781, when he was fifty-seven, it was clear to him and to many others that we cannot know theoretically *that* God is. It is true that we can and must know *as what* God can be conceived, since otherwise we could not distinguish him even from the devil. But in pure theory we cannot know whether God is.

Scientific *proofs of God* therefore are *not possible*. Since they are dependent on intuition, no scientific judgments can be made about God, who is not in space and time and thus not an object of intuition. Scientific judgments must express a truth that is both necessary (*a priori*) and "new" (synthetic). This means that synthetic, *a priori* judgments, which do not rest on a new sense experience (*a priori*) and yet widen our knowledge (synthetic) and do not merely elucidate it (analytic), according to Kant, are possible only in mathematics and natural science, but not in traditional metaphysics, which seeks to be a science of the suprasensible and consequently produces a logic of illusion. This logic of illusion, Kant submits to an annihilating critique in his "Transcendental Dialectic."[10] He reduces all conceivable proofs of God to three and criticizes especially the ontological, to which he also traces back both the teleological and the cosmological. In this way, Kant proves that God's existence cannot be proved. We have already gotten to know his essential counterarguments: the invalidity of the inference from thought to reality, the limitation of reason to the world of appearances, the impossibility of substantiating a universal principle of causality. The proofs of God, according to Kant, have not only failed in practice; they are theoretically quite impossible: "All those conclusions of ours which profess to lead us beyond the field of possible experience are deceptive and without foundation."[11]

## God as main idea

This, of course, is not Kant's last word on matters of belief in God. The destruction of the proofs of God does not mean destruction of belief in God, but is in fact the only way to make this belief possible. In the same breath, Kant insists "that human reason has a natural tendency to transgress these limits, and that transcendental ideas are just as natural to it as the categories are to understanding."[12] What does this mean?

For Kant, experience is primarily experience of nature, experience of natural science as Newton experienced it. But this *pressure to go beyond the limits of the world of experience in space and time*, according to Kant, is really a kind of *metaphysical need*, deeply rooted in man's character as a natural disposition. For man's drive for knowledge cannot be satisfied by pure knowledge of experience, by the purely relative. Human reason is oriented to a unity. Consequently it presses on through a process of reasoning toward an absolute, toward pure, *a priori* concepts, concepts of reason, basic concepts, which—according to Kant, with Plato—are rightly called *ideas*, three of them from the very beginning having been the great themes of philosophy:

the *psychological idea* of the systematic unity of the thinking subject, the idea of the *self* (or soul), which is the object of rational psychology;

the *cosmological idea* of the systematic unity of all appearances, the idea of the *world*, which is the object of rational cosmology;

the *theological idea* of the systematic unity of all objects of thought as a whole, the idea of God as the ideal of pure reason, which is the object of rational theology.

Thus God becomes the main idea, the leading idea. According to Kant, this idea of God makes it possible for our reason to consider all events, both external and internal, as the work of God, without, however, in any way knowing or understanding God on that account. Consequently, God

would be that on which everything that exists depends. Like the idea of
the self and of the world, therefore, the idea of God is not merely invented; it is not a fiction. It is a concept of reason or a heuristic rule (*a
priori* or transcendental) necessarily regulating thought: that is, a regulative principle that cannot in any case be made into a constitutive principle with a corresponding real object. Meaningful as this *main idea* is, of
itself it *does not imply any reality*. Even the theoretical assumption of a
real soul in rational psychology leads to wrong conclusions (paralogisms),
of a real world in rational cosmology to contradictions (antinomies). And
so, too, the theoretical assumption of a real God leads in rational theology
to invalid proofs. That which is merely ideal for theoretical reason is then
objectivized, afterward hypostatized, and eventually personalized. Against
all this, Kant hoped he had shown once and for all that reason spreads its
wings in vain if it tries by the power of thought to reach beyond the
world of experiences to "things in themselves" (which are conceptually
necessary but not perceptible) or, still more, tries to advance to the real
God. No, man cannot build towers reaching to heaven, but only dwelling
houses just spacious enough and high enough for what we have to do on
the plane of experience.

Of course, Kant thus likewise *rejects*—and he has not always been given
due credit for this—*the claims of atheism*. For the idea of God is not a
contradiction. And those who want to prove that God does not exist are
even more wrong: "The same grounds" that prove the incapacity of
reason to establish the existence of God also suffice, according to Kant,
"to prove the invalidity of all counter-assertions. . . . For from what
source could we, through a purely speculative employment of reason,
derive the knowledge that there is no supreme being as the ultimate
ground of all things . . . ?"[13] The idea of God is indeed a necessary theoretical borderline concept, which, like a distant star, cannot be reached in
the process of knowing, but nevertheless can be aimed at as an ideal goal.
As we need the concept of the soul (self) and of the world (as embodiment of all appearances), in order to regulate and systematize our
psychological and cosmological knowledge, we need in principle also the
idea of God, in order to combine harmoniously internal and external
events in a comprehensive unity, even though we reach no definitive result in this respect. God, that is, as "a mere *ideal*, yet *an ideal without a
flaw*, a concept which completes and crowns the whole of human knowledge. Its objective reality cannot indeed be proved, but also cannot be
disproved, by merely speculative reason."[14]

The great question remains: How can an objective reality ever legitimately correspond to the purely regulative idea of God? Kant's answer is
that this is possible not through theoretical but only through *practical
reason*; not in science, but in morality. By theoretical reason, I know what
*is* there (the objects of knowledge); by practical reason, what *ought* to be
there (the motives of the will). But practical reason has priority, in so far

as all interest is ultimately practical and in so far as even theoretical reason is complete only in practical realization. The theoretical idea of God is the presupposition for a moral knowledge of God: "It is morally necessary to assume the existence of God."[15] What is involved here?

Kant, a courageous reinterpreter but careful in his expressions, without sudden inspirations and determined not to be rushed, regarded his life task as consisting in patient and tenacious working out of problems and accepting the most varied suggestions. In his epoch-making new orientation, he was obviously concerned neither with politicoreligious restoration nor (although he approved of the French Revolution throughout his life) with agitatory political revolution. What did concern him—particularly at the time of the renewal of the politically reactionary system in Prussia after the death of Frederick the Great in 1786—was a revolution of thought and sentiment. Against the commonplace, rationalist calculation of blessedness, he appealed to moral consciousness and a harsh ethic of duty and disposition, excluding any sort of eudaemonistic ethic of pleasure or utilitarian ethics. It is a question of doing good for its own sake. Kant emphasized more strictly than ever law, duty, virtue, morality, conscience, but at the same time also man's freedom, which represents—despite all natural causality—the center of interest even of cosmology. How does Kant combine law and freedom in his thought?

Man should be *autonomous*, a law to himself in theory and practice, science and morality. Reason is seen as freedom. In *theory*: Pure theoretical (scientific) reason is—as we learned—tied only to its own pure forms, which it carries within itself, that is, the ideas of space and time and the basic concepts of the understanding (categories). In *practice*: Practical (moral) reason is tied only to its own absolute, universal, formal principles for reasonable action, to the normative "maxims," which are self-evident. Thou shalt—without any ifs and buts: so runs the imperative, which is not hypothetical but categorical, that is, absolute. This imperative is not an external precept that suppresses freedom; neither is it something purely accidental, lacking binding force, but something that follows necessarily from the internal moral law and requires man's freedom. It is precisely this absolute precept of conscience which presupposes the freedom of the human will, a freedom that cannot in fact be proved by theoretical reason but must be postulated by practical reason for the sake of man's morality. *Human freedom*, then, is *the first postulate of practical reason*.

But what is the meaning of such an absolute moral law in man if the latter—as experience shows—can never in his life completely fulfill his duty and can at best turn it to virtue but not to holiness, to good but not to perfection? The absolute "thou shalt" demands infinite progress from man. But this—and not speculation about future rewards—presupposes the continuing existence of man in the infinite, something, again, that cannot be proved but must be postulated for the sake of morality. *The immortality of the soul* is consequently *the second postulate of practical reason.*

But man would also like to be happy, and this is precisely what the moral law cannot guarantee. For—as we know from experience—duty and inclination are often incompatible, and the wicked, who merely follow their own inclinations, often succeed more than the good in getting just what they want. How, then, is an equilibrium to be established between the moral law, which must be observed unconditionally, and the striving for beatitude, which looks for absolute fulfillment? According to Kant, this "supreme good" ("kingdom of God") can be guaranteed only by a supreme legislator endowed with understanding and will, who is also author of all nature and who thus, as omniscient, omnipresent and omnipotent, is able in the last resort to combine virtue, morality—that is, worthiness for happiness—with beatitude. God himself is seen as the authentically "supreme good." None of this can be proved, but it can be postulated for the sake of morality. Hence the *existence of God is the third postulate of practical reason.*

*Postulates are not imperatives.* We are not ordered to believe in God, in the immortality of the soul, in man's freedom. But neither are they arbitrary conventions: the reasons for their justification are not simply unfathomable. No, they are necessary requirements of practical reason, on which the whole of Kant's ethics rests. And on them also is based his religion, which deliberately does not progress "from grace to virtue but rather . . . from virtue to pardoning grace," as Kant summarily expresses it at the end of his work on the philosophy of religion.[16] Kant's religion— and Christianity as far as it is reasonable—is reduced to a new attitude of mind, to morality.[17] It must now have become clear that for Kant this was no facile reduction. Kant was very serious about his religious attitude. In his youth, he had begun with cosmological investigations and a "theory of the heavens" and later progressed through all the epistemological questions up to the substantiation of ethics and religion, and he had maintained in both spheres the same sense of awe: "Two things fill the mind with ever new and increasing admiration and awe, the oftener and more steadily we reflect on them: *the starry heavens above and the moral law within.*"[18]

At the age of seventy-four, Kant still stood up, in his *Streit der Fakultäten* ("Conflict of the Faculties"),[19] for the rights of philosophy even against theology. He now returned to the ideas—mentioned at the beginning of this section—of his precritical period but could now formulate them afresh in the light of a much greater depth of thought: "*God* and *eternity* with their *awful majesty*"—this is his Calvinistic heritage—could not "stand unceasingly *before our eyes.*"[20] For that reason, Kant approves the mystery: "It is a good thing that we do not know, but believe, that there is a God."[21]

## Critique of Kant

Many philosophers and theologians have gratefully accepted Kant's moral proof of God without, however, taking equally seriously its theoretical assumptions. Here Kant will not be theologically appropriated either in his theoretical or in his practical philosophy, but—at a distance of two hundred years—critical questions will be raised about both.

1. *Did Kant's theory of knowledge gain acceptance?* Is it really possible to say that all our knowledge is tied to preliminary (transcendental) conditions, tied to the intuitive forms of space and time, tied to the thought forms of our categories of understanding? Do we actually know only that which becomes objective in these forms: the object (*ob-jectum*) not as it is in itself (the "thing in itself") but as it shows itself for us, as it "appears" (the "phenomenon")? In the present context, we can deal only briefly with these problems.[22]

At an earlier stage, when defining the relationship between the self and reality, we made a distinction:[23]

The idea that all basic categories of the world can be traced back to pure human subjectivity *has not been* accepted; in modern physics, space, time, causality are not understood as *a priori* conditions of human reason.

The idea, however, that there is no purely objective but only a subjectively colored objective knowledge *has been accepted*; that which today constitutes the world of physics cannot be defined in the light of pure objectivity, regardless of any subject.

We have to deal, therefore—and here Kant is right—with the world not in itself but as it appears to us. But, as distinct from Kant—the philosopher Walter Schulz has expounded these problems historically and systematically against the background of the most recent philosophical-scientific discussions—we must observe that, together with Kant's "pure subjectivity," his "thing in itself" has also become problematic: "If one of the two fixed points becomes questionable, then the other cannot remain unquestionably valid. Hence, quite apart from the fact that no modern physicist would imagine—as Kant did in practice—that things as such behind the appearances 'affect' us, the elimination of transcendental subjectivity as a solid embodiment of legal provisions brings about *also* the elimination of the thing in itself as the 'ground' of the appearances."[24] Referring to C. F. von Weizsäcker and W. Heisenberg, Schulz then concludes: "For modern physics the formative consciousness and the objectifiable content are no longer unquestionable factors. For the physicist, the formative subject is not a timeless authority, for the subject is involved in the very process of investigation; and the objectifiable content as such is not a world in the sense of a true reality lying behind and causing the appearances"; it is clear "that the classical interpretation of knowledge, the characteristic feature of which is that we can give unambiguous conceptual expression to the existent as it really is, that is, in itself . . . belongs to the past."25 Thus, for Schulz, physics is merely one example that shows that a new "dialectical" concept of reality is required: "Reality is neither a previously existing world of objects nor is it something posited by the subject. Reality is an interconnection of happenings in which object and subject are interwoven with each other and reciprocally conditioned; the subject is determined by the object, just as the object is determined by the subject. This happening represents a process of which the basic characteristic is *dialectic*."26

2. And yet, no matter how we judge Kant's inspired global solution of the scientific, ethical, aesthetic and religious problems in their totality and in detail and no matter how we may criticize his far too systematic antinomies, when it comes to our *problems in regard to the knowledge of God*, it must be admitted:

In questions concerning knowledge of God, Kant is right in principle to appeal not to "theoretical" but to *"practical"* reason, which is manifested in man's actions. It is not a question of pure scientific perception and critical brooding but of man's moral action and his awareness of this. Kant argues from man's understanding of himself as a moral, responsible being; it is a question not only of being but of what ought to be, not of knowledge but of morality.

As distinct from the purely rational proofs of God, Kant rightly rejects in principle any neutralizing, any elimination of concrete human existence in the course of the argument. That is why he speaks of a *"postulate,"* by which he means not a proposition necessarily inferred by theoretical reason but one necessarily required by practical reason. For man, it is a question not only of theoretical inference but of practical challenge.

In a kind of negative theology, Kant rightly proves in principle that *God's existence cannot be proved but likewise cannot be refuted;* that is, it cannot be known theoretically but only "believed" in practice.

In fact, Kant speaks in this connection of "faith," "purely rational faith,"27 "a faith of pure practical reason."28 Whatever we may make of his "denial" of "knowledge," he wanted to win a place for this faith. We noted his words: "I have therefore found it necessary to deny *knowledge,* in order to make room for *faith.*"29 This is the very thing that must not be misunderstood. Kant's view is often said to be that there cannot be any experience of God, since the latter is a pure concept of reason, a regulative principle, to which there can be no corresponding experience. But, as against this, according to Kant, "an experience of God is possible, not in the sense that experience would make known to me the God whom I could not know without it, but in the sense that I can experience God if I already know him."30 This is not a vicious circle, for—as we learned—according to Kant, God's existence is already certain from another source. In his critique of practical reason, too, he does not look "outward" or "upward" to what is beyond (to a "transcendent"), but backward, behind himself, as it were inwardly, to the preliminary condition of possibility (to the "transcendental"). God, then, is the condition of the possibility of morality and happiness. While Descartes saw God especially as perfect being and infinite substance, Spinoza as sole substance or God as nature, and Leibniz as the infinite monad, Kant started out not from natural things but from man as a moral being, and in the light of this—as a result not of theoretical but of practical necessity—postulated God as supreme moral being and originator of the world.

3. Of course, critical questions arise here, too. Kant's transcendental argumentation even in its practical aspect has met with justified *criticism*, as dogmatic Kantians themselves had to admit, in two respects.

The *first* buttress of his reasoning is the *categorical imperative*, as in the proposition: "Act so that the maxim of thy will can always at the same time hold good as a principle of universal legislation."[31] Is it still possible today legitimately to start out from an absolute "thou shalt" implanted in every thinking being? Can we start out from a categorical imperative that is supposed to be not an object of knowledge, of proof, of inference, but simply a primordial reality of the voluntary aspect of man's mental life? Must we really accept the fact of an absolute moral commitment within us which, then, demands the existence of a supreme good, reconciling morality and happiness and thus the existence of God? In the last resort, is not such an assumption merely a relic of the old belief in God, of Christian tradition, a product now of civilized custom? Can my reason not justify actions with the aid of maxims that are ill suited to generalization? Is Kant not now involved in a vicious circle? Is not the absoluteness of the obligation of "thou shalt" first postulated and then the postulate of the existence of God justified only by another postulate? Does not the assumption of an apodictically certain moral law within us, as expressed in the categorical imperative, itself presuppose the moral impetus, the question of morality or even the resolution to live a moral life, which—as Nietzsche's immoralism, beyond good and evil, has shown—can take a very different form? Has good really an advantage over evil? Does not expediency suggest doing good at one time and evil at another? Unlike Kant, must we not today take nihilism of values seriously?

The *second* buttress of his reasoning is the *striving for happiness*, which is certainly peculiar to all men. But, on what basis can we assume that it is fulfilled? On what basis can we assume that duty and inclination, worthiness for happiness and actual happiness, must be brought into harmony with each other? Why must someone who obeys the moral law necessarily gain happiness? How do I know that there is such a thing as final bliss? Might not man's quest for happiness turn out to be in vain, an expression of the absurdity of human existence, as Camus, for instance, so insistently declares?

The concept of "postulate" itself points to the fact that it is impossible to draw conclusions in theory about God without any preliminary assumptions; God must be presupposed if we want to live a truly moral life at all. Here, then—in the very midst of the modern process of secularization and emancipation—is Kant's great idea: God is to be understood as the condition for the possibility of man's moral autonomy. Kant rightly refuses to allow the contradictions, the antinomies of pure reason to invade the sphere of the realization of human existence and thus lead man to sink into the abyss of absurdity. But ought we not to go farther back here than in the transcendental argumentation? On the basis of fundamental trust in reality, might not a start be made on a broader front?[32] *Theoretical and practical reason cannot be* so clearly *separated* from the very outset. Kant has always been accused of an abstract formalism in ethics ("Thou shalt, purely and simply"). Recently, however, Jürgen Habermas has shown[33] that Kant—in virtue of his own assumptions—should have taken seriously the unity he himself affirmed between theoretical and practical reason. For theoretical reason is in fact not solely responsible for the structure of the world as it appears to us in knowledge; there are also rudimentary practical attitudes to the world which guide our knowledge from the outset and which Habermas, with reference to Kant, calls "interests guiding knowledge." What is meant by this?

As indicated at an earlier stage,[34] even supposedly purely theoretical reason (or theoretical knowledge) is secretly *determined by interests*: it is not disinterested, but guided by interests, interested knowledge. On the other hand, even supposedly purely practical reason (or morality) is equipped with knowledge: it is not unknowing, but guided by knowledge, knowledgeable willing, and action. Thus, practical reason is always involved in theoretical knowledge and, conversely, practical reason is not without theoretical knowledge. But the unity of theoretical and practical reason is important not merely—as with Habermas—for the theory of knowledge and for social theory but also for the problems of freedom, immortality and God, which Habermas, because of his materialistic-Marxist involvement, unlike Kant must of course tone down. At the same time, according to Habermas, the question in particular "what may I hope?"— the third of Kant's great questions, which, as is well known, is directed to religion—shows this unity of theoretical and practical reason: it is "both practical and theoretical."[35] Instead of hope, we would prefer, anyway, to speak here of trust, which as a practical attitude, because it is rationally justifiable, likewise clearly gives expression to this unity.

## The condition for the possibility of reality

There is no question here of a retrogression to precritical realism. The problems of Kant's transcendental argumentation are not to be passed over so that we can take refuge in a dogmatic metaphysics. In the course of our reflections, these *problems* have been *radicalized.* For the question about the conditions of the possibility of knowledge itself presupposes the reality of knowledge and the reality (identity, meaningfulness, value) of reality as a whole. And there—especially in the discussion with nihilism[36]—we had to reflect closely as to how far a fundamental certainty is possible at all, whether reality is actual, fundamentally identical, meaningful and valuable. In that sense, the nihilistic problems—the question of the conditions of the possibility of this thoroughly uncertain reality as a whole —can be seen to be the more radical, the fundamental problems. On this, we may briefly recapitulate:

First, with reference to *Nietzsche:* It is not by a theoretical proof of reason, but only by a practically realized (but completely rationally justifiable) fundamental trust on the part of the whole person, that I become certain that this *uncertain reality* is real, that is, in principle identical, meaningful and valuable. In that sense, we observed with W. Stegmüller, both confirming and surpassing Kant: "We must first believe something, in order to be able to speak at all of knowing and knowledge."[37] In order to forestall any confusion with religious belief, we prefer, however, to use the term "fundamental trust" rather than the expression "belief."

Then, with reference to *Descartes:* It is not by a theoretical proof of reason, but only by a practically realized (but completely rationally justifiable) fundamental trust on the part of the whole person, that I become certain that the *external world* in particular—this objective world of things and my fellow men, which so often puts me off but to which I continue to cling, which both inhibits and encourages, restricts and sustains me—is actual, real, and not merely dreamed or imagined.

Finally, with reference to Kant: It is not by a theoretical proof of reason, but only by a practically realized (but completely rationally justifiable) fundamental trust on the part of the whole person, that I become certain that the *self,* human *freedom* and perhaps also *God* are not merely ideas, but "realities." All these basic questions must be answered not on the basis of pure theory but on that of living and considered practice. It is not through the theoretical activity of pure reason, nor, however, through irrational feelings or mere moods, but through my practical, positive fundamental decision and fundamentally trusting attitude—which determine my whole experience, behavior and action—that I experience despite all doubts what at first is so easily taken for granted, the being-real of reality, that is, the fundamental identity, value and meaning of that which is.[38]

In the light of this fundamental and completely reasonable basis of trust, it should be understandable that we are starting out not only from a moral obligation, a stern moral law within us, a rigorous categorical imperative, but, as hitherto, from the whole reality of the world and man as concretely experienced, and that we shall ask about the condition of the

possibility of this wholly and entirely uncertain reality. Kant shattered the
proofs of God as conclusive arguments, but—as already explained—did
not liquidate their religious content. What, then, do we want?

- *God cannot be known like an already existing object within us. It cannot be proved in a universally convincing way that God exists. But still
  less can it be proved in a universally convincing way that God does not
  exist. For pure reason, which demands proofs, God does not seem to be
  more than idea without reality, a thought without actuality.*
- *It seems impossible, therefore, to deduce God by theoretical reason
  from this experienced reality of the world and man, in order to demonstrate his reality by logical reasoning.*
- *On the other hand, an inductive lead does not seem impossible, attempting to throw light on the experience of uncertain reality, which is
  accessible to each and everyone, in order thus—as it were, by way of
  "practical reason," of the "ought," or (better) of the "whole man"—to
  confront man as thinking and acting with a rationally justifiable decision that goes beyond pure reason and demands the whole person.*

Here, then—and this is how that last sentence is to be elucidated—there
can be no purely theoretical but only a completely practical, "existential,"
integral task of reason, of the reasonable human being: a meditative
reflection with a practical intention, accompanying, deciphering, illuminating the concrete experience of reality. On what kind of experience are
we to reflect here?

### Indirectly verified by experience

We are not concerned merely with a purely internal, personal experience like that expressed in the title of a book by the Frenchman André
Frossard, *God Exists. I have met him.*[39] A purely *inward, personal experience*, claimed only by a single individual (perhaps in prayer), may indeed
be an impressive testimony and may possibly be an invitation to others to
believe. It need not be disputed, for a person can genuinely believe in
God without being able to provide a rationally convincing justification of
his belief. But, in order to avoid any disrespectful or thoughtless
identification of human experience with the reality of God, it will be better to make a theological distinction. We can speak not of the experience
of God in the sense of directly "seeing" him but, more cautiously, in the
sense of the experience of his presence, closeness, radiance (what the
Bible means by "glory" as the form of manifestation, the brightness, the
reflection of God) or of the experience of his power and might ("Spirit of
God," "Holy Spirit"). This is an experience that, anyway, presupposes
faith and cannot be passed on at will but can only be attested. It is an experience that is not universally accessible; it is in no way verifiable and

can easily be dismissed as a projection. "God does not exist, for I have never met him": this might well be the reaction of many people today.[40]

Neither are we going to consider here a purely *external sense experience* that any neutral observer might have. It is completely adequate to justify statements about physical happenings, but, as we saw in detail,[41] in itself it is not a suitable basis for statements about a "meta-empirical," "metaphysical" reality.

Consequently we *cannot* be concerned with an *experience of God* in the strict sense, whether external or internal: that is, not with God's reality in its immediacy and totality. *But* we are concerned with a *knowledge of God related to experience*, by which is meant not only sense experience but also mental (inward, emotional, interpersonal, intellectual) experience so far as this is universally accessible: that is, a knowledge of God that is supported by concrete experience of the reality of the world and man and is proved right by this experience. The reference to experience, then, is not eliminated, but the experience is deciphered and interpreted.[42]

Does this mean, after all, that God's existence can be *verified?* It depends on what is understood by verification.

Undoubtedly, God cannot be verified by a *narrowly understood, empiricist criterion of verification.* God's *existence is not empirically ascertainable*, it is not there to be discovered in space and time; God would not be God if man could perceive and observe him with his own senses at certain places and certain times. If, then, that alone is to be really meaningful which is empirically meaningful, that is, can be directly related to what is accessible to sense, then God is certainly not verifiable. We have seen that this empiricist criterion of verification may be used, at best, for the demarcation of mathematical-scientific and metaphysical propositions but is completely unsuitable to decide between the meaningless and the nonmeaningless even in the field of natural science. Even the nonempirical and in this sense "meta-physical" can be completely meaningful.

There is a *more broadly understood, universal hermeneutical criterion of verification*—which was used in a wider sense in the early phases of positivism—in the light of which God can be verified. *God's existence* can be *made understandable.* Even if someone does not believe in God, he can understand the proposition "God exists" and must not describe it from the outset as sheer nonsense. If, then, that is to be meaningful which is understandable at all, God is verifiable. But this hermeneutic verification criterion is too broad in as much as it is possible with its aid to judge the meaning or absurdity of the word "God," of the proposition "God exists," but not to decide the actual existence or nonexistence of God. Even that which is completely understood, like a "golden mountain," does not necessarily exist.

Consequently we shall apply here a verification criterion that is neither as narrow as the empiricist criterion (which is merely confirmatory) nor as broad as the hermeneutical (which is all-understanding). Ours is an *indirect criterion of verification*. This means that God as the supposedly all-determining reality will be verified by *the experienced reality of man and the world*. What the universally accessible experience of the concrete reality of the world and man offers will be conceptually deciphered and given expression in language. Statements on God will be verified and tested against the background of our experience of life: not in conclusive deduction from a supposedly obvious experience that renders unnecessary a decision on man's part, but in a clarifying illumination of the always problematical experience that invites man to a positive decision. Only when talk of God is supported by concrete experience of the world and man, related to this and conveyed together with it, is its credibility established.

With the aid of such an indirect verification, it should be possible to continue the discussion with atheistic interpretations of reality, as we tried to do in regard to Feuerbach, Marx, Nietzsche and Freud: in competition for a better, deeper, more comprehensive understanding of experienced reality. Through such indirect verification, it should be possible to give an account of belief in God that will stand up to any kind of criticism and to make clear the relevance of belief in God to the reality of man and the world. This is not only a challenge but also an assurance for belief in God.

Precisely through the indirectness of the verification, the *peculiarity of our knowledge of God's existence* remains assured. Does God exist? Is there a God? "A God who is there, is not God." This saying of Dietrich Bonhoeffer,[43] a theologian who never spoke ambiguously about the question of God, must of course not be misused in order to evade a clear answer to the question of the existence of God.[44] But this saying makes it absolutely clear that God is not there to be discovered, not ascertainable and knowable, as are the things of this world. It is actually a question of the knowledge of a quite different reality.

Are we therefore pursuing metaphysics here? The word is not important; it has been understood and misunderstood, used and misused. "Metaphysics" was first used to describe the books that had to be studied "after physics."[45] Consequently, "meta-physics" is what comes "after physics" (after the science of nature) and yet is not logic or ethics. It is, then, the necessary complement to physics, which Aristotle himself calls "theology."

If today "metaphysics" is understood as a human "projection" (Feuerbach), an ideological "superstructure" (Marx), an ideal "afterworld" (Nietzsche), an unreal "wishful world" (Freud), or even if "metaphysics" is understood simply as "true reality" in the sense of Plato's world of ideas, set apart from present reality, all of which must be at the expense of this reality of ours, then we are not pursuing metaphysics.

If, however, "metaphysics" means that the purely empirical cannot be sustained from its own resources and must be surpassed in an approach to a meta-empirical that does not lie behind, beyond, above, outside this reality, but—so to speak—constitutes the inner aspect of present reality, then we are pursuing "metaphysics" or—a word that may be preferred in order to avoid misunderstandings—*ontology* ("theory of being"). What is important is to understand the thing properly; we need not trouble about the word.[46]

# IV. God exists

Who is God? Where is God? Does God exist?
Again and again people have asked about God.
Again and again people have had doubts about God.
Again and again people have denied God.
Again and again people have struggled about God, believed in God, prayed to God.

One thing must be said in advance. We are not bound to believe in God. Can we justify belief in God?

## 1. Introduction

As we saw in some detail, all arguments for an end of religion based on the philosophy of history and civilization have turned out in the last resort to be *unsubstantiated extrapolations into the future*. The facts are clear.

Instead of an "abolition of religion" by atheistic humanism, as announced in Feuerbach's projection theory,[1] there are now (despite all secularization) in many places believers in God with a new theoretical and practical humanism. But the atheistic-humanistic belief in the goodness of human nature has itself come to be suspected as a projection.

Instead of a "withering away" of religion brought about by atheistic socialism, as proclaimed in Marx's opium theory,[2] there is now (despite all repression and violent suppression) frequently a new religious revival particularly in socialist countries. But the atheistic-materialistic belief in the coming socialist society seems today to innumerable people in West and East to be itself a consolation serving vested interests.

Instead of an "elimination of religion" by atheistic science, as prophesied in Freud's illusion theory,[3] there is now (despite all the hostility to religion in certain sectors of science) a new understanding of ethics and religion. And the atheistic-scientistic belief in the solution of all problems by rational science is itself regarded by many today as something like an infantile illusion.

## New openness

Can the fact be overlooked that, despite continuing mutual mistrust, the *relationship between religion and science* has slowly improved toward a new openness? The picture of the relationship of science and religion is of course very uneven and, if we are to avoid misunderstandings, from the very beginning we must not lose sight of three aspects.

a. The scientist as such does not have a specific relationship with religion. There are only scientists of various types and therefore with a variety of personal attitudes to religion, which for the most part are not and should not be expressed in their scientific work.

b. Beyond all the individual differences even in the various scientific disciplines, there are various attitudes to religion. In the newer human sciences, there is a more negative attitude than in the long-established natural sciences, but the latter, again, are presumably more negative in their approach than some of the mental sciences.

c. On the whole, militant atheism may have lost ground among the scientists, but this does not mean automatically that belief in God has gained ground.

These trends are most striking with *physicists*. Many today see the inadequacy of the materialistic-positivistic world view and understanding of reality and also the relativity of their own methods. Particularly among physicists, we find now very few militant atheists, even though there are still many agnostics. The invention of the atom bomb, in the first place, but increasingly also the negative consequences of scientific and technical progress as a whole, have raised at the present time especially among atomic physicists the question of responsibility in scientific and technical activity and consequently the question of ethics. But ethics implies the question of discovering meaning, of a scale of values, of models and—for their justification—of religion. "Where there are no models to mark out the way, with the disappearance of the scale of values the meaning of our action and suffering also vanishes and in the end there can only be negation and despair. Religion is therefore the foundation of ethics and ethics is the presupposition of life. For we must make decisions every day and we must know or at least surmise the values which are to govern our action." This is what *Werner Heisenberg*, author of the quantum theory and Nobel prizewinner, said in 1973.[4] Long before this, in 1927, in his "First Discussions on the Relationship of Natural Science and Religion," he had appealed to the statements about faith by the great physicists Albert Einstein, Max Planck and Niels Bohr, and reacted against the classical arguments of religious criticism (projection, opium, illusion, etc.) as taken up by Paul Dirac, at the same time describing natural science as "the foundation of technically appropriate action, religion as the foundation of ethics."[5]

The situation is different with those engaged in the human sciences, especially with *psychologists* and psychotherapists, who are continually observing in their practice the disastrous connection between religion and certain obsessive neuroses, infantile fixations, repressions, self-deceptions, attempts at flight from reality. But the attitude of Adler and Jung, and particularly that of Frankl, toward religion was much more positive than —for instance—Freud's. And even in the psychoanalytical school—as we also saw[6]—the positive function of religion for the psyche, its self-discovery and healing, has been discovered. Such modern psychoanalysts as Erik Erikson and Rollo May have observed a significant connection between the decline in religiousness and an increasing lack of orientation, lack of norms, lack of meaning, typical neuroses of our time. Numerous conversations between theologians and psychotherapists have led to a convergence on many questions that would not have been considered possible in Freud's time.

An unmistakable sign of this rapprochement is a recent book by *Erich Fromm*, who—as we saw[7]—in his earlier works could not perceive any irreconcilable opposition between a humanitarian religion and a psychoanalysis concerned about human individuality and integrity. Fromm has gone more deeply into this question in the present work, which has gained the respect also of theologians: *To Have or to Be?* Starting out from the failure of the "great promise" that the increase of material goods by technology, industry and economic planning would produce happiness for men, Fromm attempts "the analysis of the two basic modes of existence: the *mode of having* and the *mode of being*." The mode of having, in particular, he regards as a basic evil of our technological-industrial age. It is expressed predominantly in the striving for possession of things and material goods, for power and domination, in wanting to control and regulate. A person who has nothing is nothing. The mode of being, on the other hand, "means to renew oneself, to grow, to flow out, to love, to transcend the prison of one's isolated ego, to be interested, to give."[8] According to the theologian Rainer Funk, with this having or being alternative Fromm has found *the* key to the understanding of all human reality, including the religious and the ethical.[9]

Great minds of history again and again have thought out and exemplified this being-mode of human existence: Buddha, Aristotle, even Jesus. For Fromm, Jesus is "the hero of love, a hero without power, who did not use force, who did not want to rule, who did not want to *have* anything. He was a hero of being, of giving, of sharing."[10] Yet even in religion, particularly in the Christian religion, according to Fromm, the estrangement between having and being is reproduced. Behind the façade of Christianity, "industrial religion" has developed, a religion that is "incompatible with genuine Christianity." "It reduces people to servants of the economy and of the machinery that their own hands built."[11] It is the same with "cybernetic religion," in which men have made machines divine and—with their technical capacity for a "second creation"—made themselves equal to God. Against this is raised Fromm's "humanist protest," nourished from the roots of Christian and philosophical humanism (Eckhart, Spinoza) and Jewish prophetical Messianism (Maimonides, carried on further today by Ernst Bloch), which he sees taken up also by an atheistic philosopher (Karl Marx) and by a Christian humanist (Albert Schweitzer). According to Fromm, then, Christianity can play an important role in understanding such figures as Meister Eckhart and Albert Schweitzer: "There is a remarkable kinship in the ideas of the Buddha, Eckhart, Marx and Schweitzer: their radical demand for giving up the having orientation; their insistence on complete independence; their metaphysical skepticism; their godless religiosity, and their demand for social activity in the spirit of care and human solidarity."[12]

## Secular quasi-religiousness

An aggressive approach to anything religious is still widespread among ideologically critical social scientists confronted by religion especially in the institutionalized form of churches, with their claim to power, their doctrinalism and their conservatism in public life. Yet here, too, there are a number of social scientists who are beginning to take a different view of the phenomenon of "religiousness." Today the tendency is increasingly to start out once more from the recognition of the permanence of man's religious needs, needs of course that might be satisfied in a "secular" way. In this case it would be better, anyway, to speak of "quasi-religiousness."

In the sixties, the American cultural philosopher *Theodore Roszak*[13] drew attention to the extent to which the "counter culture" of the hippies and the flower children in their opposition to the technocratic society bore ideological, quasi-religious features; in the meantime, many of the former hippies have joined religious groups. And at the end of the sixties, sociologists and political scientists wanted to discover in the protest movements of the "New Left" quasi-religious features, evaluating them of course critically and largely negatively. On account of the deep commitment and fanaticism of their charismatic leaders, the doctrines of salvation and dogmas disguised as science, the eschatological passion of their criticism of society, the more or less violent attempts to convert people to their revival movement, militant "New Left" supporters in the whole world came to be called the "Anabaptists of the affluent society" and their movement a "substitute rebellion with secular formulations of theological questions."[14]

The sociologist *Helmut Schelsky,* in his latest publication, sees likewise the spreading of "a new 'secularized' religiousness, a *'sociological religion'* in the class struggle and the priestly domination of the intellectuals": "We may therefore see the attitude that supports the claims to political domination on the part of this new class of 'mediators of salvation and meaning' not only as political ideology but as a more far-reaching, fundamental vital claim, as a basic relationship to reality, determining a person's whole conduct, which cannot be described as other than 'religious.' In fact, the concepts of a metaphysics long assumed to be obsolete seem to be the only appropriate forms under which this attitude can be understood. It is clear that we are faced with a religious attitude different from that of the Christian faith and indeed that this *new* religiousness can only be understood as the durability of basic religious needs after the acid of enlightenment and secularization has replaced the specifically Christian content and split it off from this religious need of salvation."[15] For Schelsky, it is clear that this new religiousness has little to do with traditional Christian attitudes. On the contrary, it is the result precisely of enlightenment and secularization and has taken the place of the traditional Christian outlook.

The Munich educationist *Richard Schwarz* is similarly skeptical in regard to the continuance of the traditional Christian religiousness. He speaks of an almost total "de-Christianizing" of our modern society, of the "decline of the sacred," of an "indeterminate faith."[16] Schwarz defends himself against the charge of making religious capital out of modern man's fear of self-destruction, out of his unease in the face of the "limits of growth," a procedure that may not be entirely unpopular among theologians and preachers today: "But the question again discussed today still seems completely open, as to whether the 'limits of growth,' the obvious discontent with the negative results of scientific progress, in face of environmental problems or the dehumanized, technicized world of work, with the inhuman organization of medicine, might not also be a discontent with the emptiness of life, a revived awareness of the unstable 'marginal situations' of our existence, a disquiet in regard to the questions of the meaning of death and life as a whole. The new 'primordial dread' of the atom roused no religious experiences but only vital fear. Nor have symptoms of the crisis of technocratical-rational authenticating systems yet been able to produce effective new religious signals."[17] Schwarz concludes: "We do not see any special signs of a fresh attempt today to raise the question of meaning in a religious sense. This age lives on an awareness of the perfection of all the means together with the absence of any ends in regard to the question of human life. We are conscious of living in the midst of a cosmic process the trend and goal of which are unknown."[18] And yet, is not such a view far too one-sided? Other social scientists see things differently; they can see "signs of transcendence."

## Rediscovery of transcendence

It is true that the American sociologist of religion *Peter Berger*, who created a sensation some years ago with his book *A Rumor of Angels*,[19] has no illusions about the survival of religion as a mass phenomenon: "It is a fairly reasonable prognosis that in a 'surprise-free' world the global trend of secularization will continue. An impressive rediscovery of the supernatural, in the dimensions of a mass phenomenon, is not in the books. At the same time, significant enclaves of supernaturalism within the secularized culture will also continue."[20] Unlike Schwarz, Berger invites the theologians to "seek out what might be called *signals of transcendence* within the empirically given human situation. And I would further suggest that there are *prototypical human gestures* that may constitute such signals."[21] At the same time, for Berger, these "prototypical human gestures" are "certain reiterated acts and experiences that appear to express essential aspects of man's being, of the human animal as such."[22]

Berger, then, finds "signs of transcendence"—for instance—in man's propensity for order. *Faith in order*, he thinks, is "closely related to man's fundamental trust in reality."[23] We may recall here what was developed at length in connection with *fundamental trust*:[24] "Man's propensity for order is grounded in a faith or trust that, ultimately, reality is 'in order,' 'all right,' 'as it should be.' Needless to say, there is no empirical method by which this faith can be tested. To assert it is itself an act of faith."[25] And "the most fundamental of ordering gestures, that by which a mother reassures her anxious child," is for Berger a sign of transcendence: "The content of this communication will invariably be the same—'Don't be afraid—everything is in order, everything is all right.'" The child's "trust in reality is recovered, and in this trust he will return to sleep."[26]

Even in *play*, man transcends his reality, ordinary life, the mechanical uniformity of society, when he partly nullifies the familiar setting in space and time and its limits, setting up a world of meaning of his own with its own rules. Berger sees these ciphers of transcendence also in the "argument from *hope*" (where he follows Bloch), in the argument from *damnation*, that is, in man's longing for a justice transcending earthly justice (we are reminded of Horkheimer), or in the "argument from *humour*," which can rise above man's most wretched reality, seen as not definitive.

Seen in this way, the rediscovery of transcendence means "a regaining of openness in our perception of reality. . . . The principal moral benefit of religion is that it permits a confrontation with the age in which one lives in a perspective that transcends the age and thus puts it in proportion. This both vindicates courage and safeguards against fanaticism. To find courage to do what must be done in a given moment is not the only moral good. It is also very much a moral good that this same moment does not become the be-all and end-all of one's existence, that in meeting its demands one does not lose the capacity to laugh and to play."[27]

Almost at the same time, the American Charles A. Reich, a professor at Yale, in a book that also became popular, *The Greening of America*,[28] anticipated a new consciousness looking beyond establishment and revolution—a "Consciousness III"—and demanded an awareness of transcendence. This would mean, in the midst of this technological world, a liberating transcendence of existing conditions through the choice of a new life-style: the development of new capacities, the development of a new independence and personal responsibility, of sensitivity, of aesthetic feeling, of the power to love, of possibilities of new forms of living together and working together, in order to control the technological machinery. Reich demands therefore a new definition of values and priorities and thus also a new reflection on religion and ethics, so that a really new humanity and a new society may become possible: "The power of the new consciousness is not the power of manipulating procedures or the power of politics or street fighting, but the power of new values and a new way of life."[29]

For *Daniel Bell*, too, the Harvard sociologist, a "great renewal of religion" is possible in the postindustrial age. The essential question today is whether man in the conflict of culture and technology can find an "Archimedean principle" in order to understand or judge his existence. In this respect, in addition to nature and history, religion acquires a decisive importance.[30] Bell shares the view of Talcott Parsons: "Religion is as much a human universal as language."[31] And he quotes with approval the saying of Max Scheler (and Max Weber): "Every finite spirit believes either in God or in idols."[32] Clearly dissociating himself from "contemporary political religions, and the claims of 'the possessed' for final truths," he recognizes as the central question: "Who is God and who is the devil?"[33] Bell, then, sees that "despite the shambles of modern culture, some religious answer surely will be forthcoming." Religion "is a constitutive part of man's consciousness: the cognitive search for the pattern of the 'general order' of existence; the affective need to establish rituals and to make such conceptions sacred; the primordial need for relatedness to some others, or to a set of meanings which will establish a transcendent response to the self; and the existential need to confront the finalities of suffering and death."[34]

Can these tasks be fulfilled only by *new religions?* Bell is skeptical. For every religion needs, in addition to rites of liberation in a new sense, also rites of incorporation into a community and ties with both past and future: "In this sense, religion is the awareness of a moment of transcendence, the passage out of the past, from which one has to come (and to which one is bound), to a new conception of the self as a moral agent, freely accepting the past (rather than just being shaped by it), and returning to tradition in order to maintain the continuity of moral meanings."[35] The *former religions*, too, would thus have the opportunity of a "great renewal" for the "future of the Western world."[36]

Youth, as always, will make its own decision about this opportunity. The latest analysis by *Klaus Mehnert, Jugend im Zeitbruch. Woher— wohin?*[37] can offer some hope in this respect. After thorough investigations in both the U.S.A. and Germany, it shows how many young people today ask basic religious questions: "Science and technology? Yes, they can split and fuse the atom and annihilate millions of human beings in a few seconds, they can construct giant supersonic airplanes, land on the moon and even on the nearest planets. But they cannot answer a single one of the real problems of human beings. Is there a God? Where do we come from? Where are we going? How shall we live? Even the established Churches have lost much of their attraction and people are seeking truth increasingly by other ways."[38]

## Future for religion

Whatever we may think of the details of the observations and attempted interpretations by Berger, Reich, Bell, Mehnert and others, one thing cannot be disputed. Despite the great advance of secularization, there is an abundant response today particularly among the younger generation to the call for new standards of values, models, priorities and ideals, for a new view of life and a new way of life, and thus also for ethics and religion. The "one-dimensional man" is seeking—often unconsciously—another dimension of life and not only by transcending the present in a forward movement to the Great Revolution or—after its failure—to the "Great Refusal" (Marcuse[39]) but—likewise in metaphorical terms—to the heights or depths of a true transcendence, enabling man to rise to new life and action. There is evidence of this not only in essentially religious stirrings—from Jesus movements and charismatic movements to the interest in Eastern religion and mysticism (and all forms of superstition, including devil worship)—but also in the commitment to the civil and human rights movement in East and West, North and South. It is the same with movements against poverty and for national independence in the Third World, especially in Africa and South America. Formerly, the extensive and direct influence of religion on society was undoubtedly greater, while today its intensive and indirect influence is perhaps more important.

It is difficult even for futurologists to extrapolate exactly the future of religion. For religion by its very nature eludes statistical expression (in terms, for instance, of Sunday observance). Religious faith, hope and action simply cannot be measured by doctrines, rites, modes of behavior and structures. But in the light of all the reflections of experts and the religious phenomena just mentioned, it seems improbable that the process of secularization will develop uninterruptedly toward a universal atheistic secularism; even the religious statistics provide no excuse for such prognoses.[40] On the other hand, of course, we can scarcely expect secularization to be reversed as a result of a reestablishment of religion; for this, all the preconditions are lacking, and the religious signals mentioned above are hardly sufficient to suggest it. Secularization will presumably continue—by no means to the detriment of religion—in a modified form. This third prognosis—by Thomas Luckmann—appears to be the most likely.[41]

It is possible to regard the important factor for religion mainly as membership in a community (as a sociologically integrating factor in Dürkheim's sense) or mainly as being placed within a system of interpretation (as a factor giving meaning and rationalizing values in Weber's sense). Religion may be important in less sacral forms in the future, for interpersonal relationships (Thomas Luckmann, Peter Berger) or even—without abandoning sacral forms—indirectly for social institutions and structures (Talcott Parsons, Clifford Geertz, Daniel Bell) or finally—combining the functions of integrating and giving meaning—for the formation of progressive elites in the pluralistic societies (Andrew Greeley[42]). In this respect, at any rate, sociologists of religion are agreed that religion —like art—will always exist. At the same time, religion is no more to be identified with the ecclesiastical, institutional, sacral, irrational aspects than is secularization with unchurching, desacralization, rational disenchantment.

What, then—looking back over the long road from Bloch and Horkheimer up to the modern human and social scientists—is to be retained in view of the future of religion?

- *The common conviction of both believers in God and atheists that the existing world with its injustice is not in order keeps alive in mankind the yearning for a wholly Other: an ultimate reality which—however it is to be understood—is different from the apparent, obvious, intrinsically contradictory world.*
- *The serious problems of man, society and science, at the present time and in the future, raise the question of standards of value, norms, priorities, of view of life and way of life, and thus the question of ethics, while ethics for its own part—with regard to its justification and absoluteness—raises the question of religion.*
- *We can wholly approve the modern process of secularization and the autonomy of secular institutions and sciences even for the future and yet decisively reject the ideologies of atheistic secularism—of that religionless Weltanschauung which links the secularity of the world, of its institutions and sciences, with fundamental godlessness.*
- Religion *means a particular social realization of a relationship to an ab-*

solute ground of meaning, to an absolutely final concern, to something with which I am unconditionally involved.

- Genuine religion, however, is found only where this ground of meaning, this absolutely final concern, that with which I am unconditionally involved, is not something merely of this world (secular) but something that is in the broadest sense "divine" ("absolute," "holy").
- Where the nondivine is set up as ground of meaning, as absolutely final concern, as that with which I am unconditionally involved—the nation in nationalism, the people in National Socialism, the race in rascism, the party in Leninism-Stalinism, science in scientism, the material world in materialism—it would be better to speak of quasi religion (Paul Tillich) or substitute religion.

Here the theologian must try to speak as unequivocally as possible. Unlike the psychologist or sociologist, he has to deal with religion not only as an individual and social problem but with the *truth* of religion and belief in God, and he cannot dispense with further questioning. Only when we get beyond talking in general about religion and religiousness and answer the question about God, does the question of religion also find a theologically unequivocal answer. For:
All "signs" and "ciphers" of transcendence (Berger) are inadequate to *substantiate* transcendence.
All demands for a new consciousness, a new definition of values and a new reflection on religion (Reich) fail to prove *any necessity* for religion.
All needs of religion (Bell) still do *not* show *the truth* of religion.
All questions of the whence and whither (Mehnert) provide *no indications of the possibility of an answer.*
And with reference to Horkheimer, Marcuse and Bloch, the question may be given a more acute form:
Yearning for the wholly Other? Yes. But is the wholly Other a reality corresponding to this yearning?
Absoluteness in ethics? Yes. But is there actually an absolute moral authority?
Transcendence beyond the one-dimensionality of human existence? Yes. But must all this necessarily mean a Yes to God?
If God is supposed to be the answer to all man's yearnings, hopes and questions, then an absolutely unequivocal answer must first be found to the basic question: Does God exist at all?

## 2. God as hypothesis

In Brecht's *Geschichten vom Herrn Keuner* ("Stories of Herr Keuner") we read: "Someone asked Herr K. if there is a God. Herr K. said: 'I advise you to consider whether your conduct would change in the light of your particular answer to this question. If it would change, then I can help you at least to this extent, that I say, you have already decided. You need a God.' "[43]

Theologians are accustomed to evade such shrewdly worded alternatives by similar astute statements. One example of this is the statement above mentioned: "A God who is there, is not God." This (in Bonhoeffer's sense) means that there is not a God in the same way as there is a Lake Geneva, or the Matterhorn, or love between two human beings. But it is not an answer to the precise question about the existence of God. Others —with reference to Brecht—might vary the statement a little: "A God whom one needs, is not needed." This idea, too, is correct in the sense that God can never be a function or a means to an end (for the education of children, for politics, Church and so on), if he is to remain God. But, again, it is not an answer to the clear question about God's existence.

Are there not enough of our contemporaries who believe in the existence of God (or at least in a "higher being") but in practice in their ordinary life do not let any of this be known? And conversely are there not many contemporaries who do not believe in the existence of God but in practice live as if he did exist? Consequently, Brecht's statement of the question demands an unequivocal answer: If God exists, does this imply any change in man's conduct or not? Yes, something is changed: this must be our clear and unequivocal answer, although we must take care not to moralize in regard to the question. Those who believe in God are not *ipso facto* better people.

## What would be different if. . . .

We might make it easy for ourselves and answer briefly with the negative hypothesis as formulated by Dostoevsky and described by Jean Paul Sartre as the "starting point of existentialism": "If God did not exist, everything would be permitted,"[44] "everything," of course, being open to various interpretations. But we shall take on the more difficult task and develop the positive hypothesis (bearing in mind that it *is* a hypothesis). The obvious thing is to start out from the questions that have been raised in the course of this chapter. From this standpoint we can say:

*If* God exists:

then this life—which *Kurt Tucholsky* found "somewhat noisy" and did not rightly understand—is not all; then a liberating ascent, a transcending of "one-dimensional man" into another dimension, a real alternative— although in a fundamentally different form from that which *Herbert Marcuse* demands—is even now possible;

then the basic question of *Gottfried Wilhelm von Leibniz:* "Why is there

something rather than nothing?" might perhaps find an answer, just like that of Martin Heidegger about the "marvel of marvels": "Why is there any Being at all—why not, far rather, Nothing?"
then there is no need to be content—like Heidegger—with invoking the vanished gods;
then the infinite yearning of man, who—according to *Ernst Bloch*—is restless, unfinished, never fulfilled and always setting out again on his way, making further demands, gaining more knowledge, seeking further, continually reaching out for what is different and new—this yearning has a meaning and would not in the end be left unsatisfied;
then, in experimenting in the laboratory of the world not only is a "possible salvation" projected, but for both the individual and society there will be brought about an "actual salvation" which the world— capitalist or socialist—cannot itself give;
then the ancient hope of a new life, the Utopian omega, the fulfilled moment, the kingdom of God is truly—that is, by God himself—assured, and a reconciliation also between man and nature, logos and cosmos, is not an illusion;
then even all the inescapable sufferings that, according to advocates of the Critical Theory, cannot be canceled out by abstract arguments, unhappiness, pain, age and death of the individual, and also the menacing final stage of boredom in a wholly managed world—all these are not the last word but point to a wholly Other;
then *Max Horkheimer*'s yearning for perfect justice, for absolute meaning and eternal truth, is not unrealistic but in the end open to fulfillment, to infinite fulfillment;
then the signs and symbols of transcendence (Berger), the demands for a new consciousness and a new definition of values (Reich), the needs of religion (Bell), the questions of the whence and whither (Mehnert), would point not to nothing but to the most real reality.

These are man's great questions of life for the future and the present, which have to be answered and which—since they are concerned with the totality of things—can be answered only in the light of the question of God; the answer varies fundamentally according to whether God exists or not. They can be summed up in three questions:

"*Who are we?*" Defective beings who are not what they might be. Expectant, hoping, yearning beings who are continually excelling themselves. But why are we like this? What explains this strange urge continually to transcend ourselves? What explains it, not only factually, provisionally, but ultimately, definitively? Is there no answer to this? Or is the question even permissible?
*If* God exists, then there is an answer to the great question why we are

very finite, defective beings and yet infinitely expectant, hoping, yearning beings.

"*Where do we come from?*" We can go back over the chain of causes, finding one cause after another. But the series breaks down when the whole has to be explained. What, then, is the cause of all causes? Do we not come up against nothingness at this point? But what is the explanation of nothing, except—precisely—nothing? Or are we to be satisfied with matter, to which divine attributes, eternity and omnipotence, are ascribed? Or perhaps even hydrogen, which in particular raises the question of whence? Is there no answer to this? Or is the question even permissible?

*If* God exists, then there is an answer to the great question where do hydrogen and matter come from, where does the world and where does man come from?

"*Where are we going?*" We can aim at one goal after another. But one goal after another is attained and we are still no nearer to finding the meaning of the whole, of the totality of human life and of human history. What, then, is the goal of all goals? Is nothingness perhaps both the beginning and the end? But nothingness no more explains the end than it does the beginning. Is the end to be a totally technicized or radically revolutionized society, both of which today are more questionable than ever? Is there no answer to this? Or is the question even permissible?

*If* God exists, then there is an answer to the great question, Where is man and where is humanity going, Where is human life and where is human history going?

## Ground, support and goal of reality

It is possible to recapitulate everything in those other three famous questions in which—according to Kant—the whole interest of human reason is concentrated and which show that the last questions are also the first. "What can I know?" sums up questions about truth. "What ought I to do?" questions about the norm. "What may I hope?" questions about meaning.

In concrete life, everything is interconnected: "functional" and "essential" questions, technically rational and totally personal questions; both man's existential "authenticity" and "unauthenticity" in Heidegger's sense and social "alienation" and "liberation" in Marx's sense. Of course, in the concrete human being, the essential questions about meaning and truth, norms and values, can be concealed and suppressed—more than ever under the soporific influence of the affluent society. That is, until they are revived on a large or small scale, by reflection or even more by "fate," and startle man out of his more or less naïve fundamental trust in reality.

We may recall the fact that, even for the person who assents in fundamental trust to the reality of the world and man, the *thoroughgoing uncertainty of reality* in the ontic, noetic and ethical senses persists. Trust in uncertain reality does not eliminate its radical uncertainty. Reality, which can justify a fundamental trust, appears itself to be mysteriously *unjustified*; sustaining though *not* itself *sustained*; evolving but *without a goal* of its own. Reality is there as a fact, but enigmatically, utterly lacking in any manifest ground, support or purpose. That is why the question of reality, of being or not-being, of fundamental trust or nihilism, can emerge again at any time.[45]

What is involved, then, is the question of where the believer in God stands in competition, in theoretical and practical discussion, with the nonbeliever: who, then, can give a convincing explanation of man and the world today, of reality as a whole? This was what concerned us when we ventured on the discussion with modern atheism, especially with Feuerbach and Marx, Nietzsche and Freud. We are concerned with the fundamental question of the *source* of the explanation of utterly uncertain reality. What makes it possible? What, then, is the *condition of the possibility of this uncertain reality?*

In this respect, we shall take completely seriously Bonhoeffer's exhortation and "speak of God not on the boundaries but at the centre, not in weaknesses but in strength."[46] That is to say, the general question about the source of reality, its ground, support and goal, is admittedly only *one* way of access to God; but, in the light of the all-embracing modern complex of problems and against the background of nihilism and atheism, it is the way that stands out. In concrete life, however, there are innumerable ways of access to God. The dissident in Moscow and the President in Washington, the socially committed head of an industrial concern and the convinced trade union leader, the mountain guide in the Alps of the Valais and the woman missionary doctor in South India, the worker-priest in the Paris suburbs and the Pope in the Vatican—all these have their own particular reasons for believing in God. But the reasons are always connected in one way or another with the grandeur and misery of man and the world; in other words, with this uncertain reality.

If a person does not want to forgo an understanding of himself, of the world, of reality as a whole, he cannot permit himself to be held up by any prohibition of questioning, no matter who has issued it (usually with very obvious interests). These ultimate questions—which are also primary —call inescapably for an answer. For—in particular—from the quite concrete experience of life's insecurity, the uncertainty of knowledge and man's manifold fear and disorientation, which we were able to follow from the time of Descartes and Pascal throughout the whole of modern times, there arises the irrecusable question: *What is the source* of this radically *uncertain reality,* suspended between being and not-being, meaning and meaninglessness, supporting without support, evolving without aim?

On our long road through modern times, we have now at last reached that point which had to be our starting point in the earlier book *On Being a Christian.*[47] It is here that the reader will see particularly clearly how little these two books can be separated from each other, how they overlap and are bound to overlap in order to complement and illuminate each other, particularly in regard to the decisive questions of reality and God. And this holds not only for the question of access to God but—as we shall see later—also for both the Old Testament and the specifically Christian understanding of God. The coherence and consistency of the whole conception will be underlined—incidentally, making it easier for the reader—by the fact that, particularly with reference to God as hypothesis and as reality, we are taking up again here the essential theses of *On Being a Christian.* These theses, however, have been illustrated and appropriately justified from all aspects, both historically and systematically, in a way quite different from that adopted in the earlier book. Similarities therefore are not only intended but also inevitable.

Does God exist? Here we want to address expressly even the unbeliever. For even someone who does not think *that* God exists could at least agree with the *hypothesis* of which the inner meaning has become clear in the previous section and which nevertheless by no means settles the question of the existence or nonexistence of God. The hypothesis runs: *If* God exists, then a fundamental solution of the riddle of persistently uncertain reality is indicated, in the sense that a fundamental answer— obviously needing to be developed and interpreted—will have been found to the question of the source of reality. This hypothesis, of which the implications have become clear from our thoroughgoing discussion with atheism and nihilism, can be set out in a very succinct form:

- *If God exists, then the grounding reality itself is not ultimately groundless. Why? Because God is then the primal ground of all reality.*
- *If God exists, then the supporting reality itself is not ultimately unsupported. Why? Because God is then the primal support of all reality.*
- *If God exists, then evolving reality itself is not ultimately without aim. Why? Because God is then the primal goal of all reality.*
- *If God exists, then reality suspended between being and nonbeing is not ultimately under suspicion of being a void. Why? Because God is then the being itself of all reality.*

When we recall in particular Nietzsche and what was said about the scholastic "transcendentals" (the one, true and good),[48] this hypothesis can be stated more precisely both positively and negatively with reference to

the ambivalent reality of the world and man. First the *positive* questions
will be raised, and every word should be noted:
Why, *if* God exists, can we assume with absolutely reasonable fundamental trust that in all disunion there is ultimately a hidden unity, in all
meaninglessness ultimately a hidden meaningfulness, in all worthlessness
ultimately a hidden value of reality? Because God is the *primal source,
primal meaning, primal value* of all that is.
Why, *if* God exists, can we assume with absolutely reasonable fundamental trust that in all the void there is ultimately a hidden being of reality? Because God himself would be the *being itself* of all reality. It should
of course be understood that reality does not then by any means lose its
actual hollowness. But a reason would be indicated why, despite the
hollowness, man can commit himself to reality and rely upon it.

And now the *counter test!* If God exists, then the *negative* aspect of
reality, its hollowness, can also be understood:
Why does the grounding reality of the world and man appear itself to be
ultimately groundless, supporting reality that is itself ultimately unsupported, evolving reality that is itself ultimately without aim? Why, then,
is its unity repeatedly threatened by disunion, its meaningfulness by
meaninglessness, its value by worthlessness? Why is reality, suspended between being and nonbeing, ultimately under suspicion of being unreality
and hollowness?
The basic answer is always the same: Because uncertain reality is itself
*not God.* Because the self, society, the world, cannot be identified with
their primal ground, primal support and primal goal, with their primal
source, primal meaning and primal value, with being itself.


## Ground, support and goal of human existence

The same hypothesis can be applied even more pointedly to the special
uncertainty *of my human existence.* It would then run: *If* God exists,
then an answer *has* been found at least in principle to the riddle of my
persistently uncertain human existence. Which means for me: If God
exists,

- *then, despite all the menace of fate and death, I can with good reason
  confidently affirm the unity and identity of my human existence. Why?
  Because God is the primal source also of my life;*
- *then, despite all the menace of emptiness and meaninglessness, I can
  with good reason confidently affirm the truth and meaningfulness of my
  existence. Why? Because God is the ultimate meaning of my life;*
- *then, despite all the menace of sin and damnation, I can with good
  reason confidently affirm the goodness and value of my existence. Why?
  Because God is then the all-embracing hope of my life;*

- *then, against all the menace of nonbeing, I can with good reason confidently affirm the being of my human existence: God is then the being itself in particular also of human life.*

Anyone who wants to do so can apply a *counter test* also to this hypothetical answer:

Why are the unity and identity, truth and meaningfulness, goodness and value, of my own human existence still menaced? By fate and death, by emptiness and meaninglessness, by sin and damnation? Why is the being of my existence still menaced by nonbeing?

The fundamental answer consistently is always one and the same: Because man *is not* God. Because my human self can *not* be identified with its primal source, primal meaning, primal value, with being itself.

It can scarcely be disputed therefore that, *if* God exists, then the condition of the possibility of this uncertain reality also exists, its "whence" (in the widest sense) explained. *If!* But there is an old proposition of logic: *Ab esse ad posse valet illatio, non autem viceversa.* We can conclude from reality to possibility, but not conversely. That is, we cannot conclude from the hypothesis of God to the reality of God. How, then, are we to get from the hypothesis to the reality? The answer can now be given.

## 3. God as reality

If we are not to draw hasty conclusions, we must proceed step by step. What are the alternatives? If—as in the question of fundamental trust—the positions are set out antithetically, this does not mean that we are dividing human beings into good ("God fearers") and bad ("godless") or that we want to pass moral judgments on the decision for or against God. However obvious the ethical aspect of the question of God may be, all the more must the alternative be first brought out in a fundamental confrontation.

## Both denial and affirmation of God are possible

The discussion with Feuerbach, Marx, Freud and Nietzsche has shown[49] that there is one thing that can never be disputed in regard to atheism:

- *It is possible to deny God. Atheism cannot be eliminated rationally. It is irrefutable.*

Why? It is the experience of the radical uncertainty of any sort of reality which over and over again provides atheism with sufficient excuse to assert and to maintain the assertion that reality has no primal ground, primal support, primal goal at all. Any talk of a primal source, primal meaning, primal value, must be rejected. We simply cannot know any of these things—this is the claim of agnosticism with a tendency to atheism. Indeed, perhaps chaos, absurdity, illusion, appearance, and not being but nonbeing, are the last word—this is the claim of atheism with a tendency to nihilism.

Hence there are actually no positive arguments for the *impossibility* of atheism. If someone says that there is no God, this cannot be positively refuted. Neither a strict proof nor an indication of God can prevail against such an assertion. For this negative statement rests in the last resort on a *decision*, a decision that is connected with the fundamental decision for reality as a whole. The denial of God cannot be refuted purely rationally.

The discussion with Feuerbach, Marx, Freud and Nietzsche[50] has, however, revealed something else:[51] atheism, for its own part, cannot positively exclude the other alternative.

● *Affirmation of God is also possible. Atheism cannot be rationally established. It is undemonstrable.*

Why? It is the *reality* in all uncertainty which provides sufficient excuse for risking not only a confident affirmation of this reality, its identity, meaningfulness and value, but over and above this also an affirmation of that without which reality in all substantiation seems to be ultimately unsubstantiated, in all supporting ultimately unsupported, in all evolution ultimately aimless: a confident affirmation, that is, of a primal ground, primal support and primal goal of uncertain reality.

Hence there is actually no conclusive argument for the *necessity* of atheism. And if someone says that there is a God, this, too, cannot be positively refuted. Atheism, for its own part, cannot prevail against such confidence imposed on us in the light of reality itself. The affirmation of God also rests, in the last resort, on a *decision*, which, again, is connected with the fundamental decision for reality as a whole. This, too, is rationally irrefutable.

## God—a matter of trust

The alternatives have become clear. Both affirmation and denial of God are possible. Are we not therefore faced with a stalemate, with indecision?

It is just at this point that we find the knot which is decisive for the solution of the question of the existence of God, a solution we have prepared in extensive discussions on the natural theology of Vatican I,[52] on the dialectical theology of Barth and Bultmann[53] and Kant's theology of moral postulates.[54] We can briefly recapitulate here:

● *If God is, he is the answer to the radical uncertainty of reality.*
● *The fact that God is, can be assumed*

*not strictly in virtue of a proof or indication of pure reason (natural theology),*

*not unconditionally in virtue of a moral postulate of practical reason (Kant),*

*not exclusively in virtue of the biblical testimony (dialectical theology),*

*but only in a* confidence *rooted in reality itself.*

This trusting commitment to an ultimate ground, support and meaning of reality—and not only the commitment to the Christian God—is itself rightly designated in general usage as *"belief"* in God, as *"faith in God."* Corresponding to "fundamental trust," we might also speak in a general way of "trust in God," if this term were not too theologically and emotionally charged. In order not to permit the term to fall completely out of use, we shall sometimes deliberately make use of the analogy between "fundamental trust" and *"trust in God."* At the same time, it is obviously a question of genuine belief, albeit in a wide sense, in as much as such a belief must not necessarily be prompted by the Christian proclamation but is possible also for non-Christians (Jews, Muslims, Hindus and so on).[55] People who profess such a belief—whether Christians or non-Christians—are rightly described as "believers in God." On the other hand, atheism in so far as it is a refusal to trust in God is, again, quite rightly described in general usage as *"unbelief."*

It has been shown therefore that man *cannot evade* a free, although not arbitrary, *decision,* not only in regard to reality as such but also in regard to a primal ground, primal support and primal goal of reality. Since reality and its primal ground, primal support and primal goal are not imposed on us with conclusive evidence, there remains scope for man's freedom. Man must decide without intellectual constraint but also without rational proof. Both atheism and belief in God are therefore ventures, they are also risks.[56] The critique of the proofs of God[57] itself shows that belief in God has the character of a decision, and—conversely—a decision for God has the character of belief.

The question of God therefore involves a decision that must of course be faced on a deeper level than the decision—necessary in view of nihilism—for or against reality as such. As soon as the individual becomes aware of this ultimate depth and the question arises, the decision becomes unavoidable. As with fundamental trust, so, too, with the question of God, not to choose is in fact a choice: the person has chosen not to choose. To abstain from voting in a vote of confidence in regard to the question of God means a refusal of confidence, a vote of mistrust. If at this point a person does not—at least factually—affirm God, he denies him.

Yet unfortunately the "depth" (or "height") of a truth and the certainty with which it is accepted by man are in inverse ratio.[58] The more banal the truth ("truism," "platitude") the greater the certainty. The more significant the truth (for instance aesthetic, moral and religious truth by comparison with arithmetical) the slighter the certainty. For the "deeper" the truth is for me, the more must I lay myself open to it, inwardly prepare myself, attune myself to it intellectually, voluntarily, emotionally, in order to reach that genuine "certainty" which is somewhat different from assured "security."[59] A *deep* truth, for me outwardly uncertain, menaced by doubts, which presupposes a generous commitment on my part, can possess much more cognitive value than a certain—or even an "absolutely certain"—*banal* truth $(2+2=4)$.

### Belief in God as ultimately justified fundamental trust

But does it not follow from the possibility of affirming or denying God that the choice is a matter of indifference? By no means.

● *Denial of God implies an* ultimately unjustified *fundamental trust in reality. Atheism cannot suggest any condition for the possibility of uncertain reality. If someone denies God, he does not know why he ultimately trusts in reality.*

This means that *atheism is nourished*, if not by a nihilistic fundamental mistrust, then at any rate *by an ultimately unjustified fundamental trust.* By denying God, man decides against a primary ground, deepest support, an ultimate goal of reality. In atheism the assent to reality turns out to be ultimately unjustified: a freewheeling, nowhere-anchored and therefore paradoxical fundamental trust. In nihilism, on account of its radical fundamental mistrust, an assent to reality is completely impossible. Atheism cannot suggest *any condition for the possibility of uncertain reality.* For this reason it lacks not perhaps all rationality but certainly a radical rationality, which lack, of course, it often disguises by a rationalistic but essentially irrational trust in human reason.

No, it is not a matter of indifference whether we affirm or deny God. *The price paid by atheism for its denial* is obvious. It is exposed by an ultimate groundlessness, unsupportedness, aimlessness, to the danger of the possible disunion, meaninglessness, worthlessness, hollowness of reality as a whole. When he becomes aware of this, the atheist is exposed also quite personally to the danger of an ultimate abandonment, menace and decay, resulting in doubt, fear, even despair. All this is true, of course, only if atheism is quite serious and not an intellectual pose, snobbish caprice or thoughtless superficiality.

For the atheist, there is no answer to those ultimate and yet immediate, perennial questions of human life, which are not to be suppressed by being prohibited—questions that arise not merely in marginal situations but in the very midst of personal and social life. To return once more to Kant's questions:

What can we *know?* Why is there anything at all? Why not nothing? Where does man come from and where does he go to? Why is the world as it is? What is the ultimate ground and meaning of all reality?

What ought we to *do?* Why do what we do? Why and to whom are we ultimately responsible? What deserves forthright contempt and what love? What is the point of loyalty and friendship, but also what is the point of suffering and sin? What is really decisive for man?

What may we *hope?* Why are we on earth? What is the meaning of the whole? Is there something that sustains us in all the hollowness, which never permits us to despair? Is there something stable in all change, something unconditioned in all that is conditioned? Is there an absolute in the relativity experienced everywhere? What is left for us: death, which makes everything pointless at the end? What will give us courage for life and what courage for death?

These are really questions in which we are wholly involved. They are questions not only for the dying but for the living. They are not only for weaklings and uninformed people but precisely for the informed and committed. They are not excuses for avoiding action but incentives to action. They are all questions that atheism, in the last resort, leaves unanswered. Now the other thesis:

- *Affirmation of God implies an* ultimately justified *fundamental trust in reality. As radical fundamental trust, belief in God can suggest the condition of the possibility of uncertain reality. If someone affirms God, he knows why he can trust reality.*

*Belief in God is nourished by an ultimately justified fundamental trust.* In affirming God, I decide confidently for a primary ground, deepest support, an ultimate goal of reality. In belief in God, my assent to reality turns out to be ultimately justified and consistent: a fundamental trust anchored in the ultimate depth, in the cause of causes, and directed to the goal of goals. My trust in God as genuine, radical, fundamental trust can therefore suggest the *condition for the possibility of uncertain reality.* In this sense, unlike atheism, it displays a radical rationality, which, however, must not simply be confused with rationalism.

No, there is no stalemate between belief in God and atheism. The *price received by belief in God for its assent* is obvious. Since I confidently decide for a primal ground instead of groundlessness, for a primal support instead of unsupportedness, for a primal goal instead of aimlessness, I can now with good reason perceive in all disunion a unity, in all worthlessness a value, in all meaninglessness a meaning of the reality of the world and man. And in all the uncertainty and insecurity, abandonment and exposure, menace, decay and finiteness even of my own existence, in the light of the ultimate primal source, primal meaning and primal value, I am granted—*given*—a radical certainty, assurance and stability. This is not simply an abstract security, in isolation from my fellow men, but always involves a concrete reference to the human "thou." How otherwise is the younger person in particular to learn what it means to be accepted by God, if he is not accepted by any single human being?

In this way, those ultimate and immediate questions of man receive at least a fundamental answer with which he can live: an answer from the very last and very first reality of God. And to measure the whole import of the answer, it would be helpful to read over again the section: "What would be different if. . . ."

## Belief in God rationally justified

After all this, it is obvious that there can be no question of a stalemate, of remaining undecided between belief in God and atheism. It is clear, then, that man is not simply indifferent in regard to the choice between atheism and belief in God. He is handicapped from the start. Essentially he would like to understand the world and himself, to respond to the uncertainty of reality, to perceive the condition for the possibility of uncertain reality; he would like to know of a primary ground, a deepest support and an ultimate goal of reality; he would like to know the primal source, primal meaning and primal value. Here are the roots of religion as a primordial fact.

Yet here, too, man remains free—within limits. He can say "No." He can adopt a skeptical attitude and ignore or even stifle any dawning confidence in an ultimate ground, support or goal:

he can, perhaps utterly honestly and truthfully, declare his inability to know (agnosticism with a tendency to atheism);

or he can assert a complete hollowness, a groundlessness and aimlessness of the reality that is uncertain anyway (atheism with a tendency to nihilism).

As with fundamental trust, so, too, here, without preparedness there is no understanding, without open-mindedness no reception. And even if I affirm God, denial of him remains a continual temptation.

But, like fundamental trust, so, too, trust in God is by no means irrational. If I do not close my mind to reality but remain open to it, if I do not try to get away from the very last and very first ground, support and goal of reality, but dare to apply myself and give myself up to it, then I know, *not* indeed *before, nor* yet *only afterward,* but *by the very fact* of doing this, that I am doing the right thing, and even what is absolutely the most reasonable thing. For what cannot be proved *in advance* I experience *in the accomplishment, in the very act of acknowledging what I perceive.* Reality can manifest itself in its proper depth; its primary ground, deepest support, ultimate goal, its primal source, primal meaning, primal value, are laid open to me as soon as I lay myself open. At the same time, in all the uncertainty, I experience a *radical reasonableness of my own reason.* Fundamental trust in reason is therefore not irrational. It is rationally justified. The last and first reality, God, is thus seen more or less as the *guarantor of the rationality of human reason.*

If man, by believing in God, is doing what is absolutely the most reasonable thing, what kind of rationality is involved here? This rationality is similar to that of fundamental trust:

- It is not an outward rationality, *which could not produce an assured security. God's existence is not first proved or demonstrated by reason and then believed, thus guaranteeing the rationality of belief in God. There is not first a rational knowledge and then confident acknowledgment of God. The hidden reality of God is not forced on reason.*
- It is an inward rationality, *which can offer a fundamental certainty. In the accomplishment, by the "practice," of boldly trusting in God's reality, despite all temptations to doubt, man experiences the reasonableness of his trust, based as it is on an ultimate identity, meaningfulness and value of reality, on its primal ground, primal meaning, primal value.*[60]

Has not the *connection between fundamental trust and belief in God* now become obvious? From the material standpoint, fundamental trust is related to reality as such (and to my own existence), while trust in God is related to the primal ground, primal support and primal goal of reality. Nevertheless, from the formal standpoint, fundamental trust and trust in God display an analogous structure that has its roots in the material connection (despite all the differences) of fundamental trust and trust in God. For, *like fundamental trust, belief in God, too, is*

- *a matter not only of human reason but of the whole concrete, living man, with mind and body, reason and instinct, in his quite particular historical situation, in his dependence on traditions, authorities, habits of thought, scales of values, with his interests and in his social involvement. Man cannot talk of this "matter" and at the same time* keep out of the "matter";
- *therefore superrational: as there is no logically conclusive proof for the reality of reality, neither is there one for the reality of God. The proof of God is no more logically conclusive than is love. The relationship to God is one of trust;*
- *but not irrational: there is a reflection on the reality of God emerging from human experience and calling for man's free decision. Belief in God can be justified in the face of a rational critique. It has a basis in the experience of uncertain reality itself, which raises the first and last questions about the condition of its possibility;*
- *not, then, a blind decision, devoid of reality, but one that is grounded in and related to reality and rationally justified in concrete life. Its rele-*

vance to both existential needs and social conditions becomes apparent from the reality of the world and of man;

- realized in a concrete relationship with our fellow men: without the experience of being accepted by men, it seems difficult to experience acceptance by God;

- not grasped once and for all, but constantly to be freshly realized: belief in God is not secured against atheism unassailably and immune from crises by rational arguments. Belief in God is continually threatened and—under pressure of doubts—must constantly be realized, upheld, lived, regained in a new decision: even in regard to God himself, man remains in insoluble conflict between trust and mistrust, belief and unbelief. But, throughout all doubts and precisely in this way, the affirmation of God is proved in fidelity to the decision once made: it becomes a tried and tested belief in God.

## Belief in God as gift

Belief in God is man's confident decision, it is my deed. This has nothing to do with rationalism or Pelagianism. For, as already indicated, it is not in advance—in virtue of a proof or demonstration—but only when I confidently commit myself to it, that reality itself lays open to me its primary ground, deepest support, its ultimate goal. That is why it is right to say that without preparedness for confident acknowledgment of God (with its practical consequences), there is no rationally meaningful knowledge of God. As with fundamental trust, so also with trust in God, I am expected to make an advance, to venture, to take a risk.

But also like fundamental trust, trust in God cannot simply be decided on, willed, extorted or produced. I cannot simply create or produce ultimate certainty, security, stability, for myself. God—as we saw[61]—is not an object of immediate experience; he is not part of existing reality, he is not among the objects available to experience; no intuition or speculation, no direct experience or immediate perception, can provide a "view" of him. It is just because of this that belief in God is seen as a *gift*:

It is enigmatic reality itself that invites and challenges me—often contrary to appearances—to commit myself in principle to a primal ground, a primal support, a primal goal in it, and which thus makes possible my trust in God.

It is enigmatic reality itself—with which, as it were, the initiative lies—that manifests to me the hidden primal source, primal meaning and primal value also of my own existence.

It is enigmatic reality itself that provides me with a basis of trust for that "vote of confidence" that ought to be cast for God's reality in the reality of this world.

It is enigmatic reality itself that makes it possible for me to see that, in all doubt, in all fear and despair, patience in regard to the present, gratitude in regard to the past, hope in regard to the future, are justified in the last resort. Hence:

- *Belief in God is a* gift. *Reality exists before me. If I do not cut myself off, but open myself entirely to reality as it opens out to me, then I can accept in faith its primary ground, its deepest support, its ultimate goal: God, who* reveals *himself as primal source, primal meaning and primal value.*

Reveals? Is it theologically permissible, in connection with the general—and certainly not specifically Christian—knowledge of God, to talk of "revelation"? We explained above that, in the Christian understanding, God can be known by all men, even by non-Jews and non-Christians.[62] This is taken for granted by the whole of the Old and New Testaments, by the entire Catholic, Orthodox and Reformation tradition (with the exception of dialectical theology) and also confirmed by the history of religion. And the Apostle Paul in particular—who otherwise can pass an overall negative judgment on the pagans as a group—in the Letter to the Romans, not only assumes on the part of the pagans an actual knowledge of God derived from knowledge of the world but speaks forthrightly of "revelation," of God making it plain to them: "For *what can be known about God is perfectly plain* to them since God himself has *made it plain.* Ever since God created the world his everlasting power and deity—however invisible—have been there *for the mind to see* in the things he has made. That is why such people are without excuse: they *knew* God and yet refused to honour him as God or to thank him."[63] This is confirmed in the prologue to John's Gospel and especially—while excusing the pagans and their ignorance—in the Acts of the Apostles. God exists: it is legitimate to speak here of revelation and also of grace.

## 4. Consequences

The findings of opinion polls are illuminating. According to a poll by the Gallup Institute in 1975, only 6 percent of all the Americans questioned were atheists or agnostics, 94 percent believed in God (69 percent in a life after death); the percentages in 1948 had been more or less the same.[1] According to a poll by the EMNID Institute in 1967, commissioned by the news magazine *Der Spiegel,* to research the "belief of Germans," 10 percent were atheists or agnostics;[2] 90 percent of the Germans questioned believed in "God" (68 percent) or in a "higher being" (22 percent). The numbers of those who believed in a "higher being," rather than "God," increased according to the educational level of the people questioned. We are reminded of one of the best of Heinrich Böll's satires,

"Doktor Murkes gesammeltes Schweigen" ("Dr. Murkes' collected si-
lences"),[3] about the unmasking of a "cultural philosopher" who "had
been converted in the religious enthusiasm of 1945" but began to have
misgivings in the postwar period and subsequently replaced the word
"God" wherever it appeared in one of his radio lectures, smuggling onto
the tape a supposedly more philosophical formulation: "that higher being
which we venerate." These are problems linked perhaps not with the idea
of God as such but with the God of the Bible.

## For dogmatics: natural theology after all?

First of all, we shall look back over this whole chapter. Did we, after
all, go in for natural theology?[4] To recapitulate:

a. We certainly did not go in for *dialectical theology*. Methodologically—
despite all genuinely dialectical theological statements—we never started
out, as it were, "vertically from above." On the contrary, we approached
the questions as consistently as possible, continually "from below": in the
light of man's immediate questions, of human experience. All this with a
view to a rational justification of faith today. For:

● Vis-à-vis nihilism, the fundamental problems of the uncertainty of reality as a whole and of human existence cannot be dismissed with an appeal to the Bible.
● Vis-à-vis atheism, the reality of God may not be merely asserted by invoking the Bible.

As we saw, the phenomena of religion, of philosophy, of the universally
human preconception, require an adequate answer. We have not yet, of
course, given a complete answer. The analysis made in the light of human
experience must later be critically interpreted in the light of the Christian
message.

b. Neither did we go in for *natural theology*. Although we started out
with man's natural questions and needs, we did not first build—so to
speak—a ground floor (as the basis of a higher, supernatural level), where
reason alone would be competent.

● We did not assume an autonomous reason capable of demonstrating a
foundation of faith but having nothing to do with faith itself. On the
contrary, it was shown that even the preliminary questions of Christian
faith—the reality of uncertain reality and the reality of God—can be
known not by pure reason but only in a believing trust or a trusting belief (in the broad sense of the term).
● There is, then, no continuous, gradual, rational ascent of man to God.

*But it is a question of a constantly renewed venture and risk in freedom and trust.*

- *Nor did we attribute any arbitrary power to man, enabling him to replace God. On the contrary, man was expected to lay himself open to reality, to respond to its appeal and demand, to accept its identity, meaningfulness and value, to acknowledge its very last and very first ground, support and goal.*

- *All things considered, then, we do not look to any "praeambula fidei" as the rational substructure of dogmatics, established by the rational arguments of pure reason. But we suggested that modern man should start his quest from the point at which he is actually living, in order to relate what he knows of God to things that move him.*

From this standpoint, theologically speaking, there are two possibilities.[5] On the one hand, we can do justice theologically to the *primacy* of God: in the reality of the world, God is experienced as real, because he reveals himself and opens himself out only to believing trust. On the other hand, we can do justice critically to the various "ideological" *positions of non-Christians:* the diverse positions of the nihilist, the atheist, the agnostic, and also of the non-Christian believer in God (in the world religions or in a secular context) are taken seriously and not theologically reinterpreted. We have already seen how important this is for ethics, and we can now underline the fact in the light of the reality of God.

## For ethics: theologically justified autonomy

If God does not exist, is everything really permitted? Formulated in this general way, the statement is undoubtedly false, for our remarks on fundamental trust as the basis of ethics showed that even an atheist, in virtue of this trust, can lead an authentically human, a humane and in this sense a moral life. This is the very way in which man's intramundane autonomy is manifested: his self-legislation and self-responsibility for his self-realization and the organization of the world.[6]

One thing, however, the atheist cannot do, even if he accepts absolute moral norms. He can scarcely justify the *absoluteness* of his obligation. Certainly there are numerous human pressures and necessities that can justify claims, duties, precepts—in brief, norms. But why should I observe these norms unconditionally? Why should I observe them even when they are completely at variance with my interests? In the end, in all these obligations, it is a question only of finitenesses, relativities, of my human existence. And from these it is quite impossible to deduce an absolute, "categorical" obligation.[7]

Not only man's individual necessities but even his universal "rational nature" are unable to justify any universally binding norms. Certainly in regard to Kant, who tried in the light of this universal "rational nature" of man to justify the absolute value and inviolable dignity of the individual human person,[8] it must be admitted that every human being must obviously realize his own nature. But, in this way, my egoism and that of others can be justified without providing a basis for an objective universal norm. A normative, universal human nature above and apart from myself and others is as much an abstraction as the idea of humanity, which Kant declares to be an end in itself. Why should such a hypostatized abstract human nature bind me absolutely to anything at all? It is the same with the claim made today, in East and West, that humanity must survive— this is absolutely binding. But what is to stop a power holder, a criminal, a group, a nation, a power bloc from acting against humanity if this serves their interest?

Is there any way of escaping from this dilemma between absolute and relative? We can now start out from the reality of God accepted in trust. By definition, God is not finite or conditioned, but the infinite, unconditioned, absolute, which can justify an unconditional, absolute claim.[9] We can state the thesis in this way:

- *The unconditionality of the ethical claim, the unconditionality of the obligation, can be justified only in the light of an* unconditioned: *of an* absolute *that can convey an overall meaning and that cannot be man as individual, as human nature or as human community, but only God himself.*

Not even the human community? *Jürgen Habermas*[10]—taking up again Kant's ideas and those of the Frankfurt School, from which he comes— within the scope of his critical theory of behavior and society, which he claims is also a theory of knowledge and practical philosophy, has attempted in the light of the human communication and argumentation community to develop norms that are unconditionally binding. Habermas rightly dissociates himself from a science, supposedly free of values and disinterested, that is understood only as a system of true and effective propositions and not as a kind of human enterprise, governed by interests, that must be seen in its sociopolitical and total historical context.[11] As against communication distorted by violence, he rightly defends reason as the principle of a nonviolent communication and pleads—against any kind of "suppressed dialogue"—for discussion, for unconstrained understanding and for rational decision. Against the Critical Theory's universal suspicion of ideology (infatuation context), he also stresses the importance of the ideal speech situation for communication and also the necessity of anticipating assent and agreement.

Formerly, Habermas had not avoided the very same mistake of which he accused the positivists: an absolutization of reason. Not indeed the positivist but the sociocritical reason, which declares everything outside its form of rationality and reality to be *ipso facto* irrational, irrelevant, ultimately unreal. This is therefore not a scientistic but a sociocritical profession of faith in emancipation and humanity, which avoids coping with nihilism, which does not enter into questions of ultimate values, goals, meaning, and is quite unable to grasp theoretically such other, similarly primitive experiences and social realities as work, language, dominion.[12]

It is worth noticing, however, that Habermas recently has been able to appreciate the problem of religion more positively than he did in his earlier publications. As recently as 1973, he was convinced that "in view of the individual's risks in life, a theory that could explain away the facticities of loneliness and guilt, sickness and death, would not even be *conceivable*; the contingencies that are linked inseparably with the bodily and moral constitution of the individual can be raised into consciousness only *as* contingencies: we have to live with them—in principle, disconsolate."[13] In principle, disconsolate? Only a year later, in a discussion with theologians on the present importance of religion, Church and theology, Habermas was able positively to appreciate the aspect of religion as consolation for the individual: "It seems to me that perhaps we may not be able to dispense with theologians for our own enlightenment about the conditions that make for a decent human life. . . . They still have a language with appellative and metacommunicative qualities that we as social scientists can no longer manage. Perhaps this language can set in motion that which would have to be set in motion in order to prevent the spread of self-objectivizing systems of interpretation. The other dimension in which theologians perhaps cannot be replaced—I cannot say much about this—is the field of individual consolation. And the third field is perhaps a form of quasi-political practice."[14]

Has not Habermas in these statements himself formulated indirectly the essential defect of his ideal communication community? Although his initiative is important, a number of questions arise. Do not an ideal speech situation and the anticipation of assent and agreement presuppose an enormous trust, which has to be carefully considered? For an ideal communication community, would not other dimensions, values and ideas of meaning have to be considered? Do not theology and religion here reach down to other depths of human and social reality? Cannot theology and religion by their language and truth move and really console human beings, really effect changes even in the political sphere quite differently, bind people absolutely to live a decent human life even more differently, from what Habermas can do with his appeal for rational, uncontrolled discourse? It will scarcely be disputed that no universal claim can be justified as absolutely binding in the light of a communication and argumentation community such as Habermas demands. For a claim of this kind always rests on a voluntary decision to take part in this community. Which means that such a claim, too, is merely hypothetical and based on human interest. Here, too, human obligation is deduced from human volition. H. Krings rightly observes: "Both Habermas' universal pragmatism and

Apel's transcendental language grammar presuppose a willingness without which accepted rules could be ascertained purely as behavior-conditioning but not identified as demands to be realized. There is no excuse for permitting these assumptions of validity to be regarded purely as a fact of communicative reason."[15]

Certainly Habermas has analyzed as basic orientations (and not merely casual needs of man) technical interest (of the empirical-analytical sciences), practical interest (of the historical-hermeneutical sciences) and emancipatory interest (of the critically oriented behavior sciences). But the legitimate human interest in truth (instead of mere convention) and in happiness (instead of mere communication) comes off badly.[16] But, in the appearance of a universal agreement of all men, in which the alienation of the individual is supposed to be really removed, is there anything more than the pure Utopia of an uncontrolled discourse? Is there not a hope expressed here that cannot be fulfilled by any purely human community but only by a genuine absolute—in that kingdom of freedom that is God's kingdom?

The Catholic moral philosopher Franz Böckle writes: "In principle, an immanent humanism can lead only to a hypothetical requirement."[17] This can be expressed more precisely. Of course, even an immanent humanism can stand for absolute requirements and provide motivations for them. Its appeal to freedom and human dignity is fascinating and can provide a variety of ethical incentives. Every immanent humanism, when it comes to ethics and fundamental trust, tends to evade the question of its ultimate justification. In the last resort, it remains unjustified. To be more exact, it cannot adequately justify the absoluteness of its ethical requirements. The *sole absolute* in all the relative is that primal ground, primal support, that primal goal, that we call God.

What does this mean for ethics, for any science of human behavior? An anchorage in a very last and very first ground, support, goal, not identical with the reality of man but embracing and surpassing this, does not mean alien determination or a heteronomy of man. On the contrary, such an anchorage makes possible for man a true self-being, self-action, a self-legislation and self-responsibility—a genuine moral autonomy. We may really draw the conclusion that, whenever even in atheistic humanism—in the light of man's autonomy, freedom, maturity, self-being, openness to the future—something like an absoluteness of obligation is postulated, the dimension of an ultimate absoluteness is in fact indicated as the condition of possibility, even though it is not called such: the unconditioned in all that is conditioned, which the believer describes by the name of "God." Here lies the justification of Kant's postulate of the existence of God because of man's morality:

● *The very last and very first reality, God, must be assumed if a person in the last resort wants to live a meaningful moral life. God's reality is the condition of the possibility of a moral autonomy of man in secular society.*[18]

Here, then, it is not a question of man's renewed moral subjection under an alien law and alien interests, but of his *true enlightenment, emancipation, of his becoming truly human.* For

only the bond with the infinite releases a person for freedom in regard to all that is finite, conditioned, restricted;

only such an ultimate justification of ethical values in God goes beyond the mere critical comparison of systems of ethics (and beyond the separation of "objective, neutral" science from subjective value judgments);

only such an ultimate justification of ethical values in God permits us to see the justification of that inviolable value, that unassailable dignity and indispensable freedom of man that a free society must simply assume if it is not to decline in the nihilism of a free-for-all or to turn into a totalitarianism.[19]

It may be asked if such an ultimate justification of ethics may not be dangerous. Is it not possible to deduce from it that even the *individual* norm, the particular precept or prohibition, being from God, is absolutely binding and that man is again subjected to individual norms regarded as absolute (we may recall the papal prohibition of contraceptives)?

Leading Catholic moralists, however, agree today that individual interpersonal norms of all kinds (priorities, rules of conduct, conventions, laws, customs) can claim intersubjective universal validity and can interpret a demand ultimately justified as from God as binding in the particular situation. Nevertheless, *individual norms cannot claim absolute validity for the interpersonal sphere;* they are not unconditionally and without exception valid in every situation.[20]

At the same time, no one would claim that the former, unfree, heteronomous legalism—which insisted solely on the law regardless of the situation—should be replaced today by some kind of libertinism, based on the principle of living for the moment and orienting oneself solely to the situation. Ethics is neither merely theoretical nor merely tactical. Neither the law alone nor the situation alone should be the dominant factor. Norms without the situation are empty; the situation without norms leaves us blind. *The norms should illuminate the situation, and the situation should determine the norms.* That is:

- *What is good and moral is not simply good and right in the abstract but what is concretely good and right for this person or this group: what is appropriate.*
- *It is only in the particular situation that the obligation becomes concrete, but the obligation in a particular situation (which of course can be judged only by the person involved) can become unconditional.*

*Our duty is related to the situation; but, in a particular situation, duty can become absolute, categorical.*

Every situation therefore is characterized by one factor that is absolute and another that must be weighed and considered: that is, a universal normative constant linked with a particular variable dependent on the situation.

It should by now have become clear that the problems of finding and justifying ethical norms involve the consistent application of the principles involved in dealing with the problems of the knowledge of God and of reality to the field of human conduct:

● *The acceptance for man of autonomous norms with an absolute—that is, theologically justified—claim is the ethical expression of that fundamental trust in reality (and human existence) that is determined by an ultimate primal ground, primal meaning, primal goal: the ethical expression, that is, of trust in God, of belief in God. Without this rationally justified trust in God, no absolute claim of any kind of autonomous ethical norms can be accepted as ultimately justified.*

*It must be admitted that all we have said up to now about God sounds very, very abstract—as abstract as the cultural philosopher's substitute for God in Böll's satire, "that higher being which we venerate." It will be possible to give more concrete expression to our ideas only if we turn again from the God of the philosophers to the God of the Bible and thus take up once more what we anticipated in connection with Hegel, Teilhard and Whitehead in regard to the modern understanding of God in his secularity and historicity.*

# G. YES TO THE CHRISTIAN GOD

"What do you think of God?" One answer to this question, raised in an opinion poll, was given by the writer Wolfgang Koeppen:

"The question about what I think of God scared me at first. It scared me when I began to think about it. Spontaneously I might have answered: 'I think well of God.' After a little reflection, however, I must say that I don't know. Is it possible at all to say what one thinks of God? If I enter into a relationship with God as with a person of whom I may think well or ill, then I believe in the existence of that person and therefore in God's existence; and if I believe in God, then his greatness is so different from my littleness that I can only say: 'I am his creature.' That is, if I believe in God at all. Well, then, I do believe.

"But an experience of God, a revelation, like that which happened to Pascal and which he recorded in the famous *Memorial* of 1654, 'God of Abraham, God of Isaac, God of Jacob, not of philosophers and scholars': such a revelation was not vouchsafed to me. I have had no burning sense of the presence of God. It may sound blasphemous in the ears of strict believers, but—if I am to answer the question sincerely—I am on friendly terms with God. I have had many a favor from him, he has protected me in distress and danger, I have thanked him in my thoughts but not in my prayers, I have thanked him at odd moments, here and there, in the crowded street, sometimes in his house. I was baptized and confirmed as a Protestant, but I have no contact with the Church. I do not attend any services, I have no desire for a sermon, I don't miss the pastor, I don't need a mediator.

"My dialogue with God is close. Sometimes I open the door of a Catholic church, at any time of the day, I smell incense from the last Mass, I enjoy the lovely interior and I think in a friendly way of my Creator. He is indeed the God of Pascal—'God of Abraham, God of Isaac, God of Jacob, not of philosophers and scholars'—but I am on terms of friendship with him, and he, I think, speaks in a friendly way to me. Don't be offended, you theologians! I know: HE is present. I always thought that people who consistently denied God were stupid. (Skeptics like Gide of course can be very shrewd.)

"When science believed in progress, in this alone, only in the small brain of man, only in the seventy years of earthly life, it became boring

and advanced into the void. The new physics (for me, the most important intellectual phenomenon of our time) is now living again in harmony with God (the atom bomb does not contradict God, even if it
comes from the devil). I would like to close with a reference to
Kierkegaard. He writes that the pastors appointed by the churches are serious people. And then he adds: 'The Apostle Paul was not a serious person.' Neither am I a serious person."[1]

Yes, what do we think of God? What do we think of the "God of
Abraham, Isaac and Jacob," of the biblical, the Christian God? What
do we think of him—here Koeppen speaks for many—if we have not had
an experience of him as dramatic as that of Pascal and yet want to cling to
him? How are we to speak of him, how experience him in various conditions?

We started out with Pascal from the "God of Abraham, the God of
Isaac, the God of Jacob," and we must now therefore turn again to that
God.[2] But, before that, there is one thing that cannot be overlooked: Judaism and Christianity are confronted today more than ever with the
religions of the world. Hence our first question must be: What must we
make of the God of the non-Christian world religions?

# I. The God of the non-Christian religions

Is it permissible for us Westerners and Christians still to talk about God as if our understanding of him is the only one possible? From the standpoint of the comparative study of religions—whether theologians like it or not—Christianity is one religion among others. Is it not a sign of provincialism if we raise universal claims from a very particular viewpoint? Might it not be evidence of a higher universalism if we remained continually aware of our own sociocultural limitations and restrictions even in the field of religion?

The religious experiences, forms, structures and ideas of humanity are infinitely rich; the problems they raise are infinitely complex.[3] It would be presumptuous to attempt to describe here even merely the diverse images of God: their divergences and convergences, distinctions and blendings are incalculable.[4] But even a small contribution to a better understanding of ideas of God that we find strange and thus also of our own ideas can be of great advantage for discussion and comparison. What we want therefore is not a pointless and fruitless collision, with the Christian once more wrongly assuming that he can prove the superiority of his God, but a genuine and fruitful encounter in which the non-Christian religions might be stimulated to tell us of their best and most profound elements.[5] We want to recognize, respect and appreciate the truth of other conceptions of God, but without relativizing the Christian faith in the true God or reducing it to general truths. In this way, mutual contempt might give way to mutual appreciation, disregard to understanding, attempts at conversion to study and dialogue.[6]

## 1. The many names of the one God

Many Christians are not at all aware of the fact that the *term* "God," taken for granted in the European languages, *has a long history behind it* and cannot without more ado be translated into other languages. "God" is a pre-Christian, universally Germanic word (Gothic *guth*). It is explained, by analogy with the ancient Indian *huta* (*puruhuta* = the much invoked = the god Indra), as "being which is invoked" or—from the root *giessen*, "to cast" (as of an image or statue)—"to which sacrifice is offered."[7] On the other hand, the question of the etymology of the Greek word for God—*theos*—used by Plato for the first time to coin the word *theologia*, can scarcely be regarded as settled. It is used in a very broad sense and—whether as subject or as predicate—means any overwhelming experience, especially the overpowering, mighty, gladdening Presence known to the primitive cults.[8] The ancient Greek religion had many gods, just like the Roman in which *deus* meant the "heavenly" (*sub divo* = under the open sky) and to which there corresponds the ancient Indian *devas* (hence in the Romance languages *Dio, Dios, Dieu*).

We cannot, however, overlook the fact that outside Christianity there are not only primitive but highly developed religions, not only mythological but enlightened, not only polytheistic or pantheistic but also expressly henotheistic or monotheistic religions: religions in which a supreme god (henotheism) or even one sole God (monotheism) is venerated and worshiped. Whatever may be the explanation of the origin of religion,[9] in the history of religion generally we speak of "God" only when there is an acceptance of the Holy as a person, of powers as beings endowed with form and will. By contrast with "spirits"—which are also powers—the term "God" has a more individual stamp: *numen* becomes *nomen*, God receives a name. Sometimes, in fact, God—as expression of power—even has countless names and sometimes of course (especially in highly developed mystical religions)—as the expression of his transcendence—no name at all (the nameless, inexpressible God, *deus ineffabilis*).[10]

## God's many names in Chinese religion

The whole complexity of the religious, theological and political problems presented by the world religions in their relationship to Christianity is reflected in the one apparently simple question: *How is God's name to be translated?* It is a question that first became an important issue at the time of the great controversy about translating the name of the Christian God for a different cultural background—that of China—at the dawn of the modern age (the period of Descartes and Pascal, from which we started out) and has remained relevant up to the present time. History itself has made the Chinese religion a typical case (in this connection we might also have discussed Hinduism or Buddhism).

Western Europe and Eastern Asia were scarcely known to one another until well into modern times and were able to interpret anything alien only in terms of their own self-understanding.[11] For China, which regarded and still regards itself even geographically as "Land of the Center," everything Western was described as "Buddhist" and the Portuguese settlers in Macao in the sixteenth century were seen as "Buddhist sects." Conversely, Nestorian Christians in the seventh and ninth centuries and Franciscan missionaries who traveled to China by the continental route in the thirteenth century scarcely noticed China's own original philosophical and religious tradition. Marco Polo also, on his Chinese journey in the same century, described the Chinese simply as "pagans." It was the Jesuit missionaries of the sixteenth and seventeenth centuries who first discovered Confucianism for Europe and brought its meaning home to the European mind. At first, as they went around preaching, they even dressed and behaved like Buddhist monks. Popular Buddhism, with its particular doctrines and deified beings, its ethic of compassion, its monastic asceticism and belief in a life after death, seemed at first closer to Christianity than Confucianism, which had grown out of the earlier Chinese religion and which concentrated more pragmatically on interpersonal relationships, saying little about man's relationship to a superhuman reality.

The founder of the modern mission to China, the Italian Jesuit *Matteo Ricci*, worked there from 1583 onward and from 1601 was allowed to stay even in Peking, the imperial city. As a result of conversations with people and the study of the Confucian classical writers, he came to the conclusion that the dominant Chinese world view was not Buddhism but Confucianism, which, precisely because of its lack of dogma, its lofty ethic and its reverence for a supreme being (without a heaven inhabited by gods and without fables about the gods), might be a better ally for Christianity than popular Buddhism, with its belief in idols and problematic doctrine of transmigration. In his famous catechism "The True Idea of God" (*T'ien-chu shih-i*),[12] Ricci explained that the original Confucian texts, not yet influenced by Buddhism or anti-Buddhism, contained in a very rudimentary form concepts analogous to those of God and life after death. But Ricci's interpretation and adoption of traditional Chinese cultural and ethical values was soon to lead to a violent controversy with the institutional Church and official theology. This was known as the "rites controversy," although in reality the controversy was less about rites than about names.

Today research by scholars has shown that the ancient Chinese actually believed in a personal God whom they venerated under two names: "Supreme Lord" and "Heaven." Presumably this *duality of names for God*—analogous to that in the Old Testament ("Yahweh" and "Elohim")—which there provides a basis for the distinction of sources in the Pentateuch, the five books of Moses—emerged from two cultic traditions, behind which were two ethnic groups:[13]

*"Supreme Lord"* ("Shang-ti") is the God of the Shang dynasty (from about 1766 B.C.).

*"Heaven"* ("T'icn")—originally written as an ideograph of a man with a large head—is the God of the Chou dynasty, which came from the West and conquered the Shang state (about 1111–249 B.C.).

The mingling of the two cults was reflected in the Confucian classics, especially in the *Book of Odes* and the *Book of Records*, where the two names alternate in the same prayers. But, in the course of time, the term *"heaven"* acquired *also other ethical and ontological meanings.* It could be used for the dualistic view of a Yin-Yang universe (with feminine and masculine principles representing earth and heaven); and it could also be used for a pantheistic or panentheistic view of the Absolute as expressed in the "Tao" of Lao-tse or in the "Li" ("principle") and "T'ai-chi" (the ultimate reality) of neo-Confucian philosophy. In addition, there were also undoubtedly atheistic interpretations, denying any sort of religious significance to "heaven."

All this complicated the situation for the Jesuit missionaries, since they arrived in China at a time when neo-Confucianism had reached its zenith and was regarded generally as the orthodox interpretation of the early classics. What was to be done in view of the diverse conceptions of God or the Absolute among the classical writers themselves and their later commentators? Ricci and the Jesuits declared themselves in favor of a return to the former Chinese idea of a personal God. But, at the same time, they kept to the practice of Christian missionaries from apostolic times and used such heavily loaded terms as *Theos, Deus,* "God," for Yahweh, the one true God of Israel and of Jesus Christ. So they adopted the usual Chinese terms for the Deity: "Shang-ti" ("Supreme Lord," then used only in the annual imperial cult of heaven) and the (admittedly ambiguous) term "T'ien" ("Heaven"); an additional expression came into use; "T'ien-chu" ("Lord of Heaven").[14]

Matteo Ricci, in the course of a decade, with his mathematical and astronomical studies in Peking, had attracted numerous leading mandarins and intellectuals. In 1610, at the age of fifty-eight, he collapsed prematurely under the strain of his missionary work and was honored by the Emperor with a solemn state funeral. It was only after his death that the tragedy began that eventually, a hundred years later, led to the prohibition of his missionary methods and thus for a long time blocked the way for Christianity to the soul of Asiatic man.

After complaints from recent Japanese converts, Niccolo Longobardi, Ricci's successor, decided against the continued use of the Chinese names of God and wanted to avoid misunderstandings by taking over the *Latin terms* into the Chinese. Francis Xavier—who died at the age of forty-six, in 1552, the year of Ricci's birth, on a small island in view of the Chinese coast—had introduced the adapted Latin term *Deusu* for God; he must have learned very soon that the Buddhist bonzes connected *Deusu* with the similar sounding *dai-uso,* which in Japanese meant—of all things— "great lie." Subsequently in Japan concern for orthodox doctrine led to the use of Latin forms not only for the three Persons of the Trinity ("*Deusu Patere, Deusu Hiiryo,* and *Deusu Supiritsu Santo*) but also such theological key words as *persona* ("person"), *susutanshija* ("substance"), *garasa* ("grace") and even *diidesu* ("faith"), about fifty altogether. Hence

—as contrasted with Ricci's missionary method—the message of the Christian God was bound to seem to the Asians like a completely alien, Latin-European import. It did not occur to anyone that it would have been more consistent to adopt the primordial Hebrew or Greek terms of the Bible.[15]

But, in the end, Longobardi could not prevail among the Jesuits in China; Ricci's practice continued to be maintained. The great controversy —the real rites controversy—only broke out when Spanish Dominicans and Franciscans began in 1634 to carry out their mission in China.[16] They first attacked the veneration of ancestors and of K'ung-fu-tse, then the use of the traditional names of God. In the subsequent discussion, undoubtedly rivalry between the orders and among the various nationalities often played a greater part than theological arguments. In any case, the Jesuits were denounced in Rome by their rivals, and once more endless negotiations began in the "Holy Office of the Most Holy Inquisition," now rechristened "Congregation for the Doctrine of the Faith." In France especially, where the Jansenists regarded any argument good enough against the Jesuits, the controversy became a political affair; a flood of rejoinders —some of them from the sharp pen of the Jansenist Antoine Arnauld, mentioned earlier[17]—spread over Europe.

Meanwhile the mission in China had made unexpected progress. Emperor K'ang-hsi in 1692 had issued an edict of tolerance permitting the preaching of the gospel in China, and some Jesuits at the imperial court were hoping for his conversion; the great philosopher and diplomat Leibniz from that time onward regarded him as the greatest prince in the world.[18] Because of the Jesuits' increasing difficulties in Rome with regard to the Chinese rites and names, Emperor K'ang-hsi sent to the Pope the official answer of the Chinese rites tribunal, for which he had been asked; this reached Rome in 1701. The answer made it quite clear that K'ung-futse was venerated not as a god but as a teacher; that ancestor veneration was a commemoration and not an act of worship; that the names T'ien and Shang-ti did not mean the physical heavens, but the Lord of heaven and earth and all things.

In the Holy Office, however, they thought they knew better than the Emperor of China and his scholars and decided eventually, under Clement XI in 1704: that the ancient Chinese had been idolaters and that the modern Chinese were atheists; that K'ung-fu-tse himself had been publicly an idolater and privately an atheist; that the Chinese rites were consequently forbidden to Christians; that the two traditional names of God, "Shang-ti" and "T'ien," were no longer permitted and only the modern Christian expression "T'ien-chu" could be used. Even Ludwig von Pastor, a historian otherwise friendly toward the papacy, could not suppress a critical undertone when describing these events: "For all that the prohibition of the rites was a decision of incalculable consequences. Things were forbidden to the Chinese Christians which, in their estimation, were de-

manded by decency and good manners, and on the basis of an interpretation which was at variance with that given by the Emperor K'ang-hsi
and the Chinese scholars."[19] In 1710, despite the protest of the Chinese
Apostolic Vicars and the Jesuits, all this was confirmed and tightened by a
new decree of the Roman Inquisition; and the penalty of excommunication threatened at that time against all authors of publications on
rites has never been formally revoked up to the present time. Once again,
is the teaching office unteachable?

The Roman decision proved to be an absolute catastrophe for Christianity in China. The Chinese reaction took shape gradually under Emperor K'ang-hsi. In 1717, the judgment of the nine supreme courts of
China was issued: expulsion of the missionaries, prohibition of Christianity, destruction of churches, compulsory renunciation of the Christian
faith. It was only five years later, after K'ang-hsi's death, that the long period of persecutions began. Nobody in Rome learned anything from this.
In 1742, the energetic Benedict XIV confirmed the earlier decisions of the
Inquisition with the bull *Ex quo singulari* and "definitively" prohibited
the Chinese rites and two years later also the special Indian (Malabar)
rites and thus the missionary method likewise formerly permitted the
Jesuit Robert de Nobili, who adopted in India the procedure that Ricci
had adopted in China.

When, in the late-nineteenth century, under political pressure—in the
train of conquerors and merchants and as an expression of political, racial,
cultural and religious European colonialism—Christian missionaries again
came to China, the Protestant missionaries opted for "Shang-ti" ("Supreme Lord"), while the Catholics stuck to "T'ien-chu" ("Lord of
Heaven"). As a result, Catholicism and Protestantism even up to the present time seemed to the Chinese (and even to many Christians) to be
two religions with two different Gods. Catholics were described as "T'ien-
chu believers," Protestants "Shang-ti believers" and Christians generally
"Chi-tu believers."

## Consequences for Christianity

It was in 1940, three hundred and fifty years after Ricci's death, that
Pius XII revised those "definitive" papal decisions and produced decrees
of toleration, approving the usages advocated by Ricci and de Nobili.[20]
But their execution was deliberately delayed in China for many years;
there were other things to worry about there: at first, resistance to the
Japanese invaders and then the inexorable rise of Chinese communism
under Mao Tse-tung. Instead of Christianity, Marxism-Leninism thus became the religion, or quasi-religion, of the 800 million Chinese (in the
form of Maoism) and their neighbors. Only in Hong Kong, Taiwan,
South Korea and Southeast Asia has Christianity been able to make any
progress in the past decades.[21] Would it not have been possible, in the six-

teenth and seventeenth centuries, to settle in a positive sense the question of the Chinese rites and names for God? This seems to have been proved not only by the courageous Jesuit missionaries in China but also by a number of European intellectuals, from the English deists to Voltaire and the encyclopedists, who discussed this question (in connection also with Spinozism) passionately. Among the philosophers, Malebranche, Leibniz and Wolff in particular devoted serious studies to Chinese thought.

First of all, *Nicolas de Malebranche,* the French Oratorian, published a "Conversation of a Christian philosopher with a Chinese philosopher" (1708),[22] in which he interpreted the Chinese "Li" ("principle" or "being") as—in his opinion—meaning divine being. The polymath *Gottfried Wilhelm Leibniz,* who was also in contact with the Jesuits, read both Malebranche's work and other works of supporters and opponents of the Chinese rites (among them the above-mentioned Niccolo Longobardi). The rites controversy contributed not a little to the darkening of the last years of his life. Only a few months before his death, he wrote his "Treatise on the Natural Theology of the Chinese" (1716),[23] in which he defended neo-Confucianism against the charge of atheism. With surprising accuracy and great empathy, he interpreted the various meanings of the ancient terms "Shang-ti" and "T'ien" and also the more philosophical terms "Li" ("principle" or "being") and "T'ai-chi" ("the ultimate," "ultimate reality"). The last two terms, he interpreted much more precisely than Malebranche as philosophical ideas of God that had developed from the earlier, more personal understanding of God and in which he found to some extent the reflection of his own idea of God as supreme monad. In this way, he produced an effective defense of the proclamation practice of the Jesuits in China. It is well known that Leibniz was actively committed to the reconciliation of the Christian churches, and he was equally desirous of a reconciliation of Eastern and Western cultures. As Christian missionaries had instructed the Chinese in the gospel and in modern sciences, so—he thought—Chinese missionaries in Europe should teach Europeans natural religion, ethics and political organization. In 1711, when he met the Czar in Torgau, he suggested that Russia could act as a connecting link in this respect. He was the first European and perhaps the first person ever to perceive the pluralist structure of humanity, consisting of races and cultures of equal value: a fact that became generally recognized only in the twentieth century.[24]

Leibniz' student and friend *Christian Wolff* was also interested in Chinese philosophy. In 1721, a few years after Leibniz' death, he was given forty-eight hours to leave the University of Halle and Prussian territory on pain of death, because a lecture he had given defending the practical philosophy of the Chinese[25] had offended not this time the Roman Inquisition but the Protestant Pietists. But none of this could stifle the sympathy of the men of the Enlightenment for everything Chinese. As in the eighteenth century a special affinity of the Enlightenment for sober, rational Chinese thought became apparent, so, too, in the nineteenth century a special affinity was seen between Romanticism and Indian thought.

If we are to take this opportunity to deduce some guiding principles from the controversy on rites and divine names, so disastrous for Christianity in the Far East, then, for the sake of a better understanding of God in the future, we must demand:[26]

- Not a God whose arrogant domination *is upheld by an exclusive missionary approach, contemptuous of freedom. For a narrow-minded, conceited, exclusive particularism that condemns all other religions globally in the name of the one God, a proselytism that goes in for unfair competition, pays too little attention not only to the religions but also to the gospel.*
- Not *the syncretist mingling of all gods, however much they contradict one another, harmonizing them and reducing the differences, and thus evading the question of truth. For a crippling, dissolvent, agnostic-relativistic indifferentism, approving and confirming the other religions and gods indiscriminately, at first perhaps has a liberating and gladdening effect, but in the last resort is too monotonous to satisfy thinking people, because it has abandoned all fixed standards and norms.*
- But *an independent, unselfish* proclamation of the one true God for all men in the various religions: *with an open-mindedness that is more than patronizing accommodation; that does not lead us to deny our own faith but also does not extort any particular answer; that turns criticism from outside into self-criticism and at the same time accepts everything positive; that destroys nothing of value in the religions, but also does not incorporate uncritically anything worthless. Christianity, with its God, should therefore perform its modest, unpretentious service among the world religions in a dialectical unity of recognition and rejection, as* critical catalyst and crystallization point *of their religious, moral, meditative, ascetic and aesthetic values.*[27]

All the discussions in both Asia and Europe have made it abundantly clear that the controversy about the names of God is about much more than words. In the last resort, what is involved is the question, still pending even today, as to whether God is to be understood in a more personal or a more impersonal sense. Might it not perhaps be far better to interpret God more as superpersonal and consequently not to give him a name at all? This is a view—and we can use it as a typical instance—that is found in Buddhism.

## The nameless God in the Buddhist religion

Buddhism seems to take up a position that is the very opposite of the Christian understanding of God. It has shown its great strength in the course of centuries: not only by its survival in an increasingly secularized world and its adaptability to sociological development but also by the fascination it has exercised and is again exercising today on Western intellectuals (we may recall Schopenhauer's interest[28] and we could see parallels in Heidegger[29]). Some Buddhists even claim that their more impersonal, negatively expressed view of the Absolute is more suitable than the Western view of a personal God for making the secularized, technological world of Japan, Europe and America aware of background experiences, of the deeper meaning and interpretation of reality.[30]

Nevertheless, the *difficulties of understanding Buddhism* seem almost unsurmountable:

In the first place, many terms in the East have a meaning somewhat different from that which they have in the West. In the controversy about being or not-being, Western philosophers and theologians are more inclined to take their stand on the side of being, the Easterns on the side of not-being. Yet in the East "not-being," "not-self," "nonego," "nothingness," "void," "silence," do not have at all the negative sound that they have in the West.

Secondly, many interpretations of the same terms and ideas are much more divergent than they are in the West. The contrasting interpretations of the "Lesser Vehicle" (Hinayana Buddhism) and of the "Greater Vehicle" (Mahayana Buddhism) have frequently led to contradictory doctrines and practices, ranging from crude idolatry to the most sublime philosophy. And Buddhist subjectivity, with its stress on individual enlightenment, has not exactly made it easier to produce a uniform answer.

Must we, then, from the very outset despair of a *Christian-Buddhist agreement?* It is said[31] that the Protestant theologian Paul Tillich, on the occasion of his visit to Japan in 1960, did not receive any satisfactory answers to the basic questions he had prepared for his Buddhist interlocutors: partly because of translation difficulties, partly because of the differing standpoints within Buddhism itself. Nevertheless, Tillich found dialogue particularly between Christianity and Buddhism so important that, on his return from Japan, he wrote his book *Christianity and the Encounter of the World Religions* (1962).[32] Mircea Eliade, the expert on the science of religion, says that Tillich had wanted to write a new "Systematic Theology," with a view to dialogue on the history of religions, but was prevented by his death, in 1965.

It is, however, *on the question of God* in particular that *the difficulties are concentrated.* In Western philosophy, God is seen in thoroughly positive terms and is given many positive titles: the Absolute, pure act, being itself, to say nothing of the specifically Christian expressions (for example, "God is love"). Is there any point in entering into discussion particularly on this question with a religion that is wholly and entirely oriented to the very opposite: to the non-Absolute, to nonbeing, to nirvana, the void, even to absolute nothingness? And this is precisely what happens in the Eastern religions and philosophies, especially in those inspired by certain schools of Mahayana Buddhism (Zen, for instance).

*Buddhism,* however, is *interested* more *in the question of man's salvation* than in the question of God. For Buddha's teaching aims at a practical way of liberation from the suffering of this life caused by man's craving for life, selfishness, self-assertion: the way to nirvana. Consequently, Buddhism at its center tends in both theory and practice to be nontheistic: it has no concept of God as First Cause, Creator, Almighty Father. . . . With reference to the metaphysical question, the historical Buddha—who personally never wrote anything down and of whom we have knowledge only from very much later witnesses—preserved a strict silence. According to him, it is pointless to bother a person who has been wounded by a poisoned arrow with questions about caste, family, what his assailant looked like. It would be equally pointless to expect suffering man to answer questions about eternity or noneternity, the finiteness or the infinity of the world, or about life after death. Such questions do not help man to reach the state he ought to reach: withdrawal from the world, passionlessness, dissolution, stillness, higher knowledge, enlightenment; in a word, nirvana.[33] Nirvana? Void? Nothingness? What is the meaning of these basic concepts of Buddhism?

1. *Nirvana:* Is it not right that Buddhism should very often have been described not only as atheistic but even as nihilistic? But what does "nirvana" mean? It means (from the Sanskrit root *va* = "blow out") being "blown away," "extinguished," into an eternal repose, without desire, without suffering, without consciousness—as a candle is blown out or as a drop of water is absorbed in the sea. Anyone who does not overcome his craving for life during his lifetime condemns himself to rebirth (transmigration) after death. Anyone who conquers the craving for life and acquires enlightenment, thus reaching the waning of desire and a state of mental repose, may experience nirvana—albeit incompletely—in his lifetime. And a person who dies thus enlightened is freed from the necessity of rebirth, entering into perfect nirvana. At this point, however, the *differences* between the later philosophies and schools begin to appear.[34]

For the earlier, dualistic Buddhism of the "Lesser Vehicle" (Hinayana), which radically separated the Transcendent-Absolute from the world, *nirvana was the diametrical opposite of "samsara,"* the life of suffering in the empirical world. Nirvana is qualified in an essentially negative fashion as an indescribable, unknowable, immutable state of the abolition of all suffering.

For the later, monistic Buddhism of the "Greater Vehicle" (Mahayana) and especially for Zen, *"nirvana" and "samsara" are merely differing aspects of the sole real and one Absolute,* as opposed to which everything individual and secular is nothing but appearance, sham, illusion.

Nirvana is understood in a supremely positive sense as the ultimate reality, not known, possessed already, but still concealed, as long as complete knowledge through enlightenment has not yet dawned.

Hence nirvana is not understood wholly negatively in any of the Buddhist schools: as nothingness purely and simply. It is true that nirvana in general has no cosmological function, even for Mahayana Buddhism. The world is not God's good creation, but emerged as a result of man's defection from the Absolute in cupidity and stupidity. Nevertheless, Buddhists are convinced "that Nirvana is permanent, stable, imperishable, immovable, ageless, deathless, unborn and unbecome, that it is power, bliss and happiness, the secure refuge, the shelter, and the place of unassailable safety; that it is the real Truth and the supreme Reality; that it is the Good, the supreme goal and the one and only consummation of our life, the eternal, hidden and incomprehensible Peace. Similarly, the Buddha, who is, as it were, the personal embodiment of nirvana, becomes the object of all those emotions which we are wont to call religious."[35]

In the influential Amitabha Buddhism—as Amida Buddhism, the most widespread form in Japan—nirvana is described even as a paradise of personal bliss, of the "Pure Land" into which we enter not by our own power, as in early Buddhism, but by trust—as in Christianity—in the promise and power of Buddha, the Buddha of light and mercy ("Amida"). There can be no doubt that in Buddhism also there is an awareness of an ultimate, supreme reality, an Absolute; that in Buddhism also there is the tension between a more personal and a more impersonal religious attitude.

2. *The void:* The term "void" (Sanskrit "sunyata"), as used for the Absolute especially by the South Indian philosopher *Nagarjuna*,[36] the founder of the Madhyamika School, and largely adopted by Mahayana Buddhism, as also by Zen, is not to be understood (any more than nirvana) as a purely negative idea. Nagarjuna, included by Karl Jaspers among his "great philosophers,"[37] but with a specifically Buddhist religious attitude—deliberately following Buddha and as opposed to Hinduism—defended a "middle way" (= Madhyamika) not only between the extremes of hedonism and asceticism (like Buddha) but also between affirmation and negation. It is only by way of the "void"—by abandoning all particular intentions, standpoints, categories—that man reaches nirvana.

Why? For Nagarjuna, the Absolute itself is "void": beyond all concepts and terms, which—since they are, one and all, relative—can never comprehend the Absolute. About the Absolute, the sole Real, nothing may or can be stated. *Neither positive nor negative predicates:* neither substance nor movement, neither causality nor relationship, neither unity nor multiplicity, and indeed neither being nor not-being. If being were to be attributed to the Absolute, it would mean attributing to it—as to all that is—coming to be and passing away. If not-being were attributed to it, that would mean attributing to it cessation and destruction.

The Absolute, then, is without any names or predicates; it is itself "void" ("sunyata"): neither a particular existent nor simply nothing. But neither is it outside the world of appearances; it is in fact identical with the appearances of the world. That is, it is the *reality of the appearances of the world*, their true nature. By discovering and removing the false reality of the appearances, the true nature of the Absolute is revealed. "Void," then, is the description of its true nature. It is the Indeterminate *par excellence* and consequently inaccessible to objectifying reason, accessible only to "wisdom" ("Prajna"), becoming intuitively one with it. Negation is thus merely a means of discovering the subterranean reality, the transcendent ground of all things and at the same time the true nature of things as norm for true and false. Without this ultimate reality, there would be no release from samsara, without sunyata no nirvana. T. R. V. Murti, professor at the Hindu university in Benares and the most important interpreter of Nagarjuna, therefore can say of the "central philosophy of Buddhism": "The Buddhist of the Middle Way (Madhyamika) is not a nihilist; only, he resists all attempts to determine what is essentially Indeterminate. The Absolute cannot even be identified with Being or Consciousness, as this would be to compromise its nature as the unconditioned ground of phenomena. The Tattva, however, is accepted by the Madhyamika as the Reality of all things, their essential nature. It is uniform and universal, neither decreasing nor increasing, neither originating nor decaying. The Absolute alone is in itself. . . . The Madhyamika holds that the Absolute is cognised in a non-dual intuition—Prajna. *It is that intuition itself.*"[38]

3. *Nothingness:* In Buddhist philosophy, even the term "nothingness" cannot be understood in a nihilist sense, a fact made clear particularly in the Japanese Kyoto School and by its head, *Kitaro Nishida* (1870–1945), who is frequently called the founder of modern Japanese philosophy and who was involved particularly in coping with modern secularization and science, with atheism and nihilism. The Kyoto School represents the Japanese attempt to develop a philosphical synthesis of East and West. In his works, Nishida deals with many Western philosophers: with Leibniz, Kant, Fichte and Hegel, and equally with Nicholas of Cusa, Descartes and Spinoza. He writes in a style that is more meditative and evocative than clear and precise. His philosophy culminates in the concept of absolute "Nothingness" (Japanese, *mu*). But this concept has nothing to do with a philosophical nihilism in Nietzsche's sense or with an existential atheism in Sartre's sense. In Nishida's work, it can be understood only against the background of his Taoist and Buddhist faith; despite all the Western influences, Nishida's philosophy is deeply rooted in his Eastern way of life and world vision. What does "Nothingness" mean here?

By "nothingness," Nishida does not mean simply "no thing," but *Absolute Nothingness*, which embraces what exists and relative nothingness. Rooted in the Buddhist idea of the "void," this concept is in some ways similar to the Christian idea of God in the *theologia negativa*. Hence Nishida can make his idea clear by referring to the work of Nicholas of Cusa *De docta ignorantia:* "In what form does God exist? Seen from one viewpoint, God, as such men as Nicholas of Cusa have said, is all negation, for that which one specifies or must affirm, i.e., that which must be seized, is not God, for if He is that which is specific and must be seized, He is already finite, and is unable to perform the infinite function of unifying the universe. (*De docta ignorantia*, Cap. 24.) Seen from this point, God is absolute nothingness. However, if one says that God is merely nothingness, this is certainly not so. . . . God is the unifier of the universe. . . . He is the basis of reality, and only because He is able to be nothingness, is there no place whatsoever where He does not operate."[39] Here there are also similarities to the later Heidegger, and these are certainly known to the Kyoto School: "Heidegger's words about the revelation of Being in human existence through 'Nothing' appear familiar to Japanese thinkers. Once man has reached the transcendent and transcendental unity, he has surpassed all antithetic opposites."[40]

This does not mean, of course, that, for Nishida, his own notion of God is identical with the Western, Christian idea. For God means, for him, not a personal deity but the God of the mystics. The true God is the "void" of Mahayana Buddhism in Nagarjuna's sense. For Nishida, the Absolute is both transcendent and immanent. Here he sees the "weak point in present-day dialectical theology. The truly absolute God must both transcend and embrace us."[41] In certain important statements, Nishida even speaks of faith and love: "God is not someone who must be known according to analysis and reasoning. If we consider that the essence of reality is a personal thing, God is that which is most personal. Our knowing God is possible only through the intuition of love or faith. Therefore, we who say we do not know God but who only love Him and believe in Him are the ones who are most able to know God."[42]

A further question arises here with regard to this Absolute, which is Absolute *Nothingness* and yet is not nothing. Certainly the Christian understanding of the Absolute is not of any existent, not even of the supreme existent. But why should we not be allowed to say that the Absolute is Absolute *Being* or *Being itself*? In this way, we would certainly not—as Nagarjuna thinks—attribute to the Absolute coming to be and passing away, but pure, stable and eternal being. The Japanese Buddhist Masao Abe, in the spirit of Nishida, insisted, against Tillich, that God must be seen not only as beyond essence and existence, the personal and the impersonal, but also as beyond being and not-being.[43] Here, however, there is an essential difference. What is there beyond being and not-being? Beyond this, the very last of all alternatives, there is literally . . . nothing. Beyond being is only not-being; beyond not-being is only being. And Abe also says that Absolute Nothingness (nirvana as absolute *mu*) is absolute negation—that is, "negation of negation"—and therefore "absolute affirmation" (according to Hegel, from whom these terms are taken, negation of negation is even the power of life). The question arises as to why absolute affirmation should be described as "nothingness" if, again, it is not nothing? With all respect for the concerns of Buddhism and of a negative theology—to which we shall return immediately—would it not be less misleading to say that the Absolute is (at least) also Absolute Being or Being itself? Is it perhaps only Buddhist tradition that leads its supporters to cling to a purely negative term, although nirvana and the Absolute for a long time now have not really been understood in the originally purely negative sense of extinction, but in a supremely positive sense: as the real truth and supreme reality, the good and the sole fulfillment of our life?

## Mutual challenge

It has become clear that "Absolute Nothingness" means absolutely notnothing. It means essentially empty being, detached, ab-solved from all concepts, categories, ideas and images. This, at any rate, is the way in which it would be described in the West. For much of what is *really* said in Buddhism—even though in contrary *terms*—can also be said in the West. A trans-lation of the main terms—whether "being" ("fullness") in the West or "Nothingness" ("void") in the East—is in any case necessary: necessary on both sides. In this respect, among Nishida's friends, D. T. Suzuki and K. Nishitani,[44] and on the Christian side H. Dumoulin deserve special recognition.[45]

The challenge in any case is mutual, and assistance also could be mutual: assistance by critical diagnosis of one's own position and that of the others. In simple terms, the East, with its drive for *unity*, could assist the West, because, without unity, analyses would be bound to lead to disintegration. Conversely the West, with its drive for *distinctions*, could assist the East, because we cannot do without distinctions either in the field of being or in that of obligation (good and bad, ethical decisions). And if Western *affirmations* particularly on the question of God may be important for the East, the Eastern *negations* may be no less important for the West. At the same time, it must be remembered that the West also is well aware of the importance of negation in regard to the question of God. The great tradition of *theologia negativa*, descending from Neoplatonism, is found not only in the work of Pseudo-Dionysius, Scotus Erigena and Meister Eckhart but also in that of Nicholas of Cusa (to which Nishida rightly attaches importance) and even that of Aquinas (of which Nishida seems to be less aware).

With *Aquinas* (1225–74), too, any determination applied to God by analogy with man or the world requires a negation: the negation of any sort of human or worldly limitation and imperfection. With Aquinas also, God's real nature remains hidden, inaccessible to human reason. In this respect, Aquinas agrees with Pseudo-Dionysius: "Hence in the last resort all that man knows of God is to know that he does not know him, since he knows that what God is surpasses all that we can understand of him."[46]

It was above all the great humanist and theologian Cardinal *Nicholas of Cusa* (1401–64) who insisted that God is accessible only to "instructed ignorance."[47] For him, any kind of purely affirmative theology without negative theology turns God into a creature of our mind and worship of God into idolatry. In God, the origin without origin, all opposites coincide; as maximum he is also the minimum and thus transcends minimum and maximum. He is the inexpressible and infinite: "From the standpoint of negative theology nothing but infinity is found in God. In that sense he cannot be known either in this world or in the future, since any creature is darkness by comparison with the infinite light, which it cannot grasp; that light is known only to itself."[48] It is clear, then, that "in theological statements negations are true and affirmations inadequate, but those negations which deny imperfections in the most perfect are truer than others."[49] Nicholas was continually working over and bringing out in its varied meanings the basic idea of *De docta ignorantia* (1440),* his early and main work, until the very late work where God is defined in a highly dialectical style in his identity and in his difference from all other beings as "Not other" (*Non aliud*[50]) and for that very reason as "center of the center, end of the end, name of the name, the being of being and the nonbeing of nonbeing."[51]

Whatever individual expressions we use in talking about God, we shall have *to consider the concerns of the East* also in the light of the Western tradition of a negative theology from Pseudo-Dionysius to Heidegger:

- *God cannot be grasped in any concept, cannot be fully expressed in any statement, cannot be defined in any definition: he is the incomprehensible, inexpressible, indefinable.*
  *Neither does the concept of being embrace him; nor can his nature be completely deduced in the light of being: he is nothing of that which is; he is not an existent: he transcends everything.*
  *Thus human thought enters into a sphere where positive statements ("God is good") prove to be inadequate and indeed always need at the*

---

* In his excellent little *Sketch of Mediaeval Philosophy* (Sheed & Ward, London, 1946), D. J. B. Hawkins suggests (p. 125) that this title "may be paraphrased as the nescience which transcends knowledge." Translator.

*same time a negation, if they are to be true ("not good" in a human, finite way) and thus to be translated into the infinite ("God is the good purely and simply").*

- God transcends all concepts, statements, definitions; but he is not separate from the world and man; he is not outside all that is; inherent in the world and man, he determines their being from within. He must be understood in the light of the ontological difference between being and the existent: God is, but he is not an existent, he is the hidden mystery of being; being itself as ground and goal of all that is and of all being: he is immanent in everything.

  *Thus human knowledge enters into a sphere where negative statements in particular ("God is not finite") can signify something eminently positive ("God is infinite").*

- God thus transcends the world and man and at the same time pervades them: infinitely distant and yet closer to us than we are to ourselves; not perceptible even when his presence is experienced; present even when his absence is experienced.

  *He is inherent in the world and yet not absorbed in it; he embraces it and nevertheless is not identical with it. In God therefore transcendence and immanence coincide.*

  *Every statement on God therefore must come through the dialectic of affirmation and negation, every experience of God must come through the ambivalence of being and not-being.*

  *Before God, all talk emerges from listening silence and leads to speaking silence.*

The East supplies Christianity with forms of thought and figures, structures and models, with the aid of which Christianity could be conceived and lived as easily as in the West. In any case, in the one world of tomorrow—which will be less than ever merely a Western world—Christianity will have a *future* only:

if there emerges from the Asian and African countries themselves a Christian proclamation that, while wholly alert to the danger of syncretist indifference, involves tolerance; while claiming absolute validity, is prepared to revise its own standpoint whenever the latter proves to be in need of revision;

if, then, a genuine Indian, Chinese, Japanese, Indonesian, Arabic, African Christianity will be possible and actual;

if in the end there is a living ecumenism not only in the narrow, denominational-ecclesiastical sense but in a universal Christian sense; based not on a triumphalist conquest of the other religions but in a missionary presence and service among the other religions, self-critically listening to their concerns, identifying with their needs and at the same time bearing living witness of its own faith in word and deed.

## 2. *The two main types of religious experience*

In addition to doctrines, rites, institutions, religion has its subjective aspect: religiousness, religious experience. And this—as we saw in connection with Freud[52]—can be examined psychologically. It was *William James* (1842–1910), son of an eccentric Swedenborgian father and brother of the writer Henry James, trend-setting representative, together with Charles S. Peirce and John Dewey, of American pragmatism, who brought out in advance of others "the varieties of religious experience" in his early standard work on the subject.[53] In that book, he defined religion as "the feelings, acts and experiences of individual men in their solitude, so far as they apprehend themselves to stand in relation to whatever they may consider the divine."[54] Like Friedrich Schleiermacher at the beginning of the nineteenth century, James stood for the priority of religious experience, by comparison with which he regarded all conceptual interpretation in doctrine and dogma as secondary. Like the influential Protestant theologian Albrecht Ritschl toward the end of the nineteenth century, James also rejected an intellectualist-rational metaphysic but had a higher regard than Ritschl for mysticism. James distinguished between a serene, optimistic religion ("the religion of healthy-mindedness") and a gloomy, pessimistic religion ("the sick soul"): a distinction that—according to James —corresponds to that between the "religion of the once-born" and the "religion of the twice-born (through conversion)."[55]

But, in Sweden, Nathan Söderblom (1866–1931), the distinguished theologian and historian of religion—afterward Archbishop of Uppsala and inspirer of the first ecumenical conference for practical Christianity ("Life and Work") in Stockholm—had distinguished, a few years before James and more deeply and correctly, two other main types of religion in a subjective sense: personality-denying and personality-asserting mysticism; emotional cosmic religion of redemption and volitional prophetic religion (religion of revelation).[56] These two main types were then closely analyzed and documented by Söderblom's friend *Friedrich Heiler* (1892–1967), the theologian (at first Catholic, then Lutheran) and historian of religion, in his monumental study of the history and psychology of religion, *Das Gebet*.[57] At first he spoke of mystical and prophetic piety, but later—under the influence of Rudolf Otto—of mysticism and piety of faith.[58]

### Mystical or prophetic religion?

Many Christians and Jews are far too little aware of the fact that there is a type of personal piety that is the very opposite of that of the Old and New Testaments. The latter may be described as "prophetic religion,"

"religion of revelation" or "piety of faith," and it is opposed by mystical religion, which, however, has only rarely been consistently developed, as in the Upanishads, in Sankara's strictly monotheistic Hindu system, in Hinayana Buddhism and also in the work of the Neoplatonist Plotinus. Within Christianity, it is found especially in the work of the extremely influential theologian of the end of the fifth or the beginning of the sixth century known as Pseudo-Dionysius and assumed for a long time to be Paul's disciple Denis the Areopagite. It was he who introduced this Neoplatonic piety into Christianity and who was responsible, with his work *Mystike Theologia,* for the term "mysticism."

"Mystical" will not be used here—as is customary today even with reference to "political theology"—as a vague slogan for a modern-sounding religiousness. To be more precise, "mystical" comes from the Greek *muein* (= "to close the lips"). The "mysteries" consequently are "secrets," "secret teachings," "secret cults," not to be mentioned to the uninitiated. Hence, that form of religiousness is "mystical" in which the lips are sealed, the mysteries hidden from profane eyes. Indeed, in mystical religion the senses are closed altogether against the whole external world, so that salvation can be sought in the depths of one's own soul. To be more precise, "mysticism is that form of intercourse with God in which the world and self are absolutely denied, in which human personality is dissolved, disappears and is absorbed in the infinite unity of the Godhead."[59] It is a fact that mysticism has developed mostly as a late form of religion in periods of advanced civilization to satisfy the longing to withdraw from the world into one's inner self, as a reaction to a sophisticated religion that forms part of the prevailing cultural pattern. So it was in Egypt or—under Taoism—in China; it was the same in Greece with Orphism or Neoplatonism (persisting in various forms even today) or in the India of the Upanishads.

Piety of faith, on the other hand, as personified in the great prophetic figures—for instance, Zarathustra, Moses or Mohammed—emerged from the primitive religion of nomadic tribes, raised by these outstanding leaders to the level of a monotheistic belief in God. There are admittedly personal elements of piety also in certain more personalistic forms of mysticism: for instance, in Chinese Taoism, in Hindu Bhakti, in the Hellenistic mystery religions, in the work of the Jew Philo, in Islamic Sufism and in Christian mysticism. But, no matter how the forms are mingled, the two main types must be distinguished in principle. What are the most important *structural differences* in the light of Heiler's exposition, with its detailed documentation? There are differences especially in the psychic basic experience, the basic attitude and the understanding of God.

a. The psychic *basic experience* is different as shaped by a different historical genesis·

What is the basic experience of mystical piety? It is "the denial of the impulse of life, a denial born of weariness of life, the unreserved surrender to the Infinite, the crown and culmination of which is ecstasy."[60]

What is the basic experience of prophetic piety? It is "an uncontrollable will to live, a constant impulse to the assertion, strengthening, and enhancement of the feeling of life, a being overmastered by values and tasks, a passionate endeavour to realize these ideals and aims."[61]

b. In the light of the different form of basic experience, there is a difference in the basic attitude that leads to a diversity of approach to history, authority, sin, salvation, ethics, society, culture and the hereafter:

The basic attitude of mystical piety is "passive, quietist, resigned, contemplative. . . . The mystic aims at the extinction of the emotional and volitional life, for the delight of ecstasy can be purchased only at the price of killing the will to live. . . . The mystic is one who renounces, resigns, is at peace."[62]

The basic attitude of prophetic piety is "active, challenging, desiring. . . . In prophetic experience, the emotions blaze up, the will to live asserts itself, triumphs in external defeat, and defies death and annihilation. Born of a tenacious will to live, faith, immovable confidence, reliance and trust firm as a rock, bold, adventurous hope break forth at last out of the bosom of tribulation and despair. . . . The prophet is a fighter who ever struggles upwards from doubt to assurance, from tormenting uncertainty to absolute security of life, from despondency to fresh courage of soul, from fear to hope, from a depressing consciousness of guilt to the blessed experience of grace and salvation."[63]

c. Finally—and this is the root of all differences—the *understanding of God* is different:

The *God of mystical piety* is the *hidden God* (*Deus absconditus*), the *God always at rest* (*Deus semper quietus*); the concept of God at least of the consistent mysticism of infinity—we are leaving personalist mysticism aside here—is nothing but the *speculative interpretation of the experience of ecstasy:*

"In ecstasy the mystic experiences himself as a complete unity; so also the God of mysticism is an undifferentiated unity, . . . the One without a second. . . .

"In ecstasy all the variety of psychic experience as also of the external world ceases. For the mystic who awakens out of the bliss of ecstasy, out of the experience of unity to the normal, conscious life, the objective world in its diversity is deception and illusion, maya or at least the dim emanation or dark shadow of the only genuine reality.

"Ecstasy is the final stage in the depersonalizing achieved in the mystical life; the God of the speculative mystic is nonpersonal, wholly devoid of anthropomorphic features.

"The ecstatic condition is perfectly empty of all concrete content, 'perfect emptiness,' 'unconditioned negation.' The absolute Unity is also completely without any quality; one can assert nothing of it; it is the 'No, No,' as it is called in the Upanishads, 'exalted above being,' as Plotinus says.

"Ecstasy is a hidden, incomprehensible mystery. It can never be grasped in thought and described in words, since it is beyond conscious experience. The divine likewise is exalted above all speech, unnamable and inexpressible, the 'Abyss,' the 'Silence,' as the Gnostics say. 'It is,' says Lao-tsze, 'something hidden, with no name to describe it, an Unfathomable, nay, the absolutely Incomprehensible.'

"The ecstatic stands in solitary quiet and unmoving fixity, having come, as it were, to a standstill; the God of the mystic is also at a standstill, 'actionless,' 'beyond activity,' 'the unchanging Light,' as Augustine says.

"The ecstatic experiences an infinite Value, the Supreme Blessedness; the God of the mystic is, therefore, the Highest Good, the *Summum Bonum*, a term which was coined by Plotinus following Plato and which, through Augustine, became most frequently used as descriptive of God. It meets us also in the Song of Songs of Indian mysticism, the *Bhagavadgita*, nay, even in the *Tao-teh-King* of Lao-tsze."[64]

The *God of prophetic piety* is the *revealed God (Deus revelatus)*, the *ever-active God (Deus semper agens); the idea of God particularly in biblical religion is* the reflex of the voluntarist experience of faith:

"God is not the immobile, infinite Unity, but the living, energizing Will, not the quiet Stillness but the active Energy, not always at rest but ever in action, not the highest Being but the supreme Life,—so run the contrasting terms of Augustine.

"The experience of the mighty power of God becomes in prophetic spirits an anxious dread before the inescapable wrath of the living God. . . . On the power of the living God prophetic spirits feel themselves absolutely dependent; in His hands are weal and woe, blessing and cursing, life and death. . . .

"But trustful faith, immovable confidence, produces the wonderful paradox that the angry, jealous, and judging God is at the same time the giving and forgiving God, the Helper and Deliverer, that the Almighty Power in its inmost essence is nothing but wisdom, compassion and goodness."[65]

Hence: "Extreme mysticism strips the idea of God of all personal attributes until it arrives at the 'bare,' 'pure' Infinite. The God of prophetic spirits, on the contrary, has unmistakably the features of a human personality, in whom primitive anthropomorphism lives on, spiritualized indeed, but in all its original power. God is Lord, King, Judge, and when trust has cast out all fear, He is Father."[66]

If we consider all these very briefly described structural differences in detail, we cannot fail to be made startlingly aware of the historical relativity of our own standpoint. And in view of the "varieties of religious experience" (described by William James), in view of the vast spectrum of religion and religious attitudes, the question is thrust upon us: Is not everything relative in the field of religion? Are not all religions equally true? With their religious experiences, have they not all always a part of the truth?

## All equally true?

In his book *Eastern Religions and Western Thought*,[67] Sarvepalli Radhakrishnan, once president of India, recalls a story that might be typical not only of Buddhism and Hinduism but also of other beliefs of non-Christians in Asia: "Once upon a time, Buddha relates, a certain king of Benares, desiring to divert himself, gathered together a number of beggars blind from birth and offered a prize to the one who should give him the best account of an elephant. The first beggar who examined the elephant chanced to lay hold on the leg and reported that the elephant was a tree-trunk; the second, laying hold of the tail, declared that an elephant was like a rope; another, who seized an ear, insisted that an elephant was like a palm-leaf; and so on. The beggars fell to quarrelling with one another, and the king was greatly amused. Ordinary teachers who have grasped this or that aspect of the truth quarrel with one another, while only a Buddha knows the whole. In theological discussions we are at best blind beggars fighting with one another. The complete vision is difficult and the Buddhas are rare. Asoka's dictum represents the Buddhist view: 'He who does reverence to his own sect while disparaging the sects of others wholly from attachment to his own, with intent to enhance the splendour of his own sect in reality, by such conduct inflicts the severest injury on his own sect.' "[68] We can certainly agree with the last sentence.

Nevertheless, it must again be asked: What if a blind man takes a tree trunk for an elephant? Some people think that Radhakrishnan's tolerance is influenced less by Vedanta than by Western idealism and the theological liberalism of the nineteenth century. But what is more important for us is that this kind of tolerance is now typical of many people in East *and* West and must be taken seriously. In one way or another, many Europeans and Americans would subscribe to Gandhi's words: "I believe in the Bible as I believe in the Gita. I regard all the great faiths of the world as equally true with my own. It hurts me to see any one of them caricatured as they are today by their own followers."[69] Let us not be too hasty, then.

Must Christians immediately start to complain of relativism and indifference? Is it so easy to deny that this point of view shows great breadth and depth, magnanimity and philanthropy, that it is fundamentally opposed to all the numerous religious prejudices, misunderstandings, religious conflicts and even the terrible religious wars in Christendom—the last of these being continually cited in the East as an argument against Christians? Behind such a viewpoint, can there not be an image of God that is grander, more noble, more religious than the image of God of those who want to regard him merely as the God of *one* party, of the party of *one* religion?

Nevertheless, with all respect for the generously tolerant Reformed Hinduism of Sarvepalli Radhakrishnan, it has to be said that everything is not ultimately one and everything is not simply equal. Certainly we must admire the absolute sincerity and the assimilation of alien ideas, the quest for infinity and the capacity for development on the part especially of Hinduism. But anyone who knows the concrete reality of the Hindu religion—the disastrous consequences of the cult of the cow, advocated even by Gandhi, of the caste system impossible to break down by any legislation, of the shocking superstition and so on—cannot regard all things as equal, and it may perhaps dawn upon him up to a point what Christian faith can mean for men by way of enlightenment and liberation, demythologization and de-demonizing, interiorization and humanization. Radhakrishnan and others have rightly observed a genuine inward, mental experience of the Absolute (spiritual experience), despite all the infinite variety of the religions, of their ideas, forms and languages. They rightly see here a concealed harmony that makes possible a far-reaching communication between radically opposed religions, even between Christianity and Hinduism. But, at the same time, the harmony must not be generalized, the differences must not be ironed out, the completely ambiguous inward experience cannot be made absolute. Or are really all statements that can be made, all revelations and creeds, authorities and churches, rites and phenomena, supposed to be equally valid in view of this inner religious experience?

Radhakrishnan speaks of tolerance. But, with him, it is a question of a specifically Hindu tolerance (based on the authority of Vedanta). For Hinduism represents (differently, of course, from the prophetic religions) an exclusive claim: conquest as it were by embrace in so far as it seeks not to exclude but to include all other religions.[70] Is not traditional Hinduism itself—with its immense power of absorption—more a package of (mutually contradictory) religions than a single religion: alongside primitive mythological polytheism and orgiastic rituals, very strict asceticism and meditation (Yoga) and also highly intellectual philosophy (Sankara)? Over and above this, Reformed Hinduism tries to utilize numerous Western and Christian ideas and thus to incorporate the other religions also into its system.

But are all gods equal? Can even merely the great personalities in the history of religion, the "archetypal men"—Buddha, K'ung-fu-tse, Socrates, Jesus—be integrated simply as a part into a totality of truth? Against this, Karl Jaspers rightly says: "They stand disparately alongside one another and are not to be united in one individual person who would go all their ways at once."[71] Only a naïve ignorance of the facts could overlook or level down the peculiarity of each individual person. We would not do justice to any one of these "archetypal men" if we were to regard him as a personification of a universal religious experience, merely as a cipher for a religion for everybody, merely as a label for an older or a newer syncretism.

Neither would we want to agree with the Dutch missionary and theologian Hendrik Kraemer[72] in his advocacy, together with Karl Barth, Emil Brunner and Friedrich Gogarten, in the spirit of dialectical theology, of a strict opposition between religion and Christian faith, or in his demand for a "radical separation" and a "radical displacement" even in the cultural sphere. Nor, on the other hand, could we agree with the British universal historian Arnold Toynbee[73] or with the American philosopher William E. Hocking,[74] in their opposition to Kraemer in the spirit of an objective idealism and liberal pragmatism, insisting on a "religious experience" common to all religions and looking forward to a single "secular faith." While Kraemer and his associates are too pessimistic, the others seem too optimistic. And all this assimilation, abstraction and generalization scarcely advance theological thought; the smoothing out of differences in a federation of religions (now perhaps a matter of interest to a few intellectual eclectics) has hitherto completely failed to touch the various religions. No, we cannot and may not spare ourselves the sober, modest task of elucidation. Neither with the religions of the West nor with those of the East can the *question of truth* be excluded or minimized.[75]

But do the psychological or historical facts form an adequate criterion of truth? Anyone who thought that the last word on the question of religious truth could be found in the psychology or history of religion would be overestimating the potentialities of both sciences. In both East and West, religion promises to lead men beyond the limits of human subjectivity and the relativity of human history into true reality—that of God or of "Absolute Nothingness." Religion thus claims to provide truth—not merely psychological, subjective or conceptual, abstract, but objective truth, in fact, absolute, ultimate and primary truth. In religion, then, it is a question of *the* truth.

## Truth through practical decision?

Even William James (on whom Hocking falls back),[76] for all his empiricism, did not think that the question of truth could be decided merely in psychological terms. He preferred to decide it *pragmatically*. For him, the "final test of a belief is not its origin but *the way in which it works on the whole.*[77] In order to know the truth, we must ask: "In what facts does it result? What is its cash-value in terms of particular experience?"[78]

We must immediately agree with James, of course, that reason by itself

can scarcely attempt to demonstrate faith, nor can it absolutely guarantee
faith. We had ourselves to carry out a critique of the proofs of God.[79] But
must we on that account expect to get at the truth only by applying the
"principle of pragmatism," first formulated by the physicist and philosopher Charles Sanders Peirce[80] and propagated especially by James (and
John Dewey[81])? James thinks so: "To attain perfect clearness in our
thoughts of an object, we need then only consider what sensations, immediate or remote, we are conceivably to expect from it, and what conduct
we must prepare in case the object should be true. Our conception of
these practical consequences is for us the whole of our conception of the
object, so far as that conception has positive significance at all."[82] According to James, only the moral attributes of God (holiness, omnis-
cience, justice, love) but not what are known as the metaphysical attributes (necessity, immateriality, simplicity, felicity) can "make any
definite connection with our life."[83]

But can the "heart of the matter" really be expressed so simply as
Leuba thought when—as cited by James—he defended the thesis that
people did not trouble themselves very much about the exact definition of
the nature of God or about the proofs of his existence, as long as they
needed God: "*God is not known, he is not understood; he is used*—sometimes as meat-purveyor, sometimes as moral support, sometimes as friend,
sometimes as an object of love. If he proves himself useful, the religious
consciousness asks for no more than that. Does God really exist? How
does he exist? What is he? are so many irrelevant questions. Not God, but
life, more life, a larger, richer, more satisfying life, is, in the last analysis,
the end of religion. The love of life, at any and every level of development, is the religious impulse."[84]

Does God really exist? What is he? Are these really irrelevant questions
as long as God "functions," "is useful"? This can also be the cynical
standpoint of rulers—or the skeptical, aloof attitude of intellectuals.
James himself of course does not mean to be cynical or skeptical and
aloof. He emphatically defended the rights of religious faith. The world,
he maintained, is richer than traditional science is prepared to admit. At
the beginning of his book, he insisted incidentally that the "only available
criteria" by which genuine religion could be judged were "*immediate
luminousness, philosophical reasonableness* and *moral helpfulness.*"[85] But
what does "philosophical reasonableness" mean in this connection? The
"pragmatic principle" is scarcely adequate here. As many critics (especially Bertrand Russell and A. O. Lovejoy) have pointed out, the pragmatic principle is too ambiguous. What does it mean to say that something "works"? What is the meaning of "true" here? Is it not too
commercial to make success the test of truth? The criterion is too difficult
in its application and it is useless in practice. It is easier to decide whether
Rousseau's social contract is a myth than to decide what were the effects
of his teaching. "How are we to determine whether the effects of believ-

ing in Roman Catholicism are on the whole good or bad? 'It is far easier, it seems to me,'" wrote Russell, "'to settle the plain question of fact: Have Popes always been infallible? than to settle the question whether the effects of thinking them infallible are on the whole good.'"[86] We had to observe with reference to *theory and practice:*[87]

that belief in God must certainly be proved in practice, but that the criterion of the truth of belief in God is not simply practice;

that truth cannot be equated with practical utility or sacrificed if necessary to tactics;

that even a theory that is not followed up can be true, that even a message that commands little or no belief can still be right.

Certainly—and in this sense James is right—it is ultimately a *decision of faith:* whether we regard as decisive the mystic's *experience of identity* when he strives to be absorbed in the monistic All-One (understood as "Nothing" or "All") *or* the prophet's experience of confrontation with God not as absorption in God but as obedient response to his call. Whether therefore—as in the mystical religions—we understand God as *passive,* in regard to whom man is active, by absorption, immersion, ascent, union, *or* whether we understand God—whom even the purest cannot discover for himself—as the really *active* partner who acts on man and thus brings the latter into activity. Whether we thus give preference to the great religious personalities and ascetics who have attained perfect inwardness *or* to the simple servants of the word who want to be obedient to it in faith.

This is always a decision of faith, but—as we have repeatedly stressed—a decision that it should be possible to *justify at the bar of reason.* For what we said about the God of the philosophers—looking at the whole range of the world religions from Hinayana Buddhism to Christianity—must also be said about the God of the religions. This faith of the religions turns out to be ambiguous and inconsistent. It calls for clarification. Belief in an Absolute, in an ultimate reality, in God, is certainly a "religious experience" or—better—a total experiential insight. But this insight—as James also admits—can be given conceptual expression in extremely diverse ways. The explanation is often superficial, unbalanced, perhaps wrong. Consequently, man has had repeatedly and still has to seek in thoughtful reflection amplification, clarification and assurance of this truly full and vital but often inadequate religious experience. Only in thoughtful reflection is the total experience conceptually explicated; only here does it become transparent; only in this way is it clearly communicable to others. To recapitulate:

- *Both pragmatism and intellectualism see only one aspect of religious reality; experience and reflection go together.*
- *Without religious experience, religious reflection is empty; reflection lives by experience.*

● *Without religious reflection, religious experience is blind; experience needs the critical illumination and assurance of reflection.*

It is precisely the apparently merely "metaphysical" question about the nature of God, as discussed between East and West, precisely the question about the personal or nonpersonal nature of God, that decides what practical attitude toward him is possible: whether—to recall Heidegger— we can pray and offer sacrifice to him, kneel in awe before him, sing and dance before him.

# II. The God of the Bible

The conflict between the "God of the philosophers" and the "God of Abraham, Isaac and Jacob"—as Pascal formulated it against Descartes and others—has remained open up to now. Can it really be settled at all?

## 1. The living God

One of Nietzsche's most aggressive texts against "meta-physics," the Platonic "real world," takes up one short page of *Twilight of the Idols* (published only after Nietzsche's mental breakdown): "How the 'Real World' at Last Became a Myth."[1] Here, in the most concise form, the history is outlined of the dissolution of the "real world" as set up by Plato and postponed to the future by Christianity, then deflated by Kant and left aside as an unknown factor by positivism, and in the end completely abolished by nihilism and creatively overcome by the Dionysian Yes to all that is dubious. All this was provided with a subtitle by Nietzsche: "History of an Error."

## History of an error?

"1. The real world, attainable to the wise, the pious, the virtuous man— he dwells in it, *he is it.*

(Oldest form of the idea, relatively sensible, simple, convincing. Transcription of the proposition 'I, Plato, *am* the truth.')
"2. The real world, unattainable for the moment, but promised to the wise, the pious, the virtuous man ('to the sinner who repents').

(Progress of the idea: it grows more refined, more enticing, more incomprehensible—*it becomes a woman*, it becomes Christian. . . .)
"3. The real world, unattainable, undemonstrable, cannot be promised, but even when merely thought of a consolation, a duty, an imperative.

(Fundamentally the same old sun, but shining through mist and scepticism; the idea grown sublime, pale, northerly, Königsbergian.)
"4. The real world—unattainable? Unattained, at any rate. And if unat-

tained also *unknown*. Consequently also no consolation, no redemption, no duty: how could we have a duty towards something unknown?

>(The grey of dawn. First yawnings of reason. Cockcrow of positivism.)

"5. The 'real world'—an idea no longer of any use, not even a duty any longer—an idea grown useless, superfluous, *consequently* a refuted idea: let us abolish it!

>(Broad daylight; breakfast; return of cheerfulness and *bon sens*; Plato blushes for shame; all free spirits run riot.)

"6. We have abolished the real world: what world is left? The apparent world perhaps? . . . But no! *with the real world we have also abolished the apparent world!*

>(Mid-day; moment of the shortest shadow; end of the longest error; zenith of mankind; INCIPIT ZARATHUSTRA.)"

Is this an end . . . or a turning point? A succession of scenes sparkling and scintillating with wit, irony and malice, provoking us to reverse the series? Might it not be possible to turn Nietzsche's "history of an error" back to front—so to speak—into a new future? The new title might be: "*The* (future) *history of a* (newly discovered) *truth*":

6. The idea of God—it cannot be abolished. Humanity never reached that peak. Zarathustra turned out to be a myth.

>(Twilight of the superman—end of the briefest error; no replacement of religion by science.)

5. The idea of God, of no further use, no longer binding, even superfluous, shows signs of new life.

>(Nihilism—particularly for the *bon sens* of the truly liberated spirits—an unproved idea. Joy among the angels. Red faces among the devils.)

4. The idea of God, certainly unattainable by pure reason and unknown in its reality, nevertheless begins again to be consoling, redeeming, binding.

>(The gray of dawn. The last yawnings of reason as it becomes aware of itself; positivism awakes from its illusions.)

3. The idea of God not only as imperative à la Königsberg or as feeble consolation for the weak.

>(Fundamentally the same old sun, but shining afresh through mist and skepticism as reality and great promise: no remythicization.)

2. The idea of God now attainable, not only for the virtuous, the pious, the wise, but also for the culpable, the irreligious, the "sinners."

>(Progress of the idea; bright day; enlightenment of the world by faith; return of the Christian reality. The idea of God becomes more comprehensible, more straightforward, more concrete, more human.)

1. The idea of God perceptible, relatively simple and convincing: the God of Israel. Oldest form of the idea. He, Jesus, dwells in it, *he is it*. Transcription of the proposition: "I *am* the way, the truth and the life."

(Noon; moment of the briefest shade; beginning of eternal truth; peak of humanity. INCIPIT REGNUM DEI.)

Hence: not only the God of philosophers and scholars in the pallor of thought (Descartes). But the living God as the "Not-other" (Nicholas of Cusa) and yet "wholly Other" (Barth, Horkheimer), as the truly "more divine God" (Heidegger); not only a *causa sui* (Spinoza) but "the God of Abraham, Isaac and Jacob, the God of Jesus Christ" (Pascal).

Thus in the end truth could become myth and myth truth. A turning away from the atheistic antithesis to a new "theistic," Judeo-Christian synthesis. A vision? A projection? An illusion? A suggestion? A hope—not more, but also not less?

## The one, sole God

It is impossible to understand the Christian God without the Jewish, for the Jewish is in fact the Christian God. And perhaps the Christian God—better understood—could also be the Jewish. If the God of the New Testament in present-day proclamation has often become so innocuous, feeble and powerless, is it not because we can no longer sense behind him the force and power of the God of the Old Testament?

Surprisingly enough, even a man like Nietzsche had respect for the Old Testament. In *Beyond Good and Evil*, he wrote: "In the Jewish 'Old Testament,' the book of divine justice, there are men, things and speeches of so grand a style that Greek and Indian literature have nothing to set beside it. One stands in reverence and trembling before these remnants of what man once was and has sorrowful thoughts about old Asia and its little jutting-out promontory Europe, which would like to signify as against Asia the 'progress of man.' To be sure: he who is only a measly tame domestic animal and knows only the needs of a domestic animal (like our cultured people of today, the Christians of 'cultured' Christianity included . . .) has no reason to wonder, let alone to sorrow, among those ruins; the taste for the Old Testament is a touchstone in regard to 'great' and 'small.' "[2]

A touchstone for "great" and "small," certainly. But also a touchstone in regard to the understanding of God himself. That is, of a God who is described in the Old Testament—as Nietzsche says that man is described—in the grand style, so that Greek and Indian literature have nothing to set beside it: a God before whom we stand in reverence and trembling, too much for measly tame domestic animals—Christian or non-Christian—with their animal needs, to digest. This God is the *one, sole God*. That is the message conveyed by the forty-five books of what Christians call the Old Testament, not only to Jewry but also to Christianity and Islam and

—indirectly by the strengthening of monotheistic tendencies, for instance, in Hinduism (Reformed Hinduism)—to the world religions.

Does this mean that *monotheism* alone should be made the criterion of the truth of religion? Not at all. The historical question about the origin of monotheism in Israel and thus about the priority of monotheism among the world religions long ago lost most of its explosive force.[3] A monotheistic religion is not by any means the more inwardly rich, more profound, more comprehensive. Religions are not merely logical systems of ideas. What would have become of the God of Israel if he had been prematurely seized on by rational reflection? Certainly he would not have become the living God who made history. What would have emerged would have been a universal principle or universal being, a universal force or some other kind of pale abstraction, like the monotheistic conceptions of Brahma in India, of the first mover in Greece or—at an earlier stage— of the sun god Aton in Egypt, all acquired by thinking.

What *history* has this God of Israel made? It would be presumptuous here to attempt to trace the extraordinarily extensive, dense and complex history of God with man, as presented in the books of the Old Testament. No more than the basic features can be described here. But they should give the reader courage to penetrate deeper himself, perhaps also again—and this would count as a success for the present book—by renewing his preoccupation with Scripture.[4]

At least a century before Moses, in the eighteenth dynasty of the Pharaohs and, at any rate, in the fourteenth century B.C., that dreamy, idealistic "heretic" king Akhenaton, husband of Nefertiti—famous even today because of her incomparable portraits—wanted to carry out a bold monotheistic revolution from above: to bring down the official god Amon and his retinue and to establish the rule of the one God Aton, whose visible symbol was the radiant sun. But Akhenaton, with his abstract religion, failed as a result of the hatred of the priests and the resistance of the people. Egyptian monotheism remained merely an episode.

It was not great and mighty Egypt but small, weak Israel, jammed between the great powers, to which the world owes the unambiguous, programmatic, exclusive, one-God faith. At any rate, it was not as if Israel's God had revealed such a belief at the beginning as a dogma or as theoretical truth at all. Also, the strict one-God faith developed slowly. As we can see from a number of passages in the Old Testament (exegetes today are agreed on this), Israel's ancestors had also been idolaters. The one-God faith emerged not as a result of theoretical reflection but from practical behavior: first of all as a *"practical" monotheism* in the forms of veneration and worship (monolatry). The Israelite tribes for a long time accepted without embarrassment the existence of other gods and understood the first commandment ("You shall have no gods except me") merely as forbidding them to worship gods other than the one they were already worshiping. In the latter, they saw the *God of the Fathers, the God of Abraham,*[5] *the God of Isaac,*[6] *the God of Jacob*[7] (known also as Israel).

This faith received a decisive stamp, presumably in the thirteenth century B.C., from the small "Moses troop," that insignificant group of unpaid workers who had been brought to Egypt as cheap labor for the gigantic buildings of the Pharaohs. They considered themselves under obligation to a God whom they venerated under the name of Yahweh, alongside whom Moses himself would not tolerate other gods and whom he experienced with his followers as (very different from the other gods around them) a "jealous" God, brooking no rivals;

to whose leadership they had entrusted themselves in the journey across the desert, until, after other tribes of the later Israelitic tribal federation, they became settled in Canaan;

whom they there identified with the Canaanite El—the supreme God of a heavenly array of gods—and then defended against the increasing pressure from the god Baal (Lord, heavenly Baal) and the baals (agricultural divinities), rivals of the one God Yahweh;

whom, in the end, in the struggle against Baal, against the Canaanite and then the Phoenician, Assyrian Babylonian gods and the syncretist popular religion, the later prophets proclaimed as not only one but the sole God of Israel.

"Yahweh is God." It was a long road from this slogan of the prophet Elijah,[8] enveloped by legend, in the ninth century B.C., who left nothing in writing but who was undoubtedly the great implacable fighter for Yahweh against Baal and the nature and fertility religion;

a long road by way of the great writing prophets, Isaiah in the eighth and Jeremiah at the end of the seventh centuries, for whom the gods (*elohim*) of the great powers (and especially those of the Neo-Assyrian kingdom) are "nothings" (*elihim*),[9] "not-gods" (*lo-elohim*)[10] and "worthless breath" (*hebhel*);[11]

a long road until at the end the clear hymnic confession of the second Isaiah (Deutero-Isaiah), who was active in the sixth century B.C. among the exiles in the Babylonian captivity and there proclaimed the one, sole God Yahweh as salvation of all nations: "There is no other god besides me, a God of integrity and a saviour."[12]

Monotheism in principle and not only in practice had thus been established. From the Babylonian Captivity onward, the basic creed of Judaism, which devout Jews profess up to the present time, is found in the *Sh'ma*, the morning and evening prayer and the prayer for the dying: "Listen (*sh'ma*), Israel: Yahweh our God is the one Yahweh."[13] Yes, for Israel God is the sole God and this in three respects:

*No other deities*—as in all other religions—around him: not even in private worship, where in other religions there was greater indulgence than in the state cult, could other gods be honored with images, amulets, song and dance.

No *feminine partner deity*, as otherwise with all Semitic high gods. In Hebrew there was not even a word for "goddess."

No *evil rival God*, as particularly in the Persian religion. Not even during the period of Persian hegemony was it possible for the "antagonist" or "accuser" (Hebrew *satan*, Greek *diabolos* (= "slanderer" and hence "devil") to prevail alongside the good principle as a second, equal principle.[14]

So, then, the God of the Fathers, the God of Abraham, Isaac and Jacob, the God of the people of Israel, is the one, sole God, alongside whom there are no higher, equally high or lower gods: no other gods at all. He is not only the highest, but the incomparable. This God is not responsible only for particular spheres of life, like the gods of the pagans (a god for the fertility of the soil, a god for success in war, a god for the moods of fate, a goddess for the perils of love, and so on). No, this one God is Lord over all. He gives everything, all life, all goodness, he may also expect man's whole surrender, his whole love.[15]

This strict, living, passionate, uncompromising, one-God faith was and remained the distinctive mark of Israel among the nations and at the same time Israel's gift to the nations. Any Christian trinitarian doctrine that claims to be more than empty assertion and speculation must be tested by this one-God belief; so, too, must any neopagan call for the return of the gods, which turns out to be not an alienation of a genuine yearning for God, but mythology. This one-God faith has important *consequences for the individual and society.* Only two points need to be stressed here:

● *Faith in the God of Abraham, Isaac and Jacob is common to Jews, Christians and Muslims.*
*Instead of the scandalous struggle with one another, which hitherto has characterized their common history, today precisely in the light of their common faith, cooperation is imperative.*

In both the Old and the New Testaments, as also in the Koran, Abraham is credited with faith in the one God who acts in history. This faith could form the basis of a better understanding and a deeper solidarity between the three great monotheistic religions, so often in conflict in the course of history, none of which can understand its own nature without reference to the other two. Hence they should never see the others as "unbelievers" (Jews and Muslims for Christians) or as "apostates" (Christians and Muslims for Jews) or "obsolete" (Jews and Christians for Muslims), but as "sons" and "daughters," "brothers" and "sisters," under one and the same God. If this common faith were to be really effective in the Near East—between Israel and the Arabs and in Lebanon between Muslims and Christians—it could be the opening of a new epoch of peace. For many political conflicts have been and are profoundly influenced by hostile religious feelings.

● *Faith in the one God of Abraham, Isaac and Jacob means the fall of both ancient and modern gods. It prevents both the deification of natural powers and the turning of political powers and rulers into idols.*

The one-God faith of course does not involve a social program, but it has incisive social consequences. It dethrones the divine world powers in favor of the one true God. In primitive societies, it means the radical repudiation of the deified natural forces in the ever-recurring cosmic dying and coming-to-be. But even in our apparently atheistic age, it means a radical repudiation of the many gods without divine titles that are worshiped by men today: of all earthly agencies with divine functions, on which man thinks that everything depends, in which he hopes and which he fears more than anything else in the world. In all of which, it is of no importance whether modern man—sometimes a monotheist, at others a polytheist—addresses his

> Holy God, we praise thy name;
> Lord of all, we bow before thee

to the great God Mammon or the great God Sex, to the great God Power or the great God Science, the great God Nation or the great God Party. The one-God faith is utterly opposed to any quasi-religion. It throws down all false gods.


## The God of liberation

*What is God like?* People have always asked this question. It is particularly serious for someone who is certain of God's existence, but even more for someone who doubts this. For whether God exists depends for many on what he is like. It is by no means *a priori* certain what is involved in the cause of causes, what is waiting in the end of ends. Is the primal ground a bright ground of light or a dark chasm? Is the primal support a real support or seductive illusion? Is the primal goal ultimate fulfillment or definitive failure? How is man to know for certain whether the primal meaning is not, in the last resort, nonsense, the primal value, in the last resort, of no value?

What is God like? Hidden, ambivalent, double-faced, like the Roman god Janus, the god of both spatial and temporal access and passage (giving his name to "January," the opening of the year)? Or enigmatic, like the sphinx, the "strangler" who brings death to passersby? Or capricious and incalculable, like Tyche/Fortuna, goddess of fortune and misfortune, as divine power of fate at the helm steering the world? In a word, if God exists, is he really for or against human beings? What does he signify? Fear or assurance, unhappiness or happiness, oppression or liberation?

For the people of Israel, these questions had long been answered. Obscure as the details of its history are for us today, that small Moses troop —probably in the thirteenth century B.C.—had had its faith formed by experience. As nomads with their livestock, flocks of goats and sheep, they had been threatened by drought and famine in the eastern plains bordering on Egypt, had sought refuge in the fertile Nile Delta, and were then recruited for forced labor on Egypt's buildings and border fortifications. In their freshly awakened longing for their old freedom, they began to recognize in trust and faith that their God, to whom they cried in their distress, was at their side, was for them, for poor, oppressed human beings. Their God was not a slave owner, but a God of freedom: *the God of liberation.*

Thence, also, the later Israelitic tribes received this message in faith and transmitted it over the centuries—parents to children, priests to pilgrims, traveling singers and storytellers to their listeners—at first orally, only at a late stage in writing:

This God of liberation called and appointed Moses—the story of whose birth in the Nile Delta was embellished (like that of other important individuals in antiquity) with a legend of preservation[16]—as his great charismatic leader.[17]

This God of the Exodus, presumably at the time of the Pharaoh Rameses II (1292–1225 B.C.), led the small, oppressed crowd of "Hebrews" (a pejorative expression for an inferior racial minority), in the face of difficulties and under special circumstances, out of Egyptian power[18] (the "ten plagues"[19] are stylized narratives about natural disasters not unusual in Egypt and Palestine).

This caring God had them celebrate as a paschal sacrifice[20] the ancient nomadic spring feast at which the wandering shepherds in a sacrificial and blood ritual had warded off demons and placed the new life of their flocks under the protection of their god: from that time onward, this feast was to recall the life of freedom granted them by God.

This rescuing God finally saved the departing Hebrews from the Egyptian troop pursuing them, who were surprised at the sea lagoon as the waters flowed back: an event experienced as a "mighty deed" of God and continually proclaimed from generation to generation afterward.[21]

Here, then, lie the historical beginning and, in the first place, the objective core of the Old Testament. From this point comes the primordial creed of Israel, the *primordial profession of faith in the one God,* "who brought Israel out of Egypt."[22] However small in numbers the troop of Moses may have been—probably a few clans and large families—this profession was later also the foundation for the tribes already settled in Canaan. In other words, the basis of unity was not at first the common policy and state organization (which existed for Israel as a whole only under the kings Saul, David and Solomon), but the cultic veneration of that one God who had liberated Israel out of Egypt. Israel's religion, then, is entirely originally the religion of the exodus, the emigration, of being spared, rescued, liberated.

## The one God with a name

This liberation was brought about by the one God, who was not nameless but had made his *name* known. In the Book of Exodus—the second of what are known as the "Five Books of Moses" (Pentateuch)—in the (perhaps later) context of the story of Moses' calling at Sinai, we are told " '*Yahweh*' *is his name.*" Yahweh (abbreviated form "Yah") is written in Hebrew only with consonants, the Tetragrammaton, YHWH. Only at a very much later time, when people regarded him with too much awe to pronounce Yahweh's name (from the third century B.C.), were the vowels of the name "Adonai" ("Lord") added to the four consonants, with the result that the medieval theologians (and Jehovah's Witnesses today) read "Jehovah" instead of "Yahweh."[23]

What is Yahweh supposed to mean? In the whole of the Old Testament, where the name occurs more than sixty-eight hundred times, there is only the enigmatic answer that Moses received from the burning bush at Sinai: *Ehyeh asher ehyeh.* How is this statement, about which a small library of books has been written,[24] to be translated?

For a long time, people kept to the Greek translation of the Old Testament (called Septuagint, because of the legend of its production by seventy translators): "I am who am." This translation can be maintained now as before. For the word *hayah* means—admittedly in the rarest cases—"to be." Mostly it means "to be present, to take place, to turn out, to happen, to come to be." And since Hebrew has the same form for both present and future, we can translate: "I am present as I am present" or "I am present as I will be present." Or we can follow the great Jewish translator of the Old Testament, Martin Buber, who has "I will be present as I will be present." But what does this enigmatic name mean?

*It is not an explanation of God's nature*, as the Fathers of the Church and medieval and modern scholastics assumed: not a revelation of a metaphysical essence of God, which would have to be understood in the Greek sense as static being (*ipsum esse*), in which, according to the Thomist theory, essence and existence would coincide.

*It is, rather, a declaration of God's will*, as leading Old Testament exegetes interpret it today: God's presence, his dynamic existence, being present, being real, being effective, giving security, find expression here, allowing no scope for objectification, determination or consolidation.

"Yahweh," then, means "I will be present": I will be present, guiding, helping, strengthening, liberating. What this means concretely is seen in the saying of Yahweh proclaimed to the people on Sinai: "I am Yahweh. I will free you of the burdens which the Egyptians lay on you. I will release you from slavery to them and with my arm outstretched and my strokes of power I will deliver you. I will adopt you as my own people, and I will be your God. Then you shall know that it is I, Yahweh your God, who have freed you from the Egyptians' burdens."[25]

Thus the God of the Fathers, who had borne no name, made known his proper name. And perhaps no exegete could have paraphrased better its meaning also for our post-Marxist, post-Freudian society than the Jewish philosopher Ernst Bloch: "The Exodus God is differently constituted; he proved in the prophets his hostility to masters and to opium. Above all, he is not statically constituted like all the pagan gods before him. For the Yahweh of Moses at the very beginning gave himself a definition, a continually breathtaking definition, which makes all staticism pointless: 'God spoke to Moses: I will be who I will be' (Exodus 3:14). . . . In order to judge the singularity of this passage, we should compare it with another interpretation, the later commentary on another name of a god, that of Apollo. Plutarch tells us (De EI apud Delphos, Maralia III) that over the door of the temple of Apollo at Delphi there is carved the sign EI; he attempts to give the two letters the meaning of a mystic number, but in the end comes to the conclusion that EI grammatically and metaphysically means the same thing: that is, 'Thou art' in the sense of timelessly unchanging divine existence. Ehyeh asher ehyeh, on the other hand, on the very threshold of the Yahweh manifestation, sets up a God of the end of time, with the future as his state of being. This End and Omega God would have been a nonsense in Delphi, as in any religion where God is not a God of the Exodus."[26]

The God of the Bible is indeed a God of historical dynamism. But can God be the end-and-omega God if he is not first of all the beginning-and-alpha God? The Exodus God and the Creator God are not opposed to one another in the Old Testament, as Bloch thinks. It is a question of one and the same living God in one and the same history of Israel.


Man's answer

Thus in the course of time there developed in Israel a singular, spacious and even—seen as a whole—historical way of thinking. The past remained present and helped people to cope with the actual situation and to catch sight of the future. Israel's credo is not a philosophical, speculative, but a historical, credo: centered on the God of liberation, "who brought Israel out of Egypt." And this primordial profession of faith made by the faith-and-cult community of Yahweh worshipers is man's one answer to God's self-revelation given in history. Closely linked with it is praise, the *praise* of God and his deeds that fills the Old Testament as a whole: beginning with what are probably the oldest songs about Yahweh, who threw the Egyptian horses and riders into the sea[27] and gave the victory to the heroine Deborah,[28] going on to the hymns of praise of Deutero-Isaiah, who announced liberation during the Babylonian exile, and to the psalms of praise of the people or of the individual, as also to the mighty hymns to the Creator God.

But is this not merely one aspect? Israel's understanding of God must not be optimistically minimized. There is little vain jubilation in the Old Testament. In addition to praise, there is always *blame*. Modern man's anxiety about God, about his absence, incomprehensibility, ineffectiveness, are not alien to the Old Testament. The suffering of both the nation and the individual—that great argument against God and his goodness—is continuously present and often cries to heaven. They cried to God even in Egypt, when they scarcely knew him. The nation cried to him and individuals cried to him when they had settled in the Promised Land, then in the Babylonian exile, finally under the alien power of Rome —in all possible situations of distress and sin.

It is more or less typical of this God that people can cry to him in any situation. And when, in ancient times, was this done in a more challenging way than in that great work of world literature of the fifth to fourth centuries B.C. in which that completely isolated and wretched man Job, in endless, groundless suffering, is continually torn hither and thither between indignation and resignation? The basic attitude of Old Testament man toward his God is more clearly manifested in him than anywhere else.

Here we are not going to talk about the position of God in regard to suffering. This question has been dealt with at length elsewhere.[29] But this much can be recapitulated here, and it amounts to the Old Testament answer to the question about man's answer to God. Suffering, doubting, despairing man—so closely akin to modern man in the face of nihilism and atheism—does not find an ultimate support with the keys of pure reason, seeking to solve the riddle of suffering and evil. Not by psychological, philosophical or moral arguments, which are meant to transform into light the darkness of suffering and evil and which, again, are too abstract and too general to be of much help in concrete suffering. Not in the optimistic logic of a rationalist apologetic and "justification of God" (known as "theodicy" since the time of the great Leibniz), which seeks inquisitively to get behind God's mystery and world plan.

Suffering, doubting, despairing man finds an ultimate support only in the forthright admission of his incapacity to solve the riddle of suffering and evil; in the calm renunciation of any claim to be a neutral and supposedly innocent censor pronouncing judgment on God and the world; in the decisive rejection of mistrust, as if God were not really good to man. Positively, in that certainly unsecured and yet liberating venture, in doubt, suffering and sin, in all inward distress and all outward pain, in all fear, anxiety, weakness, temptation, in all emptiness, desolation, anger, simply and straightforwardly to show an *absolute and unreserved trust* in the incomprehensible God. Yes, to cling to him even in an absolutely desperate situation, simply empty and burnt out, when all prayer dies out and not a word can be spoken: a *fundamental trust of the most radical kind,* which does not externally appease anger and indignation but encompasses and embraces them, and which also puts up with God's permanent incomprehensibility.

Only when—despite everything—we say explicitly or implicitly "Amen" ("so be it," "that is right"), can suffering be, if not explained, at least sustained. "Saying Amen" is the translation of the Old Testament noun "faith" (*he'emin*).[30] It is on God's account that the world, with its riddle, its evil and suffering, can be accepted. Not otherwise. The mystery of the Incomprehensible in its goodness encompasses also the wretchedness of our suffering.

But is such an absolute and unshakable trust or faith so simple? The New Testament will throw fresh light on it. And yet it remains true that this is the one God and this is faith in him, *as attested in the most diverse forms and modes of speech:* in poetry and prose, in self-reports and historical narratives, legal statutes and cult regulations, prophetic threats and promises, hymns and lamentations, sagas and legends, stories and parables, oracles, proverbs and theological tenets. All these diverse genres are obviously characterized by their wholly concrete "setting in life" and were shaped and developed at a certain place: in the large family, in worship or in legal practice, at court, in war or in the schools of theology.[31] However and whenever it occurs, God is attested with increasing clarity as he who is: the liberating Lord and Ruler of history, the Creator of the world, Legislator of the people and finally the Judge and Finisher.

## The one God and the many Gods

Before we turn to the relationship of God to his world, to him as Creator, Ruler and Finisher, let us briefly look back. How is this God of Abraham, Isaac and Jacob, the God of Israel, related to the God of the philosophers and to the God of the religions? It is not easy to be fair to all sides at the same time, to take the path between intolerance and assimilation, and not to evade the question of truth despite all broad-mindedness.

a. The *God of the philosophers* is *nameless.* For that very reason, it is possible to ask whether in the history of philosophy God has been understood at every turn as something completely different. And the answer must be: not something different but not simply the same; something cognate. As the philosopher Wilhelm Weischedel observes at the end of his historical study: "The divine of the early Greek thinkers in his immediate presence in the world is not the same as the Creator God of the Christian type of philosophical theology. God as the final end of all striving in reality, as Aristotle conceives him, is distinguished from Kant's God, guaranteeing the moral law and final bliss. The God of Aquinas or Hegel, apprehensible by reason, is different from the God of Dionysius the Areopagite or of Nicholas of Cusa, retreating to the realm of the unnamable. Neither is the purely moral God, attacked by Nietzsche, the same as the supreme Being sustaining reality, as Heidegger understands the God of metaphysics. And yet always and everywhere by the name 'God' something cognate is understood: that which, as pervading or transcendent principle, determines all reality."[32]

The history of philosophy itself calls for a clarification. But it also raises doubts as to whether it is able to produce a clarification. According to the Acts of the Apostles, the Greeks honored a *Theos agnostos*, an unknown God.[33] Does it belong to the essence of the God of philosophy to remain unknown, to be without a name? A decision can scarcely be avoided. In any case, the difference from the God of Abraham, Isaac and Jacob is unmistakable:

- *On the whole, the philosophers' concept of God is abstract and indeterminate:*
  *The God of the philosophers remains nameless.*
  *He does not reveal himself.*
- *The biblical faith in God is concrete and determinate.*
  *The God of Israel bears a name and demands a decision.*
  *He reveals himself in history as he who is: as he who will be, guiding, helping, strengthening.*

b. The *God of the religions is not nameless*. For the religions were always more than philosophy, more than a doctrine of God, a theory of God, a thinking of God. Religions do not emerge from conceptual reflection, still less from strictly argued rational proof. And certainly not—as former historians of religion thought—from the purely irrational, unintellectual strata of the human psyche. No, they are rooted—and there is a large measure of agreement on this—in the experiential unity of knowing, willing and feeling, which, however, should not be understood as one's own achievement, but as an answer: an answer to an encounter with or an experience of God (or the Absolute), whatever form it may have taken. Most religions appeal to an illumination or a manifestation of God (or the Absolute), who is in himself hidden and ambivalent.[34]

But, despite all convergences among the religions, there are fundamental differences; despite all similarities, far too many contradictions. The God of the religions has *many names*.[35] In view of the innumerable gods of the religions in history and at the present time, in view of the divine natural forms and natural forces, of plant, animal and human gods, of deities equal in rank or arranged in hierarchies, the question is thrust upon us inescapably: Which is the true God? Is he to be found in the original, primitive religions or in the highly developed? In those which have grown slowly or in those which have been instituted? In the mythological or in the enlightened religions? Are there many gods: polytheism? Or a single supreme god among many gods: henotheism? Or even one sole god: monotheism? Is God above or outside everything: deism? Or is God everything: pantheism? Or all in all: panentheism? Distinctions and decisions cannot be avoided. It is not, however, a question of an arbitrary decision, but of a decision of faith justified at the bar of reason. For we cannot simply "make" a religion. With all respect for the other religions, we have stated the reasons why we decide for the God of Israel, the God of the Bible, and this will become still clearer later.

- *The understanding of God on the part of the religions as a whole is definite but not coherent.*
  *The gods of the religions display many contrasts in names and natures. They contradict and refute one another; it is impossible to believe in all of them at the same time.*
  *A rationally justifiable decision is required.*
- *The biblical faith in God is in itself coherent, is also rationally justifiable and has proved itself historically over many thousands of years.*
  *The God of Israel is for believers the one, sole God who has no other gods beside him.*
  *He bears unmistakably the one name of Yahweh; man is to believe in him alone.*

c. And yet the religions—if not the nature religions, then at least the ethical higher religions—start out from the *same unending questions* of man that open up behind the visible and palpable and behind any individual's span of life: Where does the world and its order come from, why are we born and why must we die, what decides the fate of the individual and of mankind, what is the explanation of moral consciousness and the existence of ethical norms? And all religions seek to go beyond the interpretation of the world in order to make possible a *practical way* to salvation out of distress and torment. Do they not all regard lying, theft, adultery and murder as culpable? Do they not uphold a universally valid practical criterion something like a "golden rule" (do not do to others what you would not have done to yourself)? Were, then, Buddha, K'ung-fu-tse, Lao-tse, Zarathustra, Mohammed, not concerned with the same great ultimate questions and hopes?

It cannot be denied that in the other world religions also it is known that the Deity, however close, is remote and hidden and must itself bestow closeness, presence and manifestness. In the world religions also it is known that man cannot approach God quite naturally assuming his own innocence, that he needs purification and reconciliation, that sacrifice is needed to wipe out sin, that he reaches life only by passing through death; in fact, that man, in the last resort, cannot redeem and liberate himself but is dependent on God's all-embracing love.[36] Hence, in virtue of what we have now said about the God of the Fathers and formerly about the salvation of pagans, it must be observed:

- *Not only Muslims in Allah, but also Hindus in Brahma, Buddhists in the Absolute, Chinese in heaven or in the Tao, are seeking one and the same absolutely first, absolutely last reality, which for Jews and Christians is the one true God.*
- *The religions of the world can perceive not only the alienation, enslavement and need of redemption on man's part but also the goodness, mercy and graciousness of the one God.*
- *Because of this truth—despite many untruths, despite polytheism, magic, natural forces and superstition—people in the world religions can gain eternal salvation.*

In that sense, the other world religions can also be ways of salvation.[37] *The question of salvation must therefore be distinguished from the question of truth.* And if the question of salvation is settled positively, this by no means renders superfluous the question of truth. For, however much truth can be seen in detail in the world religions that can be accepted by Jews and Christians, they do not provide *the* truth for Jews and Christians. Only the one true God of Israel, known by faith, is *the* truth for Jews and Christians. Neither Jew nor Christian could claim that he might just as well be a Muslim, or even a Buddhist, Hindu or Confucian.


## 2. *God and his world*

"What is the meaning of human life, or of organic life altogether? To answer the question at all implies a religion. Is there any sense, then, you ask, in putting it? I answer, the man who regards his own life and that of his fellow-creatures as meaningless is not merely unfortunate but almost disqualified for life."[1] The words are those of the most eminent physicist of the twentieth century, *Albert Einstein* (1879–1955), inaugurator of the special theory of relativity (1905), of the law of the universal equivalence of mass and energy (1907), and finally of the general theory of relativity (1914–16). He confessed that he was "a deeply religious man"[2] and asserted the same of other great physicists of his generation. In what sense was Einstein religious? This question to the Jew Albert Einstein will lead us back to the problem as stated in the Old Testament.

## Does God play dice? Albert Einstein

For Albert Einstein and for not a few whose interest is mainly in natural science, religious feeling is "a knowledge of the existence of something we cannot penetrate, of the manifestations of the profoundest reason and the most radiant beauty which are only accessible to our reason in their most elementary forms."[3]

Einstein, strongly influenced in his Weltanschauung by Schopenhauer, declared himself not only against any form of primitive "religion of fear" but also against any "moral religion" as found in "the Jewish scriptures" and then also in the New Testament.[4] Against this he argued firmly for a "cosmic religious feeling" to which "no anthropomorphic conception of God corresponds."[5] He thinks that the beginnings of such a cosmic religious feeling are found in "many of the Psalms of David and in some of the Prophets," but much more strongly "in Buddhism, as we have learnt from the wonderful writings of Schopenhauer."[6] Appealing to such "heretics" as Democritus, Francis of Assisi and especially Spinoza,[7] Einstein thought that the religious geniuses of every age had been distinguished by this sort of religious feeling, without dogmas, church, or a priestly caste, "which knows . . . no God conceived in man's image."[8] He described himself as a "follower of Spinoza" and answered the telegraphic inquiry of an American rabbi as to whether he believed in God: "I believe in Spinoza's God who reveals himself in the orderly harmony of what exists, not in a God who concerns himself with the fates and actions of human beings."[9] *Einstein's conviction of the strictly causal regularity of all happenings was justified on religious grounds, based—that is—on Spinoza's work.*

According to the inspired scholar, this cosmic religious feeling is "the strongest and noblest incitement to scientific research."[10] So it was in the past, so it is at the present time: "What a deep conviction of the rationality of the universe and what a yearning to understand, were it but a feeble reflection of the mind revealed in this world, Kepler and Newton must have had to enable them to spend years of solitary labour in disentangling the principles of celestial mechanics. . . . Only one who has devoted his life to similar ends can have a vivid realization of what has inspired these men and given them the strength to remain true to their purpose in spite of countless failures. It is cosmic religious feeling that gives a man strength of this sort. A contemporary has said, not unjustly, that in this materialist age of ours the serious scientific workers are the only profoundly religious people."[11] According to Einstein, it is the function in particular of art and science "to awaken this feeling and keep it alive in those who are capable of it."[12]

Why, then, are we still faced even today with this antagonism between religion and science that Einstein, with his cosmic religious feeling, was absolutely determined to overcome? It is the principle of cause and effect ruling in science, the universal *law of causality*, that excludes any divine intervention in world events: "The man who is thoroughly convinced of the universal operation of the law of causation cannot for a moment entertain the idea of a being who interferes in the course of events—that is, if he takes the hypothesis of causality really seriously."[13] And it is not only the unenlightened religion of fear, but also moral religion, that cannot accept this universal causality: "A God who rewards and punishes is inconceivable to him for the simple reason that a man's actions are determined by necessity, external and internal, so that in God's eyes he cannot be responsible, any more than an inanimate object is responsible for the motions it goes through."[14] Man, then, is a living being, without free will, acting in accordance with external and internal necessity.

After his experience of National Socialism and the terrible consequences of the atom bomb—initiated by him indirectly in a letter to President Roosevelt in 1939[15]—must Einstein not have been forced to reconsider his theory of the nonexistence of free will and his view of religion, which was connected with it? There are no indications of this. In the latter part of his life, little was heard of Einstein. This was mainly because physics had taken a new, epoch-making turn with *quantum mechanics,* a development in which Einstein, with his rigid, determinist Weltanschauung, neither would nor could take part.

Few had contributed as much as he to the emergence of the quantum theory—a circumstance that Thomas S. Kuhn has shown to be not infrequently paralleled in the history of science. When Werner Heisenberg and Erwin Schrödinger, in 1925, independently of each other made the great theoretical breakthrough and Max Born and Pascual Jordan supplied the essential statistical interpretation, Einstein firmly rejected their conclusions. Can we no longer predict with certainty (deterministically), but only with probability (statistically), what a light quantum—paradoxically behaving both as a swiftly flying small particle and as a wave—will do? Can we decide what it will do only as a rule, what it will most probably do? Such purely statistical probability, such "vagueness," such an "uncertainty principle" (Heisenberg), decisively contradicted Einstein's determinist-Spinozist faith that nothing is left to chance as in dice-playing. He wrote at the time to the physicist Max Born: "Quantum mechanics is certainly imposing. But an inner voice tells me it is not yet the real thing. The theory says a lot, but does not really bring us any closer to the secret of the 'old one.' I, at any rate, am convinced that *He* is not playing at dice."[16] And again, in 1944, he wrote to Born: "We have become Antipodean in our scientific expectations. You believe in a God who plays dice, and I in complete law and order in a world which objectively exists, and which I, in a wildly speculative way, am trying to capture."[17] Einstein remained in fact—and this was apparently concealed even from Born (who had become a Quaker)—a captive of Spinoza's conception of God and nature. As he wrote in 1932: "Spinoza was the first to apply with true

consistency to human thought, feeling and action, the idea of the deterministic constraint of all that occurs."[18]

Max Born, the teacher of Heisenberg and Jordan, however, took the
very opposite view. He was not in the least disturbed by Heisenberg's uncertainty principle or by the particle/wave duality of the light quanta. On
the contrary, he saw in all this something more profound, playing a role
not only in physics but in the whole field of natural science and indeed
far beyond it in man's interpretation of reality as a whole: the inability of
concepts to discern the whole; the necessity of the complementation of
two differing aspects, what Niels Bohr called "complementarity." Only in
this way can light, energy, matter, be understood; only in this way is it
possible also to combine the strict system of laws of nature with ethical
freedom.

And *God?* Perhaps he, too, is predicable only in a "complementary"
sense. The more the physicists probed into matter, so much the more
opaque did it become, so much more inadequate the language. And the
more they advanced to the limits of the universe, the more inconceivable
everything became, expressible only with the aid of abstract formulas. As
Werner Heisenberg himself learned: "In the end we do succeed in understanding this world, by representing its organizational structures in mathematical forms; but when we want to talk about them, we must be content
with metaphors and analogies, almost as in religious language."[19]

There is nothing to be said against a properly understood cosmic
religious feeling. Certainly it has behind it a great Judeo-Christian tradition (up to Teilhard de Chardin) and has been far too much neglected
by an existential theology in the present century.[20] But an acosmic existentialism is not an answer to a cosmological scientism:

● *Belief in God is not merely a matter of human existence and historicity,
  but also of the cosmos and its history. It has necessarily a cosmic dimension.*

The problems of the relationship between natural science and belief in
God cannot be solved simply by unconnected coexistence. The question
therefore arises: Could there not be such a "complementarity" also between the "God" of Einstein and the God of the Bible? Is not God, according to Nicholas of Cusa, the *complexio oppositorum?* In the light of
this complementarity—or, better, dialectic—could we not also better understand how in God both necessity and freedom, rationality and morality, generality and particularity, impersonal and personal, are mutually
inclusive? This does not mean, however, that Einstein's questions are yet
answered. It is worthwhile to pursue these a little in this chapter. Is God
merely a universal reason or is he an actual person? Did he create the
world? What was there at the beginning? What comes at the end? Does
he intervene in world events? Let us consider these questions once more

in the light of the Old Testament. What has to be discussed today is not so much the exegetical findings set out in all the commentaries, but the confrontation with modern critical awareness and especially with the natural sciences. In all this, it is important to note that we are dealing with those groups of questions that were taken over from the Old Testament into the New and which are therefore common to both Jews and Christians.

## Is God a person?

There is no doubt that one of the main difficulties—and not only on the part of Albert Einstein—of believing today in the God of Israel, the God who is Creator and Finisher, lies in the fact that he is presented from the start even in the Old Testament as a person. Does not this sort of thing belong to the sphere of precritical thinking, to mythology? In this respect, theologians have good reason to practice self-criticism. Even if people have for a long time seen through the disastrous stereotype of God as an old man with a long white beard, how many ineradicable false ideas of an all-too-human God, above the clouds, in heaven with his royal household of angels and saints, have been dragged through the centuries up to the present time? How often were the products of Christian art, especially Renaissance and Baroque—as such often quite splendid—uncritically misused by theologians and preachers to describe a world that by its very nature is unimaginable, invisible? How often have people made an image of him who does not fit into any image and taken this image for reality, without taking seriously at least in spirit the Old Testament prohibition of images? To express our question more precisely: May we and must we conceive God as a person and can we do this against the background of modern awareness without lapsing into an uncritical-traditional mythologizing or even a hypercritical-radical demythologizing?

Whether God can be called "person" is a question that we must take seriously as coming from the East—in this sense, Einstein was right to appeal not only to Spinoza but also to Schopenhauer and to Buddhism. For, at the beginning, this was by no means obvious even in the West. In the Bible, at any rate, it is easy to ascertain that God is never called "person" or "personal." Nor did this term play any part even in Greek philosophy. The Greek word for person, *prosopon* (Latin *persona*), comes from the language of the theater. It means the mask worn by the actor in ancient drama, the role he played, and later, more generally, the countenance.

But early Christian theology found itself compelled to describe the relationship of the Father first to Jesus as the Son and then to the Holy Spirit in ontological terms. In a very involved process of interpretation, there were endless arguments in both Greek and Latin as to whether and how far the term "person" (*persona, prosopon, hypostasis*)—now increasingly understood as intellectual individuality—could be applied to God. It was only in the fourth and fifth centuries that an orthodox trinitarian doctrine was finally established, and even here God was not simply described as a person but as "one (divine) nature in three persons" (Father, Son and Spirit). Conversely, Jesus Christ is not a human person but "a (divine) person in two natures" (divine and human). So Jesus is not a human person? And yet there are three divine persons? Is it surprising that this manner of speaking has become obviously misleading and even unintelligible in modern times, when the original sense of the terms is no longer known? People today understand the term "person" not ontologically as formerly, but psychologically. "Person" today means self-consciousness and "personality," the character acquired by an individual in the attitudes he takes to events in the course of his life. The terms "person," "personhood," "personal" and "personality" have all acquired a different meaning. It is not surprising, then, that the traditional doctrine of three persons has come to be understood by ordinary people to a large extent as a doctrine of three Gods (tritheism), to which there are parallels in many Eastern religions (for instance, the Indian "Trimurti" of Brahma, Vishnu and Siva), but which for many Jews and Muslims has become the most offensive aspect of Christianity.

From all this, it follows that we should not argue about words either with Hindus and Buddhists or with Christians and not with those who speak of cosmic religious feeling. Whether "person" or "nonperson," it is the reality that matters. And that is complex enough. We shall therefore try to make some distinctions.

We have observed that God is not an infinite—and still less a finite— *alongside* or *above* the finite. He is the infinite *in* all finite, being itself in all that is. If Einstein speaks of cosmic reason or if Eastern thinkers speak of "nirvana," "void," "absolute nothingness,"[21] this must be understood as an expression of reverence before the mystery of the Absolute, as opposed to all-too-human "theistic" ideas of God. For the same reason, even Christian theologians speak of God as the Deity, as the supreme good, as *the* truth and *the* good, as love itself, being itself, the ocean, the inexpressible, the mystery. . . . As we saw, even the most positive human qualities are inadequate to describe God. Consequently, in every affirmation they need to be negated and then raised to the level of the infinite. With regard to the use of the term "person," this means:

● *God is not a person as man is a person. The all-embracing and all-penetrating is never an object that man can view from a distance in order to make statements about it. The primal ground, primal support and primal goal of all reality, which determines every individual existence, is not an individual person among other persons, is not a superman or superego. The term "person" also is merely a cipher for God. God is not the supreme person among other persons. God transcends also the concept of person. God is more than person.*

But we have also seen that the positive human qualities in particular, if they are affirmed while finiteness is denied and if at the same time they are raised to infinity, can be predicated of God. Only in this way does the Absolute remain for us not absolutely nothing—nor is it supposed to be such even according to the Buddhist advocates of "Absolute Nothingness." And could a God without mind or understanding, freedom or love, be a God? As the Old Testament itself observes: Can he who created the ear be deaf, he who created the eye be blind, he who created the mouth be dumb? Could God, the cause of all human individuality and personality, be an impersonal "It" and not a personal "Thou," open to man's trustful approach, an approach that is not intrusive but maintains a respectful distance? How otherwise could God have founded mind and freedom, freedom and love, in the world and in man?

- *A God who founds personality cannot himself be nonpersonal. Just because God is not a "thing," just because—as is stressed in the East—he cannot be seen through, controlled, manipulated, he is not impersonal, not infrapersonal. God transcends also the concept of the impersonal. God is also not less than a person.*

No, an insensitive geometry or harmony of the universe based on a system of necessary laws of nature, as the physicist with his special and limited methods is tempted to assume, cannot explain reality as a whole. This, at any rate, is the view of the Bible. Ultimate reality is more than a universal reason, more than a great, anonymous consciousness, more than thought turned in on itself, thinking itself, more than the supreme idea, more than the sheer beauty of the cosmos and certainly more than the blind justice of history. The ultimate reality is not something that remains indifferent and leaves us indifferent, but something that involves us absolutely, liberating us and making demands on us:

- *God is not neuter, not an "it," but a God of men, who provokes the decision for belief or unbelief. He is spirit in creative freedom, the primordial identity of justice and love, one who faces me as founding and embracing all interhuman personality. If, with the religious philosophers of the East, we want to call the absolutely last and absolutely first reality the "void" or "Absolute Nothingness," then we must also call it "being itself," which manifests itself with an infinite claim and with infinite understanding. It will be better to call the most real reality not personal or nonpersonal but—if we attach importance to the terminology —transpersonal or suprapersonal.*[22]

But, once again, the terms are not really important. We might make use here of Niels Bohr's notion of complementarity and say that, as in quantum mechanics, whether the answer in an experiment refers to the wave or the corpuscle depends on the way the question is put, so, too, in philosophical and theological discussion, whether we call God personal or nonpersonal depends on the statement of the question. It is part of the completely incommensurable nature of God that he is neither personal nor nonpersonal, since he is both at once and therefore transpersonal.

The decisive thing is that God is not below our level. Which means that, even though we can speak of God only in analogical terms, metaphors, images, ciphers and symbols, we can nevertheless *speak to* him meaningfully with human words. This much should be clear to us from the Bible. We need not try to think out in precise terms the reality of God, but we should squarely face that reality. Man should not lose his power of speech at this point, but should stand up and speak out in a genuinely human way. From the first to the last page of the Bible, the talk is not only of and about God but continually also to and with God, praising and lamenting, praying and protesting. From the first page to the last—here Feuerbach was undoubtedly right[23]—God in the Bible is subject and not predicate: it is not that love is God, but that God is love. This means:

- *The Bible shows that there is someone who faces us as benevolent and absolutely reliable: not an object, not an empty, unechoing universe, not a merely silent infinite, not an indefinable, nameless Gnostic chasm, not an indeterminate, dark abyss that might be confused with nothingness, still less an anonymous interpersonal something that could be mistaken for man and his very fragile love. God is* one who faces me, whom I can address.

Where others perceived only infinite silence, Israel heard a voice. Israel was permitted to discover for itself and for others that the one God can be heard and addressed: that he comes among men saying "I," making himself a "thou" for them, one who speaks to us and to whom we can speak. And in being addressed by this one, man learns the dignity of his own person, which is such as has scarcely ever been recognized in the East but which also cannot be guaranteed by any Western secular humanism or by any cosmic religious feeling: a dignity that cannot permit man ever to be used as fodder for bombs and experiments or as fertilizer for evolution. The fact that the West has not exemplified this kind of Christianity to the East (and to Jews) has done more to discredit belief in the one true God than all arguments of the atheists.

God can be addressed. Despite all the successive corrections of the understanding of God in the Bible, on this central point there is no development. "Spiritualization," here, would be volatilization, removing the basis of genuine prayer and worship. No matter how the Bible speaks of God—mythically or unmythically, imaginatively or conceptually, prosaically or poetically—the relationship to God as to one who faces us and can be addressed, as to a thou who may be called person and personal or even suprapersonal and transpersonal, or what you will, is a basic constant factor of the biblical faith in God that can never be abandoned, but always needs to be interpreted afresh. This question is of decisive importance particularly for prayer.

## What was there at the beginning?

"In the beginning God created the heavens and the earth." This first verse of Genesis is the very first statement in the Bible. Was God there at the beginning? Can this statement about a divine creation of the world be scientifically verified?

If natural science today claims to be able to reconstruct the vast course of the history of the world in its decisive phases, stretching over billions of years, the theologians will have to face up to this challenge. But we are not in a position here to outline any cosmology or theology of creation, together with the necessary exegesis of the Old Testament. Nevertheless, within the already sufficiently wide framework in which we are seeking to answer the question of God in modern times, we shall not try to avoid a response to the questions of the beginning, progress and end of world history. For this very reason, many people have serious difficulties in believing in God. Here we propose some ways of approaching the question that may be helpful.

The question of the beginning of "heaven and earth," of the world, of the cosmos, of the universe, in the light of the present state of scientific research, may be expressed more or less in this way: Is the point of time of the "big bang"—with which, in the opinion of leading scientists, our world began—identical with the point of time of the creation of the world out of nothing by divine omnipotence? Let us first glance quite briefly at some astrophysical facts and cosmological theories.

Cosmology—for a long time neglected by natural science and touched on (even, for instance, by Popper) only marginally in the philosophy of science[24]—has become the center of interest in the past decade, particularly in physics, because in the question of origins the physics of the very large—the macrocosm—meets the physics of the very small, the elementary particle—the microcosm. Here, too, we find confirmation of Thomas Kuhn's theory of scientific revolutions.[25] Even in this field, where, indirectly, ideological and religious questions also play a large part, the progress of science has not by any means taken a purely rational course. Such a leading German physicist as Reimar Lüst observes: "The fact that now, in 1977, we are so much more certain that there really was a beginning of the universe and that we can even date this beginning, is something we owe to a discovery in 1965, the observation of cosmic background radiation in the millimeter wave range. The manner in which it was first proved is exciting in itself, but equally fascinating is the fact that this radiation might have been discovered very much sooner if we had taken more seriously a theoretical idea of the origin of the cosmos, what we now call the 'big-bang.' Scientific discoveries do not by any means always develop logically."[26] In fact, it was a little over fifty years ago (1927) that the often misunderstood Belgian priest and professor in Louvain, Georges Lemaître (1894–1966), within the framework of the general theory of relativity and in harmony with the Hubble effect, developed the model of an expanding universe and put forward the "big bang" hypothesis. As against all others, this idea has now been so widely accepted that it is described (by Weinberg)[27] as the "standard model." What does it look like?

Einstein had developed at an early stage a *new model of the universe* completely different from the infinite universe of Newton's classical physics.[28] Such a universe could be deduced from the fundamental equations of the general theory of relativity put forward by Einstein. In this theory, gravitation is understood as the result of the curvature of the nonobservable "space-time continuum," that is, of a four-dimensional space, which is formed by non-Euclidean geometry from space and time coordinates. This geometry is determined by the distribution of matter in outer space. Assuming that, macroscopically, no point in the universe stands out from another—the "cosmological principle"—the result is a spatially curved universe. In view of all this, how can such a model of the universe be more precisely conceived? Outer space must be thought of as unlimited, but it can have a finite volume. An analogy might be found in the three-dimensional (not four-dimensional) space of the surface of a sphere, which has a finite area content and yet no boundary.

For the time being, even Einstein regarded the universe as static, but later—at first with Friedmann in 1925 and Lemaître in 1927—a dynamic view came to prevail. The model that corresponds best to the observations is that of the "big bang." As early as 1929, after many years of research, the American physicist Edwin P. Hubble concluded, from the red shifts of the spectral lines of galaxies, the continuing expansion of the universe.[29] The galaxies outside our own Milky Way are moving away from us with a velocity that is proportional to their distance from us. But when did all this start? It cannot have been from infinite time. There must have been a beginning at which all radiation and all matter was compressed in a scarcely describable primordial fireball with the smallest possible circumference and the greatest possible density and temperature. With a gigantic cosmic explosion (easier to imagine after the explosion of what we now regard as the "small" atom bomb), with a big bang—at a temperature of a hundred billion degrees Celsius and a density of about four billion times that of water—some thirteen billion years ago, the still continuing, homogeneous (and isotropic) expansion of the universe began.

In the very first seconds, out of the extremely high-energy photons, both heavy elementary particles—especially protons and neutrons and their antiparticles—and light elementary particles—electrons and positrons—must have been formed. After that, helium nuclei were soon constructed by nuclear processes out of protons and neutrons, and some hundreds of thousands of years later also hydrogen and helium atoms. And at a very much later date—with the relaxation of the pressure of the originally high-energy light quanta—the gas could condense by gravitation into lumps and finally, as a result of progressive compression, into galaxies and stars. Radiation in the decimeter and centimeter range (cosmic microwave or background radiation), discovered by A. A. Penzias and R. W. Wilson in 1964, is now generally assumed to be what remains of the radiation resulting from the big bang, which has been reduced by the expansion of the universe to a very-low-temperature radiation.

It is not surprising that naïve Christians appealed to the big-bang theory as a *proof of the truth of a creation of the world.* "God said, 'Let there be light,' and there was light . . . the first day."[30] Is not this sudden act of creation rather like a big bang? According to this theory, which corresponds to a large number of observations, the big bang took place a very long time ago but still within a finite period of time. The universe therefore has a definite age: presumably about thirteen billion years. But, now as before, it is still uncertain whether the expansion of the universe will continue indefinitely or will one day come to an end and be replaced by contraction. This can be decided only by further observations, and on these also depends the conclusion whether the universe is open or closed, whether—that is—outer space is infinitely large or has a finite volume. While, however, observations up to recently led to the assumption of a universe that would contract again after expanding, the latest discussions about the data of observation available now suggest a permanently expanding universe. But the question of the correct model of the universe cannot yet be definitively answered. For this, more sophisticated observations—which may be expected in the very near future—would be required.

Advocates of dialectical materialism, in the light of their beliefs, had violently condemned Einstein's model of the universe at an early date as "idealistic." To them, it did not seem to confirm their dogma of the infinity and eternity of matter. When, at the end of the 1940s, the attempt was made in books on Christian apologetics actually to identify the point of time of the big bang with that of a divine creation of the world, even non-Marxists were disturbed. The German astronomer Otto Heckmann, who had played a leading part in the investigation of the expansion of the universe, tells us: "Some younger scientists were so upset by these theological trends that they resolved simply to block their cosmological source. They produced the 'steady state cosmology,' the cosmology of the expanding but nevertheless unchanging universe."[31] But this theory, of Bondi,[32] Gold and Hoyle, of a stationary universe, had to assume a spontaneous generation of matter and seemed to be contradictory; after the discovery of cosmic microwave radiation and also quasars (1962–63) and pulsars (1967), the theory has scarcely any prospect of being accepted.[33]

We do not want to adopt a partisan attitude here, and we must raise the self-critical question as to whether it is really possible to speak of a scientific confirmation of the biblical statements about the beginning of the cosmos. Hoimar von Ditfurth, in his widely read book *Im Anfang war der Wasserstoff* ("In the Beginning Was Hydrogen"),[34] rightly reproaches the theologians for misusing God, far too much as a stopgap, in order to explain the hitherto inexplicable, and thus themselves contributing to what the zoologist Haeckel had caustically described as the "homelessness of God." Theology really cannot retreat to what remains unexplained in the world and attempt from that point to prove the existence of God. With each new scientific explanation, God then becomes more dispensable and in the end dies the death of a thousand qualifications. "If—as the religions hold—there is a Creator of the world, then his existence cannot be affected by the question of the exact position that molecular biology happens to have reached on earth."[35]

On the other hand, von Ditfurth speaks very seriously to those natural scientists who argue the other way around and commit the same mistake as the theologians: "With every advance they made, with every new piece of knowledge acquired, it seemed to them increasingly improbable that there could be any transcendent reality at all hidden behind the façade of visible appearances."[36] What we said in principle about atheism is confirmed here: "If a scientist maintains an atheistic standpoint, he has a perfect and indisputable right to do so. No one has any means available to refute him. But if the man thinks he can substantiate his belief with his scientific insights, he is simply falling a victim—Nobel prizewinner or not—to the fallacy here discussed."[37] Wanting to stick only to what can be weighed and measured, even outside natural science, says Ditfurth, is a "professional neurosis" or an occupational disease of people who "think they have to convince themselves" that "there are no other fields of reality at all" outside the field of things that can be weighed and measured.[38]

The question about God and creation is not only the question of an initial event but about the fundamental relationship as such between the world and God. With reference to the *beginning of the world*, we can only set out in the form of propositions some ideas that presuppose an exegesis of the texts of Genesis:[39]

- *The fact that—from the standpoint of natural science—our universe is probably finite in space and time, as competent scientists assume today, is of no little importance—even from the theological standpoint—for our understanding of the world and ourselves.*

- *But even an infinite universe could not restrict the infinite God in all things. Belief in God is compatible with both models of the world.*

- *The question, however, of the ultimate origin of the world and man— what was before the big bang and before hydrogen—the question why there is something and not nothing, is one of man's basic questions, which the natural scientist—who is not competent beyond the horizon of experience—cannot answer but may not for that reason dismiss as vain or even pointless.*

- *The two biblical accounts of creation—the first written about 900 B.C. and the second about 500 B.C.—do not provide any scientific information about the origin of things, but they do amount to a testimony of faith about the ultimate source of the universe, which natural science can neither confirm nor refute: at the beginning of the world is God.*

- *To say that God created the world "out of nothing" does not mean that nothing has a kind of independent existence before or alongside God, but is a theological expression of the fact that the world and man, together with space and time, owe their existence to God alone and to no other cause.*

- *The testimony of faith of the biblical account stresses*
  *that God is the origin of each and every thing; that he is not in competition with any evil or demonic counterprinciple;*
  *that the world as a whole and in detail, that matter also, the human body and sexuality, are fundamentally good;*
  *that man is the great goal of the process of creation and the center of the cosmos;*
  *that God's creation itself implies his gracious turning to the world and man.*

Thus the Bible in the metaphors and analogies of its time answers questions that are infinitely important also for people today—in metaphors and analogies, it must be noted. *The language of the Bible is not a scientific language of facts, but a metaphorical language of images.* The Bible does not produce scientific facts, but explains them. The two planes of language and thought must always be clearly separated if disastrous misunderstandings of the past are to be avoided on both sides. With the language of the Bible—as Werner Heisenberg expresses it—it is a question of a kind of language "that makes possible an understanding of the coherence of the world perceptible behind the appearances, a coherence without which there could be no ethics and no scale of values. . . . This language is more closely related to the language of poetry than to that of science, which aims at precision. Hence the same words often have different meanings in the two languages. The heavens of which the Bible

speaks have little to do with the heavens into which airplanes and rockets
are sent. In the astronomical universe, the earth is merely a tiny speck of
dust in one of the innumerable galaxies, but, for us, it is the center of the
universe—it is really the center of the universe. Natural science attempts
to give its terms an objective meaning. But religious language must avoid
particularly the cleavage of the universe into its objective and subjective
aspects; for who could maintain that the objective aspect is more real
than the subjective? We must not mix up the two languages; we must
think more subtly than has hitherto been the case."[40]

Whether the primordial fireball or hydrogen atoms or merely a few—
perhaps even only two—neutrons were there at the beginning, the question always arises: "Where did they come from?" The manuals of astrophysics provide no answer to this. They begin—one might say—at the
second day of creation. And even the "standard model" is not entirely satisfactory: "Just as in the *Younger Edda*, there is an embarrassing vagueness about the very beginning, the first hundredth of a second or so."
This is "an era that is still clothed in mystery—the first hundredth of a
second, and what went before."[41] And after questioning some of the best-
known astronomers in the U.S.A., the American news magazine *Time*
came to the conclusion: "To the ultimate question—what existed before
the big bang—most of modern science is mute."[42] But a radically understood rationality in particular demands an answer to the question: "Why
is there anything at all and not nothing?" Are not too many scientists (or
those who think they are scientists) content with the laconic answer that
these questions are unanswerable and there is no point in answering
them? Are not such irrational reactions connected with the centuries-old
prejudices between religion and science, which today can be overcome in
principle?[43] Ought not the scientist—perhaps not *as* scientist, but as a
rational, responsible human being—to think again, to think more subtly,
as Heisenberg said, and take the risk of speaking out? "If, from the indubitable fact that the world exists, someone wants to infer a cause of this
existence, his inference does not contradict our scientific knowledge at any
point. No scientist has at his disposal even a single argument or any kind
of fact with which he could oppose such an assumption. This is true, even
if the cause—and how could it be otherwise—obviously has to be sought
outside this three-dimensional world of ours."[44]

With reference to the beginning of the universe, then, what point can
there be today in speaking not only—scientifically—about a big bang,
models of the universe, theories of the cosmos, but also with a perfect
right—theologically—about a *God who created heaven and earth:* a God
whom people, particularly Christians and Jews, have acknowledged over
and over again in the light of the Old Testament? Certainly my age is
nothing in comparison with the age of mankind; but the age of mankind
is nothing by comparison with the thirteen billion years of this cosmos.

And this earth of ours is a speck of dust in comparison with the totality of the Milky Way, which includes some hundred billion individual stars, one of them being the sun. And, again, this Milky Way of ours is a speck of dust by comparison with galactic clusters, some of which contain ten thousand galaxies, so that the number of observable galaxies may well amount to a hundred million.[45] The more, then, I reflect on the amazing conclusions of astrophysics and, again, like human beings from time immemorial, look up into the clear night sky, am I not to wonder what it all means, where it all comes from? To answer, "Out of nothing," is no explanation. Reason cannot be satisfied with that. The only serious alternative—which, like so many other things, pure reason admittedly cannot prove, since it transcends its horizon of experience—is that *the whole stems from that first creative cause of causes, which we call God and indeed the Creator God.* And even if I cannot prove him, I can with good reason affirm him: in that reasonable, tested and *enlightened trust* in which I have already affirmed his existence. For if the God who exists is truly God, then he is not only God for me here and now, but God at the beginning, God from all eternity.

Could this be merely an illusion, could it be suspected of being a projection, as Feuerbach and Freud suggested? Do I make this existing Creator God for myself because I am afraid to be alone in the universe, because I feel the horror of a vacuum, because I fear to draw the harsh conclusion that man is abandoned to nothingness? Does not believing in God mean remaining always a child and never growing up—as Freud expressed it? As we saw, there can be no knowledge without some projection. Obviously, projection is involved in my knowledge of the Creator God. Even someone who affirms a nothingness likewise links a projection with nothingness. And yet I have every reason to assume that my projection is not merely a projection, but that a reality corresponds to it, that the reality of the Creator God meets my image of it, confirming, correcting, infinitely surpassing it. What, then, does it mean to believe in the Creator God?

Believing in the Creator of the world does not mean believing in any sort of myths; neither does it mean imagining God as Creator in the form depicted—for instance—by Michelangelo as artist when he painted him in a completely human way on the ceiling of the Sistine Chapel. At this point, all representations come to an end. Nor does believing in God as Creator of the world mean deciding for one or another of the varying models of the universe produced by leading scholars. This is impossible simply because we are here concerned with what is presupposed to all models and to the universe as a whole. Believing in the Creator of the world means affirming in enlightened trust that the world and man do not remain inexplicable in their ultimate source, that the world and man are not pointlessly hurled from nothing into nothing, but that in their totality they are meaningful and valuable, not chaos but cosmos; that they find their security first and last in God their primal ground, originator, creator. Nothing forces me into this faith. *I can decide for it absolutely freely.* Once I have decided, then this faith changes my position in the world, my attitude to the world; *it establishes my fundamental trust and gives concrete shape to my trust in God.*

Since I believe in God as Creator, I can also affirm the world and man as God's creation: respect men as my fellow men (and not as inferior beings); respect and care for nonhuman nature—especially animals—as my environment (and not as my natural enemies, not as material for arbitrary exploitation). It is not although, but because, I am God's creature, because my fellow men and my environment are also God's creatures, that I and my fellow men acquire and that my environment also—despite all differences—acquires a dignity that has to be respected. The "subdue the earth" of the creation story can never be a license for uninhibited exploitation and destruction of nature and the environment: a principle that does not apply only at a time when we are increasingly aware of the "limits of growth." Believing in the Creator God of the world thus means accepting with greater seriousness, greater realism and greater hope my responsibility for my fellow men and for the environment and the tasks assigned to me. Is it not appropriate to make such a decision of faith in the Creator God for myself? *Credo in Deum omnipotentem, creatorem caeli et terrae.*


## Does God intervene?

Many people today have fewer difficulties in believing in a Creator than they have in believing in a Ruler of all things; fewer difficulties with the biblical creation story (now largely understood metaphorically) and the work of the six days than with the subsequent history of salvation and the biblical miracle stories. Many wonder if the history of the world from beginning to end is not in itself a coherent, consistent development in which everything is governed by the law of—intramundane—cause and effect and in which every step obviously follows from the previous one. What scope can remain for a special intervention, for God to "intervene," to "come between"? For world history cannot be understood today merely as the history of mankind (a few hundred thousand years), but must be understood as the history of the actual world, of perhaps thirteen billion years from the big bang onward. Of course, we cannot deal here with the old theological questions such as man's original state and original sin, evil and the devil, sin and reconciliation; but we must go into the one question of the intervention of God in the history of the world and of mankind, since it has the character of a test.

Over and over again, theologians have attempted to give a name to decisive turning points coming even before the history of mankind and the miracles of the Old Testament, where the causal sequence was interrupted and an unmediated "supernatural" intervention of God supposedly became necessary in the otherwise natural progress of history. As already noted,[46] this of course took the form of a continual withdrawal strategy. And today it is admitted that at least both the cosmos as a whole and man in his bodily nature developed "naturally." Then the further question arises as to whether we should really continue to insist that in fact the human mind ("soul") or at least life as such emerged as a result of a direct intervention of the Creator. For reasons of space, we shall concentrate on the question of the origin of life; the question of the origin of the human mind could be answered in a similar way.[47]

Precisely with reference to the *origin of life*, the biology of the past decades can now record such sensational results that it is possible to regard Darwin's evolutionary theory—discussed earlier in its traditional form[48]— as practically physically substantiated and experimentally tested, not only on the plane of the living cell but also on that of the molecule. This has come about through *molecular biology*, which, although not the only biological approach, represents from midcentury onward the new basis of biology. Darwin himself had expressed the hope that the principle of life would one day be recognized as part or as a result of a universal law. But what seemed to be a dream a few decades ago has now become reality. The molecular biology of our time seems to have found this law; and thus biology has been revolutionized just as physics was at an earlier stage by quantum mechanics.

What was discovered in bacteria and viruses holds also for higher organisms and presumably for all life on this planet. The rudimentary bearers of life are two classes of macromolecules: nucleic acids and proteins. The chain molecules of the nucleic acids (DNA and RNA), mainly in the nucleus of the cell, form the control center. They contain in coded form (according to a "genetic code" consisting only of four "letters") the complete structural and functional plan drawn up for every living being and transmit it from cell to cell, from generation to generation. The proteins (many-sided structures of amino acids) take up this "information." They carry out the functions of the living cells assigned to them by this structural and functional control. In this way, life functions and is propagated: a marvelous world on the most rudimentary level, where molecules carry out their permutations in the smallest possible space, often in a millionth of a second.

In retrospect, we might perhaps put it this way. At some time billions of years ago, two molecules must have come together for the first time and thus given something like an initial spark to life and biological evolution. All life thus goes back possibly to a single root, even though it is today so indescribably varied and complex that any definition breaks down in face of its abundance and even the transitions from the inanimate to the animate cannot be clearly marked off. But however this transition to life is explained in detail, it rests on the above-described *self-organization of matter*, of the molecule. For why does evolution ascend at all? This is the great discovery. Even on the plane of the molecule—here, of course, we must avoid an all-too-systematic application of the thermodynamic approach to biological systems[49]—what rules is the principle, first observed by Darwin in the plant and animal worlds, of "natural selection" and the "survival of the fittest," driving evolution inexorably upward at the expense of the less healthy molecules. In the light of these latest biophysical conclusions it is impossible to see any need precisely at this point for a special intervention of the Creator God. In the existing material preconditions, the origin of life is a determinate happening; the transition from the inorganic to the organic took place continuously—almost continuously.

For we find here the same kind of problems as in quantum mechanics: an indeterminateness, a haziness, *contingency in the individual processes*. But one thing is certain, that the course of biological evolution as a whole is necessary and controlled by laws. But, frequently, evolution to a higher stage came to a crossroads, and often nature took both ways—as, for instance, both to insects and to mammals. The individual events are not determined in their chronological sequence. The ways that evolution takes in detail are not laid down from the outset. The abrupt, microscopically small mutations, out of which, through immense accumulation or upward thrusting, sudden changes and new manifestations result also in the macroscopic field, are accidental. Hence at one and the same time both chance and necessity are involved. The Greek philosopher and atomist Democritus (about 470–380 B.C.), wrote: "All that exists in the universe is the fruit of chance and necessity." This motto was adopted in our time by the late French molecular biologist and Nobel prizewinner Jacques Monod (1910–76) in his well-known book *Chance and Necessity*, but giving the priority decisively to chance: "pure chance, absolutely free but blind, at the very root of the stupendous edifice of evolution."[50]

*Is everything, then, due to chance* and, for that very reason, is there no necessity for a creator and conserver of this structure? In two respects, Monod is right:

He *rightly* argues against the assumption by Teilhard (and the vitalists) of an evolutionary force or energy existing from the outset (ultimately to be ascribed to the Creator God), which is supposed to explain the evolutionary ascent and to lead to an omega point. This "force" or "energy," stemming from the nineteenth-century belief in progress (as, for instance, with Herbert Spencer[51]), represents an "animistic projection"[52] that is not justified scientifically.

Monod—a former communist—*rightly* argues also against Marxist biology, which from Engels to Althusser likewise ascribed to an eternal matter (supposedly evolving in dialectical leaps) an unknown and unknowable force: here, too, there is an "animistic projection" and an "anthropocentric illusion" that is incompatible with science and clearly illustrates "the epistemological disaster that follows the 'scientific' use of dialectical interpretations."[53]

*But* is Monod right in arguing also against a Creator God whom, in his theory, he wanted to exclude as radically as he excluded creative matter?

The German biophysicist *Manfred Eigen*, likewise a Nobel prizewinner, in the book *Das Spiel* ("The Game"), which he published in collaboration with Ruthild Winkler, formulated the opposite thesis, largely supported by biologists today. The subtitle itself is programmatic: "Natural Laws Control Chance."[54] Or, as Eigen writes in the Preface to the German edition of Monod's book: "However much the individual form owes its origin to chance, the process of selection and evolution is equally an inescapable necessity. No more than that. There is, then, no mysterious inherent 'vital property' of matter that, in the last resort, would determine the course of history. But no less than that. There is not *merely* chance."[55]

To Einstein's arguments—mainly based on religious considerations—against an indeterminateness or vagueness in the rudimentary physical processes, which obviously apply also to the biological, the answer of the biologists as formulated by the Viennese *Rupert Riedl*, following Eigen, runs: "A God who only played dice would be a gambler. None of his products would have any meaning. This is what disturbed Einstein. But a God who never played dice would have constructed a machine and none of his products would be free. 'Does God play dice, then?' asks Manfred Eigen, 'Certainly. But he also follows his rules for the game.' And only the gap between the two provides both meaning and freedom."[56]

Hence, to explain evolution, the "strategy of genesis," chance and necessity, indetermination and determination, even materialism and idealism, are false alternatives. "Only by thinking in systems can we see the strategy of genesis. Gigantic systems of hierarchically organized internal and external causes interact on one another. In all this, *genesis* operates with the supremely ambivalent antagonism between necessary contingency and contingent necessity. Through all its strata it preserves what begins as chance, as indetermination, but ends as creativity, as freedom. And there is a continual growth of what emerges as necessity, as determination, but ends as law and order, as a sense of direction, as the meaning of possible evolution. Until finally a meaning without freedom for us is meaningless, just as a freedom without meaning would not be freedom. . . . A *world* resulting from this strategy is neither a pure product of chance, nor is it planned in advance; man is neither meaningless, as Jacques Monod with the existentialists asserts, nor was he aimed at, as Teilhard with the vitalists thought. He neither failed to acquire meaning because of the freedom of evolution nor did he lose freedom by the growth of laws. And the harmony of the world is neither a fiction nor is it

prestabilized. Its harmony is poststabilized; it is a consequence of its growing systems. When it emerges, its meaning is a consequence of the strata
of the conditions of its form. This world is neither deterministic nor inde-
terministic, neither materialistic nor idealistic. And consequently materialism cannot cure idealism, nor can idealism cure materialism. Half-truths
as they are, they could not do more than become entrenched in the incompatibility of the ideologies, divide the world in the middle and bring
it to the state in which it is today."[57]

But if God thus plays dice within the rules, the question still arises as
to whether it is really *God* who is playing at all. Does not self-organizing
matter, self-regulating evolution, render God superfluous? Monod, with
his negative view, is certainly not alone among biologists. What is the answer? A distinction must be made:

It is an *unjustified assumption*—here we would have to agree with
Monod—on the basis of the transition from the inorganic world to the
biosphere or even on the basis of molecular indeterminateness, *to postulate the existence of God*. This would, again, be a stopgap God.[58] Here
the biologist Eigen agrees with the biologist Monod: "The 'origin of life'
—that is, the evolution of the macromolecule to the microorganism—is
only one step among many, like the step from the elementary particle to
the atom, from the atom to the molecule, . . . or even the step from the
unicellular organism to the organic compound and in the end to man's
central nervous system. Why should we regard this particular step, from
the molecule to the unicellular organism, with greater reverence than any
of the others? Molecular biology has brought to an end the creation mysticism that was maintained for centuries; it has completed what Galileo
began."[59] Whether the step from the macromolecule to the first cell is not
very much more important, is disputed by biologists. What is important
for us, however, is whether the rejection of a "creation mysticism," which
Monod and Eigen saw still at work in Teilhard's system, itself involves
the rejection of a creator and ruler of the world.

It is likewise an *unjustified assumption*—and here Monod must decidedly be opposed—to *exclude God's existence* in the light of the molecular biological findings. Here, then, the biologist Eigen rightly opposes the
biologist Monod: "In Monod's demand for an 'existential attitude to life
and society' we see an animistic revaluation of the role of 'chance.' It
largely disregards the complementary aspect of regularity. The critique of
the dialectical overestimation of 'necessity'—justified, in my opinion—
should not lead to the complete denial of its quite obvious influence. We
can wholly agree with Monod when he says that ethics and knowledge
cannot be unconnected; but, for us, this implies a commitment to the
great religions and not simply a condemnation of them. . . . However little the natural sciences can do to produce a proof of God, they still do
not postulate that man 'has no need of a belief in God.' An ethic—how-

ever much it must be in harmony with objectivity and knowledge—should be oriented more to the needs of humanity than to the behavior of matter. Nor do we think that an ethical order can be absolute. It will always have a variety of aspects and cannot simply be cut off from its historical roots."[60] The rejection of a creation mysticism, therefore, does not by any means imply the rejection of a creator and ruler of the world.

The Protestant theologian E. C. Hirsch is quoted with approval by Eigen and Winkler[61] as drawing the conclusion from a series of interviews with physicists and biologists that "the origin of life is no longer the mysterious point at which God could be found more easily than elsewhere. Either we believe in God or—even here—we do not believe in him. There is no proof of God. The old question remains: 'Why is there anything at all and not nothing?' And thus the mystery of life is shifted back to the mystery of matter. Where does the matter come from, which has the property (under appropriate conditions) of giving rise to life?"[62] This view is wholly in agreement with our own.

The biologist also is faced here with an *existential alternative:* meaninglessness and desolation or . . . God:

*Either we say No* to a primal ground, primal support and primal goal of the whole process of evolution and then we must put up with the meaninglessness of the whole process—Monod invokes at the very beginning the Sisyphus depicted by Camus—and the total desolation of man: "If he accepts this message in its full significance, man must at last wake out of his millenary dream and discover his total solitude, his fundamental isolation. He must realize that, like a gipsy, he lives on the boundary of an alien world; a world that is deaf to his music, and as indifferent to his hopes as it is to his suffering or his crimes."[63]

*Or we say Yes* to a primal ground, primal support and primal goal and then the fundamental meaningfulness of the whole process admittedly cannot be proved from the process itself but can be trustingly assumed. The question raised by Eigen and Winkler would then be answered: "Now as before, knowing the connections does not produce any answer to the question raised by Leibniz: 'Why is there something and not nothing?'"[64] Then the biologist also—like Riedl—can have the courage to acknowledge the helplessness of science and at the same time the necessity of faith: "Even the atheist, mechanist, monist, of our time, has only to put back the question of the causes of this world behind the big bang and he will have to admit that—with all our science—he is in the same helpless state that he may have been foolish enough to ridicule as a cause of bear worship. In my opinion, no one can think without metaphysical premises. Certainly it is possible not to be aware of them. But it is impossible to take a step into the unknown without including expectations that are meta-physical and that go beyond the things we already know. Faith and its children—religion, philosophy and world vision—are indispensable to any civilization. Faith is the irreplaceable framework for the inexplicable."[65]

Of course, we should avoid mixing scientific conclusions with religious beliefs. Our (quite laudable) ethical and religious impulses should not lead us to ascribe to the evolutionary process the orientation to a definite final state, omega, and thus give it a meaning that can come only from religious faith and not from science.[66] We have argued for a Yes to an "alpha" as "ground" of all things, and we shall also argue for an "omega" as "goal." But it must remain clear that this is a question of a Yes "beyond science,"[67] actually of a Yes of faith.

Does God, then, intervene? It has now become clear what our answer to the question can be and what must be said concisely in answer to Monod's challenge:

- *In the opinion of leading biologists, a direct supernatural intervention of God at the origin of life—and similarly also at the origin of the human mind—appears more than ever to be unnecessary.*[68]
- *From the standpoint of natural science, the evolutionary process as such neither includes nor excludes a creator and ruler (an alpha) and an ultimate meaning and end (an omega).*
- *But even for the natural scientist there arises the existential question of the origin and the ultimate meaning and end of the whole process, which he cannot evade even though as a scientist he cannot answer it.*
- *For the natural scientist, it is a question of deciding in faith whether to assume an ultimate groundlessness, unsupportedness and meaninglessness or a primal ground, primal support and primal meaning of everything, a creator, ruler and finisher of the evolutionary process.*
- *Only an assent in faith to a primal ground, primal support and primal meaning can answer the question of the origin, support and goal of the evolutionary process and so produce for man an ultimate certainty and security. Seen in this way, radical rationality is the mark not of the No —which leads to meaninglessness—but only of the Yes.*

There remains, however, the positive question: If we are to avoid a supernatural intervention of God in the laws of nature, *how is God's controlling activity to be conceived?* The question cannot be dealt with at length here, but a lengthy treatment is not necessary.
For:
a. In Part A, on reason and faith, and in Parts E and F, on fundamental trust and belief in God, we showed that the two-floor theory of nature and supernature had been proved untenable as a result of the development of both modern science and theology itself.
b. In Part B, in dealing with Hegel, Comte, Teilhard and Whitehead, we made it clear how God must be thought of in the light of a modern understanding of reality: God in the world and the world in God, transcendence in immanence.

Thinking that is based on faith will be able therefore to put forward the following statements about God's controlling action in the world:

- *God operates in the world not in the fashion of the finite and relative but as the infinite in the finite and the absolute in the relative.*
- *God does not operate on the world from above or from outside as unmoved mover, but from within as the dynamic, most real reality in the process of the evolution of the world, which he makes possible, directs and completes. He does not operate* above *the world process, but* in *the world process: in, with* and *among human beings and things. He is himself source, center and goal of the world process.*
- *God operates not only at particular, especially important points or gaps in the world process but as the creating and consummating primal support and thus as the world-immanent, world-transcendent Ruler of the world—ubiquitous (omnipresent) and all-powerful (omnipotent)— fully respecting the laws of nature, of which he is himself the source. He is himself the all-embracing and all-controlling meaning and ground of the world process, who can of course be accepted only in faith.*

World or God—this is not an alternative: there is neither the world without God (atheism) nor God without the world (pantheism). There are God and the world, *God and man, but not as two competing finite causalities alongside each other,* with the one gaining what the other loses. If God is really the infinite primal ground, primal support and primal meaning of the world and man, it is clear that God loses nothing when man gains, but that God gains in so far as man gains. And in as much as this God must be understood according to the Bible as absolute freedom, he is not threatened by man's freedom; for God himself makes that freedom possible, authorizes and releases it. And in as much as man is relative freedom, he is not crushed by God's freedom; for man lives wholly and entirely by God's freedom. Thus the situation is very opposite of that in which there are two competing finite causes, with the one gaining at the expense of the other. The more justice is done to God, so much the more may justice be done also to man; and the more justice is done to man, so much the more may justice be done to God.[69]

## Miracles?

What is the situation, however, with God's direct interventions in man's history? What are we to make of the miracle stories—for a start— in the Old Testament: the ten plagues of Egypt, the burning bush that was not burned up, the smoke, the earthquake and thunder at Mount Sinai, the raining down of manna and quails, the collapse of the walls of Jericho at the sound of the trumpets, the sun and the moon standing still, the healing of the sick and raising from the dead, Elijah's fiery chariot taking him up to heaven? And the miracles continue in the New Testament.[70] Must we believe all this? Even though God did not intervene in the evolutionary process, did he not intervene at least in the history of Israel to produce a miracle, in the strict modern sense, in the form of a violation of the laws of nature? Is this not a part of belief in a creator and ruler of the world? Without going into detail, we can suggest only some brief points for consideration: points on which leading exegetes particularly of the Old Testament largely agree.[71] But here, too—as in many similar situations—no one who links belief in God with miracles is to be disturbed in his religious feelings. The sole aim here is to provide a helpful answer to modern man for whom miracles are a hindrance to his belief in God.

If we are to do justice historically and hermeneutically to the accounts of miracles in the Bible, we must be clear about the *fundamental difference between the biblical and the modern understanding of reality*. The people of the Bible were simply not interested in what so greatly interests modern man, the man of the rational and technological age: the laws of nature. People did not think scientifically and consequently did not take miracles to be infringements of the laws of nature, as a breach in the continuity of the causal sequence. In the Old Testament, no distinction was made between marvels that were in accordance with the laws of nature and those that broke them. Any event by which Yahweh revealed his power was regarded as a miracle, as a sign, as Yahweh's great and mighty deed. As primordial cause and creator, God is at work everywhere. People can experience miracles everywhere: from the creation and conservation of the world to its consummation, in small things and in great, in both the history of the nation and in the rescue of the individual from deep distress. . . . That is to say:

- *In biblical usage a "miracle" ("sign") does not by any means imply a violation of the laws of nature by a direct divine intervention, but everything that arouses man's wonder, including the creation and conservation of the world and even man himself. The Bible knows nothing of laws of nature in the modern sense, but "naïvely" attributes natural happenings to the power of God (or to an evil principle).*
- *Historical criticism has shown that many strange events that presented no problem to the faith of people at that time (for example, in connection with the departure from Egypt) can be understood as natural happenings frequently experienced in Palestine and the neighboring countries and that do not involve any suspension of natural causality.*
- *Literary criticism has shown that the miracle stories are not meant to be straightforward records of historical events: that often differing traditions of the same event (for instance, the passage through the sea)[72] are brought together, with the later tradition heightening the miraculous character; that the differences between the various literary genres—*

*for instance, between a hymn, a folk narrative and a court chronicle—
are fundamental and that stories of sun miracles,[73] wonderful feedings
and raisings from the dead by the prophets Elijah and Elisha,[74] or of
Jonah in the fish's stomach,[75] have the character of legend.*

From all this it is clear that miracles recorded in the Bible cannot be
proved historically to be violations of the laws of nature; and if anyone
thinks they can, the burden of proof lies with him. For the Bible in its
miracle stories is not primarily concerned with the event actually narrated
but with the reality behind the narrative, not so much with the form of
the statement as with its content. The miracle stories are meant not to
provide descriptions but to arouse admiration. They are lighthearted popular narratives intended to provoke admiring faith. They are meant to be
signs of God's power: God has done great things to us. These stories are
meant to interpret God's word and to strengthen faith; they are an aid to
the proclamation of Yahweh's power and goodness. Faith in the existence
of miracles is not required; neither is anyone required to believe that this
or that event is actually a miracle. What is expected is faith in God, who
is at work in the person who does such things and for whose operation the
marvelous deeds are significant, that is, "signs." What was important was
not the shaking of the mountain but the message that Moses perceived on
that occasion. The plagues of Egypt were not the important thing but the
testimony to God, who had demonstrated his power. The important thing
was not the crossing of the sea but the message of God, whom the people
had experienced as a God of liberation.

It follows that the miracle stories are not intended to be proofs of God
but *pointers to his action in the world:* pointers, however, that acquire an
unequivocal character only by belief in him (and not in a second, evil
principle). The message of these stories is aimed at man in all his dimensions: space and time, individual and society, body and mind. What do
they proclaim? They proclaim not a God detached from the world and
from history, apathetically leaving the world to its fate, but a God who
gets completely "involved" in what happens in the world, commits himself to it and even to its history. They proclaim a God who does not leave
the world alone, who does not let history become a gloomy, tragic fate for
man but a connection of events perceptible in faith. They tell of a God
who acts in the world in order to give a different direction to the course
of events, so that the world does not remain left to itself but can be
changed in the great hope of a future fulfillment.

The history of the world and of mankind does not proceed according to
a preconceived, fixed plan. In their fine book *Das Spiel,* Manfred Eigen
and Ruthild Winkler brought out in all their variety the various forms of
play and at the same time showed that playing was not an invention of
man. Playing is a natural phenomenon, which guided the course of the

world from the very beginning: even the formation of matter, still more its organization into living structures, and all the rest, right up to man's social behavior. The basic elements of playing—chance and law—determine every kind of happening in the universe; equilibrium, growth and evolution, are the result of chance and law: "All that happens in the world is like a great game in which nothing but the rules are laid down from the outset."[76]

Not only theologians would like to have an answer to the question as to who invented this great, marvelous game, at the very beginning. *Who laid down its rules?* With all due respect for the frontiers between religion and natural science, we have attempted to answer this question, and it would be tempting to expand on the theme of *Deus ludens,* to which the patrologist Hugo Rahner, stimulated by Aquinas and Jan Huizinga's book *Homo ludens,* devoted an impressive brief chapter in the spirit of the Greeks and the Church Fathers. Plato at an early stage had called man a *paignion theou,* "God's toy."[77] But here we must concentrate.

The whole great game is *God's playing with and on the world,* with and on man, which he has himself set in motion and for which he has laid down from the outset nothing but the rules. Without playing its game with God, sustained by him, the world should be able to play its own game; man should not be God's toy, but his free partner in the game.

This means that, in order to confront man as a free partner in this game, God is not forced to present a great spectacular show of "miracles," outside the rules of the game. God's greatness consists not in the fact that he can or must be able to do this, but in the fact that he has no need of it, that he can do without spectacular effects. For God is really not a supermagician, forced to stage public appearances in order to gain self-confidence and recognition. And in his game, is not the cosmos itself in macrocosm and microcosm the most impressive drama that can be concretely imagined: in the last resort—and particularly for the natural scientist—truly admirable, marvelous, wonderful?

But we must avoid oversimplification. If playing is also an aesthetic category, the reality to which it points is by no means to be taken lightheartedly. How often has man been not only a free partner in the game but an involuntary victim of the game; how often has he not played but been played with, played with in an evil way? There is no doubt that evolution and what has been attained by it are by no means perfect, but often fragmentary, provisional, inconsistent. How very much are sickness, feeblemindedness, the often so undignified degeneration of the personality in old age, a part of this regulated game of chance. And the *fundamental law of evolution* in particular—the selection of the strong who survives, at the expense of the weak who perishes—is a *cruel game* that can astound and horrify us and whose pitilessness has led men of such deep faith as –for instance—Reinhold Schneider to become doubters in regard to their Lord.[78] But here, too—the believer can say—God has bound himself by laws that, while justifying everything, are justified in him.

But could not everything be different, perhaps better? Surely, God can do all things. And yet this argument is of very limited use when I move within the framework established by him, the laws of this cosmos. Physically, a supernatural intervention by God in the world would be nonsense. Physically, the consequences would be unthinkable if God were to suspend even for a moment the rules of that system which he himself laid down. But, even so, the question of God and suffering has not been answered. We shall return to it later.

In order to confront man in this game, God can certainly act in a different and at the same time special way. Despite all determination, even man can freely decide and act; we have spoken about this limited but real human freedom.[79] But what is conceded to man cannot be denied to God. God, who is absolute freedom, can also act freely; indeed, he can act without any kind of miracle, without breaking the causal sequence. He can "address" man and in this (not supernatural) sense also "intervene." This is an intervention and action that occurs in secret, that is not objectively available and presentable, that can be perceived as real only in trusting self-commitment. Thus man can be addressed by God in his particular individual and social situation; he can understand with the utmost caution and reserve an idea or decision as a real inspiration of God for his life. Rudolf Bultmann, who firmly dismissed miracles as infringements of the laws of nature in his demythologizing program, expressed the same opinion: "By faith I can understand an idea or a decision as a divine inspiration, without detaching the idea or decision from its link with its psychological justification."[80]

Where do we stand in regard to the question of *providence*? Can the fact of providence be established? In this connection, the story of Moses is particularly helpful. After the Sinai revelation—in the midst of all his difficulties, struggles and doubts—it was not sufficient for him that God had promised to go before him on his way: in order to gain certainty in his distress, he wanted now to see God face to face. But he received the answer: "You cannot see my face, for man cannot see me and live."[81] But Moses was allowed to stand in a narrow cleft of rock, God covering him with his hand as he passed by so that Moses could not see him. Only after passing by did God remove his hand. Moses could then look toward his departing figure, seeing God as it were only from the back.

Is this not also our profoundly human way? I would indeed like to see the one to whom I am committing myself, on whom I am to set my hope. I would like to be able to see my life as ordered, planned, controlled and not as confused, unplanned, chaotic; I would like to see the upper side of the carpet, with its well-formed patterns and structures, and not the underside, with its jumble of threads and knots. I long for Providence to come upon me in the history of the world and of mankind, look impatiently for certainty about my vocation and the way that I have still to go, do not want to relax until I see his guidance in all the windings of my fate, nor to act in the light of mere promises but to see him face to face, in order to know exactly where I stand with him.

But, for us as for Moses, it is always only in retrospect that we can know and understand in faith how what often seemed so difficult was really for our good. Believing, I can perceive in my life, with all its twists and turns, a dispensation, perhaps even a guiding power. Here I do not need to project anything into it; faith permits me to read at least in some important points and lines what was already there. It is only afterward that I can see what had been the deeper meaning from the beginning. I do not see God from the front, but I do not need to see him from the front. I rely on his promise and do not expect any spectacular demonstrations. He is too great for me to be able to make such demands on him. *Deus semper major*—he is the always greater God, who is always greater than our ideas of him and the wishes we might put to him. To look on him is not granted to us at the present time, but it is promised for the future; there is no seeing here and now, but a yearning, as Paul expressed it in the First Letter to the Corinthians: "For our knowledge is imperfect and our prophesying is imperfect; but once perfection comes, all imperfect things will disappear. . . . Now we are seeing a dim reflection in a mirror; but then we shall be seeing face to face. The knowledge that I have now is imperfect; but then I shall know as fully as I am known."[82]

## What comes at the end?

"For now I create new heavens and a new earth." The book of the prophet Isaiah—the third part, written by an unknown prophet of salvation ("Third Isaiah") after the Babylonian Exile—ends with this triumphant promise of a new universe.[83] During the Babylonian Exile, the Second Isaiah had already proclaimed the passing of heaven and earth: "The heavens will vanish like smoke, the earth wear out like a garment, and its inhabitants die like vermin."[84] Even here, however, the promise follows: "But my salvation shall last for ever and my justice have no end."[85] According to the prophetic statements, which could easily be multiplied from both the Old and the New Testaments, what will come at the end of time will be the decline of the world and the ascent of the new world.

Here, too, the question arises for many people: Can these *biblical statements about the end of the world* possibly *be scientifically confirmed* by certain cosmological theories?

In fact, on the basis of the empirically established, still continuing expansion of the universe, it is possible to draw the conclusion that our world is anything but stable, unchangeable or, still less, eternal. It had a beginning and (in all probability) will also one day have an end. An end —but how? This depends on the model of the universe from which we start out. We heard of two models of the universe that are discussed among scientists today.

*The one model of the universe:* Expansion will one day begin to slow down. It will come to a stop and turn into a contraction, so that in a process lasting billions of years the universe will again contract and the galaxies, with their stars, will with increasing rapidity, collapse in on themselves, until possibly—it is said, about eighty billion years after the original big bang—the atoms and the nuclei will disintegrate into their elements and there will be a new big bang. After that—this is pure hypothesis—there might be a new explosion and the beginning of a new world. This is a rough sketch of the theory of a "pulsating" or "oscillating" universe.

*The other model of the universe,* on which there is increasing agreement today: Expansion will go on and on, without turning into contraction. Here, too, the stars will go through their evolution. After a transitory increase in brightness, the sun will be extinguished. The end stages of the evolution of the stars emerge, depending on the size of the individual star, the feebly radiating "white dwarfs" or—after an explosive ejection of matter—"neutron stars" or possibly "black holes." And if, out of the matter transformed inside the stars and then ejected, new stars and generations of stars are to be formed, then in the latter also nuclear processes will occur in which the matter inside the stars will finally be burned to "ashes." Coldness will slowly spread in the cosmos: death, silence, absolute night. . . . Do we not hear, as in the prophet Joel[86] so too in the New Testament, that in the final tribulation the sun will be darkened, the moon will lose its brightness, the stars will fall from heaven and the powers in the heavens will be shaken?[87]

Uncannily exact visions? Nevertheless, hasty theological conclusions about the end of the world must be avoided just as much as hasty conclusions about the beginning of the world. Here, too, theology must correct some things that led to understandable prejudice among natural scientists. We must begin with the assumption that, while biblical protology cannot be a report on events at the beginning, neither can biblical eschatology be a prognosis of events at the end. And as the biblical narratives of God's work of creation were drawn from the milieu of the time, the biblical narratives of God's work at the end were taken from contemporary apocalyptic. Here again it must be remembered with reference to *biblical language:*

*Images are not to be taken literally;* otherwise faith becomes superstition.
*But neither are images to be rejected* merely because they are images; otherwise faith becomes a religion of reason. Images may not be eliminated

or reduced to concepts and ideas, as if man consisted only in reason and not in imagination and emotions, in the capacity for the sensible, symbolic, aesthetic as a whole.

*But images must be correctly understood.* They have their own reason, represent reality with their own logic, are meant to open up the dimension of depth, the coherent meaning of reality. It is necessary therefore to transfer the reality they represent out of the framework of understanding and imagery of that time into that of the present.

Despite the fact that they are called "apocalyptic" or "revealing," these images—which cannot be harmonized with each other—cannot be understood today, at any rate as revelation or information about the chronological sequence of the "last things" at the end of world history. They do not provide a script for the last act of the human tragedy. It is not a question of special divine "revelations." Despite his understandable curiosity, man simply does not learn here the details of what will happen to him or the concrete shape of things to come. Even the picture of the general judgment of all mankind—that is, of billions upon billions of men— remains no more than a picture. Here, too, then, with reference to the *end of the world*, the essentials must be clearly set out, as concisely as possible and in the light of the relevant exegesis:[88]

- *There is neither an unambiguous scientific extrapolation nor an exact prophetic prognosis of the definitive future of humanity and the cosmos.*

- *Neither the "first things" nor the "last things," neither "primordial time" nor the "end time," are accessible to any direct experience. There are no human witnesses. Poetic images and narratives represent what is unsearchable by pure reason, what is hoped for and feared.*

- *The biblical statements about the end of the world have authority not as scientific statements about the end of the universe but as faith's testimony to the way the universe is going, which natural science can neither confirm nor refute. We can therefore give up any attempt to harmonize the biblical statements with the various scientific theories of the end.*

- *The biblical testimony of faith sees the end essentially as the completion of God's work on his creation. Both at the beginning of the world and at its end, there is not nothing, but God.*

- *The promised end may not be equated without more ado with a cosmic disaster and a cessation of mankind's history. The termination of the old, transitory, incomplete or even evil, in the last resort, is not to be understood as a simple ending, but as completion and fulfillment.*

The theologian, then, has no reason to favor either the one or the other scientific model of the universe, but he has reason to make God understandable as originator and finisher of the world and man. Here again the scientist is also a human being who is faced—whether he will admit it or not—with decisions of faith. And it is of no help to his science when certain improbable models of the universe, as we heard from Otto Heckmann, are devised mainly to evade this—admittedly often misunderstood —decision of faith. Steven Weinberg also says: "Some cosmologists are philosophically attracted to the oscillating model, especially because, like the steady-state model, it nicely avoids the problem of Genesis."[89] Neither can he deny that "it is almost irresistible for humans to believe that we have some special relation to the universe, that human life is not just a more-or-less farcical outcome of a chain of accidents reaching back to the first three minutes, but that we were somehow built in from the beginning."[90] It is a pity, then, that Weinberg—seeing human life as "a little above the level of farce" and having "some of the grace of tragedy"—at the end of his book discusses the ideological aspect only in terms of the giants and the cow of the Edda myth. He does not examine the unmythological message of the Bible about the beginning and the end. It is not surprising that the result of these reflections of an otherwise so rational scientist is scarcely rational: "The more the universe seems comprehensible, the more it also seems pointless."[91] There are more rational answers, not only for the beginning of the world but also for the end.

*What point*, then, can it still have for me, with reference to the end of the world, to speak not only—scientifically—of an end bang or of a disintegration of the universe but also, with a perfect right—theologically—of a *God who will bring to perfection the world and man*, as men have acknowledged again and again from time immemorial? I ask this in the midst of a great and sublime but also infinitely cruel history of the cosmos, with its disasters, disasters that have so often struck also human beings. I ask this in the midst of a history of humanity that is so often a history of blood, sweat and tears, a slaughter block of the nations, as Hegel says, a history of saints and gangsters, of exploiters and exploited. The more I reflect on the history of the world and humanity, must I not, again and again, in astonishment and horror, also ask: What is the meaning of the whole? Where is it all going to? Into nothingness? Does this explain anything? Is reason satisfied with this? All that I treasure and love to end in nothingness, people around me, with all their thoughts and great desires, ideas, plans, all their work, life and love, all music, art and learning, all faith and final hope—all for nothing? Is nothingness to be the end also of the world of animals, of plants, of mountains and seas; is nothing the end of the stars, solar systems, galaxies, the whole cosmos? Is all this to come to nothing, to count for nothing? Can anyone blame me for thinking that almost any other alternative seems better, more human, more reasonable, than this single great unreason? What can the alternative be?

The only serious *alternative*—which pure reason, of course, cannot prove to me, because it transcends reason's horizon of experience—is that *the whole is oriented to that last end of ends, which we call God, in fact God the Finisher.* And if I cannot prove him any more than I could prove the Creator God, I can still with good reason affirm him: in that trust which for me is so reasonable, tested, enlightened, in which I have already affirmed his existence. For if the God who exists is truly God, he is God not only for me here and now, not only at the present time, but God also at the end, God for all eternity.

Is all this, however, perhaps merely an empty consolation? Am I perhaps hoping for a final consummation only to compensate for my frequently cruel lot on earth? Am I—as Marx thought—merely adorning my chains with flowers instead of doing what I could as an inhabitant of the world to change what ought to be changed, for the sake of the humanity of man and of society? No. Precisely because we look for the consummation, it is essential to remain faithful to the earth. I ought not simply to await my end and the end of the world, but, in the light of the expected consummation, creatively to undertake my part in the world and in history. Called to freedom, I should cooperate in giving to the inexorable evolution of the cosmos a meaning that only man can give to it. The expectation of the consummation does not condemn me to passivity, but—in virtue of my belief and trust in an end that cannot but be good—demands a fearless, philanthropic activity. This hopeful trust cannot be dismissed either as suspected projection—as we saw[92]—or as illusory consolation. It involves not a flight into the future but—despite all the continually threatening doubt and despair—deeds of hope. It is in view of the future consummation that I can make my contribution to the fight for justice, freedom and peace: against the powers of evil, of injustice, of servitude, of desolation, of unkindness and death. What, then, does it mean to believe in God the Finisher?

Believing in the Finisher of the world does not mean imagining the consummation in the form of the "Last Judgment" as engraved indelibly in the Sistine Chapel by Michelangelo, or as the heaven depicted by Raphael in the Vatican Palace. Here, too, all images cease. Neither does believing in God as Finisher of the world mean deciding for one or the other of the cosmological theories of the end of the universe. The reason is that we are here concerned with what precedes all theories of the universe and even the actual universe itself. Believing in the Finisher of the world means affirming in enlightened trust that the final orientation of the world and man does not remain inexplicable; that the world and man are not hurled pointlessly from nothing into nothing, but that as a whole they are meaningful and valuable, not chaos but cosmos; that in God, their primal ground and primal goal, their originator and designer of their purpose, their Creator and Finisher, they have a first and last security and a lasting home. Nothing forces me to believe this. *I can decide for him in absolute freedom.* When I have decided, this faith changes my position in the world, my attitude to the world; it *establishes my fundamental trust and gives concrete shape to my belief in God.*

This means that, since I believe in God as Finisher, in the last resort I need not judge my life and that of my fellow men, nor do I need to leave the judgment on these to any other human tribunal. On me, my fellow men and the world as a whole, the last word has not yet been spoken. Since I believe in God as Finisher, both my own opaque and ambivalent existence and the profoundly discordant history of humanity as a whole will one day become definitively transparent and the question about the meaning of history one day be definitively answered. Or am I, with Marx, to believe in the kingdom of freedom only here on earth or with Nietzsche in the eternal recurrence of what is always the same? Or am I, finally, to take up the attitude of a pessimistic skeptic and, with Jakob Burckhardt, to contemplate history in stoic-Epicurean aloofness, or in a culture-critical spirit deplore, with Oswald Spengler, not only the decline of the West but also that of my own existence?

No. Believing in God as Finisher of the world means coolly and realistically—and even more, without succumbing to the violent benefactors of the people—to work for a better future, a better society, in peace, freedom and justice, and at the same time to know without illusions that this can always only be sought but never completely realized by man. Believing in God as Finisher of the world means to know that this world is not the ultimate reality, that conditions will not remain the same forever, that all existing things—including religious and ecclesiastical traditions, institutions, authorities—have a provisional character, that the division into classes and races, rich and poor, rulers and ruled, is temporary, that the world is changing and changeable. Believing in God the Finisher of the world, then, means continually giving fresh meaning to my life and the life of others in virtue of the hope that my life will reach fullness of meaning, that human history will become completely transparent, the individual and human society be truly fulfilled, only in the encounter with the evident ultimate reality of God. There can be a true consummation and a true happiness of mankind only when not merely the last generation, but all men, even those who suffered and bled in the past, come to share in it. Not a kingdom of man, but only the kingdom of God, is the kingdom of perfection, the kingdom of fulfilled justice, of unbroken love, of liberated freedom, of universal peace, of eternal life. *Credo in vitam venturi saeculi.*

## God's law and human rights

"Honour your father and mother, you shall not kill, you shall not commit adultery, you shall not steal, you shall not bear false witness, you shall not covet your neighbour's house, your neighbour's wife, or anything that is his." These are—slightly abbreviated[93]—the directives in regard to our fellow men, based on the belief in one God, as Israel—according to the Sinai tradition—had received them on the way through the desert in a mighty revelation of God on Mount Sinai, when Yahweh descended "in the form of fire":[94] the "ten commandments," as they are generally known, the "ten sayings" or "ten words," as they are called in the Book of Deuteronomy[95] and there quoted in a slightly different form.

We are not betraying any secrets now when we say that *the ten commandments have a history*. The ethical directives of the Old Testament did not fall from heaven any more than the narratives about the beginning and end of the world. Old Testament study[96] has largely proved this not only for the later ethos of the prophets and the even later—very secular—ethos of the wisdom literature but also and particularly for the early ethos of the Mosaic Law. For the whole long Sinai history[97] contains some very complex material by way of divine ordinances from very diverse periods of time. And the ten commandments also, presumably inserted in this precise form as the heart of the Sinai history and very diversely dated by various exegetes from Moses' time (thirteenth century B.C.) up to the sixth century B.C., have a long prehistory. The directives of the "second tablet," for interpersonal relationships, go back in any case to the moral and legal traditions of pre-Israelitic, seminomadic customs; they have numerous counterparts in the Near East. It was a long time before these norms were put into practice, before they were sharpened and proved, before they became so universal in content and form that they could be regarded as an adequate expression of the will of Yahweh. This does not exclude the possibility that a series of easily remembered basic directives for the Yahweh people was brought by Moses' troop from the desert and bequeathed to Israel as a whole.[98]

But, whatever the origin of the ten commandments may have been, these fundamental minimal requirements for human life together had their origin before the Yahweh faith and—compared with the ethos of the nations between Egypt and Mesopotamia—are not specifically Israelitic. What, then, is *specifically Israelitic?* The specifically Israelitic element is that *these requirements are put under the authority of the God of the covenant*, to whom the duties of the "first tablet," especially the fundamental commitment to Yahweh alone to the exclusion of other deities, are related.

What are the consequences for the ethos prevailing up to that time? The same norms now acquire a different character. Like other sets of precepts, so far as they were compatible with the Yahweh faith, they summarize, with the greatest possible brevity, Yahweh's will, Yahweh's claims on men. They have now acquired a different authority. It is now Yahweh himself who uses his commandments to supervise man's basic human existence, as secured in the "second tablet," with reference to respect for parents, protection of life, of marriage, of property, of one's neighbor's honor. Hence:

● *The peculiarity of Old Testament morality consists not in the fact that new ethical norms had been found but in the fact that traditional directives were placed under the legitimizing and protecting authority of the one true God and his covenant.*

● *For Israel now, the norms emerging on the basis of human experience are not part of nonbinding human law or a merely general law of God, but the categorical requirements of the one true God of the Fathers known from history.*

● *God's law alone guarantees the absolute validity of human rights: no human rights without God's law, no law of God without human rights. God's law aims at the protection of human rights, at social behavior; conversely, human rights are rooted in God's law.*

● *The acceptance of the existing ethos into the new relationship with God involves a new motivation, dynamism and transparency of morality.*

The consequences of the religious integration of the ten commandments into the idea of the covenant with God are inestimable:[99]

*New motivation of morality:* Gratitude, love, longer life, assured freedom, become the decisive motives.

*New dynamism of morality:* The existing norms are perfected and corrected—even though not consistently in all areas (for instance, marriage and the position of women)—in the light precisely of this God and his covenant. Together with older, pre-Israelitic norms, new, extra-Israelitic norms are adapted—increasingly but, again, not always completely—in the new relationship to God; new moral and legal norms are developed, and yet a significant concentration and uniformity are achieved. From being minimal ethical requirements, the "ten words" now become terse statements of God's will, absolutely binding, significant in principle and representative for wider areas.

*New transparency of morality:* The precepts and prohibitions—unrenounceable postulates of humanity—now become in a new way transparently religious. Yahweh himself appears as advocate for humanity, and the fulfillment of the law becomes an expression of faith in him as man's covenant partner.

The religious foundation now provided for ethics thus presupposes the historical development of ethical norms, but at the same time sets these in motion. In principle, then, *three legitimate forms of ethics* can be distinguished:

*autonomous ethics,* which has its basis in *fundamental trust* but is not able or is not meant adequately to justify the absoluteness of norms;[100]

*theologically justified autonomous ethics,* which has its basis in *general*

*trust in God* and in this light is able adequately to justify the absoluteness of its norms;[101]
*theologically justified autonomous ethics given concrete historical shape,* which has its basis in the *biblical* faith in God and is able to give concrete historical shape to its absolute norms.

*What point,* then, can it have, even in the face of all relativity, to commit myself to the *historical-concrete ethos of the Bible?* Why not in fact renounce, with Einstein and many others, the concrete religious foundation of ethics? Admittedly, from an empirical, rational standpoint, there are evidently several ways and not merely one of living a life of human dignity that is right and good, in accordance with conscience. The obligations resulting from the demands of reality can be very diversely articulated and human necessities and urgencies very diversely defined. But is it not just this which creates the difficulty: the far too great generality, indeterminateness and noncommittal character of ethical norms?

It is obviously not at all easy to discern what is truly human, humane. And if we did not at least tacitly orient ourselves to the Judeo-Christian standards of value, it would be still more difficult to justify even merely the basic human rights. Why in fact should not tyrannizing and domineering be truly human, as the superman morality of all times—and quite specially that of Nazism—has maintained? Or why should not pleasure-seeking and consuming be truly human, as the more or less sophisticated hedonism of all times—and that of the affluent society in particular—has maintained? And is not the prevailing morality mostly the morality of the rulers, as Marx and Marxism bring out in their criticism of the morality of a class society?

In this respect, the prophets of the Old Testament are powerful allies of critics of society, from Marx and Engels to Bloch and many religious socialists. As against the powerful in their own times, they stood for God's law—but for God's law for the sake of man's rights. They protected the oppressed against exploitation, the helpless against despotism, the ignorant from being swindled. They accused both kings and priests, both judges and landowners; they both criticized their own liturgy of sacrifice and opposed alien cults.

Since rights and norms are so difficult to justify purely rationally, traditions and authorities are readily invoked for the justification of ethics. Even with such basic questions as love and hate: it is possible to ask how we can really justify loving and not hating. Considered scientifically (and often also economically), is hatred simply worse than love? Horkheimer was right: "There is no logically conclusive reason to show why I should not hate as long as this does not put me at a disadvantage in social life."[102] Why should war not be as good or as bad as peace, freedom as good or as bad as oppression? "For how is it possible to prove exactly that I should not hate if I feel like doing so? Positivism cannot find any authority transcending men to distinguish between helpfulness and greed, kindness and cruelty, avarice and selflessness. Logic, too, remains dumb; it allows no priority to moral conviction."[103]

It must now be clear that, just as the understanding of God established by way of rational reflection in the light of the reality of this world and of man remains *ambivalent,* so, *too, do the norms deduced rationally and abstractly from this reality.* They, too, are nowhere immediately evident and given objective expression. Hence they remain ambiguous and, *in the last resort, undefined* both for each individual and for the community, for behavior and action in concrete situations. It is particularly difficult to perceive how far in their thoroughgoing relativity anything truly absolute can find expression.

In view therefore of the nonevidence, uncertainty, indeterminateness of the norms and hence of the scarcely surprising pluralism of ethics, it might be asked: Would not too much be required of man if each in isolation had to find norms for himself? Where would we stand if there had not always been before us those who tested, lived through and experienced in a variety of ways the meaning, the concrete function and the human value of these norms? If the child had not been *told* again and again what he had to do, what is truly human? Where would the family, the social group, even the state, be if it were not possible to *say*—with all possible means and media—what we ought to do, by what we must absolutely abide, which is the right, the good, the truly human way?

Even the most critical and independent person does not orient himself merely to the norms that he alone has rationally discovered and justified. I, too, never start out from zero. I live in a community, within a tradition. The knowledge of the good, its norms, models, signs, was also brought home to me socially. Would I not therefore do well to make use, for my individual and social behavior, of the experiences and maxims of a community, of the great human and religious traditions, of the treasury of experience of my ancestors, in order to throw light on my own problems, the questions of the organization of my own life, or norms and motivations?

Certainly I shall never be able to get away from my personal responsibility for my conduct and for my life's maxims. But, for that very reason, it is extraordinarily important for me to decide *who* is to tell me anything, who is *to be allowed to tell me what is essential.* And after all that has been said, is it not rationally justifiable for me to let what is ultimately decisive for practical action to be told me *by the God of the Fathers,* by *the God of the Bible?*

I would have liked to finish here, too, with a credo. But the Church's Credo says nothing about its ethos. Anyway, we do not believe in an ethos. Obviously the ethos should follow from faith. Belief in God is an eminently practical affair.

We have, then, discussed sufficiently the ethical factor of belief in God, in so far as it is determined in particular in the light of the Old Testament belief in God. For the epistemological factor, which we have likewise discussed in other chapters,[104] we may refer to biblical and especially Old Testament hermeneutics.[105] On the other hand, after all that we have heard, a summary comparison between the God of the philosophers and the God of the Fathers is now imperative.

## God of the philosophers—God of the Bible

We are now sufficiently prepared to attempt a fundamental answer to that question with which—as we saw—the modern age has been pre-occupied at least since Descartes and Pascal, but which has also continually created difficulties from patristic times and the Middle Ages: "The God of the philosophers and scholars" *or* "the God of Abraham, Isaac and Jacob, the God of the Fathers"? If we could answer this question, a possible answer might well be suggested to Heidegger's question about the more divine God. Basing ourselves therefore on all that has been worked out up to the present, we shall attempt cautiously to formulate a summary answer by asking three times in three stages in the light of the God of the philosophers about the God of the Bible, this time bringing the New Testament also into the discussion.

a. If, in the light of the God of the philosophers, we ask in regard to the God of the Bible whether God is not also for the Bible the *primal ground* of all reality, the answer runs:

- *Yes. God is the primal ground of reality, in which the world, man and all things have their ground. He is not another.*
- *On the other hand, No. God is the wholly Other. God is not a primordial nature principle, he is not a cosmic ground, not an abstract causality of the universe. Still less is he a dark abyss.*
- *More exactly, God is the Creator of the world and man, transcendently founding and immanently determining everything. That is,*
  *The biblical God is not a God of solitude, but a God of partnership, of the covenant: a God who acts in the space-time of human history, who makes himself known in world events, who shows himself in a human way, makes possible encounter, association, intercourse with him—a God of historical revelation.*

b. If, in the light of the God of the philosophers, we ask in regard to the God of the Bible whether God is not also for the Bible the *primal support* of all reality, the answer runs:

- *Yes. God is the primal support of reality, in which the world and man and all things have their support. He is not another.*

- *On the other hand, No. God is the wholly Other. God is not an anonymous primordial power; he is not a cosmic law, not an abstract normativity of the universe. Still less is he a delusive, sham support.*
- *More exactly, God is the* Ruler *of the world and man, transcendentally determining and immanently supporting everything. I.e.,*
  The biblical God is not a God who keeps out of everything, remaining rigidly aloof in a heavenly transcendence, untouched by the suffering of the world and of man, but a God who takes an active part and is secretly involved in their dark history—a God initiating reconciliation.

c. If, in the light of the God of the philosophers, we ask in regard to the God of the Bible whether God is not also for the Bible the *primal goal* of all reality, the answer runs:

- *Yes. God is the primal goal of reality, in which the world, man and all things have their goal. He is not another.*
- *On the other hand, No. God is the wholly Other. God is not merely an outwardly attracting force, he is not a cosmic power, not an abstract finality of the universe. Still less is he a frustrating final end.*
- *More exactly, God is the* Finisher *of the world and man, transcendentally sustaining and immanently fulfilling everything. I.e.,*
  The biblical God is not a God without feeling, incapable of suffering, apathetic in regard to the vast suffering of the world and man, but a sym-pathetic, com-passionate God, who, in the future, changing everything, by liberation from sin, suffering and death, leads to infinite justice, to unbroken peace and to eternal life—a God of final redemption.

All this could be illustrated in a variety of ways. In this respect, the biblical material is almost inexhaustible. We could see—for example—how it is confirmed in the prophetical proclamation where Yahweh appears—as we saw—not only as liberator from Egypt, escort through the desert and donor of the land but also as father, shepherd, king, as lover and spouse of his people—all metaphors for the reality under consideration here. And again, all this could be confirmed by the *priestly tradition,* by the *wisdom teachings* of the Hellenistic period and finally by the *eschatological expectation* of the apocalyptic literature of the period before Christ's birth.[106]

But it would also be possible to reflect quite differently on the *predicates of God* or divine attributes, so important for man's relationship to God, in order to show that the Bible, although it confirms the predicates deduced in the spirit of Greek metaphysics by a process of inference from the existing world, also denies them in a restrictive sense, in order finally concretely to surpass them. We might perhaps reflect that, according to Scripture, God's "eternity" is certainly not to be understood as involvement in time and transience, but neither is it a Platonic timelessness: it is a powerful, active simultaneity with all times. And if his "immutability" is certainly not incompleteness and superficiality, neither is it a rigid, natural, dead immobility, but must be understood as essential fidelity to himself in all his active vitality. In the same way, it would be possible to speak of God's ubiquity, omnipotence, spirituality, justice, goodness, incomprehensibility. But also of the negatively qualified attributes: of "jealousy," for instance, that is not the product of envy and fear but the expression of his uniqueness, which is incompatible with other deities existing alongside him; the consequence of his will, which—for man's well-being—absolutely insists on his directives and consequently displays —as the expression of his hostility to evil—hatred, horror, revenge, but also repentance and forgiveness.

Should we, then, be put off by all the *anthropomorphisms,*[107] the human forms in which God is presented in the Bible? They are not intended simply to humanize God, but to bring him close to men as the living God. Philosophically abstract definitions of the divine nature leave us cold. The divine, in all its passionate vitality, must enter into consciousness so that a person may encounter God as intensively and concretely as he encounters another human being: a face that lights up for us, a hand that guides us. What more noble, what greater, deeper metaphors, ciphers, symbols, ideas, concepts than the human has man at his disposal in order to reach out to God? The biblical God is wholly and entirely essentially a *God with a human face.*

We have been reflecting once more, then, on the God of the Bible without adopting a biblicist attitude and ignoring the conclusions of philosophy. And we have reflected again on the God of the philosophers without stopping at metaphysics:

- *It proved to be an overhasty reaction simply to dissociate the God of the philosophers from the God of the Bible, as "dialectical theology" attempted to do.*
- *It proved to be superficial simply to harmonize the God of the philosophers and the God of the Bible, as natural theology did.*
- *The important thing was and is to see the relationship in a truly dialectical way. In the God of the Bible, the God of the philosophers is in the best, threefold sense of the Hegelian term* "sublated"\*—at one and the same time affirmed, negated and transcended.

*This God is the more divine God,* before whom modern man, now grown so critical—without ever having to give up his reason—"can pray and offer sacrifice, again fall on his knees in awe and sing and dance before him."

---

\* *aufgehoben.*

# III. The God of Jesus Christ

"Everything the Father has is mine," says Jesus, according to John's Gospel.[1] Is it really true, as Ernst Bloch thinks, that in Christianity the Son of man, Jesus, as Son of God, has taken the place of God, so that in the end nothing remains of God himself? This would mean that Christianity prepared the way for atheism, in its idea of God becoming man, of *Deus homo factus est*. As Bloch puts it: "*Deus homo factus est*, this final biblical phase of the biblical Exodus, gave a new appearance to the apocalyptic day, Yahweh's day of triumph at the end of time, changing the face of Yahweh and revealing a wholly different countenance: ours, the face of the son of man."[2] In the enigmatic term "son of man" and its implications—as Bloch continues, wholly in the spirit of Feuerbach—"the good treasures, which had been squandered on a hypostatized Father-heaven, were invested in a very hermetic *humanum*." Thus the "Day of Yahweh," at the end of time, became a day "of the son of man, who is without Yahweh, utterly *a-kyrios*, that is, at the same time, *a-theos*, in the true sense of the *Cur deus homo*."[3] In the end, then, it comes about, as Bloch had already said in *Das Prinzip Hoffnung*, "that no God remains on high, since no one anyway is or ever was there."[4] This is Bloch's thesis of the *christologically determined "atheism in Christianity,"* which in the 1960s was likewise defended by individual "death of God" theologians: God is dead, long live Jesus, the Son of man; yes, long live Man!

It is of course legitimate to accuse Bloch of misunderstandings, wrong interpretations and making up conclusions, in short of a "wild exegesis,"[5] in his remarks. But the danger of a popular piety that identifies Christ completely with God here becomes as obvious as that of a high dogmatic christology that has not taken enough precautions in this respect. This criticism must anyway be taken seriously as a warning sign: to that extent, not only devout Jews but also Christians could agree with Bloch, the atheist of Jewish provenance.

## 1. God as Father

Bloch's thesis on atheism in Christianity is dependent on a view of the Old Testament that was widely propagated during the time between the wars[6] and that gives a somewhat gloomy picture of the Yahwistic prehistory.[7] Bloch's opinion—always very forcefully stated—that in the oldest strata of the Old Testament, Yahweh had been a demon hostile to man and therefore opposed by man, only subsequently being turned into a moral God, is one that scarcely any exegete accepts today. Nevertheless this aspect has perhaps been too little considered in recent times. But, as early as 1924, the Protestant Tübingen exegete Paul Volz wrote very decidedly about "the demonic in Yahweh," an aspect that is apologetically minimized by so distinguished an Old Testament scholar as Walter Eichrodt,[8] and by many others completely suppressed.

Just fifty years later, a Tübingen Catholic exegete, Herbert Haag, who deserves great credit for his theological struggle against an un-Christian belief in demons, wrote very discriminatingly but clearly about the "wreckage of environmental belief in demons," which could be integrated only with difficulty into the Yahweh faith: "This integration could occasionally come about by revaluing a demon and turning him into an 'angel' or even into Yahweh himself. The process of integration can be observed especially in the postexilic period, from which we can conclude that the other measures had not proved effective enough."[9] And with reference to the work of Volz, Haag writes: "Anyway, Yahweh undertook not merely the functions of demonic beings but also those of the mischief-making gods of the underworld, such as the Egyptian Seth, the Babylonian pestilence gods Erra and Nergal, the Canaanite Resheph."[10]

At this juncture a confrontation between the Old and the New Testaments is important.


## A tyrannical God?

Is it, then, so obvious that the same holy God of Israel and God of liberation in the ancient sagas

calls upon Abraham to sacrifice his son and holds back the knife only at the very last moment;[11]

attacks Jacob at the ford, wrestles with him throughout the night and leaves him behind wounded;[12]

in the Exodus history encounters man as a god of pestilence, a bloodthirsty god and a destroying angel,[13] even attacks Moses as a bloodthirsty demon and seeks to kill him[14] and later, after the dancing around the golden calf, has three thousand men massacred;[15]

in his own words, is benevolent to whom he will and shows mercy to whom he will;[16]

is the cause of both the unintended deathblow, and the plague striking the whole country;[17]

at the time of the judges meets no opposition when he has Jephthah sacrifice his daughter for Yahweh;[18]

at the time of the kings is responsible for Saul's unfair suspicion of David and for David's unjustified census involving punishment later;[19]
in the ninth century has four hundred prophets of Baal killed in his name by Elijah and brings the Omri dynasty to a fall by Elisha in a bloody revolution;[20]
even in the eighth century, according to the prophet Amos, is responsible for all man's misfortunes?[21]

Certainly it can be said that these narratives are partially reproducing older traditions, which no longer correspond to what the editors want to say. Nevertheless all this has been written and should not be suppressed or minimized. If we cannot talk here simply of an arbitrary God and despot, must we not at least up to a point speak of a God with arbitrary, despotic, *demonic features*—in this respect not unlike the pagan gods in their capriciousness? It can of course be said that the prophet Hosea condemned the bloody revolution that overthrew the Omri dynasty,[22] that the prophets from the eighth century onward no longer use force and there is no further report of human sacrifices. God keeps to his law, punishes offenses and rewards obedience to the law, does not ruthlessly demand penance and does not always insist on payment of the penalty to the very end.

And yet these features of Yahweh have been reflected both in the Israelitic ethos—for instance, of the holy war and the treatment of enemies—and in the cruel, imprecatory psalms. And even the *God of the law* possesses features that, if they are no longer expressions of despotic arbitrariness and a cruel demonic nature, can be understood as a heightening of earthly authority and as a theocracy of an oppressive, tyrannical God. Undoubtedly—and this must be repeated against overhasty negative judgments on the part of Christians—the law of Israel must be understood as expression of the grace and benevolence of the covenant God. For the foundation of Israel's faith is originally not the law but God's covenant with his people. The law exists for the sake of the covenant with God; it is the grace of the God of the covenant. But the casuistic laws of communal life and the cultic directives were increasingly equated with the apodictic law of God, as crystallized in the decalogue, and regarded as equally decisive for the understanding of God. Thus it came about, after the Babylonian exile, at the reorganization of the community by Ezra (about 400 B.C.), that the now rigid law became the basis of the understanding of God and an autonomous authority: the norm for membership of the people of God, for being pleasing to God,[23] for human well-being.[24] The law, giving life to the devout, becomes the object of veneration and love and is celebrated in hymnic form in the psalms.[25] Nothing was added to it or changed; it was only interpreted as it stood. Even what was no longer understood had to be maintained; and what had been intended for different situations had to make do for new questions.[26]

It can scarcely be disputed, then, that the *legalism* (nomism) characteristic of early Judaism at the time of Jesus had been established, even though often criticized, in the Old Testament. The law as written down in its full extent in the Pentateuch and elucidated in detail in the light of tradition by the scribes was now regarded as exclusively the revealed will of God, to be observed unconditionally right down to the last regulation for the Sabbath, food, purity, prayer and worship. It was taken for granted that the law could be fulfilled, and it not only regulated the whole course of the day but also involved separation from non-Jews in the daily life of the community.

These legal regulations developed in tradition were later recorded in Mishnah and Talmud and characterize up to the present time orthodox Judaism, which follows the law literally, rejects all innovations and adaptations of conservative and still more of liberal Jews and in the modern industrial, democratic state of Israel fights for the reintroduction of the old theocracy. A religious minority certainly, but—exercising considerable influence through the exclusively orthodox state synagogue and through political parties—it attempts in the Jewish state even today to bring both private and public life exclusively under the law, the Torah. In Israel today, there are increasingly violent struggles about the observance of the Sabbath rest (stones thrown and roads closed to cars), food regulations (against pork, for kosher cooking in the army, in hospitals and in prisons), marriage laws (on divorce, the position of women), positions of authority for the scribes (chief rabbinate), the question of "Who is a Jew?" (naturalization, mixed marriages, children of mixed marriages). All this recalls only too clearly the discussions between Jesus himself and his contemporaries. And at that time as at the present, one and the same problem was involved: that of the understanding of God himself.

If, however, *Jesus* preached as living and close this one and sole God, well known from Israel's history, as he had spoken in the experiences of men and had been addressed in their answers and questions, this God with the human face; if, then, he had merely grasped Israel's understanding of God with special purity, consistency and urgency, why was there a conflict?

There is no doubt that *Jesus saw God differently.* Not, of course, in the sense that he proclaimed a bourgeois, inoffensive, unassuming God, as we all too readily create him in our own image: a God without unpleasant features and uncomfortable demands, who would be content merely with the recognition of his existence; who satisfies our religious needs fairly and squarely and yet does not bind us to anything; who takes us just as we are and does not require us to be converted; who understands everything and pardons everything. . . . No. A God of this kind, who would be a deity of our own making, is not the God that Jesus proclaimed. In this sense, he did not want to proclaim a new God, but wholly and entirely the God of Israel, the Creator and Judge of the world. Like many people of his own time, he, too, saw the turning point of the world and the judgment of the world coming, the new heaven and the new earth, the world of God, which replaces the present world abandoned to evil: the kingdom of God. And like John, his precursor, whose baptism he had accepted, Jesus also preached repentance in view of the coming kingdom of God. His preaching on God's judgment must not be eliminated for the sake of a preaching of God's grace and love: too many passages refer to the judgment. The situation is serious: it is possible to miss God's kingdom. And yet, for Jesus, the judgment is differently evaluated. Where the Baptist spoke of anger and rejection, Jesus' message is one of salvation and mercy. Unlike the gloomy threat of judgment by the ascetic John, his message from the very beginning is a friendly, joyous message of the goodness of the approaching God and of his kingdom of justice, of joy and peace. Instead of tidings of menace, we have tidings of joy: the kingdom of God is not primarily judgment, but grace for all.

When Jesus speaks of God and when he acts in God's name, he makes clear what was vague in the Old Testament, *he makes unambiguous what there seemed ambiguous*. His message of the irrevocable closeness of God and his kingdom of course does not imply any new revelations of his nature, any new concept of God. Jesus does not reflect at all on God's innermost nature; he is not interested in metaphysical speculations on God as he is in himself. He speaks of God in parables, not speculating, not arguing, but telling a story. For him, God is the concrete partner of his believing trust and devout obedience. For this one God, he declares himself; it is this one God who is to be loved by man with his whole heart. He insists on love of God together with love of neighbor, which is rooted in it —already required in the Old Testament—as the all-embracing main commandment.

- *This God of Jesus has no despotic, demoniacal features. God is unambiguously good, never demoniacally evil; he loves men and is never indifferent.*

Jesus calls him merciful, good, alone good. But these attributes, for him, are important not as objective predicates but as active qualities for man and the world: what God is, not in himself or for himself but for man and the world, how he acts on man and the world. They are predicates not of his nature "in itself" but of his relationship to us. For it is only in God's activity that his reality is revealed: in his action on man and the world, so that whenever there is talk of God there must also be talk of man.

In this respect, it is important to note that, for Jesus, God never operates merely in a "supernatural" sphere. He is at work in the midst of the world and in this way provides for man's great and small world, rendering superfluous any anxiety about one's own needs. At the same time, Jesus does not draw conclusions by inference from the world to God. Instead, he sees the whole world in the light of God: a great symbol that points at once to the Creator and to the Finisher of the world. Thus the world is understood—as it could be understood at that time—without causality or a concept of nature and yet in such a way that it is possible to live in it in practice: to live in it as God's good world but spoiled by man. This God, then, is in his great range both here *and* hereafter, near *and* distant, intramundane *and* supramundane, present *and* future. God is oriented to the world: there is not a God without the world. And the world is wholly related to God: there is not a world without God.

## God—masculine?

Even today, it is often said that Jesus was the first to proclaim God *as the Father* and men as his children. But the history of religion has shown that God can be called "father" in a great variety of religions. In Israel's vicinity, the Greeks had learned from Homer's epics that Zeus, son of Chronos, was the father of the family of gods; in stoic philosophy, the Deity was regarded in cosmological terms as father of the reason-permeated cosmos and of human beings endowed with reason, related to him and cared for by him.

But the very fact that God can be called "father" in the pagan religions should make us cautious about using this title. And this particularly in an age of women's emancipation, which has, again, made us sharply aware of the problems involved. There is no doubt that the conception of God as Father very often had to serve as a religious justification of a sociological paternalism at the expense of women and especially as a means of permanently suppressing the feminine element in the Church. For this father ideology is, again, the basis of an exclusively male Son Christology, which in turn is misused—as in one of the more recent Roman Catholic documents[27]—with the aid of abstruse biblical arguments for continuing to refuse ordination to women.[28]

In general, the gods in the history of religion appear as sexually differentiated, although at the very beginning there might have been bisexual or sexually neutral beings and, later, bisexual features continued to be displayed. But is it not striking that in the matriarchal cultures, in place of the Father God there is the "Great Mother," out of whose fertile womb all things and beings emerged and into which they return? This throws a light on the historical relativity of a masculine deity. From a historical standpoint, it is quite possible—even though now, as formerly, disputed among historians—that matriarchy is older than patriarchy. In that case, the cult of the mother deity—which exercised some influence, for instance, in Asia Minor on the cult of Mary—would also have preceded chronologically that of the Father God.

In the Old Testament also, the designation of "father" for God is not determined solely by the uniqueness of Yahweh. It appears also to be sociologically conditioned, bearing the imprint of a male-oriented society. But, however the historical questions may be decided, *God is certainly not simply male.* Even in the Old Testament, with the prophets, God displays also feminine, maternal features. And it is this very thing that must be seen more clearly from the modern standpoint, for the sake of the urgently needed revaluation of women in the churches; for Christianity—and even more, the other world religions—is a man's religion that, however, in practice is largely sustained by women. Consequently one thing must never be forgotten:

- *The designation of "father" for God is misunderstood if it is taken as the opposite of "mother" instead of symbolically (analogically). "Father" is a patriarchal symbol—but also with matriarchal traits—for a transhuman, transsexual, absolutely last/absolutely first reality.*

God, then, is not masculine and must not be seen through the screen of the masculine-paternal, as an all-too-masculine theology did. The feminine-maternal element must also be recognized in him.

It is helpful in this reflection to note that God, even in the Old Testament, is never regarded, like Zeus, as the physical father of gods, demigods and heroes. Nor, of course, is he ever simply called the father of all men. For:

Yahweh is the Father of the people of Israel, which is called God's firstborn son.[29]

Yahweh is in particular the father of the king of Israel, who is regarded as son of God par excellence, a fact that is important for the later understanding of Jesus' title of "Son of God." The verse of the psalm, later applied to Jesus, "You are my son, today I have become your father,"[30] does not mean a miraculous procreation, but the installation of the king taking over his rights as son.[31]

Yahweh in later Judaism is promised also as father of the devout individual[32] and of the chosen people of the end time.[33]

Everywhere here—without any sexual implications and without religious paternalism—the *positive aspects of the father symbol,* which cannot be renounced even today, find expression. It means power and at the same time closeness, protection as much as solicitude, both dependence and security.

### Father of the lost

Jesus never relates the fatherhood of God to the people as such. Even for John the Baptist, membership in the chosen people no longer represents any guarantee of salvation. But Jesus relates fatherhood—and in this he differs from the Baptist—also to the wicked and unrighteous and in this light justifies love of enemies, which was so typical for him.[34] This is the striking thing.

Obviously, even before his death on the cross, Jesus was aware of all the evil in the world, all the injustice, wickedness, cruelty, all the suffering, all the pain, all the grief. But, in the face of all the evil, Jesus did not give any philosophical or theological justification of God, any theodicy. His answer has a practical orientation; it points to God as Father:

God as the Father who in his active providence and solicitude looks after every sparrow and every hair,[35] who knows our needs before we ask him,[36] makes our worries seem superfluous;[37]

God as the Father who knows about everything in this far from perfect world and without whom nothing happens, whom man can absolutely trust and on whom he can completely rely even in suffering, injustice, sin and death.

This, then, is Jesus' *practical answer to the question of theodicy*, about life's riddles, suffering, injustice, death in the world. This is not a God at an ominous, transcendent distance, but close in incomprehensible goodness; he is a God who does not make empty promises about the hereafter or minimize the present darkness, futility and meaninglessness. Instead, in darkness, futility and meaninglessness, he invites us to the venture of hope. In regard to him, man does not have to protect his freedom. God's rule and man's activity are not mutually exclusive. The problem—much discussed by theologians—of the "cooperation" (*concursus*) of divine predestination and human freedom of choice, of the divine and the human will, is obviously no problem for Jesus.[38] Nor—incidentally—was it a problem for his contemporaries. Where precisely did the problem lie?

It may be helpful to introduce the point of conflict with the well-known parable of Jesus that often enough is misunderstood as innocuous instead of being taken seriously in its novelty: the parable in which the main figure is not really the son, but the father. For it is the father who lets his son go freely, neither chasing nor following him. It is the father who sees him returning from exile before he is seen by the son, who runs toward him, interrupts his confession of guilt and accepts him without demanding an explanation, without a period of probation, without preliminary conditions. It is the father who then has a great feast prepared—to the scandal of the upright son who remained at home.[39]

Here we see exactly what this "friend of tax collectors and sinners"—who thought he had to seek and to save the lost and the disreputable—expressed also in other parables. For he speaks of God as the woman (!) or the shepherd, rejoicing at finding what had been lost, as the magnanimous king, the generous lender, the gracious judge. He committed himself also quite practically to moral failures, irreligious and immoral people, gave them preferential treatment and assured them—to the general scandal—of forgiveness of their sins on the spot.

- *Jesus represents God expressly as father of the "prodigal son" and indeed as father of the lost.*
- *The true God of Jesus is the God of Israel . . . freshly understood.*

This God—and Bloch has brought out the differences here—is not the theocratic God of despotism or of law. He is a God who is evidently more than that omniscient being, dictating and centrally directing everything from above, who strives relentlessly to achieve his plans, even by "holy wars" on a great or small scale and by the eternal damnation of his opponents. This God is also more than the supreme guarantor of a law to be accepted without question—even though it can perhaps be adroitly manipulated. Today this means that this Father God is not the kind of God feared by Marx, Nietzsche and Freud, terrifying man from childhood onward into fears and feelings of guilt, continually moralizingly pursuing him: a God who is in fact only the projection of instilled fears, of human domination, lust for power, arrogance and vindictiveness. Such a God can actually give the impression of being only a "corruption" of God.[40] No, this Father God will not be a tyrannical god who might serve as an excuse —if only indirectly—for the representatives of totalitarian systems, whether pious/ecclesiastical or impious/atheistic, who attempt to take his place and to exercise his sovereign rights: they then become holy or unholy gods of orthodox teaching and absolute discipline, of law and order, of dictatorship and planning, contemptuous of human beings.

*He is not, then, the all-too-masculine God of despotism or law.* He is not a God created in the image of kings and tyrants, of hierarchs and schoolmasters. But he is the God of love—we must not make light of that familiar word—who commits himself unreservedly to men, to their needs and hopes:

who does not demand but gives, does not oppress but raises up, does not wound but heals;

who spares those who impugn his holy law and consequently himself, who forgives instead of condemning, liberates instead of punishing, leaves grace to rule instead of law;

who rejoices at the return of a single unrighteous person more than over ninety-nine righteous, who prefers the prodigal son to the one who stayed at home, the tax collector to the Pharisee, the heretic to the orthodox, the prostitutes and adulterers to their judges, the lawbreakers and outlaws to the guardians of the law. This preaching of Jesus is certainly offensive and scandalous, not only for that time but particularly also for today; nor was he content with words, going on to practice, to an equally offensive, scandalous practice, to fellowship with sinners.

Can it still be said here that the name of father is merely an echo of experiences of fatherhood in this world? That it is a projection that serves to transfigure the circumstances of earthly fatherhood and domination? No. *This Father God is different:*

- Not a God of the hereafter at the expense of the here and now, at the expense of man and his true greatness (Feuerbach's projection theory).[41]
- Not a God of the ruling classes, of the unjust social conditions, of a distorted consciousness and of empty promises (Marx's opium theory).[42]
- Not a God produced from resentments, not the supreme head of a pitiful loafers' morality of good and evil (Nietzsche's resentment theory).[43]
- Not a tyrannical superego, the product of wishful thinking based on illusory infantile needs, a God of obsessive ritual arising from a guilt-and-father complex (Freud's illusion theory).[44]

For the justification of his own scandalous talk and behavior, therefore, Jesus appeals to a quite different Father God: a strange God and—as it seemed to many of his contemporaries and especially to those in power—even a dangerous, a really impossible God:

- A God who sets himself above the righteousness of the law, has a "higher" righteousness proclaimed and justifies the lawbreakers.
- A God who makes the existing legal order and with it the whole social system—even the temple and divine worship—purely relative.
- A God who makes man himself the measure of his commandments; who wants to see the natural frontiers removed between comrades and noncomrades, strangers and neighbors, friends and enemies, good and bad, as a result of endless forgiveness, service regardless of rank, renunciation without any return, as a result of love; who thus identifies himself with the weak, sick, poor, underprivileged, oppressed, even with the irreligious, immoral and godless.

This seemed like an *unparalleled revolution in the understanding of God;* here, in the last resort, lie the roots of the controversy about Jesus, the roots of his conflict with his religiopolitical milieu, a conflict that it is not necessary to consider again in detail.[45] This was what mattered: a new God, who seemed to have abandoned his own law, a God not of the devout observers of the law but of the lawbreakers and even—we might say with very slight exaggeration—a *God* not of the God-fearing but *of the godless.*

Here, then, was a revolt against the God of devout believers. Could it really be assumed, could it really be believed, that God himself, the true God of the Fathers, was behind such an unprecedented innovator, someone who was more revolutionary than all the revolutionaries, setting himself above law and temple, above Moses, kings and prophets, and even making himself judge over sin and forgiveness? Would not God be contradicting himself if he had such an advocate? If such a person could rightly claim God's authority and will against God's law and temple, if he could rightly assume authority for such talk and action? A God of the god-less and a blasphemer as his prophet?

It did not help Jesus—and this could be historically established[46]—that he addressed God with the *far from obvious form of "Father"*; this offensively familiar-sounding name, *abba,* more or less equivalent to our "Daddy," seemed scandalous to his hearers. It was of no avail that in all his life and action he seemed to be impelled and illumined by this father of his, that he was living wholly and entirely from this reality. In the conflict about the system, law and order, cult and customs, ideology and practice, about the ruling norms, the limits to be respected and the people to be avoided, in the conflict about the official God of the law, the temple, the nation, the hierarchy—he was the loser. He, who had announced publicly, before the whole world, the closeness and the advent of God his Father, *died completely forsaken by man and God:* "My God, my God, why have you deserted me?"[47]

## 2. God through Jesus Christ

"Why, that picture might make some people lose their faith."[1] This is the horrified cry of Prince Myshkin in front of the picture of the Crucified in Dostoevsky's novel *The Idiot.* It is based on Dostoevsky's experience a short time before in Basel, when he barely avoided an epileptic fit after looking at Hans Holbein's picture of the Crucified.[2] Yes, it is possible to lose one's faith on seeing the cross. This is something to think about when today the slogan is propagated: "God is dead. Long live Jesus." For if God is dead, that is the end of Jesus. In that case, it is impossible to understand how this Jesus would still have had something really essential and unconditional to say to us; he would have been merely one more of the best men in world history who had to die a violent death for the sake of their good cause. But, conversely, it is true that if we are at an end with Jesus, we are also at an end with this God. In that case, it is impossible to understand what this God—whose closeness he had proclaimed but who made his end into a fiasco—could have had to say to us. "Speech of the dead Christ from the roof of the world that there is no God": this was Jean Paul's dreadful vision during the decade of the dethronement of God at Notre Dame in Paris.[3]

But . . . did God really forsake him? Had God in this way repudiated himself?

## Death—and afterward?

The first community that—surprisingly enough—represented the beginning of that so successful Jesus movement that proclaimed in a truly reckless way this heretical teacher, false prophet, seducer of the people and blasphemer, allegedly judged by God, as Messiah of God, as Lord, Son of Man and Son of God: this primitive community had a different opinion. Its Easter faith—whatever there might be in it—is a world-historical fact and alone explains the emergence of Christianity. What had to be said about the dramatic story of the origin of the Easter faith and thus about the emergence of Christianity, need not be repeated here.[4] With reference to the Easter faith, we should not think simply of the variety of time-conditioned concrete expressions and elaborations, the enlargements related to the situation and legendary embellishments of the various Easter presentations and Easter accounts—for instance, of the empty tomb, of the descent into hell and the ascension into heaven.[5] These do not tell us the essentials. For the essentials, we must look to the one great Easter message, to the one simple Easter faith. Despite all the discrepancies of the various traditions with regard to place and time, persons and course of events, the various primitive Christian witnesses, Peter and Paul, James, the Letters, the Gospels, the Acts and Revelation, agree on one thing: that *Jesus lives, he lives through and with God.* Since he lives through and with God, he lives forever—as a sign of hope and obligation for us. And since he lives through and with God, the God for whom he stood in life and death is also justified. What was seen as a positive possibility—eternal life of the individual human being with God, of mankind at the end of the world or at least of the good—only toward the end of the Old Testament (the Book of Daniel) and in the intertestamentary period (apocryphal literature, especially the Book of Henoch), has been fulfilled in this one person: this is the testimony of the first Christian witnesses.[6] However they learned of it themselves,[7] they were convinced of it and—in a final, sustaining confidence, without fear of contempt, persecution and death—they brought to the people as "good news" (*euangelion*) the scandalous news of the new, eternal life of someone executed on a cross.

But is not all this, anyway, irrational? Can man in the twentieth century justify such a belief at the bar of reason? Can we put our faith solely in this one man? Certainly in the twentieth century, less than ever can we think of *resurrection or raising up*—both metaphorical expressions (awakening from sleep) for an unimaginable, undepictable reality—primitively and naïvely uncritically. For the resurrection just does not mean a return to this life in space and time. Death is not canceled, but definitively conquered. Neither does it mean a continuation of this life in space and time. The very expression "after death" is misleading; eternity is not characterized by "before" and "after."

- *"Resurrection" means* a life that bursts through the dimensions of space and time in God's invisible, imperishable, incomprehensible domain. *This is what is meant by "heaven"—not the heaven of the astronauts, but God's heaven. It means going into reality, not going out.*

Resurrection therefore means positively that Jesus did not die into nothingness, but in death and from death died into that incomprehensible and comprehensive absolutely last/absolutely first reality, was indeed taken up by that most real reality, which we designate by the name of God. And it is this very fact that the first witnesses regard as having universal importance, as having importance also for me.

After all the objections we have heard from critics of religion, how are we to believe this sort of thing in the twentieth century? The answer is that we are faced here with a fundamental *alternative* that faces everyone, even the atheist. And even Ernst Bloch, a convinced atheist, did not want to exclude the positive answer completely. At this point, he retained a small *peut-être*, since he still wanted to see what nothingness or the wholly Other might look like.[8] Hence:

*Either I die into nothingness:* If it is upheld with sincere conviction, this attitude must be respected; those who have decided on the negative answer are not the smallest minds in history. Like everything connected with atheism and nihilism, it cannot be refuted, but neither can it be positively proved. There has never been anyone who proved that we die into nothingness. All the same—recalling what was said about the end of the world[9]—this possibility does not seem in any way reasonable to me.

*Or I die into that absolutely last reality,* which is, then, also the absolutely first, the incomprehensible, comprehensive, most real reality, which we call *God.* This possibility—like everything connected with God[10]—cannot be positively and rationally proved, but neither can it be refuted. But I can rely upon it in an absolutely reasonable, enlightened trust. It seems more reasonable, it seems reasonable every time, that I should die not into nothingness but into God.

*How can I justify such trust at the bar of reason?* If I believe in some kind of "resurrection," I am not believing in some sort of unverifiable curiosity. I believe in God and I know why I believe. The fact that God—for believers—did not leave Jesus of Nazareth in death, but raised him up, justifies the confidence I have in him also on my own account. For the risen Jesus Christ shows what trust can be placed in this God. And here it seems to me only logical not to stop halfway, but with this trusting faith in God to continue consistently to the end. For if God really exists and if this existing God is really God, then he is not the God only of the beginning but also the God of the end, he is not only alpha but also omega, he is both my Creator and my Finisher. I can therefore rely with absolutely reasonable confidence on dying—like Jesus of Nazareth—in death, with death, out of death, into God; or—better—on being taken up by him. For death is my affair; raising up to life can only be God's affair. It is by God himself that I am taken up, called, brought home into him as the incomprehensible, comprehensive, last and first reality, and thus finally accepted and saved. All this occurs in death or—better—out of death, as an event of my own, based on God's deed and fidelity. This is the hidden, unimaginable, new creative deed of him who calls into existence the things that are not. And for this reason—and not as a supernatural "intervention" contrary to the laws of nature—it is for me a genuine gift and a true miracle.

Since in this new life it is a question of the ultimate reality, of God himself, it is also obvious to me from the outset that this is a matter of *faith*. For it is a question of an event of the new creation, which breaks through death as my last frontier and thus through the horizon of my world and thought as a whole. It means the definitive breakthrough of one-dimensional man into the truly other dimension: into the evident reality of God. And the less banal and the deeper the truth, so much more easily can it be doubted. There is no doubt that "pure reason" is here faced with an impassable frontier. At this point, I can only agree with Kant. I cannot verify empirically the passing from death into God any more than the entry into nothingness can be empirically verified. Going to God is something that is not to be expected and not to be proved, but to be hoped for in faith. Neither has Jesus' resurrection been proved by historical arguments (for example, the "empty tomb"): traditional apologetics always broke down at this point. Since we are dealing here with God and by definition this means with the invisible, incomprehensible, uncontrollable, only one form of behavior is appropriate and required: believing trust, trusting faith, but a faith and trust tested and enlightened by reason. There is no way to eternal life that bypasses faith. Even the resurrection of Jesus was not an authenticating miracle; it is itself the object of faith.

In faith, I entrust everything to this God, even the ultimate, even the conquest of death. The almighty Creator, who calls from nonbeing to being, can also call out of death to life. The Creator and Conserver of the universe and man, and he alone, can be trusted, even at death and as we are dying, beyond the limits of everything hitherto experienced, to have still one more word to say: to have the last word as he had the first. Anyone who seriously believes in the eternal and living God believes also in God's eternal life, in his own eternal life. If I begin my Credo with belief in God, "the almighty Creator," I may be content to end it with belief in "eternal life."

## Son of God

It was through Jesus of Nazareth—this is indisputable—that this great hope was given to men. Is it surprising, then, that these experiences of faith, vocations to faith, conclusions of faith in regard to the living Jesus exercised an influence on what Christians believed about him? One thing was clear: that in the light of Jesus, God could be understood quite differently; it became apparent who God is; God showed his true countenance. And this also became increasingly clear: that in the light of God, Jesus, too, can be understood quite differently. In all his preaching and actions, Jesus was interpreting God. But was not Jesus, then, bound to appear in a different light, thrown on him by this God proclaimed differently by him? In fact, the peculiarly new proclamation of God and way of addressing God as Father threw their light back upon the one who proclaimed and addressed him in such a peculiarly new way. And as at that time it was impossible to speak of Jesus without speaking of this God and Father, it was difficult subsequently to speak of this God and Father without speaking of Jesus. This means that our attitude to Jesus determines where we stand with God, how we regard God, what kind of God is ours.

This is the christological question: the *relationship of Jesus to God.* Here the question of God reaches its ultimate depth. The ultimate depth? Is not this the very point at which many people today have difficulties? Jesus? Yes. God? Right. But God's Son? Are these not mythological ideas, virtually impossible for modern thought to reconstruct? On the one hand, there are those who fear the repetition of the old formularies of faith, which they no longer understand, on the other those who fear the abolition of these formularies in which they have always believed. In *On Being a Christian,* I tried as far as possible to help both sides and—well aware of my own fallibility—to make the old formularies freshly intelligible in the light of the original Christian message; an effort that, on the whole, has been gratefully recognized.[11] Here we shall make a similar effort to summarize a few important points on the christological problems in connection with the question of God.

It is not true that the official Church—as distinct from popular preaching and piety—ever put Jesus in place of God and so abolished God in practice, as Ernst Bloch—here pursuing his own interests—exaggeratedly suggested. Orthodox trinitarian teaching in particular never simply identified God and Jesus; here especially the real distinction between God and Jesus was maintained. There are, however, serious reasons why early Christendom saw the risen Jesus at God's side, "seated at the right hand of the Father." For, according to ancient Eastern custom, the one who sits at the right hand of the king is his son or representative. And this is precisely how he now appeared to his community: he who even in his lifetime had spoken and acted in the light of an ultimately inexplicable experience of God, presence of God, certainty of God, and even unity with God, his Father, and now is "exalted" to God. With him who had identified himself with God, even unto death, God now, for his own part, identifies himself in the new life.

Apart from the ambiguous "Son of Man" title, Jesus himself—this view has largely come to prevail among leading New Testament scholars—probably never used any messianic titles. But the application of these titles to Jesus fitted in with his preaching and action on earth. And now, after the experience of his resurrection and what it had meant to them, no title was too high for the community to regard it as unfitting for him. Son of Man, Lord, Messiah, Christ, Son of David, Servant of God, Saviour, Son of God, Word of God—more than fifty names are given to him in the New Testament. The decision for or against the kingdom of God, to which he had summoned people during his earthly life, now became a decision for or against him who had already entered into that kingdom and personified it. The one who had called men to faith became the content of faith, Jesus' gospel became the gospel of Jesus as the Christ. People now believed not only like him, they believed in him. With his proclamation, his action and his whole fate, he became the standard for those who believed in him, for their relations with their fellow men, with society and especially with God.

In the course of time, as a result of theological reflection, the profession of faith in Christ began to be elaborated and some of the titles dropped out of use. Like the title "Son of Man," used frequently in the Gospels but not in the profession of faith, they were no longer intelligible. Other titles came to the fore and acquired a wider meaning. The Jewish title "Messiah" (anointed)—for instance—translated by the Greek *Christos*, even coalesced with the name "Jesus" and became an unmistakable proper name, "Jesus Christ." "Christ" is used for Jesus about five hundred times in the New Testament.

Hence, although there was only one Jesus and faith in the one Christ, even in the New Testament we find a variety of titles of Christ, images of Christ and Christologies. In this respect, "Son of God" displayed a dynamism that belonged to no other title. At the same time, it was not by any means originally an invention of the Christian community. As we saw, even in the Old Testament, the people of Israel were called "Sons of God" and the name was given especially to Israel's king, who was appointed as "Son of Yahweh" when he ascended the throne. This title was now applied to Jesus. By his resurrection and exaltation—as we read in one of the oldest, pre-Pauline professions of faith at the opening of the Letter to the Romans—Jesus of Nazareth "was proclaimed Son of God in all his power"[12] or—with an allusion to the psalm about ascending the throne, quoted above—on Easter day "begotten."[13] What is meant here is undoubtedly not descent but a juridical and authoritative position of Jesus, not a physical sonship as with the pagan sons of the god and heroes but an election and authorization by God.

"Son of God," more than other titles, made clear to the people of that time how much Jesus of Nazareth belongs to God, how much he stands at God's side: no longer in the community, in the world, but confronting the community and the world, subordinate only to the Father and to no one else. As definitively ascended to God, he is now in the definitive and comprehensive sense—"once and for all" unreachable, unsurpassable—in regard to men God's mandatory, plenipotentiary, advocate, spokesman, agent, also legate, trustee, confidant, friend, indeed representative, deputy, delegate of God.[14] The titles are many. And all are implied in the use of this innately extremely complex title of Son of God. The same ideas also find expression in other New Testament statements, of a different color. Jesus is the redeemer and reconciler, the one mediator and high priest of the New Covenant between God and men; he is the way, the truth and the life.

These reflections inevitably raise the question: Is the risen Christ not also the earthly? But if the risen Christ is the same as the earthly, must there not have been concealed in the earthly Chist that which is now laid bare? And if we say not only that the risen Christ is with God but that the earthly Jesus came from God, had his origin in God, must not this earthly one have always been with God? As Son with God? Even before his baptism, before his birth? In fact, in other New Testament books, the point of time of his appointment to the sonship of God is put back to an earlier date: to his baptism, as the beginning of his public activity,[15] or to his birth,[16] and even before his birth, to God's eternity.[17] Jesus Christ is not merely God's Son but God's Son from all eternity.

What is meant by "God's Son from all eternity"? We have explained more precisely elsewhere what Jesus' eternal preexistence in the light of the New Testament can mean for us today.[18] Here we can be content to recall what it meant for the first generation of Christians.

- *For someone who commits himself to Jesus, what happened in and with him is not explained solely from the course of human history: in its first source, it is explained only in the light of the eternal God.*
- *From eternity, there is no other God than the one who manifested himself in Jesus.*
- *Since there is no God other than the one revealed in Jesus, then, in the light of this universal God, Jesus himself has a universal significance.*
- *Every man is thus summoned, in believing trust, to go beyond the world and its time into another, eternal dimension. In Jesus, God's call goes out to men. It is in this fact, even for today, that the unique and authoritative significance of Jesus lies for the understanding of God and his relations with men.*

All this can be expressed more precisely. "The mission of the Son," says the Catholic New Testament scholar Wilhelm Thüsing, obviously in agreement with Karl Rahner (and here we cannot but agree with both), "does not assume that the one to be sent existed as such before being sent, that he was preexistent in the temporal sense. In my opinion the 'mission of the Son' in the Pauline sense and in the sense of the New Testament elsewhere can certainly imply the creation of the man Jesus."[19] According to Thüsing, it is possible to wonder if "the code word 'preexistence' might not be differently translated today"; for we "cannot avoid reflecting on the traditional notion of preexistence and reconsidering its nucleus of truth and its protective function."[20] Invoking the Catholic dogmatic theologian Wilhelm Breuning, of Bonn, he relates Jesus' preexistence to the "preexistence" of all men whom God chose in Christ before the beginning of the world and predestined according to his gracious will: "This does not mean reducing the unique foundation in God himself of the mission of the absolute mediator of salvation to the 'preexistence' granted by God's predestination and election to the 'many' to be saved."[21] Franz Mussner, also a Catholic New Testament scholar, quotes Thüsing with approval and concludes: "The christological doctrine of preexistence in regard to the man and prophet Jesus of Nazareth proclaims nothing other than *Yahweh's* always, 'from eternity,' present *being-there-for*, which was definitively revealed in the man Jesus of Nazareth—'revelation' incidentally being understood in the strictest sense of the word."[22]

Admittedly, in textbook theology—and not only Catholic—the preexistence idea has often been wrongly understood, even after the exegetical findings had been freshly assessed. Consequently the Catholic exegete Karl Hermann Schelkle delivers an unmistakable warning: "A curtailment of Christology may arise if the latter is developed from the idea of preexistence, as perhaps the general consciousness of faith and also textbook dogmatics may be tempted to do. Christology is then concentrated on the Incarnation, in the wonderful birth of Christ. The revelatory significance of Jesus' historical path falls into the background. The resurrection reveals the meaning of the birth event. The eschatological expectation of the second coming and the consummation becomes irrelevant."[23]

In fact, a curtailment of Christology must be avoided with reference to both the preexistence idea and also the understanding of the Incarnation. The name and concept of "incarnation" (*in-carnatio, en-sarkosis*, "becoming flesh," "becoming man") was strongly suggested especially by the hymn of John's prologue. Here alone in the New Testament is found that idea of the divine "Logos," or "Word"—preexisting from eternity with God and as God in God's being—which becomes "flesh" for men: the divine Word becomes man as God's *revelation*—life, light, truth—in the world.[24] But, already in the pre-Johannine, Pauline and deutero-Pauline books, we can distinguish not a few statements on the incarnation of the Son of God all of which are composed in the form of professions of faith[25] or as hymns[26] and may well largely go back to pre-Pauline formularies.[27] The incarnation of the Son of God is here understood mainly as *emptying*, abasement, as a justification of Christian love and unselfishness.

The distinction of the Son of God from God the Father, his obedience and subordination to the Father, is of course upheld everywhere in the New Testament. The Father is "greater" than he is and there are things that are known only to the Father and not to him.[28] Neither is there any mention anywhere in the New Testament of the incarnation of God himself. It is always a question of God's Son or Word who became man, whose identification with God the Father is admittedly increasingly stressed by the transference of divine attributes. In the New Testament, however, the term "God" (*ho theos*) in practice always means the Father.[29] Jesus is almost never directly called "God" and never at all by Paul himself. Apart from John's Gospel, written fifty years later—in the cry of the unbelieving Thomas, "My Lord and my God"[30]—Jesus is designated directly as "God" in only a few, all likewise late, Hellenistically influenced, exceptional cases.[31] These findings—to avoid all misunderstandings—make it advisable for us also today to call Jesus "Son of God" and not simply "God."

If we want to speak quite plainly, then, about the *incarnation* of the Son of God, this cannot be related only to the mathematical or mystical point of the birth or conception of Jesus, but must be related to *Jesus' life and death as a whole.*

- *God's becoming man in Jesus means that in all Jesus' talk, in his whole proclamation, behavior and fate, God's word and will have assumed a human form. In all his talking and action, suffering and death, in his whole person, Jesus proclaimed, manifested, revealed God's word and will. He, in whom word and deed, teaching and life, being and action, completely coincide, is in person, is in human form, God's Word, will, Son.*

Functional statements—which are undoubtedly to the fore—and ontological statements must not be torn apart. In this comprehensive—not speculative but historical—perspective it can be made understandable even today that Jesus before Paul and then also in the Pauline tradition is understood as the revelation of God's power and wisdom,[32] as head and lord of creation,[33] as image, true image of God,[34] as the Yes of God.[35] In this light, it can also be understood and accepted that Jesus is described by John not only as God's Word[36] but also indirectly as equal to God,[37] even as Lord and God.[38] And in this perspective we can understand such difficult and sublime statements as that in Christ lives the fullness of divinity,[39] that God's Word became flesh.[40] This, at any rate, is what we mean when we speak of "God in Jesus Christ." And in this sense, we agree also with the Council of Nicea, in 325, when it speaks of Jesus Christ as "God from God, Light from Light, true God from true God, begotten, not made, of one Being with the Father."[41]

Such statements must be safeguarded against *misunderstandings*. According to the New Testament, the relationship between Father and Son may not be understood as a doctrine of two gods (bitheism). God is the one and only; and we may speak neither of God simply as we speak of man nor of man simply as we speak of God. But, according to the New

Testament, neither is there a simple identity between Father and Son, as was suggested in the heretical trends of the first centuries (Monarchianism, Sabellianism). The Son is not simply the Father and the Father is not simply the Son. Positively, according to the New Testament, it can be said that,

- *for believers, the true man Jesus of Nazareth is the real revelation of the one true God and, in this sense, his Word, his Son.*

*John's Gospel* in particular has made clear this *unity of revelation* between Father and Son. Since the Father knows the Son and the Son the Father,[42] since the Father is in the Son and the Son in the Father,[43] since, then, Father and Son are one,[44] it is true that he who sees the Son also sees the Father.[45] What all this means is not mythology or mysticism or metaphysics, but is summed up in the prosaic but fundamental statement: *God himself encounters us in a unique and definitive way in the activity and the person of Jesus.* For the person who commits himself trustingly to Jesus and believes in him, God manifests himself—but not in a way perceptible to the neutral observer.

What does all this mean for me *today?* After all that had to be said about the God of the religions and the philosophers, I am aware of one thing: that if I want to answer adequately the question of God in modern times, I cannot do without the Judeo-Christian tradition. However grand, the God of the philosophers remains unsatisfying intellectually and emotionally; he remains pale and abstract; here I can only agree with Heidegger. The God even of the Old Testament—though I need not on that account give up my philosophical insights—is the more divine God, the concrete God with qualities, with a human face. And it is the man Jesus of Nazareth who shows, manifests and reveals to me this face of God, still hidden and sometimes ambiguous in the Old Testament. He does this in his whole being and conduct, speaking and acting, also in his suffering and dying. When I look to Jesus, I have the extraordinarily consoling certainty that, despite the infinite distance, in the presence of this God, I need not shudder and tremble in fear, degrade myself and stoop down; I do not need to brood on God's enigmatic decrees or to grope in the darkness for the meaning of his will. And I can be grateful to those who made known to me not a "corruption of God," but a "more friendly God."[46] I know that where Jesus is, there is God; that he tells me what is God's will; that where Jesus acts and talks, God is at his side; that where Jesus suffers and dies, there is God's hidden presence.[47]

I can therefore call him the face, or countenance, of God, and also Word or Son of God. All these metaphors serve to express the unique relationship of God to Jesus and of Jesus to God, his significance as God's revealer. Is it not now obvious why I can grasp only in the light of God what Jesus is and means at the deepest level; why he in particular should have this unique and authoritative significance for mankind and also for myself; why he in particular and no other of the great men—not Buddha, K'ung-fu-tse or Mohammed, nor even Marx or Freud—can call me with absolutely binding authority to discipleship? *In Jesus, the one true God of the Fathers himself calls me to the way.* At this point, I can understand Blaise Pascal only too well, and this could be the decisive thing also for me. For whether incidentally we describe this relationship between God and Jesus in theological terms more functionally or ontologically, whether we start out more from abstract statements about essences or from concrete statements about salvation, is really secondary and need not, anyway, be a contradiction. We may prefer functional statements and yet say that Jesus functions; he not only functions for me as God's Word and Son, he *is* this and he is so not only for me but also in himself.

Some today would prefer not to make use of the Hellenistic terminology for the expression of their faith. At that time, it was scarcely possible to talk of Jesus Christ except in such terms as hypostasis, person, nature, essence, of the same nature or of similar nature. But, today, we can express the same thing differently. I am bound not by the terminology but by the reality attested in the New Testament: Jesus Christ himself. It is not the literal sense of the terms used—for instance at the first ecumenical council, of Nicea—that is essential. What is essential about the definition of the "consubstantiality" (*homoousia*) of Jesus with God his Father, against Arius, is that it prevented a concealed polytheism from being introduced into Christianity, with Jesus made into a second god or a demigod; it made clear that the one true God was wholly present and active in him. With the Fathers of Nicea, we are convinced that our whole salvation depends on the fact that in Jesus we are concerned with the one God, who is truly, really and alone God: in Jesus as his Son made evident.

The Council of Chalcedon, in 451, stressed, along with the sameness of nature with the Father, also the sameness of nature with us men: that with Jesus it was a question of *both the true God and the true man.* Jesus of Nazareth in fact has, in the last resort, no decisive meaning for me unless he is proclaimed as the Christ of God. Nor, anyway, does the divine Christ mean much to me unless he is identical with the man Jesus. As against an untheological "Jesusology" and an unhistorical Christology, the name "Jesus" coalescing with the title of "Christ" to become a proper name expresses for me the fact that for the New Testament the true Jesus is the Christ of God and the true Christ is the man Jesus of Nazareth, both in a true and real unity: "Jesus Christ."

Saying, "Lord, Lord," is as unimportant to me as saying, "Son of God, Son of God." What is important, however, is the fact that in the story of Jesus Christ, man and God are truly involved. In the light of the New Testament, I could not justify any interpretation of the story of Jesus Christ that made him merely man: merely a preacher, prophet or sage, even merely a symbol or cipher for a universally human basic experience.

But neither can I justify—in the light of the same New Testament—any interpretation of the story of Jesus Christ that made him only God or simply God: a God walking the earth, free from human defects and weaknesses. Positively expressed, this means two things:

For me, Jesus of Nazareth is the *Son of God*. For the whole significance of what happened in and with him lies in the fact that in Jesus—who appeared to us men as God's advocate, deputy, representative and delegate, and who, as crucified and raised to life, was authenticated by God—the God who loves men is *himself present and active: through him, God himself has spoken, acted, definitively revealed himself.* The mythological, semimythological and legendary embellishments, I need not accept here any more than I accepted them in my faith in a Creator God or a Finisher God. But I want to maintain firmly the uniqueness, underivability and unsurpassability of his person and the appeal, offer and claim there made articulate. Since God himself definitively speaks and acts through him, he is for me the Christ of God, his revelation and his likeness, his Word and his Son. He and no other, he as the only one, "only-begotten," *unigenitus!*

For this very reason, against all pious attempts at deification, I can maintain firmly that Jesus precisely as Son of God, without any qualifications and with all the consequences, was *wholly and entirely man,* could suffer just like other men, felt loneliness and insecurity, was not free from temptations, doubts and errors. But, as distinct from myself and all other human beings (including saints and founders of religions), he is not a mere man, but *the* true man precisely as God's Word and Son. As the true man, in whom theory and practice, being and action, teaching and life, form a unity, by his proclamation, his behavior and his whole fate, he is for me a model of being human. If I trustingly rely constantly on this model, it enables me to discover and realize the meaning of my being human and of my freedom in existing and involving myself for my fellow men. As authenticated by God, he represents for me the permanent, reliable, final criterion of being human. Christology or Christ theory may be important, but faith in Christ and the following of Christ are more important. What matters is being a Christian, and this he—Jesus Christ—makes possible for me. And for that reason, I venture without hesitation to declare: *Credo in Jesum Christum, filium Dei unigenitum.*

### The Christian aspect of the Christian God

What we were able to say here about the Son of God is important, but it still does not amount by any means to a definition of the specifically Christian feature. What distinguished Jesus of Nazareth at that time from so many heroes and demigods, who were also sons of gods, was not that he was a Son of God; as Son of God, Jesus could easily have been a part of the Hellenistic, syncretist pantheon with innumerable sons of gods, heroes and genii, divinely begotten kings and emperors. So what was it that really distinguished him from all the others; what made him unique and unmistakable?

Even the first evangelist, Mark, when he produced his "Gospel"—a hitherto unknown literary genre—did not begin, as he really ought to have, according to traditional dogmatics, with the preexistence, miraculous conception and birth of the Son of God. None of this interested him at all. He never mentioned these "facts of salvation," but began his account of Jesus, the Son of God, with John the Baptist and Jesus' baptism. For Mark, then, the divine sonship rests not on a miraculous birth or conception but on the mandate of God, who calls Jesus at his baptism to follow a definite path. According to Mark also, the fact that Jesus is the Messiah and Son of God is concealed from the public until the passion, when Jesus acknowledges the title "Son of God" but does not use it himself even at that point. It is only at his death—by the voice of the pagan centurion—that the mystery of Jesus is openly proclaimed.[48] In a word, according to Mark, it is only the passion of Jesus that makes him God's Son, evident as God's Son; only in the light of the cross is divine sonship rightly understood. It is the cross, then, that distinguishes Jesus from other "sons of gods."

Twenty years before Mark, this was expressed still more clearly by the Apostle Paul, with whom an infancy story with miraculous conception and birth likewise plays no part. For Paul, the specific feature of his proclamation was not Jesus Christ as "Son of God." As he said: "The only knowledge I claimed to have was about Jesus, and only about him as the crucified Christ."[49] At that time, the cross was anything but a pious symbol, still less an ornament. It was the outlaws' gibbet, the punishment of criminals and slaves. Paul sensed here quite clearly the force of the opposition. To Roman citizens, a crucified person seemed an outright disgrace; to educated Greeks, barbaric foolery; to devout Jews, God's curse. But he also saw that, for those called to believe, the cross was the power and wisdom of God.[50] There is no doubt that, for Paul, the one crucified by men is also the one raised to life by God. And consequently the sign of shame is for him a sign of victory, of liberation and salvation, a call to abandon a life of selfishness. What seems strong to men is weak in the sight of God. What is announced here—as Nietzsche rightly perceived in his invective against Christianity—is a revaluation of all values. Certainly this is not a way of constraint, of feeble self-abasement, as sometimes practiced by Christians and rightly attacked by Nietzsche.[51] But—as boldly undertaken by innumerable people subsequently up to the present time—a life without fear even in the presence of dangerous risks, through struggle, suffering and death, firmly trusting and hoping in the goal of true freedom, love, humanity, of eternal life.

This crucified and living Christ, then, is for believers the foundation already laid, which, according to Paul, cannot be replaced by any other.[52] The Crucified as the living one is the ground of faith, the criterion of freedom. He is the center and norm of what is Christian.

What does this imply in regard to the *difference between the Old and the New Testament conception of God?* As against the abstract, indeterminate philosophers' concept of God and the inconsistent views held by the religions, the Old Testament faith in God proved to be concrete, definite and consistent, but nevertheless, in the last resort, ambiguous.[53] We can now say:

- *As opposed to the admittedly concrete, definite and consistent but still, in the last resort, ambiguous Old Testament faith in God, the New Testament faith in God is concrete, definite, consistent and at the same time unambiguous and veritably personalized in a human form.*
  *The God of the New Testament has a name and a face. He is the God of Israel, who is also the Father of Jesus Christ. The God of the New Testament reveals himself not only in the history of the nation but in an individual human form in which God's Son, Word, will and love assumed flesh.*

The whole of this last chapter is concerned with the Yes to the *Christian God.* But what really is the specifically Christian feature of this God? The decisive factor should now be clear. The *Christian* aspect of this God is not anything of a merely general character, like justice, love or mercy—all this and a great deal besides is found in the Old Testament and is also attributed to the God of Israel. No, the *Christian feature of this God is something historical:*

- *The Christian feature of the Christian God is this* Christ himself, *through whom believers know this God, the one God of the Fathers, through whom this God reveals himself for believers.*

But what prevents us from confusing this Christ with other religious or political messiahs, Christ figures, gods?

- *The Christian feature of this God is precisely the Christ who is identical with the real, historical Jesus of Nazareth: in the concrete, then, this Christ* Jesus.

But what prevents us from confusing this historical Christ with false images of Jesus and of God?

- *The Christian feature of this God—and thus the ultimate distinguishing feature of Christianity as a whole—according to Paul is quite literally "Jesus and as the* crucified *Christ."*[54]

We should not of course speak of a "crucified God."[55] That would suggest that God the Father, and not the Son, had been crucified: a view held by the Patripassians, who did not make an adequate distinction between Father and Son and whose heresy was closely linked with that of Monarchianism and Sabellianism. But we can and may certainly speak of a "hidden God revealed in the Crucified." Paul says of him: "With God on our side who can be against us? Since God did not spare his own Son, but gave him up to benefit us all, we may be certain, after such a gift, that he will not refuse anything he can give. . . . I am certain of this: neither death nor life, no angel, no prince, nothing that exists, nothing still to come, not any power, or height or depth, nor any created thing, can ever come between us and the love of God made visible in Christ Jesus our Lord."[56]

## The criterion of Christian ethics

All these definitions would remain abstract and ineffective if no conclusions for Christian practice were drawn from them. The fundamental question, then, is, What is Christian practice, Christian ethics?

After what we said about ethics in connection with fundamental trust,[57] general belief in God,[58] concrete historical (Old Testament) faith in God,[59] no further reflection on the *foundation of a Christian ethic* is necessary here. In *On Being a Christian*,[60] particularly in connection with the Christian faith in God, we dealt at length with specifically Christian norms, which obviously did not come down from heaven any more than did those of the Old Testament; a question, however, that has hitherto scarcely been adequately considered by writers on theological ethics. Over and over again in comments on the justification of ethics, an appeal is made to insufficiently considered theologoumena of traditional dogmatics, on God, grace, creation, redemption, consummation in heaven. Over and over again, on the other hand, it is thought possible to deduce from the Sermon on the Mount—casually leaving aside cross and resurrection—direct norms for today. As if there were no need to reflect on how these norms worked out in Jesus' own life. As if Jesus himself had not failed with the proclamation of his ethos and for that reason was liquidated. As if without faith in Jesus' new life these norms would even have been recorded. No, unlike the situation with Plato or Marx, with Jesus the teaching forms such a unity with his living and dying, with his fate, that a collection of abstract, general ideas and norms could never indicate what he really means for us. The authentic meaning of the Gospels, the "teaching," the message of Jesus, his Sermon on the Mount, can be understood only if these are seen in the light of his life, death and new life.

For Christians, Jesus is certainly a teacher, but also essentially more. As crucified and raised to life, he is in person the living, authoritative embodiment of his cause: the cause of God and the cause of man. This living Christ in particular does not call for ineffective adoration, still less to mystical union. But neither does he call for mere imitation. What he does is to call for personal *discipleship, for response and correlation*; he calls me to commit myself to him wholly and entirely, while going my own way—each has his own way—according to his directions. This is a great opportunity, which was regarded from the very beginning not as what must be done but as what might be done, as an unexpected chance and true gift, a genuine grace. A grace that presupposes nothing more than this one thing: that we seize on it with trust and faith and adapt our life to it; a new attitude to life, which consequently makes possible a new life-style.

In ethics, too, it is pointless to look for the *distinguishing Christian feature* in any kind of abstract idea or principle, in any kind of sentiment, generally in a horizon of meaning, in a new disposition or motivation. "Forgiveness," "love," "freedom"? Indispensable as these are for the Christian, they are not specific. Others, too, live and act according to these ideas. Acting in the light of "creation" or "consummation"? This, also, others can do: Jews, Muslims, humanists of the most varied kinds. The criterion of what is Christian, the distinctive Christian feature—this holds both for dogmatics and consistently also for ethics—is not an abstract something, neither is it a Christ idea, a Christology or a Christocentric system of ideas, but it is *this concrete, crucified Jesus as the living Christ*, as the standard.

We have dealt in detail with his person elsewhere.[61] Jesus as a concrete historical person possesses an impressiveness, audibility and realizability that are missing in an eternal idea, an abstract principle, a universal norm, a conceptual system. Even for people today, he can in many ways represent a realizable basic model of a vision of life and a practice of life. He is, in person, both positively and negatively the invitation ("you may"), the appeal ("you ought"), the challenge ("you can"), for both the individual and society. For people today, faced with lack of orientation, absence of norms, meaninglessness, drug addiction and violence, he makes possible in the concrete what they are calling for on all sides: a new basic orientation and basic attitude, but also new motivations, dispositions, enterprises, and in the end a new horizon of meaning and a new definition of the goal.

In his light, it is possible also to give an answer to the fundamental questions of Horkheimer: why man should act just in one way and not in another, why he should love and not hate, why peace is better than war. Yes, in his light it is possible to answer even the question to which—as we saw—even Freud could find no answer: "When I ask myself," said Freud, "why I have always aspired to behave honourably, to spare others and to be kind wherever possible, and why I didn't cease doing so when I realized that in this way one comes to harm and becomes an anvil because

other people are brutal and unreliable, then indeed I have no answer."[62]
The Crucified gives me the answer.

It can be brought out here in the form of propositions:

● *The criterion of Christian ethics, then, is discipleship of Christ. This Christ Jesus is in person the living, authoritative embodiment of his cause: embodiment of a new attitude to life and a new life-style. As a concrete, historical person, Jesus Christ possesses an impressiveness, audibility and realizability that are missing in an eternal idea, an abstract principle, a universal norm or a conceptual system.*

## The God of love

We did not use the word "love" thoughtlessly in connection with God. What theologians say about love sometimes feels like cold water running down one's back. It is, however, appropriate here to reflect a little more and to face a new and perhaps the deepest aspect: the meaning of life—even in a negative sense, in suffering and dying.

Simone de Beauvoir, the companion of Jean Paul Sartre, growing old, finished the third volume of her memoirs, *Force of Circumstance* (1963), with a review of the life she had so passionately affirmed: "Yet I loathe the thought of annihilating myself quite as much now as I ever did. I think with sadness of all the books I've read, all the places I've seen, all the knowledge I've amassed and that will be no more. All the music, all the paintings, all the culture, so many places: and suddenly nothing. . . . If it had at least enriched the earth; if it had given birth to . . . what? A hill? A rocket? But no. Nothing will have taken place, I can still see the hedge of hazel trees flurried by the wind and the promises with which I fed my beating heart while I stood gazing at the gold-mine at my feet: a whole life to live. The promises have all been kept. And yet, turning an incredulous gaze towards that young and credulous girl, I realize with stupor how much I was gypped."[63]

Are we perhaps all gypped? Is there a meaning not only for youth but also for age, not only for periods of happiness but also for periods of unhappiness, for periods of suffering?

There are many witnesses to the fact that *suffering* is actually the *crucial test* of fundamental trust and trust in God, of both Old Testament and New Testament faith in God. At this point, particularly when the innocent are affected, the question continually arises as to why God could not prevent this evil. Why? Either he cannot—is he, then, really all-powerful? Or he will not—is he, then, the good God in whom I should put my trust? Or he cannot and will not—is he not, then, powerless and ill-disposed? Is he not a despot, a swindler, a gambler, an executioner?

In the face of the overwhelming reality of suffering in human life and in the history of mankind is there any *alternative* to Simone de Beauvoir's hopelessness? An alternative to the indignation—for instance—of an Ivan Karamazov against this world of God which he found unacceptable?[64] Or to the rebellion of a Camus, who points, like Dostoevsky, to the suffering of the innocent creature?[65] Instead of rising up defiantly against the power of the gods, like emancipated, autonomous Prometheus, or constantly rolling the rock up the mountain only to see it roll down again, like Sisyphus, we can adopt—as we saw—the attitude of Job.[66] Despite all the suffering of this world, we can place an absolute, unshakable trust in the incomprehensible God. But the question still recurs: What sort of God is this, disinterested, above all suffering, who leaves men sitting, struggling, protesting, perishing, or simply being acquiescent and dying in their immense misery? This, for many, is an excuse for atheism.

Of course, this question, too, could be reversed. Is God really so much elevated above suffering as we imagine him in our human way and as we always assume in all our protests, as philosophers in particular think of him? It can certainly be said that, if we look at the infinite suffering of the world, we cannot believe that there is a God. But, conversely, can it not also be said that only if there is a God is it possible to look at this infinite suffering of the world at all? We are thinking of the more divine God. Does not God appear *in a different light precisely in the life and suffering of Jesus?*[67] Beyond all God's incomprehensibility, which Job so painfully experienced, did not a definitive redemption by the incomprehensible God become evident in Jesus' life and suffering, transforming suffering and death into eternal life and into the fulfillment of all yearning? It is true that, in the light of Jesus, the fact of suffering cannot be reversed; a residue of doubt remains possible. Only one thing—but it is decisive—can be said in the light of the life and suffering of this one man to those who are apparently pointlessly living and dying. Even obviously pointless human life and suffering *can* have a *meaning,* can *acquire* a meaning.

A *hidden* meaning: I cannot myself attach a meaning to my living and suffering, but I can accept it in the light of the completed life and suffering of this one man. There is no automatic endowment of meaning. No human wishful thinking will be satisfied, no transformation of suffering proclaimed, no psychic tranquilizers, no cheap consolation provided. But an *offer of meaning* that remains free. Here, too, I must decide. I can reject this (hidden) meaning, in defiance, cynicism or despair. I can also accept it, in believing trust in him who gave meaning to the pointless suffering and dying of Jesus. It renders my protest unnecessary; my indignation, frustration, do not occur. Despair is at an end. *Trust in God as the root of fundamental trust here reaches its greatest depth.*

This offer of meaning implies quite concretely that, however desolate, pointless, desperate my situation may be, God is here too. Not only in light and in joy, but also in darkness, grief, pain and sadness, I *can* encounter him. What is asserted by Leibniz and obscurely perceived by Dostoevsky is confirmed to Job and definitively made evident and certain in the light of the risen Crucified. My suffering, too, is encompassed by *God*, my suffering, too—despite Godforsakenness—can *become* the point of encounter with God. Thus I do not know a way around suffering, but I do know a way through it: in the last resort, unperturbed, actively indifferent in the face of suffering and for that very reason prepared to fight against suffering and its causes. With an eye on the one Sufferer and in believing trust in him who is secretly present in his and my suffering and who himself sustains and supports me in the utmost peril, meaninglessness, nullity, abandonment, loneliness and emptiness: with all this I can know that here is a God who stands alongside men as also involved, a *God who identifies himself with men*. No cross in the world can refute the offer of meaning that was made on the cross of him who was raised to life.

Nowhere more clearly has it become manifest to me than in Jesus' life and work, suffering and dying, that this God is a God for men, a God who is wholly on our side. Not a fear-creating, theocratic God "from above," such as we can still observe—with Bloch—in the Old Testament, but a *benevolent, com-passionate God* "with us below." No, the God who has manifested himself to me in Jesus is not a cruel, despotic, legalistic God, such as may still be found in the Old Testament, but a God encountering me as redeeming love, a God who has identified himself with me in Jesus, who does not demand but bestows love: *who is himself wholly love:* "God is love. God's love for us was revealed when God sent into the world his only Son so that we could have life through him."[68]

I can rebel against a God enthroned, above all suffering, in undisturbed bliss or apathetic transcendence. But not against the God who has revealed to me in Jesus' passion all his com-passion. I can rebel against an abstract justice of God and against a universal harmony preestablished for the present or postulated for the future. But not against the love of the Father of the abandoned, made manifest in Jesus, in its unconditional boundlessness embracing also my suffering, reducing my indignation to silence, overcoming my frustration and making it possible for me to endure all the continuing distress and finally to be victorious.

God's love does not protect me *from* all suffering. But it protects me *in* all suffering. Thus, what is to be completed only in the future does indeed begin for me in the present: the *definitive victory of the love of a God*, who is not a disinterested, unloving being whom suffering and wrong cannot move, but who himself has assumed and will assume men's suffering in love. The victory of the love of God as Jesus proclaimed and manifested it, as the final, deciding power—this is the kingdom of God. For Bloch's and Horkheimer's yearning and the yearning of countless others in the history of mankind for justice in the world, for genuine transcendence, for "the wholly Other," the hope "that the murderer will not triumph over the innocent victim"[69]—all this will be fulfilled. As it is promised—beyond all critical theory and critical theology—in the last pages of Scripture: "He will be their God; his name is God-with-them. He will wipe away all tears from their eyes; there will be no more death, and no more mourning or sadness. The world of the past has gone."[70]

### 3. God in the Spirit

Although, as a result of charismatic and pneumatic movements around the world—whether in the Church or outside it—it is becoming increasingly the fashion to talk of the Holy Spirit, there is no doubt that the Spirit still remains, for many, theologically absolutely unintelligible. How is it, then, that, in addition to the articles of faith on the Father and the Son, there is still a third: on the Holy Spirit? Does not this make faith unnecessarily difficult, often incredible? Are we not imposing on modern man a burden of faith that many are no longer prepared to bear and imposing it perhaps also only because in the Church and in theology there were those who took an immense interest in both the number three and intellectual speculations that few really understood even at that time? On the other hand, although in the earliest creeds of the New Testament only binitarian formularies on Father and Son are found, there is no doubt that, at an early date, trinitarian forms came to prevail in the profession of faith. At an early date, then, profession of faith in the Spirit was regarded as indispensable for Christians whenever there was talk of God and of Jesus. What, then, can be the meaning of "Holy Spirit"? How can we understand this today?

## What is the meaning of "Holy Spirit"?

In the light of the beginnings, our problem might be more precisely stated in this way: How was the fact to be expressed in early Christendom, how is it to be expressed today, that the invisible, incomprehensible God, that Jesus Christ raised up to him, is truly close to believers, to the community of faith: entirely, actually present and effective? To this, the writings of the New Testament give a unanimous response. God, Jesus Christ, are *close in the Spirit* to the believer, to the community of faith; present in the Spirit, through the Spirit and indeed as Spirit. They are not present, then, through our subjective recollection or through faith. They are there through the spiritual reality, presentiality, efficacy of God and Jesus Christ himself encountering us. The presence of God and Jesus Christ here and now is a spiritual reality. What, then, is the meaning of "Spirit" here?[71]

Perceptible and yet not perceptible, invisible and yet powerful, real like the energy-charged air, the wind, the storm, as important for life as the air we breathe: this is how people in ancient times frequently imagined the

"Spirit" and God's invisible working. According to the beginning of the creation account, "spirit" (Hebrew *ruah*, Greek *pneuma*) is the "roaring," the "tempest" of God over the waters. "Spirit" as understood in the Bible means—as opposed to "flesh," to created, perishable reality—the *force or power proceeding from God:* that invisible force of God and power of God that is effective, creatively or destructively, for life or judgment, in creation and history, in Israel and later in the Church. It comes upon man powerfully or gently, stirring up individuals or groups to ecstasy, often producing extraordinary phenomena, active in great men and women, in Moses and the "judges" of Israel, in warriors and singers, kings, prophets and prophetesses.

This Spirit is not—as the word itself might suggest—the spirit of man. He is the Spirit of God, who as the *Holy* Spirit is distinguished from the unholy spirit of man and his world. In the light of the New Testament, he is not—as often in the history of religion—he is not any sort of magic, substance-like, mysterious, supernatural aura of a dynamistic character or a magical being of an animistic kind. The Spirit is *no other than God himself.* He is God himself close to man and the world, as the comprehending but not comprehensible, the bestowing but not controllable, the life-creating but also judging, power and force.

This is important. The Holy Spirit is not a third party, not a thing between God and men, but God's personal closeness to men. Most misunderstandings of the Holy Spirit arise from the fact that he is mythologically separated from and made independent of God. In this respect, the symbol of the dove has often given rise to false associations. The Council of Constantinople, in 381, to which we owe the expansion of the Nicene Creed to include the Holy Spirit, expressly stresses the fact that the Spirit is of one nature with the Father and the Son.

*What, however, does it mean* for us today *to believe in the Holy Spirit, the Spirit of God?* It means to accept in forthright trust the fact that God himself can become present to me inwardly in faith, that as gracious power and force he can gain dominion over my innermost being, my heart, my person. At the same time, I can trust in faith that the Spirit of God is not an enslaving spirit, that he is no other than the Spirit of the one taken up to God, the Spirit of Jesus Christ. And since Jesus is the one taken up to God, he is in the Spirit the living Lord, the standard for both the individual Christian and the ecclesial community. In the light of this concrete standard, I can also test and discern the spirits. No hierarchy, no theology, no fanaticism seeking to invoke the "Spirit" without regard to Jesus, to his word, his behavior and his fate can in fact lay claim to the Spirit of Jesus Christ. Here, then, any obedience, any agreement, any participation reaches its limits.

Believing in the Holy Spirit, the Spirit of Jesus Christ, means knowing —and this must be remembered particularly now in view of the many charismatic and pneumatic movements—that the Spirit is never my own possibility, but always the force, power and gift of God. He is not an unholy spirit of man, spirit of the age, spirit of the Church, spirit of office, spirit of fanaticism; he is always the Holy Spirit of God, who moves where and when he wills and does not permit himself to be used to justify absolute power of teaching and ruling, to justify unsubstantiated dogmatic theology, pious fanaticism and false security of faith. No one—no bishop, no professor, no priest and no layman—"possesses" the Holy Spirit. But everyone can pray over and over again for the Spirit. And our prayer might be phrased in the words of the incomparable hymn *Veni Sancte Spiritus*, which Stephen Langton, Archbishop of Canterbury, wrote about the year 1200 and which describes the variety of the effects of the Spirit of God and of Jesus Christ:

> *O Holy Ghost,*
> *Come down from heaven's height,*
> *Give us Thy light.*
> *O Father of the poor,*
> *All gifts to men are Thine*
> *Within us shine.*
> *O Comforter beyond man's comforting,*
> *O stranger sweet*
> *Our hearts await Thy feet.*
> *In passion Thou art peace,*
> *Rest for our labouring,*
> *Our cooling spring.*
> *O solace of our tears,*
> *Upon the secrets of our sins and fears,*
> *Pour Thy great light.*
> *Apart from Thee,*
> *Man has no truth unfeigned,*
> *No good unstained.*
> *Our hearts are dry.*
> *O River, flow Thou through the parched ground,*
> *Quicken those near to die.*
> *Our hearts are hard,*
> *O bend them to Thy will, Eternal Lord,*
> *To go Thy way.*
> *Thy sevenfold power*
> *Give to Thy faithful folk*
> *Who bear Thy yoke.*
> *Give strength to endure,*
> *And then to die in peace*
> *And live for ever in Thy blessedness.*[72]

Receiving the Holy Spirit, then, does not mean submitting to a magical happening, but opening myself inwardly to the message and thus to God and his crucified Christ, permitting myself, then, to be seized by the Spirit of God and of Christ. Believing in the Holy Spirit, the Spirit of God and of Jesus Christ, means not least believing in the *Spirit of freedom*. For "where the Spirit of the Lord is," says Paul, "there is freedom."[73] A freedom from sin, legalism and death, a freedom in the world and in the Church, a freedom for action, for love, for life in peace, justice, joy, hope and gratitude. All this despite opposition and constraints in society and Church, despite all shortcomings and failures. And I know, too, that, just like innumerable unknown people in their great and small decisions, fears, dangers, forebodings and expectations, I can continue to find again courage, support, strength and comfort, in this freedom of the Spirit. The Spirit of freedom, then, as Spirit of the future, directs me and my fellow men forward: not to the hereafter of empty promises but to the here and now of probation in the midst of ordinary secular life until the consummation for which we now have only a "pledge" in the Spirit.[74] In regard to the Church, since I set my hope on this Spirit, I have good reason to believe not indeed *in* the Church but certainly in the Spirit of God and of Jesus Christ also *in* this Church of men. I can believe *the* Church (*credo sanctam ecclesiam*). And because I base my trust on this Spirit, I can confidently say even now: *Credo in Spiritum Sanctum.*[75]

## Triune God

The dogma of the triune God, of the Trinity—the word comes from the third century and the classical formulation of the doctrine from the fourth—is stressed by some as the central mystery of Christianity and rejected by others as Hellenistic speculation alien to Scripture. After a long resistance to a separate liturgical development on Gallic soil, the Feast of the Trinity was inaugurated by the Avignon Pope John XXII only in 1334 for the Church as a whole. It is a feast on which even in Catholic churches it is frequently possible to hear either a scarcely intelligible explanation of traditional teaching or a deafening silence. There is a story about a Bavarian parish priest who announced to his congregation on the Feast of the Trinity that this was so great a mystery, of which he understood nothing, that there would unfortunately be no sermon. Actually in both Catholic and Protestant churches sermons explicitly on the Trinity are very rare. But must it necessarily be so?

In the Acts of the Apostles, by the Evangelist Luke, we find an account —substantially historical but embellished with legend—of the execution in Jerusalem of the first Christian martyr, the Hellenist Stephen, who was said—in words echoing the charges against Jesus—to have been "using blasphemous language against Moses and against God, . . . against this Holy Place and the Law."[76] In his defense speech, probably edited by Luke himself on the basis of the material, Stephen gives a general description of Israel's salvation history from the call of Abraham to the prophets and, as a justification of his Christian faith, appeals expressly to "the God of your ancestors, the God of Abraham, Isaac and Jacob," who appeared to Moses. Only in the last two sentences does he mention—without naming him—the murder of Jesus. Immediately after the condemnation—just before his own death—he had a vision: "Stephen, filled with the Holy Spirit, gazed into heaven and saw the glory of God, and Jesus standing at God's right hand. 'I can see heaven thrown open,' he said, 'and the Son of Man standing at the right hand of God.' "[77]

Here, then, Father, Son and Holy Spirit are mentioned together, or—as Luke puts it—God, Jesus and the Holy Spirit. But Stephen does not see—as is so often depicted in Christian art—a triangle in heaven or even a three-faced Deity (*trikephalos*) and still less the repeatedly produced representation—despite the warnings of Benedict XIV (1754)—in later times of three men with the same figure. No, the Holy Spirit is at his side, in Stephen himself. The invisible force and power proceeding from God fills him entirely and thus opens his eyes: in the Spirit, heaven is shown to him. But God himself remains hidden. Only—quite in the Old Testament sense—his "glory" (Hebrew *kabod*, Greek *doxa*) is visible: God's brightness and power, the brilliance of the light that proceeds from him. But Jesus does not sit; he stands, not of course in front of God but *at his right hand*: that is, in the same power and glory. As Son of God exalted and taken up into God's eternal life, he is representative of God and at the same time as man representative of men.

It was the Apostle Paul who reflected more closely, as the first Christian theologian, on the nature and operation of the Spirit[78] and described the relations between Father, Son and Spirit. For Paul, not only are man's more or less extraordinary individual deeds or experiences (as, for instance, ecstasy or vision) determined by the Spirit but also the very existence of the believer, his day-to-day existence. Paul sees the Spirit wholly in the light of that turning point which was decisive for him: the death and resurrection of Jesus. Since it was revealed there that God himself acted in Jesus, the Spirit of God can now rightly be understood also as the Spirit of Jesus taken up to God.

With regard to "discernment of spirits," which is often so difficult, this means that God's Spirit can no longer be misused as an obscure, nameless and easily misinterpreted divine power, as understood in Gnosticism. No, *God's Spirit* is wholly unequivocally and identifiably *the Spirit of Jesus Christ*, of the Son.[79] Now it can be understood why God and the risen Jesus, although clearly distinguished by Paul as "persons," are seen as one in their operation. God effects salvation *through* Jesus *in* the Spirit. God's power, force, Spirit, are now so completely possessed by Jesus as the Lord exalted to God that he not only has power and control over the Spirit but, in virtue of the resurrection, can even be understood himself as Spirit. Jesus "has become a life-giving Spirit."[80] Paul even says: "This Lord is the Spirit."[81]

What is the meaning in particular of this enigmatic statement, which in this form simply does not fit into the solid structure of the traditional teaching on the Trinity? It means, as already indicated, that there is no absolute identity of two personal agencies, but that *the Lord raised up to God is now in the existence and mode of operation of the Spirit.* He appears to be identical with the Spirit as soon as he is considered not in himself but in his action on the Church and on individuals. The Jesus now taken up to God acts at the present time through the Spirit, in the Spirit, as Spirit. In the Spirit, the risen Christ is himself present: in the life of the individual, in the life of the community of faith, and especially in the liturgy, in the eucharistic celebration in memory of him. Thus the identification of the Lord with the Spirit and the subordination of the Spirit to the Lord can coexist.[82] So, too, the expressions "in the Spirit" and "in Christ" or even "the Spirit in us" and "Christ in us" can be regarded as parallels and in practice as interchangeable. In the encounter of "God," "Lord" and "Spirit" with the believer, it is in the last resort a question of one and the same encounter, of the one action of God himself: "The grace of the Lord Jesus Christ, the love of God and the fellowship of the Holy Spirit be with you all."[83]

We could speak in the same way of Father, Son and Spirit in the farewell discourses in John, where the Spirit is given the personal characteristics of an "advocate" and "helper" (this and not "comforter" is the meaning of "the other paraclete"[84]). The Spirit is—so to speak—the representative on earth of the risen Christ. He is sent by the Father in the name of Jesus. So he speaks not of himself but merely recalls what Jesus himself said.[85]

This is what we can draw directly from New Testament sources. Is it not more understandable, more illuminating, than the many speculations of later times—often very remote from the New Testament and little more than pure philosophizing—on the one divine nature (*physis, ousia, essence, substance*) in the three divine persons (*hypostases, subsistences, prosopa, relations*)? We discussed all this elsewhere.[86] Might not preaching, too, perhaps be better if it were based on what is said in Scripture about this God who forms with Jesus a unity in the Spirit?

It is essentially a question of the *right coordination of God, Jesus* (Son, Word, Christ) *and Spirit* that brings out both the real distinction and the undivided unity. The attempts at interpretation based on Hellenistic ideas and the resultant dogmatic formulations of this coordination are not always helpful today. Like all formulations, they are time-conditioned and not simply identical with the basic biblical statements. This is not a reason for thoughtlessly rejecting them. But neither should they be thoughtlessly repeated. They must be discriminatingly interpreted in the light of the New Testament for the present time.[87]

*God is revealed by the Son in the Spirit.* It is important to see the *unity* of Father, Son and Spirit as *revelation event and revelation unity.* At the same time, what really matters is never to put in question the unity and uniqueness of God, not to cancel the diversity of the "roles" of Father,

Son and Spirit; not to reverse the "sequence" and in particular never to lose sight for a moment of Jesus' humanity. The trinitarian question has developed out of the christological question. The relationship of God and Jesus was considered with reference to the Spirit; a Christology without pneumatology (theology of the Spirit) would be incomplete. As we saw, *as Son the true man Jesus of Nazareth is the true revelation of the one true God.* Hence the question arose: How does he become present for us? The answer ran: not physically and materially and yet not in an unreal way, but *in the Spirit,* in the Spirit's mode of existence, as spiritual reality. The Spirit is the presence of God and of the risen Christ for the community of faith and for the individual believer. In this sense, *God himself is manifest through Christ in the Spirit.*

It is, then, only logical if—conversely—prayers, as in the classical Roman liturgy, are always addressed "through" the Son "in" the Holy Spirit[88] to God, the Father. It must not be forgotten that the Trinity originally was an object not of theoretical speculation but of the profession of faith and the act of praise of God's "glory": "doxo-logy." And there is no finer expression of the original understanding of the Trinity than in the great closing doxology of the Roman Canon: "Through him, with him, in him, in the unity of the Holy Spirit, all glory and honor is yours, almighty Father, forever and ever. Amen."


*Does God exist?*
After the difficult passage through the history of the modern age from the time of Descartes and Pascal, Kant and Hegel,
considering in detail the objections raised in the critique of religion by Feuerbach, Marx and Freud,
seriously confronting Nietzsche's nihilism,
seeking the reason for our fundamental trust and the answer in trust in God,
in comparing finally the alternatives of the Eastern religions,
entering also into the question "Who is God?" and of the God of Israel and of Jesus Christ:
after all this, it will be understood why the question "Does God exist?" can now be answered by a clear, convinced Yes, justifiable at the bar of critical reason.

Does God exist? Despite all upheavals and doubts, even for man today, the only appropriate answer must be that with which believers of all generations from ancient times have again and again professed their faith. It begins with faith—*Te Deum, laudamus,* "You, God, we praise"—and ends in trust: *In te, Domine, speravi, non confundar in aeternum!* "In you, Lord, I have hoped, I shall never be put to shame."

# Notes

EDITOR'S NOTE: A *superior number after the year of publication indicates the edition of the work.*

## A. REASON OR FAITH?

### A.I. *I think; do I therefore exist? René Descartes*

1 René Descartes, *Discours de la méthode pour bien conduire la raison et chercher la vérité dans les sciences. Plus la dioptrique, les météores et la géométrie, qui sont les essais de cette méthode,* Leyden, 1637. We shall take over from this original edition the subdivision into numbered paragraphs, but we shall follow the critical edition of Descartes's works by C. Adam and P. Tannery, Vols. I–XIII, Paris, 1897–1913, for quotations (AT, with volume and page). The essential texts of Descartes (the Latin works being translated into French) can be found in A. Bridoux, *Descartes. Oeuvres et lettres,* Paris, 1952 (Vol. 40 of the "Bibliothèque de la Pléiade"). The quotation is from *Discours* I, 10 = AT VI, 7. (The best-known English translation of Descartes's philosophical works is that by E. S. Haldane and G. T. Ross, in two volumes, Cambridge, 1911–12, reprinted 1931–34. For the present work, I have used *Descartes: Philosophical Writings,* edited and translated by Elizabeth Anscombe and Peter Thomas Geach, first published in 1954 in the Nelson Philosophical Texts Series, revised for Nelson's University Paperbacks, 1970, reprinted in 1971, Thomas Nelson, London/Melbourne/Don Mills, Ontario. References will be to AG, followed by page number. The quotation is from AG, p. 11. Translator.)
2 *Discours,* I, 4 = AT VI, 3–4. (AG, p. 8.)
3 *Discours* I, 14 = AT VI, 9. (AG, p. 13.)
4 René Descartes, *Regulae ad directionem ingenii,* Amsterdam, 1701.
5 Regula I = AT X, 359. (AG, p. 153.)
6 Regula II = AT X, 362. (AG, p. 153.)
7 Regula III = AT X, 366. (AG, p. 153.)
8 Regula IV = AT X, 371. (AG, p. 157.)
9 Bonaventure, *De reductione artium ad theologiam.* This was probably a lecture before the students assembled from the University of Paris between the years 1248 and 1256.
10 René Descartes, *Meditationes de prima philosophia in Quibus Dei existentia, et animae humanae a corpore distinctio, demonstrantur,* Paris, 1641. The quotation is from the Synopsis prefaced to the Meditations = AT VII, 12. (Not in AG.)
11 *Discours* II, 4 = AT VI, 16. (AG, p. 19.)
12 Cf. *Discours* VI, 2 = AT VI, 62. (AG, pp. 45–46.)
13 *Discours* II, 7 = AT VI, 18. (AG, p. 20.)
14 Cf. F. Dessauer, *Der Fall Galilei und wir,* Linz, 1943, esp. Ch. VII.
15 Cf. N. M. Wildiers, *Wereldbeeld en teologie,* 1972; German translation, *Weltbild und Theologie, Vom Mittelalter bis heute,* Zürich/Einsiedeln/Cologne, 1974, esp. pp. 233–91.

16 René Descartes, letter (presumably to Plempius in August 1638) in AT II, 348.
17 René Descartes, *Le monde ou le traité de la lumière*, Paris, 1664; also *L'homme et un traité de la formation du foetus*, Paris, 1664. These are in AT XI, 3–118, 119–215.
18 René Descartes, letter to Mersenne, March 1636, in AT I, 338–42.
19 Cf. n. 10.
20 René Descartes, *Principia philosophiae*, Amsterdam, 1644.
21 René Descartes, *Les passions de l'âme*, Paris, 1649.
22 *Discours* III, 6 = AT VI, 29. (AG, p. 28.)
23 We must agree with Ferdinand Alquié, *Descartes. L'homme et l'oeuvre*, Paris, 1956, who links the historical presentation (order of time) with the systematic (order of the system) (cf. his Introduction). On the differences between the metaphysics of the *Discours* and that of the *Meditationes*, see esp. Ch. 3, *La métaphysique*. Cf. also H. Gouhier, *La pensée métaphysique de Descartes*, Paris, 1962. On the other hand, M. Gueroult, *Descartes selon l'ordre des raisons*, Paris, 1953, interprets Descartes strictly according to the claims of a logical-mathematical system. This book, together with Gouhier's earlier book *La pensée religieuse de Descartes*, Paris, 1924, and J. Laporte, *Le rationalisme de Descartes*, Paris, 1946, is reviewed by I. Fetscher, "Das französische Descartesbild der Gegenwart," in an Appendix to the German edition of Alquié's *Descartes* (Stuttgart, 1962), pp. 127–58.
24 *Meditationes* I, 1 = AT VII, 17. (AG, p. 61.)
25 Ibid.
26 Cf. *Discours* III, 1–5 = AT VI, 22–28. (AG, pp. 24–27.)
27 Cf. *Discours* II, 5 = AT VI, 16–17. (AG, p. 19.)
28 *Meditationes*, Synopsis = AT VII, 12. (Not in AG.)
29 *Meditationes* I, 2 = AT VII, 18. (AG, p. 61.)
30 Cf. *Meditationes* I, 3 = AT VII, 18. (AG, p. 62.)
31 Cf. *Meditationes* I, 5 = AT VII, 19. (AG, p. 62.)
32 Cf. *Meditationes* I, 9 = AT VII, 21. (AG, p. 63.)
33 *Meditationes* I, 11–12 = AT VII, 22–23. (AG, p. 65.)
34 Ibid.
35 *Meditationes* II, 1 = AT VII, 23–24. (AG, p. 66.)
36 *Discours* IV, 1 = AT VI, 32. (AG, pp. 31–32.)
37 *Meditationes* II, 3 = AT VII, 25. (AG, p. 67.)
38 Cf. *Meditationes* II = AT VII, 23–34. (AG, pp. 66–75.)
39 Cf. *Meditationes* III = AT VII, 34–52. (AG, pp. 76–91.)
40 Cf. *Meditationes* V, 7–16 = AT VII, 65–71. (AG, pp. 103–8.)
41 *Meditationes* III, 39 = AT VII, 52. (AG, p. 91.)
42 Cf. *Meditationes* V–VI = AT VII, 63–90. (AG, pp. 101–24.)
43 G. W. F. Hegel, *Vorlesungen zur Geschichte der Philosophie*, in Werke (ed., Glockner), Vol. XIX, p. 328. (E.t., *Lectures on the History of Philosophy*, Kegan Paul, Trench, Trübner, London, three volumes 1892–95, Vol. III, p. 217.)
44 Cf. n. 23.
45 M. Leroy, *Descartes le philosophe au masque*, Paris, 1929.
46 Karl Jaspers, *Descartes und die Philosophie*, 1937, 4th ed., Berlin, 1966. Ch. 3: "Der Charakter der cartesischen Philosophie im Ganzen," esp. pp. 89–93 ("Descartes' Wesen.") (E.t. in *Leonardo, Descartes, Max Weber. Three Essays*, Harcourt Brace Jovanovich, New York, 1964/Routledge, Kegan Paul, London, 1965, Ch. 3: "The Character of Cartesian Philosophy as a Whole," esp. pp. 165–70 ["Descartes' Personality"].)
47 W. Weischedel, *Die philosophische Hintertreppe. 34 grosse Philosophen in Alltag und Denken*, Darmstadt, 1973, pp. 136–48: "Descartes oder der Philosoph hinter der Maske."
48 The account, by A. Baillet, is quoted in A. Bridoux (ed.), *Descartes. Oeuvres et lettres*, Paris, 1953, p. 1412. Baillet's *La Vie de Monsieur Descartes* (1691) is the essential source for Descartes's life, even though too much a work of edification and sometimes unreliable on details. On this, cf. C. Adam, *Vie et oeuvres de Descartes* = AT XII, and, by the same author, *Descartes. Sa vie, son oeuvre* (Paris, 1937). For our purposes the works of H. Gouhier and F. Alquié, supra, are more important.

49 I. Fetscher, "Das französische Descartesbild," in the German ed. of Alquié's *Descartes*, Stuttgart, 1962, p. 158.
50 Regulae III, 9 = AT X, 370. (AG, p. 157.)
51 *Meditationes* IV, 8 = AT VII, 57–58. (AG, pp. 95–96.)
52 These have been very closely analyzed by H. Gouhier, *La pensée religieuse de Descartes*, pp. 207–60. We shall follow him here on the place of Descartes in the history of tradition (cf. pp. 263–86). At this point, I would like to express my sincere thanks to Henri Gouhier and also to my teachers at the Sorbonne, especially Maurice de Gandillac, Jean Wahl and Ferdinand Alquié, for crucial suggestions during my student days.
53 Augustine, *De Civitate Dei* XI, 26. CC 48, p. 345.
54 Cf. H. Gouhier, *La pensée religieuse de Descartes*, pp. 279–80.
55 René Descartes, letter (without addressee's name), Sept. 12, 1638, in AT II, 378.
56 René Descartes, letter to Mersenne, Dec. 31, 1640, in AT III, 274.
57 Aquinas, *De Veritate* q.14 a.1. See also *Summa Theologiae* II/2 q.2 a.1. On the influence of the Thomist tradition on Descartes, cf. H. Gouhier, *La pensée religieuse de Descartes*, pp. 270–80. E. Gilson, *Études sur le rôle de la pensée médiévale dans la formation du système cartésien*, Paris, 1951, pp. 281–98, also confirms Gouhier's interpretation with reference to Thomism on the relations between faith, philosophy and theology, but in other respects attaches more importance to Augustinian influences.
58 For a historical and critical study of Thomism, see D. H. Pesch, "Thomismus," in *Lexikon für Theologie und Kirche*, Vol. X, Freiburg, 1965, cols. 157–67.
59 J. Kleutgen, *Theologie der Vorzeit*, cited in F. Malmberg, "Analysis Fidei," in *Lexikon für Theologie und Kirche*, Vol. I, Freiburg, 1957, col. 478.
60 M. Schmaus, *Katholische Dogmatik*, Vol. I, Munich, 1960, p. 184.
61 A great influence was exercised concerning this question by the apologetic study of M. de Elizalde, *Formae verae religionis quaerendae et inveniendae*, Naples, 1662. There it was claimed that the motives of credibility could provide *evidentia reductive metaphysica* ("what amounts to metaphysical evidence") of the fact of revelation.
62 On these and other important historical links, see H. Küng, *Unfehlbar? Eine Anfrage*, Zürich/Einsiedeln/Cologne, 1970, Ch. IV, 2: "Der rationalistische Ursprung des Erkenntnisideals von klaren Sätzen." (E.t., *Infallible? An Inquiry*, Doubleday, Garden City, N.Y./Collins, London, 1971, Ch. IV, 2: "Rationalist origin of the theory of clear propositions as the ideal of knowledge.")
63 Cf. DS 3015–20, 3041–45.
64 DS 3026; cf. 3004.
65 For a critique, cf. H. Küng, *Unfehlbar? Eine Anfrage*, esp. Ch. II: "Sichere Grundlagen?" (E.t., *Infallible? An Inquiry*, esp. Ch. II: "Firm Foundations.") On the outcome of the discussion, H. Küng (ed.), *Fehlbar? Eine Bilanz*, Zürich/Einsiedeln/Cologne, 1973, esp. Ch. E: "Eine Bilanz der Unfehlbarkeitsdebatte." On the interpretation of the definition of infallibility, see the recent important work by A. B. Hasler, *Pius IX (1846–1878), Päpstliche Unfehlbarkeit und 1. Vatikanisches Konzil. Dogmatisierung und Durchsetzung einer Ideologie*, 2 vols., Stuttgart, 1977.
66 Code of Canon Law, Canon 1366 §2.
67 F. Morandini, S.J., *Logica Major. Ad usum auditorum*, Rome, 1946. Father Morandini was my own teacher at the Gregorian University. Even today I remain sincerely grateful to him and to others who taught Neo-Thomistic philosophy and theology with a clarity and consistency that encouraged discussion with the traditional teaching.
68 F. Morandini, op. cit., cf., however, the consistent use of the Cartesian method in starting out from consciousness, as in J. de Vries, *Denken und Sein. Ein Aufbau der Erkenntnistheorie*, Freiburg, 1937, esp. Ch. 1–2.
69 Cf. also H. Küng, *Unfehlbar? Eine Anfrage*, Ch. IV, 2, as in n. 62. (E.t., see n. 62.)
70 G. W. von Leibniz, letter to C. Rödeken in Berlin (1708), in *Die philosophische Schriften*, ed. C. J. Gerhardt, Vol. VII, Leipzig, 1931, p. 32. On Leibniz's treat-

ment of these problems as a whole, see *Scientia generalis. Characteristica* (pp. 3–247) and here esp. *Specimen calculi universalis* (pp. 218–77) and his essays on calculation with concepts that are described in mathematical sign language (pp. 228–47).

71 H. Hermes, *Aufzählbarkeit, Entscheidbarkeit, Berechenbarkeit. Einführung in die Theorie der rekursiven Funktionen*, Berlin, 1961, p. vi (Preface). On the difficulties of the transition from conversational language to the formalistic language of mathematics and logic, cf. the same author, *Einführung in die mathematische Logik. Klassische Prädikatenlogik*, Stuttgart, 1969.

72 Ibid.

73 These are the words of Morris Kline, the American mathematician, in "Les fondements des mathématiques," in *La Recherche*, No. 54, March 1975, pp. 200–8; quotation, p. 208; cf. the same author's *Mathematical Thought from Ancient to Modern Times*, New York, 1972.

74 Cf. H. Weyl, quoted in Kline's article (n. 73), p. 208.

75 A. Arnauld, *Objectiones quartae*, in AT VII, 214. There is an extensive substantiation of the objections to both the causal and the ontological arguments in W. Weischedel, *Der Gott der Philosophen. Grundlegung einer Philosophischen Theologie im Zeitalter des Nihilismus*, 2 vols., Darmstadt, 1971, Vol. I, p. 173.

76 V. Caterus, *Objectiones primae*, in AT VII, 99.

77 Cf. N. M. Wildiers, *Weltbild und Theologie*, pp. 60–146.

78 Immanuel Kant, "Beantwortung der Frage: Was ist Aufklärung?" in *Werke*, Vol. VI, ed. W. Weischedel, Darmstadt, 1964, pp. 53–61; quotation, p. 53.

79 Karl Jaspers, *Descartes und die Philosophie*, p. 76. (*Leonardo, Descartes, Max Weber*, Harcourt Brace Jovanovich, New York, 1964/Routledge and Kegan Paul, London, 1965, pp. 149–52.)

## A.II. *I believe; do I therefore exist? Blaise Pascal*

1 Cf. "La vie de Monsieur Pascal, écrit par Madame Périer, sa soeur," in *Pascal, Oeuvres complètes*, ed. J. Chevalier, Paris, 1954, pp. 3–34; see also pp. 35–41, the account by his niece: "Mémoire sur la vie de M. Pascal, écrit par Mademoiselle Marguerite Périer, sa nièce."

2 Chevalier's edition of Pascal's works, which appeared as Vol. 34 of the Bibliothèque de la Pléiade, will be used here for all references in works other than the *Pensées*. In the German original of the present book, the *Pensées* have also been translated from Chevalier's more reliable French text (which also makes use of the corrections in the editions of the *Pensées* by Z. Tourneur [1938–42] and L. Lafuma [1952]). The best-known edition of the *Pensées* is by Léon Brunschvicq, in his *Oeuvres de Blaise Pascal, suivant l'ordre chronologique*, Paris, 1897. There is no completely satisfactory arrangement of the *Pensées*, and Brunschvicq's numbering is usually indicated even in editions that adopt a different arrangement. (In the English translation, Brunschvicq's number will be given first, followed by the number in A. J. Krailsheimer, *Pascal: Pensées*, Introduction and translation, Penguin Books, Baltimore/Harmondsworth, 1966. Thus the reference here is to B 347/K 200. All quotations from the *Pensées* will be from Krailsheimer's translation. Other English translations include Martin Turnell, *Pascal's Pensées*, Harvill Press, London, 1962, and *Blaise Pascal, Pensées*, transl. John Warrington, 1960, Introduction and notes by H. T. Barnwell, 1973, J. M. Dent & Sons, Ltd., London, pub. in U.S.A. by arrangement with J. M. Dent. Translator.)

3 B. Pascal, "Réponse au très bon Révérend Père Noël, Recteur de la Société de Jésus, à Paris"; cf. also "Lettre de Pascal à M. le Pailleur, au sujet du Père Noël, Jésuite" in *Oeuvres complètes*, pp. 370–77 and 377–91. With reference to the "truth" of physics, Pascal anticipates Popper's principle of falsification: even verified hypotheses are not, properly speaking, true. Cf., on this subject, L. Schäfer, "Pascal und Descartes als methodologische Antipoden," in *Philosophisches Jahrbuch* 81 (1974), pp. 314–40.

4 Blaise Pascal, "Préface pour le traité du vide," in *Oeuvres complètes*, pp. 529–35.
5 *Pensées* B 3/K 751.
6 Cf. *Pensées* B 6/K 814.
7 *Pensées* B 277/K 423.
8 *Pensées* B 282/K 110.
9 Ibid.
10 Ibid.
11 Ibid.
12 *Pensées* B 1/K 512.
13 Ibid.
14 Ibid.
15 *Pensées* B 76/K 553.
16 An early precursor of Catholic fideism, as developed systematically in nineteenth-century France by L. de Bonald and F. de Lamennais and then by A. Bonnetty, was the Bishop of Avranches, P.-D. Huet, who had begun as an enthusiastic Cartesian and ended as a radical opponent of Cartesianism. His work *Traité philosophique de la faiblesse de l'esprit humain* was published posthumously in Paris in 1722 (also in Amsterdam, 1723).
17 *Pensées* B 144/K 687.
18 *Pensées* B 66/K 72.
19 *Pensées* B 206/K 201.
20 *Pensées* B 72/K 199.
21 Ibid.
22 *Pensées* B 347/K 200.
23 Ibid.
24 *Pensées* B 140/K 522.
25 *Pensées* B 139/K 136.
26 *Pensées* B 131/K 622.
27 *Pensées* B 194/K 427.
28 *Pensées* B 210/K 165.
29 *Pensées* B 127/K 24.
30 *Pensées* B 397/K 114.
31 *Pensées* B 398/K 116.
32 *Pensées* B 78/K 887.
33 See esp. the long fragment B 434/K 131.
34 Ibid.
35 Ibid.
36 Ibid.
37 Ibid.
38 Ibid.
39 Ibid.
40 B. Pascal, "Memorial," in *Oeuvres complètes*, pp. 553–54. (English version in Krailsheimer, pp. 309–10. Ernest Mortimer, *Blaise Pascal*, Methuen & Co., London, 1959, also gives a translation, on pp. 123–24, and the original French on pp. 224–25.)
41 On the parchment sheet there is an explicit reference to both Exodus 3:6 and Matthew 22:32.
42 Psalm 119:16. (English as in Krailsheimer's translation.)
43 *Pensées* B 278/K 424.
44 *Pensées* B 272/K 182.
45 *Pensées* B 267/K 188.
46 *Pensées* B 269/K 167.
47 *Pensées* B 77/K 355.
48 *Pensées* B 527/K 192.
49 An illuminating collection of the very varied reactions to Pascal on the part of philosophers, theologians and writers in the periods of the Enlightenment and Romanticism and in the late-nineteenth and the twentieth centuries is provided in Part V of J. Steinmann, *Pascal*, new, rev. and enl. ed., Paris, 1961. The quotation (from Mauriac) is on p. 338. (The English translation, London, 1965, does not include Part V.)

50 *Pensées* B 253/K 183.
51 *Pensées* B 268/K 268.
52 *Pensées* B 73/K 76.
53 *Pensées* B 82/K 44.
54 Ibid.
55 *Pensées* B 365/K 756.
56 *Pensées* B 260/K 505.
57 Ibid.
58 *Pensées* B 234/K 577.
59 *Pensées* B 233/K 418.
60 Ibid.
61 *Pensées* B 242/K 781.
62 *Pensées* B 243/K 463.
63 *Pensées* B 242/K 781.
64 *Pensées* B 543/K 190.
65 *Pensées* B 547/K 189.
66 *Pensées* B 22/K 696.
67 F. Strowski, *Pascal et son temps*, Vols. I–III, Paris, 1907–8; quotation, Vol. I, Preface, p. ii.
68 B. Castiglione, *Il Cortegiano*, Venice, 1528.
69 Pascal's will, in *Oeuvres complètes*, pp. 51–53; quotation, p. 51.
70 Cf. *Pensées* B 61/K 694; *Pensées* B 338 (not in K).
71 B. Pascal, "Lettre à M. et Mme. Périer, à Clermont," in *Oeuvres complètes*, pp. 490–501.
72 *Pensées* B 869/K 517.
73 On Pascal's position in the theological tradition, cf. J.-E. d'Angers, *Pascal et ses précurseurs. L'apologétique en France 1590–1670*, Paris, 1954.
74 *Pensées* B 233/K 418.
75 Cf. Romano Guardini, *Christliches Bewusstsein. Versuche über Pascal*, Munich, 1956, pp. 185–96.
76 Augustine, *Contra epistolam Manichaei quam vocant fundamenti*, cap. 5 in CSEL 25/1, p. 197.
77 Augustine, "Sermo 43, 9," in CC 41, p. 512.
78 Ibid. The *intellege, ut credas* is, of course, only *verbum meum* (of Augustine), but the *crede, ut intellegas* is the *verbum Dei*.
79 Pascal refers here to Augustine, *Epistolae 120 (ad Consentium)*. Whatever the importance of reason, the objective priority of faith is clearly brought out here: *Si igitur rationabile est, magnam quandam, quae capi nondum potest, fides antecedat rationem, procul dubio quantulacumque ratio, qua hoc persuadet, etiam ipsa antecedit fidem* ("Epistolae 120,3" in CSEL 34/2, pp. 706–7).
80 *Pensées* B 270/K 174.
81 *Pensées* B 234/K 577.
82 Augustine, *De Civitate Dei* XI, 2 in CC XLVIII, p. 322.
83 Cf. Concilium Carisiacum 853 (DS 621).
84 Cf. Council of Constance Session VIII (May 4, 1415) in *Conciliorum oecumenicorum decreta*, ed. by J. Alberigo and others, Basel, 1962, pp. 187–92.
85 Cf. C.II. *God—a consolation serving vested interests? Karl Marx.*
86 Cf. D.II.2. *What Christians can learn.*
87 Gerhard Ebeling deals thoroughly with these problems in his inaugural lecture in Tübingen, Jan. 12, 1967: "Gewissheit und Zweifel. Die Situation des Glaubens im Zeitalter nach Luther und Descartes," in his collection of essays *Wort und Glaube*, Vol. II, Tübingen, 1969, pp. 138–83.
88 S. Kierkegaard, " 'Guilty?'/'Not Guilty?' " in *Stages on Life's Way*, Oxford University Press, Oxford/Toronto, 1940, pp. 179–444. References to Feuerbach and Pascal, pp. 415–16. "Suffering is the natural state of the Christian" (p. 416).
89 S. Kierkegaard, *Johannes Climacus or De omnibus Dubitandum Est*, transl. by T. H. Croxall, A. & C. Black, London, 1958.
90 Ibid., p. 181.
91 Ibid., pp. 101–2.

92 Ibid., p. 188. For a further survey of the reception of the *cogito* in the English, French and German Enlightenment, in German Idealism and in post-Hegelian and contemporary philosophy and history of philosophy, cf. M. Hagmann, *Descartes in der Auffassung durch die Historiker der Philosophie. Zur Geschichte der neuzeitlichen Philosophiegeschichte*, Winterthur, 1955.

93 "Theologische Erklärung zur gegenwärtigen Lage der deutschen evangelischen Kirche," in *Bekenntnisschriften und Kirchenordnungen der nach Gottes Wort reformierten Kirche*, ed. W. Niesel, Zöllikon/Zürich, 3rd ed., n.d., pp. 333–37; quotation, p. 335.

94 Karl Barth, *Kirchliche Dogmatik*, Vols. I–IV, Zöllikon/Zürich, 1932–70. (E.t., *Church Dogmatics*, T. & T. Clark, Edinburgh/Charles Scribner's Sons, New York, 1936–69.)

95 *Kirchliche Dogmatik* III/1, pp. 401–15; cf. pp. 395–401. (E.t., *Church Dogmatics* III/1, pp. 350–63; cf. pp. 344–50.)

96 Barth mentions Pascal twice, merely incidentally: *Kirchliche Dogmatik* IV/2, pp. 11, 837. (E.t., IV/2, pp. 12, 737.)

97 *Kirchliche Dogmatik* III/1, p. 414. (E.t., III/1, p. 362.)

98 *Kirchliche Dogmatik* III/1, p. 415. (E.t., III/1, p. 362.)

99 *Kirchliche Dogmatik* III/1, p. 400. (E.t., III/1, p. 349.)

100 Pius V, bull *Ex omnibus afflictionibus*, Oct. 1, 1567 (DS 1901–80), confirmed by Gregory XIII in the bull *Provisionis nostrae*, Jan. 29, 1579.

101 The decree is mentioned in a brief history of the controversies on grace preceding DS 1997.

102 C. Jansenius, *Augustinus seu doctrina S. Augustini de humanae naturae sanitate, aegritudine, medicina adversus Pelagianos et Massilienses*, Vols. I–III, Louvain, 1640.

103 Cf. the book by a student of mine, G. Kraus, *Vorherbestimmung. Traditionelle Prädestinationslehre im Licht gegenwärtiger Theologie*, Freiburg/Basel/Vienna, 1977, pp. 34–41.

104 Innocent X, constitution *Cum occasione*, May 31, 1653 (DS 2001–5).

105 B. Pascal, "Les Lettres Provinciales," in *Oeuvres complètes*, pp. 659–904.

106 A. Escobar y Mendoza, *Liber theologiae moralis, viginti et quatuor Societatis Jesu doctoribus reseratus*, Lyons, 1644. There were forty-two editions.

107 Alexander VII, constitution *Ad sacram beati Petri Sedem*, Oct. 16, 1656 (DS 2012).

108 "Factum pour les curés de Paris," in *Oeuvres complètes*, pp. 906–45.

109 "Écrits sur la grace," in *Oeuvres complètes*, pp. 948–1004.

110 This formulary was afterward imposed also by Rome in the constitution *Regiminis apostolici*, Feb. 15, 1665 (DS 2020).

111 Racine's publications on the famous "Querelles des imaginaires," against Nicole, assistant of Saint-Cyran in Port-Royal, from the year 1666, are found in J. Racine, *Oeuvres complètes*, Édition l'Intégrale, Paris, 1962, pp. 307–14. Later, however, he writes very positively about Port-Royal: *Abrégé de l'histoire de Port-Royal*, pp. 315–61.

112 Cf. Clement XI, dogmatic constitution *Unigenitus*, Sept. 8, 1713 (DS 2400–2501).

113 Cf. Alexander VII, decrees of Sept. 24, 1665, and Mar. 18, 1666 (DS 2021–65); Innocent XI, decree of Mar. 4, 1679 (DS 2101–67).

114 Cf. the fragments "Sur l'obéissance due à l'Église et au pape" and "Écrit sur la signature," in *Oeuvres complètes*, pp. 1072–77.

115 Ibid., p. 1073.

116 On the further development of these problems, cf. H. Küng, *Christ sein*, esp. C.I.3: "Emigration?"; D.III.2: "Die Bewältigung des Negativen." (E.t., *On Being a Christian*, New York, 1976/London 1977, esp. C.I.3: "Emigration?"; D.III.2: "Coping with the negative side.")

117 Cf. *Pensées* B 330/K 26.

118 Cf. H. Küng, *Christ sein*, esp. C.III: "Die Sache des Menschen"; D.III: "Christ sein als radikales Menschsein." (E.t., *On Being a Christian*, esp. C.III: "Man's cause"; D.III: "Being Christian as being radically human.")

119 *Pensées* B 4/K 513.
120 Baruch Spinoza, *Tractatus theologico-politicus,* "Hamburg" (actually Amsterdam), 1670.
121 Richard Simon, *Histoire critique du Vieux Testament,* Paris, 1678; with a new Preface, Amsterdam, 1685.
122 These later works included a critical history of the New Testament (1689), of the translations of the New Testament (1690), and of the more important commentaries on the New Testament (1693), all published in Amsterdam.
123 Robert Boyle, *The Sceptical Chymist,* London, 1661.
124 J. O. de La Mettrie, *L'homme machine,* Leyden, 1748.
125 P.-H. d'Holbach, *Système de la nature ou des loix du monde physique et du monde moral,* "London" (in fact, Amsterdam), 1770.
126 P.-S. de Laplace, *Traité de la Mécanique Céleste,* Vols. I–V, Paris, 1805–25.

A.III. *Against rationalism for rationality*

1. *The epistemological discussion*

1 The best survey is that of the philosopher and logician Wolfgang Stegmüller, *Hauptströmungen der Gegenwärtsphilosophie. Eine kritische Einführung,* Vol. I, Stuttgart, 1969[4], Ch. 9–11; Vol. II, Stuttgart, 1975, Ch. 1–2, 5. (E.t., *Main Currents in Contemporary German, British and American Philosophy,* D. Reidel Publishing Company, Dordrecht, Holland, 1969. The chapters are differently arranged in the English edition, there is an additional chapter on Wittgenstein, and everything is contained in a single volume.) Critical accounts have also appeared, particularly by theologians: among Protestant theologians, Wolfhart Pannenberg, *Wissenschaftstheorie und Theologie,* Frankfurt, 1973, Part I (E.t., *Theology and the Philosophy of Science,* Darton, Longman & Todd, London, 1976, Part I); among Catholic theologians, H. Peukert, *Wissenschaftstheorie—Handlungstheorie —Fundamentale Theologie. Analysen zu Ansatz und Status theologischer Theoriebildung,* Düsseldorf, 1976, Part I.
2 L. Wittgenstein, *Tractatus Logico-Philosophicus,* completed in 1918, first published in 1921, 2nd, improved ed., 1933. It was included in Vol. I of the author's works (*Schriften*), pp. 7–83, Frankfurt, 1960. (Bilingual translation with English and German on facing pages, with same title, published by Routledge & Kegan Paul, International Library of Psychology, Philosophy and Scientific Method, London, first pub. 1922, 2nd, corrected impression, 1933. The 9th impression, 1962, is used here.)
3 *Tractatus,* Preface. (E.t., p. 27.)
4 *Tractatus* 6.53. (E.t., p. 189.)
5 *Tractatus* 4.003. (E.t., p. 63.)
6 *Tractatus,* Preface. (E.t., p. 27.)
7 *Tractatus,* 6.52. (E.t., p. 187.)
8 *Tractatus* 6.522. (E.t., p. 187.)
9 *Tractatus* 6.44. (E.t., p. 187.)
10 *Tractatus* 6.41. (E.t., p. 183.)
11 *Tractatus* 6.42. (E.t., p. 183.)
12 *Tractatus* 6.4312. (E.t., p. 185.)
13 *Tractatus* 6.432. (E.t., p. 186.)
14 N. Malcolm, "Wittgenstein" in The Encyclopedia of Philosophy, ed. by Paul Edwards, Vol. VIII, Macmillan Co., New York/Collier Macmillan, London, 1967, pp. 327–40; quotation, p. 331.
15 Ibid.
16 L. Wittgenstein, *Tractatus* 4.0031. (E.t., p. 63.)
17 *Tractatus* 6.54. (E.t., p. 189.)
18 *Tractatus* 7; cf. Preface. (E.t., p. 189, cf. p. 27.)
19 Cf. F.I.2: "God—a meaningful term: Ludwig Wittgenstein."
20 Cf. Moritz Schlick, *Gesammelte Aufsätze 1926–1936,* Vienna, 1938; on the com-

plex (not entirely antimetaphysical) personality of Schlick, cf. Friedrich Waismann's memorial address reprinted as a Preface to Schlick's book. Schlick invoked Leibniz, Frege, Russell and especially Wittgenstein when he announced in 1930 "the turning point of philosophy" (ibid., pp. 31–39).

21 In addition to Moritz Schlick and Rudolf Carnap, among the foremost members of the Vienna Circle were Herbert Feigel, Philipp Frank, Kurt Gödel, Hans Hahn, Victor Kraft, Karl Menger, Otto Neurath, Friedrich Waismann (linked with Hans Reichenbach in Berlin). Cf. V. Kraft, *Der Wiener Kreis. Der Ursprung des Neopositivismus. Ein Kapitel der jüngsten Philosophiegeschichte*, Vienna, 1950. The manifesto had been composed by the logician Carnap, the mathematician Hahn and the economist Neurath as a welcome to Schlick on his return from lecturing as a visitor to Stanford, California. In the review *Erkenntnis*, ed. R. Carnap and H. Reichenbach, the program of the Vienna Circle was summed up thus: "The intellectual world of the Vienna Circle, under the influence of Mach, Poincaré, Frege, Russell, Wittgenstein and others, is opposed to all forms of metaphysical and theologican attitudes" (*Erkenntnis* I [1930], p. 74, Chronik Verein "Ernst Mach," Vienna).

22 On the differences between Wittgenstein and the logical positivism of the Vienna Circle, cf. N. Malcolm, op. cit., pp. 333–34.

23 W. Stegmüller, *Hauptströmungen*, Introduction, p. xxxvi. (E.t., pp. 9–10.)

24 R. Carnap, *Der logische Aufbau der Welt*, Berlin, 1928; a new ed. (Hamburg, 1961) includes the essay "Scheinproblemen in der Philosophie. Das Fremdpsychische und der Realismusstreit." (E.t., *The Logical Structure of the World*, incl. "Pseudoproblems in Philosophy: The Heteropsychological and the Realism Controversy," Copyright © Regents of the University of California, 1967/Routlege & Kegan Paul, London, 1967.)

25 A. N. Whitehead and B. Russell, *Principia mathematica*, Vols. I–III, Cambridge, 1910–13; 2nd ed., 1925–27.

26 R. Carnap, *Der logische Aufbau der Welt*; cf. esp. Ch. III.C.1: "Die Grundelemente." (E.t., Part III, Ch. C.1: "The Basic Elements.")

27 Cf. Ch. IV: "Entwurf eines Konstitutionssystems." (E.t., Part IV: "Outline of a Constructional System."

28 Ibid., p. 139. (E.t., p. 158.)

29 Recent French structuralism pursues similar trends, even though it is less interested in mathematical-logical problems, carrying out comparisons of structure, style and motif in very diverse fields: ethnology (Claude Lévi-Strauss), psychoanalysis (Jacques Lacan), linguistics (Roland Barthes), history (Michel Foucault) and Marx interpretation (Louis Althusser). For a survey, with texts, see G. Schiwy, *Der französische Strukturalismus. Mode, Methode, Ideologie*, Hamburg, 1969.

30 Carnap, p. xix. (E.t., p. xvii.)

31 Ibid. (E.t., ibid.)

32 Ibid., p. xx; cf. pp. 246–47. (E.t., p. xvii; cf. p. 282.)

33 Ibid., pp. 246–47. (E.t., p. 282.)

34 Ibid., p. 226. (E.t., p. 261.)

35 Ibid. (E.t., ibid.)

36 Ibid., pp. 256–58. (E.t., pp. 292–94.)

37 Ibid., p. 257. (E.t., p. 293.)

38 Ibid., p. 258. (E.t., p. 294.)

39 R. Carnap, *Scheinprobleme in der Philosophie*, Berlin, 1928, p. xv.

40 R. Carnap, *Der logische Aufbau der Welt*, p. 331. (E.t., p. 339.)

41 This is the title of the two basic articles of Carnap in *Erkenntnis* 2 (1931), pp. 219–41, 432–65. On "metaphysical pseudostatements" particularly of Heidegger, see pp. 229–33.

42 B. Russell, *An Inquiry into Meaning and Truth*, London, 1940. On Russell's development, see his *Autobiography*, London, 3 vols, 1967–68.

43 A. J. Ayer, *Language, Truth and Logic*, London, 1936; 2nd, rev. ed., London, 1946.

44 R. Carnap, *Der logische Aufbau der Welt*, p. xx. (E.t., p. xviii.)

45 Carnap's first large work to be published in the U.S.A. was *Introduction to Semantics and Formalization of Logic*, Harvard University Press, Cambridge, Mass., 1942 (two vols. in one, 1959). To this he added as an appendix a long list of modifications of certain sections of his earlier work *The Logical Syntax of Language*, Harvard University Press, Cambridge, Mass./Routledge & Kegan Paul, London, 1937 (German original, *Logische Syntax der Sprache*, Vienna, 1934).

According to the later Carnap, the logic of science is not identical with logical syntax. Logic of science as analysis and theory of the language of science embraces
1. syntax, which is concerned only with the purely formal structures of linguistic expressions;
2. semantics, which investigates the meaning of relations between expressions and objects or concepts (and therefore also the truth of a statement).
3. pragmatics, which goes farther and considers the psychological and sociological relationships between the speakers.

46 Cf. Carnap's monumental work *Logical Foundations of Probability*, University of Chicago Press/Routledge & Kegan Paul, London, 1950.
47 W. Schulz, *Philosophie in der veränderten Welt*, Pfullingen, 1972, p. 14. On critical questions, see the whole section on logical positivism (pp. 29–67).
48 R. Carnap, "Überwindung der Metaphysik," in *Erkenntnis* 2, p. 227.
49 P. Wust, *Die Auferstehung der Metaphysik*, Leipzig, 1920; esp. Ch. 4, on the metaphysics of life of Nietzsche, Bergson and Dilthey, also Ch. 5, on E. Troeltsch and G. Simmel.
50 G. Patzig, *Nachwort zu R. Carnap, Scheinprobleme in Philosophie*, Frankfurt, 1966, pp. 85–135; quotation, pp. 97–98.
51 Ibid., p. 120.
52 W. Stegmüller, *Hauptströmungen*, I, p. 422. (E.t., p. 315.)
53 K. R. Popper, *Logik der Forschung*, Vienna, 1934, 6th, rev. ed., Tübingen, 1976, p. 24. (E.t., *The Logic of Scientific Discovery*, Hutchinson, London/New York, 1959, p. 51.)
54 Cf. A.1.4: "Consistent mathematics?"
55 K. R. Popper, *Logik der Forschung*, p. 11. (E.t., p. 36.)
56 Ibid. (E.t., ibid.)
57 Ibid. (E.t., ibid.)
58 K. R. Popper, *Conjectures and Refutations. The Growth of Scientific Knowledge*, Routledge & Kegan Paul, London, 1963, 3rd, rev. ed., 1969, pp. 15–17. The historical-systematic problems as Popper sees them are explained in detail in H. Albert, *Traktat über kritische Vernunft*, Tübingen, 1968, 1975³, esp. Ch. I: "Das Problem der Begründung."
59 H. Albert, op. cit., pp. 13–15, varies this scheme in the form of the "Münchhausen Trilemma": infinite regress—vicious circle—breaking off the proceedings or dogmatism.
60 K. R. Popper, *Conjectures and Refutations*, p. vii.
61 Cf. Popper's more recent work *Objective Knowledge. An Evolutionary Approach*, Oxford University Press, 1972 (reprinted with corrections, 1973).
62 K. R. Popper, *Logik der Forschung*, p. 211. (E.t., *Logic of Scientific Discovery*, p. 265.)
63 Ibid., p. 225. (E.t., p. 280.)
64 Cf. K. R. Popper, *Unended Quest. An Intellectual Autobiography*, Collins, London, 1976, p. 18.
65 K. R. Popper, *Logik der Forschung*, p. xiv. (E.t., *Logic of Scientific Discovery*, p. 15.)
66 Ibid. (E.t., ibid.)
67 Ibid. (E.t., ibid.)
68 Ibid., p. xix. (E.t., p. 19.)
69 Ibid., p. 223. (E.t., p. 278.)
70 Ibid. (E.t., ibid.)
71 Ibid. (E.t., p. 279.)
72 Ibid., p. 225. (E.t., p. 281.)

73 Cf. K. R. Popper, *The Open Society and Its Enemies,* 2 vols., Routledge & Kegan Paul, 1945; 5th, rev. ed., 1966. The relevance of Popper's sociological-political ideas is clear from the volume *Kritischer Rationalismus und Sozialdemokratie,* ed. G. Lührs, T. Sarrazin, F. Spreer, M. Tietzel, with a Preface by the Federal Chancellor, Helmut Schmidt. On the discussion about Popper, cf. esp. P. A. Schilpp (ed.), *The Philosophy of Karl Popper,* 2 vols., La Salle, Ill., 1974: This contains the original version of Popper's autobiography, with descriptive and critical essays on his philosophy and finally his detailed answer to critics, and a comprehensive bibliography. A recent work from the Frankfurt School also deserves to be mentioned: E. Nordhofen, *Das Bereichsdenken im Kritischen Rationalismus. Zur finitistischen Tradition der Popperschule,* Freiburg/Munich, 1976.

74 K. R. Popper, *Logik der Forschung,* p. xxv.

75 Ibid.

76 J. Passmore, "Logical Positivism," in The Encyclopedia of Philosophy, ed. P. Edwards, New York/London, Vol. V, 1967, p. 56.

77 K. R. Popper, *Unended Quest,* p. 87.

78 Ibid., p. 88.

79 Ibid., p. 90.

80 Thomas S. Kuhn, *The Structure of Scientific Revolutions,* University of Chicago, 1962; 2nd, enl. ed., 1970. Other essays by Kuhn are found in Frederick Suppe (ed.), *The Structure of Scientific Theories,* Urbana, Ill., 1971–72.

81 On the discussion between Kuhn and his critics among Popper's followers, cf. esp. I. Lakatos and A. Musgrave (eds.), *Criticism and the Growth of Knowledge,* London, 1970.

82 T. S. Kuhn, *The Structure of Scientific Revolutions,* p. 10.

83 M. Masterman, "The Nature of a Paradigm," in Lakatos and Musgrave, op. cit., attempts to show that Kuhn has given twenty-two meanings to "paradigm" and divides these into three main groups. Kuhn, in his "Postscript-1969," distinguishes between two of the meanings indicated here on p. 175; cf. pp. 181–91.

84 T. S. Kuhn, *The Structure of Scientific Revolutions,* p. 36.

85 Ibid., p. 65.

86 Ibid., p. 77. On falsification in virtue of a new paradigm, cf. pp. 146–49.

87 Kuhn, op. cit.

88 Cf. ibid., p. 184.

89 Cf. in Lakatos and Musgrave, op. cit., K. Popper, "Normal science and its dangers" (pp. 51–58), and I. Lakatos, "Falsification and the methodology of scientific research programmes" (pp. 91–195). Popper and Lakatos claim that Kuhn makes science a subjectivist, relativist and irrationalist enterprise. Against them, Kuhn strongly defends himself, in "Reflections on my critics" (pp. 231–78); cf. also Kuhn's "Postscript," in *The Structure of Scientific Revolutions.* Popper's answer to Kuhn's new paradigm for explaining the progress of science itself provides an interesting proof of Kuhn's theory.

90 Cf. P. K. Feyerabend, *Against Method. Outline of an anarchistic theory of knowledge,* London, 1975, Thesis 1, p. 23.

91 Among the authors of the Critical Theory, cf. esp. the inaugural lecture at Frankfurt by J. Habermas, "Erkenntnis und Interesse" (1965), pub. in his collection *Technik und Wissenschaft als "Ideologie,"* Frankfurt am Main, 1968, pp. 146–68.

92 These ideas are developed in a larger work by J. Habermas, *Erkenntnis und Interesse,* Frankfurt am Main, 1968. I owe important insights into the problems of the theory of knowledge, especially in regard to its criticism, to my colleague at Tübingen Ludger Oeing-Hanhoff. Together, we conducted a very fruitful seminar on "Theory of Knowledge and Theology" in the summer term of 1977 in the faculty of theology at Tübingen. I also owe to him valuable suggestions particularly with reference to the chapters on Descartes and Paul. Cf. also L. Oeing-Hanhoff, "Descartes und das Problem der Metaphysik. Zu F. Alquiés Descartes-Interpretation," in *Kant-Studien,* 51 (1959–60), pp. 196–217; the same author, "Der

sogenannte ontologische Gottesbeweis bei Descartes und Bonaventura," in *Die Wirkungsgeschichte Anselms von Canterbury. Akten der ersten Internationalen Anselm-Tagung,* Bad Wimpfen, Sept. 13–16, 1970, ed. H. Kohlenberger, Frankfurt am Main, 1975, pp. 211–20.

93 Cf. A.II.3: "Augustinian heritage."
94 Cf. A.I.3: "Thomistic heritage."
95 Quoted in Kuhn, *The Structure of Scientific Revolutions,* p. 83.
96 Ibid., p. 84.
97 Ibid., p. 158.
98 Max Planck, *Scientific Autobiography and Other Papers,* New York, 1949, pp. 33–34; quoted by Kuhn, p. 151.
99 Kuhn, p. 84.
100 Ibid., p. 85.
101 Ibid., p. 137.
102 Ibid., p. 169.
103 Ibid., p. 169.
104 Ibid., cf. p. 170.
105 Ibid., p. 164.
106 Ibid.
107 Ibid., p. 171.
108 Ibid., p. 173.
109 Ibid.
110 Ibid.

## 2. Interim results I: Theses on modern rationality

1 H. Küng, *Christ sein,* Munich, 1974, A.I.3: "Humanität durch technologische Evolution?" (E.t., *On Being a Christian,* Doubleday, Garden City, N.Y., 1976/Collins, London, 1977, A.I.3: "Humanity through technological evolution?")
2 Cf. ibid.: "Clarity as ideal of theology."
3 T. S. Kuhn, *The Structure of Scientific Revolutions,* pp. 178–79.
4 N. M. Wildiers, *Wereldbeeld en teologie,* 1972. German translation: *Weltbild und Theologie vom Mittelalter bis heute,* Zürich/Einsiedeln/Cologne, 1974, pp. 250–91.
5 Cf. H. Haag, *Biblische Schöpfungslehre und kirchliche Erbsündenlehre,* Stuttgart, 1966; K. Schmitz-Moormann, *Die Erbsünde. Überholter Vorstellung—bleibender Glaube,* Olten, 1969; U. Baumann, *Erbsünde? Ihr traditionelles Verständnis in der Krise heutiger Theologie,* Freiburg/Basel/Vienna, 1970. On the discussion, cf. H. Haag, "Die hartnäckige Erbsünde. Überlegungen zu einigen Neuerscheinungen," in *Theologische Quartalschrift* 150 (1970), pp. 358–66, 436–56.
6 Cf. H. Küng, *Unfehlbar? Eine Anfrage,* Zürich/Einsiedeln/Cologne, 1970, Ch. I: "Unfehlbares Lehramt?" (E.t., *Infallible? An Inquiry,* Doubleday, Garden City, N.Y./Collins, London, 1971, Ch. I: "Infallible Teaching Office?")
7 Cf. H. Küng, "Thesen zur Stellung der Frau in Kirche und Gesellschaft," in *Theologische Quartalschrift* 156 (1976), pp. 129–32. English in New York Times, May 23, 1976. This article, "Women in Church and Society," was reproduced in Hans Küng, *Signposts for the Future,* Doubleday, Garden City, N.Y., 1978, pp. 158–59.
8 On this, cf. K. Erlinghagen, *Katholisches Bildungsdefizit in Deutschland,* Freiburg, 1965.
9 G. Ebeling, "Gewissheit und Zweifel. Die Situation des Glaubens im Zeitalter nach Luther und Descartes," in *Wort und Glaube,* Vol. II, Tübingen, 1969, pp. 138–83; quotation, pp. 176–77.
10 Cf. W. Hochkeppel, *Mythos Philosophie,* Hamburg, 1976, Ch. V.
11 Cf. A.II.4: "Questions of science: scientific atheism?"
12 W. Hochkeppel, *Mythos Philosophie,* p. 177.
13 W. Weischedel, "Was heisst Wirklichkeit?" in *Festschrift für Ernst Fuchs,* ed G. Ebeling, E. Jüngel, G. Schunack, Tübingen, 1973, pp. 337–45; quotation, pp. 343–44.

14 J. Moltmann, "Theologie in der Welt der modernen Wissenschaften," in *Perspektiven der Theologie. Gesammelte Aufsätze*, Munich/Mainz, 1968, pp. 269–87. Quotation, pp. 275–76. (E.t., "Theology in the World of Modern Science," in *Hope and Planning*, S.C.M. Press, London, pp. 200–22; quotation, p. 207.)

## B. THE NEW UNDERSTANDING OF GOD

### B.I. *God in the world: Georg Wilhelm Friedrich Hegel*

1 Cf. H. Küng, *Menschwerdung Gottes. Eine Einführung in Hegels theologisches Denken als Prolegomena zu einer künftigen Christologie*, Freiburg/Basel/Vienna, 1970. We shall be largely following this book in the present section on Hegel. It contains also an extensive bibliography on Hegel (pp. 671–83).

2 Material on these authors from the theological standpoint will be found in Karl Barth, *Die protestantische Theologie im 19. Jahrhundert. Ihre Vorgeschichte und ihre Geschichte*, Zollikon/Zürich, 1946, 2nd ed., 1952 (E.t., *Protestant Theology in the Nineteenth Century. Its Background and History*, S.C.M. Press, London, 1972); E. Hirsch, *Geschichte der neueren evangelischen Theologie im Zusammenhang mit den allgemeinen Bewegungen des europäischen Denkens*, Vols. IV–V, Gütersloh, 1949, 2nd ed., 1960.

3 G. C. Storr, *Dissertatio de sensu historico*, Tübingen, 1778; the same author, *Neue Apologie der Offenbarung Johannis*, Tübingen, 1783; the same author, *Doctrinae christianae pars theoretica e sacris litteris repetita*, Stuttgart, 1793.

4 Edmund Burke, *Reflections on the Revolution in France*, London, 1790.

5 Cf. F. Hölderlin to Hegel in *Briefe von und an Hegel*, in Werke XXVII, p. 9. For the most part, the authoritative edition of Hegel's works, by Lasson and Hoffmeister, will be cited here as Werke, with the number of the volume in Roman numerals and the page in Arabic.
The lectures on aesthetics and history of philosophy are not in the critical edition by Lasson and Hoffmeister. These will be cited from the jubilee edition of Hegel's collected works, ed. H. Glockner. These volumes will be indicated by G followed by the volume number and page.
For the youthful writings, we are using the well-known collections of H. Nohl, *Theologische Jugendschriften, nach den Handschriften der Kgl. Bibliothek in Berlin*, Tübingen, 1907 (quoted as N with page number) and J. Hoffmeister, *Dokumente zu Hegels Entwicklung*, Stuttgart, 1936 (quoted as H with page number).
("Wherever possible, published translations of Hegel in English will be quoted in the present edition with details of place and date of publication. Translator.)

6 G. W. F. Hegel, H 37.

7 N 20.

8 N 12.

9 N 15.

10 P. de Mendelssohn, "Sass Baruch Spinoza jemals vor Rembrandts Staffelei? Mutmassungen über die Verbindung zwischen dem bankrotten Maler und dem verdammten Ketzer von Amsterdam," in *Frankfurter Allgemeine Zeitung*, Feb. 26, 1977.

11 B. Spinoza, *Tractatus theologico-politicus*, Hamburg, 1670. (E.t., Vol. I of *The Chief Works of Benedict de Spinoza*, in two vols., pub. in Bohn's Philosophical Library, George Bell, London, 1906–9. This translation has been reprinted, also in two vols., and pub. by Dover Publishers, New York/Constable, London, 1955.)

12 B. Spinoza, *Ethica ordine geometrico demonstrata*, 1677 (no place indicated). (E.t., Vol. II, pp. 45–271.)

13 G. W. F. Hegel, *Vorlesungen zur Geschichte der Philosophie*, in Werke G XIX, p. 376. (E.t., *Lectures on the History of Philosophy*, Kegan Paul, Trench, Trübner, London, 1895, Vol. III, pp. 257–58.)

14 F. H. Jacobi, Über die Lehre des Spinoza in Briefen an den Herrn Moses Mendelssohn, Breslau, 1785.

15 J. G. Fichte, "Aphorismen über Religion und Deismus" (1790), in Sämtliche Werke, Vol. V (ed. J. H. Fichte, Berlin, 1845; reprinted Berlin, 1965), pp. 1–8.

16 J. G. Fichte, "Grundlage der gesamten Wissenschaftslehre" (1794), in Werke, Vol. I, ed. F. Medicus, Leipzig, 1911 (reprinted Darmstadt, 1962), pp. 275–603. (E.t., Science of Knowledge, Century Philosophy Source Book, Appleton-Century-Crofts, New York, 1970.)

17 Cf. the philosophical works on the atheism conflict in Fichte, Werke, Vol. III (ed. Medicus), pp. 151–415; in the same volume, "Über den Grund unseres Glaubens an eine göttliche Weltregierung," pp. 119–33; quotation, p. 130.

18 On this, cf. E. Hirsch, Geschichte der neueren evangelischen Theologie, Vol. IV, Gütersloh, 1949, 2nd ed., 1960, pp. 351–64.

19 J. G. Fichte, "Appellation an das Publikum" (1799), in Werke, Vol. III (ed. Medicus), pp. 151–98.

20 J. W. Goethe, Faust, I, in Werke, Vol. III, Hamburg, 1964, p. 110. (E.t. by Philip Wayne, Penguin Books, Harmondsworth, Middlesex, England, 1949, p. 153.)

21 F. Schiller, "Worte des Glaubens," in Werke, Vol. I, ed. J. Petersen and F. Beissner, Weimar, 1943, p. 379.

22 Quoted by H. Knittermeyer, art. "Atheismusstreit," in Religion in Geschichte und Gegenwart, Vol. I, Tübingen, 1957³, p. 678.

23 J. G. Fichte, "Die Bestimmung des Menschcn" (1800), in Werke, Vol. III (ed. Medicus), pp. 261–415. (E.t., "The Vocation of Man," in The Popular Works of Johann Gottlieb Fichte, Trübner & Co., London, 1889, Vol. I, pp. 321–478.)

24 F. Nietzsche, "Die fröhliche Wissenschaft," in Werke, Vol. III (ed. K. Schlechta), Munich, 1955, p. 127. (E.t., The Gay Science, Vintage Books, Random House, New York, 1974, p. 181.)

25 G. W. F. Hegel, "Glauben und Wissen oder die Reflexionsphilosophie der Subjektivität, in der Vollständigkeit ihrer Formen, als Kantische, Jacobische und Fichtesche Philosophie" (1802), in Werke I, pp. 223–346; quotation, p. 345.

26 G. W. F. Hegel, "Über das Wesen der philosophischen Kritik überhaupt, und ihr Verhältnis zum gegenwärtigen Zustand der Philosophie insbesondere" (1802), in Werke I, pp. 117–30; quotation, p. 128.

27 G. W. F. Hegel, "Glauben und Wissen," in Werke I, p. 232.

28 Ibid., p. 230.

29 Ibid., pp. 345–46.

30 Ibid., p. 345.

31 Ibid.

32 Ibid., p. 346.

33 Ibid.

34 Ibid.

35 Ibid.

36 A number of books on death-of-God theology may be mentioned, differing considerably in their approach. G. Vahanian, The Death of God. The Culture of Our Post-Christian Era, New York, 1961; P. M. van Buren, The Secular Meaning of the Gospel. Based on an Analysis of its Language, London, 1963; W. Hamilton, The New Essence of Christianity, New York/London, 1966; T. J. J. Altizer, The Gospel of Christian Atheism, Philadelphia, 1966; T. J. J. Altizer and W. Hamilton, Radical Theology and the Death of God, Indianapolis/New York, 1966; D. Sölle, Stellvertretung. Ein Kapitel Theologie nach dem "Tode Gottes," Stuttgart/Berlin, 1965; the same author, Atheistisch an Gott glauben, Beiträge zur Theologie, Olten/Freiburg in Breisgau, 1968; T. J. J. Altizer (ed.), Towards a New Christianity. Readings in the Death of God Theology, New York, 1967, which includes a section on Hegel by J. N. Findlay.

On the discussion in America, cf. J. Bishop, Die Gott-ist-tot-Theologie, Düsseldorf, 1968. B. Murchland (ed.), The Meaning of the Death of God. Protestant, Jewish and Catholic Scholars Explore Atheistic Theology, 2 vols., New York, 1967; C. W. Christian and G. R. Wittig (eds.), Radical Theology: Phase Two, Essays on the Current Debate, Philadelphia/New York, 1967.

On the discussion in Germany, cf. J. Moltmann, *Theologie der Hoffnung*, Munich, 1964, pp. 150–55 (E.t., *Theology of Hope*, S.C.M. Press, London, 1967, pp. 165–72, particularly illuminating on Hegel); G. Hasenhüttl, "Die Wandlung des Gottesbildes," in *Theologie im Wandel*, Festschrift for the 150 years of the Catholic faculty at Tübingen, Munich/Freiburg, 1967, pp. 228–53; H. Fries, "Theologische Überlegungen zum Phänomenon des Atheismus," in *Theologie im Wandel*, pp. 254–79; H. Fries and R. Stählin, *Gott ist tot? Eine Herausforderung. Zwei Theologen antworten*, Munich, 1968; H. Mühlen, *Die abendländische Seinsfrage als der Tod Gottes und der Aufgang einer neuen Gotteserfahrung*, Paderborn, 1968; H. Thielicke, *Der evangelische Glaube*, Vol. I, Tübingen, 1968, pp. 305–565; M. Seckler, "Kommt der christliche Glaube ohne Gott aus?" in H. J. Schultz (ed.), *Wer ist das eigentlich—Gott?* Munich, 1969, pp. 188–92.

Some contributions from the *Marxist-communist* side are important, notably R. Garaudy, *Dieu est mort. Étude sur Hegel*, Paris, 1962, and V. Gardavsky, *Gott ist nicht ganz tot* (with an Introduction by J. Moltmann), Munich, 1968. In discussing recent literature on Hegel, W. Kern provides a penetrating analysis of the relationships between atheism, Christianity and emancipated society: "Atheismus-Christentum-emanzipierte Gesellschaft. Zu ihrem Bezug in der Sicht Hegels," in *Zeitschrift für katholische Theologie* 91 (1969), pp. 289–321. The same author has now provided a collection of his articles: *Atheismus-Marxismus-Christentum. Beiträge zur Diskussion*, Innsbruck/Vienna/Munich, 1976.

37 *Atheistisch an Gott glauben*, p. 54.
38 D. Bonhoeffer, *Widerstand und Ergebung. Briefe und Aufzeichnungen aus der Haft*, Munich, 1951, p. 241. (E.t., *Letters and Papers from Prison*, ed. Eberhard Bethge, S.C.M. Press, London, 1967, 3rd ed., rev. and enl., p. 196.)
39 G. W. F. Hegel, "Glauben und Wissen," in Werke I, p. 346.
40 Ibid.
41 G. W. F. Hegel, "Wie der gemeine Menschenverstand die Philosophie nehme" (1802–3), in Werke I, pp. 143–60; quotation, p. 149.
42 G. W. F. Hegel, "Glauben und Wissen," in Werke I, p. 233.
43 G. W. F. Hegel, "De orbis planetarum," in Werke I, pp. 347–401; cf. "Disputation über 12 entsprechende Thesen mit Schelling," in Werke I, pp. 403–5.
44 G. W. F. Hegel, "Jenenser Logik. Metaphysik und Naturphilosophie," in Werke XVIII; "Jenenser Realphilosophie I–II, in Werke XIX–XX.
45 F. W. J. von Schelling, *System des transzendentalen Idealismus* (1800), in Werke, ed. M. Schröter, Munich, 1927, 2nd ed., 1958, Vol. II, pp. 327–634; quotation, p. 601.

## B.II. God in history

1 "Briefe von und an Hegel," in Werke XXVII, p. 120.
2 G. W. F. Hegel, *Phaenomenologie des Geistes* (1807), in Werke II (the German text as in the 5th ed., by Hoffmeister, 1949, which has been closely compared with the 1st ed. of the *Phaenomenologie*). (E.t., *The Phenomenology of Mind*, transl. J. B. Baillie, 2nd rev. ed., 1931, Allen & Unwin, London/Macmillan Co., New York.) Literature on this work will be found in H. Küng, *Menschwerdung Gottes. Eine Einführung in Hegels theologisches Denken als Prolegomena zu einer künftigen Christologie*, Freiburg/Basel/Vienna, 1971, pp. 243–44.
3 "Phänomenologie des Geistes," in Werke II, p. 67. (E.t., p. 135.)
4 Ibid. (E.t., ibid.)
5 M. Heidegger, "Hegels Begriff der Erfahrung," in *Holzwege*, Frankfurt am Main, 1950, pp. 105–92.
6 Cf. K. Rosenkranz, *G. W. F. Hegels Leben. Supplement zu Hegels Werken*, Berlin, 1844, reprinted Darmstadt, 1963, p. 204.
7 Hegel, "Phänomenologie des Geistes," in Werke II, p. 20. (E.t., p. 81.)
8 "Briefe von und an Hegel," in Werke XVII, p. 240; cf. p. 239.
9 Hegel, "Wissenschaft der Logik" (1812–13), in Werke III–IV. (E.t., *Hegel's*

*Science of Logic*, transl. W. H. Johnston and L. G. Struthers, Allen & Unwin, London/Macmillan, New York, 2 vols., 1929, new impression 1951.) For literature on this work, see H. Küng, *Menschwerdung Gottes*, pp. 313–14.

10 Hegel, Enzyklopädie der philosophischen Wissenschaften im Grundrisse. Zum Gebrauch seiner Vorlesungen (1817), in Werke V. The 1949 edition of Hoffmeister is used here, which includes Hegel's additional notes. (Parts I and III of the Encyclopaedia were translated by W. Wallace and published by the Oxford University Press in 1892 and 1894 and have recently been reproduced as separate volumes. Details of these editions will be given as they are quoted. Translator.) For literature on the Encyclopaedia, see Küng, note 9, pp. 333–34.

11 "Briefe von und an Hegel," in Werke XXVIII, p. 31.

12 Cf. Karl Barth, *Die Protestantische Theologie im 19. Jahrhundert*, Zollikon/Zürich, 1952, p. 343. (E.t., *Protestant Theology in the Nineteenth Century*, S.C.M. Press, London, 1972, p. 384.

13 Cf. Hegel, Enzyklopädie, in Werke V, pp. 46–47; likewise, "Wissenschaft der Logik," in Werke IV, pp. 500–4. (E.t., *Hegel's Logic. Being Part One of the Encyclopaedia of the Philosophical Sciences*, Oxford University Press, 1975, p. 19; *Hegel's Science of Logic*, transl. Johnston and Suthers, London/New York, 1951, pp. 482–86.)

14 Enzyklopädie, in Werke V, p. 46. (E.t., p. 20.)

15 Ibid., pp. 51–104. (E.t., pp. 25–296.)

16 On the differences between the *Greater Logic* and the Encyclopaedia, see John McTaggart, *A Commentary on Hegel's Logic*, Cambridge, 1910, pp. 150–54.

17 Hegel, Enzyklopädie, in Werke V, pp. 203–325.

18 Enzyklopädie, in Werke V, pp. 326–490. (E.t., *Hegel's Philosophy of Mind. Part III of the Encyclopaedia of the Philosophical Sciences*, Oxford University Press, 1971.)

19 Hegel, Inaugural Address, Oct. 22, 1818, in Berlin, in Werke XXII, p. 8.

20 Hegel, *Grundlinien der Philosophie des Rechts* (1821), in Werke VI. (E.t., *Hegel's Philosophy of Right*, transl. with notes by T. M. Knox, Oxford University Press, London/New York/Toronto/Melbourne, 1942, rev. ed. 1945.) For literature on the *Philosophy of Right*, see Küng, *Menschwerdung Gottes*, pp. 356–81 (including an analysis of the work).

21 Hegel, *Vorlesungen über die Philosophie der Weltgeschichte*, in Werke VIII–IX. (E.t., *The Philosophy of History*, London, 1894, reproduced by Dover Books, New York, 1956. A new and more complete translation of the Introduction, by H. B. Nisbet, *Lectures on the Philosophy of World-History. Introduction: Reason in History*, appeared in 1975, Cambridge University Press, London/New York/Melbourne. Since all the references are to the Introduction, this translation will be used in the present work. Translator.) For literature, see Küng, *Menschwerdung Gottes*, p. 394.

22 *Philosophie der Weltgeschichte*, in Werke VIII, p. 31. (E.t., p. 29.)

23 Ibid., p. 38. (E.t., p. 35.)

24 Ibid., pp. 181–82. (E.t., p. 150.)

25 *Phänomenologie des Geistes*, in Werke II, p. 564. (E.t., Baillie, p. 808.)

26 *Philosophie der Weltgeschichte*, in Werke VIII, p. 48. (E.t., p. 43.)

27 Ibid., p. 78. (E.t., p. 67.)

28 Cf. esp. Hegel's Introduction to the *Philosophy of World-History*.

29 Cf. "Philosophie der Weltgeschichte," in Werke VIII, pp. 123; 124–35. (E.t., pp. 101; 101–13.)

30 Hegel, *Vorlesungen über die Aesthetik*, in Werke X (*Die Idee und das Ideal*), G XII–XIV. (E.t., *Aesthetics. Lectures on Fine Art by G. W. F. Hegel*, transl. by T. M. Knox, Oxford University Press, 2 vols., 1975.) Analysis and literature in Küng, *Menschwerdung Gottes*, Ch. VII, 3: "Christus in der Kunst."

31 Hegel, *Vorlesungen über die Philosophie der Religion*, in Werke XII–XIV. (E.t., *Lectures on the Philosophy of Religion*, 3 vols., Kegan Paul, Trench, Trübner, London, 1895.) Analysis and literature in Küng, *Menschwerdung Gottes*, Ch. VII.4: "Christus in der Religion."

32 Hegel, *Vorlesungen über die Geschichte der Philosophie*, in Werke XV (Intro-

duction: System and History of Philosophy); G XVII–XIX. (E.t., *Lectures on the History of Philosophy*, Kegan Paul, Trench, Trübner, London, 3 vols., 1892–95.) Analysis and literature in Küng, *Menschwerdung Gottes*, Ch. VII, 5: "Christus in der Philosophie."

33 *Geschichte der Philosophie*, in Werke XV, p. 252. (E.t., Vol. I, p. 110.)
34 Ibid., G XIX, p. 684. (E.t., III, p. 545.)
35 Ibid., G XIX, p. 685. (E.t., III, p. 546.)
36 Ibid. (E.t., ibid.)
37 Cf. H. Küng, *Menschwerdung Gottes*, Ch. VII, 6: "Gott der Zukunft?"
38 F. Rosenzweig, *Hegel und der Staat*, 2 vols., Munich/Berlin, 1920; quotation, Vol. II, p. 237.
39 K. Fischer, *Hegels Leben, Werke und Lehre*, 2 vols., Heidelberg, 1901; quotation, Vol. I, p. 201.

## B.III. Secular and historical God

1 Hegel, *Wissenschaft der Logik*, in Werke IV, p. 218. (E.t., *Hegel's Science of Logic*, transl. Johnston and Suthers, Allen & Unwin, London/Macmillan, New York, Vol. II, p. 215.)
2 R. Kroner, *Die Selbstverwirklichung des Geistes. Prolegomena zur Kulturphilosophie*, Tübingen, 1928, p. 224; cf. p. 222 and the critical observations of the work by K. Nadler (who invokes Kroner), *Der dialektische Widerspruch in Hegels Philosophie und das Paradoxon des Christentums*, Leipzig, 1931, pp. 130–43.
3 J. Möller, *Der Geist und das Absolute. Zur Grundlegung einer Religionsphilosophie in Begegnung mit Hegels Denkwelt*, Paderborn, 1951, pp. 155–56; there are similar criticisms by E. Przywara, T. Litt, I. Iljin, H. Niel, E. Coreth, H. Ogiermann, P. Henrici, among others.
4 W. Kern, "Das Verhältnis von Erkenntnis und Liebe als philosophisches Grundproblem bei Hegel und Thomas von Aquin," in *Scholastik* 34 (1959), pp. 394–427. Cf. also N. Rüfner, "Die zentrale Bedeutung der Liebe für das Werden der Hegelschen Philosophie" in *Erkenntnis und Verantwortung*, Festschrift for T. Litt, Düsseldorf, 1960, pp. 346–55.
5 Hegel, *Philosophie der Weltgeschichte*, in Werke VIII, p. 80. (E.t., pp. 68–69.)
6 Ibid., p. 81. (E.t., p. 69.)
7 Cf. R. F. Beerling, *De List der Rede in de Geschiedenisfilosofie van Hegel*, Arnhem, 1959.
8 Cf. I. Iljin, *Die Philosophie Hegels als kontemplative Gotteslehre*, Berne, 1946, pp. 330–39.
9 Cf. Beerling, op. cit., pp. 80–152.
10 For what follows, cf. Iljin, op. cit., p. 360.
11 Ibid., p. 358.
12 Cf. P. Hünermann, *Der Durchbruch des geschichtlichen Denkens im 19. Jahrhundert. Johann Gustav Droysen, Wilhelm Dilthey, Graf Paul Yorck von Wartenburg. Ihr Weg und ihre Weisung für die Theologie*, Freiburg/Basel/Vienna, 1967.
13 Hegel, Enzyklopädie, in Werke V, p. 47. (E.t., *Hegel's Logic. Being Part One of the Encyclopaedia of the Philosophical Sciences*, Oxford University Press, 1975, p. 20.)
14 Cf. H. Blumenberg, "Kant und die Frage nach dem 'gnädigen Gott,'" in *Studium Generale* 7 (1954), pp. 554–70; quotation, p. 555.
15 Karl Barth, *Die protestantische Theologie im 19. Jahrhundert*, p. 378. (E.t., *Protestant Theology in the Nineteenth Century*, S.C.M. Press, London, 1972, p. 421.)
16 Ibid. (E.t., ibid.)
17 A. Comte, *Cours de philosophie positive*, 6 vols., Paris, 1830–42.
18 Cf. A.III.1: "Logic and theory of knowledge against metaphysics? Rudolf Carnap."

19 P. Teilhard de Chardin, "Comment je vois" (1948), in *Les directions de l'avenir*, Oeuvres de Pierre Teilhard de Chardin, Vol. XI, Paris, 1973, pp. 177–223; quotation, p. 181. (E.t., "My Fundamental Vision," in *Toward the Future*, Collins, London, 1975, pp. 162–211; quotation, p. 164.)

20 Ibid. (E.t., ibid.)

21 S. Daecke, *Teilhard de Chardin und die evangelische Theologie. Die Weltlichkeit Gottes und die Weltlichkeit der Welt*, Göttingen, 1967, pp. 186–200.

22 Ibid., p. 191.

23 P. Teilhard de Chardin, "Comment je vois," in Oeuvres XI, p. 213. (E.t., "My Fundamental Vision," in *Toward the Future*, Collins, London, 1975, p. 198.)

24 Ibid. (E.t., ibid.)

25 P. Teilhard de Chardin, "Comment je crois" (1934), in Oeuvres de Pierre Teilhard de Chardin, Vol. X, Paris, pp. 115–52; quotation, p. 117. (E.t., "How I believe," in *Christianity and Evolution*, Collins, London, pp. 96–132; quotation, p. 96.)

26 Ibid., pp. 117–18. (E.t., ibid., pp. 96–97.)

27 P. Teilhard de Chardin, "Le Dieu de l'évolution," in Oeuvres de Pierre Teilhard de Chardin, Vol. X, Paris, 1969, pp. 283–91; quotation, p. 285. (E.t., "The God of Evolution," in *Christianity and Evolution*, Collins, London/Harcourt Brace Jovanovich, New York, 1971, pp. 237–43; quotation, p. 237.)

28 Ibid., p. 288. (E.t., p. 239.)

29 Ibid. (E.t., p. 240.)

30 Ibid., p. 291. (E.t., p. 243.)

31 Ibid., p. 292. (E.t., p. 244.)

32 P. Teilhard de Chardin, "Comment je vois," in Oeuvres XI, pp. 181–82. (E.t., "My Fundamental Vision," in *Toward the Future*, p. 165.)

33 Ibid., p. 182. (E.t., p. 165.)

34 Cf. P. Teilhard de Chardin, "Hymne à la Matière," in *Hymne de l'univers*, Paris, 1961, pp. 71–75. (E.t., "Hymn to Matter," in *Hymn of the Universe*, Collins, London/Harper & Row, New York, 1965, pp. 63–66.)

35 There is an account of Rome's censuring of Teilhard in secret in the Canadian Jesuit review *Relations* (Montreal), No. 212, of August 1958. On June 30, 1962, a public *monitum* appeared in the *Osservatore Romano*. Professor Dr. K. Schmitz-Moormann's paper on Teilhard and Whitehead, delivered at a colloquium for doctoral candidates, was a great help to me in preparing my account of these two authors. Schmitz-Moormann deserves great credit not only for his editing and translation of Teilhard's books into German but also for his French edition of the diaries.

36 Cf. F. H. Bradley, *Appearance and Reality*, London, 1908, esp. Ch. 26, "The Absolute and Its Appearances," pp. 455–510.

37 A. N. Whitehead, *Process and Reality. An Essay in Cosmology*, 1929, new ed., 1960, Macmillan, New York/Cambridge University Press, p. viii.

38 Whitehead, *Religion in the Making*, 1926, new ed., 1960, Macmillan, New York/Cambridge University Press. Cf. pp. 66–68; quotation, p. 68. On Whitehead's metaphysics, cf. esp. W. A. Christian, *An Interpretation of Whitehead's Metaphysics*, New Haven, 1959, esp. Part III: "God and the World." On Whitehead's philosophy in general, see esp. P. A. Schilpp (ed.), *The Philosophy of A. N. Whitehead*, 1941, new ed., New York, 1951, esp. C. Hartshorne, "Whitehead's Idea of God," pp. 513–59.

39 Whitehead, *Religion in the Making*, p. 147.

40 Cf. Whitehead, *Process and Reality*, p. 524.

41 Cf. ibid., pp. 521–26.

42 Ibid., p. 521.

43 Ibid.

44 Ibid., p. 524.

45 Ibid., pp. 524–26.

46 Ibid., p. 532.

47 Ibid., pp. 520–21.

48 Ibid., p. 521.

49  Ibid., p. 527.
50  Ibid.
51  Ibid., p. 528.
52  On American *Process Theology*, which often invokes Teilhard de Chardin in addition to Whitehead, cf. the numerous publications especially of Charles Hartshorne but also of Bernard E. Meland, Bernard M. Loomer, Daniel D. Williams, Schubert M. Ogden, John B. Cobb, Walter E. Stokes, W. Norman Pettinger and also the young Henry N. Wieman. By way of introduction, cf. the collections of D. Brown, R. E. James and G. Reeves (eds.), *Process Philosophy and Christian Thought*, Indianapolis/New York, 1971, and of E. H. Cousins (ed.), *Process Theology. Basic Writings*, New York, 1971. The discussion has been continued in the periodical *Process Studies*, eds. J. B. Cobb and L. Ford. Important contributions to the discussion are contained in S. M. Ogden, *The Reality of God and Other Essays*, New York, 1963. As against process theologians of the strict observance, Langdon Gilkey and David Tracy especially have tried to integrate also other philosophical and theological traditions. The present-day problem of God was discussed and suggestions for a renewal in ways of speaking about God were made at an early stage by L. Gilkey, *Naming the Whirlwind. The Renewal of God-Language*, Indianapolis/New York, 1969. One of the most recent works to come from the University of Chicago, the center of process theology, deserves careful consideration: D. Tracy, *Blessed Rage for Order. The New Pluralism in Theology*, New York, 1975. As against the earlier orthodox, liberal, neo-orthodox and radical theologies, Tracy suggests programmatically a "revisionist model" of theology that—although I do not like the term itself because of its association with the idea of political revisionism—will find some confirmation in both the method and the content of this book. There are clarifications—especially with reference to the concept of God in process theology (dipolarity) in Ch. 8: "The Meaning, Meaningfulness, and Truth of God-Language."
53  K. R. Popper, *The Open Society and Its Enemies*, Vol. II, *The High Tide of Prophecy*, Routledge & Kegan Paul, London, 5th, rev. ed., 1966, p. 247.
54  Ibid., p. 249.
55  Cf. A.III.1: "The universal claim of scientific thought? Karl Popper."
56  E. Bloch, *Subjekt-Objekt. Erläuterungen zu Hegel*, 1951; enl. ed., Frankfurt am Main, 1962, p. 327.
57  On Fichte, see E. Coreth, "Vom Ich zum absoluten Sein. Zur Entwicklung der Gotteslehre Fichtes," in *Zeitschrift für katholische Theologie* 79 (1957), pp. 257–303, esp. p. 273; cf., the same author, "Zu Fichtes Denkentwicklung. Ein problemgeschichtlicher Durchblick," in *Bijdragen. Tijdschrift voor Filosofie en Theologie* 20 (1959), pp. 229–41; see also E. Hirsch, *Geschichte der neueren evangelischen Theologie im Zusammenhang mit den allgemeinen Bewegungen des europäischen Denkens*, Vol. IV, Gütersloh, 1949, 1960², pp. 364–75. On Schelling, see W. Kasper, *Das Absolute in der Geschichte. Philosophie und Theologie der Geschichte in der Spätphilosophie Schellings*, Mainz, 1965, pp. 10–11; cf. pp. 181–215.
58  More specific details on Plato, Aristotle and Plotinus will be found in H. Küng, *Menschwerdung Gottes*, Ch. VIII.2: "Die Geschichtlichkeit Gottes"; also in Excursus III, on the dialectic of the attributes of God.
59  D. Bonhoeffer, *Widerstand und Ergebung. Briefe und Aufzeichnungen aus der Haft*, Munich, 1951, p. 182. (E.t., *Letters and Papers from Prison*, S.C.M. Press, London, 1967, p. 155.)
60  On the further implications of the *secularity* of God, cf. H. Küng, *Menschwerdung Gottes*, Ch. VIII.2: "Die Geschichtlichkeit Gottes," and also Excursus III, on the dialectic of the attributes of God.
61  On the further implications of the *historicity* of God, cf. H. Küng, *Menschwerdung Gottes*, Ch. VIII.2: "Die Geschichtlichkeit Gottes," and also Excursus IV, on the immutability of God, and V, on the recent attempts at a solution of the old problems. See also the works of Karl Rahner, H. U. von Balthasar, M. Löhrer, on the Catholic side, and of Karl Barth, D. Bonhoeffer, E. Jüngel, K. Kitamori, J. Moltmann, on the Protestant side. Cf. also W. Kasper, "Unsere Gottes-

beziehung angesichts der sich wandelnden Gottesvorstellung," in his collected pieces, *Glaube und Geschichte*, Mainz, 1970, pp. 101–43; the same author, "Die Gottesfrage als Problem der Verkündigung," in J. Ratzinger (ed.), *Die Frage nach Gott*, Freiburg/Basel/Vienna, 1972, pp. 143–61; J. Moltmann, *Der gekreuzigte Gott. Das Kreuz Christi als Grund und Kritik christlicher Theologie*, Munich, 1972. (E.t., *The Crucified God. The Cross of Christ as the Foundation and Criticism of Christian Theology*, S.C.M. Press, London, 1974.)

## C. THE CHALLENGE OF ATHEISM

1 Cf. A.II.4: "Tracks of atheism."

### C.I. God—a projection of man? Ludwig Feuerbach

2 F. Engels, "Ludwig Feuerbach und der Ausgang der klassischen deutschen Philosophie" (1888), in Marx-Engels-Werke, Vol. 21, Berlin, 1962, p. 272.

3 In general we shall keep to the most recent critical editions: a) L. Feuerbach, Werke (4 vols. to date), ed. E. Thies, Frankfurt, 1975 onward, quoted as Werke; b) L. Feuerbach, Gesammelte Werke, ed. by W. Schuffenhauer, 10 vols., Berlin, 1967–72, quoted as Gesammelte Werke. Texts not contained in these editions will be quoted from earlier editions: the first, ed. by Feuerbach himself, Sämtliche Werke, Leipzig, 1846–66; enl. ed., inadequate from the point of view of scholarship, by W. Bolin and F. Jodl, 10 vols., Stuttgart, 1903–11; 2nd ed. of this, by H. M. Sass had three supp. vols., Stuttgart, 1959–64.
Letters are quoted from various collections with an indication of the source: K. Grün, *Ludwig Feuerbachs philosophische Charakterentwicklung. Sein Briefwechsel und Nachlass 1820–1872*, Vols. I–II, Leipzig/Heidelberg, 1874; A. Kapp (ed.), *Briefwechsel zwischen Ludwig Feuerbach und Christian Kapp*, Leipzig, 1876; P. Nerrlich (ed.), *Arnold Ruges Briefwechsel und Tagebuchblätter aus den Jahren 1825–1880*, 2 vols., Berlin, 1886; W. Bolin (ed.), *Ausgewählte Briefe von und an Ludwig Feuerbach*, Leipzig, 1904; W. Schuffenhauer (ed.), *Ludwig Feuerbach, Briefwechsel*, Leipzig, 1963.
For the *Wesen des Christentums* we are using the separate edition by W. Schuffenhauer, Berlin, 1956. (E.t., by George Eliot (1854); new ed., *The Essence of Christianity*, with an Introduction by Karl Barth, Harper Torchbooks, Harper & Row, New York/London, 1957.)

4 Cf. H. Arvon, "Engels' Feuerbach kritisch beleuchtet," in H. Lübbe and H. M. Sass (eds.), *Atheismus in der Diskussion. Kontroversen um Ludwig Feuerbach*, Munich/Mainz, 1975, pp. 109–19. But F. Richter, H. M. Sass, and W. Schuffenhauer took the other side in the discussion. Cf. also H. Arvon, *Feuerbach. Sa vie, son oeuvre, avec un exposé de sa philosophie*, Paris, 1964.

5 For our problems the following monographs are particularly useful: K. E. Bockmühl, *Leiblichkeit und Gesellschaft. Studien zur Religionskritik und Anthropologie im Frühwerk von Ludwig Feuerbach und Karl Marx*, Göttingen, 1961; E. Kamenka, *The Philosophy of Ludwig Feuerbach*, London/New York, 1970; M. Xhauflaire, *Feuerbach et la théologie de la sécularisation*, Paris, 1970; H. J. Braun, *Ludwig Feuerbachs Lehre vom Menschen*, Stuttgart/Bad Cannstatt, 1971; A. Schmidt, *Emanzipatorische Sinnlichkeit. Ludwig Feuerbachs anthropologischer Materialismus*, Munich, 1973. A bibliography of works on Feuerbach 1960–73 is provided by H. M. Sass in *Atheismus in der Diskussion*, pp. 264–80. Important contributions on the acceptance of Feuerbach in Protestant theology and in Marxist and non-Marxist philosophy in the twentieth century are included in E. Thies (ed.), *Ludwig Feuerbach*, Darmstadt, 1976. (Among the contributors are theologians K. Barth, R. Lorenz, and H. M. Barth, and philosophers E. Bloch, K. Löwith, A. Kosing, H. Arvon, A. Schmidt, and G. Rohrmoser.)

6 K. Barth, *Protestantische Theologie im 19. Jahrhundert*, Zollikon/Zürich, 1952[2],

pp. 484–89. (E.t., *Protestant Theology in the Nineteenth Century*, S.C.M. Press, London, 1972, pp. 534–40.)

7 Cf. M. Buber, "Das Problem des Menschen," in *Werke*, Munich/Heidelberg, 1962, Vol. I, pp. 309–47; esp. pp. 339–43.

8 Cf. K. Löwith, *Das Individuum in der Rolle des Mitmenschen*, Munich, 1928, pp. 5–13; the same author, *Gesammelte Abhandlungen. Zur Kritik der geschichtlichen Existenz*, Stuttgart, 1960, pp. 37–44.

9 On Feuerbach's *critique of religion*, cf. esp. G. Nüdling, *Ludwig Feuerbachs Religionsphilosophie. "Die Auflösung der Theologie in Anthropologie,"* Paderborn, 1936, 1961²; M. von Gagern, *Ludwig Feuerbach. Philosophie- und Religionskritik*, Munich/Salzburg, 1970; H. J. Braun, *Die Religionsphilosophie Feuerbachs. Kritik und Annahme des Religiösen*, Stuttgart/Bad Canstatt, 1972; E. Schneider, *Die Theologie und Feuerbachs Religionskritik*, Göttingen, 1972; J. T. Bakker, H. J. Heering and G. T. Rothuizen, *Ludwig Feuerbach—Profeet van het atheisme. De mens, sijn ethiek en religie*, Kampen, 1972.

10 L. Feuerbach, "Fragmente zur Charakteristik meines philosophischen curriculum vitae," in *Gesammelte Werke*, ed. W. Schuffenhauer, Berlin, 1971, Vol. X, p. 178.

11 On Feuerbach's development, cf. K. Grün, *Ludwig Feuerbachs philosophische Charakterentwicklung. Sein Briefwechsel und Nachlass 1820–1872*, 2 vols., Leipzig/Heidelberg, 1974; quotation, Vol. I, p. 12. On the development of the young Feuerbach to the publication of the *Essence of Christianity*, cf. the dissertation by W. Schuffenhauer, published in a corrected version as an Introduction to Schuffenhauer's critical edition of Feuerbach's *Wesen des Christentums*, pp. v–cx.

12 L. Feuerbach, letter to L. Noack (1846), in K. Grün, *Ludwig Feuerbach*, Vol. I, p. 16.

13 From Feuerbach's unpub. work in K. Grün, *Ludwig Feuerbach*, Vol. I, p. 387.

14 Ibid.

15 L. Feuerbach, *De infinitate, unitate atque communitate rationis. Disputatio inauguralis.* Feuerbach allowed his Latin dissertation to be printed only in the revised and considerably enlarged version prepared for his qualifying examination. There is a new German translation, by Manfred Hiller, in *Werke*, Vol. I, pp. 15–76.

16 L. Feuerbach, letter to Hegel Nov. 22, 1828, in *Werke*, Vol. I, pp. 353–57.

17 L. Feuerbach (anonymously), *Gedanken über Tod und Unsterblichkeit aus den Papieren eines Denkers, nebst einem Anhang theologisch-satyrischer Xenien, herausgegeben von einem seiner Freunde*, Nuremberg, 1830, in *Werke*, Vol. I, pp. 77–349.

18 Letter to Helene von Dobenegg, née Feuerbach, 1833, in W. Schuffenhauer (ed.), *Feuerbachs Briefwechsel*, p. 78.

19 K. Grün (ed.), *Feuerbach in seinem Briefwechsel*, Vol. I, p. 256.

20 L. Feuerbach, *Geschichte der neuern Philosophie von Bacon von Verulam bis Benedict Spinoza* (Ansbach, 1833), in *Gesammelte Werke*, ed. W. Schuffenhauer, Vol. II, Berlin, 1969.

21 Feuerbach, *Geschichte der neuern Philosophie. Darstellung, Entwicklung und Kritik der Leihnizschen Philosophie* (Ansbach, 1837), in *Gesammelte Werke*, ed. W. Schuffenhauer, Vol. III, Berlin, 1969.

22 L. Feuerbach, *Pierre Bayle, nach seinen für die Geschichte der Philosophie un Menschheit interessanten Momenten dargestellt und gewürdigt* (Ansbach, 1838), in *Gesammelte Werke*, ed. W. Schuffenhauer, Vol. IV, Berlin, 1967.

23 L. Feuerbach, "Pierre Bayle," in *Gesammelte Werke*, Vol. IV, p. 3.

24 Ibid., pp. 7–8.

25 Cf. especially P. Bayle, *Dictionnaire historique et critique*, 2 vols., Rotterdam, 1696–98; the same author, *Pensées diverses*, in *Oeuvres diverses*, Vol. III, Hildesheim, 1966 (photographic reprint of the edition, The Hague, 1727), pp. 1–147.

26 Cf. Feuerbach's reviews of works by K. Bayer, J. Sengler, C. F. Bachmann, and F. Dorguth in the *Halle Yearbooks* (from 1838), in Gesammelte Werke, Vol. VIII, Berlin, 1969.

27 L. Feuerbach, "Der wahre Gesichtspunkt, aus welchem 'der Leo-Hegelsche Streit' beurteilt werden muss," in the *Hallesche Jahrbücher*, Mar. 12–13, 1839; later published as a separate brochure with the title *Über Philosophie und Christentum in Beziehung auf den der Hegelschen Philosophie gemachten Vorwurf der Unchristlichkeit*, in Werke, Vol. II, pp. 261–330.

28 L. Feuerbach, *Zur Kritik der Hegelschen Philosophie*, in Werke, Vol. III, pp. 7–53. At an earlier stage, Feuerbach had defended Hegel, against C. F. Bachmann's *Antihegel*, in Werke, Vol. II, pp. 63–128, and against H. Leo's *Die Hegelingen*, in Werke, Vol. II, pp. 261–330.

29 Werke, Vol. III, p. 52.

30 D. F. Strauss, *Das Leben Jesu, kritisch bearbeitet*, 2 vols., Tübingen, 1835–36, reprinted Darmstadt, 1969, Vol. II, pp. 732–38. (E.t., George Eliot, *The Life of Jesus Critically Examined*, 1846. The 2nd ed., 1892, has been reproduced by Peter C. Hodgson, with Introduction and notes, Fortress Press, Philadelphia, 1972/S.C.M. Press, London, 1973. The section on Christology is on pp. 777–81.)

31 Ibid., pp. 734–35. (E.t., p. 780.)

32 Ibid., p. 736. (Not in the E.t.) On the complex relationship between Hegel and Strauss and the turning from a speculative Christology "from above" to a historical Christology "from below," cf. H. Küng, *Menschwerdung Gottes*, Ch. VIII.3: "Die Geschichtlichkeit Jesu," esp. pp. 567–73.

33 Cf. A. Schweitzer, *Von Reimarus zu Wrede. Eine Geschichte der Leben-Jesu-Forschung*, Tübingen, 1906, Appendix I, pp. 410–13. (The E.t., *The Quest of the Historical Jesus*, A. & C. Black, London, 1911, does not contain this Appendix.)

34 As explained in note 3, we are using the critical edition of *Das Wesen des Christentums*, by W. Schuffenhauer, Berlin, 1956. (E.t., *The Essence of Christianity*, 1854, and Harper & Row, New York/London, 1957.) For the interpretation of the book in the light of Feuerbach's own thought, we are using especially two works that continue the theme of *The Essence of Christianity*: *Vorläufige Thesen zur Reformation der Philosophie*, 1843 (Werke III, pp. 223–43), and *Grundsätze der Philosophie der Zukunft*, 1843 (Werke III, pp. 247–322). On the double confrontation mentioned above, cf. the Preface to the 1st ed. of *Das Wesen des Christentums*, 1841, pp. 1–2. (Not in E.t.)

35 L. Feuerbach, letter to W. Bolin, Oct. 20, 1860, in K. Grün, *Ludwig Feuerbach*, Vol. II, p. 120.

36 A. Ruge, letter to Stahr, Sept. 8, 1841, in P. Nerrlich (ed.), *Arnold Ruges Briefwechsel und Tagebuchblätter aus den Jahren 1825–1880*, Berlin, 1886, p. 239.

37 L. Feuerbach, *Wesen des Christentums*, p. 51. (E.t., p. 12.)

38 Ibid., p. 408; cf. Preface, p. 6. (E.t., p. 336.)

39 L. Feuerbach, *Grundsätze der Philosophie der Zukunft* (1843), in Sämtliche Werke, eds. W. Bolin and F. Jodl, 2nd ed. by H. M. Sass, Vol. II, p. 245.

40 *Wesen des Christentums*, p. 15. (E.t., p. xxxiv.)

41 Ibid., p. 22. (E.t., p. xxxix.)

42 Ibid., p. 94; also Ch. 9 and 11. (E.t., p. 44 and Ch. 8, on the "Mystery of the Cosmogonical Principle in God," and Ch. 10, on the "Mystery of Providence and Creation out of Nothing.")

43 Ibid., p. 148. (E.t., p. 82.)

44 Ibid., pp. 17–18. (E.t., p. xxxv.)

45 Ibid., p. 37. (E.t., pp. 2–3.)

46 Ibid., p. 41. (E.t., p. 5.)

47. Ibid., pp. 76–77. (E.t., pp. 30–31.)

48 Cf. ibid., pp. 81–95. (E.t., pp. 33–43.)

49 Cf. ibid., pp. 95–100. (E.t., pp. 44–49.)

50 Cf. ibid., pp. 101–3. (E.t., pp. 50–58.)

51 Ibid., p. 53. (E.t., p. 14.)

52 Ibid., p. 541. (E.t., p. 339.)

53 Ibid., p. 18. (E.t., p. xxxvi.)
54 Ibid., p. 4. (Not in E.t.)
55 Ibid., p. 21. (E.t., p. xxxviii.)
56 L. Feuerbach, letter to A. Ruge (1843), in P. Nerrlich (ed.), *Arnold Ruges Brief-wechsel*, Vol. I, p. 304.
57 L. Feuerbach, *Vorlesungen über das Wesen der Religion* (delivered 1848–49 in Heidelberg), in Gesammelte Werke, Vol. VI, Berlin, 1967, pp. 30–31.
58 A. Ruge, letter to Ludwig Feuerbach, Mar. 8, 1842, in K. Grün, *Ludwig Feuer-bach*, Vol. I, p. 352.
59 Cf. A. Schmidt (of the neo-Marxist Frankfurt School), *Emanzipatorische Sinn-lichkeit. Ludwig Feuerbachs anthropologischer Materialismus*, Munich, 1973.
60 Cf. the theses of A. Schmidt, "Erfordernisse gegenwärtiger Feuerbach-Interpreta-tion," in *Atheismus in der Diskussion*, pp. 166–67, and in the same volume the opposite positions of W. Schuffenhauer, "Feuerbach statt Marx—Emanzipation wessen?" (pp. 168–73), and F. Richter, "Ludwig Feuerbach und der wis-senschaftliche Kommunismus" (pp. 174–83), also the contributions to the discus-sion by F. Richter, W. Schuffenhauer, H. Lübbe, M. Prucha, and H. M. Sass (pp. 184–96).
61 Cf. M. Xhaufflaire, "L'Évangile de Sinnlichkeit et la théologie politique," in *Atheismus in der Diskussion*, pp. 36–56.
62 Cf. M. Xhaufflaire in his contribution to the discussion, pp. 65–67.
63 Cf. the rather inconclusive discussion on Xhaufflaire's contribution, pp. 67–71. Fundamentally different evaluations of Feuerbach's philosophy of religion are found especially in the works above mentioned by K. E. Bockmühl, G. Nüdling, M. von Gagern, H. J. Braun, and E. Schneider.
64 L. Feuerbach, *Wesen des Christentums*, p. 36. (E.t., p. 2.)
65 Ibid., pp. 37–38. (E.t., p. 3.)
66 M. Stirner, *Der Einzige und sein Eigentum*, Leipzig, 1845. (E.t., *The Ego and His Own*, Harper & Row, New York, 1974.)
67 We can agree with H. Arvon's revaluation of Stirner—but not with his devalua-tion of the importance of the *Essence of Christianity* for Marx—in his comments in *Atheismus in der Diskussion*, pp. 109–19.
68 L. Feuerbach, *Notwendigkeit einer Reform der Philosophie* (1841), Sämtliche Werke, eds. Bolin and Jodl, Vol. II, Stuttgart, 1904, p. 217.
69 Ibid., Vol. II, pp. 218–19.
70 L. Feuerbach, *Wesen des Christentums*, pp. 29–30. (E.t., p. xliv.)
71 M. Baumotte, in his contribution in *Atheismus in der Diskussion*, p. 71.
72 L. Feuerbach, *Vorlesungen über das Wesen der Religion*, in Gesammelte Werke, Vol. VI, p. 262.
73 L. Feuerbach, *Wesen des Christentums*, p. 136. (E.t., p. 73.)
74 L. Feuerbach, *Vorlesungen über das Wesen der Religion*, in Gesammelte Werke, Vol. VI, p. 262.
75 E. von Hartmann, *Geschichte der Metaphysik*, 2 vols., Leipzig, 1900; reprinted Darmstadt, 1969; quotation, Vol. II, p. 444.
76 L. Feuerbach, *Nachgelassene Aphorismen*, in Sämtliche Werke, eds., Bolin and Jodl, Vol. X, Stuttgart, 1911, p. 345.
77 L. Feuerbach, letter to Christian Kapp, Mar. 11, 1841, in A. Kapp (ed.), *Brief-wechsel zwischen Ludwig Feuerbach und Christian Kapp*, p. 134.
78 Cf. L. Feuerbach, "Die Naturwissenschaft und die Religion," in *Blätter für die lit-erarische Unterhaltung* Nr. 268, Nov. 8, 1850 (in connection with an adver-tisement of J. Moleschott's book *Lehre der Nahrungsmittel. Für das Volk*, Erlan-gen, 1850). The article is reproduced in K. Grün, *Ludwig Feuerbach*, Vol. II, pp. 73–92 (quotation, p. 90); cf. also the correspondence with Moleschott in K. Grün, Vol. II, pp. 60–70, 196–98.
79 L. Feuerbach, "Gespräch mit G. Struve," quoted in Sass (ed.), Sämtliche Werke, Vol. XII, Stuttgart, 1964, p. 121. This statement of Feuerbach's is guaranteed—as W. Schuffenhauer kindly informed me—by the account in Dodel-Port's biography of Deubler: *Konrad Deublers Lebens- und Entwicklungsgang*, Leipzig, 1886, pp. 216–17.

80 L. Feuerbach, *Vorlesungen über das Wesen der Religion*, in Gesammelte Werke VI.
81 L. Feuerbach, letter to A. Ruge, June 20, 1843, in K. Grün, *Ludwig Feuerbach*, Vol. I, p. 358.
82 L. Feuerbach, diary note, in K. Grün, *Ludwig Feuerbach*, Vol. II, p. 4.
83 L. Feuerbach, "Nachgelassene Aphorismen," in K. Grün, *Ludwig Feuerbach*, Vol. I, p. 137.
84 Ibid., p. 138.
85 A. Scholl, address at the graveside for Ludwig Feuerbach, Sept. 15, 1872, in K. Grün, *Ludwig Feuerbach*, Vol. II, p. 114.
86 E. Feuerbach, letter to L. Feuerbach, Aug. 3, 1842, in K. Grün, *Ludwig Feuerbach*, Vol. I, p. 355.
87 L. Feuerbach, letter to E. Feuerbach, Aug. 18, 1842, in K. Grün, *Ludwig Feuerbach*, Vol. I, p. 356.
88 Address of thanks by the Heidelberg *Arbeiter-Bildungs-Verein* to Ludwig Feuerbach, Mar. 16, 1849, in K. Grün, *Ludwig Feuerbach*, Vol. I, pp. 385–86.
89 Ildephonsus Müller, letter to Ludwig Feuerbach, Oct. 11, 1867, in Grün, *Ludwig Feuerbach*, Vol. II, pp. 193–94.
90 Ibid., p. 194.
91 Cf. B.III.1: "The irremovable difference."
92 M. Buber, *Das Problem des Menschen*, p. 341.
93 Karl Barth, *Die protestantische Theologie im 19. Jahrhundert*, p. 489. (E.t., *Protestant Theology in the Nineteenth Century*, S.C.M. Press, London, 1972, pp. 539–40.)

## C.II. God—a consolation serving vested interests? Karl Marx

1 We shall mainly use Karl Marx, Werke-Schriften-Briefe, eds. H. J. Lieber and P. Fürth, Vols. I–VII, Darmstadt, 1962 onward. This edition will be cited as Werke. For texts not included there, we shall use K. Marx and F. Engels, Historisch-kritische Gesamtausgabe, eds. D. Rjazanov and V. Adoratsky for the Marx-Engels Institute, Moscow, pub. at Frankfurt am Main, 1927–32 (cited as MEGA). Anything else will be quoted from K. Marx and F. Engels, Werke, ed. in 39 vols. with supp. vols., by the Institute for Marxism-Leninism in East Berlin, 1956–71 (cited as MEW). The quotation is from Werke I, p. 109; MEGA I, Section I/1, p. 175; MEW I, p. 27. (For the English translation, we shall use mainly Karl Marx and Frederick Engels, Collected Works, published in several volumes from 1975 onward by Lawrence & Wishart, London/International Publishers Company, New York [quoted as Collected Works]. Other reliable translations will be used when convenient and full details given on each occasion.)
2 L. Feuerbach, *Vorläufige Thesen zur Reformation der Philosophie* (1843), in Werke III, pp. 223–43.
3 This was first substantiated by H. M. Sass, "Feuerbach statt Marx. Zur Verfasserschaft des Aufsatzes 'Luther als Schiedsrichter zwischen Strauss und Feuerbach,'" in *International Review of Social History* 12 (1967), pp. 108–19.
4 As in the E. Thies edition of Feuerbach, Werke III, pp. 244–46; notes on the reasons for ascribing the article to Feuerbach are on pp. 368–72.
5 K. Marx, letter to L. Feuerbach, Aug. 11, 1844, in MEW Vol. 27, p. 425. (E.t., Collected Works, Vol. 3, p. 355.)
6 *Die Differenz der demokritischen und epikureischen Naturphilosophie*, in Werke I, pp. 18–76; cf. the preparatory materials in I, pp. 77–106. (E.t. in Collected Works, Vol. I, pp. 25–107; preparatory materials in I, pp. 403–509.)
7 A. Künzli, *Karl Marx Eine Psychographie*, Vienna/Frankfurt/Zürich, 1966, pp. 504–5. In addition to the numerous biographies of Marx, the following recent monographs on his critique of religion should be noted: G. M. M. Cottier, *L'athéisme de jeune Marx. Ses origines hégéliennes*, Paris, 1969; W. Post, *Kritik der Religion bei Karl Marx*, Munich, 1969; J. Kadenbach, *Das Religionsverständnis von Karl Marx*, Munich/Paderborn/Vienna, 1970; K. Farmer and W. Post,

*Marxistische Religionskritik*, Stein/Nuremberg, 1972; B. Casper, *Wesen und Grenzen der Religionskritik: Feuerbach-Marx-Freud*, Würzburg, 1974.

8 K. Marx, "Betrachtung eines Jünglings bei der Wahl eines Berufes," in Werke I, pp. 1–6. (E.t. in Collected Works, Vol. I, pp. 3–9.)

9 Ibid., p. 5. (E.t., ibid., p. 8.)

10 K. Marx, "Die Vereinigung der Gläubigen mit Christo nach Jo. 15, 1–14, in ihrem Grund und Wesen, in ihrer unbedingten Notwendigkeit und in ihren Wirkungen dargestellt," in MEGA I, Sec. I/2, pp. 171–74. (E.t., Collected Works, Vol. I, pp. 636–39.)

11 Ibid., p. 173. (E.t., ibid., p. 639.)

12 H. Marx, letter to K. Marx in Berlin, Dec. 9, 1837, in MEGA I, Sec. I/2, pp. 223–28; quotation, p. 226. (E.t., Collected Works, Vol. I, pp. 685–91; quotation, p. 689.)

13 A. Ruge, letter to Stahr, Sept. 8, 1841, in *Arnold Ruges Briefwechsel und Tagebuchblätter aus den Jahren 1825–80*, ed. P. Nerrlich, Vol. I, Berlin, 1886, p. 239.

14 K. Marx, *Die Differenz der demokritischen und epikureischen Naturphilosophie*, in Werke I, p. 62. (E.t., Collected Works, Vol. I, p. 68.)

15 B. Bauer, *Die Posaune des jüngsten Gerichts über Hegel den Atheisten und Antichristen. Ein Ultimatum*, Leipzig, 1841.

16 The occasion for this was Bauer's *Kritik der Synoptiker (Critique of the Synoptists)*, Vols. I–II, Leipzig, 1841. Vol. III appeared in Brunswick in 1842.

17 M. Hess, letter to Berthold Auerbach, Sept. 2, 1841, in MEGA I, Sec. I/2, p. 261.

18 K. Marx, letter to A. Ruge, Nov. 30, 1842, in MEGA I, Sec. I/2, p. 286. (E.t., Collected Works, Vol. I, p. 395.)

19 M. Hess, *Die europäische Triarchie*, 1841. Three articles date from Marx's time in Paris: "Sozialismus und Kommunismus," "Philosophie der Tat" and "Die eine und ganze Freiheit," all included in M. Hess, *Philosophische und sozialistische Schriften 1837–1850. Eine Auswahl*, eds. A. Cornu and W. Mönke, Berlin, 1961.

20 K. Marx, *Die heilige Familie oder Kritik der kritischen Kritik. Gegen Bruno Bauer und Consorten*, in Werke I, pp. 667–925. (E.t., Collected Works, Vol. IV, pp. 5–211.)

21 K. Marx, *Zur Kritik der Nationalökonomie. Ökonomisch-philosophische Manuskripte* (1844), in Werke I, pp. 506–665; quotation, p. 658. (E.t., Collected Works, Vol. 3, pp. 229–346; quotation, p. 341.)

22 Cf. F. Engels, "Umrisse zu einer Kritik der Nationalökonomie," which appeared in the first and only issue of the *Deutsch-Französische Jahrbücher* (Paris, 1844), eds. Marx and Ruge, in MEW I, pp. 499–524. (E.t., "Outlines of Political Economy," in Collected Works, Vol. 3, pp. 418–43.) On the biography of Engels, see esp. G. Mayer, *Friedrich Engels. Eine Biographie*, 2 vols., The Hague, 1934.

23 K. Marx, "Zur Kritik der Hegelschen Rechtsphilosophie. Einleitung" (appeared first in the *Deutsch-Französische Jahrbücher*), in Werke I, pp. 488–505. The article "Zur Judenfrage" (not particularly friendly toward Jews) appeared also as an answer to Bruno Bauer in the *Jahrbücher* and is found in Werke I, pp. 451–87. (E.t., Collected Works, "Contribution to the Critique of Hegel's Philosophy of Law," Vol. 3, pp. 3–129.)

24 K. Marx, "Auszug aus dem letzten Kapitel von Hegels *Phänomenologie des Geistes*" (known as the fourth manuscript of the "Economic and Philosophical Manuscripts"), in Werke I, pp. 958–64.

25 K. Marx, *Kritik der Hegelschen Dialektik und Philosophie überhaupt* (also part of the "Economic and Philosophical Manuscripts"), in Werke I, pp. 637–65. (E.t., *Critique of the Hegelian Dialectic and Philosophy as a Whole*, Collected Works, Vol. 3, pp. 326–46.)

26 K. Marx, *Kritik des Hegelschen Staatsrechts* §§261–313 in Werke I, pp. 258–426.

27 Art. "Atheismus," in Grosse sowjetische Enzyklopädie, Moscow, 1950, Vol. III, p. 351. (The article on atheism in the English ed., Great Soviet Encyclopedia, Moscow, 1970 [Macmillan, New York/Collier and Macmillan, London], pp. 458–59, does not contain anything like this sentence.)

28 On this, cf. esp. the above-mentioned manuscripts *Zur Kritik des Hegelschen Staatsrechts* and *Kritik der Hegelschen Dialektik und Philosophie überhaupt.*
29 K. Marx, *Kritik der Hegelschen Dialektik*, in Werke I, p. 639. (E.t., Collected Works, Vol. 3, p. 328.)
30 Ibid. (E.t., ibid.)
31 K. Marx, *Kritik der Hegelschen Rechtsphilosophie*, in Werke I, p. 488. (E.t., Collected Works, Vol. 3, p. 175.)
32 Ibid. (E.t., ibid.)
33 Ibid. (E.t., ibid.)
34 K. Marx, letter to L. Feuerbach, Aug. 11, 1844, in MEW Vol. 27, p. 425. (E.t., Collected Works, Vol. 3, p. 354.)
35 K. Marx, *Thesen über Feuerbach*, in Werke II, 2–3. (E.t, *Theses on Feuerbach*, in Karl Marx and Frederick Engels, *Selected Works*, one vol., Progress Publishers, Moscow/International Publishers Inc., New York/Lawrence & Wishart, London, 1968 [reprinted 1973], p. 29.)
36 Ibid. (E.t., ibid.)
37 Ibid., II, p. 1. (E.t., ibid., p. 28.)
38 K. Marx, "Kritik der Hegelschen Rechtsphilosophie," in Werke I, p. 488. (E.t., Collected Works, Vol. 3, p. 175.)
39 Ibid. (E.t., ibid.)
40 Cf. E. Bloch, *Atheismus im Christentum. Zur Religion des Exodus und des Reichs*, Frankfurt am Main, 1968.
41 K. Marx, "Kritik der Hegelschen Rechtsphilosophie," in Werke I, p. 488. (E.t., Collected Works, Vol. 3, p. 175.)
42 Ibid. (E.t., ibid.)
43 M. Hess, "Die eine und ganze Freiheit" (1843), in *Schriften*, pp. 227–28.
44 L. Feuerbach, *Wesen des Christentums*, ed. by Schuffenhauer, Berlin, 1956, pp. 200–1. (E.t., *The Essence of Christianity*, Harper & Row, New York/London, 1957, p. 122.)
45 K. Marx, "Kritik der Hegelschen Rechtsphilosophie," in Werke I, p. 489. (E.t., Collected Works, Vol. 3, p. 176.)
46 Ibid. (E.t., ibid.)
47 Ibid., p. 497. (E.t., ibid., p. 182.)
48 Ibid., p. 498. (E.t., ibid.)
49 Ibid., p. 504. (E.t., ibid., p. 186.)
50 Ibid., p. 505. (E.t., ibid., p. 187.)
51 K. Marx, *Thesen über Feuerbach*, in Werke II, p. 4. (E.t., *Selected Works*, p. 30.)
52 K. Marx, *Kritik der politischen Ökonomie*, in Werke VI, p. 840. (E.t., *A Contribution to the Critique of Political Economy*, with an Introduction by Maurice Dobb, Progress Publishers, Moscow/International Publishers Inc., New York/Lawrence & Wishart, London, 1971, p. 32.)
53 K. Marx, *Die Deutsche Ideologie. Kritik der neuesten deutschen Philosophie in ihren Repräsentanten Feuerbach, B. Bauer und Stirner, und des deutschen Sozialismus in seinen verschiedenen Propheten.* This was first published in MEGA in 1932 and at the same time in the selection of early writings by S. Landshut and P. J. Mayer, Werke II, pp. 5–655. (E.t., *The German Ideology. Critique of Modern German Philosophy. According to Its Representatives Feuerbach, Bruno Bauer and Stirner, and of German Socialism. According to Its Various Prophets*, Progress Publishers, Moscow/International Publishers Inc., New York/Lawrence & Wishart, London, 1965.)
54 K. Marx and F. Engels, *Manifest der Kommunistischen Partei*, in Werke II, pp. 813–58; quotation, p. 816. (E.t., *The Communist Manifesto*, with an introduction by A. J. P. Taylor, Penguin Books Ltd., Harmondsworth, Middlesex, England/Penguin Books Inc., Baltimore, Md., U.S.A., 1967 [frequent reprints], p. 78.)
55 Ibid., p. 846. (E.t., p. 107.)
56 Ibid., p. 840. (E.t., pp. 102–3.)
57 Ibid., p. 841. (E.t., p. 103.)

58 Ibid., p. 858. (E.t., pp. 120–21.)
59 K. Marx, "Die standrechtliche Beseitigung der *Neuen Rheinischen Zeitung*," in *Neue Rheinische Zeitung*, May 19, 1849, reproduced in MEW Vol. 6, p. 505.
60 K. Marx, *Zur Kritik der politischen Ökonomie* (first part), in Werke VI, pp. 837–1029, esp. the Preface, pp. 837–42. (E.t., *A Contribution to the Critique of Political Economy*, Moscow/New York/London, 1971, Preface, pp. 19–27.)
61 K. Marx, *Das Kapital. Kritik der politischen Ökonomie. Erster Band. Erstes Buch: Der Produktionsprozess des Kapitals*, in Werke IV, pp. 46–63. (E.t. *Capital*, 2 vols., Everyman Library, Dent, London/Dutton, New York, 1957, Vol. I, pp. 43–58.)
62 Ibid., p. 48. (E.t., pp. 45–46.)
63 Ibid., p. 57. (E.t., pp. 53–54.)
64 F. J. Raddatz's *Karl Marx. Eine politische Biographie* (Hamburg, 1975) is often provocative and has been adversely criticized by W. Harich in *Der Spiegel* No. 17 (1975), but in many points it provides a necessary "demythologization" of the Marx image and a correction not only of the orthodox communist Marx historiography but also of the official social-democratic biography by F. Mehring, *Karl Marx. Geschichte seines Lebens. Gesammelte Schriften*, Vol. 3, Berlin, 1960. Cf. also the discussion between G. Grass and W. Harich in *Der Spiegel* Nos. 20 and 21 (1975).
65 K. Marx, *Der achtzehnte Brumaire des Louis Bonaparte* (1852), in Werke III, pp. 266–87. (E.t., *The eighteenth Brumaire of Louis Bonaparte*, in *Selected Works*, pp. 94–179.)
66 K. Marx, "Inauguraladresse und Statuten der Internationalen Arbeiterassoziation" (1864), in Werke III, pp. 866–81.
67 K. Marx, *Adresse des Generalrates über den Bürgerkrieg in Frankreich 1871*, in Werke III, pp. 897–953. (E.t., *The Civil War in France. Address of the General Council of the International Working Men's Association*, in *Selected Works*, pp. 271–307.)
68 Foundation of the Universal German Workers' Union by F. Lassalle, 1863; foundation of the German Social Democratic Workers' Party by A. Bebel and K. Liebknecht, 1869; union of the two parties as the Socialist Workers' Party of Germany at the party congress in Gotha, 1875. Marx submitted the Gotha program to a severe criticism, but this was published only after his death. Cf. K. Marx, "Randglossen zum Programm der Deutschen Arbeiterpartei" (together with an accompanying letter to Wilhelm Bracke, May 5, 1875), in Werke III, pp. 1014–38.
69 F. Engels, *Herrn Eugen Dührings Umwälzung der Wissenschaft* ("Anti-Dühring"), 1878, new ed., Berlin, 1948. (E.t., *Anti-Dühring: Herr Eugen Dühring's Revolution in Science*, Progress Publishers, Moscow/Lawrence & Wishart, London, 1969.)
70 Ibid., pp. 393–95. (E.t., pp. 374–76.)
71 Cf. B.III.2: "Progress without God? Auguste Comte."
72 F. Engels, *"Anti-Dühring,"* pp. 125 and 426–27. (E.t., pp. 128, 407.)
73 J. Dietzgen, "Die Religion der Sozialdemokratie," in *Volksstaat* (1870ff.), quoted from Gesammelte Schriften, 3 vols., Berlin, 1930, pp. 98 and 103. I. Fetscher has brought out clearly the differences between Marx's critique of religion and the later Marxist Weltanschauung in an article in *Concilium* ("Developments in the Marxist Critique of Religion," in the English-language edition of *Concilium*, June 1966) and more recently in his volume *Karl Marx und der Marxismus. Von der Philosophie des Proletariats zur proletarischen Weltanschauung*, Munich, 1973[3], pp. 200–17. Fetscher has collected the most important Marxist texts on philosophy, ideology, economics, sociology and politics in a large volume, *Der Marxismus. Seine Geschichte in Dokumenten*, Munich, 1973[2]. Important works on the development of Marxism include P. Vranicki, *Geschichte des Marxismus*, 2 vols. (transl. from Serbo-Croat ed., Zagreb, 1967–71), Frankfurt am Main, 1972–74; L. Kolakowski, *Die Hauptströmungen des Marxismus. Entstehung-Entwicklung-Verfall*, 3 vols. (transl. from Polish ed., Paris, 1976), Munich, 1977ff.
74 V. I. Lenin, *Religion*, Lawrence & Wishart, London, 1932, pp. 11–12.
75 Ibid., p. 14.

76 Ibid.
77 Ibid., p. 54.
78 Pope Leo XIII, encyclical letter *Quod Apostolici Muneris*, Dec. 28, 1878. Extracts in DS 3130–33.
79 G. Wetter, *Der Dialektische Materialismus. Seine Geschichte und sein System in der Sowjetunion*, Vienna, 1952.
80 Cf. G. A. Wetter, op. cit., pp. 574–80. See also H. Küng, *Kirche in Freiheit*, Einsiedeln, 1944, pp. 7–9. (E.t., "The Freedom of the Church," appears as a chapter in *Freedom Today*, Sheed & Ward, New York, 1966.)
81 Cf. H. Küng, *Christ sein*, Munich, 1974, Ch. A.I.3: "Humanität durch politisch-soziale Revolution?" (E.t., *On Being a Christian*, New York, 1976/London, 1977, Ch. A.I.3: "Humanity through politico-social revolution?")
82 Ibid.
83 A new phenomenon is the increasing criticism of Marx on the part of formerly Marxist young French intellectuals who are dissociating themselves not only from Marxism-Leninism but also from Marx himself. The group of the *Nouvelle Philosophie* around André Glucksmann consists of philosophers who were among the militant champions of Marxism even up to 1968 but who now proclaim the death of socialism. Cf. A. Glucksmann, *La Cuisinière et le mangeur d'hommes*, Paris, 1975; the same author, *Les maîtres penseurs*, Paris, 1977; C. Jambet and G. Lardreau, *Ontologie de la révolution*, Vol. I, "L'ange," Paris, 1976; announced as Vol. II, L'âme"; as Vol. III, "Le monde"; B. H. Lévy, *La barbarie à visage humain*, Paris, 1977. Lévy is the editor of the collection Figures, in which F. Lévy's *Marx. Histoire d'un bourgeois allemand* is shortly to appear.
84 Marx's position in regard to Hegel's dialectic is made particularly clear in his postscript, written in 1873, to the 2nd ed. of the 1st vol. of *Das Kapital*, in Werke IV, p. xxxi.
85 Karl Marx, "Ökonomische Studien," in MEGA 1, Sec. III, pp. 546–47.
86 K. Marx and F. Engels, *Die deutsche Ideologie. Kritik der neuesten deutschen Philosophie in ihren Repräsentanten Feuerbach, B. Bauer und Stirner, und des deutschen Sozialismus in seinen verschiedenen Propheten*, in Werke II, pp. 5–655; quotation, p. 36. (E.t., *The German Ideology*, Lawrence & Wishart, London/Progress Publishing, Moscow, 1965, pp. 44–45.)
87 K. Marx, *Kapital*, in Werke IV, p. 57. (E.t., *Capital*, J. M. Dent, London/Dutton, New York, 1930, reprint 1967, pp. 53–54.)
88 K. Marx and F. Engels, *Manifest*, in Werke II, p. 843. (E.t., *The Communist Manifesto*, Penguin Books, Harmondsworth/Baltimore, 1967, p. 105.)
89 On what follows, see F. Borkenau, "Praxis und Utopie," Introduction to *Karl Marx. Auswahl*, Frankfurt, 1956, pp. 7–37, especially 25–30.)
90 Cf. H. Prosa, "Überleben des Kapitalismus? Mitwirkung der Unternehmer an der Verbesserung der Wirtschaftsverfassung," in *Sonderdruck der Arbeitsgemeinschaft Selbständiger Unternehmer*, pub. on the occasion of the annual conference of employers in Munich, May 31, to June 2, 1973, pp. 15–20.
91 For the past and present of the Marxist-Leninist *Soviet system*, cf., in addition to the novels of Alexander Solzhenitsyn, the publications of prominent Russian critics of the regime, esp. the letter of Professors A. D. Sakharov, W. F. Turtshin and R. A. Medvedev in 1968 to the Central Committee of the Communist Party of the Soviet Union, printed in the *Neue Zürcher Zeitung*, Apr. 22, 1970; A. D. Sakharov, *Wie ich mir die Zukunft vorstelle*, Zürich, 1969; the same author, "Ein Memorandum an den General-Sekretär der KPdSU, L. I. Breschnew," 1971, printed in *Die Zeit*, July 21, 1972; the same author, "Interview," in *Der Spiegel*, 1973, No. 18; the same author, *Mein Land und die Welt*, Vienna/Munich, 1975; A. Amalrik, *Will the Soviet Union Survive until 1984?*, London, 1970/New York, 1971; P. I. Jakir, *Kindheit in Gefangenschaft*, Frankfurt, 1972; A. Solzhenitsyn, *An Open Letter to the Soviet Leaders*, New York Times, Sept. 1973; "Live not by lies" (Feb. 12, 1974), in Leopold Labetz (ed.), *Solzhenitsyn. A Documentary Record*, Penguin Books, Harmondsworth/Baltimore, 1974, pp. 375–79. Also informative is the investigation by R. Bernheim. *Die sozialistischen Errungen-*

*schaften der Sowjetunion,* Zürich, 1972. See, too, the study by the correspondent of the New York *Times* H. Smith, New York: Quadrangle Books, 1976.

92 A. Solzhenitsyn, Lenten Letter to the Patriarch of Moscow, in the New York *Times,* Apr. 9, 1972. Abridged version in Labetz, op. cit., pp. 296–98.

93 Cf. the information from the Moscow Patriarchate, according to *Der Spiegel,* 1974, No. 17.

94 T. Luckmann, Introduction to the German edition of B. Malinowski, *Magie, Wissenschaft und Religion,* Frankfurt, 1973. Some impressive observations against the Marxist thesis on the dying out of the Christian religion can be found in L. Kolakowski, "Die sogenannte Krise des Christentums," in the *Frankfurter Allgemeine Zeitung,* Apr. 17, 1976; reprinted in the Kolakowski anthology *Leben trotz Geschichte,* Munich/Zürich, 1977, pp. 175–86.

95 Cf. A.II.4: "Questions of politics: political atheism?"

96 This was expressly affirmed by the synod in its resolutions on the Church and the workers. See *Synode. Amtliche Mitteilungen der Gemeinsamen Synode der Bistümer in der Bundesrepublik Deutschland,* 1976, fascicle 2, pp. 73–101, esp. Ch. 1: "Ein fortwirkender Skandal."

97 K. Marx, in *Deutsche-Brüsseler Zeitung,* Sept. 12, 1847, in MEGA 1, Sec. VI, p. 278.

98 Cf. O. Nell-Breuning, "Auseinandersetzung mit Marx und seiner Lehre. Anmerkungen zu einer Kontroverse um das Synodendokument 'Kirche und Arbeiterschaft,' " in *Stimmen der Zeit,* 101 (1976), pp. 173–82.

99 K. Marx, letter to F. Engels, Sept. 25, 1869, in MEGA 3, Sec. IV, p. 227.

100 In connection with G. F. Daumer's assertions in his book *Die Geheimnisse des christlichen Altertums,* according to a report on a lecture by Marx at the London Workers' Educational Association, Nov. 30, 1847, in MEGA 1, Sec. VI, pp. 639–40.

101 Cf. H. Küng, *Christ sein.* (E.t., *On Being a Christian,* New York, 1976/London, 1977.) The same author, *Die Kirche,* Freiburg/Basel/Vienna, 1967. (E.t., *The Church,* London/New York, 1967.)

102 This is rightly stressed by W. Bienert (although his theology is often too apologetic in style), *Der überholte Marx. Seine Religionskritik und Weltanschauung kritisch untersucht,* Stuttgart, 1974, esp. Ch. 3: "Karl Marx' Kritik am Sozialversagen der Kirche, pp. 93–131; see also pp. 295–96.

103 H. Lübbe, "Diskussionsbeitrag," in *Atheismus in der Diskussion. Kontroversen um L. Feuerbach,* eds. H. Lübbe and H. M. Sass, Mainz, 1975, p. 189.

104 A. Schmidt, *Emanzipatorische Sinnlichkeit. Ludwig Feuerbachs anthropologischer Materialismus,* Munich, 1973; the same author, "Erfordernisse gegenwärtiger Feuerbach-Interpretation," in *Atheismus in der Diskussion,* pp. 166–67.

105 V. I. Lenin, "Materialismus und Empiriokritizismus," in *Werke,* Vol. 14, Berlin, 1968, p. 120. (E.t., "Materialism and Empirio-Criticism," in *Collected Works,* Lawrence & Wishart, London/Foreign Languages Publishing House, Moscow, 1962, pp. 17–388; quotation, pp. 125–26.)

106 V. I. Lenin, *Religion,* Lawrence & Wishart, London, 1932, p. 19.

107 On relations between Christianity and Marxism, first from the *Christian standpoint:* J. L. Hromádka, *Evangelium für Atheisten,* Berlin, 1957; H. Gollwitzer, *Die marxistische Religionskritik und der christliche Glaube,* Hamburg, 1965; M. Reding, *Die Glaubensfreiheit im Marxismus. Zum Verhältnis von Marxismus und christlichen Glauben,* Vienna/Frankfurt/Zürich, 1967; G. Girardi, *Marxismo e cristianesimo,* Assisi, 1967; F. J. Adelmann, *From Dialogue to Epilogue. Marxism and Catholicism,* The Hague, 1968; I. Fetscher and W. Post, *Verdirbt Religion den Menschen? Marxistischer und christlicher Humanismus. Ein Interview,* Düsseldorf, 1969; H. Aptheker, *The Urgency of Marxist-Christian Dialogue,* New York, 1970; J. M. Lochman, *Church in a Marxist Society. A Czechoslovak View,* New York, 1970; D. Sölle, "Christentum und Marxismus. Bericht über den Stand des Gesprächs," in *Das Recht ein anderer zu werden,* Neuwied/Berlin, 1971; F. v. d. Oudenrijn, *Kritische Theologie als Kritik der Theologie. Theorie und Praxis bei Karl Marx—Herausforderung der Theologie,* Munich/Mainz, 1972; J. P.

Miranda, *Marx y la Biblia. Crítica a la filosofía de la opresión*, Salamanca, 1972; A. Stüttgen, *Kriterien einer Ideologiekritik. Ihre Anwendung auf Christentum und Marxismus*, Mainz, 1972; J. M. Lochman, *Marx begegnen. Was Christen und Marxisten eint und trennt*, Gütersloh, 1975.
On relations between Christianity and Marxism *from the Marxist standpoint*: E. Bloch, *Das Prinzip Hoffnung*, 2 vols., Frankfurt, 1967[2]; the same author, *Thomas Münzer als Theologe der Revolution*, Frankfurt, 1962; the same author, *Atheismus in Christentum. Zur Religion des Exodus und des Reichs*, Frankfurt, 1968; M. Machoveč, *Marxismus und dialektische Theologie. Barth, Bonhoeffer und Hromádka in atheistisch-kommunistischer Sicht*, Zürich, 1965; the same author, *Jesus für Atheisten*, Stuttgart, 1972 (E.t., *Jesus for Atheists. A Marxist looks at Jesus*, London, 1976); R. Garaudy, *Marxisme du XXième siècle*, Paris/Geneva, 1966; V. Gardavsky, *Gott ist nicht ganz tot. Betrachtungen eines Marxisten über Bibel, Religion und Atheismus*, Munich, 1968; L. Kolakowski, *Geist und Ungeist christlicher Traditionen*, Stuttgart, 1971; I. Fetscher and M. Machoveč (eds.), *Marxisten und die Sache Jesu*, Mainz, 1974.
On relations between Christianity and Marxism, *Dialogue*: E. Kellner (ed.), *Christentum und Marxismus—heute. Gespräche der Paulus-Gesellschaft*, Vienna/Frankfurt/Zürich, 1966, cf. esp. the contributions by W. Dantine, G. Girardi, J. B. Metz, K. Rahner, M. Reding, O. Schreuder, G. A. Wetter, R. Garaudy, R. Havemann, L. Lombardo-Radice; R. Garaudy, *De l'Anathème au Dialogue*, Paris, 1965 (E.t., *From Anathema to Dialogue*, with an Introduction by Karl Rahner and Epilogue by J. B. Metz, translated from German, London, 1967; the translation of the French text was published in New York, 1966); M. Stöhr (ed.), *Disputation zwischen Christen und Marxisten*, Munich, 1966; B. Bosnjak and W. Dantine and J. Y. Calvez, *Marxistisches und christliches Weltverständnis*, Freiburg, 1966; H. J. Girock (ed.), *Partner von morgen? Das Gespräch zwischen Christentum und marxistischem Atheismus*, Stuttgart/Berlin, 1968, with contributions by J. Hromádka, C. Luporini, E. Moss, J. B. Metz, J. Makowski, G. Jacob, H. Gollwitzer, M. Machoveč; C. Link, *Theologische Perspektiven nach Marx und Freud*, Stuttgart, 1971; K. Farner and K. Marti, *Dialog Christ-Marxist*, Zürich, 1972; I. R. Romić, *De dialogo inter marxistas et christianos in marxisticis de religione fontibus fundato. Ratio atque aestimatio progressus obtenti in primis tribus congressibus internationalibus* (1964–65) *de dialogo prosequendo*, Rome, 1972; L. Bedeschi, *Cattolici e comunisti. Dal socialismo cristiano ai cristiani marxisti*, Milan, 1974; M. Spieker, *Neomarxismus und Christentum. Zur Problematik des Dialogs*, Paderborn, 1974; H. Rolfes (ed.), *Marxismus—Christentum*, Mainz, 1974; L. Boisset, *La théologie en procès. Face à la critique marxiste*, Paris, 1974; A. Ancel, *Pour une lecture chrétienne de la lutte des classes*, Paris, 1975; J. M. Lochmann, *Marx begegnen. Was Christen und Marxisten eint und trennt*, Gütersloh, 1975.
108 D. Sölle and K. Schmidt (eds.), *Christentum und Sozialismus. Vom Dialog zum Bündnis*, 2 vols., Stuttgart, 1974–75; the same authors, *Christen für den Sozialismus*, 2 vols., Stuttgart, 1975.
109 Cf. H. Küng, *Christ sein*, D.III.1: "Keine politische Kurzschlüsse." (E.t., *On Being a Christian*, D.III.1: "No political short cuts."
110 On the various types of socialism, see No. 5 of *Concilium* 13 (1977), eds. J. B. Metz and J. P. Jossua, on Christianity and socialism.
111 Cf. G. Girardi, *Marxismo e cristianesimo*, Ch. 1.
112 H. Küng, *Christ sein*, D.III.1: "Keine unkritischen Identifikationen." (E.t., *On Being a Christian*, D.III.1: "No uncritical identifications.")
113 Cf. H. F. Steiner, *Marxisten-Leninisten über den Sinn des Lebens. Eine Studie zum kommunistischen Menschenbild*, Essen, 1970; cf. esp. the documents translated from the Russian on the discussion in Soviet periodicals, pp. 309–63.
114 A. Schaff, *Marxismus und das menschliche Individuum*, Vienna/Frankfurt/Zürich, 1965.
115 M. Machoveč, *Jesus für Atheisten*, Stuttgart/Berlin, 1972, pp. 15–30. (E.t., *Jesus for Atheists*, London, 1976, pp. 18–38; the same author, *Vom Sinn des*

*menschlichen Lebens*, Freiburg, 1971; cf. also E. Bloch, *Religion im Erbe. Eine Auswahl aus seinen religionsphilosophischen Schriften*, Munich/Hamburg, 1967.
116 I. Fetscher, *Karl Marx und der Marxismus. Von der Philosophie des Proletariats zur proletarischen Weltanschauung*, Munich, 1967, p. 117.
117 Cf. A.III.2. *Interim results: Theses on modern rationality*.

## C.III. God—an infantile illusion? Sigmund Freud

*1. Psychoanalytic atheism*

1 L. Feuerbach, *Die Naturwissenschaft und die Revolution* (1850), in E. Thies's edition of Feuerbach's works, to be completed in six volumes. Vols. I–IV, Frankfurt, 1975–76, Vol. IV, pp. 243–65; quotation, pp. 253–54.
2 Ibid., pp. 249–50.
3 R. Wagner, *Menschenschöpfung und Seelensubstanz. Ein anthropologischer Vortrag, gehalten in der ersten öffentlichen Sitzung der 31.Versammlung deutscher Naturforscher und Ärzte zu Göttingen am 18.September 1854*, Göttingen, 1854; cf. also the same author, *Über Wissen und Glauben mit besonderer Beziehung auf die Zukunft der Seelen*, Göttingen, 1854.
4 K. Vogt, *Köhlerglaube und Wissenschaft*, Giessen, 1854.
5 J. Moleschott, *Der Kreislauf des Lebens. Physiologische Antworten auf Liebig's Chemische Briefe*, Mainz, 1852.
6 L. Büchner, *Kraft und Stoff. Empirisch-naturphilosophische Studien*, Leipzig, 1855.
7 Most of Freud's works quoted here can be found in S. Freud, Studienausgabe, eds. A. Mitscherlich, A. Richards and J. Strachey, Vols. I–IX, Frankfurt, 1969–75. Texts not contained in that edition can be found in S. Freud, Gesammelte Werke, edited in chronological sequence by A. Freud and others, Vols. I–XVIII, Frankfurt, 1960–68. Basic for Freud's biography is his own *Selbstdarstellung*, in Gesammelte Werke, Vol. XIV, pp. 31–96; see also his postscript (*Nachschrift*) to that work, written in 1935, in Gesammelte Werke XVI, pp. 29–34. (Except where otherwise indicated, all quotations in the present translation will be taken from the Standard Edition of the Complete Psychological Works of Sigmund Freud, 24 vols., 1953 onwards, published by Hogarth Press and the Institute of Psycho-Analysis, London/Clarke Irwin, Toronto. References to this edition will be indicated by S.E., followed by volume, date and page. An Autobiographical Study is in Vol. XX, 1959, pp. 2–70, followed by Postscript, pp. 71–74. Translator.)
8 Feuerbach, *Über Spiritualismus und Materialismus, besonders in Beziehung auf die Willensfreiheit*, in Sämtliche Werke, Leipzig, 1846–66, Vol. X, pp. 37–204; quotation, p. 119.
9 Ernest Jones, *Sigmund Freud. Life and Work*, Hogarth Press, London/Clarke Irwin, Toronto, 3 vols. 1953–57. Editions used here are Vol. I, 1956; Vol. II, 1958; Vol. III, 1957. The quotation is from I, p. 22; cf. also III, pp. 372–73.
 On recent psychological and theological discussion of Freud, cf. the following monographs: W. G. Cole, *Sex in Christianity and Psycho-Analysis*, London, 1956; J. Scharfenberg, *S. Freud und seine Religionskritik als Herausforderung für den christlichen Glauben*, Göttingen, 1970; the same author, *Religion zwischen Wahn und Wirklichkeit, Gesammelte Beiträge zur Korrelation von Theologie und Psychoanalyse*, Hamburg, 1972; A. Plé, *Freud et la religion*, Paris, 1968; P. Homans, *Theology after Freud. An interpretative Inquiry*, New York, 1970.
 Informative symposia on the subject include: P. Homans (ed.), *The Dialogue between Theology and Philosophy*, Chicago, 1968; H. Zahrnt (ed.), *Jesus und Freud. Ein Symposion von Psychoanalytikern und Theologen*, Munich, 1972, with contributions by the psychoanalysts T. Brocher, A. Görres, M. Hirsch and E. Wiesenhütter, and the theologians H. Fries and J. Scharfenberg. Particularly enlightening is E. Nase and J. Scharfenberg (eds.), *Psychoanalyse und Religion*, Darmstadt, 1977, with articles by authors belonging to the various stages of the

present century. A very up-to-date and comprehensive bibliography, compiled by E. Nase, on psychoanalysis and religion, can be found in pp. 387–435. Surveys of the discussion are provided by K. Birk, *Sigmund Freud und die Religion*, Münsterschwarzach, 1970, and by E. Wiesenhütter, *Freud und seine Kritiker*, Darmstadt, 1974.

Among recent helpful interpretations of Freudian thought may be mentioned P. Ricoeur, *De l'interprétation. Essai sur Freud*, Paris, 1964; W. Loch, *Zur Theorie, Technik und Therapie der Psychoanalyse*, Frankfurt, 1972; A. Mitscherlich, *Der Kampf um die Erinnerung. Psychoanalyse für fortgeschrittene Anfänger*, Munich, 1975.

10 Jones, op. cit., I, p. 21; cf. also Vol. I, Ch. 2 ("Boyhood and Adolescence") also Vol. III, Ch. 13 ("Religion").
11 Quoted by Jones, op. cit., I, pp. 21–22.
12 Ibid., p. 22.
13 S. Freud, *Die Traumdeutung*, in Studienausgabe II, p. 215. (*The Interpretation of Dreams*, in S.E. IV, 1953, p. 205.)
14 Freud, "Selbstdarstellung" in I. Grubrich-Simitis (ed.), *Schriften zur Geschichte der Psychoanalyse*, Frankfurt, 1971, p. 40. This sentence is lacking in the first edition of the *Selbstdarstellung* of 1925 (Gesammelte Werke XIV, p. 34) and was added only in 1935. (*An Autobiographical Study*, in S.E. XX, 1959, p. 8.)
15 Jones, op. cit., I, p. 183.
16 Cf. E. Wiesenhütter, *Freud und seine Kritiker*, pp. 31–35.
17 Freud, "Eine Kindheitserinnerung aus 'Dichtung und Wahrheit,'" in Gesammelte Werke XII, p. 26. ("A Childhood Recollection from *Dichtung und Wahrheit*," in S.E. XVII, 1955, pp. 145–56; quotation, p. 156.)
18 Marie Bonaparte, Anna Freud and Ernst Kris (eds.), *Aus den Anfängen der Psychoanalyse*, London, 1950, p. 236.
19 S. Freud, "Zwangshandlungen und Religionsübungen," in Studienausgabe VII, pp. 11–21. ("Obsessive Actions and Religious Practices," in S.E. IX, 1959, pp. 115–27.)
20 Ibid., p. 21. (S.E. IX, pp. 126–27.)
21 *Die Traumdeutung*, in Studienausgabe II, p. 208. (*The Interpretation of Dreams*, in S.E. IV, p. 197.)
22 S. Freud, *Selbstdarstellung*, in Gesammelte Werke XIV, p. 34. (*An Autobiographical Study*, in S.E. X, p. 9.)
23 S. Freud, "Nachwort zur 'Frage der Laienanalyse,'" in Gesammelte Werke XIV, p. 290. ("The Question of Lay Analysis. Postscript," in S.E. XX, 1959, p. 253.)
24 Ibid. (E.t., ibid.)
25 S. Freud, *Selbstdarstellung*, in Gesammelte Werke XIV, p. 35. (*An Autobiographical Study*, in S.E. XX, 1959, p. 9.)
26 S. Freud in a letter to his fiancée, Martha Bernays, quoted by Jones, op. cit., I, p. 45.
27 Ibid.
28 S. Freud, *Psychoanalyse*, in Gesammelte Werke XIV, p. 301. (*Psycho-Analysis*, in S.E. XX, 1959, p. 265.)
29 S. Freud, "Klinische Studie über die halbseitige Cerebrallähmung von Kindern" (1891), in *Beiträge zur Kinderheilkunde*, ed. M. Kassowitz, No. III, Vienna, 1891
30 Cf. Jones, op. cit., I, pp. 158, 358.
31 S. Freud and J. Breuer, *Studien über Hysterie* (1895), in Gesammelte Werke I, pp. 75–312. (*Studies in Hysteria*, in S.E. II, 1955.)
32 S. Freud, "Entwurf einer Psychologie" (1895), first pub. 1950 in M. Bonaparte, A. Freud and E. Kris (eds.), *Aus den Anfängen der Psychoanalyse*, London, 1950, pp. 371–466. Cf. W. Salber, *Entwicklungen der Psychologie Freuds*, Vol. I, Bonn, 1973, esp pp. 106–33.
33 S. Freud, *Selbstdarstellung*, in Gesammelte Werke XIV, p. 86. (*An Autobiographical Study*, in S.E. XX, 1959, p. 59.)
34 G T Fechner, *Elemente der Psychophysik*, 2 vols., Leipzig, 1860.
35 S. Freud, *Die Zukunft einer Illusion*, in Studienausgabe IX, pp. 135–89; quota-

tion, p. 164. (*The Future of an Illusion*, in S.E. XXI, 1961, pp. 5–56; quotation, p. 30.)

36 S. Freud, "Entwurf einer Psychologie," in *Aus den Anfängen der Psychoanalyse*, London, 1950, p. 424.

37 S. Freud, *Die Traumdeutung* (1900), in Studienausgabe II. (*The Interpretation of Dreams*, in S.E. IV and V, 1953.)

38 Cf. Jones, op. cit., I, pp. 356–60.

39 S. Freud, *Drei Abhandlungen zur Sexualtheorie* (1905), in Studienausgabe V, pp. 37–45. (*Three Essays on the Theory of Sexuality*, in S.E. VII, pp. 123–246.)

40 Cf. S. Freud, *Vorlesungen zur Einführung in die Psychoanalyse* (1916–17), in Studienausgabe I, pp. 33–445. (*Introductory Lectures on Psychoanalysis*, in S.E. XV and XVI, 1963.)

41 S. Freud, *Neue Folge der Vorlesungen zur Einführung in die Psychoanalyse* (1933), in Studienausgabe I, pp. 446–608. (*New Introductory Lectures on Psycho-Analysis*, in S.E. XXII, 1964, pp. 3–182.)

42 S. Freud, *Selbstdarstellung*, in Gesammelte Werke XIV, p. 34. (*An Autobiographical Study*, in S.E. XX, 1959, p. 8.)

43 H. Spencer, *The Principles of Psychology*, London, 1855; the same author, *First Principles*, London, 1862, which appeared as Vol. I of *A System of Synthetic Philosophy*.

44 E. B. Tylor, *Primitive Culture. Researches into the Development of Mythology, Philosophy, Religion, Art and Customs*, 2 vols., London, 1871.

45 W. Wundt, *Völkerpsychologie. Eine Untersuchung der Entwicklungsgesetze von Sprache, Mythus und Sitte*, 2 vols., Leipzig, 1905–9. Vol. II, "Mythus und Religion."

46 R. R. Marett, *The Threshold of Religion*, London, 1909, 1914.

47 W. Robertson Smith, *Lectures on the Religion of the Semites*, Edinburgh, 1898.

48 W. Mannhardt, *Der Baumkultus der Germanen und ihrer Nachbarstämme*, Berlin, 1875; the same author, *Antike Wald- und Feldkulte aus nordeuropäischer Überlieferung*, Berlin, 1877.

49 J. G. Frazer, *The Golden Bough. A Study in Comparative Religion*, 2 vols., London, 1890; the same author, *Totemism and Exogamy. A Treatise on Certain Early Forms of Superstition and Society*, 4 vols., London, 1910.

50 C. G. Jung, *Wandlungen und Symbole der Libido*, Vienna, 1912; 4th, rev. ed., with the title *Symbole der Wandlung* (1952), in Gesammelte Werke, Vol. 5, Zürich/Stuttgart, 1972. (E.t., *Symbols of Transformation*, transl. from the 4th German ed., in Collected Works, Vol. 5, Routledge & Kegan Paul, London/H. Wolff, New York, 1956.)

51 S. Freud, *Totem und Tabu. Einige Übereinstimmungen im Seelenleben der Wilden und Neurotiker* (1912–13), in Studienausgabe IX, pp. 287–444. (*Totem and Taboo*, in S.E. XIII, 1957, pp. 1–161.)

52 Ibid., p. 363. (E.t., ibid., p. 72.)

53 Quoted by Jones, op. cit., II, p. 394.

54 S. Freud, *Selbstdarstellung*, in Gesammelte Werke XIV, pp. 93–94. (*An Autobiographical Study*, in S.E. XX, p. 68.)

55 Ibid., p. 94. (E.t., ibid.)

56 S. Freud, *Der Mann Moses und die monotheistische Religion*, in Studienausgabe IX, p. 580. (*Moses and Monotheism. Three Essays*, in S.E. XXIII, pp. 3–137; quotation, p. 136.)

57 S. Freud, *Eine Kindheitserinnerung des Leonardo da Vinci*, in Studienausgabe X, p. 146. Cf., the same author, *Totem und Tabu*, in Studienausgabe IX, pp. 430–31. (*Leonardo da Vinci and a Memory of his Childhood*, in S.E. XI, p. 123. Cf. *Totem and Taboo*, in S.E. XIII, pp. 141–42.)

58 S. Freud, "Nachschrift" (1935) to *Selbstdarstellung*, in Gesammelte Werke XVI, p. 32. ("Postscript" to *An Autobiographical Study*, in S.E. XX, p. 72.)

59 S. Freud, *Das Unbehagen in der Kultur* (1930), in Studienausgabe IX, pp. 191–270. (*Civilisation and Its Discontents*, in S.E. XXI, pp. 59–145.)

60 S. Freud, *Der Mann Moses und die monotheistische Religion* (1939), in Studienausgabe IX, pp. 455–581. (*Moses and Monotheism*, in S.E. XXIII, pp. 3–137.)

61 S. Freud, *Neue Folge der Vorlesungen zur Einführung in die Psychoanalyse* (1933), in Studienausgabe I, pp. 447–608, esp. Lecture 35, "Über eine Weltanschauung." (*New Introductory Lectures on Psycho-Analysis*, in S.E. XXII, pp. 1–182, esp. Lecture 35, "The Question of a Weltanschauung.")

62 S. Freud, *Die Zukunft einer Illusion*, in Studienausgabe IX, p. 159. (*The Future of an Illusion*, in S.E. XXI, p. 25.)

63 Ibid., p. 161. (E.t., ibid., p. 27.)

64 Ibid., p. 164. (E.t., ibid., p. 30.)

65 S. Freud, letter to Wilhelm Fliess, Dec. 12, 1897, in *Aus den Anfängen der Psychoanalyse*, p. 252.

66 S. Freud, *Die Zukunft einer Illusion*, in Studienausgabe IX, p. 164. (*The Future of an Illusion*, in S.E. XXI, p. 30.)

67 Ibid., pp. 151–52. (E.t., ibid., pp. 17–18.)

68 Ibid., p. 167. (E.t., ibid., p. 33.)

69 Ibid. (E.t., ibid.)

70 Ibid., p. 172. (E.t., ibid., p. 38.)

71 Ibid., p. 183. (E.t., ibid., p. 50.)

72 Ibid., p. 188. (E.t., ibid., p. 55.)

73 Ibid., p. 189. Cf. also Freud's comments in *Das Unbehagen in der Kultur*, in Studienausgabe IX, p. 206. (E.t., ibid., p. 56; cf. also *Civilisation and Its Discontents*, in S.E. XXI, p. 70.)

74 S. Freud, *Neue Folge der Vorlesungen zur Einführung in die Psychoanalyse*, in Studienausgabe I, p. 608. (*New Introductory Lectures on Psycho-Analysis*, in S.E. XXII, p. 181.)

75 Ibid., p. 588. (E.t., ibid., p. 160.)

76 Ibid., pp. 588–89. (E.t., ibid., p. 161.)

77 Ibid., p. 589. (E.t., ibid.)

78 Ibid., p. 595. (E.t., ibid., p. 168.)

79 Ibid., p. 608. (E.t., ibid., p. 182.)

## 2. Critique of Freud

1 S. Freud, *Die Zukunft einer Illusion*, in Studienausgabe IX, p. 170. (*The Future of an Illusion*, in S.E. XXI, p. 36.)

2 Ibid., pp. 170–71. (E.t., ibid., pp. 36–37.)

3 A. Adler, "Zur Kritik der Freudschen Sexualtheorie des Seelenlebens" (1911), in Adler and C. Fortmüller, *Heilen und Bilden. Ein Buch der Erziehungskunst für Ärzte und Pädagogen*, new ed. by W. Metzger, Frankfurt, 1973, pp. 94–113.

4 Adler, *Über den nervösen Charakter. Grundzüge einer vergleichenden Individual-Psychologie und Psychotherapie*, Wiesbaden, 1912, 4th ed., 1928, reprinted Frankfurt, 1972. (E.t., *The Neurotic Constitution. Outline of a Comparative Individualistic Psychology and Psychotherapy*, Kegan Paul, London/Moffat-Yard, New York, 1917.)

5 Adler, *Studie über Minderwertigkeit von Organen*, Vienna, 1907. (E.t., *Study of organ inferiority and its psychical compensation: a contribution to clinical medicine*, Nervous and Mental Disease Publishing Co., New York, 1917.)

6 Cf. Adler, *Über den nervösen Charakter*, Frankfurt, 1972. (E.t., *The Neurotic Constitution*, London/New York, 1917.)

7 Cf. also Adler, *Menschenkenntnis*, 1927, reprinted Frankfurt, 1966, and the same author, "Vorträge zur Eisführung in die Psychotherapie für Ärzte, Psychologen und Lehrer," pub. under the title *Praxis und Theorie der Individualpsychologie*, 1930, new impression Darmstadt, 1965. (E.t., *Understanding Human Nature*, Greenberg, New York/Allen & Unwin, London, 1928, new impression, 1968; *The Practice and Theory of Individual Psychology*, Harcourt Brace, New York, 1924/Routledge & Kegan Paul, London, 1923, 2nd, rev. ed., 1929, new impression, 1964.)

8 Cf. C. G. Jung, "Über die Psychologie der Dementia praecox. Ein Versuch" (1907), now published as "Frühe Schriften II," in Studienausgabe, Olten, 1972. Cf. in the same edition "Frühe Schriften I" ("Psychiatrie und Okkultismus") and "Frühe Schriften III" ("Zur Psychoanalyse"). (E.t., "The Psychology of Dementia Praecox," pp. 1–151 in *The Psychogenesis of Mental Disease*, Vol. 3 of

Collected Works, Routledge & Kegan Paul, London/Pantheon, New York, 1960; "On the Psychology and Pathology of So-called Occult Phenomena," pp. 3–88 in *Psychiatric Studies*, Vol. I of Collected Works, London/New York, 1957; "Concerning Psychoanalysis," pp. 78–81 in *Freud and Psychoanalysis*, Vol. 4 of Collected Works, London/New York, 1961.)

9  Jung, "Wandlungen und Symbole der Libido," Vienna, 1912; 4th, rev. ed. under the title *Symbole der Wandlung* (1952), in Gesammelte Werke, Vol. 5, Zürich/Stuttgart, 1973. (E.t., *Symbols of Transformation*, in Collected Works, Vol. 5, London/New York, 1956.)

10  Jung, *Psychologische Typen* (1920), 9th, rev. ed., in Gesammelte Werke, Vol. 6, Zürich/Stuttgart, 1960. (E.t., *Psychological Types*, in Vol. 6 of Collected Works, Routledge, London/University Press, Princeton, 1971.)

11  Cf. R. Wollheim, *Sigmund Freud*, London, 1971, Ch. 7.

12  Adler, "Religion und Individualpsychologie," in Adler and E. Jahn, *Religion und Individualpsychologie. Eine prinzipielle Auseinandersetzung über Menschenführung*, 1933, new impression, Frankfurt, 1975, pp. 68–98; quotation, p. 70. Cf. Adler, *Der Sinn des Lebens*, 1933, new impression, Frankfurt, 1973, esp. the last chapter. (E.t., "Religion and Individual Psychology," in Adler, *Superiority and Social Interest*, Routledge & Kegan Paul, London, 1965, pp. 271–308; quotation, p. 277. Cf. Adler, *Social Interest*, Faber, London, 1949.)

13  Adler, *Religion und Individualpsychologie*, p. 69. (E.t., *Superiority and Social Interest*, p. 276.)

14  Ibid., p. 73. (E.t., p. 280.)

15  Ibid., p. 98. (E.t., pp. 307–8.)

16  Ibid., p. 70. (E.t., p. 277.)

17  Ibid. (E.t., pp. 277–78.)

18  E. Jahn in an epilogue to *Religion und Individualpsychologie*, p. 99. (Jahn's epilogue is not contained in the English version.)

19  Adler, *Religion und Individualpsychologie*, p. 70. (E.t., p. 277.)

20  Ibid.

21  Ibid., p. 100.

22  Jung, "Psychoanalyse und Seelsorge" (1928–29), in *Psychologie und Religion*, in Studienausgabe, Olten, 1971, pp. 155–61; quotation, p. 156. (E.t., "Psychoanalysis and the Cure of Souls," in *Psychology and Religion*, pp. 348–54 of Vol. 11 of Collected Works; quotation, p. 349.)

23  Ibid., p. 160. (E.t., p. 353.)

24  Cf. esp. Jung, "Das Wandlungssymbol in der Messe" (1940–41), in *Psychologie und Religion*, in Studienausgabe, Olten, 1971, pp. 163–267. (E.t., "Transformation Symbolism in the Mass," in *Psychology and Religion*, pp. 201–96 of Vol. 11 of Collected Works.)

25  Jung, "Psychologie und Religion" (1939), in *Psychologie und Religion*, in Studienausgabe, Olten, 1971, pp. 11–127; quotation, p. 12. (E.t., "Psychology and Religion," pp. 3–105 in *Psychology and Religion*, Vol. 11 of Collected Works; quotation, p. 6.)

26  E. Fromm, *Psychoanalysis and Religion*, Yale University Press, New Haven, 1950, pp. 15–16.

27  Jung, op. cit., p. 267. (E.t., p. 296.)

28  Jung, *Briefe*, ed. A. Jaffé with the collaboration of G. Adler, 3 vols., Olten/Fribourg, 1973, Vol. III, pp. 322–23. (E.t., *Letters*. Selected and edited by Gerhard Adler in collaboration with Aniela Jaffé, 2 vols., Routledge & Kegan Paul, London/University Press, Princeton, 1973–75, Vol. 2, 1975, p. 575.)

29  E. Durkheim, *Les formes élémentaires de la vie religieuse. Le système totémique en Australie*, Paris, 1912, 5th ed., 1968.

30  Andrew Lang, *The Making of Religion*, London, 1898; the same author, *Magic and Religion*, London, 1901.

31  Wilhelm Schmidt, *Der Ursprung der Gottesidee*, 12 vols., Münster, 1912–55. (E.t., abridged, *The Origin and Growth of Religion*, London, 1931.)

32  Adolf E. Jensen, *Mythos und Kult bei Naturvölkern*, Wiesbaden, 1951. (E.t., *Myth and Cult among Primitive Peoples*, University of Chicago Press, London/Chicago, 1963.)

33 M. Dhavamony, *Phenomenology of Religion*, Rome, 1973, p. 49.
34 On these common features, cf. V. Grønbach and J. Prytz Johansen, "Primitive Religion," I–II in J. P. Asmussen and J. Laessøe in association with C. Colpe (eds.), *Handbuch der Religionsgeschichte*, Vol. I, Göttingen, 1971, pp. 11–151.
35 Cf. R. Benedict, *Patterns of Culture*, New York, 1948/London, 1949 (first published, 1934).
36 Cf. B. Malinowski, *Magic, Science and Religion. And Other Essays*, Beacon Press, Boston, Mass., 1948.
37 Ibid., p. 7.
38 M. Eliade, "Cultural Fashions and the History of Religions," in J. M. Kitagawa (ed.), *The History of Religions. Essays in the Problem of Understanding*, Chicago/London, 1967, pp. 21–38; quotation, p. 24.
39 Ibid.
40 S. Freud, *Die Zukunft einer Illusion*, in Studienausgabe IX, p. 169. (*The Future of an Illusion*, in S.E. XXI, p. 35.)
41 Cf. A. Görres, "Alles spricht dafür, nichts Haltbares dagegen. Kritische Reflexionen eines Analytikers über den christlichen Glauben," in H. Zahrnt (ed.), *Jesus und Freud. Ein Symposion von Psychoanalytikern und Theologen*, Munich, 1972, pp. 36–52.
42 Freud, *Die Zukunft einer Illusion*, in Studienausgabe IX, p. 187. (*The Future of an Illusion*, in S.E. XXI, p. 54.)
43 Ibid., p. 188. (E.t., ibid., pp. 54–55.)
44 Ibid. (E.t., ibid.)
45 Ibid., p. 189. (E.t., ibid., p. 56.)
46 Cf. A.III.2. *Interim results I: Theses on modern rationality.*
47 Cf. C.I.2: "The end of Christianity?"
48 Cf. C.II.2: "Future without religion?" "Promise without fulfillment?"
49 G. R. Taylor, *The Doomsday Book*, London, 1970; S. Kirban, *Die geplante Verwirrung*, Wetzlar, 1972; G. Ehrensvärd, *Nach uns die Steinzeit. Das Ende des technischen Zeitalters*, Berne, 1972; D. Widener, *Kein Platz für Menschen. Der programmierte Selbstmord*, Frankfurt, 1972; E. E. Snyder, *Todeskandidat Erde. Programmierte Selbstmord durch unkontrollierten Fortschritt*, Munich, 1972; M. Lohmann (ed.), *Gefährdete Zukunft*, Munich, 1973; H. Gruhl, *Ein Planet wird geplündert. Die Schreckensbilanz unserer Politik*, Frankfurt, 1976.
50 In this connection, cf. S. Freud, *Das Unbehagen in der Kultur* (1930), in Studienausgabe IX, pp. 191–270. (*Civilisation and Its Discontents*, in S.E. XXI, pp. 56–145.)
51 Freud, "Selbstdarstellung," in I. Grubrich-Simitis (ed.), *Schriften zur Geschichte der Psychoanalyse*, Frankfurt, 1971, p. 40. ("An Autobiographical Study," in S.E. XX, p. 8.)
52 Cf. Jones, op. cit., Vol. I, pp. 32–33, 38, 67, 324, 327, 382, 421; Vol. II, p. 394.
53 Freud, letter to W. Fliess, Jan. 1, 1896, in *Aus den Anfängen der Psychoanalyse*, p. 152. (E.t., *The Origins of Psycho-Analysis*, Imago Publishing Company, London, 1954, p. 141.)
54 Freud, letter to W. Fliess, Apr. 2, 1896, in S. Freud, *Briefe 1873–1939*, ed. E. L. Freud, Frankfurt, 1960, p. 227. (E.t., *Letters of Sigmund Freud 1873–1939*, ed. Ernest L. Freud, Hogarth Press, London, 1961, p. 241.)
55 Max Schur, *Freud: Living and Dying*, The Hogarth Press and the Institute of Psycho-Analysis, London, 1972.
56 Ibid., p. 26.
57 Ibid., p. 98.
58 Ibid., p. 109.
59 Ibid., p. 529.

## 3. Critique of the Critique

1 Paul Ricoeur, "The Atheism of Freudian Psychoanalysis," in *Concilium*, June 1966 (Vol. 6, No. 2), pp. 31–37; quotation, p. 36.
2 S. Freud, *Die Zukunft einer Illusion*, in Studienausgabe IX, p. 166. (*The Future of an Illusion*, in S.E. XXI, p. 12.)

3 Ibid.
4 Ibid., p. 167. (E.t., ibid., p. 32.)
5 Ibid., p. 170. (E.t., ibid., p. 36.)
6 Cf. A.III.2. *Interim results I: Theses on modern rationality.*
7 Freud, *Die Zukunft einer Illusion*, in Studienausgabe IX, p. 162. (S.E. XXI, p. 28.)
8 Ibid. (E.t., ibid.)
9 Ibid. (E.t., ibid.)
10 Ibid. (E.t., ibid., pp. 28–29.)
11 Ibid., p. 163. (E.t., ibid., p. 29.)
12 Cf. H. Küng, *Christ sein*, Munich, 1974, D I: "Die Praxis der Kirche." (E.t., *On Being a Christian*, New York, 1976/London, 1977; D I: "The Practice of the Church.")
13 H. M. Gauger, "Sprache und Sprechen im Werk Sigmund Freuds," in *Neue Rundschau* 85 (1974), pp. 586–90.
14 Ibid., p. 577.
15 Ibid., p. 582.
16 Cf. Ricoeur, op. cit., p. 31.
17 Cf. E. Wiesenhütter, *Freud und siene Kritiker*, Darmstadt, 1974. The author provides a comprehensive survey of the criticism of Freud on the part of four groups: psychotherapists, psychiatrists, scholars in the fields of the humanities, and theologians. A useful survey of theological reactions to Freud is provided by P. Homans, *Theology after Freud. An Interpretative Inquiry*, Indianapolis/New York, 1970, esp. the chapters on R. Niebuhr, P. Tillich, N. O. Brown, D. Bakan, P. Rieff.
18 Cf. P. Bjerre, *Psychosynthese*, Stuttgart, 1971; A. Maeder, "Psychosynthese-Psychagogik," in *Handbuch der Neurosenlehre und Psychotherapie*, Vol. III, Munich/Berlin, 1959, pp. 391–412.
19 A. Hoche, *Zentralblatt für die gesamte Neurologie und Psychiatrie* 55 (1930), p. 206.
20 R. A. Spitz, *La première année de la vie de l'enfant*, Paris, 1959. (E.t., Spitz and G. W. Cobliner, *The First Year of Life. A psychoanalytic study of normal and deviant development of object relations*, International Universities Press, New York, 1965, reprint 1973, p. 13.)
21 W. Loch, *Zu Theorie, Technik, und Therapie der Psychoanalyse*, Frankfurt, 1972, p. 142. I am particularly grateful, for a number of fruitful suggestions, to Wolfgang Loch, my colleague in Tübingen, professor of psychoanalysis and psychotherapy, who was kind enough to read the whole section on Freud.
22 C. G. Jung, "Über die Beziehung der Psychotherapie zur Seelsorge" (1932), in *Psychologie und Religion*, Olten, 1971, pp. 129–52; quotation, p. 139. (E.t., "Psychotherapists or the Clergy," in *Psychology and Religion: West and East*, Collected Works, Routledge & Kegan Paul, London/Pantheon Books, New York, Vol. 11, pp. 327–47; quotation, p. 335.)
23 Ibid., p. 138. (E.t., ibid., p. 334.)
24 Ibid., p. 134. (E.t., ibid., pp. 330–31.)
25 Ibid., p. 135. (E.t., ibid., p. 331.)
26 Ibid., p. 142. (E.t., ibid., p. 338.)
27 Ibid., p. 143. (E.t., ibid., p. 339.)
28 Ibid., p. 148. (E.t., ibid., p. 344.)
29 Erich Fromm's *Psychoanalysis and Religion*, Yale University Press, New Haven, 1950, is fundamental to our themes. Cf. also Fromm's later work for the development in his attitude to the problems of religion: *The Sane Society*, Routledge & Kegan Paul, London, 1956/Holt, Rinehart & Winston, New York, 1955; *The Dogma of Christ and Other Essays on Religion, Psychology and Culture*, Holt, Rinehart & Winston, 1963; *You Shall Be as Gods. A Radical Interpretation of the Old Testament and Its Tradition*, Holt, Rinehart & Winston, New York, 1966/Cape, London, 1967.
30 Fromm, *The Crisis of Psychoanalysis. Essays on Freud, Marx and Social Psychology*, Cape, London, 1971.
31 Fromm, *Psychoanalysis and Religion*, Ch. IV: "The Psychoanalyst as 'Physician of the Soul,'" pp. 65–98.

32 Fromm, *Man for Himself. An Inquiry into the Psychology of Ethics*, Holt, Rinehart & Winston, New York, 1947/Routledge & Kegan Paul, London, 1949.
33 Fromm, *Psychoanalysis and Religion*, Ch. V: "Is Psychoanalysis a Threat to Religion?" pp. 99–119.
34 Ibid.
35 Ibid., p. 108.
36 Ibid., p. 109.
37 Ibid., p. 118.
38 V. E. Frankl, *Der unbewusste Gott. Psychotherapie und Religion*, 1947, revised and expanded edition, Munich, 1974, pp. 45–53, 55. (E.t., *The Unconscious God*, Simon & Schuster, New York, 1975/Hodder & Stoughton, London, 1977, pp. 51–58, 60.) Cf. also, by the same author, *Ärztliche Seelsorge. Grundlagen der Logotherapie und Existenzanalyse*, 1946, 8th, rev. ed., Vienna, 1971. (E.t., *The Doctor and the Soul. From Psychotherapy to Logotherapy*, Alfred A. Knopf, New York, 1955, 1965/Souvenir Press, London, 1969.) *Der Wille zum Sinn*, Berne/Stuttgart/Vienna, 1972. (E.t., *The Will to Meaning. Foundations and Applications of Logotherapy*, New American Library-The World Publishing Company, New York, 1970/Souvenir Press, London, 1971.)
39 Frankl, *Der unbewusste Gott*, pp. 48–50. (E.t., *The Unconscious God*, pp. 53–55.)
40 This is the approach of others also from the Viennese school: W. Daim, *Umwertung der Psychoanalyse*, Vienna, 1951; I. A. Caruso, *Psychoanalyse und Synthese der Existenz. Beziehungen zwischen psychologischer Analyse und Daseinswerten*, Freiburg, 1952; J. Rudin (following Jung more closely), *Psychotherapie und Religion*, Olten, 1960.
41 E. H. Erikson, *Childhood and Society*, New York, 1950, rev. and enl., 1963; *Identity and the Life Cycle*, New York, 1959; *Insight and Responsibility*, New York, 1964; *Identity, Youth and Crisis*, New York, 1968.
42 Rollo May, *The Meaning of Anxiety*, New York, 1950; *Man's Search for Himself*, W. W. Norton, New York, 1953/Souvenir Press, London, 1975; *Love and Will*, W. W. Norton, New York, 1969/Souvenir Press, London, 1970; *Power and Innocence*, New York, 1972.
43 May, *Man's Search for Himself*, p. 14.
44 Ibid., p. 24.
45 Ibid.
46 May, *Love and Will*, p. 26.
47 Wiesenhütter, *Kritik an Freud*, p. 87; cf. the same author, *Therapie der Person*, Stuttgart, 1969.
48 S. Freud and O. Pfister, *Briefe 1909–1939*, Frankfurt, 1963, p. 33.
49 Cf. Fromm, *The Anatomy of Human Destructiveness*, New York, 1973/London, 1974. Appendix, "Freud's Theory of Aggressiveness and Destructiveness," pp. 439–78.
50 Freud, *Das Unbehagen in der Kultur*, in Studienausgabe II, p. 268. (*Civilisation and Its Discontents*, in S.E. XXI, p. 143.)
51 S. Freud, "Warum Krieg?" in Studienausgabe IX, p. 283. ("Why War?" in S.E. XXII, p. 212.)
52 S. Freud, letter to J. J. Putnam, July 8, 1915, quoted in Ernest Jones, op. cit., Vol. 2, p. 465.

### 4. Interim results III: Theses on atheism

1 T. W. Adorno, "Vernunft und Offenbarung," in *Stichworte Kritische Modelle 2*, Frankfurt, 1969, p. 20.
2 Ibid.
3 Ibid., p. 21.
4 We shall return in a different context to Popper and such other critics of religion as Heidegger, Sartre, Bloch, Russell and Ayer.
5 M. Horkheimer, *Notizen 1950 bis 1969 und Dämmerung, Notizen in Deutschland*, ed. W. Brede, Frankfurt, 1974. The Introduction, by A. Schmidt (pp. xix–lxx), is important for the interpretation of the *Notizen*.

6 Horkheimer, "Bemerkungen zur Liberalisierung der Religion," in *Sozialphiloso-phische Studien*, Frankfurt, 1972, p. 131.
7 Ibid., p. 132.
8 Cf. C.II.2: *Critique of Marx*.
9 Horkheimer, "Bemerkungen zur Liberalisierung der Religion," p. 132.
10 Horkheimer, *Notizen*, p. 96.
11 Horkheimer, "Theismus-Atheismus," in *Zur Kritik der instrumentalen Vernunft. Aus den Vorträgen und Aufzeichnungen seit Kriegsende*, ed. A. Schmidt, Frankfurt, 1974, p. 217.
12 Adorno deals sharply with revolutionary actionism in an article published posthumously, "Marginalien zu Theorie und Praxis," in his book *Stichworte. Kritische Modelle 2*, pp. 169–91.
13 Cf. H. Küng, Preface to *Die Kirche*, Freiburg/Basel/Vienna, 1967. (E.t., *The Church*, London/New York, 1967.)
14 Cf. Küng, *Christ sein*, Munich, 1974, Ch. C.VII.4: "Der grosse Auftrag." (E.t., *On Being a Christian*, New York, 1976/London, 1977, Ch. C.VII.4: "The great mandate.")
15 Adorno, "Vernunft und Offenbarung," p. 22.
16 Ibid.
17 Horkheimer and Adorno, *Dialektik der Aufklärung. Philosophische Fragmente*, Amsterdam, 1947, new ed., Frankfurt, 1969. (E.t., *Dialectic of Enlightenment*, New York, 1972/London, 1973.)
18 Adorno, "Vernunft und Offenbarung," p. 23.
19 Ibid.
20 Ibid., p. 24.
21 Ibid., p. 25.
22 Cf. A.III.2. *Interim results I: Theses on modern rationality*.
23 Cf. C.I.2: The end of Christianity?
24 Cf. C.II.2: "Future without religion?" "Promise without fulfillment?"
25 Cf. C.III.2: "Faith in science?"
26 Cf. C.I.2: "God—wish or reality?"
27 Cf. C.II.2: "Is religion a human fabrication?"
28 Cf. C.III.2: "Religion—merely wishful thinking?"
29 Cf. C.I.1. *Anthropological atheism*.
30 Cf. C.II.1. *Sociopolitical atheism*.
31 Cf. C.III.1. *Psychoanalytic atheism*.
32 Cf. A.III.2: "Correcting course."
33 Particular Council of Cologne, 1860, in *Collectio Lacensis* V, 292; cf. later the answer of the Pontifical Biblical Commission of 1909 on the historical character of Genesis and the special creation of man (DS 3514). Documents relating to the procedures against individual theologians have not been published.
34 Pius XII, address to the Pontifical Academy of Sciences, Nov. 30, 1941. This inconvenient text is not included in recent editions of Denzinger's *Enchiridion Symbolorum*. In the 1952 ed., it is No. 2285.
35 Pius XII, encyclical *Humani Generis*, Aug. 12, 1950 (DS 3896).
36 Anthony Flew, "Theology and Falsification" (1950), in *New Essays in Philosophical Theology*, eds. Flew and A. McIntyre, S.C.M. Press, London, 1955, p. 97.
37 H. Albert, *Traktat über kritische Vernunft*, Tübingen, 1968; enl. ed., 1975, p. 115.
38 Ibid.
39 Ibid., pp. 115–16.
40 Adorno, "Vernunft und Offenbarung," p. 27.
41 Cf. A. REASON OR FAITH? and esp. A.III.2. *Interim results I: Theses on modern rationality*.
42 Cf. B.III.3. *Interim results II: Theses on the secularity and historicity of God*.
43 H. Albert, *Traktat über kritische Vernunft*, p. 116.
44 Ibid., pp. 116–18.
45 Ibid., p. 118.
46 Ibid.

47 Albert, *Theologische Holzwege. Gerhard Ebeling und der rechte Gebrauch der Vernunft*, Tübingen, 1873, p. 86.
48 Albert, *Traktat über kritische Vernunft*, pp. 118–19.
49 F. Buri, *Wie können wir heute noch verantwortlich von Gott reden?* Tübingen, 1967, p. 28.
50 Albert, *Traktat über kritische Vernunft*, p. 119.
51 Ibid.
52 Albert, *Theologische Holzwege*, p. 88.
53 Albert, *Traktat über kritische Vernunft*, p. 120.
54 Albert, *Theologische Holzwege*, p. 88. Cf. H. Küng, *Unfehlbar? Eine Anfrage*, Zürich/Einsiedeln/Cologne, 1970 (E.t., *Infallible? An Inquiry*, New York/London, 1971); the same author, *Fehlbar. Eine Bilanz*, Zürich/Einsiedeln/Cologne, 1973.
55 G. Ebeling, "Kritischer Rationalismus? Zu Hans Alberts 'Traktat über kritische Vernunft,'" in *Zeitschrift für Theologie und Kirche* 70 (1973), Supp. 3. Cf. H. Albert, *Theologische Holzwege*, Preface and pp. 104–7.
56 Albert, *Theologische Holzwege*, pp. 88–89.
57 Ibid., p. 90.
58 Cf. Luke 10:41–42.
59 This is the title of a book by Albert continuing the argument of the *Traktat* with special reference to theology: *Plädoyer für kritischen Rationalismus*, Munich, 1971.
60 Horkheimer, *Theismus-Atheismus*, p. 227.
61 Ibid., p. 228.
62 Ibid.
63 Ibid.
64 Ibid.
65 Ibid.
66 Ibid.
67 Ibid.
68 Among recent theological works on atheism see especially C. Fabro, *Introduzione all'ateismo moderno*, Rome, 1964; H. Fries, *Abschied von Gott? Eine Herausforderung—Versuch einer Antwort*, Munich, 1968; G. M. M. Cottier, *Horizons de l'athéisme*, Paris, 1969; E. Coreth and J. B. Lotz, *Atheismus kritisch betrachtet. Beiträge zum Atheismusproblem der Gegenwart*, Munich/Freiburg, 1971; A. Esser (ed.), *Atheismus. Profile und Positionen der Neuzeit*, Cologne, 1971; V. P. Miceli, *The Gods of Atheism*, New Rochelle, N.Y., 1971; E. Biser, *Theologie und Atheismus. Anstösse zu einer theologischen Aporetik*, Munich, 1972; W. Schmidt (ed.), *Die Religion der Religionskritik*, Munich, 1972; C. Tresmontant, *Les problèmes de l'athéisme*, Paris, 1972; H. Desroche, *Les dieux rêvés. Théisme et athéisme en utopie*, Paris, 1972; R. Caporale and A. Grumelli (eds.), *Religione e ateismo nelle società secolarizzate. Aspetti e problemi della cultura della non credenza*, Bologna, 1973; C. Chabanis (ed.), *Dieu existe-t-il? Non*, Paris, 1973; H. Schwarz, *The Search for God. Christianity, Atheism, Secularism, World Religions*, Minneapolis, 1975; W. Kern, *Atheismus—Marxismus—Christentum. Beiträge zur Diskussion*, Innsbruck/Vienna/Munich, 1976; R. Boon, *Het Christendom op de tocht. Een onderzoek naar de opkomst van het westeuropese atheisme*, Kampen, 1976. On the history of atheism, see esp. F. Mauthner, *Der Atheismus und seine Geschichte im Abendland*, 4 vols., Stuttgart, 1921–23; H. Ley, *Geschichte der Aufklärung und des Atheismus*, 3 vols., Berlin, 1966–71.

## D. NIHILISM—CONSEQUENCE OF ATHEISM

### D.I. The rise of nihilism· Friedrich Nietzsche

1 We shall use here Karl Schlechta's edition of Nietzsche, Werke, 3 vols., with an index volume, Munich, 1954–65, quoted as Werke, followed by vol. and p. nos.

But, for the later work and the letters, other editions should be consulted: Nietzsches Werke, ed. Nietzsche-Archiv, 19 vols. in 3 secs., with an index volume, Leipzig, 1894–1912; F. Nietzsche, Gesammelte Briefe, 5 vols., Leipzig, 1905ff.; F. Nietzsche, Werke und Briefe. Historisch-Kritische Gesamtausgabe, 5 vols. of works and 4 vols. of letters (not completed), Munich, 1933–42; F. Nietzsche, Werke: Kritische Gesamtausgabe, ed. G. Colli and M. Montinari, 30 vols., planned in 8 secs., Berlin, 1967ff. (Until recently, the best-known English-language translation of Nietzsche was The Complete Works, in 18 vols., ed. Oscar Levy, first published, from 1909 onward, by Allen & Unwin, London, and Macmillan [reissued 1964 by Russell & Russell, New York] and running to several editions. These have been severely criticized, and many of his books have now been published in more up-to-date translations, esp. Random House [Vintage Books], New York, and Penguin Books, New York and Harmondsworth. The later translations will mostly be used here, full details being given in each case.) Translator.

2 F. Nietzsche, *Ecce Homo. Wie man wird, was man ist* (1889), in Werke II, pp. 1063–1159; quotation in *Ecce Homo (Die Unzeitgemässen* 2), in Werke II, p. 1114. (E.t., *On the Genealogy of Morals and Ecce Homo*, Random House [Vintage Books], New York, 1969, pp. 278–79.) Apart from the reminiscences of Elisabeth Förster-Nietzsche, Franz Overbeck (in Bernoulli's study), Paul Deussen and others, *Ecce Homo* and the letters are of fundamental importance for the understanding of Nietzsche.

3 Nietzsche, *Der Antichrist. Fluch auf das Christentum* (1888) in Werke II, pp. 1161–1235; quotation, *Antichrist* 8, in Werke II, p. 1169. (E.t., *Twilight of the Gods* and *The Antichrist*, Penguin Books, New York/Harmondsworth, p. 119.) On the more recent philosophical and theological discussion about Nietzsche: K. Löwith, *Nietzsches Philosophie der ewigen Wiederkunft des Gleichen*, Berlin, 1935; K. Jaspers, *Nietzsche und das Christentum*, Munich, 1952; the same author, *Nietzsche. Einführung in das Verständnis seines Philosophierens*, Berlin, 1950; R. M. Thompson, *Nietzsche and Christian Ethics*, New York, 1951; H. Heimsoeth, "Metaphysische Voraussetzungen und Antriebe in Nietzsches 'Immoralismus,'" in *Abhandlungen der geistes- und sozial-wissenschaftlichen Klasse der Akademie der Wissenschaften und Literatur in Mainz*, 1955, pp. 475–539; E. Benz, *Nietzsches Ideen zur Geschichte des Christentums und der Kirche*, Leiden, 1956; G. G. Grau, *Christlicher Glaube und intellektuelle Redlichkeit. Eine religionsgeschichtliche Studie über Nietzsche*, Frankfurt, 1958; M. Heidegger, *Nietzsche*, 2 vols., Pfüllingen, 1961; E. Biser, "Gott ist tot." *Nietzsches Destruktion des christlichen Bewusstseins*, Munich, 1962; M. Kaempfert, *Säkularisation und neue Heiligkeit. Religiöse und religionsbezogene Sprache bei Friedrich Nietzsche*, Berlin, 1971; W. Müller-Lauter, *Nietzsche. Seine Philosophie der Gegensätze und die Gegensätze seiner Philosophie*, Berlin/New York, 1971; W. Weischedel, *Der Gott der Philosophen. Grundlegung einer philosophischen Theologie im Zeitalter des Nihilismus*, Darmstadt, 1971, pp. 429–57; E. Diet, *Nietzsche et les métamorphoses du divin*, Paris, 1972; E. Fink, *Nietzsches Philosophie*, Stuttgart, 1973; H. Steffen (ed.), *Nietzsche. Werk und Wirkungen*, Göttingen, 1974; M. Balkenohl, *Der Antitheismus Nietzsches. Fragen und Suchen nach Gott. Eine sozialanthropologische Untersuchung*, Münster, 1976.

4 Nietzsche, *Antichrist* 8, in Werke II, p. 1169. (E.t., *Twilight of the Idols* and *The Antichrist*, Penguin Books, New York/Harmondsworth, 1968, p. 119.)

5 Ibid. (E.t., ibid.)

6 *Antichrist* 4, in Werke II, p. 1166. (E.t., p. 116.)

7 Unpublished work from the eighties in Werke III, p. 632.

8 Charles Darwin, *On the Origin of Species by Means of Natural Selection*, London, 1859.

9 Darwin, *The Descent of Man*, London, 1871.

10 Cf. C.III.1: "What is the source of religion?"

11 T. R. Malthus, *An Essay on the Principles of Population*, London, 1798

12 E. Haeckel, *Generelle Morphologie der Organismen. Allgemeine Grundzüge der organischen Formen-Wissenschaft, mechanisch begründet durch die von Charles Darwin reformierte Deszendenz-Theorie*, 2 vols., Berlin, 1866.

13 Cf. esp. A.II.5: Correcting course; C.III.4: Theology and Natural Science.

14 Cf. A.III.2. *Interim results I: Theses on modern rationality;* C.III.4: *Interim results III: Theses on atheism.*
15 Cf. B.III.3. *Interim results II: Theses on the secularity and historicity of God.*
16 *The Life and Letters of Charles Darwin,* first published in 1887, is shorter by about six thousand words than *The Autobiography of Charles Darwin,* published by his granddaughter Nora Barlow in 1958. Here we are using the latest, complete and corrected edition, by G. de Beer, containing also the autobiography of T. H. Huxley: *Charles Darwin, Thomas Henry Huxley, Autobiographies,* Oxford University Press, London/New York/Toronto, 1974.
17 Ibid., p. 54.
18 Haeckel, *Natürliche Schöpfungsgeschichte. Gemeinverständliche wissenschaftliche Vorträge über die Entwicklungslehre im Allgemeinen und diejenige von Darwin, Goethe und Lamarck im Besonderen, über die Anwendung derselben auf den Ursprung des Menschen und andere damit zusammenhängende Grundfragen der Naturwissenschaft,* Berlin, 1868.
19 Haeckel, *Die Welträtsel. Gemeinverständliche Studien über Monistische Philosophie,* Bonn, 1899. (E.t., *The Riddle of the Universe,* Watts & Co., London, n.d.)
20 Ibid., p. 23. (E.t., p. 8.)
21 Ibid., p. 333. (E.t., p. 102.)
22 Ibid., p. 336. (E.t., p. 103.)
23 Ibid. (E.t., ibid.)
24 Ibid., p. 439. (E.t., p. 135.)
25 Ibid., pp. 357–58. (E.t., pp. 109–10.)
26 Nietzsche, *Unzeitgemässe Betrachtungen. Erstes Stück: David Strauss, der Bekenner und der Schriftsteller* (1873) in Werke I, pp. 137–207. (E.t., *Thoughts out of Season,* Part I, "David Strauss, the Confessor and the Writer," T. N. Foulis, Edinburgh/London, 1909, pp. 1–197.)
27 D. F. Strauss, *Der alte und der neue Glaube. Ein Bekenntnis,* Leipzig, 1872.
28 Ibid., p. 94.
29 Ibid., p. 146.
30 Nietzsche, *Unzeitgemässe* I, 9 in Werke I, p. 182. (E.t., *Thoughts out of Season,* p. 72.)
31 Ibid., I, 4, 7 in Werke I, pp. 153, 166. (E.t., pp. 28, 48–51.)
32 Ibid., I, 9 in Werke I, p. 182. (E.t., pp. 72–73.)
33 Ibid., I, 6 in Werke I, p. 165. (E.t., p. 46.)
34 Ibid., I, 6 in Werke I pp. 165–66. (E.t., p. 47.)
35 Ibid., I, 7 in Werke I, pp. 166–67. (E.t., p. 50.)
36 Ibid., I, 7 in Werke I, p. 167. (E.t., p. 50.)
37 Ibid., I, 9 in Werke I, p. 181. (E.t., p. 70.)
38 Ibid., I, 7 in Werke I, p. 167. (E.t., p. 50.)
39 Ibid., I, 7 in Werke I, p. 168. (E.t., p. 52.)
40 Ibid., I, 7 in Werke I, p. 169. (E.t., p. 52.)
41 Ibid., I, 7 in Werke I, pp. 169, 171. (E.t., pp. 53, 55.)
42 Ibid., I, 7 in Werke I, p. 171. (E.t., pp. 56–57.)
43 Ibid., I, 8 in Werke I, p. 173. (E.t., p. 59.)
44 Ibid., I, 8 in Werke I, p. 174. (E.t., pp. 60–61.)
45 Ibid., I, 8 in Werke I, p. 175. (E.t., pp. 61–62.)
46 Ibid., I, 10 in Werke I, p. 189. (E.t., pp. 82–83.)
47 F. Overbeck, writing at Nietzsche's request to Treitschke, Sept. 1, 1873. Cf. C. A. Bernoulli, *Franz Overbeck und Friedrich Nietzsche. Eine Freundschaft,* Vol. I, Jena, 1908, p. 84.
48 F. Engels, *Entwicklung des Sozialismus von der Utopie zur Wissenschaft,* Berlin, 1882.
49 Nietzsche, *Die fröhliche Wissenschaft* (1882), in Werke II, pp. 7–274. Quotation, *Fröhliche Wissenschaft* 125, in Werke II, p. 127. (E.t., *The Gay Science,* Random House [Vintage Books], New York, 1974, p. 181.)
50 P. Deussen, *Erinnerungen an Friedrich Nietzsche,* Leipzig, 1901, p. 4.
51 F. A. L. Nietzsche, *Gamaliel oder über die immerwährende Dauer des Christen-*

*tums zur Belehrung und Beruhigung bei der gegenwärtigen Gärung in der theologischen Welt,* Leipzig, 1796; the same author, *Beiträge zur Beförderung einer vernünftigen Denkensart über Religion, Erziehung, Untertanenpflicht und Menschenleben,* Weimar, 1804.

52 K. Jaspers, *Nietzsche,* Introduction, p. 41.

53 Quoted by R. Blunck, *Friedrich Nietzsche. Kindheit und Jugend,* Munich/Basel, 1953, pp. 76–77. In this book there are also useful details about Nietzsche's religious development.

54 K. A. von Hase, *Das Leben Jesu. Ein Lehrbuch, zunächst für akademische Vorlesungen,* Leipzig, 1829; the same author, *Kirchengeschichte. Lehrbuch für akademische Vorlesungen,* Leipzig, 1834.

55 F. Nietzsche, *Werke und Briefe. Historisch-Kritische Gesamtausgabe* II, p. 428. (E.t., *Twenty German Poets,* ed., transl and intro. by Walter Kaufmann, Random House, New York, 1962, p. 143.)

56 F. Nietzsche, *Werke und Briefe. Historisch-Kritische Gesamtausgabe* V, p. 471.

57 F. Nietzsche, *Antichrist* 28, in *Werke* II, p. 1190. (E.t., *Twilight of the Idols* and *The Antichrist,* Penguin Books, New York/Harmondsworth, 1968, p. 140.)

58 F. Nietzsche, *Autobiographisches aus den Jahren 1856–1869:* "Rückblick auf meine zwei Leipziger Jahre," in *Werke* III, p. 133.

59 Thomas Mann, *Betrachtungen eines Unpolitischen,* Berlin, 1918, new ed., Frankfurt, 1968, p. 53.

60 André Gide, *The Journals,* II, Secker & Warburg, London/Alfred A. Knopf, New York, 1948, p. 365.

61 A. Schopenhauer, *Sämtliche Werke,* ed. W. von Löhneysen, Vols. I–V, Darmstadt, 1961–65, quoted as *Werke.* Vols. I–II contain *Die Welt als Wille und Vorstellung.* (E.t., *The World as Will and Idea,* 3 vols., Kegan Paul, Trench, Trübner, London, 1906.) For the biographical background cf. W. von Gwimmer, *Schopenhauer's Leben,* Leipzig, 1910.

62 F. Nietzsche, *Autobiographisches* in *Werke* III, p. 133.

63 F. Nietzsche, *Ecce Homo* (*Die Unzeitgemässen* 2), in *Werke* II, p. 1114. (E.t., *On the Genealogy of Morals* and *Ecce Homo,* Random House [Vintage Books], New York, 1969, p. 279.)

64 Schopenhauer, *Die Welt als Wille und Vorstellung,* Preface, 2nd ed., in *Werke* I, p. 18. (E.t., Vol. I, p. xxi.)

65 Schopenhauer, *Die Welt als Wille und Vorstellung,* in *Werke* I, p. 31. Cf. the whole of the first book in *Werke* I, pp. 29–47. (E.t., Vol. I, p. 3; first book in pp. 1–120.)

66 *Die Welt als Wille,* in *Werke* I, p. 164. (E.t., Vol. I, p. 136.)

67 *Die Welt als Wille,* in *Werke* I, p. 33; cf. the discussion of this principle in the second book in *Werke* I, pp. 149–241. (E.t., Vol. I, p. 5; second book in Vol. I, pp. 121–215.)

68 *Die Welt als Wille,* in *Werke* I, p. 380. (E.t., Vol. I, p. 354.)

69 *Die Welt als Wille,* in *Werke* I, p. 237. (E.t., Vol. I, p. 211.)

70 *Die Welt als Wille,* in *Werke* I, p. 380. On Schopenhauer's argument with Kant, see the appendix *Kritik der kantischen Philosophie,* in *Werke* I, pp. 559–715. (E.t., Vol. I, p. 354. *Criticism of the Kantian Philosophy,* in Vol. II, pp. 1–159.)

71 Cf. also Schopenhauer, *Die Welt als Wille und Vorstellung,* Vol. II (supplements to the 4 books of Vol. I) = *Werke* II. (E.t., Vols. II–III contain these supplements.)

72 *Ibid.,* *Werke* I, p. 241. (E.t., Vol. I, p. 215.)

73 *Ibid.,* p. 428. (E.t., Vol. I, p. 403.)

74 *Ibid.,* pp. 377–78. (E.t., Vol. I, p. 351.)

75 *Ibid.,* p. 379. (E.t., Vol. I, p. 353.)

76 *Ibid.,* *Werke* II, p. 569. (E.t., Vol. III, p. 226.)

77 Cf. the whole third book in *Werke* I, pp. 243–372. (E.t., "The World as Idea—Second Aspect. The idea independent of the principle of sufficient reason and the Platonic Idea: the object of art." Vol. I, pp. 217–346.)

78 *Die Welt als Wille,* in *Werke* I, pp. 356–72. (E.t., Vol. I, pp. 330–46.)

79 Cf. the fourth book in Werke I, pp. 373–558. (E.t., *The World as Will—Second Aspect. The assertion and denial of the will to live when self-consciousness has been attained,* Vol. I, pp. 347–532.)
80 *Die Welt als Wille,* in Werke I, pp. 550–51. (E.t., Vol. I, p. 524.)
81 Ibid., p. 530. (E.t., Vol. I, p. 504.)
82 Ibid., p. 557. (E.t., Vol. I, p. 531.)
83 Ibid., p. 558. (E.t., Vol. I, p. 532.)
84 Schopenhauer, *Über den Willen in der Natur,* in Werke III, pp. 299–479. (E.t., *On the Fourfold Principle of Sufficient Reason* and *On the Will in Nature,* George Bell, London, 1903. The second work is contained in pp. 192–380 and is described by the author as "an account of the corroborations received by the author's philosophy since its first appearance, from the empirical sciences.")
85 Schopenhauer, *Die beiden Grundprobleme der Ethik, behandelt in zwei akademischen Preisschriften,* in Werke III, pp. 481–815.
86 Schopenhauer, *Parerga und Paralipomena. Kleine philosophische Schriften,* 2 vols., in Werke IV and V. (E.t., *Parerga and Paralipomena. Short Philosophical Essays,* Clarendon Press, Oxford, 2 vols., 1974; cf. also the translation of selections from this work, *Schopenhauer: Essays and Aphorisms,* Penguin Books, Harmondsworth/New York, 1970.)
87 Schopenhauer, *Aphorismen zur Lebensweisheit,* in Werke IV, pp. 373–592. (E.t., "Aphorisms on the Wisdom of Life," in *Parerga and Paralipomena,* Oxford, 1974, Vol. I, pp. 311–497.)
88 W. von Gwimmer, *Schopenhauers Leben,* p. 393.
89 Ibid.
90 F. A. Lange, *Geschichte des Materialismus und Kritik seiner Bedeutung in der Gegenwart,* Iserlohn, 1866.
91 F. Nietzsche, letter to E. Rohde, Nov. 9, 1886, in Werke III, p. 999.
92 Cf. C. A. Bernoulli, *Franz Overbeck und Friedrich Nietzsche. Eine Freundschaft,* 2 vols., Jena, 1908.
93 Cf. C. Wagner, *Die Tagebücher,* Vol. I, 1869–77, eds. M. Gregor-Dellin and D. Mack, Munich/Zürich, 1976. Vol. II, 1878–83, Munich/Zürich, 1977, describes especially Wagner's reaction to Nietzsche's *Human, All-Too-Human* (pp. 87, 88, 92, etc.).
94 F. Nietzsche, *Die Geburt der Tragödie aus dem Geiste der Musik,* in Werke I, pp. 19–134. (E.t., *The Birth of Tragedy* and *The Case of Wagner,* Random House [Vintage Books], New York, 1967.)
95 U. von Wilamowitz-Möllendorff, *Zukunftsphilologie! Eine Erwiderung auf Friedrich Nietzsches "Geburt der Tragödie,"* Berlin, 1872. Nietzsche's friend Erwin Rohde had to help out with a rejoinder, *Afterphilologie. Zur Beleuchtung des von dem Dr. phil. U. v. Wilamowitz-Möllendorff herausgegebenen Pamphlets: "Zukunftsphilologie!" Sendschreiben eines Philologen an R. Wagner,* Leipzig, 1872. Cf. the new edition of the contributions to the controversy: *Der Streit um Nietzsches "Geburt der Tragödie." Die Schriften von E. Rohde, R. Wagner, U. v. Wilamowitz-Möllendorff. Zusammengestellt und eingeleitet von K. Gründer,* Hildesheim, 1969. Wagner himself reacted with an open letter, "An Friedrich Nietzsche," in the *Norddeutsche Allgemeine Zeitung,* June 23, 1872 (ibid., pp. 57–64); Wilamowitz-Möllendorff's reply to Rohde (1873) is given in pp. 113–35.
96 In his diary (Dec. 31, 1871) F. W. Ritschl wrote: "brilliant buffoonery" (*geistreiche Schwiemelei*), quoted by K. Schlechta in Werke III, p. 1363.
97 F. Nietzsche, *Schriften der Studenten- und Militärzeit 1864–1868,* eds. H. J. Mette and K. Schlechta, in *Werke und Briefe, Historisch-Kritische Gesamtausgabe,* Werke III, Munich, 1935, p. 360.
98 Ibid., p. 353.
99 F. Nietzsche, *Menschliches, Allzumenschliches. Ein Buch für freie Geister,* in Werke I, pp. 435–733. Quotation, p. 519. (E t., *Human, All-Too-Human,* Vol. I, T. N. Foulis, Edinburgh/London, 1910, p. 115.)
100 R. Wagner, *Die Kunst und die Revolution,* Berlin, 1849.
101 F. Nietzsche, *Nietzsche contra Wagner* ("Wie ich von Wagner loskam" 1), in

Werke II, p. 1054. (E.t., "Nietzsche contra Wagner," in Walter Kaufmann (ed.), *The Portable Nietzsche*, Viking Press, New York, 1954, 1968/Chatto & Windus, London, 1971, pp. 661–83; quotation, p. 676.)

102 F. Nietzsche, *Menschliches, Allzumenschliches. Ein Buch für freie Geister* (1878), in Werke I, pp. 435–733. A second volume with the same title appeared in 1886 containing "Miscellaneous Maxims and Opinions" and "The Wanderer and his Shadow," in Werke I, pp. 735–1008. (E.t., *Human, All-Too-Human. A book for free spirits*, 2 vols., Edinburgh/London, 1910.)

103 Cf. the detailed description in K. Jaspers, *Nietzsche. Einführung*, pp. 91–118.

104 Cf. the documents in R. Blunck, *Nietzsche*, pp. 160–62.

105 P. Rée, *Psychologische Beobachtungen*, Berlin, 1875.

106 F. Nietzsche, *Ecce Homo (Menschliches, Allzumenschliches 1)*, in Werke II, p. 1118. (E.t., *On the Genealogy of Morals* and *Ecce Homo*, Random House [Vintage Books], New York, p. 283.)

107 G. Benn, quoted in I. Frenzel, *Friedrich Nietzsche in Selbstzeugnissen und Bilddokumenten*, Reinbek, 1966, p. 138.

108 Cf. H. H. Stuckenschmidt, "Nachruhm als Missverständnis. Richard Wagner," in the same author's collection of essays *Die Musik eines halben Jahrhunderts. 1925–1975. Essay und Kritik*, Munich/Zürich, 1976, pp. 263–72.

109 F. Nietzsche, *Menschliches, Allzumenschliches*, I, 26, in Werke I, p. 467. (E.t., *Human, All-Too-Human*, Vol. I, p. 42.)

110 *Menschliches, Allzumenschliches*, I, 5, in Werke I, p. 450. (E.t., Vol. I, p. 18.)

111 These are the themes of the main sections of the first volume, published independently in 1878.

112 *Menschliches, Allzumenschliches*, Preface, 1, 3, in Werke I, pp. 437, 440. (E.t., Vol. I, pp. 1–2, 6.)

113 F. Nietzsche, *Morgenröte. Gedanken über die moralischen Vorurteile* (1881), in Werke I, pp. 1009–1279. (E.t., *The Dawn of Day*, Edinburgh/London, 1911.)

114 F. Nietzsche, *Ecce Homo* ("Morgenröte" 1), in Werke II, pp. 1124–25. (E.t., *On the Genealogy of Morals* and *Ecce Homo*, Random House [Vintage Books], New York, 1969, pp. 290–91.)

115 F. Nietzsche, *Die fröhliche Wissenschaft* ("la gaya scienza") (1882), in Werke II, pp. 7–274. (E.t., *The Gay Science*, Random House [Vintage Books], New York, 1974.)

116 *Fröhliche Wissenschaft* IV, 341–42, in Werke II, pp. 202–3. Cf. in the appendix the poem *Sils-Maria*, II, p. 271. (E.t., pp. 273–75; the poem is on p. 371.)

## 2. The counterreligion

1 F. Nietzsche, *Fröhliche Wissenschaft* V, 343, in Werke II, p. 205. (E.t., p. 279.)

2 Ibid. (E.t., ibid.)

3 Ibid., pp. 205–6. (E.t., p. 280.)

4 Ibid., p. 205. (E.t., p. 277.)

5 *Fröhliche Wissenschaft* V, 357, in Werke II, p. 227. (E.t., p. 306.)

6 Ibid. (E.t., p. 307.)

7 Ibid., p. 228. (E.t., p. 308.)

8 Ibid., p. 229. (E.t., p. 309.)

9 Ibid., p. 228. (E.t., p. 308.)

10 *Fröhliche Wissenschaft* III, 125, in Werke II, pp. 126–27. (E.t., p. 181.)

11 Ibid., p. 127. (E.t., p. 181.)

12 Ibid. (E.t., ibid.)

13 Ibid. (E.t., ibid.)

14 This is how E. Biser approaches it in *"Gott ist tot." Nietzsches Destruktion des christlichen Bewusstseins*, Münster, 1962; the same author, "Nietzsches Begriff des christlichen Gottesbegriffs und ihre theologischen Konsequenzen," in *Philosophisches Jahrbuch* 78 (1971), pp. 34–65, 295–305.

15 This answer to Biser is given by P. Köster, "Nietzsches Beschwörung des Chaos," in *Theologische Quartalschrift* 153 (1973), pp. 132–63. See also E. Biser, "Ant-

wort auf P. Köster," same journal, pp. 164–66; P. Köster, "Replik auf E. Biser," same, pp. 167–68.
16 Cf. C. III.4. *Interim results III: Theses on atheism.*
17 *Fröhliche Wissenschaft* V, 357, in Werke II, pp. 227–28. (E.t., p. 307.)
18 Ibid., p. 227. (E.t., ibid.)
19 *Fröhliche Wissenschaft* III, 125, in Werke II, p. 127. (E.t., p. 181.)
20 Ibid. (E.t., ibid.)
21 Ibid. (E.t., ibid.)
22 Ibid. (E.t., ibid.)
23 Ibid. (E.t., p. 182.)
24 Ibid., pp. 127–28. (E.t., p. 182.)
25 Ibid., III, 108; in Werke II, p. 115. (E.t., p. 167.)
26 Ibid. (E.t., ibid.)
27 Ibid., III, 109; in Werke II, p. 115. (E.t., pp. 167–68.)
28 *Fröhliche Wissenschaft* III, 265–75, in Werke II, pp. 159–60. (E.t., pp. 219–20.)
29 F. Nietzsche, *Also sprach Zarathustra. Ein Buch für Alle und Keinen* (1884–85), in Werke II, pp. 275–561. (E.t., *Thus Spoke Zarathustra*, Penguin Books, New York/Harmondsworth, 1961.)
30 Letter to Peter Gast, Feb. 19, 1883, in Werke III, p. 1201.
31 Nietzsche, *Ecce Homo* ("Also sprach Zarathustra" 3), in Werke II, p. 1131. (E.t., p. 300.)
32 *Ecce Homo* ("Warum ich ein Schicksal bin" 3), in Werke II, p. 1154. (E.t., p. 328.)
33 F. Nietzsche, *Zarathustra* ("Vorrede" 3), in Werke II, p. 279. (E.t., p. 41.)
34 Ibid., pp. 279–80. (E.t., p. 42.)
35 Ibid., p. 280. (E.t., p. 42.)
36 Ibid. (E.t., ibid.)
37 *Zarathustra* ("Vorrede" 3, 4), in Werke II, pp. 280–81. (E.t., pp. 42–44.)
38 *Zarathustra* II ("Von der Selbst-Überwindung"), in Werke II, p. 371. (E.t., pp. 137–38.)
39 Nietzsche, *Ecce Homo* ("Also sprach Zarathustra" 1), in Werke II, p. 1128. (E.t., p. 295.)
40 Nietzsche, *Fröhliche Wissenschaft* IV, 341, in Werke II, p. 202. (E.t., pp. 273–74.)
41 Ibid. (E.t., p. 274.)
42 Ibid., pp. 202–3. (E.t., ibid.)
43 Nietzsche, *Zarathustra* III ("Vom Gesicht und Rätsel" 2), in Werke II, pp. 408–9. (E.t., pp. 178–79.)
44 *Zarathustra* III ("Der Genesende" 1), in Werke II, p. 462. (E.t., p. 233.)
45 Ibid. (E.t., ibid.)
46 *Zarathustra* III ("Der Genesende" 2), in Werke II, p. 463. (E.t., p. 234.)
47 Ibid., p. 466. (E.t., p. 237.)
48 Ibid., p. 465. (E.t., p. 236.)
49 Ibid., pp. 465–66. (E.t., pp. 236–37.)
50 *Zarathustra* III ("Das andere Tanzlied" 3), in Werke II, p. 473 (the strokes of the midnight bell come between the lines). (E.t., p. 244.)
51 *Zarathustra* III ("Die sieben Siegel oder: das Ja- und Amen-Lied 1"), in Werke II, pp. 473–74. (E.t., pp. 244–45.)
52 *Zarathustra* IV ("Das trunkne Lied 12"), in Werke II, p. 558. (E.t., p. 333.)
53 *Zarathustra* IV ("Das Zeichen"), in Werke II, p. 561. (E.t., pp. 335–36.)
54 Nietzsche, letter to E. Rohde, Feb. 22, 1884, in Werke II, p. 1136.
55 Nietzsche, *Ecce Homo* ("Also sprach Zarathustra" 6), in Werke II, p. 1136. (E.t., p. 306.)
56 *Ecce Homo* ("Also sprach Zarathustra" 5), in Werke II, p. 1133. (E.t., p. 303.)
57 *Ecce Homo* ("Also sprach Zarathustra" 8), in Werke II, p. 1139. (E.t., pp. 308–9.)
58 *Ecce Homo* ("Also sprach Zarathustra" 8), in Werke II, p. 1140. (E.t., p. 309.)

### 3. What is nihilism?

1 F. Nietzsche, *Ecce Homo* ("Jenseits von Gut und Böse" 1), in Werke II, p. 1141. (E.t., p. 310.)
2 Nietzsche, *Der Fall Wagner. Ein Musikanten-Problem* (1888), in Werke II, pp. 901–38; quotations in Werke II, pp. 912, 925 (E.t., *The Birth of Tragedy* and *The Case of Wagner*, Random House [Vintage Books], New York, 1967, pp. 164, 172.)
3 Nietzsche, *Nietzsche contra Wagner. Aktenstücke eines Psychologen* (1889), in Werke II, pp. 1035–61 (E.t., "Nietzsche contra Wagner Out of the Files of a Psychologist," in Walter Kaufmann [ed./transl.], *The Portable Nietzsche*, The Viking Press, New York, 1954; rev., 1968, Chatto & Windus, London, 1971, pp. 681–83.)
4 Nietzsche, *Jenseits von Gut und Böse. Vorspiele einer Philosophie der Zukunft* (1886), in Werke II, pp. 563–759. (E.t., *Beyond Good and Evil*, Penguin Books, New York/Harmondsworth, 1973.)
5 Nietzsche, *Ecce Homo* ("Jenseits von Gut und Böse" 2), in Werke II, p. 1141. (E.t., p. 310.)
6 Cf. A.II.3: "Neither freethinking nor Thomism."
7 Nietzsche, *Ecce Homo* ("Jenseits von Gut und Böse" 2), in Werke II, p. 1141. (E.t., p. 310.)
8 *Ecce Homo* ("Der Fall Wagner" 3), in Werke II, p. 1149. (E.t., p. 322.)
9 Nietzsche, *Jenseits* 191, in Werke II, pp. 648–49. (E.t., *Beyond Good and Evil*, p. 96.)
10 Ibid., p. 649. (E.t., ibid.)
11 Cf. A.I.1. *The ideal of mathematical certainty.*
12 Cf. Nietzsche, *Menschliches, Allzumenschliches* II ("Vermischte Meinungen und Sprüche" 408), in Werke I, p. 870. (E.t., *Human, All-Too-Human*, T. N. Foulis, Edinburgh/London, Vol. II, 1910, p 178.)
13 Nietzsche, letter to G. Brandes, Nov. 20, 1888, in Werke III, p. 1335.
14 Nietzsche, *Ecce Homo* ("Warum ich so klug bin" 3), in Werke II, p. 1088. (E.t., p. 243.)
15 Nietzsche, *Antichrist* 5, in Werke II, p. 1167. (E.t., p. 117.)
16 Nietzsche, *Jenseits* 229, in Werke II, p. 694. (E.t., p. 141.)
17 *Jenseits* 16, in Werke II, p. 579. (E.t., p. 27.)
18 *Jenseits* 16, in Werke II, pp. 579–80 (E.t., pp. 27–28.)
19 *Jenseits* 16, in Werke II, p. 580. (E.t., p 28.)
20 *Jenseits* 19, in Werke II, pp. 581–82. (E.t., p. 30.)
21 *Jenseits* 11, in Werke II, p. 575. (E.t., pp. 23–24.)
22 *Jenseits* 12, in Werke II, p. 577. (E.t., p. 25.)
23 Ibid. (E.t., ibid.)
24 *Jenseits* 14, in Werke II, p. 578. (E.t., p. 26.) Cf. also, on the erroneousness of the world: *Jenseits* 34, in Werke II, pp. 598–600. (E.t., pp. 46–48.)
25 *Jenseits* 1, in Werke II, p. 567. (E.t., p. 15.)
26 *Jenseits* 2, in Werke II, p. 568. (E.t., p. 16.)
27 Ibid. (E.t., ibid.)
28 Ibid. (E.t., ibid.)
29 *Jenseits* 4, in Werke II, p. 569. (E.t., p. 17.)
30 *Jenseits* 23, in Werke II, p. 587. (E.t., p. 35.)
31 Ibid. (E.t., p. 36.)
32 Ibid. (E.t., p. 35.)
33 Ibid. (E.t., ibid.)
34 Nietzsche, *Genealogie der Moral. Eine Strettschrift* (1887), in Werke II, pp. 761–900. (E.t., *On the Genealogy of Morals* and *Ecce Homo*, Random House [Vintage Books], New York, 1969.)
35 F. Nietzsche, *Ecce Homo* ("Genealogie der Moral"), in Werke II, p. 1143. (E.t., p. 312.)
36 Ibid. (E.t., ibid.)
37 Ibid. (E.t., ibid.)

38 Ibid. (E.t., p. 313.)
39 F. Nietzsche, *Götzen-Dämmerung oder Wie man mit dem Hammer philosophiert* (1889), in Werke II, pp. 939–1033. (E.t., *Twilight of the Idols* and *The Antichrist*, Penguin Books, New York/Harmondsworth, 1968.)
40 *Götzen-Dämmerung* (Preface), in Werke II, p. 941. (E.t., p. 22.)
41 Nietzsche, *Ecce Homo* ("Götzen-Dämmerung" 1), in Werke II, p. 1144. (E.t., p. 314.)
42 Nietzsche, *Götzen-Dämmerung* ("Moral als Widernatur" 4), in Werke II, p. 968. (E.t., p. 45.)
43 Ibid. (E.t., ibid.)
44 *Götzen-Dämmerung* ("Moral als Widernatur" 4), in Werke II, p. 967. (E.t., p. 45.)
45 *Götzen-Dämmerung* ("Moral als Widernatur" 6), in Werke II, p. 969. (E.t., p. 46.)
46 *Der Antichrist. Fluch auf das Christentum* (1888), in Werke II, pp. 1161–1235. (E.t., *Twilight of the Gods* and *The Antichrist*, Penguin Books, New York/Harmondsworth, 1968.)
47 *Antichrist* 62, in Werke II, p. 1235. (E.t., pp. 186–87.)
48 *Antichrist* 35, in Werke II, p. 1197. (E.t., p. 147.)
49 Nietzsche, *Nachlass*, in Werke III, p. 658. (As noted in the text, Nietzsche's unpublished works were used after his death to construct a book called *Der Wille zur Macht*. The English translation of this work edited by Walter Kaufmann, Random House [Vintage Books], New York, 1968, will be used here for the passages cited in the text, indicated as WP, with paragraph number. So here the reference is WP 168.)
50 Nietzsche, *Antichrist* 18, in Werke II, p. 1178. (E.t., p. 128.)
51 Nietzsche, *Ecce Homo* ("Warum ich ein Schicksal bin" 2), in Werke II, p. 1153. (E.t., p. 327.)
52 *Ecce Homo* ("Warum ich ein Schicksal bin" 1), in Werke II, p. 1152. (E.t., p. 326.)
53 Ibid. (E.t., pp. 326–27.)
54 Ibid. (E.t., p. 326.)
55 Nietzsche, *Der Wille zur Macht. Versuch einer Umwertung aller Werte*, in Nietzsches Werke, pub. by the Nietzsche-Archiv, Vol. XV, pp. 129–489; Vol. XVI, pp. 1–412, Leipzig, 1911. (E.t., see n. 49, above.)
56 Cf. K. Schlechta, "Nachwort," in Werke III, pp. 1433–52; the same author, *Der Fall Nietzsche. Aufsätze und Vorträge*, Munich, 1958; esp. his treatment of the criticism of Rudolf Pannwitz, pp. 99–115.
57 Cf. E. F. Podach, *Friedrich Nietzsches Werke des Zusammenbruchs*, Heidelberg, 1961, pp. 9–12. This edition contains the works "Nietzsche contra Wagner," "Der Antichrist," "Ecce Homo" and "Dionysus-Dithyramben," but not the unpublished material.
58 Nietzsche, *Aus dem Nachlass der achtziger Jahre*, in Werke III, pp. 415–925.
59 F. Würzbach, *Das Vermächtnis Nietzsches* (1940), now in paperback with the title *Umwertung aller Werte*, 2 vols., Munich, 1969.
60 Schlechta, "Nachwort," in Werke III, p. 1433.
61 Cf., e.g., the very clear presentation by W. Weischedel, *Der Gott der Philosophen*, Vol. I, pp. 429–57.
62 Nietzsche, *Nachlass*, in Werke III, p. 530. (WP 25.)
63 *Nachlass*, in Werke III, p. 779. (WP 40.)
64 F. Nietzsche, *Menschliches, Allzumenschliches* I ("Vorrede" 3), in Werke I, p. 440. (E.t., *Human, All-Too-Human*, Edinburgh/London, Vol. I, 1910, p. 6.)
65 F. Nietzsche, *Fröhliche Wissenschaft* III, 125, in Werke II, p. 127. (E.t., *The Gay Science*, New York, 1974, p. 181.)
66 *Fröhliche Wissenschaft* V, 346, in Werke II, pp. 210–12. (E.t., pp. 285–87.)
67 *Fröhliche Wissenschaft* V, 375, in Werke II, pp. 250–51. (E.t., p. 337.)
68 As by H. Wein, "Zur Rechtfertigung des Nihilismus. Aus Anlass seines 100.Geburtstags" (1963), in D. Arendt (ed.), *Der Nihilismus als Phänomen der Geistesgeschichte in der wissenschaftlichen Diskussion unseres Jahrhunderts*, Darmstadt, 1974, pp. 195–209.

69 As W. Vordtriede suggests, "Das nihilistische Geburtstagskind" (1963), in Arendt, pp. 210–12. H. Thom, "Wie alt ist der Nihilismus" (1964), in Arendt, pp. 213–20, sees the origin of nihilism in far too general terms in Christianity.

70 Quotation and commentary by O. Pöggeler, "Hegel und die Anfänge der Nihilismus-Diskussion" (1970), in Arendt, pp. 307–49. Pöggeler points to the fact that D. Jenisch, three years before Jacobi, had described absolute transcendental idealism as nihilism.

71 On the relationship of idealism to nihilism, in addition to Pöggeler, compare W. Müller-Lauter, "Nihilismus als Konsequenz des Idealismus. F. H. Jacobis Kritik an der Transzendental Philosophie und ihre philosophiegeschichtliche Folgen," in A. Schwan (ed.), *Denken im Schatten des Nihilismus. Festschrift für Wilhelm Weischedel zum 70. Geburtstag*, Darmstadt, 1975, pp. 113–63.

72 Nietzsche, *Nachlass*, in Werke III, p. 557. (WP 2.)

73 *Nachlass*, in Werke III, p. 567. (WP 3.)

74 *Nachlass*, in Werke III, p. 634. (WP, Preface, n. 2.)

75 *Nachlass*, in Werke III, p. 881. (WP 1.)

76 *Nachlass*, in Werke III, p. 635. (WP, Preface, n. 4.)

77 *Nachlass*, in Werke III, p. 678. (WP 12 B.)

78 *Nachlass*, in Werke III, p. 679. (WP 7.)

79 Ibid. (WP ibid.)

80 *Nachlass*, in Werke III, p. 738. (WP 461.)

81 *Nachlass*, in Werke III, p. 887. (WP 707.)

82 *Nachlass*, in Werke III, p. 661. (WP 39.)

83 *Nachlass*, in Werke III, p. 686. (WP 252.)

84 Nietzsche, *Jenseits* ("Vorrede"), in Werke II, p. 566. (E.t., *Beyond Good and Evil*, Penguin Books, New York/Harmondsworth, 1973, p. 14.)

85 Nietzsche, *Nachlass*, in Werke III, p. 826. (WP 251.)

86 Nietzsche, *Antichrist* 18, in Werke II, p. 1178. (E.t., *The Antichrist*, New York/Harmondsworth, 1968, p. 128.)

87 Nietzsche, *Nachlass*, in Werke III, p. 638. (WP 153.)

88 Nietzsche, *Antichrist* 18, in Werke II, p. 1178. (E.t., *The Antichrist*, p. 128.)

89 Nietzsche, *Nachlass*, in Werke III, p. 880. (WP 18.)

90 *Nachlass*, in Werke III, p. 554. (WP 20.)

91 *Nachlass*, in Werke III, p. 881. (WP 19.)

92 *Nachlass*, in Werke III, pp. 491–92. (WP 69.)

93 *Nachlass*, in Werke III, pp. 881–82. (WP 1, n. 3.)

94 *Nachlass*, in Werke III, pp. 893–94. (WP 8.)

95 *Nachlass*, in Werke III, p. 881. (WP 1, n. 1.)

96 Ibid. (WP 1, n. 2.)

97 *Nachlass*, in Werke III, p. 675. (WP 598.)

98 *Nachlass*, in Werke III, p. 679. (WP 36.)

99 *Nachlass*, in Werke III, p. 549. (WP 585 A.)

100 *Nachlass*, in Werke III, p. 621. (WP 28.)

101 *Nachlass*, in Werke III, p. 911. (WP 29.)

## Was Nietzsche a nihilist?

1 F. Nietzsche, *Nachlass*, in Werke III, p. 558. (WP 23.)

2 Ibid. (WP 23.)

3 *Nachlass*, in Werke III, p. 557. (WP 22.)

4 Ibid. (WP ibid.)

5 Ibid. (WP 23.)

6 *Nachlass*, in Werke III, p. 558. (WP 23.)

7 *Nachlass*, in Werke III, p. 555. (WP 15.)

8 Ibid. (WP ibid.)

9 *Nachlass*, in Werke III, p. 670. (WP 24.)

10 *Nachlass*, in Werke III, p. 533. (WP 26.)

11 *Nachlass*, in Werke III, p. 478. (WP 405.)

12 *Nachlass*, in Werke III, p. 634. (WP, Preface, n. 4.)

13 *Nachlass*, in Werke III, p. 560. (WP 462.)
14 *Nachlass*, in Werke III, p. 834. (WP 1041.)
15 Nietzsche, *Götzendämmerung* ("Was ich den Alten verdanke" 5), in Werke II, p. 1032. (E.t., *Twilight of the Idols*, New York/Harmondsworth, 1968, p. 110.)
16 Nietzsche, *Nachlass*, in Werke III, p. 480. (WP 254.)
17 *Nachlass*, in Werke III, p. 917. (WP 1067.)
18 *Nachlass*, in Werke III, p. 556. (WP 1005.)
19 *Nachlass*, in Werke III, p. 453. (WP 91.)
20 *Nachlass*, in Werke III, p. 634. (WP, Preface, n. 3.)
21 Quoted by C. A. Bernoulli, *Franz Overbeck und Friedrich Nietzsche. Eine Freundschaft*, Vol. I, Jena, 1908, p. 250.
22 Nietzsche, *Dionysus-Dithyramben*, "Zwischen Raubvögeln," in Werke II, pp. 1249–52; quotation, pp. 1251–52.
23 *Dionysus-Dithyramben*, "Klage der Ariadne," in Werke II, pp. 1258–59. (E.t., in *Thus Spoke Zarathustra*, New York/Harmondsworth, 1961, p. 267.)
24 Nietzsche, *Ecce Homo* ("Also sprach Zarathustra" 8), in Werke II, pp. 1138–39. (E.t., *Ecce Homo*, New York, 1969, p. 308.)
25 Nietzsche, letter to Malvida von Meysenburg, Jan. 14, 1880, in Werke III, p. 1161.
26 Cf. C. A. Bernoulli, *F. Overbeck und Friedrich Nietzsche*, Vol. II, pp. 202–57; E. F. Podach, *Nietzsches Zusammenbruch. Beiträge zu einer Biographie auf Grund unveröffentlichter Dokumente*, Heidelberg, 1930; important references to the person of Ariadne are found on pages 57–58 and 88–94. (E.t., *The Madness of Nietzsche*, Putnam, London/New York, 1931, pp. 101–3, 142–51.)

## D.II.  Conquest of nihilism?

1 F. Nietzsche, *Ecce Homo* ("Der Fall Wagner" 4), in Werke II, p. 1151. (E.t., *Ecce Homo*, p. 324.)
2 W. Jens, "Friedrich Nietzsche. Pastor ohne Kanzel," in *Frankfurter Allgemeine Zeitung*, Feb. 6, 1974; reprinted in his collection *Republikanische Reden*, Munich, 1976, pp. 101–12.

## 1. Critique of Nietzsche

3 Nietzsche, letter to Jakob Burckhardt, Jan. 6, 1889, in Werke III, p. 1351. (E.t., Walter Kaufmann [ed. and transl.], *The Portable Nietzsche*, Viking Press, New York, 1954; rev. 1968, Chatto & Windus, London, 1971, p. 685.)
4 J. Hirschberger, *Geschichte der Philosophie*, Vol. II, "Neuzeit und Gegenwart," Freiburg/Basel/Vienna, 1952, p. 477.
5 Ibid., cf. pp. 478–82.
6 Cf. M. Heidegger, "Nietzsches Wort 'Gott ist tot,'" in *Holzwege*, Frankfurt, 1950, pp. 193–247; the same author, *Nietzsche*, 2 vols. (lectures and articles, 1936–46), Pfullingen, 1961.
7 W. Müller-Lauter deals with these problems at greater length in *Nietzsche. Seine Philosophie der Gegensätze und die Gegensätze seiner Philosophie*, Berlin/New York, 1971.
8 K. Schlechta, *Der Fall Nietzsche. Aufsätze und Vorträge*, Munich, 1958, p. 92.
9 W. Weischedel, *Der Gott der Philosophen*, Darmstadt, 1971–72, Vol. II, pp. 451–52.
10 Nietzsche, *Nachlass*, in Werke III, p. 853. (WP 55.)
11 L. Andreas-Salomé, *Friedrich Nietzsche in seinen Werken*, Vienna, 1894, pp. 222–23.
12 Ibid., p. 224.
13 Ibid., p. 225.
14 K. Jaspers, *Nietzsche. Einführung in das Verständnis seines Philosophierens*, 1935, Berlin, 1950³, pp. 350–63.
15 Jaspers, *Nietzsche und das Christentum*, 1947, Munich, 1952, p. 69.

16 M. Eliade, *Le Mythe de l'Eternel Retour. Archétypes et répétition*, Paris, 1949. (E.t., *The Myth of the Eternal Return*, Routledge & Kegan Paul, London, 1955, pp. 112–13.)
17 Ibid., p. 123.
18 M. Čapek, "Eternal Return," in The Encyclopedia of Philosophy, New York/London, 1967, Vol. III, pp. 61–63; quotation, p. 63.
19 Nietzsche, *Nachgelassene Werke*, in Nietzsches Werke, Vol. XII, Leipzig, 1901, p. 415.
20 Ibid., p. 169.
21 Nietzsche, *Antichrist* 16, in Werke II, p. 1176. (E.t., *The Antichrist*, New York/Harmondsworth, 1968, p. 126.)
22 *Antichrist* 15, in Werke II, p. 1175. (E.t., p. 125.)
23 Nietzsche, *Morgenröte* 95, in Werke I, pp. 1073–74. (E.t., *The Dawn of Day*, T. N. Foulis, Edinburgh/London, 1911, p. 94.)
24 Nietzsche, *Nachlass*, in Werke III, p. 747. (WP 135.)
25 Nietzsche, *Zur Genealogie der Moral* II, 22 in Werke II, p. 833. (E.t., *On the Genealogy of Morals*, Random House [Vintage Books], New York, 1969, p. 92.)
26 Nietzsche, *Antichrist* 47, in Werke II, pp. 1211–12. (E.t., *The Antichrist*, pp. 162–63.)
27 Nietzsche, *Nachlass*, in Werke III, p. 853; cf. p. 496. (WP 55.)
28 *Nachlass*, in Werke III, p. 585. (WP 639.)
29 Nietzsche, *Zarathustra* II ("Auf den glückseligen Inseln"), in Werke II, p. 344. (E.t., *Thus Spoke Zarathustra*, p. 110.)

## 2. What Christians can learn

1 F. Nietzsche, *Ecce Homo* ("Der Fall Wagner" 2), in Werke II, p. 1148. (E.t., *Ecce Homo*, p. 320.)
2 The positive statements are stressed—perhaps overstressed—by Karl Jaspers, *Nietzsche und das Christentum*, pp. 8–10.
3 Nietzsche, *Antichrist* 31, in Werke II, p. 1192. (E.t., *The Antichrist*, p. 143.)
4 *Antichrist* 31, in Werke II, p. 1193. (E.t., p. 143.)
5 Ibid. (E.t., ibid.)
6 *Antichrist* 28, in Werke II, p. 1190. (E.t., p. 140.)
7 *Antichrist* 29, in Werke II, pp. 1190–91; cf. *Antichrist* 27, in Werke II, p. 1189. (E.t., pp. 141, 140.)
8 *Antichrist* 29, in Werke II, p. 1191. (E.t., p. 141.)
9 *Antichrist* 33, in Werke II p. 1195. (E.t., p. 145.)
10 *Antichrist* 34, in Werke II, pp. 1196–97. (E.t., pp. 146–47.)
11 *Antichrist* 35, in Werke II, p. 1197. (E.t., pp. 147–48.)
12 *Antichrist* 37, in Werke II, p. 1198. (E.t., p. 149.)
13 *Antichrist* 40, in Werke II, p. 1202. (E.t., p. 153.)
14 *Antichrist* 39, in Werke II, p. 1200. (E.t., p. 151.)
15 Ibid. (E.t., ibid.)
16 Cf. the description in *Ecce Homo* ("Why I am a destiny" 8), in Werke II, pp. 1158–59. (E.t., pp. 333–34.)
17 This is how *Ecce Homo* ends: Werke II, p. 1159. (E.t., p. 335.)
18 Cf., on the whole subject, H. Küng, *Christ sein*, esp. D: "Die Praxis." (E.t., *On Being a Christian*, D: "Practice.")

## 3. What non-Christians can learn

19 F. Nietzsche, *Nachlass*, in Werke III, p. 491. (WP 856.)
20 Nietzsche, *Antichrist* 51, in Werke II, p. 1217. (E.t., *The Antichrist*, pp. 168–69.)
21 Nietzsche, *Nachlass*, in Werke III, p. 621. (WP 28.)
22 Cf. C.III.3: "The importance of religion for Jung, Fromm, Frankl."
23 Nietzsche, *Nachlass*, in Werke III, p. 562. (WP 903.)
24 Cf. *Nachlass*, in Werke III, p. 610. (WP 891.)
25 *Nachlass*, in Werke III, p. 554. (WP 901.)

26 *Nachlass*, in Werke III, pp. 505–6. (WP 954.)
27 *Nachlass*, in Werke III, p. 432. (WP 982.)
28 For early evidence of this, see H. Rauschning, *Gespräche mit Hitler*, Zürich, 1940. (E.t., *Hitler Speaks. A Series of Political Conversations with Adolf Hitler on his Real Aims*, Thornton Butterworth, London, 1939.)
29 Nietzsche, *Nachlass*, in Werke III, p. 708. (WP 864.)
30 Ibid. (E.t., ibid.)
31 W. Jens, "Friedrich Nietzsche. Pastor ohne Kanzel," in *Frankfurter Allgemeine Zeitung*, Feb. 6, 1974; reprinted in his collected articles, *Republikanische Reden*, Munich, 1976, pp. 101–12.
32 Nietzsche, *Nachlass*, in Werke III, p. 630. (WP 888.)
33 *Nachlass*, in Werke III, p. 629. (WP 866.)
34 *Nachlass*, in Werke III, p. 708. (WP 864.)

### 4. *Interim results IV: Theses on nihilism*

35 Cf. First Vatican Council, Dogmatic Constitution, "Dei Filius," on the Catholic faith, Apr. 24, 1870 (DS 3000–3045).
36 Cf. W. Kamlah and P. Lorenzen, *Logische Propädeutik. Vorschule des vernünftigen Redens*, Mannheim, 1973, Ch. 4, §3: "Sachverhalt und Tatsache"; quotation, p. 138.
37 Ibid.
38 Ibid., p. 144.
39 Cf. A.III.1. *The epistemological discussion.*
40 Kamlah and Lorenzen, op. cit., p. 140.
41 Ibid., pp. 140, 138.
42 On the question of the transcendentals, cf. P. Dezza, *Metaphysica generalis*, Rome, 1948, pp. 61–98. A more detailed treatment, with numerous indications of primary and secondary works on the subject, is found in J. B. Lotz, *Ontologia*, Barcelona/Freiburg/Rome, 1963, pp. 69–97, 117–28, 133–47. Similar views are defended in the neoscholastic works on metaphysics or ontology by R. Arnou, L. de Raeymaeker, A. Marc, F. van Steenberghen, E. Coreth, P. Descoqs, S. Cuesta, C. Nink, A. Brunner.
43 F. Nietzsche, *Nachlass*, in Werke III, p. 677. (WP 12 A.)
44 Ibid. (WP 12 A.)
45 Ibid., p. 678. (WP 12 A.)
46 Ibid. (WP 12 A.)
47 Ibid., p. 676. (WP 12 A.)
48 Ibid., p. 568. (WP 599.)
49 Ibid., p. 896. (WP 617.)
50 Ibid., p. 678. (WP 12 A.)
51 Ibid., p. 557. (WP 13.)
52 Ibid., pp. 677, 678. (WP 12 A.)
53 Ibid., p. 896. (WP 617.)
54 Ibid., p. 678. (WP 12 A.)
55 Ibid. (WP 12 A.)
56 Ibid. (WP 12 B.)
57 Ibid., p. 566. (WP 298.)
58 Ibid., pp. 582–83. (WP 272.)
59 D. Arendt, "Die Überwindung des Nihilismus," in *Der Nihilismus als Phänomen*, pp. 350–54. Note also Arendt's Introduction, pp. 1–17.
60 On nihilism, cf. also F. Leist, *Existenz im Nichts. Versuch einer Analyse des Nihilismus*, Munich, 1961. A. Caracciolo, *Pensiero contemporaneo e nichilismo*, Naples, 1976: especially Ch. I (on Kant and nihilism) and Ch. III (on Heidegger and nihilism). See also the articles not already mentioned in the collection *Der Nihilismus als Phänomen* by L. Landgrebe, H. Schaeder, G. Cloege, T. Süss, W. Kohlschmidt, H. Rauschning, K. Hübner, W. Hof, L. Kofler.

## E. YES TO REALITY—ALTERNATIVE TO NIHILISM

1 W. Stegmüller, *Metaphysik, Skepsis, Wissenschaft,* 1954, 2nd ed., with new Introduction, Berlin/Heidelberg/New York, 1969, pp. 1–2.

### E.I. The basic attitude

2 Cf. Aquinas, *Summa Theologiae* I–II, q.9 a.1; q.12 a.1; q.13 a.1; *De Malo,* q.VI a.unicus.

3 Cf. F. Dorsch, art. "Wille," in F. Dorsch (ed.), *Psychologisches Wörterbuch,* Berne/Stuttgart/Vienna, 1976, p. 667.

4 Cf. A.III.1: "Scientific revolutions: Thomas S. Kuhn."

5 Cf. P. Ricoeur, "L'homme faillible," in *Finitude et Culpabilité,* Paris, 1960.

6 Fyodor Dostoevsky, *The Brothers Karamazov,* Heinemann, London, 1912, new impression 1965, p. 241.

7 J. P. Sartre, *Huis clos,* Sc. 5, in J. P. Sartre, *Théâtre,* Paris, 1947. (E.t., *In Camera,* Hamish Hamilton, London, 1946, new impression 1965; in the same volume is *The Flies.*) The negative aspect of personal relationships (in connection with the American race problem) is treated in *La putain respectueuse,* also in J. P. Sartre, *Théâtre,* Paris, 1947.

8 Sartre, *L'être et le néant. Essai d'ontologie phénoménologique,* Paris, 1943; cf. esp. Part III: "Le pour-autrui." (E.t., *Being and Nothingness,* Philosophical Library, Inc., New York/Methuen, London, 1957; cf. esp. Part III: "Being-for-others.")

9 Cf. R. Dahrendorf, "Homo Sociologicus: Versuch zur Geschichte, Bedeutung und Kritik der Kategorie der sozialen Rolle" (1957), incl. in Vol. I of his collected works, *Pfade aus Utopia. Arbeiten zur Theorie und Methode der Soziologie,* Munich, 1967, pp. 128–94. On the discussions about this term, cf. pp. 384–85.

10 C. G. Jung, "Über die Beziehung der Psychotherapie zur Seelsorge" (1932), in *Psychologie und Religion,* Studienausgabe, Olten, 1971, p. 143. (E.t., "Psychotherapists and the Clergy," in *Psychology and Religion,* Collected Works XI, Routledge & Kegan Paul, London/Pantheon Books, New York, 1958, p. 339.)

11 R. Guardini, *Die Annahme seiner selbst,* Würzburg, 1960, p. 13.

12 Cf. W. Schulz, *Philosophie in der veränderten Welt,* Pfullingen, 1972, pp. 125, 135.

13 On the concept of *Einstellung* ("attitude," "approach") cf. esp. E. Roth, *Einstellung als Determination individuellen Verhaltens. Die Analyse eines Begriffes und seiner Bedeutung für die Persönlichkeitspsychologie,* Göttingen, 1967; the same author, *Persönlichkeitspsychologie. Eine Einführung,* Stuttgart, 1969, pp. 104–14. Cf. also R. Strohal, U. Claesges and P. Janssen, art. "Einstellung," in J. Ritter (ed.), *Historisches Wörterbuch der Philosophie,* Vol. II, Basel/Darmstadt, 1972, pp. 417–22.

14 Sartre, *Les mouches,* Act III, Sc. 2, in *Théâtre,* p. 100. (E.t., *The Flies,* in J. P. Sartre, *Two Plays,* Hamish Hamilton, London, 1946, 1965, p. 95.)

15 Sartre, *L'existentialisme est un humanisme,* Paris, 1946, pp. 36–37. (E.t., *Existentialism and Humanism,* Methuen, London, 1948, reprinted 1970, p. 34.) Sartre's philosophy first appeared important to the present author in connection with his work for the licentiate in philosophy under Professor Alois Naher, S.J., at the Gregorian University, Rome: *Der existentialistische Humanismus Jean-Paul Sartres,* Rome, 1951. Although I can still keep to the presentation of Sartre's philosophy as given there, I would have to correct in a number of ways the answer I gave at that time.

16 G. W. F. Hegel, *Phänomenologie des Geistes,* in Werke II, p. 419. (E.t., *Phenomenology of Mind,* transl. by J. B. Baillie, Allen & Unwin, London/Macmillan Company, New York, 1931, p. 606.)

17 Sartre, *L'être et le néant*, p. 516; cf. pp. 516–18. (E.t., *Being and Nothingness*, p. 441; cf. pp. 441–43.)

18 Cf. Sartre, *L'existentialisme*, pp. 67–72. (E.t., *Existentialism and Humanism*, pp. 45–48.)

19 Sartre, *Les mouches*, Act III, Sc. 2, in *Théatre*, p. 101. (E.t., *The Flies*, in *Two Plays*, p. 97.)

20 Sartre, *L'existentialisme*, p. 22; cf. *L'être et le néant*, p. 516. (E.t., *Existentialism and Humanism*, p. 28; cf. *Being and Nothingness*, pp. 440–41.)

21 *L'existentialisme*, pp. 23–24. (E.t., *Existentialism and Humanism*, pp. 28–29.)

22 Cf. Sartre, *L'être et le néant*, p. 660; cf. pp. 518–21. (E.t., *Being and Nothingness*, pp. 571–72; cf. pp. 442–45.)

23 Ibid., p. 539. (E.t., p. 461.)

24 Cf. p. 539. (E.t., pp. 461–62.)

25 Cf. esp. *L'être et le néant*, pp. 651–63. (E.t., pp. 565–75.)

26 Cf. C. von Bormann, art. "Entscheidung," in *Historisches Wörterbuch der Philosophie*, Vol. II, pp. 541–44.

27 S. Kierkegaard, *Either/Or, A Fragment of Life*, Princeton University Press/Oxford University Press, 1946, Vol. II, pp. 179–80.

28 Kierkegaard, *Tagebucher*, Vol. II in Gesammelte Werke, ed. H. Gerdes, Düsseldorf/Cologne, pp. 104–5.

29 B. F. Skinner, *Beyond Freedom and Dignity*, New York, 1971.

30 K. Lorenz, *Das sogenannte Böse. Zur Naturgeschichte der Aggression*, Vienna, 1963; the same author, *Über tierisches und menschliches Verhalten. Aus dem Werdegang der Verhaltenslehre. Gesammelte Abhandlungen*, 2 vols., Munich, 1965. (E.t., *On Aggression*, Methuen, London, 1966; *Studies in Animal and Human Behaviour*, Methuen, London, Vol. I, 1970, Vol. II, 1971.) A good survey is provided by I. Eibl-Eibesfeldt, *Grundriss der vergleichenden Verhaltensforschung. Ethologie*, Munich, 1972.

31 I. Eibl-Eibesfeldt, *Der vorprogrammierte Mensch. Das Ererbte als bestimmender Faktor im menschlichen Verhalten*, Vienna/Munich/Zürich, 1973, pp. 271–72.

32 K. Jaspers, *Der philosophische Glaube*, Frankfurt, 1958, p. 54.

33 Ibid., pp. 54–55.

34 Ibid., p. 55. On Jaspers' specific view of will and (existential) freedom, cf. his basic work, *Philosophie*, 3 vols., 1932, new ed., Berlin/Göttingen/Heidelberg, 1956, esp. Vol. II, "Existenzerhellung," second main section: "Selbstsein als Freiheit."

35 Cf. A.II.3: "Conflict of faith with faith: Jansenism."

36 Cf. A.II.3: "Reasonable reason—credible faith?"

37 Sartre, *L'existentialisme*, p. 37. (E.t., *Existentialism and Humanism*, p. 34.)

38 Cf. A.III.1: The universal claim of scientific thought? (On Karl Popper and Hans Albert.)

39 K. R. Popper and H. Marcuse, *Revolution oder Reform? Eine Konfrontation*, ed. F. Stark, Munich, 1971, pp. 38–39.

40 Popper, *The Open Society and Its Enemies*, 2 vols., 5th, rev. ed., Routledge & Kegan Paul, London, 1966; quotation, Vol. II, p. 230.

41 Ibid., p. 231.

42 Ibid., p. 232.

43 Ibid., p. 224.

44 Popper, *Logik der Forschung*, 1934, 6th, rev. ed., Tübingen, 1976, p. 12. (E.t., *The Logic of Scientific Discovery*, Hutchinson, London/New York, 1959, p. 38.)

45 Cf. Popper, *The Open Society*, Vol. II, pp. 233–40. We can agree with what Popper says also on the importance of the consequences of all "proposals" and "conventions" in *Logik der Forschung*, pp. 12–13. (E.t., *The Logic of Scientific Discovery*, p. 38.)

46 Popper, *The Open Society*, Vol. II, p. 231. Hans Albert has kindly drawn my attention to the fact that, in his "Addenda" to the 4th ed. (Vol. II, p. 369–90), Popper himself opposes the "irrationalist view of decisions," regarding it as "an exaggeration as well as an over-dramatization," the decision itself being "a leap in the dark, which we take with closed eyes" (pp. 380–81). In this respect he is ab-

solutely right. But, then, there should be no more talk of an "irrational faith in reason" or of a "priority of irrationalism," perhaps not even of "rationalism"; the term "rationality" is to be preferred. This critique of ours is confirmed by Popper's superficial treatment of the problems of nihilism (pp. 381–83) and his emotional remarks about Hegel's philosophy (pp. 393–95).

47 K. R. Popper, *Logik der Forschung*, p. 76. (E.t., *The Logic of Scientific Discovery*, p. 111.)

48 Ibid., pp. 75–76. (E.t., p. 111.)

## E.II. Fundamental mistrust or fundamental trust?

1 Dag Hammarskjöld, *Markings*, Knopf, New York/Faber, London, 1964, p. 169.

### 1. Confrontation

2 Peter Wust, *Ungewissheit und Wagnis*, 1937, 7th ed., Munich, 1962, pp. 63, 68–69, 65.

3 Wust recognizes in particular his debt to three works: B. Rosenmüller, *Religionsphilosophie*, Münster, 1932; J. Pieper, *Über die Hoffnung*, Leipzig, 1935; and K. Jaspers, *Vernunft und Existenz*, Groningen, 1935. Wust's moral qualification of the fundamental decision of the subject can scarcely be avoided if "the principle of universal intelligibility (*ens et verum convertuntur*)" is assumed as "the true primordial and first principle of philosophy," the truth of which is "radiantly evident" to the mind of the philosopher: "the clarity of ontological truth penetrating everything" (pp. 150–51).

4 Cf. J. P. Sartre, *L'existentialisme*, pp. 80–82; *L'être et le néant*, pp. 85–111. (E.t., *Existentialism and Humanism*, p. 51; *Being and Nothingness*, pp. 47–70).

5 The importance of fundamental trust, rarely considered by theologians, which is prior to all belief in God, is seen by S. M. Ogden (who calls it "basic existential faith") in his essay on "The Task of Philosophic Theology," in R. A. Evans (ed.), *The Future of Philosophical Theology*, Philadelphia, 1971, pp. 55–85, esp. pp. 56–59. At the same time, however, the possible alternative of fundamental mistrust, of nihilism, is not considered. Ogden's reflections (and those of I. Ramsey and F. Ferré) are taken up by D. Tracy, *Blessed Rage for Order. The New Pluralism in Theology*, New York, 1975, Ch. 7: "The Question of God: Metaphysics Revisited," esp. pp. 153–56. Also important is Tracy's argument with A. Nygren in *Meaning and Method. Prolegomena to a Scientific Philosophy of Religion and a Scientific Theology*, Philadelphia, 1972.

6 H. Albert, *Traktat über kritische Vernunft*, Tübingen, 1966, 2nd ed., 1975, p. 13.

7 Ibid., pp. 13–14.

8 Cf. the quotation from Stegmüller at the beginning of this Chapter E, to which we shall have to return.

9 Cf. the quotation from Popper analyzed in E.I.2: "The fundamental alternative"

10 G. W. F. Hegel, Inaugural address, Oct. 22, 1828, in Berlin, in Werke XXII, ed. J. Hoffmeister, p. 8. In the original, the words quoted are italicized.

11 Albert, *Traktat über kritische Vernunft*, p. 35.

12 Ibid., p. 33.

13 Ibid.

14 H. Hülasa, "Baron Albert im Trilemma," in *Studia Philosophica* 36 (1977), p. 84.

15 Dag Hammarskjöld, *Markings*, Knopf, New York/Faber, London, 1964, p 110

16 N. Luhmann, *Vertrauen. Ein Mechanismus der Reduktion sozialer Komplexität*, Stuttgart, 1968, p. 21.

17 Ibid., p. 41.

18 Cf. ibid., pp. 44–57.

19 Cf. Gabriel Marcel, *Homo Viator. Prolégomènes à une métaphysique de l'espérance*, Paris, 1944.

20 Cf. O. F. Bollnow, *Neue Geborgenheit. Das Problem einer Überwindung des Existentialismus*, Stuttgart, 1955, 1972³; the same author, *Wesen und Wandel der Tugenden*, Frankfurt/Berlin, 1958, esp. Ch. XII, "Das Vertrauen."

21 Cf. H. Hauke, *Die anthropologische Funktion des Vertrauens und seine Bedeutung für seine Erziehung*, Tübingen, 1956 (as dissertation); C. Narowski, *Vertrauen. Begriffsanalyse und Opera tionalisierungsversuch*, Tübingen, 1974 (as dissertation).

22 The neglect of this basic human phenomenon even in the encyclopedias is significant. To take some examples at random: In *Der Grosse Herder*, Freiburg, 1956, Vol. IX, col. 673, we find "Vertrauensarzt, -bruch, -frage, -mann, -schaden," but nothing about "Vertrauen" (trust) as such. "Vertrauen" is also absent from the Evangelisches Kirchenlexikon, Vol. III, Göttingen, 1959; Handbuch Theologischer Grundbegriffe, Vol. II, Munich, 1963; Handbuch Philosophischer Grundbegriffe, Vol. VI, Munich, 1974; Lexikon der Psychologie, Vol. III, Freiburg, 1972; Wörterbuch der Soziologie, ed. W. Berndorf, Stuttgart, 1962; Lexikon zur Soziologie, eds. W. Fuchs and others, Opladen, 1973; Staatslexikon. Recht-Wirtschaft-Gesellschaft, Vol. VIII, Freiburg, 1963. There is one column on the subject in the Lexikon der Pädagogik, Vol. IV, Freiburg, 1955, cols. 803–4, and one in the Lexikon für Theologie und Kirche, Vol. X, Freiburg, 1965, cols. 751–52. There are two substantial columns in Die Religion in Geschichte und Gegenwart, Vol. VI, Tübingen, 1962, cols. 1386–88.

23 Cf. P. Kerans, *La confiance selon E. F. Bollnow. Un essai de dépassement de l'existentialisme*, Strasbourg, 1966 (as dissertation).

24 Bollnow, *Wesen und Wandel der Tugenden*, p. 182.

25 Ibid., p. 182–83.

26 Cf. C.II.3: *Critique of the critique*.

27 William Shakespeare, *Hamlet, Prince of Denmark*, Act III, Sc. 1.

28 Ibid., Act I, Sc. 5.

## 2. Concretion

29 Cf., on the psychology of personality, esp. C. R. Rogers, *On Becoming a Person. A Therapist's View of Psychotherapy*, 1961. Among German works, see J. Herzog-Dürck, *Zwischen Angst und Vertrauen. Probleme und Bilder aus de psychotherapeutischen Praxis*, Nuremberg, 1957.

30 For instance, the social psychology of the "factor climate," small group studies on the style of leadership and on group-dynamical processes, with study of the relationship of teacher and pupil in lessons instruction.

31 Cf. C. Narowski, *Vertrauen*, pp. 145–218 (in discussion with E. Höhn, M. Deutsch, L. H. Strickland, F. J. di Vesta, D. L. Meyer, J. Mills, R. and A. Tausch and B. Fittkau).

32 R. A. Spitz, "Hospitalism," in *The Psychoanalytic Study of the Child*, 2 vols., 1945–46, and other special studies. More comprehensive is the same author's *Genèse des premières relations objectales*, Paris, 1954; 2nd, rev. ed., with the title *La première année de la vie de l'enfant*, Paris, 1963; German transl., *Die Entstehung der ersten Objektbeziehungen*, Stuttgart, 1973. The same author (in collaboration with W. Godfrey Cobliner), *The First Year of Life. A Psychoanalytic Study of Normal and Deviant Development of Object Relations*, International Universities Press, New York, 1965. (*The First Year of Life* is, in effect, a revised and expanded edition of the French book *Genèse des premières relations objectales*, containing the same material treated at greater length and in different words. But, since the French book was not available to me and the American book does not contain the exact quotations used by Dr. Küng, I have simply translated these as they appeared in the German version (*Die Entstehung der ersten Objektbeziehung*), keeping in mind the American terminology. Where Dr. Küng quotes from the German translation of *The First Year of Life*, I have of course reproduced the original passage. Translator.) Other studies, by H. Durfee and K. Wolf, L. Bender and H. Yarnell, L. B. Lowrey, W. Goldfarb, J. Bowlby and J. Robertson, could also be cited.

33 Spitz, *Die Entstehung der ersten Objektbeziehungen*, p. 114.

34 Ibid., p. 128.

35 Ibid., p. 66.

36 Spitz, *The First Year of Life*, pp. 289–90. It should be noted that E. H. Erikson

and T. Benedek have expressed in a somewhat different form—"basic trust" or "confidence"—what Spitz is talking about here.

37 At an early date, anthropologists and ethnologists such as M. Mead, R. Benedict, A. Kardiner and R. Redfield pointed to the close link between the mother-child relationships and the forms of cultural institutions and modes of behavior on the part of adults in certain primitive populations.

38 F. Renggli, *Angst und Geborgenheit. Soziokulturelle Folgen der Mutter-Kind-Beziehung im ersten Lebensjahr. Ergebnisse aus Verhaltensforschung, Psychoanalyse und Ethnologie,* Hamburg, 1974, p. 32.

39 Cited by Renggli, *Angst und Geborgenheit,* pp. 28–29.

40 Cited by Renggli, op. cit., p. 29.

41 A. Nitschke, "Angst und Vertrauen," in *Das verwaiste Kind in der Natur. Ärztliche Beobachtungen zur Welt des jungen Menschen,* Tübingen, 1962, pp. 10–17; quotation, pp. 13–14. Cf. the recent work by H. Müller-Braunschweig, *Die Wirkung der frühen Erfahrung. Das erste Lebensjahr und seine Bedeutung für die psychische Entwicklung,* Stuttgart, 1976.

42 Cf. C.III.3: "Critique and countercritique."

43 Renggli gives a detailed account of the treatment of infants among apes (Ch. 2), in evolution (Ch. 3) and among certain primitive peoples (Ch. 6–9).

44 On the development of the modern "thou" philosophy, cf. M. Theunissen, "Du," in Historisches Wörterbuch der Philosophie, Vol. II, Basel/Darmstadt, 1972, cols. 295–97; the same author, *Der Andere. Studien zur Sozialontologie der Gegenwart,* Berlin, 1965; also H. H. Schrey, *Dialogisches Denken,* Darmstadt, 1970.

45 Cf. L. Feuerbach, "Grundsätze der Philosophie der Zukunft" (1843), in Werke, 6 vols., ed. E. Thies, Vol. III, Frankfurt, 1975, pp. 321–22.

46 Cf. E. Rosenstock, *Angewandte Seelenkunde. Eine programmatische Übersetzung,* Darmstadt, 1924.

47 Cf. F. Ebner, "Das Wort und die geistigen Realitäten. Pneumatologische Fragmente" (1918–19), in *Schriften,* ed. F. Seyr, Vol. I, Munich, 1963, pp. 75–342.

48 Cf. Martin Buber, *Ich und Du* (1923), in Werke, Vol. I: *Schriften zur Philosophie,* Munich/Heidelberg, 1962, pp. 77–170. (E.t., *I and Thou,* T. & T. Clark, Edinburgh, 1937); the same author, "Zur Geschichte des dialogischen Prinzips," in Werke, Vol. I, pp. 291–305.

49 Cf. G. Marcel, *Journal métaphysique,* Paris, 1927.

50 Bollnow, *Wesen und Wandel der Tugenden,* p. 175.

51 F. Nietzsche, *Götzen-Dämmerung,"* in Werke, Vol. II, p. 960. (E.t., *Twilight of the Idols,* Penguin Books, Harmondsworth/New York, 1968, p. 38.)

52 To his "beloved friend Lou," quoted by C. A. Bernoulli, *Franz Overbeck und Friedrich Nietzsche. Eine Freundschaft,* Vol. I, Jena, 1908, p. 333.

53 Cf. C.III.3: "Critique and countercritique."

54 H. E. Richter, *Flüchten oder Standhalten,* Hamburg, 1976.

55 E. H. Erikson, *Identity and the Life Cycle,* W. W. Norton, New York, 1959. The second article in *Identity and the Life Cycle* called "Growth and Crises of the 'Healthy' Personality" was asked for by the preparatory commission of the conference on Childhood and Youth at the White House in 1950 and concentrates on the question of the healthy personality, which Erikson dealt with only marginally in his book *Childhood and Society,* Norton, New York, 1963.

56 Erikson, in *Identity and the Life Cycle,* p. 61, prefers the word "trust" (or "mistrust"), "because there is more naïveté and more mutuality in it," in preference to the more precise "confidence." Theodor Schumacher, professor of German philology at Tübingen, has drawn my attention to the fact that Vertrauen ("trust") and Trost ("comfort") have the same root as the Gothic trausti ("treaty," "alliance") and the old Norse traust ("trust," "confidence," "assurance").

57 Cf. esp. diagrams B, C and D in Erikson, *Identity and the Life Cycle,* also his third essay, "The Problem of the Ego Identity."

58 I. Eibl-Eibesfeldt, *Liebe und Hass. Zur Naturgeschichte elementarer Verhaltensweisen,* Munich, 1970, p. 251.

59 Erikson, *Identity and the Life Cycle,* p. 55.

60 Ibid., pp. 55–56.
61 Ibid., p. 56.
62 Ibid. Here Erikson refers to F. Fromm-Reichmann, *Principles of Intensive Psychotherapy*, Chicago, 1950.
63 Erikson, *Identity and the Life Cycle*, p. 56.
64 Ibid., pp. 60–61. Recently the importance of fundamental trust has been recognized also by German behavioral scientists: cf. I. Eibl-Eibesfeldt, *Liebe und Hass* Ch. 10, "Die Entwicklung persönlicher Bindung und des Urvertrauens."
65 On all this, Richter makes some useful suggestions, esp. with reference to initiative groups as positive alternative models to the dehumanized practice of the world of work (cf. esp. Ch. 11–14).
66 Richter, *Flüchten oder Standhalten*, p. 18.
67 A. M. Greeley, *The Friendship Game*, Doubleday, Garden City, N.Y., 1970, pp. 152–53.

## 3. *Explication*

1 Cf. A.III.1. *The epistemological discussion*.
2 K. R. Popper, *The Logic of Scientific Discovery*, Hutchinson, London/New York, 1959, p. 53.
3 Ibid., p. 108, this is in connection with acceptance of basic statements by agreement.
4 Cf. E.I.2: "The fundamental alternative."
5 R. Carnap, *The Logical Syntax of Knowledge*, Routledge & Kegan Paul, London, 1937, 3rd impression, 1951, p. xv.
6 Ibid.
7 Ibid., cf. p. 51.
8 Ibid., p. xv.
9 Ibid., p. xvi.
10 Thomas S. Kuhn, *The Structure of Scientific Revolutions*, University of Chicago, 1970, p. 42.
11 Ibid., p. 184.
12 W. Kamlah and P. Lorenzen, *Logische Propädeutik. Vorschule des vernünftigen Redens*, Mannheim/Vienna/Zürich, 1973, p. 24.
13 J. Habermas, "Gegen einen positivistisch halbierten Rationalismus," in T. W. Adorno et al., *Der Positivismusstreit in der deutschen Soziologie*, Darmstadt-Neuwied, 1969, p. 236.
14 W. Pannenberg, *Wissenschaftstheorie und Theologie*, Frankfurt, 1973, First Part. (E.t., *Theology and the Philosophy of Science*, Darton, Longman & Todd, London, 1976.)
15 H. Peukert, *Wissenschaftstheorie-Handlungstheorie-Fundamentale Theologie*, Düsseldorf, 1976.
16 W. Stegmüller, *Metaphysik, Skepsis, Wissenschaft*, 1954, rev. ed., Berlin/Heidelberg/New York, 1969, pp. viii–ix. Cf., the same author, *Glauben, Wissen und Erkennen*, 1956, new impression, Darmstadt, 1965.
17 Stegmüller, *Metaphysik, Skepsis, Wissenschaft*, p. 2.
18 Ibid.
19 Ibid.
20 Ibid., pp. 2–3.
21 Ibid., p. 13.
22 Ibid.
23 Ibid., pp. 222–307.
24 Ibid., p. 307.
25 Ibid., p. 168.
26 Ibid., pp. 168–69.
27 Ibid., p. 169.
28 Ibid.
29 Ibid.
30 Ibid., p. 28.
31 Ibid.

32 Ibid., p. 31.
33 Ibid.
34 Ibid., p. 33.
35 Ibid., pp. 210–11.
36 Ibid., p. 211.
37 Ibid.
38 Ibid., pp. 211–12.
39 Ibid., p. 212.
40 Ibid., p. 169.
41 Ibid., p. 456.
42 Cf. E.II.1: "No stalemate."
43 H. G. Gadamer, *Wahrheit und Methode. Grundzüge einer philosophischen Hermeneutik*, Tübingen, 1960, 2nd ed., 1965. (E.t., *Truth and Method*, Seabury Press, New York/Sheed & Ward, London, 1975.)
44 On the critique of Gadamer, see the volume *Hermeneutik und Ideologiekritik*, Frankfurt, 1971, with contributions by K. O. Apel, C. von Bormann, R. Bubner, Gadamer, H. J. Giegel, Habermas.
45 Gadamer, *Wahrheit und Methode*, p. 465. (E.t., *Truth and Method*, p. 446.) Theologians, too, are beginning to pay attention to the real problem of the basis of epistemology as developed here. We referred earlier to S. M. Ogden and D. Tracy. In his Hamburg dissertation, which appeared recently, the Protestant theologian S. Scharrer, after an analysis of the epistemological problems, reaches conclusions that—we are glad to say—largely agree with those put forward here: "Empirical science cannot work unless it risks this trust. Behind the trust there is no static evidence valid once and for all but evidence that might be refuted and that is subject to historical change. The foundation is shaky, 'science does not rest on rock bottom, but rises above a swamp with its bold construction of theories' (Popper). What remains for us? 'If we *hope* that they will sustain the building, we decide for the time being to be content with the firmness of the piles' (Popper). This hope therefore presupposes trust in the carrying power of the basis. Can we produce a proof? Yes, if we have a basic statement. Have we a guarantee of its validity? No? Can we even begin to prove it? Yes, we must decide for one statement. Have we a firm ground for this decision? No. We hover, but we trust." The words are those of Scharrer, *Theologische Kritik der Vernunft*, Tübingen, 1977, p. 83, with a preface in which Helmut Thielecke expresses his approval. We are less happy with Scharrer's identification of biblical "truth" and "trust" (cf. pp. 93–106). He himself defines trust as a *"human* attitude" and on several occasions identifies trust and "faith" (pp. 100, 106, 107). I can therefore trust in truth. But, for that very reason, truth and trust should not be identified with each other.
46 Cf. D.II.3. *What non-Christians can learn.*
47 Cf. C.III.4: "The question of truth."
48 H. Sachsse, quoted by H. Aichelin, "Abschied von der Aufklärung? Zu den Anzeichen einer neuen Religiosität," in *Information* Nr. 44, pub. by the Protestant Central Office for Weltanschauung Questions, Stuttgart, 1970, p. 6. These ideas are developed in Sachsse, *Technik und Verantwortung. Probleme der Ethik im technischen Zeitalter*, Freiburg, 1972, pp. 29–48.
49 On this, cf. W. Korff, *Norm und Sittlichkeit. Untersuchungen zur Logik der normativen Vernunft*, Mainz, 1973, pp. 189–94. I owe a number of suggestions for this section especially to my colleagues in Tübingen concerned with theological ethics, Prof. Alfons Auer and Prof. Wilhelm Korff. Prof. Franz Böckle, the Bonn moral philosopher, also provided me with new, stimulating ideas about questions on the foundations of ethics.
50 Cf. H. Küng, "Die Glaubwürdigkeit," in *Frankfurter Allgemeine Zeitung*, Dec. 24, 1976. The results of this inquiry on "The foundations of our society. Have our ideas of value changed?" carried out among politicians, educationists, psychologists, historians, philosophers, artists, theologians, were very revealing and, despite all the differences, showed a clear agreement in approving values for the modern pluralist society.
51 On the problems of investigating political decisions, see H. Lübbe, "Zur Theorie

der Entscheidung" (1965), in his collected essays *Theorie und Entscheidung. Studien zum Primat der praktischen Vernunft*, Freiburg im Breisgau, 1971, pp. 7–31.

52 B. Russell, *Autobiography*, Vol. I, Allen & Unwin, London, 1967, p. 13.

53 Russell, *Why I Am Not a Christian and Other Essays on Religion and Related Subjects*, Allen & Unwin, London, 1957.

54 Ibid., p. 44.

55 Ibid., p. 49.

56 E. Bloch, *Das Prinzip Hoffnung*, 3 vols., Frankfurt, 1967; quotation, Vol. I, p. 7.

57 Ibid., p. 519.

58 A. Camus, *L'Homme révolté*, Paris, 1951. (E.t., *The Rebel*, Penguin Books, Harmondsworth/New York, 1971, esp. the last chapter, "Beyond Nihilism.")

59 Camus, "L'incroyant et les chrétiens," in *Actuelles I. Chroniques 1944–1948*, Paris, 1950. (E.t., "The Unbeliever and Christians," fragments of a talk given at the Dominican Monastery of Latour-Maubourg in 1948, in *Resistance, Rebellion and Death*, Hamish Hamilton, London, 1961, pp. 47–53; quotation, p. 50.)

60 Ibid., p. 52.

61 Ibid.

62 Camus, *The Rebel*, p. 269.

63 Ibid., p. 268.

64 Ibid.

65 Ibid., p. 269.

66 On this subject, see the general works on Christian ethics. Among recent Catholic works on ethics, the following may be mentioned: F. Tillman (ed.), *Handbuch der katholischen Sittenlehre*, 4th ed., Düsseldorf, 1953; J. Stelzenberger, *Lehrbuch der Moraltheologie. Die Sittlichkeitslehre der Königsherrschaft Gottes*, Paderborn, 2nd ed., 1965; B. Häring, *Das Gesetz Christi. Moraltheologie*, Freiburg, 1954; J. de Finance, *Ethica generalis*, Rome, 1959; J. Mausbach and G. Ermecke, *Katholische Moraltheologie*, 3 vols., Münster, 1959–61; F. Böckle, *Grundbegriffe der Moral. Gewissen und Gewissensbildung*, Aschaffenburg, 1967; W. Korff, *Theologische Ethik. Eine Einführung*, Freiburg/Basel/Vienna, 1975. For a philosophical treatment, see H. E. Hengstenberg, *Grundlegung der Ethik*, Stuttgart, 1969. Among recent Protestant works on ethics: E. Brunner, *Das Gebot und die Ordnungen. Entwurf einer protestantisch-theologischen Ethik*, Tübingen, 1932; A. de Quervain, *Ethik*, 2 vols., Zollikon/Zürich, 1945–56; D. Bonhoeffer, *Ethik*, ed. E. Bethge, Munich, 1949, 1963[6] (E.t., *Ethics*, S.C.M. Press, London, 1955; Collins Fontana Library, 1964); W. Elert, *Das christliche Ethos. Grundlinien der lutherischen Ethik*, Hamburg, 1961[2]; N. H. Soe, *Christliche Ethik*, Munich, 1949, 1965[3]; P. Ramsey, *Basic Christian Ethics*, New York, 1952; H. van Oyen, *Evangelische Ethik*, 2 vols., Basel, 1952–57; K. Barth, *Kirchliche Dogmatik* II/2 (§§36–39), III/4; H. Thielicke, *Theologische Ethik*, 3 vols., Tübingen, 1958–64; W. Trillhaas, *Ethik*, Berlin, 1959; P. L. Lehmann, *Ethics in a Christian Context*, New York, 1963; O. A. Piper, *Christian Ethics*, London, 1970.

67 Cf. Hans Küng, *On Being a Christian*, New York, 1976, London, 1977, D.II.1: Norms of the human. For what follows, important titles include: A. Auer, *Autonome Moral und christliche Glaube*, Düsseldorf, 1971; the same author, "Die Aktualität der sittlichen Botschaft Jesu," in *Die Frage nach Jesus*, ed. A. Paus, Graz, 1973, pp. 271–363; F. Böckle, "Was ist das Proprium einer christlichen Ethik?" in *Zeitschrift für Evangelische Ethik* 11 (1967), pp. 148–57; the same author, "Theonomie und Autonomie der Vernunft," in W. Oelmüller, ed., *Fortschritt wohin? Zum Problem der Normenfindung in der pluralen Gesellschaft*, Düsseldorf, 1972, pp. 63–86; the same author, "Unfehlbare Normen?" in H. Küng (ed.), *Fehlbar? Eine Bilanz*, Zürich/Einsiedeln/Cologne, 1973, pp. 280–304; the same author, "Ethik und Normenbegründung," in the symposium *Vatican III: the work which needs to be done*, published by *Concilium* and the Catholic Theological Society of America, at the University of Notre Dame, Ind., in May 1977; J. Fuchs, "Gibt es eine spezifisch christliche Moral?" in *Stimmen der Zeit* 185 (1970), pp. 99–112; J. Gründel and H. van Oyen, *Ethik ohne Normen? Zu den Weisungen des Evangeliums*, Freiburg/Basel/Vienna, 1970; W. Korff, *Norm und Sittlichkeit. Untersuchungen zur Logik der normaitven Vernunft*,

Mainz, 1973; the same author, "Wie kann der Mensch glücken? Zur Frage einer ethischen Theorie der Gesellschaft," in *Theologische Quartalschrift* 153 (1973), pp. 305–22; D. Mieth, "Die Situationsanalyse aus theologischer Sicht," in A. Hertz (ed.), *Moral*, Mainz, 1972, pp. 13–33; B. Schüller, "Zur Problematik allgemein verbindlicher ethische Grundsätze," in *Theologie und Philosophie* 45 (1970), pp. 1–23; the same author, *Die Begründung sittlicher Urteile. Typen ethischer Argumentation in der katholischen Moraltheologie*, Düsseldorf, 1973; E. McDonagh, *Gift and Call. Towards a Christian Theology of Morality*, Dublin, 1975; H. Rotter, *Grundlagen der Moral. Überlegung zu einer moral theologischen Hermeneutik*, Zürich/Einsiedeln/Cologne, 1975; J. Sauer (ed.), with contributions from A. Auer, J. Gründel, R. Hofmann, A. K. Ruf, B. Stoeckle, *Normen im Konflikt. Grundlagen einer erneuerten Ethik*, Freiburg/Basel/Vienna, 1977. The convergence of Catholic moral theologians on the question of the justification of norms becomes very clear in No. 12 of *Concilium* 12 (1976), ed. by F. Böckle and J. M. Pohier, on value insight and norm substantiation, with contributions from J. Gründel, D. Mieth, G. Sala, F. Böckle, B. Schüller, R. Simon, R. McCormick, C. Curran.

68 It is illuminating that the distinguished logician P. Lorenzen, of Erlangen, in his *Normative Logic and Ethics*, Mannheim, 1969, p. 74, in order to justify particular norms, assumes moral "supernorms" or "principles" that themselves are not in their turn rationally justified but can only be accepted in an "act of faith." Obviously this does not mean religious faith but "the acceptance of something which has not been justified." We might consider of course whether the justification could come not before the accomplishment of this act of faith but in its accomplishment—similarly to the justification explained earlier of "inner rationality." In this way, the charge of making everything depend on arbitrary decisions would be without substance.

69 On what follows, see A. Auer, *Die Aktualität der sittlichen Botschaft Jesu*, p. 281 (invoking H. Rombach and G. Meyer); W. Korff, *Theologische Ethik*, pp. 24–26.

70 Fundamental trust as interpreted here is not identical therefore with an assent to the existing sociopolitical reality or still less with a "plea for our system," as developed on the basis of a political liberalism (undoubtedly diagnosing a great deal correctly) by K. Steinbuch in *Ja zur Wirklichkeit*, Munich, 1976.

71 Cf. C.III.4: "Atheism to be taken seriously."

72 K. Jaspers, *Der philosophische Glaube*, Frankfurt, 1958, esp. the first lecture, "Der Begriff des philosophischen Glaubens."

73 Cf. R. Guardini, *Die Annahme seiner selbst*, Würzburg, 1960, pp. 16–18.

74 Cf. W. Weischedel, *Der Gott der Philosophen*, Vol. II, Darmstadt, 1972, pp. 185–206. A different method of argument against Weischedel is adopted by W. Weidlich, "Befragung der philosophischen Theologie der radikalen Fraglichkeit," in *Zeitschrift für Theologie und Kirche* 70 (1973), pp. 226–43.

75 B. Staehelin, *Urvertrauen und zweite Wirklichkeit. Das Ftan ist nie krank*, Zürich, 1973, p. 67.

76 Ibid., pp. 9–10.

77 Ibid., pp. 15, 40.

78 Ibid., p. 10.

79 Ibid., p. 53; cf. p. 20.

80 Cf. also two earlier works by Staehelin: *Haben und Sein. Ein medizinpsychologischer Vorschlag als Ergänzung zum Materialismus der heutigen Wissenschaft*, Zürich, 1969; *Die Welt als Du. Betrachtungen aus der Medizinpsychologie über Zeitgeist, Mystik, Unbehagen des Einzelnen, Unruhe der Jugend. Unzulänglichkeit der Wissenschaft und Anregungen für eine allfällige Änderung*, Zürich, 1970, together with a recent lecture, "Europas Zukunft," in *Civitas* 31 (1976), pp. 319–35. R. Schottlaender, *Theorie des Vertrauens*, Berlin, 1957, traces the causes of the present decline of trust (esp. pp. 38–64) and maintains the opinion that, as against "evil" or the "Antichrist," without "the religious way to the supernatural," all that remains of trust in the world and oneself is merely "the muted self-confidence of a single person or of a community" (p. 18).

81 E. H. Erikson, *Identity and the Life Cycle*, p. 64.
82 Ibid.
83 Ibid.
84 Ibid.
85 Ibid., pp. 64–65.
86 Ibid., p. 65.
87 On what follows, cf. O. F. Bollnow, *Neue Geborgenheit. Das Problem einer Überwindung des Existentialismus*, Stuttgart, 1955, 3rd ed., 1972, pp. 45–56.
88 Bollnow, *Wesen und Wandel der Tugenden*, Frankfurt/Berlin, 1958, p. 181.

## F. YES TO GOD—ALTERNATIVE TO ATHEISM

1 One of Tucholsky's last entries in his "scribbling book," which was never published. Quoted in E. Worbs (ed.), *In die Ewigkeit gesprochen. Letzte Gedanken. Eine tröstliche Anthologie*, Munich, 1970, p. 265. In his farewell letter to his divorced wife, Mary, Tucholsky wrote: ". . . The reason for fighting, the bridge, the inner link, the *raison d'être*, is lacking . . ."; quoted in M. Gerold-Tucholsky (ed.), *Kurt Tucholsky hasst—liebt in Prosastücken, Gedichten und Briefen*, Hamburg, 1957, p. 252.

### F.I. Multidimensional man

*1. Transcendence?*

2 C. F. von Weizsäcker, *Die Verantwortung der Wissenschaft im Atomzeitalter*, Göttingen, 1957, pp. 11–12. On the recent philosophical discussion on the question of God, see: K. Jaspers, *Der philosophische Glaube*, Munich, 1948; W. Schulz, *Der Gott der neuzeitlichen Metaphysik*, Pfullingen, 1957; J. D. Robert, *Approche contemporaine d'une affirmation de Dieu. Essai sur le fondement ultime de l'acte scientifique*, Bruges, 1962; M. E. Marty, *Varieties of Unbelief*, New York/Chicago/San Francisco, 1964; W. Strolz, *Menschsein als Gottesfrage. Wege zur Erfahrung der Inkarnation*, Pfullingen, 1965; K. Kremer, *Gott und Welt in der klassischen Metaphysik. Vom Sein der "Dinge" in Gott*, Stuttgart, 1969; E. Fontinell, *Toward a Reconstruction of Religion. A Philosophical Probe*, New York, 1970; J. N. Findlay, *Ascent to the Absolute*, London, 1970; W. Weischedel, *Der Gott der Philosophen. Grundlegung einer Philosophischen Theologie im Zeitalter des Nihilismus*, 2 vols., Darmstadt, 1971–72; G. Hasenhüttel, *Gott ohne Gott. Ein Dialog mit J. P. Sartre*, Graz/Vienna/Cologne, 1972; G. D. Kaufman, *God the Problem*, Cambridge, Mass., 1972; J. Splett, *Gotteserfahrung im Denken. Zur philosophischen Rechtfertigung des Redens von Gott*, Freiburg/Munich, 1973; C. Bruaire, *Die Aufgabe, Gott zu denken. Religionskritik—Ontologischer Gottesbeweis—Die Freiheit des Menschen*, Freiburg/Basel/Vienna, 1973; R. Schaeffler, *Religion und kritisches Bewusstsein*, Freiburg/Munich, 1973; the same author, *Die Religionskritik sucht ihren Partner. Thesen zu einer erneuerten Apologetik*, Freiburg/Basel/Vienna, 1974; M. M. Olivetti, *Filosofia della religione come problema storico. Romanticismo e idealismo romantico*, Padua, 1974; B. Welte, *Zeit und Geheimnis: Philosophische Abhandlungen zur Sache Gottes in der Zeit der Welt*, Freiburg/Basel/Vienna, 1975; D. Rössler, *Die Vernunft der Religion*, Munich, 1976.
   In addition, there are the numerous, mostly neoscholastic (or Thomistic) treatises on natural theology: among others, R. Arnou, *Theologia naturalis*, Rome, 1947; C. Nink, *Philosophische Gotteslehre*, Munich, 1948; M. Rast, *Welt und Gott. Philosophische Gotteslehre*, Freiburg, 1952; M. R. Holloway, *An Introduction to Natural Theology*, New York, 1959; M. Grison, *Théologie naturelle ou théodicée*, Paris, 1959; W. Brugger, *Theologia naturalis*, Pullach, near Munich, 1959; J. Donceel, *Natural Theology*, New York, 1962; J. F. Anderson, *Natural Theology. The Metaphysics of God*, Milwaukee, 1962; T. Gornall, *A Philosophy of God. The Elements of Thomist Natural Theology*, London, 1962.

Other works, esp. Anglo-American, will be cited in connection with the problems of linguistic analysis.

3 Cf. H. Küng, *On Being a Christian*, New York, 1976/London, 1977, Ch. A.I.3: "Between nostalgia and reformism."

4 H. Marcuse, *One-Dimensional Man. Studies in the Ideology of Advanced Industrial Society*, Boston/London, 1964.

5 E. Bloch, *Tübinger Einleitung in die Philosophie*, 2 vols., Frankfurt am Main, 1963–64; quotation, Vol. I, p. 11.

6 Ibid., Vol. I, p. 13.

7 Bloch, *Das Prinzip Hoffnung* (1959), spec. ed., in 3 vols., Frankfurt, 1967, Vol. I, p. 1.

8 Bloch, "Kann Hoffnung enttäuscht werden?" inaugural lecture at Tübingen, 1961, in *Auswahl aus seinen Schriften*, selected and introduced by H. H. Holz, Frankfurt, 1967, pp. 176–81; quotation, p. 177.

9 Bloch, *Prinzip Hoffnung*, Vol. I, p. 5.

10 Bloch, "Kann Hoffnung enttäuscht werden?" in *Auswahl aus seinen Schriften*, p. 181.

11 Bloch, *Prinzip Hoffnung*, Vol. I, p. 16.

12 Bloch, *Atheismus im Christentum. Zur Religion des Exodus und des Reichs* (1968), paperback, Frankfurt, 1973, p. 13.

13 Cf. esp. *Prinzip Hoffnung*, Ch. 53, and *Atheismus im Christentum*, Parts III, IV and V.

14 Bloch, *Atheismus im Christentum*, p. 13.

15 Ibid.

16 Bloch, *Prinzip Hoffnung*, Vol. III, p. 1523.

17 Cf. esp. the last chapter of *Atheismus im Christentum*. I found important confirmation on this point in a discussion with Ernst Bloch, in which Jürgen Moltmann and our assistants also took part, on Bloch's ninetieth birthday, in Tübingen.

18 Cf. B.III. *Secular and historical God*.

19 On the extensive theological discussion with Bloch, cf. esp. Jürgen Moltmann, " 'Das Prinzip Hoffnung' und die 'Theologie der Hoffnung.' Ein Gespräch mit Ernst Bloch," in *Theologie der Hoffnung*, Munich, 1964, 3rd ed., 1965, pp. 313–34 (this discussion is not included in the English translation of Moltmann's book *Theology of Hope*, London, 1967). Cf. also the Festschrift for Bloch's eightieth birthday, ed. S. Unseld, *Ernst Bloch zu ehren. Beiträge zu seinem Werk*, Frankfurt, 1965.

20 Cf. C.I. *God—a projection of man? Ludwig Feuerbach*; C.II. *God—a consolation serving vested interests? Karl Marx*.

## 2. The other dimension

21 M. Horkheimer, *Dialektik der Aufklärung. Philosophische Fragmente*, Frankfurt, 1969; T. W. Adorno, *Negative Dialektik*, Frankfurt, 1966.

22 Cf. H. Küng, *On Being a Christian*, A.I.3: "Humanity through politico-social revolution?"

23 Cf. Horkheimer, *Die Sehnsucht nach dem ganz Anderen* (an interview with a commentary by H. Gumnior), Hamburg, 1970.

24 Horkheimer, "Theismus—Atheismus," in *Zur Kritik der instrumentellen Vernunft. Aus den Vorträgen und Aufzeichnungen seit Kriegsende*, ed. A. Schmidt, Frankfurt, 1974, pp. 216–28; quotation, p. 227.

25 Horkheimer, *Die Sehnsucht nach dem ganz Anderen*, p. 60.

26 Ibid.

27 Ibid., pp. 60–61.

28 Ibid., p. 69.

29 Ibid., p. 67.

30 Ibid., p. 75.

31 Ibid., pp. 61–62.

32 Horkheimer, "Bemerkungen zur Liberalisierung der Religion," in W Brede (ed ), *Sozialphilosophische Studien. Aufsätze, Reden und Vorträge 1930–72* (with an

appendix on university and study), Frankfurt, 1972, pp. 131–36; quotation, p. 135.

33 Ibid.
34 Ibid.
35 Ibid., p. 136.
36 F. Brentano, *Von der mannigfachen Bedeutung des Seienden nach Aristoteles*, Freiburg im Breisgau, 1862.
37 M. Heidegger, *Frühe Schriften*, Frankfurt, 1972, p. x.
38 Heidegger, *Was ist Metaphysik?* Inaugural lecture, Freiburg, 1929. Postscript to the 4th ed., 1941. Introduction to the 5th ed., 1949, Frankfurt, 1975[11], p. 38. (E.t., "What is Metaphysics?" in Martin Heidegger, *Existence and Being*, Vision Press, Saxone House, 74a Regent Street, London, W.1, 1968[3], pp. 353–92; quotation, p. 374.)
39 Cf. O. Pöggeler, *Philosophie und Politik bei Heidegger*, Freiburg/Munich, 1972.
40 Cf. E.I.2: "Freedom within limits."
41 J. P. Sartre, *L'existentialisme est un humanisme*, Paris, 1946. (E.t., *Existentialism and Humanism*, Methuen, London, 1948, reprint 1970.)
42 Heidegger, *Über den Humanismus* (expanded text of a letter written to Jean Beaufret in Paris, autumn 1946), Frankfurt, 1949. (E.t., "Letter on Humanism," in *Martin Heidegger. Basic Writings*, Harper & Row, New York/Routledge & Kegan Paul, London, 1977.)
43 From the indications in *Vom Wesen der Wahrheit* (actually written 1930–31), Frankfurt, 1943, and *Über den Humanismus*, Frankfurt, 1946, to *Identität und Differenz*, Pfullingen, 1957, the book on Nietzsche (lectures and essays 1936–46), 2 vols., Pfullingen, 1961, and the lecture given in Freiburg Jan. 31, 1962, with the title significantly reversed: "Zeit und Sein," in *Zur Sache des Denkens*, Tübingen, 1969, pp. 1–25.
44 Heidegger, *Über den Humanismus*, p. 29. (E.t., *Basic Writings*, p. 222.)
45 Ibid. (E.t., p. 221.)
46 Ibid., p. 19. (E.t., p. 210.)
47 Ibid., p. 22. (E.t., p. 213.)
48 Heidegger, *Identität und Differenz*, p. 51; cf. *Was ist Metaphysik?* p. 19. (E.t., p. 356.)
49 Cf. Heidegger, *Nietzsche*, 2 vols., Pfullingen, 1961.
50 Heidegger, *Holzwege*, Frankfurt, 1950, p. 233.
51 Heidegger, *Identität und Differenz*, p. 59.
52 W. Jens, "Nachruf der Akademie der Künste Berlin," in G. Neske (ed.), *Erinnerungen an Martin Heidegger*, Pfullingen, 1977, pp. 149–53; quotation, p. 149.
53 Heidegger, *Über den Humanismus*, p. 19. (E.t., *Basic Writings*, p. 210.)
54 Heidegger, *Identität und Differenz*, p. 70.
55 Ibid., p. 51.
56 Heidegger, *Über den Humanismus*, p. 26. (E.t., *Basic Writings*, p. 218.)
57 Heidegger, "Zeit und Sein," in *Zur Sache des Denkens*, Tübingen, 1969, pp. 1–25; quotation, p. 21.
58 W. Weischedel, *Der Gott der Philosophen. Grundlegung einer Philosophischen Theologie im Zeitalter des Nihilismus*, 2 vols., Darmstadt, 1971–72, Vol. I, p. 494.
59 Ibid.
60 Cf. C. Grossner, *Verfall der Philosophie. Politik deutscher Philosophen*, Hamburg, 1971.
61 Quoted by H. G. Gadamer, "Anrufung des entschwundenen Gottes. Das Denken Martin Heideggers zwischen Metaphysik und technischer Welt," in *Evangelische Kommentare* 10 (1977), p. 204.
62 Cf. O. Pöggeler, *Der Denkweg Martin Heideggers*, Pfullingen, 1963, pp. 36–45; likewise K. Lehmann, "Christliche Geschichtserfahrung und ontologische Frage beim jungen Heidegger," in O. Pöggeler (ed.), *Heidegger. Perspektiven zur Deutung seines Werks*, Cologne/Berlin, 1969, pp. 140–68, esp. pp. 141–45.
63 Cf., for instance, Heidegger, *Was heisst Denken?* (lectures, 1951–52), Tübingen, 1954, 2nd ed., 1961, p. 44; the same author, "Sprache im Gedicht," in *Unterwegs zur Sprache*, Pfullingen, 1959, 3rd ed., 1965, pp. 75–76.

64 Heidegger, *Was ist Metaphysik?* p. 42. (E.t., "What is Metaphysics?" in *Existence and Being*, Vision Press, London, 1968, p. 380.)
65 Ibid., p. 47. (E.t., p. 386.)
66 Ibid., p. 49. (E.t., p. 389.)
67 G. W. Leibniz, *Principes de la nature et de la grace*, Paris, 1714, n. 7. (E.t., "Principles of Nature and of Grace," in *Leibniz: Philosophical Writings*, Dent, London, 1973, pp. 195–204; quotation, p. 199.)
68 Heidegger, *Was ist Metaphysik?* p. 40. (E.t., *Existence and Being*, p. 377.)
69 Heidegger, "Interview," in *Partisan Review*, April 1948, p. 511. Quoted by H. Kuhn, *Begegnung mit dem Nichts*, Tübingen, 1950, p. 151.
70 Heidegger, "Aus einem Gespräch von der Sprache. Zwischen einem Japaner und einem Fragenden," in *Unterwegs zur Sprache*, pp. 83–155; quotation, p. 96.
71 Heidegger, *Über den Humanismus*, p. 26. (E.t., *Basic Writings*, p. 218.)
72 Ibid., p. 47. (E.t., p. 242.)
73 Cf. H. Küng, *Unfehlbar? Eine Anfrage*, Zürich/Einsiedeln/Cologne, 1970 (E.t., *Infallible? An Inquiry*, New York/London, 1971); the same author, as editor, *Fehlbar? Eine Bilanz*, Zürich/Einsiedeln/Cologne, 1973.
74 Cf. the editorial introduction to B. Welte, "Denken und Sein. Gedanken zu Martin Heideggers Werk und Wirken," in *Herder Korrespondenz* 30 (1976), pp. 373–77.
75 Heidegger, *Nietzsche*, Vol. II, p. 396.
76 These questions are briefly analyzed by L. Weber, "Gott—verborgener als das Sein," in *Alte Fragen und neue Wege des Denkens. Festschrift für Josef Stallmach*, Bonn, 1977, pp. 39–46. H. Danner has produced a comprehensive study (but in the light of dialectical theology) in *Das Göttliche und der Gott bei Heidegger*, Meisenheim, 1971.
77 Heidegger, *Holzwege*, p. 240.
78 Cf. Aquinas, *Summa Theologiae* I q.4 a.2: *ipsum esse per se subsistens*; I q.3 a.4: *ens per essentiam*; I q.3 a.2: *purus actus*; I q.3 a.3: *sua essentia vel natura*.
79 L. Weber, *Gott—verborgener als das Sein*, pp. 45–46. On Heidegger's importance for theology, cf. esp. the collection made by J. M. Robinson and J. B. Cobb, *Der spätere Heidegger und die Theologie*, Zürich/Stuttgart, 1964; G. Noller (ed.), *Heidegger und die Theologie. Beginn und Fortgang der Diskussion*, Munich, 1967.
80 Cf. Heidegger, *Nietzsche*, Vol. I, p. 324.
81 Cf. A.III.1. *The epistemological discussion.*
82 A. J. Ayer, *Language, Truth and Logic*, Gollancz, London, 1936. In the introduction to the 2nd ed., in 1946, Ayer speaks with more reserve but does not substantially change his position. Cf., more recently, *The Central Questions of Philosophy*, London, 1973, esp. Ch. X: "The Claims of Theology."
83 A. Flew, "Theology and Falsification," in A. Flew and A. McIntyre (eds.), *New Essays in Philosophical Theology*, S.C.M. Press, London, 1955, pp. 96–103. Flew also published on the same theme a "Silver Jubilee Review" in a volume of collected essays, *The Presumption of Atheism and Other Philosophical Essays on God, Freedom and Immortality*, London, 1976, pp. 71–80.
84 Cf. A.III.1: "Logic and theory of knowledge against metaphysics? Rudolf Carnap." In the Preface to the 1st ed., 1935, Ayer admits that he depends less on G. E. Moore—who in England based analytical philosophy on ordinary language—than on the philosophers of the Vienna Circle, "with whom I am in the closest agreement," especially Rudolf Carnap.
85 Cf. A.III.1: "The universal claim of scientific thought? Karl Popper."
86 Some of the essays important in this connection are to be found in collections: S. M. Cahn (ed.), *Philosophy of Religion*, New York/Evanston/London, 1970, esp. Ch. II; B. Mitchell (ed.), *The Philosophy of Religion*, Oxford, 1971, with contributions from A. Flew, R. M. Hare, B. Mitchell, I. M. Crombie, J Hick, R. B. Braithwaite, J. L. Mackie, A. Platinga, D. Z. Phillips, H. H. Price, R W. Hepburn, T. Penelhum
87 R. B. Braithwaite, *An Empiricist's View of Religious Belief*, Cambridge, 1955

88 R. M. Hare, "Theology and Falsification," in A. Flew and A. McIntyre (eds.), *New Essays in Philosophical Theology*, S.C.M. Press, London, 1955, pp. 99–103.

89 "Blik" is a word invented by Hare to describe certain quasi-metaphysical fundamental attitudes.

90 Paul van Buren, *The Secular Meaning of the Gospel. Based on an Analysis of its Language*, New York: Macmillan and Penguin Books, Harmondsworth, England, 1963.

91 Anglo-American literature on the contemporary discussion of philosophy of religion includes the Philosophy of Religion Series, ed. John Hick. New York: Seabury Press, Inc., esp. J. Hick, *Arguments for the Existence of God*, 1971; H. P. Owen, *Concepts of Deity*, 1971; K. Nielsen, *Contemporary Critiques of Religion*, 1971; W. A. Christian, *Oppositions of Religious Doctrines. A Study in the Logic of Dialogue among Religions*, 1972; M. J. Charlesworth, *Philosophy of Religion. The Historic Approaches*, New York; T. Penelhum, *Problems of Religious Knowledge*, 1972; B. Mitchell, *The Justification of Religious Belief*, 1973; N. Smart, *The Phenomenon of Religion*, 1973; H. D. Lewis, *The Self and Immortality*, 1973. Cf. also, from the Catholic viewpoint, L. Dupré, *The Other Dimension. A Search for the Meaning of Religious Attitudes*, Doubleday & Company, Inc.: Garden City, N.Y., 1972. From the Protestant viewpoint, J. E. Smith, *Reason and God. Encounters of Philosophy with Religion*, Yale University Press: New Haven/London, 1961; the same author, *Experience and God*, Oxford University Press: New York, 1968; the same author, *The Analogy of Experience. An Approach to Understanding Religious Truth*, New York, 1973.

92 Cf. A.III.1: "The empirical and the 'mystical': Ludwig Wittgenstein."

93 L. Wittgenstein, *Philosophical Investigations*, transl. G. E. M. Anscombe, Bilingual Edition, Basil Blackwell, Oxford, 1968.

94 Ibid., p. 47e, n. 109.

95 A brief description of the basic features and paradoxes of Wittgenstein's later philosophy, with reference to the theological problems, is given by H. Peukert, *Wissenschaftstheorie*, Düsseldorf, 1976, pp. 145–53; in addition, there are reflections on the theory of linguistics (esp. on N. Chomsky and J. L. Austin), on the foundations of the social sciences (the controversy over positivism between Popper and Albert on the one hand and Adorno and Habermas on the other), and on epistemology, pp. 153–205.

96 A useful survey of the whole development in the Anglo-American sphere is provided by M. J. Charlesworth, *Philosophy of Religion*. Cf. also the same author's collection of texts in *The Problem of Religious Language*, Englewood Cliffs, N.J., 1974. Also F. Copleston, *Contemporary Philosophy. Studies of Logical Positivism and Existentialism*, London/New York, 1956, 6th ed., 1972.

97 Cf. F.III.2: "Indirectly verified by experience."

98 M. J. Charlesworth, *Philosophy of Religion. The Historic Approaches*, New York/Macmillan, London, 1972, p. 174. Cf. also the critical presentation by F. Ferré, *Language, Logic and God*, London, 1962.

99 P. Engelmann, *Ludwig Wittgenstein. Briefe und Begegnungen*, Munich, 1970, p. 121.

100 David Pears, *Wittgenstein*, Fontana Modern Classics, Collins, London, 1971, pp. 88–89.

101 Ibid., p. 89.

102 With reference to religion and ethics, see the noteworthy essay by G. Brand, *Die grundlegenden Texte von Ludwig Wittgenstein*, Frankfurt am Main, 1975, pp. 185–95.

103 Wittgenstein, *Notebooks 1914–1916*, eds. G. H. von Wright and G. E. M. Anscombe, transl. G. E. M. Anscombe (bilingual ed.), Basil Blackwell, Oxford, 1961, pp. 72e–73e.

104 Ibid., p. 74e.

105 David Pears, *Wittgenstein*, pp. 174–75.

106 Norman Malcolm, *Ludwig Wittgenstein. A Memoir*, Oxford University Press, London/New York/Toronto, 1958, p. 100; cf. G. Pitcher, *The Philosophy of Wittgenstein*, Englewood Cliffs, N.J., 1964, p. 138. A recent study by J. Track,

*Sprachkritische Untersuchungen zum christlichen Reden von Gott*, Göttingen, 1977, deals with the problem of God in analytical philosophy.

107 C. Grossner, *Verfall der Philosophie. Politik deutscher Philosophen*, Hamburg, 1971.
108 W. Hochkeppel, *Mythos Philosophie*, Hamburg, 1976.
109 Ibid., pp. 150–51.
110 M. Buber, "Gottesfinsternis. Betrachtungen zur Beziehung zwischen Religion und Philosophie," in Werke, Vol. I, *Schriften zur Philosophie*, Munich/Heidelberg, 1962, pp. 503–603; quotation, pp. 508–10.

## F.II. Theological discussions

### 1. Catholic or Protestant approach?

1 Bertrand Russell, *Why I Am Not a Christian and Other Essays on Related Subjects*, Allen & Unwin, London, 1957, p. 3.
2 Ibid.
3 First Vatican Council, Dogmatic Constitution on Catholic Faith, 1870, DS 3026.
4 On the history of the First Vatican Council, in addition to the collections of documents of Mansi and the *Collectio Lacensis*, see T. Granderath, *Geschichte des Vatikanischen Konzils*, 3 vols, Freiburg im Breisgau, 1903–6; Cuthbert Butler, *The Vatican Council 1869–1870*, first published 1930, new ed., rev. by Christopher Butler, Collins/Harvill Press, London, 1962; R. Aubert, *Le pontificat de Pie IX*, Paris, 1952 (Vol. 21 of Fliche-Martin, *Histoire de l'Église*). On the infallibility debate, cf. A. B. Hasler, "Pius IX (1846–1878)," *Päpstliche Unfehlbarkeit und 1 Vatikanisches Konzil. Dogmatisierung und Durchsetzung einer Ideologie*, Stuttgart, 1977.
5 So he said in his first mention of the plan to the cardinals, Dec. 6, 1864. *Collectio Lacensis*, Vol. VII, Freiburg, 1890, p. 1013.
6 Proclamation of the Council, June 26, 1967, in *Collectio Lacensis*, Vol. VII, p. 1032.
7 Pius IX, *Syllabus seu Collectio errorum in diversis Actis Pii IX proscriptorum*, Dec. 8, 1864. (DS 2901–80.)
8 Ibid. (DS 2980.)
9 Cf. A.I.3: "Clarity as ideal of theology."
10 Gregory XVI, Brief *Dum acerbissimas*, Sept. 26, 1835 (DS 2738–40); see also the Index Decree of 1836. For the process against Hermes and his supporters, H. H. Schwedt, *Das römische Urteil über Georg Hermes (1775–1831)*, a dissertation that appeared in Rome, 1976, is very informative; cf. also A. Franzen, *Die Katholisch-Theologische Fakultät Bonn im Streit um das Erste Vatikanische Konzil. Zugleich ein Beitrag zur Entstehungsgeschichte des Altkatholizismus am Niederrhein*, Cologne/Vienna, 1974.
11 Pius IX, Brief *Eximian tuam*, to the Archbishop of Cologne, June 15, 1857 (DS 2828–31).
12 First Vatican Council, Dogmatic Constitution on Catholic Faith, 1870, DS 3025, 3035–36.
13 Gregory XVI, encyclical *Singulari nos*, June 25, 1834 (not in DS, see older editions of Denzinger, 1617).
14 Gregory XVI, theses accepted by Louis Bautain, Sept. 8, 1840 (DS 2751–56).
15 Cf. Pius IX, Decree of the Congregation of the Index, June 11, 1855 (DS 2811–14).
16 Cf. First Vatican Council, Dogmatic Constitution on Catholic Faith, 1870, DS 3004, 3026.
17 Ibid. (DS 3015.)
18 Ibid. (DS 3017–18.)
19 Ibid. (DS 3019.)
20 Expressed in theological and traditional terms, not human nature in a particular concrete real of hypothetical state or status (*natura elevata, lapsa, reparata,*

*glorificata*) but human nature in general existing in every state (*natura humana abstracte* or *absolute spectata*).

21 Createdness in the meaning of *res creatae* is not logically presupposed to the knowledge of God, as W. Weischedel (*Der Gott der Philosophen*, Vol. II, pp. 44–45) thinks, which would be a vicious circle ("creature" is understood here in the very general sense).

22 What is asserted is not the *factum* or *exercitium* of the natural knowledge of God, but the *potentia* (*activa*).

23 It is a question here not of being able to demonstrate the existence of God but only of being able to know God.

24 Cf. B. Greco, *Evangelium und Kirche. Das Kirchenbild Ernesto Buonaiutis* (a dissertation that appeared in Tübingen, 1978).

25 Pius X, Motu proprio, *Sacrorum antistitum*, Sept. 1, 1910 (DS 3538).

26 K. Barth, *Der Römerbrief*, Berne, 1919/Munich (2nd ed.), 1922. (E.t., *The Epistle to the Romans*, Oxford University Press, 1935.)

27 Cf. A.II.3. *Faith as the basis of reason*.

28 W. Niesel (ed.), *Bekenntnisschriften und Kirchenordnungen der nach Gottes Wort reformierten Kirche*, Zollikon/Zürich, 1938, p. 335.

29 Barth, *Die Kirchliche Dogmatik*, Vols. I/1–IV/4, Zürich, 1932–67; quotation, I/1, p. viii. (E.t., *Church Dogmatics*, Vols. I/1–IV/4, T. & T. Clark, Edinburgh, 1936–69; quotation, I/1, p. x.)

30 E. Brunner, *Natur und Gnade. Zum Gespräch mit Karl Barth*, Zürich, 1934, 2nd ed., 1935. (E.t., *Natural Theology*, comprising "Nature and Grace," by Emil Brunner, and the reply "No," by Karl Barth, Geoffrey Bles, London, 1946.)

31 The dramatic struggle about the question of God in the Protestant theology of the present century is nowhere better described than in Heinz Zahrnt, *Die Sache mit Gott. Die protestantische Theologie im 20. Jahrhundert*, Munich, 1966. (E.t., *The Question of God*, Collins, London/Harcourt, Brace & World, New York, 1969.) Texts also in H. Zahrnt (ed.), *Gespräch über Gott. Die protestantische Theologie im 20. Jahrhundert. Ein Textbuch*, Munich, 1968. With reference directly to present problems, the same author, *Gott kann nicht sterben. Wider die falschen Alternativen in Theologie und Gesellschaft*, Munich, 1970; the same author, *Wozu ist das Christentum gut?* Munich, 1972. Zahrnt's survey in retrospect of his life as a theologian has now appeared: *Warum ich glaube. Meine Sache mit Gott*, Munich/Zürich, 1977.

32 Barth, *Kirchliche Dogmatik*, II/1, p. 86. (E.t., *Church Dogmatics* II/1, p. 79.)

33 Ibid. (E.t., ibid.)

34 Ibid., II/1, p. 87. (E.t., II/1, p. 80.)

35 Ibid., II/1, p. 88. (E.t., II/1, p. 80.)

36 Ibid. (E.t., II/1, p. 81.)

37 Ibid., II/1, p. 91. (E.t., II/1, p. 83.)

38 Barth, *Kirchliche Dogmatik*, I/2, p. 343; cf. pp. 328–35. (E.t., I/2, p. 352; cf. pp. 337–44.)

39 Ibid., I/2, p. 343; cf. pp. 335–43. (E.t., p. 352; cf. pp. 344–52.)

40 R. Bultmann, *Glauben und Verstehen. Gesammelte Aufsätze*, Vol. I, Tübingen, 1954[2], pp. 1–25, 26–37, 294–312. (E.t. *Faith and Understanding*, S.C.M. Press, London, 1969, pp. 28–52, 53–65, 313–31.)

41 On the lines of Barth, see H. Gollwitzer in discussion with W. Weischedel, *Denken und Glauben. Ein Streitgespräch*, Stuttgart, 1965; J. Moltmann, *Der gekreuzigte Gott. Das Kreuz Christi als Grund und Kritik christlicher Theologie*, Munich, 1972; esp. Ch. I, 3; VI, 2. (E.t., *The Crucified God. The Cross of Christ as the Foundation and Criticism of Christian Theology*, S.C.M. Press, 1974, Ch. I, 3; 6,2.) On the lines of Bultmann, see esp. G. Ebeling, *Das Wesen des christlichen Glaubens*, Tübingen, 1959; the same author, *Wort und Glaube*, Tübingen, 1960. I am grateful for the seminar on natural theology in Barth's *Church Dogmatics*, which I shared with Eberhard Jüngel, professor of systematic theology in the faculty of Protestant theology at the University of Tübingen, and which gave me the opportunity to reexamine my views on the subject. Cf. E. Jüngel, "Das Dilemma der natürlichen Theologie und die Wahrheit ihres Prob-

lems. Überlegungen für ein Gespräch mit Wolfhart Pannenberg," in the *Festschrift* for W. Weischedel, ed. A. Schwan, *Denken im Schatten des Nihilismus*, Darmstadt, 1975, pp. 419–40. As a result of the seminar, Jüngel has published "Gelegentliche Thesen zum Problem der natürlichen Theologie," in *Evangelische Theologie* 37 (1977), pp. 485–88. Jüngel sees the problem that faces us here and, from his markedly Barthian standpoint, can formulate it as a thesis: "Since God is secretly present in every event of true love, since therefore in every event of human love the *Absolutely Reliable* is present, there is in this world a well-founded *fundamental trust* which would not be possible without the experience of love. In this sense the *identity* of God and love is the basis of *trust* as a whole, while the *revelation* of the identity of God and love is the basis of *faith* as true trust in God" (p. 488).

2. *Controversy on natural theology*

42 This holds also for the work of Michael Schmaus, *Katholische Dogmatik*, 5 vols., Munich, 1937ff., which is typical of German Catholic dogmatics in the preconciliar period.

43 H. de Lubac, *Le Surnaturel. Études historiques*, Paris, 1946.

44 Pius XII, encyclical *Humani Generis*, Aug. 12, 1950 (DS 3890–91). Cf. Vitus de Broglie, *De fine ultimo humanae vitae. Tractatus theologicus, pars prior positiva*, Paris, 1948.

45 Cf. B.III.2: "The God of evolution: Pierre Teilhard de Chardin."

46 Yves Congar's great work *Vraie et fausse réforme dans l'Eglise*, Paris, 1950, suppressed soon after its publication, may be regarded as typical.

47 Hans Urs von Balthasar, *Karl Barth. Darstellung und Deutung seiner Theologie*, Cologne, 1951. (E.t., *The Theology of Karl Barth*, Holt, Rinehart & Winston, New York, 1972.)

48 Cf. H. Küng, *Rechtfertigung. Die Lehre Karl Barths und eine katholische Besinnung*, Einsiedeln, 1957, 4th, exp. ed., 1964. (E.t., *Justification*, Thomas Nelson, New York/Burns & Oates, London, 1964.)

49 J. Ratzinger in a review of Küng's book in *Theologische Revue* 54 (1958), pp. 30–35; quotation, p. 34. A survey of the discussion on the book is offered by C. Hempel, *Rechtfertigung als Wirklichkeit. Ein katholisches Gespräch: Karl Barth—Hans Küng—Rudolf Bultmann und seine Schule*, Frankfurt am Main/Berne, 1976.

50 Ibid.

51 Lubac, *Le mystère du surnaturel*, Paris, 1965. (E.t., *The Mystery of the Supernatural*, Geoffrey Chapman, London/Dublin/Melbourne, 1967.)

52 R. Bultmann, "Das Problem der 'natürlichen Theologie,'" in *Glauben und Verstehen*, Vol. I, pp. 294–312; quotation, p. 295. (E.t., *Faith and Understanding*, p. 314.)

53 Rm 1:20. On the exegesis of Rm 1:18–32, cf. O. Kuss, *Der Römerbrief*, first fascicle, Regensburg, 1957, 2nd ed., 1963, pp. 26–56; E. Käsemann, *An die Römer*, Tübingen, 1973, pp. 32–47.

54 Rm 3:9–20.

55 Rm 3:21–31.

56 Rm 2:10–11.

57 Rm 2:13.

58 Rm 2:15.

59 Rm 2:14. On the exegesis of Rm 2:12–16, cf. O. Kuss, *Der Römerbrief*, pp. 67–82; E. Käsemann, *An die Römer*, pp. 56–63.

60 Ac 14:8–18.

61 Ac 17:16–34.

62 Cf. Ac 14:15; 17:30–31.

63 Ac 14:16.

64 Ac 17:30.

65 Ac 14:17.

66 Ac 17:22.

67  Ac 17:23.
68  Ac 17:24.
69  Ac 17:25.
70  Ac 17:29.
71  Ac 17:30-31.
72  Ac 17:26.
73  Ac 17:27-28.
74  Heb 11:4.
75  Heb 11:5.
76  Heb 11:31.
77  Jn 1:4-5.
78  Jn 1:9.
79  Jn 1:10.
80  K. Barth, *Kirchliche Dogmatik*, IV/3, p. 95. (E.t., *Church Dogmatics*, IV/3, p. 86.)
81  Ibid., IV/3, p. 122. (E.t., p. 111.)
82  Cf. ibid., I/1, pp. 89-128; I/2, pp. 505-98, 831-48; IV/3, pp. 122-28. (E.t., I/1, pp. 98-134; I/2, pp. 457-537, 743-58; IV/3, pp. 113-17.)
83  Ibid., IV/3, p. 157. (E.t., IV/3, p. 139.)
84  Ibid., IV/3, p. 158. (E.t., IV/3, p. 140.)
85  On the other hand, we may note with respect Jürgen Moltmann's public correction of his theological devaluation of the world religions—even as late as *Der gekreuzigte Gott*, in 1972 (E.t., *The Crucified God*, 1974)—in his *Kirche in der Kraft des Geistes. Ein Beitrag zur messianischen Ekklesiologie*, Munich, 1975 (E.t., *The Church in the Power of the Spirit*, S.C.M. Press, London, 1977). Here he asks for the *"indigenization* [of Christianity] in another culture and religion" and also "the charismatic activation of cultural and religious forces in the interests of the messianic future" (p. 185 [E.t., p. 163]). The other religions will not be "extinguished" but "charismatically absorbed and changed." "They will not be ecclesiasticized . . . nor will they be Christianized either; but they will be given a messianic direction towards the kingdom" (ibid.). Of course, it cannot be subsequently asserted that criticism of religion by dialectical theology was "only directed against the Christianity which had become 'religious,' . . . not against the world religions" (p. 176 [E.t., p. 154]). On this, cf. Barth, *Kirchliche Dogmatik*, I/2, pp. 372-79 (E.t., I/2, pp. 340-44), in a critique of Bhakti Hinduism and of Japanese Amida Buddhism. By contrast to this, Moltmann now demands (as suggested in my book *On Being a Christian*) not only "a truly Indian, Chinese, Japanese, Indonesian, Arabic and African Christianity" but over and above this "a Buddhist, Hindu, Moslem, animist, Confucian, Shintoist Christianity" (pp. 184-85 [E.t., p. 162]). But are the world religions here adequately distinguished as cultural and as religious phenomena and are they taken sufficiently seriously as religions? For obviously the meaning cannot be that both Buddha and Christ are to be followed in a "Buddhist Christianity."

## F.III. Proving God?

### 1. Arguments for and against

1  There is an immense literature on individual proofs of God as advocated by various authors. Among more recent surveys of the proofs of God and of criticism of these are Q. Huonder, *Die Gottesbeweise. Geschichte und Schicksal*, Stuttgart, 1968, and W. Weischedel, *Der Gott der Philosophen. Grundlegung einer philosophischen Theologie im Zeitalter des Nihilismus*, Vol. I: "Wesen, Aufstieg und Verfall der philosophischen Theologie," Darmstadt, 1971. J. Hick provides a collection of texts with a commentary, from Anselm to analytical philosophy, in *The Existence of God*, London/New York, 1964. Among more recent monographs defending the proofs of God are J. Schmucker, *Die primären Quellen des Gottesglaubens*, Freiburg im Breisgau/Basel/Vienna, 1967; the same author, *Das Problem der Kontingenz der Welt. Versuch einer positiven Aufarbeitung der Kri-*

tik *Kants am kosmologischen Argument*, Freiburg/Basel/Vienna, 1969; W. Cramer, *Gottesbeweise und ihre Kritik. Prüfung ihrer Beweiskraft*, Frankfurt, 1967; H. Ogiermann, *Sein zu Gott. Die philosophische Gottesfrage*, Munich/Salzburg, 1974; J. Fellermeier, *Die Philosophie auf dem Weg zu Gott*, Paderborn/Vienna, 1975.

2 Aquinas, *Summa Theologiae* I q.2 a.3.
3 H. Ogiermann, *Sein zu Gott*, p. 26.
4 J. Schmucker, *Die primären Quellen des Gottesglaubens*, p. 8.
5 Cf. D.II.4: "Reality in doubt."
6 Cf. A.I.4: "Conclusive proof of God?"
7 K. Jaspers, *Der philosophische Glaube*, Munich, 1948, paperback ed., Frankfurt am Main, 1958, p. 33.

## 2. More than pure reason: Immanuel Kant

1 References to Kant's works will be made to the edition in six volumes by W. Weischedel, Frankfurt am Main/Darmstadt, 1956–64, abbreviated as *Werke*. For the *Kritik der reinen Vernunft* (= *Werke* II), we shall also indicate the pages as in the 2nd ed., of 1787, revised by Kant himself, as B followed by the page number. The quotation here is from *Kritik der reinen Vernunft* (first pub., 1781), Preface to the 2nd ed. (1787), B xvi = *Werke* II, p. 25. (Wherever possible, English translations of Kant will be quoted and details of title, place and date of publication and page reference given in the notes. Norman Kemp Smith's translation, *Immanuel Kant's Critique of Pure Reason*, Macmillan, London/St. Martin's Press, New York, 1929, rev. 1933, reprint 1964, will be indicated here by KS followed by page number. This quotation is in KS, p. 22.)
2 I. Kant, *Allgemeine Naturgeschichte und Theorie des Himmels, oder Versuch von der Verfassung und dem mechanischen Ursprunge des ganzen Weltgebäudes nach Newtonischen Grundsätzen abgehandelt* (1755), in *Werke* I, pp. 219–400.
3 Kant, *Der einzig mögliche Beweisgrund zu einer Demonstration des Daseins Gottes* (1763), in *Werke* I, pp. 617–738.
4 Kant, *Der einzig mögliche Beweisgrund*, in *Werke* I, p. 738.
5 Kant, *Träume eines Geistersehers, erläutert durch Träume der Metaphysik* (1766), in *Werke* I, pp. 919–89.
6 Kant, *Die Religion innerhalb der Grenzen der blossen Vernunft* (1793), in *Werke* IV, pp. 645–879. (E.t., *Religion within the Limits of Reason Alone*, Harper & Row, New York/Evanston, 1960.)
7 Cf. J. Bohatec, *Die Religionsphilosophie Kants in der "Religion innerhalb der Grenzen der reinen Vernunft,"* Hamburg, 1938; H. G. Redmann, *Gott und Welt. Die Schöpfungstheologie der vorkritischen Periode Kants*, Göttingen, 1962
8 Kant, *Kritik der reinen Vernunft*, B xxx = *Werke* II, p. 33. (KS, p. 29.)
9 Ibid., B 858 = *Werke* II, p. 694. (KS, p. 650.)
10 Ibid., B 349–732 = *Werke* II, pp. 308–605. (KS, pp. 297–570.)
11 Ibid., B 670 = *Werke* II, pp. 563–64. (KS, p. 532.)
12 Ibid., B 670 = *Werke* II, p. 564. (KS, p. 532.)
13 Ibid., B 668–69 = *Werke* II, pp. 562–63. (KS, p. 531.)
14 Ibid., B 669 = *Werke* II, p. 563. (KS, p. 531.)
15 Kant, *Kritik der praktischen Vernunft* (1788) = *Werke* IV, pp. 103–302; quotation, A 226 = *Werke* IV, p. 256. (E.t., *Kant's Critique of Practical Reason and Other Works on the Theory of Ethics*. Transl. Thomas Kingsmill Abbott, 6th ed., Longmans, Green, London/New York/Toronto, 1909, reprinted 1954, indicated here by Abbott followed by page number; the quotation is from Abbott p. 222.) Cf. on the *Critique of Practical Reason* L. W. Beck, *Kants "Kritik der praktischen Vernunft." Ein Kommentar*, Munich, 1974.
16 Kant, *Die Religion innerhalb der Grenzen der blossen Vernunft*, in *Werke* IV, p. 879. (E.t., *Religion within the Limits of Reason Alone*, Harper & Row, New York/Evanston, 1960, p. 190.)
17 For a more detailed treatment of Kant's critique of religion, see H. Küng, *Menschwerdung Gottes. Eine Einführung in Hegels theologisches Denken als*

*Prolegomena zu einer künftigen Christologie*, Freiburg/Basel/Vienna, 1970, pp. 102–19.

18 Kant, *Kritik der praktischen Vernunft*, A 288 = Werke IV, p. 300. (Abbott, p. 260.)

19 Kant, *Streit der Fakultäten* (1978), in Werke VI, pp. 261–393.

20 Kant, *Kritik der praktischen Vernunft*, A 265 = Werke IV, p. 282. (Abbott, p. 245.)

21 Kant, *Reflexionen zur Metaphysik*, Nr. 4996 in *Kants handschriftlicher Nachlass*, Vol. V, Berlin/Leipzig, 1928, p. 55. This can be found in Kant's collected works published by the Prussian Academy of Sciences, Vol. XVIII.

22 A survey of the various recent philosophical reactions to Kant's theory of knowledge (his theory of synthetic *a priori* judgments) is provided by W. Stegmüller, *Hauptströmungen der Gegenwartsphilosophie. Eine kritische Einführung*, Stuttgart, 1969, pp. xvii–xxxix.

23 Cf. E.I.1: "Which reality?"

24 W. Schulz, *Philosophie in der veränderten Welt*, Pfullingen, 1972, p. 115.

25 Ibid.

26 Ibid., p. 841.

27 Kant, *Kritik der praktischen Vernunft*, A 227 = Werke IV, p. 257. (Abbott, p. 223.)

28 Ibid., A 259–60, 263 = Werke IV, pp. 278, 280. (Abbott, pp. 242, 244.)

29 Kant, *Kritik der reinen Vernunft*, B xxx = Werke II, p. 33. (KS, p. 29.)

30 This is the interpretation given by W. Bröcker, *Kant über Metaphysik und Erfahrung*, Frankfurt am Main, 1970, pp. 135–36.

31 Kant, *Kritik der praktischen Vernunft*, A 54 = Werke IV, p. 140. (Abbott, p. 119.)

32 Cf. E.II.1: "Yes to reality."

33 J. Habermas, *Erkenntnis und Interesse*, Frankfurt am Main, 1968, pp. 235–62.

34 Cf. A.III.1: "Scientific revolutions: Thomas S. Kuhn."

35 Habermas, *Erkenntnis und Interesse*, p. 251.

36 Cf. D.II.4. *Interim results IV: Theses on nihilism*. Also Ch. E as a whole.

37 Cf. E.II.3: "Fundamental trust as basis of science."

38 An attempt to reflect on God in the context of a transcendental philosophy of freedom, in the light of Kant's work, has been made by H. Krings, "Freiheit. Ein Versuch Gott zu denken," in *Philosophisches Jahrbuch* 77 (1970), pp. 225–37; cf. the same author's article "Freiheit," in *Handbuch philosophischer Grundbegriffe*, eds. H. Krings, H. M. Baumgartner and C. Wild, Vol. I, Munich, 1973, pp. 493–510.

39 A. Frossard, *Dieu existe. Je l'ai rencontré*, Paris, 1969. (E.t., *God Exists. I Have Met Him*, Collins, London/Doubleday, Garden City, N.Y., 1970.) Frossard's account of his sudden encounter with God in a chapel in Paris must be respected, but its credibility is not heightened by the total acceptance of all the teachings of the Roman Catholic Church, which he connects directly with that experience: "The teaching of the Church was true and I took pleasure in all its details" (p. 123).

40 Cf. the collection edited by C. Chabanis, *Dieu existe-t-il? Non*, Paris, 1973, where God's existence is questioned by a variety of French authors. Or, among recent reactions to the question of mystical experience, in the English-speaking countries, A. J. Ayer, *The Central Questions of Philosophy*, London, 1973.

41 Cf. A III.1: "The universal claim of scientific thought? Karl Popper."

42 Cf. K. Riesenhüber, *Existenzerfahrung und Religion*, Mainz, 1968, esp. Ch. I.2. On the theological problems of verification, cf. H. Häring, "Zur Verifikation von Glaubenssätzen," in H. Küng (ed.), *Fehlbar? Eine Bilanz*, Zürich/Einsiedeln/Cologne, 1973, pp. 232–48.

43 D. Bonhoeffer, *Akt und Sein. Transzendentalphilosophie und Ontologie in der systematischen Theologie*, 1931, 2nd ed., Munich, 1956, p. 94: "Einen Gott, den 'es gibt,' gibt es nicht." But the sentence that follows is not often quoted: "God 'is' in relation to persons, and his being is being a person."

44 Cf. C.III.4: "For a serious theology."

45 There is a widespread legend to the effect that the expression "metaphysics" originally served the editor of the Aristotelian works, Andronicus of Rhodes, three
hundred years after Aristotle (c. 70 B.C.), as a planning device. But this is rightly
criticized as a mere legend by H. Reiner, "Die Entstehung und ursprüngliche
Bedeutung des Namens Metaphysik," in *Zeitschrift für Philosophische Forschung*
8 (1954), pp. 210–37; 9 (1955), pp. 77–79.
46 On the discussion of the problems of metaphysics in the English-speaking countries, cf. D. Tracy, *Blessed Rage for Order. The New Pluralism in Theology*, New
York, 1975, Ch. 7, "The Question of God: Metaphysics Revisited," and Ch. 8,
"The Meaning, Meaningfulness and Truth of God-Language," esp. pp. 172–75.

## F.IV. God exists

### 1. Introduction

1 Cf. C.I.2: "The end of Christianity?"
2 Cf. C.II.2: "Future without religion?"
3 Cf. C.III.2: "Faith in science?"
4 W. Heisenberg, *Der Teil und das Ganze. Gespräche im Umkreis der Atomphysik*,
Munich, 1969, pp. 116–30; cf. pp. 279–95.
5 Heisenberg, "Naturwissenschaftliche und religiöse Wahrheit" (an address before
the Catholic Academy in Bavaria on receiving the Guardini prize, Mar. 23, 1973),
in *Schritte über Grenzen. Gesammelte Reden und Aufsätze*, pp. 335–51. Cf also
P. Jordan, *Der Naturwissenschaftler vor der religiösen Frage. Abbruch einer
Mauer*, Oldenburg/Hamburg, 1964.
6 Cf. C.III.3: "The importance of religion for Jung, Fromm, Frankl."
7 Cf. ibid.
8 Erich Fromm, *To Have or to Be?* Harper & Row, New York/Jonathan Cape,
London, 1976, p. 88.
9 R. Funk, *Mut zum Menschen. Erich Fromms Denken und Werk unter besonderer Berücksichtigung seiner humanistischen Religion und Ethik*, Dissertation,
Tübingen, 1976, esp. Part IV, "Humanismus als Wissenschaft und als religiöses
Ethos bei Erich Fromm."
10 E. Fromm, *To Have or to Be?* p. 141.
11 Ibid., p. 146.
12 Ibid., p. 163.
13 T. Roszak, *The Making of a Counter Culture. Reflections on the Technocratic
Society and Its Youthful Opposition*, New York, 1968.
14 E. K. Scheuch (ed.), *Die Wiedertäufer der Wohlstandsgesellschaft. Eine kritische
Untersuchung der "Neuen Linken" und ihrer Dogmen*, Cologne, 1968; quotation,
p. 12.
15 H. Schelsky, *Die Arbeit tun die anderen. Klassenkampf und Priesterherrschaft der
Intellektuellen*, Opladen, 1975, p. 15. This book scarcely gives an objective description of the role of intellectuals and theologians.
16 R. Schwarz, "Die Rolle der Religion im modernen Existenzverständnis," South
West German Radio talk, May 22, 1977; quotation, p. 16.
17 Ibid., pp. 13–14.
18 Ibid., p. 16.
19 P. L. Berger, *A Rumor of Angels. Modern Society and the Rediscovery of the Supernatural*, Doubleday, Garden City, N.Y., 1969/Allen Lane, London, 1970.
20 Ibid., p. 41.
21 Ibid., p. 70.
22 Ibid.
23 Ibid., p. 71.
24 Cf. E.II. *Fundamental Mistrust or Fundamental Trust?*
25 Berger, op. cit., pp. 71–72.
26 Ibid., p. 72.
27 Ibid., pp. 119–20.

28 Charles Reich, *The Greening of America*, New York, 1970/London, 1971.
29 Ibid., New York, p. 327/London, p. 223.
30 Daniel Bell, *The Cultural Contradictions of Capitalism*, Basic Books, New York/ Heinemann, London, 1976, p. 162.
31 Ibid., p. 166.
32 Ibid., p. 169.
33 Ibid.
34 Ibid.
35 Ibid., p. 170.
36 This is a translation of the German title of Bell's book.
37 K. Mehnert, *Jugend im Zeitbruch. Woher—wohin?* Stuttgart, 1976.
38 Ibid., p. 106.
39 H. Marcuse, *One-Dimensional Man*, Boston: Beacon Press/London: Routledge & Kegan Paul, 1964, p. 257.
40 Cf. A. M. Greeley, *Religion in the Year 2000*, New York, 1969, Ch. 3: "The Data."
41 Cf. T. Luckmann, "Verfall, Fortbestand oder Verwandlung des Religiösen in der modernen Gesellschaft?" in O. Schatz (ed.), *Hat die Religion Zukunft?* Graz/ Vienna/Cologne, 1971, pp. 69–82.
42 Greeley, *The Persistence of Religion*, London, 1974.

## 2. God as hypothesis

43 B. Brecht, *Geschichten vom Herrn Keuner*, in Gesammelte Werke, Vol. 12, Frankfurt am Main, 1967, p. 380.
44 J. P. Sartre, *L'existentialisme est un humanisme*, Paris, 1946, p. 36. (E.t., *Existentialism and Humanism*, Methuen, London, 1948, reprint 1970, p. 33.)
45 Cf. E.II.3: "The persistent basic riddle of reality."
46 D. Bonhoeffer, *Widerstand und Ergebung*, Munich, 1951, p. 182. (E.t., *Letters and Papers from Prison*, S.C.M. Press, London, 1967, p. 155.)
47 Cf. H. Küng, *Christ sein*, Munich, 1974, Ch. A.II.2: "Die Wirklichkeit Gottes." (E.t., *On Being a Christian*, New York, 1976/London, 1977, Ch. A.II.2: "The reality of God.")
48 Cf. D.II.4: "Reality in doubt."

## 3. God as reality

49 On Feuerbach, cf. C.I.1. *Anthropological atheism*. On Marx, C.II.1. *Sociopolitical atheism*. On Freud, C.III.1. *Psychoanalytic atheism*. On Nietzsche, D.I.2. *The counterreligion*.
50 Cf. C.I.2. *Critique of Feuerbach*; C.II.2. *Critique of Marx*; C.III.2. *Critique of Freud*; D.II.1. *Critique of Nietzsche*.
51 Cf. C.III.4. *Interim results III: Theses on atheism*; D.II.4. *Interim results IV: Theses on nihilism*.
52 Cf. F.II.1: "Knowledge of God by reason: Vatican I."
53 Cf. F.II.2. *Controversy on natural theology*.
54 Cf. F.III.2. *More than pure reason: Immanuel Kant*.
55 Cf. F.II.2: "Non-Christians' knowledge of God."
56 It is interesting to note that William James at an early stage in his "The Will to Believe," first published in *New World* in June 1896 and now included in the paperback William James, *Pragmatism and Other Essays*, New York, 1963 (pp. 185–213), started out with hypotheses and—with a reference to Pascal's wager— brought out clearly the character of faith as decision in his main thesis: "Our passional nature not only lawfully may, but must, decide an option between propositions, whenever it is a genuine option that cannot by its nature be decided on intellectual grounds; for to say under such circumstances, 'Do not decide, but leave the question open,' is itself a passional decision—just like deciding yes or no—and is attended with the same risk of losing the truth" (p. 200). The character of faith as decision is also clearly brought out by F. Ferré, *Language, Logic and God*, London, 1961, esp. pp. 224–33. E. Fontinell refers to William James and John

Dewey, as well as Process Philosophy, in his attempt to outline a pragmatic theory of religion: E. Fontinell, *Toward a Reconstruction of Religion. A Philosophical Probe*, New York, 1970.

57 Cf. F.III. *Proving God?*
58 Cf. H. E. Hengstenberg, "Wahrheit, Sicherheit, Unfehlbarkeit. Zur 'Problematik' unfehlbarer kirchlicher Lehrsätze," in H. Küng (ed.), *Fehlbar? Eine Bilanz*, Zürich/Einsiedeln/Cologne, 1973, pp. 217–31.
59 Cf. A.II.1. *The relativity of mathematical certainty.*
60 J. Hick, *Arguments for the Existence of God*, New York, 1971, insists on the necessity of the rationality of belief in God. "Eschatological verification," developed also by I. M. Crombie and often criticized, would have to be based on an intrinsic rationality verifiable at the present time. Cf. also Hick, *Faith and Knowledge*, London, 1957, and *Philosophy of Religion*, Englewood Cliffs, N.J., 1963.
61 Cf. F.III.2: "Indirectly verified by experience."
62 Cf. F.II.2: "Non-Christians' knowledge of God."
63 Rm 1:19–21.

## 4. Consequences

1 Cf. *Frankfurter Allgemeine Zeitung*, Aug. 6, 1976.
2 The results of the EMNID poll were published in W. Harenberg (ed.), *Was glauben die Deutschen?* Munich/Mainz, 1968.
3 H. Böll, "Doktor Murkes gesammeltes Schweigen" (1955), in his volume *Nicht nur zur Weihnachtszeit. Satiren*, Munich, 1966, pp. 87–112.
4 Cf. F.II.2. *Controversy on natural theology.*
5 Cf. H. Küng, *Christ sein*, Ch. A.II.2: "Die Aufgabe der Theologie." (E.t., *On Being a Christian*, New York, 1976/London, 1977, Ch. A.II.2: "The task of theology.")
6 Cf. E.II.3: "Fundamental trust as basis of ethics."
7 On the critique of the categorical imperative, see F.III.2: "Critique of Kant."
8 Cf. I. Kant, "Grundlegung zur Metaphysik der Sitten" (1785), in Werke, ed. W. Weischedel, Vol. IV, Darmstadt, 1956, pp. 60–61. (E.t., *The Moral Law. Kant's Groundwork of the Metaphysic of Morals*, translated and analyzed by H. J. Paton, Hutchinson, London/Toronto/New York, 1948, pp. 90–91.)
9 Cf. the bibliography given in E.II.3 ("Fundamental trust as basis of ethics") on the justification of ethical norms. In almost all the works listed, the problems of autonomy or theonomy are discussed, esp. in those by A. Auer, F. Böckle, W. Korff.
10 Cf. J. Habermas, *Erkenntnis und Interesse*, Frankfurt am Main, 1968, esp. the new postscript to the 2nd ed., 1973; the same author, *Theorie und Praxis. Sozialphilosophische Studien*, Frankfurt, 1963, esp. the Introduction to the new ed. of 1971; the same author, *Technik und Wissenschaft als "Ideologie,"* Frankfurt, 1968; the same author, "Vorbereitende Bemerkungen zu einer Theorie der kommunikativen Kompetenz," in J. Habermas and N. Luhmann, *Theorie der Gesellschaft oder Sozialtechnologie—Was leistet die Systemforschung?* Frankfurt, 1971, pp. 101–41; the same author, *Legitimationsprobleme im Spätkapitalismus*, Frankfurt, 1973; the same author, "Wahrheitstheorien," in H. Fahrenbach (ed.), *Wirklichkeit und Reflexion*, Pfullingen, 1973, pp. 211–65. In this connection, K. O. Apel's program of a "transformation of philosophy" toward a "transcendental pragmatic thought" deserves consideration. His contributions belonging to various periods are collected in K. O. Apel, *Transformation der Philosophie*, 2 vols., Frankfurt, 1971, esp. Vol. II, "Das Apriori der Kommunikationsgemeinschaft," pp. 358–435. On the discussion, cf. K. O. Apel (ed.), *Sprachpragmatik und Philosophie*, Frankfurt, 1976, with contributions also by J. Habermas, S. Kannengiesser, H. Schnelle, D. Wunderlich.
11 Cf. A.III.1: "Scientific revolutions: Thomas S. Kuhn"; F.III.2: "Critique of Kant."
12 On the theological discussion with Habermas and Apel, see W. Pannenberg, *Wissenschaftstheorie und Theologie*, Frankfurt, 1973, pp. 90–105 (esp. with regard to

the questions of meaning), pp. 185–206 (with regard to sense experience and dialectic) (E.t., *Theology and the Philosophy of Science*, Darton, Longman & Todd, 1976, pp. 88–102, 185–205); H. Peukert, *Wissenschaft—Handlungstheorie—Fundamentale Theologie. Analysen zu Ansatz und Status theologischer Theoriebildung*, Düsseldorf, 1976, esp. Part III; F. Böckle, "Ethik und Normenbegründung," a lecture at the Symposium on Vatican III, "The work that needs to be done," organized by *Concilium* and the Catholic Theological Society of America at the University of Notre Dame, Ind., in May 1977. Important in this connection is the critique of Habermas by Niklaus Luhmann, "Systemtheoretische Argumentation. Eine Entgegnung auf Jürgen Habermas," in J. Habermas and N. Luhmann, *Theorie der Gesellschaft*, pp. 291–405.

13 J. Habermas, *Legitimationsprobleme im Spätkapitalismus*, Frankfurt, 1973, p. 165.
14 H. E. Bahr (ed.), *Religionsgespräche. Zur gesellschaftlichen Rolle der Religion*, Darmstadt/Neuwied, 1975, p. 29; contributions by Dorothee Sölle and Jürgen Habermas, among others.
15 H. Krings, *Reale Freiheit. Praktische Freiheit*, a lecture at the University of Tübingen in the framework of a series on the theme of "freedom." I am grateful to my Munich colleague for a copy of this lecture, which also contains important comments on the use of the term "ideal."
16 Wolfhart Pannenberg, *Wissenschaftstheorie und Theologie*, pp. 42–43 (E.t., *Theology and the Philosophy of Science*, pp. 41–42), rightly draws attention to the fact that Habermas too hastily opposes truth as object (correspondence theory) to truth as consensus (consensus theory), as mutually exclusive, with the result that he is unable to explain the difference between consensus on truth and a mere prevailing convention.
17 F. Böckle, "Unfehlbare Normen," in H. Küng (ed.), *Fehlbar? Eine Bilanz*, pp. 280–304; quotation, p. 291.
18 Cf. F.III.2: "Critique of Kant"; F.III.2: "The condition for the possibility of reality."
19 Cf. W. Korff, *Norm und Sittlichkeit. Untersuchung zur Logik der normativen Vernunft*, Mainz, 1973, pp. 192, 199 (citing A. Gehlen).
20 Cf. B. Schüller, "Zur Problematik allgemein verbindlicher ethischer Grundsätze," in *Theologie und Philosophie* 45 (1970), pp. 1–23.

## G. YES TO THE CHRISTIAN GOD

### G.I. *The God of the non-Christian religions*

1 W. Koeppen, "Sein Geschöpf," in *Die Welt*, Dec. 24, 1951. On the work of Wolfgang Koeppen from the theological standpoint, cf. K. J. Kuschel, *Jesus in der deutschen Gegenwartsliteratur*, Einsiedeln/Zürich/Cologne, 1978, esp. Ch. B.II.2c: "Das Wunder der Christwerdung." The book discusses interpretations of the person of Jesus by numerous contemporary German writers.
2 From the immense theological literature on the question of God, in addition to the philosophical works listed at the beginning of F.I.1 and the manuals of dogmatics on the Catholic side (M. Schmaus, and articles in *Mysterium Salutis* by H. U. von Balthasar, A. Deissler, J. Pfammatter, M. Löhrer, K. Rahner) and on the Protestant side (P. Althaus, K. Barth, E. Brunner, H. Diem, H. Ott, H. Thielicke, P. Tillich), the systematic monographs: H. Gollwitzer, *Die Existenz Gottes im Bekenntnis des Glaubens*, Munich, 1963; J. A. T. Robinson, *Honest to God*, London, 1963; J. C. Murray, *The Problem of God. Yesterday and Today*, New Haven/London, 1964; E. Jüngel, *Gottes Sein ist im Werden Verantwortliche Rede vom Sein bei Karl Barth. Eine Paraphrase*, Tübingen, 1965; the same author, *Gott als Geheimnis der Welt. Zur Begründung der Theologie des Gekreuzigten im Streit zwischen Theismus und Atheismus*, Tübingen, 1977; S. M. Ogden, *The Reality of God and Other Essays*, New York, 1966; H. Engelland, *Die Wirklichkeit Gottes und die Gewissheit des Glaubens*, Göttingen,

1966; H. Zahrnt, *Die Sache mit Gott. Die Protestantische Theologie im 20. Jahrhundert*, Munich, 1966 (E.t., *The Question of God. Protestant Theology in the Twentieth Century*, London, 1969); the same author, *Gott kann nicht sterben. Wider die falschen Alternativen in Theologie und Gesellschaft*, Munich, 1970; F. Leist, *Nicht der Gott der Philosophen*, Freiburg/Basel/Vienna, 1966; C. H. Ratschow, *Gott existiert. Eine dogmatische Studie*, Berlin, 1966; J. Macquarrie, *God and Secularity*, Philadelphia, 1967; F. Gogarten, *Die Frage nach Gott. Eine Vorlesung*, Tübingen, 1968; J. B. Cobb, Jr., *God and the World*, Philadelphia, 1969; G. Ebeling, *Wort und Glaube*, Vol. II, Tübingen, 1969; E. Schillebeeck, *God the Future of Man*, London/Sydney, 1969; L. Gilkey, *Naming the Whirlwind. The Renewal of God-Language*, Indianapolis/New York, 1969; E. R. Baltazar, *God within Process*, New York, 1970; W. Kasper, *Glaube und Geschichte*, Mainz, 1970, esp. pp. 101–43; R. G. Smith, *The Doctrine of God*, London, 1970; H. Küng, *Menschwerdung Gottes. Eine Einführung in Hegels theologisches Denken als Prolegomena zu einer künftigen Christologie*, Freiburg/Basel/Vienna, 1970; H. Ott, *Gott*, Stuttgart/Berlin, 1971; H. Braun, *Wie man über Gott nicht denken soll. Dargelegt an den Gedankengängen Philos von Alexandria*, Tübingen, 1971; J. C. Barreau, *Qui est Dieu*, Paris, 1971; W. Pannenberg, *Gottesgedanke und menschliche Freiheit*, Göttingen, 1972; E. Biser, *Theologie und Atheismus. Anstösse zu einer theologischen Aporetik*, Munich, 1972; J. Moltmann, *Der gekreuzigte Gott*, Munich, 1972 (E.t., *The Crucified God*, London, 1974); H. M. Barth, *Die christliche Gotteslehre. Hauptprobleme ihrer Geschichte*, Gütersloh, 1974; C. Wackenheim, *Christianisme sans idéologie*, Paris, 1974; F. Mildenberger, *Gotteslehre. Eine dogmatische Untersuchung*, Tübingen, 1975.

Symposia on the question of God: A. Schaefer (ed.), *Der Gottesgedanke im Abendland*, Stuttgart, 1964; N. Kutschki (ed.), *Gott heute. Fünfzehn Beiträge zur Gottesfrage*, Mainz/Munich, 1967; H. Zahrnt (ed.), *Gespräch über Gott. Die protestantische Theologie im 20. Jahrhundert. Ein Textbuch*, Munich, 1968; T. C. de Kruijf and others, *Zerbrochene Gottesbilder*, Freiburg/Basel/Vienna, 1969; H. J. Schultz (ed.), *Wer ist das eigentlich-Gott?* Munich, 1969; E. Castelli (ed.), *L'analyse du langage théologique. Le nom de Dieu*, Paris, 1969; the same author, *La philosophie de la religion. L'herméneutique de la philosophie de la religion*, Paris, 1977; K. Krenn (ed.), *Die wirkliche Wirklichkeit Gottes. Gott in der Sprache heutiger Probleme*, Paderborn/Vienna, 1974; A. Graner-Haider, *Gott*, Mainz, 1970; J. Blank et al., *Gott-Frage und moderner Atheismus*, Regensburg, 1972; J. Ratzinger (ed.), *Die Frage nach Gott*, Freiburg/Basel/Vienna, 1972; J. Kopperschmidt (ed.), *Der fragliche Gott. Fünf Versuche einer Antwort*, Düsseldorf, 1973; K. Rahner (ed.), *Ist Gott noch gefragt? Zur Funktionslosigkeit des Gottesglaubens*, Düsseldorf, 1973.

3 For information on the world religions, see—from the immense amount of literature—especially the recent large symposia: M. Gorce and R. Mortier (eds.), *Histoire générale des religions*, 5 vols., Paris, 1947–52; C. Clemen (ed.), *Die Religionen der Erde*, Munich, 1949; F. König (ed.), *Christus und die Religionen der Erde. Handbuch der Religionsgeschichte*, 3 vols., Vienna, 1951; M. Brillant and R. Aigran (eds.), *Histoire des religions*, 3 vols., Paris, 1953–55; M. Eliade and J. M. Kitagawa (eds.), *The History of Religions*, Chicago, 1959; C. M. Schröder (ed.), *Die Religionen der Menschheit*, Stuttgart, 1960ff. (36 vols. planned); J. P. Asmussen and J. Laessoe (ed.), *Illustreret Religionshistorie*, Copenhagen, 1968; T. Ling, *A History of Religion East and West. An Introduction and Interpretation*, London, 1968; C. J. Bleeker and G. Widengren (eds.), *Historia Religionum. Handbook for the History of Religions*, 2 vols., Leiden, 1970; P. Tacchi Venturi and G. Castellani, *Storia delle Religioni*, 5 vols., Turin, 1971.

A brief orientation is provided by A. Bertholet and H. von Campenhausen, *Wörterbuch der Religionen*, Stuttgart, 1952; H. von Glasenapp, *Die nichtchristlichen Religionen*, Frankfurt, 1957; G. Günther (ed.), *Die grossen Religionen*, Göttingen, 1961; H. Ringgren and A. V. Ström, *Die Religionen der Völker. Grundriss der allgemeinen Religionsgeschichte*, Stuttgart, 1959; R. C. Zaehner,

*The Concise Encyclopedia of Living Faiths*, London, 1959; E. Dammann, *Grundriss der Religionsgeschichte*, Stuttgart, 1972; G. Mensching, *Die Weltreligionen*, Darmstadt, 1972; E. Brunner-Traut (ed.), *Die fünf grossen Weltreligionen*, Freiburg/Basel/Vienna, 1974. All these contain bibliographies including books on individual religions.
The subject is treated at greater length by P. D. Chantepie de la Saussaye, *Lehrbuch der Religionsgeschichte*, 2 vols., Tübingen, 1925; J. Finegan, *The Archeology of World Religions*, Princeton, 1957; H. von Glasenapp, *Die fünf grossen Religionen*, Düsseldorf/Cologne, 1951–52. There are paperbacks in various languages giving texts from the nonbiblical religions, especially of Indian and Chinese wisdom.

4 On the phenomenology of religion: after the important early works of R. Otto, H. Pinard de la Boullaye and N. Söderblom, cf. G. van der Leeuw, *Phänomenologie der Religion*, Tübingen, 1933, 1956²; the same author, *Einführung in die Phänomenologie der Religion*, Haarlem, 1948, Darmstadt, 1961²; G. Widengren, *Religionsphänomenologie*, Berlin, 1969; G. Mensching, *Vergleichende Religionswissenschaft*, Heidelberg, 1949; the same author, *Die Religion. Erscheinungsformen, Strukturtypen und Lebensgesetze*, Stuttgart, 1959; H. von Glasenapp, *Die Religionen der Menschheit. Ihre Gegensätze und Übereinstimmungen*, Vienna, 1954; M. Eliade, *Patterns of Comparative Religion*, London, 1958; J. Wach, *The Comparative Study of Religions*, New York, 1958; K. Goldammer, *Die Formenwelt des Religiösen*, Stuttgart, 1960; F. Heiler, *Erscheinungsformen und Wesen der Religion*, Stuttgart, 1961; G. Lanczkowski, *Begegnung und Wandel der Religionen*, Düsseldorf/Cologne, 1971.

5 On relations between Christianity and the world religions, in addition to the works, already cited, by K. Barth, E. Brunner and H. Kraemer, as also by K. Rahner, H. R. Schlette and H. Küng: E. Troeltsch, *Die Absolutheit des Christentums und die Religionsgeschichte*, Tübingen, 1929; O. Karrer, *Das Religiöse in der Menschheit und das Christentum*, Frankfurt, 1934; F. Heiler, "Die Frage der 'Absolutheit' des Christentums im Lichte der vergleichenden Religionsgeschichte," in *Eine heilige Kirche* 20 (1938), pp. 306–66; W. Holstein, *Das Evangelium und die Völker. Beiträge zur Geschichte und Theorie der Mission*, Berlin, 1939; the same author, *Das Kerygma und der Mensch*, Munich, 1953; T. Ohm, *Die Liebe zu Gott in den nichtchristlichen Religionen*, Munich, 1950; the same author, *Asiens Nein und Ja zum westlichen Christentum*, Munich, 1960; H. H. Farmer, *Revelation and Religion. Studies in the Theological Interpretation of Religious Types*, London, 1954; E. Benz, *Ideen zu einer Theologie der Religionsgeschichte*, Mainz, 1960; S. Niell, *Christian Faith and other Faiths. The Christian Dialogue with Other Religions*, London, 1961; R. C. Zaehner, *At Sundry Times. An Essay in the Comparison of Religions*, London, 1958; the same author, *The Catholic Church and World Religions*, London, 1964; P. Tillich, *Christianity and the Encounter of World Religions*, New York, 1962; J. A. Cuttat, *Hemisphären des Geistes. Der spirituelle Dialog von Ost und West*, Stuttgart, 1964; the same author, *Asiatische Gottheit—Christliche Gott. Die Spiritualität der beiden Hemisphären*, new, rev. ed., Einsiedeln, 1971; R. Panikkar, *Religionen und die Religion*, Munich, 1965; G. Thils, *Propos et problèmes de la théologie des religions non chrétiennes*, Tournai, 1966; J. Heilsbetz, *Theologische Gründe der nichtchristlichen Religionen*, Freiburg/Basel/Vienna, 1967; G. Rosenkranz, *Der christliche Glaube angesichts der Weltreligionen*, Berne/Munich, 1967; J. Neuner (ed.), *Christian Revelation and World Religions*, London, 1967; O. Wolff, *Anders an Gott glauben. Die Weltreligionen als Partner des Christentums*, Stuttgart, 1969; R. Girault, *Évangile et religions d'aujourd'hui*, Paris, 1969; U. Mann, *Das Christentum als absolute Religion*, Darmstadt, 1970; the same author, *Die Religion in den Religionen*, Stuttgart, 1975; R. D. Young, *Encounter with World Religions*, Philadelphia, 1970; *Religions. Fundamental Themes for a Dialogistic Understanding*, published by the secretariat for non-Christians, Rome, 1970; S. J. Samartha, *Dialogue between Men of Living Faiths*, Geneva, 1971; the same author (ed.), *Living Faiths and Ultimate Goals. A Continuing Dialogue*, Geneva, 1974; M. Seckler, *Hoffnungsversuche*, Freiburg/Basel/Vienna, 1972, pp. 13–46;

V. Hernández Catalá, *La expresión del divino en las religiones no cristianas*, Madrid, 1972; I. H. Dalmais, *Shalom. Chrétiens à l'écoute des grandes religions*, Paris, 1972; V. Boublik, *Teologia delle religioni*, Rome, 1973; W. Kasper, "Der christliche Glaube angesichts der Religionen. Sind die nichtchristlichen Religionen heilsbedeutsam?" in H. Feld and J. Nolte (eds.), *Wort Gottes in der Zeit*, Düsseldorf, 1973, pp. 347–60; J. Hick, *Truth and Dialogue in World Religions. Conflicting Truth Claims*, Philadelphia, 1974; G. Evers, *Mission, nichtchristliche Religionen, weltliche Welt*, Münster, 1974; R. Friedli, *Fremdheit als Heimat. Auf der Suche nach einem Kriterium für den Dialog zwischen den Religionen*, Fribourg, Switzerland, 1974; T. Paul (ed.), *The Emerging Culture in India*, Alwaye, India, 1975; W. Trutwin, *Licht vom Licht. Religionen in unserer Welt*, Düsseldorf, 1976. Additional titles up to 1960 are given in E. Benz and M. Nambara, *Das Christentum und die nichtchristlichen Hochreligionen. Begegnung und Auseinandersetzung. Eine internationale Bibliographie*, Leiden, 1960. Recent surveys of the solutions offered by Protestant and Catholic theology, in addition to the work of G. Rosenkranz already mentioned, are found in Beyerhaus, "Zur Theologie der Religionen im Protestantismus," and W. Bühlmann, "Die Theologie der nichtchristlichen Religionen als ökumenisches Problem," both in *Freiheit in der Begegnung* (Festschrift for Otto Karrer), Frankfurt/Stuttgart, 1969, pp. 433–78.

6 On the general problems, see H. Küng, *Christ sein*, Munich, 1974, Ch. A.III. (E.t., *On Being a Christian*, New York, 1976/London, 1977, Ch. A.III: "The Challenge of the World Religions.")

7 Cf. F. Kluge, *Etymologisches Wörterbuch der deutschen Sprache*, rev. by W. Mitzka, Berlin, 1963, p. 265; H. Paul, *Deutsches Wörterbuch*, rev. by W. Betz, Tübingen, 1966, p. 269.

8 Cf. W. Burkert, "Gott," in *Historisches Wörterbuch der Philosophie*, Vol. III, Darmstadt, 1974, pp. 721–25.

9 Cf. C.III.1: "What is the source of religion?"

10 Cf. B. Gladigow, "Götternamen und Namen Gottes," in H. von Stietencron (ed.), *Der Name Gottes*, Düsseldorf, 1975, pp. 25–31. The same volume also contains informative articles on the names of God in a variety of religions.

11 In all this section G.I, I owe many valuable insights, corrections and additional bibliographical details to conversations with Julia Ching, professor of Chinese philosophy at Yale University. On Chinese religion, cf. her book *Confucianism and Christianity*, Tokyo, 1977.

12 M. Ricci, *T'ien-chu shih-i* (the first version may have been completed in 1594, but the date of publication is given as Aug. 22, 1603); Latin translation, *De Deo Vero Disputatio* (completed in 1597 and released for publication by the ecclesiastical censors in 1601).

13 Cf. W. Eichhorn, "Der 'Name Gottes,' in religiösen Strömungen des alten China," in H. von Stietencron (ed.), *Der Name Gottes*, pp. 66–74.

14 Cf. A. S. Rosso, *Apostolic Legations to China of the Eighteenth Century*, South Pasadena, Calif., 1948, pp. 77–79.

15 The contemporary Catholic writer Shushako Endo in his novel, *Silence*, Tokyo, 1969, has described how Japanese Christians during the persecution died for a God whom they really did not know.

16 On the history of the rites controversy, cf. L. von Pastor, *Geschichte der Päpste*, Vol. XV, Freiburg/Rome 1961[8]. (E.t., *The History of the Popes*, Vol. XXXIII, Kegan Paul, Trench, Trübner, London, 1941.)

17 Cf. A.II.3: "Conflict of faith with faith: Jansenism."

18 Cf. T. Grimm, "China und das Chinabild von Leibniz," in *Studia Leibnitiana Sonderheft* 1 (1969), pp. 60–61.

19 L. von Pastor, *Geschichte der Päpste*, Vol. XV, p. 309. See pp. 309–27 for a vivid account of the ignorance and arrogance of the papal legate Tournon after the prohibition of the Chinese names and rites. (E.t., *History of the Popes*, Vol. XXXIII, pp. 428–46.)

20 S. Congregatio de Propaganda Fide. "Instructio circa quasdam ceremonias et juramentum super ritibus Sinensibus," in *Acta Apostolicae Sedis* 32 (1940), pp.

24–26; "Decretum de juramento super ritibus Malabaricis a missionariis in Indiis orientalibus praestando," in *Acta Apostolicae Sedis* 32 (1940), p. 379.

21 On the whole complex of problems of the mission to the world in past and present, with a comprehensive new conception, see the excellent book by W. Bühlmann, *Wo der Glaube lebt. Einblicke in der Lage der Weltkirche*, Freiburg/Basel/Vienna, 1974.

22 N. de Malebranche, *Entretien d'un philosophe chrétien et d'un philosophe chinois sur l'existence et la nature de Dieu*, ed. A. Le Moine, Marseilles, 1936.

23 G. W. von Leibniz, *Lettre sur la philosophie chinoise à Nicolas de Remond*. A German translation of this letter is included in R. Loosen and F. Vonessen (eds.), *Zwei Briefe über das binäre Zahlensystem und die chinesische Philosophie*, Stuttgart, 1968, pp. 39–125.

24 Cf. T. Grimm, *China und das Chinabild von Leibniz* pp. 60–61. Leibniz met Peter the Great three times: 1711 in Torgau, 1712 in Karlsbad, 1716 in Bad Pyrmont. On this, cf. E. M. Kunik (ed.), *Briefe von Christian Wolff aus den Jahren 1719–1753*, St. Petersburg, 1860, new ed., Hildesheim, 1971, p. ix.

25 C. Wolff, *Oratio de Sinarum philosophia practica vom 12. Juli 1721*, Frankfurt am Main, 1726.

26 Cf. H. Küng, *Christ sein*, Ch. A.III.4. (E.t., *On Being a Christian*, Ch. A.III.4: "Not exclusiveness, but uniqueness.")

27 Jürgen Moltmann also approves the model of "the critical catalyst" in his book *Kirche in der Kraft des Geistes*, Munich, 1975, pp. 180–81 (E.t., *The Church in the Power of the Spirit*, London, 1977, pp. 158–59), but he does not see it (as suggested in *On Being a Christian*) as based on dialogue. On the other hand, I have maintained that the idea of a "critical catalyst" emerges from the dialogue with other religions, expressly presupposes and includes this dialogue, that it also involves a "common quest for truth" and in particular a "critical testing" of our own position (cf. *On Being a Christian*, A.III).

28 Cf. D.I.1: "Schopenhauer's pessimism."

29 Cf. F.I.2: "Silence before God?"

30 Cf. M. Doi, "Dialogue between Living Faiths in Japan," in J. Samartha, *Dialogue between Men of Living Faiths*, pp. 32–46; cf. p. 36.

31 M. Abe, "In Memory of Dr. Paul Tillich," in *The Eastern Buddhist*, New Series I/2 (1966), pp. 128–31.

32 P. Tillich, *Christianity and the Encounter of the World Religions*, New York, 1962; on the comparison between the Buddhist nirvana and the Christian kingdom of God, see Ch. 3, §§3–4. M. Abe provides a critique from the Buddhist standpoint in "Christianity and the Encounter of the World Religions," in *The Eastern Buddhist*, New Series I/1 (1965), pp. 109–22.

33 Cf. E. Conze, *Buddhism. Its Essence and Development*, Oxford University Press, 1953, p. 16.

34 Cf. H. von Glasenapp, *Unsterblichkeit und Erlösung in den indischen Religionen*, Halle, 1938; the same author, "Nirvana," in *Die Religionen in Geschichte und Gegenwart*, Vol. IV, Tübingen, 1960³, cols. 1498–99.

35 Conze, op. cit., p. 40.

36 T. R. V. Murti, *The Central Philosophy of Buddhism. A Study of the Madhyamika System*, Allen & Unwin, London, 1955, pp. 50–51, 87–89.

37 K. Jaspers, *Die grossen Philosophen*, Vol. I., Munich, 1957, pp. 934–56.

38 Murti, op. cit., pp. 235–36.

39 Kitaro Nishida, *A Study of Good*, Printing Bureau, Japanese Government, Tokyo, 1960, pp. 88–89. Cf. H. Waldenfels, *Absolutes Nichts. Zur Grundlegung des Dialogs zwischen Buddhismus und Christentum*, Freiburg, 1976. Here there is a description—both understanding and understandable—of Nishida's philosophy (pp. 48–64) and especially that of his student Keiji Nishitani (pp. 65–154).

40 Nishida, *Intelligibility and the Philosophy of Nothingness. Three Philosophical Essays*, transl. and intro. by Robert Schinzinger, Maruzen Co. Ltd., Tokyo, 1958; the quotation is from Schinzinger's Introduction, p. 16.

41 Nishida, "Towards a Philosophy of Religion with the Concept of Pre-Established Harmony as Guide," in *The Eastern Buddhist*, New Series, Vol. III, No. 1, June 1970, p. 35.

42 Nishida, *A Study of Good*, p. 189.
43 Cf. M. Abe, "Christianity and the Encounter of the World Religions," in *The Eastern Buddhist*, New Series I/1 (1965), pp. 109–22, esp. pp. 116–17; cf. also K. Nishitani, "The Personal and the Impersonal in Religion," in *The Eastern Buddhist*, New Series III/1 (1970), pp. 1–18; III/2 (1970), pp. 71–87.
44 Cf. D. T. Suzuki, *Mysticism: Christian and Buddhist*, London, 1957, and various articles in *The Eastern Buddhist*; K. Nishitani, "Der Buddhismus und das Christentum," in *Nachrichten der Gesellschaft für Natur- und Völkerkunde Ostasiens* 88 (1960), pp. 5–32.
45 Cf. H. Dumoulin, *Zen. Geschichte und Gestalt*, Berne, 1959; the same author, *Östliche Meditation und christliche Mystik*, Freiburg/Munich, 1966; the same author, *Christianity meets Buddhism*, La Salle, Ill., 1974; cf. also H. Dumoulin (ed.), *Buddhismus der Gegenwart*, Freiburg/Basel/Vienna, 1970, with contributions from Christian and Buddhist experts including H. Bechert, E. Benz, H. Dumoulin, A. Fernando, A. M. Fiske, H. Hoffmann, J. M. Kitagawa, H. Nakamura, Y. Raguin, F. Reynolds, D. K. Swearer, Vu Duy-Tu, H. Welch.
46 Thomas Aquinas, *De potentia* q.7 a.5 ad 14.
47 Nicholas of Cusa, *De docta ignorantia* I, 1440, in Nicolai de Cusa, *Opera Omnia*, Vol. I, Heidelberg, 1932.
48 Ibid., Ch. 26, pp. 55–56.
49 Ibid.
50 Nicholas of Cusa, *Directio speculantis seu de non aliud* (1462), in *Opera Omnia* XIII, Leipzig, 1944.
51 Ibid., p. 87 (Prop. 5).
52 Cf. C.III.1: "What is religion?"
53 William James, *The Varieties of Religious Experience*, Longmans, Green, London/New York/Toronto, 1902.
54 Ibid., p. 31.
55 Cf. ibid., Lectures IV–VII.
56 N. Söderblom, "Uppenbarelse religion" (1903) with "Tre livsformer," under the title *Till mystikens belysning*, ed. H. Akerberg, London, 1975.
57 F. Heiler, *Das Gebet*, Munich, 1918, 5th ed., 1923. (E.t., *Prayer. A Study in the History and Psychology of Religion*, Oxford University Press, New York, 1932, Galaxy Books, 1958.)
58 Cf. Heiler, Preface to the 5th German ed., 1923, p. viii.
59 Heiler, *Das Gebet*, p. 249. (E.t., p. 136.)
60 Ibid., p. 255. (E.t., p. 142.)
61 Ibid. (E.t., ibid.)
62 Ibid. (E.t., pp. 142–43.)
63 Ibid. (E.t., pp. 142–43.)
64 Ibid., pp. 259–60. (E.t., pp. 146–48.)
65 Ibid., pp. 261–62. (E.t., pp. 148–49.)
66 Ibid., p. 262. (E.t., p. 149.)
67 S. Radhakrishnan, *Eastern Religions and Western Thought*, Oxford University Press, London/New York, 1939.
68 Ibid., pp. 308–9. On this, cf. the criticism by Indian Christian theologians in M. M. Thomas, *The Acknowledged Christ of the Indian Renaissance*, Madras, 1970, Ch. VII.
69 M. Gandhi, in *Harijan* quoted by Radhakrishnan, op. cit., p. 313.
70 G. Lanczkowski, *Begegnung und Wandel der Religionen*, Düsseldorf/Cologne, 1971, pp. 111–12, 115–16. Cf. G. Mensching, *Toleranz und Wahrheit in der Religion*, 1955, paperback, Munich/Hamburg, 1966.
71 K. Jaspers, *Die massgebenden Menschen*, Munich, 1971, p. 206.
72 H. Kraemer, *The Christian Message to a Non-Christian World*, London, 1938; the same author, *Religion and the Christian Faith*, London, 1956.
73 A. J. Toynbee, *An Historian's Approach to Religion*, London, 1956; the same author, *Christianity among the Religions of the World*, London, 1958.
74 W. E. Hocking, *Living Religions and a World Faith*, New York, 1940.
75 On the fruitful Hindu-Christian discussion in India, cf., in addition to the above-mentioned book by M. M. Thomas, esp. K. Baago, *Pioneers of Indigenous Christianity*, Bangalore, 1969; the same author, *Bibliography of Indian Christian Theol-*

ogy, Madras, 1969; R. H. S. Boyd, *An Introduction to Indian Christian Theology*, Madras, 1969; Robin Boyd, *What Is Christianity?* Madras, 1970. Among Indian Christian theologians, the following should be mentioned: Joshua Marshman, Nehemiah Goreh, M. C. Parekh, C. F. Andrews, S. K. Rudra, P. D. Devanandan, P. Chenchiah, D. G. Moses, J. R. Chandran, Surjit Singh, M. Sunder Rao.

76 Cf. W. E. Hocking, *The Meaning of God in Human Experience. A Philosophic Study of Religion*, New Haven/London/Oxford, 1912.

77 William James, *The Varieties of Religious Experience*, p. 19.

78 Ibid., p. 443.

79 Cf. F.III. *Proving God?*

80 The foundations were laid in C. S. Peirce's article "How to make our Ideas Clear," in *The Popular Science Monthly*, January 1878. See also C. S. Peirce, *Collected Papers*, Harvard, 1931.

81 John Dewey's *A Common Faith*, New Haven, 1934, has gone through many editions and has been influential for a humanistic-naturalistic understanding of religion. Here faith in God seems to be replaced by "faith" in human values and relationships.

82 James, op. cit., pp. 444–45.

83 Ibid., p. 445.

84 Ibid., pp. 506–7.

85 Ibid., p. 18.

86 On this, see the survey by G. Ezorsky, "Pragmatic Theory of Truth," in *The Encyclopedia of Philosophy*, Vol. VI, London/New York, 1967, p. 428.

87 Cf. C.III.4: "Correcting course."

## G.II. The God of the Bible

### 1. The living God

1 F. Nietzsche, *Götzen-Dämmerung* ("Wie die 'wahre Welt' endlich zur Fabel wurde"), in *Werke* (ed., K. Schlechta) II, p. 963. (E.t., *The Twilight of the Idols*, Harmondsworth/New York, 1968, pp. 40–41.)

2 Nietzsche, *Jenseits von Gut und Böse* 52, in *Werke* II, pp. 614–15. (E.t., *Beyond Good and Evil*, Harmondsworth/New York, 1973, pp. 61–62.)

3 Cf. C.III.1: "What is the source of religion?"

4 An excellent generally understandable introduction to the Old Testament in historical perspective is H. M. Lutz, H. Timm and E. C. Hirsch (eds.), *Das Buch der Bücher. Altes Testament, Einführungen. Texte. Kommentare*, Munich, 1970. A more academic background to this book is provided by what is now a classic on the subject: G. von Rad, *Theologie des Alten Testaments*, 2 vols., Munich, 1957 and 1960. (E.t., *Old Testament Theology*, S.C.M. Press, 2 vols., London, 1965.) On the understanding of God, see, again, the Old Testament theologies by W. Eichrodt, G. Fohrer, P. Heinisch, E. Jacob, P. van Imschoot, L. Köhler, J. L. McKenzie, W. Zimmerli. There is a useful survey by C. Westermann, "Der Gott Israels," in *Neues Glaubensbuch. Der gemeinsame christliche Glaube*, eds. H. Feiner and L. Vischer, Freiburg/Zürich, 1973, pp. 114–31. (E.t., *The Common Catechism. A Christian Book of Faith*, Search Press, London/Seabury Press, New York, 1975, pp. 104–20.) In addition to the large numbers of commentaries, the various introductions to the Old Testament by J. A. Bewer, O. Eissfeldt, A. Feuillet, G. Fohrer, O. Kaiser, W. U. Oesterley, R. H. Pfeiffer, T. H. Robinson, A. Weiser, are important for individual books (esp. for the Pentateuch). H. Haag (ed.), *Das Bibellexikon*, Einsiedeln/Zürich/Cologne, 2nd ed., 1968, can be recommended as a very full and informative work of reference. A helpful introduction to the literary genres of the Bible is provided by G. Lohfink, *Jetzt verstehe ich die Bibel. Ein Sachbuch der Formkritik*, Stuttgart, 1973. Monographs on the Old Testament understanding of God include B. M. F. van Iersel, *Der Gott der Väter im Zeugnis der Bibel*, Salzburg, 1965; W. H. Schmidt, *Alttestamentlicher Glaube und seine Umwelt. Zur Geschichte des alttestamentlichen Gottesverständnisses*, Neukirchen, 1968; J. S. Chesnut, *The Old Testament Understanding of God*,

Philadelphia, 1968; G. Fohrer, *Geschichte der israelitischen Religion*, Berlin, 1969; A. Deissler, *Die Grundbotschaft des Alten Testaments. Ein theologischer Durchblick*, Freiburg/Basel/Vienna, 1972.

5 Gn 31:53; cf. 26:24; 28:13; 32:9.

6 Gn 28:13; cf. 32:9; 46:1.

7 Ex 3:6, 15, 16: the comprehensive formula of the three is found only here. On the development of the Yahweh religion, cf. esp. G. Fohrer, *Geschichte der israelitischen Religion*, particularly Part I.

8 1 K 18:39; cf. 18:21–37.

9 Is 2:8, 18; 10:10; 19:3.

10 Jr 2:11; 5:7.

11 Jr 2:5; 10:8; 14:22.

12 Is 45:21.

13 Dt 6:4.

14 Cf. H. Haag, *Abschied vom Teufel*, Zürich/Einsiedeln/Cologne, 1969; the same author, *Teufelsglaube*, with contributions from K. Elliger, B. Lang, and M. Limbeck, Tübingen, 1974, Part II: "Dämonen und Satan im Alten Testament" (pp. 141–69). I am grateful to Professor Haag, my colleague in Tübingen, professor of Old Testament in the faculty of Catholic theology, for looking through this chapter, G.II, on the God of Israel, and for many useful suggestions.

15 Cf. Dt 6:4, 5 (cf. Mk 12:29, 30 and parallels).

16 Cf. Ex 2:1–10.

17 Cf. Ex 3 and 4.

18 Cf. Ex 5 to 15.

19 Cf. Ex 7 to 11.

20 Cf. Ex 12.

21 Cf. Ex 13 and 14; Ex 15 (Israel's song of victory).

22 G. von Rad, *Theologie des Alten Testaments*, Vol. I, Munich, 1958, pp. 127–28. (E.t., *Old Testament Theology*, S.C.M. Press, London, 1965, Vol. I, p. 121.)

23 One of the four anonymous written sources (representing differing strata of tradition) of the five "books of Moses" (the Pentateuch), belonging to the time of King Solomon, introduces the name "Yahweh" already in the stories of the patriarchs and consequently is known as the "Yahwist" source (J—from the German form). But today it is generally assumed that "Yahweh" became the proper name of God ("El," "Elohim") only from Moses' time onward. The second source, about two centuries later, is known as the Elohist (E) because of its use of the older name. The third source, concerned mainly with the organization of worship and the priesthood and therefore known as the priestly code (P), is much later than the first two and provides the framework for the final version. In addition, there is the Deuteronomic historical work, which comprises the books from Deuteronomy to Kings and thus embraces the whole period from Mosaic times to the beginning of the Babylonian exile.

24 The problems of the name of God are discussed both comprehensively and concisely by H. Gese, "Der Name Gottes im Alten Testament," in H. von Stietencron (ed.), *Der Name Gottes*, pp. 75–89. Cf. also the commentaries on Exodus.

25 Ex 6:6–7.

26 E. Bloch, *Das Prinzip Hoffnung*, Vol. III, pp. 1457–58.

27 Cf. Ex 15.

28 Jg 5.

29 Cf. H. Küng, *Gott und das Leid*, Einsiedeln/Zürich/Cologne, 1967; the same author, *Christ sein*, Ch. VI.2. (E.t., *On Being a Christian*, Ch. VI.2.)

30 Cf. A. Weiser, "Pisteuo," in *Theologisches Wörterbuch zum Neuen Testament*, founded by G. Kittel, ed. G. Friedrich, Vol. VI, Stuttgart, 1959, pp. 182–97.

31 All this becomes particularly clear in G. von Rad's *Old Testament Theology*, with its analysis of the various traditions.

32 W. Weischedel, *Der Gott der Philosophen. Grundlegung einer Philosophischen Theologie im Zeitalter des Nihilismus*, Vol. I, Darmstadt, 1971, pp. 494–95.

33 Ac 17:23.

34 Cf. the list under G.I.1. n.4. of works on the phenomenology of religion.

35 Cf. the contributions of P. Beyerhaus, A. Böhlig, H. Brunner, H. Cancik, W. Eichhorn, J. van Ess, H. Gese, B. Gladigow, M. Hengel, W. Kasper, M. S. Laubacher, J. Simon and H. von Stietencron, in H. von Stietencron (ed.), *Der Name Gottes.*

36 As against Karl Barth's (also Rudolf Bultmann's and Karl Heim's) Christian exclusiveness, which can be understood in the light of the history of theology, the truth content of the world religions is admitted by many Protestant theologians. These include Ernst Troeltsch and other theologians interested in the history of religion, who come from the school of Ritschl; others take similar views in the light of the Old and New Testaments, among them A. Schlatter (and W. Lütgert) and later P. Tillich, P. Althaus, C. H. Ratschow, W. Pannenberg. A good survey of the problems is found in P. Althaus, *Die christliche Wahrheit*, esp. §5 and §16. On the recent tendencies, cf. P. Knitter, "What is German Protestant Theology Saying About the Non-Christian Religions?" in *Neue Zeitschrift für systematische Theologie und Religionsphilosophie* 50 (1973), pp. 38–64.

37 Cf. F.II.2: "Non-Christians' knowledge of God."

## 2. God and his world

1 A. Einstein, *Wie ich die Welt sehe* (1930), in C. Seelig (ed.), *Mein Weltbild*, Berlin, 1955, pp. 7–45; quotation, p. 10. (E.t., *The World as I see it*, Watts & Co., London, 1935, in Thinkers Library, 1940, 3rd impression, 1949, p. 1.)

2 Ibid. (E.t., p. 5.)

3 Ibid. (E.t., ibid.)

4 Einstein, "Religion und Wissenschaft," in *Berliner Tagblatt*, Nov. 11, 1930; incl. in C. Seelig, op. cit., pp. 15–18; quotation, pp. 15–16. (E.t., "Religion and Science," op. cit., pp. 24–28; quotation, p. 25.)

5 Ibid., p. 16. (E.t., p. 26.)

6 Ibid. (E.t., ibid.); cf. D.I.1: "Schopenhauer's pessimism."

7 Ibid. (E.t., pp. 26–27.); cf. B.I.1: "All in God: Spinoza and his influence."

8 Ibid. (E.t., p. 26.)

9 Banesh Hoffmann, with the collaboration of Helen Dukas, *Albert Einstein. Creator and Rebel*, Granada Publishing Company, New York, 1972/Hart-Davis, Mac-Gibbon, London, 1973, p. 95. Hoffmann is a former student and scientific assistant of Einstein. Helen Dukas was Einstein's secretary from 1928 until his death, in 1955.

10 Einstein, "Religion und Wissenschaft," p. 17. (E.t., p. 28.)

11 Ibid., pp. 17–18. (E.t., p. 28.)

12 Ibid., p. 17. (E.t., p. 27.)

13 Ibid. (E.t., p. 27.)

14 Ibid. (E.t., p. 27.)

15 Letter to F. D. Roosevelt, Aug. 2, 1939, in Jeremy Bernstein, *Einstein*, Collins Fontana, London, 1973, pp. 180–81.

16 Einstein, letter to Max Born, Dec. 4, 1936, in Albert Einstein, Hedwig Born and Max Born, *Briefwechsel 1916–1955*, Munich, 1969, pp. 129–30; cf. also pp. 118–19. (E.t., *The Born-Einstein Letters*, with commentaries by Max Born, Macmillan, London/New York, 1971, p. 91; cf. pp. 84–85.)

17 Letter to Max Born, Sept. 7, 1944, in *Briefwechsel 1916–1955*, p. 204. (E.t., p. 149.)

18 Letter, in 1932, quoted by J. Bernstein, op. cit., p. 95.

19 W. Heisenberg, "Naturwissenschaftliche und religiöse Wahrheit" (address given to the Catholic Academy in Bavaria on receiving the Guardini prize, Mar. 23, 1973), in *Schritte über Grenzen. Gesammelte Reden und Aufsätze*, Munich, 2nd, enl. ed., 1973, pp. 333–51; quotation, p. 349.

20 Cf. The critique of H. Albert in C.III.4: Theology and natural science.

21 Cf. G.I.1: "The nameless God in the Buddhist religion."

22 On the analysis of being a person (as "mutuality," "being able to say 'thou,'" "being able to answer," "between") and its application, cf. H. Ott, *Gott*, Stuttgart/Berlin, 1971, esp. Ch. IV and V. This work includes a discussion with advocates of a "posttheistic" understanding of God; the same author, *Wirklichkeit und*

*Glaube*, Vol. II, "Der persönliche Gott," Göttingen/Zürich, 1969, esp. Ch. III–VI. Cf. also Paul Tillich, *Systematic Theology*, University of Chicago Press, Chicago, 1951/Nisbet, London, 1953, Vol. I, pp. 270–72. There is a useful survey of the present state of the discussion in *Concilium* 13 (1977), No. 3, "Ein persönlicher Gott?"

23 Cf. C.I.1: "God as reflection of man."
24 Cf. A.III.1: "The universal claim of scientific thought? Karl Popper."
25 Cf. A.III.1: "Scientific revolutions: Thomas S. Kuhn."
26 R. Lüst, in a Preface to the German translation of Steven Weinberg's *The First Three Minutes*. I am particularly grateful to my colleague Gerhard Elwert, professor of theoretical astrophysics at the University of Tübingen, for looking through this section, on the origin and the end of the world, and for his suggestions on more exact expressions.
27 On what follows, cf. the generally understandable account by the American physicist Steven Weinberg, *The First Three Minutes. A Modern View of the Universe*, New York, 1977/Andre Deutsch, London 1977. In his "historical diversion" (Ch. VI) and in his Bibliography, Weinberg mentions Gamow but, oddly enough, not the "father of big-bang cosmology," Lemaître, who, however, did not associate—as Gamow did—the early stage with the origin of the elements. See also Weinberg's work *Gravitation and Cosmology. Principles and Applications of the General Theory of Relativity*, New York, 1962. On the problems of the origin of the universe, see also H. von Ditfurth, *Im Anfang war der Wasserstoff*, Hamburg, 1972; O. Heckmann, *Sterne, Kosmos, Weltmodelle. Erlebte Astronomie*, Munich/Zürich, 1976; H. W. Woltersdorf, *Die Schöpfung war ganz anders. Irrtum und Wende*, Olten/Freiburg im Breisgau, 1976.
28 Cf. A. Einstein, *Über die spezielle und die allgemeine Relativitätstheorie*, 1917, 21st ed., Brunswick, 1973, esp. pp. 30–32; "Betrachtungen über die Welt als Ganzes."
29 Cf. E. Hubble, *The Realm of the Nebulae*, New Haven, 1936.
30 Gn 1:3–5.
31 O. Heckmann, op. cit., p. 37.
32 Cf. H. Bondi, *Cosmology*, London, 1952, esp. Part 3, "Cosmological Theories."
33 Cf. P. Jordan, *Der Naturwissenschaftler vor der religiösen Frage. Abbruch einer Mauer*, Oldenburg/Hamburg, 1963, Preface to the new edition of 1968; 6th ed., 1972.
34 H. von Ditfurth, *Im Anfang war der Wasserstoff*, Hamburg, 1972.
35 Ibid., p. 142.
36 Ibid., p. 140.
37 Ibid., p. 142.
38 Ibid., p. 49.
39 Cf. the commentaries on Genesis by G. Aalders, U. Cassuto, J. de Fraine, H. Gunkel, B. Jacob, H. Junker, F. Michaeli, J. Morgenstern, G. von Rad, A. van Selms, J. Skinner, E. A. Speiser, R. de Vaux, C. Westermann.
40 Heisenberg, "Naturwissenschaftliche und religiöse Wahrheit," in *Schritte über Grenzen*, p. 348.
41 Weinberg, op. cit., pp. 8–9.
42 *Time Magazine*, Dec. 27, 1976.
43 Cf. Ditfurth, op. cit., p. 47.
44 Ibid., p. 49; cf. also Heckmann, op. cit., p. 108.
45 Cf. H. Elsässer, "Galaxien und Kosmologie," in *Sterne und Weltraum* (1971), No. 5, pp. 123–28.
46 Cf. A.III.2: Theology and natural science.
47 Cf. the popular scientific presentation by S. E. Luria, *Life—The Unfinished Experiment*, Charles Scribner's Sons, New York, 1973/Souvenir Press, London, 1976, Ch. 11 ("Mind"); H. von Ditfurth, *Der Geist fiel nicht vom Himmel. Die Evolution unseres Bewusstseins*, Hamburg, 1976.
48 Cf. D.I.1: "Darwin's evolutionary thinking."
49 Cf., for instance, the objections against the application of the law of entropy raised by H. Metzner, *Physical Chemistry of Living Systems*, London/New York,

1977, Introduction. I am grateful to my colleague at Tübingen Helmut Metzner, professor of chemical physiology of plants, for reading this section and suggesting important corrections.

50 J. Monod, *Le hasard et la nécessité*, Paris, 1970. (E.t., *Chance and Necessity*, Collins, London, 1972, p. 110.) Cf. Luria, op. cit., p. 120: "Man is but one product, albeit a very special one, of a series of blind chances and harsh necessities." The basic attitude of the American cancer researcher and Nobel prizewinner is not, however, existentialist and pessimistic, like that of Monod, but American and optimistic: cf. pp. 7–8, 148–50. The prediction of Genesis "Ye shall be as gods, knowing good and evil," which Luria sees fulfilled in the progress of science, is, incidentally, uttered by the *serpent*.

51 Cf. D.I.1: "Darwin's evolutionary thinking."

52 Cf. Monod, op. cit., p. 40.

53 Cf. ibid., pp. 40–50.

54 M. Eigen and R. Winkler, *Das Spiel. Naturgesetze steuern den Zufall*, Munich/ Zürich, 1975. E. Schoffeniels, *L'anti-hasard*, Paris, 1973, is less balanced.

55 M. Eigen in a Preface to the German ed. of Monod, *Zufall und Notwendigkeit*, Munich, 1973 p. xv.

56 R. Riedl, *Die Strategie der Genesis. Naturgeschichte der realen Welt*, Munich/ Zürich, 1976, p. 122.

57 Ibid., pp. 10–11.

58 God's activity may not be located in chance, in the scope for play within the system of nature's laws, as it is by P. Jordan, op. cit., pp. 158–59: "To see all that happens as pervaded by divine activity has only now become logically possible, as a result of the discovery of nondetermining laws of nature that are sufficiently wide-meshed to leave scope for play everywhere in the most subtle happenings, from which determining influences are exercised also on crude happenings." In the postscript to his important book, Jordan rightly insists on the necessity of distinguishing between the *"examination* of logical, objective circumstances" and religious *"professions of faith"* (p. 349). Cf. the account in E. C. Hirsch, *Das Ende aller Gottesbeweise? Naturwissenschaftler antworten auf die religiöse Frage*, Hamburg, 1975.

59 Eigen, Preface to German ed. of Monod, *supra*, p. xv.

60 Eigen and Winkler, op. cit., pp. 13, 197.

61 Cf. ibid., p. 224.

62 E. C. Hirsch, *Das Ende aller Gottesbeweise*, pp. 83–84.

63 Monod, op. cit., p. 160.

64 Eigen and Winkler, op. cit., pp. 190–91.

65 Riedl, op. cit., pp. 294–95.

66 This is the danger in the challenging book of the Freiburg geneticist C. Bresch *Zwischenstufe Leben. Evolution ohne Ziel*, Munich/Zürich, 1977: Bresch ascribes to the evolutionary process an orientation to a *Monon*, to which—according to him—there is no "logical alternative" (p. 272). Quite apart from Bresch's interpretation of the second law of thermodynamics, which may be disputed by experts, it seems to me difficult to exclude any other logical possibility. Bresch is right, however, in his arguments against scientists who either do not raise certain fundamental questions about the great whence and whither or even—consciously or unconsciously—allow their dogmatic atheistic beliefs to enter into their scientific theories (cf. pp. 275, 284–86).

67 See Bresch's Epilogue, pp. 296–99.

68 This is also what Bresch says, rejecting, like Eigen and Winkler, the alternative of chance or necessity (cf., e.g., p. 293).

69 On the relationship between divine and human freedom, cf. G. Kraus, *Vorherbestimmung. Traditionelle Prädestinationslehre im Licht gegenwärtiger Theologie*, Freiburg, 1977.

70 Cf. H. Küng, *Christ sein*, Munich, 1974, Ch. C.II.2: "Wunder?" (E.t., *On Being a Christian*, New York, 1976/London, 1977, C.II.2: "Miracles?")

71 A comparison between two articles on miracles is revealing. These are by the Catholic exegete H. Haag in *Lexikon für Theologie und Kirche*, Vol. X, Freiburg/

Basel/Vienna, 1965, cols. 1252–54, and by the Protestant Old Testament scholar
W. Vollborn in *Religion und Geschichte und Gegenwart*, Vol. VI, Tübingen,
1962, cols. 1833–34.

72 Cf. Ex 13:17–22; 14:1–31.
73 Cf. Jos 10:12–13.
74 Cf. 1 K 17:7–16, 17–24; 2 K 4:18–37, 42–44.
75 Cf. Jon 2.
76 Eigen and Winkler, op. cit., p. 11.
77 Cf. H. Rahner, *Der spielende Mensch*, Einsiedeln, 1960, p. 15. (E.t., *Man at
Play*, Burns & Oates, London, 1965, p. 16.) More recently, G. Gilch, *Das Spiel
Gottes mit der Welt. Aspekte zum naturwissenschaftlichen Weltbild*, Stuttgart,
1968.
78 R. Schneider, *Winter in Wien*, Freiburg, 1958.
79 Cf. E.I.2: "Freedom within limits."
80 R. Bultmann, "Jesus Christus und die Mythologie," in *Glauben und Verstehen*,
Vol. IV, Tübingen, 1965, pp. 141–89; quotation, p. 174. Cf. also H. Jonas, "Im
Kampf um die Möglichkeit des Glaubens," in O. Kaiser (ed.), *Gedenken an
Rudolf Bultmann*, Tübingen, 1977, pp. 41–70. The difficult and complex problem
of revelation really needs separate consideration, which would have to be based on
the ideas put forward here.
81 Ex 33:20.
82 1 Co 13:9–10, 12–13.
83 Is 65:17; cf. 66:22.
84 Is 51:6.
85 Ibid.
86 Cf. Jl 3:15–16.
87 Cf. Mk 13:24–25 and par.
88 Cf. the commentaries on Third Isaiah by A. Bentzen, B. Duhm, G. Fohrer, S. C.
Thexton and I. Y. Muckle, P. Volz, C. Westermann.
89 Weinberg, op. cit., p. 154.
90 Ibid.
91 Ibid.
92 Cf., on Feuerbach, C.I.2: "God—wish or reality?" On Marx, C.II.2: "Is religion a
human fabrication?" On Freud, C.III.2: "Religion—merely wishful thinking?"
93 Cf. Ex 20:1–17.
94 Cf. Ex 19:18.
95 Dt 4:13; 10:4; cf. Ex 34:28.
96 Of the Old Testament theologians, cf. esp. W. Eichrodt, *Theologie des Alten Testaments*, Vol. III, Stuttgart/Güttingen, 1961, §22 (E.t., *Theology of the Old
Testament*, S.C.M. Press, London, Vol. 2, 1967, Ch. 22); G. von Rad, *Theologie
des Alten Testaments*, Vol. I, Munich, 1957, pp. 188–202 (E.t., *Old Testament
Theology*, S.C.M. Press, London, Vol. I, 1965, pp. 187–203); W. Zimmerli,
*Grundriss der alttestamentlichen Theologie*, Stuttgart, 1972, §11; J. L. McKen-
zie, *A Theology of the Old Testament*, New York, 1974, Ch. II.2. In addition, see
H. van Oyen, *Ethik des Alten Testaments*, Gütersloh, 1967. The following provide
basic reading on the decalogue: A. Alt, *Die Ursprünge des israelitischen Rechts*,
Leipzig, 1934; then, in addition to the various articles in encyclopedias, J. J.
Stamm, *Der Dekalog im Lichte der neueren Forschung*, Berne, 1962; H.
Reventlow, *Gebet und Predigt im Dekalog*, Gütersloh, 1962; H. Haag, "Der
Dekalog," in J. Stelzenberger (ed.), *Moraltheologie und Bibel*, Paderborn, 1964,
pp. 9–38; G. Fohrer, "Das sogenannte apodiktisch formulierte Recht und der
Dekalog," in *Kerygma und Dogma* 21 (1965), 49–74; G. O. Botterweck,
"Form and Growth of the Decalogue," in *Concilium* No. 1, 1965, Vol. 5, pp.
33–44; E. Niclsen, *Die Zehn Gebote*, Copenhagen, 1965; J. Schreiner, *Die Zehn
Gebote im Leben des Gottesvolkes*, Munich, 1966; H. Gese, "Der Dekalog als
Ganzheit betrachtet," in *Zeitschrift für Theologie und Kirche* 64 (1967), pp.
121–38; N. Lohfink, "Die zehn Gebote ohne den Berg Sinai," in his collection of
essays *Bibelauslegung im Wandel*, Frankfurt am Main, 1967, pp. 129–57; A. M.
Greeley, *The Sinai Myth*, New York, 1972; W. Stählin, *Die Urordnung des*

*Lebens. Ein Versuch, die zehn Gebote ausgelegt für unsere Zeit*, Hamburg, 1973;
H. Schüngel-Straumann, *Der Dekalog, Gottes Gebote?* Stuttgart, 1973.
97  Exodus 19 to Numbers 10.
98  Cf. A. Deissler, *Die Grundbotschaft des Alten Testaments*, pp. 75–81.
99  On these consequences from the Old Testament findings, cf. A. Auer, *Autonome Moral und christlicher Glaube*, Düsseldorf, 1971, pp. 63–68.
100  Cf. E.II.3: "Fundamental trust as basis of ethics."
101  Cf. F.IV.4: "For ethics: theologically justified autonomy."
102  M. Horkheimer, *Die Sehnsucht nach dem ganz Anderen*, ed. H. Gumnior, Hamburg, 1970, p. 60.
103  Ibid., pp. 60–61.
104  Cf. A.III.1. *The epistemological discussion*; E.II.3: "Fundamental trust as basis of science"; F.I.2: " 'God'—a meaningful term: Ludwig Wittgenstein."
105  Cf. A. H. Gunneweg, *Vom Verstehen des Alten Testaments. Eine Hermeneutik*, Göttingen.
106  Cf. the brief and impressive survey by A. Deissler, *Die Grundbotschaft des Alten Testaments*, pp. 97–150.
107  On the anthropomorphisms, cf. P. van Imschoot, *Théologie de l'Ancien Testament*, Vol. I, Paris/Tournai, 1954, pp. 28–30; W. Eichrodt, *Theologie des Alten Testaments*, Stuttgart, 1957, Vol. I, pp. 134–41 (E.t., *Theology of the Old Testament*, Vol. I, S.C.M. Press, London, 1961, pp. 210–17); E. Jacob, *Théologie de l'Ancien Testament*, Neuchâtel, 1955, pp. 28–32 (E.t., *Theology of the Old Testament*, Hodder & Stoughton, London/Sydney/Auckland/Toronto, 1958, 1974², pp. 39–41); T. C. Vriezen, *Theologie des Alten Testaments in Grundzügen*, Neukirchen-Moers, 1956, pp. 144–47 (E.t., *An Outline of Old Testament Theology*, Basil Blackwell, Oxford, 1958, pp. 171–73); G. von Rad, *Theologie des Alten Testaments*, Vol. I, Munich, 1957, pp. 217–18 (E.t., *Old Testament Theology*, Vol. I, S.C.M. Press, London, 1965, pp. 218–19); J. Jeremias, *Die Reue Gottes. Aspekte alttestamentliche Gottesvorstellung*, Neukirchen, 1975.

## G.III.  The God of Jesus Christ

1  Jn 16:15.
2  E. Bloch, *Atheismus im Christentum. Zur Religion des Exodus und des Reiches*, Frankfurt am Main, 1973, p. 174.
3  Ibid., p. 180.
4  Bloch, *Das Prinzip Hoffnung*, 3 vols., Frankfurt am Main, 1967, Vol. III, p. 1524.
5  Cf. H. Donner, " 'Wilde Exegese.' Ein Argument zum Problem der Scheinmodernität des Alten Testaments," in *Wege zum Menschen* 23 (1971), pp. 417–24.

### 1. God as Father

6  In addition to Julius Wellhausen, cited by Bloch, he uses especially—without quoting him—E. Sellin, *Alttestamentliche Theologie auf religionsgeschichtlicher Grundlage*, 2 vols., Leipzig, 1933. My attention was drawn to this by my Tübingen colleague Professor Bernhard Lang, *Ernst Bloch als Leser des Alten Testaments*, a lecture given in the colloquium for the ninetieth birthday of Ernst Bloch in Tübingen, 1975.
7  Cf. Lang, op. cit.
8  Cf. W. Eichrodt, *Theologie des Alten Testaments*, Vol. I, Stuttgart, 1957, pp. 168–76, esp. p. 170. (E.t., *Theology of the Old Testament*, S.C.M. Press, London, 1967, Vol. II, pp. 223–28, esp. p. 225.)
9  H. Haag, *Teufelsglaube* (with contribs. by K. Elliger, B. Lang and M. Limbeck), Tübingen, 1974, p. 180.
10  Ibid. n. 65; on a despotic God, cf., in the present work, B.III.1: "Everything necessary?"
11  Cf. Gn 22:1–12.
12  Cf. Gn 32:24–31.

13 Cf. Ex 9:1–12; 7:14–25; 11:1–10.
14 Cf. Ex 4:24–26.
15 Cf. Ex 32:25–29.
16 Cf. Ex 33:19.
17 Cf. Ex 21:13; cf. 1 S 6:5 with 6:9.
18 Cf. Jg 11:30–40.
19 Cf. 1 S 26:13–25; 2 S 24.
20 Cf. 1 K 18:22–40; 2 K 9–10.
21 Cf. Am 3:6.
22 Cf. Ho 1:4–5.
23 Cf. Is 56:1–8.
24 Cf. Ps 1; Ps 37.
25 Cf. Ps 119.
26 There is a brief summary of the problems by E. Würthwein and E. Lohse, "Gesetz" II–III, in *Religion in Geschichte und Gegenwart*, Vol. II, Tübingen, 1958, cols. 1513–17.
27 Congregation for the Doctrine of the Faith, *Declaration on the Admission of Women to the Ministerial Priesthood*, Oct. 15, 1976. (E.t., *Women and the Priesthood*, Catholic Truth Society, London, 1976.)
28 Cf. H. Küng, "Thesen zur Stellung der Frau in Kirche und Gesellschaft," in *Theologische Quartalschrift* 156 (1976), pp. 129–32. (E.t., "Feminism: A New Reformation," in the New York *Times Magazine*, May 23, 1976. Reproduced as "Women in Church and Society," in Küng, *Signposts for the Future*, Doubleday, Garden City, N.Y., 1977–78, pp. 155–59.) See also H. Küng and G. Lohfink, "Keine Ordination der Frau," in *Theologische Quartalschrift* 157 (1977), pp. 144–46.
29 Cf. Ex 4:22–23; Jr 31:9; Is 63:16.
30 Ps 2:7. Cf. H. Haag, "Sohn Gottes im Alten Testament," in *Theologische Quartalschrift* 154 (1974), pp. 223–31.
31 Cf. ibid., p. 230: "The mythically based idea of a physical divine procreation was clearly transformed in Israel into a divine sonship based on *election*." Cf. W. Schlisske, *Gottessöhne und Gottessohn im Alten Testament. Phasen der Entmythisierung im Alten Testament*, Stuttgart, 1973, esp. Part 2.
32 Cf. Si 4:10; Ws 2:16–18.
33 Cf. The Book of Jubilees 1:24.
34 Cf. Mt 5:44–48.
35 Cf. Mt 10:29–31.
36 Cf. Mt 6:8.
37 Cf. Mt 6:32.
38 G. Kraus, *Vorherbestimmung. Traditionelle Prädestinationslehre im Licht gegenwärtiger Theologie*, Freiburg, 1977, pp. 334, 336.
39 Cf. Lk 15:11–32.
40 To this extent, but only to this extent, the psychoanalyst T. Moser is right with his indictment *Gottesvergiftung*, Frankfurt, 1976.
41 Cf. C.I.3: "What remains of Feuerbach's critique of religion?"
42 Cf. C.II.3: "What is left of Marx's critique of religion?"
43 Cf. D.II.2: "Being Christian and being Human?"
44 Cf. C.III.3: "What remains of Freud's critique of religion?"
45 Cf. H. Küng, *Christ sein*, Munich, 1974, Ch. C.IV.2. (E.t., *On Being a Christian*, New York, 1976/London, 1977, Ch. C.IV.2: "The debate on God.")
46 Cf. ibid. Not an obvious form of address.
47 Mk 15:34 (Ps 22:2); Mt 27:46. On the trial and death of Jesus, see *On Being a Christian*, C.IV.3: "The end."

## 2. God through Jesus Christ

1 F. M. Dostoevsky, *The Idiot*, Heinemann, London, 1913, p. 212.
2 *The Diary of Dostoevsky's Wife*, edited by R. Fülop-Miller and F. Eckstein, London, 1928, p. 419.
3 J. Paul, *Siebenkäs*, in Werke, Vol. II, ed. G. Lohmann, Munich, 1959, pp. 7–565;

pp. 266–71: "Rede des toten Christus von Weltgebäude herab, dass kein Gott sei."

4 With regard to all this, see H. Küng, *On Being a Christian*, Ch. C.V.1: "The beginning."

5 Cf. *On Being a Christian*, Ch. C.V.1: "Clarifications, Legends?"

6 On the difference between the Jewish and the Christian understanding of the resurrection, cf. *On Being a Christian*, C.V.1: "The ultimate reality."

7 On the question of the appearances, cf. *On Being a Christian*, C.V.1: "*Origin of faith.*"

8 Cf. W. Jens, *Ein Segel in eine andere Welt* (memorial address for Ernst Bloch), in *Die Zeit*, Aug. 12, 1977.

9 Cf. G.II.2: "What comes at the end?"

10 Cf. F.IV.3: "Belief in God rationally justified."

11 This was not the attitude of the German Bishops' Conference. In its second press statement, Mar. 3, 1977, it imputed to the author the opinion that Jesus Christ is "only an exemplary human being" and "merely God's spokesman and advocate." This I reject as an incomprehensible misrepresentation of my ideas. The same holds for the assumption that I had in fact denied the christological statements of the Nicene Creed. On the contrary, my aim was to make it intelligible to people today. One may wonder what was the point of all one's readiness for discussion, all the clarifying ideas and correspondence with bishops, in face of an apparently unteachable teaching office. It must be asked, in this situation, to whom the charge of "wrongly orienting and confusing the readers" really applies. The volume of contributions by selected theologians, with the deceptive title *Diskussion um Hans Küngs "Christ sein,"* supported with various flanking measures, launched in 1976 with the knowledge of the German Episcopate's commission on faith, turned out to be less a discussion than a series of misunderstandings, misinterpretations, disparagements, imputations, without offering any countersuggestions and—as in the infallibility debate—without giving the author the opportunity of a response in this volume. This made an "Answer to my Critics," in the *Frankfurter Allgemeine Zeitung* of May 22, 1976, absolutely necessary. But people today expect bishops to stand up in a credible way not only for a dogmatic system and an institution but also for the cause of God and of Christ in modern society; they, too, are expected to proclaim the message intelligibly and to carry out long-overdue practical reforms. If these things were done, perhaps public condemnations of theologians would not be necessary.

When the manuscript of *Existiert Gott?* had gone to print, the third statement of the Bishops' Conference against *Christ sein* appeared, together with documents. As the person involved, not only do I find it intolerable to have had to make a sharp protest against the publication, without my consent, of personal letters to the president of the German Bishops' Conference, but especially the fact that the Conference could not wait until the technical theological questions in dispute in this book had been taken up again, deepened and—I hope—clarified. All this I pointed out in several letters to the German Bishops' Conference. I thus found myself compelled, for my own part, to agree to the publication of documents that would contain the whole truth: *Um nichts als die Wahrheit. Deutsche Bischofskonferenz contra Hans Küng. Eine Dokumentation*, ed. Walter Jens, Munich, 1978; this includes my "Appeal for Understanding."

The further theological and biographical context is made clear in H. Häring and K. J. Kuschel (eds.), *Hans Küng. Weg und Werk*, Munich, 1978. (E.t., *Hans Küng. His Work and His Way*, London, 1979.)

12 Rm 1:3–4.

13 Cf. Ac 13:33 (Ps 2:7).

14 A good summary of the New Testament statements on the "Son of God" is found in M. Hengel, *Der Sohn Gottes. Die Entstehung der Christologie und die jüdisch-hellenistische Religionsgeschichte*, Tübingen, 1975, pp. 143–44.

15 Cf. Mk 1:9–11.

16 Cf. Lk 1:32, 35.

17 Cf. Ga 4:4; Jn 3:16.

18 Cf. H. Küng, *On Being a Christian*, C.VI.3: "True God and true man."
19 W. Thüsing and K. Rahner, *Christologie—systematisch und exegetisch. Arbeitsgrundlagen für eine interdisziplinäre Vorlesung*, Freiburg/Basel/Vienna, 1972, p. 250.
20 Ibid., pp. 250–51.
21 Ibid., p. 251.
22 F. Mussner, "Ursprünge und Entfaltung der neutestamentlichen Sohneschristologie. Versuch einer Rekonstruktion" in *Grundfragen der Christologie heute*, ed. L. Scheffczyk, Freiburg/Basel/Vienna, 1975, pp. 77–113; quotation, p. 103.
23 K. H. Schelkle, *Theologie des Neuen Testaments*, Vol. II, Düsseldorf, 1973, pp. 189–90. Cf. also D. Wiederkehr, "Entwurf einer systematischen Christologie," in J. Feiner and M. Löhrer (eds.), *Mysterium Salutis* 3, 1, Einsiedeln, 1970, pp. 477–648; on preexistence, pp. 534–40, esp. p. 534. The problem of the preexistence of the Son of God is being investigated at the present time by my assistant K. J. Kuschel from the standpoint of both exegesis and systematic theology for his qualifying dissertation.
24 Cf. Jn 1:14.
25 Cf. Rm 1:3–4; 2 Tm 2:8.
26 Cf. Ph 2:6–11; 1 Tm 3:16.
27 Cf. what must be the earliest recorded text on the Incarnation, Ga 4:4; then 2 Co 8:9; Rm 8:3 and finally Tt 2:11; 3:4. There is an analysis of these texts in K. H. Schelkle, *Theologie des Neuen Testaments*, Vol. II, pp. 151–68.
28 Cf. Jn 10:29; 14:28; Mk 13:32.
29 Cf. K. Rahner, "Theos im Neuen Testament," in his *Schriften zur Theologie*, Vol. I, Zürich/Einsiedeln/Cologne, 1954, pp. 91–167. (E.t., *Theological Investigations*, Vol. I, London, 1961, pp. 79–148.)
30 Jn 20:28.
31 Jn 1:1, the preexistent Logos, and Jn 20:28, Thomas' confession; certainly in Heb 1:8, perhaps also in 2 Th 1:12; Tt 2:13; 2 P 1:1.
32 Cf. 1 Co 1:30.
33 Cf. 1 Co 11:3; 8:6; Col 1:15–18; 2:10; Ep 4:15–16.
34 Cf. 2 Co 4:4, 6; Rm 8:29; Col 1:15.
35 Cf. 2 Co 1:20.
36 Cf. Jn 1:1–14.
37 Cf. Jn 5:18–19; 10:33–38; 19:7.
38 Cf. Jn 20:28; 1 Jn 5:20.
39 Col 2:9.
40 Jn 1:14.
41 Nicene Creed (DS 125).
42 Cf. Jn 10:15, 38.
43 Cf. Jn 10:38; 14:10–11, 20; 17:21–23.
44 Cf. Jn 10:30.
45 Cf. Jn 14:9; 12:45; 5:19.
46 Cf. T. Moser, *Gottesvergiftung*, Frankfurt, 1976. The motto of this book is "Rejoice if your God was more friendly"; cf. pp. 22, 100.
47 Cf. H. Küng, *On Being a Christian*, Ch. C.VI.2: "God and suffering."
48 Cf. Mk 15:39 and parallels.
49 1 Co 2:2.
50 Cf. 1 Co 1:23–24.
51 Cf. D.II.2. *What Christians can learn*.
52 Cf. 1 Co 3:11.
53 Cf. G.II.1: "The one God and the many Gods."
54 I Co 2:2.
55 Cf. J. Moltmann, *Der gekreuzigte Gott. Das Kreuz Christi als Grund und Kritik christlicher Theologie*, Munich, 1972. (E.t., *The Crucified God*, London, 1974.) It is significant that the title of the important Ch. VI contains these words in quotation marks: "The 'crucified God.'"
56 Rm 8:31–32, 38–39.
57 Cf. E.II.3: "Fundamental trust as basis of ethics."

58 Cf. F.IV.4: "For ethics: theologically justified autonomy."
59 Cf. G.II.2: "God's law and human rights."
60 Cf. H. Küng, *On Being a Christian*, D.II.2: "Specifically Christian norms?"
61 Cf. *On Being a Christian*, Ch. C. *The program*.
62 S. Freud, letter to J. J. Putnam, July 8, 1915, in Ernst L. Freud (ed.), *Sigmund Freuds Briefe 1873–1939*, Frankfurt, 1906, p. 305. (E.t., see Ernest Jones, *Sigmund Freud. Life and Work*, Hogarth Press, London/Clarke Irwin, Toronto, Vol. 2, 1958, p. 465.)
63 Simone de Beauvoir, *La Force des Choses*, Gallimard, Paris, 1963, p. 686. (E.t., *Force of Circumstance*, Penguin Books, Harmondsworth/New York, 1968, p. 674.)
64 F. M. Dostoevsky, *The Brothers Karamazov*, Heinemann, London, 1912, new impression 1965, Ch. 5.
65 Cf. A. Camus, *Le Mythe de Sisyphe*, Paris, 1942 (E.t., *The Myth of Sisyphus*, Hamish Hamilton, London, 1955); the same author, *L'homme révolté*, Paris, 1951 (E.t., *The Rebel*, Penguin Books, Harmondsworth/New York, 1971). On the suffering of children, cf. esp. Camus's remarks in a lecture to the Paris Dominicans, 1948, transl. in Albert Camus, *Resistance, Rebellion and Death*, Hamish Hamilton, London, 1961, "The Unbeliever and Christians," pp. 47–53.
66 Cf. G.II.1: "Man's answer."
67 On the question of theodicy, cf. H. Küng, *Gott und das Leid*, Zürich/Einsiedeln/Cologne, 1967; J. Moltmann, "Gott und Auferstehung. Auferstehungsglaube im Forum der Theodizeefrage," in *Perspektiven der Theologie*, Munich/Mainz, 1968, pp. 36–56; the same author, *Der gekreuzigte Gott*, Munich, 1972, esp. Ch. VI.3 (E.t., *The Crucified God*, London, 1974); H. Gollwitzer, *Krummes Holz-aufrechter Gang. Zur Frage nach dem Sinn des Lebens*, Munich, 1970, esp. Ch. VII and XI; J. B. Metz, "Erlösung und Emanzipation," in *Erlösung und Emanzipation*, ed. L. Scheffczyk, Freiburg/Basel/Vienna, 1973, pp. 120–40. Cf. also the issue of *Concilium*, ed. J. B. Metz, June 1972, on "The God Question."
68 Cf. 1 Jn 4:8–9.
69 Cf. M. Horkheimer, *Die Sehnsucht nach dem ganz Anderen* (an interview with a commentary by H. Gumnior), Hamburg, pp. 61–62.
70 Rv 21:4.

## 3. God in the Spirit

71 On the biblical understanding of the Spirit, see among the articles in encyclopedias H. Kleinknecht, F. Baumgärtel, W. Bieder, E. Sjöberg, and esp. E. Schweizer, in *Theologisches Wörterbuch zum Neuen Testament*, Vol. VI, Stuttgart, 1959, pp. 330–453; E. Käsemann in *Religion in Geschichte und Gegenwart*, Vol. II, Tübingen, 1958, cols. 1272–79; F. Mussner, in *Lexikon für Theologie und Kirche*, Vol. VIII, Freiburg, 1963, cols. 572–76; among the theologians of the New Testament see esp. Rudolf Bultmann. Important among recent monographs are C. K. Barrett, *The Holy Spirit and the Gospel Tradition*, London, 1947; E. Schweizer, *Geist und Gemeinde im NT*, Munich, 1952; S. Zedda, *L'adozione a figli di Dio e lo Spirito Santo*, Rome, 1952; H. von Campenhausen, *Kirchliches Amt und geistliche Vollmacht in den ersten drei Jahrhunderten*, Tübingen, 1953; N. Q. Hamilton, *The Holy Spirit and Eschatology in Paul*, London, 1957; I. Hermann, *Kyrios und Pneuma*, Munich, 1961; K. Stalder, *Das Werk des Geistes in der Heiligung bei Paulus*, Zürich, 1961; M. A. Chevallier, *Esprit de Dieu, paroles d'hommes. Le rôle de l'esprit dans les ministères de la parole selon l'apôtre Paul*, Neuchâtel, 1966; H. Küng, *Die Kirche*, Freiburg/Basel/Vienna, 1967, Ch. C.II.2 (E.t., *The Church*, London, 1967); E. Brandenburger, *Fleisch und Geist. Paulus und die dualistische Weisheit*, Neukirchen, 1968; D. Moody, *Spirit of the Living God. The Biblical Concepts Interpreted in Context*, Philadelphia, 1968; W. D. Hauschild, *Gottes Geist und der Mensch. Studien zur frühchristlichen Pneumatologie*, Munich, 1972.
72 Translation of the *Veni Sancte Spiritus* by Helen Waddell, *More Latin Lyrics*.

*From Virgil to Milton*, ed. Dame Felicitas Corrigan, Gollancz, London, 1976, pp. 298–301.
73  2 Co 3:17.
74  2 Co 1:22.
75  Among recent systematic studies may be mentioned H. U. von Balthasar, *Spiritus Creator. Skizzen zur Theologie* III, Einsiedeln, 1967; H. Mühlen, *Der Heiliger Geist als Person in der Trinität, bei der Inkarnation und im Gnadenbund: Ich-Du-Wir*, Münster, 1967; H. Berkhof, *Theologie des Heiligen Geistes*, Neukirchen, 1968; W. Fitch, *The Ministry of the Holy Spirit*, Grand Rapids, Michigan, 1974; C. Heitmann and H. Mühlen (eds.), *Erfahrung und Theologie des Heiligen Geistes*, Hamburg/Munich, 1974; J. de Goitia, *La fuerza del espíritu: Pneuma-Dynamis*, Bilbao, 1974; *El Espíritu Santo, ayer y hoy*, Salamanca, 1975.
76  Ac 6:11; cf. 6:8–15; 7:1–60.
77  Ac 7:55–56.
78  Among recent monographs on the Trinity, cf. E. Haible, *Trinitarische Heilslehre*, Stuttgart, 1960; B. Lonergan, *De Trinitate. Pars analytica*, Rome, 1961; the same author, *De deo trino*, Vol. I, *Pars dogmatica*, Rome, 1964, Vol. II, *Pars systematica*, Rome, 1964; F. Bourassa, *Questions de théologie trinitaire*, Rome, 1970; M. F. Sciacca, *Ontologia triadica e trinitaria*, Stresa, 1972; R. Panikkar, *The Trinity and the Religious Experience of Man. Icon, Person, Mystery*, New York/London, 1973; J. Daniélou, *La Trinité et le mystère de l'existence*, Paris, 1973; M. Durrant, *Theology and Intelligibility. An Examination of the Proposition That God Is the Last End of Rational Creatures and the Doctrine That God Is Three Persons in One Substance. "The Doctrine of the Holy Trinity,"* London/Boston 1973; A. Brunner, *Dreifaltigkeit. Personale Zugänge zum Mysterium*, Einsiedeln, 1976. Cf. also the volumes of the "Semanas de estudios trinitarios": *La Santísima Trinidad, fuente de salvación en la constitución sobre la Iglesia*, Salamanca, 1968; *La Trinidad, hoy. El tratado sobre la Santísima Trinidad en el neuvo ordenamiento de los estudios teológicos*, Salamanca, 1971; *La Trinidad en la Biblia. Cristo, revelador del Padre y emisor del Espíritu en el Nuevo Testamento*, Salamanca, 1973; L. Oeing-Hanhoff, "Hegels Trinitätslehre. Zur Aufgabe ihrer Kritik und Rezeption," in *Theologie und Philosophie* 52 (1977), pp. 378–407. Among the numerous manuals of dogmatics, see especially the sections in *Mysterium Salutis*. Unfortunately I was not able to make use in the present work of E. Jüngel's large book on the question of God: *Gott als Geheimnis der Welt. Zur Begründung der Theologie des Gekreuzigten im Streit zwischen Theismus und Atheismus*, Tübingen, 1977.
79  Cf. 2 Co 3:18; Ga 4:6; Rm 8:9; Ph 1:19.
80  1 Co 15:45.
81  2 Co 3:17.
82  Cf. 2 Co 3:17–18.
83  2 Co 13:13; cf. 1 Co 12:4–6; Ga 4:4–6; Rm 5:1–5; Mt 28:19.
84  Cf. Jn 14:16.
85  Cf. Jn 14:26. On the Johannine pneumatology, cf. G. Johnston, *The Spirit-Paraclete in the Gospel of John*, London, 1970; F. Porsch, *Pneuma und Wort. Ein exegetischer Beitrag zur Pneumatologie des Johannesevangeliums*, Frankfurt, 1974.
86  Cf. H. Küng, *On Being a Christian*, C.VII.2: "Trinity"; cf. also H. Küng, *Menschwerdung Gottes. Eine Einführung in Hegels theologisches Denken als Prolegomena zu einer künftigen Christologie*, Freiburg/Basel/Vienna, 1970: Excursus I, "Der Weg zur klassischen Christologie."
87  Among more recent systematic studies, cf. J. S. Vos, *Traditionsgeschichtliche Untersuchungen zur paulinischen Pneumatologie*, Assen, 1973; O. Knoch, *Der Geist Gottes und der neue Mensch. Der Heilige Geist als Grundkraft und Norm des christlichen Lebens in Kirche und Welt nach dem Zeugnis des Apostels Paulus*, Stuttgart, 1975.
88  On the historical development, cf. A. Jungmann, "Die Abwehr des germanischen Arianismus und der Umbruch der religiösen Kultur im frühen Mittelalter," in *Li-*

*turgisches Erbe und pastorale Gegenwart,* Innsbruck/Vienna/Munich, 1960, pp. 3–86. On the New Testament data, cf. G. Lohfink, "Gab es im Gottesdienst der neutestamentlichen Gemeinden eine Anbetung Christi?" in *Biblische Zeitschrift,* NF 18 (1974), pp. 161–79; quotation, p. 172. For his scrutiny of G.III. *The God of Jesus Christ* and for various improvements, I am grateful to my colleague Gerhard Lohfink, professor for New Testament at Tübingen.

# Index of Names

Where a specific author is discussed at length, the page numbers are in **boldface.** All other references in the text are in Roman type. References to the author in the notes are printed in *italics.*

# Index

References in the text are in roman type. References in the notes are in italics.